educational
psychology

educational psychology

effective teaching
effective learning

second edition

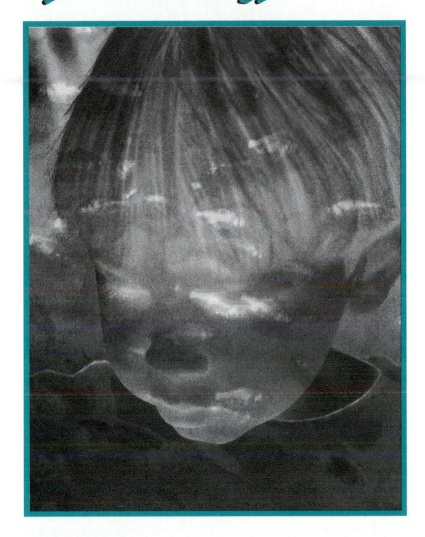

Stephen N. Elliott
University of Wisconsin–Madison

Thomas R. Kratochwill
University of Wisconsin–Madison

Joan Littlefield
University of Wisconsin–Madison

John F. Travers
Boston College

Brown & Benchmark
PUBLISHERS

Madison   Dubuque, IA   Guilford, CT   Chicago   Toronto   London
Caracas   Mexico City   Buenos Aires   Madrid   Bogota   Sydney

Book Team

Executive Publisher *Edgar J. Laube*
Managing Editor *Sue Pulvermacher-Alt*
Developmental Editor *Suzanne M. Guinn*
Production Editor *Gloria G. Schiesl*
Proofreading Coordinator *Carrie Barker*
Designer *Jeff Storm*
Art Editor *Rachel Imsland*
Photo Editor *Leslie Dague*
Permissions Coordinator *Mavis M. Oeth*
Production Manager *Beth Kundert*
Production/Costing Manager *Sherry Padden*
Marketing Manager *Katie Rose*
Copywriter *Jennifer Smith*

Basal Text *10/12 Garamond Light*
Display Type *Memphis, Universe Black Extended*
Typesetting System *Macintosh/QuarkXPress*
Paper Stock *50# Mirror Matte*

President and Chief Executive Officer *Thomas E. Doran*
Vice President of Production and Business Development *Vickie Putman*
Vice President of Sales and Marketing *Bob McLaughlin*
Director of Marketing *John Finn*

 A Times Mirror Company

The credits section for this book begins on page 615 and is considered an extension of the copyright page.

Cover image © Lance Hidy/SIS

Copyedited by Beth Bulger; proofread by Paula Gieseman

Library of Congress Catalog Card Number: 95–76282

ISBN 0–697–17485–9

Printed in the United States of America by Times Mirror Higher Education Group, Inc., 2460 Kerper Boulevard, Dubuque, IA 52001

10 9 8 7 6 5 4 3 2 1

To Anita, Dustin Rhodes, and Andrew Taylor, who all continue to provide love
and support and are a source of great pride.

Stephen N. Elliott

To my family, Carol, Tyler, and Rudy, and especially in loving memory
of the late Donna Ehrler Ryan, my sister-in-law.

Thomas R. Kratochwill

To Greg Cook, for his unfailing love and support; to Andy and Will Cook, for their daily joys and challenges; and to
Margaret and Philip Littlefield, for their example of lifelong love of learning.

Joan Littlefield

To my wife, Barbara, whose love, support, and encouragement have been
a source of inspiration through the years.

John Travers

brief contents

section 1
introduction to educational psychology

1 Educational Psychology: Teaching and Learning 2

2 Research and Educational Psychology 26

3 Diversity in the Classroom: Culture, Class, and Gender 50

section 2
the development of students

4 Cognitive and Language Development 78

5 Psychosocial and Moral Development 118

6 Exceptional Students 150

section 3
learning theories and practices

7 Behavioral Psychology and Learning 198

8 Cognitive Psychology and Learning 236

9 Thinking Skills and Problem-Solving Strategies 278

10 Motivation in the Classroom 328

section 4
design and management of classroom instruction

11 Planning for Essential Learning Outcomes 366

12 Effective Teaching Strategies and the Design of Instruction 394

13 Classroom Management: Organization and Control 432

14 Teaching and Technology 476

section 5
assessing learning and evaluating education

15 Teacher-Constructed Tests and Performance Assessment Methods 518

16 Standardized Tests and Rating Scales in the Classroom 558

Free Copy

contents

Preface xv

section 1

introduction to educational psychology

1 Educational Psychology: Teaching and Learning 2

How to Use This Book 4
So You Want to Teach 6
  What It Means to Teach 6
  Who Becomes a Teacher? 8
  Teaching and Educational Issues 8
Teaching as an Art and as a Science 11
  Teaching as an Art 11
  Teaching as a Science 12
  Questions That Teachers Ask 13
  Our Multicultural Classrooms 14
Effective Schools 17
  A Place Called School 18
  Effective Schools—Effective Teachers 19
Educational Psychology: The Core
  Concepts 20
  Educational Psychology and the
  Classroom 21

*Issues and Answers: Is Total Quality Management
  the Solution for Effective Schools? 17*
Teacher-Student Interactions: Relating to Students 19

Applications and Reflections
Chapter Highlights 23
Connections 24
Getting the Picture and Drawing
  Relationships 25
Personal Journal 25
Key Terms 25

2 Research and Educational Psychology 26

Research and Effective Schooling 28
  Sources of Knowledge 28
The Emergence of Research on Children 30
  Baby Biographies 30
  Case Studies 31
  Scientific Influences 32
Major Research Methods 34
  Historical Research 34
  Descriptive Research 34
  Correlational Research 35
  Comparative Research 36
  Experimental Research 36
Techniques Used by Researchers 37
  Surveys 37
  Interviews 39
  Observation 41
  Cross-Sectional and Longitudinal
    Research 41
  Cross-Cultural Research 42
  Single-Case Research 43
Primary, Secondary, and Meta-Analysis 44
Ethical and Legal Considerations in
  Research in Education 47

Focus: Rival Hypotheses 31
Focus: The Case Study 33
Focus: Understanding the Research Article 35
*Issues and Answers: Should Teachers Use Single-Case
  Designs to Evaluate Their Interventions with
  Students in Classrooms? 46*

Applications and Reflections
Chapter Highlights 47
Connections 48
Getting the Picture and Drawing
  Relationships 48
Personal Journal 49
Key Terms 49

3 Diversity in the Classroom: Culture, Class, and Gender 50

Culture and the Schools 52
  Merging Cultures 52
  Cultures and Cognitive Development 53
  Our Changing Classrooms 55
  Interactions in the Classroom 57
  Cultural Differences and Testing
    Practices 58

Social Class and Academic Achievement 59
  The Children of Poverty 60
  Social Class and Education 60
  Teaching, Learning, and Social Class 61

Gender, Development, and the Classroom 64
  Becoming Boys and Girls 66
  Gender Stereotyping 69
  Gender and Classroom Achievement 70
  Gender and the Curriculum 72
  Teacher-Student Relationships:
    A Summary 74

Focus: Checking Your Relationships with Students 58
*Teacher-Student Interactions: Teaching Students
  Social Skills* 64
*Teacher-Student Interactions: The Value of Your
  Relationships with Students* 74

Applications and Reflections
Chapter Highlights 75
Connections 76
**Getting the Picture and Drawing
  Relationships** 76
Personal Journal 76
Key Terms 76

section 2

the development of students

4 Cognitive and Language Development 78

The Meaning of Development 80
  Vygotsky and Mental Development 82

Piaget and Cognitive Development 83
  Key Concepts in Piaget's Theory 84
  Piaget's Four Stages of Cognitive
    Development 86
  Criticisms of Piaget 96
  For the Classroom 98
  Alternatives to Piaget 100

Language Development 102
  Language Accomplishments 102
  The Language Components 102

Language Development in Infancy 104
  Speech Irregularities 105
Language Development in
  Early Childhood 106
  Metalinguistic Awareness 107
  The Whole Language Movement 107
  Bilingualism 108
Language Development in
  Middle Childhood 110

Theories of Language Acquisition 111
  Lenneberg's Biological Explanation 111
  Piaget and Language Development 112
  Chomsky and Psycholinguistics 113

Language and the Classroom 113

*Focus: What African American Children
  Consider Important* 83
Teacher-Student Interactions: The Sensorimotor Period 89
*Teacher-Student Interactions: The Preoperational
  Period* 92
*Teacher-Student Interactions: The Concrete
  Operational Period* 94
*Teacher-Student Interactions: The Formal
  Operational Period* 97
*Issues and Answers: Should Piaget's Theory of Cognitive
  Development Drive Public School Curricula?* 101
*Issues and Answers: Should Non-English-Speaking
  Students Be Educated in a Bilingual
  Educational System?* 109
*Teacher-Student Interactions: Activities to
  Facilitate Language Skills* 114

Applications and Reflections
Chapter Highlights 114
Connections 115
**Getting the Picture and Drawing
  Relationships** 116
Personal Journal 117
Key Terms 117

5 Psychosocial and Moral Development 118

Psychosocial Development 120
Erikson's Eight Stages 120
  Stage 1: Trust Versus Mistrust 120
  Stage 2: Autonomy Versus Shame
    and Doubt 121
  Stage 3: Initiative Versus Guilt 123
  Stage 4: Industry Versus Inferiority 126
  Stage 5: Identity Versus Identity
    Confusion 130
  Stage 6: Intimacy Versus Isolation 134
  Stage 7: Generativity Versus Stagnation 135
  Stage 8: Integrity Versus Despair 135
  For the Classroom 135

Moral Development 136
Kohlberg's Theory of Moral Development 137
   Level 1: Preconventional Morality 138
   Level 2: Conventional Morality 138
   Level 3: Postconventional Morality 140
   Criticisms of Kohlberg's Theory 141
   For the Classroom 142
   Using Moral Dilemmas 143
   The Teacher's Role 144

Teacher-Student Interactions: Erikson's Early Stages 127
Teacher-Student Interactions: Erikson's Elementary School Years 128
Issues and Answers: Equal Education for All— Does That Include Girls? 131
Teacher-Student Interactions: Erikson's Adolescent Years 134
Teacher-Student Interactions: Moral Development— The Early Years 139
Issues and Answers: Schools, Violence, and Moral Education 140
Focus: The Moral Dilemma 143
Focus: Schools and Character Development 144
Teacher-Student Interactions: Moral Development— The Later Years 147

Applications and Reflections
Chapter Highlights 146
Connections 148
Getting the Picture and Drawing Relationships 148
Personal Journal 149
Key Terms 149

6   Exceptional Students   150

Children Who Are Exceptional in the Classroom 152
   Children at Risk 152
   Ability Grouping 153
The Categories of Exceptionality 155
   The Gifted/Talented 156
   Sensory Handicaps 162
   Communication Disorders 165
   Physical and Health Impairment 166
   Behavior Disorders 167
   Learning Disabilities 171
   Cognitive Disabilities 174
The Assessment and Classification of Children 176
Mainstreaming 178
   What Is Mainstreaming or Inclusion? 178
   Classroom Support for Mainstreamed Students 180
   Some Results of Mainstreaming 186
Education and Exceptionality: A Model 187
Multicultural Students and Special Education 188

Bilingual Education and Bilingual Children 190

Focus: Thinking About Individual Differences 152
Focus: A Pioneer in Special Education 154
Teacher-Student Interactions: Students Who Are Exceptional 157
Focus: Genetic Studies of Genius 160
Teacher-Student Interactions: Working with the Gifted and Talented 162
Teacher-Student Interactions: Working with the Visually Impaired 163
Teacher-Student Interactions: Working with the Hearing Impaired 164
Teacher-Student Interactions: Working with Students Who Are Physically or Health Impaired 167
Teacher-Student Interactions: Working with Students Who Have Behavior Disorders 168
Teacher-Student Interactions: Working with Students Who Are Mildly Mentally Retarded 176
Issues and Answers: Should Children Be Labeled to Receive Special Education Services? 177
Focus: Teachers and the Referral Process 179
Focus: The Special Education Process 181
Focus: The Regular Education Initiative 185

Applications and Reflections
Chapter Highlights 192
Connections 193
Getting the Picture and Drawing Relationships 194
Personal Journal 195
Key Terms 195

section 3

learning theories and practices

7   Behavioral Psychology and Learning   198

Classical Conditioning 200
   Pavlov's Work 200
   Features of Classical Conditioning 201
Thorndike's Connectionism 202
   The Law of Readiness 202
   The Law of Exercise 202
   The Law of Effect 204
Operant Conditioning 204
   Skinner's Views 204
   Skinner and Reinforcement 205
   The Nature of Reinforcement 206
   Skinner and Punishment 209
   Categories of Punishment 210
   How Punishment Works 211
   For the Classroom 212

Social Cognitive Learning	216
An Explanation of Modeling	217
Multicultural Models	220
For the Classroom	220
Behavioral Theories and Teaching	222
Techniques to Increase Behavior	222
Techniques to Decrease Behavior	224
Techniques to Maintain Behavior	227
Techniques of Self-Control	228
Behaviorism and the Future	230
Applying Behavior Analysis to Schooling	230
Skinner's Suggestions	232

Teacher-Student Interactions: Using Classical Conditioning in the Classroom	*203*
Focus: The Keller Plan	*208*
Focus: Don't Rely on Punishment	*212*
Focus: Skinner and the Reluctant Mathematician	*213*
Teacher-Student Interactions: Using Operant Conditioning in the Classroom	*215*
Teacher-Student Interactions: Social Cognitive Learning in the Classroom	*221*
Issues and Answers: Alternatives to Punishment	*225*
Focus: Recording Student Behavior	*231*

Applications and Reflections
Chapter Highlights	**233**
Connections	**234**
Getting the Picture and Drawing Relationships	**234**
Personal Journal	**235**
Key Terms	**235**

8 Cognitive Psychology and Learning 236

The Meaning of Cognitive Psychology	238
The Emergence of Cognitive Psychology	241
The Influence of the Gestaltists	241
Bartlett and the Schema	242
For the Classroom	244
Some Major Approaches in Cognitive Psychology	245
Meaningful Learning	245
The Contribution of Jerome Bruner	247
The Brain and Thinking	249
Brain and Mind: The Relationship	249
Lateralization	250
Pattern Matching	252
Learning	252
The Importance of Information Processing	253
The Meaning of Representation	253
How We Represent Information	253
The Role of Perception	255
Explanation of the Perceptual Process	255
For the Classroom	256

How Students Categorize	259
Forming Categories	261
For the Classroom	262
Memory at Work	263
New Directions in Memory Studies	264
Recognition, Recall, and Forgetting	265
For the Classroom	268
Metacognition	269
Metacognitive Knowledge	269
Metacognitive Experiences	270
Decision Making and Reasoning	270
Representativeness	270
For the Classroom	271
Cognition Across Cultures	274

Focus: How Much Do You Remember?	*239*
Issues and Answers: The Role of the Computer	*240*
Focus: Would You Make a Good Eyewitness?	*243*
Teacher-Student Interactions: Classroom Implications of Cognitive Psychology	*248*
Focus: Structure and Memory	*259*
Teacher-Student Interactions: Information Processing in the Classroom	*260*
Focus: What Would You Do?	*269*
Teacher-Student Interactions: Cognition in the Classroom	*271*

Applications and Reflections
Chapter Highlights	**275**
Connections	**276**
Getting the Picture and Drawing Relationships	**276**
Personal Journal	**277**
Key Terms	**277**

9 Thinking Skills and Problem-Solving Strategies 278

Thinking Skills	280
Critical Thinking: A Definition	280
Intelligence and Thinking	280
Sternberg's Triarchic Model of Intelligence	281
Gardner and Multiple Intelligences	282
Perkins' Thinking Frames and Enculturation of Mindware	284
Thinking Skills: An Analysis	285
The Bloom Taxonomy	286
Costa and Thinking Skills	289
Thinking Skills and Multicultural Students	290
Selected Thinking Skills Programs	291
Practical Intelligence for School	291
Instrumental Enrichment	294
The CoRT Thinking Program	295
Problem Solving	296
Problem-Solving Strategies	300
The Good Problem Solver	301

Different Cultures—Different
Perspectives   302
The DUPE Model   303
Determining the Nature of a Problem   303
Understanding the Nature of the
Problem   306
Planning the Solution   312
The Role of Memory   313
Evaluating the Solution   316
The Creative Student   318
Teaching Problem-Solving Techniques   319
Helping Students to Transfer Their
Learning   319
For the Classroom   321

*Teacher-Student Interactions: Intelligence and
Thinking Skills Exercises*   *292*
*Teacher-Student Interactions: Teaching Students
to Construct Graphic Representations*   *308*
Focus: Social Problem Solving   *320*
*Teacher-Student Interactions: Using Problem-Solving
Strategies in the Classroom*   *323*

Applications and Reflections
Chapter Highlights   **324**
Connections   **325**
**Getting the Picture and Drawing
Relationships**   **326**
Personal Journal   **327**
Key Terms   **327**

**10 Motivation in the
Classroom**   **328**

Motivation: Meaning and Myths   330
What Are the Myths About Motivation?   330
Motivation to Learn   331
Intrinsic and Extrinsic Motivation   332
What Causes Motivation?   334
Humanistic Psychology and Motivation   334
Cognitive Psychology and Motivation   336
Achievement and Motivation   336
Attribution Theory and Motivation   337
Behavioral Psychology and Motivation   339
Social Cognitive Learning and
Motivation   340
What Affects Students' Motivation?   342
Anxiety   342
Attitudes   344
Curiosity   346
Locus of Control   347
Learned Helplessness   348
Self-Efficacy and Motivation   350
Cooperative Learning and Motivation   354
Motivation and Multicultural Students   355
Educational Implications of Motivation   357
The Beginning of Learning   357
During Learning   359
When Learning Ends   360

*Issues and Answers: Should Teachers Be Generous
When Grading Their Students' Work?*   *333*
Teacher-Student Interactions: Motivation and Learning *342*
*Issues and Answers: Will a Multicultural Curriculum
Better Motivate Minority Children?*   *356*
Teacher-Student Interactions: Motivation and Learning *358*

Applications and Reflections
Chapter Highlights   **361**
Connections   **362**
**Getting the Picture and Drawing
Relationships**   **363**
Personal Journal   **364**
Key Terms   **364**

section 4

design and management
of classroom instruction

**11 Planning for Essential
Learning Outcomes**   **366**

Educational Standards   368
Standards for Disciplines   368
Deciding on Educational Objectives   368
Classroom Objectives   369
What Place Schooling?   370
The Role of Objectives in Instruction   371
Why Bother with Objectives   371
Descriptions, Goals, and Objectives   373
Goals and Multicultural Students   374
What Are Good Objectives?   376
Writing Acceptable Objectives   377
Sources of Objectives   378
Instructional Objectives and School
Subjects   380
Reading   381
Mathematics   385
Science   388

Focus: High-Achieving African American Schools *370*
Focus: An Example of Task Analysis   *374*
Focus: Teachers, Students, and Objectives   *375*
Teacher-Student Interactions: Thinking About Objectives *381*
Focus: How Clear Objectives Can Help   *382*
*Issues and Answers: Should Schools Replace a Skills
Approach to Teaching Reading with a Whole
Language Approach?*   *384*
*Teacher-Student Interactions: Objectives in the
Classroom*   *391*

Applications and Reflections
Chapter Highlights   **391**
Connections   **392**
**Getting the Picture and Drawing
Relationships**   **393**
Personal Journal   **393**
Key Terms   **393**

12 Effective Teaching Strategies and the Design of Instruction   394

The Meaning of Teaching   396
What Makes an Effective Teacher?   396
Direct Instruction   399
Indirect Instruction   403
Teaching and Subject Matter   408

The Design of Instruction   410
Skinner and the Technology
of Teaching   411
Markle and Programed Instruction   414
Gagne and Instructional Design   415

Adapting Instruction to the Individual
Differences of Learners   418
Bloom and School Learning   418
Students and Study Skills   421
The Role of Homework   424
Adapting Instruction in a Multicultural
Classroom   425
Teacher Expectations   427

Focus: Multicultural Teaching   398
Issues and Answers: Will Reflective Teaching Lead
to Higher Student Achievement Scores?   401
Focus: To Be "Hunterized" or Not?   403
Focus: Teaching and Learning—Bruner in the
Classroom   407
Focus: The Instructional Environment   409
Teacher-Student Interactions: The Functions
of Teaching   416
Issues and Answers: Can Homework Bring Home
and School Closer Together?   426
Teacher-Student Interactions: Adapting Your Teaching   428

Applications and Reflections
Chapter Highlights   429
Connections   430
Getting the Picture and Drawing
Relationships   430
Personal Journal   431
Key Terms   431

13 Classroom Management: Organization and Control   432

Management Concerns in the Classroom   434
Preventing Classroom Problems   434
Time and Teachers: The Carroll Model   435
Developmental Tasks and Classroom
Management   436
Management and Control of Problem
Students   438

Life in the Classroom   439
When You Close the Classroom Door   439
Classroom Activities   441
The QAIT Model   443
Classroom Contexts   445

Managing the Classroom   447
Rule Setting and Classroom
Procedures   447
Rules and Classroom Activities   448
Management and Control   449
Aggression in the Classroom   449
Searching for the Causes of Classroom
Problems   451

Methods of Control   451
Misbehavior in the Classroom   452
Multicultural Students and Discipline   453
Effective Teacher Behaviors   454
Using Behavior Modification   455

Don't Cause Any Problems Yourself   467
Teacher-Parent Collaboration   468
You Are Not Alone   469

Focus: Classroom Activities to Manage   435
Focus: Student Engagement During Class   442
Focus: The Native American Student: Core Values
and the Teaching Process   446
Focus: The Bully   450
Issues and Answers: Do Discipline Programs
Promote Ethical Behavior?   452
Focus: Using Behavior Modification   461
Focus: Glasser's Control Theory   463
Teacher-Student Interactions: Maintaining
Order in the Classroom   471

Applications and Reflections
Chapter Highlights   472
Connections   473
Getting the Picture and Drawing
Relationships   474
Personal Journal   475
Key Terms   475

14 Teaching and Technology   476

What Is Educational Technology?   478
Questions to Answer When
Considering Technology   478

A Brief History of Technology
in Education   480

How Is Technology Currently Used
in Classrooms?   481
Quantitative Aspects   481
Qualitative Aspects   484
Why Don't More Teachers
Use Technology?   485

Students' Perceptions of Technology
in the Classroom   488
Attitude Surveys   488
Novelty Effects?   488
Gender Differences in Attitudes   489

Types and Uses of Technology
in Education   489
Administrative and Managerial Uses   491

Audiovisual Aids for Instruction 491
Teaching of the Technology 493
Computer-Assisted Instruction 494
Using Technology to Teach Thinking 498
Intelligent Tutoring Systems 501
Multimedia Uses 503
Recent Developments in Educational
Technology 506

Issues in Technology Use 509
Access 509
Security 509
Role of the Teacher 510
Selection of Hardware and Software 511
Classroom Set-Up of Technology 511
Effect of Computers on Social
Interactions 512
Consideration of Individual Differences 512

Focus: A Computer Glossary 479
Focus: A Brief History of Educational Technology 482
*Issues and Answers: Are Today's Teachers Prepared to Teach
in a Technological Classroom?* 486
*Issues and Answers: Will the "Information Superhighway"
Change the Nature of Teaching and Learning?* 508
*Issues and Answers: Will Increased Emphasis on Educational
Technology Further Widen the Technology Gap?* 510
Focus: Selection of Software 512

Applications and Reflections
Chapter Highlights 513
Connections 515
**Getting the Picture and Drawing
Relationships** 515
Personal Journal 516
Key Terms 516

section 5

assessing learning
and evaluating education

**15 Teacher-Constructed
Tests and Performance
Assessment Methods** 518

Assessment: Terminology
and Assumptions 520
Uses and Users of Classroom
Assessment Information 521
Multicultural Students and Testing 522

Integrating Learning and Assessment 522
Teachers and Testing 523

Methods and Technical Issues in the
Assessment of Students 524
Teacher-Constructed Tests 525
Planning a Teacher-Constructed Test 529

Alternative Methods and New
Assessment Trends 536
Behavioral Assessment Fundamentals 537
Curriculum-Based Assessment (CBA) 539
Authentic/Performance Assessment 540

Using Data From Teacher-Constructed
Tests and Classroom Assessments 547
Marking 548
Grading 549
Reporting 551

Research on Teachers' Judgments of
Students' Achievement 552

Helping Students Take Tests 552

*Focus: A Teacher's Professional Role and
Responsibilities for Student Assessment* 524
Focus: Essay Tests—Pros and Cons 533
*Teacher-Student Interactions: Helping Students
Prepare for Essay Tests* 535
*Teacher-Student Interactions: Helping Students
Prepare for Objective Tests* 537
Focus: Conducting a Classroom Observation 540
Focus: Writing Comments on Tests 550

Applications and Reflections
Chapter Highlights 553
Connections 556
**Getting the Picture and Drawing
Relationships** 556
Personal Journal 557
Key Terms 557

**16 Standardized Tests
and Rating Scales
in the Classroom** 558

A School's Testing Program 560

Standardized Tests 561
Developing a Standardized Test 562

Types of Standardized Tests 564
Standardized Achievement Tests 564
Standardized Aptitude Tests 566
Behavior Rating Scales 573
Preschool Screening 576

Interpreting Standardized Test Scores 579
Kinds of Scores 579

Using Standardized Tests 583
Educational Applications
of Standardized Testing 583
Multicultural Students and
Standardized Testing 584
Common Criticisms of Standardized
Tests 584
Best Practices 585

Focus: Testing Young Children 568
*Teacher-Student Interactions: Communicating
Test Results* 585

Applications and Reflections

Chapter Highlights	**586**
Connections	**587**
Getting the Picture and Drawing	
Relationships	**587**
Personal Journal	**588**
Key Terms	**588**
Appendix: The Code of Fair	
Testing Practices in Education	**589**

Glossary   591
References   599
Credits   615
Name Index   617
Subject Index   623

Free Copy

preface

Teaching and learning are complex and exciting processes that bring people together in ways that can change their lives. Educational psychologists have been at the center of teaching-learning interactions for nearly a century. Their theoretical and applied work has provided educators significant guidance toward the goals of effective teaching and effective learning.

Individuals entering the education profession are often both excited and anxious, and they may have many questions and many ideas about teaching and learning. What shall I teach? How shall I teach it? Will my students like me? What if I have a discipline problem right away? Even experienced teachers approach that first class meeting of a new year with similar, though perhaps less intense, feelings and concerns.

We are aware that a dynamic field such as educational psychology must not only incorporate vital facts, but also offer teachers data and teaching suggestions for the changes that any society inevitably experiences. Because more children of widely different backgrounds are entering our classrooms, teachers must be prepared to recognize and understand the values, beliefs, and behaviors of these students and their families. Thus, with this second edition of *Educational Psychology: Effective Teaching, Effective Learning,* we have added an entire chapter on diversity in the classroom (chapter 3), and continue to weave throughout most chapters material on multicultural issues and teaching applications. We also believe that technology in the form of computers, videodisks, and hypermedia is impacting teaching and learning in many classrooms. Therefore, we have added to this new edition an entire chapter on technology and teaching (chapter 14).

Educational psychology textbooks provide insights into the teaching-learning process and student behavior, as well as research data, theory, and illustrations, all concerned with actual classroom application of psychological principles. Consequently, individuals taking an educational psychology course and reading an educational psychology textbook should enter a classroom with greater confidence in their ability to teach and their understanding of the learning process.

To accomplish these goals, we have presented the basic principles of effective teaching and effective learning in a book that has a balanced (cognitive and behavioral) theoretical orientation. Becoming a successful teacher depends to a considerable extent upon acquiring an understanding of students, of how they learn, and of the most effective means of teaching. Since teaching is reaching, that is, reaching students, we—the authors of *Educational Psychology: Effective Teaching, Effective Learning*—have attempted to present the latest and most pertinent data available, to apply those theories that best explain particular classroom situations, and to consistently illustrate with classroom examples how these theories and data "work." In this way, we provide readers with a practical and useful book, based largely on empirical research, that will provide knowledge and guidance now and in the future when teaching others is their priority!

Organization of the Text

Writing an educational textbook that is both practical and useful demands that certain decisions be made. What is to be presented and how is it to be organized? Answering these questions forced us to select and organize the most pertinent and critical data around the core concepts of educational psychology. These core concepts, which are the heart of educational psychology, and the chapters that include them are as follows:

Introduction to Educational Psychology
1. Educational Psychology: Teaching and Learning
2. Research and Educational Psychology
3. Diversity in the Classroom: Culture, Class, and Gender

The Development of Students
4. Cognitive and Language Development
5. Psychosocial and Moral Development
6. Exceptional Students

Learning Theories and Practices
7. Behavioral Psychology and Learning
8. Cognitive Psychology and Learning
9. Thinking Skills and Problem-Solving Strategies
10. Motivation in the Classroom

Design and Management of Classroom Instruction
11. Planning for Essential Learning Outcomes
12. Effective Teaching Strategies and the Design of Instruction
13. Classroom Management: Organization and Control
14. Teaching and Technology

Assessing Learning and Evaluating Education
15. Teacher-Constructed Tests and Performance Assessment Methods
16. Standardized Tests and Rating Scales in the Classroom

Note the emphasis on students, learning, and teaching. We believe that this organization helps the reader to focus on *the learner* and development, *the learner* and learning, *the learner* and teaching, and the assessment of *the learner* by teachers. Thus, the book stresses the interactions between students as learners and teachers and contextualizes these interactions in an increasingly diverse, technological place called school.

Content of the Text

Any text's content must not only present the basic principles of the discipline, but also reflect changes in the field. To address both of these concerns, we have presented in five sections what we think are the most important elements of educational psychology. *Section one* is an overview of the field and demonstrates the important link between educational psychology and teaching. We have also included a strong research component to help readers evaluate the studies that appear throughout the book and judge the value of the suggestions that have been made about improving schools and instruction. To conclude this section, we offer a **NEW** chapter on diversity. This chapter highlights the important role that diversity can play in the schooling process and takes a close look at issues associated with class, culture, and gender differences. Many of these issues are discussed in the remainder of the book.

Section two is devoted to a careful analysis of how students develop, from the early years that can be so important to those later years in which they prepare for higher education or an occupation. Teachers are often told to present material that is "biologically and psychologically appropriate." We help readers follow this guideline by introducing cognitive, linguistic, moral, and psychosocial data on various age levels. We then use these developmental perspectives to examine important school relationships, for example, those between students and teachers, students and students, and teachers and parents. Finally, given the current emphasis on the inclusion of students with disabilities in virtually all classrooms, we conclude this section with a detailed chapter on childhood exceptionalities.

Section three takes the reader into the world of learning, in both theory and practice. Here we examine the details of behavioral and cognitive theories of learning and their implications for the classroom. A major portion of this section is devoted to methods of teaching students how to improve their thinking skills, essential both to improving their academic performance and to transferring classroom learning to their daily lives. As part of the chapter on thinking skills, we present a problem-solving model (called DUPE) that provides students a meaningful method to attack problems they meet in and out of the classroom. Needless to say, little or no learning will occur without motivated students; therefore, we conclude this section with a chapter focusing on several pertinent motivational theories and practices for the classroom.

Section four concentrates on teaching and classroom management. In a sense, *Educational Psychology: Effective Teaching, Effective Learning* represents a hierarchy: knowing how students develop helps teachers to select appropriate materials and learning techniques. Teachers can then encourage their students to become more effective thinkers and problem solvers, and can base their teaching strategies and methods of classroom management upon this knowledge. The section opens with a discussion of instructional objectives, since clearly formulated, precise objectives lead to meaningful teaching. Once teachers have a firm idea of what they want to accomplish and what they think their students should achieve, they can then devise suitable teaching strategies. Teaching strategies are effective to the extent that both teachers and their students know what is expected (for class work and for personal behavior). This leads us to an analysis of the most productive means of managing a classroom. Successful classroom management is most likely to occur when teachers are aware of the individual differences of their students, from slow to gifted, from withdrawn to outgoing. In addition to managing both students and instructional content, educators today are expected to use technology (e.g., computers, videotapes, hypermedia, etc.) to enhance communication and instruction. Thus, the last chapter of this section, **NEW** for this edition, focuses on teaching with technology.

In the final section of the book, we address the issue of assessment, both teacher-made and standardized. Given some of the controversy surrounding testing in our classrooms and society, we have included both traditional and innovative methods of assessment, presenting as wide a range of options as possible. Since assessment is a critical part of good teaching and learning, readers should know the best techniques available for the optimal assessment of their students. In the two final chapters, readers are provided current information on performance assessment, preschool screening, and classroom observations.

Pedagogical Features of the Text

The most important pedagogical goal of our work has been to help readers master the contents of this text in as uncomplicated and meaningful a manner as possible. To accomplish this task, we have built a number of helpful features into each chapter.

• *A chapter outline.* The major topics of each chapter are presented initially, so that readers may quickly find the subject they need. This tactic also aids retention and is an efficient method for reviewing content.

• *Boxes.* Rather than present boxed material randomly, we have designed three types of boxed material that expand on the text under discussion in a manner calculated to aid student retention. The three types of boxes are as follows:

1. Focus boxes
2. Teacher-Student Interaction boxes
3. Issues and Answers boxes

The Focus boxes provide opportunities to share specific teaching tips, applications of theory and research to classroom activities, and updates on a wide range of multicultural and technical issues associated with teaching, learning, and the schooling process.

The Teacher-Student Interaction boxes are often located at the ends of chapters, after discussion of major topics. These boxes suggest techniques for applying the text's content to classroom situations. Important statements from a chapter are repeated, and specific examples are given of ways that content could be used at various grade levels. We believe these boxes can help readers understand how the chapter's theoretical and factual material can be translated into classroom usage.

The Issues and Answers boxes highlight alternative perspectives on issues such as grading, use of punishment, and use of intelligence tests. The purpose of these boxes is to stimulate students to think about the range of reasoned perspectives that exists on salient issues in education and psychology.

• *Embedded Questions*. **NEW** to the second edition: Throughout each chapter, in the margins, readers will be confronted with five or six questions designed to stimulate them to think about how they would use certain knowledge or how they feel about a particular issue or teaching technique. In most cases, there are no "right" answers to these questions; they are designed to encourage readers to personalize the material they are reading by invoking their own perspectives concerning a number of issues.

• *Applications and Reflections*. **NEW** to the second edition: At the end of each chapter, readers will find a section designed to stimulate integration of information and summarization of major points. This section is called Applications and Reflections and consists of five subsections: Chapter Highlights, Connections, Getting the Picture and Drawing Relationships, Personal Journal, and Key Terms. The Chapter Highlights subsection provides lists of summary statements that are grouped according to the major topics of the chapter. This subsection enables readers to review the chapter quickly and thoroughly by turning to the chapter outline and then checking this against the chapter highlights, to determine how successful they have been in recalling the pertinent material of the chapter and how it could be used in the classroom. The Key Terms subsection provides readers a list of terms that are essential to understanding the chapter's ideas and suggestions. These terms are highlighted when used in the context of the chapter, and also appear in the book's glossary. The other three subsections of the Applications and Reflections section are designed to stimulate readers to apply and summarize information they have read by writing, outlining, or drawing it. The more readers are able to personalize what they have read, the more meaningful and memorable the information is likely to be for them!

Supplementary Materials for the Instructor

We have worked with the publisher and a group of very talented individuals to put together a quality set of supplementary materials to assist instructors and students who use this text. These include

• *Instructor's Manual.* The key to this teaching package was created by Joan Littlefield, one of the text's authors. This flexible planner provides a variety of useful tools to enhance your teaching efforts, reduce your workload, and increase your enjoyment of teaching. For each chapter of the text, the manual provides an outline, overview, learning objectives, and key terms. These items also are contained in the Student Study Guide. The manual also contains lecture suggestions, classroom activities, discussion questions, integrative essay questions, suggestions for using the Educational Psychology video series, a film list, and a transparency guide.

• *The Test Item File* was constructed by James Wollack and Mark Szymanski, with contributions from Joan Littlefield. This comprehensive test bank includes over one thousand multiple choice and true/false questions that are keyed to the text and learning objectives.

• *The Student Study Guide* was also created by Joan Littlefield. For each chapter of the text, the student is provided with an outline, an overview, learning objectives, key terms, a guided review, study questions (with answers provided for self-testing), and integration and application questions. The study guide begins with a section on developing good study habits, to help students study more effectively and efficiently.

• *The Educational Psychology Transparency Set* also is available to adopters of this text in the Instructor's Manual. The set consists of 40 transparency masters of key tables and graphics from the text. The images have been carefully chosen to provide comprehensive coverage of the major topics in *Educational Psychology* and to aid the instructor in explaining intricate and complex concepts presented in the text.

• *Brown & Benchmark MicroTest 3.0* is a powerful but easy-to-use test-generating program by Chariot Software Group. MicroTest is available for DOS, Windows, and Macintosh. With MicroTest, instructors can easily select questions from the Test Item File and print tests and answer keys. Instructors can also customize questions, headings, and instructions; add or import their own questions; and print tests in a choice of printer-supported fonts. Contact your local Brown & Benchmark sales representative for more information.

• *Brown & Benchmark customized Psychology and Education Reader,* developed by authors Stephen Elliott and Thomas Kratochwill, allows instructors to select journal or magazine articles from a menu of over 60 articles. These readings can be custom printed and bound into an attractive 8.5- by 11-inch book, giving instructors an opportunity to create their own student readers. Many of the articles in this customized package are referenced in *Educational Psychology,* and thus it provides an efficient way to extend the depth of coverage of a particular area.

• *Our custom publishing service* will also allow you to have your own notes, handouts, or other classroom materials printed and bound for your course use very inexpensively. See your Brown & Benchmark representative for details.

• *Annual Editions: Educational Psychology* is designed to provide current, carefully selected articles from some of the most respected magazines, newspapers, and journals published. Includes articles by psychologists, educators, researchers, and writers. Articles from this source are referenced by an icon in the text margin, so instructors can easily find additional reading material for students in targeted areas.

• *Videotapes.* The final component of the supplementary materials package for *Educational Psychology* is its newest and most exciting component: an integrative series of five videotapes produced by Tim Connell and Robert Clasen in cooperation with the authors. These videotapes draw upon the book's knowledge base, and bring to life the content from each of the major sections of the text. The videotapes provide students with opportunities to observe a variety of classroom practices and to hear from some of the leading educational psychology researchers in the country. The Instructor's Video Guide, written by Joan Bissell, helps instructors use the videos in the most effective ways possible.

Acknowledgments

We would particularly like to express our thanks to our editors, Sue Pulvermacher-Alt and Suzanne Guinn, for their insights and support during the writing of this book. We would also like to thank the many others at Brown & Benchmark who contributed their expertise, and the reviewers of the text.

Reviewers

Mark E. Ehrlich
University of Wisconsin–Madison

Etta B. Miller
Taylor University

Timothy Reagan
University of Connecticut

Marianne K. Dove
Youngstown State University

Joan S. Bissell
University of California–Irvine

Robert Lucking
Old Dominion University

Thomas G. Getso
Northern Arizona University

David S. Dungan
Emporia State University

Malinda Hendricks Green
University of Central Oklahoma

Iva W. Trottier
Concordia College

Hunter Downing
Southeastern Louisiana University

Mary Ann Chapko
Indiana University Northwest

David Larry Smith
Florida Atlantic University

Brian E. Butler
Queen's University

Karen D. Carpenter
Coastal Carolina University

Dale Schunk
University of North Carolina–Chapel Hill

Douglas L. Herbster
Montana State University

Marianne K. Dove
Mount Union College

Joyce Alexander
Indiana University

Lawrence R. Rogien
Indiana University

Libby Street
Central Washington University

section 1

introduction to educational psychology

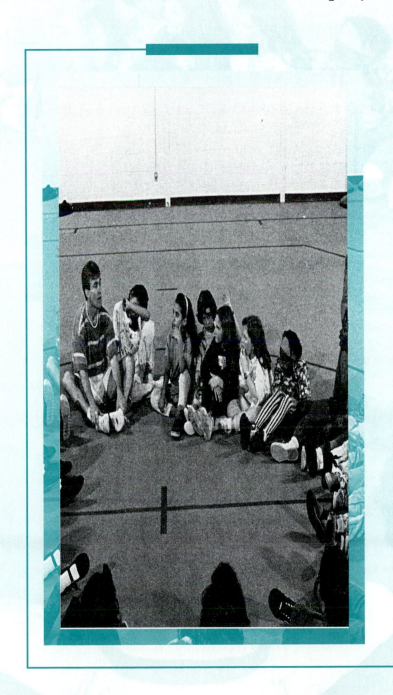

Donna Peterson was nervous. In spite of repeated warnings to herself to relax, her stomach was churning and her legs were shaking. Classes were to begin the day after tomorrow and her anxiety level was rising with each day. She had reported to her school, the Junior High West, for a day of orientation meetings. She had been pleased to see that construction in the cafeteria had been completed and that everything had been freshly painted. She had listened as her principal, Joseph Allen, described the changing nature of the school population.

The Junior High West was a medium-sized school located in a large suburban town (population 60,000) about ten miles away from the

rant, but I'd love to know what kinds of problems they have with their students."

The meeting was held in an attractive classroom on the first floor. It was a congenial group, with the veteran teachers trying to put the new arrivals at ease. Kim Fraser smiled at them and said, "You heard what Joe Allen said yesterday: our numbers are growing and reflect our changing population. So, in a sense, we're all beginners this year."

"Before we begin talking about any issues you want to raise, I'd like to mention that there will be a series of workshops devoted to cultural affairs beginning in the first week of October. We're all agreed that the more we know

chapter 1

educational psychology: teaching and learning

state capital. Mr. Allen had explained that the student body was changing. The school had been predominantly white, with a small percentage of African Americans. Now, there were more Hispanic and Asian students and an increasing number of African American students, while the number of white students remained fairly constant.

"Well, here I am," she thought, "female, white, 22 years old, a graduate of what is considered an excellent teacher preparation university, with a major in social studies." Donna had achieved high grades in her program and completed a particularly satisfying practicum (student teaching assignment). "With all of this, why am I nervous?" she asked herself. "At least tomorrow should help."

The next day, the day before the opening of school, four experienced teachers with excellent reputations would meet at the principal's request with the new teachers. The experienced teachers were Kim Fraser, who taught English; Pete Johnson, a science teacher; Alice West, another social studies teacher; and Kevin Roche, who taught math.

Donna had enjoyed the classroom when she did her student teaching; this was different, however. Now she was on her own, with no regular teacher who could step in if needed. She loved teaching and working with young people and wanted to do well in her new job. "What should I ask them? I don't want to seem too igno-

about our students' backgrounds, the better we'll understand them."

"Now, what about some specific topics you'd like to discuss?"

Donna was the first to reply: "I know that I've thought a lot about myself as a teacher— but what about the students' learning process? Can you really tell when learning happens? I don't mean just test scores."

Kevin Roche looked at Donna for a moment and said, "You know, Donna, you're one of the few beginning teachers I've seen over the years who has thought at all about students as learners. Usually new teachers are just concerned with themselves."

Donna flushed at the praise and told Kevin, "Well, it finally dawned on me that I won't be the only one in that classroom. I would really like to feel that I'm accomplishing something worthwhile."

Alice West, another of the senior teachers, joined in and said, "One approach you might consider, Donna, is to keep in mind that you want your students to *understand*. Not just repeat facts."

The other teachers responded enthusiastically, and Kim Fraser made several suggestions. Try to explain things at their level; clarify as much as possible; give your students open-ended tasks that force them to use in a different manner what they've learned."

"Right," said Pete Johnson. "If we've all learned anything in our course work, it's that

How to Use This Book 4
So You Want to Teach 6
What It Means to Teach 6
Who Becomes a Teacher? 8
Teaching and Educational
  Issues 8

Teaching as an Art and as a
Science 11
Teaching as an Art 11
Teaching as a Science 12
Questions That Teachers
  Ask 13
Our Multicultural
  Classrooms 14

Effective Schools 17
A Place Called School 18
Effective Schools—Effective
  Teachers 19

Educational Psychology: The
Core Concepts 20
Educational Psychology and the
  Classroom 21

Applications and
Reflections 23

educational psychology *The
application of psychology to
the study of development,
learning, motivation,
instruction, and related issues.*

children don't all learn the same way; they're at various developmental levels. And they're motivated by different things. Ask yourself this question: What's the best way to bring your students into this process and make it exciting for them?"

As Pete talked, Donna noticed the other teachers nodding agreement and she was struck by their sincerity and their desire to help their students. ▪

Donna Peterson's thoughts mirror the concerns of most beginning teachers. Worried about the opening of classes, they focus on several common problems of inexperienced teachers: classroom management, school routine, working with parents, and particularly, discipline. Will students like me? Will I be able to control them? Is it possible to do both? Can I help students with backgrounds different from mine?

The beginning teacher realizes that contemporary culture affects the education of our youth. Today's teachers must be prepared to work competently and harmoniously with a growing number of multicultural students entering our classrooms, who have unique experiences that influence their educational lives. This range of educational settings serves to make teaching in the nineties both complex and challenging.

It is an exciting time to teach; our nation wants good teachers in the classroom to improve the quality of education for a rapidly changing population. To have an idea of the cultural backgrounds of America's students, consider these facts. The national population grew by 9.8 percent during the 1980s, but in that period the number of African Americans increased by 13.2 percent, that of Native Americans by 37.9 percent, that of Hispanics by 53 percent, and that of Asian-Pacific Islanders by 107.8 percent (Hodgkinson, 1993). Thirty percent of our school-age children are members of a racial or ethnic minority group.

Pointing to a need for teachers to rethink their strategies, Hodgkinson (1993) noted that children come to school today with different diets, different religions, different individual and group loyalties, different music, different interests, and different languages. The excitement, the challenges, and the opportunities leap out at us. One of the goals of your work in educational psychology is to help you to be so well-prepared to teach that you can be sufficiently flexible to develop strategies to meet the needs of your diverse students.

Before delving into teaching and learning, we want to share key features of this book that will facilitate your learning. We then begin to address these issues by examining what it means to teach. Good teaching doesn't just happen. You must be part artist and part scientist. Next we look at what today's schools are like. Finally, you will be asked to think about educational psychology by exploring the link between educational psychology and teacher effectiveness.

Speculating about the definition of educational psychology, Harre and Lamb (1983) stated that it is too simple to say that educational psychology is the psychology of learning and teaching in school. Rather, it is concerned with the development and education of children from birth to adulthood. For nearly a century there has been no common agreement on a definition of educational psychology. The most widely accepted definition is that **educational psychology** involves the application of psychology to the study of development, learning, motivation, instruction, and any related issues that occur in educational settings. After a review of the historical literature in educational psychology, Glover and Ronning (1987, p. 14) suggested that educational psychology includes topics that span human development, individual differences, measurement, learning, motivation, and humanistic views of education, and is both data- and theory-driven.

When you finish your reading of this chapter, you should be able to

- define educational psychology
- identify the major issues facing teachers today
- describe qualities that contribute to excellent teaching
- assess your expectations for teaching
- compare the views of teaching as an art and as a science
- evaluate the relationship between effective teachers and effective schools

How to Use This Book

We have designed this book to influence your learning and to stimulate your thinking. And although you have read about the many features of *Educational Psychology: Effective Teaching, Effective Learning* in the preface, we want to be certain that you obtain everything you need from reading this text. Consequently, at this point, we ask you to return to the Preface and once again familiarize yourself with the organization of each chapter. In particular, note the relevant vignettes in the chapter opening that lead into the subject of the chapter. While they are fictional, they represent actual incidents that we have experienced in our teaching careers. Note also how you can use the organizational features of each chapter that are shown here. The Applications and Reflections section at the end of each chapter helps students summarize and apply chapter content. In chapter 1, this section begins on page 23.

Visuals

Visuals placed throughout the book help readers understand and apply concepts presented in the text. Visuals include line art, photographs, tables, and cartoons

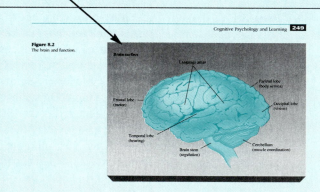

Figure 8.2
The brain and function.

THE BRAIN AND THINKING

Annual Edition

We begin by asking a fundamental question: Can there be learning, developing, and thinking without a biological substrate? Although no one would argue against this premise, considerable controversy arises when we speculate about the relationship between brain and mind, that is, thinking and cognition. For an overview of basic brain anatomy, examine figure 8.2, noting the relationship of location in the brain to function. Also note the basic brain areas, identified by lobe; function has also been assigned to the various areas.

Brain and Mind: The Relationship

Until recently, extreme positions have been the rule when it comes to discussing the brain-mind relationship. Philosophical advocates virtually have ignored the existence of the brain, and more currently physiologists and biologists have insisted that the mind is nothing more than a system of connecting neurons. Rose (1987) raised this question: How are data transformed as they pass in a series of electrical signals along particular nerves to central brain regions, where they interact with one another, thus producing certain kinds of responses? One attempt to answer this question was made by Alexander Luria.

Luria's Work

The Russian neuropsychologist Alexander Luria (1980) proposed a less extreme but still neurological view. Intellectual activity begins with analyzing the conditions of the task and then identifying its most important elements. In an example, Luria (1973) traced the thinking process through several stages.

- Thinking begins only when a person is motivated to solve a problem for which there is no ready solution. When students recognize problems and realize that they have the tools to solve them, their motivation remains high.
- The second stage is not an attempt to solve the problem immediately. Rather, it entails the restraint of impulsive responses. The individual must carefully investigate any possible solutions. We have commented previously on the need to identify a problem's basic elements.

Icons

You'll notice *icons* in the margin; they reference other materials that are available for additional information. For example, you may be referred to an article in the current *Annual Edition of Educational Psychology,* or a segment in the videos available with the text.

Key terms

Definitions of key terms are in the margins. Be sure to read these definitions. Think of them as a vocabulary that will help you to grasp the full meanings of the topics under discussion.

Boxes

The Focus boxes and Issues and Answers boxes involve you with the chapter's contents and help you examine topics from different perspectives. For example, the Issues and Answers box in this chapter discusses Total Quality Management (TQM), a topic that some educators endorse and others question. Our intent is to cause you to think about the quality of our schools by introducing a novel viewpoint. The Teacher-Student Interaction boxes suggest specific ways for you to actually implement the topics you're reading about in the classroom. All these aids should help you in your understanding of teaching and learning.

(Sample page 17 excerpt)

Educational Psychology: Teaching and Learning **17**

EFFECTIVE SCHOOLS

TQM (Total Quality Management)
Name for a conceptual framework for understanding the complexity of systems.

As mentioned earlier in the chapter, "quality," "quality education," and "quality schools" are terms that appear more and more frequently in any discussion of our schools. Sometimes referred to as **TQM (Total Quality Management)**, this concept is usually linked to the work of W. Edwards Deming in Japan following World War II. Deming helped Japanese business leaders move from carelessly turning out shoddy products to a level of quality production that inspired worldwide envy. With the present concerted effort to improve our schools, more and more educators are turning to TQM.

The TQM approach, however, cannot simply be applied as a panacea for all educational problems (Bonstingl, 1992). Deming himself warned those interested in TQM against merely imitating what worked in a business setting and applying these ideas without modification to an educational setting. There are, nevertheless, aspects of TQM that are particularly relevant to educational psychology: acknowledgment of the importance of intrinsic motivation, an emphasis on process, and recognition of individual differences. All of these attitudes contribute to effective teaching and effective schools.

(Note: At several points in each chapter, we introduce current issues that are demanding the attention of today's teachers and educational psychologists. For example, the issue of TQM, discussed in the following box, concerns both teachers and educational psychologists because of its implications for teaching, learning, and motivation. In such boxes we present positive and negative arguments with the expectation that you and your instructor can use them as a basis for discussion.)

Issues & Answers

Is Total Quality Management the Solution for Effective Schools?

As the search for answers to questions about the effectiveness of our schools continues, more and more educators are turning to new ideas: cooperative learning, authentic assessment, portfolio assessment, thinking skills, and, more recently, Total Quality Management. Some educators are attracted to this last concept because it offers a conceptual framework that helps them to understand a complex system (Brandt, 1992). Educational psychologists are examining it carefully because of its implications for programs that address individual differences, intrinsic and extrinsic motivation, and methods of assessments.

Issue
TQM is just another of the "fads" that intrigue educators.

Answer: Pro To follow the principles of TQM, teachers must change many traditional practices. For example, they must abandon their dependence on grades. Many teachers will find this difficult, if not impossible. Will administrators be willing to devote time and precious resources to the commitment that must be made? Although there may be potential in the plan, the many obstacles it faces make it unlikely that TQM will succeed.

Answer: Con Our schools cannot continue as they are now. TQM can provide many of the answers that we are

presently searching for. It has succeeded in business and, with modifications, can improve the quality of learning in our schools. There will be problems; there will be delays. A key element obviously is the teaching force. If our teachers can be persuaded of its value through workshops, seminars, and modeling, then TQM has an excellent chance of bringing change to our schools.

Issue
TQM lends itself to a greater understanding of how motivation functions in a classroom.

Answer: Pro Total quality management would lead to a lessening of teachers' reliance on extrinsic motivation (stars, grades, etc.), and place much more emphasis on intrinsic motivation. Extrinsic motivation can be destructive because it fosters competition and hurts those who are excluded.

Answer: Con Reliance on intrinsic motivation quickly leads to a lack of attention, faulty classroom control, and poor learning. The assumption that students will come to every class enthusiastic and eager to learn is simply not realistic. A carefully planned sequence of rewards that addresses specific behaviors can lead eventually to intrinsic motivation.

(Sample page 83 excerpt)

Cognitive and Language Development **83**

Focus — What African American Children Consider Important

Although students attend to both the physical and the social aspects of their environments, they seem to prefer one more than the other, and their preference depends on the guidelines of their culture (Wigginton, 1992; Banks & Banks, 1993). The urban environment and the social milieu in which African Americans develop seem to predispose them toward the social elements of their environment; this then affects their school performance. Understanding the influence of this orientation on the achievement of these students, we need to examine the mechanisms by which students organize their lives.

Three categories seem to be significant:
- the physical environment that a family uses to shape a child's interactions with symbols and objects;
- the interpersonal relations that provide feedback to students for their expectations and performances;
- the emotional and motivational climate that influences a student's personality and behavior (Shade, 1987).

Within these categories, visual forms and family interaction patterns are particularly relevant. For example, research suggests that the visual forms within African American homes are usually those of people (Martin Luther King, Jr., Jesse Jackson, John and Robert Kennedy). Middle-class white homes seem to display more abstract paintings, pictures of flowers, and landscape scenes (Shade & New, 1993).

Interpersonal relationships within the family play a large role in the socialization of African American children, with the ultimate goal of helping children to function independently within and outside the family (Banks, 1993). Parents attempt to prepare their children for interactions with both peers and teachers and teach them how to act in social situations. Thus, parents are trying to provide a set of guidelines for behaving in novel situations (Shade, 1987).

With regard to the impact on personality and behavior, these socialization practices point to the importance of people to African American students. For example, both white and black adolescents were asked to take photographs that they thought best portrayed their school. Most of the pictures taken by the African American students were of people (Hale-Benson, 1986). Other studies indicate that teachers of African American students concentrate on classroom management and reinforce these students for personable behavior, while rewarding white children for their academic performance (Shade, 1987).

To avoid this discrepancy (importance of people versus importance of classroom management) in teaching African American students, then, it is helpful to remember the importance they place on social interactions, and to try to structure the classroom environment in a way that encourages the social dimensions of learning.

Give an instance in which you might use Vygotsky's zone of proximal development theory in working with students. How would you decide where to begin?

Vygotsky's ideas of mental development stand in contrast to those of Jean Piaget. While both theorists used a cognitive interpretation of mental development, Vygotsky, as we have seen, turned to social stimulation to explain a child's cognitive development. Piaget, on the other hand, believed that children construct their own ideas on how the world around them "works"; they function as "little scientists." Their ideas about the world and its objects change as they pass through four identifiable stages. Teachers following Vygotsky's ideas would address those functions in students' zones of proximal development, while teachers using Piaget's ideas would encourage more independent work.

PIAGET AND COGNITIVE DEVELOPMENT

Probably no one has influenced our thinking about cognitive development more than Jean Piaget. Born in Neuchatel, Switzerland in 1896, Piaget was trained as a biologist; his biological training made a major impact upon his thinking about cognitive development. Piaget insisted upon calling himself a "genetic epistemologist," a term that reflected his interest in how the manner in which individuals acquire knowledge changes as they develop. He became fascinated by the processes that led children to make incorrect answers in reasoning tests and turned his attention to the analysis of children's developing intelligence. Until his death in 1980, Piaget remained active in his research into cognitive development. Many believe that he was responsible for the resurgence of interest in cognitive studies.

Personal questions

You will also find personal questions in the margins. *Stop and take the time to answer them.* We have carefully prepared these questions to encourage you to interact with the text to bring your ideas to what you are reading.

SO YOU WANT TO TEACH

We have recently seen a spate of *joy* books: *The Joy of Cooking, The Joy of Running, The Joy of Shopping.* Most experienced teachers would also endorse a book entitled *The Joy of Teaching.* Will you have your down days? Of course; you cannot escape that in any profession. But you probably have been attracted to teaching by one, or a combination, of the following reasons: you enjoy working with young people; you like a particular subject; you enjoy being in an environment where people want to learn. Before examining how educational psychology can help your teaching and your students' learning, let's look at what it means to teach.

School environments vary greatly and influence learning and attitudes about the importance of learning.

What It Means to Teach

What do we mean by **teaching?** There are many different definitions of teaching, but all seem to include several common critical attributes. For example, Anderson and Burns (1989, pp. 7–8) stated that *teaching can be considered a process,* since teaching involves action. You perform when you teach. *Teaching can also be regarded as an interpersonal activity,* since a teacher interacts with one or more students. The interaction can be bidirectional (teachers influence students and students influence teachers). This is also known as reciprocal interaction. Finally, *teaching is intentional.* When you teach, you do so with a purpose or purposes.

Considering these attributes, Anderson and Burns (1989) provided the following useful definition of teaching: "Teaching is an interpersonal, interactive activity, typically involving verbal communication, which is undertaken for the purpose of helping one or more students learn or change the ways in which they can or will behave" (p. 8). These authors then presented several generalizations that they drew from more than fifty years of research on teachers, teaching, and instruction. They noted that the generalizations are fairly conservative and should stimulate discussion and innovation among researchers and practitioners. These generalizations appear in table 1.1. As you read them, remember that these topics will be discussed in greater detail in subsequent chapters. Decide now if you agree or disagree with the points. When you have completed your reading of this book, return to these points and determine if your agreements and disagreements remain the same.

The acquisition of teaching skills is a complex process, but one that can be mastered. Any course or book on educational psychology should strive to provide education students and readers with insights into the teaching-learning process. Such insights involve both knowledge and understanding of the students, what teaching is, how learning occurs, how classrooms are run, and, in general, what schools are all about.

These insights should help you to meet the challenges posed by changing conditions in the schools. More and more authority is being returned to the schools and to

teaching *Those actions designed to help one or more students learn.*

Table 1.1

Generalizations About Teachers, Teaching, and Instruction	
Category	**Generalization**
Teachers	Teachers assume a very central, directive, and active role in the classroom.
	Differences in individual teaching behaviors are not reliably associated with differences in student achievement.
	Teacher characteristics do not impact directly on student achievement.
	Teachers progress through a fairly predictable set of qualitatively distinct stages as they move from novice to expert status.
Teaching	If teaching behaviors are to be reliably associated with student achievement, then patterns, groupings, or clusters of these behaviors must be identified. Furthermore, experimental or quasi-experimental studies may be necessary to produce the variation in these behavioral clusters that is needed to properly examine the relationships between teacher behavior and student achievement.
	Considering teaching from a functional, rather than a behavioral, point of view is more likely to result in a greater understanding of teaching in general and effective teaching in particular.
Instruction	The subject matter being taught impacts on some, if not all, of the other components of instruction.
	Even when the academic demands on students tend to be fairly slight, the greater the emphasis is on these demands and the students' need to meet them, the greater is student achievement in the basic skills.
	Lecture, recitation, and seatwork predominate in classrooms; there is little if any evidence that changes in format would result in higher levels of student achievement.
	Although most teaching and learning take place in whole-class settings, there is increasing evidence that grouping within the classroom is beneficial for student learning.
	Instructional time, content coverage, and pacing are associated with higher levels of student achievement.

From L. W. Anderson and R. B. Burns, *Research in Classrooms: The Study of Teachers, Teaching, and Instruction*. Copyright © 1989 Butterworth/Heinemann Group, Oxford, England. Reprinted by permission.

teachers, a change which is vital if quality education is to be attained. As Murphy (1993) noted, teaching is a job that requires judgment; given the authority, teachers have a growing opportunity to exercise their judgment and take responsibility for the results.

You will find yourself teaching in a time when "quality" has become a magic word, a fact that should only heighten your expectations. When you realize that you are teaching to the best of your ability, several things happen: you feel good about yourself; you know your efforts are targeted to the individual needs of your students; you take pride in your work. These are reliable markers for quality teaching.

In discussing the search for quality in our schools, Bonstingl (1992) argued that schools must think of their students as customers who should receive the best educational services possible. In this way, students learn to communicate effectively and demand quality in their own lives. They should also become devoted to lifelong learning. This text will help you to apply the principles of educational psychology to a variety of learning environments, extending from those of young childhood to those of adulthood. But, first, who are the individuals entering the classrooms to teach our nation's children?

Annual **Edition**

Who Becomes a Teacher?

Discussions about education frequently focus on teaching, learning, or new instructional methods. Equally as interesting, however, is what we know about those who are attracted to teaching.

Characteristics of Beginning Teachers

One of the best ways to learn more about students attracted to teaching is to analyze those whom Brookhart and Freeman (1992) called *entering teacher candidates* (students enrolled in their first teacher preparation course). Today's students chose teaching for a variety of reasons, such as the desires to work with others and to help young people (Brookhart & Freeman, 1992). The authors also found that most students in teacher preparation programs were confident of their ability to teach successfully. When the students began their student teaching, however, and during their first two years of teaching, they indicated some anxiety about their ability to maintain discipline and worried whether their students liked them. With experience, teachers' concerns shifted from merely dispensing the correct information to the achievement of their students.

The changes in teachers' concerns that occur with experience are well documented. Principals have reported that beginning teachers have a tendency to spend too much time on chores, with the result that students become restless. They assume too much responsibility and worry excessively about student approval. Extremes in the behavior of beginning teachers are often apparent: excessive teacher control can cause fear in younger students, while ignoring disruptive behavior can lead to chaos (Cooledge, 1992). In looking back at their careers, veteran teachers speak of these problems and usually remember gratefully a fellow teacher or principal who supported them in their down days (Kane, 1992). Knowing that time will bring confidence and increasing expertise will help you in your first days as a teacher.

Considering the nation's positive attitude toward bettering our schools and improving the quality of teaching in the classrooms, one can be optimistic about the future of teachers and teaching in the years ahead. But what of you as an individual? What are some issues that could involve you, at either the elementary or the secondary level?

When you decided to enter the teaching profession, you probably had several ideas about teaching and what you hoped to accomplish. These ideas are known as teacher expectations. As you have learned more about teaching, have you found your expectations to be realistic? Why? Why not? Have they changed?

Teaching and Educational Issues

You undoubtedly will be involved in making decisions about many sensitive issues. These issues are likely to involve students who possess a wide range of abilities; teaching and classroom management techniques; evaluation and grading of students; communication with parents; and the use of research to guide teaching and interaction with students. Let us examine several specific issues that we will address in greater detail in later chapters.

Language

A major change in the teaching of reading and writing is the use of a concept known as **whole language.** With a whole language approach, students are not taught phonics isolated from meaning; rather, they learn to read by obtaining the meanings of words from context, with phonics introduced as needed. For example, if while reading a story, one of your pupils had difficulty with the word *dish,* you would have the student stop to sound it out. Students don't use basal readers; they read appropriate-level literature about themes that interest them and then write about these ideas. Teachers who

whole language *A technique in which all language processes are studied in a natural context (as a whole, and not as a series of possibly unrelated facts).*

have begun to use this new technique believe that it motivates their pupils better than the older methods. Not everyone agrees with this approach, however; we will discuss this hotly contested issue in greater detail in chapter 4.

Mathematics

Results of international tests measuring mathematics achievement have repeatedly shown American students to be at or near the bottom. As a result, the country will soon experience another wave of publicity about a revision of the mathematics curriculum. You may have heard about the "new math" of the 1960s, followed a few years later by the "back-to-basics" movement. One of the reasons that the new math was not an unqualified success was that public school teachers had little to say about its implementation. It was simply imposed on them.

Today's emphasis is less on skills for their own sake and more on thinking about and understanding the meaning of numbers. Mathematician J. Paulos (1988) gave an example of the usefulness of this second ability. Paulos quoted a couple as saying they were not going to Europe because of the dangers they would face there from all the terrorists. Paulos pointed out that in 1985, only 17 of the 28 million Americans who traveled abroad were killed by terrorists. That same year, 45,000 people were killed on American highways. That is, motorists in the United States had 1 chance in 5,300 of being killed in a car crash. Understanding the numbers involved would help individuals like the couple mentioned above to evaluate which situation truly contained the greatest potential danger.

The National Council of Teachers of Mathematics recommends that students use calculators at all times, and urges teachers to emphasize problem-solving skills (see chap. 9) and the practical side of mathematics. The goal is to make mathematics seem less threatening and more useful.

Science

Estimates are that fewer than 10 percent of high school graduates have the skills necessary to perform satisfactorily in college-level science courses. Attempting to combat this trend, many science educators are today turning to a more "hands-on" approach to their teaching. Instead of having their students memorize lengthy formulas, they have them do experiments starting in the early grades. For example, instead of reading about the principle of buoyancy, students make lumps of clay into various shapes, put them in plastic bags, and discover which shapes float and which ones sink.

You may argue that there's nothing new in this technique; good teachers have been doing it for years. There are differences, however. Where this approach has been successful, teachers have acted as facilitators, not directors. Teachers need not teach a specific amount of material; in a sense, teaching less can result in teaching more. That is, by teaching generalizable problem-solving strategies along with the concepts of basic subject matter, and by emphasizing that learners should know themselves, teachers can prepare students for a lifetime of learning. Also, these school systems have been strongly committed to scientific discovery from the elementary grades through high school.

Retention in Grade

Consider this possible future scenario. You are meeting with the parents of one of your students and they ask you if their child should be retained in third grade. What would you say to them? Making pupils repeat a year's work has come under heavy attack recently, with opponents claiming that it usually doesn't work. After reviewing studies comparing the education of students who were retained with students of comparable achievement and maturity who were promoted, Holmes (1990) concluded that retained students were no better off than those who went on to the next grade. Retention, because of either immaturity or lack of achievement, is a common practice in our schools, one which raises many questions (Medway & Rose, 1986).

- Does grade retention produce academic achievement superior to that found in comparable students who are promoted?
- Do students who have been retained drop out of school more frequently than comparable students who were promoted?
- Does a policy of retention discriminate against particular groups of students?
- What evidence does a school use in its decision to retain?
- Does eliminating grade retention mean a return to a policy of social promotion?
- What are the legal ramifications of grade retention?

Although evidence is accumulating that retention has not been a uniformly successful policy, the issue today is widely debated.

Homework

Homework, that in-and out-of-favor subject, is once again enjoying renewed acceptance. (Homework usually refers to school-assigned academic work that is to be completed outside of school, usually in the home. At the turn of the twentieth century, homework was considered vital. Its popularity declined in the 1940s, reemerged in the 1950s (after Sputnik), fell into disfavor in the 1960s because it was seen as a form of useless pressure, and now, with reports of the poor achievement of American students, is once more viewed as essential. Research shows that for high school students, two or more hours of homework nightly increases achievement, that junior high school students benefit from one to two hours of homework, and that there seems to be a slight relationship between homework for elementary school pupils and improved achievement (Cooper, 1989). Homework at the elementary school level does have the recognized benefit, however, of bringing home and school closer together, and also encourages pupils to realize that they can learn on their own. Homework should not be a burden for students and their parents, but should be assigned to meet demonstrated needs.

"I'm only attending school until it becomes available on CD-ROM."

© Martha F. Campbell.

The point of introducing these selected but representative issues at this stage of your work is to make you aware of how educational psychology can help you reach decisions. For example, reading about language and development should help you with any questions about whole language programs (see chap. 3). The details of problem solving that you will read about in chapter 8 should help you in judging science and math methods. Understanding possible alternatives to retention in grade helps in weighing the pros and cons of this controversial practice. You can better assess the value of homework by using your knowledge of development and learning.

To use educational psychology most effectively to address these and other issues, you must act as both artist and scientist.

The joy of teaching comes from interacting with the students, which demands the intuition of the artist and the precision of the scientist.

TEACHING AS AN ART AND AS A SCIENCE

Although teachers have always needed professional skills to be successful in the classroom, perhaps few periods in history have dictated a greater need for teachers who are competent, thoughtful, and imaginative. A combination of factors, ranging from changing social conditions to a continuing knowledge explosion, demands teachers who possess abilities that go beyond the sheer mechanics of teaching.

Teaching as an Art

You must know your subject; this implies that you grasp not only the material that you currently are presenting in class, but also the core of the subject, and what researchers are discovering at the frontiers of the discipline. In an age devoted to empirical research, the expansion of knowledge necessitates ongoing independent study to prevent personal obsolescence.

Teachers will avoid such work unless they like their subject and enjoy interacting with students. To devote hours of study beyond the demands of duty requires a commitment to a discipline and the company of the young, both of which can be provocative masters. You have already made a commitment that reflects a love of study and pleasure in working with youth. These categories actually mirror two basic themes that are at the heart of this book: the teacher as a professional and the teacher as a person.

Musing about the art of teaching, Cohen (1992) described the lives of five veteran secondary school teachers and concluded that common to them all was a passion and enthusiasm for the subjects they taught. Particularly interesting was her finding that they were not locked into any single teaching style. They had developed their own unique and, for them, effective styles, which they constantly modified. In many ways, they never lost the perspective of a novice: always wanting to try something new, to seek constantly for improvement. As Cohen noted, they were "originals."

A Modern Art of Teaching

In a modern version of *The Art of Teaching* (a graceful overview of teaching originally written by Gilbert Highet in 1950), Flinders (1989), after observing public school teachers, noted that the concept of professionalism in education failed to capture the "artistry of teaching." Flinders believes that such skills as the way that teachers use body language to communicate a message and their use of silence to motivate, reveal the grace, subtlety, and drama of everyday teaching.

Analyzing these behaviors, Flinders suggested several categories that capture the art of teaching. The first is **communication,** which goes beyond speaking or writing. It includes body language, the use of space (stepping toward a pupil, for example), voice intonation, and eye contact. All of these nonverbal cues are coordinated to convey a message of caring about students.

communication *Imparting of a message not only verbally, but also through body language and use of space, voice intonation, and eye contact. Vital in teaching as an art.*

The next quality is **perception:** teachers read cues that describe the emotional context of the group, and then adapt their methods to the "mood" of the class. How many times have you heard teachers talk about the "vibes" they pick up from a class? Perception, then, reflects a sensitivity to students and a capacity (and willingness) to adapt.

perception *Insight of teachers into the moods of their classes, prompting them to adapt their methods.*

Flinders' next category is **cooperation.** Any classroom functions more smoothly when teachers and students get along well with each other. Working *with* students is much more effective than talking *to* them. To encourage cooperation, Flinders recommended several strategies. The teacher can use humor to promote solidarity between teacher and students, and can allow students to choose activities. The teacher should also work at providing opportunities for pupil recognition, and try to create pockets of time for one-to-one contact.

cooperation *Situation in which students and teachers get along well together, so that a classroom functions smoothly.*

The final category is **appreciation.** While appreciation is not something teachers "do," it is an important part of job satisfaction. Appreciation, then, is a product of artistry: knowing you have done a good job.

appreciation *Knowing when you have done a good job in your teaching.*

In no sense did Flinders diminish the professionalism of teaching: the knowledge that teachers possess, their ability to apply various teaching strategies, and their skill at achieving different kinds of pupil learning. Rather, he urged a recognition of those principles that Highet expressed so well many years ago.

As an individual with your own needs, characteristics, strengths, and weaknesses, you will adopt certain techniques and styles in the classroom that you decide are best suited to you. Your students will in turn respond to your classroom style. These reciprocal interactions of teacher and student will eventually culminate in a relationship. The quality of the relationship, positive or negative, goes far in determining your success as a teacher. A section of each chapter in this book will illustrate teacher-student interactions as they relate to the chapter's topic.

One of the objectives of this text is to present a range of ideas, theories, and research that will enable you to apply the best and most recent data about teaching and learning to your own needs and characteristics. To make these decisions, you must be familiar with data concerning teacher characteristics, student characteristics, teaching, and learning. As we shall see, such knowledge defines the field of educational psychology. The remaining chapters of this book are designed to facilitate effective teaching and learning.

Teaching as a Science

Considering teaching strictly as an art, however, is too limiting. Given the knowledge that researchers have acquired about the nature of instruction and about the methods of inquiry into any discipline, we should explore the notion that teaching can also be considered a science.

Most teachers, knowingly or not, adopt—and adapt—the scientific method in their work. Teachers may adopt the role of experimenter as they try new instructional methods and classroom procedures (even things as simple as changing the seating arrangement). Any scientific analysis will include the following four steps.

1. *Identifying the problem.* For teachers, this means deciding exactly what they want their students to learn.
2. *Formulating a logical series of steps to reach a goal.* For teachers, this means deciding not only which topic to present but how they will do so.
3. *Gathering the data.* For teachers, this means deciding just what student behavior is to be measured, and then the best means of measurement.
4. *Interpreting the data.* For teachers, this means deciding if the students' performance (the results of the teacher's strategy and testing) has achieved the desired goal.

By following the "scientific method" in their instruction and by their involvement at various levels of scientific inquiry, teachers act as scientists: they identify objectives, devise strategies, gather and evaluate their data, and communicate their results.

In a thoughtful attempt to bridge the gap between teaching as an art and teaching as a science, Gage (1977, 1985) urged that we distinguish between a science of teaching and a scientific basis for the art of teaching. He noted that the idea that teaching is a science is probably erroneous, because we cannot predict that good teaching inevitably follows from an adherence to rigorous laws that yields high predictability and control. (As we shall see later in our work, some psychologists who have applied their work to teaching and learning, notably B. F. Skinner, might disagree with Gage's conclusion.)

Gage (1985) argued, however, that it is possible to develop a scientific base for teaching. For example, in teaching, as in any science, the laws and trends relating any two variables are subject to modification by the influence of additional variables. Gage then gave the example of the relationship between teacher criticism and student achievement. It may be negative for students with lower academic orientation and positive for students with higher academic orientation. Thus the relationship between teacher criticism and student achievement is influenced by a third variable: the pupil's degree of academic orientation.

The assertion that teaching has a scientific basis means that educational researchers have accumulated, carefully and painstakingly, a body of knowledge concerning regular, nonchance relationships about teaching and learning. This type of research is difficult and time-consuming; yet, "in the long run, the improvement of teaching—what is tantamount to the improvement of our children's lives—will come in large part from the continued search for a scientific basis for the art of teaching" (Gage, 1977, p. 41). So we conclude as we began: teaching is both art and science, a needed combination for changing classrooms. At this point, there are undoubtedly some questions about teaching you would like to ask.

Questions That Teachers Ask

How can educational psychology help you to recognize your own needs and also help you to become a true professional? This discipline can help you answer the following and other questions:

When you consider the relationship between teaching and learning, are there other questions you would add to the list?

- *When are students ready for certain experiences?* Are there developmental data that provide clues to the ideal time and circumstances for teaching different subjects? (Reading instruction is a good illustration.)
- *Are there particular teaching techniques that are better suited to some students than to others?* For example, do some students learn best when they are required to discover things for themselves (with guidance), and others when they receive more direct instruction?
- *Does a knowledge of learning theory help in the classroom?* For example, does understanding the fundamentals of memory enable teachers to help students retain their learning and transfer it to other subjects?

Diversity in the classroom can only enrich students' daily experiences.

- *Does knowing the details of test construction really matter?* For example, if we understand the theory behind test making, does it help us to be more certain about the extent and quality of a student's learning?
- *What does the latest research say about classroom discipline?* This question usually is the first one asked by students and beginning teachers. Students need a happy blend of firmness and freedom—but how do we arrive at this happy medium?

These are practical questions that have direct classroom application, and that we attempt to answer in this text. When you complete your reading, if you are a beginning teacher, you should face the first day with more confidence. If you are an experienced teacher, you should have new ideas to test, new techniques to try. You may also be concerned that you will be teaching students from different cultures.

Our Multicultural Classrooms

America today is welcoming great waves of immigrants; therefore, many immigrant and minority children will be in our classrooms. Cultural diversity can bring a special strength and vitality to the classroom, as to the whole society. **Multicultural classrooms** will be discussed in each chapter; you should be aware of the meanings of the terms used in these discussions. We realize there may not be complete agreement with the definitions we offer; we suggest that readers use those meanings with which they are most comfortable. As one example, Matsumoto (1994) has commented that any definition of culture is "fuzzy": there are no hard and fast rules to determine what a culture is or who belongs to that culture. (If you wish to pursue further definitions and explanations, good sources include Banks & Banks, 1993; Lonner & Malpass, 1994; Matsumoto, 1994.)

Culture commonly refers to those values, beliefs, and behaviors characteristic of a large group of people—for example, those of Hispanic origin. The term *ethnic,* however, usually applies to distinctive national or linguistic backgrounds which can be included within a larger culture, such as that of Mexican Americans. *Race,* on the other hand, does not refer to nationality, culture, or language, but is identified by bloodtype, such as African. Anthropologists have identified nine major racial groups: African, American Indian, Asian, Australian, European, Indian, Melanesian, Micronesian, Polynesian (Tiedt & Tiedt, 1990).

Schools across the country are now welcoming a growing number of multicultural students. Enjoying your work with young people is a necessity for good teaching. For many prospective—and veteran—teachers, this means knowing and understanding an increasing number of multicultural students. National concern with minority students

multicultural classrooms
Classrooms with students and teachers from different ethnic or cultural groups.

Figure 1.1

U.S. immigration rate by decade.

Source: U.S. Immigration and Naturalization Service, 1992 Statistical Yearbook (1993).

Period	Total number ('000s)	Rate per 1,000 U.S. pop.
1820–30	152	1.2
1831–40	599	3.9
1841–50	1,713	8.4
1851–60	2,598	9.3
1861–70	2,315	6.4
1871–80	2,812	6.2
1881–90	5,247	9.2
1891–1900	3,688	5.3
1901–10	8,795	10.4
1911–20	5,736	5.7
1921–30	4,107	3.5
1931–40	528	0.4
1941–50	1,035	0.7
1951–60	2,515	1.5
1961–70	3,322	1.7
1971–80	4,493	2.1
1981–90	7,338	2.9
1991–92	2,801	1.1

has ebbed and flowed through the years, but the successes of the Civil Rights movement and a growing awareness of the effects of poverty have produced a renewed interest in multicultural matters.

To give you some idea of the changes in our population, which are reflected in the classroom, figure 1.1 illustrates U.S. immigration rates for the years 1820 to 1992.

This is the *third* great immigration we have seen in this country. The first occurred in the middle of the nineteenth century, with the arrival of immigrants from England, Ireland, Germany, and Scandinavia. The second movement took place between 1900 and 1920, and was dominated by immigrants from Russia, Italy, Hungary, and Poland. In 1907 alone, 1.3 million immigrants entered the United States (Kellogg, 1988). The third major migration began in the late 1960s and still continues. The regions of origin of these new immigrants are as follows (Kellogg, 1988): Asia, 34 percent; Latin America, 34 percent; Europe, 16 percent; and other regions, 16 percent. In 1985, 80 percent of all immigrants came from Mexico and Asia.

Among the most important characteristics of the members of this new group with direct implications for the schools are the following: (a) *they are young* and will be in our educational system for many years; (b) *they have remarkable language diversity*, a fact that points to the need for definite policy decisions in the schools; and (c) *many of the children have not yet mastered their own first languages*.

As an example of what these figures mean, consider the various birth rates. While Americans as a whole now average 1.7 children per lifetime, African Americans average 2.4 children per lifetime, Cambodian Americans average 7.4, Laotian Americans average 4.6, Vietnamese Americans average 3.4, and Mexican Americans average 2.9. The populations in our schools will shift to reflect these figures.

There are growing numbers of minority children in our classrooms. Children will have increasing opportunities to interact with peers of great cultural diversity.

Kellogg (1988) reported that the class of 2001 (which started kindergarten in September 1988), mirrors the changing face of America. For example, minority enrollment ranges from 70 percent to 96 percent in the nation's fifteen largest school systems.

What can we conclude from this brief summary? Our public schools will be serving an ever-growing number of immigrant students. In Lowell, Massachusetts, for example, the number of Southeast Asian students jumped from 98 in 1980 to 2,000 in 1994. The same phenomenon is happening across the country.

Of the four major minority groups—African American, Asian American, Hispanic American, and Native American—the greatest amount of research has been done with African Americans. Attention to this group remains high because of the declining developmental and educational status of a significant number of African American children (McLoyd, 1990). Researchers studying any of the minority groups, however, should be alert to the danger of the "race-comparative" design: noting how minority children differ from Anglo-American children and then interpreting these differences as deficits. This strategy has been particularly true of some studies of African American children that ignore the developmental paths of these youngsters, their individual differences, and the ways some children deviate from the norms of development within the group (McLoyd, 1990).

Students with varied backgrounds, languages, and cultures pose a challenge to all of us as teachers. As McBay (1990) noted, the primary mandate for teachers, administrators, and curricula is to meet the individual needs of multicultural students. For now, the best advice is this: Work diligently to understand *all* the students in your classroom.

One State's Experience

It is often said that as California goes, so goes the nation. In fact, many of the issues that California is now addressing will soon be faced by other localities around the country. Consequently, the way that California's educators have faced the problems associated with increased immigration may provide insights for the nation as a whole.

One in six California students is foreign born; *one in four* public school students comes from a non-English-speaking home. Thus, educators must address the need for new teaching techniques and new programs that are appropriate for a multiethnic, multiracial, and multilingual student population. Most of these new immigrants come from the Pacific Rim countries of Asia, Mexico, and Central America (Olsen, 1988).

For example, the Asian American population grew by 70 percent from 1980 to 1988, a growth rate seven times that of the general population. From 3.8 million in 1980, the Asian American population grew to 6.5 million in 1988. One-third of these settled in California (Takaki, 1989).

This influx has been accompanied by the usual problems: schools caught unaware, uncertainty about needed changes, resistance to change, hostility to the new. One project—California Tomorrow—has arranged interviews with immigrant children, their parents, teachers, administrators, policymakers, and community advocates in an attempt to identify unmet needs. Since these pupils have a dropout rate of from 50 to 70 percent, the problem is real, immediate, and growing.

Only about one in four of the foreign born students begin their American education in the elementary grades; this means that many of the older children lack the necessary basics. To meet these needs, some schools have turned to new assessment techniques, such as centralized centers that test basic academic skills in a child's native language, perform health screening, and test English proficiency. In the schools themselves, American students are often assigned as helpers to immigrant students. To reduce misunderstandings and feelings of hostility, some schools (especially at the secondary level) use videotapes in which both immigrant and American-born students speak of an immigrant's difficulties in a new land.

These are merely a few of the innovations that schools and teachers have devised to meet new challenges in their quest for effective schools (Olsen, 1988).

EFFECTIVE SCHOOLS

TQM (Total Quality Management)
Name for a conceptual framework for understanding the complexity of systems.

As mentioned earlier in the chapter, "quality," quality education," and "quality schools" are terms that appear more and more frequently in any discussion of our schools. Sometimes referred to as **TQM (Total Quality Management),** this concept is usually linked to the work of W. Edwards Deming in Japan following World War II. Deming helped Japanese business leaders move from carelessly turning out shoddy products to a level of quality production that inspired worldwide envy. With the present concerted effort to improve our schools, more and more educators are turning to TQM.

The TQM approach, however, cannot simply be applied as a panacea for all educational problems (Bonstingl, 1992). Deming himself warned those interested in TQM against merely imitating what worked in a business setting and applying these ideas without modification to an educational setting. There are, nevertheless, aspects of TQM that are particularly relevant to educational psychology: acknowledgment of the importance of intrinsic motivation, an emphasis on process, and recognition of individual differences. All of these attitudes contribute to effective teaching and effective schools.

(Note: At several points in each chapter, we introduce current issues that are demanding the attention of today's teachers and educational psychologists. For example, the issue of TQM, discussed in the following box, concerns both teachers and educational psychologists because of its implications for teaching, learning, and motivation. In such boxes we present positive and negative arguments with the expectation that you and your instructor can use them as a basis for discussion.)

Issues & Answers

Is Total Quality Management the Solution for Effective Schools?

As the search for answers to questions about the effectiveness of our schools continues, more and more educators are turning to new ideas: cooperative learning, authentic assessment, portfolio assessment, thinking skills, and, more recently, Total Quality Management. Some educators are attracted to this last concept because it offers a conceptual framework that helps them to understand a complex system (Brandt, 1992). Educational psychologists are examining it carefully because of its implications for programs that address individual differences, intrinsic and extrinsic motivation, and methods of assessment.

Issue
TQM is just another of the "fads" that intrigue educators.

Answer: Pro To follow the principles of TQM, teachers must change many traditional practices. For example, they must abandon their dependence on grades. Many teachers will find this difficult, if not impossible. Will administrators be willing to devote time and precious resources to the commitment that must be made? Although there may be potential in the plan, the many obstacles it faces make it unlikely that TQM will succeed.

Answer: Con Our schools cannot continue as they are now. TQM can provide many of the answers that we are presently searching for. It has succeeded in business and, with modifications, can improve the quality of learning in our schools. There will be problems; there will be delays. A key element obviously is the teaching force. If our teachers can be persuaded of its value through workshops, seminars, and modeling, then TQM has an excellent chance of bringing change to our schools.

Issue
TQM lends itself to a greater understanding of how motivation functions in a classroom.

Answer: Pro Total quality management would lead to a lessening of teachers' reliance on extrinsic motivation (stars, grades, etc.), and place much more emphasis on intrinsic motivation. Extrinsic motivation can be destructive because it fosters competition and hurts those who are excluded.

Answer: Con Reliance on intrinsic motivation quickly leads to a lack of attention, faulty classroom control, and poor learning. The assumption that students will come to every class enthusiastic and eager to learn is simply not realistic. A carefully planned sequence of rewards that addresses specific behaviors can lead eventually to intrinsic motivation.

Consistent findings support the conclusion that differences among schools are related to different levels of student performance, even beyond those that would be expected because of the individual variation of pupils. During the past twenty to twenty-five years, educational research has quite clearly identified those characteristics that mark an effective school. Schools whose students achieve well and where morale is high possess identifiable attributes.

For example, *good instructional leadership* is critical. This means that principals, teachers, students, and parents agree on goals, methods, and content. Good leadership produces *an orderly environment* in which positive discipline encourages academic achievement and personal fulfillment. Positive conditions lead to *collegiality among teachers* in which they work together to aid student achievement and adjustment. Teachers have *realistic but high expectations for all of their students.* In other words, teachers are efficient and caring (Pulido, 1991).

Attempts have also been made to identify defective schools. *Faulty communication* seems to be a major cause of problems. *Special interest groups* flourish and *favoritism* is obvious. There is *no sense of a democratic atmosphere,* no discussion of issues; decisions are rendered from above, and there is a *lack of control in the daily functioning of the school.* Finally, there is *little, if any, parental involvement* (Gilman, 1992).

We turn now to this question: What do we know about the circumstances in which you find—or will find—yourself?

A Place Called School

In his studies and reflections on American education (1984, 1991), John Goodlad has commented on the results of a sweeping survey of American schools. Intended to further our understanding of our schools and the problems that face them, Goodlad presented a timely picture of what is happening in the nation's classrooms. He and his investigators were impressed with several important and persistent aspects of classroom life.

Regardless of the type of organization, *the total group* is the vehicle for teaching and learning. Much of what occurs in a classroom depends on the orderly relationship among all its members. It is within this total organization that individual students work and achieve. Goodlad also noted that *teachers are the strategic figures in this group.* They determine the activities, their sequence, and the tone of the classroom. As Goodlad stated, the teacher is virtually autonomous with respect to classroom decisions (1984, p. 123).

Goodlad and his researchers also found that *the classroom group* behaves in a manner calculated to maintain the teacher's strategic role. Even when the class is divided into smaller groups, those groups tend to do those things previously determined by the teacher. Finally, they discovered that the emotional tone of the classroom tends to be level. Goodlad described students as "passively content," that is, they felt generally positive about peers and teachers and usually liked subjects and activities. These findings are almost identical with those reported by Philip Jackson almost 30 years ago (1968), and are a positive sign that the vast majority of students are prepared to like schools and teachers.

After reviewing the many findings of the survey, Goodlad (1991) asserted that the two major functions of the schools are to socialize children into a social and political democracy and to help students develop their thinking skills for productive participation in the life of the community. To attain these goals, teachers must acquire what Shulman (in Brandt, 1990) called "pedagogical content knowledge." Any profession has its own unique body of knowledge, and teachers need to master the essential content, skills, and techniques required for effective teaching. (See chap. 12.) Goodlad stressed that schools should pursue equity and excellence for all.

How did teachers in Goodlad's survey react to the current educational scene?

What Do Teachers Say?

Earlier in this chapter, the topic of teacher needs and characteristics was mentioned as a subject of concern in this text. When questioned on why they had decided to teach, the majority of teachers in Goodlad's survey (57 percent) stated that their decisions had to

Given today's emphasis on group activities and cooperative learning, do you agree with Goodlad's conclusion that the teacher remains the strategic figure in the group? Or do you see the teacher remaining more in the background, quietly guiding students? In which role do you think you would function more effectively?

teacher – student

interactions

Relating to Students

You have read about teaching and the schools in this chapter. Let's assume that as part of a test on educational psychology, you are asked to list the qualities of a good teacher.

A. List ten of the most desired qualities of a good teacher.
1.   6.
2.   7.
3.   8.
4.   9.
5.   10.

Can you group these qualities in any way? Are some personal characteristics? Are others professional? Which would help you to relate more positively to your students?

B. In a 1987 report on a survey of four hundred high school students, Bragstad and Stumpf (1984) found

that the students' descriptions of important teacher characteristics could be grouped into personal and instructional qualities. Among the personal qualities most valued were those of being caring (understanding, patient), having a sense of humor (relaxed but effective), and being fair. The most valued instructional qualities included being interesting (varying style), knowledgeable, well organized, and enthusiastic.

C. Reinforcing what is stressed in this chapter concerning teacher-student relations, remember:
- a teacher's ability to relate to students is positively related to student achievement
- a teacher's ability to relate to students is positively related to enhanced student self-concept

---

do with the nature of teaching itself. For example, 22 percent wanted to teach in general or to teach a particular subject; 18 percent saw teaching as a desirable profession; and 17 percent felt a desire to serve others. Fifteen percent of the elementary and 11 percent of the secondary teachers stated that liking children was their primary reason.

The teachers who had entered the profession because of its inherent value, a desire to teach a specific subject, or a liking for children felt that their expectations had been fulfilled. They also stated that they would choose a teaching career if starting again. Those whose choices had been influenced by compensation felt least fulfilled. In all, 74 percent of the teachers questioned stated that their career expectations had been fulfilled. Finally, the teachers in the survey perceived themselves to be competent, autonomous, and influential regarding classroom decisions. In other words, most teachers think they are well prepared to teach.

There were, however, several subject areas for which teachers felt less prepared. At the secondary level, science seemed to be more of a concern than other subjects, with the exception of special education, where greater teacher support at this level seems to be needed. Elementary teachers felt inadequately prepared in art, physical education, home economics, science, and foreign languages. These survey results provide us with an agenda for improving the academic preparation of teachers, and also helping the schools to become more effective.

(Note: At various points in each chapter, boxes entitled Teacher-Student Interactions will appear. These are specifically designed to help you translate the theory and research you have been reading about into classroom practice.)

Effective Schools—Effective Teachers

Schools are effective to the extent that they are staffed by effective teachers. As you continue your reading, you will find several chapters directed to an analysis of teaching and classroom management. Here, however, it would help to mention briefly what research has discovered about effective teachers. In this way, you can see more clearly the link between teacher characteristics (both personal and professional) and a smoothly functioning classroom that contributes to students' achievement.

Studies indicate that superior teachers are flexible and maintain close personal relationships with their students (Agne, 1992). When it comes to discipline, expert teachers are constantly alert to the behavioral cues of their students and have thought about

Annual Edition

a wide variety of techniques (see chap. 13). They also spend more time analyzing the cause of a problem than beginning teachers do (Swanson, 1990). A general conclusion of these studies is that expert teachers expect every student in their classrooms to learn, and take measures to *ensure* that learning occurs. The most important of these measures is to try to increase their students' sense of competence (Robinson & Magliocca, 1991).

We know also that effective teachers maintain good classroom organization, playing a major role in the classroom but also involving students in planning and organizing (see chap. 13). Having a structured curriculum and setting high goals that are communicated to students are important qualities in positive classroom management. These are the teachers who set and maintain clear rules and consistently apply them, using positive reinforcement.

A teacher's persistence in seeking goals, following a daily schedule, selecting appropriate content and teaching methods, and involving students is also an important feature. Research (to be discussed in chap. 2) indicates that good teachers also insist on student responsibility.

A teacher's personal characteristics are likewise significant. The qualities of being well organized, efficient, task oriented, knowledgeable, fluent, and alert to student differences were characteristics frequently mentioned in analyses of effective teachers. These were coupled with such other characteristics as clarity, enthusiasm, self-confidence, friendliness, warmth, and an encouraging and supportive manner.

In addition to professional and personal characteristics, the relationships that teachers have with the parents of their students can do much to enrich the teaching—learning interaction. Improving parental involvement is one of the most challenging tasks facing educators today (Vandegrift & Greene, 1991). Improved parental involvement doesn't occur merely because a school offers activities to which parents are invited. Teachers need to meet parents "where they (the parents) are." Vandegrift and Greene gave the example of a school that provided adult English as a Second Language (ESL) courses after interviews with parents revealed that the parents wanted to learn English. The parents came in large numbers, felt comfortable around the school, and were excited about being able to read with their children. We see, then, that the secret to successful home-school relationships is to personalize home-school communication.

The blend of teacher, student, and school characteristics needed to produce optimal learning is one that we will refer to constantly throughout this book. Figure 1.2 illustrates teacher, student, and school variables that have a powerful influence on learning.

Much more will be said throughout this book about the variables that affect learning and teaching . Up to this point we have emphasized the importance of excellent teaching to encourage student learning. We now turn our attention to the specific role of educational psychology in helping to improve both teaching and learning.

EDUCATIONAL PSYCHOLOGY: THE CORE CONCEPTS

Thus far we have stressed the notion of teachers as persons and professionals leading their students to higher levels of excellence. As you can well imagine, whenever discussions about teaching and learning occur, they are invariably accompanied by different interpretations. For example, *behaviorists* emphasize the importance of studying behavior and linking that behavior to environmental causes; *cognitive theorists* stress the significance of thinking and problem solving; finally, *humanistic psychologists* use the concept of personal growth and freedom to explain many of the topics we will discuss.

Another more recent interpretation is the *contextual* (also referred to as cultural or sociocultural). Here the emphasis is on culture, ethnicity, and gender to explain behavior. We make particular mention of the contextual interpretation because psychologists are becoming more sensitive to the impact of culture, ethnicity, and gender on all aspects of behavior, including teaching and learning. In discussing the many topics associated with educational psychology throughout the remainder of our work, we will attempt to illustrate the importance of cultural context to teaching and learning.

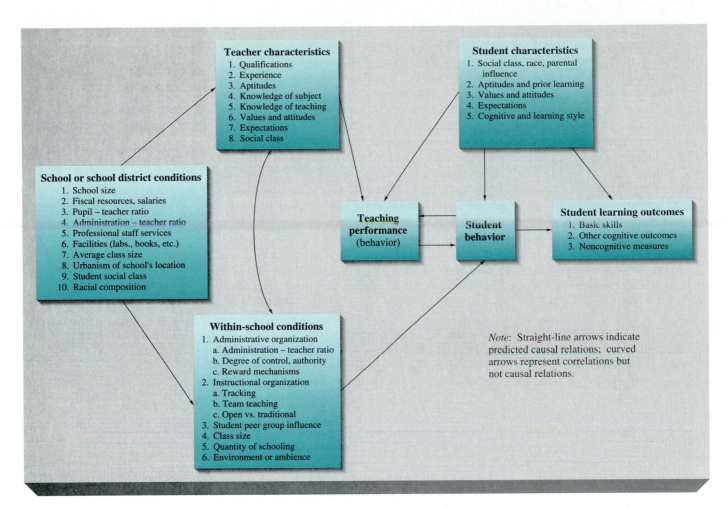

Figure 1.2

Structural model of school and teacher variables influencing student learning outcomes.

From Centra and Potter, "School and Teacher Effects: An Interrelational Model" in Review of Educational Research, *1980. Copyright © 1980 American Educational Research Association, Washington DC. Reprinted by permission of the publisher.*

Recognizing that each of these different interpretations of behavior has its own strengths, in this text we will apply pertinent ideas from each to the topics we discuss (teaching, learning, motivation, etc.). As Mayer noted (1992, p. 553), some of the great debates in modern psychology are occurring within the field of education, and educational psychology is playing a central role as a testing ground for psychological theories. To understand this critical function, consider the core concepts of educational psychology and their relationship to the classroom. Each of these five concepts provides the topic for a section of this book.

Educational Psychology and the Classroom

The first key concept in educational psychology is that it is important to understand what it means to teach. We hope that as a result of reading chapter 1, you have a better grasp of "life in the classroom." You must, however, have a basis from which to make decisions about your teaching. To help you with these decisions, chapter 2 presents a careful analysis of the research techniques that support the studies mentioned in this book. If you understand these methods, you can feel confident that by adopting (and perhaps adapting) the suggestions offered here, you are following the most recent and carefully researched teaching techniques now available. As mentioned in chapter 1, today's student population reflects the changing face of the country; the more you know about your students, the more effective you will be in the classroom. Consequently, chapter 3 presents a more detailed assessment of the impact of culture, and also stresses the need for clarity of communication.

The second core concept is the belief that if you are to teach effectively, you must have as much knowledge about your pupils as possible: their needs, characteristics, and differences. Chapter 4 is devoted to tracing the cognitive and language development of children, while chapter 5 focuses on their psychosocial and moral development. If you become a regular classroom teacher, you will come into contact with one or more students who are exceptional. There are many different types of exceptional student, including the gifted and talented, as well as students experiencing sensory handicaps, communication disorders, physical and health impairments, behavior disorders, learning disabilities, and mental retardation. Chapter 6 provides valuable information about the typical characteristics of those students who are exceptional.

The third priority in educational psychology is the commitment to understanding the learning process, which guides all else, since students are in school to learn. Chapters 7 and 8 focus on behavioral and cognitive explanations of learning, and provide numerous examples of how these theoretical explanations of learning can be translated into classroom practice. Chapter 9 has been written to help you turn students into better thinkers and problem solvers by presenting many techniques and "tips" that have proven helpful. Motivation, the subject of chapter 10, is so essential that we can safely state that without it, learning will not occur.

The fourth key concept is the function of instruction, beginning with the objectives that teachers wish to attain. Chapters 11 and 12 concentrate on those instructional strategies that research has shown to be effective. Learning, however, does not occur in a vacuum. You must understand and facilitate as fully as possible the best circumstances in which learning can occur. Consequently, chapter 13 presents in some detail successful strategies for managing a classroom, focusing on those techniques shown by both theory and research to be effective. For example, psychologists and educators now realize that many of the problems teachers experience in the classroom can be prevented, thus reducing the need for teachers to use specific control techniques. Today's effective teacher also requires skill and competence in managing a technological classroom. Given the increasing importance of this topic to the modern teacher, we will devote chapter 14 to the impact of technology on teaching and learning.

As a fifth tool for teachers, educational psychology provides techniques that can be used to determine how successful students have been in attaining objectives. Today, perhaps more than ever, assessing students' knowledge and skills is a central issue in schools. From a teacher's perspective, two of the most relevant purposes of assessment are (a) to identify students who are in need of educational or psychological assistance, and (b) to provide information to teachers that will help them develop instructional programs to facilitate students' functioning. Assessment involves the use of many tools and techniques, which will be examined in detail in chapters 15 and 16.

This text, then, seeks to give you a basis from which to make decisions about your teaching and your students' learning. Table 1.2 summarizes the relationship between the core concepts of educational psychology and the chapters of this text.

Throughout this text you will constantly find suggestions for maintaining good relationships with your students. Understanding pupil characteristics, using techniques for enhancing motivation, and applying recommendations for improving the learning atmosphere all contribute to your establishing warm interactions with your students.

The circle is now complete: extensive study of the characteristics of effective teaching have resulted in the core concepts of educational psychology, which, in constituting the structure of this book, can be used to make you a more effective teacher.

Have you thought about the individual differences of the students you'll teach? Which student characteristics do you think are most important for successful teaching and learning? Why?

Table 1.2

Core Concepts and Chapter Coverage	
Core concepts	**Chapters**
Introduction to Teaching	1. Educational Psychology: Teaching and Learning 2. Research and Educational Psychology 3. Diversity in the Classroom: Culture, Class, and Gender
The Development of Students	4. Cognitive and Language Development 5. Psychosocial and Moral Development 6. Exceptional Students
Learning Theories and Practices	7. Behavioral Psychology and Learning 8. Cognitive Psychology and Learning 9. Critical Thinking Skills and Problem-Solving Strategies 10. Motivation in the Classroom
The Design and Management of Classroom Instruction	11. Planning for Essential Learning Outcomes 12. Effective Teaching Strategies and the Design of Instruction 13. Classroom Management: Organization and Control 14. Teaching and Technology
Assessing Learning and Evaluating Education	15. Teacher-Constructed Tests and Performance Assessment Methods 16. Standardized Tests and Rating Scales in the Classroom

APPLICATIONS AND REFLECTIONS

Chapter Highlights

So You Want to Teach
- Teachers have their own unique expectations as they enter the classroom.
- Teachers are intimately involved with the changes shaping America's schools today.
- Teaching, as an art and as a science, is today recognized as one of the most exciting and important professions an individual could enter.
- Today's changing classrooms reflect the population's multicultural mix.
- Educational psychology today is concerned with the development and education of individuals from birth to adulthood.

Teaching as an Art and as a Science
- Definite characteristics mark the effective school.
- Teachers must be masters of their subject matter, of both core knowledge and current research.
- As teachers gain experience, they develop their own unique teaching styles, which are most effective for them.
- Teaching involves a series of reciprocal interactions: What you do with your students changes them. As a result of the changes in them, you also change.
- Researchers have acquired a systematic body of knowledge about teaching and learning.

Effective Schools

- As society becomes more complex and technological, students need quality education more than ever.
- Characteristics of effective (and defective) schools have been identified.
- In their personal education and teaching experience, teachers acquire a pedagogical content knowledge that can lead them to mastery.
- Most individuals become teachers because they find pleasure in teaching, in their subject matter, and in working with young people.
- Expert teachers have characteristics that are discernible and that can be modeled by novices.

Educational Psychology: The Core Concepts

- Educational psychology, as a discipline, is intended to clarify and improve the interaction between teaching and learning.
- In pursuing this mission, educational psychologists have developed a body of empirical research and theoretical insights that contributes to effective teaching and learning.

Connections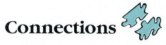

1. Think about how you learn and describe how one of the major concepts discussed in this chapter is part of your learning activities or approach.

2. Identify at least one learning situation (classroom instruction, self-study, taking a test, small-group work) and describe how you would apply one of the key concepts examined in this chapter *if you were a teacher*.

Getting the Picture and Drawing Relationships

Think about the various learning concepts and variables discussed in this chapter.
Create pictures, graphics, or figures that highlight the relationships among key
components.

Personal Journal

What I really learned in this chapter was _____

_____

_____

_____

What this means to me is _____

_____

_____

_____

Questions that were stimulated by this chapter include _____

_____

_____

_____

_____

Key Terms

appreciation	12	multicultural classrooms	14	TQM (Total Quality	
communication	12	perception	12	Management)	17
cooperation	12	teaching	6	whole language	8
educational psychology	3				

chapter 2

research and educational psychology

Paul Anderson, one of the third-grade teachers at Northside Elementary School, had made up his mind that he would talk to his fellow teachers about the new *Assertive Discipline* program that the school board was adopting for all the elementary classrooms in the district. In fact, the board had adopted the program, and Northside's principal, Mrs. Ramirez, had already ordered material for dissemination. Soon letters would be sent out to parents informing them of the school policy and components of the program.

When Paul arrived at the faculty lounge, he met Mary Sisco. Paul opened the conversation. "Mary, do you know about the new discipline program?" Mary noted that she had heard some of the teachers talking about the program after the faculty meeting last week, which Paul had missed. Paul, further curious about the program, asked, "Did the principal say anything about research to support the program? Is it effective with students? Does it really help?" Mary noted that little had been said about research on the program, but that it was being used in many schools across the country. Many teachers at Northside had said that given the rise in discipline problems recently, they would like to see the program in their school.

Paul was still concerned about adopting this program. He recently had enrolled in a classroom management class at the local university. The program introduced at Northside School was not one of those the professor had identified as having considerable research support. Paul was skeptical about this program's chances of ultimately improving student academic skills. He wanted the school to consider other programs that involved preventing classroom management problems. Mary, who was always trying to get Paul to do more than just talk about school issues, said, "Perhaps you could get involved with folks at the University and do some research on the effectiveness of the program. I bet that Mrs. Ramirez would support the project." ■

Paul Anderson was raising some important questions that you will often face once you have entered the teaching profession. The question here is one of research support for a particular program implemented at Northside School and in other schools around the country. Paul was recognizing the important role that research can play in making critical decisions on behalf of students, teachers, and parents. In this chapter we will explore the role that various forms of scientific research can play in educational psychology.

Here we see an example of the need to obtain solid data before making any decisions that could affect the well-being of students, teachers, and parents. It is not, however, enough to collect isolated pieces of information that may or may not be useful. Carefully designed studies are needed that will provide pertinent and reliable information to guide decision making.

Consequently, in this chapter you will discover the vital relationship between research and effective schooling. You also will explore the various methods used to obtain data and the specific purposes for which each method is intended. Finally, you will be asked to think about an issue that is becoming increasingly critical for those of us who work with other human beings: the ethical and legal aspects of research.

When you finish reading this chapter, you should be able to

- identify the sources of knowledge that lead to educational decisions
- distinguish the various types of research methods
- describe the techniques used by educational researchers
- classify the various types of research methods according to the purposes for which they are intended

Research and Effective Schooling 28
Sources of Knowledge 28

The Emergence of Research on Children 30
Baby Biographies 30
Case Studies 31
Scientific Influences 32

Major Research Methods 34
Historical Research 34
Descriptive Research 34
Correlational Research 35
Comparative Research 36
Experimental Research 36

Techniques Used by Researchers 37
Surveys 37
Interviews 39
Observation 41
Cross-Sectional and Longitudinal Research 41
Cross-Cultural Research 42
Single-Case Research 43

Primary, Secondary, and Meta-Analysis 44

Ethical and Legal Considerations in Research in Education 47

Applications and Reflections 47

RESEARCH AND EFFECTIVE SCHOOLING

Teachers are always concerned about the effectiveness of their methods, and they like to try different techniques. Teachers who are alert to the latest research and the methods that are appropriate for them to use become increasingly more skillful in their classroom instruction. This chapter is designed to acquaint you with the ways in which educational research is conducted, and the ways in which it contributes to our understanding of schools, teaching, and learning. *Research answers questions.* Most research is designed to answer questions about causation, relationships, or effectiveness. Examples of such questions relevant to many educators include these: What effect do teachers' oral questions have on students' attention and comprehension of material? What is the relationship between the amount of time spent on homework and classroom test performance? Which social skills program, Program A or Program B, is most effective with regard to increasing students' cooperation skills?

"Okay—who asked it about the chicken and the egg?"

H. Schwadron in Phi Delta Kappan.

Sources of Knowledge

Much of the systematic knowledge we have about human behavior has resulted from the application of scientific methods to the study of certain events. A major goal of scientific study is to explain, predict, and/or control these events. Yet, the application of scientific procedures is a relatively recent happening in history. It is also true that although scientific study has contributed greatly to human understanding of ourselves and others, knowledge is obtained from many sources (see table 2.1).

Authority

Individuals in a position of status or authority have provided people or societies with the so-called "truth." One prominent example was the belief that the earth was flat. Scholars and mapmakers proclaimed this "fact" with absolute confidence. As you can see, depending on this type of knowledge can lead to trouble if the so-called authority is incorrect. The information conveyed to others will be in error. Of course, authority may not be incorrect in all cases.

Identify the sources of knowledge that you believe lead to educational decisions, and provide an example of how each source could be utilized in decision making.

Table 2.1

Common Sources of Knowledge About People and the Environment	
Source	**Example**
Authority	The earth is flat.
Tradition	Children should begin school at 6 years of age.
Expert opinion	Detention of student is unlikely to improve academic functioning.
Personal experiences	Mothers should breast-feed.
Documentation	More children attend school today than did so in 1900.
Scientific research	Some forms of mental retardation are genetic in origin.

Should you change your answers on multiple-choice tests? Students' common sense would say no. You have probably heard the folk wisdom, "Don't change your answers on exams, because you'll be more likely to change a right answer to a wrong answer than to change a wrong answer to a right answer." You might be surprised that scientific research has consistently found that students are slightly more likely to change a wrong answer to a right answer than to change a right answer to a wrong answer (Skinner, 1983).

Tradition

Knowledge is also obtained from tradition. Did you begin your formal education around the age of 6 years? If you did, you were one of millions of children who started school at 6 (in either kindergarten or first grade) because traditionally, this has been the appropriate age to begin formal schooling. Moreover, American schools have had a tradition of closing for the summer for agricultural reasons. Such a rationale is no longer relevant, but tradition has prevailed. Knowledge based on tradition can also be inaccurate. Formal educational experiences often begin much earlier than age 6. In fact, many children in the United States begin some type of formal education by age 2 or 3. This example illustrates the considerable debate over tradition as a source of knowledge.

Expert Opinion

Another influential source of knowledge is the opinion of experts. Certain individuals may take positions that dramatically influence people's beliefs. Many readers of this book may have been reared according to the practices suggested by Dr. Benjamin Spock in his book *Baby and Child Care* (1957). There have been many other popular books (e.g., *How to Parent,* by Fitzhugh Dodson, 1970; *How to Raise Independent and Professionally Successful Daughters,* by Rita and Kenneth Dunn, 1977; *How Children Fail,* by John Holt, 1964) that have influenced the thinking and behavior of parents and teachers. The thinking of many young Americans on the birth process may have been influenced by the writings of Lamaze and his followers on natural childbirth. Many attitudes now in vogue are the ideas of various experts and have had a tremendous impact on child-rearing and social practices.

Personal Experience

Human beings gain a considerable amount of knowledge from personal experience, although not all of it is accurate. In many instances we may change our beliefs through knowledge from different sources. A teacher might adopt a classroom management program because personal experiences with the techniques suggest that it will likely be effective with the students. However, the approach may have little or no research support. Some limitations of personal experience are that certain evidence may be omitted and that individuals may be too subjective in their beliefs.

Documentation

Another knowledge source is the documentation of events, in which records are kept of various events or phenomena. Today, there is rather extensive documentation of data, easily accessible through the use of computer technology. For example, we can document that a specific number of children in a large city have received inoculations against a certain disease. Documentation is a relatively new source of information and knowledge. In many cases, we must speculate about certain events in history, because important documentation is incomplete or fragmented. Documentation is a good source of knowledge, but has its limitations. People can be biased in providing certain information. Nevertheless, documentation is a step in the right direction: scientific data as a source of knowledge.

Scientific Research

The final source of information is scientific research. "Scientific research is the systematic, controlled, empirical, and critical investigation of hypothetical propositions about the presumed relations among natural phenomena" (Kerlinger, 1973, p. 11). This definition implies that scientific investigation is an orderly endeavor, so that the researcher can have confidence in the outcomes. Scientific research typically is carried out under controlled conditions. Educational researchers make available both the procedures and findings of research to outside evaluation or criticism.

With procedures, findings, and conclusions available, other reviewers of a study may propose rival hypotheses or different interpretations of the data from those drawn by the original researchers (Huck & Sandler, 1979). In this chapter, we will present a study as summarized by Huck and Sandler (1979), along with a rival hypothesis. After you have read the summary of the study, suggest an alternative; then, read what the authors had to say about the research. (You will find this in the focus box entitled "Rival Hypotheses.")

Although the scientific form of investigation generally is regarded as an important method of generating knowledge, there is considerable disagreement over which ones are the best methods. Scientific methods of investigation have evolved over a considerable period of time. In the next section, we review some of the historical features of scientific research.

THE EMERGENCE OF RESEARCH ON CHILDREN

Long before people developed systematic experimental procedures to study children, an interest was evolving in the documentation of child behavior. Some of these procedures, such as baby biographies and individual case studies, were dominant forms of investigating aspects of child development. Although both of these techniques are still used in educational psychology, they generally have been replaced by more credible strategies based on principles of scientific research.

Baby Biographies

Maintaining records of one's children is a relatively common practice and has likely existed since written communications began. However, it was not until the end of the eighteenth century that some individuals began to share formally and publicly their observations on children. For example, in 1774 Johann Pestalozzi, a Swiss educator, published observations on the development of his 3½-year-old son, in which he affirmed

Focus ◄ Rival Hypotheses

Modeling Clay

Jean Piaget is a well-known Swiss psychologist whose ideas have transformed the field of developmental psychology over the past few decades. Many students associate him with conservation tasks, such as how a child learns that 200 cc of water is the same in a tall skinny glass as in a short fat glass, despite the difference in the water level. A similar task involving a clay ball and a clay cylinder (each with the same volume of clay) was one of a number of conservation tasks used in a study comparing modeling and nonmodeling instructions given to 6-year-olds.

In this study, a random sample of twenty-eight Chicano children were drawn from the first grade of a school located in a *barrio* area of Tucson, Arizona. The children were all from Spanish-speaking homes and were in their first few months of school (median age was 6.3 years). The children were randomly assigned to one of two groups; each group included seven boys and seven girls. Some children (those in the modeling group) were allowed to watch the experimenter transform an object from one shape to another while listening to another child (the model) answer the experimenter's questions about the transformation. Those in the nonmodeling instructions group were not shown the transformation process but were instead presented with

"before" and "after" objects. This group was told that the objects were equivalent. Analysis of variance showed significant differences between the two groups, with the modeling group showing superiority on the conservation tasks. Furthermore, according to the authors, the nonmodeling instructions produced no reliable changes.

What do you think? Do you agree that the modeling approach is clearly superior? Before continuing your reading, write your reasons for either agreeing or disagreeing with the authors' conclusions.

Rival Hypothesis

Although we are generally sympathetic towards social learning theory and its methods (including modeling), we have difficulty accepting this study as evidence in its favor. Though the authors are to be commended for the design (true random selection and assignment) and analysis (appropriate use of the analysis of variance,) we wonder about the effectiveness of English instructions being given to children for whom Spanish is a first language. We would have recommended that the entire experiment be conducted in Spanish to eliminate the plausible rival hypothesis that the nonmodeling instructional group received its instructions in a foreign language.

Selected excerpt from Rival Hypotheses: Alternative Interpretations of Data-Based Conclusions *by Schuyler W. Huck and Howard M. Sandler. Copyright © 1979 by Schuyler W. Huck and Howard M. Sandler. Reprinted by permission of HarperCollins Publishers.*

the innate goodness of the child. In 1787, Dieterich Tiedeman published his observations of an infant during the first 2½ years of life, in which aspects of sensory motor, language, and intellectual growth were reported.

Systematic observation of children continued into the nineteenth century. Two important publications were instrumental in promoting a long series of observational studies of children. In 1877, Charles Darwin published *A Biographical Sketch of an Infant,* an account of his infant son. Likewise, in 1882, William Preyer published a book on his son's first four years of life. The involvement of these professionals facilitated the proliferation of the baby biography as a method of child study. These biographies also focused attention on important aspects of child development and created interest in child study in general.

Despite these positive contributions of the baby biography in child study, the method is not held in high regard in the scientific community. There are several reasons for this conclusion. First, the biography represents a subjective description of events and cannot be independently evaluated and replicated by others. Second, typical observations made by individuals are unsystematic and may be made at irregular intervals. Third, the descriptions of behavior may represent the bias of the individual who holds certain conceptions about human development. Fourth, it is difficult to generalize data from biographies as a result of the aforementioned problems.

Case Studies

case study *The evaluation and report of research on an individual subject, usually of an anecdotal nature.*

The **case study** is a methodology of investigation that is characterized by uncontrolled reporting of some experience, treatment, or phenomenon. The typical case study lacks the usual controls that are a part of scientific experiments. Case studies have played an important role in research investigations throughout the history of psychology and education, and are still used in psychology and psychiatry. As a form of research methodology, the case study evolved as individuals of various theoretical orientations became involved in treating people with personality and behavior problems. Though case studies commonly are used in reporting therapeutic interventions with children and adults, they also have been used widely in psychology and education. Professional journals have often reported using "case study" methods (Kazdin, 1982), which remained a primary form of methodology of clinical investigations through the first half of this century. The case study reported in the focus box illustrates its usefulness in a contemporary school setting.

Case study investigation has been useful in advancing knowledge, particularly in psychotherapy. Barlow and Hersen (1984) noted that case studies can (a) foster clinical innovation, (b) cast doubt on certain theoretical positions, (c) permit study of uncommon problems, (d) develop new technical skills, (e) support theoretical views, (f) promote refinement in various techniques, and (g) provide data that can be used to design more highly controlled research. For example, Dukes (1965) reviewed over two hundred case studies over a twenty-five-year period from many areas of psychology, noting that in many instances the reports provided evidence of findings that changed the course of future study.

Despite positive features, case studies, like baby biographies, have many problems and generally are not regarded as reliable research procedures. Case studies typically are characterized by subjective impression, bias, and inadequate description of the procedures used to treat a person, and they are difficult to replicate. Replication is a key concern. Thus, case study methods are increasingly being replaced by single-case time-series research strategies that are designed to make replication possible. These strategies are described later in the chapter.

THE FAR SIDE By GARY LARSON

"No doubt about it, Ellington—we've mathematically expressed the purpose of the universe. Gad, how I love the thrill of scientific discovery!"

THE FAR SIDE © 1984 Universal Press Syndicate. Reprinted with permission. All rights reserved.

Scientific Influences

Researchers embarking on the systematic study of education have many techniques to use in this endeavor. Contemporary research in educational psychology is guided by scientific methods. We use the term "methods" because there is no one scientific method. Scientific research generally is guided by the following five steps shown in figure 2.1, used to study a particular topic or problem. We will examine these steps in the context of an applied educational problem that was investigated by researchers in a preschool setting (Twardosz, Cataldo, & Risley, 1974).

- *Step 1: Research problem identification.* A first step in conducting scientific research involves the identification of a problem or question. There is great interest in knowing how the physical environment influences the behavior and learning of children (Dunn, 1987). One aspect of the problem identified in the study by Twardosz et al. (1974) was determining how an open day-care environment influenced the sleep of infants and toddlers.
- *Step 2: Research problem clarification.* Researchers must analyze the specific aspects of the problem and identify the nature, scope, and specifics of the situation. In the Twardosz et al. study, they had the problem of how to examine the variables that might influence sleep. Any ideas? If you choose the conditions of noise and light versus quiet and darkness, you are on the right track.

Focus

The Case Study

The following case study is a direct and brief account of the efforts of a public school speech therapist who, by working with a classroom teacher, a school principal, and the parents, was able to help a boy, LeRoy, overcome his fear of speaking in public situations.

LeRoy, who had never spoken in school, was referred to the speech therapist during the second semester of first grade. The boy showed good comprehension, did all his silent work, was careful with minute details, and was very good in art; but he had never read aloud nor taken part in rhythmic work and singing. LeRoy's intelligence was average, and his score on the Detroit First Grade Reading Test was 92, well above average.

His parents said that LeRoy talked with his family and played well alone. He would never play with other children or go to their homes. His speech with the family was normal. The only reason his mother could give for his behavior was that he was bashful. But the speech therapist felt this remark had been made so often that LeRoy had been encouraged to develop his antisocial tendencies rather than to overcome his natural shyness.

The speech therapist was called in because, by school rules, LeRoy could not advance to second grade until he could read aloud. The first session showed almost no progress, although, of course, the speech therapist did not wish to rush the child. He obviously could hear well and take directions; vocabulary and memory were no problem to him, as his comprehension and seat work showed. At the second session, the therapist began to gain his confidence, and when asked, LeRoy timorously showed both his tongue and his teeth.

During the third session, he uttered his first word in school. Knowing his interest in coloring, the therapist had brought some attractive colored pictures of animals and children. His interest in these was used as the first step in breaking through his withdrawal and silence. To see the pictures, LeRoy repeated "come" and then other first-grade reading words.

At the next meeting, he read a book for the therapist. He read well, and was, of course, praised generously. Later he agreed to "surprise the principal" by reading aloud for her, and also for his teacher, although he would stop if anyone else came into the room.

He remained completely withdrawn from peers, although he would read for a few adults. At an outdoor picnic the following September, he held his ice cream cone in his hand while it melted, and he did not move until he was told to throw his soggy cone away—which he did. He watched the other children having fun but showed no indication that he was enjoying himself.

As LeRoy's second grade year progressed, the therapist encouraged him to read for, and later play with, two neighbor boys who were in his schoolroom. After she suggested that he visit one of them to watch television, LeRoy did so. He had never before gone to another child's house to play. His conversation then was in one-word sentences, but he had no speech defects.

One day the therapist suggested that LeRoy's two friends each bring another boy to be surprised at how well LeRoy read. He assented. His classroom teacher, who was very cooperative, was asked to send first the boys, then the girls, one at a time, at about two-minute intervals. The children came, one by one, and the group moved to a larger room, but LeRoy continued to read for them. They all moved back to the classroom, where everyone could have a seat. And there LeRoy walked to the front of the room, sat in the teacher's chair, and read to the children of his class.

The next day he stayed home; the shock must have been too much for him. The speech therapist went to his home, and he returned eagerly to school with her. When he arrived, his classmates had chosen colored paper to make Easter baskets. He was asked what color he wanted, and he answered "green." The following day LeRoy's teacher noted that he had read aloud in class and that the children had chosen him for games, although he would not participate in the poems or rhythmic actions.

Three weeks later, just before his second grade ended, his teacher reported that he was participating more and that "he beams," whereas before he had shown no facial expression. His withdrawal and silence were rapidly breaking down, and his behavior appeared to be that of a normal, happy child.

Interview script courtesy of Dr. John R. Bergan.

- *Step 3: Implement research plan.* In this step, researchers state the problem and test the plan and program implemented to answer the question. The researchers measured the percentage of sleeping and crying repeatedly over 47 days under the conditions of noise and light (door was left open and light entered the room) and quiet and darkness (door was closed and light was shut out).
- *Step 4: Research plan evaluation.* This step involves making decisions based upon the data collected from the study. The data may or may not support the hunches (hypotheses) of the researchers. Any guesses as to how the Twardosz et al. study (1974) turned out? The researchers found *no* differences in the effects of noise and light and quiet and darkness (i.e., none of the children's sleep was adversely affected by noise and light).

Examine the five steps of the scientific method in the context of an educational problem that you have identified.

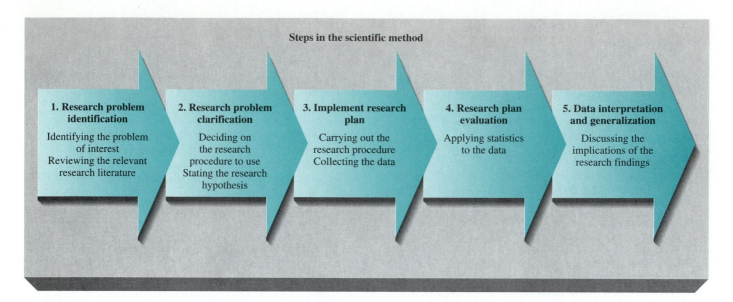

Steps in the scientific method

1. Research problem identification
Identifying the problem of interest
Reviewing the relevant research literature

2. Research problem clarification
Deciding on the research procedure to use
Stating the research hypothesis

3. Implement research plan
Carrying out the research procedure
Collecting the data

4. Research plan evaluation
Applying statistics to the data

5. Data interpretation and generalization
Discussing the implications of the research findings

Figure 2.1
The scientific method.

- *Step 5: Data interpretation and generalization.* The final step involves interpretation and generalization of the researcher's findings into a larger body of knowledge related to the problem under study. Results may be integrated into existing knowledge or suggest topics for future research. How would you explain the findings of our study? Perhaps the conditions of noise and light were not strong enough to make a difference. Would you generalize the results of the study by telling people that noise and light have no effect on a child's sleep patterns? You may be "going beyond the data" to suggest this; as you will see in later chapters, research data in educational psychology are sometimes misrepresented in just such a way.

MAJOR RESEARCH METHODS

To a greater or lesser degree, all the above steps are involved in the major types of research conducted in schools and about schooling. These approaches to research include (a) historical, (b) descriptive, (c) correlational, (d) comparative, and (e) experimental research.

Historical Research

As the name implies, **historical research** involves studying, understanding, and explaining past events. A major purpose of historical research is to formulate conclusions about causes, effects, or trends of past events that help to either explain current events or anticipate future events. Typically, individuals conducting historical research do not gather data by administering tests or observing behavior. Rather, they use data that are already available. For example, if educational researchers wanted to examine the factors that influence academic achievement of children in orphanages, they would conduct a search of the literature of follow-up studies of achievement of children in this type of institution.

historical research *The study, understanding, and explanation of past events.*

Descriptive Research

In qualitative or **descriptive research,** the investigator examines and reports things the way they are in an effort to understand and explain them. In this type of study, the researcher collects data to test a hypothesis or answer questions concerning the status of some issue or problem. Instruments such as surveys, questionnaires, interviews, and observation may be developed for this type of investigation. The year-round school is an educational alternative being examined by many public school systems. If you were interested in studying the students, parents, and teachers participating in a year-round

descriptive research *Research in which the investigator examines and reports things the way they are.*

Focus **Understanding the Research Article**

As you continue your reading and work in educational psychology, your instructor will probably ask you to review pertinent articles that shed light on the topic you're studying. Many of these articles will present the results of an experiment that reflects the scientific method.

The typical research article contains four sections: the *Introduction,* the *Method* section, the *Results* section, and the *Discussion* (Moore, 1983). We'll review each of these sections using a well-designed study— "The Effects of Early Education on Children's Competence in Elementary School," published in *Evaluation Review* (Bronson, Pierson, & Tivnan, 1984)—to illustrate each of the four parts.

The Introduction

The introductory section states the purpose of the article (usually as an attempt to solve a problem) and predicts the outcome of the study (usually in the form of hypotheses). The introduction section also contains a review of the literature. In the introductory section of the Bronson et al. article, the researchers state that their intent is to coordinate the effects of early education programs on the performance of students in elementary school. They concisely review the pertinent research and suggest a means of evaluating competence.

The Method Section

The method section informs the reader about the subjects in the experiment (Who were they? How many? How were they chosen?), a description of any tests that were used, and a summary of the steps taken to carry out the study. In the Bronson et al. study, the subjects were 169 second-grade children who had been in an early education program and 169 other children who had not been in the preschool program. The outcome measure was a classroom observation instrument. The authors then explained in considerable detail how they observed the pupils.

The Results Section

Here the information gathered on the subjects is presented, together with the statistics that help us to interpret the data. In the article we are using, the authors presented their data in several clear tables and discussed differences between the two groups, using appropriate statistics.

Discussion

Finally, the authors of any research article discuss the importance of what they found (or didn't find) and relate their findings to theory and previous research. In the Bronson et al. article, the authors reported that the students who had experienced any early education program showed significantly greater competence in the second grade. The authors concluded by noting the value of these programs in reducing classroom behavior problems and improving students' competence.

---

school, you might observe a select sample of children, their parents, and teachers. Such a study would be an example of qualitative research.

Correlational Research

correlational research *Research in which the researcher attempts to determine if a relation exists between two or more variables.*

In **correlational research,** the researcher attempts to determine if a relation exists between two or more variables. Variables can refer to a range of human characteristics, such as height, weight, sex, intelligence, and so forth. For example, a researcher may be interested in examining the relation between intelligence and creativity. But the finding that there is a relation between intelligence and creativity does not mean that intelligence "causes" creativity. A high correlation indicates only that most people with high intelligence have higher creative behavior, and that most people with lower intelligence have lower evidence of creativity. Thus, the finding that two variables are highly related (correlated) does not mean that one has caused the other; a third variable may cause or strongly influence both variables. Or, in our example, it may be that some degree of intelligence is necessary to, but not the only requirement for, creativity.

The degree of relation between two or more variables generally is expressed as a correlation coefficient (labeled "r"), represented by a number between .00 (no relation) and 1.00 (perfect relation). Of course, two variables can be negatively related, a situation that occurs when a high score on one variable is accompanied by a low score on the other variable. The closer the coefficient is to 1.00, the better the researcher is able to make a prediction. Most correlations are less than 1.00; thus, prediction is far from perfect. Nevertheless, predictions based on known relations are useful in understanding the nature of child behavior.

Comparative Research

In **comparative research** the investigator searches for causal relations among variables that are compared with each other. Typically, comparative research involves the comparison of groups that are different before the study begins. For example, if researchers are interested in examining the effect of socioeconomic status (SES) on drug abuse in adolescents, they might form several different groups on the basis of SES (i.e., the nonmanipulated independent variable). Much research in educational psychology is conducted in this fashion, but the scientific community does not regard this type of research to be as reliable and credible as studies in which variables are manipulated directly. Since there is no manipulation of or control over extraneous events, the causal relations established in comparative research must remain tentative. Thus, in the above example, we would have to consider that variables other than SES accounted for different patterns of drug abuse. Although comparative research is not as predictable as experimental research, it has the following advantage: Many variables cannot be manipulated or controlled by the educational researcher; thus this form of research provides an option. The alternative might be no study at all.

comparative research *Research in which the investigator searches for direct relations among variables that are compared with one another.*

Experimental Research

Experimental research involves the active manipulation of an independent variable to observe changes in the dependent variable. In experimental research, the **independent variable** frequently is called the experimental, or treatment, condition. Treatment conditions may be compared with each other or with a control condition: a condition in which no treatment is administered, although the group is the same as the treatment group in all other respects. The most important feature of experimental research is that researchers are able to manipulate variables and to control sources of influence that could affect the results. Thus, researchers attempt to make the groups as equal as possible on all variables except the independent variable.

experimental research *Research in which the researcher actively manipulates an independent variable to observe changes in the dependent variable.*

independent variable *The experimental or treatment condition variable.*

One type of experimental research occurs when an investigator forms two groups by assigning subjects randomly to these conditions. In random assignment, any individual going into one of the two groups has an equal chance of ending up in either group. Thus, no bias is introduced into the experiment by having more subjects with specific characteristics, such as a specific age, a specific gender, and so forth, in one group than in the other. For example, let's assume that you, the researcher, want to discover the effectiveness of a new method of teaching reading. You have decided that you are interested in discovering the effects of a new type of reading instruction for fifth-graders. Thus, you have selected the independent variable. One of the criteria for a true experiment has been met. You next randomly assign each fifth-grade student to one of two groups: the first group receives reading instruction according to the new method, while the second group continues with the traditional method. You have now met *both* of the criteria for experimental research: *control of the independent variable* and *random assignment of subjects*. If the study is carefully done, by meeting these two criteria, the researcher can point to a cause and effect relationship. That is, the researcher can state that the new type of reading instruction did cause an improvement in pupils' reading scores, if the average scores for the students in the group that were taught by the new reading method were higher than those of the students in the group that were taught by the traditional method.

The variable (here, reading method) that is manipulated or directly controlled is, as we have seen, the independent variable. The experimental subjects must perform some task (here, a reading test) that is selected to determine the effect of the independent variable. The way in which the subjects respond (here, test performance) is the **dependent variable.** The design is as follows:

$$Eb-X-Ea$$
$$Cb-X-Ca$$

dependent variable *The variable on which subjects respond to the manipulation of the independent variable.*

In this illustration, E is the experimental group, C is the control group, X is the independent variable, b is before, and a is after the experiment. If the study has been carefully controlled, any differences on the reading test should be the result of X, the new method of teaching reading.

In experimental research, the investigator is interested in determining if a relationship exists between the independent and the dependent variable, and how widely the relationship applies. Krathwohl (1993) labeled these two criteria as the *internal validity* and *external validity* of research, respectively. To determine if a relationship exists, *internal validity* (LP) is examined, where LP represents the *linking power* of the variables in the relationship. To determine how widely the relationship applies, Krathwohl refers to the *external validity* (GP), where the GP represents the *generality power* of the research findings. Consider our example of the reading experiment to understand both types of validity. To determine the linking power, the investigator would be interested in ruling out variables that might link the new reading instruction to obtained improvements in reading. What variable might reduce the linking power? What would you expect if it were determined that the teachers in the new method didn't like it and used the procedure only occasionally during the study? Such a conclusion would surely reduce the linking power. In the case of generality power we could consider a number of criteria that might influence the degree to which we could generalize our findings. We conducted our reading experiment with fifth-grade students. Would the same results be expected with third-grade children? Maybe not! Results may not generalize to this group.

Which type of research is best? Many educational researchers believe that experimental research is the most useful form of scientific investigation. Since experimental research allows control of many factors that potentially bias results, it is preferred in the scientific world. However, determining which method of research is best for a particular study depends on numerous factors, such as the problem under investigation, subjects to be studied, instruments used to collect data, and previous work in the field. The purpose of the research helps to determine if correlational, comparative, or well-controlled experimental studies are to be conducted. For example, when one is interested in reviewing historical events that led to some current school practice, historical research is the most appropriate.

Thus, many factors must be examined to decide which research method is best under which circumstances; no single research method is always the best. The five types of research we have discussed are summarized in table 2.2.

TECHNIQUES USED BY RESEARCHERS

Researchers in the field of educational psychology use many different approaches to gather data. In the following sections, we review some of the more common techniques and procedures used in research. These techniques include surveys, interviews, and observations, and the procedures to be highlighted are cross-sectional and longitudinal methods. Time-series and cross-cultural research are also discussed.

Surveys

surveys *A research technique in which the investigator asks subjects questions about a particular issue, usually with structured questionnaires.*

In survey research the investigator asks a group of individuals questions about a particular issue. Survey research often is used to study teachers, particularly their attitudes, beliefs, opinions, and behavior. **Surveys** actually are conducted through a variety of methods, such as interviews, questionnaires (called "direct administration"), the telephone, and mail (Fraenkel & Wallen, 1990). Regardless of the method, the heart of good survey research is the development of a meaningful survey tool—one that clearly communicates questions or concerns in an unbiased fashion, can be completed in a

Table 2.2

Classification and Description of Major Research Methods	
Classification	**Description**
Historical research	Involves studying, understanding, and explaining past events.
	Example: Factors leading to the development and growth of the use of teaching machines.
Descriptive research	Involves collecting data to test hypotheses or answer questions related to the current status of a problem.
	Example: How new parents share responsibilities in child rearing. New parents would be observed for a period of time and results could be reported as percentages (e.g., Feeding: Mother 60%, Father 40%; Diaper changing: Mother 95%, Father 5%; etc.).
Correlational research	Involves determining whether, and to what extent, a relation exists between two or more variables.
	Example: The relation between intelligence and achievement. Scores on an intelligence test would be obtained from each individual in a certain group. The two sets of scores would be correlated, and the resulting correlation coefficient would indicate the degree of relation between intelligence and achievement.
Comparative research	Involves establishing a direct relation between variables that are compared, but not manipulated, by the researcher.
	Example: The effect of preschool attendance on achievement at the end of first grade. The independent variable (or presumed cause) is preschool attendance; the dependent variable (or effect) is measured achievement at the end of first grade. Groups of first-graders would be identified—some that had attended preschool and some that had not—and the achievement would be compared.
Experimental research	Involves actual manipulation by a researcher of at least one independent variable to observe the effect on one or more dependent variables.
	Example: The effect of positive reinforcement on the number of math problems completed by second-grade children. The independent variable is the reinforcement (praise statements by teachers); the dependent variable is the number of problems completed. Two groups would be exposed to essentially the same experiences, except for the reinforcement. After some time, their output on math problems would be compared.

time-efficient manner, and can be scored or interpreted reliably. Each of these methods has various advantages and disadvantages, as can be observed in table 2.3.

Before examining an illustration of the proper use of the survey method, let us begin by agreeing that few topics have caused as much controversy in American public schools as the use of corporal punishment. You might wonder how often corporal punishment is used in schools. Who administers the punishment? Is it used equally across the grades? These are but a few of the questions that Rose (1984) was able to address in a school discipline survey that was mailed to 324 principals in eighteen randomly selected states representing the nine U.S. Census districts. Table 2.4 displays several items from the actual questionnaire and the frequency and percentage of responses to each item. Rose found that 74.1 percent of the principals responding to the survey used corporal punishment with their students! Corporal punishment was used more frequently

List five major research methods and provide an example of each type of research in a school setting.

Table 2.3

	Direct administration	Telephone	Mail	Interview
Comparative cost	Lowest	About the same	About the same	High
Facilities needed?	Yes	No	No	Yes
Require training of questioner?	Yes	Yes	No	Yes
Response rate	Very high	Good	Poorest	Very high
Group administration possible?	Yes	No	No	Yes
Allow for random sampling?	Possibly	Yes	Yes	Yes
Require literate sample?	Yes	No	Yes	No
Permit follow-up questions?	No	Yes	No	Yes
Encourage response to sensitive topics?	Somewhat	Somewhat	Best	Weak
Standardization of responses	Easy	Somewhat	Easy	Hardest

From J. R. Fraenkel and N. E. Wallen, *How to Design and Evaluate Research in Education.* Copyright © 1990 McGraw-Hill, Inc., New York, NY. Reprinted by permission of McGraw-Hill.

with male students than with female students. If you look closely at the table, you can also observe other interesting trends in the study. Do you think the results would be different today?

Survey research like that performed in the Rose (1984) study has the advantage of wide scope, in that a great deal of information can be obtained from a large population (e.g., principals in the United States). Generally, survey research provides a good representation of sources of information. But survey research also has disadvantages. First, survey methods may not allow very detailed information on the issue being researched, because the survey questions are so general. Second, survey research can be expensive and time-consuming. Third, one may introduce into the study sampling error that can bias the results. Perhaps all states should have been sampled in the Rose study, for example. Fourth, survey research is subject to faking responses and bias in responding to questions. Even with these limitations, however, the survey method can provide useful information in research.

Interviews

interviews *A research method in which an investigator asks another individual questions designed to obtain answers relevant to a research problem.*

Although **interviews** are used often in survey research, they are used in many other forms of research as well. Have you ever been interviewed by someone who was conducting a study on some problem or issue? If so, you were exposed to another common method of obtaining information for research purposes. The interview procedure involves a face-to-face situation in which an interviewer asks another individual questions designed to obtain answers relevant to the research problem. Of course, interview procedures are used for purposes other than research, such as those interviews usually conducted to fill job openings.

In research, interviews are typically categorized as either *structured* (also called *standardized*) or *unstructured* (also called *unstandardized*). In a standardized interview, the interviewer asks questions in which the sequence and wording are fixed. Thus, the interviewer has little freedom to depart from a prepared script. In contrast, unstandardized interviews are more flexible and open, in that the interviewer determines what will be asked. Thus, the unstandardized, nonstructured interview has an open format, whereas the standardized, structured interview has a closed format.

Interview strategies allow the researcher to obtain a great deal of information, particularly when the situation is open. The interview can also be made flexible, to

Suppose that you conducted a survey of U.S. teachers' attitudes about grade retention. What would be some advantages and disadvantages of using the survey techniques?

Table 2.4

Frequencies and Percentages of Responses to Questionnaire Items in the Rose Survey

Item	Frequency	Percentage
Demographic		
1. Approximate size of community in which your school is located:		
A. Rural, unincorporated	14	6.0
B. Incorporated, under 1,000	12	5.2
C. 1,000–5,000	36	15.5
D. 5,000–10,000	31	13.4
E. 10,000–50,000	50	21.6
F. 50,000–100,000	25	10.7
G. 100,000–500,000	46	19.8
H. 500,000 or more	18	7.8
2. Number of students in your school:		
A. 0–300	46	19.8
B. 301–600	84	36.2
C. 601–900	58	25.0
D. 901–1,200	20	8.6
E. 1,200 or more	24	10.3
Discipline		
7. Is corporal punishment used in your school?		
A. Yes	172	74.1
B. No	60	25.9
If Question 7 is yes, please complete the remainder of the questionnaire.		
8. Who administers corporal punishment?		
A. Referring teacher	6	3.7
B. Principal	34	21.0
C. Other teacher	0	-
D. Other administrative personnel (e.g., assistant principal)	16	9.9
E. Combination	106	65.4
For the following three items, circle the number of students in each category who received corporal punishment in the last month.		
14. Male:		
A. 0–5	69	44.8
B. 6–10	35	22.7
C. 11–15	28	18.2
D. 16–20	8	5.2
E. 21–25	2	1.3
F. 26 or more	12	7.8
Do you feel that corporal punishment is effective in:		
18. Maintaining the general level of discipline in your school?		
A. Yes	130	83.3
B. No	26	16.7
19. Reducing specific behavior problems for specific students?		
A. Yes	141	88.1
B. No	19	11.9
20. Maintaining teacher morale?		
A. Yes	111	73.0
B. No	41	27.0
21. Demonstrating your support of your teachers?		
A. Yes	141	73.1
B. No	42	26.9
22. List the offense that most often leads to corporal punishment (categorized subsequent to responses).		
Fighting	72	51.4
Disruptive in class	30	21.4
Disrespect for authority	19	13.5
Disobedience	9	6.4
Truancy	6	4.3
Miscellaneous	4	2.8

From T. L. Rose, "Current uses of corporal punishment in American public schools" in *Journal of Educational Psychology,* 76, 427–441, 1984. Copyright © 1984 American Psychological Association, Washington DC. Reprinted by permission.

meet the needs of the situation, problem, and person. This flexibility is an advantage with children, since questions can be reworded so that a child can understand the question. Interviews are often used as adjunct methods, to probe individuals after an experiment, or to follow up on written survey responses. On the negative side, interviewee responses can be faked, are subject to interpretation, and can take a lot of time.

Observation

observation *A research method in which trained observers assess individuals in as natural a setting as possible.*

One of the most common ways we obtain information is through **observation.** Systematic observation also has evolved as a basic scientific tool for gathering data in research on teaching (Evertson & Green, 1986). As noted earlier in the chapter, many early researchers made observations of their own children. A special branch of psychology called *ecological psychology* was developed out of naturalistic observational techniques used by Barker (1968, 1978). In this form of observation, teams of observers view children throughout a typical day's activities. The observers may literally follow the child for the entire day, recording virtually every event.

The observational form of research has opened many new possibilities in the field of educational psychology. It also has been useful for studying children and adolescents in their natural environments. But observational research is expensive and time-consuming, both in training observers and in conducting the observations in the natural environment.

Cross-Sectional and Longitudinal Research

cross-sectional research *Research involving data collection at one point in time from a sample containing two or more subgroups that are then compared on variables of interest.*

Two broad, contrasting approaches are used to study students in schools: cross-sectional and longitudinal. A main feature of **cross-sectional research** is the selection of different groups of children at a variety of age levels for study. Typically, a researcher separates the children into different age levels and studies the problem of interest. Following is an example. Have you ever wondered when children are able to judge age accurately? Kratochwill and Goldman (1973) noted that previous research had found that it is not until approximately age 9 that children are able to judge age accurately. Kratochwill and Goldman believed that results in previous studies had been influenced by the ambiguity of the drawings used (cartoon characters were used in previous research); their study was designed to investigate children's judgments of age when more realistic stimuli (photographs) were used.

The primary focus of the study was on evaluating a cross-section of children (ages 3, 4, 5, 6, 7, 8, and 9 years) on developmental changes in judgments by relating people's ages with their physical sizes. The photographs consisted of males and females at four age levels: infant, child, adolescent, and middle-aged adult. Each photograph (and thus each human figure) was reproduced in two sizes. Using a paired-comparison procedure, experimenters presented a cross-section of children from ages 3 through 9 years (there were 16 children at each age level) with either the male or the female photographs. (See female photographs in fig. 2.2 for one example of the paired comparison). The authors found that the accuracy of children's judgments increased in a generally orderly fashion, improving from 47 percent at age 3 to 59 percent at age 6, and to 100 percent at age 9. In comparison to a previous study (Looft, 1971) that had used cartoon-like drawings, Kratochwill and Goldman's use of photographs improved the children's accuracy in age judgments. In contrast with previous research (Looft, 1971), the errors children made in the Kratochwill and Goldman study were primarily the result of basing age judgments on size.

A major advantage of cross-sectional research is that data can be collected across a wide age range in a relatively short time period. Kratochwill and Goldman (1973) evaluated age judgments within a few days. They did not have to measure 3-year-olds at 1-year intervals for 6 years to examine the same problem. The advantage is even more apparent when the comparisons involve longer age periods. The major disadvantage of cross-sectional research is that it yields no information about the history of age-related changes. Thus, knowing how specific children in cross-sectional research would have responded at earlier ages is impossible.

A second form of educational research is called **longitudinal research** because the subjects are assessed repeatedly over a longer period of time. Technically, one could study the same individuals from birth to death, but this strategy would likely involve more than one team of researchers. An example of the longitudinal method of research is the Fels study, begun in 1929 at the Fels Research Institute in Ohio. Initially, 89 subjects (44 males and 45 females) were enrolled to participate in the study. In the Fels study, children repeatedly were weighed, measured, and assessed to identify various developmental changes. For example, at least twice a year, from each child's birth to age 6, a trained interviewer visited the parents' home for half a day. For the six years thereafter, researchers interviewed mothers annually to assess their attitudes toward their children. Most children between the ages of 2 and 2 ½ also attended the Institute's nursery for two 3-week sessions, and researchers observed peer interaction at the Fels day camp in children ages 6 to 10. Such measures as achievement, aggression, conformity, dependency, imitation, language, sex role, and sociability were rated repeatedly. This study was later followed up by Kagan and Moss (1962), who brought back 71 of the original 89 Fels subjects (who were then between 20 and 29 years old). Thus, longitudinal studies can extend for a long time, even beyond the period originally intended by the initial research team.

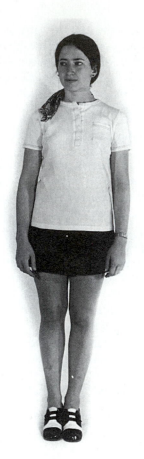

Figure 2.2
Actual photographs from the Kratochwill and Goldman (1973) study depicting an adolescent and an adult in two sizes. Children under the age of 7 generally indicated that the adolescent on the left was older because she was taller.

A major advantage of the longitudinal research approach over cross-sectional research is that the researcher can study the *same* subjects at each stage or age interval, to record the patterns of an individual's behavior. In this way, a researcher can assess the influence of early events on later behavior. There are also some disadvantages. The longitudinal approach is very expensive and time-consuming. Subjects also may leave the study as a result of such factors as moving, illness, death, and loss of motivation to participate. When the sample of subjects changes dramatically, the researcher cannot be sure that subjects who have left the study are similar to those who remain. This problem could cause a bias in the results. Some of the major features of cross-sectional and longitudinal methods of educational research are summarized in table 2.5.

longitudinal research *A research method in which subjects are assessed repeatedly over a lengthy period of time.*

Cross-Cultural Research

Many of the studies cited in this text present research that took place within the context of "mainstream" American culture. Yet, as many educational researchers recognize, **cross-cultural research** should be conducted to determine which factors are related to a particular culture. For example, people from a traditional Euro-American culture differ considerably from people from Asian cultures in the way they behave, think, and approach problems. Consider our earlier example of children's judgment of age. From research conducted in the United States, researchers have found that children living in the United States become aware sometime during the first 2 or 3 years of life that there is a correlation between the physical size of people and their age. Looft, Raymond, and Raymond (1972) attempted to determine the characteristics of age judgments by children in a non-American culture: Sarawak, of the Federation of Malaysia. Children in the study made age judgments on cartoon drawings of four different male figures (infant, child, adolescent, and adult). The procedures were much the same as those described earlier in the Kratochwill and Goldman (1973) study.

cross-cultural research *Research conducted across different cultures to determine which factors are related to a particular culture.*

Table 2.5

	Cross-Sectional and Longitudinal Development Research Strategies Compared	
Characteristics	**Design type**	
	Cross-sectional	*Longitudinal*
Research procedure	Measurement of several groups on different development dimensions (e.g., age) simultaneously over a short time period	Repeated measurement of the same group over long periods of time
Time investment	Short time to conduct (i.e., days, weeks, months)	Long time to conduct (i.e., years, decades)
Expense	Typically inexpensive	Typically expensive
Resources	Relatively few researchers needed	Typically many researchers or research teams needed, depending on the time period
Major advantage	Relatively large amounts of data can be gathered on a large age span within a short period of time	Researchers can study individual developmental changes within groups
Major disadvantage	Analysis of individual change is obscured	Requires considerable time and resources; subjects may leave study

Looft and his associates found that as in the American studies, the older children in the sample were more accurate than the younger children in determining the older of the two persons on each stimulus card. However, the children's explanations for their judgments varied greatly between the two cultures. Fifty-five percent of the Sarawak children used the word "stronger" in their explanations for their judgments; this rationale was never offered by U.S. children in comparable research (Kratochwill & Goldman, 1973; Looft, 1971). Also, 64 percent of the Malaysian children mentioned the degree of fatness or thinness in their responses, whereas in the American research, descriptions almost always pertained to height.

To account for these cultural differences, Looft et al. (1972) noted that they reflect the occurrence and status of obesity in Sarawak. A fat person was regarded as one who has accumulated considerable wealth—enough to allow that person to eat well and not work hard. In contrast to Americans, most people associate fatness with older individuals, since fat people would presumably live longer. Thus, a young child would commonly judge the infant, whose drawing showed a protruding belly, to be older than the adolescent figure, and explain that the infant was "bigger and fatter."

Single-Case Research

A research approach that is similar to the longitudinal methods discussed above is called single-case design. Like the repeated measurement feature of the longitudinal design, **single-case research** emphasizes the repeated analysis of a group or individual subject over a definite time period. However, in the single-case research strategy, the repeated measurement is taken at more frequent intervals (i.e., hours, days, weeks) over a relatively short period of time (several weeks or months). At some point in the data series, an intervention is introduced and the researcher evaluates the effect. Single-case designs can involve any number of subjects, ranging from one to one million.

Single-case designs are used most commonly in psychological research in behavioral or operant psychology (see chap. 7). However, the designs are not limited to this

single-case research *Research designed to evaluate the effect of an intervention on a single case, usually one individual.*

orientation and are used currently in psychology, sociology, medicine, and education (Kratochwill, 1978; Kratochwill & Levin, 1992). The major advantage of single-case research is that formal measurement takes place, some credible design is used to evaluate treatments, and reliable data are gathered.

Many single-case designs are used in applied settings where the researcher wishes to demonstrate that some treatment was effective with an identified problem. Single-case designs have often been recommended in evaluation of practice in educational settings (Barlow, Hayes, & Nelson, l984). However, their most common application is in research. Narayan, Heward, and Gardner (1990) demonstrated the use of single-case time-series methodology in their investigation of a strategy to increase active student responding in the classroom. Based on educational research that has shown a positive relationship between active student responding and academic achievement, the authors were looking for a time- and cost-efficient way to increase student responding. Traditionally, a teacher would call upon one student at a time to respond. As an alternative, the authors devised a response card that can be held up simultaneously by every student in the class to respond to a question by the teacher.

To evaluate their strategy, Narayan and associates selected a regular fourth-grade classroom in an urban public elementary school. There were 20 students in the class and 6 were chosen to participate. The authors measured four dependent variables in the study: (1) teacher presentation rate, (2) number of student responses, (3) accuracy of student responses, and (4) daily quiz scores. The study consisted of two independent variables, hand raising and write-on response cards, that were alternated in a replication type design. During the baseline, the teacher called upon one student, who raised a hand in response to a teacher question. In the response-card condition, each student in the class was presented with a white laminated board on which to write one- or two-word answers in response to teacher questions.

The results of the study for each of the 6 selected students are presented in figure 2.3. As you can observe from the graphs, the rate of active student responses during instruction was higher with the use of response cards than with hand raising. Also, most of the students scored better on daily quizzes following the sessions in which the response cards were used than they did on quizzes following sessions that used hand raising. What do you think the students had to say about the procedure? Interestingly, 19 of 20 students in the class preferred the response cards over hand raising.

PRIMARY, SECONDARY, AND META-ANALYSIS

Have you ever wondered how educational researchers draw conclusions from a body of research evidence? The process of drawing conclusions is not as straightforward as you might think. After the researcher completes the data-gathering phase of the investigation, the data are analyzed in some manner. Typically, some form of statistical test is applied to the data. The first or original analysis of the data that takes place is called *primary analysis*. This primary analysis is usually done by the individual who designed and conducted the research. Following the analysis and discussion of the results, the researcher may share the findings with the scientific community. Once the results are published, they may influence future research, practice, or even public policy.

Not all published research is accepted at face value. Sometimes other researchers wish to reexamine the original data analysis. This procedure is called *secondary analysis* (Cook, 1974). Secondary analysis refers to the reanalysis of data to clarify the original research questions with better statistical procedures, or to answer new questions with old data. For example, a researcher may want to examine some early research data on the effect of class size on student achievement. Perhaps the reanalysis will pose some new issues or even different conclusions from those reached by the original researcher's data analysis. Secondary analysis depends greatly on the availability of the original data. Such data are not always easy to come by. Sometimes they are lost, or coded so that it is difficult to understand the original analysis scheme.

Figure 2.3

Number of academic responses and hand raises by students 1–6 during hand-raising (HR) and response-card (RC) conditions. Breaks in data paths indicate student absences.

From J. S. Narayan, et al., "Using response cards to increase student participation in an elementary classroom" in Journal of Applied Behavior Analysis, *23,483–490, 1990, Copyright © 1990 JABA. Reprinted by permission.*

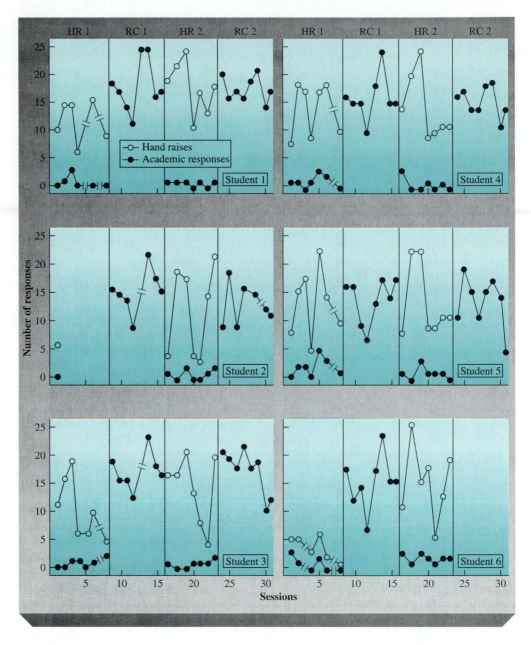

meta-analysis *A statistical technique used to synthesize and interpret the results of multiple data-based studies.*

Another form of analysis is called **meta-analysis**: the analysis of analyses (Glass, McGaw, & Smith, 1981). Meta-analysis refers to the statistical analysis of a large collection of analysis results from individual studies, for the purpose of integrating the findings. Meta-analysis is a relatively recent procedure, first coming into prominence during the mid-1970s. It was designed to replace narrative review of research studies, something that most of us have done as students when writing term papers. Some authors have recommended that traditional narrative review be combined with meta-analysis (e.g., Slavin, 1991b), a strategy called "best-evidence synthesis."

Applications of meta-analysis have been quite controversial. For example, Smith and Glass (1977) coded and integrated statistically the results of nearly 400 controlled evaluations of psychotherapy and counseling. Their findings provided convincing evidence of the effectiveness of psychotherapy. Specifically, the individual receiving therapy was better off than 75 percent of untreated individuals. In another study, Smith and Glass (1980) conducted a meta-analysis of research on class size and its relationship to attitudes. They found that advantages of reduced class size are greater in classes whose sizes range from 1 to 15 than in classes of larger sizes (i.e., only small differences occur

Should Teachers Use Single-Case Designs to Evaluate Their Interventions with Students in Classrooms?

Over the past decade there have been increasing calls for evaluation of student performance outcomes in education. Such a trend is not unlike that in the clinical psychology field, where there are increasing demands for accountability in the provision of mental health services (Barlow, Hayes, & Nelson, 1984; Kazdin, 1993). Increasingly, we will live in a climate of accountability. Single-case research designs have been recommended as a strategy to evaluate practice. However, use of these designs in educational settings has been controversial.

Issue

Should single-case designs be used by teachers to evaluate student performance in the classroom?

Answer: Pro Teacher evaluation of student performance using single-case designs will help evaluate the efficacy of instructional and management programs. Such evaluation will increase the quality of instruction in terms of better information for making instructional decisions.

Answer: Con Teachers do not need to use any formal designs to evaluate the efficacy of instructional and management programs. Nearly every teacher knows how a student is performing without imposing rigid design structure on the teaching and learning process.

Answer: Pro Measurement of student progress is a necessary but not a sufficient tactic to evaluate student progress.

Use of single-case design adds an element of validity to the process because the teacher can determine if the instructional program is *responsible* for the observed change in student performance. Such a design structure can promote good thinking about the presumed variables that contribute to student performance change.

Answer: Con Imposing the design structure of single-subject research on the teaching process is too intrusive in an already busy and complex teacher-student relationship. Teachers do not have the time to wait for student behavior to change to meet the requirements of certain designs, such as withdrawal and multiple-baseline designs.

Answer: Pro Use of single-case designs is one way to teach in an ethical and professional manner. Formal application of designs would allow the teacher to make decisions that are in the best interests of students and student learning.

Answer: Con The structure of many single-case designs necessitates withholding instruction or waiting for lengthy time periods during which no instruction occurs, in order to meet the design stipulations. Such lack of instruction during these periods may not be in the best interest of students and would not be considered the best ethical and professional behavior of teachers.

---

in the attitudes of students whose class sizes range from 20 to 60). Recently, several meta-meta-analyses have appeared in the psychological and educational literature. These papers are reviews of individual meta-analyses in various areas. For example, Lipsey and Wilson (1993) reviewed the efficacy of psychological, educational, and behavioral treatments. The authors found that the effects were overwhelmingly positive for the interventions reviewed, including those with an educational focus. More recently, Wang, Huertel, and Walberg (1994) reviewed the literature to identify and estimate the influence of various educational, psychological, and social variables on learning. Evidence was obtained from 61 research experts, 91 meta-analyses, and 179 chapters and narrative reviews. Thus, meta-analysis was combined with other literature review methods. The authors found that proximal variables (such as psychological, instructional, and home environment variables) exerted more influence

H. Schwadron *in* Phi Delta Kappan.

on learning than distal variables (such as demographic, policy, and organizational variables). Despite such interesting findings, some researchers have been especially critical of meta-analysis, because in making general statements about a particular research topic, it does not discriminate between good and poor studies (Levin, 1994). The future, however, will likely see more of the meta-analysis research strategy used in educational psychology (Asher, 1990; Walberg, 1986; Wang et al., 1994).

ETHICAL AND LEGAL CONSIDERATIONS IN RESEARCH IN EDUCATION

Research with human subjects carries with it special responsibilities for the educational researcher. A major goal of research is to generate knowledge that will be useful in advancing the human condition. Increasingly, ethical and legal guidelines have been advanced for individuals conducting research with children and adults. The American Psychological Association (APA) undertook one such effort in its formulation of a code of "Ethical Standards for Research with Human Subjects" (APA, 1982). The guidelines provide researchers with direction when undertaking scientific investigation.

APPLICATIONS AND REFLECTIONS

Chapter Highlights

Research and Effective Schooling
- One of the most important sources of knowledge about human behavior is scientific research.
- Research answers questions about the effectiveness of educational practices.
- Scientific research is systematic, controlled, empirical, and involves a critical study of some issue or problem.
- Scientific research has been subjected to many and varied influences.
- Scientific research typically follows a series of steps that consists of identifying, clarifying, implementing, evaluating, and interpreting procedures.

Major Research Methods
- Research into educational problems may be historical, descriptive, correlational, comparative, or experimental.
- Historical research involves studying, understanding, and explaining past events.
- Descriptive, or qualitative, research involves collecting data to test hypotheses or answer questions related to the current status of a problem.
- Correlational research involves the process of determining whether, and to what degree, a relation exists between two or more variables.
- Comparative research involves establishing a direct relation between variables that the researcher compares, but does not directly manipulate.
- Experimental research involves a study in which the researcher actually manipulates at least one independent variable to observe the effect on one or more dependent variables.

Techniques Used by Researchers
- The more common research techniques used today are surveys, interviews, observation, and cross-sectional and longitudinal studies.
- Research can be conducted with large groups of subjects or with a single subject.
- Cross-cultural research helps to explain differences in how individuals behave, think, and attempt to solve problems.
- Meta-analysis, the analysis of the results of a large number of individual studies, is increasingly popular today.
- No one research method is always best; the research question and issues investigated often determine the method that the researcher will use.

Connections

1. Think about how you learn and describe how one of the major concepts discussed in this chapter is a part of your learning activities or approach.

_____

_____

_____

_____

_____

2. Identify at least one learning situation (e.g., classroom instruction, self-study, taking a test, small-group work) and describe how you would apply one of the key concepts examined in this chapter *if you were a teacher*.

_____

_____

_____

_____

_____

Getting the Picture and Drawing Relationships

Think about the various learning concepts and variables discussed in this chapter. Create pictures, graphics, or figures which highlight relationships among the key components.

Personal Journal

What I really learned in this chapter was _____

_____

_____

_____

_____

What this means to me is _____

_____

_____

_____

_____

Questions that were stimulated by this chapter include _____

_____

_____

_____

_____

Key Terms

case study	31	descriptive research	34	longitudinal research	42
comparative research	36	experimental research	36	meta-analysis	45
correlational research	35	historical research	34	observation	41
cross-cultural research	42	independent variable	36	single-case research	43
cross-sectional research	41	interviews	39	surveys	37
dependent variable	36				

Sara Anders was excited to get the offer to teach at Winfield Middle School. She had loved living in a large city as a college student and had always wanted to work in an urban school. She was excited by the opportunity to teach in a school that had a history of academic and athletic excellence, although during the past few years, Winfield Middle School's status had diminished somewhat. Alissa Jones, the principal at Winfield, had indicated during Sara's interview that the enrollment for the school had been enlarged in 1991 to include several low-income apartment complexes on the south side of the city. As a result, the school's population

learning styles that students might have. Finally, she mentioned that she was concerned about communicating with parents of a culturally diverse class and would benefit from some of the senior staff members' experiences.

Summer was nearly over and school was about to start. Sara was anxious to meet her new students and a bit nervous about how they would react to her. She did look young, and she would be one of the few Anglo teachers in the school. To calm herself, she thought, "I am more like my students than different from them, and I have always enjoyed learning from others. This is going to be an exciting year!" ■

chapter 3

diversity in the classroom: culture, class, and gender

had increased by 250 students, of which 35 percent were Hispanic and 25 percent were African American.

During Sara's interview, Alissa Jones and Zollie Stevens, the director of instruction for the school district, had both asked her about her ability to work with a diverse population of students. They were very interested in her knowledge of cultural differences and in how she would react as a young, Anglo female to some of the tensions that can occur in an inner-city school. Sara had been forthright in her responses. First, she indicated that she had not previously taught classes with more than one or two minority students, but she had been very involved in the development of an ESL program for Hispanic students. In fact, last year she had relearned much of her high school Spanish so she could communicate more effectively with the parents and grandparents of one of her students. Second, she told them that during the past summer, she had taken a course at the university on instructional accommodations for at-risk students. She believed that some of the students from low-income families would be considered at risk for educational failure and would gain from the "Reading Rescue" and "Study Skills" programs she had researched. Sara also indicated that she recognized that many students learn differently; she felt it was her responsibility to accommodate a variety of

It should be apparent that to function effectively in today's classroom, you as a teacher must be aware of the individual differences that your students bring to school. These are not only differences in levels of cognitive functioning, but also variations in child-rearing practices, cultural beliefs and values, social class distinctions, and gender. The manner in which you adapt to these differences, both personally and professionally, has strong implications for your teaching success. Consequently, your work in this chapter should alert you to the manner in which culture, class, and gender interact to influence academic achievement.

When you finish your reading, you should be able to

- apply your knowledge of cultural differences to the methods and materials you introduce into your classroom
- identify any sources of bias in classroom interactions, curriculum, and materials
- analyze the ways in which social class differences can affect a student's behavior and achievement
- detect any gender biases that influence participation, classroom success, and testing results
- evaluate the relationships between you and your students on the basis of culture, class, and gender

Culture and the Schools 52
Merging Cultures 52
Cultures and Cognitive
    Development 53
Our Changing Classrooms 55
Interactions in the
    Classroom 57
Cultural Differences and Testing
    Practices 58

**Social Class and Academic
Achievement 59**
The Children of Poverty 60
Social Class and Education 60
Teaching, Learning, and Social
    Class 61

**Gender, Development, and the
Classroom 64**
Becoming Boys and Girls 66
Gender Stereotyping 69
Gender and Classroom
    Achievement 70
Gender and the Curriculum 72
Teacher-Student Relationships:
    A Summary 74

**Applications and
Reflections 75**

CULTURE AND THE SCHOOLS

As our nation continues to change, we all will interact with others from quite different backgrounds from our own, especially in the classroom. The manner in which we respond to others who seem different can have a serious impact on success in school, work, and harmonious relationships with others. It is important to remember that "different is not deficient." Cultural differences imply the transmission of ideas from generation to generation by significant members of older generations (parents, teachers, religious leaders, business managers). Few would challenge the view that the Japanese, for example, place great value on formal education. Japanese children, through their experiences, internalize this value. They probably always will remember the educational programs that start at the end of their regular school days. British children will likewise always be aware of the class differences reflected in the distinction between public and private schools. These and countless other socialization experiences, once internalized, help children to become accepted members of their adult societies (Brislin, 1990).

The expression "different is not deficient" has received wide acceptance. When you think of your friends who have a cultural background that differs from yours, do you understand why this concept needs to be emphasized? Explain your answer.

Merging Cultures

Members of one group—Irish American, Italian American, African American—can use standards from their own cultural backgrounds to form opinions about those from other cultures. If people can understand *why* those from other groups behave as they do, there is less of an inclination to conclude that "different is deficient." For example, when meeting people from another culture, we are initially struck by differences in behavior, speech, clothing, food. If these differences aren't too sharp, we accept the people; if they are, we judge them unfavorably. It is helpful to remember that if you were a member of some other group, you would probably behave just as its current members do (Triandis, 1990).

If we take the time and make the effort to understand these differences, our relationships with others can move to a level of mutual understanding in all settings. As an illustration, think of the way children and teachers from many different cultures are now coming together in our changing American classrooms. Many minority children have had to make major adjustments to the dominant culture in the classroom. Teachers who are aware of the differences between a child's home culture and that of the school can do much to insure that these children succeed academically and personally to the extent of their potential.

A good example of this kind of endeavor can be seen in Kim's description (1990) of Hawaiian children's school experiences. Many Hawaiian children achieve at the lowest academic level and are labeled as lazy and disruptive by some teachers. Yet these same children are remarkably responsible at home, cooking, cleaning, taking care of their brothers and sisters. In the home setting, they demonstrate considerable initiative and a high performance level. When something needs to be done, they get together and make a group effort to do whatever is necessary. When they find themselves in an individualistic, competitive classroom, however, their performance suffers. In a series of experiments, teachers were encouraged to model desired behaviors and not assign specific tasks to students. Kim reported that by the end of the academic year, the third-grade students would begin the day by examining the schedules of their learning centers and then divide themselves into groups that assigned tasks to individual members, obtained materials, and used worksheets. Their achievement scores improved significantly. However, once the students were returned to regular classrooms for the fourth grade, a familiar pattern of behaviors appeared.

The classroom is not the only milieu in which cultures merge. The business world now has people of various cultures working side by side, and also has those designated as minorities—women, African Americans, Asian Americans, Hispanic Americans—assuming leadership positions in which members of the dominant culture report to them. As companies become more global and as the number of international markets increases steadily, the workplace is beginning to resemble the classroom as a meeting place of cultures (Brislin, 1990).

Annual **Edition**

Our goal in urging you to adopt a multicultural perspective in your classroom is to help you develop a greater understanding of those who seem "different." If you adopt this perspective, you will come to realize that different people have different world views that decisively influence their thinking (Shweder, 1991). In this way, you can work, play, or study more congenially with others, thus fostering more positive relations in our society. People from different cultures do *not* all think alike. As we have stressed, these differences are not deficits. Recognizing how diverse people are in their thinking and behavior will help you to identify and comprehend variations in how students are raised, how they think, and how they become functioning members of their cultures. This is particularly true of cognitive development.

Cultures and Cognitive Development

Any discussions of social-cultural influences on development stress that cultures differ in their views of acceptable child-rearing practices. As a result of these different parenting beliefs, children of various cultures may think and act differently and carry these differences into the classroom. We also know that the effects of culture, health, socioeconomic status, and biological factors interact with each other to produce varying, although normal, developmental outcomes. As Bruner (1990) noted, culture has become the major factor in giving form to the minds of those under its sway. The Russian psychologist Vygotsky argued in a similar manner that mental functioning can be understood only by examining the surrounding social and cultural processes (Wertsch & Tulviste, 1992).

Vygotsky and Mental Growth

Born in Russia in 1896, Vygotsky was educated at Moscow University and quickly turned his attention to educational psychology, developmental psychology, and psychopathology. He was particularly concerned with applying psychological data to the practical problems facing the Russian schools. Although his career was abruptly terminated by his death from tuberculosis in 1934, his work has attracted considerable recent attention because of the central role that he allotted social processes in cognitive development. As a result, many of his writings have been translated into English.

Vygotsky's work (1962, 1978) reflected a belief that the clues to understanding mental development lie in children's social processes, that is, that cognitive growth depends on children's interactions with those around them. The adults around children interact with them in a way that emphasizes those things that a culture values. For example, a child points to an object; those around the child respond in a way that conveys information not only about the object, but also about how the child should behave. To understand cognitive growth, we need to concentrate on the social processes by which these higher mental forms are established, *not* on the products of development.

The Zone of Proximal Development   Commenting on the relationship between learning and development, Vygotsky (1978) noted that learning, in some way, must be matched with a pupil's developmental level, which is too frequently identified by an intelligence test score. Vygotsky believed, however, that we cannot be content with the results of intelligence testing, which provides information only on a student's present developmental level. For example, after administering a Stanford-Binet intelligence test, we might find that a pupil's IQ on this test is 110, which we would consider that student's current level of mental development. We might then assume that the pupil could work only at this level. Vygotsky argued, however, that with a little help, pupils might be able to do work that they were unable to do on their own.

We know that pupils who have the same IQ are quite different in other respects. Motivation, interest, health, and a host of other conditions produce different achievement levels. For example, our student with an IQ of 110 might be able to deal effectively with materials of various levels of difficulty. That is, this student might be able only to do addition problems when working alone, but to solve subtraction problems with the teacher's help.

Vygotsky believed that cognitive development was closely linked to children's interactions with those around them. Teachers, as significant adults in children's lives, play a critical role in mental growth.

To explain this phenomenon, Vygotsky introduced his notion of the **zone of proximal development.** He defined the zone of proximal development as the distance between a child's actual developmental level, as determined by independent problem solving, and that child's higher level of potential development, as determined by problem solving under adult guidance or in collaboration with more capable peers (Vygotsky, 1978). This is the difference between what pupils can do independently and what they can do with help. For Vygotsky, children depend on social interactions to develop cognitively (Rogoff, 1990).

Vygotsky's ideas are similar to Bruner's explanation of the role of symbols in cognitive development.

zone of proximal development
The distance between a child's actual developmental level, as determined by independent problem solving, and that child's potential developmental level, as determined by problem solving under adult guidance or in collaboration with more capable peers.

Language as an Example

In much the same manner, Bruner (1990) argued that culture shapes cognitive development by imposing its symbolic systems—language, for example—on a child's developing mind. Turning to language, Bruner urged that we not be swept away by biological interpretations, since children need considerable interactions with others in acquiring their language. As he stated, learning language is learning how to do things with words.

Healthy children come into the world able to acquire their language, but it is the context that gives their language shape and meaning. For example, Choi (1991) found in a study of the responses of children 15 to 39 months old to yes-no questions that there were many similarities and some important differences in the way that English, French, and Korean children used their native answering systems. In all three languages, the same answering system applies to affirmative questions, but the answering systems for negative questions differ among the three languages.

Choi used the examples of an affirmative question—"Is this a cat?"—and a negative question—"Isn't this a cat?" All the children from all three countries had learned the interpretative-functional meaning of yes-no questions before the truth-functional meaning. They differed in the way they responded to negative questions because of their interpretation of the questions, which seemed to be a cultural phenomenon. In English, negative questions are used when the questioner believes the positive, that is, they have a rhetorical function. For example, "Wasn't John at the party?" implies that the questioner believes John *was* at the party. Neither Korean nor French children reacted this way; in those languages, negative questions are rarely used rhetorically. The Korean and French children interpreted the question to indicate doubt about its truthfulness: John was *not* at the party.

Another example of cultural influence on cognitive and language development is offered by Tobin, Wu, and Davidson (1989). Studying 4-year-old children in China, Japan, and the United States, they noted that adults in both China and the United States believe that preschool experiences should help children develop their language skills and learn appropriate ways to express themselves. In Japan, however, the preschool language experience is seen less as a vehicle for self-expression than as a way of developing and expressing group solidarity and shared social goals.

While these views about the powerful influence of culture on learning and development probably come as no surprise to you, you may well ask how these ideas translate into improved teaching and learning. Although the rest of this chapter is devoted to specific answers to this question, in the next section we'll speak generally of the importance of understanding the role of culture in academic achievement.

Our Changing Classrooms

Increasingly, children from different cultures are interacting with each other, thus presenting parents and educators with unique opportunities for further understanding across cultures. Given these circumstances, is it any wonder that our classrooms have become the focus of efforts to achieve such understanding? The old cliche that the school reaches all the children of all the people is as true today as it ever was. Helping children of various cultures to achieve as fully as possible, while simultaneously adapting to each other, demands innovative strategies on the part of parents, teachers, and administrators.

An example of the need for these new strategies was offered by Rogoff (1990), when she noted that the different techniques that students use for classification reflect their cultures. For example, children with an agricultural background may see logical analysis and paper problems, tasks with which other children are comfortable, as a waste of time.

Rogoff (1990) offered another excellent example of the need for cultural understanding and adaptation in teaching. The behavior used to define intelligence may range from an ability to remember facts (Chinese) to a slow, careful approach to a problem (Ugandan). In a similar manner, the way in which problems are attacked varies according to culture. With some groups, problem solving is seen as demanding a group effort. With other groups, using a companion is seen as cheating. These are differences that teachers must be alert to if they are to promote cultural harmony. One rule of thumb for educators to remember is that children may be socialized to think and behave one way at home and another at school.

Grant and Sleeter (1993, p. 51), for example, urged educators not to think of a student in the classroom as just Asian American, but also as male and middle-class. Thus, a student who is a member of an oppressed minority may also be a member of a dominant gender and social class group. This student's view of the world is probably quite different from that of a middle-class Asian American girl or a lower-class Asian American boy.

These are important distinctions to make; otherwise, Banks' grim observation in 1993 will continue to remain true: in the early years, the classroom achievements of the various cultural groups (African American, Asian American, Native American, Hispanic American) are about the same as those of white students, but the longer they remain in school, the more their achievement lags behind that of white students.

Any such achievement lag can affect students in several ways. One example would be a lack of adequate preparation for work. As the economic goals of nations become more international, the need for an intelligent, productive, and competitive work force has become critical. This issue is addressed by two new federal reports, released by the U.S. Secretary of Labor's Commission on Achieving Necessary Skills (SCANS) and the National Council of Educational Standards and Testing (NCEST). Recent legislation, the Perkins Act (P. L.103–392), is intended to fund and shape vocational education (Pullin, 1994, p. 33). Its goal is to facilitate school efforts to prepare individuals for the workplace by integrating academic and vocational education. The Perkins Act has powerful equity requirements to protect students and workers from gender, racial, ethnic, and disability discrimination. The challenge for teachers, then, becomes one of preparing students to benefit from this new emphasis. The answer may lie in the notion of cultural compatibility.

Cultural Compatibility

In a wide-ranging and pertinent essay, Tharp (1989) identified several psychocultural variables that link cultural compatibility to teaching and learning. Beginning with the inescapable fact that students from some cultural groups (Chinese, Japanese) have done better in North American schools than those from other groups (Native American, Hispanic American, African American), Tharp traced the changes that have recently come about in attitudes toward those students experiencing school difficulty: From a "cultural deficit" belief, today's focus, which recognizes the strengths of many cultures, has moved to an appreciation of cultural differences. This changed perspective brings with it changed experiences and expectations for better student achievement.

The force behind these changed attitudes is the **cultural compatibility** hypothesis: When instruction is compatible with cultural patterns, learning improves. There are several variations of this hypothesis, but the most widely adopted holds that some schools have students who are less westernized and industrialized and who have a crucial incompatibility with their schools. If schools are to be compatible with and effective for these cultures, they need to have models unlike that of the standard school.

We should pause here to identify, as Tharp has done (1989), the different interests of the various cultural groups. For example, the energy and efforts of African Americans have been directed to such issues as desegregation and equal educational opportunity for all students; Hispanic Americans have been concerned about bilingual programs; and Asian Americans have concentrated on desirable parent-child relationships. The result of a positive interaction between culture and school is seen in the twenty-year-old Kamehameha Early Education Program (KEEP), which was mentioned in chapter 1 (Kim, 1990). Recall our statement that generally, Hawaiian children don't do well in typical schools. Students in the KEEP program, however, reached national norms on standard achievement tests. What happens in these culturally compatible classrooms?

cultural compatibility
Compatibility of instruction with the cultural patterns of students.

Some individuals have stated that concern with cultural compatibility is just another fad. Students will learn, regardless of their culture. How do you respond to this.

Pertinent Psychocultural Variables

Tharp (1989) identified four variables that have been manipulated to bring about greater compatibility between the classroom experience and different cultures: social organization, sociolinguistics, cognition, and motivation.

One of the keys to successful educational design is to make teaching, learning, and performance compatible with the social organization of students. In a typical classroom, for example, Hawaiian children show low attention to teachers and a high level of attention seeking from their peers. When the social structure of the classroom was changed in ways similar to those of the KEEP program (to collaboration and cooperation), achievement scores and motivation increased noticeably.

When the KEEP program was introduced into Navajo classrooms, the results were also good, but the Navajo children were more independent, neither seeking nor giving assistance; this is not surprising given their tradition. While the Hawaiian children worked better with others in mixed-sex groups, Navajo children interacted more in same-sex groups. Another example of cultural influences on classroom dynamics was the behavior of African American children, whose peer interactions were more intense and sensitive. Their physical expressiveness and behavior caused some teachers to label them as disruptive. Other teachers, however, capitalized on these behaviors by having the students give performances in front of the class that were related to the subject under discussion, while their "audience" watched intently to detect mistakes and thus be able to take their place. These and similar culture-compatible techniques were found to heighten motivation and lead to higher achievement.

Discernible differences also exist in the conversational, or sociolinguistic, practices of the classroom. Children of certain cultures have different language expectations, which influence their classroom speech and can cause them to be labeled "low verbal ability." For example, observations of Anglo and Navajo teachers of the same students demonstrate that Navajo teachers give their students longer wait-times (the time students take to respond). Anglo teachers, thinking that a student has completed a response, interrupt what to the students was only a pause. Consequently, if the rhythm of the teacher's speech is not compatible with that of the students, fewer interactions occur, resulting in lower teacher-student rapport. Children from some cultures, such as Hawaiian, resent being confronted directly; this affects performance. When sociolinguistic compatibility exists, children are more comfortable, participate more, and display their abilities appropriately (Tharp, 1989, p. 352).

We have spoken enough throughout our work of Tharp's third variable—cognition—to be able to treat it briefly here. Children whose patterns of cognitive functioning are compatible with the school's are usually successful; children whose cognitive patterns do not match the school's usually do poorly. A good example can be seen in the work of Stevenson et al. (1990). Studying 1,440 Chinese and Japanese first- and fifth-grade students in the public schools of Minneapolis, Stevenson and his colleagues tested the children on reading and mathematics, interviewed the mothers, interviewed the principals, and administered a questionnaire to the teachers.

The interviews with the mothers revealed that the Chinese and Japanese mothers paid greater attention to their children's academic abilities than did American mothers. The Chinese and Japanese mothers also viewed academic achievement as the most important part of their children's lives. American mothers were less interested in academic achievement than in their children's general cognitive growth. American mothers also tended to overestimate their children's academic abilities, while the Chinese and Japanese mothers held higher academic standards for their children. In this example, you can see that the Chinese and Japanese mothers surpassed their American counterparts in their adherence to the traditional school model.

Annual **Edition**

Tharp's final variable is motivation. We know that one of the major contributions teachers can make to the successful integration and accomplishments of multicultural students is to provide an understanding, supportive environment. For example, in attempting to heighten the motivation of African American males to succeed, teachers should publicly recognize the successful academic experiences of young African American men, thus helping them to grow in self-concept, self-esteem, and academic confidence.

As an illustration of strategies that help to meet the needs of multicultural students, Gary and Booker (1992) suggested several techniques to empower African American students to achieve academic success. These students should be helped in establishing goals early in life. Adults who recognize and foster children's early interests help them to engage in long-term thinking, and also help them to avoid seeking immediate gratification. It is useful also to remember that many African American students learn best in an environment that encourages human interaction and verbal dialogue.

Interactions in the Classroom

For some children, the path to understanding and esteem can be difficult. As Billingsley (1992) noted, many African American families are caught between conflicting tensions: the economic, physical, social, psychological, and spiritual demands of their members on the one hand, and the demands of a dominant society on the other. That is, the struggle for better housing and schools, higher incomes, and more satisfying occupations requires adjustment to a different lifestyle (Jaynes & Williams, 1989).

Garbarino and Benn (1992) asserted that a child's single most important psychological necessity is self-esteem. It is clear that rejection can only frustrate the development of a positive self-regard. The notion of rejection as an obstacle to the development of healthy self-esteem is not confined to rejection by individuals, that is, a mother's rejection of her child or a father's rejection of his child. Rejection because the child is a member of a particular group can work in exactly the same way.

When children interact with individuals from other cultures, their experiences help them to accept those with different customs, languages, and ideas. While this may sound idealistic, helping youngsters to achieve this objective is the social goal of multicultural education. Children are encouraged to form positive cultural, racial, and class

Focus — Checking Your Relationships with Students

By pausing for a moment and considering the implications of the types of interactions you have with your pupils, you can better understand how a particular relationship has developed. For example, you work with either a group or individuals. You provide correction and feedback. You answer questions. We could create a lengthy list of your activities; in all of these, you are interacting with students. Do you ever step back to analyze the interactions you engage in with your students? By doing so, you could improve both relationships and achievement.

Occasionally during the year, once your rules are in place and your class knows what is expected, why not try something like this? Ask your students to complete a checklist about you like the one that follows, including these or similar topics. (Make it as easy as possible for students to fill out.) Put a check on the line where you think your teacher [*name*] belongs.

High   *Low*

1. Fair
2. Plays Favorites
3. Firm
4. Easy
5. Helpful
6. Ignores pupils
7. Friendly
8. Aloof
9. Concerned
10. Disinterested

Obviously, you can include many additional or different items, to obtain an appraisal of your relationships with your pupils. Whether you decide to use this checklist technique or another one, it's a good idea to evaluate yourself; if a negative profile emerges, you can assess what is wrong and take corrective measures.

identities; this in turn leads to high self-esteem and the ability and willingness to interact with diverse others. Ultimately, then, children develop a sense of social responsibility and an active concern for the welfare of others. This is both an idealistic and an attainable outcome (Ramsey, 1987).

Those working with students of various cultures have a unique opportunity to further a positive multicultural perspective during these years of enthusiasm and rapid learning. As an example of steps that could be taken, Yao (1988) offered several suggestions for adults working with Asian immigrant parents. She began by urging them to take the time to familiarize themselves with the social, cultural, and personality traits that make these children and their parents unique. Teachers should ask themselves questions such as these:

- Do I have any prejudices toward this group?
- What stereotypes do I associate with Asian Americans? (for example, they're all superior in math and science)
- What do I know about their culture?
- Will there be any conflict between my values and theirs?

These and similar questions can act as guidelines to help us adapt to those of different cultures, and also to help these children adapt to rules and procedures that may seem strange to them. Positive interactions with your multicultural students will also help them to improve their test performance in the classroom.

Cultural Differences and Testing Practices

A child's ability to take tests often powerfully influences the results of a test. This is especially true of intelligence tests. Tests can frighten students or cause them anxiety. Whatever the reason for test anxiety—parental pressure, their own concerns, or the testing atmosphere—merely taking a test can affect performance. This is especially true for those pupils with different cultural experiences from the majority. Language, reading, expectations, and behavior all may be different for these students, and may influence test performance (Stigler et al., 1990).

In an effort to insure equity in testing, a new national system of authentic assessment has been proposed (Madaus, 1994). These tests supposedly engage students in real-world

When children, especially those whose cultural background differs from that of the classroom, understand what is expected of them in their test-taking, they tend to perform at a level that more accurately reflects their abilities.

tasks rather than multiple-choice tests (Darling-Hammond, 1994). For example, President Clinton's Goals 2000: Educate America Act rests on the assumption that the federal government can help state and local communities in their striving for educational reform by specifying goals, providing financial support to attain these goals, and establishing a voluntary assessment mechanism for accountability (Pullin, 1994). The intent is to ensure that *all* students will be competent in the core academic subjects; this can occur only if each disadvantaged group has an effective and complete opportunity to learn.

The goals are clear; the task itself is difficult. As Madaus noted (1994, p. 79), since social and cultural groups differ in the extent to which they share the values that underlie testing and the values that testing promotes, any national testing system raises questions of equity. The values of the test-makers and the test-takers aren't necessarily identical. For example, various cultural groups may have specific experiences that tests (of any design) may not measure. A good example of this is seen in the publication *New Voices: Immigrant Students in U. S. Public Schools* (1988), which describes many immigrant pupils as having experienced wars, political oppression, economic deprivation, and long, difficult journeys to come to the United States.

That children of different cultures want to succeed is reflected in interviews with many of them: almost 50 percent were spending one to two hours on homework every night. (Twenty-five percent of the Southeast Asian students reported spending more than three hours each night.) We have spoken throughout our work of the need for sensitive responsiveness. Here is an instance in which sensitivity to the needs of multicultural children (in this case, recognition of previous hardships) can only aid their adjustment and achievement in school.

When children feel comfortable, they perform better. This is particularly true of test-taking. Multicultural children need information about why a test is being given, when it is being given, what material will be tested, and what kinds of test items will be used. These are just a few topics to consider. Language should not be a barrier to performance. For example, students need to understand the terms in the directions of a test: what "analyze" means; what they should do when asked to "compare"; what "discuss" means.

Helping multicultural students in this way means extra time and effort for teachers. But it is teaching, just as teaching English or history is teaching. As more and more multicultural students become users of classroom tests, they must not be allowed to do poorly simply because they don't understand the mechanics of the tests. These same issues apply to economically deprived students who arrive at school with, perhaps, a different sense of values from those of their middle-class teachers.

SOCIAL CLASS AND ACADEMIC ACHIEVEMENT

Before discussing the relationship between social class and academic achievement, it would be well to examine briefly the conditions under which some children live. First, however, we would like to emphasize that although we have separated this chapter into the topics of culture, class, and gender for discussion purposes, these three factors are almost impossible to separate in reality. African Americans, Hispanics, and women are overly represented at the poverty level.

Given the undisputed differences between social classes, it is surprising that there aren't greater differences between them in attitudes, values, and parenting practices. Differences that do appear relate to feelings about power and self-direction versus helplessness and obedience to the demands of others. For example, middle-class parents encourage curiosity, internal control, the ability to work for distant goals, and a sensitivity to relationships with others; lower-class parents place greater emphasis on respectability and obedience to authority (Hetherington & Parke, 1993). What else do we know about disadvantaged children?

The Children of Poverty

The children of poverty experience more health problems, many of which can be traced to prenatal difficulties. More of these children die in the neonatal and infancy periods; they simply lack adequate health care. They suffer more accidents than more fortunate children and are exposed to greater stress: occupational, financial, housing, neighborhood. We know that parental stress can often translate into poor parenting practices (depression, irritability, abuse), which can lead to behavioral and emotional problems and academic difficulty for the children. Finally, as we know from the daily news, these children often witness and are the targets of violence, such as physical assault, rape, and shootings. The danger in all of this, of course, is that poverty becomes a self-perpetuating cycle (Sroufe, Cooper, & DeHart, 1992). The conditions we have described put children at an immediate disadvantage: they are subject to school difficulties (perhaps culminating in their dropping out), low self-esteem, troublesome behavior, limited occupational opportunities, and encounters with the law. Erratic employment contributes to poverty, and the cycle commences again.

Analyses of families in poverty typically focus on income, education, occupation, and social status, yet other, potentially more powerful, psychological forces are also at work. For example, can children living in poverty avoid feelings of powerlessness? It doesn't take them long to perceive that in comparison to more fortunate classmates, they have little influence in their society, have access to fewer societal opportunities, and are more likely to have their lives directed by others.

How do these facts translate into meaningful differences in the classroom? One example relates to scores on standardized intelligence tests. Although our interpretation and use of intelligence tests has changed dramatically (see chap. 15), these tests remain an indicator of achievement. Today children at a lower socioeconomic level score 10 to 15 IQ points below middle-class children; these differences not only are *present by the first grade,* but persist throughout the school years. Profiles drawn from the data suggest that higher social class seems to cause an increase in scores, but that the general pattern of intellectual ability is similar. That is, when profiles of lower-class children were drawn, they showed the children to be like the middle-class children, but to score lower on all abilities (Hetherington & Parke, 1993).

It is clear that socioeconomic status remains a reliable predictor of school achievement and suggests that students from the same social class will perform in a remarkably similar manner. For example, in a study of eighth-graders, low-SES white children were as likely as African American and Hispanic American students to have poor grades. In this same study, low-SES Asian American students did not achieve much better than other low-SES students (Weiss, Farrar, & Petrie, 1989). These and similar results testify to the conclusion that socioeconomic status, more than any other single variable, predicts educational functioning.

Social Class and Education

As the importance of education in our society has increased, a shared belief has developed that every American child should graduate from high school. Given this belief, our schools' high dropout rate has become a matter of national concern, especially in those schools serving the poor and minorities. In some school districts, particularly in urban and rural communities, the dropout rate ranges from 20 percent to 40 percent. What this says about the future of these students is evident. For example, salaries for dropouts who are between 18 and 24 years of age average no more than $6,000 per year (Hayes, 1992). Since one in five children is poor, if our concerns about the relationship between poverty and education are correct, the chances of these children for productive employment in a technological society are starkly limited.

In her thoughtful commentary, Renyi (1993) noted that Americans have been firm believers that schools in poverty areas are the means for students to turn their lives around. But, too many poor (and minority) students continue to attend schools that don't address their needs and in which they learn little. The idea that all students should graduate from high school, however, has radically altered current views of teaching and learning.

Attempting to identify the causes behind high school dropout rates, failure, and low achievement, Renyi (1993, p. 14) discovered that the differential success rate for white and black populations is closely related to the economic success of the population as a whole in a particular school building. As she stated, the critical difference for any child was whether that child attended a school with others who were affluent. For example, a poor black child in a white middle-class school had a better chance of academic success than a rich white child in a school in which the majority of the children were poor.

Given the goal of a high school education for all, not every student could adjust to the role of white middle-class American. In other words, everyone would go to school, but the schools themselves would remain the same, dedicated to white, middle-class goals. The constant calls for school reform have ignored the nature of the *total* school population; this helps to explain why about 15 percent of our students continue to drop out.

Renyi (1993) analyzed this 15-percent group, composed of the poor and minority students of today, compared it to similar groups in previous generations, and concluded that in the past, children of the poor were not expected to complete high school. They were expected to leave school before graduation and get a job offering a living wage. But now members of this same group are expected to finish high school and eventually assume the status of middle-class citizens—a task easier to talk about than to accomplish. Children who come to school hungry and listless, often carrying memories of violence, are not overly concerned about academic achievement.

In school districts with much poverty, the schools themselves tell a similar story: not enough texts for all students; limited, perhaps nonexistent, materials; metal detectors at school entrances. One of the authors, early in his career, shifted from teaching secondary school biology in the suburbs to teaching in the upper grades of an urban elementary school. Materials were so limited that the teachers used their own money to buy paper, crayons, and workbooks. (This concern of teachers for their students will never be forgotten; such generosity is a quality we hear about too infrequently.) How does this type of educational environment affect the classroom performance of both teachers and students?

Teaching, Learning, and Social Class

In his biting commentary on current conditions in America's schools, Kozol (1991) drew some vivid comparisons. In schools populated with children of the poor, students are crowded into small, squalid spaces, and in some cities overcrowding is so bad that some schools function in abandoned factories. In one school, students eat their lunches in what was once the building's boiler room. Reading classes are taught in what used to be a bathroom; there are no microscopes for science classes; one counselor serves 3,600 students in the elementary grades. In the high school of the same district, there is a single physics section for 2,200 students; two classes are being taught simultaneously in one classroom.

For more details of these student's lives, here are Kozol's words:

> The city was so poor there had been no garbage pickup for four years. . . . On the edge of the city is a large chemical plant. There is also a very large toxic waste incinerator, as well as a huge sewage treatment plant . . . The city has one of the highest rates of infant mortality in Illinois, the highest rate of fetal death, and also a very high rate of childhood asthma.

Do you agree with the statement that since all students are expected to graduate from high school, schools must adapt to their changing populations to lower the dropout rate? Why or why not?

The opportunities provided by different educational enviroments can affect, negatively or positively, the achievement of students.

The schools, not surprisingly, are impoverished. . . . The entire school system had been shut down after being flooded with sewage from the city's antique sewage system. "I did meet several wonderful teachers in the school, and I thought the principal of the school was excellent. The superintendent is also a very impressive person." (Kozol, 1993, p. 5)

A high school in a more affluent district in the same state presents a different picture. There is a greenhouse for students interested in horticulture; the physical sciences department offers fourteen courses; there are eighteen biology electives. The school's orchestra has traveled to the former Soviet Union. Beautifully carpeted hallways encourage students to sit and study; computers are everywhere. The ratio of counselors to students is one to 150. Parents of these students recently raised money to send the school choral group to Vienna.

Given these different conditions, is it any wonder that different educational outcomes are inevitable? If, as frequently described, the school is a middle-class institution staffed mainly by white middle-class teachers, then students from different social classes immediately begin their schooling at a disadvantage (Hetherington & Parke, 1993). From everything we have said, you can understand that middle-class teachers can be expected to have different values and expectations than their economically deprived students.

These conditions can be either improved or made worse by a family's attitude toward education. As Garbarino and Benn noted (1992), parents may not be present in the classroom, but they have a profound influence on the ways their children view school and learning. The extent to which the parents support the school's objectives directly affects their children's academic performance. Too often, low parental expectations for their children reflect the parents' own educational experiences. If parents themselves encountered difficulties in school, they may exercise a negative impact on their children's attitudes, expectations, and performance. The reverse also holds true.

These conclusions are particularly significant for immigrant students. Frequently coming from crushing poverty and often from wartime conditions, they have backgrounds which can be almost impossible for American teachers to understand. The economic hardships these immigrants previously lived with may continue here, and they undoubtedly face a bleak economic future in the United States, especially when we realize minorities reach the poverty level at an ever-increasing rate (*New Voices*, 1988). You may well ask at this point: Is there any positive side to these facts?

Head Start

Conceived as part of President Lyndon Johnson's War On Poverty, **Head Start** was originally headed by Sargent Shriver, who had been astounded on examining the distribution of poverty in the United States. Data indicated that about one-half of the nation's 30 million poor were children, most of these were under 12 years of age. Shriver's main objective became the preparation of poor children for entrance into the first grade. As Hauser-Cram et al. (1991) noted, Head Start was intended to provide educational and developmental services to preschool children from low-income families. Improving

Head Start *An intervention program intended to provide educational and developmental services to preschool children from low-income families.*

children's health became a primary goal: children received pediatric and neurological assessments, plus two nutritious meals a day (Zigler & Muenchow, 1992). Head Start programs had six components: preschool education, health screening and referral, mental health services, nutrition education and hot meals, social services for the child and family, and parental involvement (Zigler & Styfco, 1994). Since its beginning, more than 13 million children have been served by Head Start.

Unfortunately, some of the early claims about the gains to be realized from Head Start programs revolved around changes in IQ; some proponents stated that as a result of participation in Head Start, a child's IQ would increase one IQ point a month. In the mid-1960s, critical evaluations of intelligence tests had not reached today's level of sophistication. Edward Zigler, a member of the Head Start planning committee, deplored reliance on increases in IQ scores as the means of evaluating Head Start.

His fears were quickly justified, as follow-up studies of Head Start children showed a "fadeout effect." That is, although graduates of these preschool programs showed immediate gains in intelligence and achievement test scores, after several months in the public schools, the Head Start children seemed to lose these cognitive benefits (Zigler & Styfco, 1994, p. 128). Nevertheless, even if Head Start graduates do not maintain *academic* gains, they have improved their readiness for school, and the advantages of Head Start extend to other parts of their lives.

For example, Lazar and Darlington (1982) studied the long-term results of twelve Head Start programs and reported significant effects on school competence, families, and attitudes about self and school. Among the techniques employed by the various programs were constant communication with parents, training of mothers in the use of educational activities in the home, and periodic home visits. Pooling the data from these studies, Lazar and Darlington discovered that children who had attended these programs were less likely to be retained in grade and more likely to meet their schools' requirements. They also attained higher IQ scores than their controls, demonstrated higher self-concepts, and were proud of their school accomplishment. The mothers of program graduates were more satisfied with their children's school performance than were control mothers; they also had higher occupational aspirations for their children than did control mothers. These results were obtained several years after the children had left the Head Start program, and suggest the benefits of positive parental involvement in school affairs.

Today, with the rapid increase in the number of working women and the stunning rise of children living in poverty, the need for early intervention programs to aid these children seems more compelling than ever. In her summary of the need for greater support of preschool programs, Kassebaum (1994) pointed out that 21 percent of all American children live in poverty; 25 percent of all children live with a single parent; 25 percent of all babies are born to unmarried mothers; every night at least 100,000 children are homeless; the United States ranks 20th in the world with regard to infant mortality.

These statistics cry out for attention because the children they represent not only suffer educational disadvantages, but also face other developmental difficulties. For example, as we have seen, children of these families are more frequently born premature; their families suffer devastating and widespread deprivation; the children themselves are more subject to physical illness and lowered cognitive performance. As more of these children enter the public schools, is it any wonder they are unable to meet the ordinary demands of the classroom (Hauser-Cram et al., 1991)? It is in meeting some of the many needs of these children that we see the value of programs such as Head Start, with its hope of bringing the children successfully into the mainstream of school life and the wider community. If we are to succeed, we must identify the skills, both academic and social, that our students need.

We turn now to the final subject in our analysis of diversity and the classroom: the role that gender plays in academic achievement.

teacher – student

Teaching Students Social Skills

Teaching children social skills involves many of the same methods used to teach academic concepts. Effective teachers of both academic and social skills model correct behavior, elicit an imitative response, provide corrective feedback, and arrange for opportunities to practice the new skills.

Elliott and Gresham (1991), the authors of the *Social Skills Rating System,* recently published the *Social Skills Intervention Guide* to facilitate a link between assessment results and interventions for children who have social skills deficits. The following skill training unit on "Responding to Teasing from Peers" illustrates a basic instructional sequence that can be used to successfully teach students appropriate social skills.

Domain: Self-Control

Subdomain: Anger Control

Skill: Responds to teasing from peers appropriately

Definition of Skill: Student responds to teasing from peers by ignoring, changing the subject, making a joke, or complimenting other person.

Learning Objective: The student will appropriately respond to teasing or name-calling from peers.

Tell Phase

1. Introduce skill by asking questions such as these:
   - Have you ever been teased by your peers? How does this make you feel?
   - Why do you think people sometimes like to tease others? (it makes them feel better, they like to see other people squirm, etc.)
   - What have you done when you were teased by others?
   - What happened? How did you feel afterwards?
   - What are some ways you could respond to being teased? (get mad; get feelings hurt; ignore it; change the subject; make a joke; compliment other person)

2. Read definition of skill to be taught and discuss it to ensure understanding by students (key terms are noted below).
   - Key terms: teasing, name-calling, being butt of jokes, complimenting, changing the subject.
3. Give rationales for importance of skill:
   - Sometimes you can get people to stop teasing you by ignoring them. They don't enjoy teasing if you don't get upset by it.
   - Many times you can stop being teased by just changing the subject.
   - Often, if you compliment people who are teasing you, they will stop.
   - Sometimes making a joke about yourself takes the fun out of teasing.
4. Outline in performing the skill:
   a. Decide if you are being teased.
   b. Try to understand why you are being teased.
   c. Choose a strategy (ignoring, making a joke, complimenting, changing the subject).
   d. Implement a strategy.
   e. Evaluate how you did and how other person reacted.

Show Phase

1. Have group leader (teacher or a delegated student) model the skill:
   a. Positive modeling: Use steps identified in stage 4 above.
   b. Negative modeling: Model inappropriate ways of performing the skill, such as teasing back, showing that your feelings are hurt, yelling or screaming, pushing or shoving other person.
2. Have group leader model skill again, but this time emphasizing and commenting on each step as it is performed.

GENDER, DEVELOPMENT, AND THE CLASSROOM

Another issue that has attracted the attention of educational psychologists is that of gender and schooling. A basic question is this: Are females receiving the support they need, particularly in the classroom, to fulfill their potential? Or is their development being frustrated by a form of discrimination so subtle and sophisticated that it has become part of their daily lives? Before beginning our analysis of the relationship between gender and classroom achievement, we should have an idea of the issues involved.

Let's begin by defining terms that we can use in a consistent manner. For several years psychologists, responding to Unger's plea (1979), have urged that we use the terms *sex* and *gender* more carefully. In this new context, *sex* would refer to *biological* maleness or femaleness (for example, the sex chromosomes), while *gender* would suggest *psychosocial* aspects of maleness and femaleness (for example, changing

3. Have group leader role-play skill with other students. Read the following vignette and role play:
   - Julie is climbing on the monkey bars during recess. A couple of kids behind her yell at her to get off. They say, "Hurry up and get off, fatso. You're no good at climbing." They continue to call her "fatso."
4. Have group leader lead a discussion of alternative ways the person could have performed the skill. Decide if students need another role play. If so, choose one of the following vignettes and role-play it:
   - (optional)
     Anthony is playing on the playground with his class. Several students from another class taunt and tease Anthony by saying, "You're in the stupid kid class. You're retarded."
   - (optional)
     Donna is in a wheelchair. Some girls yell at her when she goes down the hall, "Where did you get those wheels, crippo?"
   - (optional)
     Bill has struck out for the third time during the softball game. His teammates say, "You're a bad player, four-eyes. You can't even see the ball."

Do Phase

1. Ask students to define skill verbally. Have at least half the group provide definitions. Refine and clarify definitions as needed.
2. Ask students to provide rationales for performing skill. Ask group members who do not provide a definition to provide rationales.
3. Ask students to list critical steps in performing skill. List steps in proper sequence on chalkboard or flip chart.
4. Ask students to model the behavior. Use vignettes not used in "Show" Phase for role plays.

5. Have students generate new or novel situations in which skill could be performed. Then have them act out these student-directed role plays.
   a. Ask nonparticipating students to provide feedback on role plays.
   b. Have group leader provide informative feedback on individual student performances.

Follow-Through and Practice Phase

1. Periodically review and practice steps in performing the skill. Watch for instances of teasing and for appropriate as well as inappropriate uses of skill.
2. Have students generate a list of things that kids get teased about and discuss how they could respond.
3. Make a list of "good-natured" teasing incidents and discuss how this form of teasing is not something to get upset or feel bad about.
4. Have students monitor the times they are teased for one week. Be sure they answer "who, what, when, and where", questions about the incidents, and tell how they responded.

Generalization Phase

1. Teach self-instructional strategy for responding to teasing and name-calling. Have students write down steps for skill performance on note cards. Have them memorize steps, verbalize steps aloud, whisper them, and finally use the steps.
2. Role-play different situations in which children are teased. Use situations generated in stage 2 of the "Follow-through" Phase for role plays.
3. Role-play situations in which children are teased by familiar and unfamiliar peers.
4. Discuss and role-play alternative ways that students could appropriately respond to teasing. Use ways generated in stage 4 of the "Show" Phase for this activity.

gender roles). Although no absolute distinction is possible—we can't completely separate our ideas about gender from a person's body—this distinction can help us to focus on the major forces contributing to the acquisition of gender identity. Within this framework, we can now distinguish among gender identity, gender stereotypes, and gender roles.

gender identity *The conviction that one belongs to the sex of birth.*

gender stereotypes *Beliefs about the characteristics associated with males or females.*

gender role *Culturally acceptable sexual behavior.*

- **Gender identity** is a conviction that one belongs to the sex of birth.
- **Gender stereotypes** reflect those beliefs about the characteristics associated with male or female.
- **Gender role** refers to culturally acceptable sexual behavior.

Studies of gender have taken distinctive paths: theoretical explanations, research into gender similarities and differences, and studies of gender stereotypes. We will analyze these topics throughout this text in an attempt to discover how gender roles affect classroom achievement. Here, it is instructive to mention a few signs that indicate the changing status of women in our society.

Recent census figures (Bureau of the Census, 1992) reveal that 18.7 percent of females 25 years or older had completed 4 or more years of college, compared to 24.3 percent of males. For women, this is a substantial increase from the 3.8 percent who had completed 4 or more years of college in 1940. During the 1980s, the number of women on campus increased by 17 percent; today's estimates are that women constitute about 53 percent of the post-high school population (Sadker & Sadker, 1994).

As concern about gender equity has received more publicity, stereotypes about males and females are slowly eroding. If despite this trend, however, people are treated according to stereotypical characteristics, then their potential is immediately limited. Although gender stereotyping is only one part of gender development, it illustrates the importance of the relationship between gender, schooling, and development. At an early age, children construct social categories from the world around them, attach certain characteristics to these categories, and then label the categories. This process may be positive, since it helps children to organize their world. It may also be negative, if the characteristics associated with a particular category are limiting: "Girls just can't do math" (Serbin et al., 1993).

One of the first categories children form is sex related; there is a neat division in their minds between male and female. Children then move from the observable physical differences between the sexes and begin to acquire gender knowledge about the behavior expected of males and females. Although its content varies according to the source of this knowledge, gender role stereotyping has commenced, and attitudes toward gender are being shaped. As Serbin and her colleagues (1993) noted, despite the societal changes we have seen in acceptable gender roles, gender role stereotypes have remained relatively stable in the culture. What do we know about the acquisition of gender identity?

Becoming Boys and Girls

We find clues to identifying and understanding the current status of women in our schools by examining the processes by which boys and girls acquire their sense of gender identity. Both biology and the environment contribute to this in a complex, interactive manner. The first component of the heredity-environment interaction is biology.

Does Biology Count?

Individuals with various perspectives on issues of gender identity agree on one premise: parts of the sexual agenda are biologically programmed. John Money (1980), working in a Johns Hopkins clinic devoted to the study of congenital abnormalities of the sex organs, observed that sexual differentiation seems to occur in four stages. The first stage determines *chromosomal sex*. The biological sexual program is initially carried by either the X or the Y sex chromosome. Formed second is *gonadal sex,* in which the XX or XY combination passes on the sexual program to the undifferentiated gonads, or reproductive glands (testes or ovaries). Third, *hormonal sex* develops. Once the gonads are differentiated, they begin to produce chemical agents called sex hormones. Males produce more of the sex hormones called androgens than females, while females produce more estrogen (the female sex hormone). Fourth to develop is *genital sex*. A baby's sex is determined not only by chromosomes and hormones, but also by its external sex organs. As you can well imagine, it is genital or morphological sex that determines how society regards a new born baby. With these as the biological givens, we turn now to the role of socialization.

Does the Environment Count?

Most psychologists today believe in a *reciprocal interaction* model of development to explain behavior. That is, we respond to those around us and they change; their responses to us then change, and we in turn change, in an ongoing process. Clearly, then, the reactions of others to ideas of gender, particularly if they are stereotypical, can influence children's gender identity, and also their behavior. If girls are told, "Girls don't make good scientists," then it is possible that their achievement in science classes will suffer.

It doesn't take children long to discover which behavior "fits" girls and which "fits" boys (Fagot, Leinbach, & O'Boyle, 1992). Children have the cognitive competency to acquire their own gender identity by 2 to 3 years of age; in this light, their rapid assignment of appropriate behavior to either male or female is understandable. Lott (1989) reported that by preschool age, most children are well aware of their own gender, of which parent they are most like, and of the gender of family members and peers (Martin & Little, 1990).

How soon do children begin to make decisions about appropriate behavior based on sex? Lott (1989) reported the result of a study that required children from 2 to 7 years of age to assign various occupations to either a male or a female doll. As early as 2 years of age, they assigned traditionally male occupations to male dolls. For example, 67 percent of 2- and 3-year-olds chose the male doll to be a doctor.

In an attempt to explain these and similar findings, Martin, Wood, and Little (1990) found a developmental sequence to the appearance of gender stereotypes. In the first stage, children learn what kinds of things are associated with each sex (boys play with cars; girls play with dolls). From the ages of 4 to 6 years, children move to the second stage, where they begin to learn the more complex associations for their own sex (e.g., different kinds of activities associated with a toy). By the third stage (roughly 6 to 8 years), children make the same types of associations for the opposite sex. Where do these ideas come from? Among the most influential of the socialization agents are family, peers, and the media.

Family

Evidence clearly suggests that parents treat girl and boy babies differently from birth. Adults tend to engage in rougher play with boys, give them stereotypical toys (cars and trucks), and speak differently to them. By the end of the second year, parents respond favorably to what they consider gender-appropriate (that is, stereotypical) behavior, and negatively to cross-sex play (boys engaging in typically girls' play, and vice versa). For example, Fagot (1985; Fagot & Hagan, 1991), who observed toddlers and their parents at home, discovered that both mothers and fathers differentially reinforced their children's behavior. That is, they reinforced girls for playing with dolls and boys for playing with blocks, girls for helping their mothers around the house and boys for running and jumping.

Lips (1993) believes that parents are unaware of the extent to which they engage in this type of reinforcement. In a famous study (Will, Self, and Datan, 1976), 11 mothers were observed interacting with a 6-month old infant. Five of the mothers played with the infant when it was dressed in blue pants and called "Adam." Six mothers later played with the same infant when it wore a pink dress and was called "Beth." The mothers offered a doll to "Beth" and a toy train to "Adam." They also smiled more at Beth and held her more closely. The baby was actually a boy. Interviewed later, all the mothers said that boys and girls were alike at this age and *should be treated identically*.

Siblings also influence gender development. Brothers and sisters differ markedly in personality, intelligence, and psychopathology, in spite of shared genetic roots. Since about 80 percent of children have siblings and they spend considerable time with one another, these relationships exercise an important influence (Dunn, 1983). A younger sister watching her older sister play with dolls; an older brother showing a younger brother how to hold a bat; quarreling among siblings—each of these examples illustrates the impact that sibling relationships have on gender development.

Perhaps no one has summarized the importance of this differential treatment of daughters and sons better than Block (1983). Noting the reality of this parental behavior, Block states that males and females grow up in quite different learning environments, with important psychological implications for development. Peers are an important part of these different learning environments.

Peers

When children start to make friends and play with them, these activities foster and maintain sex-typed play. Studies show that by the age of 3, children reinforce each other for gender-typed play (Langlois & Downs, 1980). When they engage in "gender-inappropriate" play (girls with footballs, boys with dolls), their peers immediately criticize them and tend to isolate them. This tendency increases with age, until most adolescents react with intense demands for conformity to stereotypical gender roles.

Here, again, we see the influence of imitation and reinforcement. During development, youngsters of the same sex tend to play together, a custom called **sex cleavage** and encouraged by parents and teachers. If you think back on your own experiences, you can probably remember your childhood friends as either all male or all female. In adolescence, despite dating and opposite-sex attraction, both females and males want to live up to the most rigid interpretations of what their group thinks is ideally female or male. Imitation, reinforcement, and cognitive development all come together to establish firmly which traits children view as masculine or feminine (Dunn, 1983).

sex cleavage *The tendency of children of the same sex to play together.*

The Media

Another influence on gender development, one that carries important messages about what is desirable for males and females and one that reaches into the home, is the media, especially television. Television has assumed such a powerful place in the socialization of children that it is safe to say that it is almost as significant as family and peers. What is particularly bothersome is the stereotypical behavior that it presents as both positive and desirable. As Lips (1993) stated flatly, television teaches gender stereotypes. The more television children watch, the more stereotypical is their behavior.

Programs such as *Murphy Brown* and *Murder, She Wrote* are the exception. The rule is that the central characters of shows are much more likely to be male than female, themes of such male-dominated programs are action oriented, and the characters typically engage in stereotypical behavior (women are the housewives and secretaries; men are the executives and leaders). Much the same holds true for television commercials. There is little doubt that children notice the different ways television portrays females and males and that this affects their views of gender behavior. When asked to rate the behavior of males and females, children aged 8 to 13 responded in a rigidly stereotypical manner: males were brave, adventurous, and intelligent, and made good decisions. Females, on the other hand, cried easily and needed to be protected (Lips, 1993).

These distinctions apply to other, much more subtle, features of television programming. To understand a television program, children must know something about story form: how stories are constructed and presented. They must use their general knowledge of the world and of situations and events in order to grasp television's content; what they are watching often reinforces this prior understanding. They must also have knowledge of television's forms and conventions to help them understand what is happening on the screen. Such things as music and visual techniques, including camera angles, all convey information (Liebert et al., 1988).

In other words, children learn more than the contents of a program from television. Among other things, they learn the many cues that signal "male" or "female". Loud music, rapid scene changes, multiple sound effects, and frequent cuts mean just one thing: a male-oriented show. Shows designed for females have soft background music, gentle cuts, and soothing sound effects. Children as young as 6 years can use these cues to identify which shows are intended for males and which for females (Lips, 1993). Children understand television programs according to their level of development, and their development is affected by their television viewing, with all that implies for gender development. We now turn our attention to several theories that attempt to explain gender development.

Theories of Gender Development

Several theories of gender development have generated most of the research during the past ten years: social learning theory, cognitive-developmental theory, and gender schema theory. Proponents of *social learning theory* believe that parents, as the

Both biological and environmental forces contribute to gender-related behaviors.

distributors of reinforcement, reinforce appropriate gender role behaviors. By their choice of toys, by urging "boy" or "girl" behavior, and by reinforcing such behavior, parents encourage their children to engage in gender-appropriate behavior. If the parents have good relationships with their children, they become models for their children to imitate, encouraging them to acquire additional gender-related behavior. Thus children are reinforced or punished for different kinds of behavior. They also learn appropriate gender behavior from other male and female models (such as those in television shows).

A second explanation, quite popular today, is found in *cognitive-developmental theory,* which derives from Kohlberg's speculations about gender development (1975). We know from Piaget's work that children engage in symbolic thinking by about 2 years of age. Using this ability, children acquire their gender identity and then, Kohlberg believes, they begin the process of acquiring gender-appropriate behavior.

gender schema *A mental blueprint for organizing information about gender.*

A newer, and different, cognitive explanation is called **gender schema** theory. A schema is a mental blueprint for organizing information, and children develop a schema for gender. Such a schema helps a child to develop gender identity and formulate an appropriate gender role. Consequently, children develop an integrated schema, or picture, of what gender is and should be.

This very brief examination has shown that both biological and environmental forces contribute to gender, and that several theories attempt to explain the process. What happens once gender stereotypes are formed?

Gender Stereotyping

In the section of this text on the relationship of gender to classroom achievement, gender stereotyping is defined as the beliefs humans hold about the characteristics and behavior associated with males and with females. From an early age, people form ideas of what males and females should be, beginning to accumulate characteristics that they consider male and female, and assigning labels to those categories. This process certainly simplifies the ability to deal with the world. Obviously, that rough, noisy person is a boy, and that gentle, soft-spoken, obedient person is a girl. (As a result of such stereotyping, the "feminine" boy or "masculine" girl often has difficulties with peers.)

Several problems exist with this process, however. One occurs when the characteristics associated with a particular gender have a negative image. A second occurs when a unique individual is assumed to have all the characteristics associated with his or her gender. Both problems are reflected in these comments: "Oh, girls can't do math; girls can't do science; girls are always crying; girls can't be leaders." The attitudes behind such comments hold some potential pitfalls, especially for teachers. Why should a teacher who believes a girl "can't do science" call on girls or give them attention in a science class? (For an excellent summary of the place of women in education, see Sadker & Sadker, 1994, pp. 15–41.)

Although sexual equality is widely accepted today—legally, professionally, and on a personal level—gender stereotyping is still alive and well. But are males and females actually that different?

Gender Similarities and Differences

As knowledge about gender behavior increases, there is a growing consensus that the differences between the sexes are not so great as they were once thought to be. In a benchmark study of gender differences published in 1974, Maccoby and Jacklin did conclude that males were superior in mathematical and visual-spatial skills, while females had better verbal skills. (Recent studies have continued to identify gender similarities and differences; for a summary of this research, see Berk, 1994.) We can capsulize recent research by stating that there are many similarities between males and females, and that any differences that do exist are not necessarily caused by biological forces.

The recent work of Pinker (1994) helps to give a balanced perspective on differences between any human beings. Pinker noted that anthropologists frequently stress differences between peoples (the "strange behaviors" of others) and often understate the many similarities among all humans. Pinker specifies such universal human characteristics as humor, insults, fear, anger, storytelling, laws, dreams, words for common objects, binary distinctions, measures, common facial expressions (happy, sad, angry, fearful), crying, displays of affection, among others. Pinker identifies these attributes as complex interactions between a universal human nature and the conditions of living in a human body on this planet (Pinker, 1994, p. 415). Obviously, the point for our purposes is that humans are quite similar, regardless of any male-female distinctions.

Nevertheless, differences do exist, as seen in table 3.1. It is important to point out that these differences are not fixed. That is, changes in our understanding occur as more sophisticated research techniques produce new data. One example of this is the realization that differences in mathematical abilities are not so great as they were once thought to be.

With these ideas in mind, we turn now to how gender impacts classroom performance.

Gender and Classroom Achievement

The relationship of gender to classroom performance has inspired considerable research that has taken a definite direction. Teacher-student and student-student interaction patterns, curricular content, and testing have all been scrutinized in an effort to detect gender bias. Achieving gender equity in the classroom means equally recognizing and rewarding the achievements of both boys and girls. Let's begin by looking at interaction patterns.

Interaction Patterns

Before examining how gender may possibly affect teacher-student interactions, we should pause to consider the importance of interactions in general. Do the interactions that take place between teacher and student constitute a relationship? A focus box earlier in this chapter implied that a relationship develops from a pattern of intermittent interactions over an extended period of time. Certainly, this describes what constantly occurs in the classroom during the school year.

Table 3.1

Observed Gender Differences	
Characteristic	**Gender difference**
Physical differences	Although almost all girls mature more rapidly than boys, by adolescence, boys have surpassed girls in size and strength.
Verbal ability	Girls do better on verbal tasks beginning in the early years, a superiority that is retained. Boys also exhibit more language problems than girls.
Spatial skill	Boys display superiority on spatial tasks, a superiority that continues throughout schooling.
Mathematical ability	There is little, if any, difference in the early years; boys begin to demonstrate superiority during the high school years.
Science	Gender differences seem to be increasing; females are falling behind, while the performance of males is increasing.
Achievement motivation	Differences here seem to be linked to task and situation. Boys do better in stereotypically "masculine" tasks (math, science), and girls in "feminine" tasks (art, music). In direct competition between males and females, beginning around adolescence, girls' achievement seems to drop.
Aggression	Boys appear to be innately more aggressive than girls, a difference that appears early and is remarkably consistent.

Do any clues exist as to why the quality of interactions with teachers can vary so widely from student to student? An examination of the way teachers interact with different types of students may yield additional insights into classroom relationships. If we accept the notion of reciprocal interactions, no longer can we believe merely that active teachers do something to passive students. As we now know, changes in one participant in a relationship produce changes in the other. A teacher changes as the result of changes in the pupils. It also seems clear that teachers give more attention and different attention to some students than to others. And one of the ways they make these distinctions is along gender lines.

As we have indicated, many teachers treat boys differently from girls. The elementary school has frequently been characterized as a feminine domain, more conducive to the needs and interests of girls than to those of boys. But several interesting issues arise upon examining the data more carefully. Although girls, in general, do better than boys in the elementary grades, girls lose this achievement edge in secondary school, especially in such subjects as science and mathematics. Why? One reason may be an extension into the classroom of stereotypic attitudes toward gender: boys are reinforced for intellectual pursuits, girls for nurturing activities. Teachers more frequently attribute failure in boys to lack of motivation, while girls more frequently are seen as lacking ability.

How teachers interact with their students has long intrigued researchers. One finding has been consistent: regardless of the level at which they are teaching, teachers pay more attention to boys than to girls. Frequently, boys simply demand more attention than girls. These findings are particularly applicable to math and science classes. Teachers reported to researchers that they had similar expectations for boys and girls; yet, when the same teachers were observed in class, they questioned the boys as much as 80 percent more than the girls. Also, in science classes, it was much more common to have the experiments demonstrated by a boy (Bailey, 1993).

The Sadkers (1994) reported that although teachers believed they held all of their students accountable to classroom rules (e.g., raising their hands when they want to speak), their observed behavior was quite different. In the give-and-take of the classroom, boys quickly dominated any discussion; males called out 8 times more often than girls (Sadker & Sadker, 1994, p. 43). An interesting finding associated with this research is that even when the boys called out comments that were irrelevant, teachers still responded to them. When girls, on the other hand, called out, teachers frequently reminded them of the calling-out rules, a clear sign of differential treatment.

Gender differences also appear in the nature of the teacher-student interactions, that is, the types of comments teachers use when they are interacting with boys as compared with girls. Identifying four types of teacher comments (praise, acceptance, remediation, and criticism), the Sadkers (1994) found that males received more of *all* types of comments, but particularly more praise, criticism, and remediation, which are more useful kinds of comments. In other words, boys received more precise teacher reactions. As you might imagine, these findings were particularly applicable to math and science classes.

Will this kind of treatment scar girls for life? Hardly. Yet there are subtle consequences of gender inequality in the classroom. For example, in your reading of the literature on motivation, you will come across terms such as learned helplessness and attribution. Do girls acquire a sense of academic helplessness and lose their scholarly initiative as a result of differential treatment? Do they attribute feelings of powerlessness in the classroom to their perceived lack of ability? These are difficult questions to answer, yet ones that research must continue to address (AAUW, 1992). Similar issues appear in any examination of the relationship between gender and the curriculum.

Gender and the Curriculum

If we wanted to learn from one document alone about a classroom's, school's, district's, or state's views on a particular issue, we would do well to look at its curriculum. At a cursory glance, a curriculum might seem to address only the academic subjects. But a closer look would reveal some important underlying assumptions. One of the messages that a curriculum contains is a particular position on matters of culture, class, and gender. For example, certain attitudes toward women are reflected in a course in American history in which there is little, if any, mention of outstanding American women of the particular period being studied.

Most state curriculum guides identify the philosophies that undergird specific curriculum content. A state curriculum should also give suggestions for adapting content to special groups, helping teachers highlight, for example, the role of American women in education, as physicians, as business executives, and in the armed forces. A school system uses state guidelines and applies them to the local population (Borich, 1992). Then the individual instructor takes the state and school district suggestions, examining them for specific resources that address a particular issue (such as gender and achievement). Do these materials offer help in determining definite units of study and daily lesson plans? Are there illustrations of the tangible accomplishments of outstanding women, as for example, Nadine Gordimer, the South African woman who won the Nobel Prize for Literature in 1991, or the psychologist Eleanor Gibson, who won a National Medal of Science in 1992? Illustrations such as these are easily woven into a curriculum and can only produce positive results.

A teacher who wanted to teach specific contributions of women in history could collect stories, books, videotapes, and films that illustrated and supported this objective, as well as the larger goal of increasing regard for the role of women in general. The teacher could also ask leading women of the community to come to the classroom to explain the nature of their work. This is a sure and simple way to raise the self-esteem of the girls in the class, and to offer them some outstanding women as role models.

Banks (1993) offered a helpful framework for including gender material (as well as cultural and class content) in a curriculum. He identified four levels of integration, the first of which is the *contributions approach*. This typically is the initial step used by teachers and school systems, and involves using heroic figures as curricular illustrations (for example, Rosa Parks, whose refusal to move to the back of the bus triggered the overt activities of the American Civil Rights movement). The curriculum remains the same except for the inclusion of the heroic figures.

The second level is the *additive approach*. Here, various themes and perspectives are added to the curriculum without changing its overall structure. Something new is brought to the curriculum, such as material about pioneer women, or a book such as *The Color Purple*.

The third level of integration is the *transformational approach,* in which the goals, structure, and perspectives of the curriculum are changed. Banks (1993, p. 203) gives the example of the study of the American revolution: to acquire a balanced, comprehensive view of it, the perspectives of the revolutionaries, the loyalists, women, African Americans, Native Americans, and the British all need to be considered.

At the fourth and final level, in the *social action approach,* students make decisions and take actions that incorporate the changes of the transformational level into their own lives. The goal is to encourage students to undertake social criticism and social change by teaching them decision-making skills. At this level, these and similar questions can guide teachers' efforts to introduce positive gender concepts in the classroom: Why are women discriminated against? What causes this discrimination? Does it occur in the classroom? What can be done about it?

Efforts are being made, on the state, local, and classroom levels, to eliminate gender bias in curricula. Another concern is the possibility of gender bias in testing.

Test Bias

An important aspect of the relationship between curriculum and gender is evaluation. Do the same issues apply to testing that we have seen with regard to other school activities? To put it simply, is gender bias evident in school testing? The intent here is not to analyze the strengths and weaknesses of various types of evaluation; that will be done in chapters 15 and 16. In this section, we call attention to the inherently powerful role that testing plays in determining the future of students, and to explore the ways some testing seems to be biased in favor of males.

In a statement concerning the place of assessment in helping to attain equity, Madaus (1994, p. 77) asserted that one role of assessment is to be a large-scale, high-stakes policy tool, used to drive reform of schools and curricula and to make important decisions about individuals. It is in the "important decisions about individuals" that the possibility of bias exists. Pullin (1994, p. 46) argued that the potential for gender differences resides in almost any testing or assessment program, especially if the testing involves mathematical skills. For example, an examination of the scores on the Scholastic Achievement Test (SAT) reveals that performance is consistently higher for males than for females.

If gender bias in testing exists, it must be addressed. As Pullin (1994) noted, any allegation of gender bias in assessment could be subject to legal challenge, given the provisions of Title IX, which bars any form of sex discrimination in all educational programs and activities conducted by recipients of federal financial aid. These safeguards are intended to insure access to equal educational opportunity, both in schools and the workplace. The rationale behind this directive is that assessment programs should be used to survey the possibilities for student growth, and not just to designate students as ready or not ready to profit from standard instruction.

Is there any basis for these concerns? To answer this question, we turn once again to the notion of equal access to opportunity. One example was offered by Rosser (1989), who pointed out that girls are more likely than boys to go to college, but that scholarships based on test scores are twice as likely to go to boys. Another example of possible bias is the use of SAT scores to predict college success. SAT scores underpredict women's success and overpredict men's (AAUW, 1992). When researchers examined the SAT scores of men and women who received the same grades in the same college courses, they discovered that the women's SAT scores had been 35 points below the men's. Finally, the National Commission on Testing and Public Policy (1990) reported that women averaged 56 points lower than men on the SAT. (Incidentally, relative to whites, African Americans averaged 92 points lower, Puerto Ricans 90 points lower, Mexican Americans 63 points lower, and Asian Americans 37 points lower.)

What can a teacher do to help reverse the discrepancy between male and female scores? Just an awareness of the differences that appear in math and science scores, for example, suggests certain techniques. Make sure your questions and comments are evenly distributed to girls and boys; involve girls in math and science cooperative learning activities. If you are particularly concerned about the differences in performance you may discover, provide a setting in which girls (and any boys experiencing problems) can study math and science topics with guidance before they are covered in

teacher – student

The Value of Your Relationships with Students

Hinde's statement (1979) that relationships are the most important part of our lives applies as forcefully to the classroom as to any other setting, and we may add that the quality of your relationships with your students will determine the success of your instruction, your management, and your student's learning.

1. Teacher-student relationships are crucial for learning and development.
   - Work hard at recognizing your students as persons; they must not be merely "faces in the crowd." Don't be blinded by the stereotypes we have discussed in this chapter. Give students personal attention when they return from an illness or if something has gone wrong at home. Recognize publicly their achievements; if they have accomplished something significant—in or out of class—let them talk about it to the rest of the class.
   - Although we will stress the need for rules and routine in later chapters, once you come to know your students well, there will be times when you must react individually to a child. For example, if you sense that a good pupil is upset and likely to explode, send this pupil on an errand or talk to the child individually about some unrelated matter.
   - Don't take any student for granted. Your daily interactions will vary because of the many influences acting on pupils, both in and out of class. Get to know your pupils; be sensitive to any clues of possible problems, and act appropriately.

2. A teacher's interactions with students determine the value of the relationship.
   - Fairness is a teacher characteristic that students cherish and that affects teacher-student relationships. Check your behavior often in this regard. Keep these questions in mind: Am I fair to all of my pupils, regardless of culture, social class, or gender? Do I treat them all in the same way?
   - Remember to use humor in your interactions with your pupils. Don't attempt to be a stand-up comic, but do remember that students appreciate it when you react humorously to some light-hearted incident in class or when you joke about an innocent mistake in class.
   - Remember to treat *all* of your students with dignity and respect. If you treat them courteously, the majority of students will respond in kind. In any survey of desirable teacher characteristics, students usually say something like this: "The teacher always acted nice toward us; you feel good as a person." Dignity, respect, and courtesy are remarkably powerful forces in a relationship.
   - Remember that students take their cues from you. In their interactions, they are assessing your tone of voice, facial expressions, and behavior. If you are sensitive to them, they also are sensitive to you; if you are usually patient but on this occasion seem to be abrupt, the interactions change, and pupil behavior is affected, perhaps for the whole day.

3. Strive for a "goodness of fit" in your relationships with your students.
   - Be clear in your own mind about how you feel a teacher should act, that is, your role. Try not to be blinded by the "teacher-as-authority" role. You certainly are the authority figure, but you also want your pupils to see you as a real person. Acting with dignity, using humor, and perhaps using a few personal examples can be quite helpful. Be yourself.
   - To help you and your pupils define your roles in the classroom, put a VENN diagram (one which contains two overlapping circles) on the board. Label one large section *Teacher*, the other large section *Students*, and the area where they overlap *Both*. Now with your students, fill in the appropriate roles for each person or group.
   - When the "goodness of fit" is lacking and you find it difficult to relate to a pupil, don't deny it. Face up to this and watch your own behavior. Don't overlook any misbehavior in the student, but when you can, force yourself to take the extra step; furnish as much positive reinforcement as you can. Usually this helps, and the logic of reciprocal interactions take over: as you change, the pupil changes.

class. These and similar practices can help girls feel more at ease with science and mathematics and gradually help them to improve their test scores.

Teacher-Student Relationships: A Summary

Finally, it is important to remember that regardless of a student's actual ability, teachers, using a number of variables (including cultural, social, and gender), form certain expectations for their students. They then, subtly or otherwise, communicate these feelings to individual students who quickly grasp the messages and react to them accordingly. Students begin to see themselves as bright or slow, as persons of whom much is expected or those of whom little is expected.

The telling impact of reciprocal interactions is easy to observe. You, the teacher, behave toward a student in a certain way; the student reacts to your behavior; you react in turn. The norms are set and the student performs in a manner consistent with the interactions that have shaped the relationship between the two of you. In this chapter, we have stressed that teacher and students each bring givens with them—their culture, their social class, and their gender—and that the resulting interactions of the distinct personalities affect the classroom atmosphere and are the basis of teacher-student relationships.

Put them all together, and the resultant complex mixture of interactions identifies the classroom atmosphere. If you think about your role as teacher and how you visualize your instruction, you should become more sensitive to the reasons for your reactions to specific pupils. As you do, try to assess your interactions with those pupils: are they good, positive, too negative, too infrequent? If you decide that a change in a particular relationship is necessary, focus on the specific interactions with that student in an attempt to determine why you (and the student) are acting as you do. Are you reacting to a stereotype? Have you formed prior expectations? Such self-analysis will help you to achieve healthy and respectful interactions and relationships that result in better learning for your students.

From your own classroom experiences, would you agree that there is a difference in how boys and girls are treated?

APPLICATIONS AND REFLECTIONS

Chapter Highlights

Culture and the Schools
- Cultural differences imply the transmission of ideas from generation to generation by significant members of older generations. Differences are not deficits, nor do differences imply something "wrong" or "bad."
- Vygotsky, a Russian psychologist, emphasized cultural processes as one of the major influences on the cognitive development of children.
- Vygotsky introduced the notion of the zone of proximal development, which he defined as the distance between a child's actual developmental level, as determined by independent problem solving and the child's higher level of potential development, as determined by problem solving under adult guidance or in collaboration with a more capable peer.
- Bruner argued that culture shapes cognitive development by imposing its symbolic systems, such as language, on a child's developing mind.
- The cultural compatibility hypothesis suggests that when instruction is compatible with cultural patterns of problem solving, learning improves.
- Four variables that have been manipulated to bring about greater compatibility of classroom experience with different cultures are social organization, sociolinguistics, cognition, and motivation
- Although assessment of learning is not highly reliable, researchers have reported some typical approaches to learning among African Americans, Mexican Americans, and Native Americans.

Social Class and Academic Achievement
- Socioeconomic status (SES) is a reliable predictor of school achievement and suggests that students from the same social class will perform in a similar manner.
- Parents can have a profound influence on their children's view of school and learning.

Gender, Development, and the Classroom
- Gender refers to psychosocial aspects of maleness and femaleness, whereas sex refers to biological maleness and femaleness.
- Gender identity is a conviction that one belongs to the sex of birth.
- Gender stereotypes reflect those beliefs about the characteristics associated with being male or female.
- Gender role refers to culturally acceptable sexual behavior.
- Researchers have consistently reported that teachers pay more attention to boys than to girls. These findings are particularly applicable to math and science classes.
- The quality of the relationships between teachers and students will influence the success of instruction, classroom management, and students' learning.

Connections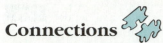

1. Think about how you learn. Describe how one of the major concepts discussed in this chapter is part of your learning activities or approach.

_____

_____

_____

2. Identify at least one learning situation (classroom instruction, self-study, taking a test, small-group work) and describe how you would apply one of the key concepts examined in this chapter *if you were a teacher*.

_____

_____

_____

Getting the Picture and Drawing Relationships

Think about the various learning concepts and variables discussed in this chapter. Create pictures, graphics, or figures that highlight the relationships among key components.

Personal Journal

What I really learned in this chapter was _____

_____

What this means to me is _____

_____

Questions that were stimulated by this chapter include _____

_____

Key Terms

cultural compatibility	56	gender schema	69	sex cleavage	68
gender identity	65	gender stereotypes	65	zone of proximal	
gender role	65	Head Start	62	development	54

section 2

the development of students

Michelle Johnson, a 15-year-old sophomore at Patriot High School, was in Jane Conley's history course. She consistently did work that was average or a little above average in her classes. She rarely volunteered in class and appeared uneasy when called on; she was also reluctant to express her ideas. Her teacher wasn't sure if this was because she was uncomfortable speaking before her peers or because she had difficulty conceptualizing her thoughts.

Michelle was a member of a social group of sophomores and tended to be a follower who trailed after the others. She seemed to have satisfactory relationships with her parents; she had one younger brother. She didn't have an

and almost always pleasant. She's doing "okay" in the American literature course, but sometimes I wonder if she's an overachiever."

"An interesting observation," said Jane. "What makes you say that?"

"Well, her marks are a little above average. As long as we're talking about the facts—what we discussed in her class, or the readings—she's fine. But when I ask what they think about something, she never has an answer. I think she studies hard to master the facts, and is fine if that's all the class has to do. But if the discussion moves beyond facts, she seems lost."

"I agree," said Jane. "What can we do about it?" ■

chapter 4

cognitive and language development

after-school job. Her health was good and she seldom missed school. There were no outstanding problems.

The teacher noticed, however, that Michelle struggled with some of the concepts the class was discussing. For example, in its work on World War II, the class had finished the reading and had examined a wide range of topics: causes of the war, crucial battles, leadership, and political consequences.

At the beginning of one of the class sessions she used to summarize the material, the teacher asked the students to write what they think would have happened if Germany had been victorious and Hitler had become the most powerful leader in the world. While most of the other students obviously saw the question as an enjoyable challenge, really an opportunity to demonstrate their newly acquired knowledge and to speculate about the unknown, Michelle sat there as if stunned. When the teacher walked down the aisle and asked her what was wrong, Michelle looked at her and asked, "What do you want me to do?"

It wasn't the first time Michelle had reacted in this way. In talking to Barbara Cotter about their classes, Jane asked her if she had noticed anything about Michelle. (The two teachers were good friends and often discussed school matters with each other; Barbara Cotter had a good relationship with her students; they both liked and respected her.) "Not really," Barbara replied. "She's very nice

Both teachers were searching for clues that would help them work with Michelle and improve her ability to grapple with abstract ideas. And the clues were there, as you can tell from the conversation. Their first task, however, was to identify the level of cognitive development at which Michelle functioned most easily. You will face similar situations with your students.

To interpret students' behavior, you must understand the normal path of development that your students follow, which will help you to adapt your instruction to meet their needs. In this chapter you will first explore cognitive development, emphasizing the work of Jean Piaget. Since cognition and language are so tightly intertwined, our discussion will then turn to the language development of your students.

When you finish reading this chapter, you should be able to

- apply your knowledge of cognitive development to the classroom through the appropriate selection of materials and the perceptive use of instructional methods
- use your classroom as a means of providing needed opportunities for the cognitive and linguistic achievement of your pupils
- use language data for the purpose of improving your students' entire range of language behavior : reading, writing, speaking, listening, and spelling

The Meaning of Development 80
Vygotsky and Mental
    Development 82

Piaget and Cognitive Development 83
Key Concepts in Piaget's
    Theory 84
Piaget's Four Stages of Cognitive
    Development 86
Criticisms of Piaget 96
For the Classroom 98
Alternatives to Piaget 100

Language Development 102
Language Accomplishments 102
The Language Components 102

Language Development in Infancy 104
Speech Irregularities 105

Language Development in Early Childhood 106
Metalinguistic Awareness 107
The Whole Language
    Movement 107
Bilingualism 108

Language Development in Middle Childhood 110

Theories of Language Acquisition 111
Lenneberg's Biological
    Explanation 111
Piaget and Language
    Development 112
Chomsky and
    Psycholinguistics 113

Language and the Classroom 113

Applications and Reflections 114

THE MEANING OF DEVELOPMENT

Annual **Edition**

An excellent way to think about development is to consider it as a "call to order" (Bjorklund & Bjorklund, 1992), that is, a tendency for mind and body to function as well as possible. Development certainly includes physical development: an increase in size and physical abilities. But for a psychologist, development also means an increasing ability to understand abstract ideas (cognitive development) and to get along with others (social development).

As figure 4.1 illustrates, physical, cognitive, and social development do not occur at the same rate. Your students may be all the same chronological age, but their growth ages (physical, cognitive, psychosocial) will vary. Some will be tall for their age, and some will be short; others may be mentally delayed or accelerated.

If you are aware of the processes of development, you can reassure a self-conscious adolescent whose growth in height is slightly delayed but whose weight is normal. You can look for opportunities to reinforce the social skills of a student whose mental growth has outpaced her social growth. Or you may realize that several members of your eighth-grade civics class are floundering because they haven't fully acquired the ability to think abstractly, and so provide additional "hands-on" assignments for the class. In these and other ways, familiarity with developmental theory and characteristics will enable you to determine appropriate techniques and content to match individual differences.

Although the various facets of development take different forms and proceed at different rates, several common trends are apparent. For example, orderly changes over time and certain new and improved behaviors appear in predictable sequence. Children crawl and then they stand and walk; they babble and then they talk; they act impulsively and then they learn to control their behavior. These new behaviors enable them to adapt to their environments.

Within the overall developmental pattern reflected in these universal accomplishments, however, there is considerable variation that affects children's school performance. For example, some children are reading by the time they enter school; others immediately display unusual mathematical ability; still others seem more mature socially than their classmates. These differences will influence their achievements in the

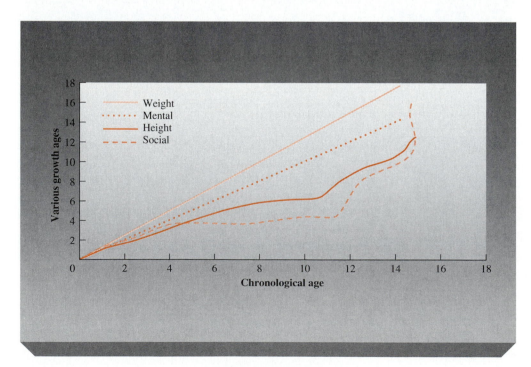

Figure 4.1
The complexity of development.

The young child's development of fine motor coordination reflected in the ability to hold a pencil. (*a*) The toddler grabs the whole crayon and is able to make only crude markings with it. (*b, c*) During early childhood, the child uses fewer arm and shoulder movements and more finger movements. (*d*) By the end of early childhood, the child has learned to use the fingers and wrist to manipulate the tip rather than the whole pencil (Goodman, 1979, p. 96).

a. b. c. d.

classroom. The more you, the teacher, know about development, the better you can adjust your curriculum and methods to such students' individual needs.

Today psychologists have accumulated considerable data about the development of children; the work of the cognitive and language theorists discussed in this chapter offers teachers a wealth of information that you can integrate and apply to the classroom. As you read their ideas, here are several questions that will guide your thinking and help you to form classroom applications.

In what way does the age group you are teaching (or plan to teach) see the world differently from you? Students entering kindergarten and first grade are still quite egocentric, that is, they tend to think everything relates directly to them. (You will certainly not be surprised to learn that adolescents react in much the same way.) Knowing this can help you to make adjustments in your teaching methods.

How can you recognize signs of developmental growth in students and use these signs to determine their readiness to acquire new skills? Educational psychologists like to use the expression "developmentally appropriate methods" to explain this type of teaching. For example, a secondary school teacher who realizes that a student is bright and understands scientific concepts when explained but also has a reading problem can reach this student by using high-interest but low-vocabulary reading material.

Do the theorists you are about to study provide any insights into the relationship between the abilities of your students and their classroom performance? As you read this chapter, try to discover how each theorist's interpretation of development can help you to improve your teaching. Piaget, for example, has made us more aware that students need a carefully structured sequence of materials and ideas (moving from the more concrete to the more abstract) to develop their abilities to engage in abstract thinking.

One theorist who thought deeply about cognitive development and whose ideas about the role of culture in development have direct classroom application is Lev Vygotsky, the Russian psychologist discussed in chapter 3 who specialized in educational psychology, developmental psychology, and psychopathology.

Vygotsky and Mental Development

As we mentioned in chapter 3, Vygotsky's work (1962, 1978) reflected his belief that the clues to understanding mental development lie in children's social processes, that is, that cognitive growth depends on children's interactions with those around them. The adults around children interact with them in a way that emphasizes those things that a culture values. For example, a child points to an object; those around the child respond in a way that conveys information not only about the object, but also about how the child should behave. To understand cognitive growth, we need to concentrate on the social processes by which these higher mental forms are established.

Vygotsky's argument continues by introducing a belief in qualitative shifts in development. Biological explanations can account for only so much of development, and then social forces become a powerful factor. Consequently, no single explanation of development suffices; rather, we must search for multiple influences that help to explain the nature of developmental change (Wertsch, 1985).

Vygotsky also made a distinction between "elementary" and "higher" mental processes. For example, children use a practical intelligence during their preverbal days by using their bodies and the objects around them. They will pull themselves up using a chair or table to obtain an attractive object. As soon as speech appears, their actions are transformed. They can ask for that same object, and as they do, they initiate verbal relationships with those around them.

Speech thus helps children in their efforts at mastery, producing new, verbal relationships with the environment. Control of these developing higher mental functions gradually shifts from the environment to the individual. Children then use inner speech, for themselves, to solve problems, for example, and for others, to enhance interpersonal relations (Vygotsky, 1978, p. 25). An interesting question here is whether learning can facilitate the shift.

The Zone of Proximal Development

Commenting on the relationship between learning and development, Vygotsky (1978) noted that learning must be matched in some way with a pupil's developmental level, which is too frequently and inaccurately identified by an intelligence test score. Vygotsky argued that with a little help, a student of a given developmental level (as measured by an intelligence test) might be able to do more difficult work that the child could not do alone. That is, this student might be able to do only addition problems when working alone, but to solve subtraction problems with the teacher's help.

To explain this phenomenon, Vygotsky introduced his notion of the **zone of proximal development.** He defined the zone of proximal development as the distance between a child's actual developmental level, as determined by independent problem solving, and the higher level of potential development, as determined by problem solving under adult guidance or in collaboration with more capable peers (Vygotsky, 1978). It is the difference between what pupils can do independently and what they can do with help.

As Vygotsky noted (1978), instruction is effective only when it proceeds ahead of development. That is, teaching awakens those functions that are already maturing and that are in the zone of proximal development. Although teaching and learning are not identical to development, they can act to stimulate developmental processes.

zone of proximal development
The distance between a child's actual developmental level and a higher level of potential development with adult guidance (between what children can do independently and what they can do with help).

Focus   ◄ What African American Children Consider Important

Although students attend to both the physical and the social aspects of their environments, they seem to prefer one more than the other, and their preference depends on the guidelines of their culture (Wigginton, 1992; Banks & Banks, 1993). The urban environment and the social milieu in which African Americans develop seem to predispose them toward the social elements of their environment; this then affects their school performance. Understanding the influence of this orientation on the achievement of these students, we need to examine the mechanisms by which students organize their lives.

Three categories seem to be significant:

- the physical environment that a family uses to shape a child's interactions with symbols and objects;
- the interpersonal relations that provide feedback to students for their expectations and performances;
- the emotional and motivational climate that influences a student's personality and behavior (Shade, 1987).

Within these categories, visual forms and family interaction patterns are particularly relevant. For example, research suggests that the visual forms within African American homes are usually those of people (Martin Luther King, Jr., Jesse Jackson, John and Robert Kennedy). Middle-class white homes seem to display more abstract paintings, pictures of flowers, and landscape scenes (Shade & New, 1993).

Interpersonal relationships within the family play a large role in the socialization of African American children, with the ultimate goal of helping children to function independently within and outside the family (Banks, 1993). Parents attempt to prepare their children for interactions with both peers and teachers and teach them how to act in social situations. Thus, parents are trying to provide a set of guidelines for behaving in novel situations (Shade, 1987).

With regard to the impact on personality and behavior, these socialization practices point to the importance of people to African American students. For example, both white and black adolescents were asked to take photographs that they thought best portrayed their school. Most of the pictures taken by the African American students were of people (Hale-Benson, 1986). Other studies indicate that teachers of African American students concentrate on classroom management and reinforce these students for personable behavior, while rewarding white children for their academic performance (Shade, 1987).

To avoid this discrepancy (importance of people versus importance of classroom management) in teaching African American students, then, it is helpful to remember the importance they place on social interactions, and to try to structure the classroom environment in a way that encourages the social dimensions of learning.

Give an instance in which you might use Vygotsky's zone of proximal development theory in working with students. How would you decide where to begin?

Vygotsky's ideas of mental development stand in contrast to those of Jean Piaget. While both theorists used a cognitive interpretation of mental development, Vygotsky, as we have seen, turned to social stimulation to explain a child's cognitive development. Piaget, on the other hand, believed that children construct their own ideas on how the world around them "works"; they function as "little scientists." Their ideas about the world and its objects change as they pass through four identifiable stages. Teachers following Vygotsky's ideas would address those functions in students' zones of proximal development, while teachers using Piaget's ideas would encourage more independent work.

PIAGET AND COGNITIVE DEVELOPMENT

Probably no one has influenced our thinking about cognitive development more than Jean Piaget. Born in Neuchatel, Switzerland in 1896, Piaget was trained as a biologist; his biological training made a major impact upon his thinking about cognitive development. Piaget insisted upon calling himself a "genetic epistemologist," a term that reflected his interest in how the manner in which individuals acquire knowledge changes as they develop. He became fascinated by the processes that led children to make incorrect answers in reasoning tests and turned his attention to the analysis of children's developing intelligence. Until his death in 1980, Piaget remained active in his research into cognitive development. Many believe that he was responsible for the resurgence of interest in cognitive studies.

Piaget's analysis of cognitive development can help you match curriculum to the abilities of your pupils. Say, for example, you are working with an eleven- or twelve-year-old student who seems to be having trouble with comprehension (both verbal and mathematical). Piaget's ideas would suggest that you should provide more concrete examples and more tangible materials, because most preteens are not yet ready to do much abstract thinking.

Key Concepts in Piaget's Theory

After many years of observing children of all ages, Piaget concluded that cognitive development has four stages, each of which builds on the previous one. Cognitive functioning begins in the form of responses to concrete phenomena: babies know only what they can touch, taste, or see. The ability to use symbols and to think abstractly increases with each subsequent stage, until adults are able to manipulate abstract concepts and consider hypothetical alternatives. How did Piaget explain these accomplishments?

Functional Invariants

Piaget (1952) stated that human beings inherit a method of intellectual functioning that enables us to respond to our environment by forming cognitive structures. (Piaget believed that intelligence is essentially a form of organization; by **structures,** he meant the organizational properties of intelligence.) He suggested that two psychological mechanisms, adaptation and organization, are responsible for the development of our cognitive structures. Because we use these same two mechanisms constantly throughout our lives, Piaget named them **functional invariants.**

Adaptation Piaget believed that **adaptation** consists of **assimilation** and accommodation. When we assimilate something, we incorporate it; that is, we take it in. This process is similar to that of eating. We take food into the structures of our mouths and change it to fit the structures of our mouths, throats, and digestive tracts. We take objects, concepts, and events into our minds in a similar way: we incorporate them into our mental structures, changing them to fit those structures just as we change food to fit our physical structures.

For example, you are now studying Piaget's views on cognitive development. These ideas are unique, and require effort to be understood. You are attempting to comprehend them by using the cognitive structures you now possess. You are assimilating Piaget's ideas; you are mentally taking them in and shaping them to fit your existing cognitive structures.

But human beings also change as a result of assimilation; that is, we accommodate to what we have taken in. The food we eat produces biochemical changes; likewise, the stimuli we incorporate into our minds produce mental changes. We change what we incorporate; we are also changed by it. As you read this chapter, not only are you taking in Piaget's ideas, but they are changing your views on intelligence and cognitive development. Your cognitive structures are changed; if you understand Piaget's concepts, you will never look at your students in quite the same way again. The change in your cognitive structures will produce corresponding behavioral changes. This is the process of **accommodation.**

The adaptive process is the heart of Piaget's explanation of learning. Students begin by trying to "fit" new material into existing cognitive structures, to assimilate the material, in a process called **equilibration.** Like all other humans, students try to strike a balance between assimilation and accommodation. That is, students are continually assimilating new information into their cognitive structures. In this process, they do make mistaken judgments, but by continued interaction with the environment, they correct their mistakes and change their cognitive structures (they have accommodated). But these mental activities do not occur randomly; they are organized.

Jean Piaget (1896–1980), one of the most influential developmental psychologists, who has significantly influenced educational theories and practices.

structures   *Piaget's term for the psychological units of the mind that enable us to think and know.*

functional invariants   *Piaget's term for the cognitive mechanisms of adaptation and organization.*

adaptation   *Piaget's term for one of the two psychological mechanisms used to explain cognitive development (organization is the other). Refers to the two complementary processes of assimilation and accommodation.*

assimilation   *Piaget's term to describe the way human beings take things into their minds; one part of adaptation.*

accommodation   *Piaget's term for a change in cognitive structures that produces corresponding behavioral changes; one part of adaptation.*

equilibration   *Piaget's term for the balance between assimilation and accommodation.*

Organization   The cognitive structures that we form enable us to engage in ever more complex thinking. Physical structures can again provide an analogy for Piaget's ideas on **organization.** In order to read this text, you are balancing it, turning the pages, and moving your eyes. All of these physical structures are organized so that you can read. Likewise, for you to understand the material the text contains, your appropriate cognitive structures are organized so that they assimilate and accommodate.

organization   Piaget's term for the connections among cognitive structures.

If some stimulus is radically different from what you are accustomed to (for example, written in another language), you may be unable to assimilate it because you do not have the necessary cognitive structures; the material remains meaningless. This has important implications for the classroom. The teacher must not permit students merely to memorize material and then repeat it on demand with little, if any, comprehension. Such "learning" will persist only for a brief moment and students will not relate it to other topics; it will not expand or enrich their knowledge. We can see from this example that although Piaget was primarily interested in the development of thinking, his work has great value for teachers, providing insight into comprehension, transfer, and problem-solving ability.

Schemes   Organization and adaptation are inseparable. As Piaget stated (1952), they are two complementary processes of a single mechanism. Every intellectual act is related to other similar acts; this introduces Piaget's notion of scheme. **Schemes** are organized patterns of thought and action, that is, the cognitive structures and behavior that help us to adapt to our environment. They may best be thought of as the inner representation of our activities and experiences. A scheme is named by its activity: the grasping scheme, the sucking scheme, the kicking or throwing scheme.

schemes   Piaget's term for organized patterns of thought.

For an idea of how schemes develop, consider a baby reaching out and touching something, such as a blanket. The child immediately begins to learn about the material—its heaviness, its size. In other words, the child is forming a cognitive structure about the blanket. Piaget called the child's combination of knowledge about the blanket with the act of reaching for it a scheme—in this case, the grasping scheme.

How do these concepts "work" in Piaget's theory? It may help to think of his theory in this way. Stimuli come from the environment and are filtered through the functional invariants. The functional invariants, adaptation and organization, use the stimuli to form new structures or to change existing structures. (For example, you may have had your own idea of what intelligence is, but now be changing your structures relating to intelligence because of your new knowledge about Piaget's ideas.) Your **content,** or behavior, now changes because of the changes in your cognitive structures. The process is as follows:

content   Piaget's term for behavior.

Environment
(filtered through)
Functional Invariants
(produces)
Cognitive Structures
(which combine with behavior to form)
Schemes

One of Piaget's classic experiments illustrates the process. To replicate this experiment, you'll need a 5-year-old child (in Piaget's preoperational stage), a 7-year-old child (in Piaget's concrete operational stage), 6 black tokens, and 6 orange tokens. Make a row of the black tokens. If you give the 5-year-old child the orange tokens with instructions to match them with the black tokens, the child can easily do it. When the tokens are in a one-to-one position, a 5-year-old can tell you that both rows have the same number.

But if you spread the 6 black tokens to make a longer row, the 5-year-old will tell you that the longer row has more tokens!

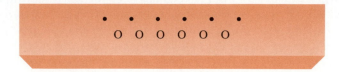

Even when Piaget put the tokens on tracks and let the child move and match them, the younger child still believed the longer row had more tokens.

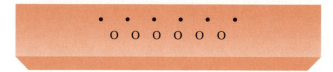

If you present the 7-year-old with the same problem, the child will think it is a trick: both rows obviously still have the same number.

These and related experiments hold an important lesson for teachers: cognitive structures change with age. Consequently, subject matter must be presented in a form that matches the cognitive structures of pupils. For example, a kindergarten teacher often has to show pupils how to hold paper, grasp a pencil, and print on the line. By the time these pupils are in the third grade, they immediately know how to adjust the paper, hold the pencil, and print on the line.

Piaget's Four Stages of Cognitive Development

For Piaget, cognitive development meant passage through four stages or periods: *sensorimotor, preoperational, concrete operational,* and *formal operational* (see table 4.1). The age at which children reach the four stages varies, but the sequence of the stages does not vary. In other words, Piaget's theory is stage invariant, age variant. Every child must pass through the sensorimotor stage before the preoperational, the preoperational stage before the concrete operational, and the concrete operational stage before the formal operational.

As you read about Piaget's stages of cognitive development, keep in mind four interacting influences that aid passage through the stages: maturation, experience, social interactions, and equilibration (Piaget & Inhelder, 1969). *Maturation* means just what its name implies: physical development, especially that of the muscular and nervous systems. Piaget believed that there are two types of *experience.* One involves acting on objects to learn about them: to determine which of two objects is heavier, we pick them up and compare their weights. The second type of experience refers to what we learn from simply using objects. For example, a child arranges 10 pebbles in a row, then in a circle, and discovers that in both configurations, there are always 10 pebbles.

Social interactions refers to the knowledge that children acquire from others in their culture: parents read them books; teachers instruct them in subject matter; they model their behavior on other children. Finally, *equilibration,* as we have already seen, refers to a process of self-regulation in which there is constant interplay between assimilation and accommodation. For example, students learn something new in their science class (they assimilate); after studying it, discussing it, and reading about it, they accommodate. But in the next class, they learn something else, and the equilibration process continues.

Table 4.1

The Four Periods of Intellectual Development

The cognitive periods and approximate ages

1. The sensorimotor period (birth to 18–24 months)
2. The preoperational period (2 to 7 years)
3. The concrete operational period (7 to 11 years)
4. The formal operational period (over 11 years)

Note: This is a "stage invariant" theory, which means that the order of the stages does not vary; everyone passes through these stages in this sequence. It is not an "age invariant" theory, which means that a child's age may vary at any one of the periods. For example, although most children reach the concrete operational period at 7 years, others may not reach it until 8 or 9 years.

We can picture these interactive forces working as follows.

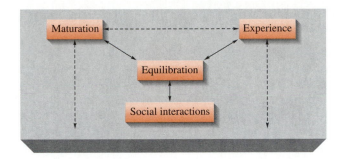

The Sensorimotor Period

The *sensorimotor* period extends from birth to about 2 years. The cognitive development of infants and toddlers comes mainly through their use of their bodies and their senses as they explore the environment; hence the label *sensorimotor*.

Infants "know" in the sense of recognizing or anticipating familiar, recurring objects and happenings, and they "think" in the sense of behaving toward these objects and events with mouth, hand, eye, and other sensory-motor instruments in predictable, organized, and often adaptive ways (Flavell, 1985). A good example of this behavior can be seen in the way a baby follows its mother with its eyes, and in how it often smiles at its mother's face, expecting pleasant consequences.

For Piaget, development is a continuous creation of more complex forms. Piaget described development as occurring in four stages: (*a*) sensorimotor, (*b*) preoperational, (*c*) concrete operational, and (*d*) formal operational.

a.

b.

c.

d.

Features of the Sensorimotor Period

There are several characteristics of the sensorimotor period that help to explain how an infant thinks. Among these are the following.

- *Egocentrism.* The child's universe is initially egocentric, entirely centered on self. Piaget used **egocentrism** here in a cognitive sense in contrast to egocentric adults, who know there are other viewpoints but disregard them, Piaget's egocentric children are simply unaware of any other viewpoint. Very young children lack social orientation: they speak *at* rather than *to* each other, and two children in conversation will discuss utterly unrelated topics. Through cognitive development in the sensorimotor period, however, they begin to learn that others exist, that there is a world beyond themselves.

- *Object permanence.* An infant initially does not have a sense of **object permanence.** This means that an object or person removed from an infant's field of vision ceases to exist for the infant. If the toy an infant is playing with is put behind a chair and thus out of sight, the child simply stops searching for it. This explains the pleasure infants manifest when someone plays peek-a-boo with them. The face no longer exists when it is hidden, since the child has not yet acquired a sense of object permanence, which gradually develops during the sensorimotor period.

- *Concepts of space and time.* Gradually, as children begin to crawl and walk, they realize that there is distance between the objects that they are using to steady themselves. Think of how many times you have seen infants pull themselves up to a chair, drop to the floor, crawl some distance, and then pull themselves up to a table. By moving from object to object, they learn about space and the time it takes to move from object to object.

- *Causality.* As children use their growing sensorimotor intelligence, they begin to find order in the universe. They begin to distinguish their own actions as causes, and they begin to discover events that have their causes elsewhere, either in other objects or in various relationships between objects (Piaget and Inhelder, 1969). For example, an infant will push a toy, perhaps a truck, and watch it roll. The child gradually comes to realize that its own actions caused the truck to roll.

Infants pass through six subdivisions of the sensorimotor period (see table 4.2). As they do so, they progress from reliance on reflex actions (such as sucking and grasping) to a basic understanding of the world around them and the beginnings of the ability to represent the world through language.

egocentrism *Piaget's term for children's tendency to see things as they want them to be.*

object permanence *Piaget's term for an infant's ability to realize that an object or person not within sight still exists.*

Educational Implications

Piaget's analysis of infant cognitive development not only is important for day-care staff and others who care for infants, but also has implications for the classroom. What happens during the first two years of life provides the foundation for more formal work. Children's cognitive achievements during the sensorimotor period enable them eventually to go on to the use of symbols (such as those used in language and mathematics).

If you work with infants in a day-care setting, remember Piaget's suggestions for furthering cognitive development (1969).

- *Provide multiple objects of various sizes, shapes, and colors for them to use.* Think about the label *sensorimotor* for a moment. What meanings do you attach to it? One meaning undoubtedly includes the active use of the senses or body; through bodily use (reaching, touching, creeping), infants learn about the environment. Consequently, parents and day-care centers should furnish toys and objects that are both circular and square, both soft and hard, both stationary and mobile. (These needn't be expensive: blocks of wood, rubber balls, pieces of fruit are perfectly satisfactory.) By manipulating these simple objects, children use physical actions to form the cognitive groundwork of their lives.

teacher – student

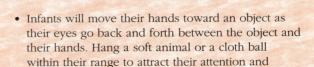

The Sensorimotor Period

1. Piaget believed that infants learn about other human beings from the way they are treated from birth.
   - A parent or day-care provider's face is the most exciting plaything an infant experiences. It changes, makes noises, and responds to the baby. Use pictures of faces in magazines, photographs, or even circles with features drawn on them to help infants respond positively to those around them.
   - Talk *to* infants, not *at* them. Infants find adult speech, properly used, one of the most stimulating parts of their environment.
2. Children are active processors of information from birth.
   - Since newborns can see to a distance of only about 10 inches, place objects such as mobiles and rattles within that range.
   - Have them look at colorful objects with high contrast (red, black and white, navy and white).

- Infants will move their hands toward an object as their eyes go back and forth between the object and their hands. Hang a soft animal or a cloth ball within their range to attract their attention and stimulate movement.
3. Infants use their bodily actions to discover cause-effect relationships.
   - Use toys that are fun to touch for their texture but also make noises when squeezed or shaken.
   - Toward the end of the first year, offer real toys or homemade ones like plastic cups of varying sizes, wooden spoons, or measuring spoons, so that infants can learn how things work. For example, encourage them to stack the cups and discover the differences in sound when they bang the wooden or the metal spoons.

Table 4.2

Outstanding Characteristics of the Sensorimotor Period
The six subdivisions of this period
Stage 1 During the first month, children exercise the native reflexes, for example, the sucking reflex. Here is the origin of mental development, for states of awareness accompany the reflex mechanisms.
Stage 2 Piaget refers to stage 2 (from 1 to 4 months) as the stage of *primary circular reactions*. Infants repeat some act involving the body, for example, finger sucking. (*Primary* means first; *circular reaction* means repeated actions.)
Stage 3 From 4 to 8 months *secondary circular reactions* appear; that is, the children repeat acts involving objects outside themselves. For example, infants continue to shake or kick the crib.
Stage 4 From 8 to 12 months, children coordinate secondary schemata. Recall the meaning of scheme: behavior plus mental structure. During stage 4, infants combine several related schemata to achieve some objective. For example, they remove an obstacle that blocks some desired object.
Stage 5 From 12 to 18 months, *tertiary circular reactions* appear. Now children repeat acts, but not only for repetition's sake; now they search for novelty. For example, children of this age continually drop things. Piaget interprets such behavior as expressing their uncertainty about what will happen to the objects when they release them.
Stage 6 At about 18 months or 2 years, a primitive type of *representation* appears. For example, one of Piaget's daughters wished to open a door but had grass in her hands. She put the grass on the floor and then moved it back from the door's movement so that it would not blow away.

- *If infants are to develop cognitively as fully as their potential permits, they must actively engage environmental objects.* They must touch them, push them, pull them, squeeze them, drop them, throw them, and perform any other conceivable action on them, because infants learn through sensory and motor activity. The ball the infant pushes and watches roll; the square block that makes different sounds when it falls on the wooden floor or on a rug; the different sounds that come from kicking the rungs of the crib and then the solid front and back—interaction with all these things furthers cognitive development.

The Preoperational Period

When Piaget referred to **operations** (as in the term *preoperational*), he meant actions that we perform mentally in order to gain knowledge (Ginsburg & Opper, 1988). To know an object is to act on it. An individual mentally compares it, changes it, and then returns it to its original state. According to Piaget (in Ripple & Rockcastle, 1964), *knowledge is not just a mental image of an object or event.* It is not enough to look at that object or event, to picture it. A person must modify the object, that is, do something to it.

An individual might compare the object with other objects, noting similarities and differences; place it in a particular order in a series; measure it; or take it apart and then put it back together. Piaget believed that mental actions are reversible. By this he meant that humans can think in opposite directions: we add, but we can also subtract; we join things mentally, but can also separate them. For example, a human being can add 2 to 2, with the result of 4; but a person can also take 2 away from 4, so that the original 2 results.

The term *preoperational,* then, refers to a child who has begun to use symbols, but is not yet capable of mentally manipulating them in the ways described above. Children who cannot yet take something apart and put it together again; who cannot return to the beginning of a thought sequence (that is, who cannot comprehend how to reverse the action of 2 + 2); who cannot believe that water poured from a short, fat glass into a taller, thinner one retains the same volume—these children are at a level of thinking that precedes operational thought. To help students, particularly at the kindergarten and first-grade levels, teachers should encourage the manipulation of materials (especially in math and science), and as many hands-on experiences as possible.

operations   Piaget's term for actions that we perform mentally in order to gain knowledge.

Features of Preoperational Thought

Although symbolic activity steadily develops during the preoperational period, several important limitations still exist.

- **Centering,** or concentrating on only part of an object or activity. Children ignore the relationships among the various parts. Recall Piaget's experiment with the tokens. When the tokens were spread out, preoperational children could not relate the spaces between tokens to the number of tokens.
- **Egocentrism.** This is a central characteristic of the preoperational as well as the sensorimotor period. For preoperational children, things can be only as they want them to be; other opinions are meaningless. For example, children may believe that the moon follows *them* around; everything focuses on them.
- **Irreversibility,** or the inability to reverse one's thinking. Preschoolers cannot return to an original premise. They may have learned that 2 + 2 = 4, but they cannot yet grasp that 4 – 2 = 2.

centering   Piaget's term for a child's tendency to concentrate on only part of an object or activity.

irreversibility   Piaget's term for children's inability to reverse their thinking.

Between the ages of 2 and 7, children are starting to recognize that there is a world "out there" that exists independently of them. Recognizing the abilities of young children and also the cognitive limitations that we have just discussed, we can identify the following features of preoperational thought: realism, animism, artificialism, and transductive reasoning.

- **Realism,** or distinguishing and accepting the "real world," thus identifying both an external and an internal world. This ability develops slowly during this period. Piaget believed that youngsters initially confuse internal and external; they confuse

realism   Piaget's term for a child's growing ability to distinguish and accept the real world.

thought and matter. The confusion disappears at about 7 years. For example, a young child who is jealous of a newborn sibling gradually realizes that parents can't "take it back."

animism *Piaget's term for a child's tendency to attribute life to inert objects.*

- **Animism,** or considering a large number of objects that adults consider to be inert as alive and conscious. For example, a child who sees a necklace wound up and then released explains that it is moving because it "wants to unwind." Children overcome this cognitive limitation as they recognize their own personalities. They then refuse to accept personality in things. Piaget believed that comparison of one's own thoughts with the thoughts of others—social intercourse—slowly conquers animism, as it does egocentrism. Piaget identified four stages of animism:

  a. almost everything is alive and conscious;
  b. only those things that move are alive;
  c. only those things that manifest spontaneous movements are alive;
  d. consciousness is limited to the animal world.

artificialism *Piaget's term for a preoperational child's tendency to assume that everything is the product of human creation.*

- **Artificialism,** or assuming that everything is the product of human creation. For example, when asked how the moon began, some of Piaget's subjects replied, "because we began to be alive." As egocentrism decreases, youngsters become more objective, and they steadily assimilate objective reality to their cognitive structures. They proceed from a purely human or divine explanation to an explanation that is half natural, half artificial: the moon comes from the clouds, but the clouds come from people's houses. Finally, at about 9 years they realize that human activity has nothing to do with the origin of the moon. (Realism and artificialism are examples of a growing ability and a declining limitation of preoperational thought. The decline of artificialism parallels the growth of realism.)

transductive reasoning *Piaget's term for a preoperational child's reasoning technique: moving from particular to particular in a non-logical manner.*

- **Transductive Reasoning,** or reasoning that is neither deductive nor inductive. Rather, reasoning moves from particular to particular. The following are examples of transductive reasoning:

  The sun won't fall down because it's hot.
  The sun stops there because it's yellow.

Educational Implications

Certain activities typical of preoperational children reflect their use of internal representation (Piaget & Inhelder, 1969).

1. *Deferred imitation.* Preoperational children can imitate some object or activity that they have previously witnessed; for example, they might walk like animals that they have seen at the zoo earlier in the day.
2. *Symbolic play.* Children enjoy pretending that they are asleep, or that they are someone or something else.
3. *Drawing.* Children of this age project their mental representations into their drawings. Highly symbolic, their art work reflects the level of their thinking and what they are thinking. Encouraging children of this age to talk about their art is a fruitful practice for the adults caring for them.
4. *Mental images.* Preoperational children can represent objects and events, but they cannot change, or anticipate change in, their thinking. Recall Piaget's experiment with the 5-year-old who thought there were more tokens in a row when they were spaced farther apart.
5. *Language.* For preoperational children, language is becoming a vehicle for thought. Parents, teachers, and other care providers should let them have ample opportunities to talk with adults and with one another.

For teachers working with children of this age, the cognitive accomplishments described above suggest several kinds of activities. A teacher could take pictures from magazines, brochures, or newspapers and have the children tell stories about what they see. This would not only help in assessment of their language ability, but also would reveal much about their cognitive development. For example, how egocentric are they (in

teacher – student

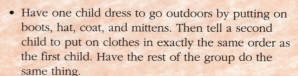

The Preoperational Period

1. Preoperational children learn through active explorations and interactions with adults, other children, and materials.
   - Help kindergartners to make short story books with such titles as *What's on My Street?* Use vocabulary words that they have already learned and have them illustrate their stories. Then have the children take their stories home and read them aloud to their parents.
   - Toward the end of the preoperational period, use role plays and similar activities. For example, when teaching a unit on the solar system to second-graders, have the children play the role of the planets, the satellites, and the sun. Cut large circles from poster board, label them, and attach strings so that the students can hang them around their necks, indicating what they represent. The pupils can then act out their roles.
2. The great accomplishment of the preoperational period, Piaget believed, is a growing ability to represent.
   - Put a series of circles and lines on the board. Give pupils a few minutes to study the sequence, then erase it. Have them write the circles and lines in the same sequence on their papers.

- Have one child dress to go outdoors by putting on boots, hat, coat, and mittens. Then tell a second child to put on clothes in exactly the same order as the first child. Have the rest of the group do the same thing.
- Provide opportunities for pupils to tell jokes. They like to do this, and it promotes socialization, improves memory, and aids in more pragmatic skills, such as social interactions with their peers.

3. Preoperational pupils are egocentric.
   - Have students play games such as *Simon Says,* in which they learn that they can't always be the winner.
   - Rotate special, and usually desired, duties such as teacher's helper, so that pupils learn that they must take turns.

Piaget's terms)? Is their ability to represent at an appropriate cognitive level? Or, a teacher could group 10 circular objects (coins, chips, marbles) in a circle, then put 10 objects of the same type in a straight line, then ask them which grouping contained more objects. Their reactions would be revealing. Would they immediately point to the straight line? Would some hesitate? Why? These and similar activities can furnish clues to children's cognitive development as they approach the concrete operational period.

The Concrete Operational Period

Children at the *concrete operational* stage are strikingly different in their thinking from children at the preoperational stage. Between 7 and 11 or 12 years of age, children overcome the limitations of preoperational thinking and accomplish true mental operations. Students are now able to reverse their thinking and to group objects into classes.

There are still limitations at the concrete operations stage, however. Children can perform mental operations only on concrete (tangible) objects or events, and not on verbal statements. For example, if they are shown blocks A, B, and C, concrete operational children can tell you that A is larger than B, that B is larger than C, and that, therefore, A is largest of all. But if they are told that Liz is taller than Ellen, who is taller than Jane, they cannot tell who is tallest of all (especially in the early years of the period). These results explain why Piaget designated the period "concrete operational."

Features of Concrete Operational Thought

Several notable accomplishments mark this period.

1. **Conservation,** or the realization that the essence of something remains constant, although surface features may change. In Piaget's famous water jar problem, children observe two identical jars filled to the same height. While they watch,

conservation *Piaget's term for the realization that the essence of something remains constant, although surface features may change.*

Figure 4.2

Different kinds of conservation appear at different ages.

From John F. Travers, The Growing Child. *Copyright © 1982 Harpercollins College Publishers, Glenview, Illinois. Reprinted by permission.*

Conservation of	Example		Approximate age
1. Number	Which has more?		6–7 years
2. Liquids	Which has more?		7–8 years
3. Length	Are they the same length?		7–8 years
4. Substance	Are they the same?		7–8 years
5. Area	Which has more room?		7–8 years
6. Weight	Will they weigh the same?		9–10 years
7. Volume	Will they displace the same amount of water?		11–12 years

the contents of one container are poured into a taller and thinner jar, so that the liquid reaches a higher level. By the age of 7, most children will state that the contents are still equal; they *conserve* the idea of equal amounts of water by decentering, that is by focusing on more than one aspect of the problem. They can now reverse their thinking; they can mentally pour the water back into the original container.

Different types of conservation appear at different times during the concrete operational period, as figure 4.2 shows.

Piaget (1973) believed that youngsters use three arguments to conserve:

a. *The argument of identity.* Concrete operational children say that since no water has been removed or added to either jar, it is still the "same thing." By 8 years of age, children are amused by the problem, not realizing that a year earlier they probably would have given a different answer.

b. *The argument of reversibility.* Concrete operational children state that you just have to pour the water back to see that it is the "same thing."

c. *The argument of compensation.* Concrete operational children say that although the water is higher in the taller beaker, it is narrower. That is, these youngsters compensate for the height increase by noting the circumference decrease, thus realizing that the water in both beakers is the "same thing."

seriation *Piaget's term for the ability to arrange objects by increasing or decreasing size.*

2. **Seriation,** or the ability to arrange objects by increasing or decreasing size. As we noted above, concrete operational children can arrange concrete objects, such as blocks. If, however, the operation is in pure language, such as the word problem mentioned earlier comparing the heights of three girls, it becomes more complicated, and the concrete operational child cannot solve it.

classification *Piaget's term for the ability to group objects with some similarities within a larger category.*

3. **Classification,** or the ability to group objects with some similarities within a larger category. If a preoperational child is shown a picture of 6 roses and 6 tulips, the child will be able to correctly answer questions about the number of tulips and the number of roses, but when asked, "Are there more roses than flowers?" the child will answer, "Yes." The concrete operational child, however, is able to classify both roses and tulips as flowers.

teacher – student

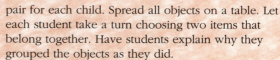

The Concrete Operational Period

1. Concrete operational pupils can conserve, reverse their thinking, and classify.

    Begin to have students compare, contrast, and classify using materials that offer hands-on learning.

    • Have students construct objects or replicas of events they have studied and relate them to their reading. Ask them to write about their experiences, and then discuss the topics with them and their classmates. In short, constantly blend the concrete with the abstract, to develop a readiness for increasingly abstract material.

    • Have students design floats made from shoeboxes about the states (or countries) they are studying. Ask them to print their states' mottoes on the sides of their floats. On a separate piece of paper, have each student illustrate the specific state, including the state's emblem. Also have each student prepare an outline of the state's outstanding features.

2. Concrete operational students are developing classification skills.

    • Have pupils play a classification game by pairing common household objects like a knife and a fork, a towel and a bar of soap, a toothbrush and toothpaste, a brush and comb. Include some pairs that are obvious and some that are not. Have one pair for each child. Spread all objects on a table. Let each student take a turn choosing two items that belong together. Have students explain why they grouped the objects as they did.

    • Celebrate with a "food fest" in social studies. Assign two students to explore research materials about a particular country, perhaps the country from which their families originated. Locate recipes and types of food. Enlist the parents' help to cook the food. Make decorations and costumes, and provide music for your celebration.

    • Have students list all the activities they engage in during the week. Then work with them to develop categories, such as Home, School, Play. Finally, have them put their activities into the appropriate categories.

3. Concrete operational students are able to reverse their thinking.

    • Use origami (Japanese paperfolding) techniques to have pupils design shapes such as birds and flowers. Then ask them how they would get the paper back to its original shape.

    • Look at an island on a map. Tell students to imagine that they can fly there, but that then their plane will become disabled. Ask them how they would return.

In a classic experiment illustrating mastery of classification, Piaget showed children at both the preoperational and the concrete operational levels 20 wooden beads, 16 of which were brown and 4 of which were white. When he asked, "Are there more brown beads than wooden beads?" the preoperational children typically answered, "Yes," while the older children answered correctly.

4. **Number concept,** which is not the same as the ability to count. As Piaget's previously mentioned experiment with the two rows of tokens showed, even though the preoperational child can count, "one" isn't always "one." When the 5 tokens in one row were spread out, the child was convinced that it contained more than 5 tokens. Only after children acquire the concepts of seriation and classification are they able to understand the "oneness of one": that one boy, one girl, one apple, and one orange are all "one" of something.

number concept   *Piaget's term for the ability to understand numbers.*

These thought systems of the concrete operational child, which Piaget refers to as cognitive operations, gradually come into a well-organized equilibrium. When children reach this phase of cognitive development, they are on the threshold of adult thought, or formal operations. Consequently, we can see that middle childhood pupils have experienced an intellectual revolution. Their thinking has become logical and more abstract, their attention is improving, and their memory is becoming more efficient as they develop new strategies.

Educational Implications

Are youngsters capable of meeting the problems they face in the classroom? Yes and no. They can assimilate and accommodate the material they encounter, but only at their level. Elementary school youngsters up to the age of 10 or 11 are capable of representational thought, but only with the concrete, the tangible. Consequently, we cannot expect them to comprehend fully any abstract subtleties.

A striking example of concrete operational thinking was evident in a science project involving sixth-graders. While discussing the fishing industry off the coast of Massachusetts, the teacher had the students construct topographical ocean zone maps. Each student put many class hours into the project. They cut and positioned as many as twenty-five layers of ocean bottom before completing their maps. In the end, each student had sore hands, but a thorough understanding of the varying ocean depths that influenced fishing off the coast of Massachusetts.

If you are a teacher of concrete operational children, provide opportunities for your students to engage in tasks that will help them at this level. For example, take the common objects in your classroom (pencils and pens) and ask your students to group them. Then ask them why they put certain things together. Have them look at the various pieces of glass in the classroom (in doors and windows) and ask them to group these by size. Are there more large glass windows than small glass windows? Why? Have your students explain their answers.

The Formal Operational Period

According to Piaget, the *formal operational* period, during which the beginnings of logical, abstract thinking appear, commences at about 11 or 12 years of age. During this period, youngsters demonstrate an ability to reason realistically about the future and to consider possibilities that they actually doubt. Teenagers look for relations; they separate the real from the possible; they test their mental solutions to problems; they feel comfortable with verbal statements (Manaster, 1989). In short, the period's great achievement is a release from the restrictions of the tangible and the concrete (Ginsburg & Opper, 1988).

Piaget and Inhelder (1969) summed up the difference between concrete operations and formal operations with an example from their research: when younger children were asked to assume that coal is white, they replied that coal had to be black, whereas adolescents accepted the unreal assumption and reasoned from it.

Remember, though, that some students at this age may still be concrete operational, or only into the initial stages of formal operations in their cognitive processes. Many adolescents have just recently consolidated their concrete operational thinking and continue to use it consistently. Unless they find themselves in situations (such as science and math classes) that demand formal operational thinking, they continue to be concrete operational thinkers. Estimates are that only about 1 in 3 young adolescents think at the formal operational level (Santrock, 1995). With these pupils, teachers must continue to blend concrete and abstract materials.

Another interesting feature of adolescent thought is what Elkind (1981) referred to as *adolescent egocentric thinking.* He stated that adolescents assume that everyone else thinks as they do and shares their concerns. This is due to the changes occurring in their bodies and their sensitivity to others, which leads to intense concentration on themselves. "But why is everyone looking at me?" They thus create an *imaginative audience.*

Features of Formal Operational Thought

There are several essential features of formal operational thinking.

1. *The adolescent's ability to separate the real from the possible,* which distinguishes the concrete operational from the formal operational child. The adolescent tries to discern all possible relations in any situation or problem and then, by mental experimentation and logical analysis, attempts to discover which ones are true. Flavell (1963) noted that there is nothing trivial in the adolescent's accomplishment: it is a basic and essential reorganization of thought processes that permits the adolescent to exist in the world of the possible.

2. *The adolescent's thinking is propositional.* This means that adolescents use not only concrete data, but also statements or propositions that contain the concrete data. Dealing with abstract concepts no longer frustrates them. For example, a history teacher can ask a class, "What were the real reasons for our struggle with the Japanese in World War II?" and expect that the students will be able to respond.

3. *Adolescents attack a problem by gathering as much information as possible and then making all the possible combinations of the variables that they can.* They proceed as follows. *First,* they organize data by concrete operational techniques (classification, seriation). *Second,* they use the results of concrete operational techniques to form statements or propositions. *Third,* they combine as many of these propositions as possible. (These are hypotheses, and Piaget often refers to this process as hypothetico-deductive thinking.) *Fourth,* they then test to determine which combinations are true.

Educational Implications

There are many practical applications of Piaget's work to the classroom of adolescents. Teachers can aid their students' cognitive development by analyzing their content (what they do) in order to infer the type of underlying cognitive structure that is being used, and then using methods and materials that will help their students to assimilate and accommodate. If Piaget's statement that children construct their own world is true, then students must manipulate material as much as possible.

Although most adolescents are comfortable with formal operational materials and activities, teachers should be careful not to exaggerate students' abilities. They should provide as many concrete examples as they think necessary before asking students to formulate general principles. Teachers should also try to discover how students sequence materials and activities, in order to match their developmental levels. The activities should challenge students' thinking, but should not be so difficult as to frustrate and cause failure. Students should concentrate upon the activities and not the teacher, thus permitting the teacher more time to observe and to guide.

In the case study presented at the chapter's opening, for example, the student (Michelle Johnson) did not know how to combine propositions and speculate about the future. This ability could not be forced on her, but she could learn to improve her thinking. The teacher could lead Michelle from reciting concrete facts to considering more abstract conclusions and possibilities. Such a sequence of questions could take the following form in the history class already mentioned:

"Let's review again the major battles of World War II. What is the significance of each of the great battles?" "What if the outcomes of particular battles had been reversed? How would that have affected other events in the war?" "How might these changed events have affected each nation involved?"

In other words, teachers should try first to have the student *understand* the facts and the causes for them, and then to *guide* the student to draw implications from the data.

Criticisms of Piaget

Although Piaget has left a monumental legacy, his ideas have not been unchallenged. Piaget was a believer in the stage theory of development. Such a theory sees development as a sequence of distinct stages, each of which entails important changes in the way a child thinks, feels, and behaves (Scarr et al., 1986). Theorists such as Rest (1983), however, argue that the acquisition of cognitive structures is gradual rather than abrupt, and is not a matter of "all or nothing"; for example, a particular child is not completely in the preoperational or the concrete operational stage. A particular manifestation of a child's level of cognitive development seems to depend more on the nature of a task than on a rigid classification system.

By changing the nature of the task (for example, reducing the number of objects children must manipulate—see Gelman & Baillargeon, 1983); by allowing children to

teacher – student

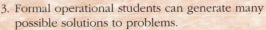

The Formal Operational Period

1. Formal operational students can engage in propositional thinking. Teachers can now use verbal materials in their instruction.
   - After presenting the basic facts about the end of the Cold War, have the students adopt opposing positions about the actual causes. Then set up debating teams; have students act as the political or military leaders of the time in their debates.
2. Adolescents gather as much information as possible about a problem.
   - Ask your students to list what they think are the major environmental problems caused by advanced technology: nuclear waste disposal, nuclear weapons, air and water pollution, energy shortages, depletion of natural resources, etc. Now ask students how many of these problems affect all nations. Have them comment on how the fact that nations share these problems illustrates our interdependence.

3. Formal operational students can generate many possible solutions to problems.
   - Ask your students how *they* could actively participate in solving some of the problems discussed above.
   - Discuss with your students how things would be different today if the following imaginary events had occurred:
   a. In 1492, Christopher Columbus sailed west into an area known as the Bermuda Triangle and mysteriously disappeared.
   b. Martin Luther King was not assassinated in 1968.
   c. George Washington proclaimed himself king of the United States of America instead of its first president.

From your knowledge of children, do you think Piaget's stages give a realistic picture of a child's cognitive development? Why or why not?

practice (for example, teaching children conservation tasks—see Field, 1987); and by using materials familiar to children, researchers have found that children can accomplish specific tasks at earlier ages than Piaget believed (see Halford, 1989). Such criticisms have led to a more searching examination of the periods during which children acquire certain cognitive abilities.

For example, Piaget believed that infants retrieve an object that is hidden from them in stage 4, at 8 to 12 months of age. Before this age, if a blanket is thrown over a toy that the infant was looking at, the child stops reaching for it as if it doesn't exist. Tracing the ages at which the concept of object permanence appears, Baillargeon (1987) devised an experiment in which infants between 3½ and 4½ months old were seated at a table on which a cardboard screen could be moved back and forth. It could be tilted forward (toward the baby) until it lay flat on the table, or backward (away from the baby) until its back touched the table.

Baillargeon then placed a painted wooden block behind the cardboard screen, so that the infant could see the block when the screen was in a forward, flat position. But when the screen was tilted backwards, it came to rest on the block, removing it from the infant's sight. Occasionally, Baillargeon secretly removed the block so that the screen continued to tip backwards until it rested flat on the table. The 4½-month-old infants showed surprise at the change by looking at the screen longer; even some of the 3½-month-olds seemed to notice the "impossible" event. These findings suggest that infants may develop the object permanence concept earlier than Piaget originally thought.

In a wide-ranging review of hundreds of studies that have tested Piaget's ideas, Gelman and Baillargeon (1983) also questioned the idea of broad stages of development, although they supported the notion of cognitive structures that assimilate and accommodate the environment. The idea of stages with no overlap seems to lack empirical evidence to support it.

In a typical Piagetian experiment, a doll was placed at different positions around a model of three mountains; children were then asked how the mountains looked to the doll at each position. Children under 6 reported their own views, not the doll's. Yet when Gelman and Baillargeon (1983) showed cards with different pictures on each side to 3-year-old children, the children correctly reported what they had seen and what the tester would see.

As we end our study of Piaget's analysis of cognitive development, what can we conclude? Two major contributions of Piaget come immediately to mind. First, thanks to Piaget, we have a deeper understanding of children's cognitive development. Second, he has made us more alert to the need for greater comprehension of *how* children think (the processes that they use), and not just *what* they think (the products of their thinking).

Piaget's research has been criticized because it was done using middle-class Swiss children. Consequently, we may ask if Piaget's ideas cross cultures. On this point, there are mixed reviews.

Piaget Across Cultures

Piaget's is an interaction theory, and therefore assumes that the experiences students have can help or hinder passage through the stages of cognitive development. We can expect, then, that culture will affect how students do with Piagetian tasks. For example, conservation appears at different times in different cultures, a fact that suggests that cognitive tasks must reflect a child's culture if that child's level of cognitive development is to be accurately assessed (Rogoff, 1990).

Most cross-cultural research has attempted to discover if all children develop and use the cognitive structures and the sequence of developmental stages that Piaget outlined (Bullinger & Chatillon, 1983). Results indicate that almost all children demonstrate behavior that confirms the sensorimotor and preoperational stages. Many adolescents and adults of non-Western cultures, however, do not demonstrate concrete and/or formal operational behavior (Fischer & Silvern, 1985). While almost all adults in Geneva, Paris, London, and New York display concrete operational thinking on conservation tasks, many adults in Third World capitals do not (Stigler et al., 1990). But the tests of cognitive functioning may be at fault, because they were designed for Western European children. Tests that use culturally familiar tasks do yield findings of concrete and formal operational behavior (Irvine, 1978; Rogoff, 1990).

Do you think Piaget placed enough emphasis on culture in his explanation of cognitive development? Think about this and try to form a list of reasons that support your answer.

A review of the major Piagetian studies of cognitive development in several African nations provides evidence of the impact of cultural factors upon the testing situation (Malone, 1984). As one example, Malone found that African children who have gone to school show more advanced cognitive development on Piagetian tests than do comparable children who have not attended school. Given the nature of Piagetian tasks, we would expect this conclusion, because schools emphasize the search for general rules, rely heavily on verbal instructions, and teach specific skills intended to obtain specific information. Consequently, we must know more about how tasks are interpreted in the light of cultural variables before we can reach definite conclusions about the universality of Piaget's ideas.

For the Classroom

Knowledge of Piaget's theory helps teachers to assess the levels of students' cognitive development. By observing students closely, the teacher can link behavior to cognitive level and utilize appropriate subject matter. For example, curriculum planners can profit from Piaget's findings by attempting to answer two questions. Are there ideal times for the teaching of certain subjects? Is there an ideal sequence for a subject that matches Piaget's sequence of cognitive development?

Piaget's work provides data for the formulation of optimal learning conditions. For example, during the first two periods (sensorimotor and preoperational), youngsters should constantly interact physically with their environments. During the concrete operational period, pupils should be able to use as many tangible objects as possible. Finally, adolescents should encounter verbal problems, master learning strategies, and test their solutions.

As we conclude our work on Piaget, here are some general suggestions to keep in mind for your teaching. Remember that Piaget always insisted that his theory stressed the interaction between the individual and the environment.

Allow students to "operate" on curricular materials. For example, adolescents with reading problems must have materials that are appealing and that actively involve them in skill development and comprehension.

Carefully consider how much direction and guidance each of your pupils needs. A youngster who has a language problem requires prompt assistance to prevent a persistent speech deficit. But a student who has the necessary formula to solve a math problem should be permitted to make a few mistakes and to discover the correct solution rather than being told.

Be careful concerning the materials that you use. If you encourage interactive learning, what you have your pupils "operate on" must be appropriate for them physically (can they physically manipulate the materials?) and cognitively (can they understand what they are supposed to do?).

Use instructional strategies appropriate to your students' ethnic and racial backgrounds (Rogoff, 1990). For example, studies of Hispanic students have shown that they tend to be influenced by personal relationships and praise or disapproval from authority figures. Pueblo Indian children from the American Southwest show higher achievement when instruction utilizes their "primary learning patterns" (those that occur outside the classroom). These students respond well when instruction incorporates the concerns and needs of the community. For such students, tasks like measuring the amount of rainfall (in inches) per year and relating it to crop production can be used in math classes.

Cognitive Development and AIDS Prevention

Piaget's ideas on cognitive development have also been used to formulate programs in related fields, such as health and AIDS prevention. For example, Walsh and Bibace (1990, 1991) have proposed a developmentally based program that attempts to educate, not merely inform, students about the reality of AIDS. Knowledge about AIDS is growing, but mere information is not education, and does not induce behavioral change.

One method of reaching schoolchildren has been suggested by Walsh and Bibace (1990). Arguing that the schools will inevitably be drawn into the struggle to contain the spread of AIDS, these researchers urge that HIV/AIDS programs be included at every school level. To be most effective, such programs should be developmentally based, since children understand themselves and their world according to their level of cognitive development. With this caution goes another: program designers should remember that not all students of the same age are at the same level of cognitive development.

One technique for designing an AIDS education program is to base its content and methodology on the processes children use to develop their ideas of illness. Three types of explanation have been identified by Walsh and Bibace (1990).

1. *Explanations based on association.* Children describe an illness according to specific, external situations with which they have linked the sickness. This is a highly personal explanation in which they pay little attention to the cause of an illness. "You know; it's poison ivy, that itchy stuff. It comes by magic."
2. *Explanations based on sequence.* Children's explanations include both internal and external symptoms, and they tend to identify something concrete, often "bad," that caused the illness. They realize that this bad "something" can appear in a variety of situations; thus, they now have the ability to generalize their conclusions. Their explanations also include a mechanism or sequence of events to explain the cause: "You know, Billy touched those bushes and then he got that itchy rash"; "Of course Maddy got sick; she got wet in the rain and stayed outside in wet clothes to play. The cold got on her and went inside her nose and throat and now she's sneezing all over the place."

3. *Explanations based on interactions.* Children describe illness as a bodily malfunction whose ultimate outcome depends on the interplay of a variety of factors: time, body condition, medical care, and environmental conditions. "When you touch a poison ivy plant, it leaves an oil trace on your body or clothes. The oil gets into your skin and causes a rash to appear; it makes little blisters that break; and then the itch hits you. Remember: Leaves of three; leave them be."

Children seem to follow a similar pattern in understanding AIDS. For example, Walsh and Bibace (1990) state that young children (about 4 or 5 years old) remain quite egocentric, with a tendency to focus on external events, and don't show much concern for cause and effect. They define AIDS by something with which they are familiar. It's a "bad" sickness, and anyone who is seriously ill can have AIDS. Those working with children at this level should be concerned with the fears that they have about the illness. Reassurance and correcting any erroneous views are probably the best techniques to use.

Children who are older (about 7 to 11 years old) and at a concrete level of cognitive development can differentiate more accurately and interpret AIDS according to specific bodily symptoms. They initially interpret cause in concrete terms: "A bug caused it"; "Using someone else's straw." At a later stage in this level, they begin to describe the cause of AIDS in a more sequential manner: "A bug gets inside your blood, infects you, makes you sick, and then you die." Those working with children at this level should appeal to their ability to make distinctions: for example, doing drugs with dirty needles can transmit the virus.

Older children (11 years and older) are capable of more complex thinking, and can understand the possibility that many interacting elements may be at work in the disease. For example, they realize that AIDS may be caused by sex and/or dirty needles, but that these behaviors may not always cause AIDS (Walsh & Bibace, 1990).

Such a program goes a long way to answering a pertinent question raised by Quackenbush and Villarreal (1988): What do teachers need to know in order to talk about AIDS? As these authors noted, to be comfortable in discussing this sensitive topic with students, you need familiarity with the following.

- *Child development.* You should be prepared to give appropriate answers to their questions about health, personal relationships, and sexuality. "Appropriate" in this sense describes a discussion or program based on the ideas suggested by Walsh and Bibace (1990).
- *Basic AIDS information.* To answer students' questions accurately, you need to be knowledgeable about the transmission, prevention, and path of AIDS. In other words, before you shape your answers to a child's cognitive level, you need to have mastered the fundamental information so that you don't either overinform or misinform.
- *The types of questions that students of different ages and stages will ask.* For example, "What is AIDS?" "How do people get AIDS?" "What does 'sharing needles' mean?" (For an excellent overview of this topic, see Quackenbush & Villarreal, 1988, pp. 27–42).
- *Timing.* You should know students well enough to realize when the time is right to introduce the topic and how much time is needed for adequate coverage.

Alternatives to Piaget

As you can well imagine, other cognitive theorists have offered insights into cognitive development that have different emphases and different interpretations. Those advocating an information processing perspective believe that cognitive development is better understood by breaking down a child's solution to a problem into small, detailed steps. Kurt Fischer (Fischer & Silvern, 1985), for example, has proposed an elaborate theory of cognitive development from infancy to adulthood that encompasses ten stages: three at the sensorimotor level, three at the representational level, and four at the abstract level. Unlike Piaget, Fischer believes that development is much more uneven than it was previously considered to be.

Issues & Answers

Should Piaget's Theory of Cognitive Development ➤ Drive Public School Curricula?

American schools are varied and diverse. There is no one overarching philosophy or methodology of education in the tens of thousands of schools across our fifty states. While most educators accept, in general, Piaget's stages of cognitive development, teachers and school systems are not required to demonstrate a curriculum sensitive to developmental considerations for learning.

Issue

Teaching methods and the subject matter should demonstrate a developmental approach.

Answer: Pro   While there are disagreements about the particulars of Piaget's theory of cognitive development, the progression through successively sophisticated levels of cognitive development is widely supported. The ways in which students learn, marked by definite clues at different levels of development, give us great insight into how to best present subject matter in order to maximize a student's learning.

Answer: Con   A commitment to any one approach to learning limits opportunities to try something new. All teachers know that students learn in many different ways and at different rates. Even the same learner may be on different cognitive levels in different subjects. In Piaget's theory, students are constructors of their own knowledge through experiential learning, but the reality of the classroom dictates that teachers be free to use whatever style best suits the needs of their students on any given day.

Issue

Hands-on experience should be the cornerstone of the curriculum.

Answer: Pro   Through direct experience students come to an understanding of the material. Comprehension is necessary for authentic meaning to be achieved.

Answer: Con   While sometimes there are hands-on experiences that help students "see" a concept or make a connection, teachers cannot always provide their learners with this kind of experience. With ten units to get through in social studies, for example, the class does not have time to use experience to go to the same depth with each unit. Also some students, or entire classrooms, seem unable to settle in or settle down easily. For these learners, any departure from a teacher-directed activity is an invitation to chaos.

Issue

A report card should evaluate a child's level of cognition and reasoning capabilities, as well as content learning.

Answer: Pro   Letter grades are insufficient, telling us little about where our children are as learners. They most often reflect specific content learning. What does a C – tell us? Is the problem one of reasoning, understanding, or memory? A complete assessment provides an evaluation of the child's level of cognitive development and reasoning capabilities, as well as one of content learning.

Answer: Con   ABC grades have for many years been the accepted and the expected measure of a child's school progress. Having come through this system themselves, today's parents know how to gauge their children's progress using these measures. A developmental evaluation might inform a future teacher of the child, but would be of little value to a student or a parent.

Another theorist who has elaborated on Piaget's ideas is Robbie Case (1985). Believing that development proceeds by the use of ever improving cognitive strategies, Case presented a construct called the *M-space,* or mental space. This is essentially a memory concept: the M-space holds the number of schemes that a student has available for a specific task. As these schemes are used more and more frequently and as the student ages, the schemes become more automatic and free up more M-space. This increase in memory capacity is the major mechanism for cognitive development. The *total* capacity for memory does not change, but the *available* capacity at any given time can increase because of more efficient functioning (Miller, 1989).

Changes in cognitive development occur as children find themselves in problem situations. Relying on what Case calls *executive control structures,* children identify goals and the strategies needed to reach the goals by using their innate processing abilities. That is, children determine what is needed to solve a problem, activate appropriate mental structures, and then evaluate the results. For example, in solving a word problem, children may decide that they must find the cost of one orange by applying their knowledge of division, then multiply by the number of oranges to find the total cost that the problem calls for. Once students learn to apply their mathematical knowledge automatically in problems like this one, they can go on to more difficult problems.

As you see, Piaget has had a great influence on other cognitive theorists, and his ideas on cognitive development have had wide impact. Piaget has also proposed a theory of language development. Before we examine his and other theories of language development, however, let us first trace the path by which children acquire language.

LANGUAGE DEVELOPMENT

Children quickly acquire their native languages, a task of such scope and intricacy that its secrets have eluded investigators for centuries. They proceed from hesitant beginnings to competent usage—that is, the use of language to control their environment—by the age of 6 or 7 years. Children do not learn to speak by merely imitating adults, nor do most parents reward their children for good grammar (deCuevas, 1990).

Language Accomplishments

All children, whether they live in a ghetto or in a wealthy suburb, manifest similar patterns of speech development at about the same age. Within a short span of time and with almost no direct instruction, children completely analyze their languages. Although refinements are made between the ages of 5 and 10, most children have completed the greater part of the process of language acquisition by the age of 4 or 5. Recent findings have also shown that when children acquire the various parts of a given language, they do so in a set order. For example, in English, children learn *in* and *on* before other prepositions, and they learn to use *ing* as a verb ending before mastering other endings such as *ed* (Gleason, 1985).

This is a tremendous accomplishment. You may have tried to learn a foreign language as an adult; recall how difficult it was to acquire vocabulary and to master rules of grammar and the subtleties of usage. Yet preschool children do just this with no formal training. By the time they are ready to enter kindergarten, most children have a vocabulary of about eight thousand words; can use questions, negative statements, and dependent clauses; and have learned to use language in a variety of social situations (Gleason, 1985). They also have discovered that there are rules for recombining sounds into words, and that individual words have specific meanings. In addition, they have come to realize that there are rules for recombining words into meaningful sentences and that there are rules for participating in a dialogue.

From production of the first random sounds, through the precise and direct expressions of the first-grader, to the sophisticated conversation of the teenager, language offers definite clues to personality, intelligence, education, and occupation. By the time children reach the age of 6, they have acquired their language and are able to use language to control their environments. Instead of leaving the table, walking to the refrigerator, and taking out the milk, they may simply ask someone else to do it for them.

We tend to take language acquisition for granted, but closer inspection of this accomplishment testifies to the enormity of the task. Children seem to be programmed to talk and to use all forms of language to adjust to their environments. The form that the particular language takes—whether it is English, Arabic, or Chinese—is incidental. From birth, children tune into the language that they hear around them and feed these sounds into their unique ability to master language.

The Language Components

When linguists examine a language, they identify four major components: **phonology** (or sound), **syntax** (or grammar), **semantics** (or meaning), and **pragmatics** (or usage).

phonology *The use of sounds to form words.*

syntax *The grammar of a language; the system used to put words together to form sentences.*

semantics *The meaning of words; the relationship between ideas and words.*

pragmatics *The ability to take part in a conversation, using language in a socially correct manner.*

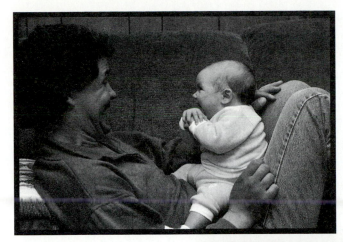 

Children acquire the basics of language easily and continue to refine it, using language to adapt to and control their environments.

Phonology

phonemes *The distinctive, fundamental sounds of a language.*

morpheme *The smallest unit of language to have meaning; may be a whole word or part of a word (old,er).*

Every language possesses certain distinctive, fundamental sounds, which are the **phonemes** of that language. These are the smallest language units. For example, the words *thin* and *shin* sound alike, but the initial sounds differ sufficiently to distinguish the words; this qualifies the initial sounds as phonemes.

The smallest unit of language to have meaning is the **morpheme.** Morphemes may be whole words or parts of words that signify meaning, such as the endings *er, ed,* and *ing.* The word *older* has two morphemes: *old,* signifying age, and *er,* signifying comparison. Morphemes are composed of a series of phonemes (the morpheme *er* consists of two phonemes, while *old* consists of three phonemes).

Syntax

Morphemes are arranged in the grammar, or *syntax,* of a language. The task of any syntax is to arrange morphemes in meaningful sentences. Grammatical studies have repeatedly shown that any speaker can say and any listener can understand an infinite number of sentences. As was previously mentioned, children learn the syntactic rules of their languages with little adult instruction.

Semantics

Grammar seems to be designed to convert ideas into word combinations. The relationship between ideas and words is the source of meaning, or *semantics*. To integrate language elements, children must be able to represent various kinds of knowledge, to combine them, and to evaluate their relevance in context.

As teachers, it is important to remember that it can be difficult to understand the precise meaning that a student gives a word. Although young children can understand the meaning of most of what is said to them, they may be reacting to environmental cues: a parent may be pointing to a toothbrush while speaking about it, for example. Only over time do children slowly acquire understanding of the adult meaning of words (Pease & Gleason, 1985).

Pragmatics

Children must also learn how to use language; this requires the development of *pragmatic* skills. Language is a remarkably sophisticated developmental accomplishment, one aspect of which is the increasing success children have in making their communication clear.

All children, regardless of their native tongue, manifest similar patterns of language development. The basic sequence of language acquisition is as follows:

- *At about 3 months* children use intonations similar to those of adults;
- *At about 1 year* they begin to use recognizable words;
- *At about 4 years* they have acquired the complicated structures of their native tongues;
- *At about 6 or 7 years* they speak and understand sentences that they have never previously used or heard.

Table 4.3 reviews these developmental changes during the early years.

Table 4.3

The Sequence of Infant Language Development

Language	Age
Crying	From birth
Cooing	2–4 months
Babbling	4–6 months
Single words	12 months
Two-word phrases	18 months
Longer phrases	2 years
Short sentences and questions	2–3 years

LANGUAGE DEVELOPMENT IN INFANCY

Infants tune into the speech they hear and immediately begin to discriminate distinctive features. They also seem to be sensitive to the context of the language they hear; that is, they identify the *affective* nature of speech. The origins of language appear immediately after birth, in infants' gazes and vocal exchanges with those around them. Although these are not specific language behaviors, they are an integral part of the language continuum.

Neonates vocalize by crying and fussing, which are forms of communication. At about the sixth to the eighth week, *cooing* (production of sounds that resemble vowels and consonants) appears. These precursors of language blend into *babbling,* which then merges into the first words; then language development continues with the appearance of two-word phrases, longer phrases, and sentences. The sequence is as follows.

At about 4 months, children begin to babble, that is, to make sounds that approximate speech. For example, you may hear an "eee" that makes you think that the infant is saying "see." It seems, however, that babbling does not depend on external reinforcement: deaf as well as hearing children babble. However, deaf children continue to babble past the age when hearing children begin to use words. Babbling probably appears initially because of biological maturation.

Late in the babbling period, children use consistent sound patterns to refer to objects and events. These sound patterns are called *vocables,* and seem to indicate that children have discovered that meaning is associated with sound. For example, a child may hear the doorbell and say "ell." The use of vocables may be a link between babbling and the first intelligible words. These speechlike sounds increase in frequency until about the age of 1 year, when children begin to use single words. At this stage, babbling is still interspersed among the single words.

At about 1 year, the first words appear. (The age can vary markedly, however, depending on how the proud parents or other observers define what qualifies as a word.) Often called *holophrastic* speech, these first words are difficult to analyze. They are usually nouns, adjectives, or self-invented words, and they may even represent multiple meanings. "Ball" may mean not only the ball itself, but also "Throw the ball to me." Children's first words show a phonetic similarity to adult words, and children consistently use these words to refer to the same objects or events.

The single-word period flows into the use of multiple words and the development of grammar. Between the ages of about 1 year and 18 months, *children begin to use these single words to convey multiple meanings.* At first, "ball" refers to a round, moving object. Gradually, "ball" acquires the meaning of "give me the ball," "throw the ball," or "watch the ball roll." "Ball" now means much more than a round object. When toddlers begin to use their words to convey these more complex ideas, they are getting ready to move to the next stage of language development.

When the two-word stage appears, at about 18 months, youngsters initially struggle to devise some means of indicating tense and number, and typically experience difficulty with grammatical correctness. At first they employ word order to suggest meaning. They do not master inflections (plurals, tenses, possessives) until they begin to form three-word sentences. A youngster's effort to inject grammatical order into language is a good sign of normal language development.

At about 2 years of age, children's vocabularies expand rapidly, and simple sentences, or telegraphic speech, appear. Research indicates that the amount of maternal speech is closely related to a child's vocabulary growth (Huttenlocher, Haight, Bryk, Seltzer, & Lyons, 1991). Although young children use primarily nouns and verbs (rather than adverbs, conjunctions, prepositions), their sentences demonstrate definite syntactic structure. While the nouns, adjectives, and verbs of children's sentences differ from those of adults, the same organizational principles are present. **Telegraphic speech,** like holophrastic speech, contains considerably more meaning than the sum of its words. For example, "milk gone" means "my milk is all gone."

telegraphic speech *The use of two- or three-word phrases to convey more sophisticated meanings ("milk gone" means "my milk is all gone").*

Once syntactic structure emerges in two-word sentences, inflection soon appears, usually with three-word sentences. The appearance of inflections seems to follow a pattern: first the plurals of nouns, then tense and person in verbs, and then possessives.

Vocabulary constantly expands. As their symbolic activity increases and becomes more abstract, youngsters learn that everything has a name, and their vocabulary expands at an enormous rate (which explains why these months are often called the time of the *language explosion*). Between the ages of 1 and 2, a toddler's vocabulary grows by at least 2500 percent, even by as much as 6000 percent. The growth rate in the subsequent years of early childhood is less spectacular, but quite remarkable. Estimates of vocabulary are extremely tentative, however, since youngsters know more words than they articulate.

Speech Irregularities

When should a teacher be concerned about the possible existence of a language problem? Youngsters who consistently miss the language milestones mentioned above should receive detailed examinations. Speech/language pathologists, professionals who are trained to diagnose and help correct speech and language problems, are often available in the schools, and should be contacted if teachers have any questions. But teachers should not confuse a serious language problem (such as lack of comprehension) with temporary setbacks or with speech irregularities that are a normal part of development.

As speech emerges, certain irregularities appear that are quite normal and to be expected. For example, *overextensions* mark children's beginning words. A child who has learned the name of the family pet—"doggy"—may for a while use that label for a cat, a horse, a donkey, a cow, or any other animal with a head, a tail, a body, and four legs. As children learn about their world, they quickly eliminate overextensions.

Overregularities are a similar fleeting phenomenon. As youngsters begin to use two- and three-word sentences, they struggle to convey more precise meanings by mastering the grammatical rules of their language. For example, many English verbs add *ed* to indicate past tense.

I wanted to play ball.

Some verbs, however, form the past tense by a change in the root.

Daddy came home.

Most children, even after they have mastered the correct forms of such verbs as *come, see,* and *run,* still add *ed* to the original forms. That is, youngsters who know that the past tense of *come* is *came* will still say this:

Daddy comed home.

This tendency to overregularize persists only briefly. It is another example of the close link between language and thought. We know that from birth children respond to patterns. Infants look longer at the human face than they do at diagrams because the human face is more complex. Once children have learned a pattern such as adding *ed* to signify past tense, they have considerable difficulty in changing the pattern.

LANGUAGE DEVELOPMENT IN EARLY CHILDHOOD

Children will not speak before they are about 1 year old; this is a biological given and nothing will change it. But once language appears, it is difficult to retard its progress. Usually only some traumatic event such as brain damage or dramatically deprived environmental conditions will hinder development.

To encourage language development during the early childhood years, Hendrick (1992) recommended that teachers give students something real to talk about, and then listen to their stories (really paying attention to what they are saying). Since students of this age are beginning to use more socialized speech, try to encourage as much conversation as possible—between teachers and students, between students, and with other adults. (Urge their parents to have children discuss their days during the evening meal, asking them questions that require more than one-word answers.)

Children proceed from hesitant beginnings to almost complete acquisition of their native languages by the time they are about 7 years old. They manifest similar patterns of speech development whether they live in ghettos or in wealthy suburbs. A particular culture has little to do with language emergence, although it has everything to do with the shape that language assumes. Children in France and in Spain, for example, may use different words for the same objects, but the appearance of single words, two-word sentences, and other achievements follows the same developmental pattern. All children likewise begin to realize that they are language users and understand what this means for interacting with their environments. This is referred to as metalinguistic awareness.

Metalinguistic Awareness

Metacognition refers to children's ability to step back and look at the various cognitive skills that they have developed. One of these cognitive skills is language, and probably nothing reveals the close link between cognitive and language development more than a youngster's acquisition of metalinguistic awareness (Dash & Mohanty, 1992). At about the age of 6, youngsters acquire this ability to "look at language and not through it."

The stages in the acquisition of metalinguistic awareness have been summarized as follows by Bullinger and Chatillon (1983).

For 4-year-olds, words exist on the same plane as the things to which they refer. "Train is a long word because a train has a lot of cars."

From 5 to 6 years, children identify words with the activity of speaking. "A word is when you talk."

From 6 to 7 years, children differentiate words from what they represent. Youngsters now begin to show an understanding of language.

An example of how understanding their language affects children's accomplishments is found in the work of Dresher and Zenge (1990) on the relationship between metalinguistic awareness and reading success. After studying 65 first-graders, they found that the students with greater metalinguistic ability at that age became superior readers in the third and fifth grades. These researchers concluded that metalinguistic awareness is a good predictor of later reading success.

The Whole Language Movement

Building on a growing knowledge of language development, many educators, long dissatisfied with the teaching of reading and writing, have adopted a new strategy. Called **whole language,** it is a movement that is sweeping the country and refers to a technique by which all language processes (speaking, listening, reading, and writing—including spelling and handwriting) are studied in a more natural context, as a whole and not as a series of facts (Symons, Woloshyn, & Pressley, 1994).

whole language *A technique in which all language processes are studied together in a natural context (as a whole, and not as a series of facts).*

The whole language movement rests on the basic premise that infants learn language by actually using it, and that this should be the acquisition model for reading and writing (Giddings, 1992). This premise leads to several educational guidelines. For example, oral and written language are best acquired through actual use in meaningful situations. Instruction should be guided by the needs and interests of the learners, and real literature should be used as much as possible (Giddings, 1992).

The proponents of whole language believe that it is consistent with Piaget's theory of human development, because the individual child's use of language materials matches that child's level of cognitive development. Proponents also claim that it is consistent with Vygotsky's work because of the important role that context plays in a child's attempts to master reading and writing (McCaslin, 1989). Still others believe that the whole language movement is a natural outgrowth of several earlier educational beliefs, such as the emphasis on the integrated curriculum and individualized reading (Goodman, 1989).

Explaining the Whole Language Concept

The shift from dependence on a basal language series to whole language requires teachers to rethink their assumptions about literature and language learning. Many teachers using a whole language approach work with themes: friendship, loyalty, honesty. First, students read a story that illustrates the theme. This is known as *experiencing the literature.* Next, the teacher may read a related story or poem; pupils are *listening to the literature.*

Now the teacher may attempt to *expand* the concepts that the pupils experienced in their literature and simultaneously work on vocabulary using various techniques.

Next, students may read the selection cooperatively (taking turns with their partners, or reading aloud about a particular character in the story). They can then discuss the characters in the story.

Then, students may *respond* to the literature by filling out a story form (completing sentences with missing words, explaining the beginning and ending, telling how the story's problem was solved). The teacher may ask them to evaluate the characters' actions in the story or give their own opinions about the story. Some pupils may explore language at this point: if they need help with vocabulary or phonics, or with general reading strategies, they are guided to appropriate activities.

The students then shift from reading to writing. For example, they may write a paragraph explaining a particular part of the story. They apply the words they have learned in their reading to their writing. They can be taught how to proofread and to revise in this phase.

With their reading and writing experiences completed, and if time permits, students may *extend their reading experiences*. That is, if the theme of their work was friendship, they may do independent research that could include examples of friendship in stories, friendship between leaders of nations, or friendship between people of different cultures.

The ideal time for the introduction of whole language is during the early childhood period. Children of this age are experiencing a rapid natural growth of language and enjoying the newfound power that language confers. It seems to be an ideal time to harness this exuberance and use it to further their learning.

Can Language Learning Be Easy?

Supporters believe that when language learning is meaningful and relevant to pupils in such a way that they actually use it for their own purposes, the teaching of language becomes simpler and more appealing. Meaningful language learning helps students to make sense out of their worlds, because while they are learning language, they are also learning *through* language. That is, comprehension of meaning is always the goal of readers, and expression of meaning is always the goal of writers (Giddings, 1992).

One way of motivating pupils to search continually for meaning is to turn to literature. Literature has proven to be a superb vehicle for developing, enhancing, and enriching lifelong, active literacy (Chaney, 1990). There are many reasons for using literature as the foundation for a reading and writing program. *Literature encourages meaning*. Children beginning to read immediately search for meaning, and stories that make sense are easy for them to discuss and recall. *Literature has pupils focus on reading as a whole* (a natural process), rather than on an isolated series of parts (an unnatural one). Finally, *literature encourages language development* by exposing pupils to a variety of correct, creative, and imaginative language that aids comprehension and vocabulary development.

Bilingualism

You have just entered your first classroom to meet your pupils. Much to your surprise, several students whom you will be teaching this year do not speak or write English as their primary language. This situation is becoming more and more common in our schools. All evidence points to the conclusion that our country is more diverse ethnically and linguistically today than ever before. For example, while the country's population increased by 11.6 percent between the years 1970 and 1980, the number of Asian Americans increased by 233 percent, that of Native Americans by 71 percent, that of Hispanic Americans by 61 percent, and that of African Americans by 17.8 percent. Moreover, estimates are that at least 3.4 million pupils have limited English-language skills in a school system designed primarily for those who speak English (Lindholm, 1990).

Issues & Answers

Should Non-English-Speaking Students Be Educated in a Bilingual Educational System?

By the turn of the century, about 40 percent of public school students will be from ethnically diverse backgrounds, and many of these students may be at risk because of an English-language deficit. Bilingual education offers these students course instruction in their native languages while they study English separately. It is a major commitment, since academic fluency takes about seven years.

Issue
Bilingual education is the way American public schools should educate non-English-speaking students.

Answer: Pro Students in bilingual education are not penalized because of a language deficit. They are able to stay current with their studies because subjects are taught in their native languages; this helps to maintain students' self-esteem while they gain proficiency in English.

Answer: Con Bilingual education is not very helpful to these students. Students who eventually succeed in the marketplace are proficient in English. Bilingual education wastes valuable time reinforcing students' native languages instead of teaching them English.

Issue
English as a second language (ESL) is a good alternative program to bilingual education.

Answer: Pro ESL is a desirable program because most of a student's coursework is in English, with separate time allotted for specific English-language instruction. Students are grouped according to grade level, and the ESL teacher uses the student's classroom curriculum.

Answer: Con ESL does not give students support in their native languages. In spite of English language training, these students fall behind. Older students in particular may have difficulty with this technique.

Issue
Since English is the official language of government and commerce in the United States, classroom instruction in public school classrooms should be in English.

Answer: Pro One of the goals of public school education is fluency in spoken and written English. If students are in an environment where only English is spoken, they will learn the language more quickly. These students may have initial difficulty, but once they have acquired English proficiency, they typically catch up.

Answer: Con Non-English-speaking students are often put into classes with students younger than themselves while they gain English proficiency. Or if they are put in with their peers, they suffer because they cannot keep up with the coursework. Both of these conditions result in a loss of self-esteem for the students, which can then affect total academic performance and may cause them to drop out of school altogether.

---

bilingualism *The condition of using, with facility, two or more languages.*

Issues related to **bilingualism** are clearly of increasing concern to school districts across the nation. The rights of language-minority students have come increasingly under analysis, with specific implications for the schools and the professionals who work in them. Some of the rights of these students are as follows (Garcia Coll, 1990):

- There is a legally acceptable procedure for identifying all students who have problems speaking, understanding, reading, or writing English.
- Once these pupils are identified, there are minimal standards for the educational program that is provided for them. For example, some courts have noted that the teacher must have special training in working with these students and that the students must receive adequate time to acquire English skills.
- A school district is advised, but not compelled, to offer instruction in the student's native language as well as in English.
- A school system may not deny services to a student because the district contains only one or a few students who speak the student's specific language.

Many misconceptions have surrounded the educational progress of those students with an ability to speak two or more languages. For example, introducing a second language does *not* hurt the development of a student's primary language. Bilingual students

Table 4.4

Some Typical Language Accomplishments	
Age (years)	**Language accomplishments**
6	Has vocabulary of about several thousand words
	Understands use and meaning of complex sentences
	Uses language as a tool
	Possesses some reading ability
7	Is improving in motor control; is able to use pencil
	Can usually print several sentences
	Begins to tell time
	Is losing tendency to reverse letters (b, d)
8	Is improving in motor control; has more graceful movements
	Is able to write as well as print
	Understands that words may have more than one meaning (ball)
	Uses total sentence to determine meaning
9	Can describe objects in detail
	Has little difficulty in telling time
	Writes well
	Uses sentence content to determine word meaning
10	Describes situations by cause and effect
	Can write fairly lengthy essays
	Likes mystery and science stories
	Masters dictionary skills
	Possesses good sense of grammar

will *not* become confused by the use of two languages. In the past, a common practice has been to emphasize English and minimize the student's primary language. This practice has caused McLaughlin (1990) to note the following:

> **Educational programs that do not attempt to maintain the child's first language deprive many children of economic opportunities they would otherwise have as bilinguals. This is especially true of children who speak world languages used for international communication such as Spanish, Japanese, Chinese, and the like. If these children's first languages are not maintained, one of this country's most valuable resources will be wasted. (p. 74)**

As the classroom teachers of today and the future, you will continue to work with students of growing ethnic and linguistic diversity. Learn as much about your pupils as possible, and search constantly for the most effective means of communicating with them.

LANGUAGE DEVELOPMENT IN MIDDLE CHILDHOOD

As youngsters mature, their vocabularies (both speaking and comprehension) increase enormously to match their expanding cognitive activities. For example, children aged 6 to 11 recognize sarcastic remarks; although they probably understand more from intonation than from context, they do grasp the intent of such statements (Capelli et al., 1990). It now becomes increasingly difficult to continue to match age with language accomplishment. Table 4.4 illustrates general language achievements for the preteen years.

This is an interesting chart: it encompasses almost all aspects of development for these years. Note the steady progression in motor skills: from acquiring the ability to grasp a pencil and print at about age 7 to writing lengthy essays just three years later. Increasing visual discrimination is apparent in the ability to describe events accurately and the elimination of letter reversals (for example, b for d). Growth in cognitive ability is seen in the ability to detect cause and effect, and the appeal of science and mystery stories.

For children between 6 and 10, the relationship of language development (in the sense of mastering a native tongue) to reading is crucial. Everywhere they turn—from signs on buses and streets as they go to school to an educational curriculum that is overwhelmingly verbal—children must interpret the written word. In our society the functional illiterate faces a daily battle for survival.

THEORIES OF LANGUAGE ACQUISITION

Many of the language achievements that we take for granted are actually amazing accomplishments and defy easy explanation. Imitation, although a powerful linguistic force, does not seem to be the sole explanation for a youngster's intuitive grasp of grammar, since a child hears so many incorrect utterances. Imitation also does not explain the manner by which thoughts are translated into words.

"No use debating environmental versus genetic causes. Either way, it's your fault."

© Martha F. Campbell

Lenneberg's Biological Explanation

Linguistic achievements that cannot be explained as the results of imitation or some other process have led some to a biological interpretation of language.

And what else but an innate capacity for language can explain the innovative nature of language? Children do not merely imitate those around them. If you listen carefully to young children, you will distinguish unique combinations of words, combinations that the children have never heard before. They may have heard the words *man, doll,* and *walk,* but never the combination, "Man walk doll." Such novel utterances testify to the creative aspects of language. The work of Eric Lenneberg (1967) offers insights into the biological bases of the capacity for language.

The Language Spurt

Lenneberg's initial premise is that at a certain time in development, children show an amazing spurt in the ability to name things. There is a rapid increase in vocabulary between the ages of 14 and 30 months. At the end of the third year, children have a speaking vocabulary of about one thousand words, and probably understand thousands of other words. This explosion in vocabulary occurs at about the same age for every normal child in the world.

The specific causal elements and the underlying cerebral mechanisms for the language explosion are still unknown. Lenneberg believes that imitation, conditioning, and reinforcement—all external factors—are inadequate explanations for language development, and that anatomical and physiological agents—internal factors—play a major part.

Language and Behavior

In normal children, there is initially nothing to show that the various steps of language development are about to occur. And rapid vocabulary growth is only one of the amazing features that we have yet to explain. Without instruction, youngsters are also learning the rules of language, so that by the age of 4, they have acquired the essentials of adult speech. The sheer mechanisms of speech production demand a high order of interpretation and an entire complex of special physiological adaptations.

Table 4.5

Piaget on Language and Thought		
Period (age in years)	**Outstanding characteristics**	**Language equivalent**
Sensorimotor (0–2)	1. Egocentrism 2. Organization of reality by sensory and motor abilities	1. Language absent until final months of period
Preoperational (2–7)	1. Increasing symbolic ability 2. Beginnings of representation	1. Egocentric speech 2. Socialized speech
Concrete operations (7–11)	1. Reversibility 2. Conservation 3. Seriation 4. Classification	1. Beginnings of verbal understanding 2. Understanding related to concrete objects
Formal operations (over 11)	1. Development of logico-mathematical structures 2. Hypothetico-deductive reasoning	1. Language freed from the concrete 2. Verbal ability to express the possible

Lenneberg postulated that language development follows a biological schedule that is activated when a state of "resonance" exists; that is, when children are "excited" in accordance with the environment, the sounds that they have been hearing suddenly assume a new, meaningful pattern.

Language development parallels motor and cognitive ability. Standing, walking, and general muscular coordination approximate the appearance of certain language characteristics. Motor, cognitive, and language schedules seem to follow genetically programmed instructions: first to manifest steady, sometimes spectacular, development, then to level off, and slowly to decline. Consequently, if children of an appropriate age are placed in any language community, they will immediately and with little difficulty acquire that language.

Piaget and Language Development

Piaget believed that language emerges not from a biological timetable such as Lenneberg suggested, but rather from existing cognitive structures and in accordance with the child's needs. Piaget's basic work on language, *The Language and Thought of the Child* (1926), begins by asking what the needs are that a child tends to satisfy by talking. In other words, what is the function of language for a child? Piaget answered this question by linking language to cognitive structures. Thus, he saw language function as differing at each of the four cognitive levels (see table 4.5).

Recording the speech of two 6-year-old children, Piaget identified two major speech categories of the preoperational child: egocentric speech and socialized speech. Children engage in *egocentric speech* when they do not care to whom they speak, or whether anyone is listening to them (Piaget, 1926, p. 32). There are three types of egocentric speech:

1. *repetition,* which children use for the sheer pleasure of talking and which is devoid of social character;
2. *monologue,* in which children talk to themselves as if they were thinking aloud;
3. *collective monologue,* in which other children are present but not listening to the speaker.

Children engage in *socialized speech* when they exchange views with others, criticize one another, ask questions, give answers, and even command or threaten. Piaget estimated that about 50 percent of the 6-year-old's speech is egocentric and that what is socialized is purely factual. He also warned that although most children begin to communicate thought at between 7 and 8 years of age, their understanding of each other is still limited.

Seven or 8 years of age sees the slow but steady disappearance of egocentrism, except in verbal thought, in which traces of egocentrism remain until about 11 or 12 years of age. Usage and complexity of language increases dramatically as children pass through the four stages of cognitive development. Piaget insisted that the striking growth of verbal ability does not occur as a separate developmental phenomenon, but reflects the development of cognitive structures.

Chomsky and Psycholinguistics

Language Acquisition Device (LAD) *Chomsky's term for the mechanism in humans that, he believes, gives them an innate knowledge of language.*

psycholinguistics *The combined study of psychology and linguistics; refers most often to Chomsky's work on language development.*

Similarly to Lenneberg, Noam Chomsky (1928–) a professor of linguistics at the Massachusetts Institute of Technology trained in mathematics and philosophy as well as linguistics, believes that all humans have an innate capacity to acquire language as a result of our biological inheritance. Chomsky goes farther than Lenneberg in his views: for Chomsky, not only do we have a biological predisposition for language, but we also have an innate knowledge of language. He calls it our **Language Acquisition Device (LAD).** Chomsky (1965, 1985) also stated that no one acquires a language by learning billions of sentences of that language. Rather, a child acquires a *grammar* that can generate an infinite number of sentences in the child's native language.

Chomsky's work is usually referred to as **psycholinguistics,** a combination of psychology and linguistics. Linguistics is the study of the rules of any language, while psychology studies the causes of an individual's behavior. Linguists assume that the rules of language are part of our knowledge; psychologists have attempted to discover how children learn and understand these rules. The combination of the two approaches has produced the field of psycholinguistics (Gardner, 1982).

Children possess an innate competence for language acquisition, just as they possess an innate capacity for walking. No one has to tell children *how* to walk or talk: they do both without consciously knowing how they do so. Although all normal children possess approximately the same language competence, their performance, or use of language, varies increasingly as they grow older. This variation is due largely to differences in opportunities to learn how to use language, which involves not only speaking but also listening, writing, and reading. Thus, even though all preschoolers may have roughly the same linguistic abilities, the language abilities of adults vary widely.

The view of language as an unfolding of innate capacities, as seen in the work of Chomsky and others, offers clues as to the teaching of second languages. For example, teachers have long worried that the acquisition of a first language may interfere with the learning of a second. Recent research suggests that the native language does not in any significant way interfere with the development of the second language. The acquisition of both seems to be guided by common language principles that are a part of the human cognitive system. In fact, success in the acquisition of a second language is closely related to proficiency level in the first language; this indicates that languages share a common base (Hakuta, 1986).

How would you use the heredity-environment controversy to explain language development? In other words, do you think language development is chiefly biological? Or is it learned? Or is there yet another explanation?

LANGUAGE AND THE CLASSROOM

Are you satisfied with the explanations of language development offered by the various theorists? Why? Do you think any of the theories you have read about gives a full explanation?

As we conclude our analysis of language development, it is possible to see the classroom impact of the various theories we have discussed, especially with regard to current curriculum changes. The whole language concept, which is an approach to teaching reading that focuses on meaning, is a good example. The whole language technique incorporates all aspects of language—listening, speaking, reading, writing, spelling, thinking—by using children's literature and trade books across the curriculum. The meaning that pupils derive from such involvement is, in turn, related to cognitive ability, reflecting Piaget's belief that language development depends on cognitive development.

teacher – student

interactions

Activities to Facilitate Language Skills

1. Language is an integral part of instruction in the content areas; this emphasizes its importance to students.
   - Ensure access to a wide range of appropriate books.
   - Schedule class time for independent reading.
   - Encourage class discussion of the books that the students read.
   - Devise activities that focus on a story or an author; for example, role-play an author, imagining how and why that author wrote a story, or turn a story into a classroom play.

2. Understanding the spoken word and using a variety of words in their own speech prepares children for meeting words on the printed page. Use these activities to promote pupils' language development.
   - Encourage children to make place associations with this game. Tell your pupils that for the next minute they are to name everything they can think of that they might find in a grocery store, on a farm, or in a sports shop. Encourage pupils to use specific names for people and objects.
   - Show pupils pictures of everyday objects, such as a bicycle, a toothbrush, an umbrella, and so on. Ask pupils to describe how the objects are used and what they are used for.
   - Pose problems for children to solve on their own or by acting out the situations with puppets. For example, give pupils the following scenario: Four friends were going to go on a picnic, but it has started to rain and they have to stay inside. What can they do now to have fun? Insist that pupils use complete sentences as they make up their dialogues.

- Test language skills and creativity by having pupils tell a story in the round. Seat the class in a circle on the floor. Begin a story; then, after several minutes, tap the child next to you and say, "Please continue." The child now adds to the story for a few minutes, then taps the next child. Continue around the circle, asking the last child to make up an ending.
- See how well pupils listen and understand what they hear by giving children verbal directions for drawing a mystery object on paper. Have a picture of the object ready for pupils to check against their own drawings.
- Check problem-solving abilities and language skills by giving pupils a story problem, but omitting vital information needed to solve it. Ask pupils to pinpoint what else they need to know before they can figure out the answer.

3. As children acquire language, they must also learn to use it properly.
   - Read aloud to your pupils as often as possible. Children like to listen; as they do, they are learning about language as communication. This technique also increases their motivation to read.
   - Ask children to retell stories in their own words. This is a procedure that aids sequencing, helps in learning about story structure, and aids comprehension.
   - Use prompts such as these: "What comes next?" "What problems did they face?" "How did they overcome them?"

Chomsky's ideas on the relationship of performance to competence can be seen in the occasions for teaching language skills that the whole language technique offers across the curriculum. Language activities become an integral part of instruction in content areas, thus assuming a more meaningful and functional place in a pupil's life.

APPLICATIONS AND REFLECTIONS

Chapter Highlights

The Meaning of Development

- Vygotsky's concept of a zone of proximal development offers insight into the relationship among learning, development, and social processes.
- Knowledge of cognitive development aids in instructional decisions.

Piaget and Cognitive Development

- Piaget's basic ideas help teachers to decide on developmentally appropriate materials and instructions.
- Piaget's theory aids us in understanding that "children think differently from adults."
- His stages of cognitive development help us to comprehend what we can expect cognitively from pupils of different ages.
- Piaget's belief that students must interact with the environment for learning to occur has classroom implications.

Language: Theories and Development

- Like other cognitive processes, language development follows a predictable sequence in children of all cultures and native languages.
- Several different explanations of language acquisition—biological, cognitive, and innate—have led to the formulation of specific theories.
- Language acquisition offers definite clues to a pupil's developmental progress, which can aid teachers in working with pupils.

Connections

1. Think about how you learn and describe how one of the major concepts discussed in this chapter is part of your learning activities or approach.

2. Identify at least one learning situation (classroom instruction, self-study, taking a test, small-group work) and describe how you would apply one of the key concepts examined in this chapter *if you were a teacher*.

Getting the Picture and Drawing Relationships

Think about the various learning concepts and variables discussed in this chapter. Create pictures, graphics, or figures that highlight the relationships among key components.

Personal Journal

What I really learned in this chapter was _____

_____

_____

_____

What this means to me is _____

_____

_____

_____

_____

Questions that were stimulated by this chapter include _____

_____

_____

_____

_____

Key Terms

accommodation	84	functional invariants	84	psycholinguistics	113
adaptation	84	irreversibility	90	realism	90
animism	91	Language Acquisition		schemes	85
artificialism	91	Device (LAD)	113	semantics	102
assimilation	84	morpheme	103	seriation	93
bilingualism	109	number concept	94	structures	84
centering	90	object permanence	88	syntax	102
classification	93	operations	90	telegraphic speech	105
conservation	92	organization	85	transductive reasoning	91
content	85	phonemes	103	whole language	107
egocentrism	88	phonology	102	zone of proximal	
equilibration	84	pragmatics	102	development	82

Bill Brown, who was in the eighth grade at the Junior High West, kept staring at the ground in the school's parking lot. Although all the students in the school were milling around, talking and trying to discover the exact location and cause of the fire, Bill stayed by himself. With a troubled expression he watched the firemen quickly extinguish the small blaze. He knew who had set the fire.

Earlier in the day, Jim Weston, another eighth-grader, had said to him, "It's time we had a little excitement around here. It's been pretty dull lately. Watch what happens in science today."

years ago. Bill had overheard his own parents talking quietly about the possibility of Jim's parents divorcing.

"Maybe that's it," Bill muttered to himself. "Maybe he just feels left out. Still, if that fire had gotten out of control, people could have been seriously hurt. Why, Jim even told me something would happen, just to make sure somebody would know," thought Bill. "If I tell Mr. Johnson what I know, maybe he could straighten him out. But he could be in a lot of trouble, maybe even expelled."

Bill stood there not sure what to do next. ■

chapter 5

psychosocial and moral development

"What's up, Jim? You're not going to try anything in Johnson's class, are you?" (Pete Johnson was the eighth-grade science teacher.) Bill had continued, "He's a pretty good guy."

"What difference does that make? Let's liven things up."

When the officials from the fire department gave the all clear and the students returned to the building, Bill walked by the science lab and saw the damage caused by the small fire. He liked Mr. Johnson; he had been Bill's Little League coach and had always been fair to him.

Pete Johnson saw him standing at the doorway and said, "This is a tough one, Bill. The fire inspector said it was set. I can't believe anyone would do this. Think of the damage and what could have happened to some of the students. Who could possibly do something like this?"

It was a hard decision for Bill. His parents, while not overly strict, had firm ideas about right and wrong, and he had been brought up to tell the truth. "Great," said Bill to himself. "It's too bad nobody told me anything about volunteering the truth, especially if it could hurt a friend."

Bill looked at the teacher. He knew that Jim Weston wasn't really bad; he just didn't think that others really liked him, so he was always looking for attention. It must be something in his family, Bill thought. He had heard stories about trouble between Jim's mother and father a few

Torn between loyalty to a friend and the knowledge that his friend's actions were wrong, Bill is faced with a dilemma that has strong implications for his psychosocial and moral development. If he decides to confide in the teacher whom he respects, what will the rest of his friends think? Peer influence at this age is a powerful motivator of behavior. Yet, as we realize from studying Piaget in chapter 4, a pupil of this age *knows* when something is wrong. Will Bill reconcile his behavior with what he thinks is right, and hope that at the same time he can keep the trust of his friends? Or will he compromise what he believes to be right to stay "in" with his friends?

Teachers would be concerned not only with what Bill Brown should do, but also with Jim Weston's background, with discovering something that might help to explain his behavior. And of course, Jim's teachers would want to find ways to help him grow in his relations with others and in making moral choices.

This chapter aims to help you address these issues. First, the chapter will explore the dimensions of psychosocial development, primarily through the work of Erik Erikson. Erikson has traced this aspect of development through eight stages, several of which have important implications for the classroom. Second, we will explore moral issues such as the ones faced by both boys using Lawrence Kohlberg's insights into the path of moral development. Kohlberg's

Psychosocial Development 120

Erikson's Eight Stages 120
Stage 1: Trust Versus
    Mistrust 120
Stage 2: Autonomy Versus
    Shame and Doubt 121
Stage 3: Initiative Versus
    Guilt 123
Stage 4: Industry Versus
    Inferiority 126
Stage 5: Identity Versus Identity
    Confusion 130
Stage 6: Intimacy Versus
    Isolation 134
Stage 7: Generativity Versus
    Stagnation 135
Stage 8: Integrity Versus
    Despair 135
For the Classroom 135

Moral Development 136

**Kohlberg's Theory of Moral
Development 137**
Level 1: Preconventional
    Morality 138
Level 2: Conventional
    Morality 138
Level 3: Postconventional
    Morality 140
Criticisms of Kohlberg's
    Theory 141
For the Classroom 142
Using Moral Dilemmas 143
The Teacher's Role 144

**Applications and
Reflections 146**

ideas, which have been directly applied to the classroom, should help you to understand the reasoning behind your students' behavior.

When you complete your reading of this chapter, you should be able to

- interpret students' behaviors according to Erikson's stages of psychosocial development
- appeal to the strengths of each stage, and help students prepare for the crises that await them

- use developmental knowledge to encourage and maintain a secure and free classroom atmosphere
- use developmental knowledge to establish positive relationships with students
- apply Kohlberg's ideas to your classroom, having a firmer idea of the type of moral thinking students are capable of
- formulate moral education techniques through Kohlberg's use of moral dilemmas
- use your ideas of moral development to establish a moral classroom environment

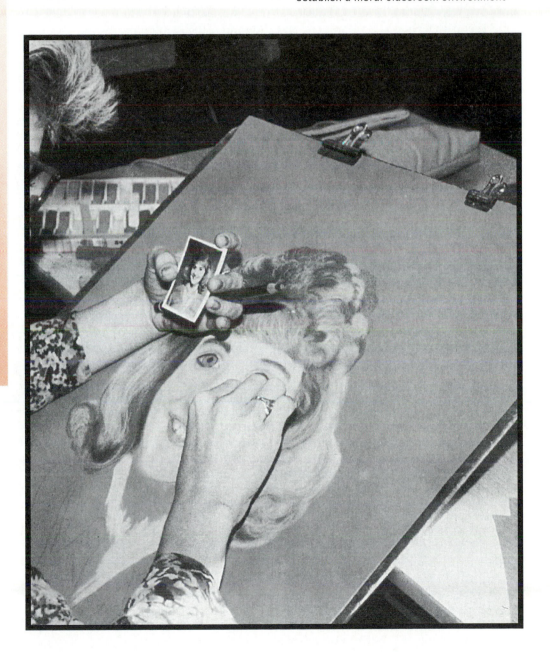

PSYCHOSOCIAL DEVELOPMENT

We are intensely aware today that children are deeply affected by the social agents (family, school, peers, the media) that surround them. By linking children's development to the interactions and interrelationships with the critical agents in their environment, Erik Erikson has dramatically called our attention to the significance of social context (Isenberg, 1987).

Born in Frankfurt, Germany in 1902, Erikson became interested as a young man in both education and psychoanalysis. He came to the United States in 1933 and settled in Boston, where he was the first child psychoanalyst in the city. His work with American Indian tribes and World War II veterans helped Erikson to realize that many emotional problems were due to identity confusion.

Erikson's views on development and the search for identity are widely popular today. He proposed a series of stages of psychosocial development, during each of which an individual has to establish changing concepts of self and reality. During the "working out" of the psychosocial stages, students must grapple with both positive and negative influences as they strive for self-identity.

ERIKSON'S EIGHT STAGES

Erikson believed that personality emerges from a series of inner and outer conflicts that, if resolved, result in a greater sense of self. These crises arise at each of eight stages of life identified by Erikson. Each crisis results in a period of increased vulnerability and heightened potential, and can lead to either maladjustment or increased psychic strength. During the adolescent years, for example, teenagers are besieged by self-doubt—about their bodies, their abilities, their popularity—yet with patience and proper guidance, they can acquire positive self-identities.

In his famous *Childhood and Society* (1950), Erikson stated that *personality develops according to one's ability to interact with the environment.* Society invites this interaction with the environment and encourages and safeguards the successive appearance of the eight stages, the first of which occurs in the first year of life. (The crises, strengths, and major environmental influences that characterize each stage are outlined in table 5.1.)

Erik Erikson, whose psychosocial theory of human development offers insights into the challenges that people face at various stages of their lives.

Stage 1: Trust Versus Mistrust

Erikson believed that a healthy personality requires a sense of trust toward oneself and the world, a trust that develops during the first year of life. Infants derive security and comfort from warm relationships with their parents. Cold parental care and rejection cause mistrust and affect all later development (for an exhaustive summary of human studies, see Rutter, 1980).

As infants develop greater control over their bodies (e.g., more accurate grasping of objects), they learn to trust their bodies as well, thus increasing their psychological sense of security. The world becomes a safe and orderly place as children take their first steps toward personal mastery.

Table 5.1

Erikson's Eight Stages: Crises, Strengths, Influences

Age (years)	Stage	Psychosocial crisis	Psychosocial strength	Environmental influence
1	Infancy	Trust vs. mistrust	Hope	Maternal
2–3	Early childhood	Autonomy vs. shame, doubt	Willpower	Both parents or adult substitutes
4–5	Preschool, nursery school	Initiative vs. guilt	Purpose	Parents, family, friends
6–11	Middle childhood	Industry vs. inferiority	Competence	School
12–18	Adolescence	Identity vs. identity confusion	Fidelity	Peers
18–35	Young adulthood	Intimacy vs. isolation	Love	Partners: spouse/lover friends
35–65	Middle age	Generativity vs. stagnation	Care	Family, society
Over 65	Old age	Integrity vs. despair	Wisdom	All humans

Source: Data from Erik Erikson, *Childhood and Society,* 1950.

Attachment

attachment *Behavior intended to keep a child (or adult) in close proximity to a significant other.*

Development during the first year of life can have long-term consequences, since research demonstrates that attachment (usually to the mother) appears during the last half of the first year (Bowlby, 1969; Ainsworth, 1979). If **attachment** is not nurtured by the mother or other caregiver, children may not develop the trust necessary to establish lasting relationships with others.

Although relationships with parents are a key element in the development of attachment, other developmental factors also contribute to it. For example, a child's inborn temperamental tendency to be fearful or relaxed in unfamiliar situations affects that child's behavior. In other words, children are psychologically different from each other from birth, a fact that has been ignored in the attachment studies (Kagan, 1989). Infants in Erikson's first stage, Trust versus Mistrust, have as much influence on surrounding adults as the adults have on them; this phenomenon is known as **reciprocal interactions.**

reciprocal interactions *Process in which we respond to those around us and they change; their changed behavior then causes changes in us. In the classroom, emphasizes a student's active involvement in teacher-student interactions; that is, students are not merely passive recipients in any exchange.*

Stage 2: Autonomy Versus Shame and Doubt

For Erikson, the theme of the second stage, which usually occurs during toilet training (between the ages of 2 and 3), is **autonomy** versus shame and doubt. During this period, personality is shaped by the child's learning of the meaning of self-control. These years are decisive for establishing a proper balance between standing on one's own feet, and being protected from shame and doubt (Erikson, 1950, p. 223). Parental reactions are crucial, since the objective of this stage is the child's development of self-control with no loss of self-esteem. Loss of self-control because of parental overcontrol results in self-doubt and shame.

autonomy *Erikson's term for a child's growing sense of independence. Attained in stage 2 (Autonomy versus Shame and Doubt).*

Although children need to maintain a sense of trust in a manner calculated to further self-confidence, adults (parents, day-care providers, and nursery school teachers) must also introduce restraints that will help youngsters develop self-control, competence, and maturity. For example, youngsters of this age, when playing in a sandbox, have a tendency to throw sand in the faces of other children. They need to learn not to do things that can hurt other children, even when they are provoked. For many children, these lessons are learned away from home, for these years see the beginning of day care.

Day Care

Almost two-thirds of women with children under 14 and more than one-half of mothers with children under 1 year of age are in the labor force. In fact, the single largest category of working mothers is that of mothers with children under 3 years old (Zigler & Lang, 1991). What happens to these children while their mothers are at work? Obviously, someone must be taking care of these youngsters. It is precisely here that questions are raised about day care. How competent are the individuals who offer day-care services? Is a given day-care center healthy and stimulating? Is it safe? What are the long-term developmental consequences of day-care placement? In light of recent exposés about the sexual abuse of children in some centers, America's parents are demanding answers to these questions.

The development of self-control and the learning of respect for the rights of others requires sensitive parental reactions that must strike a balance among love, understanding, and being firm.

Facts About Day Care   There are about thirty-five to forty thousand "places" providing day-care services (whose principal income is from offering child care) in this country. "Places" is perhaps the best way to describe them, because of the wide variety of circumstances that exist. For example, one mother may charge another mother several dollars to take care of her child. A relative may care for several children in the extended family. Churches, businesses, and charities may run large operations. Some centers may be sponsored by local or state governments as an aid to the less affluent. Others are run on a pay-as-you-go basis. Almost everyone agrees that the best centers are staffed by teachers who specialize in day-care services; about 25 percent of day-care personnel fall into this category.

Developmental Outcomes of Day Care   Regardless of what you may have heard or read, there are no definite conclusions concerning the long-term developmental consequences of day care. One reason is that careful follow-up studies of children who have been in day care are not yet available (Clarke-Stewart, 1993). Such studies are only beginning to appear. Belsky and Rovine (1988) reported on the results of two longitudinal studies of infants and their families. They found that when infants who had received 20 or more hours of nonmaternal care per week reached the age of 12 or 13 months, some of them were insecurely attached. These same infants were more likely to be aggressive and tend to withdraw. Yet this report also contains puzzling data. Over one-half of the infants who received 20 hours weekly of nonmaternal care were securely attached.

These data testify to the uncertainty of our present knowledge, and reinforce the conclusion that we must be careful about making either positive or negative statements concerning day care. Another obstacle in studying the effects of day care has been the use of university-sponsored research centers to do so. These centers are usually lavishly equipped and overstaffed. They simply do not reflect the national norm.

What is your position on day care? Do you think there are both positive and negative outcomes for children as a result of day-care placement? What is the youngest age you think a child should be placed in a day-care center? Why?

Some conclusions about what is needed for quality day care, however, are beginning to come to light. Day-care settings should facilitate the growth and development of young children playing and working together. The equipment and play materials should be attractive and educationally appropriate to help youngsters acquire necessary skills. Finally, instructors need to be sufficiently skilled to aid children in their language and social development.

Educational Implications

Ideally, youngsters should achieve considerable self-control as well as control of their bodies during these years. To accomplish this goal, adults working with young children must make every effort to protect them from injury and to prevent them from harming others. At the same time, children of this age need opportunities to exercise and develop their talents; this will help them to acquire sufficient self-mastery to understand both their limitations and their opportunities.

"Miss Cobb, there's something you should know. We were having a contest to see who could lean out the window the farthest, and Tommy Bishop won."

© Glenn Bernhardt.

How you accomplish these objectives will depend on your individual style of interacting with others and the unique personality of each child. From Erikson's perspective, it is important never to humiliate a child, either physically or verbally, when you must impose restrictions. Your use of firm but tactful restraint will have the result that youngsters recognize and respect you as an authority figure while retaining their sense of autonomy and initiative.

Young children require consistent and reasonable discipline. Since children of this age are so attuned to adult authority, any adult behavior that confuses them can have a lasting impact. As they grow older, they will need to abide by rules; these years are the time for them to acquire respect for reasonable rules reasonably administered. They won't always obey, of course; when you must reprimand, do so, and then as soon as possible offer a warm response to their acceptable behavior.

Children of this age need opportunities to do things for themselves, such as arranging furniture, obtaining materials, and helping around a room. Any such activities that you can devise will help them to gain mastery over themselves and their surroundings, thus contributing to their autonomy.

Young children also need good models. At this age, they love to imitate, so you will have many pertinent opportunities. Use your behavior (as a model) to protect them from unwarranted fears. Because young children have a limited cognitive capacity as well as an aptitude for fantasy, they may become subject to unreasonable anxieties and fears (Morris & Kratochwill, 1983). Table 5.2 lists some common fears that children experience.

Although children experience many normal fears, unreasonable punishment or, conversely, excessive permissiveness can cause them to become unduly fearful of a parent or a teacher, and that fear may transfer to other adults. Your best reaction to a child's unwarranted fear is to listen, to explain, and to set a positive example.

Stage 3: Initiative Versus Guilt

initiative *Erikson's term for children's ability to explore the environment and test their world. Attained in stage 3 (Initiative versus Guilt).*

Children in Erikson's third stage (ages 4 to 5 years) show greater freedom of movement, perfection of language, and expansion of imagination. A sense of **initiative** emerges that will serve as a basis for realistic ambitions and purposes. As Erikson

Table 5.2

Common Fears in Children	
0–6 months	Loss of support; loud noises
7–12 months	Fear of strangers; fear of sudden, unexpected, and looming objects
1 year	Separation from parent; toilet; injury; strangers
2 years	A multitude of fears, including loud noises (vacuum cleaners, sirens/alarms, trucks, and thunder); animals (e.g., large dogs); dark room; separation from parent; large objects/machines; change in personal environment
3 years	Masks; dark; animals; separation from parent
4 years	Parent separation; animals; dark; noises (including at night)
5 years	Animals; "bad" people; dark; separation from parent; bodily harm
6 years	Supernatural beings (e.g., ghosts, witches, "Darth Vader"); bodily injuries; thunder and lightning; dark; sleeping or staying alone; separation from parent
7–8 years	Supernatural beings; dark; fears based on media events; staying alone; bodily injury
9–12 years	Tests and examinations in school; school performance; bodily injury; physical appearance; thunder and lightning; death; dark (low percentage)

From R. J. Morris and T. R. Kratochwill, *Treating Children's Fears and Phobias.* Copyright © 1983 Simon & Schuster International, Hemel Hempstead, Herts, United Kingdom.

noted, the indispensable contribution of this stage to later identity development is to free the child's initiative and sense of purpose for adult tasks that promise fulfillment of human capacities.

Erikson notes that preschoolers realize who they are, have a lively imagination, are mobile, and have a good grasp of language. Their world challenges them to master new tasks, such as learning to read, adapting to school, and dressing themselves. Their growing symbolic ability, which was discussed in chapter 4 in the section on Piaget's preoperational stage, enables them to meet the tasks that Erikson identifies for these years. Parents who encourage children to do things (play, help in the home, etc.) encourage a sense of initiative. Scoffing at children's ideas and efforts produces in them a sense of guilt.

Another interesting development during this stage is the emerging *role of conscience*. Children now have the ability to cope with the environment, but they are also encountering yes and no reactions from their parents. Consequently, they experience guilt feelings when they know they have done something of which parents or teachers disapprove. If children face too many restrictions, they can acquire emotional problems early in life; this fact testifies to the role of play in helping children of this age to adjust.

Annual Edition

The Importance of Play

Play has many benefits for young children. *Play aids cognitive development.* Through play, children learn about the objects in their world; what these objects do (balls roll and bounce), what they consist of (toy cars have wheels), and how they work. To use Piaget's term, children "operate" on objects through play, and also learn behavioral skills that will be of future use. *Play also helps social development.* Playing with others demands a give-and-take that teaches young children the basics of forming relationships. Why are some 4- and 5-year-olds more popular with their classmates than others? Watching closely, you can discover the reasons: decreasing egocentrism, recognition of the rights of others, and a willingness to share. Finally, *play provides an*

The role of play in the early childhood years is especially important because of its influence on physical, cognitive, social, and emotional development.

emotional release. There is not the right-or-wrong, life-and-death feeling that accompanies interactions with adults. Children can be creative without worrying about failure. They frequently release emotional tensions through play.

Youngsters in early childhood have many different experiences that contribute to their socialization. For example, family conditions may change; these changes have different effects on children's development, some more significant than others (Scarr, 1992). A growing problem in our society is the number of homeless children, the majority of whom are under 5 years of age.

Homeless Children

Homelessness has become a serious problem in our society. The homeless today represent a different population from the alcoholic men who once clustered together on skid row. The new homeless population is younger and much more mixed: it includes more single women, more families, and more minorities. Families with young children may be the fastest-growing segment of today's homeless. On any given night, one hundred thousand children in this country will be homeless (Walsh, 1992). These children are also characterized by few social contacts, poor health, and a high level of contact with the criminal justice system. When you realize that 30 percent of the homeless population in the cities is composed of families, you appreciate the impact that homelessness can have upon the development of many children.

The Impact of Homelessness on Development   It is no exaggeration to say that the well-being of children who are homeless is seriously threatened. Defining the homeless as those in emergency shelter facilities with their families, Rafferty and Shinn (1991) stated that these children are particularly vulnerable to a variety of problems. For example, homeless children seem to suffer more than typical children from depression, anxiety, and behavioral problems. We lack the data that enable us to identify the particular aspect of homelessness that causes a child's anxiety or depression. We must certainly consider that parental depression affects children and that children's problems may reflect the parents' feeling of helplessness.

These psychological problems typically translate into educational underachievement. Little research has been done on this issue, other than to show that homeless children do poorly on reading and mathematics tests. This finding should come as no surprise, given that these children have difficulty in finding and maintaining free public education for substantial periods. Missing educational opportunities is bad enough; because of the frequent moves their families make, these children also miss the remedial work they so urgently need. As Rafferty and Shinn (1991) noted, school is an especially critical environment for homeless children, because it can produce a sense of stability that is otherwise lacking.

In her interviews with homeless children, Walsh (1992) noted that children, because of their status and lack of power, cannot directly solve the problem of homelessness. Instead, they concentrate on coping with the emotions that arise from becoming homeless, perhaps by restructuring the circumstances surrounding their homelessness. Younger children, for example, may unrealistically attribute their problems to some external event that is unrelated to them or their parents. Older children may try to explain away the cause, especially if it pertains to a parent. For example, rather than blame a parent's alcoholism or drug use, a youngster may say that the parent is sick or has problems.

The Changing Family

The number of single mothers in our society is growing, but as governmental support increases, there will undoubtedly be more and better day-care services, additional after-school programs for older children, and perhaps greater flexibility in the work schedules of working parents. Children cannot escape the results—positive or negative—of the twists and turns of family living. *Divorce,* particularly, is a phenomenon that a growing number of children of this age are experiencing.

Children of Divorce   Divorce, an increasingly common aspect of family life, affects children in many ways. Not only is their physical way of life changed (perhaps through a move to a new home, or a reduced standard of living), but their psychological lives are also touched (Hetherington et al., 1985). In about two or three years following the divorce, most children have adjusted to living in a single-parent home. This adjustment, however, can once again be shaken by a parent's remarriage. For many children, one change follows another: they lose one parent in the divorce, then they adapt to life with the remaining parent, and then they must adapt again to the addition of at least one family member in a remarriage (Hetherington & Clingempeel, 1992).

Studying the long-term effects of divorce on children, Hetherington and her colleagues (1985, 1989) concluded that divorce has more adverse, long-term effects on boys. Remarriage of a mother who has custody of the children, however, is associated with an *increase* in girls' behavior problems and a slight *decrease* in boys' problems (Hetherington, 1991). The transition period in the first year following the divorce is stressful economically, socially, and emotionally. Conditions then seem to improve, and children in a stable, smoothly functioning home are better adjusted than children in a nuclear family riddled with conflict. Nevertheless, *school achievement may suffer, and impulsivity increases* (Wallerstein & Blakeslee, 1989).

The consequences of divorce inevitably follow children into classrooms, and may take many different forms. Some children may withdraw; others may become aggressive. While you must deal with any of these problems in an evenhanded manner, try to understand the causes of the behavior and offer as much support as possible.

Educational Implications

The characteristics of preschool children have led to a concern for *developmentally appropriate curricula.* The National Association for the Education of Young Children, in a series of papers (Calvert, 1986), has urged greater attention to "learning through active exploration and interaction with adults, other children, and materials." Teachers of these children, as active observers, prepare the environment to be developmentally appropriate. They make sure that the children have toys or objects that will match and challenge their muscular development and coordination as they feel, handle, and manipulate them. Children at the beginning of this period, for example, need to use large crayons when drawing. The best advice for dealing with children of this age is to meet them *on their level,* but still challenge them.

Youngsters who acquire a sense of initiative will bring to the classroom a healthy desire to face challenges. These are the pupils who will try to read a sentence, who will attempt a new activity, who are undaunted by facing the computer. Young children have much to learn about the world, and a well-structured environment—including appropriate objects in a wide variety of colors, plants, and animals—helps them to label and order their world, thus extending cognitive, language, and psychosocial development. Schooling at this level must capitalize on a child's spontaneous learning, thus aiding the development of competence and security, two of the great objectives of this period.

Stage 4: Industry Versus Inferiority

Erikson's next stage occurs between the ages of 6 and 11 years. Children now possess a sense of being able to do things well; they want to win recognition by producing things through their own **industry.** Youngsters in elementary school are coming into

industry   *Erikson's term to describe a child's sense of being able to do things well and desire to win recognition in this way. Attained in stage 4 (Industry versus Inferiority).*

teacher – student

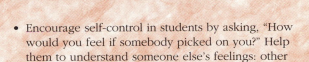

interactions

Erikson's Early Stages

1. A healthy personality requires a sense of trust, toward oneself and the world.
   - If you find yourself working with infants in a day-care setting, have as much physical contact with the infants as possible. For infants, physical contact helps to establish a sense of security and trust.
   - Once separation anxiety appears, be careful of the way that you leave infants. Although you can't be with each child every minute, you can contribute to their psychological comfort and trust in those around them by doing such simple things as putting a familiar toy with a child before you leave.
   - When children are from 1 to 2 years old, think of yourself as a learning consultant. For example, play games that help them acquire a better understanding of the world; take their questions seriously and answer them carefully.
2. For healthy development, children must acquire not only control over their bodies but also self-control.
   - Help students who tend to lose their tempers easily to change. Talk to them and remind them of any times when they maintained control: "Do you remember last week when Jimmy pushed you? You didn't scream; you acted very grown-up. You told him to stop or you would tell me."
   - Stress to your pupils that everybody gets mad and wants to strike out. The difference is, however, that not everybody does strike out. Use examples of children in the class who do not yell or scream every time something goes wrong.
   - Encourage self-control in students by asking, "How would you feel if somebody picked on you?" Help them to understand someone else's feelings: other students don't feel very good when someone constantly tells them they're wrong.
   - Explain to children who "go off the wall" too frequently that they might have to back away from arguments. Nobody likes a "sore loser." Encourage self-esteem in the classroom by occasionally allowing these children to be your helpers. In this way, they can still feel good about themselves even when they lose an argument.
3. With developing control, children begin to manipulate their environments, thus acquiring feelings of competence. (More is said about teaching self-control to students in chap. 6.)
   - Encourage children who have difficulty controlling their emotions to engage in physical activities (such as bike riding, throwing a ball, or running) in which they have physical control.
   - Help children to eliminate jealousy. If others get better grades, remind them of their past accomplishments. You might even put these on special cards as a reminder.
   - Help children to avoid keeping things that annoy them to themselves to the point that they become preoccupied with them. Encourage them to talk to others about those things that bother them.

"Your teacher tells me you've become the class clown."

© Mike Shapiro.

their own: they sense their growing competence, both physical and mental, and if challenges match their abilities, they feel fulfilled. Horizons widen as children encounter a wide variety of people, tasks, and events.

During these years the school becomes a proving ground. Can they establish positive relationships with their teachers? Can they do well in subjects? Are they able to form friendships? Some degree of success contributes to both personal adjustment and social acceptance. Conversely, children who despair of their skills and their status with their peers can easily acquire a sense of inadequacy.

Erikson's ideas of industry and inferiority are particularly relevant for multicultural students. Entering a classroom in which language and customs may seem strange, these pupils may feel overwhelmed by self-doubt. If you encourage them to bring elements of their cultures into the classroom, you help to enhance their self-esteem by accepting their identity as members of particular groups.

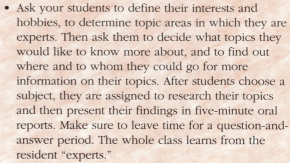

teacher – student

interactions

Erikson's Elementary School Years

1. Elementary school children need to acquire a sense of accomplishment.
   - Congratulate your students out loud for their successes; help students in your class not only to feel proud individually but also to feel proud of one another.
   - Arrange a table in your room labelled "All About Me." This could hold a week-long display of items that are special to a particular child (collections, sports mementos, photos, baby toys, etc.), things that the child brings from home. On Friday, the spotlight child shares what he or she has brought.
   - Ask each child to write a compliment about another child on a white piece of paper with a white crayon. The "invisible ink" papers are then delivered to the designated persons. The recipients paint their papers with watered-down tempera paint. As the students paint, messages appear (as well as smiles on the students' faces as they see the messages).
   - Take a picture of each child on the first day of school. Mount the pictures on a bulletin board. Keep the display up all year long. Outside the hall or in the classroom, reserve a bulletin board as a "brag board." When a child wins an award, writes an outstanding paper, etc., put that child's snapshot on the board. Put the photos in a scrapbook at the end of the year.

   - Ask your students to define their interests and hobbies, to determine topic areas in which they are experts. Then ask them to decide what topics they would like to know more about, and to find out where and to whom they could go for more information on their topics. After students choose a subject, they are assigned to research their topics and then present their findings in five-minute oral reports. Make sure to leave time for a question-and-answer period. The whole class learns from the resident "experts."

2. During these years, children acquire knowledge about the world beyond their families.
   - Ask your children to participate in a "world project" to track down the origins of foreign products. Have students check their clothing labels to find manufacturing locations. Locate these places on a world map and encourage children to speculate about how the items arrived in your area. Next, ask pupils to look through their kitchen cupboards at home. Are any food products from out of the country? Mark these spots on your map, too. And finally, investigate the origins of their toys, appliances, even cars. Help the children develop a growing awareness of how they are "connected" to the rest of the world.
   - Ask children how they got their names. You may discover that some are named after grandparents

Your behavior thus sets an example for your students and motivates multicultural students to participate more fully in classroom activities. You can then use their strength as competent members of their cultures as a bridge to successful classroom work in this new environment, with its challenging tasks (Tiedt & Tiedt, 1990).

Milestones of Middle Childhood

The successful mastery of several developmental tasks guides elementary school children in their quest for growth, fulfillment, and self-identity. One of these tasks is *to sustain self-esteem*. Given their relationships with parents, peers, and teachers, children of this age have varied opportunities either to enhance or to reduce feelings of self-esteem.

Developmental psychologists, educators, parents, and almost everyone who works with children have come to accept the vital role that a child's self-esteem plays in development. What do we mean by self-esteem? A simple definition would be that self-esteem is the way children feel about themselves, or the way they value themselves. The girl who realizes that she is not just a student but a good student and the boy who realizes that he is not just a basketball player but a good basketball player both have good self-esteem.

At about 7 or 8 years of age, children begin to identify their competence in particular activities; this suggests that there are developmental changes in self-esteem. A child coming from a supportive home typically has an inflated sense of self-esteem before beginning school. It isn't until the second grade that pupils' estimation of themselves matches the opinions of those around them, that is, that children's estimations correlate with teacher ratings, test scores, and direct observations (Berk, 1994).

from other countries, or that some received their names simply because of the way they looked when they were born.

- Ask parents to cook ethnic dishes to share with the class while they talk about their countries of origin. Have children bring in items common to their heritage and wear native costumes to school as you study different cultures.
- Have children study folktales from other countries. Discuss common themes and point out differences.
- Explore local history. Visit historical houses; discuss how children lived in earlier days as compared to today.
- Develop ways your pupils can keep in touch with the community: take field trips to manufacturing plants, museums, hospitals, community centers, nursing homes, etc.
- Celebrate Grandparents' and Senior Citizens' Days, when older residents are invited to spend a day at school. Build a unit around these visits—perhaps called "Living History"—and search for ways to record and publish the information you gather (perhaps in a local paper).
- Adopt a downtown building and learn as much as you can about it and its present and former inhabitants. With scissors, rulers, and paints, create a replica of Main Street. Have the project supervised by local shopkeepers.

3. In the elementary school years, children learn from almost everything that they do.
- Have your students share a cooking experience to promote social interaction and language skills. As they feel successful in completing (and eating) a cooking project, their self-images are enhanced.
- After a tour or a field trip, use dramatics to encourage your children to reenact what they observed.
- Encourage creative thinking during your pupils' free time by setting up centers where students may write and "publish" their own books; make puppets and write short skits; design posters; or create their own "inventions."
- Plan a celebration like a fiesta or a fair to study other times or countries. Relate your language arts activities to the celebration. Include food, art, handicrafts, and songs.
- Explore science through nature walks. Write a class journal about the experiences of your walks. Have the children make clay models or drawings of what they see on their walks. Design murals with your class about what they observe.
- Invite the children to bring in their insect collections from home. Review the life cycle of the monarch butterfly. Make a hands-on bulletin board or devise an activity in which pupils can demonstrate the scientific words they have learned.

Children's self-esteem is enhanced by their ability to acquire a *sense of physical safety*. Children who feel physically secure aren't afraid of being harmed. This experience helps them to develop feelings of confidence. These feelings of physical security then contribute to a *sense of emotional security*. Children who aren't humiliated or subjected to sarcasm feel safe emotionally, and this security then translates into a willingness to trust others. Children who know "who they are," that is, who possess a *sense of identity,* have achieved a degree of self-knowledge that enables them to take responsibility for their actions and relate well with others (Parker & Asher, 1993). Finally, they acquire a *sense of competence* that helps them to feel confident in their growing abilities and makes them willing to try to learn to do new things and persevere until they achieve mastery.

Educational Implications

Erikson aptly described the elementary school years in this way: "I am what I learn." For youngsters at this stage, learning occurs in almost everything they do. They learn through play, from their peers, in sports and other activities, and, of course, in school.

Elementary school youngsters understandably are eager to use the abilities that they developed during their first 6 or 7 years. This eagerness means that they will inevitably encounter failure as well as success, especially in their schoolwork. The balance between these two outcomes will decisively affect a child's self-esteem. Your task is to channel the child's energy and talent in positive directions.

Teachers can do much to help pupils gain a sense of mastery over the environment by matching content with ability (or level of cognitive development, as emphasized by

Piaget) so that they can achieve at their own levels. Predicting what your pupils can do from their behavior (recall Piaget's understanding of *content*), from tests, and from their classroom work, you can direct them to tasks that are challenging but within their range of ability. Children can gain a feeling of competence, a sense of being capable, if their performance meets tangible goals.

Moreover, achievement and acceptance go hand in hand in this socially significant stage. Youngsters of this age who do well in the spelling bees, who become team leaders in subject matter areas, and who read well usually are popular. Thus your efforts to match content with cognitive level—*for all pupils*—have intellectual, emotional, and social consequences.

Stage 5: Identity Versus Identity Confusion

Erikson's fifth stage (from ages 12 to 18 years) sees the end of childhood and the beginning of adulthood. Youngsters become concerned with what others think of them, and peer opinion plays a large part in how they think of themselves. If uncertainty at this time results in *identity confusion,* a bewildered youth may withdraw, run away, or turn to drugs. Youngsters faced with the question "Who am I?" may be unable to answer. The challenges are new; the tasks are difficult; the alternatives are bewildering. Needless to say, adults must have patience and understanding.

The complexity of modern society raises challenging issues in an adolescent's search for identity. The support of family, school, and friends can be a positive, even decisive, force in this process.

Minority children may be particularly susceptible to these concerns. To help them cope with their search for identity, Spencer and Markstrom-Adams (1990) recommended that everything possible should be done to keep these youths in school, attempt to make them more health conscious, identify potential social support systems, help them develop a sense of group pride, and, finally, sensitize teachers to their needs.

According to Erikson, the young in our society are searching for something or someone to be true to. They yearn for stability in an age of change, and their search may lead to extremes. But the search is a time for testing both self and the world.

The Search for Identity

Adolescence is the period Erikson is most often associated with, mainly because of his speculations about the adolescent **identity crisis.** Faced with a combination of physical, sexual, and cognitive changes joined with heightened adult expectations and peer pressure, adolescents understandably feel insecure about themselves—who they are and where they're going. By the end of adolescence, those who have resolved their personal crises have achieved a sense of identity. They know who they are. Those who remain locked in doubt and insecurity experience what Erikson calls **identity confusion.** Erikson's views on identity have generated considerable speculation, theorizing, and research.

identity crisis *Erikson's term for those situations, usually in adolescence, that cause humans to make major decisions about their identities.*

identity confusion *The state of human beings who experience doubt and uncertainty about who they are.*

Equal Education for All—Does That Include Girls?

In the introduction to a report commissioned by the American Association of University Women, *How Schools Short-change Girls* (1992), the authors wrote:

> There is clear evidence that the educational system is not meeting girls' needs. Girls and boys enter school roughly equal in measured ability. On some measures of school readiness, such as fine motor control, girls are ahead of boys. Twelve years later, girls have fallen behind their male classmates in key areas such as higher level mathematics and measures of self-esteem. Today's students are tomorrow's citizens, parents and workers. It is they who will bear the responsibility for maintaining a vital and creative society. To leave girls on the sidelines in discussions of educational reform is to deprive ourselves of the full potential of half of our work force, half of our citizenry and half of the parents of the next generation.

Issue

Many educators attribute the drop in self-esteem to the negative message the curriculum delivers over and over to girls: Men's lives count for more. Curriculum developers should be sensitive to this criticism, and mediators of the curriculum should strive to "correct" it whenever possible.

Answer: Pro

In reviewing their curriculum content and materials, teachers can ask themselves if females are being adequately represented and justly portrayed. Is the reading list for the year authored mostly by men? Are the stories about boys' adventures? Are the masterpieces for discussion all, or mostly all, works by males? Are the scientists and mathematicians cited all male? Teachers should take the time to make necessary adjustments to represent the interests of all their learners.

Answer: Con

The realities of the curriculum are such that students are responsible for knowing certain information. If women are included in the curriculum that is well and good, but a teacher cannot dismiss the scope of a curriculum based on any one issue. Teachers have barely enough time as it is to do their work. They cannot be expected to spend all the hours it would take to revamp curricula and to supplement the students' lessons with additional information.

Issue

Interactions within the classroom are as important as the curriculum for contributing to lowered self-image in girls. Studies have shown that boys receive more precise teacher comments than do girls, for both scholarship and conduct (Jones, 1989). Teachers should be trained in classroom interaction strategies in order to establish more equitable classroom environments.

Answer: Pro

Teachers have the power to create a classroom community where all learners are valued equally. But teachers are not always aware of the way they interact with their students; thus, in-service training sessions would benefit teachers and all of their students.

Answer: Con

Teachers have to be able to respond to the needs of the classroom quickly. When teachers are asking questions or commenting on behaviors, they do not always have the time or presence of mind to reflect and consider whether it is a boy or a girl who has a hand up or is misbehaving. Teachers cannot be expected to keep mental tallies of how many times they have responded to boys versus how many times they have responded to girls. Most teachers try to make sure they are responding to the individual needs of their students, regardless of gender.

Issue

There are several strategies that have been identified as promoting a more gender-equitable learning environment. One of these is single-sex cooperative learning groups (Gross, 1993). Teachers should experiment with different groupings within their classrooms, keeping the gender issue in the front of their minds.

Answer: Pro

Teachers often rearrange their students for different subjects. It is very easy to add the gender dimension to the thinking that goes into forming these groups.

Answer: Con

There is not always the luxury of making ideal groups. In the lower grades especially, the socialization that takes place within the classroom is as important as academic work. What kind of message would the teacher be sending to encourage these children to sit only with other boys or other girls? We must teach our students to work together.

For example, Marcia (1966, 1980) concluded from a series of studies that adolescents seem to respond to the need to make choices about their identity (particularly regarding career, religion, or politics) in one of four ways:

1. **Identity diffusion,** or the inability to commit themselves to choices; the lack of a sense of direction.
2. **Identity foreclosure,** or the making of a commitment only because someone else has prescribed a particular choice; the condition of being "outer-directed."
3. **Identity moratorium,** or the desire to make a choice at some time in the future but the inability to do so now.
4. **Identity achievement,** or the commitment of themselves to choices about identity and the maintaining of those commitments under all conditions.

Educational psychologists have been increasingly concerned about the connection between emotional well-being and success in school. Consequently, you should be alert to those students who appear to have low self-esteem. Fortunately, there are programs in which students can participate to cultivate their self-esteem and improve their academic functioning. The school's work in reaching troubled students early can prevent many problems, such as the eruption of violent behavior.

Schools and Violence

On June 3, 1986, the state of Florida charged 9-year-old Jeffrey Bailey with murder. Making sure that no one else was around, he had pushed a 3-year-old boy who couldn't swim into a pool, then pulled up a chair to watch the boy drown. Later, when the police had pieced together the circumstances of the murder, they arrested Jeffrey, who was described as calm, nonchalant, and enjoying the attention (Magid & McKelvey, 1987).

This startling story is true, and others like it are appearing with increasing frequency in our nation's newspapers. Are these children in our classrooms? Yes, and teachers are often the first to identify potential problems, as early as preschool and kindergarten. Before we examine the phenomenon of violence, especially school violence, however, we would be well advised to avoid the dramatic. Jeffrey's case, while true, is exceptional. As Wilson (1993) noted, one of the reasons that these stories are so sensational is that they are *unusual*. They are also shocking, and so inevitably attract attention. For example, although 1.75 million juveniles were arrested in 1990 (Uniform Crime Reports, 1991), almost all these arrests were for out-of-school offenses such as purse snatching or car theft.

The Roots of Violent Behavior   In their massive study of crime and human nature, Wilson and Herrnstein (1985) noted that there is clear evidence of the positive association between past and future criminal behavior, giving rise to the maxim that the best predictor of crime is past criminal behavior.

Some of the causes of crime include *biological and psychological causes* (physical appearance, psychopathology), *behavioral causes* (impulsivity, attitudes, values), *home and family conditions* (broken homes, family tensions), *peers* (gangs), and *the media* (especially television). This abbreviated list illustrates the meaning of the statement that the causes of crime are multiple, complex, and interactive. Family conditions may cause criminal behavior in one child but not in another; that is, one child may experience the environment quite differently than another does. Surveys have repeatedly shown educators to agree that a major cause of their students' problems is the lack of parental involvement in their children's lives (Bobbitt & Rohr, 1993).

Today's criminologists believe that a tendency to commit crime is established early in life, perhaps as soon as the preschool years (Nagin & Farrington, 1992). The single best predictor of adolescent criminal behavior is a history of early school antisocial be-

Did you experience any sense of "identity confusion" when you were an adolescent? If so, what caused it? If not, how did you avoid it?

identity diffusion   *An inability to commit oneself to choices; the lack of a sense of direction.*

identity foreclosure   *The making of a commitment under pressure, not as the result of the resolution of a crisis.*

identity moratorium   *The desire to make a choice but the inability to do so.*

identity achievement   *Committing oneself to choices about identity and maintaining that commitment.*

havior. In studies of delinquent youths, another important finding was that during the middle years (ages 7 to 12), troublesome students tend to form groups that encourage antisocial acts (Walker & Sylwester, 1991).

These findings about the initial appearance of delinquent behavior lead to the conclusion that most intervention programs come too late (Zigler, Taussig, & Black, 1992). For example, in their study of fifth-grade antisocial boys, Walker & Sylwester (1991) found that by the seventh grade, 21 of the 40 most antisocial boys had been arrested 68 times for criminal behavior. These authors suggested that three simple measures would have predicted the later problems of these boys:

• teachers' ratings of social skills;
• negative playground behavior of the boys and their playmates;
• disciplinary contacts with the principal's office.

You can see, then, that by the time children are identified and placed in programs in the late middle and adolescent years, they are well on the way to serious trouble. This fact has increased the interest in early childhood programs. By seeing the child as part of a system of social institutions (family, school, community), well-designed programs can help parents to interact with these institutions and secure needed help, in such forms as health care, assistance in improving child-rearing practices, and counseling (Burke, 1991).

Educational Implications

For teachers working with adolescents, helping students to integrate the physical, sexual, and cognitive changes of adolescence and focus on particular and clearly defined goals becomes the crucial task, one whose successful attainment leads to healthy feelings of identity in the students. Teachers can help their students acquire psychosocial maturity by treating them as *almost adult,* providing them with independence, freedom, and respect. Give them the chance to discuss, argue, and present their own views, always within the framework of classroom control. *Challenge them* with realistic goals, coordinating classroom activities with college and career choices. For example, have them research ways in which the math or science that they are studying in class relates to job skills.

Be sure to use materials that are both biologically and psychologically appropriate. If you have a student who has difficulty reading at the secondary level, for example, try to find reading material that is interesting but not too difficult (high in interest, low in vocabulary); a student like this would resist using a reader from an obviously lower level. With students of this age, *constantly recall the issue of identity versus identity confusion.* Help your students to discover their strengths and weaknesses through their classroom work. For example, suggest they read stories in which the characters work out personal problems, and in so doing find out about themselves.

Finally, if you find yourself involved with disruptive students, encourage, support, and participate in pertinent intervention programs. Walker and Sylvester (1991) identified several core elements in worthwhile intervention programs. These include *the school's leadership role in establishing the program* as soon as students' antisocial behavior begins to appear (the earlier the better). The program should include instruction in critical personal, academic, and social skills that these at-risk students need for school success; a vital aspect of this instruction would be the interest and help of peer and teacher mentors. Also important is *a brief training program for parents* that emphasizes awareness of their children's activities and the parents' appropriate involvement in their children's lives. Among other things, such a training program would stress the skillful use of praise and rewards (stressing the positive), coupled with fair discipline.

The United States Senate recently approved a crime bill that authorized the spending of *three billion dollars* to finance the building of ten regional prisons, and *another*

teacher – student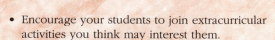

Erikson's Adolescent Years

1. During the adolescent years, teenagers engage in excruciating self-scrutiny.
   - Consider giving your teenage students "free time." Have an interesting classroom full of learning aids, with interest areas (containing books, microscopes, educational games, etc.) easily accessible to students. Let students use the items at their discretion. Establish a few rules for "free time": only a certain number are allowed in any one area at a time; when the teacher says time is up, students must clean up the areas in which they are working. Then, as students work independently, you walk around, talking, explaining when asked, but mainly listening. During this time you demonstrate your trust in the students; they in turn reveal the academic areas in which they are weak. They may also reveal personal problems, as well as topics that interest them.
   - Have each student write a journal entry and submit it to you. Tell students they can write about anything they wish. Many will write about personal problems. After all are submitted, you write back, answering their questions and commenting on the information in the entries.
   - Develop communication strategies like rap sessions and pep talks. If students are upset about something, get them to ask: Is this really worth getting upset about? Present hypothetical situations similar to their experiences and have the students judge whether those matters warrant such strong reactions. If students feel that they do, ask why. Help them to see other solutions to the situations.
   - Encourage your students to give themselves a pat on the back when they handle personal situations competently.
2. Rapidly occurring developmental changes—physical, sexual, cognitive, social—can lead to an identity crisis in an adolescent.
   - Develop your own sensitive responsiveness towards students' emotional needs.
   - Encourage your students to join extracurricular activities you think may interest them.
   - Coordinate programs with guidance and career counselors that will help them plan for their futures.
   - Keep in touch with parents by telephone or by personally inviting them to school programs.
3. Through classroom work, teachers can help students to acquire a needed sense of identity.
   - Develop academic units that will highlight their expertise. You may have a student in your class who has traveled to a country you are studying. If so, in a social studies class, encourage the student who has travelled to share experiences with the class.
   - Stress the skill of communication. By being able to express how they feel in groups and with individuals and by learning how to listen, teenagers will realize that they are not the only human beings who are confused. They will also learn numerous ways to deal with their fears.
   - Encourage teenagers to be assertive. In highly stressful situations, they can identify and relieve their stress by asking questions and expressing their needs.
   - Teach them problem-solving strategies. Show them how to break a problem down into a series of steps so that it no longer seems mountainous. Problem solving also involves thinking about alternative ways to deal with a situation, realizing that it is not necessary to respond in the same way every single time something happens.
   - Be sympathetic to the student who is not doing well, who is showing signs of buckling under accumulated pressures, or is withdrawing from situations. Teenagers often need a confidant in such cases.

three billion dollars for boot camps and other programs for young offenders. In that light, the cost-effectiveness as well as the need and the potential for success of early school-sponsored programs is enormous (Herbert, 1993).

Stage 6: Intimacy Versus Isolation

Erikson's sixth stage, Intimacy versus Isolation, encompasses the years of young adulthood (ages 18 to 35). Erikson believes that a sense of **intimacy** goes beyond being

intimacy *Erikson's term for the ability to be involved with another without fearing a loss of self-identity. Attained in stage 6 (Intimacy versus Isolation).*

Sharing the experience of different generations enriches development.

generativity *Erikson's term for productive and creative responsibility for the next generation. Attained in stage 7 (Generativity versus Stagnation).*

integrity *Erikson's term for the ability to look back and see meaning in life. Attained in stage 8 (Integrity versus Despair).*

sexual, and involves the capacity to develop a true and mutual psychosocial intimacy with friends, the ability to care for others without fearing a loss of self-identity. Young people of this age continue to develop their identity by close relationships with others. If the young adult fails to acquire a sense of intimacy with others, a sense of isolation may appear. Relationships are avoided, and there is a refusal to commit to others.

Stage 7: Generativity Versus Stagnation

During middle age, from about ages 35 to 65 years, individuals think about the future of both society and their own children. An outstanding characteristic of this period is care for others, which implies an obligation to guide the next generation by passing on desirable social values. If a sense of **generativity** (which is similar to productivity and creativity) is lacking, individuals may stagnate, suffering from morbid self-concern. Basic to a sense of generativity is care: individuals assume responsibility for the well-being of the next generation.

Stage 8: Integrity Versus Despair

Erikson's eighth stage is attained in old age (65 years and over). As Erikson (1950) stated, those individuals who have taken care of things and people over the years and have adapted to the triumphs and disappointments of life are the people who reap the harvest of the first seven stages. These persons, able to view their lives with satisfaction and accept their ups and downs, have achieved a sense of **integrity.** This term implies that an individual looks back and sees meaning in life. No despair over age, failure, or missed opportunities clouds this outlook. Basic to a sense of integrity is the quality of wisdom, a detached yet active concern with life and its meaning.

For the Classroom

In a thoughtful commentary on the role of schools, Erikson (1968) stated that children require systematic instruction. He believed that good teachers, those who are trusted and respected by the community, know how to alternate play with work, games with study. They also know how to work well with those students to whom school is just not important right now, something to endure rather than enjoy.

Effective teachers know how to pace their instruction to maximize learning. (This topic is discussed in greater detail in chap. 12.) When we link the importance of pacing to Erikson's comments, we can see that optimal scheduling and time on task demand a good knowledge of students: their attention spans, interests, and motivation.

Regardless of the level at which you teach, your students will be on the move. Elementary school students may move from room to room for special projects, assignments, and special classes (reading, music, art, science, and physical education, among others). At the secondary level, students move from class to class and to various locations for study periods, lunch periods, and free periods.

Teachers quickly become aware of the classroom implications of these activities and build their techniques around them. For example, pupils coming into the classroom from recess need a few minutes to settle down. Adolescents returning from a lunch period usually are not ready to immerse themselves instantly in a subject; they must be led into it through questions, announcements, or other activities that set the tone for instruction.

Remember that student attitudes toward school itself will affect your pacing. In the early grades, pupils tend to be swept up in the academic life of the school. It is why they are there. At the secondary level, however, new dimensions are added to the school experience; learning must compete with friendships, peer pressure, and rivalries. Good teachers accept these facts of school life and build them into their planning.

Erikson's message is clear: Make every effort possible to understand your students, and the teacher-learner interaction can be both productive and enjoyable for you and your students.

MORAL DEVELOPMENT

What do we mean by the term *moral?* The very use of the word can cause heated debate. Consequently, educators approach the topic cautiously, if at all. However, in a time of terrorism, assassinations, nuclear arms, war, and a burgeoning drug culture, moral education deserves consideration.

What is the school's role in moral education? Some believe that moral issues do not belong in the classroom; others state that moral education goes on in every classroom every day. Students learn about and discuss revolution (including its "moral causes") in history classes. As they discuss current events, they must address the issue of honesty in government leaders. Other moral concerns arise in class after class. Given these realities, many schools have felt the necessity to address the role of moral development through education.

Even if your school has not initiated any formal program, you will find it useful to be aware of the theory and research that attempt to describe the moral development of your students (Stigler et al., 1990). Teachers are faced with an unavoidable fact: they make moral decisions every day on such real issues as stealing, lying, and cheating. Schab (1991), interviewing thousands of adolescents from 1969 to 1989, found that the students themselves were pessimistic about the increase in cheating in school.

Jean Piaget was one of the first psychologists to consider the moral development of children. He formulated his ideas on moral development from observations of children playing a game of marbles. Watching the children, talking to them, and applying his cognitive theory to their actions, he identified the following stages of moral development: how children actually conform to rules.

- *Stage 1.* Young children simply play, making no attempt to conform to rules. Piaget (1965) referred to this as the *stage of motor rules.*
- *Stage 2.* Between about 3 and 6 years of age, children seem to imitate the rule behavior of adults, but they still play by themselves and for themselves. Piaget called this the *egocentric stage.*
- *Stage 3.* During the seventh and eighth years, children attempt to play by rules, even though the rules are only vaguely understood. This is the *stage of incipient cooperation.*
- *Stage 4.* Finally, between the ages of 11 and 12, children play strictly by the rules. Piaget called this the *stage of codification of rules.*

After youngsters reach stage 4, they realize that rules emerge from the shared agreement of those who play the game, and that therefore rules can be changed by mutual agreement. They gradually understand that intent is an important part of determining right and wrong, and their decreasing egocentrism permits them to see how

Table 5.3

	Kohlberg's Stages of Moral Development	
Level	**Description**	**Stage**
I. Preconventional (about 4–10 years)	Children respond mainly to cultural control to avoid punishment and attain satisfaction. There are two stages:	**Stage 1** Punishment and obedience. Children obey rules and orders to avoid punishment; there is no concern about moral rectitude.
		Stage 2 Naive instrumental behaviorism. Children obey rules but only for pure self-interest; they are vaguely aware of fairness to others but only for their own satisfaction. Kohlberg introduces the notion of reciprocity here: "You scratch my back, I'll scratch yours."
II. Conventional (about 10–13 years)	Children desire approval, both from individuals and society. They not only conform, but actively support society's standards. There are two stages:	**Stage 3** Children seek the approval of others, the "good boy–good girl" mentality. They begin to judge behavior by intention: "She meant to do well."
		Stage 4 Law-and-order mentality. Children are concerned with authority and maintaining the social order. Correct behavior is "doing one's duty."
III. Postconventional (13 years and over)	If true morality (an internal moral code) is to develop, it appears during these years. The individual does not appeal to other people for moral decisions; they are made by an "enlightened conscience." There are two stages:	**Stage 5** An individual makes moral decisions legalistically or contractually; that is, the best values are those supported by law because they have been accepted by the whole society. If there is conflict between human need and the law, individuals should work to change the law.
		Stage 6 An informed conscience defines what is right. People act, not from fear, approval, or law, but from their own internalized standards of right or wrong.

From L. Kohlberg, "Moral Stages and Moralization: The Cognitive Developmental Approach" in *Moral Development and Behavior: Theory, Research, and Social Issues,* edited by Thomas Lickona. Copyright © 1976 Holt, Rinehart & Winston, Inc. Reprinted by permission of Thomas Lickona.

others view their behavior. Peers help here, because in the mutual give-and-take of peer relations, they are not forced to accept an adult view. This is referred to as the *morality of cooperation.*

KOHLBERG'S THEORY OF MORAL DEVELOPMENT

Fascinated with the study of a child's moral development during his doctoral work at the University of Chicago, Lawrence Kohlberg (1927–1987) attempted to apply Piaget's cognitive rationale to moral development. His doctoral dissertation forced a rethinking of the traditional ideas on moral development. After teaching at the University of Chicago for six years, Kohlberg accepted an invitation to join the Harvard faculty, where he continued his longitudinal studies of moral development until his death.

Kohlberg believed that moral stages emerge from a child's active thought about moral issues and decisions (Kohlberg, 1975; Colby et al., 1983). Kohlberg's theory of moral development describes the behavior of human beings from about 4 years of age through adulthood, and traces moral development through three levels that encompass six stages in all. (Be sure to distinguish stages from levels as you read this section; if you feel any confusion, be sure to check table 5.3.) Passage through the six stages occurs by successive transformations of a child's cognitive structures. The six stages are grouped into three levels: *preconventional* (4 to 10 years), *conventional* (10 to 13 years), and *postconventional* (13 years and over).

Kohlberg believed that moral judgment requires us to weigh the claims of others against self-interest. Thus youngsters must overcome their egocentrism before they can legitimately make moral judgments. Children who still believe that the world centers on them can't recognize the legitimate claims of others. Also, the level of moral development (what one knows) may differ from the content of moral judgment (what one does). That is, people may know what is right but do things they know are wrong.

Kohlberg's six stages of moral development are illustrated in table 5.3.

Level 1: Preconventional Morality

Moral development begins during infancy when children are rewarded for what their parents believe is right and punished for wrongdoing. With cognitive growth, moral reasoning appears and control, as we have seen, gradually begins to shift from that based on external sources to a more internal self-control.

For youngsters at Kohlberg's **preconventional level** (approximately ages 4 to 10), punishment and obedience still determine what is right or wrong. As their abstract abilities increase, however, youngsters begin to understand that if they do action A, they will be punished, while action B will bring something pleasant. Not concerned with moral correctness, children basically try to avoid unpleasant consequences.

preconventional level
Kohlberg's first level of moral development, from about 4 to 10 years of age, when children respond mainly to rewards and punishment.

Educational Implications

Because young children are highly dependent on adults for their ideas of right and wrong, they are particularly susceptible to being taught, both directly and by example, basic moral principles such as honesty, trustworthiness, and cooperativeness. Try to *reinforce examples of desired behavior:* praise a child in front of the other children for returning money found in the room. *Encourage young children in higher-order thinking.* Have them talk things over with you, giving you the chance to specify what is right or wrong, but also to explain why. "Why shouldn't you take your brother's money from the table?" "Yes, you probably would be punished; but you wouldn't want anyone to steal from you, would you?" *Teach directly;* set an example; use stories, movies, school plays, and where possible, urge your students to think about *why* actions are right or wrong.

To teachers and parents meeting youngsters at stage 2 in this first level, Lickona (1983) suggested tolerance of the youngster's changed concept of the adult-child relationship, that is, children's awareness that *they* have their own ideas. Also, adults can possibly use this changed concept to reason with youngsters: if I do something that pleases you, isn't it right that you should do something to please me?

Elementary school children obey because they either expect something in return or want to avoid punishment. Urge them, when you can, to move beyond this level of moral reasoning by helping them to be more sensitive to the feelings of others. When they hurt a brother, sister, or friend, talk about this with them and help them to understand what has happened. Appeal to your expectations for them, rather than have them concentrate on rewards and punishment.

Level 2: Conventional Morality

Moral development during the middle childhood years continues to develop from the merger of two influences, authority and mutuality (Kohlberg, 1975). Children at the **conventional level** of moral development are still susceptible to authority, but cognitive and psychosocial changes are beginning to produce differences in outlook. For example, youngsters realize that the opinions and feelings of others matter: "What I do might hurt someone else."

By the end of the period, children clearly include intention in their thinking. For the typical 6-year-old, stealing is bad because "I might get punished"; for the 11- or

conventional level *Kohlberg's second level of moral development, from about 10 to 13 years of age, when children desire approval from both others and society.*

teacher – student

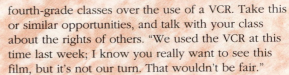

Moral Development—The Early Years

1. Moral development occurs because of a child's active thought about moral issues and decisions, and interactions with others about these matters.

   - Pose a situation for your class in which each class member pretends to be the teacher. The teacher in the story is upset because he knows that someone in his class is breaking bottles on the playground, but no one will admit it. The teacher must decide if he should punish the whole class or ask class members if they know who did it. Have each of the pupils write down what they would do if they were the teacher. After they have done this, use their answers for class discussions.

   - Ask your pupils what they would do in this situation. You have just seen your best friend cheat on an important test that will decide who receives the class prize. Should you tell the teacher? Should you pretend you didn't see it? What will you say to your friend later? If you were the teacher and discovered it, what would you do? Why?

   - You probably will want to structure situations in which boys and girls work together. Ask your class what they would do if, while the class was working in teams of two boys or two girls, one of the girls was sick and couldn't come to school. Should a team of two boys work with the girl who was in school? Do you think the girl would want to work with the boys? Shouldn't boys and girls work together?

2. Moral judgments necessitate weighing the claims of others against self-interest.

   - It may happen that two of your students constantly are "at each other." The tension between them may even flow into your classroom. Have a discussion with them in which you act as moderator. Try to get each of them to see the other's point of view and work out a plan so that when one irritates the other, they won't start to fight immediately.

   - You will inevitably be faced with a situation in which your pupils can only think of themselves. It may be as simple as a time conflict between two

fourth-grade classes over the use of a VCR. Take this or similar opportunities, and talk with your class about the rights of others. "We used the VCR at this time last week; I know you really want to see this film, but it's not our turn. That wouldn't be fair."

   - One way of getting your pupils to think about the needs and wishes of others is to form groups that must solve individual problems. As pupils work together, they are forced to take the viewpoints of others into consideration.

   - Elementary school children love to use the telephone. This is an excellent way to introduce a language lesson, perhaps on pragmatics. As you do, you can emphasize that other family members may also like to use (or need to use) the phone.

3. Moral reasoning can be advanced by challenging children to think of moral issues at a higher level.

   - Use classic stories (such as *Huckleberry Finn,* in which the relationship between Huck and Jim changed as Huck moved beyond mere self-interest to a concern for Jim).

   - Engage a student in a role play in which the character acts on moral principles higher than those of the student. Have the student identify those qualities in the character's personality that are most admired.

   - History is a great teacher. Have two of your students portray a parent and son discussing the son's desire not to serve in Vietnam. Have them answer questions such as these: Why should I go? Is it better (morally) to serve or not to go? (This activity correlates well with almost any historical period.)

   - Opportunities to discuss ways of improving race relations are an integral part of most social studies curricula. Involve your students in a discussion of busing as a means of insuring racial equality in the schools. Use questions like these: "Why do some people oppose having their children bused?" "Why are others in favor of it?" "Why do people become part of a mob?"

Do you think cheating is a serious problem in our schools? Or do you believe that "everyone does it," so we shouldn't worry about it?

12-year-old, stealing may be bad because "it takes away from someone else." During the elementary school years, children move from judging acts solely by their enormity or the degree of punishment they incur to judging intention and motivation.

A new level of moral reasoning—wanting to be a good person to please others—appears in the middle to late elementary school years and lasts into the teens (Kohlberg, 1975). This turn to adult authority is marked, and a youngster's developing conscience is shaped mainly by parents. Toward the end of the period, peers also become influential.

These two sources of influence for elementary school children—adults and peers—can cause a frustrating dilemma when the actions of either come into conflict with what a child's changing cognitive capacity determines is wrong. Again, we are reminded that a youngster's understanding of moral right or wrong is no guarantee of appropriate moral action.

Educational Implications

We can draw certain conclusions about moral development from the cognitive and psychosocial characteristics of elementary school children. For example, *they can reason about their actions,* although their level of moral reasoning may not be an accurate indication of their moral behavior. *They also are influenced strongly by both adults and peers.* These conclusions may point a teacher in different directions in the effort to improve the children's moral reasoning: you can appeal to their reason and also influence them by your own attitude.

Teachers can use discussions of moral dilemmas (see Issues & Answers, above) to assess children's level of moral reasoning and to enable them to test the limits of that reasoning. To an 8-year-old child, for example, you might pose the following dilemma: "You need money for a ticket to a skating party and you find a wallet with $10.00 in it, but the wallet also contains the owner's name and address." Question the child about returning the wallet: "You found it, so would keeping the money be stealing?" "Why should you return it?" "What if you don't get a reward?" If the child says, "I might get into trouble," you have identified a stage I child.

By varying your questions, you will discover the range of the child's moral reasoning. Your knowledge of the upper limits is a yardstick for measuring that child's behavior and a help to you in motivating the child to act at the appropriate level.

Level 3: Postconventional Morality

Controversy surrounds Kohlberg's **postconventional** level: Do people actually reach and pass through this level? As youths move into the teenage period, they seem to be equally divided between Kohlberg's stage 2 and stage 3; that is, they retain elements of both preconventional and conventional moral reasoning (Colby et al., 1983). By the

postconventional level
Kohlberg's third level of moral development when individuals act according to an enlightened conscience.

end of adolescence, most are solidly entrenched in stage 3, in the conventional level. Teenagers want to do the "right thing," but their reasoning remains clouded by their dependence on others. Adults, primarily teachers and parents, may advise behavior that is the opposite of what their peers advise, and this can lead to conflict. For example, adolescents whose friends are saying, "Well, the clubs are open till two o'clock, so it must be okay to stay out" may have trouble with parents who are saying, "One o'clock and no later." It is in these situations that treating adolescents as "almost adults" by reasoning with them can prove valuable.

Although "other-directedness" characterizes adolescents' judgments, their thinking represents a more abstract and sophisticated mode of thought. Cognitive subtleties appear in stage 3 thinking: no longer bound solely by personal concerns, adolescents consider the reactions of others.

Educational Implications

The developmental changes of the teenage years explain many of the conflicts that seem to buffet stage 3 youth. Frequently, in critical self-examination, they dislike what they see; they become desperate to be popular and retreat into "everybody's doing it" excuses. Working with teenagers requires some special strategies, such as the need to *maintain as positive a personal relationship as possible.* Reason with them by trying to explain your thinking; talk things over with them as often as seems feasible; don't dictate to them.

Help adolescents to form a good self-image. Stress their strengths and absolutely refuse to compare them to others. As you do, be aware of the opportunity to *try to teach moral values by example.* In spite of apparent unconcern, teenagers are impressed by displays of fairness and honesty. Provide a classroom atmosphere in which honesty prevails, and you will have taken a major step toward enlisting class cooperation. Conversations with high school teachers reinforce this point. Secondary school teachers believe that today's students have few heroes, but do look up to and admire fair, honest teachers.

Finally, *balance independence and control.* Your task will be to have students accept your control. Fairness in dealing with your students, when accompanied by appropriate opportunities for their independent action, help to establish a harmonious, healthy classroom climate. Remember: you are dealing with "almost adults" (Lickona, 1983).

After reading about Kohlberg's stages, decide what level best suits you. What behaviors helped you to decide this?

Criticisms of Kohlberg's Theory

Several commentators have expressed concern about Kohlberg's use of an all-male group. Most notably, Gilligan (1977, 1982, 1988) has questioned the validity of Kohlberg's theory for women. Gilligan believes the qualities the theory associates with the mature adult (autonomous thinking, clear decision making, and responsible action) are qualities that have been traditionally associated with "masculinity" rather than "femininity." The characteristics that define the "good woman" (gentleness, tact, concern for the feelings of others, display of feelings) all contribute to a different concept of morality.

As a result, Gilligan (1988, p. 7) argued that different images of self lead to different interpretations of moral behavior. Females, raised with the belief that attachment is desirable, develop along a path of inequality; males, raised with the belief that separation is desirable, develop along a path of independence. Yet dependence, commonly associated with attachment, is part of the human condition; properly interpreted, it implies helping, caring, and the ability to have an effect on others (Gilligan, 1988, p. 16).

Consequently, because women's moral decisions are based on an *ethic of caring* rather than a *morality of justice,* Gilligan argues for a different sequence for the moral development of women. For males, *separation from mothers* is essential to the development of masculinity, whereas for females, femininity is defined by *attachment to mothers.* Male gender identity is threatened by attachment, whereas female gender identity is threatened by separation. Women define themselves through a context of human relationships and judge themselves by their ability to care (Gilligan, 1982, p. 17). As a result of her studies, Gilligan formulated a developmental sequence, with three levels, based on the ethic of care, as outlined in table 5.4.

Table 5.4

Gilligan's Theory of Moral Development for Women
Level I: Orientation to Individual Survival

Decisions center on the self and concerns are pragmatic.
    First Transition: From Selfishness to Responsibility
    As attachment to others appears, self-interest is redefined in the light of "what one should do."

Level II: Goodness as Self-Sacrifice

A sense of responsibility for others appears (the traditional view of women as caretakers).
    Goodness is equated with self-sacrifice and concern for others.
    Second Transition: From Goodness to Truth
    Women begin to include concern for self with their concern for others. Is it possible to
    be responsible to oneself as well as to others? The answer requires knowledge; hence,
    there is a shift from goodness to truth. Recognizing one's needs is not being selfish, but
    rather being honest and fair.

Level III: The Morality of Nonviolence
Resolution of the conflict between concern for self and concern for others results in a guiding principle of nonviolence. Harmony and compassion govern all moral action involving self and others. Level III defines both femininity and adulthood.

Gilligan does not argue for the superiority of either the male or the female sequence, but urges that we recognize the difference between the two. As she notes, by recognizing two different modes, we can accept a more complex account of human experience, which acknowledges the importance of separation and attachment in the lives of men and women, and discover how these events appear in different modes of language and thought.

For the Classroom

Schools are in the moral education business, either directly or indirectly. Whatever they do to influence how students think, feel, and act regarding matters of right and wrong is a matter of moral education. Some districts have well-planned moral education programs. In others, the curriculum in morality is unwritten. It is reflected, for example, in the attitudes of teachers toward minority and handicapped students, and in the attitudes of the community toward academics and athletics (Benninga, 1988, p. 415).

Teachers of adolescents cannot avoid moral issues in the classroom. They will face ethical and value questions in almost every class. Classroom work designed to facilitate moral development can be divided roughly into two types: *informal* and *formal*.

The *informal* treatment of moral issues occurs in those communities where no commitment has been made to introduce moral education into the curriculum. In these situations, teachers become moral educators by the manner in which they interact with their students, by the type of classroom atmosphere they create, and by their handling of sensitive curriculum issues (such as race relations, religion, and aggression).

In a more *formal* setting, specific class time is designated for moral instruction as part of the curriculum. This moral instruction usually entails the discussion of moral dilemmas. Without dominating the discussion, instructors ask students to explain the reasons for their positions, always gently urging them to a higher state of reasoning and encouraging them to listen to each other, question each other, respond to each other. These formal programs seem to be effective in raising students' levels of moral reasoning.

Focus   The Moral Dilemma

Kohlberg devised a modified clinical technique—the moral dilemma, a scenario containing conflict that asks subjects to justify the morality of their choices—to discover the structures of moral reasoning and the stages of moral development. Here is an example of the types of moral dilemmas Kohlberg (1976) presented.

A woman needs a miracle drug to save her life. The druggist is selling the remedy at an outrageous price, which the woman's husband cannot meet. He collects about half the money and asks the druggist to sell it to him more cheaply or allow him to pay the rest later. The druggist refuses. What should the husband do: steal the drug, or permit his wife to die rather than break the law?

Note: You project your own views in your answer.

Using Moral Dilemmas

moral dilemma   *A conflict causing subjects to justify the morality of their choices.*

Many teachers are now using **moral dilemmas** in their classrooms. These are thought-provoking dialogues that probe the moral bases for people's thinking. They are real or imaginary conflicts involving competing claims, for which there is no clear, morally correct solution.

Since most students have had little experience in resolving moral dilemmas, teachers should initially be active during the discussion, and only later introduce more complex issues that require resolution at the stage above the student's present moral level. Certain strategies will help you make classroom discussions of moral dilemmas most effective.

Ask why, to help students identify the dilemma and discover their level of moral reasoning. Ask students why theirs is a good solution.

Complicate the circumstances to add a new dimension to the problem. Pose this problem: Imagine an official in the Cuban government with family in the United States. He is torn between trying to retain power in Cuba and moving to the United States to rejoin his family. A teacher could begin by discussing loyalty, then gradually introduce complications, such as civil conflict, family ties, or regional or national commitment, and then ask, "What would you have done?"

Present examples based on incidents at school, such as that of the pupil who surreptitiously sets off an alarm that disrupts the entire school. The teacher threatens to punish the whole class unless the offender confesses. His friend knows who did it. When the offender doesn't admit his guilt, what should his friend do: let the innocent class be punished or tell on his friend?

Finally, *alternate real and hypothetical dilemmas,* so that students are encouraged to live by their beliefs. For example, it can be difficult for a pupil to befriend another student who is being mocked by classmates because of differences in language or customs. But if pupils have encountered similar situations in literature and in moral dilemma discussions, they are more likely to stand by their principles.

Effective discussions of moral dilemmas also require an atmosphere conducive to moral instruction which can be encouraged by the teacher's attention to the following four points.

1. You must create an atmosphere of trust and fairness, in which students are willing to reveal their feelings and ideas about the moral dilemma with which the group is wrestling. In the lower grades, teachers can avoid becoming the authority when resolution of an issue remains elusive; in the upper grades, teachers must work to bring older students to the point where they will share their beliefs with others.

Focus ◀ --------- Schools and Character Development

Addressing the issue of a troubled society and the role of our schools in that society, Lickona (1991, 1993) argued that the schools cannot be ethical bystanders. With the realization that young people experience difficult times, schools are beginning to become concerned once more with the issue of character development. As educators cautiously commence work on this topic, they are attempting to avoid the controversies that surrounded the values clarification movement of the 1960s, whose programs were intended to help children clarify their own values. Today's efforts are directed at identifying and building into programs such universal values as honesty, kindness, responsibility, and respect, all concepts that teachers have traditionally introduced into their work (Brooks & Kann, 1993).

As Lickona (1993) noted, character development in the classroom takes many forms: a teacher treats students with love and respect; makes sure that students treat one another with care and concern; involves students in a democratic classroom (helping them to accept responsibility); and encourages students to extend these ideas beyond the classroom. In a similar manner, Brooks and Kann (1993) urged teachers to be sure their students understand the meaning of the concepts they are trying to instill in their students. For example, do students really know what *courage, responsibility,* and *respect* mean?

Because there is no way to really know what another person is thinking, we can identify good character only by watching and listening to our students (Wynne, 1988). Therefore it makes sense for schools to encourage and reward the good conduct of their students. For example, the *For Character* program developed in the Chicago area publicly acknowledges the good conduct and academic efforts of its students, including such character-building activities as tutoring peers or students in other grades, serving as crossing guards, acting as student aides, acting as class monitors, and joining school or community projects.

The program also provides public recognition to motivate students, through awards and ribbons presented at school assemblies, and through mention over the school's public address system and in school bulletins. Such recognition is given to individual pupils, groups of students, and entire classes.

2. Such an atmosphere results from respecting your students and valuing their opinions. Teachers who are decent and fair in their relations with their students and who respect their pupils can do much to create a positive atmosphere for moral instruction.

3. An atmosphere of trust does not appear overnight. Students need time to evaluate you, to judge how you react to them as persons. They also need time to decide how you will handle sensitive discussions and to feel secure that they will not be ridiculed or humiliated by their peers or by you.

4. You must be sensitive to what your students are experiencing. You must especially be alert to students who find the discussion painful, for whatever reason. Make every effort to provide a forum—within the group or in private conversation—for them to express their feelings *on their terms.*

The Teacher's Role

Meaningful discussion of moral issues requires careful preparation. For example, a teacher described by Lickona (1983) was determined to foster such desirable moral qualities in her students as justice, truth, and fairness. So she initiated discussions involving these qualities (using the moral dilemma technique) and encouraged her pupils to search for them and talk about them in their group meetings. When she later observed their behavior in typical class situations, she discovered that nothing had happened !

Analyzing her own behavior, she realized that her pupils searched for what they thought *she* wanted. She felt that she had conveyed the impression that only she had the wisdom to answer the question; thus, discussion within the group had been limited. After this honest self-evaluation, she reduced the size of discussion groups to six, frequently adopted a devil's advocate position on issues, and encouraged interaction among the children.

She also began to use classroom dilemmas that both had moral dimensions and were personally meaningful to the children. Why were two boys fighting? Should a pupil tell the teacher when a class member was cheating on a test? These in-school dilemmas gradually led to the discussion of issues that occur outside the classroom.

With a talented teacher, the moral and academic curriculum can be two sides of the same coin. For example, it is almost impossible to read the story of Anne Frank without commenting on the courage of the family that hid her. During a civics class, it is natural to point out the responsibility to vote, or the injustice and unfairness of treating people as unequal because of color or religion.

Talented teachers who are committed to moral education can play a major role in the process. How? *Speak up for morality.* When something is wrong, teachers should speak up forcibly—to explain, for example, that picking on a smaller child is wrong. *State your personal opinions* when you feel strongly about an issue—for example, no politician, whether mayor or president, is above the law. When expressing opinions, be sure that you allow others to be heard. *Take the time to explain rules or positions of right and wrong,* not just to announce them. In chapter 13, we'll discuss the need for classroom rules to be clearly understood so that they can work for the good of all.

With teachers and students working together to attain moral objectives, students should begin to develop such desirable characteristics as *a sense of self-respect* that emerges from positive behavior toward others. They acquire skill in *social perspective-taking,* which asks how others think and feel, and begin to engage in *moral reasoning* about the right things to do. They begin to appreciate *moral values,* such as kindness, courtesy, trustworthiness, and responsibility, and apply the social skills and habits of *cooperation.*

Moral Development and Forgiveness

forgiveness *A special application of mercy; focuses on the individual who forgives, not on the one seeking forgiveness.*

Robert Enright and his associates (in press) developed a cognitive model of **forgiveness** as a specific application of mercy. Their work focuses on the individual who forgives, and not on the one seeking forgiveness. The work is an extension of the Kohlbergian justice presentation, but there are clear differences. Enright and his colleagues presented the issues as follows.

> When we ask the fairest solution to a problem, forgiveness never enters the picture. As an example, suppose Billy runs to Mom, telling her that Jill unfairly took all the marbles. Although Mom could ignore it, she probably would engage in some form of justice reasoning. Whether she uses distributive justice, punitive justice, care reasoning, or another form, she is reasoning with a justice strategy of some kind. The parent would not think of forgiving the child in this context. On the other hand, Mom may ask Billy to forgive Jill. If so, and this is the crux of the justice-forgiveness distinction, she is abandoning her quest for the *fair* solution. Instead, she is seeking the compassionate solution, or the one beneficial to Billy's emotional health, or even the one most beneficial to Billy's and Jill's relationship (p. 136).

The forgiveness option is distinguished from the justice strategy. Enright noted that he would focus on a different aspect than would Kohlberg in the above-mentioned moral dilemma, by asking individuals what they would do if the druggist concealed the drug. The options might be to use a justice strategy to decide whether to seek retribution on their own, to use the courts to sue, or to forgive. Enright has drawn some useful distinctions between the Kohlbergian justice sequence and the stages of forgiveness (see table 5.5). To forgive is an important skill; teaching it requires both an understanding of how students reason and an awareness of their problems.

Table 5.5

Stages of Justice and Forgiveness Development		
	Stages of justice	**Stages of forgiveness**
Stage 1	Punishment and Obedience Orientation. I believe that justice should be decided by the authority, by the one who can punish.	Revengeful Forgiveness. I can forgive someone who wrongs me only if I can punish him or her to a similar degree to my own pain.
Stage 2	Relativist Justice. I have a sense of reciprocity that defines justice for me. If you help me, I must help you.	Restitutional or Compensational Forgiveness. If I get back what was taken away from me, then I can forgive. Or, if I feel guilty about withholding forgiveness, then I can forgive to relieve my guilt.
Stage 3	Good Boy/Girl Justice. Here, I reason that the group consensus should decide what is right and wrong. I go along so that others will like me.	Expectational Forgiveness. I can forgive if others put pressure on me to forgive. It is easier to forgive when other people expect it.
Stage 4	Law and Order Justice. Societal laws are my guides to justice. I uphold laws in order to have an orderly society.	Lawful Expectational Forgiveness. I forgive when my religion demands it. Notice that this is not Stage 2 in which I forgive to relieve my own guilt about withholding forgiveness.
Stage 5	Social Contract Orientation. I am still interested in that which maintains the social fabric but I also realize that unjust laws exist. Therefore, I see it as just, as fair, to work within the system to change.	Forgiveness as Social Harmony. I forgive when it restores harmony or good relations in society. Forgiveness decreases friction and outright conflict in society. Note that forgiveness is a way to control society; it is a way of maintaining peaceful relations.
Stage 6	Universal Ethical Principle Orientation. My sense of justice is based on maintaining the individual rights of all persons. Conscience rather than laws or norms determines what I will accept when there are competing claims.	Forgiveness as Love. I forgive unconditionally because it promotes a true sense of love. Because I must truly care for each person, a hurtful act on his or her part does not alter that sense of love. This kind of relationship keeps open the possibility of reconciliation and closes the door on revenge. Note that forgiveness is no longer dependent on a social context, as in Stage 5. The forgiver does not control the other by forgiving; he or she releases the other.

From R. D. Enright and the Human Development Study Group, "The Moral Development of Forgiveness" in W. Kurtines and J. Gewirtz, editors, *Handbook of Moral Development*, Volume 1, pages 123–152. Copyright © Lawrence Erlbaum Associates, Hillsdale, NJ. Reprinted by permission.

APPLICATIONS AND REFLECTIONS

Chapter Highlights

Erikson and Psychosocial Development
- Erikson's eight stages of psychosocial development provide a structure for analyzing the crises and strengths in students' lives.
- Understanding the meaning of these stages in your pupils' lives can only help to enhance and enrich teacher-learner interactions.
- Knowing the various phases of the socialization process as defined by Erikson, helps teachers in their work with students who are experiencing the divorces of their parents.

teacher – student

Moral Development—The Later Years

1. Moral development during the elementary school years can be traced to the merger of two influences: authority and a pupil's growing cognitive capacity.
   - Discuss issues of right and wrong on which there would be agreement: lying, stealing, cheating, and the like. Now ask the class to suggest ways of dealing with these problems if they should occur in the classroom.
   - Recognize that when students' moral ideas are challenged, they find it painful. Students, for example, can be scornful of "those foreigners. Why worry about their rights?" they might add. "After all, isn't this our country?" Classmates may point out that newcomers have the same rights as everyone else, and discussion can be heated. Encourage students to express their feelings of doubt and confusion as they are prodded to a higher level of moral thinking.
   - Raise such direct questions as, "Why is it wrong to cheat?" Try to get your pupils to realize that cheating is a lie (it's pretending to know what you don't know); that people will find out and won't trust you any more; and that it's not fair to all your classmates who don't cheat.
   - Try to teach pupils to think first and act later as Lickona (1983) suggested. Do this in three steps:
   a. Do I have any options?
   b. What will happen if I do any of these (the options)?
   c. What's the best decision for myself (that is, what do I think is right?) and for others?

2. An understanding of what is right or wrong is no guarantee of appropriate moral action.
   - Arrange discussion groups that will address such topics as these: "What kind of person am I?" "What kind of person would I like to become?"
   - Organize students into groups to research and talk to younger students about the effects of using drugs and alcohol.
   - Discuss how movies and television sometimes depict figures that break the law as exciting and charismatic. What effect does that have on younger students? What happens when popular actors and actresses are in such shows?
3. Students are impressed by the moral behavior of their teachers.
   - Show your students that you respect them, by listening to their opinions and acting on them when you can.
   - Be consistent in your own behavior; don't just talk about fairness and justice to all, but demonstrate these traits when you interact with all of your students, regardless of race, color, and belief.
   - Treat all of your students in the same manner: what's wrong for one should be wrong for all.
   - Ask your students to write an essay about desirable moral qualities for teachers. You will usually discover much about yourself and what students think of your behavior.

- Psychosocially, youngsters need those around them to whom they can attach, thus acquiring a sense of security about their surroundings and avoiding many of the problems plaguing today's youth. Issues about secure attachment still swirl around day-care placement.
- The number of homeless children in our society is increasing, and as it does, the range of problems associated with homelessness becomes more noticeable.
- The emergence of self-control is a critical feature of psychosocial growth as children develop their ideas of right and wrong.

Kohlberg and Moral Development

- Children begin to understand the moral consequences of their actions as they are rewarded or punished for their behavior.
- To explain this phenomenon, Kohlberg has formulated a cognitive interpretation of moral development that incorporates Piagetian thinking.
- Using the technique of moral dilemmas and analyzing an individual's reasoning, Kohlberg has traced progress through stages of moral development.
- Kohlberg's ideas have been challenged, especially by Carol Gilligan, who proposes a different path for a woman's moral development.
- Educators believe that the concepts of moral development can be translated into classroom practice.

Connections

1. Think about how you learn, and describe how one of the major concepts discussed in this chapter is part of your learning activities or approach.

2. Identify at least one learning situation (classroom instruction, self-study, taking a test, small-group work) and describe how you would apply one of the key concepts examined in this chapter *if you were a teacher*.

Getting the Picture and Drawing Relationships

Think about the various learning concepts and variables discussed in this chapter. Create pictures, graphics, or figures that highlight the relationships among key components.

Personal Journal

What I really learned in this chapter was _____

_____

_____

_____

_____

What this means to me is _____

_____

_____

_____

_____

Questions that were stimulated by this chapter include _____

_____

_____

_____

_____

Key Terms

attachment	121	identity crisis	130	intimacy	134
autonomy	121	identity diffusion	132	moral dilemma	143
conventional level	138	identity foreclosure	132	postconventional level	140
forgiveness	145	identity moratorium	132	preconventional level	138
generativity	135	industry	126	reciprocal interactions	121
identity achievement	132	initiative	123		
identity confusion	130	integrity	135		

Phyllis Allan, principal of the Brackett school, had detected an underlying current of unrest among her teachers and decided to bring it out into the open. She knew what was bothering them: they were concerned about the mainstreamed students in their classes.

At the next scheduled faculty meeting, she reviewed how the mainstreamed students had been assessed and said she felt that they were progressing nicely.

Dolores Amico, a third-grade teacher, grumbled a little. "With all we have to do—and remember, you asked us to get additional information on our students this year—I'm not sure I'm helping Joey as much as possible."

exceptionality.) Consequently, this chapter is devoted to an analysis of exceptional students and their classroom activities.

Phyllis Allan, the principal of Brackett school, was worried about both her teachers and the exceptional students in her school. Like many educators, she realized her teachers wanted to be sure that these students received the best education possible, but were worried about their abilities to provide it.

Before addressing the specific categories of exceptionality, we'll first explore the implications of **mainstreaming,** the placement of students who are exceptional in regular classrooms whenever possible. Mrs. Allan's concern

chapter 6

exceptional students

"Dolores, just your having Joey in class and doing what you can to help is a tremendous boost for him. With the aid he gets from Mary Powers (the learning resource specialist) and Ann Kline (the reading specialist), do you think he'll get through the year?"

"I suppose so, if we can keep up this level of support."

"Of course we can," snapped Mary Powers impatiently. "When he comes to me, he's happy and seems to be getting along with everyone else in the class."

"Not only that," Ann Kline joined in, "we don't have any choice; federal and state legislation provides for students like Joey."

Mrs. Allan now wanted to move the discussion to a different level. "I know you're worried that you feel you might not be prepared to do all you should. Many teachers feel this way— but your concern and your efforts, together with specialized support, can make a big difference in the lives of students like Joey."

Mrs. Allan was addressing her concern that all the staff be aware of the needs of students like Joey, who, with help, could probably meet the learning standards for his grade level. ■

In chapters 4 and 5, we have described the typical course of development for most students, tracing the manner in which they learn and best respond to instruction. We know, however, that although all students exhibit individual differences, some have been identified as *students who are exceptional.* (Note: **exceptional** is a general term referring to one or more kinds of

in the opening vignette of this chapter that her teachers felt uncertain about their work with mainstreamed children is quite real, and is present in schools—both elementary and secondary—across the country.

To help you become more familiar with this topic, we'll first turn our attention to types of exceptionality, with much of the chapter organized around the following categories:

Children who are gifted/talented

Children with sensory handicaps

Children with communication disorders

Children with physical and health impairments

Children with behavior disorders

Children with learning disabilities

Children with cognitive disabilities

When you have completed reading this chapter, you should be able to

- identify the various types of exceptionalities
- appraise the progress of mainstreamed students in your class
- discriminate the range of individual differences among your students
- contrast educational programs for specific exceptionalities
- formulate appropriate classroom techniques for students to address their specific exceptionalities

exceptional *A term that refers to one or more kinds of special needs or characteristics in children.*

mainstreaming *Integrating physically, mentally, and behaviorally handicapped students into regular classes.*

Children Who Are Exceptional in the Classroom 152
Children at Risk 152
Ability Grouping 153

The Categories of Exceptionality 155
The Gifted/Talented 156
Sensory Handicaps 162
Communication Disorders 165
Physical and Health
    Impairment 166
Behavior Disorders 107
Learning Disabilities 171
Cognitive Disabilities 174

The Assessment and Classification of Children 176

Mainstreaming 178
What Is Mainstreaming or
    Inclusion? 178
Classroom Support for
    Mainstreamed Students 180
Some Results of
    Mainstreaming 186

Education and Exceptionality: A Model 187

Multicultural Students and Special Education 188
Bilingual Education and Bilingual
    Children 190

Applications and Reflections 192

CHILDREN WHO ARE EXCEPTIONAL IN THE CLASSROOM

Individual differences fascinate and challenge the instructional skills of every teacher. There are countless individual differences among students who have been identified as exceptional learners with exceptional needs. As we attempt to meet all these needs, the students' developmental characteristics can guide us to choose appropriate curriculum materials and foster a supportive classroom atmosphere. Instruction in any subject must be adapted to students who differ in a wide range of abilities: intellectual, motor, and behavioral (Snow, 1986).

Children at Risk

Although we will focus on students that meet the criteria for accepted categories of exceptionality, there is another group of students who are considered **at risk.** These children are not currently identified as handicapped according to various criteria, but they are considered to have a high probability of becoming handicapped (Heward & Orlansky, 1988). Many of the children who fall into the at-risk group are preschoolers. Another way of characterizing these students is that they are in danger of failing to complete their educations with adequate levels of academic skills (Slavin & Madden, 1989). In fact, a number of variables lead us to predict that such students are at risk for dropping out of school. These risk factors include low academic achievement, grade retention, low socioeconomic status, social behavior problems, and poor school attendance (Slavin, 1989).

As you can imagine, a large number of programs have been designed for children at risk. In a comprehensive review of programs designed to help these children

at risk *A term used to describe those children who have a high probability of becoming handicapped.*

Focus ◄ Thinking About Individual Differences

Stop for a moment to consider the possible range of individual differences you can expect to find in the classroom. To help shape your thinking, use the following questions as a guide:

1. What kinds of student differences can you expect to find in your classroom? Try to answer the question by placing each difference into the following categories:

    Physical   Behavioral   Cognitive

2. Assume that you are a teacher in either an elementary or a secondary school and have just been asked by the school psychologist if there are some students who you think should not be in your classroom. If so, why? What are your reasons for excluding them? Where should they be placed?
3. Can you identify those students who could do well in a regular classroom but who will need some specific help? Are there students who you think should not be in a regular classroom if they are to receive the best education possible? Can you give specific examples?

When you finish your reading of this chapter, return to these questions and ask yourself if you would answer them in the same manner. If not, what would you change? Why?

You can expect to find a wide range of individual differences in schools.

succeed in school, Slavin and Madden (1989) provided the following research synthesis for what works (and what does not work) with students at risk. Does it challenge any of your beliefs?

- First-grade prevention programs that include intensive resources, tutors, and small-group instruction increase students' reading achievement.
- Cooperative learning programs and continuous-progress models accelerate the achievement of students at risk.
- Frequent assessment of student progress that results in a restructuring of instructional content characterizes effective programs.
- Effective programs are comprehensive and include teachers' manuals, curriculum guides, lesson plans, and many other supportive materials.
- Ineffective strategies include failing, which negatively affects achievement, and special pullout programs, which only keep students in the early grades from falling farther behind their regular-education peers.

Many of the instructional and behavior management procedures that have been found to be effective with at-risk students can and should be used with exceptional students. Keep these points in mind as you read the remainder of this chapter.

Ability Grouping

The task that you face in dealing with a wide range of individual differences reflects the common educational goal that all citizens will be brought to minimally acceptable levels in such subject areas as reading, writing, mathematics, and citizenship. As a teacher, however, you are also expected to help students achieve those individual goals in which all citizens realize their own maximal potential for individual development and for a specialized contribution to society (Snow, 1986, p. 1034).

One way of achieving these goals is to use skillfully the concept of **ability grouping.** There are several means of forming ability groups.

ability grouping *The technique of helping students achieve individual goals by placing those of similar ability together, either by groups in the same classroom (homogeneous grouping) or in separate classrooms (tracking).*

- Assign students to classes depending on their abilities; a good example of this technique is the use of high school "tracks," in which students are placed in "college prep" or general classes; another example is placing students in special education classes.
- Create ability groups within a single class; a good example of this technique would be assigning students to reading groups based upon their reading abilities.
- Form small, mixed-ability groups in which higher-ability students serve as peer tutors, in a form of cooperative learning. (See chap. 10.)

Research indicates that although teaching homogeneous classes may be easier with regard to planning, it is more demanding than teaching using small groups. Small-group instruction involving different ability levels requires more differentiated instruction, well-chosen assignments, and rules of conduct that all group members understand (Brophy & Good, 1986). Teachers have many ways of manipulating the organizational structure of the class; in doing so, they should ensure that grouping is short-term and does not label (Corno & Snow, 1986).

A teacher's task is clear: to establish educational environments that permit the greatest number of students to flourish to the fullest extent of their abilities. P.L. 94–142, the *Education for All Handicapped Children Act* (now called the IDEA— *Individuals with Disabilities Education Act*) provides for services for students with disabilities in the least restrictive environment, which in many cases is the classroom.

To give an idea of the dimensions of the issue, Ysseldyke and Algozzine (1990) identified the following ten categories of exceptionality used in providing services to exceptional students:

- *Blind or visually handicapped.* Less than 1 percent of the school-age population is classified in this category.

Focus — A Pioneer in Special Education

One of the outstanding individuals credited with furthering the field of special education has been Samuel Kirk (1904–). He received his doctorate from the University of Michigan, specializing in physiological and clinical psychology. Kirk has been a staunch believer in the power of the environment and consistently challenges the idea of an unchanging IQ. His work contributed to an increasing interest in the plight of disadvantaged children and influenced the nature of the Head Start program. His research into psycholinguistic deficits and learning disabilities did much to advance both fields.

Samuel A. Kirk.

- *Deaf or hard of hearing.* Less than 1 percent of the school-age population is classified in this category.
- *Deaf and blind.* Less than 1 percent of the school-age population is classified in this category.
- *Orthopedically or otherwise health impaired.* Less than 1 percent of the school-age population is classified in these two categories.
- *Mentally retarded.* About 1.4 percent of the school-age population is classified in this category.
- *Gifted and talented.* About 3 percent of the school-age population is classified in this category.
- *Learning disabled.* About 5 percent of the school-age population is classified in this category.
- *Emotionally disturbed.* About 1 percent of the school-age population is classified in this category.
- *Language impaired.* About 2.5 percent of the school-age population is classified in this category.
- *Multihandicapped or severely impaired.* Less than 1 percent of the school-age population is classified in this category.*

least restrictive environment
A learning environment or classroom situation that provides necessary support for a handicapped student's continuing educational progress while also minimizing the time the student is removed from a normalized educational environment. In many ways, it has the same philosophical base as the practice of mainstreaming.

Categories of exceptionality, however, vary across the states. For example, Massachusetts and South Dakota do not use categories for providing special education services. Other states also are moving away from this system. (We'll say more about this change later in the chapter.)

As we noted, federal law also mandates that these students be placed in the **least restrictive environment** in which they can achieve success. *Least restrictive* means that students are to be removed from the regular classroom, home, and family as infrequently as possible. Their lives should be as "normal" as possible, and intervention should be consistent with individual needs and not interfere with individual freedom any more than is absolutely necessary. For example, children should not be placed in special classes if they can be served adequately by resource teachers, and they should

* Ysseldyke, James and Robert Algozzine, *Introduction to Special Education,* Second Edition. Copyright © 1990 by Houghton Mifflin. Used with permission.

Table 6.1

Implementing Least Restrictive Environment Placements

1. Not all handicapped children benefit from being placed in the "mainstream." So-called restrictive environments such as residential institutions, resource centers, and self-contained special education classrooms in many cases offer a child developmental opportunities that would be impossible to achieve in a "less restrictive" setting.

2. Placement of handicapped children should be decided on an individual basis, based on the readiness of the special student and the preparedness of the receiving classroom to meet individual children's special needs.

3. Placement decisions should take into consideration a child's social and emotional developmental opportunities, as well as intellectual and physical development.

4. Teachers should be involved in placement decisions to ensure acceptance of the exceptional child in the classroom and to evaluate the capability of the classroom to accommodate the individual child's special needs. Regular teachers should be informed of special placements in their classes.

5. Transitional periods are often necessary to prepare both handicapped and nonhandicapped students to adjust to new situations.

6. Staff development programs to prepare teachers to work with exceptional children in their classes must be available prior to such placements, and continuous support and training are necessary to meet problems as they arise. Special education teachers specialize in certain areas and may require in-service training when assigned children with disabilities in which they have little or no expertise. In-service training also is needed for paraprofessionals and other support personnel.

7. Class sizes must be kept low in special education, whether in a "restrictive" environment or in the regular classroom, to ensure the necessary individualization of instruction.

8. Certified special education teachers must be retained to continue to meet the needs of children in special classes and to work with regular teachers in developing appropriate instructional programs for exceptional children.

9. Counselors, psychologists, psychiatrists, and other auxiliary personnel must be readily available to special and regular teachers.

10. Teachers should have regularly scheduled release time for consultations with support personnel.

11. Instructional materials, equipment, and facilities must be adapted to the needs of exceptional children in the regular classroom and throughout the school.

12. Scheduling of the educational program and buses should conform to the needs of exceptional children rather than vice versa.

13. Safeguards should exist to see that funds designated in special education follow the child, even if in a less restrictive environment, including the regular classroom.

From M. Rauth, "What Can Be Expected of the Regular Teacher? Ideals and Realities" in *Exceptional Education Quarterly,* Vol. No. 2, pp. 27–36. Copyright 1981 by PRO-ED, Inc. Reprinted by permission.

not be placed in institutions if special classes will serve their needs just as well (Hallahan & Kauffman, 1988, p. 8). Given the importance of serving handicapped students in the least restrictive environment, we offer table 6.1 as a concise summary of guidelines for implementing least restrictive services.

Let us now consider how these students are identified as exceptional.

THE CATEGORIES OF EXCEPTIONALITY

You might wonder what types of exceptional students you will encounter in school. Researchers have reported the incidence and prevalence of various categories of exceptionality to give us some idea about this. The terms *incidence* and *prevalence* are sometimes used interchangeably in discussions of exceptional children; however, they should be differentiated (Hallahan & Kauffman, 1988). *Incidence* refers to the number of new cases of exceptionality during a given period, such as one year. In contrast, *prevalence* refers to the total number of existing cases (new and old) in the population at a particular time.

When discussing students with exceptional needs, it is useful to consider prevalence by three broad divisions. First, there are *high-prevalence* categories, which typically include students with learning disabilities, gifted and talented students, and those with speech and language problems. In the *moderate-prevalence* categories are those with cognitive disabilities and those who are emotionally disturbed. A number of categories of exceptionality are considered *low-prevalence;* included in these are students with hearing and visual problems, health and orthopedic handicaps, and multiple handicaps.

The range of exceptional abilities varies widely, and any particular difficulty will affect performance in some subjects more than in others. A student confined to a wheelchair, for example, may do quite well in academic subjects but be prevented from full participation in certain motor activities. Visual problems, depending on their severity, can cause major problems in adaptive behavior, or can be erased quite simply by eyeglasses. Note also that we have included the gifted and talented among the categories, since these children are unquestionably exceptional.

The Gifted/Talented

What to do with gifted and/or talented students has perplexed educators for as long as these children have been recognized as exceptional. Even defining the term *gifted* has caused considerable controversy. Initially, the results of IQ tests were used, with some arbitrary score such as 120 or 140 used as the cut-off point. This definition, however, was too restrictive; youngsters who have exceptional talent in painting or music, or who seem unusually creative, are also gifted (Reis, 1989). As a result, the *Gifted and Talented Children's Education Act of 1978* defined these students as follows:

> **The term *gifted* refers to children and (whenever applicable) youth who are identified at the preschool, elementary, or secondary level as possessing demonstrated or potential abilities that give evidence of high performance capabilities in specific areas (which could be intellectual, creative, specifically academic, related to leadership, or related to the performing and visual arts), and who, by reason thereof, require services or activities not ordinarily provided by the school.**

Estimates are that about 3 to 5 percent of the school population fits the above definition. Recent United States government reports reflect interest in the gifted, stating that the gifted are a minority who need special attention. They are a minority, characterized by their exceptional ability, who come from all levels of society, all races, and all national origins, and who represent both sexes equally (Sternberg & Davidson, 1986).

If these children are so talented, why do they require special attention? For every Einstein who is identified and flourishes, there are probably dozens of others whose gifts are obscured. Thomas Edison's mother withdrew him from first grade because he was having so much trouble; Gregor Mendel, the founder of scientific genetics, failed his teacher's test four times; Isaac Newton was considered a poor student in grammar school; Winston Churchill had a terrible academic record; Charles Darwin left medical school.

Schools frequently fail to challenge the gifted, and their talents are lost to themselves, the professions, and society. You may wonder why extraordinary children fail in ordinary educational programs. Most schools are designed for the average student; as the slow learner has difficulty keeping up with average classmates, so the gifted one has difficulty staying behind with average classmates. The gifted lose their motivation and either reconcile themselves to mediocrity or become discipline problems (Borland, 1989).

But the curriculum is not the only issue facing these students; there are several others.

- *Failure to be identified.* In a recent survey, the U.S. Office of Education reported that 60 percent of schools reported no gifted students. Teachers and administrators simply fail or refuse to recognize them.
- *Hostility of school personnel.* Teacher hostility traditionally has been a problem for the gifted. Teachers' resentment that these students are smarter than they are, dislike for an "intellectual elite," and antagonism toward their often obvious boredom or even disruptive behavior have all occasionally produced a hostile atmosphere for the gifted.

What are the guidelines for implementing least restrictive environment (LRE) placements? Consider a child in your classroom who is experiencing a severe behavior problem. Apply the criteria of LRE to this case.

Annual **Edition**

gifted   *A term describing those with abilities that give evidence of high performance capabilities.*

teacher – student

Students Who Are Exceptional

1. Those students who are exceptional and who spend time in a typical classroom may display behaviors that require your careful attention. For example, students with learning and behavior problems may exhibit:
   - poor academic performance
   - attention difficulties
   - hyperactivity
   - difficulty with memory of symbols
   - lack of coordination
   - perception problems
   - language difficulties
   - aggression
   - withdrawn behavior
2. Watch your students; listen to them; evaluate their behavior. Then, if you're still unhappy with their performance, analyze your instruction by using the following criteria:
   - *Student motivation.* Does the classroom environment make students want to learn?

Students who are exceptional will display behaviors that require your special attention. You should evaluate their behavior to design a better instructional environment.

- *Student attention.* Does the learning environment attract students so that they will attend to the task?
- *Positive reinforcement.* Does the classroom setting challenge students and provide satisfactory rewards and feedback?
- *Modeling.* Do the students see good examples of how learning should occur?
- *Practice.* Are the students given sufficient opportunity to practice?
- *Time on task.* Are the students given the chance to learn skills until they are comfortable with them?
- *Pacing.* Am I setting the right tempo in class so that the rate and amount of material taught provide time and incentive?
- *Generalization.* Do the students have a chance to transfer their learning to other settings?

3. You may want to monitor mainstreamed students more carefully when they are in class; if so, you could try something like this (Bos & Vaughn, 1988):
   Put the student's name on a card that says:

   Student Helped (Name)

Date	Time	Comments

   Carefully mark the date and time and use appropriate comments, such as these:

   difficulty with long and short vowels

   trouble with two-place multiplication

4. You can use this technique with behavioral problems as well. Keep a close check on dates to determine if the time between incidents is improving.
   - What was the time of day?
   - Was it the same time each time the incident occurred?
   - What was the subject matter when the incident occurred?

   With these and other simple techniques, you can keep a close check on the progress of your students who are exceptional.

- *Lack of attention.* The "in and out of favor" phenomenon may reduce attention to the gifted. Estimates are that only 3 or 4 percent of the nation's gifted have access to special programs.
- *Lack of trained teachers.* There are remarkably few university programs to train teachers for these children.

In spite of a concentrated effort to ensure equality in our schools, minority students remain woefully underrepresented in programs for the gifted (Frasier, 1989). Many explanations have been offered for this phenomenon, among them low IQ test scores and the lack of stimulating socioeconomic backgrounds. Some writers have speculated that problems in identifying minority gifted adolescents are the major cause of underrepresentation of these groups (Genshaft, 1991).

Yet we are now seeing a reconsideration of the role of a student's home life in intellectual development. Research has shown that the environments of those homes that foster intellectual achievement are quite similar, regardless of income level (Frasier, 1989). R. Brown (1988), examining model youth, pointed out the considerable support for intellectual development in the African American community.

In an interesting analysis, Sue and Okazaki (1990), arguing against either heredity or environment as the explanation of high levels of achievement, turned to the concept of relative functionalism. They suggested that the behavior (including achievement) patterns of Asian Americans, for example, result from a combination of cultural values and status in society. That is, education provides an opportunity for upward mobility; it becomes increasingly functional when other avenues are blocked.

Frasier (1989) suggested that we change the screening procedures that have inherent limitations built into them for multicultural students. Why not use behavioral characteristics indicating giftedness, such as the *use* of language rather than a test question *about* language? Parents of multicultural students could help educators reword items on rating scales. Vignettes describing successful multicultural students could be used for motivational purposes.

These and similar techniques broaden the concept of giftedness in multicultural populations. Different concepts of intelligence (such as Sternberg's Triarchic Model or Gardner's Multiple Intelligences—see chap. 9) can enrich the use of intelligence as a criterion for a gifted program. Other attempts to identify potential for a gifted program could include:

- seeking nominations from knowledgeable professionals and nonprofessionals;
- using behavioral indicators to identify those students who show giftedness in their cultural traditions;
- collecting data from multiple sources;
- delaying decision making until all pertinent data can be collected in a case study.

Remember: The gifted in our schools are a diverse group.

How have the schools treated gifted students once they have been identified? Usually one of three different techniques has been adopted: acceleration, enrichment, or some form of special grouping (Eby & Smutny, 1990).

Acceleration. **Acceleration** means some modification in the regular school program that permits a gifted student to complete the program in less time or at an earlier age than usual. Acceleration can take many forms: school admission based on mental rather than chronological age, skipping of grades, combining of two years' work into one, elimination of more basic courses, and early admission to high school and college. To say that reactions to acceleration are mixed would be an understatement. Recent reactions, however, have turned more positive.

Learning for the gifted is inadequate if it omits acceleration, according to Stanley and Davidson (1986), who have worked with the mathematically precocious. Concluding that most of the gifted child research was buried with Lewis Terman in 1956, they stated that acceleration is vastly preferable to various enrichments that frequently degenerate into busywork (unrelated to the student's specific talent) or merely present advanced material earlier, guaranteeing future boredom.

Stanley and Davidson (1986) recommended that grade acceleration and subject matter acceleration should proceed simultaneously. Using an example from the Johns Hopkins program, they described a verbally and mathematically brilliant boy who took one course each semester and summer from ages 12 to 15. He also skipped the second, eleventh, and twelfth grades; combined with subject-matter acceleration, this enabled him to enter Johns Hopkins at the age of 15 years, 2 months.

Most gifted boys and girls want to accelerate, and do so with ease and pleasure (Stanley & Davidson, 1986). Of the 44 early college entrants studied by Stanley and Davidson, only one experienced initial difficulty, which he quickly conquered. Those gifted students who desired to accelerate had few social or emotional problems. Such procedures are relatively inexpensive and may actually save school systems time and

Annual **Edition**

acceleration *A change in the regular school program that permits a gifted student to complete a program in less time or at an earlier age than usual.*

money: identification of the gifted, grade skipping, some special courses, early high school graduation, and arrangement for early college placement require little extra funding.

Enrichment. **Enrichment** is a term designating different learning experiences in the regular classroom. Enrichment techniques usually follow one or more of these procedures:

- Attempt to challenge gifted students by assigning extra readings and assignments, and permit them to participate in related extracurricular activities. For example, if parents could arrange the time, they could take a scientifically advanced student to special classes at an institution such as the New England Aquarium.
- Group a school's gifted students so that they are together occasionally, enabling interested teachers to challenge their abilities through group discussions and independent research.
- Provide special offerings, such as classes in a foreign language or in advanced science.
- Employ for each school system a special teacher who could move from school to school, identify the gifted, aid regular teachers, and actually work with the gifted in seminars or group discussions.

Enrichment has advantages and disadvantages. The major disadvantage is the tendency to provide the gifted with busywork and call it enrichment. More of the same is not enrichment. Another disadvantage is that extra work, discussions, or classes may not match the talent and interests of the particular gifted child.

The chief advantage of enrichment is that it can provide challenging, meaningful work for gifted youngsters while they remain with their peers. If teachers can satisfactorily adjust their instruction, enrichment can protect gifted youngsters from social and emotional maladjustment that could accompany acceleration.

In an attempt to avoid these pitfalls, Renzulli (1986) devised the enrichment **triad model,** which entails three components: exploration, skill building, and research into real problems. *Exploration* helps students find topics and subjects that are commensurate with both the interests and the skills of a student and that are not in the basic curriculum. *Skill building* focuses on the research, data, and communication skills in particular disciplines, providing an introduction to problem-solving strategies and creative thinking. *Research into real problems* has the student investigate some actual situation and propose a novel solution.

Students involved in the triad model have been identified by Renzulli's three-ring model of giftedness: above-average ability in a subject or field (such as music or art); creative potential; and task commitment. Though Renzulli's model has proven to be popular with classroom teachers, little research is available to testify to its effectiveness.

Special Groups

Special grouping implies self-contained special classes, or even special schools, not merely the temporary groupings mentioned in our discussion of enrichment. Considerable controversy swirls around self-contained units for the gifted, some of which relate to the Jeffersonian versus the Jacksonian concepts of equality. Should a democracy encourage and establish an intellectual elite? Aside from this philosophical issue, no evidence exists indicating a clear superiority of special grouping over other techniques. Research is inconclusive, and experts remain uncertain as to the social desirability of grouping or its effect on achievement.

Developing Talent

Defining talent as an unusually high level of demonstrated ability, achievement, or skill in some special field of study or interest, Bloom (1985) investigated the development of talent in several fields: psychomotor (including athletic), aesthetic (including musical and artistic), and cognitive. Selecting Olympic swimmers and world-class tennis players,

enrichment *A method of instruction for gifted students in which they are furnished with additional, challenging experiences.*

Suppose you were presenting an in-service to novice teachers on gifted and talented students. What suggestions would you offer to teachers working with such students in their classes?

triad model *Renzulli's enrichment model for working with the gifted.*

Focus   Genetic Studies of Genius

In 1921, Lewis Terman began one of the most ambitious studies of the gifted ever undertaken, known as the *Genetic Studies of Genius*. Terman wished to identify over 1,000 children in the California schools whose IQs were so high that they placed them within the highest 1 percent of the nation's child population. Teachers were asked to name their schools' brightest children, who were then given a group intelligence test. Those who scored highest were administered an individual Stanford-Binet test. The original criterion for inclusion in the study was an IQ of 140.

This phase of the study yielded 661 subjects (354 boys and 307 girls). An additional 365 subjects came from volunteer testers in schools outside the main survey. Both of these groups consisted of subjects from the eighth grade or lower. Another 444 subjects, all junior and senior high school students, were selected by their scores on group intelligence tests. These 1,470 subjects were selected from a school population of one-quarter million. Fifty-eight more subjects were added during the first follow-up in 1927–1928, providing a grand total of 1,528 subjects.

Terman and his associates collected additional information about the subjects: developmental histories, school information, medical data, anthropometrical measurements, achievement test data, character test data, interests, books read over a two-month period, data on the nature of their play, word association tests, and, finally, home ratings. These data were eventually used to supply information about the characteristics of the gifted compared with their average peers (Terman & Oden, 1959).

What is especially interesting about Terman's work was his method of identifying the gifted—by almost sole reliance upon intelligence tests. Today, as indicated, we have broadened our definition of these children to include those who demonstrate talent across many fields.

concert pianists and sculptors, and finally research mathematicians and research neurologists, Bloom and his team subjected the participants to intensive interviewing. The team also interviewed the parents and teachers of these individuals, with the subjects' permission.

From these interviews, Bloom and his colleagues reached the following general conclusions:

• Young children initially viewed their talent as play and recreation, followed by a long period of learning and hard work, then eventually focused on one particular learning activity (math, science).
• The home environment structured the work ethic and encouraged a youngster's determination to do the best at all times.
• Parents strongly encouraged a child in a specialized endeavor in which that youngster showed talent.
• No one "made it alone"; families and teachers or coaches were crucial at different times in the development of a youngster's talent.
• Clear evidence of achievement and progress was necessary for the individual to continue learning even more difficult skills.

If talent is to flourish, strong interest and emotional commitments to a particular talent field must be accompanied by a desire to reach a high level of attainment, and a willingness to expend great amounts of time and effort to reach that high level of achievement.

Three recent trends augur well for the future of students who are gifted and talented: (1) the movement throughout the special education field for greater individualized instruction could, if also applied to the gifted, allow them to move more rapidly through both the elementary and the secondary curricula; (2) the greater interest in the gifted on the part of colleges and universities should bring more substantial financial support, more widespread academic encouragement, and better continuity to programs; and (3) multicultural efforts to identify talented men and women should help to dispel charges of elitism (Fox & Washington, 1985).

The mentally gifted. Children who are mentally gifted, like those who are mentally retarded, benefit from special educational programs to help them develop their abilities.

Finally, if you discover talented students in your class, you may find these suggestions helpful.

- *Learn to recognize the signs of giftedness.* Terman's discouraging conclusions about the failure of parents and teachers to recognize unusual talent should be a warning to everyone. As the gifted return to educational prominence, you will probably be more sensitive to these youngsters and become more capable of discovering hidden talent. If you suspect unique talent, arrange for a referral to the school psychologist or counselor. Avoid guesses; confirm your intuitions.
- *Help the gifted; do not reject them.* Once you have identified gifted students, plan to help them. This task is easier said than done; teachers busy with twenty or thirty students can consider extra work with a gifted student an imposition. Try to control such feelings and recall that these are exceptional students with deep, often unmet, needs. They may be personally difficult to work with because school bores them, or you may feel intimidated by their quickness. Be honest with yourself; recognize the reasons for your feelings. Try to challenge these students. If you succeed, follow their progress: you can take pride in a job well done.
- *Avoid hostility toward the gifted.* Discipline problems in the children and feelings of inadequacy on your part can often produce open hostility in you toward these students. Realize that feelings may exist; try to realize why you feel this way, and determine to recognize these students for what they are: youngsters with real needs who require help.
- *Remember that gifted students are similar to other students.* You should help to bring together the talented with the other students to remove feelings of isolation, or of "being different." Terman's findings that the gifted have the same interest in games and sports should be a definite help to you. Also, remember that the intellectually gifted student is not necessarily physically gifted, or that the artistically talented may not be mathematically superior. These facts should help you guide the gifted child's social and emotional development.

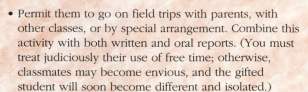

teacher – student interactions

Working with the Gifted and Talented

1. The gifted are excellent readers.
   - Outline a reading program that challenges them, keeps them interested, and encourages them in any special talents they possess.
   - Do not use reading materials that they will meet in the next grade; you only ensure future, more serious, problems, and do later teachers a disservice.
2. The gifted enjoy working with abstract materials and complex relationships.
   - Provide situations in which they work with other gifted students on some complex problem or project you have devised.
   - Encourage discussions and seminars where they can express and support their beliefs and yet be challenged by equally inquiring minds.
   - Search the Educational Resources Information Center (ERIC) for possible programs and techniques.
3. The gifted are insatiably curious.
   - Be sure to fill their free time productively when they complete assignments before their classmates; urge them to build collections of books, rocks, fish— whatever they enjoy that is educationally profitable.

- Permit them to go on field trips with parents, with other classes, or by special arrangement. Combine this activity with both written and oral reports. (You must treat judiciously their use of free time; otherwise, classmates may become envious, and the gifted student will soon become different and isolated.)
- Although they have similar interests in games and sports, their interests are more mature. For example, when most youngsters quickly acquire an interest in baseball, it centers on the physical aspects of the game. It is the gifted child who wants to know rules, who interprets disputes, or who quotes batting averages. Use this interest to motivate them to read, calculate, or even invent a board game.
4. Your state department of education may be of assistance. Know what it is doing. Is anyone coordinating efforts for the gifted? Those states that have such coordinators will offer excellent suggestions for programs, teaching techniques, and related literature.

- *Recognize where your talents lie.* As someone who has survived many years of academic trial, you possess certain talents. Recognize them and use them in your work. For example, if you like to excel in literature, you can be of enormous help in arranging reading programs for gifted students. Your knowledge of books will permit you to make pertinent suggestions for those with other talents, such as the artistic, or the scientific.
- *Watch for signs of boredom.* Recall Terman's guidelines: the gifted are usually at least two years beyond grade placement, sometimes three or four. Gifted youngsters may quickly become restless if immersed in a regular curriculum.

Sensory Handicaps

Some students will enter your classroom with visual and hearing problems, but educational and psychological assessments will have shown that they are at or above grade level in cognitive, general psychomotor, and auditory skills. Consequently, these students will spend most, if not all, of the day in the regular classroom (depending on the severity of the impairments). The visually handicapped are a good example.

Visual Impairment

The following definitions of visual impairment (Livingston, 1986) are widely used today:

- **Visually impaired.** Individuals with any type of reduction in vision are described by this general classification. When vision remains limited following intervention (prescription lenses, surgery, etc.), special services are required in order for these students to benefit from instruction, and they are considered to be visually impaired.

visually impaired *Those individuals subject to any type of reduction in vision.*

teacher – student

Working with the Visually Impaired

1. The National Society's publication, *Vision Screening in Schools,* recommends that teachers help in identifying vision problems by being aware of several symptoms:
   - Clumsiness; difficulty in walking in a new environment
   - Adopting awkward head positions in order to see
   - "Tuning out" on information written on blackboard
   - Constantly asking others to tell them what is written at a distance
   - Constant squinting
   - Constant rubbing of eyes
   - Obvious eye problems: red, swollen, crusted eyes

2. Be alert to those youngsters who complain of itchy or scratchy eyes, dizziness, headaches, or feelings of nausea following eye work.
   - Urge normally sighted classmates to respect and encourage students who are visually impaired.
   - If you have any of these students in class, remember to say aloud what you are writing on the board.
   - With regard to content, your expectations should match the potential of these students; in other words, treat them like their classmates in academic matters.

---

visually limited *Those who have difficulty seeing under ordinary conditions but who can adapt with glasses.*

legally blind *A term referring to those individuals with vision of 20/200 or less in the better eye (after correction).*

- **Visually limited.** When students have difficulty seeing under average conditions but have the condition corrected by adaptation (glasses), they are considered to be visually limited, but are classified as sighted for educational purposes.
- **Legally blind.** You probably recall from any eye examinations you may have had that normal vision is 20/20. The numerator of this fraction indicates the distance at which you can read figures on a chart (usually the Snellen). The denominator indicates the distance at which a person with normal vision could read those same letters. If for example, your vision is 20/60, that means you can read at 20 feet what the person with average vision can read at 60 feet. Legal blindness refers to those individuals with vision of 20/200 or less in the better eye (after correction).

The National Society for the Prevention of Blindness recommends that children be referred for an eye examination if their attempts to read lines on the Snellen Chart have the following results:

- 3-year-olds: 20/50 or less
- 4-year-olds through third grade: 20/40 or less
- fourth grade and above: 20/30 or less

An accurate count of visually impaired children remains elusive, since data collection varies from state to state. The most widely used figure suggests that one in every 1,000 children is either visually impaired or blind; this figure translates to a total of 55,000 visually impaired children in the United States.

Myths of the Visually Impaired We should dispel some of the myths surrounding persons who are visually impaired. They are not born with greater auditory acuity, tactile sense, or musical talent. Superior performance may result, however, from more constant use. On the other hand, visual problems do not adversely affect cognitive, language, motor, and social abilities. Such views represent the stereotypes of society.

For example, though concept development may initially be delayed, visually impaired students demonstrate normal performance during the elementary school years. Language development may also be delayed, but again, most youngsters progress to normal levels of usage during the school years. Any social problems that may arise seem to be more the result of the attitudes of others than of the impairment itself. Perhaps the best way to summarize the developmental characteristics of visually impaired children is to note that they are like other children in many more ways than they are different from them.

teacher – student

interactions

Working with the Hearing Impaired

1. Be on the lookout for those students who
   - have trouble following directions;
   - seem to be at a loss with other students;
   - do not pay attention to noises (classroom sounds, voices from the corridor, etc.).
2. Be careful of seating.
   - If you tend to remain at the front of the classroom, seat students with hearing deficits in the front row so that they can hear better and perhaps read your lips, if necessary.
   - Encourage these students to watch your face carefully.
   - Do not exaggerate your speech.
   - Discourage their use of distorted positions in order to hear better.
   - Urge the remainder of the class to speak clearly and distinctly but, again, not in any exaggerated fashion.
3. Be especially alert to the kinds of social interactions in which these students engage.
   - Don't let these students depend solely on you for social interactions.
   - Encourage other students to interact with hearing-impaired students.
   - Arrange classroom activities in which hearing-impaired students can actively participate (projects entailing art, data collection, etc.).

If your classroom is the least restrictive environment for a visually impaired student, then that student belongs there, and should be taught the same sequence of topics as students with normal vision. Students with visual impairment should be monitored carefully so that they acquire appropriate nonacademic skills, enabling them to interact with and be accepted by their peers.

Hearing Impairment

Hearing is the sense that developing students use to learn those language and speech skills necessary for social interaction and academic success. Hearing-impaired students possess the same potential for acquiring language as other children, but they lack linguistic input, the raw material of language acquisition (Lowenbraun & Thompson, 1986).

The following definitions are widely used today (Marschark, 1993): **Hearing impairment** refers to any type of hearing loss, ranging in severity from mild to profound. There are two subdivisions of hearing impairment. (a) *Deafness:* this term defines a hearing disability so acute that an individual is prevented from processing linguistic information through audition, with or without a hearing aid. (b) *Hardness of hearing:* individuals who are **hard of hearing** have sufficient hearing potential that with the use of hearing aids, they can process linguistic information through audition. (Note: Be sure to make a clear distinction between *deafness* and *hearing loss,* because deafness implies a hearing loss so severe that normal activity is impossible.)

hearing impairment *A term referring to any type of hearing loss, from mild to profound.*

hard of hearing *A term describing those individuals with sufficient hearing potential (with hearing aids) to process linguistic information through audition.*

Estimates are that about 8 percent of Americans, or over 17 million, experience some form of hearing difficulty. Within this group, approximately 100,000 preschool youngsters, 600,000 elementary and junior high students, and almost 1,000,000 high school and college students have some degree of hearing loss. About 50,000 children and youth have been educated under the conditions of P.L. 94–142.

Since most classrooms rely heavily on both spoken and written language, students with any type of hearing impairment remain at a distinct disadvantage in their learning. One of the most realistic dangers these students face is the danger of being labeled. If initially we lacked hard evidence of a hearing problem, we could too easily label a student as slow or difficult, with all the attendant problems that accompany such categorizing.

For the hearing impaired, controversy surrounds the meaning of the term *least restrictive environment* (Lowenbraun & Thompson, 1986). If interaction with peers is deemed vital, a regular classroom would seem most suitable, but also fraught with potential communication pitfalls. Most experts agree, however, that a regular classroom is most beneficial if specialized support is available.

Try to detect students with hearing impairments as soon as possible. Students with mild hearing loss (and even some with more severe loss) often adapt sufficiently to go for several years in school without being identified. They compensate in ways that cause teachers to miss the problem. But these students suffer because they cannot work to their full potential, and frequently become frustrated and anxious.

Communication Disorders

Some students have speech and language problems that are unrelated to sensory handicaps or cognitive difficulty. (Speech and language problems are high-prevalence categories of exceptionality.) These students are delayed in demonstrating language or have difficulty in expressing themselves. Under P.L. 94–142, *speech impairment* is defined as a communication disorder, such as stuttering, impaired articulation, language impairment, or voice impairment, that affects educational performance.

The terms *communication, language,* and *speech* must be distinguished, for although they are often used synonymously, they technically have different meanings. (See chap. 4 for a discussion of language.)

Communication refers to any process that transmits information (language, speech, telephone, computer). *Language,* a more restrictive term, refers to verbal or nonverbal communication between individuals. *Speech,* an even more restrictive term, refers to human usage of sound as the vehicle for conveying meaning.

What happens when students talk? Three major accomplishments are necessary. The first is encoding, in which speaker A wishes to convey some meaning to receiver B and must fit the message to the language. The message must also fit the grammar of the language before it becomes part of the sound system. This phase is referred to as *encoding*. The second process is *transmission* of the message, which commences when the brain activates the speech organs. The speech organs now produce a speech sound that generates sound waves. These reach listener B, cause ear vibrations, and eventually stimulate B's brain. The third step is *decoding,* in which the listener uses the sound and grammar of the message to interpret it. Assume that phonologically you decode a message such as "I'd like the sand which you ate," which is semantically illogical. To find the source of the problem, you return to phonological decoding; when you repeat this process, the sounds are the same. But grammatically, you can decode the message into two possible arrangements:

1. I'd like the sand, which you ate.
2. I'd like the sandwich you ate.

Now all aspects of decoding—phonological, grammatical, and semantic—are complete, and you accept the message.

You will better understand communication disorders if you remember much of what was covered in chapter 4 regarding language development. You will recall that language consists of three major elements: *sounds* (phonology), *meaning* (morphology), and *grammar* (syntax). Any language possesses certain fundamental distinctive sounds: the phonemes of that language. Think of two similar sounding words: *thin, shin.* The initial sounds differ sufficiently to be distinctive and thus qualify as phonemes.

Although phonemes affect meaning (for example, adding an *s* can change a singular word to a plural one), they possess no meaning in themselves. Morphemes, however, introduce meaning. The morpheme may be a word (a free morpheme) or part of a word (a bound morpheme). For example, *cat* and *be* are free morphemes; *s* and *ed* are bound morphemes. Morphemes allow a speaker to signal relationships: *Jack is older than Jill.* Morphemes also permit the speaker to indicate numbers, an important consideration in English—for example, *cats, pails, roses.*

Linguists believe that morphemes carry a considerable burden in the English language. *Cat,* for example, contains three phonemes, so arranged that they convey meaning: a particular animal. Morphemes combine in complex ways to carry meaning.

Consider this string of morphemes: *Jack fetch pail water.* It is not grammatical, because it lacks those additional morphemes necessary to signal relationship: *ed, a, of. Jack fetched a pail of water* is a grammatical sentence.

Morphemes are meaningfully arranged in the grammar or construction of a language, forming acceptable constructions of a language, the syntax of that language. Syntax arranges morphemes in meaningful sentences. Recent grammatical studies have shown that any speaker can say, and any listener can understand, an infinite number of sentences. Thanks to grammar, no two sentences you speak, hear, or read are identical (excluding trivia, such as "How are you?").

Students with problems in any or all of these three aspects of language will experience communication disorders, which may be divided into two categories: (a) *speech disorders,* such as *misarticulation,* which refers to difficulty with phonemes; *apraxia,* which refers to difficulty with commands to the muscles controlling speech; *voice disorders,* which are deviations of pitch, loudness, or quality; and *fluency disorders,* which usually take the form of stuttering; and (b) *language disorders,* which usually refer to difficulty in learning the native language with respect to content, form, and usage, and possibly are present in those students with delayed language development.

What are possible causes of communication disorders? They may range from neuropsychological elements that interfere with cognitive development and information-processing strategies to structural and physiological elements (such as the hearing problems just discussed), and environmental causes, such as deprived sociocultural conditions. These elements rarely act in isolation, and you must accept the reality of interaction among the causative elements. For example, hearing impairments may adversely affect peer interactions, causing a student to engage in limited attempts at communication.

Among the characteristics you should be on the alert for are the following:

1. Is there any kind of articulation delay or disorder?
2. Is there anything unusual about a student's voice (loudness, uneven pitch)?
3. Is there a smooth flow of speech?
4. Does a student use the same type of speech (similar words to describe actions, people, objects) with the same meanings as typical students do?
5. Does a student use speech to achieve goals in the same manner as other students?

To aid students with communication disorders, Bailey and Wolery (1984) suggested that teachers reinforce both verbal and nonverbal forms of communication. Encourage nonhandicapped classmates to talk to these students as much as possible and reinforce them for doing so. Also urge their peers to play with them frequently, thus increasing all forms of interaction. You should be a clear and positive model to students with communication problems as you have them use increasingly more complex speech patterns.

Physical and Health Impairment

Under the definitions used in P.L. 94–142, physical disabilities are grouped into two classes: (a) those involving *orthopedic impairment,* such as cerebral palsy, amputations, muscular dystrophy, polio, spinal cord injuries, and multiple sclerosis; and (b) those affecting *vitality,* such as heart problems, asthma, epilepsy, diabetes, and leukemia. Many of these students can function in regular classrooms once they have mastered supportive equipment such as crutches or artificial limbs. For others, transition into the regular classroom depends on other circumstances, such as the quality of support services, the availability of transportation, accessibility within and without the school, and the opportunity for individualized programs.

Once your initial anxiety is over, you will be concerned mainly with insuring that these students are able to share fully in class activities without lowering your expectations

teacher – student

interactions

Working with Students Who Are Physically or Health Impaired

Consider the following specific suggestions for integrating these students into your classroom:

- Ask students what adaptations, special equipment, or teaching procedures work best for them.
- Ask parents, therapists, or education specialists what special devices or procedures are needed to assist students.
- Allow disabled students, if possible, the opportunity to do what their peers do, even though their physical disability may cause them to seem uncoordinated.
- Have volunteers assist with physical management so that students with disabilities can go on field trips and participate in special events and projects.

- Work with able-bodied students so that they understand that characteristics such as drooling, unusual ways of talking, and physical awkwardness cannot be helped and should not be ridiculed.
- Prepare yourself and your class for helping students with special needs.
- Treat students with disabilities as normally as possible. Do not overprotect them; make them assume responsibility for themselves.

Outline guidelines that you would use for working with students who are visually and hearing impaired and students who are physically or health impaired.

for them. Familiarize yourself as fully as possible with any equipment used (braces, wheelchairs, etc.), and be aware of the characteristics of some of the more common disabilities, such as the following:

- *Asthma*. Treat students with asthma as normally as possible, since the asthma is unlikely to interfere with education.
- *Amputation*. Students with prostheses will usually function at normal levels and require little support once they have overcome the immediate effects of the traumas.
- *Epilepsy*. Seizures are serious, and you should be alert to the possibilities of their occurrence. If medication used to control seizures is particularly potent, it may affect learning.
- *Cerebral palsy*. One of the most common disabilities in this category, its severity will determine placement, in either a regular or a special class.
- *Muscular dystrophy*. The education goal for these students, again depending on the initial severity of the condition, is to maintain them in an ordinary class for as long as possible.

Behavior Disorders

Here we encounter a particularly baffling cluster of problems whose exact definition and prevalence have continually frustrated investigators. Some students in this category are unusually restless and active, to the point of disrupting a classroom; others seem to explode into tantrums at the slightest provocation; still others may be terrified of the most simple situations (such as the student who will not enter a classroom unless the lights are on). These few examples should give you a sense of the wide range of problems encompassed by the label *behavior disorders* (or *emotional disturbances*).

Characteristics of Behavior Disorders

behavior disorders *Any conditions in which environmental conflicts and personal disturbance persist and negatively affect academic performance.*

Behavior disorders include any conditions in which one or more of the following characteristics are exhibited over a long period of time and to a marked degree, adversely affecting educational performance:

- *an inability to learn* that cannot be explained by intellectual, sensory, or health factors;

teacher – student — interactions

Working with Students Who Have Behavior Disorders

1. The term *behavior disorders* encompasses a wide variety of problems that require diversified classroom strategies.
   - When possible, change pace, or even your schedule, when you anticipate a possible eruption.
   - Be sure that these students understand classroom rules. Try listing the rules on the board and reinforcing (by praise or token) when the student follows the posted rules.
   - Remove as many distractions as possible from these students so that they may focus more fully on their work.
   - Give these students needed structure, with their learning tasks carefully arranged in small, concrete steps.
   - Select several peers and ask them to ignore any disruptive behavior and reinforce positive behavior. Elementary school students are particularly good at this.
   - Above all, be consistent in your interactions with these students, which will differ according to the behavior. Ignoring acting-out behavior may be impossible because it could become disruptive; this technique may be quite effective, however, with withdrawn students.
2. There are several behaviors to avoid in working with these students.
   - Don't use sarcasm or ridicule.
   - Don't use force.
   - Don't make an issue of minor problems.
   - Don't compare one student's behavior with another's.

- *an inability to build or maintain satisfactory interpersonal relationships* with peers or teachers;
- *inappropriate types of behavior or feelings* under normal circumstances;
- *a general pervasive mood of unhappiness or depression;*
- *a tendency to develop physical symptoms or fears* associated with personal or school problems (Ysseldyke & Algozzine, 1990, p. 175).

These problems can be grouped into two general categories: environmental conflict and personal disturbance. Environmental conflict encompasses aggressive-disruptive behavior, hyperactivity, and social maladjustment; personal disturbance includes anxiety and withdrawal.

As you can well imagine, determining the causes of the problem is difficult, with assessments incorporating biological and environmental elements. These youngsters are difficult to work with, and teachers may be enormously relieved when students with behavior disorders are removed from regular classrooms. But before rendering judgment, you should keep firmly in mind the interactive nature of the factors involved.

Attention-Deficit/Hyperactivity Disorder

One of the more challenging problems that you may experience in a school setting is teaching a student diagnosed with **attention-deficit/hyperactivity disorder (ADHD).** Research shows that ADHD occurs in approximately 3 to 5 percent of U.S. elementary school students and is three times more common in boys than in girls (Braswell & Bloomquist, 1991). Although there is considerable controversy over the diagnosis of this problem (some authors discuss it as primarily a language disorder—see Lovinger, Brandell, & Seestedt-Stanford, 1991), most researchers rely on the diagnostic criteria presented by the American Psychiatric Association in its *Diagnostic and Statistical Manual of Mental Disorders* (DSM-IV, 1994). Table 6.2 presents the diagnostic criteria for ADHD from the DSM-IV.

attention-deficit/hyperactivity disorder (ADHD) *A disorder usually appearing in childhood that is characterized by various symptoms of inattention and/or hyperactivity-impulsivity.*

Table 6.2

Attention-Deficit/Hyperactivity Disorder

A. Either (1) or (2):

1. Six (or more) of the following symptoms of *inattention* have persisted for at least 6 months to a degree that is maladaptive and inconsistent with developmental level:

   Inattention
   a. often fails to give close attention to details or makes careless mistakes in schoolwork, work, or other activities
   b. often has difficulty sustaining attention in tasks or play activities
   c. often does not seem to listen when spoken to directly
   d. often does not follow through on instructions and fails to finish schoolwork, chores, or duties in the workplace (not due to oppositional behavior or failure to understand instructions)
   e. often has difficulty organizing tasks and activities
   f. often avoids, dislikes, or is reluctant to engage in tasks that require sustained mental effort (such as schoolwork or homework)
   g. often loses things necessary for tasks or activities (e.g., toys, school assignments, pencils, books, or tools)
   h. is often easily distracted by extraneous stimuli
   i. is often forgetful in daily activities

2. Six (or more) of the following symptoms of *hyperactivity-impulsivity* have persisted for at least 6 months to a degree that is maladaptive and inconsistent with developmental level:

   Hyperactivity
   a. often fidgets with hands or feet or squirms in seat
   b. often leaves seat in classroom or in other situations in which remaining seated is expected
   c. often runs about or climbs excessively in situations in which it is inappropriate (in adolescents or adults, may be limited to subjective feelings of restlessness)
   d. often has difficulty playing or engaging in leisure activities quietly
   e. is often "on the go" or often acts as if "driven by a motor"
   f. often talks excessively

   Impulsivity
   g. often blurts out answers before questions have been completed
   h. often has difficulty awaiting turn
   i. often interrupts or intrudes on others (e.g., butts into conversations or games)

B. Some hyperactive-impulsive or inattentive symptoms that caused impairment were present before age 7 years.

C. Some impairment from the symptoms is present in two or more settings (e.g., at school [or work] and at home).

D. There must be clear evidence of clinically significant impairment in social, academic, or occupational functioning.

E. The symptoms do not occur exclusively during the course of a Pervasive Developmental Disorder, Schizophrenia, or other Psychotic Disorder and are not better accounted for by another mental disorder (e.g., Mood Disorder, Anxiety Disorder, Dissociative Disorder, or a Personality Disorder).

Code based on type:

314.01 Attention-Deficit/Hyperactivity Disorder, Combined Type:
If both Criteria A1 and A2 are met for the past 6 months
314.00 Attention-Deficit/Hyperactivity Disorder, Predominantly Inattentive Type:
If Criterion A1 is met but Criterion A2 is not met for the past 6 months
314.01 Attention-Deficit/Hyperactivity Disorder, Predominantly Hyperactive-Impulsive Type:
If Criterion A2 is met but Criterion A1 is not met for the past 6 months

Coding note: For individuals (especially adolescents and adults) who currently have symptoms that no longer meet full criteria, "In Partial Remission" should be specified.

From American Psychiatric Association (1994). *Diagnostic and Statistical Manual of Mental Disorders, Fourth Edition.* Washington, DC, American Psychiatric Association, 1994.

ADHD (sometimes simply called hyperactivity) seems to be caused by a variety of factors—neurological, emotional, dietary, and/or environmental—and can encompass a range of behaviors (Greene, 1987). For example, some students may exhibit only mild and infrequent episodes, while others are chronically disruptive. Among the methods used with these students are medication, behavior modification, perceptual-motor training, and special diets.

School can become a problem for these children, since it may be the first place where they are required to demonstrate self-control and adjustment to a structured environment. In fact, parents may not realize until the time of school entrance that their child experiences what psychologists call ADHD. Previously they may have dismissed such behavior as just "part of growing up." These students may shout things out in class, demand a teacher's immediate attention, and not wait their turn. If this behavior is accompanied by emotional outbursts, those around such children may begin to suspect that they are seriously emotionally disturbed.

What can you do to help these students? Here are a few suggestions you may find helpful (Ingersoll, 1988):

- Keep your own emotions under control. Though this may be easier said than done given the demands that these students will make upon you, it's nevertheless true that you only add to the problem if you respond in anger. Remember: it's not the student who so aggravates you; it's the disorder.
- Provide structure and feedback. Because these students sometimes cannot organize their own world, you have to assist them (Ingersoll, 1988, p. 167). These students should know exactly where they are to be at all times and where things are to go. Perhaps most important of all, they must receive clear, precise instructions from you.
- Use feedback to improve their behavior. Positive feedback can be a major force in helping to improve this behavior. Reinforce often, reinforce small steps, and vary the reinforcers.
- Help these students with their peer problems. Reinforce peers for including ADHD students in their activities (but do this subtly with older students). Also try to plan activities that require mutual cooperation for success.

Most students develop normally, that is, with a minimum of difficulties. Even those who experience some emotional and behavioral problems usually do not experience serious psychiatric illness. The roots of their conditions may be traced to many sources—the student, family, school, society. This situation dramatically illustrates the importance of an interactive analysis.

It is deceptively simple to classify a student's problem along a single dimension: a disturbed personality, parental separation, or the school. But a student's behavior represents the interaction of many causal points. There is no avoiding the biological, psychological, and social consequences of a problem, either physical, emotional, or behavioral. For example, it is possible to classify many of the disorders discussed in this section as emotional. To do so is a disservice to the student who is experiencing the problem. There may well be a physical cause behind an apparent emotional problem, such as anxiety; any physical difficulty, such as asthma, can have definite, even serious emotional consequences.

Working with students who display behavior disorders requires both knowledge and patience, characteristics not always in plentiful supply. Although most educators believe that mainstreaming these students is positive, good guidelines for the best way to handle them in the regular classroom are still lacking. Figure 6.1 illustrates several behavior patterns that students might display in the classroom. Some of these are teacher-related; others are peer-related. Students who demonstrate externalizing patterns typically have more difficulty in their adjustment to the expectations of teachers. In contrast, internalizing students may not have as much difficulty with teachers, but will likely have considerable difficulty with peers, who may neglect or reject them.

What can you do to help a student with attention-deficit/hyperactivity disorder?

Figure 6.1

Interrelationships of bipolar behavior patterns and school adjustment types.

From "Behavior Disorders and the Social Context of Regular Class Integration: A Conceptual Dilemma?" by H. M. Walker and M. Bullis, p.82, in J. W. Lloyd , N. N. Singh, and A. C. Repp, eds., The Regular Education Initiative: Alternative Perspectives on Concepts, Issues, and Models. *Copyright © 1991 by Sycamore Publishing Co. Reprinted by permission of Brooks/Cole Publishing Company, a division of Thomson Publishing, Inc.*

	Behavior patterns	
Types of adjustment	**Externalizing**	**Internalizing**
Teacher–related	• Acting out, noncompliant behavior • Teacher defiance • Behavioral excesses • Low achievement • Disruption of classroom ecology • High probability of referral • Resistant to social influence tactics	• High levels of appropriate classroom behavior • Nonassertive behavior patterns • Problems with self • Performance deficits • Low achievement • Low probability of referral

Peer–related	• Variable peer status
	  - some acceptance
	  - some rejection
	• Failure to use social skills that support positive peer interactions
	• High levels of social engagement
	• High levels of negative/aggressive social behavior
		• Neglected or rejected peer status
		• Low levels of participation in peer controlled activities
		• Social isolation and withdrawal
		• Low levels of negative social behavior

Learning Disabilities

learning disabilities *A term referring to a handicapping condition characterized by a discrepancy between ability and achievement, most commonly manifested in reading, writing, reasoning, and/or mathematics.*

Annual **Edition**

Of all the categories of exceptionality we have discussed, perhaps none has caused as much difficulty in definition as **learning disabilities,** or learning disorders. Prior to 1965, special education textbooks contained no reference to the term "learning disabilities" (Myers & Hammill, 1990). Hammill (1990) reviewed 28 textbooks that included definitions of learning disabilities. There were 11 different definitions of learning disabilities, and in some cases, there was little agreement among the different definitions. Dissatisfaction with existing definitions (including that offered by the U.S. Department of Education in 1977) caused representatives of several organizations to meet and propose a new definition that has become more widely accepted. Hammill (1990) suggested that there is a growing consensus around one definition.

In 1981, the National Joint Committee for Learning Disabilities (NJCLD) proposed the following definition of learning disabilities:

> **Learning disabilities is a generic term that refers to a heterogeneous group of disorders manifested by significant difficulties in the acquisition and use of reading, writing, reasoning, or mathematical abilities. These disorders are intrinsic to the individual and presumed to be due to central nervous system dysfunction. Even though a learning disability may occur concomitantly with other handicapping conditions (e.g., sensory impairment, mental retardation, social and emotional disturbance) or environmental influences (e.g., cultural differences, insufficient-inappropriate instruction, psychogenic factors), it is not the direct result of the conditions or influences. (Hammill, Leigh, McNutt, and Larsen, 1981, p. 336)**

Recently, a special study group of the National Institute of Health expanded this definition to encompass social skills and the relationship between learning disabilities and attention-deficit disorder. Though controversy may swirl around definitions, professionals working with these students are in general agreement about the following aspects of the problem (Morsink, 1985):

• *Discrepancy.* There is a difference between what these students should be able to do and what they are actually doing.

Table 6.3

Myths and Facts About Learning Disabilities

Myth	Fact
All LD students are brain-damaged.	Learning problems occur without brain damage.
All LD students have perceptual problems.	Many students with learning disabilities show no such evidence.
Perceptual training will lead to academic gains.	Perceptual training improves perceptual skills, which may lead to academic gain.
Hyperactivity is easily controlled by drugs.	The effective use of drugs is complicated and requires the cooperation of students, teachers, parents, and physicians.
LD students do not have math problems.	Two out of three students with learning disabilities receive special instruction in math.
Knowing that a student's learning disability is the result of brain damage helps a teacher.	Such a diagnosis is of little help to a teacher (it may help staff or medical personnel).

Adapted from Hallahan and Kauffman (1988), *Exceptional Children: Introduction to Special Education.* Englewood Cliffs, NJ: Prentice-Hall.

- *Deficit*. There is some task others can do that an LD child can't do (such as listen, read, or do arithmetic).
- *Focus*. The child's problem is centered on one or more of the basic psychological processes involved in using or understanding language.
- *Exclusions*. Learning disabilities are not the direct result of poor vision or hearing, disadvantage, or cognitive disabilities, but these students still aren't learning.

Development and Learning Disabilities

An **exclusion component** is now used to identify as accurately as possible students with learning disabilities. This component means that the problems are not a result of mental retardation, visual or hearing impairment, motor handicaps, or environmental disadvantage. You have probably concluded that learning disabilities characterize the school-age child; they are difficult to detect in young children. Reading, mathematics, and language are the vulnerable subjects, with research focusing on the psychological processes that may cause the problem. Symbolic activity seems to be the basic weakness. To help you separate myth from fact, table 6.3 presents and addresses several misconceptions about learning disabilities.

Levine, Brooks, and Shonkoff (1980) attempted to link developmental characteristics and milestones with clinical dysfunction in children who evidence learning problems. They used the following categories:

- *Selective attention and activity*. Students labeled "hyperactive" or "having minimal brain dysfunction" are increasingly identified as having attention difficulties. Unless they can focus on meaningful stimuli, they will encounter adjustment problems from birth. As we have seen, infants can discriminate detail and detect differences between the familiar and the discrepant, thus facilitating cognitive development. During the preschool years attention becomes more efficient, preparing the child for more formal schooling. It is during these years that attentional problems become apparent, a discovery that is disturbing, because early academic success depends upon the capacity to select and sustain a focus.

  Attention deficits are associated with academic, social, and behavioral problems, especially for boys. Some of the signs of an attention deficit are easy distractibility, impulsivity, task impersistence, insatiability (never being satisfied), and the ineffectiveness of rewards and punishments.

Name myths and facts that you know about learning disabilities. Discuss a child that you know who may have a learning disability.

exclusion component *A means of accurately identifying students with learning disabilities.*

- *Visual-spatial and gestalt processing.* Some students have difficulty with spatial relations; this affects their performance in activities ranging from catching a ball to reading. They have difficulty in discriminating patterns or shapes, a skill that is critical for comprehending the physical world. This problem is especially evident in their attempts to master the symbols used in reading and mathematics.

- *Temporal-sequential organization and segmental processing.* It is difficult to learn something unless its parts are placed in the right order. The relationships among words and numbers as well as the steps in a task (such as tying shoes) all involve order. Most of a student's classroom activities demand sequential organization. Storage and retrieval of information is a particular problem for these youngsters, as is following directions (for example, "Open your book to page 20, do the first three problems, and then check the answers on page 132"). Since an attention deficit may be involved, teachers should offer students help in focusing upon steps, accompanied by reinforcement.

- *Perceptive language function.* Some students have difficulty in interpreting auditory stimuli and in obtaining meaning from words and sentences. The strong link between language development and academic success poses obstacles that these students must quickly overcome; if they cannot do so, educational failure can result.

- *Expressive language function.* Competent spoken language depends on a number of factors, including the capacities to retrieve relevant words from memory, to arrange these words in phrases or sentences that conform to linguistic rules, to develop ideas in meaningful sequence or narrative, and to plan and execute the highly complex motor act of speech (Levine, Brooks, & Shonkoff, 1980, p. 77). Acquiring these abilities also carries with it the potential for difficulty: poor articulation, lack of ability to convey symbolic meaning, and stuttering—all of which can affect oral work in the classroom.

- *Memory.* Smooth developmental progression relies on the storage of data, experience, and acquired skill. Retention and retrieval of this accumulated content is basic for meaningful learning. Students can't read meaningfully if they can't recall the order and meaning of words. Students with memory deficits frequently show a wide range of clinical symptoms, both behavioral and academic. For example, such students may be unable to retain directions and as a result appear lazy or poorly motivated. Weak visual memory may result in shaky word configurations, thus slowing the rate of reading.

- *Voluntary motor function.* Typical in this category are those students who say, "I know what you mean, but my body won't do what I tell it." Problems in this category include both gross and fine motor functioning, which may or may not be associated with learning difficulties. In many cases, a cycle is established in which motor difficulties lead to embarrassment, lowered self-esteem, and social withdrawal, all of which can contribute to the formation of learning disabilities. Lack of control of the fingers and hand in writing or an inability to move correctly in classroom games or physical activities could cause a tendency to avoid these potentially embarrassing situations.

- *Developmental implications.* Learning disabilities affect from 4 percent to 20 percent of school-age children, with a boy-girl ratio of between 6 and 8 to 1. Learning disorders are probably the most common of the problems that children experience. Parents and teachers are usually involved immediately, but frequently counseling is needed because of accompanying emotional or behavioral difficulties.

The Role of Previous Knowledge in Learning Disabilities

Studies of students with learning disabilities have underscored the key role of specific knowledge and skills in learning (Brown & Campione, 1986). As psychological theory has shifted to a greater cognitive emphasis, the role of previous knowledge, or the knowledge that a student brings to any topic, is critical. Consequently, it is essential to determine the extent to which a student can function effectively with the knowledge needed to perform a specific academic task. Rather than seeking underlying mental problems, teachers can help these students to acquire the necessary prerequisite knowledge and skills. Can this student move on to fractions? Does that student understand the logic behind the experiment?

Instruction, then, should focus on where the student is now, and the use of appropriate methods to match a particular level of competence. If possible, have students with learning disabilities work with expert peers who guide their efforts and carefully structure the environment for them. This strategy may help these students to adopt regulatory and structuring activities of their own. If it is successful, you will have provided considerable social support for students who are disabled.

Dimension I: Intellectual functioning and adaptive skills	**STEP 1. Diagnosis of mental retardation** *determines eligibility for supports* Mental retardation is diagnosed if: 1. The individual's intellectual functioning is approximately 70 to 75 or below. 2. There are significant disabilities in two or more adaptive skill areas. 3. The age of onset is below 18.
Dimension II: Psychological/ emotional considerations Dimension III: Physical/health/ etiology considerations Dimension IV: Environmental considerations	**STEP 2. Classification and description** *identifies strengths and weaknesses and the need for supports* 1. Describe the individual's strengths and weaknesses in reference to psychological/emotional considerations. 2. Describe the individual's overall physical health and indicate the condition's etiology. 3. Describe the individual's current environmental placement and the optimal environment that would facilitate his/her continued growth and development.
	STEP 3. Profile and intensities of needed supports *identifies needed supports* Identify the kind and intensities of supports needed for each of the four dimensions 1. Dimension I: Intellectual functioning and adaptive skills 2. Dimension II: Psychological/emotional considerations 3. Dimension III: Physical health/etiology considerations 4. Dimension IV: Environmental considerations

Figure 6.2
The three-step process: Diagnosis, classification, and systems of support.

From Mental Retardation: Definition, Classification, and Systems of Support, *9th ed. Copyright © 1992 American Association on Mental Retardation, Washington DC. Reprinted by Premission.*

Cognitive Disabilities

Much of the dramatic change in our thinking about exceptionality can be traced to the relatively recent surge of interest in mental retardation. After decades of neglect, the public has willingly supported programs designed to educate, rehabilitate, and care for exceptional children, a large number of whom are mentally retarded.

Who are the mentally retarded? A widely accepted definition was proposed by the American Association on Mental Retardation (AAMD) in 1992. That definition is as follows.

Mental retardation refers to significantly subaverage general intellectual functioning resulting in or associated with concurrent impairments in adaptive behavior and manifested during the development period (Grossman, 1983, p. 11).

In the application of this definition, three assumptions are considered essential:

mental retardation
Significantly subaverage general intellectual functioning.

1. *Those who are moderately mentally retarded* constitute about 6 percent of the mentally retarded. Although many reside in institutions, some adults may live with their families and can do household chores. Brain damage and Down's syndrome are the chief causes of moderate mental retardation.
2. *Those who are severely mentally retarded* encompass about 3.5 percent of this population. They have historically been institutionalized, requiring constant supervision; they may acquire language and self-care skills, but only after extensive training. Genetic problems and neurological damage usually cause severe mental retardation.
3. *Those who are profoundly mentally retarded* represent about 1.5 percent of the mentally retarded population. They require total care. Infant mortality is high in this group.

The current definition of mental retardation consists of a multidimensional approach that is designed to broaden the traditional conceptualization of mental retardation, to reduce or avoid the sole reliance on the use of IQ scores to assign a disability, and to feature an individual's level of support in the environment. Figure 6.2 provides a summary of the process used in diagnosis, classification, and evaluation of support systems.

Table 6.4

Definition and Examples of Intensities of Supports	
Type of support	**Definition and Examples**
Intermittent	Supports on an "as needed "basis. Characterized by episodic nature, person not always needing the support(s), or short-term supports needed during life-span transitions (e.g., job loss or an acute medical crisis). Intermittent supports may be high or low in intensity when provided.
Limited	An intensity of supports characterized by consistency over time, being time-limited but not of an intermittent nature, perhaps requiring fewer staff members and less cost than more intense levels of support (e.g., time-limited employment training or transitional supports during the school-to-adult-provided period).
Extensive	Supports that are characterized by regular involvement (e.g., daily) in at least some environments (such as work or home) and not time-limited (e.g., long-term support and long-term home living support).
Pervasive	Supports characterized by their constancy and high intensity; provided across environments; and of a potentially life-sustaining nature. Pervasive supports typically involve more staff members and intrusiveness than do extensive or time-limited supports.

From *Mental Retardation: Definition, Classification, and Systems of Support,* 9th ed. Copyright © 1992 American Association on Mental Retardation, Washington, DC. Reprinted by permission.

The evaluation of support is designed to focus on the level of needed habilitation. While the various support intensities parallel individual limitations in functioning, this analysis is not designed to be used as a traditional diagnosis. The level of support needed by an individual is typically determined by a multidisciplinary team (e.g., school psychologist, school nurse, special education teacher). Table 6.4 provides an illustration of how the concept of support intensities might be used.

A Mentally Retarded Student Who Is Adapting

Today Eddie is 19 years old, physically strong, and working in a local gas station. Usually pleasant, Eddie is perfectly capable of pumping gas, cleaning windshields, and getting coffee and donuts. It is only when you await change from a twenty-dollar bill that you notice Eddie's difficulty. If you are a new customer, one of the other attendants immediately helps; if you are known and trusted, you tell Eddie how much change to give you.

Eddie is a good example of a young mentally retarded person who is functioning satisfactorily. He experienced immediate difficulty in school and was placed in a special class when he was 11. Learning rudimentary skills, he acquired sufficient knowledge to enable him to service cars—pumping gas, adding water, charging batteries, washing cars. The station owner feels strongly about him and has given him an opportunity that many other similar youths never receive.

There is one problem: Eddie is usually pleasant, but several mechanics mock him and send him on foolish errands. This infuriates him when he realizes what they have done. Human nature being what it is, these conditions are perhaps inevitable. Still, despite this one drawback, Eddie enjoys a unique situation, where he has proven himself a valuable asset and shown the wisdom of attempts to give youths like him as normal a life as possible. Many individuals like Eddie blend into society, leading lives that are not dramatically different from the lives of those who hold similar jobs.

Common Problems of Students with Cognitive Disabilities

Mental retardation can result from many causes: genetic, prenatal, perinatal, postnatal, and cultural. These general categories encompass specific causes such as PKU

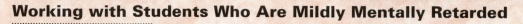

teacher – student

interactions

Working with Students Who Are Mildly Mentally Retarded

Students who are mildly mentally retarded are mainstreamed into many classes. To facilitate their adjustment and progress, teachers are encouraged to consider the following:

1. *Provide carefully guided instruction.* This will help students avoid failure, and their performance will enable you to emphasize positive features. These youngsters work best with a carefully designed, step-by-step technique. Considerable repetition is usually necessary, and you should adapt material appropriately for the slow learner. Use as much positive reinforcement as possible.

2. *Avoid any kind of competition or comparison* between mentally retarded students and their classmates. Constant failure has a damaging impact on anyone's self-concept. Cooperative groups where handicapped students work on teams with nonhandicapped peers is desirable.

3. *Discover the specific skills mentally retarded students may possess.* If possible, let them demonstrate these skills for other students.

4. *Be careful of environmental stimuli.* Too many stimuli, especially if they are similar, confuse these children. For example, in *through, thought, trough,* similar letters (*ough*) demand different responses.

5. *Be careful of both the number of things taught and the abstractness of the material.* Sheer numbers can overwhelm anyone, especially these youngsters. The more abstract the material, the greater the difficulty the low-ability youngster will have with it.

(phenylketonuria), rubella, oxygen deprivation at birth, brain injury, drugs, and economic deprivation. You should remember that in spite of being mentally handicapped, mentally retarded students have the same basic needs as the nonretarded and demonstrate considerable individual differences.

The student who is mentally retarded will exhibit difficulties at specific levels of learning. Among the more common problems are the following:

- *attention,* which may be both limited and nonselective;
- *cognitive processing,* especially with regard to organization, classification, and strategies;
- *memory,* which may be poor for short-term retention;
- *transfer,* which may be a particularly difficult task;
- *distractibility,* which results in excessive attention to incidental information.

THE ASSESSMENT AND CLASSIFICATION OF CHILDREN

Assessment is an information-gathering process central to decision making about exceptional children. It can be a complex process, and is given detailed consideration in chapters 15 and 16. The discussion of assessment in this chapter focuses on children who are exceptional. Before you commence an evaluation of a student, several issues require attention. These issues are some of those that school professionals take into account in the decision-making process (Rutter, 1975).

Identify types of mental retardation and describe characteristics of school-age children with each type. How would these characteristics influence your teaching strategies?

1. *The awareness that children are developing organisms.* Any evaluation must consider the student's developmental level, since one of the major criteria in judging the abnormality of behavior is its age appropriateness. Since students behave differently at different ages, it is important to know what behavior is typical of a given age. Students are vulnerable to different stresses at different ages. At some ages they may be particularly susceptible to an interruption of physical development whose consequences are both physical and psychological (anorexia nervosa in adolescents, for example, may disrupt development). At an

Issues & Answers

➤ Should Children Be Labeled to Receive Special Education Services?

It has been estimated that approximately 250 million standardized tests are administered to children in American schools (Ysseldyke et al., 1992). Most of the testing that is conducted is designed to make classification decisions related to special education services. Children who are labeled as learning disabled or emotionally disturbed, for example, obtain access to special services through the labeling process.

Issue

Labeling is the most effective way to get students access to special education services in our public schools.

Answer: Pro When done correctly by a qualified professional, the labeling process is a good strategy to ensure that children who need special resources have access to these resources. Such resources should change situations in which children are not learning to the best of their ability.

Answer: Con Labeling does not necessarily lead to improved educational services for children. Just being labeled does not mean that a child has improved educational services.

Answer: Pro Labeling serves as a method to organize the field of special education and therefore can guide research on a variety of childhood problems. Detailed understanding of a particular problem through research can lead to better treatment for children experiencing a certain type of problem.

Answer: Con Labels can actually produce negative effects on students, especially if those students are members of certain minority groups. Such labeling of minority students can limit their access to the opportunities that occur in the regular classroom setting.

Answer: Pro The labeling process as linked to special education services is a remarkable success story for special-needs children. Labeling has allowed millions of children access to services that have improved the quality of their lives and the lives of their families. Moreover, the labeling of children has provided documentation needed for special legislation and funding of special services.

Answer: Con There are many noncategorical methods of determining student needs, and these needs can often be met in the regular classroom. Documentation of student needs can be accomplished without using a labeling system that is useless in designing intervention programs and also harmful to students.

Where do you stand on labeling? Think about it from a teacher's perspective, a parent's perspective, and a student's perspective.

---

earlier age, interference with psychological development may have physical and psychological consequences (separation from the mother during the first months of life, for example).

2. *Epidemiological considerations.* Since any information concerning the nature and dimensions of a problem will facilitate evaluation (How often does it occur? When? In the classroom or the schoolyard?), studies that examine the distribution of the problem in the general population are usually helpful. These studies show that from 5 to 15 percent of children experience sufficiently severe disorders to handicap them in daily living. Though the precise number may vary, it is clear that except for a minority of cases, students with these disorders are not qualitatively different from their classmates.

3. *The abnormality and severity of the handicap.* Several criteria are used in assessing abnormality, the first of which is the age- and gender-appropriateness of the behavior. For example, certain behavior is normal at one age and not at another; bedwetting is common until 4 or 5 years of age, but uncommon by 10 years of age. Persistence of a problem is another criterion; a reluctance to leave home and attend school is normal in the early years, but abnormal in the later grades. Other criteria that cluster and indicate a problem are the extent of the disturbance and the intensity of the symptoms under different circumstances.

The severity of a problem can be judged by four criteria. The first is the degree of personal suffering that a student experiences (can the student function in the classroom?); the second is the social restriction involved (does the problem prevent a student from doing what is desired, such as actively participating in the classroom?); the third is whether there is any interference with development (does dependency on the parents become so intense that a student finds it impossible to form normal peer relationships?); and the fourth is whether there is an effect on others (has a student's behavior become so maladaptive that interpersonal relationships in the classroom deteriorate?).

Guidelines for Diagnosis/Classification

Using these criteria to determine that assessment is needed, we next face the issue of classification. Remember: Most problems are too intricate to be explained by one cause, and are unravelled only in a search for multiple causes. The diagnostic process is both complex and controversial, given the unreliability of the diagnostic and classification systems now available. For example, the widely used *Diagnostic and Statistical Manual of Mental Disorders* of the American Psychiatric Association (*DSM-IV*, 1994) has been faulted for yielding unreliable results in the classification of children and youth. The categories of exceptionality used in education (from P.L. 94–142) are even more unreliable, and the labels used to classify students do not convey accurate information.

For example, Rutter uses the term "minimal brain damage" to illustrate how a diagnosis can be misleading, even dangerous. There are several, brain damage syndromes, not one, and the form they take is often indistinguishable from the behavior of students without brain damage. Furthermore, brain damage does not directly lead to psychiatric disorder, although it may increase a student's vulnerability to environmental stress. For example, parental pressure to excel may precipitate a latent problem.

Potential Problems with Labeling Students

The term *exceptional* includes both persons who are talented and those who have disabilities. These students have characteristics—physical, mental, behavioral, or social—that require special attention in order for them to achieve to their potentials. Awareness of the characteristics and needs of exceptional students points to an important conclusion: A student may be considered disabled in one situation, but not in another. A student who appears at your classroom door in a wheelchair may be an outstanding scholar; a physical disability does not imply cognitive difficulties. Avoid the pitfall of stereotyping students who are exceptional.

Although labels sometimes may be necessary for identifying exceptional students and making available appropriate services, problems result from a rigid classification system. These pitfalls range from indiscriminate exclusion from a regular classroom to the very real danger that the label itself becomes a self-fulfilling prophecy. Ysseldyke, Algozzine, and Thurlow (1992) noted that labeling should be examined from the perspectives of the impact of the label on the person being labeled and the impact of the label on those who interact with the labeled person. Sensitive to these problems, today's educators emphasize the skills that a child who is exceptional possesses and attempt to improve inadequate skills.

MAINSTREAMING

Because of mainstreaming, your classroom could be the least restrictive environment for some youngsters. Mainstreaming's admirers praise it as the single greatest educational change since school integration. Its critics question it as a headlong plunge into chaos in the classroom. As usual, reality lies somewhere between these two extremes.

What Is Mainstreaming or Inclusion?

Mainstreaming or **inclusion** means integrating physically, mentally, and behaviorally handicapped children into regular classes. In the past, the vast majority of these students were educated apart from their peers for a majority of the time, but in 1975, Congress passed the *Education for All Handicapped Children Act of 1975* (P.L. 94–142), which

inclusion *The movement to place all handicapped children in regular classrooms regardless of the nature and severity of the handicaps.*

Focus

Teachers and the Referral Process

By now you realize that the teacher's role is critical in working with students who are handicapped. A teacher's responsibility often will extend to determining who is handicapped. Teachers are frequently pivotal in the identification process, since once a teacher initiates the referral process, such students are assessed and often receive some form of special help (Pugach, 1985).

Pugach investigated the referral practices of classroom teachers. She personally interviewed 39 teachers (21 elementary, 18 junior high) in a midwestern school system of 5,000 students. She divided the teachers into three groups: those making no referrals that year, those making one to three referrals, and those making four or more. The interviews focused on demographic information, problems of particular students, and the general efficiency of the school system.

Pugach found that elementary-level teachers were more likely to attempt serious intervention before referral, feeling a professional obligation to attempt to find a solution. Junior high teachers made more casual intervention efforts. Only 36 percent of the teachers used specialized help before referral, although it was available. Over 50 percent of the teachers who referred students felt it was their only choice, although they believed special placement was unnecessary. Only 27 percent referred students for the express purpose of removing them from the classroom. Of the 28 teachers who had made referrals, 64 percent cited behavioral problems as the cause; 61 percent believed that the student referred had abilities within a normal range for the child's age.

Two aspects of this study deserve our added attention. First, teachers may feel frustrated when they decide that a student needs short-term remediation. Where do they turn? In this study, we have seen that they believe they have no recourse other than to initiate a referral process that typically results in some form of special education treatment. *Know your system and the professionals who work in it. Know the services that are available before you initiate specialized procedures.* Second, teachers should be extremely sensitive to the delicate role they play in identification. Teachers exercise a decisive role in a student's future educational path.

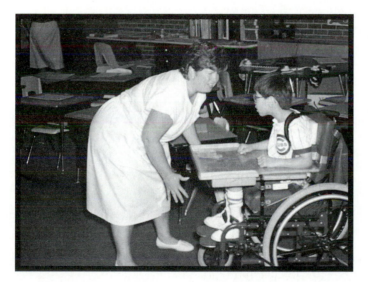

What are some of the most important issues in the special education of the handicapped?

ensures every child some form of public education. If possible, integration into regular classes as soon as possible is desirable for all but the most severely handicapped.

Mainstreaming, however, may be a mixed blessing for some exceptional children. Insensitive classmates can make life miserable for individuals who are handicapped. Teachers' organizations generally favor mainstreaming with reservations, but as we saw in Mrs. Allan's remarks about mainstreaming in the chapter opening, individual teachers feel uneasy. Administrators must designate funds to install ramps, elevators, and other special equipment; otherwise, school life could become excessively difficult for a child who is physically handicapped.

This attitude toward mainstreaming, favorable but cautious, reflects an awareness of the dangers of pendulum swings in education—for example, from enthusiasm for special classes to a rush away from them. Some believe that the current zeal for mainstreaming, resulting from excessive expectations for special classes, may in turn lead to excessive expectations for mainstreaming. Others believe that mainstreaming has been oversold and underfunded. We need both quality special education and appropriate integration of exceptional children into regular classes.

The Individuals with Disabilities Education Act

Among the chief requirements of the mainstreaming legislation are the following (Haring & McCormick, 1986):

1. *All children must be provided with a free, appropriate public education, regardless of the severity of their handicap.* The rationale for this requirement lies in our national commitment to education for all. One important feature of this stipulation addresses the financial responsibility of government at all levels: not only an exceptional child's program, but also any specialized service deemed vital, must be supported.

2. *All children who are potentially disabled must be fairly and accurately evaluated.* Historically, these children have suffered unnecessary burdens because of poor evaluation procedures that led to faulty labeling and improper program placement. One outcome of these practices was that minority students, often experiencing language difficulties and cultural bewilderment, were placed in classes for the mildly mentally retarded.

3. *The education of children who are exceptional must "match" individual capacities and needs.* One of the main features of the changed legislation was the demand that each exceptional child receive an *individualized educational plan:* the IEP. The IEP, based on the student's needs, is prepared annually by a committee that includes any needed special education teacher, a school representative, an expert on the student's disability, and the child's parents. The IEP must incorporate a statement about the student's present level of functioning, long-term goals, short-term objectives, special services needed, and any other pertinent information. Figure 6.3 illustrates a typical IEP.

4. *Children who are exceptional must be educated in the least restrictive, most normal educational environment possible.* We have previously commented on this requirement. In addition to guiding classroom placement, it also mandates the task of insuring that those students who need separate placement be brought together with nonhandicapped students for physical education (where appropriate), assemblies, and lunch periods.

5. *Students' and parents' rights must be protected throughout all stages of evaluation, referral, and placement.* Parental involvement and consent have become an integral part of the entire process. To give you an idea of the role envisioned for parents in the process, consider several measures relating to need assessment and parental involvement.

Parents are to receive a written notice in their native language about any change in identification, evaluation, or placement of their child. The legislation defines *native language* as the language normally used by a person with limited English-speaking ability. If parents remain dissatisfied with placement and education, they may initiate a due process hearing, which is conducted by someone not presently responsible for the child's education.

All participants will receive a verbatim record of the hearing. If still dissatisfied, parents or guardians may carry their grievance to the appropriate state agency and, ultimately, to the courts. While a decision is pending, children remain where they were before the appeal.

The legislation, sweeping in its scope, illustrates why some observers believe that it has produced and will continue to produce radical changes in education. Of importance here is the teacher's role in the process. Somewhere in the identification, evaluation, and placement procedure, teachers will be asked to comment on the child's classroom performance. (Some states have the teacher play a key role in presenting current and past educational information.)

Since the legislation also requires each state to develop and implement a comprehensive system of personnel development, teachers will experience changes in preservice education and in-service training. Sooner or later you will encounter the ramifications of P.L. 94–142. Mainstreaming is here to stay. Table 6.5 is a summary of the major provisions of P.L. 94–142.

Classroom Support for Mainstreamed Students

Mainstreaming, or the inclusion of exceptional children into regular classrooms, means that the mildly handicapped—of all categories—will require additional classroom support. Special education teachers will function as resource personnel, helping regular teachers to plan a student's schooling.

The scope of the federal and state special education legislation has caused educators to realize that almost 50 percent of school children experience problems, some of

Focus → The Special Education Process

Traditionally, when a teacher was concerned about a student who was experiencing an academic or behavioral problem, the first step was to refer that student for a special education evaluation. This process has changed dramatically in recent years. Due to the increasing emphasis on mainstreaming exceptional students and the concept of least restrictive environment, more and more students are being maintained in the regular classroom through prereferral intervention. Figure A illustrates the prereferral process as it would typically be implemented in a school setting.

What is a teacher's role both prior to and after the referral? The role of the regular education teacher in this decision-making process is demonstrated in table A. Note in table A the central role of the teacher in providing services to the exceptional student at the prereferral stage. In this phase, teachers have the consultation support of various school professionals in developing the prereferral intervention program.

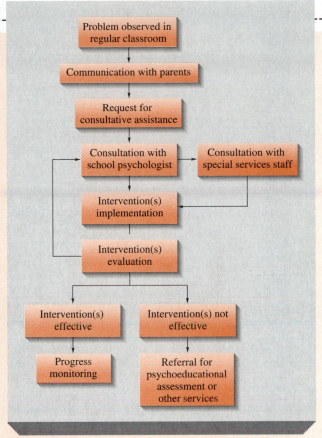

Figure A

Flow chart for prereferral consultation process.

Table A   How the Regular Classroom Teacher Participates in Special Education Decision Making

Stage	Description
Prereferral Stage: *Regular Education Process*	The teacher notices that a student is performing differently from most of the other students in the class. The teacher checks with other teachers to verify his or her observations, then checks with the student's parents to eliminate special circumstances at home that might explain the exceptional performance. The teacher tries different methods of instruction (prereferral interventions) to identify the nature of the problem, and gathers information about the student's performance in other areas. The teacher decides the prereferral intervention was effective and continues to use instructional modifications to provide special education in the regular classroom. Or, the teacher decides the student's performance is sufficiently different to warrant special services, and refers the student to the school's special education support team.
Postreferral Stage: *Special Education Process*	The teacher reviews the results of individual psychological and educational testing, then consults with other team members and compares the student's performance to established criteria for eligibility for special education. The teacher offers an opinion about the appropriate placement for the student. The teacher cooperates with other team members in providing special services and evaluating their effectiveness.

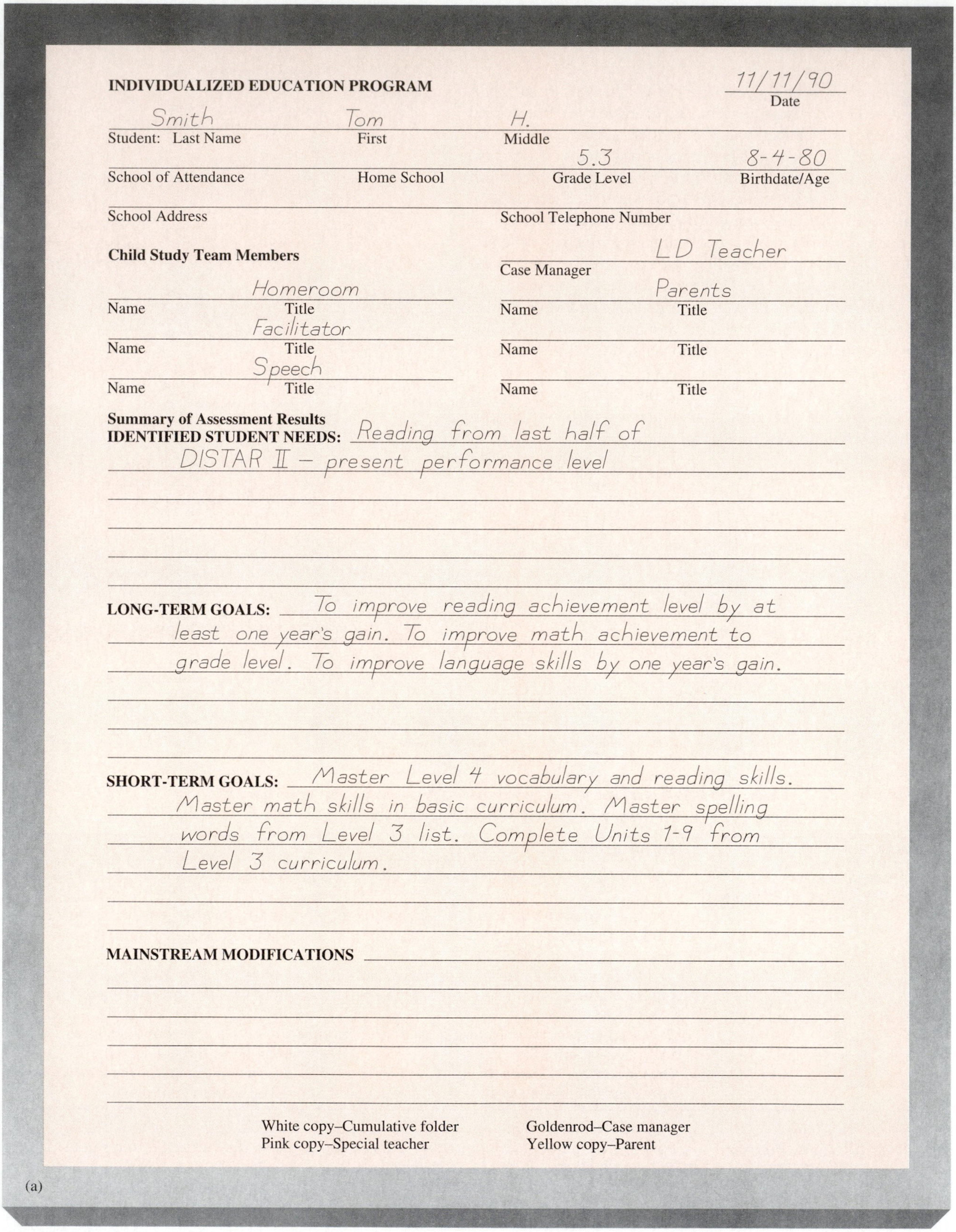

INDIVIDUALIZED EDUCATION PROGRAM

11/11/90
Date

Student: *Smith* — *Tom* — *H.*
Last Name — First — Middle

5.3 — *8-4-80*

School of Attendance — Home School — Grade Level — Birthdate/Age

School Address — School Telephone Number

Child Study Team Members

LD Teacher
Case Manager

Homeroom		*Parents*	
Name	Title	Name	Title
Facilitator			
Name	Title	Name	Title
Speech			
Name	Title	Name	Title

Summary of Assessment Results
IDENTIFIED STUDENT NEEDS: *Reading from last half of DISTAR II – present performance level*

LONG-TERM GOALS: *To improve reading achievement level by at least one year's gain. To improve math achievement to grade level. To improve language skills by one year's gain.*

SHORT-TERM GOALS: *Master Level 4 vocabulary and reading skills. Master math skills in basic curriculum. Master spelling words from Level 3 list. Complete Units 1-9 from Level 3 curriculum.*

MAINSTREAM MODIFICATIONS

White copy–Cumulative folder   Goldenrod–Case manager
Pink copy–Special teacher   Yellow copy–Parent

(a)

Figure 6.3
(a) An individualized education program; (b) description of services to be provided.

DESCRIPTION OF SERVICES TO BE PROVIDED

Type of Service	Teacher	Starting Date	Amt. of time per day	OBJECTIVES AND CRITERIA FOR ATTAINMENT
SLD Level III	LD Teacher	11-11-90	2½ hrs.	Reading: will know all vocabulary through the "Honeycomb" level. Will master skills as presented through DISTAR II. Will know 123 sound-symbols presented in "Sound Way to Reading." Math: will pass all tests at basic 4 level. Spelling: 5 words each week from Level 3 list. Language: will complete Units 1-9 of the grade 4 language program. Will also complete supplemental units from "Language Step by Step."

Mainstream Classes	Teacher	Amt. of time per day	OBJECTIVES AND CRITERIA FOR ATTAINMENT
		3½ hrs.	Out-of-seat behavior: sit attentively and listen during mainstream class discussions. A simple management plan will be implemented if he does not meet this expectation. Mainstream modifications of Social Studies: will keep a folder in which he expresses through drawing the topics his class will cover. Modified district social studies curriculum. No formal testing will be made. An oral reader will read text to him, and oral questions will be asked.

The following equipment, and other changes in personnel, transportation, curriculum, methods, and educational services will be made:

DISTAR II Reading Program, Spelling Level 3, "Sound Way to Reading" Program, vocabulary tapes

Substantiation of least restrictive alternatives: The planning team has determined the student's academic needs are best met with direct SLD support in reading, math, language, and spelling.

ANTICIPATED LENGTH OF PLAN   1 yr.   The next periodic review will be held: _____ May 1991 _____

DATE/TIME/PLACE

☒ I do approve this program placement and the above IEP
☐ I do not approve this program placement and/or the above IEP
☐ I request a conciliation conference

_____
PARENT/GUARDIAN

_____
Principal or Designee

(b)

Table 6.5

Major Provisions of P.L. 94–142	
Each state and locality must have a plan to ensure the following:	
Child identification	Extensive efforts must be made to screen and identify all handicapped children.
Full service, at no cost	Every handicapped child must be assured an appropriate public education at no cost to the parents or guardians.
Due process	The child's and parents' rights to information and informed consent must be assured before the child is evaluated, labeled, or placed, and they have a right to an impartial due process hearing if they disagree with the school's decisions.
Parent/parent surrogate consultation	The child's parents or guardian must be informed about the child's evaluation and placement and the educational plan; if the parents or guardian are unknown or unavailable, a surrogate parent to act for the child must be found.
LRE	The child must be educated in the least restrictive environment that is consistent with his or her educational needs and, insofar as possible, with nonhandicapped children.
IEP	A written individualized education program must be prepared for each handicapped child. The plan must state present levels of functioning, long- and short-term goals, services to be provided, and plans for initiating and evaluating the services.
Nondiscriminatory evaluation	The child must be evaluated in all areas of suspected disability and in a way that is not biased by the child's language or cultural characteristics or handicaps. Evaluation must be by a multidisciplinary team, and no single evaluation procedure may be used as the sole criterion for placement or planning.
Confidentiality	The results of evaluation and placement must be kept confidential, though the child's parents or guardian may have access to the records.
Personnel development, in-service	Training must be provided for teachers and other professional personnel, including in-service training for regular teachers in meeting the needs of the handicapped.
There are detailed federal rules and regulations regarding the implementation of each of these major provisions. The definitions of some of these provisions—LRE and nondiscriminatory evaluation, for example—are still being clarified by federal officials and court decisions.	

From D. P. Hallahan and J. M. Kauffman, *Exceptional Children* 4th ed. Copyright © 1988 Allyn & Bacon Inc., Reprinted by permission.

which require special help. Unless teachers possess both competence and understanding, mainstreaming simply will not achieve its desired objectives. Ultimately, then, much of the responsibility rests with teachers. Faced with this assignment, teachers may have many questions, several of which probably are similar to the following:

• How can I lessen the anxieties of exceptional students and their classmates?
• Exactly what are my obligations under mainstreaming?
• How many students who are handicapped will be in my class?
• Will I receive help in planning programs?
• What is the responsibility of resource personnel?

Focus ← The Regular Education Initiative

A recent movement among many special educators has raised questions about the extent to which P.L. 94–142 has been fully realized. Called the **Regular Education Initiative (REI),** its thrust has been to call into question the exclusion of students who are mildly handicapped (identified as the learning disabled, the seriously emotionally disturbed, and the educable mentally retarded). Supporters of REI argue that most of these students can and should receive all of their education in the regular classroom.

Descriptions of REI contain many statements with which few educators could or would disagree, such as the following:

- Better integration and coordination of services for students with handicaps is needed.
- Effective and economical methods of educating these students should be a priority.
- Students should be identified as needing special services only when necessary.
- Special education should be reserved for those students needing the most specialized help.
- Some students are labelled because of the inadequacies of regular classroom teachers (Kauffman, Gerber, & Semmel, 1988).

As the implications of REI spread throughout the educational community, it received a more searching examination, and several important issues were identified.

1. Can regular classroom teachers distribute instructional resources for all?
2. Does REI distinguish sufficiently between elementary and secondary levels?
3. Research does not support the belief that all students with handicaps should be in regular classrooms.
4. Although there are problems with identifying (labeling) such students, they nevertheless exist.

You can see, then, that REI is a hotly debated topic that cuts to the core of the controversy surrounding the effectiveness of special education services.

Services across the categories of exceptionality that we have identified do not always demonstrate the individualized instructional strategies needed for these students. Frequently, the same instructional tasks are being used with nonhandicapped students and with different types of handicapped students, which ignores the need to individualize instruction for students (Ysseldyke et al., 1989).

The issues have been defined; the lines have been drawn; the implications are far-reaching. You should be alert to the direction this controversy takes, since it can affect all classrooms. (See Lloyd, Singh, & Repp, 1991, for a review of these issues.)

Regular Education Initiative (REI)
A movement to include more of the mildly handicapped in regular classrooms.

- How can I spare the time?
- How can I learn more about special needs?

Though most teacher-preparation institutions have incorporated planning for exceptional children into their courses, you may find several professional activities helpful.

- *Classroom visitation.* Observation and demonstration by others can be invaluable. Having a skilled expert observe you, make constructive suggestions, and actively demonstrate techniques for you can substantially enhance your own expertise.
- *Teacher demonstrations.* Administrators and supervisors can schedule visits to other schools and classrooms where master teachers offer demonstration lessons. Learning theorists have amply demonstrated the persuasiveness of observational learning.
- *Meetings, institutes, and conferences.* These assemblies can be helpful if they are planned to discuss pertinent problems and permit meaningful participation.
- *Professional libraries.* Since the vast special education literature and the rapidly accumulating mainstreaming data often provide profitable suggestions, sample as many bibliographies, articles, books, and government pamphlets as possible. You will find the following journals particularly helpful:

Journal of Learning Disabilities   *American Journal of Orthopsychiatry*

Teaching Exceptional Children   *Educational Leadership*

Exceptional Children   *Behavioral Disorders*

Mental Retardation   *Journal of Special Education*

Remedial and Special Education

• *Curriculum and research.* Thoughtful school officials may encourage teachers to publish bulletins, to prepare curriculum alterations, and to cooperate in writing course objectives. Scholarships may be available; universities may offer course vouchers as a courtesy for student teacher placement; some teachers may conduct research with their classes. All of these activities promote professional growth and furnish information that may produce more efficient teaching and learning.

Some Results of Mainstreaming

In the years that have passed since P.L. 94–142 took, effect, the reactions of educators and the results of a wide variety of studies have been used to evaluate its effectiveness. The results are mixed. For example, Wang and Baker (1985/1986), in a study intended to assess the research on mainstreaming in educating disabled students, summarized the results of 11 empirical studies.

The 11 studies contained a total of 541 students highly diverse in socioeconomic status, gender, race, and geographic location. Thirty-nine percent of the children studied were primary and elementary school students, 16 percent were middle school students, 1 percent were preschool children, and in 44 percent of the comparisons, no information on grade level was provided. The categories of exceptionality broke down as follows:

• 53 percent of the students were classified as mentally retarded
• 3 percent were learning disabled
• 19 percent were hearing impaired
• 25 percent were classified as "mixed category"

Though the authors found that the mainstreamed students with disabilities outperformed nonmainstreamed students with similar educational classifications, the results were not statistically significant. Nevertheless, the positive outcomes on all measures caused the authors to conclude that mainstreaming improves performance, attitudes, and process outcomes for exceptional students.

We must be cautious in interpreting the results of studies investigating differences between segregated and mainstreamed students, particularly with regard to these factors:

• *The nature of the disability.* Emotionally disturbed students find greater difficulty in adjustment and peer acceptance in regular classes than do those students with other disabilities, such as children experiencing vision and hearing difficulties.
• *Parental warmth, acceptance, and cooperation.* These have a powerful impact on a student's locus of control and achievement.
• *Uncontrolled, multiple variables.* Some of these are sibling reaction, self-esteem, and teacher behavior.

Consequently, care must be taken before interpreting these conflicting results; the final verdict on mainstreaming has yet to be rendered. Perhaps the safest route is for our schools to follow such general guidelines as these for students who are mainstreamed:

• Students should be capable of doing some work at grade level.
• Students should be capable of doing some work without requiring special materials, adaptive equipment, or extensive assistance from the regular classroom teacher.
• Students should be capable of "staying on task" in the regular classroom without as much help and attention as they would receive in the special classroom or resource room.
• Students should be capable of fitting into the routine of the regular classroom.
• Students should be able to function socially in the regular classroom and profit from the modeling and appropriate behavior of their classmates.

- The physical setting of the classroom should not interfere with the student's functioning (or, it should be adapted to their needs).
- It should be possible to work out scheduling to accommodate the students' various classes, and the schedules should be kept flexible and be easy to change as students progress.

Neverstreaming: A New Concept

In this chapter, we have introduced you to the concept of mainstreaming. Many proposals have been offered to facilitate implementing the concept of mainstreaming, including consultation by the teacher with a professional (e.g., resource teacher, school psychologist), individualized instruction, and cooperative learning. Nevertheless, many educators in both regular and special education are not comfortable with the concept when it is put into practice. As an alternative to mainstreaming, Robert Slavin and his associates (1991) proposed a new concept, called **neverstreaming.** According to the authors, "the key focus of this approach is an emphasis on prevention and early, intensive, and continuing intervention to keep student performance within normal limits" (p. 373). The proposal is designed to keep nearly all children in the mainstream by trying to prevent academic problems. Neverstreaming is designed to be a comprehensive approach to academic skill development. One aspect of this approach that Slavin and his coworkers are investigating is teacher tutoring with children who have reading problems. Although the neverstreaming approach is just being investigated, this model is one that may have the potential to change your role as a teacher. Think about it!

neverstreaming *A term introduced by Slavin that refers to a determined effort to keep students functioning within normal limits by preventing academic problems.*

EDUCATION AND EXCEPTIONALITY: A MODEL

It is important to associate a given student's characteristics with typical developmental characteristics. How much does a student's performance vary from the norm? How does this affect adjustment? What are the educational implications of a particular student's developmental path?

We previously discussed in some detail the developmental paths that most children take, the theories that attempt to explain the various phenomena, and the research that either verifies or challenges these theories and conclusions. At this point, we suggest you review quickly the developmental norms presented in chapters 4 and 5, using table 6.6.

Although we can arbitrarily divide development into many parts, the categories in this table will help you to relate these developmental accomplishments to the potential damage resulting from a deficit in any one area. For example, extremes in cognitive development may well mean that you can have in your classroom students who are mildly mentally retarded and students who are gifted.

Study any of the eight columns of table 6.6, and you will see how deviation from these milestones can cause varied problems. For example, examining the sequence of social development and learning, you can visualize a student who—for whatever reason—is having problems with peers, causing classroom difficulties, and experiencing learning problems. As the teacher, you would have many concerns. How severe is the underlying problem? Who makes the diagnosis of the problem? Should the student be formally referred or is consultation possible? Could there be long-term effects of the problem?

These questions cannot be taken lightly, since they involve a teacher's role in the prereferral and referral processes. With students who have already been diagnosed and assigned to regular classes through mainstreaming, the questions are similar, but follow a slightly different path. Specialized help will already be available for a student, and the teacher's task will be to determine the extent to which that student can flourish in a regular classroom despite the handicap.

Table 6.6

Milestones in Development and Learning

	Physical	Cognitive	Social	Emotional
Infancy (0–2)	1. Can hear and see at birth 2. Grows rapidly in height and weight 3. Develops rapidly neurologically 4. Proceeds steadily in motor development (crawling, standing, walking)	1. Seeks stimulation 2. Has an egocentric view of the world (beginning to decrease) 3. Demonstrates considerable memory ability 4. Begins to process information	1. Needs interaction 2. Begins to smile 3. Immediately begins having reciprocal interactions 4. Develops attachment	1. Shows beginnings of emotions in first months 2. Passes through emotional milestones

Preschool (2–6)	1. Is extremely active
	2. Masters gross motor behavior
	3. Refines fine motor behavior
		1. Becomes sharper in perceptual discrimination
		2. Shows more focused attention
		3. Shows noticeable improvement in memory
		4. Is easily motivated
			1. Has formed attachments
			2. Experiences beginning of interpersonal relationships
			  a. parents
			  b. siblings
			  c. peers
			  d. teachers
			3. Experiences play as highly significant
				1. Still becomes angry at frustration
				2. Is prone to emotional outbursts
				3. Is slowly growing in emotional control
				4. Is aware of gender
				5. Has fantasies that conform more to reality
				6. May begin to suppress emotionally unpleasant memories

Middle Childhood (7–11)	1. Masters motor skills 2. Exhibits considerable physical and motor skills	1. Experiences attention becoming selective 2. Begins to devise memory strategies 3. Begins to evaluate behavior 4. Shows marked improvement in problem-solving behavior	1. Is more frequently involved in organized activities 2. Is member of same-sex group 3. Is increasingly influenced by peers 4. Usually has "best" friend	1. Takes pride in competence 2. Is confident 3. Shows growing sensitivity 4. Is volatile 5. Strives, is competitive 6. Has growing sexual awareness

You will be involved with mainstreamed students during the referral process and/or during actual instruction. By attempting to match average child development with a particular child's problem in any of the developmental phases seen in table 6.6, you can better understand both the student's problem and the need for an appropriate remedial program.

MULTICULTURAL STUDENTS AND SPECIAL EDUCATION

Of growing concern to U.S. educators is the large number of multicultural students in special education classes. Faced with both standardized tests in a language that may

| | **Developmental Theorists** | | |
Language	Piaget	Erikson	Kohlberg
1. Proceeds from cooing and babbling to words and sentences 2. Begins to use word order and inflection 3. Experiences beginning and rapid increase of vocabulary	*Sensorimotor* 1. Use of reflexes 2. Primary circular reactions 3. Secondary circular reactions 4. Coordination of secondary schemata 5. Tertiary circular reactions 6. Representation	1. Development of trust	1. Beginning of learning wrong from right
1. Moves from first speech sounds to use of sentences with conjunctions and prepositions 2. Acquires basic framework of native language	*Preoperational* 1. Deferred imitation 2. Symbolic play 3. Mental imagery 4. Drawing 5. Language	1. Growing competence and autonomy 2. Initative and purpose	1. Beginning of preconventional moral reasoning
1. Experiences rapid growth of vocabulary 2. Uses and understands complex sentences 3. Can use sentence content to determine word meaning 4. Has good sense of grammar 5. Can write fairly lengthy essays	*Concrete Operations* 1. Conservation 2. Seriation 3. Classification 4. Number 5. Reversibility	1. Industry and competence	1. Continued development of preconventional moral reasoning to 2. Conventional moral reasoning

cause them difficulty and adjustment to a new culture, many of these students experience achievement problems. Too often they are labeled as failures and assigned to special education classes.

Difficulty in identifying students in need of services remains the culprit. Is the problem a limited ability in the new language? Is it the assessment strategies used by professionals? Is it uneasiness with a new culture? Is it sheer unfamiliarity with American schools? Or is it actually some handicapping condition? If you examine these questions objectively, you probably will agree that there is a real risk that some immigrant students will be inappropriately placed in special education classes.

Students from different ethnic groups reflect their distribution in the general population most closely in the learning disability, emotional disturbances, and speech impaired categories, although Asian students are underrepresented in each of these categories. White and Asian students are underrepresented in the mental retardation category, where African Americans are overrepresented. Asian students are overrepresented in gifted and talented programs, while African American, Hispanic, and Native American students are underrepresented (Ysseldyke & Algozzine, 1990).

Frequently, a physical problem may be at the root of a student's difficulties, particularly since many of these students have undetected health problems. Occasionally, emotional problems follow the traumatic experiences of some of these students. Many school systems, wishing to avoid unwarranted special education placement, have attempted an immediate evaluation of these students.

Few linguistically and culturally appropriate assessment instruments exist for the students who speak languages other than English or Spanish, and there seems to be a limited understanding of many of the different cultures from which students come. Consequently, educators hesitate to place a newly arrived immigrant student who does not present a physical handicap into special education (First & Carrera, 1988). Nevertheless, many of these students seem to be candidates for special education. As a teacher, or potential teacher, of such students, try to determine just what is the source of any problem, so that your judgment is based as much on your background knowledge of a student as on immediate behavior.

In the United States today, educators are becoming concerned with the large number of multicultural students in special education classes. Many of these students experience achievement problems because they are faced with standardized tests in a language that may be causing them great difficulty.

After implementation of a plan that is acceptable to the family, school, and specialists, the student begins the specified program. The process does not cease here, but provides continuous evaluation to determine the program's effectiveness, and, if necessary, to devise a new plan. As we have emphasized throughout this chapter, you should prepare for involvement at two key points: helping to identify a student's needs by reporting on educational status, and working with the student and specialized personnel to implement the educational plan.

Bilingual Education and Bilingual Children

Today there are over 30 million Americans for whom English is not the primary language. Estimates are that there will be about six million American school children with "limited English proficiency" (LEP) by the year 2000. In some states (California, Texas, Florida), the linguistic-minority school population is about 25 percent, and in some large urban school districts, 50 percent of the students come from non-English-speaking homes.

bilingual education *Instruction using programs designed to help those with limited English proficiency (LEP) to acquire English by teaching them partly in English and partly in their own languages.*

What happens to students who do not speak the language of the school? Unfortunately, many will achieve below their potential and drop out of school. In an effort to combat this problem, the *Bilingual Act of 1988* stipulates that students with limited English proficiency receive **bilingual education** for three years (or up to five years, if needed) until they can use English to succeed in school.

America, as a nation of immigrant people, has long faced this problem, with our schools playing a special role in the naturalization process (Fillmore & Valadez, 1986). Schools are the places where minority children are exposed to the majority language, usually with the assumption that they'll "pick it up." Little, if any, special help has been provided traditionally to these students, and dropout rates have remained high. In a technological society, a lack of education and poor language skills combine to produce a bleak future; hence, increased attention has been given to this issue.

As research begins to accumulate about bilingual education programs, more knowledge about the students themselves is becoming available. For example, the higher the degree of bilingualism, the better is the level of cognitive attainment (Hakuta, 1986). This outcome is especially true when the native language is retained, the social climate is positive, and minority-language children are not negatively labeled.

Recent research, however, indicates that the native language does not interfere with second language development. Both first- and second-language acquisition seem to be guided by similar principles; the acquisition of languages is a natural part of our cognitive system. Also, the rate of acquisition of the second language seems to be related to the level of proficiency in the first (Hakuta, 1986). With these ideas in mind, what programs have been devised to help bilingual students?

In a landmark decision in 1974 (Lau v. Nichols, 414, U.S. 563), the U.S. Supreme Court ruled that LEP students in San Francisco were being discriminated against, because they were not receiving the same education as their English-speaking classmates. The school district was ordered to provide means for LEP students to participate in all instructional programs. The manner of implementing the decision was left to the school district under the guidance of the lower courts. This decision provided the impetus for the implementation of bilingual education programs in the United States.

Two different techniques for aiding LEP students emerged from this decision. The *English as a Second Language program* (ESL) usually has students removed from class and given special English instruction. The intent is to have these students acquire enough English to allow them to learn in their regular classes, which are taught in English. With the *bilingual* technique, students are taught partly in English and partly in their native languages. The objective here is to help students to learn English by subject matter instruction in their own language and in English. Thus, they acquire subject matter knowledge simultaneously with knowledge of English.

In today's schools, bilingual education has become the program of choice. It is important to remember that programs for LEP students have two main objectives:

• Provide these students with the same education that all children in our society have.
• Help them to learn English, the language of the school and society (Fillmore & Valadez, 1986).

Bilingual education programs can be divided into two categories. In one category are those programs (sometimes called "transitional" programs) in which rapid development of English is to occur, so that students may switch as soon as possible to all-English programs. In the second are those programs (sometimes referred to as "maintenance" programs) that permit LEP students to remain in them even after they have become proficient in English. The rationale for such programs is that students can use both languages to develop mature skills and to become fully bilingual.

The difference between these two programs lies in their objectives. Transitional programs are basically compensatory: they use the students' native languages only to compensate for their lack of English. Maintenance programs, however, are intended to bring students to the fullest use of both languages. As you can well imagine, transitional programs are the more widely used in the schools.

Since the use of two languages in classroom instruction actually defines bilingual education, several important questions must be answered.

- What is an acceptable level of English that should signal the end of a student's participation?
- What subjects should be taught in each language?
- How can each language be used most effectively? (That is, how much of each language is to be used to help a student's progress with school subjects?)
- Should English be gradually phased in, or should students be totally immersed in the second language (which, for most of the students we are discussing, would be English)?

One reason for the controversy surrounding these programs is that research has yet to grapple with many of the important variables. For example, what should be evaluated, English proficiency or subject matter success? How can the quality of the program be assessed? How alike are the children in any program (in ability, SES, proficiency in the native language, level of English on entering the program)?

Although the answers to these and other questions continue to spark controversy, bilingual programs allow students to retain their cultural identities while simultaneously progressing in their school subjects. They also offer the opportunity for students to become truly bilingual, especially if programs begin early.

Who are the exceptional students who will appear in your classroom? To close this chapter, we will review the seven categories of exceptionality mentioned at the opening of the chapter. We must again emphasize, however, that we use these "categories" only to help you organize the information available on exceptional children. Finally, remember that most exceptional students are more like "normal" students than they are different from them.

APPLICATIONS AND REFLECTIONS

Chapter Highlights

Exceptional Children in the Classroom
- You can expect to find a wide range of individual differences in your classroom: physical, cognitive, and behavioral.
- Federal law (P.L. 94–142) requires that students with handicaps be placed in the environment that is "least restrictive" for them.

The Categories of Exceptionality
- Students who are gifted and/or talented have often been overlooked in our classrooms, but today we realize they deserve special attention to further their abilities in a manner calculated to provide normal social and emotional development.
- Students with visual and hearing impairments require early detection to prevent lingering problems that may affect performance. The cognitive ability of these students will be in a normal range, so your expectations for them should be similar to those for the rest of the class.
- Students with communication disorders may experience a developmental delay in language acquisition or find difficulty in expressing themselves. Your knowledge of language development should help you to identify these students.
- Students with physical and health impairments need your help in physically adjusting to the classroom and participating in all class activities.

- Students with behavior disorders present a range of problems that are caused by some interaction of personal, environmental, and even physical factors. You will need considerable sensitivity in working with these students to help them achieve as fully as possible.
- Students with learning disabilities are now identified by applying an exclusion component; that is, the difficulty is not attributed to some other cause, such as mental retardation or a physical problem. In your work with these students, be careful that some other surface difficulty does not mask the learning disability.
- Students with cognitive disabilities will be in your class; they require a carefully sequenced program and a lack of stress as they work.
- Several support systems, ranging from a student's family to professional staff, operate to help exceptional students adjust to their placement.

The Assessment and Classification of Children

- Assessment plays a critical role in placement decisions about students.
- Any classification system of students with handicaps must avoid the dangers of labeling.

Mainstreaming

- Mainstreaming is a policy of placing students with handicaps into regular classrooms whenever possible.
- You will undoubtedly be involved at some point in educational decisions about these students: their identification, evaluation, and placement.
- Your informed input requires knowledge from reading, classroom visits, and workshops (among other sources).

Education and Exceptionality: A Model

- A thorough familiarity with normal development can provide developmental milestones to use as an aid in judging student behavior.

Multicultural Students and Special Education

- Considerable sensitivity is needed in making decisions about multicultural students, since many factors may affect their performance.

Connections

1. Think about how you learn and describe how one of the major concepts discussed in this chapter is part of your learning activities or approach.

_____

_____

_____

_____

2. Identify at least one learning situation (e.g., classroom instruction, self-study, taking a test, small-group work) and describe how you would apply one of the key concepts examined in this chapter _if you were a teacher._

_____

_____

_____

_____

Getting the Picture and Drawing Relationships

Think about the various learning concepts and variables discussed in this chapter. Create pictures, graphics, or figures which highlight relationships among the key components.

Personal Journal

What I really learned in this chapter was _____

_____

_____

_____

What this means to me is _____

_____

_____

_____

Questions that were stimulated by this chapter include _____

_____

_____

_____

_____

Key Terms

ability grouping	153	exclusion component	172	legally blind	163
attention-		exceptional	150	mainstreaming	150
deficit/hyperactivity		gifted	156	mental retardation	174
disorder (ADHD)	168	hard of hearing	164	neverstreaming	187
acceleration	158	hearing impairment	164	Regular Education	
at risk	152	inclusion	178	Initiative (REI)	185
behavior disorders	167	learning disabilities	171	triad model	159
bilingual education	191	least restrictive		visually impaired	162
enrichment	159	environment	154	visually limited	163

section 3

learning theories and practices

Alice West, the ninth-grade social studies teacher at the Junior High West, had caught one of her students, Pam Jones, smoking in the rest room that morning. She told Pam to meet her in her homeroom after school. Alice, who cared about her students, knew she had to take some action and thought seriously about what she should do.

When Pam came to her room later that day, Alice told her to sit down and then said to her, "You're lucky in one way, Pam. There was no one else who saw you smoking."

Pam looked puzzled and said, "I don't understand, Ms. West."

skillfully, teachers are bringing into the classroom a theory that has strong implications for behavior change. ■

In this chapter, as in this example, the primary focus is on behavior. The work in behavioral psychology is guided by a philosophy of science called *behaviorism*. Traditionally, individuals who embrace a behavioristic philosophy believe that studies of ideas, percepts or concepts such as those cognitive theorists propose are not highly useful to change behavior; we must work directly with behavior itself. (Certain behaviorists, such as Bandura, who are frequently called *neobehaviorists,* attempt to

chapter 7

behavioral psychology and learning

"If someone else had seen you, I'd have to make an example of you," replied Alice. "Why do you think that we have rules about smoking on school property? Did you ever think about the possibility of a fire and what could result from that? Didn't you listen to the fire marshall when he spoke to the group? He wasn't just trying to scare you."

"I know, Ms. West. But it's more of a habit now than anything else."

"OK, Pam. Let's try this. You know how you'd like to be part of the tutoring teams that visit the elementary schools; if you can go without smoking at school, I'll put you on the team."

"I won't smoke, Ms. West. I hadn't really thought of what could happen. Besides, I really like working with the kids."

In her concern for the safety of her students, Alice West turned to the use of a behavioral technique. By attempting to use reinforcement

consider cognitive processes such as motivation and intention. Some scholars would now consider Bandura a cognitive theorist, even though his early work embraced a more traditional focus on behavior.) Many of the classroom applications of behavioral psychology have been developed in the field called *applied behavior analysis.* As the name implies, applied behavior analysis is "the science in which procedures derived from the principles of behavior are systematically applied to improve socially significant behavior to a meaningful degree and to demonstrate experimentally that the procedures employed were responsible for the improvement in behavior" (Cooper, Heron, & Heward, 1987, p. 15).

To help you understand the differences among the outstanding behaviorists, we'll first examine Pavlov's *classical conditioning* and Thorndike's *connectionism.* Next we'll analyze

Classical Conditioning 200
Pavlov's Work 200
Features of Classical
     Conditioning 201

Thorndike's Connectionism 202
The Law of Readiness 202
The Law of Exercise 202
The Law of Effect 204

Operant Conditioning 204
Skinner's Views 204
Skinner and Reinforcement 205
The Nature of
     Reinforcement 206
Skinner and Punishment 209
Categories of Punishment 210
How Punishment Works 211
For the Classroom 212

Social Cognitive Learning 216
An Explanation of Modeling 217
Multicultural Models 220
For the Classroom 220

**Behavioral Theories and
Teaching 222**
Techniques to Increase
     Behavior 222
Techniques to Decrease
     Behavior 224
Techniques to Maintain
     Behavior 227
Techniques of Self-Control 228

Behaviorism and the Future 230
Applying Behavior Analysis to
     Schooling 230
Skinner's Suggestions 232

**Applications and
Reflections 233**

Skinner's *operant conditioning* and point out key differences between Pavlov and Skinner. Bandura's *neobehaviorism* deserves our attention because of its importance for learning and development. Finally, we'll turn to behaviorism's impact on the classroom, concentrating on applied behavior analysis management techniques. These theories have continuing and direct relevance for classroom teachers.

After you read this chapter, you should be able to

- distinguish between classical and operant conditioning

- recognize how students may acquire fears through classical conditioning
- explain how a theory such as Thorndike's connectionism had widespread classroom application
- identify the major elements of operant conditioning
- understand how the principles of reinforcement and punishment can be used in the classroom
- apply the principles of social cognitive theory (such as imitation and modeling) to your instructional techniques

CLASSICAL CONDITIONING

Much of the affective behavior that your students demonstrate in class can be explained by the work of the Russian physiologist, Ivan Pavlov. Many students' fears, anxieties, and joys can be traced to conditions within the classroom, frequently without the awareness of their teachers.

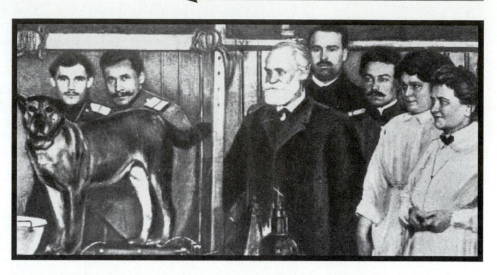

Pavlov's Work

Many years after his death, Pavlov's best-known writings, *Conditioned Reflexes* (1927) and *Lectures on Conditioned Reflexes* (1928), remain highly influential.

Ivan Pavlov (1849–1936) shown in his laboratory flanked by his assistants and one of his dogs.

His studies of digestion in animals led to an important psychological discovery: that of the **conditioned reflex.** In Pavlov's classic experiment, the anticipation of food caused the flow of saliva in dogs.

Saliva flowed at each dog's sight of the food dish or of the attendant, perhaps even at a sound the attendant usually made during feeding. We would expect the sight and smell of food to cause the flow of saliva, but other sights and sounds (such as the attendant or a bell) don't usually cause saliva to flow. Somehow, Pavlov's dogs had "learned" that these sights and sounds signalled the appearance of food, as described in figure 7.1.

Pavlov called the signal (the sight or sound) that produced saliva the **conditioned stimulus.** He next turned his attention to the planned establishment of conditioned reflexes. You may be familiar with the model he used. Food (labeled the *unconditioned stimulus*) was paired with a metronome (labeled the *conditioned stimulus*). At the beginning of the conditioning experiment, the salivary reflex (labeled the *unconditioned response*) was elicited only in the presence of the food. Pavlov repeatedly paired the food with the metronome, and found that in time, the metronome, independent of the food, elicited salivation (labeled a *conditioned response*). The sequence in **classical conditioning** is as follows:

1. US (unconditioned stimulus) produces UR (unconditioned response)

    food————saliva

2. CS (conditioned stimulus) produces no response

    metronome alone————no response

3. CS + US (conditioned + unconditioned stimulus) produces UR (unconditioned response)

    metronome plus food————saliva

4. CS (conditioned stimulus) produces CR (conditioned response)

    metronome alone————saliva

conditioned reflex *A response that is elicited by a conditioned stimulus when the unconditioned stimulus is not present.*

conditioned stimulus *A previously neutral stimulus that has acquired the power to elicit a response.*

classical conditioning *Pavlov's explanation of conditioning in which a neutral (conditioned) stimulus gradually gains the ability to elicit a response because of its pairing with a natural (unconditioned) stimulus.*

Thus, the conditioned stimulus (sound of the metronome) has come to acquire some of the response-producing potential of the unconditioned stimulus (the food). Note that the conditioned stimulus has been conditioned to the unconditioned stimulus.

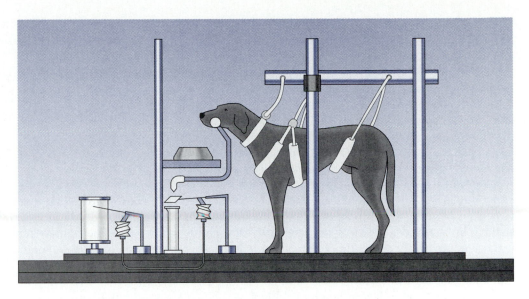

Figure 7.1

Pavlov's research apparatus. In studying the digestive process, Ivan Pavlov would present a dog with meat powder and collect saliva through a tube inserted into one of the dog's salivary glands. The amount of salivation was recorded by a stylus writing on a rotating drum. Pavlov found that dogs salivated to stimuli associated with the presentation of food, such as the mere sight of the laboratory assistant who brought the food.

From Benjamin B. Lahey, Psychology: An Introduction, *3rd ed. Copyright © 1989 Wm. C. Brown Communications, Inc., Dubuque, Iowa. All Rights Reserved. Reprinted by permission of Times Mirror Higher Education Group, Inc., Dubuque, Iowa.*

stimulus generalization *The process by which a conditioned response transfers to other stimuli.*

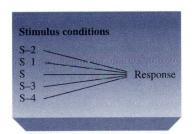

Figure 7.2

Stimulus generalization. S is some stimulus. The response—stopping—is made to S_1, red traffic light; S_2, red light over door; S_3, red stop sign; and S_4, red flag.

discrimination *The process by which we learn not to respond to similar stimuli in an identical manner.*

Features of Classical Conditioning

Before discussing the classroom implications of Pavlov's work, we should review several principles of classical conditioning that Pavlov discovered (Kalish, 1981). These include stimulus generalization, discrimination, and extinction.

Stimulus generalization refers to the process by which the conditioned response transfers to other stimuli that are similar to the original conditioned stimulus. For example, once having learned that the color red means "stop," we tend to stop or hesitate at red lights, signs, and flashing red bulbs. In figure 7.2, think of the various stimuli as different forms of the red condition meaning "stop."

Stimulus generalization is a process that lies at the heart of transfer of learning in the classroom. We want our students to be able to use the material they learn in class in a variety of circumstances. Teenagers who have learned to avoid drug usage in schools, through the use of written and visual materials, will, we hope, avoid drugs when and if they actually are offered to them on the street. Remember, though, that the less closely the stimulus resembles the conditioned stimulus, the weaker the response will be. Reading about a drug transaction is far different from being approached by someone—maybe even a friend—who is offering to sell drugs.

Generalization appears to explain the transfer of a response to a situation other than that in which the original learning occurred. A first-grade youngster terrified by a stern teacher may transfer that fear or anxiety to anything about schools: teachers, books, the school building itself. Two facts about generalization are worth noting.

- Once conditioning to any stimulus occurs, its effectiveness is not restricted to that stimulus.
- As a stimulus becomes less similar to the one originally used, its ability to produce a response lessens accordingly (Hulse, Egeth, & Deese, 1980).

Discrimination refers to the process by which we learn not to respond to similar stimuli in an identical manner. You would be well advised not to yell at a uniformed police officer as you would at a uniformed opposing football player. We make these distinctions by a process known as *discrimination,* which is just the opposite of generalization. Whereas *generalization* means responding in the same way to two different stimuli, discrimination implies responding differently to two similar stimuli.

For example, if in the morning your car absolutely refuses to start—nothing happens—you can be quite sure that the problem is electrical. It might be the battery; it might be the starter. If, however, you hear a clicking sound, the chances are good that the starter is faulty. Because of prior experiences, you have discriminated the starter as the problem. We respond differently to stimuli because of our previous experiences, in which certain of our responses were successful in the presence of certain stimuli.

Again, we can draw important classroom implications. Youngsters learning to read might have serious difficulties if they could not discriminate circles from curved lines, or horizontal from vertical lines. They then could not, or at least not consistently, discriminate the letters *v* from *u* or *b* from *d;* this could lead to reading problems. Similar discrimination challenges exist for young learners confronted with pairs of numbers such as 21 and 12, or 25 and 52. Learning to make discriminations of form and, later in life, of substance is a critical component of successful learning.

Extinction refers to the process by which conditioned responses are lost. In his experiments, Pavlov found that by presenting the sound of the metronome alone (that is, with no food), he could eliminate the conditioned response. The older brother or sister who warned a child of that "terrible Mrs. Smith" who would be next year's teacher could easily cause the younger student to associate anxiety with Mrs. Smith. After several nervous weeks at the beginning of school, however, the child's discovery that Mrs. Smith is a pleasant person gradually extinguishes the anxiety.

Behaviorists who have followed Pavlov have been interested in the consequences of the responses that students make and in deliberately shaping behavior. This leads us to the work of E. L. Thorndike.

extinction *Refers to the process by which conditioned responses are lost.*

Develop an example of classical conditioning in the classroom. Identify the sequence in classical conditioning, including naming the US, UR, CS, and CR.

THORNDIKE'S CONNECTIONISM

Edward Lee Thorndike (1874–1949) believed that all learning is explained by connections (or bonds) that are formed between stimuli and responses. These connections occur mainly through trial and error, a process Thorndike later designated as **connectionism,** or learning by selecting and connecting. Thorndike formulated laws of learning, which were not inflexible laws, but rules that learning seemed to obey. His three major laws of learning (Readiness, Exercise, and Effect) have had direct application to education.

connectionism *Thorndike's explanation of learning (by selecting and connecting).*

The Law of Readiness

When organisms, both human and animal, are ready to form connections, to do so is satisfying and not to do so is annoying. Thorndike believed that readiness is an important condition of learning, because satisfaction or frustration depends on an individual's state of readiness. He stated (1913, p. 133) that readiness is like an army sending scouts ahead of a train whose arrival at one station sends signals ahead to open or close switches. Schools can't force students to learn if they aren't biologically and psychologically prepared.

The Law of Exercise

Any connection is strengthened in proportion to the number of times it occurs and in proportion to the average vigor and duration of the connection. Conversely, when a connection is not made between a stimulus and response for some time, the connection's strength decreases. Continued experimentation and criticism forced Thorndike to revise the original law of exercise after 1930. He realized that practice alone was insufficient for improvement. There must also be a strengthening of the bond by reinforcement; that is, the law of effect must also operate. When students practice, they should be aware of the consequences of what they are doing. Otherwise, practice becomes ineffective—even harmful, if error creeps in.

Edward Thorndike (1874–1949).
Archives of the History of American Psychology, The University of Akron.

teacher – student

Using Classical Conditioning in the Classroom

1. *Generalization* is the process by which a conditioned response transfers to other stimuli that are similar to the original conditioned stimulus.
   - If you suspect that a student is nervous in your class, try to discover what circumstances triggered the anxiety; that is, try to identify the stimuli acting at the time.
   - Assume that you have found that your anxious students are relaxed elsewhere in school. Observe them carefully and identify the situations where they are most anxious (in the classroom? on the playground? walking to school?).
   - Continue to narrow your search to discover the stimuli that actually produced the anxiety. It may be a larger classmate who bullies your student on the way to and from school. With supervised activity on the playground and in the classroom, everything seems fine. Or you may discover that anxiety appears in your relationship with this student. Have **you** done something, or could this be anxiety over grades? You may find that you student's nervousness results from fear of adults or parental pressure over grades.
   - If grades are the cause, then the fear or anxiety is the unconditioned response. Take definite steps to introduce non-fear-provoking stimuli with those stimuli that cause the anxiety. You could have the student practice with tests (with reassurance that "they won't count"). Try to obtain parental cooperation: ask parents to downplay any "life and death" feelings about their youngster's grades. Help in preparing for exams by reassuring the child. Finally, without showing favoritism, help this student to succeed. (Note in all of these examples that the intent is identical: to change the circumstances.)

2. If you want students to transfer the material you are presenting, then you must provide ample opportunity for them to discover the relationship that the subject has to other situations.
   - Since you want your students to learn more about numbers than merely memorizing them, give practical examples, preferably using community sources with which the children are familiar. "When you came by Mr. Smith's store this morning, did you notice the four rows and four columns of oranges? How many were there altogether?"
   - In teaching subjects such as the American Revolution or the French Revolution, point out to students how people can live under tyranny for only so long before they rebel. Remind them of recent events in which many of the communist countries overturned their governments.

3. *Discrimination* is the process by which we learn not to respond to similar stimuli in an identical manner.
   - Stress to your students how important it is to distinguish things that seem alike but mean different things. One ring of the school bell may mean recess; continuous ringing may mean a fire drill or alarm.
   - Provide continued practice for your students so that they become accustomed to searching for differences. This is true at all grade levels. In the early grades, students must learn to look for the difference that makes a number 6 and not 9. At the secondary level, the search for differences becomes more subtle: in *Tom Sawyer,* both boys run away, but for different reasons. Encourage your students to discover the differences and discuss them.

4. *Extinction* is the process by which conditioned responses are lost.
   - Help students to make their concerns realistic. Students in California, for example, may be anxious about earthquakes. Explain to them how the school was constructed to protect them from earthquakes; show films of boys and girls leaving a school quietly and in good order; practice leaving the building while you talk to them in a reassuring manner. The same procedures can be used for other situations, such as fires or tornadoes.
   - Prevent responses encouraging misbehavior. During written work the class clown may continue to act up, even after having been reprimanded. In many cases, teachers turn away after a scene, and other students, by gesture or whisper, urge the child on. If you continue to monitor the situation, they will be unable to offer encouragement, and the behavior should cease.

The importance of classical conditioning for teachers is that awareness of its principles enables you to be more alert to the role that stimuli can play in a student's behavior.

The Law of Effect

Probably the most important of Thorndike's laws, the Law of Effect states that responses accompanied by satisfaction are more firmly connected with a situation; responses accompanied by discomfort have their connections weakened. The greater the satisfaction or discomfort, the greater is the strengthening or weakening of the bond. In 1932, Thorndike revised the law to stress that the strengthening effect of reward is much greater than the weakening effect of punishment. Pupils tend to learn more effectively (and easily), and to retain that learning longer, if it has pleasant consequences.

For many years, Thorndike had a powerful influence on educational practice because of his insistence on a scientific basis for education. For example, his explanation of the transfer of learning is still meaningful. Called *identical elements,* the theory states that learning can be applied to new situations only when there are identical elements in both situations.

Hergenhahn (1988) stated that Thorndike believed good teaching begins with knowing what you want to teach: the stimuli. You must also identify the responses you want to connect to the stimuli and the timing of appropriate satisfiers. Thorndike would say this:

- Consider the pupil's environment.
- Consider the response you want to connect with it.
- Form the connection (with satisfaction).

Thorndike's remarkable energy and drive led to an astounding number of publications and provided education with the scientific emphasis it so desired. His work with the Law of Effect was an early statement of the importance of positive reinforcement, a concept B. F. Skinner greatly expanded.

OPERANT CONDITIONING

B. F. Skinner (1904–1990) received his doctorate from Harvard, and after teaching for several years at the universities of Minnesota and Indiana, he returned to Harvard. It was there that he continued to refine the differences between classical and operant conditioning and applied his ideas to a wide range of human endeavors.

Convinced of the importance of reinforcement, Skinner developed an explanation of learning that stressed the consequences of behavior: what happens after we do something is all-important. Alice West, the teacher in the opening vignette in this chapter, decided that she would react to her student's behavior by reinforcing the desired behavior. Reinforcement has proven to be a powerful tool in the shaping and control of behavior, both in and out of the classroom.

For many years, the two Freds (Fred S. Keller and B. Fred Skinner) educated and entertained those attending the annual behavior analysis convention. This entertaining exchange was entitled "Old Friends" and occurred at the Midwestern Association for Behavior Analysis convention in Chicago in 1976.

Photo by G. K. Hare.

Skinner's Views

B. F. Skinner was in the forefront of psychological and educational endeavors for several decades. Innovative, practical, tellingly prophetic, and witty, Skinner's work has had a lasting impact. In several major publications—*The Behavior of Organisms* (1938), *Science and Human Behavior* (1953), *Verbal Behavior* (1957), *The Technology of Teaching* (1968), *Beyond Freedom and Dignity* (1971), and *About Behaviorism* (1974)—and in a steady flow of articles, Skinner reported his experiments and developed and clarified his theory. He never avoided the challenge of applying his findings to practical affairs. Education, religion, psychotherapy, and other fields have all felt the force of Skinner's thought.

Although Skinner initially made his impact during the 1930s when the classical conditioning of Pavlov was popular and influential, he demonstrated that the environment

operant conditioning *Skinner's explanation of learning, which emphasizes the consequences of behavior.*

had a much greater influence on learning and behavior than Pavlov realized. In his explanation of **operant conditioning,** Skinner argued that the environment (i.e., parents, teachers, peers) reacts to our behavior and either reinforces or eliminates that behavior. The environment holds the key to understanding behavior (Bales, 1990).

For Skinner, behavior was a causal chain of three links: (a) an operation performed upon the organism from without—a student comes to school without breakfast; (b) some inner condition—the student gets hungry; and (c) a kind of behavior—listless behavior in the classroom.

Lacking information about inner conditions, teachers should not indulge in speculation. For example, a student is listless and disinterested during class. Skinner would scoff at those who would say the student was unmotivated. He would ask, "What does this mean?" "How can you explain it behaviorally?" The teacher or counselor searching for causes has mistakenly stopped at the second link: some inner condition. The answer lies in the first link: something done to the student—here, the lack of breakfast. Physical difficulty or trouble with parents would be similar operations.

Until his death in 1990, Skinner emphasized the important effect of consequences on behavior and cautioned us about the limitation of a cognitive-oriented psychology.

> So far as I'm concerned, cognitive science is the creationism of psychology. It is an effort to reinstate that inner initiating-originating-creative self or mind which, in a scientific analysis, simply does not exist. I think it is time for psychology as a profession and as a science in such fields as psychotherapy, education, developmental psychology and all the rest, to realize that the science which will be most helpful is not cognitive science searching for the inner mind or self, but selection by consequences represented by behavior analysis.
>
> Looking back on my life—sixty-two years as a psychologist—I would say that what I have tried to do, that what I have been doing, is to make that point clearer; to show how selection by consequences in the individual can be demonstrated in the laboratory with animals and with human subjects and to show the implications of that for the world at large—in not only the profession of psychology, but in consideration of what is going to happen in the world unless some very vital changes are made. Any evidence that I've been successful in that is what I should like to be remembered by. (Skinner, 1990)

Skinner and Reinforcement

Throughout our analysis of Skinner's system, we will constantly encounter the term *reinforcement,* which Skinner considers a key element to explain how and why learning has occurred. Reinforcement is typically used as follows:

reinforcer *A consequential stimulus that occurs contingent on a behavior and increases the behavior.*

• A **reinforcer** is a *stimulus event* that, if it occurs in the proper temporal relation with a response, tends to maintain or increase the strength of a response, a stimulus-response connection, or a stimulus-stimulus connection (Hulse, Egeth, & Deese, 1980, p. 23). In our discussion of Skinner's work, it is important to distinguish between the basic principles of behavior and various behavior change procedures. Reinforcement is a *principle of behavior,* in that it describes a functional relationship between behavior and controlling variables. In contrast, a *behavior change procedure* is a method used to put the principle into practice. Praise, for example, is a procedure that may be a powerful reinforcer. If you praise a student's correct responses immediately and the student increases correct responses, praise can be identified as a behavior change procedure that functions as a reinforcer.

• The term *principle of reinforcement* refers to an increase in the frequency of a response when certain consequences immediately follow it. The consequence that follows behavior must be contingent upon the behavior. A contingent event that increases the frequency of behavior is referred to as a reinforcer (Kazdin, 1989, p. 105). Once you praise a student's correct response, you increase the probability that the student will remember the response and use it in future, similar situations.

- *Reinforcement* is not synonymous with *reward*. Nonpsychologists use the term *reward:* parents may buy a child an ice cream cone for "being good"; a basketball coach may take the squad to a pizza parlor for a "good game." These are broad statements, in which no specific behavior is identified. Psychologists, however, view reinforcement quite specifically. They believe that reinforcement becomes effective when applied to *specific* behaviors: a student receives a teacher's praise for the solution to a problem or the correct answer to a question.

The Skinnerian model attempts to link reinforcement to response as follows:
antecedents—response—reinforcement

The antecedents represent the range of environmental stimuli, the unknown antecedents acting on an organism at a given time. If we focus on what is observable (the response) and reinforce it, control of behavior passes to the environment (i.e., teachers, parents). (Note that Pavlov concentrated on conditioned stimuli, which is why his theory is called *Type S conditioning*. Skinner focused on responses, and thus his theory is called *Type R conditioning*.)

The Nature of Reinforcement

In his analysis, Skinner (1953) concentrated on behavior that affects the surrounding world because the consequences of that behavior feed back into the organism, thus increasing the organism's tendency to reproduce that behavior under similar circumstances. Once Skinner reached that conclusion, he had at his disposal a powerful tool for analyzing behavior.

Using Reinforcement

Imagine that you are a ten-year-old with a sweet tooth. Your father has prodded you all summer to mow the lawn: "Do it today"; "Do it before I get home, or else." But your mother, with a shrewd understanding of human behavior, discovers that the local variety store carries a new brand of ice cream bars that you like—but they're rather expensive. She promises you a package each week after mowing the lawn. By the end of the summer you are cutting the grass on a regular basis, with no threats, coercion, or scoldings.

This simple illustration contains all of the elements that made fervent believers of many of Skinner's readers. It also demonstrates why Skinner was dissatisfied with the Pavlovian model as a technique for explaining all of our behavior. Skinner was determined that he would work only with the observable in order to build a scientific structure of learning and behavior.

In our example, no one can identify the stimulus that caused you to mow the lawn during August. The only tangibles that we have to work with are your behavior and the reinforcers. (Remember: your father told you to do it, and you avoided the task.) Skinner began his analysis with pigeons and rats in exactly the same manner, and quickly recognized that the consequences of behavior—the reinforcers—were powerful controlling forces. Perhaps we could summarize his thinking by saying this: *Control the reinforcers, control the behavior.* We saw an example of this technique in the chapter opening. By controlling the reinforcer (the chance to tutor elementary school students), Alice West was attempting to encourage her student to obey the school's rule on smoking.

Thus far we have been discussing positive reinforcers, or events that are presented after a response has been performed and that increase the behavior or activity they follow. *Negative reinforcement* also exists; the term refers to stimulus events *removed* after a response has been performed, whose removal also increases the behavior or activity they follow (Kazdin, 1989). That is, both positive and negative reinforcement functionally *increase* behavior. Negative reinforcement should not be confused with punishment, which, as we shall see later in the chapter, decreases behavior.

Skinner (1953) noted that some event is a negative reinforcer only when its removal increases performance of the response. You can probably think of many things that are aversive in the environment. For example, if we are talking on the phone and

Table 7.1

Categories of Reinforcers		
Category	**Types**	**Usage**

Primary	1. Biological (natural)
	   a. food, liquids, sensory
	     pleasures
		Giving candy, ice cream, soft music
		(used with young or exceptional students)

Secondary	1. Social
	   a. facial expression
	   b. proximity
	   c. words
	   d. privileges
		
		Frowning, smiling
		Changing seats
		Praise
		Appointment to leadership role

	2. Activity
	   a. pleasant or "high-
	     frequency" behavior
		
		Playing a game following completion of
		class assignment

	3. Generalized
	   a. tokens
	   b. points
	   c. anything that can be used
	     to obtain pleasure
		
		Allowing student who compiles 25 points
		to select pleasant activity, such as free
		reading, playing a game, building models

close the door to reduce some noise, the stimulus (noise) is removed contingent upon a response (closing the door). There is an increased probability that in the future, we will perform the same behavior (closing the door) again. In Skinner's analysis (1974, p. 46), "A negative reinforcer strengthens any behavior that reduces or terminates it."

Negative reinforcement operates in many situations. Note that it is necessary for some aversive event to be present in order for the principle to operate. Since you want to avoid establishing aversive events in the classroom, this procedure should be used infrequently in educational programs. Nevertheless, it is important to understand the concept and its potentially strong impact on behavior.

Types of Reinforcers

As he continued to study behavior from this viewpoint, Skinner examined reinforcers more carefully and categorized them according to their power.

Provide an example of a primary, a secondary, and a generalized reinforcer. Apply use of the three types of reinforcers to a student who is learning math.

1. *Primary reinforcers* are those that affect behavior without the necessity of learning: food, water, sex. In this sense, they are natural reinforcers.
2. *Secondary reinforcers* are those that acquire reinforcing power because they have been associated with primary reinforcers. For example, if one of Skinner's pigeons pecked a disk, a green light would go on, followed a second later by the arrival of a piece of corn. The green light remained on and, after repeated trials, gradually acquired reinforcing potential of its own.
3. *Generalized reinforcers,* a form of secondary reinforcers, are those that acquire reinforcing power because they have accompanied several primary reinforcers. Money belongs in this category because it leads to the possession of food, liquids, and other positive things; it then becomes a generalized reinforcer for a multitude of behaviors. Table 7.1 illustrates the various types of reinforcers.

Schedules of Reinforcement

interval reinforcement
Scheduled reinforcement, in which the reinforcement occurs at definite established time intervals.

Skinner identified two kinds of intermittent reinforcement: interval and ratio reinforcement. **Interval reinforcement** is scheduled reinforcement, or that which occurs at definite established time intervals; for example, you may decide to praise a student who talks out only if that student remains quiet for five minutes. Following the praise, no additional reinforcement is given until another five minutes passes.

Focus The Keller Plan

Utilizing many of the behavioral principles we have just discussed, Keller (1968) devised a technique for individualized instruction. Using a **personalized system of instruction (PSI),** students proceed at their own pace through a series of self-contained curricular segments. Each student responds to written stimulation and is reinforced for a correct response. Several steps are involved.

- Decide on the material to be covered.
- Divide the material into self-contained segments.
- Determine the most efficient means of evaluation.
- Permit students to move from step to step at their own pace.

In a PSI classroom, you see students working independently at their desks and a teacher moving from student to student. Upon passing a mastery test, the student moves on to the next unit (Stallings & Stipek, 1986).

Hergenhahn (1988), summarizing the results of PSI, concludes that students seem to achieve at a superior level if the principles of learning in the system are carefully followed. Criticisms of PSI focus on the lack of reciprocal interactions between teachers and students and whether all curricular material can be so easily segmented.

Ratio reinforcement is reinforcement that occurs after a certain number of responses. For example, you may insist that one of your students complete four math problems before doing a game activity. If the ratio is slowly altered, an amazing number of responses may result from a very low number of reinforcements. Skinner also developed variable schedules for both interval and ratio reinforcement, whereby reinforcement can appear after any time interval or number of responses (Ferster & Skinner, 1957).

The importance of reinforcement and the identification of classes of reinforcers led Skinner to consider what happens to behavior that escapes constant reinforcement for some reason. You don't reinforce your students for every desired response they exhibit. Students receive periodic grades; workers receive weekly or monthly checks; but both students and workers continue to behave appropriately.

The answer lies in the effectiveness of **intermittent reinforcement,** especially the use of schedules of reinforcement. Studies of four classes of schedules (see table 7.2) have produced consistent findings.

1. **Fixed ratio,** in which reinforcement depends on a definite number of responses. If you require your students to complete thirty workbook problems before they can do something else, perhaps more exciting, you have put them on a fixed ratio schedule.
2. **Variable ratio,** in which the number of responses needed for reinforcement varies from one reinforcement to the next. Required responses may vary, and subjects never know which response will be reinforced. For example, some teachers don't want to see only completed projects. They ask to see them during various stages of their progress, and mark what has been done.
3. **Fixed interval,** in which a response results in reinforcement after a definite length of time. The sequence is as follows: reinforcement—20 seconds—reinforcement; reinforcement—20 seconds—reinforcement. Note that responses made during the 25-second interval are not reinforced. Teachers occasionally fall into a pattern in which they have students work independently, and then ask for responses perhaps ten or fifteen minutes into the work period. Students learn this pattern and start to work just before the teacher is due to call on them.
4. **Variable interval,** in which reinforcement again depends on time and a response, but the time between reinforcements varies. In the above example, rather than waiting for ten or fifteen minutes to go by, teachers ask for responses at different times: immediately, later, and in the middle of the class.

personalized system of instruction (PSI) *Kellers technique for individualized instruction.*

ratio reinforcement *Reinforcement occurring after a certain number of responses.*

intermittent reinforcement *Reinforcement in which reinforcers occasionally are implemented.*

fixed ratio *Term describing a schedule in which reinforcement depends on a definite number of responses.*

variable ratio *Term describing a schedule in which the number of responses needed for reinforcement varies from one reinforcement to the next.*

fixed interval *Term describing a schedule in which a response results in reinforcement only after a definite length of time.*

variable interval *Term describing a schedule in which the time between reinforcements varies.*

Table 7.2

Schedules of Reinforcement		
Type	**Meaning**	**Outcome**
Fixed ratio (FR)	Reinforcement depends on a definite number of responses—for example, every tenth response	Activity slows after reinforcement and then picks up
Variable ratio (VR)	Number of responses needed for reinforcement varies—ten responses, reinforcement; five responses, reinforcement	Greatest activity of all schedules results
Fixed interval (FI)	Reinforcement depends on a fixed time—for example, every thirty seconds	Activity increases as deadline nears (e.g., students must finish paper by a certain date)
Variable interval (VI)	Time between reinforcements varies	Steady activity results

What can we conclude from Skinner's analysis of reinforcement schedules?

First, continuous reinforcement produces a high level of response only as long as reinforcement persists. The lesson for teachers: don't constantly reinforce your students; they come to expect it. (You like students, or you wouldn't be teaching, and probably tend to use praise excessively; be careful.)

Second, intermittent reinforcement, although producing slower acquisition of responses, results in greater resistance to extinction (loss of response).

Third, ratio schedules can be used to generate a high level of responding, but fatigue may hinder performance. Fixed ratios are common in education; we reinforce our students for papers, projects, and examinations. However, after students respond and receive reinforcement, behavior drops off sharply and learning efficiency declines (Skinner, 1953).

Fourth, interval schedules produce the most stable behavior. Skinner (1968, p. 159) summarized the meaning of these schedules for education as follows:

The student will be less dependent on immediate and consistent reinforcement if he is brought under the control of intermittent reinforcement. If the proportion of responses reinforced (on a fixed or variable ratio schedule) is steadily reduced, a stage may be reached at which behavior is maintained indefinitely by an astonishingly small number of reinforcements.

Skinner and Punishment

Thus far we have stressed the key role of reinforcement (both positive and negative) in controlling behavior: **positive reinforcers** are those stimuli whose presentation strengthens behavior, and **negative reinforcers** are those stimuli whose withdrawal strengthens behavior. But what happens when a teacher or parent withdraws a positive reinforcer (e.g., says that a child cannot go to the movies) or introduces something unpleasant (e.g., slapping or scolding)? Skinner believed that these two types of actions constitute **punishment.**

Kazdin (1989) defined punishment more formally as follows: "the presentation of an aversive event or the removal of a positive event following a response that decreases the frequency of that response" (p. 144). Note that Kazdin mentioned two aspects of punishment.

1. *Something aversive (unpleasant) appears after a response.* This is called an *aversive stimulus.* For example, a parent may slap a child who yells at the parent; teachers may reprimand students who are talking in class. In each case, something unpleasant follows behavior.

Describe how schedules of reinforcement affect the rate and strength of responses for a child who is disruptive in your classroom.

positive reinforcers　*Those stimuli whose presentations increase the rates of responses.*

negative reinforcers　*Stimuli whose withdrawal strengthens behavior.*

punishment　*Refers to the presentation of an aversive stimulus or removal of a positive stimulus contingent upon a response which decreases the probability of the response.*

2. *Something positive (pleasant) disappears after a response.* A child who slaps another youngster while playing may be sent indoors. A teenager who violates the curfew may lose use of the car for the next weekend. In both instances, something unpleasant follows undesirable behavior.

Categories of Punishment

In behavioral programs, *punishment* refers to the presentation or removal of some event that results in a reduction in the frequency of a behavior. There are three general categories of punishment: the presentation of aversive events, the withdrawal of positive consequences, and consequences based on activity (Kazdin, 1989).

The most commonly recognized form of punishment involves presenting something aversive following the performance or response of an individual. If the event presented reduced the frequency of the behavior, it would be functionally defined as punishment. Note that certain aversive events (such as shouting) may actually increase some behavior, and therefore would be defined as reinforcers. Verbal statements such as reprimands commonly function as punishment, but may lose their effectiveness over extended applications. Other aversive events, such as physical intervention (corporal punishment), have been identified as having functional punishing effects, but should not be used except in extraordinary circumstances, and even then their use remains quite controversial.

Withdrawal of positive consequences can also serve to reduce the frequency of some behavior and may serve as punishment. The two major forms of withdrawal of positive consequences are **time out** from reinforcement and **response cost.**

Time out from reinforcement has a long history of use in educational settings. You may have heard of or seen instances in which students were involved in "time out" or "time away" by being placed in a chair in the hall or sent to the principal's office. Many of these procedures did not qualify as punishment, and may actually have led to greater misbehavior.

Time out from positive reinforcement refers to the removal of all positive reinforcers for some time period. Time out is often not effective, because not all sources of reinforcement are removed. For example, a student sent to the hallway for a time out period may actually receive considerable attention from peers who happen to be walking by. Brief time out has been found to be effective, but has some disadvantages in educational settings. First, there is a tendency for teachers and others to use time out as the sole method of discipline. During these periods, the child is often excluded from learning activities. There also is the danger that teachers might revert to longer and longer time-out periods with no real benefit to the student.

Response cost involves a loss of a positive reinforcer and, unlike time out, does not involve a period during which positive events are unavailable. Response cost most often involves a fine or penalty of some sort. For example, students given access to some reinforcer for a specified period of time may have that time taken away for inappropriate behavior. Like time out, response cost should be used with positive procedures. Indeed, response cost depends on positive events being present to work effectively.

A relatively new class of punishment techniques is based on *aversiveness following some response.* For example, requiring a person to do something that involves effort or work may reduce the response and therefore, serve as punishment. **Overcorrection** is a procedure that is included in this category. It involves a penalty for some inappropriate behavior that includes two procedures. First, restitution is involved, since the person corrects the effects of some negative action. A student who breaks another student's pencil would be required to replace it. Second, positive practice is included; this consists of repeatedly practicing an appropriate behavior. A student may be required to demonstrate the correct use of a pencil, by writing, for example. Of course, not all behaviors that a teacher is trying to reduce would be handled with both components of overcorrection.

time out *A form of punishment in which a student loses something desirable for a period of time.*

response cost *A form of punishment involving the loss of a positive reinforcer (e.g., after misbehavior, a student may no longer be a classroom monitor).*

overcorrection *A form of classroom management involving both restitution and positive practice.*

How Punishment Works

Studying the psychological mechanisms underlying punishment, researchers have identified several key elements that influence its effectiveness (Kazdin, 1989).

1. *Schedule of punishment.* Generally, punishment is more effective when it is delivered every time, rather than intermittently. However, when you discontinue punishment, recovery of a response originally punished is greater under conditions of continuous punishment than it is with intermittent applications. A teacher who reprimands a student for some rule infraction would be advised to use the reprimand each time the problem behavior occurs. Nevertheless, once a behavior has been suppressed, the punishment procedure should be used intermittently to keep it from reappearing.

2. *Intensity of punishment.* It was once believed that increasing the intensity of punishment increases its effectiveness. However, this is not the case. If punishment is to be considered, you should use mild forms.

3. *Source of reinforcement.* Punishment is usually enhanced when other sources of reinforcement that maintain the behavior are removed. It is important to recognize that behavior (both positive and negative) is maintained by various reinforcement contingencies. Therefore, punishment will be more effective when a certain behavior is not reinforced at the same time that punishment contingencies are involved. For example, when a teacher tries to use punishment in the classroom, it is common for a student's peers to reinforce the child's inappropriate behavior through laughing or clapping. Punishment would be expected to be less effective when peers reinforce the child.

4. *Timing of reinforcement.* Most student behavior consists of a series of actions that make up a response class, or group of behaviors. Punishment is usually more effective when it is delivered early in a sequence of behaviors that form a response group. Consider the student who throws spit wads in the classroom. The act of throwing spit wads is actually made up of a series of actions that lead to the final act of throwing. The child usually takes out a piece of paper, rolls it into a ball, puts the magic solution on the ball, and proceeds to toss it across the room. Punishment early in the sequence leading to the act of throwing will be more effective in breaking up the chain of problematic behaviors.

5. *Delay of punishment.* The longer the interval between behavior and punishment, the less effective is the punishment. The consequences of behavior, pleasant or painful, are most effective when they immediately follow that behavior. The explanation for the effectiveness (or not) of punishment lies in the interval between behavior and punishment: if it is lengthy, the unwanted behavior may be reinforced by something or someone else in the environment. By the time you get around to disciplining a student, he or she may have received the attention of peers, who may laugh or give the "thumbs up" signal or some other form of support that encourages additional misbehavior.

    Also, punishment becomes more effective (in a positive sense) if students know exactly why you're punishing them. Punishing an entire class for something a few may have done can produce only bad feelings and tension. Make sure students understand the what and why of punishment, and be consistent: if you punish something once, you must punish the behavior each time it appears—regardless of the offender. Otherwise, students are confused and continue to exhibit the behavior.

6. *Variation of punishment.* Kazdin (1989) noted that although punishment usually consists of a contingency applied after some behavior, varying the punishment that follows a behavior can actually enhance the effects. It is possible that some type of adaptation to the repeated effects of the same punishment occurs (e.g., always reprimanding a child will be less effective over repeated applications). Kazdin, however, was careful to point out that variation does not imply

combination. Combining several aversive events would be objectionable on ethical and practical grounds.

7. *Reinforcement of alternative behaviors.* Kazdin made two important points that must be considered in any use of punishment techniques. First, aversive events of relatively weak intensity can effectively suppress behavior if reinforcement also is provided for an alternative positive response. Second, punishment usually trains a person in what not to do, rather than in what to do. Thus, it is important that you follow up with positive reinforcement when punishment is used, because it will increase the effectiveness of punishment as a procedure, focus your attention on teaching positive behaviors to replace the negative ones you are trying to reduce, and reduce the negative side effects of using aversive strategies.

At this point you should consider two generalizations about punishment: (a) regardless of what you may personally think of punishment as a means of controlling behavior, punishment is highly effective when properly used; (b) there is little doubt that the side effects of punishment, most of which are undesirable, accompany punishment that is routinely, even thoughtlessly, applied.

For the Classroom

Skinner was a constant and critical observer of current educational practices. Using the teaching of arithmetic as an example, Skinner noted that students must learn special verbal responses—words, figures, signs—that refer to arithmetic functioning. Consequently, teachers must help their students to bring this behavior under stimulus control.

Students must learn to count, add, subtract, multiply, and divide before they can solve problems. Teaching these procedures entails the proper use of positive reinforce-

"First, she tells us how much fun reading is. Then, she assigns me three extra chapters as punishment when I snicker."

Robert Hageman. Courtesy of Phi Delta Kappan.

Try to avoid using schoolwork as a means of punishment. Think of alternatives—preferably reinforcement of an alternative desired behavior.

Focus ◀------ **Don't Rely on Punishment**

In a perceptive analysis, Skinner questioned the reasons for teaching failure and settled upon the excessive reliance upon punishment (Skinner's expression for this: *aversive stimuli*. Although corporal punishment, legal in some states, is used infrequently today, other forms of punishment that are perhaps even more damaging psychologically, such as ridicule and sarcasm, have grow more common. With these forms of aversive control, we can force students to read books, listen to lectures, and take tests; but if these activities are disliked, they are usually accompanied by unwanted by-products. In fact, some behaviorists argue that behavior problems can be solved with nonaversive strategies under virtually all conditions (LaVigna & Donnellan, 1986).

Students are ingenious in their methods of avoiding and escaping from aversive stimuli: they come late; they become truants; they develop school phobia; they feign illness; they simply "turn off" to the teacher and anything educational. They may even become abusive and destructive, turning to vandalism.

Note: There is a difference between escape and avoidance behavior.

1. *Escape behavior* occurs when a response eliminates an aversive event. Keeping a student from joining classmates in a pleasant activity until a task is completed illustrates the escape technique: when the appropriate responses are made, the aversive stimulus or punishment (in this case, isolation) is removed.

2. *Avoidance behavior* allows a student to prevent or postpone contact with something aversive. Feigning illness in the morning to stay home so as to avoid a teacher's punishment is a good example of avoidance behavior.

Attractive settings, multisensory materials, and insultingly easy material provide few, if any, answers. Students will not learn unless positive reinforcement prevails. Students remember what happened in school and transfer that learning to new situations because of the consequences of their behavior in the classroom. If we present material mechanically and don't offer students the opportunity to respond in order that we may reinforce those responses, school becomes meaningless for students.

Teaching will become more pleasant, teachers more successful, and teacher-student relationships more positive when teachers abandon aversive techniques in favor of designing personally satisfying schedules of reinforcement for students (Skinner, 1968).

Focus

Skinner and the Reluctant Mathematician

You may agree or disagree with Skinner's system, but his identification of the reluctant mathematician is at once perceptive and telling. We are all familiar with those who freeze at the sight of numbers (are you one?). Skinner, of course, argued that such behavior can be directly traced to the lack of adequate and correct contingencies of reinforcement.

If you are comfortable with figures, you should have no difficulty with these simple problems. If, however, you are one of the frozen, your reactions should be interesting.

1. Examine the following columns of figures for about thirty seconds. Don't try to add them. Just scan each column and estimate the four that have the highest totals.

```
A B C D E F G H I
3 9 5 7 1 8 3 2 3
8 0 3 7 2 5 9 8 4
3 8 8 5 3 2 1 4 3
6 2 2 4 3 6 5 1
8 7 5 4 5 6 5 7 9
5 1 2 6 6 1 5 6 3
2 1 2 6 6 1 5 7 9
7 4 9 3 8 8 7 9 6
```

2. Fill in the blanks to make this a correct multiplication problem.

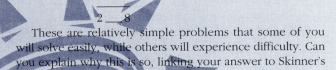

$$
\begin{array}{r}
\underline{}7 \\
\times\ 8\underline{} \\
\hline
2\underline{}8
\end{array}
$$

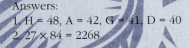

These are relatively simple problems that some of you will solve easily, while others will experience difficulty. Can you explain why this is so, linking your answer to Skinner's operant conditioning?

Answers:
1. H = 48, A = 42, G = 41, D = 40
2. 27 × 84 = 2268

---

ment, which should be immediate and frequent (particularly in the first stages of instruction). For example, Skinner estimated that during the first four school years, teachers can arrange only a few thousand behavior-reinforcement contingencies, but that efficient mathematical behavior requires at least *twenty-five thousand contingencies* during these years (Skinner, 1968). How might positive contingencies be increased?

Skinner believed that schools should search for positive reinforcers that they now have at their disposal, such as paper, paints, puzzles, and activities that students enjoy. The next step is to make their use contingent upon desired behavior. One way of combining both of these features would be the use of *teaching machines,* which divide materials to be learned into small units and reinforce successful behaviors. These devices are mechanical (which students usually like) and they provide positive reinforcement (which everybody likes). They also eliminate aversive stimuli.

There are several advantages in the use of teaching machines.

- Reinforcement for the right answer is immediate; just using these machines can be reinforcing.
- Machines make possible the presentation of carefully controlled material in which one problem can depend on the answer to the preceding problem, eventually leading to the development of complex behaviors.
- If the material lacks sufficient inherent reinforcing characteristics, other reinforcers (such as those just mentioned) can be made contingent upon completion of the program (Skinner, 1986).

Tracing the history of teaching machines, Skinner (1986) noted that teaching machines are a great asset for motivation, attention, and appreciation. Motivation is enhanced because good programs "maximize the effects of success" by having students take small steps and helping them to do so successfully (Skinner, 1986, p. 108).

Attention increases because students (like all of us) attend to those things that reinforce us. Appreciation of art, music, or a discipline is enhanced by a carefully arranged series of reinforcements.

Having students proceed, successfully, at their own rate means that some students will master many fields quickly, while those who move more slowly will, nevertheless, survive as successful students. Education can become more efficient if it utilizes the existing technology of teaching machines and moves away from those ideas that have proven fruitless for the past several decades. Today's more sophisticated teaching machines include desktop models with earphones and voice feedback, and microcomputers designed for programmed instruction.

Finally, Skinner's work has definite implications for teachers:

- *Reinforcement remains such a powerful tool in controlling behavior* that teachers should constantly be aware of the consequences they provide.
- *The well-known* **Premack principle** *has valuable classroom implications.* David Premack (1965) stated that all organisms engage in some activities more than in others. After noting a student's preferred activities, you can then use these as positive reinforcers. For example, noting that several boys who avoid anything mathematical enjoy playing ball, a shrewd teacher could promise them free time to play ball after completing their math work.
- *Aversive stimulation (punishment) may cause more problems than it solves.* Use punishment sparingly and carefully, realizing that there may be occasions when nothing else works. If you must punish, try to get the offending student to do something that you can positively reinforce—and do so as soon as possible.
- *Teachers should be alert to the timing of reinforcements.* Though it may be impossible to reinforce all desirable behaviors, when you decide that a certain behavior is critical, reinforce it immediately. Do not let time elapse.
- *Teachers should determine precisely what they want their students to learn,* and then arrange the material so that they make as few mistakes as possible.

A study of disruptive behavior in secondary school classes illustrates these ideas (McNamara, Evans, and Hill, 1986). The classes were in remedial math; one consisted of 17 pupils aged 12 to 13 years; the other had 15 pupils aged 13 to 14. Both groups were noisy and disruptive at the beginning of class; they pushed their tables together and talked loudly, making it impossible to begin the lesson.

The teacher, a 23-year-old woman, had one year of experience teaching in the school and felt she related well to the students individually but lacked group control. Several procedures were suggested to make up the intervention technique.

1. The tables were set in rows with two students at each table. (Here the teacher was attempting to structure the classroom environment to aid in her use of behavior techniques.)
2. Rules of the classroom were displayed on a large chart placed at the front of the classroom. The rules also were printed on sheets of paper and distributed to the class. The rules were these: arrive on time, work quietly, bring necessary materials, do not shout, don't bother others. (This procedure identified acceptable behavior.)
3. The teacher was asked to make evaluative statements about conduct at the end of the lesson. (Here assessment measures were introduced.)
4. If the evaluation was positive, the class could spend the final ten minutes of the lesson doing puzzles. (Recall the Premack principle.)

Premack principle *The theory that access to high-frequency behaviors acts as a reinforcer for the performance of low-frequency behaviors.*

How could the Premack principle be implemented with a child who is not paying attention in your class?

teacher – student

Using Operant Conditioning in the Classroom

1. Operant conditioning is concerned with the consequences of behavior.
   - A good general principle for teaching is this: when students respond, react to their behavior as quickly as possible, immediately if you can. Your reaction may be either positive or negative, but you can be sure that if you allow enough time to elapse between a student's response and your reaction, what you say or do will have lost much of its impact.
   - Don't assume that you know why students do or don't do something. Skinner would say that you are guessing. Work with what your students say or do and reinforce (or punish) that behavior in an attempt to shape their behavior in the desired direction.
   - Be sure that you know exactly what you want your students to do; otherwise you reinforce behavior that may or may not lead to desirable objectives. Must a student have the correct answer to receive positive reinforcement? Would a partial answer suffice? Or would a positive attitude toward the task be enough to warrant reinforcement? These are important questions that you must think about to become skillful in applying reinforcement.
2. Control the reinforcers, control the behavior.
   - Once you get to know your students, you'll be able to identify those reinforcers that they particularly like. In the chapter's opening vignette, the secondary school student liked working with the younger students. Allowing her to do so illustrates the application of a powerful reinforcer. The opposite also holds true: knowing your students well enables you to take away something pleasurable (working with younger students) or to introduce something unpleasant (extra work after school). In either case, your control of the reinforcers permits you to shape students' behavior.
   - Be sure students understand why they are being reinforced. Teachers who stand in front of a class and say "That's very good" to the entire class are reinforcing unknown behaviors, some of which may be objectionable.
   - When you apply reinforcers, remember Skinner's advice: apply them to specific behaviors. "That's good" is too vague. "Good, Billy. You got the right answer this time." By merely saying "That's good," you can't be sure of what you're reinforcing. Billy may have stopped trying to get the answer when you spoke to him.
   - If you must use punishment, be careful of how you use it and be sure that it is appropriate for the particular behavior. A secondary school teacher recently related how he had been pushing a good student ("Do you call that good work? When are you going to turn in something that you're proud of?"). The student, a good worker and usually pleasant and good-natured, turned one day and shouted at the teacher. Though there will unquestionably be times when you must punish, try not to misjudge the situation the way that this teacher did. Know your students: know what they are capable of, and what they can tolerate.
3. Be aware of the nature and timing of your reinforcements.
   - Teachers are often criticized for giving too much positive reinforcement. Decide how frequently you must reinforce a student, since the frequency will vary from student to student. Discover what individual students consider as important reinforcers; some will respond well to teacher praise, while others will need more tangible reinforcers, such as being appointed teacher's helper, leading traffic patrols, or being designated class messenger for the week.
   - Students who have a problem with their self-esteem or lack confidence in a particular subject may need frequent reinforcement. Provide as much as you think necessary and then gradually reduce it. Initially, you may reinforce their general behavior in your class (let them select the posters for the month), then restrict it to the subject matter (reinforce partially correct answers), and, finally, limit reinforcement to the necessary minimum (tests, projects).
   - Teachers who reinforce too frequently find that students work only for the reinforcement and that reinforcement becomes meaningless after awhile. If you find this happening, initiate class discussions in which you try to lead students to the realization that learning itself is satisfying and important.

5. Self-assessment consisted of the students' checking off the rules that they had followed on the sheets that had been distributed. (Here the teacher was striving for student self-control.)

The results showed a substantial improvement in student on-task behavior and a notable increase in positive teacher behavior. (We shall return to Skinner's ideas on behavior modification in greater detail in chap. 13.)

SOCIAL COGNITIVE LEARNING

Albert Bandura (1925–) received his doctorate in 1952 from the University of Iowa, where he was influenced by the learning research tradition. Applying these principles to human behavior, Bandura initiated a sweeping program of theory and research that led to the development of social learning theory. Although some scholars now consider Bandura and those who embrace his theory to be cognitive theorists, we discuss his work in this section because it has strong behavioral foundations. His theory does have many cognitive features. Considerable evidence exists that learning occurs through observing others, even when the observer does not reproduce the model's responses during acquisition and therefore receives no reinforcement (Bandura et al., 1963). For Bandura, **social cognitive learning** means that the information we process from observing other people, things, and events influences the way we act.

Children in all cultures learn and develop by observing experienced people engaged in culturally important activities. In this way, teachers and parents help students to adapt to new situations, aid them in their problem-solving attempts, and guide them to accept responsibility for their behavior (Rogoff, 1990).

Observational learning has particular classroom relevance, since children do not do just what adults tell them to do, but rather what they see adults do. If Bandura's assumptions are correct, teachers can be a potent force in shaping the behavior of their students with the teaching behavior they demonstrate in class. The importance of models is seen in Bandura's interpretation of what happens as a result of observing others.

- The observer may acquire new responses.
- Observation of models may strengthen or weaken existing responses.
- Observation of models may cause the reappearance of responses that were apparently forgotten.

If students witness undesirable behavior that either is rewarded or goes unpunished, undesirable student behavior may result; the reverse also is true. Classroom implications are apparent: positive, consistent teacher behavior contributes to a healthy classroom atmosphere. To understand the power of modeling, study the accompanying pictures carefully. Note the children's aggressive behavior after observing the model.

In a classic study, Bandura, Ross, and Ross (1963) studied the effects of live models, filmed human aggression, and filmed cartoon aggression on preschool children's aggressive behavior. The filmed human aggression portrayed adult models displaying aggression toward an inflated doll. The filmed cartoon aggression portrayed a cartoon character displaying the same behavior as the humans. The live models displayed aggression identical to that in the films. Later, all the children exhibited significantly more aggression than youngsters in a control group. Also, filmed models were as effective as live models in transmitting aggression. Research suggests that prestigious, powerful, competent models are more readily imitated than models who lack these qualities (Bandura et al., 1963).

social cognitive learning
According to Bandura's theory, the process whereby the information we glean from observing others influences our behavior.

Older siblings in the family have a strong modeling influence on younger family members.

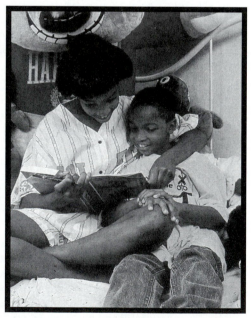

What processes are involved in observational learning? Develop a teaching strategy that uses these processes.

An Explanation of Modeling

Modeling behavior may be described as one person's observation of another's behavior and acquiring of that behavior in representational form, without simultaneously performing the responses (Bandura, 1977, 1986). Four important processes seem to be involved in observational learning.

1. *Attention*. Mere exposure to a model does not ensure acquisition of behavior. An observer must attend to and recognize the distinctive features of the model's response. The modeling conditions also must incorporate the features previously mentioned, such as attractiveness in the model and reinforcement of the model's behavior. Students who recognize these characteristics in their teachers will attend to the important features of their instructors' presentation. That our students are attracted to the compelling features of desirable models can be seen in their imitation of the clothing, hairstyles, and mannerisms of today's rock stars, athletes, actors, and actresses.

2. *Retention*. Reproduction of the desired behavior implies that a student symbolically retains the observed behavior. Bandura believes that "symbolic coding" helps to explain lengthy retention of observed behavior. For example, a student codes, classifies, and reorganizes the model's responses into personally meaningful units, thus aiding retention. What does this mean? As your students observe you, they must also form some type of image or mental schema that corresponds to what you are actually doing. (Note: they cannot form this mental picture unless they attend.) Your task is to urge them, either covertly or overtly (or both) to form this image while you are demonstrating.

3. *Motor reproduction processes*. Bandura believes that symbolic coding produces internal models of the environment that guide the observer's future behavior. The cognitive guidance of behavior is crucial for Bandura, because it explains how modeled activities are acquired without performance. But cognitive activity is not autonomous: stimulus and reinforcement control its nature and occurrence. Again, what does this mean? After observation and after urging your students to form an image of the task's solution, have them demonstrate the solution as soon as possible. Can they do it? You can then reinforce correct behavior and alter any incorrect responses. Don't be satisfied with "show and tell" on your part; have them reproduce the necessary behavior so that all of learning's mechanisms are used: stimulus—cognition—response—reinforcement.

4. *Motivational processes*. Although an observer acquires and retains the ability to perform modeled behavior, there will be no overt performance unless conditions are favorable. For example, if reinforcement previously accompanied similar behavior, the individual tends to repeat it. But vicarious reinforcement (observing a model being reinforced) and self-reinforcement (satisfaction with one's own behavior) are also powerful human reinforcers.

   Bandura introduces a subtle distinction here that helps to distinguish social learning theory from Skinner's operant conditioning. Reinforcement acts on our students' motivation to behave, and not on the behavior itself. In this way, Bandura believes, the resulting learning is stronger and longer-lasting than that produced by reinforcing behavior alone.

Self-Efficacy

As we have seen, social cognitive learning results from the interactions among behavior, environmental variables, cognitive processing, and personal factors (Schunk, 1989). These factors, especially the environment (in the form of modeling or the feedback we

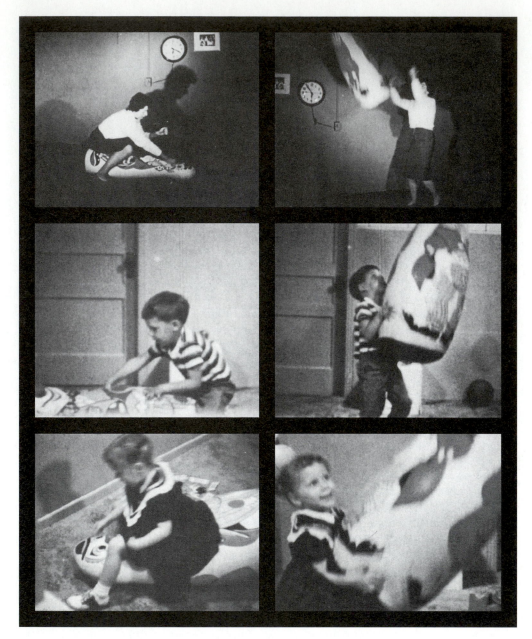

Photographs of children reproducing the aggressive behavior of the female model they had observed on film.

From Bandura, Ross, & Ross, 1963.

get from others), influence our feelings of competency on a particular task or skill. Such feelings of competency, called **self-efficacy,** develop from information conveyed by four sources (Bandura, 1981, 1986).

1. *Performance accomplishments.* We acquire personal and effective information from what we do; we learn from first-hand experience how successful we are in mastering our environments.
2. *Vicarious experience.* Watching "similar others" perform, we persuade ourselves that we can probably do an action also. The reverse is also true.
3. *Verbal persuasion.* Persuasion can lead our students into believing that they can overcome their difficulties and improve their performance.
4. *Emotional arousal.* Stressful situations constitute a source of personal information. If we project an image of ourselves as inept and fearful in certain situations, then we enhance the possibility of just that behavior. But if an admired model demonstrates "coolness under fire," that behavior reduces our tendency toward debilitating emotional behavior.

self-efficacy *Individuals' beliefs in their abilities to exert control over their lives; feelings of competency.*

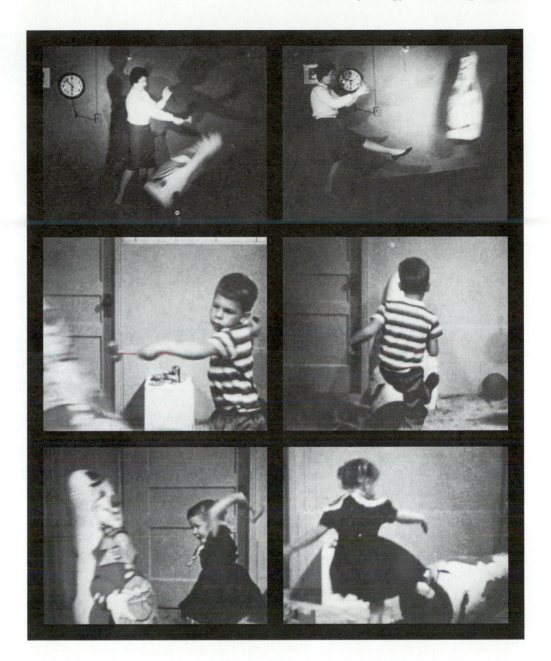

Receiving data from these sources enables us to judge the extent of our self-efficacy; that is, success raises our sense of self-efficacy, while failure diminishes it. You can see how your feedback to your students can have a powerful effect on their feelings of competency. As a respected model, your evaluations carry significant weight. When you say, "Of course you can do it, Kelly," you are providing strong verbal persuasion. You should then follow through on this encouragement by ensuring that the student's performance accomplishment meets your (and the student's) expectations.

Your instructional techniques also are important. Research has consistently shown that when students are taught how to go about a task—that is, when they are given strategy training—their performance improves (Paris, Cross, & Lipson, 1984). This in turn influences their self-efficacy: persons' belief that they know what they are doing improves their control over a situation.

Using models also can be effective in improving self-efficacy. Working with elementary school children who were experiencing difficulty in mathematics, Schunk, Hanson, and Cox (1987) had the students observe videotapes of students under different learning conditions.

- Some of the students observed a teacher helping students solve problems.
- Others observed peer models who solved the problems easily and then made positive statements reflecting self-efficacy.
- Still others observed coping models in which the students had difficulty and made mistakes, but also uttered coping statements ("I'll have to work hard on this"). The students were then seen to become more skillful.

Observation of the coping models seemed to produce the most beneficial results.

Thus far we have indicated that social cognitive learning offers pertinent suggestions for understanding our students' behavior, particularly by making us aware of the modeling power of our behavior and the importance of self-efficacy to our students' learning. How can we apply these principles to the classroom?

Multicultural Models

Our discussion of modeling provides an excellent opportunity to stress the benefits of presenting models from various cultures. Different cultures have different values, beliefs, and motives that appear in the behavior of members of those cultures. If you are able to introduce into your classroom outstanding representatives of a particular culture, you can then reinforce the characteristics, abilities, and behaviors that members of that culture hold in esteem.

The visit of Nelson Mandela to the United States is a good example. His trials and ultimate triumph have been a source of inspiration to black youths. Study of such an individual not only engenders pride in black students, but also reminds the other students of the respect and honor that a model like Mandela commands. By inviting such outstanding figures into your classroom or initiating study projects about them, you also have the chance to promote intercultural understanding. Individuals who are honored by their cultures because they further interpersonal relations teach your students an important lesson.

Self-efficacy develops from performance accomplishments, vicarious experience, verbal persuasion, and emotional arousal.

With regard to inviting models, consider these questions that can help your selection.

- Do they have status? They should possess those features that lead to status: they should be knowledgeable, educated, and admired.
- Are they competent? Probably so, or they would not have achieved status.
- Are they respected? Though we may quibble over the definition of "respect," outstanding individuals eventually must behave in a manner that elicits the respect of others.

Children from different cultures, like all of us, try to make sense of their world by developing explanatory models. By reinforcing the values and attitudes that express the best in their cultures, you help to instill pride in these students and contribute to greater intercultural understanding.

For the Classroom

Bandura's ideas have particular relevance for the classroom, especially as they furnish information about the characteristics of desirable models and the personal features of students, notably their self-efficacy. Certain characteristics of models seem to relate positively to observational learning: those who have high status, competence, and power are more effective in prompting others to behave similarly than are models of lower standing (Bandura, 1977, p. 88).

teacher – student

Social Cognitive Learning in the Classroom

1. Learning occurs from observing others even when the observer doesn't practice the observed behavior.
   - Film a video while groups of your students make social studies presentations (using maps, transparencies, models, etc.). As they watch the video, let them criticize the quality of their presentations, their methods, how they gained (or did not gain) the interest of the class, and how they would improve their presentations.
   - Show a filmstrip or a video of a favorite story. Set up groups in the class to critique the filmstrip and compare it to the story. Is it true to the book? Are the characters depicted the way they imagined they would be? What did they learn from observing the way that the characters acted?
   - Discuss the subject of "heroes" with your students. Who are they? What makes them heroes? Are they all particularly courageous? Did they take risks and overcome obstacles to achieve outstanding goals? Did they contribute something of lasting value to society? Do you believe that a person has to give up his or her life to become a hero? Under what circumstances? What is the difference between an idol and a hero? Do popular culture heroes fit the criteria of a true hero? Your class may want to make a Hall of Fame and nominate their heroes for membership.
2. Several important processes are involved in observational learning.
   - Reinforcement occurs when children reenact what they have observed after a tour or a field trip. (For example, in the early elementary classes, after a trip to a dentist, use a high stool for a dental chair and large white shirts buttoned down the front as dentists' smocks, and let the children act out what they have seen and heard.)
   - After reading a story aloud to a middle school group, select students to be the main characters, and after a brief "rehearsal," let them reproduce a scene for the class; then discuss with them the main idea, the characterization, the plot.
   - Draw high school students' attention to the sequencing of steps during a chemical experiment. Once they have seen it performed and understand the procedure, they perform the experiment themselves. Those who perform it well may help their classmates who are having difficulty. In this way, all of the students should better be able to retain and use the material.
3. For teachers who use observational learning, there are several significant sources of information available that are also excellent motivational tools.
   - Cooperative learning provides students with the opportunity to show each other how to work together to complete a project.
   - Peer tutoring is another method to encourage one child to imitate another's skill in performing a special task.

Older children help younger children to learn when they demonstrate their knowledge to them. They may present puppet shows for them, help them with their reading, play games with them in the schoolyard, assist them in using the computer, or be "buddies" to children with special needs.

The behavior of those who have achieved status and distinction undoubtedly has produced successful consequences, thus suggesting a high functional value for observers. The model's behavior, then, also furnishes information about the probable consequences of similar behavior by the observer. Thus, model characteristics attract observers not only because the models have achieved status, even adulation (as in the example of rock stars), but also because their behavior has resulted in tangible rewards, such as money and power.

As for students, Bandura (1981) has expressed concern about the development of self-knowledge, particularly the notion of self-efficacy, which he states "is concerned with judgments about how well one can organize and execute courses of action required to deal with prospective situations that contain many ambiguous, unpredictable, and often stressful, elements" (1981, p. 201).

Estimates of self-efficacy affect choices of activities and situations: we avoid situations that we fear will exceed our abilities, but confidently perform those activities that we think we can handle. They also affect the quality of our behavior and our persistence in difficult tasks. For an example of how observational learning improves task persistence, consider Craske's research.

In a study of 37 male (mean age = 11.4) and 28 female pupils (mean age = 10.11), Craske (1985) used a social learning theory strategy to increase the persistence of the subjects who had been identified as *learned helplessness* children (children who feel helpless when faced with almost any kind of challenge). Subjects were taught to attribute failure to a lack of effort rather than a lack of ability. The subjects observed an eight-minute film in which a model answered a set of 18 puzzles and was reinforced for each correct response. The model was also told that the correct answer resulted from "trying hard."

The results in the study indicated that the females were helped significantly, while the males improved, but not to the same extent. These results are particularly interesting as they relate to self-efficacy. The girls saw themselves as needing help, but the boys' judgments of themselves as competent individuals caused them to downplay any support.

The schools offer an excellent opportunity for the development of self-efficacy; consequently, educational practices should reflect this reality (Bandura, 1981). That is, materials and methods should be evaluated not only for academic skills and knowledge, but also for what they can accomplish in enhancing students' perceptions of themselves.

Finally, to translate social learning theory into meaningful classroom practice, remember:

1. Just what do you wish to present to your students (the specific behaviors to be modeled)?
2. Is this worth their doing? (What are the kinds of reinforcements available for the correct response?)
3. How are you going to tell them, show them, and urge them to visualize the desired behaviors?
4. Does the lesson possess qualities that will improve your students' self-efficacy?

BEHAVIORAL THEORIES AND TEACHING

Our objective thus far in this chapter has been to explain the theory and research that comprises behaviorism, while offering general applications. With this as a basis, we can now turn to specific illustrations of how the theory "works" in the classroom. Our discussion will include techniques for increasing, decreasing, and maintaining behavior. Also, since the use of behavioral principles has not been without criticism, we will conclude this section by considering certain ethical issues.

Techniques to Increase Behavior

In our earlier discussion of reinforcement, we emphasized that only those events that strengthen or increase behavior can be called reinforcement. Positive reinforcement is any event following behavior that increases the future rate and probability of responding. Negative reinforcement involves an increase in the probability of some behavior following the removal of an aversive event after the behavior is performed.

As we have seen, consequences must be contingent upon the appropriate behavior. The sequence in positive reinforcement is as follows:

1. You have made it quite clear to a student that the math seatwork must be finished before the student plays with a puzzle or game.
2. Your student completes an assignment.
3. The student commences play with the game.
4. There is increased probability that this student will complete seatwork in the future.

Figure 7.3 illustrates the process.

Figure 7.3
Contingency of reinforcement.

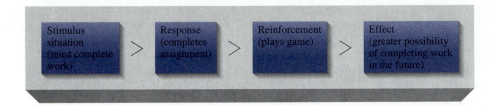

Effective Reinforcers

It is not always easy to identify positive reinforcers, because what one student reacts to well may antagonize another. Attention is a good example. Adolescents particularly can show considerable variation in their reactions to teacher attention. For a few, it is something they wish to escape from or avoid, depending upon their reinforcement history. Occasionally, when reinforcement does not seem to produce the desired result, it is not that reinforcement principles are faulty, but rather that inappropriate reinforcers have been chosen.

If you wish to use positive reinforcers (and we all do, deliberately or otherwise), then be aware of the manner in which you apply them.

One way to select appropriate reinforcers is to consult chapter 10 (on motivation). You may want to use the following list as a guide in selecting reinforcers.

- Consider the ages, interests, and needs of your students. Pieces of candy are not too motivating for adolescents.
- Know precisely the behavior you wish to strengthen and make your reinforcer sufficiently desirable.
- List potential reinforcers that you think would be desirable. The reinforcer menu could be valuable here.
- Don't forget the demonstrated effectiveness of the Premack principle.
- Vary your reinforcers.
- Keep a record of the effectiveness of various reinforcers on individual students.

Secondary Reinforcers

Earlier in this chapter we discussed the difference between primary and secondary reinforcers. (Primary reinforcers are those that have biological importance; secondary reinforcers are those that acquire their power through association with primary and/or other secondary reinforcers.) Most teachers will use secondary reinforcers frequently. These can be grouped into three major categories (Alberto & Troutman, 1986).

1. *Social reinforcers,* which typically include attention, can be verbal or nonverbal. For example, the expression on your face can carry an unmistakable message to a student. Usually, however, social reinforcers are verbal, either accompanying some other form of reinforcement ("John, you can act as class monitor because of the way you behaved in gym") or taking the form of words of praise that signal your pleasure about a specific behavior. Social reinforcers may include expression, contact, proximity, privileges, and words.

activity reinforcers *High-frequency behaviors used to reinforce low-frequency behaviors.*

2. **Activity reinforcers,** which we mentioned in discussion of the Premack principle, are high-frequency behaviors. As reinforcers they are used following low-frequency behaviors. For example, the chance to work on a ship model as a class project may appeal to a student, and can be used to reinforce the behavior of turning in an assignment when due. Again, however, be sure you know what your individual students like.

3. *Generalized reinforcers* are those associated with a variety of other reinforcers. A smile at a student, for example, has a history of being associated with a variety of pleasant experiences. Generalized reinforcers may also be things—money or tokens—that may be exchanged for other things of value.

Suggestions for Use

Positive reinforcement is a powerful principle and can be applied to great advantage in the classroom. All of us who teach, from the preschool to the doctoral level, use positive reinforcement. We must avoid, however, making students too dependent on the reinforcement we provide, particularly if we have initiated structured programs for students. *We want them to work for those reinforcers that are natural to them.*

Reducing dependence on such reinforcers as points or tokens or any other artificial reinforcers, by providing reinforcement less frequently, is called *thinning*. Greater amounts of appropriate behavior must occur before reinforcement occurs. You should realize the following benefits from thinning:

- a more constant rate of responding with appropriate behavior (your students consistently follow classroom rules);
- a lessened anticipation of reinforcement (your students learn not to rely on outside reinforcement);
- shift of control to typical classroom procedures, such as occasional praise (your students gradually acquire a sense of satisfaction from their own classroom successes);
- maintenance of appropriate behavior over longer periods of time.

Remember: the correct use of positive reinforcement demands that you present the reinforcing stimulus (praise, candy, tokens, points) as soon as the appropriate behavior appears.

Techniques to Decrease Behavior

The use of positive procedures should be your goal as often as possible. Sometimes when the goal is to reduce or eliminate misbehavior, teachers consider using punishment (aversive procedures). A word of warning: don't fall into the trap of relying on punishment. It's easy; it frequently works for a short period of time (although not so well with secondary school students); and it gives you a feeling of having established control, which is fine unless you rely exclusively on punishment as a means of maintaining order. But punishment also can destroy your rapport with students if excessively used; it produces a ripple effect that touches all students and affects your own teaching; and it may have side effects of which you are unaware.

Where do you stand on the use of punishment as a behavior change procedure? How often do you think that punishment is used in educational settings? Also, how often is punishment in a behavioral theory context confused with the use of aversive techniques that have no functional role in behavior change?

Analyzing punishment and its alternatives, Alberto and Troutman (1986) offered a sequential hierarchy with four levels as a means of reducing inappropriate behavior. This hierarchy begins at Level I with the least restrictive and least aversive methods, and gradually progresses to Level IV methods that are more restrictive and aversive. The best professional practice dictates beginning with Level I and moving to a higher level only when a student's behavior does not improve in a reasonable time period.

Level I Strategies

These procedures are designated as the preferred option, because in using them, teachers use positive techniques. They are based on the idea of *differential reinforcement;* that is, they rely on reinforcement to decrease or completely eliminate some behavior. Differential reinforcement of low rates of behavior is a technique designed

Issues & Answers

➤ Alternatives to Punishment

In recent years, there has been considerable discussion about the use of aversive techniques (see Repp & Singh, 1990, for a review of various perspectives). The use of punishment may even be associated with some myths (Donnellan & LaVigna, 1990). Consider the following issues.

Issue

Should we use punishment in schools?

Answer: Pro   Punishment is necessary. It is an effective behavior change technique and often results in immediate change in behavior.

Answer: Con   Positive reinforcement can be used as an alternative in almost all cases. Reinforcement is effective and more likely to lead to generalization than is punishment.

Answer: Pro   Punishment is more effective than other control techniques. There is strong evidence that as a technique it can control a large range of even severe behavior problems.

Answer: Con   The evidence for the effectiveness of punishment is not really any stronger than that for the effectiveness of reinforcement. Moreover, the side effects of punishment may be greater.

Answer: Pro   Punishment is easier to implement than are many other behavioral techniques.

Answer: Con   Some punishment techniques may be easier to implement than reinforcement. However, the ease with which punishment is applied may lead to its frequent use when other procedures are available.

to prevent that same behavior from becoming disruptive: for example, it would motivate students to contribute to but not dominate group discussion. In another example, you may wish to eliminate a student's talking-out behavior. Using differential reinforcement of low rates of behavior, you would select a period of time, perhaps ten minutes; when the student had remained silent, you would offer praise and time to work on a model plane. You would then gradually stretch the time period for remaining silent.

Differential reinforcement of incompatible behavior means that you reinforce some totally incompatible behavior. For example, you may decide to reinforce silent reading; a student cannot read silently while talking out.

Level II Strategies

The strategies of this category are intended to reduce misbehavior by *withholding reinforcement*. As Alberto and Troutman (1986) noted, teachers use extinction to reduce behavior that is being maintained by their attention. (Again, note the need to know what reinforces students.) Extinction is best used in conjunction with the positive reinforcement of appropriate behavior.

Don't be discouraged if the effects of extinction are not immediate, because students will be demonstrating a phenomenon called *resistance to extinction*. You may even encounter an increased rate of misbehavior before the effects of extinction become noticeable. Even after the misbehavior disappears, it may occasionally surface once again, a phenomenon called *spontaneous recovery*. (Once this happens, however, ignoring behavior causes it to disappear rapidly.)

You must be careful that other students don't pick up the misbehavior when they see you ignoring it in one of their classmates. If you are successful at identifying the source of the misbehavior (perhaps peer attention), you can usually manipulate other reinforcers to bring about a combination of extinction and positive reinforcement.

Level III Strategies

Note that Level III strategies involve the use of punishment techniques, ranging from less to more severe. In the first of the suggested strategies, *response cost,* you attempt to reduce behavior by removal of a reinforcer (Alberto & Troutman, 1986, p. 246). Once the targeted misbehavior occurs, specific reinforcers are withdrawn.

For example, telephone companies, at different times in different localities, have addressed the problem of excessive requests for information about telephone numbers. They typically provide this service free of charge, certainly a positive reinforcer for callers. When companies begin to charge for this service, the number of requests drops dramatically. Withdrawal of reinforcement (free service) acts as punishment.

You can adopt similar practices in your classroom. A technique proven to be effective combines a token reinforcement system with response cost. Students can not only earn tokens toward something desirable, but also lose tokens by misbehavior. A talking-out student acquires tokens by periods of silence, but also loses tokens by inappropriate talking.

Consider these suggestions for productive use of the response cost technique (Alberto & Troutman, 1986).

- Be sure that you actually withdraw the reinforcers when needed. It is probably best to avoid using physical action. If you move to take away candy with younger students, they may put as much as possible in their mouths and eat it. Taking tokens away from a six-foot-four football player would be considerably more difficult. Try positive reinforcement initially.
- Know what reinforces individual students.
- Be sure that students understand clearly what constitutes misbehavior and its cost.
- Don't trap yourself; be certain that you can indeed withdraw a reinforcer.
- Combine response cost with positive reinforcement for behavior.

The second of the Level III strategies entails the use of *time-out procedures,* in which students are denied reinforcement for a specific period. Again you must be sure that you know exactly what reinforces your individual students.

There are two basic time-out procedures:

1. *Nonseclusionary time out:* the student remains in the classroom but is barred from normal reinforcement. Use of the directive "Put your head on your desk for the next five minutes" prevents the student from receiving reinforcement from either the teacher or classmates. Any type of procedure that prevents reinforcement while keeping the student in the classroom belongs in this category.
2. *Seclusionary time out:* the student is removed from an activity or from the classroom itself. You may resort to this technique by seating a student alone in a remote corner of the room for some specified period. Putting a student in a separate room is a technique usually reserved for special situations and must be used with sensitivity and caution.

Level IV Strategies

This level involves the use of aversive stimuli and is what is most frequently regarded as punishment. Since we have discussed the pros and cons of punishment in considerable detail earlier in this chapter, we can conclude by stressing that regardless of the procedure used to reduce or eliminate behavior, you should remember to combine these techniques with positive reinforcement.

Techniques to Maintain Behavior

Once a student's behavior has changed, you want that student to maintain the desirable behavior over time and without programmed reinforcement. You also want students to demonstrate appropriate behavior in other classes. For example, after you have successfully reduced talking-out behavior in your history class, you also want students to talk out less in English class. In other words, teachers strive for generalization.

Strategies for Facilitating Generalization

You hope that what you teach students in your classroom will transfer to other settings and be remembered over time. Behavioral researchers have developed a technology that teachers can use in classrooms to help students generalize their knowledge and behavior. Building on some of the classic work of Stokes and Baer (1977), White and his associates (1988) presented a review and update of the strategies for facilitating generalization that is of special value to teachers. They described the following twelve strategies:

1. *Teach and hope.* In this traditional strategy, the teacher provides regular instruction and hopes that the child's behavior will generalize. For example, the teacher introduces some new vocabulary words in class, emphasizing their meaning. Some children may remember, but most likely some will not. You hope that most will remember. "Teach and hope" is actually the absence of any special techniques to facilitate generalization, and is common in many classrooms.

2. *Teach in the natural setting.* Teaching is conducted directly in at least one setting in which the skill or knowledge will actually be used. Generalization is then assessed in other, nonteaching, settings. For example, the teacher might ask parents to teach new vocabulary words at home after they are taught in the classroom. Effective teachers use this tactic quite often.

3. *Teach sequentially.* This strategy is an extension of strategy 2, in which teaching is conducted in one setting and generalization is assessed in other settings. If necessary, teaching is conducted sequentially in more and more settings, until generalization to all the desired settings is observed. For example, a teacher interested in teaching social skills might schedule the teaching of the skill in school, at home, and on the playground.

4. *Introduce students to natural maintaining contingencies.* In this strategy, the teacher ensures that the student experiences the natural consequences of a new skill, by (a) teaching a functional skill that is likely to be reinforced outside of the instructional setting; (b) teaching to a level of proficiency that makes the skill truly useful; (c) making sure that the learner actually experiences the natural consequences; and (d) teaching the learner to seek reinforcement outside of the instruction. You may consider using academic content that will be useful to students outside the classroom, such as teaching words that they will likely use when interacting with peers and adults.

5. *Use indiscriminable contingencies.* Sometimes natural consequences cannot be expected to facilitate and maintain generalization. In such cases it may be necessary to use artificial consequences. It is best that the learner cannot determine precisely when those consequences will be available. Teaching social skills to preschoolers, a teacher might praise the children after progressively greater delays rather than after each skill is demonstrated, as would be the strategy during initial teaching.

6. *Train students to generalize.* With this strategy, the student is reinforced only for performing some generalized instance of a new skill. Performance of a previously reinforced version of the skill is no longer reinforced. For example, students could be taught the names of various shapes. Reinforcement then would be provided when students named shapes that had not been taught previously in the classroom.

7. *Program common stimuli.* The teacher can select a salient, but not necessarily task-related, stimulus from the situation to which generalization is desired and include that stimulus in the teaching program. For example, students might be taught skills in the presence of their peers. These skills would then be expected to be available in other settings when the peers were present (that is, when the stimuli were present).

8. *Use sufficient exemplars.* This strategy entails the sequential addition of stimuli to the teaching program until generalization to all related stimuli occurs. Different skills may require a different number of examples to ensure generalization, and you should make this determination based on a student's performance.

9. *Use multiple exemplars.* Using this technique means that you will teach, at the same time, several examples of the stimulus class to which generalization is desired. The teacher who uses multiple examples of a concept or skill will increase the chances that a student will use the skill in a nonteaching setting.

10. *Conduct general case programming.* To use this strategy, the teacher must conduct a careful analysis of both the skill and the environment to which generalization is desired. Thereafter, the teacher selects and teaches stimuli in the presence of which the skill should be used, stimuli in the presence of which the skill should not be used, and stimuli that should not affect skill use, but could inappropriately do so. For example, in teaching high school students to use a stick shift in a driver education class, it would be useful to analyze the range of stick shift options found in most cars and trucks and teach this universe of options. One could then anticipate that good generalization to most cars in the community would occur.

11. *Teach loosely.* By "teaching loosely," we do not mean that you should become an incompetent teacher. What we mean is that you should teach in a variety of ways, so as to avoid a ritualized, highly structured, invariate program that inhibits generalization. Teaching that involves a variety of settings, materials, and reinforcers will help facilitate generalization.

12. *Mediate generalization.* This tactic involves teaching a strategy or other procedure to help the student remember when to generalize, or at least reduce the differences between the teaching and generalization settings. Students can be taught to monitor their own behavior across settings.

Each of the twelve strategies to facilitate generalization will be helpful to you in teaching your students. It is important to remember that you can use the strategies in combination to increase the chances that your students will transfer their knowledge and skills. Remember that according to behavioral educators, teaching is not enough. You must do more than teach and hope: use those strategies that facilitate generalization.

Techniques of Self-Control

Since you cannot monitor a student constantly, a major objective in working with students is to have them accept responsibility for their own behavior, that is, exercise self-control. Kazdin (1994, p. 269) offered a good definition: "Self-control usually refers to those behaviors that a person deliberately undertakes to achieve self-selected outcomes."

In aiding your students to acquire this ability, be sure that they know precisely what behavior produced reinforcement in a given instance. Encourage them to talk about why they were or were not reinforced, thus aiding them to understand their behavior. Remember: it is the students' self-control; therefore, they must be active in the process.

Once you have made them aware of the inappropriateness of some behavior and they are willing to cooperate, have them note, with your help at first, the frequency of their misbehaviors—a kind of self-recording device.

Next, involve them in the management of reinforcement: let them help decide what reinforcers should be used, when they should be given, what constitutes misbehavior, and how much each instance of misbehavior should cost them. In this way, responsibility slowly shifts from you to the student.

Teaching Students Self-Control

Some children learn to regulate their own behavior during their early years within the family. Many children, however, can benefit from learning some strategies to help them control their own behavior in social and learning settings. In recent years, psychologists have developed programs that teachers and other professionals can use to help children in their psychosocial development (Esveldt-Dawson & Kazdin, 1982; Workman, 1982). There are three components of self-control that you can use to teach your students self-control: (a) self-assessment, or self-analysis; (b) self-monitoring; and (c) self-reinforcement.

Self-assessment requires that students examine their own behavior or thinking and determine whether they have performed some behavior or thought process. To foster this, a teacher might ask one of her students if the child has been completing math assignments, for example. It is important that children have some idea or standard that they can use in self-assessment, one that often comes from the performance of significant adults and peers. Remember that all students do not routinely set self-standards, and that it is therefore helpful to teach these skills.

Self-monitoring is a procedure in which students record their performance or keep a record of what they are doing. Interestingly, the very act of recording some action has been shown to change performance. For example, if you encourage kind or positive statements from students when they interact with peers, self-monitoring of this social interaction is likely to increase. Researchers have shown that self-monitoring can increase academic performance, but may not be sufficient in itself to sustain any improvement (Piersel & Kratochwill, 1979).

Self-reinforcement refers to students' giving themselves a reward following successful completion of the activity being monitored. Self-reinforcement can be a very potent strategy for increasing the occurrence of a student's performance. Students can be taught to praise themselves or arrange some pleasant activity as a self-reward, which then acts to sustain performance.

Workman (1982) identified several advantages of using self-control strategies:

- Self-control strategies allow students to manage their own behavior in the absence of the teacher or other adults.
- Self-control strategies can help students develop responsibility for their own behavior.
- Self-control can help improve the chances that a student's behavior will transfer to other settings with other individuals.

Although some students appear to regulate their behavior quite well without formal attempts to teach this skill, others may need additional assistance to regulate their behavior. Teaching self-control strategies to these students can increase both their sense of self-efficacy and their sense of responsibility.

BEHAVIORISM AND THE FUTURE

Behaviorism, which has remained remarkably stable in its basic orientation, has recently shown signs of change. Faced with the challenge of a renewed, dynamic cognitive psychology, behaviorists have reacted by adopting several strategies. They have attempted to:

- strengthen and refine their methodology;
- accept the warnings of the ethologists concerning constraints on learning; and
- incorporate, on behavioral terms, cognitive concepts within their frameworks.

Behaviorists have made significant contributions to education. For example, behavioral studies have demonstrated that almost all students, regardless of preparedness, disabilities, or deprivation, can learn. Behaviorism also has helped to remove blocks to student learning (Sulzer-Azaroff, 1991).

Applying Behavior Analysis to Schooling

In this chapter, we have noted that many of the behavioral procedures urged by Skinner have been successfully applied to educational problems. As Skinner stated (1984), the survival of humankind depends on how well we educate. Education, however, has not widely adopted many of his suggestions. Critics of behavioral techniques (such as Brophy, 1983) have noted that behavioral procedures are often ignored because they apply to circumscribed or isolated problems in the schools.

To increase the use of behavioral procedures in the schools, Greer and his associates at Columbia University Teachers College have developed a model called the Comprehensive Application of Behavior Analysis to Schooling (CABAS) (Greer, in press; Selinske, Greer, & Lodhi, 1991). The model is designed to apply behavior analysis to the school roles of students, teachers, and supervisors. It also includes such behavioral components as direct instruction, a personalized system of instruction, programmed instruction, and an organizational behavior management component for supervision and administration. Following is a description of each of the components:

- *Application to students.* This section consists of collecting data for all instructional trials. Scripted curricula specifying the antecedent stimuli, responses, and consequences for all instruction are used. The following is an example of a one-trial teaching sequence for handicapped children:

    The student was presented with a three-dimensional object (e.g., a cube); the student felt the object and the teacher asked, "What shape?" The student had a 5-second period (for example) to produce the correct signed or vocal response. An incorrect response resulted in a correction procedure (i.e., "This is a cube."). A correct response resulted in praise and the presentation of an edible reinforcer, a token, or a brief activity period with a toy. The teacher recorded a minus for the lack of a response or an incorrect response or a plus for a correct response, and then proceeded to the next trial. (Greer, in press, pp. 109–110)

- *Application to teachers.* This section involved instructing the teachers to use the skills and terminology of behavior analysis with on-the-job training and out-of-class instruction through a personalized system of instruction. The teachers applied the behavioral principles to their work with the students.

Focus   Recording Student Behavior

Before you begin to use any form of behavior change, you must know precisely what you want to change, the best way to change it, and whether you actually can bring about the change. To accomplish these objectives you should know exactly how often the misbehavior occurs and under what circumstances. This is not as arduous as it sounds, particularly if you follow fairly simple, but proven, procedures. (For detailed discussion of observation, collection, and interpretation of data, see Alberto & Troutman, 1986; Sulzer-Azaroff & Reese, 1982; Fromberg & Driscoll, 1985; Gelfand & Hartmann, 1986.) These and similar techniques that we have mentioned help not only teaching and learning but also help to improve your relationships with your students.

You have identified the behavior you want to change and are now ready to determine just how bad things are; you must collect data. There are several ways that you can do this (Sulzer-Azaroff & Mayer, 1991):

1. *Permanent product recording*—measurement of tangible outcomes of behavior (grades, number of tasks completed, number of problems solved);
2. *Event recording*—how often the behavior occurs during a specified period (number of questions asked, number of episodes of talking out);
3. *Duration*—how long the behavior persists (does a student talk out during the entire period or only at the beginning or end?);
4. *Latency recording*—how soon after a stimulus (the start of a class) the misbehavior commences;
5. *Interval recording*—if a thirty-minute class is divided into ten-minute intervals, at what point does the behavior occur?
6. *Time sampling*—whether the behavior is occurring at specified periods (perhaps every ten minutes). This is a relatively simple procedure—easy to use, not too intrusive, and not too demanding of your time.

Let's assume you have targeted the behavior and made your observations. You now must put them in some manageable form that is readily understandable, something you can look at to judge if your efforts have been successful. Graphing data can be useful to you, students, parents, counselors, and administrators.

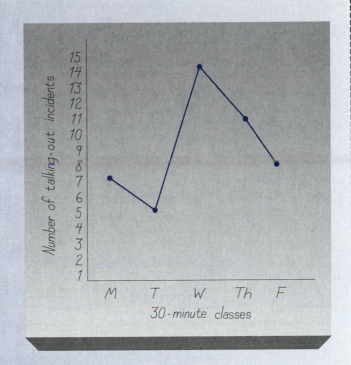

You have recorded the number of times a student has talked out during a thirty-minute class and now wish to plot your graph. Remember that the basic graph has two axes: the horizontal (abscissa or x-axis) and the vertical (ordinate or y-axis). Behavior is plotted on the ordinate; time on the abscissa.

Using your record sheets, place a dot at the proper intersection of the two axes. Now connect the dots to have a graphic illustration of this student's inappropriate behavior. Continue this practice after you begin your program, and you will have telling evidence of the success or failure of your efforts.

Collecting data in this fashion need not be confined to misbehavior. You can use the same technique to assess the effectiveness of a remedial math program for a student who is having trouble. Students, as well as teachers, like to see their progress.

• *Application to supervisors.* Supervisors were involved in the training of the teachers. Specifically, they designed the teacher modules and tutored the teachers to the point of mastery. The supervisors also maintained logs of their activities, and they themselves had to meet criteria for job performance.

Greer and his associates (Selinske et al., 1991) evaluated the CABAS program in a small school that served blind students with multiple handicaps. The program produced educationally significant increases in trials taught and correct trials; also, it identified student objectives. Teachers also evaluated the program positively. Support for the program has been modest, however, because of its limited application in a small school that serves handicapped students. Though a better test would be set in a regular public school, the program does indicate that a combination of behavioral principles has merit in teaching academic skills.

Skinner's Suggestions

As you might expect, Skinner (1984) pronounced on the state of American education and found it wanting, mainly because it neglects behaviorist principles. Skinner believed that the resurgence of humanistic and cognitive psychology has proven a major obstacle to any progress in our schools (progress, by the way, that he believes began with his work on programmed instruction).

To solve our educational dilemma, Skinner (1984) recommended a return to the principles and objectives of behaviorism.

1. *Be clear about what is to be taught.* This implies that you should concentrate on what is to be learned. For example, we don't teach "spelling"; we teach students how to spell words.
2. *Teach first things first.* You should avoid any attempt to reach the final product too quickly, since any subject and its subdivisions contain a series of steps that students must master before reaching the final stage.
3. *Teach to individual differences.* Here is one of Skinner's favorite themes: students can progress only at their own rates. To respond to this truism, Skinner long ago advocated teaching machines, programmed instruction, and computers.
4. *Program subject matter.* Unlike typical texts, individual programs induce students to do or say the things that they are to do or say. Skinner called this "priming" the behavior, and stipulated that the prompts that are built into the program must be gradually eliminated until the behavior appears without help. At that point, the reinforcing consequences of being right become highly effective in sustaining behavior.

Referring to concerns about education, Skinner stated:

There is a better way: give students and teachers better reasons for learning and teaching. That is where the behavioral sciences can make a contribution. They can develop instructional practices so effective and so attractive in other ways that no one—student, teacher, and administrator—will need to be coerced into using them." (Skinner, 1984, p. 952)

Among the accomplishments behaviorists claim are the following:

1. Although behaviorism has proven its worth in the successful education of disabled youngsters, its range of achievements also incorporates the other end of the spectrum: its carefully controlled techniques likewise have been shown to help students to learn at *advanced levels*.
2. Though behaviorism is usually thought to be effective in teaching simple topics, evidence exists that *complex behaviors* are equally as teachable. Complex procedures such as shaping, differential reinforcement, and fading have all become tools of educators.
3. Behaviorism has made clear to educators that the key to teaching complex skills is to distinguish, clearly and precisely, the *critical features* of the task: exactly what behavior is to change under what conditions. Closely allied to the careful identification of objectives is the use of effective and natural reinforcers.
4. Behaviorism has attacked the problem of individual differences in the classroom in a unique manner. If any of your students fail to achieve objectives, it may well be that *they lack the basic prerequisite skills*. Your task, then, is to divide the learning task into its component parts, including those subskills that lead to complexity. For example, you cannot expect students to solve division problems until they can add, subtract, and multiply.

If behaviorism is to continue to progress, certain barriers must be overcome.

- Many educators simply lack information about the value of behavioral strategies.

- Even those who appreciate the benefits of behavioral techniques may lack the skills to implement them.

- Current societal contingencies impede the implementation of behavioral techniques.

By working to overcome these challenges, most behaviorists feel confident about the future of their theory, both its viability and its application.

APPLICATIONS AND REFLECTIONS

Chapter Highlights

Classical Conditioning

- Pavlov's work has educational implications, especially with regard to generalization, discrimination, and extinction of behavior.
- Conditioning principles should make teachers aware of a need to use classroom stimuli sensitively.

Thorndike's Connectionism

- Thorndike was a powerful force in American psychology and his ideas remain influential even today, especially the Law of Effect.
- Thorndike's Law of Effect remained popular for years (influencing Skinner), and his views of exercise and transfer are still applicable.

Operant Conditioning

- Skinner's interpretation of conditioning has become the most accepted and widely used form of behaviorism today. Its impact is felt in education, psychology, and business.
- Skinner's ideas on reinforcement have led to broad acceptance of programmed instruction and computers as effective teaching tools.
- His views of punishment have clarified its meaning and use.

Social Cognitive Learning

- Bandura's stress on the impact of modeling has shown the potency and far-reaching effects of this type of learning.
- Observational learning attempts to include the influence of cognitive processes within a behavioral framework.
- The principles of observational learning emphasize the need for multicultural models that meet the needs of a variety of students.

Behavioral Theories

- The principles of behaviorism are widely used in today's classrooms.
- Techniques for shaping behavior can be effectively used in the classroom, if thoroughly understood and carefully applied.

Behaviorism and the Future

- The future success of behaviorism demands clear adherence to its basic principles, while introducing compatible changes from related disciplines.

Connections

1. Think about how you learn and describe how one of the major concepts discussed in this chapter is part of your learning activities or approach.

_____

_____

_____

_____

2. Identify at least one learning situation (e.g., classroom instruction, self-study, taking a test, small-group work) and describe how you would apply one of the key concepts examined in this chapter *if you were a teacher*.

_____

_____

_____

_____

Getting the Picture and Drawing Relationships

Think about the various learning concepts and variables discussed in this chapter. Create pictures, graphics, or figures that highlight relationships among the key components.

Personal Journal

What I really learned in this chapter was _____

_____

_____

_____

What this means to me is _____

_____

_____

_____

Questions that were stimulated by this chapter include _____

_____

_____

_____

Key Terms

activity reinforcers	223	intermittent reinforcment	208	ratio reinforcement	208
classical conditioning	200	interval reinforcement	207	reinforcer	205
conditioned reflex	200	negative reinforcers	209	response cost	210
conditioned stimulus	200	operant conditioning	205	self-efficacy	218
connectionism	202	overcorrection	210	social cognitive learning	216
discrimination	201	personalized system of		stimulus generalization	201
extinction	202	instruction (PSI)	208	time out	210
fixed interval	208	positive reinforcers	209	variable interval	208
fixed ratio	208	Premack principle	214	variable ratio	208
		punishment	209		

Kim Fraser, an English teacher at Junior High West, was concerned about her Modern Literature course. She too frequently felt that she was fighting a losing battle in trying to get her students interested in many of the ideas that were central to the stories she was teaching. Such concepts as loyalty and persistence, among others, seemed to escape her students. She wondered if she should look at her problem psychologically; perhaps something was at work that she hadn't identified. She decided to discuss it with her class.

At the beginning of class the next day, she mentioned her concern. "Look, I want to be very honest with you.

what's important, I'd like to make a list of my own ideas, of what qualities of a story are most important to me."

Sandra joined in from the other side of the room. "Yes, and then after each of us does that, perhaps we could put together a list of the traits of the leading characters—what's good and what's bad—and try to relate them to the story's theme."

"Right," said Alex. "That makes sense. You know, it would mean more to us and help us to remember the story better. Now that I think of it, why don't we try to develop some memory aids that will help us all?"■

chapter 8

cognitive psychology and learning

honest with you. I know you think you're working hard, and I appreciate your cooperation, but something seems to be missing."

Jake, a good student but also a bit of a class clown, asked, "Why, did someone take something, Miss Cotter?"

The teacher decided to go along with the good humor. "No, that would be the least of my problems, Jake. What's missing is some spark, some clue that you really like reading these stories. After all, reading is something that will stay with you all your life."

Andrea, a serious student, raised her hand and said, "I know what you mean. I think I'm going to enjoy one of these stories and then something seems to happen. Everything goes dead."

With that, other students began to raise their hands.

The teacher pointed to a student and said, "Okay, Alex. What do you think?"

The student hesitated a bit and said, "Well, gosh, Miss Cotter, it could be the way that we're going about this."

With this, the teacher knew that a start had been made. "What do you mean, Alex?"

"Well, you keep telling us how important these stories are—and I'm sure you're right. But maybe we should find out for ourselves."

Andrea chimed in rather excitedly. "That's right. Instead of you or the guide telling us

The conversation between this teacher and her students reflects many of the features of this chapter. If you can have your students develop their own concepts and relate them to other parts of the subject you're teaching, your work will be much easier and probably more efficient. Before teachers can hope to improve thinking skills, however, they must be knowledgeable about their students' cognitive competence and capacity to engage in abstract thought. In this chapter, which explores the relationship between cognitive psychology and learning, you will note the clear implications for the classroom.

The pace of change in cognitive work during the past two decades has been rapid, and as the field has sharpened its focus on information processing, its contribution to teaching and learning has grown noticeably. (In chap. 9 we shall discuss in greater detail the classroom applications of cognitive theory, such as mnemonics, problem-solving strategies, and other related topics.)

We'll examine the major themes of cognitive psychology in this chapter and attempt to indicate pertinent classroom application of such topics as the development of a cognitive science—from its beginnings to where it is today. Also, you'll read about the significance of mental representations in cognitive studies. Current interpretations of perception, recent

The Meaning of Cognitive Psychology 238

The Emergence of Cognitive Psychology 241
The Influence of the Gestaltists 241
Bartlett and the Schema 242
For the Classroom 244

Some Major Approaches in Cognitive Psychology 245
Meaningful Learning 245
The Contribution of Jerome Bruner 247

The Brain and Thinking 249
Brain and Mind: The Relationship 249
Lateralization 250
Pattern Matching 252
Learning 252

The Importance of Information Processing 253
The Meaning of Representation 253
How We Represent Information 253

The Role of Perception 255
Explanation of the Perceptual Process 255
For the Classroom 256

How Students Categorize 259
Forming Categories 261
For the Classroom 262

Memory at Work 263
New Directions in Memory Studies 264
Recognition, Recall, and Forgetting 265
For the Classroom 268

Metacognition 269
Metacognitive Knowledge 269
Metacognitive Experiences 270

Decision Making and Reasoning 270
Representativeness 270
For the Classroom 271
Cognition Across Cultures 274

Applications and Reflections 275

studies and speculation concerning classification, the changing status of memory work, and the logic—or illogic—of human reasoning processes will also be presented.

When you finish your reading, you should be able to

- understand the key role that representation plays in learning
- help students to construct categories to aid their learning
- distinguish between recognition and recall of material
- recognize those distractions that affect student memory
- accept that the manner in which you frame or structure your material will influence your students' thinking and decision making

Before we commence our work, however, try the simple exercise that appears on page 239 in the focus box :"How Much Do You Remember?".

THE MEANING OF COGNITIVE PSYCHOLOGY

What is cognitive psychology? Cognitive scientists are in general agreement that their work encompasses the study of memory, attention, perception, language, reasoning, problem solving, and creativity. That is, cognitive psychology is the study of the structures and components for processing information (Phye & Andre, 1986). Gardner (1985) identified five features of cognitive science: representations; computers; deemphasis on affect, context, culture, and history; belief in interdisciplinary studies; and rootedness in classical philosophical problems. Each of these key features is presented in table 8.1, along with some elaboration of their meaning. Gardner (1985) considers representations and computers to be "core assumptions," and the latter two features listed to be strategic features. With this in mind, we discuss the first two issues in greater detail in this section.

Central to cognitive psychology is a belief in **mental representations,** or the coding of external events so that they become retrievable in internal forms (Glass, Holyoak, & Santa, 1987). These internal forms are not direct copies of the external stimuli, but can be significantly altered and affected by prior knowledge, beliefs, and experiences. As you can see, this orientation is a departure from early writings on behaviorism, which we discussed in chapter 7.

Stored in memory, these mental representations have

mental representation *The coding of external events so they are retrievable in an internal form.*

Central to cognitive psychology is the concept of mental representations. External events are coded and become retrievable in internal form.

Reprinted with special permission of King Features Syndicate.

Focus ← How Much Do You Remember?

In the early 1930s, the British psychologist F. C. Bartlett became convinced that studies on memory actually ignored clues that explained much about remembering and forgetting. Read the following passage (a legend found in a Pacific Northwest Indian group.). Later in the chapter, when you again meet Bartlett's work, write the legend as you recall it.

The War of the Ghosts

One night two young men from Egulac went down to the river to hunt seals, and while they were there it became foggy and calm. Then they heard war cries, and they thought: "Maybe this is a war party." They escaped to the shore, and hid behind a log. Now canoes came up, and they heard the noise of paddles, and saw one canoe coming up to them. There were five men in the canoe, and they said:

"What do you think? We wish to take you along. We are going up the river to make war on the people."

One of the young men said: "I have no arrows."

"Arrows are in the canoe," they said.

"I will not go along. I might be killed. My relatives do not know where I have gone. But you," he said, turning to the other, "may go with them."

So one of the young men went, but the other returned home.

And the warriors went on up the river to a town on the other side of Kalama. The people came down to the water, and they began to fight, and many were killed. But presently the young man heard one of the warriors say: "Quick, let us go home: that Indian has been hit." Now he thought: "Oh, they are ghosts." He did not feel sick, but they said he had been shot.

So the canoes went back to Egulac, and the young man went ashore to his house, and made a fire. And he told everybody and said: "Behold I accompanied the ghosts, and we went to fight. Many of our fellows were killed, and many of those who attacked us were killed. They said I was hit, and I did not feel sick."

He told it all, and then he became quiet. When the sun rose he fell down. Something black came out of his mouth. His face became contorted. The people jumped up and cried.

He was dead.

From T. C. Bartlett, Remembering: A Study in Experimental and Social Psychology. *Copyright © 1932 Cambridge University Press, New York. Reprinted with the permission of Cambridge University Press.*

Table 8.1

Five Key Features of Cognitive Science

Key feature	Definition/characteristics	Example
Representations	Human cognitive activity is explained by representing cognition through internal entities.	The student has an idea or image of some event or person.
Computers	The computer serves as a model of human information processing or human thought.	The computer can be programmed to store large amounts of information in memory.
Deemphasis on affect, context, culture, and history	These concepts are not considered of primary importance in understanding mental processes.	The context that surrounds a student's thinking does not really influence the basic thinking process.
Interdisciplinary studies	There is an emphasis in cognitive psychology on interdisciplinary study to develop the field.	Researchers from psychology and neuroscience work together.
Classical philosophical problems	Traditional philosophical problems have served as a springboard for issues studied in the cognitive psychology field.	Can thinking be represented in the chemistry of the brain?

Source: H. Gardner, *The Mind's New Science.* Copyright © 1985 Basic Books, New York.

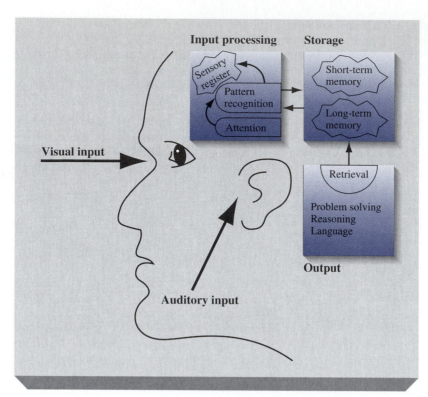

Figure 8.1
Sequence of information processing.

From H. C. Ellis and R. R. Hunt, Fundamentals of Cognitive Psychology 5th ed. Copyright © 1993 Wm. C. Brown Communications, Inc., Dubuque Iowa. All Rights Reserved. Reprinted by Permission of Times Mirror Higher Education Group, Inc., Dubuque, Iowa.

Issues & Answers

The Role of the Computer

The computer has served a central role in the development of the cognitive science field. Several authors (e.g., Ellis & Hunt, 1993; Gardner, 1985) have outlined a number of controversial issues that pervade the cognitive psychology field, including especially the use of computers in cognitive science research. An important point of controversy is whether the computer should serve as a model of human thought. Some cognitive scientists believe that the computer model of thinking is central to progress in the field. Other critics in cognitive psychology suggest that the computer model will never replace the human brain. See, for example, the book by Herbert Dreyfus, *What Computers Can't Do* (1979).

Issue

The computer should serve as a model of human thought.

Answer: Pro The computer is our best model for how the human brain operates. The computer is able to store vast amounts of information, code this information, and sort it into categories, among other information processing functions. In this regard, the computer serves as a good model for human thought.

Answer: Con The computer, like a lot of other machines, has served as a useful tool in cognitive science research, but it will never serve as a model of the human brain. The human brain is far too complex to be represented in a computer model, such as those used in studying artificial intelligence.

Answer: Pro The computer is especially useful in helping us understand the workings of the human mind, and especially is helpful in promoting research on mental representations in cognitive psychology. Much of our understanding of thinking has come from the development and programming of the computer.

Answer: Con The computer can never serve as a good model for human thinking or information processing. The reason is that the computer removes the study of these psychological processes from the context people use to process information and store it in memory. People perform in a social and cultural context, and the computer cannot take into account these variables in the study of cognition.

Do you believe that the computer is a reasonable model for the study of human cognition? Revisit the question and your answer to it after you read this chapter.

become a legitimate focus of speculation and research. Cognitive psychologists firmly, even fiercely, believe that the stimulus situation does not directly determine human behavior. For example, the way that your students think about you, your classroom, and the school influences their learning. Interposed between stimulus and response is cognitive activity. Thus, thought processes are not an accumulation of stimulus-response connections; cognition intervenes and distinctly colors human reactions.

Most cognitive scientists have been strongly influenced by the computer (Gardner, 1985). Because the computer carries out tasks that we often regard as "thinking" (e.g., transforming information, storing things in memory), it has become a model of human thinking. In other words, humans, like computers, can be viewed as "symbol manipulation devices" that code external information into internal representations, manipulate or store these internal representations in some way, and then produce some output (or response). Also, as Gardner noted, the computer is often used in research on information processing, and therefore is a valuable tool in cognitive science work. Indeed, the computer has often been used as a model to describe thinking from the cognitive perspective, and provides one way of conceptualizing information processing (Ellis & Hunt, 1993). Figure 8.1 provides the sequence of information processing that divides cognition into three components: input processing, storage, and output. Although there are many arguments against the computer model of the mind, it provides a useful introductory approach to understanding cognitive psychology.

Today, cognitive psychology enjoys great appeal and, as we noted in the chapter opening, has become a potent force in the classroom. One source of cognitive psychology's appeal is its perspective on human beings. Your students organize information into goals and subgoals in a fraction of a second and achieve remarkable results: they remember, they decide, they solve problems, they learn (Siegler, 1983). If you can aid your students in organizing and processing information, you will help them to become more competent and to improve their learning both in and out of the classroom (Glaser, 1991).

Cognitive conceptions of learning have entered the classroom with far-reaching effects. For example, psychologists and teachers have much greater awareness of the important effects of students' prior knowledge and their memory strategies on their present learning (Shuell, 1986).

But human beings also face cognitive limitations: our students, like ourselves, can simultaneously manipulate only a certain number of symbols at a time, with limits on the speed at which we can manipulate them (Kinsbourne, 1986). Consequently, students are taught or invent strategies to help them overcome these obstacles: they organize material to help them remember; they rehearse data over and over; they devise schemes to help them solve problems. The use, or lack of use, of strategies to overcome speed-to-capacity limits has been a major focus of cognitive research and has important implications for educators. (These techniques are analyzed in some depth in chap. 9.)

THE EMERGENCE OF COGNITIVE PSYCHOLOGY

The history of cognitive psychology, like that of any science, is rooted in many fields. Today's cognitive psychology flows from the conceptual framework of Gestalt psychology, especially from its emphasis on perception—an emphasis that strongly shaped the thinking of more modern cognitivists such as Jerome Bruner.

The Influence of the Gestaltists

The early Gestaltists—Max Wertheimer, Wolfgang Köhler, and Kurt Koffka—were firmly convinced that behaviorism could not account for the full range of human behavior. Consequently, they launched a determined and effective attack against early behaviorism.

Wertheimer, the founder of the movement, discovered that if two lights were turned off and on at a definite rate, a human subject reported the impression that a single light was moving back and forth. This finding, which Wertheimer called the *phi phenomenon,* could not be effectively explained by a stimulus-response model; when processing these stimuli, humans added something to the incoming sensory data to form their perception of movement.

From their academic base in Germany, the Gestaltists earned rapid acceptance from their European colleagues, but it was not until Wertheimer, Koffka, and Köhler were forced to flee Nazi Germany that Gestalt psychology was recognized as a viable psychological force in America. Given the preeminence of behaviorism in American psychology, the Gestaltists were attempting no small feat in their direct challenge to behaviorism.

With their views on perception and perceptual learning finding acceptance in many quarters, the Gestaltists widened their efforts to bring a cognitive interpretation to human development, intelligence, and especially problem solving. One of the lasting legacies of Gestalt theory has been its principles of perceptual organization, which we will discuss in the perception section of this chapter. (The Gestaltists' work still has current significance; for example, see Michael Wertheimer's proposal (1985) for a Gestaltist perspective on computer simulation of cognitive processes.)

Bartlett and the Schema

Unhappy with existing methods used to study memory, Bartlett (1932) presented exotic stories to his subjects and then asked them to recall the stories at different times. You were asked to read "The War of the Ghosts" at the beginning of this chapter. *Stop now and rewrite that story as you recall it, without again looking at it.*

Now check your story against the original. How different is it? Did you add to or subtract from the original? Is it essentially the same story? When asked to recall the story, most subjects imposed an order and organization on it that are missing from the original. With increasing time, subjects made the story even more meaningful, more logical, and more consistent with their own personal experiences. Thus, **schemata** (plural of *schema*) of events are mental frameworks that modify incoming data so that they "fit" a person's experiences and perceptions (Phye & Andre, 1986).

schemata *Mental frameworks that modify incoming data; plural of* schema.

When presenting new material, teachers quickly learn to expect a familiar refrain. One of the students will undoubtedly say, "That's like Mrs. Anderson said last year." The student is trying to fit something new into an existing cognitive framework: the schema.

Introducing the Schema

In 1967, Pompi and Lachman conducted an experiment in which subjects read stories that lacked words ordinarily associated with the themes of the stories. For example, one story concerned a surgical operation, but words such as *doctor, nurse, scalpel,* and *operation* were lacking.

After reading the story, subjects were then given a list of words that included *doctor, nurse, scalpel,* and *operation,* and asked if these words had appeared in the story. Subjects invariably stated that these words had appeared in the story.

The investigators believed that people grasp a story theme, compare it with the test words, and then match on the basis of familiarity. The stimulus for the subjects' responses must have been mental; that is, they used their knowledge of medicine and surgery in their replies, even though no such specific cues appeared in the story.

To explain this tendency toward logic and the familiar, cognitive psychologists turned to the *schema,* a term that refers to some form of abstract cognitive structure. These schemas, or schemata, are the basis of memory and result from our previous experiences, which we organize in an individual manner. The organization of information is at the heart of the concept of schema. Organization of one's knowledge is a central ingredient of learning. Consequently, organization is important at three levels: (a) orga-

Focus ◀------- Would You Make a Good Eyewitness?

The notion of schema has important consequences for many facets of our lives. As one example, consider the testimony of eyewitnesses in a court of law. The amount of reconstruction—or even creativity—in an eyewitness' account of a crime cuts to the heart of our system of justice. Repeated studies have shown that even immediately after the event has occurred, inaccuracies consistently appear in testimony. (In a recent publication of the American Psychological Association [Doris, 1991], the suggestibility of children's recollections and its implications for eyewitness testimony was discussed.)

Attorneys typically ask a set of standard questions of an eyewitness:

- Under what circumstances did the eyewitness view the defendant at the time of the crime?
- Does present testimony match any prior description (for example, one given immediately after a crime or accident)?
- Was the identification of the person (defendant) accurate?

Stressful conditions do not lend themselves to reliable testimony, and the courts have become increasingly skeptical about such accounts. Since three-quarters of all trials involve police testimony, the significance of distortion of recall cannot be ignored.

Skilled questioning can shape even the testimony of truthful witnesses. Loftus and Palmer (1974) showed students a film of a collision between two cars. They then asked their subjects one of two questions:

1. About how fast were the cars going when they hit each other?
2. About how fast were the cars going when they smashed into each other?

Students gave higher estimates of speed when answering the second question, and when asked the same question one week later, erroneously reported broken glass at the scene.

The schema and the danger of distortion of recall also have direct classroom relevance. If you have some knowledge of a topic, such as the nature of intelligence (a schema for intelligence), you use that schema in attempting to understand Piaget's views. (You may have already reacted in this way to chap. 4.) In answering examination questions, did you fuse, that is, distort, your knowledge? In these and similar conditions, cognitive psychologists have provided considerable insight into how cognitive processes affect memory (Braddeley, 1988).

nization that already exists in one's long-term memory; (b) organization that can be perceived or generated within the material to be learned; and (c) organization that links the first two levels, thus allowing new material to be integrated with one's existing knowledge (Baddeley, 1990).

For example, after listening to or reading "The War of the Ghosts," you would use your own schemata to interpret and recall the story's theme. You may have some familiarity with canoes; you may have had previous encounters with ghost stories or Indian adventure stories. If these matched corresponding parts of the story, you may recall these themes quite accurately. If, however, your schemata varied widely from the story's themes, you would probably add to "The War of the Ghosts" from your own schemata, introduce a more acceptable (to you) story theme, and distort the theme even further on additional recalls. Thus, memory is not a passive retelling of past events; rather, activity and even creativity characterize our recall. That is, memory is believed to be more of a reconstruction of past events than a literal recalling of them.

The Schema Today

Schema has remained a viable concept in cognitive psychology (Phye & Andre, 1986). Think of a schema as a unit of organized knowledge about events, situations, or objects, one that guides informational input and retrieval (Leahey & Harris, 1985). A schema may be quite specific, such as the technique used to add a column of numbers, or quite general, such as an interpretation of intelligence. In other words, the material that your students must learn will not in itself explain exactly what they do learn. The material contains potential information; that is, it possesses cues and directions that should guide students to use their own knowledge, thus obtaining the fullest possible information that they can. (We will develop this idea in our discussion of Ausubel and meaningful learning.)

The rationale for accepting the notion of schema has been a growing realization that human beings do not approach any topic totally devoid of knowledge; we have both prior knowledge and present expectations. We possess schemata that shape how we encode incoming material, and indeed, even affect how we "feel" about such material.

As an example of the way the latest theories and results from research into cognitive psychology are finding their way into the classroom, consider the following experiment. Rahman and Bisanz (1986) were interested in examining how students used a schema of stories to aid recall and in discovering how a schema affected strong reconstruction. Working on the assumption that inadequate knowledge of a story's structure could cause difficulty for poor readers, the authors were directly reflecting the most recent thinking about schema theory.

Rahman and Bisanz (1986) attempted to answer four questions.

1. Do both good and poor readers typically utilize a story schema?
2. Can both groups ignore the standard sequence of the story and retrieve information from a jumbled format?
3. Can both groups use a story schema when cued to do so?
4. Do poor readers improve when the task is repeated?

They studied 48 good readers (mean age 11.5 years) and 48 poor readers (mean age 11.8 years) from the sixth grade. The students heard a story in either standard or scrambled form. They were then told to recall and reconstruct the order of the story as they had heard it, or as it should be. The same procedure was repeated in a second phase, with one change: before hearing the story, the subjects were told about the story's format and given possible ways to rearrange it if the story's sequence were askew.

The authors were able to draw several conclusions concerning schema use.

- Both poor and good readers could recall and reconstruct a story presented in standard form, although poor readers' stories were not well developed.
- Good readers consistently used a strong schema when cued to do so on any task (both standard and scrambled), while poor readers could demonstrate a story schema only with a standard format.
- In the second phase of the experiment, poor readers improved only on the standard format.

The authors concluded that comprehension research is vital in studies of poor readers; in so doing, they emphasized the growing importance of cognitive research for the classroom. Their findings point to the need to provide poor readers with a clear structure of what they are reading. If their comprehension is to improve, then techniques such as outlining, sequencing, and finding main features must be incorporated into their programs. A given student's learning style will largely determine which techniques to use with that student (see chap. 9). The goal is to find the best way that students represent material.

For the Classroom

One way of improving your relationships with students is to help students decrease their feelings of frustration when faced with a challenging situation. As an example of how mental representations affect classroom performance, even at higher levels, consider an experiment described by deJong and Ferguson-Hassler (1986). Using evidence indicating that possession of knowledge does not necessarily lead to effective problem solving, the authors wished to investigate the problem schemata that their students used. (By "problem schemata," they meant knowledge students have that is related to and relevant for solving a problem, such as types of information likely to be needed, questions likely to be asked, relevant facts, formulas, and underlying principles.)

Experts use more adequate and complete problem schemata; that is, they attack problems according to underlying principles, while novices fixate on the surface characteristics of problems. Expert problem solvers tend to use the correct data and appropriate procedures.

Studying 47 first-year university physics students, the authors presented them with 12 problems that involved 65 elements. (The subject matter was electricity and magnetism.) The 65 elements were then printed on cards, and the students were asked to sort them into coherent piles: a card in any one pile was to be more closely connected to the other cards in that pile than to the cards in other piles.

The authors found that the good problem solvers organized their knowledge in a much more *problem-type-centered fashion* than did the poor problem solvers; they had well-developed problem schemata that allowed them to organize their information into coherent problem types in a way that showed some underlying principles. Interestingly, a high correlation was discovered between course examination scores and problem-centered scores.

Utilization of problem schemata thus appears to be an extremely efficient way both to solve problems and to do well on examinations. To encourage this ability in students, the authors urged teachers to help their students organize memory by the underlying (rather than surface-level) characteristics of a problem situation, the necessary data, and the correct procedural knowledge.

To use this information in the classroom, try to have students feel comfortable with the basic types of problems in a given subject, make sure they master the fundamental data, and ensure that they are familiar with the necessary steps to solve a problem (such as changing signs when an amount is moved from one side of an equation to another). If you work at this technique, you will help your students to form more positive attitudes toward a subject, reduce the chances of unhappiness and discipline problems, and increase learning (Foster, 1986).

Compare and contrast behavioral and traditional cognitive theories of learning and cognition.

SOME MAJOR APPROACHES IN COGNITIVE PSYCHOLOGY

Meaningful Learning

In his analysis of learning, David Ausubel (1968; 1977; Ausubel et al., 1978) made two basic distinctions: one between *reception* and *discovery learning* and the other between *rote* and *meaningful learning*. He suggested that the first distinction is significant because most of students' learning, both in and out of school, is presented to them; that is, it is reception learning. Reception learning need not be rote; it can be quite meaningful for students.

Reception learning and discovery learning pose two different tasks for students. In reception learning, the potentially meaningful material becomes meaningful as students internalize it. In discovery learning, however, students must discover what is to be learned and then rearrange it to integrate the material with existing cognitive structures.

meaningful learning *Ausubel's term to describe the acquisition of new meanings.*

Ausubel has long been an outspoken advocate of **meaningful learning,** which he defines as the acquisition of new meanings. Note: there are two important ideas contained in his definition. *Meaningful learning* implies that the material to be learned is potentially meaningful (is appropriate for the student). *The acquisition of new meanings* refers to the process by which students turn potentially meaningful material into actual meaningfulness.

Ausubel noted that meaningful learning occurs when the material to be learned is related to what students already know. If, for example, Barbara Cotter, the English teacher we meet at the chapter's opening, is teaching Hemingway's *For Whom the Bell Tolls* in her Modern Literature course, she could help her students' attempts to transfer potentially meaningful themes (such as belief in a cause or loyalty to others) into actual meaning by relating those themes to their own schemata, such as their willingness to help one of their friends or their joining a student club dedicated to fighting the use of drugs. She would then have utilized the important ideas in Ausubel's definition of new meanings.

Advance Organizers

One of Ausubel's most important ideas for teachers is that of advance organizers, which he described as a form of expository teaching, that is, explaining what is to come (Williams, 1986). Ausubel (1960, 1980) defined an **advance organizer** as an abstract, general overview of new information to be learned that occurs in advance of the actual reading. In teaching *For Whom the Bell Tolls,* for example, Barbara Cotter could summarize the major features of the novel before her students read the book. She could then lead a discussion of important concepts such as loyalty and steadfastness in terms that her students understood.

advance organizers *Ausubel's term for an abstract, general overview of new information before the actual learning is expected.*

This introductory material is intended to help students ready their cognitive structures for incorporating potentially meaningful material. Advance organizers are presented before introducing the new material and at a slightly higher level of abstraction, because meaningful material is better learned and retained if it can be subsumed under already existing relevant ideas. Your students already have their own ideas about loyalty to friends.

To help your students acquire meaning, follow Ausubel's advice: identify relevant anchoring ideas that your students already possess (in their cognitive structures). That is, attempt to relate new, potentially meaningful material to some topic with which students are familiar. You read earlier in this book (chap. 4) about Piaget's initiating this process when he described *assimilation* and *accommodation.* He often referred to biological processes: we use the structure of the mouth to eat; therefore, it is logical to assume that we use cognitive structures to think.

Advance organizers are effective when they utilize the anchoring ideas already present in the students' cognitive structures, thus helping to reduce the students' dependence on rote memorization. Ausubel summarized the principal function of advance organizers as bridging the gap between what students already know (their ideas of loyalty to their friends, for example) and what they need to know before they can successfully learn new material (the abstract notion of loyalty inherent in the novel). In this way, learners receive an overview of the material before they actually encounter it and are provided with organizing elements that are the core of the new material.

Ausubel's ideas, however, must be used with caution. Advance organizers have not always produced more efficient learning, although the results of recent research indicate that advance organizers have a consistent, moderate, and positive effect on learning (Corkill, Glover, Bruning, & Krug, 1989). Such learning variables as a student's cognitive structures and general state of developmental readiness must be taken into consideration. In other words, potentially meaningful material must be biologically and psychologically appropriate. Introducing a preschooler's story by referring to concepts such as loyalty without giving appropriate examples frustrates the entire process of meaningful learning. But by talking about the relationship between a child and a dog, a teacher could introduce the concept at the proper psychological level and then gradually help the students apply a label to it. (For additional applications of Ausubel's theory, see Smith, 1984.)

How can you help students effectively use their schemata in the acquisition of meaningful learning, yet avoid distortion? First, you must discover just what knowledge they possess about a topic, since this will guide their organization of the new material. Second, try to link the new work to specific themes in their knowledge. If you are teaching twentieth-century American history, for example, you might ask your students to link as many characteristics of Bill Clinton as they can to those of other modern presidents. Finally, be certain that your students have mastered the pertinent facts before you expect them to generalize; otherwise, you may inadvertently encourage distortion. Students must be familiar with the American presidents before they can compare them to President Bill Clinton.

discovery learning *Bruner's term for learning that involves the rearrangement and transformation of material that leads to insight.*

Although Ausubel emphasized meaningful reception learning, another famous cognitive psychologist, Jerome Bruner, concentrated his efforts on **discovery learning.** Bruner's work has also been in the forefront of the development and acceptance of cognitive psychology. Let's now turn our attention to Bruner's work.

The Contribution of Jerome Bruner

The ideas that flourished during the early years of cognitive science could not be ignored, and had a decided influence on the creative minds of such young psychologists as George Miller and Jerome Bruner. These two cognitivists continued in the tradition we have been tracing, and founded the Center for Cognitive Studies at Harvard in 1960.

We have previously mentioned the high regard in which Miller's colleagues held him. The impact of Miller's 1956 article, "The Magical Number Seven, Plus or Minus Two," was enormous. Bruner believes that if there were a retrospective Nobel Prize in Psychology for the mid-1950s, George Miller would win it on the basis of that one article. It is about the limitations on human information capacity. The "magic number" was the number of elements that a human being could keep in mind in immediate memory: seven, plus or minus two (Bruner, 1983, p. 97).

A Study of Thinking

Jerome Bruner (1915–) received his PhD from Harvard in 1941 and immediately became involved in the American war effort, especially in psychological warfare. He was a professor of Psychology at Harvard from 1945 until 1972, where from 1960 to 1972 he was also Director of Cognitive Studies. He was at England's Cambridge University from 1972 until 1979. Presently he is at the New School for Social Research in New York.

With colleagues Jacqueline Goodnow and George Austin, Bruner, published in 1956 an ingenious and important account of categorization called *A Study of Thinking*. In it they analyzed categorizing and expressed their belief that it explains why humans are not overwhelmed by environmental complexity. Bruner, Goodnow, and Austin effectively showed that their subjects actively participated in the classification process. As you can imagine, the great value of Bruner's work in the 1950s and 1960s lay in the energy it supplied to the renewed cognitive movement. Gardner (1985) noted that subjects were treated as active, constructive problem solvers, rather than as simple reactors to whatever stimuli were presented to them. The active construction of solutions to problems implies that students turn to their cultural environment for clues to aid them in their task.

The authors state that three types of concepts exist: conjunctive, disjunctive, and relational.

1. *Conjunctive concepts* rely upon the joint presence of several attributes. These attributes are abstracted from many individual experiences with an object, thing, or event. So there are categories, such as *boy, car, book,* and *orange*.

2. *Disjunctive concepts* are composed of concepts, any one of whose attributes may be used in classification. That is, one or another of its attributes enable an object to be placed in a particular category. A good example of the disjunctive category is the strike in baseball. A strike may be a ball thrown by the pitcher that is over the plate and between a batter's shoulders and knees, or a ball at which the batter swings and misses, or a ball that the batter hits as a foul (outside the playing limits of the diamond). Any one of these attributes enables the observer to classify it as a strike.

3. *Relational concepts* are formed by the relationship that exists among defining attributes. The authors illustrate this category by using income brackets. There are many income levels or classes, all of which exist because of the relationship among income, eligible expenses, and number of dependents. The combination of these properties determines an individual's income class. These are relational categories.

teacher – student

interactions

Classroom Implications of Cognitive Psychology

1. Mental representations are at the heart of cognitive psychology. Thus the use of active learning methods increases the depth of information processing and the likelihood that it will be memorable. Some suggestions to improve memory and comprehension of important material follow.
   - Have your students listen to tapes of great speeches, such as Martin Luther King's *I Have A Dream* so that they gain insight into the Civil Rights Movement.
   - Have elementary school students perform historical skits about important events, such as the discovery of America or the coming of the Pilgrims, so that they can better understand their place in American history and remember their significance for longer intervals.
   - Conduct a classroom or school-wide election to simulate state and federal elections. Help students transfer these external events into mental representations by using such memory techniques as rehearsal and urging them to compare different elections.

2. Children can be taught to monitor their own cognitive strategies.
   - Encourage upper elementary and middle school students to check their report-writing skills by having them use reference materials such as the dictionary to correct their spelling, the thesaurus to rewrite information in their own words, and the almanac to give them up-to-date facts and statistics.
   - Develop kindergarten and elementary school children's ability to monitor their own sequencing and classification skills by using such techniques as a cooking class. Emphasize that they should concentrate on the needed steps as they themselves cook. Stress the importance of paying close attention to detail and using the correct utensils.
   - Ask your high school students who are learning to write journal articles to make certain their articles answer the questions *who, what, where,* and *how.* Ask them to edit their articles before submitting them to make sure they have answered all the questions.

3. Schemata or mental frameworks, can help students not only to learn more effectively but also to recall information over longer periods of time.
   - Develop units of study about topics such as the value of water by first relating the topics to your students' prior knowledge. For children of the Northwest and Northeast, you may offer the example of snow melt, then ice backup.
   - When you develop a unit such as "Holidays," remember that children of various cultures celebrate holidays differently, but that all students have schemata for holidays to which you can relate your activities. With young children, challenge their knowledge of familiar words by using "interrupted reading." Before you read a story or a book, explain to them that when you stop, they have to think of a word the author would use. For example, "The graceful animal that came to the watering hole for a drink had only one horn. He must be a _____."

4. Meaningful learning and discovery learning pose two different tasks for students.
   - (For meaningful learning.) Before you explain a scientific fact to lower elementary school students (e.g., how a caterpillar turns into a butterfly), first discuss the importance of steps that happen in a specific order. As an advance organizer you may illustrate a sequence with pictures of a butterfly's life cycle: egg, caterpillar, chrysalis, butterfly.
   - (For discovery learning.) Explain to your children that they are going to find out how a caterpillar turns into a butterfly by watching the caterpillar as it eats the leaf, turns into a chrysalis, and finally becomes a butterfly which will be released in the playground.
   - (For meaningful learning.) Introduce the concept of career planing by discussing a recent career article in a journal or magazine. Using charts and diagrams, demonstrate how many students their age would like to study medicine, law, or education. As an advance organizer, the class may like to discuss friends or relatives who are engaged in these careers.
   - (For discovery learning.) Divide your students into small groups to take polls of their classmates to discover what careers they are interested in pursuing. Tabulate the results and make a report to the class.

Bruner, Goodnow, and Austin concluded that categorizing implies more than merely recognizing instances. Rules are learned and then applied to new situations. Students learn that a sentence—subject, object, predicate—is the basic unit in writing, in history class as well as in English class. The various categories (conjunctive, disjunctive, relational) are really rules for grouping attributes to define the positive instances of any concept.

Figure 8.2
The brain and function.

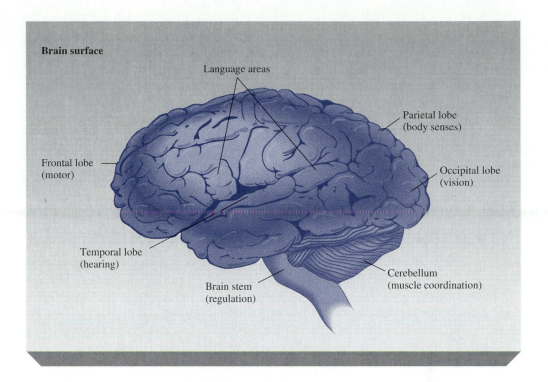

THE BRAIN AND THINKING

Annual **Edition**

We begin by asking a fundamental question: Can there be learning, developing, and thinking without a biological substrate? Although no one would argue against this premise, considerable controversy arises when we speculate about the relationship between brain and mind, that is, thinking and cognition. For an overview of basic brain anatomy, examine figure 8.2, noting the relationship of location in the brain to function. Also note the basic brain areas, identified by lobe; function has also been assigned to the various areas.

Brain and Mind: The Relationship

Until recently, extreme positions have been the rule when it comes to discussing the brain-mind relationship. Philosophical advocates virtually have ignored the existence of the brain, and more currently physiologists and biologists have insisted that the mind is nothing more than a system of connecting neurons. Rose (1987) raised this question: How are data transformed as they pass in a series of electrical signals along particular nerves to central brain regions, where they interact with one another, thus producing certain kinds of responses? One attempt to answer this question was made by Alexander Luria.

Luria's Work

The Russian neuropsychologist Alexander Luria (1980) proposed a less extreme but still neurological view. Intellectual activity begins with analyzing the conditions of the task and then identifying its most important elements. In an example, Luria (1973) traced the thinking process through several stages.

• Thinking begins only when a person is motivated to solve a problem for which there is no ready solution. When students recognize problems and realize that they have the tools to solve them, their motivation remains high.
• The second stage is not an attempt to solve the problem immediately. Rather, it entails the restraint of impulsive responses. The individual must carefully investigate any possible solutions. We have commented previously on the need to identify a problem's basic elements.

Figure 8.3
Lateralization of handedness.

- Next the person selects what seems to be the most satisfactory alternative and creates a general plan. Students must be taught to pause, use the critical elements they have identified, and take the time to plan for a solution.
- Finally, the individual must put into action the methods and operations of the proposed solution, asking these questions: Does it work? Have I reached a satisfactory solution?

Neuropsychological deficits differentiate specific aspects of the brain-mind relationship. Noting that lesions in different cerebral locations cause different types of intellectual disturbances, Luria described the impact of frontal zone lesions on the ability to formulate plans and noted that individuals suffering from them manifest an inability to form a preliminary basic plan of action. Any system of connections that arises will be random, having lost its goal-directed and selective character.

This testimony to the relationship between brain and mind establishes a firm rationale for the need to include information about brain functioning in our analysis of cognitive thinking skills. We'll now examine brain characteristics that appear particularly suited to expand our views of cognition, such as pattern matching, lateralization, and learning.

Lateralization

Which hand do you use for writing? If you were to kick a football, would you use the leg on the same side of your body as the hand you use for writing? Pick up a pencil or ruler and pretend it is a telescope. Which eye do you use? Are you using the same side of the body that you would use for writing and kicking? Your answers to these questions should give you some idea of the meaning of cerebral lateralization.

We tend to think of the brain as a single unit, but actually it consists of two halves: the cerebral hemispheres. The two halves are connected by a bundle of nerve fibers (the corpus callosum), and the left hemisphere controls the right side of the body, while the right hemisphere controls the left side of the body. Although the hemispheres seem to be almost identical, your answers to the above few questions provide clues about important differences between the two.

These differences, called *functional asymmetry,* offer insight to your brain's organization. If you are right-handed, for example, your left cerebral hemisphere is lateralized for handedness and also for control of your speech. You are "left lateralized." There is general agreement today that although there may be some rationale for the distinction between left and right hemispheric dominance, both hemispheres are involved in all activities (Caine & Caine, 1990). Figure 8.3 illustrates the relationship between one's left and right hemispheres and handedness.

Much of our knowledge of cerebral lateralization has resulted from the study of individuals with brain damage. Patients with left hemisphere damage, for example, typically encounter speech difficulties; damage to the right hemisphere frequently causes perceptual and attentional disorders. The right hemisphere often has been relegated to a "minor" position because as humans we rely so heavily on language that the left hemisphere came to be thought of as the dominant or "major" hemisphere. Today, however, psychologists place much importance in the right hemisphere's control of visual and spatial activities.

As interesting as these data are, our concern must focus mainly on developmental and educational implications. Data clearly suggest functional asymmetry in hemisphere use at various ages and between the two sexes. Rourke, Bakker, Fisk, and Strang (1983) reported an age-related shift in scanning letters from LFA (left field advantage) to RFA (right field advantage). The shift occurred between approximately 6 to 7 years and 11 to 12 years. They gave the example of presenting a 7-year-old and a 14-year-old with the same simple sentence. Rourke and his colleagues reported that these children seemed to generate different strategies to process the sentence. They also doubted that this processing occurs in the same brain structures. The authors speculated that a younger child is likely to respond to the visual configuration of the sentence, thus signalling visual-spatial predominance (involving the right hemisphere). The older reader, however, probably responds, almost automatically, with a perceptual analysis, thus indicating greater syntactical and semantic awareness (involving the left hemisphere).

Lateralization in the Classroom

Lateralization in the Classroom   Can we draw implications from the lateralization literature with regard to education? Answering this question requires two significant considerations.

1. *Are there gender differences that are definitely related to lateralization?* Without reviewing here the enormous body of literature addressing this question, we can safely state that gender differences exist in certain abilities, such as verbal and spatial skills. Females generally seem superior in anything relating to language, while males excel in spatial tasks. But these differences tell us nothing about why they exist. They may result from either biological or cultural factors, or both. The differences are too tenuous and too subject to a variety of interpretations (Caine & Caine, 1990).

    Our interest, however, focuses on one question: Should these demonstrated differences dictate different instructional practices for males and females? Though these research results should be taken into consideration, they should not be the basis for curriculum construction or different instructional techniques. For one thing, males and females are much more alike in brain functioning than they are different; some women have greater spatial ability than most men, and some men have greater language skills than most women. Also, we encourage cultivating differences and fostering unique talents.

2. *To what extent, then, should educators recognize these differences?* Since the results of lateralization studies have become known, criticism has been directed at the schools for "teaching to the left hemisphere." Reading, writing, and mathematics all favor logical, sequential processing: left hemisphere functions. Should we teach to the right hemisphere?

    Although the temptation to teach for right hemispheric involvement is great, research to date remains vague as to how much involvement of either hemisphere is present in the activities of the other—how much one interferes with the other. Perhaps we can best conclude that acceptance of current findings means accepting the reality of greater or lesser hemispheric activity in any particular activity, but also being aware that human activity, especially learning, entails the commitment of both hemispheres.

One way of integrating current knowledge of lateralization into the curriculum is to become aware of your reliance on verbal directions (Grady, 1984). Most teachers depend heavily on linear tasks, such as having students respond to specific questions or following directions. Try also to present material graphically, in visual form, and encourage students to express their understanding of a topic in a creative manner.

Pattern Matching

In this chapter, we will examine cognitive explanations of learning, making frequent reference to the pattern match between our cognitive capacities and the external world. Here we address the role of the brain in the process, since pattern detection seems to be an inherent function of the brain. In fact, some authors (Caine & Caine, 1990) believe that the brain resists having meaningless patterns imposed on it—it tries to make sense of the stimuli presented to it by seeking patterns!

Hubel (1979), discussing how the brain organizes information (by patterns), noted that at the input end, the brain is primarily preoccupied with extracting from the outside world information that is biologically interesting. At the output end, nerve impulses stimulate behavioral responses. What happens between input and output remains vague, and as Hubel stated, understanding the neural mechanisms that explain perception (pattern matching) remains a major goal.

Hart (1983), commenting on the brain's tendency to match patterns, stated that the brain detects, constructs, and elaborates patterns as a basic, built-in, natural function. He believes there is no concept, no fact in education that is more important than the brain's pattern-matching function, because it is at the heart of all learning.

Hart (1983, p. 67) summarized his thinking about the brain's pattern-matching ability as follows:

- The brain is naturally a pattern matcher, even in infants.
- Pattern matching utilizes both specific elements and relationships and is aided by the effective use of clues.
- Negative clues play an important role, since they instantly alert the brain that "something is wrong."
- The brain uses clues in a probabilistic manner; that is, we use a minimum number of clues to reach a correct decision or solution.
- Pattern matching depends on the experience an individual brings to any situation; the more clues the person recognizes, the quicker is the match.
- Patterns are continually changing to meet the demands of new experiences.

Since the human brain seems predisposed to search for patterns, you can help students to improve their classroom performance by using what we know of pattern matching. One technique is to have them develop chronological pattern guides. After students have read a story (or page or paragraph), give them a mixed series of statements and ask them to arrange these statements in the order in which they appeared in the story. Students react well to such exercises, because they are predisposed to identify patterns. Teaching that attempts to present information in a way that helps their brains to extract patterns—as is found in an integrated curriculum, thematic teaching, and the current use of whole language—helps students to make sense of what they are learning (Caine & Caine, 1990).

Learning

Regardless of hemispheric lateralization and our efforts to capitalize on current findings, we can safely state that classroom learning finds its biological base in the cerebral cortex. For the successful functioning of such complex mental processes as perception, cognition, and decision making, perfectly tuned and smoothly operating synapses are essential.

Human beings show amazing resiliency or flexibility, which is the meaning of *plasticity;* recovery from injury has been a well-documented fact of biological and psychological research. Yet there are limits to plasticity, and thus we are faced with a puzzle: under what conditions will children and adults recover from damage? As you can well imagine, the research and literature that have addressed this problem are enormous.

What seems to distinguish the human brain is the variety of specialized activities it is capable of learning. The difficulty still facing investigators lies in the unexplored gap between the psychological reality of learning and knowledge about the structure, biochemistry, and physiology of the brain. One possible approach to bridging this gap is to determine if brain cells undergo change because of learning.

Hyden (1985) discovered, that in animals, both brain cells and their synapses show an increase in protein production during and after learning. Hyden believed that a "wave of protein synthesis" pervades the brain at learning; that is, system changes occur in brain cell protein during learning. He then hypothesized that when learning begins, inner and outer stimuli cause electrical changes in the nervous system that induce the production of specific proteins in the brain. Calcium production also increases.

What also should interest us are the developmental changes that occur in brain structures—size, number of connections, and changes in such brain support systems as the glial cells. The growth of intellectual capacity in our students strongly appears to match the brain's anatomical and biochemical changes. Although this match still lacks biological proof, the fact that the brain's role in learning and cognition seems well established testifies to the need for a comprehensive theory of thinking to acknowledge a brain basis.

For example, all teachers know that some students prefer to learn with noise surrounding them, or while they move around, talk to others, or just fidget. They don't act in this manner to irritate a teacher. They are, however, responding to signals from their central nervous systems (Garger, 1990). Frequently, a student's approach to learning (for example, wanting to listen to music while studying) is a neurophysiological response.

THE IMPORTANCE OF INFORMATION PROCESSING

As we begin to examine specific aspects of cognition, the significance of information processing for both teachers and students becomes more apparent. Think of information processing as encompassing such topics as attention, perception, thinking, memory, and problem-solving strategies. Representation lies at the very heart of information processing. Its importance for teachers becomes apparent from observing student behavior. How many times have you said to yourself, "I wonder what he's thinking?" or asked yourself, "Now, how could she have arrived at that answer?"

Cognitive psychologists are attempting to discover techniques that will allow us to analyze our students' thinking, which, if successful, will have positive and far-reaching implications for both understanding learning and improving instruction. It seems reasonable to assume that our students have ideas and use symbols; however, translating these simple statements into testable situations demands that researchers explore the domain of representation: symbols, schemas, images, and ideas, and their interactions.

The Meaning of Representation

representation *The manner in which information is recorded or expressed.*

The manner in which information is recorded or expressed is a **representation** of that information (Glass, Holyoak, & Santa, 1987). The simple word *car* is a representation, since it represents a certain idea; the idea conveyed can also be represented in different ways: *auto, automobile,* or *motor car.* In each example, however, the information represented remains the same; this common represented information is called the *content* of the representation; the different ways that the information can be expressed are called the *representational codes.*

How We Represent Information

The way our students represent the material they encounter in the classroom raises important issues for both curriculum and instruction (Phillips, 1983). We appear to use two types of codes for representing information: mental imagery and verbal processing (Foster, 1986).

Mental Imagery

Stop for a moment and think about the last time you went to the beach. Were there waves? Was the beach crowded? What color was the water? Answering these questions takes you into the world of mental imagery, a world that has long intrigued philosophers and psychologists. You undoubtedly formed a "picture in your mind" to answer each of the questions. Your mental image represented or resembled the waves, the people at the beach, the color of the water. If you think about your answers, you will sooner or later question the accuracy of your image. Just how precise is it? Was the water exactly that blue-green color you recall? Though almost all of us use mental imagery, today's psychologists are concerned with the reliability of our reports.

For example, Paivio (1974) asked his subjects to imagine two clocks whose times were 12:05 and 9:15. Then he asked them on which clock the hands formed the larger angle. You think about this question for a moment. How did you answer the question? Didn't you form an image of each clock similar to the following?

Paivio's subjects reported that they had formed pictures of the clocks; they also needed more time to answer if the angles were similar, as in a comparison of 12:05 and 1:10.

Another example of mental images can be found in the work of Stephen Kosslyn (1980), who attempted to have readers get an intuitive feeling for the topic by trying to answer the following questions: What shape are a German shepherd's ears? Is a tennis ball larger than a pear? Does a bee have a dark head? Is a Christmas tree darker green than a frozen pea? Most people report that they mentally picture the named objects in the course of trying to answer these questions.

Images and Pictures

Any discussion of imagery must reckon with the widespread conviction that a visual image is a picture in our memory, much as a snapshot is stored in a photo album (Kosslyn, 1980). Yet an image is not like a picture stored in memory, waiting to be retrieved. Imagine a tiger. How many stripes does it have? You may have difficulty with this notion; it is difficult to "pull" a tiger picture from memory and count its stripes. Images are abstract, while pictures are linked to the visual properties of actual objects.

Our general knowledge can distort our images (Anderson, 1985). In one study exemplifying this, some subjects were told that a drawing of two circles connected by a straight line was a dumbbell; others, that it was eyeglasses. When asked to draw the object from memory, subjects who had been given the label "eyeglasses" often bent the connecting line. Those who were given the label "dumbbell" strengthened or doubled the connecting line. Anderson interpreted these results to indicate that the subjects' general knowledge distorted their memories of the physical properties of the objects. Reproducing an actual picture would not result in such distortions.

Thus, though *image* may be difficult to define, we can specify several properties of images (Anderson, 1985).

- Images represent continuously varying information.
- Images possess the capability of responding to certain mental operations (for example, we can "rotate" them: imagine a cat's face, now its tail).

Cognitive psychologists are attempting to discover techniques that will allow us to analyze our students' thinking, which, if successful, have positive and far-reaching implications for both understanding learning and improving instruction.

- Images are not linked to a "picture" of the object, but are part of our representational system.
- Images often change because of the knowledge that we possess (recall the dumbbell experiment).

Verbal Processing

Discuss how you could facilitate information processing in the classroom by using the techniques of mental imagery and verbal processing to represent information.

Unlike mental imagery, verbal processing does not resemble in any way what it represents. Language is a good example: in no way does the word *car* resemble an actual automobile. The distinction between mental imagery and verbal processing has classroom significance: consider that although most people use both codes, individuals typically prefer one over the other.

If you can determine which code each of your students prefers, use instructional methods that match preferred codes whenever possible. For example, several methods described in the next chapter are designed to help students with their memories. Some of these methods, such as rehearsal, appeal to verbal processes, while others, such as method of loci, appeal to mental imagery.

THE ROLE OF PERCEPTION

If you stop reading for a moment and look around, you may see some things that you recognize immediately, such as your computer or a dictionary. You may also notice something that is totally different or new—perhaps the internal mechanism of your computer, if you are seeing it for the first time (Shuell, 1986). Our ability to recognize the familiar and to realize what we do not know is **perception.** Perceiving something means that

perception *The ability to recognize familiar persons, objects, or events with meaning and expectations.*

- you can recall past experiences with this person, object, or event;
- you experience meaning;
- you have certain expectations about the person, object, or event.

Consequently, perception seems to entail more than just the ability to react to something; considerable processing is necessary to integrate multiple sources of information into a single representation.

Explanation of the Perceptual Process

Human beings do not respond to elements in our environments on an item-by-item basis. In this regard, cognitive psychologists have learned much from the early Gestaltists. For example, examine the following figure.

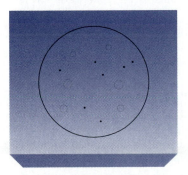

What do you see? Undoubtedly your reply would be something like, "I see a circle with dots and smaller circles inside it." You would not say, "I see one dot, and another dot, and another dot, and a small circle, and another small circle, and a big circle." You grouped the stimuli and expressed your answer in some related manner. You utilized your past experience by combining it with this present experience.

When someone asks you what time it is, do you carefully observe all of the minute markings on your watch? No. Your past experience enables you to ignore the irrelevant and concentrate on the section where the hands and numbers are.

Human beings organize the relevant stimuli, ignore the irrelevant, and move them into the background, thus creating a *figure-ground relationship.* The more prominent qualities of the stimulus pattern emerge more clearly (as a figure), while the less prominent qualities recede (into the ground). In the example of telling time, the hands resting on the minute markings representing five o'clock form the figure, while the remainder of the face of the watch is the ground.

Perception is the giving of meaning to the discrete, meaningless stimuli that initially arouse awareness. The meaning that an individual gives to any stimulus depends upon the manner in which that person patterns it. For example, a young boy hears a sound. From his past experiences he realizes that it is a whistle. As he continues to relate this stimulus to his experience, perceptual meaning becomes richer. He notes the time element; the whistle always blows at seven o'clock, morning and evening. Passing through town one evening at seven o'clock, he hears the whistle from the fire station. He has located its source. When he hears it from now on, he will identify it as the seven o'clock whistle coming from the firehouse.

The way stimuli are structured determines the quality of the percept and, ultimately, the concept. The strong reaction against history as the memorization of dates, and against geography as the memorization of places, is negative proof of the importance of perceptual meaning. When a subject is presented as a mass of sheer facts, students are unable to form patterns and establish meaningful relations among the stimuli, or to link them with their own past experiences. The result is a distorted concept of all aspects of history and geography, and a distressing tendency to avoid these subjects later in life.

Teachers should use materials that form meaningful patterns for youngsters. Only then can we hope to encourage students to see the value of a particular subject and help them to make its topics more meaningful. This in itself is no easy chore; it requires a thorough knowledge of individual students. But the effort is richly rewarded when students acquire awareness and begin to discern meaning in their schoolwork.

For the Classroom

We have emphasized that perception is a crucial element in learning. The sensory experiences that students have are not just mechanically registered and then filed away. Incoming data merge with past, similar experiences and combine with present physiological and psychological states to produce a particular perception (Speth & Brown, 1988). Perception, then, depends on both learning and maturation.

Patterns of Stimuli

Almost from birth, students react to patterns of stimuli as they perceive them at the moment. Learning, maturation, emotions, needs, and values are all intertwined in perception. In one classic study (Bruner & Goodman, 1947), several 10-year-old children from poor homes and a like number from rich homes were asked to estimate the size of coins. The experimenters first showed the youngsters coins ranging in value from a penny to a half dollar and then asked them to duplicate the coin sizes by adjusting a knob that projected circles onto a screen. The circle on the screen could be made larger or smaller. Interestingly, the poor children greatly overestimated the sizes of the coins: the value they placed on them affected their perceptions. The rich youngsters only slightly overestimated the coin sizes.

How does a student proceed from a gross reaction to a discriminated response? In figure 8.4 a gradually more detailed pattern of a face is given. Older subjects often identify it as a face as soon as they see the second figure, while some students of even third- or fourth-grade age are unable to identify it until the last line is drawn. Why? What delays the recognition? The older students, because of their experiences, added the necessary details themselves. (The ability to perform these closure tasks is a good predictor of reading readiness.)

Fantz (1961, 1963) indicated that newborn infants not only see but also have preference for certain patterns. He studied 18 infants under 5 days of age by placing them in the bottom of a test chamber. At the top of the chamber was an illuminated slot into

Figure 8.4
Gradual differentiation of a face.

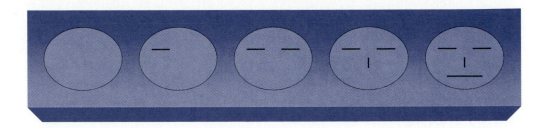

which cards could be placed, and a peephole next to the slot that enabled the investigator to observe the infant's eyes. When the image was established in the eye, the length of time the infant focused on a particular color, pattern, or form was recorded. The infant was given a range of choices: a schematic face, a patch of newsprint, a bull's eye, and a red, a white, and a yellow circle. The subjects looked longest at facial patterns, then at the newsprint, and then at the bull's eye. None looked longest at the circles.

What can we conclude from these results? We cannot conclude that there is any instinctive reaction to the human face. But the experiment seems to suggest that there are definite properties in the visual world of the infant, since visual attention focuses earlier on patterns than on color differences. If this is so (and all evidence supports this conclusion), then perceptual training should commence much earlier in life, since children show an early readiness for perception.

For classroom purposes, it is especially significant that developmental changes occur in the attainment of perceptual acuity. Your answers to the four questions next to the illustrations below will demonstrate the perceptual phenomena involved in these developmental changes.

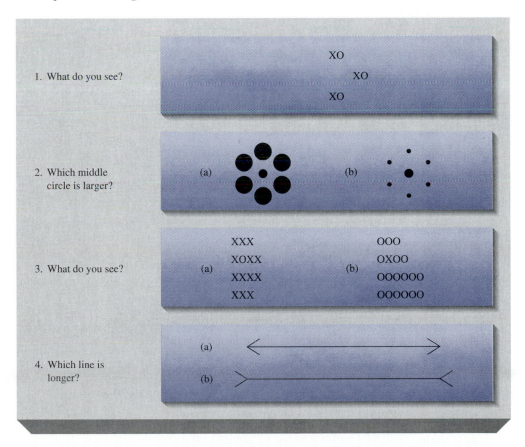

In examining these illustrations, you probably answered as follows:

• Three figures of XO (You grouped them.)
• You probably identified B as the larger. (Objective measurement reveals that they are identical; the surrounding elements affected your perception of the middle circle.)
• You probably saw an O in the first illustration and an X in the second. (The difference between the central figure and its surrounding elements is so striking that you focused on the central figure.)
• Your first reaction was probably to say line b was longer. (Measurement shows that they are the same length.)

The main point that we wish to emphasize is that internal perceptual learning allows students to make finer and finer discriminations, so that they can make more and more fine-grained analysis of stimuli. Consider the wine taster who has to learn to make minor discriminations among a variety of wines that may all taste the same to the novice. We need to help students to learn complex stimulus patterns and process new information from their environments.

Helping Students with Their Perceptual Acuity

As adults, our experience enables us to overcome our initial responses with little difficulty. Younger students are more easily confused (they may, for example, confuse *b* with *d*), but they gradually develop less susceptibility to misinterpret complex stimulus patterns. The task then becomes one of aiding them to acquire perceptual acuity as early as possible, since this is a capacity they possess almost from birth (Foster, 1986). For example, many of the skills that a child must master in school, such as reading, require accurate discriminations and competence in detecting the unchanging nature of stimulus patterns in spite of possible surface changes. A teacher's added knowledge of the perceptual process would aid in both the construction of suitable curriculum materials and the nature of instruction.

Teachers can capitalize on their students' tendency to group; that is, students want to organize and structure, and you can help them by recalling certain principles.

1. Human beings tend to group by familar objects. What do you see in the following figure?

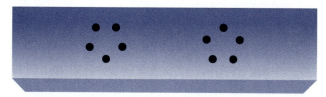

   You saw two groups of circles, not 10 isolated figures.
2. Objects that are similar form natural groups. What do you see in the following figure?

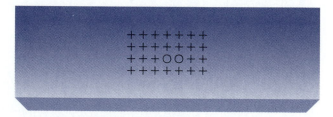

   You saw a group of crosses and two circles because you grouped similar things.

Focus ← Structure and Memory

As we have mentioned, your students learn better when material is somewhat familiar or can be organized into structures. Try this experiment yourself. It is similar to the tasks your students encounter. Memorize this list of words.

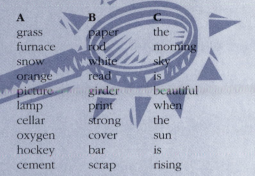

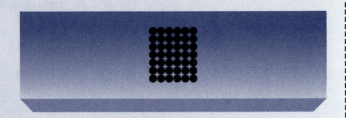

A	B	C
grass	paper	the
furnace	rod	morning
snow	white	sky
orange	read	is
picture	girder	beautiful
lamp	print	when
cellar	strong	the
oxygen	cover	sun
hockey	bar	is
cement	scrap	rising

As you attempt to recall them, certain patterns emerge. You probably had difficulty with the words in column A—they were meaningless. Column B was easier—not only did the words possess meaning, but they clustered around two key words: book and steel. Column C was probably the easiest—the words were logically organized into a meaningful structure. You thus have a dual task. You must either relate new material to what your students already know, or you must make new material as meaningful as possible.

You can help your students by following the organization principles suggested by the Gestaltists. For example, what do you see in the diagram shown above?

Most readers say that it is a square, but it is a square of circles; individual identity is absorbed by the larger unit. Four of these "circles" now become "corners."

These basic perceptual principles aid in meaningful learning because through them, students can organize material. So you should attempt:

- to use the familiar to introduce the novel
- to relate new material to some structure that the students already possess
- to stress any meaningful relations within the material

You cannot overemphasize the importance of meaning and structure to your students. Human beings often experience difficulty in thinking and problem solving because "facts" are buried by their surroundings—they are "camouflaged." Can you find the digit 4 in the following diagram? It is buried within unfamiliar shapes, so you will probably have trouble finding it. If you do have trouble, turn to the next page.

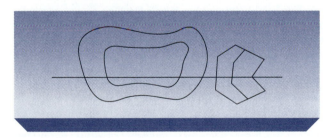

Students have exactly the same trouble discovering and finding meaning within unfamiliar subjects. Your students' past experiences should be used to form cognitive schemata in their efforts to master new materials, solve problems, and look at subjects more creatively.

HOW STUDENTS CATEGORIZE →

Students interact successfully with their environments according to their ability to organize information. Placing objects into categories and then inventing a name for the category is one of the fundamental organizing activities in which all students engage. The words *book, pupil, teacher, car, doll,* and *water* are examples of the human tendency to

teacher – student

interactions

Information Processing in the Classroom

1. The manner in which information is recorded or expressed is a representation of that information.
   - Show your students pictures or actual objects used in various occupations: paint brush, easel, stethoscope, baker's hat, spatula, wrench, etc. Have them guess how each object is used and what the typical user's career is.
   - Tell the story of the blind men and the elephant. Discuss how important perception is in the story and why the men's perception was distorted.
   - For older children, describe a hypothetical automobile accident. Ask the children to accept roles as witnesses. Ask what each witness could have seen. Point out how each person may have seen something that another did not.
   - Select a short mystery (by an author like Donald Sobel) to read to your class. Before you begin, however, ask the children to listen carefully for clues. Towards the conclusion, ask them how they think the mystery should be solved and then compare their projected solutions to the author's.
2. Students use two techniques for representing information: mental imagery and verbal processing.
   Mental Imagery
   - In kindergarten and lower grades, show students pictures of everyday objects such as a broom, comb, ball, etc., and ask your students to describe how these objects are used and what they are used for.
   - Train your students to "use their third eye" as each one takes a turn to continue the story that you begin.
   - Use a game like "Blind Man's Bluff" to teach the alphabet to young children. Have one child blindfolded. Select another to take a large oak tag letter off the wall. The blindfolded child traces around the letter with his or her hands, trying to determine which one it is.
   - In math, to determine what a problem wants you to find, ask your students to picture which facts are

present and which are missing. It is easier to decide what steps they must take to find the missing facts when they know what is present. Sometimes it helps to draw a picture of the problem. Use concrete models such as a diagram, coins, or plastic chips labeled for value to help students think a problem through using these visualization techniques.
   Verbal processing
   - For older students, organize a debate. For example, should there be a dress code? a change in academic requirements to graduate? etc.
   - Arrange a forum; invite guests knowledgeable in their fields to discuss with students current topics, e.g., should driving lessons be part of the school curriculum; should students be forced to pay a fee for sports; should there be a ban on smoking in public places?
   - For younger students, play games such as "I went to the market and brought home . . .", in which each student, using each letter of the alphabet, says one thing that the following child must repeat.
3. Perception is giving meaning to the stimuli that come from the environment.
   - Develop a keener perception in your students by having them research the various cultures that are represented in their class. Ask them to find out their traditional dress, their food, family attitudes, etc. Children who may have immaturely ridiculed or called others names should have a deeper appreciation of their classmates after completing such a project.
   - In kindergarten, select a child to be a "buddy" to another who is having difficulty. By watching the more competent child, the other child will learn more quickly how to fold a paper, hang up a jacket, put toys away, etc.
   - In upper classes, organize children into several small cooperative learning groups to help one another develop perceptual awareness.

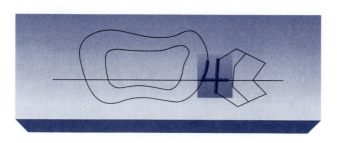

categorize. With this skill, you avoid the necessity of responding separately to each and every object in your environment. When you hear the word "book," you need not seek an actual book to ascertain its characteristics. If you have a concept of *book,* you have placed this recent utterance in a category with other similar objects that are made of bound sheets and have pages with words and illustrations. Upon hearing "book," you recall the concept that includes the common properties of that category.

Forming Categories

Bruner, Goodnow, and Austin (1956) summarized the importance of categorizing information; their insights, although dated, have stood the test of time and are worthy to be repeated today.

1. *Categorizing reduces the complexity of the environment.* Abstraction enables students to group objects, and then students gradually respond to classes of objects rather than responding to each and every thing they encounter.
2. *Categorizing permits us to identify the objects of the world.* We identify objects by placing them in a class, and when similar objects are met, we can say, "Ah, there is another one of those little redheaded Venusians."
3. *Categorizing allows humans to reduce their need of constant learning.* Each time we experience an object, we are not forced to form a new category; we merely categorize with no additional learning. This object has attributes X, Y, Z; therefore, it belongs to the category entitled *car.*
4. *Categorizing provides direction for instrumental activity.* When we see a road sign that reads *Danger Ahead,* we alter our driving to meet the anticipated conditions. We become more alert, proceed more cautiously, and drive more slowly.
5. *Categorizing encourages the ordering and relating of classes.* Since we react to systems and patterns, once we place an object in a category, we vastly increase the possibilities of establishing relationships for that particular object. For example, once students decide on the characteristics of the "good" president, they can then match any president to this category.

Recent Research

This classic view of how we organize information (form categories or concepts) has come under considerable revision, so that a more novel interpretation is widely accepted. The impetus for the assault began with research into how we name colors.

If you think about it, there is no clear rationale for the color names that we have designated, since color is actually on a continuum. We arbitrarily divide color as we see fit. A question that intrigued cognitive psychologists was: Does the manner in which we label things structure the way that we classify them? Brown and Lenneberg (1954), showed English-speaking subjects 24 colors and asked them to label the colors. Those readily named were called *codable.* Another group of subjects was shown a small set of colors and then a large set, and asked to specify which ones they had seen before. Subjects readily recognized those colors that the researchers had identified as codable.

The matter rested there until 1973, when Eleanor Rosch, studying a Stone Age tribe in New Guinea that had only two color terms (one for bright, one for dark), discovered that although her subjects had difficulty identifying by name the intermediate colors, they showed the same recognition characteristics as had the English-speaking subjects. Thus, differences in naming between the two cultures did not reflect differences in memory storage: cognitive processing determined the color categories they formed.

Upon her return to America and with continued experimentation, Rosch (Mervis & Rosch, 1981) concluded that her discoveries concerning color categories extended throughout the classification process to explain how we form all categories. The classic theory of classification described at the beginning of this section holds that a category consists of certain definite criteria. If an object possesses these criteria, it belongs to that category; if it lacks the defining criteria, it must be a member of another category.

However, all categories do not seem to possess neat, defining sets of criteria. Gardner (1985, p. 345) noted that some categories are better identified by the actions that they signify. For example, a "drinking vessel" is defined by its potential for being held and poured from. These and similar difficulties caused Rosch to propose an explanation that cuts across many natural categories. The explanatory concept she proposed is called a *prototype,* which contains not clearly defined critical attributes, but a common standard form (Glass, Holyoak, & Santa, 1987, p. 343–345). For example, though technically both chickens and robins are birds, most people would state that the robin is a more typical example of a bird; it is more natural; it is a prototype.

For the Classroom

What does this change in thinking about classification mean for teachers? It probably reinforces what teachers have been doing intuitively for years. When teaching an idea—a concept—good teachers never had their students memorize long lists of attributes that best described it. Rather, they consistently gave examples, and they compared the concept to other categories that did not include it. Macintosh and Delicious apples are both apples; an orange is not an apple. Good teachers have generally appealed to information in a child's natural world and not depended solely on artificial criteria.

Try to structure classroom experiences to provide as many rich and meaningful impressions as possible. The following principles should help:

1. *Remember that concepts are only as valuable as the meanings they convey.* Be careful that you do not accept the symbol alone as evidence that students have attained a concept. You should continually probe to guarantee that meaning is associated with the symbol. For example, students probably can define the concept, but can they describe it, give examples, and explain the various types (Wilson, 1987)?
2. *Provide varied experiences for the learner.* Students should encounter the concept under different conditions. Where possible they should see and feel and talk about it, connecting the object with as many senses as possible. Learners should occasionally encounter examples of what a concept is not. That is, some negative examples are effective, if mixed with many positive, clear instances.
3. *Utilize assorted methods of presenting the concept.* Different techniques of presentation are most efficient. You cannot be satisfied with one method, whether it is telling, discovery, or reading. A combination of methods is definitely indicated.
4. *Encourage self-activity in the search for common elements.* This principle is almost a subdivision of principle 3. All learning increases with a student's activity; that is also true of concept formation. Students should spend substantial time searching for the necessary properties of a concept. The time spent should be proportionate to the other methods you use for the acquisition of any concept. That is, you must decide, at least initially, how much time should be given to searching, and how much to telling. The concept's abstractness will unquestionably influence the teacher. For example, teaching a preschool student the concept of *ball* or another toy entails considerable self-activity. Learning about deoxyribonucleic acid demands substantial direction from you, especially in the initial phases of concept acquisition.
5. *Encourage students to apply the concept.* Once students have partially attained the concept, they should begin to use it. They should read it and explain it; they should furnish it as a missing word; they should use it to solve problems. Above all, if they are to use it outside the classroom, teachers should supply experiences that are not routinely educational. Students must realize that they can use it at home, work, or play; that is exactly what is meant by the maxim that concepts aid in the economical adjustment to the environment.
6. *Relate the concept or category to your students' prior knowledge in a systematic manner.* Encourage students to think about how they organize their knowledge about a particular set of concepts or categories. For example, if they are studying about metals such as silver and gold, have them relate this content to existing information they may have about minerals.

Summarize the importance of categorizing information for students and discuss how you should structure classroom experiences to provide meaningful learning of concepts.

Figure 8.5

A conceptual hierarchy for the concept of minerals.

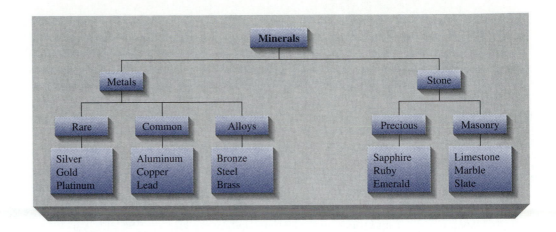

Depending on the students' prior knowledge and schemata about metals, they may find the hierarchical organization (like that illustrated in fig. 8.5) similar to their own organized schemata. If not, such a graphic organizer should facilitate further inquiries and learning. In some cases in which hierarchical organization of information is not known or readily apparent, encourage students to create their own subjective representations of information (Baddeley, 1990).

Concepts are vital to thinking, reasoning, and perceiving relationships. The quality of a student's concepts is the best measure of probable success in learning, because meaning is basic to learning. Also, concepts determine what we know, believe, and do. Concepts, then, are vital to all phases of life. They order the environment, add depth to perceptual relationships, clarify thinking, and, particularly, facilitate the entire learning process. Meaningful concepts are also a great aid to memory.

Annual **Edition**

MEMORY AT WORK

Acquiring concepts in itself is not enough; we want our students to remember what they acquire. As the reborn cognitive movement moved into the late 1960s and 1970s, the study of memory attracted considerable attention. An analysis of memory that cognitive psychologists widely accepted was the distinction made between episodic and semantic memory (Tulving, 1972).

episodic memory *The recall of personal experiences within a specific context or period of time.*

1. **Episodic memory** is recall of personal experiences within a specific context or period of time. Think of it as autobiographical; episodic memory provides an individual with a personal history. Here are some examples:

   • John and I watched the Red Sox play the Yankees last Friday night.
   • I saw Rex Harrison play Henry Higgins in *My Fair Lady* when it first opened in New York.

semantic memory *Memory necessary for the use of language.*

2. **Semantic memory** is the memory necessary for the use of language, a kind of dictionary without reference to our personal experiences that represents our general knowledge. It is the organized knowledge that a person possesses about words and other verbal symbols. Here are examples:

   • I know that Albany is the capital of New York.
   • I know that *friend* is an acceptable English word.

Note that we can verify the accuracy of semantic memory. Written testimony (geography books, state and federal listings) attest to the truthfulness of the statement that Albany is the capital of New York. No such tests exist for episodic memory.

In a particularly influential model of episodic memory, Atkinson and Shiffrin (1968) proposed a three-store system: the sensory register, the short-term store, and the long-term store. These three stores are structurally distinct because they hold information differently, for varying times, and for different purposes. The authors also stated that the three stores lose information differently. Figure 8.6 illustrates a multistore model.

The **sensory register** holds input in almost the same form as the sensory image; that is, cognitive processes do not begin to alter data until after they pass through the sensory register. Information is lost from the register in less than a second, either through spontaneous decay or through the entry of new data. The sensory register momentarily preserves information so that it can be selectively transmitted into the memory system. The selective character of the sensory register prevents us from being overwhelmed by the sensory input. For example, what attracts the attention of some students does not do so with others.

sensory register *The ability, which is highly selective, to hold information in memory for a brief period.*

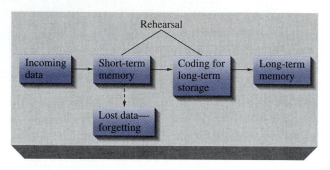

The **short-term store** is the working memory, which entails conscious processes. Input to the short-term store comes from both the sensory register and the long-term store, both of which feed data to the short-term store for conscious manipulation. Information can be held indefinitely here if attention remains constant; otherwise, decay commences and data are lost in 15 to 30 seconds. The critical nature of the short-term store lies in its conscious content; neither the sensory register nor the long-term store entails consciousness. The longer information remains in the short-term store, the greater is the chance that it will be transmitted to the long-term store (George Miller's reference to the magical number seven as our storage capacity applied to short-term memory).

Figure 8.6
An early multi-store model.

The **long-term store** holds both conscious and unconscious data. For example, you can recall how the clams tasted at a beach cookout when you were a child. You probably still talk about the smell of the kitchen when an apple pie was baking. Although information may be stored indefinitely, data still may be lost (through interference, lack of retrieval cues, perhaps even sheer decay). The significance of long-term memory lies in its survival and adaptation value; humans require an enormous amount of information to survive in modern society.

short-term store *The working memory; consciousness is involved.*

long-term store *The aspect of memory that holds both conscious and unconscious data for long periods of time; related to meaningfulness of material.*

Consequently, the more meaningful you can make material for your students, the better you will relate it to their experiences, and the more successful you are in motivating them, the greater will be their level of understanding, since they will select their information from the sensory register, keep it active in the short-term store, and transfer it to the long-term store.

Although multistore models of memory have a neatness and elegance that many find appealing, the interests of most cognitive scientists are shifting away from this view (Baddeley, 1990). Several cognitivists advocate a **levels of processing** analysis (Craik & Lockhart, 1972), which focuses on the depth of processing. Information is not transformed by moving through a series of stores. Data are processed by various operations called perceptual-conceptual analysis.

levels of processing *Describes analysis of memory focusing on the depth at which humans process information.*

The perceptual-conceptual analysis reflects an individual's attention. If you deem incoming material worthy of long-term recall, you will analyze it differently from material you judge as relatively unimportant. Whether the stimulus is processed at a shallow level or at a deeper level depends on the nature of the stimulus, the time available for processing, and the subject's own motivation, goals, and knowledge base. Thus, the operations performed during input determine the fate of the incoming information.

Consequently, the initial processing of a word will determine the length of time students remember it and which aspects are remembered. For example, if you are interested only in the color of a word's printed letters, you will not remember that word as you would if you had examined the word for its meaning (Sherry & Schachter, 1987).

New Directions in Memory Studies

Memory remains a major research interest for today's cognitive psychologists (Baddeley, 1990). A question now frequently asked is this: Should memory be studied naturally, that is, by using everyday experiences (Conway, 1991), or by using strict laboratory techniques?

"You simply associate each number with a word, such as 'lipoprotein' and 3,467,009."

© 1991 by Sidney Harris—Science Magazine.

To illustrate the value of both these techniques, Ceci and Bronfenbrenner (1991) used a 30-minute cake-baking experiment in which the children were observed while they waited for the cupcakes to bake. There were three conditions: some children did the baking in the laboratory; others did it in their homes; and others did it in a kitchen in a university building. The authors reported that the children in the lab checked the clock 30 percent more frequently than those in their own homes, but with no greater degree of punctuality. As a result, the authors urged that memory researchers adopt both techniques in the study of memory.

Yet certain basic questions remain to be answered: Why do we forget? Do all individuals experience the same types of problems with memory? Are there specific types of memory problems? Are they related? How exactly do we memorize? How can we become skillful at remembering (Neisser, 1982)?

As a result of decades of research, speculation, and common sense reasoning, certain generalizations are possible. Among them are the following:

- similarity of material can cause interference;
- meaningful material aids recall;
- time on task helps students to remember;
- rehearsal (going over something repeatedly) is an important memory strategy;
- mnemonic strategies can help students remember.

Before proceeding further, we should pause to make some basic distinctions that will help to clarify a complex topic.

Recognition, Recall, and Forgetting

storage *The act of putting information into memory.*

retrieval *The act of recognizing, recalling, and reconstructing what we have previously stored in memory.*

Distinguish between storage and retrieval, and identify measures you can adopt to aid students' storage and retrieval of information.

It is important that in the study of memory, you also distinguish between **storage** and **retrieval.** Storage implies "putting information into" memory, which occurs as a result of attending, encoding, and the use of memory strategies. Retrieval, on the other hand, implies recognizing, recalling, and reconstructing what has previously been "put in."

For example, your students may have memorized the names of the major battles of the Civil War on Monday, but on Wednesday some of the class can't recall them. You then furnish a cue. "Henry, how would you describe the tip of your pencil?" "It's sharp, Miss Smith. Oh, I get it. Sharpesville is the name." This student knew the name, but couldn't retrieve it without help. Two other topics that have special relevance for the classroom are recognition and recall.

If you think for a moment, you will quickly realize the importance of these concepts for the classroom. In your teaching you constantly appeal to your students' basic knowledge; you are asking them to recognize something familiar in a new work that you are teaching. In testing, you want them to recognize familiar cues in the questions. Academic success or failure is closely tied to both recognition and recall.

Recognition

recognition *The act of comparing an incoming representation with a representation already in memory.*

Recognition is the act of comparing a present, incoming representation with a representation already stored in memory. Is the number of your apartment 29? You have just performed a recognition task; note that you were not asked to recall the number of your apartment, but to compare it to 29.

There are three major elements involved in recognition: similarity, prior experience, and expectation and context. The need for similarity seems obvious: we probably will not recognize something we have not encountered before, or something familiar in a radically altered form—for example, a friend at a costume party. But as essential as it seems, the notion of similarity can lead to difficulty in the classroom. If you use multiple-choice questions, the alternate answers you select, if too similar to the correct one, can hinder recognition. *Prior experience* refers to the frequency and recency of encounters with the object, event, or person. Repetition exercises a strong impact upon recognition. The term *expectation and context* refers to the expectation of meeting certain things or people in certain circumstances. For example, youngsters in the early grades are almost always surprised to meet their teachers in the supermarket. They do not expect to see them in these circumstances. The expectations that arise from context, of course, are not limited to elementary school youngsters. A continuing frustration for teachers is the inability, almost refusal, of some students to recognize and apply mathematical principles anywhere but in math classes. Different context; different expectations.

Recall

What are the names of the Great Lakes? Who won the 1986 World Series? Who was the President of the United States before Lyndon Johnson? These questions force you to *recall* information. Recall goes beyond recognition, because you are not given a "copy" of the representation. Any retrieval cue is minimal; consequently, students must generate their own cues in their search for the necessary information. For a search to be effective, the information sought must have been stored in a reasonably organized manner; otherwise, the target information remains elusive and recall usually falters. Again we note the importance of a schema—or organizational property—for understanding cognitive processes.

Since the strategies to aid recall are so central to memory, learning, and problem solving, chapter 9 is devoted to their analysis.

Forgetting

Forgetting, unfortunately, is a normal process and here does not refer to an abnormal loss of memory occasioned by aging, shock, or brain injury. Under normal daily conditions, what causes your students to forget previously acquired material? Theorists have proposed several explanations (Sherry & Schachter, 1987).

forgetting *The loss of previously acquired material from memory.*

- *Forgetting as disuse or fading.* Once they have learned it, students will forget an item unless they use it. This explanation of forgetting has been referred to as the trace decay hypothesis (Ebbinghaus, 1885). Deterioration of the information develops and learning slowly fades. Though this is still a popular belief, today psychologists question it. For example, if subjects memorize a list of words to errorless recall, and then wait for various lengths of time before testing, they experience loss as illustrated in figure 8.7.

The exact details of the curve may vary depending upon the nature of the material, the degree of overlearning, and other material studied between the time of learning and the time of recall. But note two items with important implications for teaching:

- the rapid decline after initial learning; and
- the stability of retained materials with increasing time.

Other possible interpretations of the forgetting curve exist. Certain skills, such as riding a bicycle, swimming, and ice skating, show remarkable endurance. Even some verbal material is not quickly forgotten. You probably recall several lines from an elementary school play or show, while forgetting something you learned last semester; decay over time does not explain this. Other variables, such as motivation, also must influence retention. Still, time exacts its toll, and you should consider this in your teaching by conducting periodic, meaningful reviews.

- *Motivated forgetting,* or repressed forgetting. Unquestionably, you have had experiences that you try to forget because of the unpleasantness, fear, or anxiety associated with them. If experiences are sufficiently severe, amnesia—partial or total loss of memory—results. The extent of repression as a cause of normal forgetting remains unestablished because of the lack of experimental control that can be introduced.

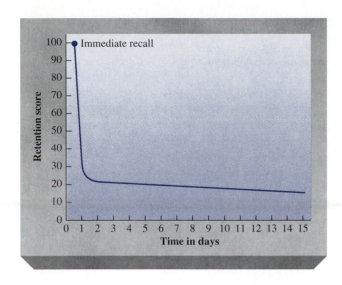

Figure 8.7
The curve of retention.

• *Forgetting because of interference.* Psychologists agree that most forgetting happens because new learning interferes with past learning. Interference can be either *retroactive* (the interference is produced by learning that occurs after the memory event) or *proactive* (it is produced by learning that occurred prior to the memory event) (Ellis & Hunt, 1993).

• *Forgetting because of extinction and reorganization.* Because of disuse and a lack of reinforcement, students forget a response. When forced to recall it, they apply newly acquired experiences and undoubtedly reshape the original response, so that it may or may not suit the original stimulus. We have seen an example of this situation in the exercise using "The War of the Ghosts."

Given the present understanding of the forgetting and retention phenomenon, what are some specific measures you can adopt to aid your students' storage and retrieval?

1. *Repeatedly urge students to remember.* This suggestion refers not to obvious exhortation, but to student self-activity, whereby material acquires both meaning and personal significance: it is organized and stored. For example, overlearning aids memory because it more sharply distinguishes the item to be stored and facilitates coding, which lowers the possibility of negative transfer and increases the possibility of positive transfer.

2. *Comprehension, not mere mastery of facts, should be the aim of your instruction.* Such understanding depends upon the kind of material presented and how you present it. Words are remembered better than nonsense syllables, and solutions of problems are better remembered than isolated facts. Try to guide students to perceive and use relationships within the material and between the topics and their own backgrounds. (Note: For verbal learning, three essentials must always be stressed: *meaning, organization, and structure.*)

Given that much of what students must remember is based on material they read, you should be aware of several strategies for increasing comprehension of written material. These include the following (Pressley & Harris, 1990):

• *summarization,* or creating a representation of the central idea;

• *imagery,* or constructing an internal visual representation of text content;

• *story grammar,* or identifying the setting, problem, goal, action, and outcome in a story;

• *prior knowledge activation,* or having students relate what they already know to the content of the text;

• *self-questioning,* or devising questions that help to integrate the content being read;

• *question-answer,* or teaching students to analyze questions carefully as a way of helping them to respond.

3. *Provide distributed rather than mass practice and insure that overlearning occurs.* It is better to teach ten foreign language words a day for five days than to force memorization of all fifty words in a single period. The periodic review of lecture notes is more effective than cramming.

4. *Conduct periodic review.* Review soon after learning and at short intervals, gradually widening the lengths of time between reviews. Review need not consist of dogmatic, formal sessions. Quizzes, assignments, and use of material are effective review techniques. Periodic reviews are especially significant considering the retention curve, which dramatically illustrated the initial loss of learning. Meaningful reviews are an excellent tool to overcome this loss.

5. *Reduce interference.* Recalling the proactive-retroactive inhibition paradigm, teachers, and especially administrators, should try to schedule subjects that reinforce and not interfere with each other. After a history period involving complicated names, dates, and places, you would probably not want to move into a discussion of *Henry V* in an English class.

For teachers, the customary method of recall is to ask students to retrieve information in its original form. If they present cues (questions) different from the form in which the information was originally stored, students experience much greater difficulty. Consequently, teachers should use questions carefully, so that they may aid students to acquire a method of problem solving or to think creatively. To demand recall in the original form is to promote *convergent* thinking (often but not always a needed and desired technique) at the expense of *divergent* or creative thinking. Try to encourage both types of thinking—convergent at the introduction of a topic, when mastery of facts is required, and divergent once facts have been acquired and problem solving and creativity can be encouraged.

For the Classroom

If students rapidly learn a large amount of nonmeaningful material, they will forget it just as quickly. The rate of loss slows when most of the material has been forgotten. But occasionally a surprising phenomenon seems to occur: after a rest period, there may be an actual gain in retention.

For example, after 30 minutes of studying 20 spelling words, students may be able to spell 15 of them correctly. Yet, the next morning, they may spell 17 correctly. This **reminiscence** is hard to explain. Is it true learning, or is it the product of faulty experimentation? There are two possible causes of reminiscence.

reminiscence *The phenomenon that after rest, memory seems to improve.*

1. Fatigue developed during the original learning and affected retention, which then improved after rest.
2. The experiment was faulty because the initial test of retention was actually another learning experience that aided performance in the next test of retention.

Another important feature of memory relates to the position of items to be memorized. Students learn items at the beginning and end of any memory task much more easily than they do the middle elements. Undoubtedly this is a function of interference; isolated items in these lists are learned more readily and retained longer. What can you do to help students with those difficult middle sections? One technique is to furnish some organization or structure to which they can relate them. For example, ask them to select two or three words in a middle section that have particular meaning for them and have them use these words as clues, or have them imagine a picture related to the section, or use some words to form pictures.

This procedure helps to reduce interference, which may produce the phenomenon seen in table 8.2.

Procedure A is the control: there is no interference. Procedure B is retroactive inhibition; that is, new material (Task 2) interferes with previously learned material (Task 1). Procedure C is proactive inhibition; that is, previously learned material interferes with the recall of new material. For example, studying the same historical period in English and history could lead to either proactive or retroactive interference, unless students have formulated a clear structure of the topic in both subjects.

Help to eliminate interference by ensuring that the material to be learned is meaningful and organized. Learning meaningful material to mastery lessens your students' susceptibility to interference. If students comprehend the meaning inherent in any content, they learn it more rapidly and retain it longer. The meaningfulness in material depends upon either some pattern that the learner recognizes (such as 1, 7, 13, 19, 25, 3l) or the familiarity of the material (such as previously learned details).

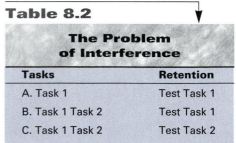

Table 8.2	
The Problem of Interference	
Tasks	**Retention**
A. Task 1	Test Task 1
B. Task 1 Task 2	Test Task 1
C. Task 1 Task 2	Test Task 2

Focus — What Would You Do?

How would you answer these questions?

1. Imagine that you have been lucky enough to obtain two tickets to the great Broadway musical *42nd St.* for $70.00. As you walk down the street to the theatre, you discover that you have lost the tickets. You can't remember the seat numbers. Would you go to the ticket window and buy another pair of tickets for $70.00?

2. Imagine that you are on the way to the theatre to buy tickets for the Broadway play, *42nd St.* They will cost you $70.00. As you approach the ticket window, you discover that you have lost $70. Would you still pay $70.00 for the tickets?

These questions, originally posed by Tversky and Kahneman (1981), usually elicit some interesting answers. How did you answer them? Among their subjects, 46 percent answered yes to question 1, while 88 percent answered yes to question 2. Note: Many more people said they would buy new tickets if they had lost the money than if they had lost the tickets. Yet the two situations are actually identical—in each instance you would have lost $70.00.

How can we explain the difference in the responses? Tversky and Kahneman believed that the way a problem is "framed" helps to explain our responses. As they stated (1981, p. 453):

The frame that a decision-maker adopts is controlled partly by the formulation of the problem and partly by the norms, habits, and personal characteristics of the decision-maker.

This latest research holds much promise for learning, instruction, and curriculum construction, because the manner in which material is packaged (books, kits) and presented (instructional techniques) goes far in determining the responses of students.

You have probably determined by now that students differ in their abilities to remember. Psychologists have become interested in the reasons for these differences and have attempted to discover whether students can learn to improve their performance. These efforts have led to the phenomenon of **metacognition,** the ability to examine one's own cognitive processes (see chap. 4).

metacognition *The ability to think about thinking.*

METACOGNITION

Although interest in metacognition is relatively recent, its content has always been with us: for example, our thoughts about a decision we have made or about how we are doing on a project all entail metacognitive processes. When we discussed Piaget's stage of formal operations (see chap.4), we were exploring metacognitive thinking about hypotheses and possibilities.

Metacognitive skills seem to be involved in many classroom cognitive activities: comprehension, evaluation, reading, writing, and problem solving, among others. Discussing metacognition, Flavell (1985) analyzed it as including two domains: metacognitive knowledge and metacognitive experiences.

Metacognitive Knowledge

metacognitive knowledge *An individual's knowledge and beliefs about cognitive matters, gained from experiences and stored in long-term memory.*

Metacognitive knowledge refers to an individual's knowledge and beliefs about cognitive matters, gained from experience and stored in long-term memory (Flavell, 1985, p. 105). Humans acquire metacognitive knowledge about people, tasks, and strategies.

- Metacognitive knowledge of people is an important concept for the classroom. You may have come to believe that a particular student just doesn't like you; a student may decide that you have little confidence in the student's ability.
- Metacognitive knowledge of tasks operates when the nature of a task forces us to think about how we'll manage. If it's difficult, perhaps we decide to allot more time, or perhaps to prepare an outline.
- When we discuss strategies, we must make a distinction between cognitive strategies (used to achieve goals) and metacognitive strategies (monitoring one's progress toward a goal; monitoring the *effectiveness* of the cognition strategies being used; monitoring one's *level of understanding*). Over time, we have all learned much about which strategies are best suited for success on particular tasks.

For example, you have a strategy for recalling what you have read in this chapter. These strategies (to be discussed in detail in chap. 9) may be simple (repeatedly going over the material) or complex (imagining that you place certain topics in different parts of your house).

Since learning strategies can be taught, you can help your students appreciate their value by having them concentrate on just what they do when they must learn. Here is an example of the importance of learning strategies (Derry, 1989). Imagine that you are a student who has arrived at school and discovered that your first period teacher is giving a test on chapter 5. You mistakenly studied chapter 4. You have fifteen minutes before the class. How would you most wisely use the time?

Derry actually assigned a reading, allowed fifteen minutes, and then tested her students. At the end of the quiz she asked them to describe in detail what they did when they studied. Not many had done well on the quiz. One student who had, stated that she initially read the chapter summary and then skimmed the chapter, concentrating on the chapter headings, looking for organization. With the remaining time, she read the topic sentences in as many paragraphs as possible. Another student, who had done poorly, said he felt panic and started to read through the chapter as fast as he could, but didn't get too far.

Here is a striking example of the difference between successful and unsuccessful learning strategies, or plans used for attaining a goal. By teaching your students how to attack a problem, you can do much to improve their achievement.

Metacognitive Experiences

Metacognitive experiences are either cognitive or affective experiences that relate to cognitive activities. For example, while you are reading this chapter, you may feel a little uncertain or doubtful about one of the topics, or you may be quite concerned that you didn't understand it. As Flavell (1985) noted, metacognitive experiences are most likely to occur when careful, conscious monitoring of your cognitive efforts is required. The uncertainty or confidence that you may feel about a topic is tied to relevant metacognitive knowledge.

metacognitive experiences
Cognitive or affective experiences that relate to cognitive activities.

You can see, then, how valuable these metacognitive experiences can be. If you are puzzled by one of these topics, then your sense of uncertainty will cause you to read the section again, discuss it with other students, or bring up questions in class.

By making students aware that they can "think about their thinking," you will also help them to improve those cognitive behaviors that result in better classroom performance. This ability becomes apparent when students—and all of us—make decisions.

DECISION MAKING AND REASONING

Do you consider yourself to be logical? How good are you at making decisions? Do you pride yourself on your accurate thinking? Although we all want to think that we are models of logical thinking, facts seem to tell us otherwise. How would you respond to the situations in the focus box entitled "What Would You Do?"

We have long believed that we think, reason, and solve problems on the basis of rational processes. Decision making has long been described as a process in which individuals examine alternatives according to their probability, utility, and value (Krouse, 1986).

Representativeness

Tversky and Kahneman appealed to the principle of representativeness to explain apparent variations in an individual's thinking; by the term, they meant the human tendency to compare things, people, or events to see how well they resemble each other. Gardner (1985) used the following example to illustrate the principle of representativeness.

Consider the case of Linda: 31 years old, single, very bright, and outspoken. As a student, she majored in philosophy, participated in antinuclear demonstrations,

teacher – student

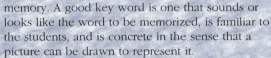

interactions

Cognition in the Classroom

1. Students will be successful—both in and out of class—to the extent that they acquire the ability to place objects in categories.

   For older students:

   - Suggest a research project about possible careers, to be divided into categories, such as those that require a college education and those that demand a high school diploma; those that require clerical skills and those that don't; those that traditionally recruit males and those that attract females.

   For younger students:

   - Encourage recycling among your students. Have them collect trash throughout the school day in a paper bag and then divide it into biodegradable, degradable, and nondegradable materials.
   - Plan an outdoor treasure hunt. Give each student a list of items to find. When the class returns, divide all the items into their proper categories.

2. Helping students improve their memory will aid their successful achievement throughout life.

   - Suggest that your students be "picture helpers"; train them to use mental pictures to keep track of a numbered series of items.
   - Show them that using key words derived from the fact to be remembered can help their long-term memory. A good key word is one that sounds or looks like the word to be memorized, is familiar to the students, and is concrete in the sense that a picture can be drawn to represent it.
   - Demonstrate how they may draw pictures illustrating their key words and show these to the class while describing them. Then encourage the students to think back to their pictures when they are trying to remember the words they have to memorize.

3. The manner in which a teacher presents material helps to shape the responses that students make.

   - Ask yourself these questions when you're presenting material:
     a. Am I a cheerful, enthusiastic speaker, or a boring predictable droner?
     b. Is the length of my lessons appropriate to my students' attention spans?
     c. Do I avoid abstractions and try to be as concrete as possible?
     d. When I realize students don't understand, do I rephrase my comments or just repeat them?
     e. Do I speak at a rate appropriate to my students' ability levels?

and was active in campus issues involving discrimination and social justice. Which of the following statements do you think is more probable?

1. Linda is a psychiatric social worker.
2. Linda is a bank teller.
3. Linda is a bank teller and is active in the feminist movement.

Which did you select? Like many readers, you probably selected the third alternative—but if you pause for a moment, you may have second thoughts. Was Linda trained as a psychiatric social worker? Nothing was mentioned except her work in philosophy. It certainly makes more sense to assume that Linda is a bank teller than that she is a bank teller and an active feminist, since the probability that a person will have one characteristic is higher than the probability that she will have two. Yet, as Gardner indicated, 80 percent of subjects (even those knowledgeable about statistics) selected item three.

Why? Representativeness is at work here. We assume that because a person has certain characteristics, others will also be present. Consequently, knowing that Linda has certain specific characteristics (activist at school, outspoken), we then add other characteristics that are representative of "this kind" of person.

For the Classroom

Annual **Edition**

If the manner in which a teacher presents a problem influences both how students process this information and their responses to it, the classroom implications are far-reaching (Tennure, 1986). An initial question that requires answering relates to the developmental characteristics of students. It is one thing to state that students use representations, through verbal processes and/or through mental imagery, or that certain organizational principles govern their perceptions. It is quite another thing to state that the nature of students' responses is influenced by the manner in which teachers **frame** material.

frame *Present material in a certain manner; here, refers to teachers.*

Students' Decision Making

Addressing this question, Krouse (1986) studied 90 students, 30 each from grades 1, 3, and 6 (48 boys, 42 girls). Using the *Concept Assessment Kit (Conservation)* and a variety of Tversky-Kahneman tasks, Krouse sought to determine if any relationship existed between children's decision-making behavior (as determined by Tversky-Kahneman tasks) and certain variables: educational level, level of cognitive development, and sex of the child.

Though no gender differences appeared and level of cognitive development was not significant, Krouse found that educational level did make a difference. Third- and sixth-graders demonstrated the same variations in decision making as adults, a particularly interesting finding in the light of cognitive theory. Recalling our discussion of attention, perception, representation, classification, and memory, we could conclude, not surprisingly, that students' processing capacities are fairly restricted during their early years. To what do young children attend? Are they capable of discriminating loss of money from loss of object, or are all types of items just "something I lost"?

Younger students (preschoolers to the early elementary grades (1, 2) could not judge their mental capabilities as accurately as could the older students; this ability gradually and consistently improves during the elementary school years. Whatever the reason, a developmental shift seems to occur around the third grade, a finding that should reinforce the concern you have for carefully framing material during instruction.

Advances in Social Cognitive Learning: Self-Regulated Training

In chapter 7 we introduced you to social cognitive learning and some of the fundamental assumptions of this theoretical approach. In this section, we will reintroduce some of the concepts in the theory and present some of the recent advances that have occurred in work in this area. First of all, however, we want to note that although Bandura's early work shared many of the basic assumptions of behavioral psychology, the current work represents a definite focus on cognition and shows how theories can evolve over time. At any rate, we regard current work in social learning a very important part of cognitive psychology and entirely relevant to work in educational psychology.

You will remember that central to social cognitive learning is that information we observe in our environment (people, things, events) influences the way we behave. Modeling, or observational learning, involves four important processes: attention, retention, motor reproduction, and motivation. Also central to social cognitive theory is the role that self-efficacy plays in human performance. Self-efficacy is influenced by four sources of information: performance accomplishments, vicarious experience, verbal persuasion, and emotional arousal. Self-efficacy plays a very important role in a student's self-regulated learning in school settings. According to Zimmerman (1989), for learning to qualify as **self-regulated,** it "must involve the use of specified strategies to achieve academic goals on the basis of self-efficacy perceptions" (p. 329). Important to the definition is the phrase "the use of self-regulated learning strategies," which refers to actions and processes used in acquiring information that involve purpose, such as seeking or transforming information (Zimmerman, 1989). In self-regulated learning, self-efficacy plays an important role, because the students' perceptions about their own capabilities influence their performance on academic tasks. A student with a high degree of self-efficacy for academic work should work harder and persist in the face of difficulty and failure (Zimmerman, 1994).

self-regulated *Describing an individual's ability to control his or her own learning or behavior through cognitive processes.*

Recently, Zimmerman (1994) developed a conceptual framework to analyze academic self-regulation according to psychological dimensions, task conditions,

Table 8.3

Conceptual Analysis of the Dimensions of Academic Self-Regulation

Scientific questions	Psychological dimensions	Task conditions	Self-regulatory attributes	Self-regulatory processes
Why?	Motive	Choose to participate	Intrinsically or self-motivated	Self-goals, self-efficacy, values, attributions, etc.
How?	Method	Choose method	Planned or automatized	Strategy use, relaxation, etc.
What?	Performance outcomes	Choose performance outcomes	Self-aware of performance outcomes	Self-monitoring, self-judgment, action control, volition, etc.
Where?	Environmental (social)	Control social and physical setting	Environmentally/socially sensitive and resourceful	Environmental structuring, help seeking, etc.

From B. J Zimmerman, "Dimensions of academic self-regulation: A conceptual framework for education. In D. H. Schunk and B. A. Zimmerman, Editors, *Self-regulation of Learning and Performance.* Copyright © 1994 Lawrence Erlbaum Associates, Hillsdale, NJ. Reprinted by permission.

self-regulatory attributes, and self-regulatory processes. The framework is presented in table 8.3. The question *why* deals with a student's motivation to self-regulate. *How* deals with the methods that students use to self-regulate their learning. The *what* issue pertains to the student's effort to self-regulate, and *where* refers to the physical and social environment in which self-regulation occurs.

There also are some essential task conditions that are necessary for self-regulation to occur. Students in your classroom are likely to engage in self-regulated learning if they are given choices to participate in learning activities, choices in the methods of learning, choices in the options for monitoring their learning (e.g., self-recording their work completion), and choices in the social and physical settings in which they want to learn. Clearly, many of our traditional classrooms do not allow students to engage in such choices for learning.

Zimmerman (1994) also suggested that there are self-regulatory attributes that must be considered in academic self-regulation. Students who display good self-regulation are more intrinsically externally motivated. For example, these students tend to study without need for the usual prompting by parents. These students also tend be more planned in their approach to learning, and their cognitive functioning becomes very automatic and less tied to conscious control. In addition, these students are quite resourceful in structuring their environments to maximize learning. Such students can be quite independent, but they also know when to get help from peers and adults.

The final category, self-regulatory processes, involves four dimensions that are known to enhance self-regulation. In fact, there is a growing literature that supports teaching the various self-regulatory processes to students. Such processes as self-efficacy and establishing goals will promote effective self-regulated learning. In addition, directly teaching students to self-regulate (i.e., using metacognitive strategies) has been shown to facilitate learning. For example, there is evidence to support the position that teaching skills associated with time management and planning can help students better self-regulate and improve their learning. With regard to the performance outcome dimension, students who have been taught to monitor their own performance, thereby increasing their self-awareness, have shown increases in their learning performance. Finally, students who are able to self-select excellent models of what they want to learn have shown increases in self-regulatory skills in learning. Students might be taught that they should model the work of excellent performers in a certain area of academic skills. Of course, this type of activity goes on often in the teaching of sports to high school students, as when the coach brings in a talented athlete or professional player to serve as a model. In self-regulatory activities, students actively seek out these models across a number of diverse tasks, both academic and social.

Cognition Across Cultures

In their classic analysis, *Culture and Thought* (1974), Cole and Scribner provided interesting observations into the cognitive differences among various cultures. Noting that perceptual variations are common among different peoples, Cole and Scribner state that our modes of responding to stimuli are not "experience-free." Rather, our reactions depend on our past histories of dealing with similar stimuli.

Stating that what children "see" in geometric patterns may be related to the actions they are asked to perform (recognize the pattern, copy it, or reconstruct it), Cole and Scribner (1974) believed that different actions require different perceptual information. Consequently, children master their perceptual worlds as they master new activities. An example of this issue can be seen in the authors' work in Liberia. They asked some subjects to sort cards and others to describe the cards. The two groups showed different preferences for stimuli, depending on whether they were asked actually to sort (preference: form) or to describe verbally (preference: color).

With regard to such conceptual processes as classifying, the authors found similar differences. The characteristic used for classifying reflected the nature of the task: how familiar it was; the source of the task (for example, animal or plant); and the form in which it was presented.

Classifying processes seem to change with experience. In the Cole and Scribner study (1974), when people moved from an isolated village to a city or town or were exposed to a Western-type education, class membership seemed more important for grouping items. Schooling also contributes in a similar manner to the way in which people describe and explain their own mental operations.

Culture influences how people think, relate, and learn. Consequently, we can too frequently misperceive and misunderstand our students' behavior when we interpret it solely from our own cultural perspective. Cognitive activities occur in cultural situations (such as the classroom) that involve interpretations and values by both teachers and students.

Students who come from racial, ethnic, or socioeconomic backgrounds different from those of their teachers and the school administrators may have values, goals, and interests that are highly acceptable to their families and communities, but not to the school community. Consequently, educators may not be able to accept behavior that the students and their parents find completely appropriate (Grossman, 1990, p. 339).

A good example of this difference can be found in the school's expectations and assumptions. Most schools and teachers expect that their students will function cognitively in a verbal and analytic manner (Tharp, 1989). Students who conform to these expectations, such as Japanese American and Chinese American students, are more likely to succeed than students who do not. Their patterns of cognitive functioning "fit" school expectations. Native Americans, on the other hand, perform better on performance and spatial tasks than on verbal ones. Consequently, their achievement may decline in traditional settings.

To offset these disadvantages, the concept of *contextualized instruction* has been introduced; in this approach, a student's personal experiences in a particular culture are used to introduce new material (Tharp, 1989). Materials that reflect the student's cultural community are utilized to provide a basis for developing school skills. These various levels of contextualization—personal, community, and cultural—seem to result in improved academic performance.

For example, Navajos reject the idea that "toughness" is at one extreme of the spectrum of appropriate behavior and "niceness" is at the other. Educators who are unaware of these beliefs can be ineffective in their methods of instruction. The Navajos resist open displays of affection but respect their children's individuality and independence. Thus, certain efforts to control behavior by punishment or obvious rewards violate cultural values, and are doomed to failure. Consequently, when teachers embed cultural values in classroom practices, they see greater student participation and higher levels of achievement (Tharp, 1989).

These ideas reflect the tendency to view mental life as consisting of two quite different methods of functioning: logical, abstract, scientific thinking, and *narrative* thinking, a much more personal kind of thinking that concentrates on people and the causes of their behavior (Bruner, 1986). Thus, stories of their particular cultures greatly influence children, and they make up stories about their own lives; that is, they interpret their lives as stories or narratives (Howard, 1991).

If you have multicultural students in your classroom, take the time to discover the outstanding features of their cultures, the ways they respond to various stimuli, and any notable cultural variations in behavior. You will find that the resulting positive relationships with these students will be well worth your effort.

APPLICATIONS AND REFLECTIONS

Chapter Highlights

The Meaning of Cognitive Psychology

- The concept of representation is basic to an understanding of cognitive psychology.
- We attend, perceive, and reason, and these cognitive activities affect our behavior.

The Emergence of Cognitive Psychology

- Cognitive psychology has a long and rich tradition, with its roots in many disciplines.
- Among modern cognitive psychologists, Jerome Bruner has been particularly influential.
- Bruner's studies on perception and thought have been landmarks in modern cognitive psychology.

The Importance of Information Processing

- Representation, which is at the heart of information processing, is the manner in which information is recorded or expressed.
- No matter how data are represented, the information remains the same; this is called the content of representation.
- The different ways that information can be expressed are called the representational codes; these codes may be either mental or verbal.

The Role of Perception

- Perceiving is an active process demanding our involvement with the objects, events, and people in our environment.
- The active process of perception helps us to receive information from our environment.
- Helping students structure, or organize, their environments aids their perceptual processes, thus furthering learning.

How Students Categorize

- The better students categorize (form classes and put information in these categories), the more efficient learners they become.

Memory at Work

- Studies of memory have long fascinated cognitive psychologists because of its critical role in thought and decision making.

Connections

1. Think about how you learn and describe how one of the major concepts discussed in this chapter is part of your learning activities or approach.

_____

_____

_____

_____

2. Identify at least one learning situation (e.g., classroom instruction, self-study, taking a test, small-group work) and describe how you would apply one of the key concepts examined in this chapter *if you were a teacher*.

_____

_____

_____

_____

Getting the Picture and Drawing Relationships

Think about the various learning concepts and variables discussed in this chapter. Create pictures, graphics, or figures that highlight relationships among the key components.

Personal Journal

What I really learned in this chapter was _____

_____

_____

_____

_____

What this means to me is _____

_____

_____

_____

_____

Questions that were stimulated by this chapter include _____

_____

_____

_____

_____

Key Terms

advance organizers	246	mental representation	238	representation	253
discovery learning	247	metacognition	269	retrieval	265
episodic memory	263	metacognitive		schemata	242
forgetting	266	experiences	270	self-regulated	272
frame	272	metacognitive knowledge	269	semantic memory	263
levels of processing	264	perception	255	sensory register	264
long-term store	264	recognition	265	short-term store	264
meaningful learning	245	reminiscence	268	storage	265

Walter Grimes, the superintendent of schools, had the assistant superintendents and principals gathered in his office for a meeting as a follow-up to the memo he had circulated concerning instituting a thinking skills program. There was unanimous support in the group for the idea. Everyone realized that given the rapid changes students faced in their daily lives, they needed help to prepare for unique challenges.

The superintendent had asked the assistants to prepare reports that would be discussed at this meeting. His only charge to them was to make sure that any program they developed was "solid." In this, he was reflecting a concern that with the growing popularity of

Administrators, teachers, and parents are not shocked to be told that we are living in an age of enormous and rapid change. In the meeting between Walter Grimes and his assistants, several issues arose that will guide our work in this chapter. As our society changes from one based on industry to one committed to an information technology, the skills that our students need to adapt to it likewise change. Unless teachers equip themselves with the ability to teach innovative skills, their students will be woefully unprepared to meet new demands. If the reports discussed in chapter 1 concerning national teaching and learning initiatives are accurate, and repeated evidence testifies to

chapter 9

thinking skills and problem-solving strategies

incorporating thinking skills in the classroom, some superficial or ineffective programs would be available.

The assistant superintendents made their presentations. Jack Cunningham spoke of the need to have any thinking skills work founded on a sound scientific, philosophical, and educational base. Harry Walker addressed the issue of relating any program to intellectual skills. Helen Ruiz talked about the various taxonomies of thinking skills currently available and the possibility of adapting them for individual usage. Finally, Zona Wilson outlined the important points of several outstanding programs.

It was a lengthy meeting, but the principals recognized the significance of the topic and began to ask specific questions. Would there be a formal program? How could they insure teacher cooperation? Had any of these programs been used elsewhere? How much time would be allotted? Were there materials available for distribution?

They all agreed that a thinking skills program could be a significant way of helping their students adapt to change. ■

their accuracy, our concerns about these new skills become more pressing.

After a general discussion of thinking skills, the topics that will occupy our attention for the remainder of the chapter are the following:

1. What are thinking skills? Why teach them?
2. Does intelligence have a special meaning for thinking skills?
3. What kind of programs have been devised to further the acquisition of thinking skills and problem solving?
4. Are there specific suggestions that will help in teaching students to be good problem solvers?

When you complete your reading of this chapter, you should be able to

- identify those strategies that help students acquire fundamental facts and skills
- apply those strategies that help students develop reasoning skills, concepts, and problem-solving processes
- suggest strategies that help students search for insights in their learning

Thinking Skills 280
Critical Thinking: A
    Definition 280

Intelligence and Thinking 280
Sternberg's Triarchic Model of
    Intelligence 281
Gardner and Multiple
    Intelligences 282
Perkins' Thinking Frames and
    Enculturation of
    Mindware 284

Thinking Skills: An Analysis 285
The Bloom Taxonomy 286
Costa and Thinking Skills 289
Thinking Skills and Multicultural
    Students 290

**Selected Thinking Skills
Programs 291**
Practical Intelligence for
    School 291
Instrumental Enrichment 294
The CoRT Thinking Program 295

Problem Solving 296
Problem-Solving Strategies 300
The Good Problem Solver 301
Different Cultures—Different
    Perspectives 302

The DUPE Model 303
Determining the Nature of a
    Problem 303
Understanding the Nature of the
    Problem 306
Planning the Solution 312
The Role of Memory 313
Evaluating the Solution 316
The Creative Student 318

**Teaching Problem-Solving
Techniques 319**
Helping Students to Transfer
    Their Learning 319
For the Classroom 321

**Applications and
Reflections 324**

- guide students in the use of those strategies that help them to learn about relationships and how to work together with humor, enthusiasm, and a tolerance for ambiguity
- help your students identify the nature of a problem
- improve your students' willingness to undertake problem solving
- teach your students the basics of a problem-solving model that they can apply both in and out of school
- identify the weaknesses in your students' problem-solving skills

Think for a moment about the high school dropout rate. Estimates for some large cities are that 25 percent of the 14- to 18-year-old population no longer attends school. These ex-students now lack the skills needed to advance in today's markets. Both the number of students dropping out and the number of students who complete high school unprepared to cope with changing conditions must be reduced by a concerted effort to have our school population equipped with those skills that will enable them to adapt to change.

THINKING SKILLS

Thinking skills (sometimes simply called *critical thinking*) have infused educators with an enthusiasm for both their ultimate value and their present utility. Since an information technology is marked by a swift proliferation of knowledge, mastery of available content will not suffice once our students leave school and attempt to become productive citizens. Rather, they need skills and strategies that will enable them to adapt to constant change. Critical thinkers are self-correcting; they discover their own weaknesses and act to remove obstacles and faults (Lipman, 1987).

As stated in the influential report *Educating Americans for the 21st Century,* schools must return to basics, but not merely the basics of the past: communication skills and problem-solving skills are the "thinking" tools needed in a technological society. An examination of thinking skills and methods of teaching students to think critically and to problem solve occupies the remainder of this chapter.

Critical Thinking: A Definition

Two definitions of **critical thinking** will be offered here as a reference for our work. The first is offered by Robert Ennis and is rooted in philosophy. "Critical thinking is reasonable reflective thinking that is focused on deciding what to believe or do" (Ennis, 1987, p. 10). Ennis believes that terms are key to this definition: *practical, reflective, reasonable, belief,* and *action.* Critical thinking is an activity, both practical and reflective, that has reasonable belief or action as its goal. When we come to investigate the skills that emerge from this definition, we'll discover that Ennis's definition includes dispositions as well as abilities.

The second definition was proposed by Robert Sternberg and reflects Sternberg's psychological concerns about thinking and intelligence. "Critical thinking comprises the mental processes, strategies, and representations people use to solve problems, make decisions, and learn new concepts" (Sternberg, 1985, p. 46). As Sternberg noted, his definition emerged from a psychological analysis of critical thinking, especially as it is related to intelligence. Tracing Sternberg's view of intelligence will help us to discover those skills that seem most closely associated with critical thinking.

"I don't get it! They make us learn reading, writing, and arithmetic to prepare us for a world of videotapes, computer terminals, and calculators!"

H. Schwadron in Phi Delta Kappan.

thinking skills *Skills and strategies that enable students to adapt to constant change.*

critical thinking *The use of mental strategies to solve problems.*

INTELLIGENCE AND THINKING

Having established in chapter 8 the connection between thinking and its biological base, the brain, we now turn our attention to the relationship between intelligence and thinking. We have all taken cognitive abilities tests and speculated about their results in comparison to our own assessments of our potential. You probably think in a similar way about your students: Are they working to their potential? How can I help them to improve their performance?

If we are to help students improve their performance on IQ tests, achieve better grades, and prepare for life's problems, we would be wise not to be trapped by traditional views of intelligence. If we hope to aid our students by directly teaching thinking skills, we must turn to a broader, more qualitative view of intelligence.

Any theory of intelligence must be able to do three things (Sternberg, 1986, 1987, 1988): (a) relate intelligence to an individual's internal world and explain what happens when a person thinks intelligently; (b) accept the relation between the external world and that person's intelligence, and explain how intelligence functions in the "real world"; and (c) relate intelligence to the individual's experiences.

With these criteria in mind, let's turn to three current interpretations of intelligence that have particular relevance for the teaching of thinking skills. These include Sternberg's triarchic model, Gardner's multiple intelligences, and Perkins' thinking frames and mindware.

Sternberg's Triarchic Model of Intelligence

Robert Sternberg, a cognitive psychologist and leading theorist concerned with human intelligence and problem solving.

triarchic theory of intelligence *Sternberg's view of intelligence as consisting of three elements: componential, experiential, and contextual.*

metacomponents *Higher-order control processes used to evaluate a planned course of action; the executive components of intelligence. A major component in Sternberg's triarchic model.*

performance components *The implementation aspect of intelligence in Sternberg's triarchic model of intelligence.*

knowledge-acquisition components *Humans' ability to acquire and use language, thus helping them solve problems. A major component in Sternberg's triarchic model.*

Sternberg believes that intellectual skills and thinking skills are inseparable, although there is more to intelligence than thinking. With this as background, Sternberg developed a **triarchic theory of intelligence,** consisting of three elements designed to explain each of his three ideas of what intelligence "should do." He labeled these three elements *componential, experiential,* and *contextual.* Let's examine each of them in some detail.

1. *Componential.* Sternberg identified three types of information-processing components that constitute the initial segment of our intelligence: metacomponents, performance components, and knowledge-acquisition components.

    a. **Metacomponents** are the executive components of intelligence, used to plan, monitor, and evaluate problem-solving strategies. Sternberg (1986) suggested ways to improve such strategies and provided sample problems to solve. Discussed later in this chapter, these suggestions are to identify the nature of a problem, select the steps necessary to solve it, devise a plan, and evaluate a solution.

    b. **Performance components** help us execute the instructions of the metacomponents; they are the implementation segment of intelligence. Among the most important of these are inferring relations, applying these relations to new stimuli, and comparing attributes of stimuli. Students must learn when to use the various components and to use them in as wide a variety of situations as possible. Inference is particularly important. You hear a friend is in the hospital and infer that she is ill or injured. But could she not have taken a job there? Students need to learn that they need as much information as possible before making any inferences. (This example should make us aware of how impulsivity can work against a student's achievement.)

    c. **Knowledge-acquisition components** refer primarily to our ability to acquire and use language, thus enabling us to seize on contextual cues in solving problems. The key here is to help students determine which facts are pertinent. Sternberg (1988) identified three crucial processes. The first is *selective encoding,* in which the individual detects relevant facts that are not immediately obvious. In the discovery of penicillin, for example, Fleming noticed that although mold had ruined his experiment, it had also killed bacteria. The second is *selective combination,* in which the individual sees a way of combining unrelated facts. The third process is *selective comparison,* in which the person combines old and new information. For example, a teacher who conducts class according to cognitive principles encounters a student who is not doing well with these methods. The instructor recalls an educational psychology course in which the instructor, while discussing behaviorism, mentioned that some students need a carefully planned reinforcement schedule.

    Sternberg notes that the three components are highly interactive: they generally act in tandem as they allow a person to plan, act, and receive feedback. Figure 9.1 illustrates the integration of these three components.

2. *Experiential.* The second aspect of intelligence Sternberg identified is experiential. Our experiences increase our ability to deal with novel tasks and to make information processing more automatic. In other words, there are times when our intelligence must deal with novelty, with new conceptual systems—times when our traditional mode of intellectual functioning is inadequate. For example, reading about an electric motor doesn't mean you can repair it. You must experience the novelty of actually taking it apart and putting it together again. These situations demand creative responses. There are other times and

situations, however, when to pause and analyze each element would retard intellectual functioning. Reading is a good example: to ponder each letter would be devastating. Needed are those automatic processes that enable us to solve complex problems.

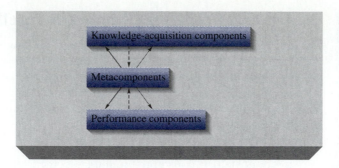

Figure 9.1
The integration of intellectual components.

3. *Contextual.* The third aspect of intelligence in Sternberg's model specifies the functions to which components are applied in coping with the external world (Sternberg, 1987, p. 198). In other words, the major thrust of contextual intelligence is adaptation. Adaptation as used here has three connotations: (a) *adaptation to existing environments,* in order to fit better into them; (b) *shaping existing environments,* or changing present environments to more suitably meet one's needs; and (c) *selecting new environments,* which involves evaluation of present environments and selection of new, more favorable environments.

If you apply these descriptions to yourself and others whom you know, you probably can identify which aspect of intelligence is predominant. For example, those who excel in analytic thinking usually do quite well on traditional IQ tests. Their componential aspect seems to eclipse the others. We can draw similar conclusions about those who exhibit high creativity (the experiential aspect dominates), or those who always seem to know "the right thing to do" (contextual intelligence is strong). Recognizing these individual differences inflicts no damage on Sternberg's insistence on the integrated nature of the triarchic model; rather, it recognizes our unique abilities as real and inevitable. Though it is too early to judge the impact of Sternberg's model, the triarchic theory offers promising insights into qualitative intelligence.

Gardner and Multiple Intelligences

A second theory linking intelligence and thinking skills is Howard Gardner's theory of **multiple intelligences** (1983, 1985, 1991). Gardner's speculations are particularly fascinating. Any model of thinking skills contains several basics that reflect intellectual ability. But this is not the whole of intelligence: the same individual who can form penetrating mathematical insights may be quite baffled by the most obvious musical clues. Gardner's ideas, though still theoretical, attempt to address this issue.

Identifying Intelligences

Gardner begins by noting that his theory of multiple intelligences accepts a cultural input into intelligence as well as a biological basis. Next Gardner explains his eight criteria for identifying any intelligence.

1. *Potential isolation by brain damage.* If brain damage can destroy a particular ability, it seems likely that this ability is not dependent on any other ability.
2. *Existence of exceptional populations.* Those individuals who exhibit outstanding but uneven abilities testify to the distinctive existence of a particular ability. For example, one child may be mathematically precocious, with other abilities not at the same level. Another example is the idiot savant, an individual who may exhibit a single prodigious ability and otherwise be mentally retarded.

Howard Gardner, a psychologist who has offered an appealing theory of multiple intelligences.

multiple intelligences
Gardner's seven relatively autonomous intelligences. These include linguistic, musical, logical-mathematical, spatial, bodily-kinesthetic, interpersonal, and intrapersonal intelligence.

3. *Core operations.* These include basic information-processing operations that are highly unique to particular abilities. The gifted athlete, for example, evaluates multiple stimuli, judges their value, and instantly communicates information to his or her body.

4. *A distinctive developmental history.* Any intelligence must possess discernible developmental stages through which individuals pass, with some remaining at low levels of expertise while others pass on to high levels of performance.

5. *An evolutionary history.* Antecedents of the intelligence should be able to be identified in other species. These may appear as discrete elements in other species and be integrated only in humans.

6. *Experimental evidence.* Precise methodology must be available to study the details of a particular intelligence. In this way, the autonomy of the intelligence may be probed to examine whether the facts support the theory.

7. *Support from psychometric findings.* Standardized tests (similar to the IQ test) offer clues as to the existence of any intelligence when test items correlate with some tasks and not others.

8. *Susceptibility to encoding in a symbol system.* There must be some means of capturing the information content in an intelligence.

The Seven Intelligences

Using the above criteria, Gardner identified seven intelligences that are relatively autonomous. He believes that human cognitive competence is best described as a set of abilities, talents, or mental skills that we call "intelligence." Everyone possesses each of these skills to some extent, but we differ in degrees of skill and in how we combine them. Here are Gardner's seven types of intelligence.

Which of Gardner's seven intelligences represents your strongest form of intelligence? Which is your least-developed form of intelligence?

1. *Linguistic intelligence.* The first of Gardner's intelligences to meet the eight criteria is language. For example, we can trace the effects of damage to the language areas of the brain; we can identify the core operations of any language: phonology, syntax, semantics, and pragmatics; its developmental history has been well-documented and supported by empirical investigations. Gardner considers language a preeminent instance of human intelligence.

2. *Musical intelligence.* One has only to consider the talent and career of Yehudi Menuhin to realize that there is something special about music. At 3 years of age, Menuhin became fascinated by music; by age 10, he had been performing on the international stage. The early appearance of musical ability suggests some kind of biological preparedness. The right hemisphere of the brain seems particularly important for music, and musical notation clearly indicates a basic symbol system. Though musical skill usually is not considered "intelligence" in most theories, it satisfies the criteria posed by Gardner, and so demands inclusion.

3. *Logical-mathematical (L-M) intelligence.* Theoreticians of intelligence have so commonly accepted scientific thinking that we may safely assume that L-M intelligence completely satisfies Gardner's criteria.

4. *Spatial intelligence.* Brain research has linked spatial ability to the right side of the brain. For example, the national system of maps requires the use of symbols based on spatial abilities and involving spatial intelligence to interpret data.

5. *Bodily-kinesthetic intelligence.* The left hemisphere's control of the body's right side and vice versa is so well known that it requires no additional comment here. The developmental schedule of bodily movements has been carefully recorded. Thus Gardner has identified the control of bodily motions and the ability to handle objects skillfully as core operations. Although the concept of "body as intelligence" may at first surprise you, Gardner notes that such reactions do not characterize other societies, which cherish harmony between mind and body.

6. & 7. *Interpersonal intelligence* and *intrapersonal intelligence.* Gardner refers to these two categories as the "personal" intelligences. Interpersonal intelligence builds on a core capacity to recognize what is distinctive in others. Intrapersonal intelligence uses a core capacity to understand one's own feelings, to discriminate among them, and to express feelings through a symbolic code. Autistic children are good examples of a deficit in this latter form of intelligence: often competent in certain skills, they may be nearly incapable of ever referring to themselves.

Gardner has focused on the educational ramifications of multiple intelligence. Beginning with the need for mastery in a technological society, Gardner traces educational needs through the early years to adolescence, when youths need to be assisted in their choices of careers.

Acceptance of the multiple-intelligence model raises some questions about career choice, although various "intelligences" may interact in any given occupation. Physicians obviously must bring their logical-mathematical intelligence to a high skill level, but they also must master interpersonal skills in treating patients and bodily-kinesthetic skills to do surgery.

For students to acquire a needed minimum in all intelligences and extraordinary proficiency in one or two, their instructional needs will vary throughout their development. The detailed instruction needed to acquire notational systems during the early years becomes inappropriate at the upper levels. Sole reliance upon a notational system for instruction during the early years is also inappropriate, since an enriched sensory environment is also suitable. Finally, Gardner believes that excessive emphasis on linguistic and logical-mathematical intelligences is short-sighted, given the role that spatial, interpersonal, and bodily skills play in many career choices. Consequently, Gardner (1987) recommended that educators become "assessment specialists": for example, they should search for strengths in students indicating high levels of spatial and personal intelligences.

Perkins' Thinking Frames and Enculturation of Mindware

Perkins (1986, 1987), believing that schools must address thinking skills, stated that any perspective on the teaching of thinking must confront the problem of intelligence, if for no other reason than to help teachers decide whether those they teach are already functioning at their intellectual "ceilings," or upper levels. Can we improve intelligence by teaching our students to think better?

Perkins urged teachers to avoid too narrow a view of intelligence, lest we become trapped by a concept of intelligence only as measured by IQ tests. He believes that the key question is this: What psychological factors contribute to a broader, more qualitative model of intelligence? Answering his own question, Perkins stated that modern psychologists have adopted one of three concepts of intelligence:

1. *a power theory of intelligence,* which is solely dependent on the neurological efficiency of the brain (a genetic interpretation);
2. *a tactical theory of intelligence,* which holds that those who think better do so because they know more tactics about how to use their minds; or
3. *a content theory of intelligence,* which reflects a view of intelligence as a rich knowledge base. Mastery of factual material is at the heart of thinking and problem solving.

David Perkins, whose studies of thinking have helped us to understand the relationship between teaching and intelligence.

Source: Harvard University

Perkins believes that no single one of these views contains all the answers about intelligence that we have been searching for; a combination of all three seems more promising. Therefore, he conceptualized intelligence in this way:

Intelligence = Power + Tactics + Content

Perkins next turned his attention to ways that teaching thinking skills can improve intelligence. Noting that the schools can do little about the power side of intelligence, and perhaps have done too much in the teaching of content, Perkins focused upon tactics, or strategies, as our best hope. Describing tactical intelligence as "a bag of tricks," he proposed the term *thinking frames* to describe the "tricks that make up tactical intelligence."

thinking frames *Perkins' term for those representations that guide the thought process.*

Thinking frames are representations intended to guide the process of thought by supporting, organizing, and activating that process (Perkins, 1986, p. 7). More simply put, they are guides to organizing and supporting thought processes (Perkins, 1987, p. 47). How can students acquire these frames? Perkins hypothesizes that humans learn thinking frames through a three-stage process involving acquisition, internalization, and transfer.

- In *acquisition,* students encounter and transfer the basics of a frame by direct instruction, or invention. The teacher's task is to help them to form a representation of the topic.
- In *internalization,* students make the process automatic. Internalization comes about through practice on simple examples until it becomes fluent and spontaneous. Memory gradually becomes an important support, only to recede as the process becomes automatic. Meaningful practice and memory aids lead to automatic processing.
- In *transfer,* students use the frame in a wide variety of contexts. Since transfer or generalization does not occur spontaneously, we must teach for it.

Perkins' recent work (Perkins, Jay, & Tishman, 1993) has focused on ways to advance instruction of thinking skills, or "mindware," as he now prefers to call it. The term *mindware* refers to learnable processes, schemata, and attitudes that foster good thinking. Although Perkins and his colleagues acknowledge that strategy-based instructional programs and expert models have been used effectively to teach thinking skills, they argue that both of these approaches can be integrated more powerfully into an approach that more fully situates learning. Perkins, Jay, and Tishman (1993) referred to their new approach to teaching thinking skills as **enculturation.**

enculturation *The broad and complex process of acquiring knowledge.*

The concept of teaching thinking skills or mindware as an enculturation process provides a broad, less top-down approach to skill development. According to Perkins, we should think of enculturation as occurring in four distinct but mutually reinforcing ways: through *cultural exemplars, direct transmission of key information, involvement in cultural activities,* and *involvement in cultural interactions. Cultural exemplars* are artifacts and people modeling or otherwise exemplifying cultural knowledge. *Direct transmission of key information* is the straightforward teaching of concepts, vocabularies, and information related to cultural knowledge. *Involvement in cultural activities* entails hands-on practice using aspects of cultural knowledge. Finally, *involvement in cultural interactions* refers to learner/learner and mentor/learner interpersonal exchange that embodies cultural knowledge. These four methods of stimulating enculturation can serve as guidelines for organizing instruction, since each element of the approach enjoins specific teaching activities.

THINKING SKILLS: AN ANALYSIS

Now that we have established neurological (in chap. 8) and intellectual bases for thinking skills programs and instructional suggestions, we can discuss several taxonomies of thinking skills that have been proposed. We'll consider two of the most widely accepted and practical taxonomies: Benjamin Bloom's Taxonomy of Educational Objectives—Cognitive Domain and Arthur Costa's Model of Critical Thinking Skills. Each of these systems offers a solid basis for the skills it proposes: Bloom's in educational objectives, and Costa's in curriculum goals.

The Bloom Taxonomy

In 1956, Benjamin Bloom and his colleagues published an enduring classification of educational goals entitled *Taxonomy of Educational Objectives, Handbook 1: Cognitive Domain*. Bloom had several goals in mind. First, he believed, the taxonomy would help in curriculum construction. Second, it would identify certain behaviors in any plan (recall, define, compare). Third, it would help in the preparation of both learning experiences and evaluation devices. Fourth, it could serve as a tool to analyze educational processes. (See chap. 15 for additional applications of Bloom's work.)

Bloom's taxonomy has enjoyed widespread acceptance and today forms the core of many thinking skills programs. The main purpose of the taxonomy is to provide a classification of the goals of our educational system (Bloom, 1956, p. 1). The taxonomy consists of three major sections covering the cognitive, the affective, and the psychomotor domains. Our concern here is with the cognitive taxonomy, which is divided into the six major classes listed below:

1. *Knowledge*—recall of specific facts
2. *Comprehension*—understanding what is communicated
3. *Application*—generalization and use of abstract information in concrete situations
4. *Analysis*—breakdown of a problem into subparts and detection of relationships among the parts
5. *Synthesis*—putting together parts to form a whole
6. *Evaluation*—using criteria to make judgments

Each category is further subdivided into other, more specific objectives. Bloom and his associates stated that these six classes represent the hierarchical order of the different classes of objectives. The objectives of each class usually depend on those of preceding classes (Bloom, 1956, p. 18). Educators have found the upper levels of the taxonomy (analysis, synthesis, and evaluation) particularly helpful in constructing a taxonomy of thinking skills.

Bloom justifies the simple-to-complex sequence of the categories by noting that a simple behavior may become integrated with other, equally simple behaviors, to form a more complex behavior. Addition, subtraction, and multiplication are needed in order to master long division. As you can see, the educational implications of the taxonomy can be quite explicit.

Educational objectives follow from the various taxonomic categories and are interpreted to specify exactly how the educative process is to change students. They answer the question, "What precisely do I want my students to learn?". A taxonomy of thinking skills provides a useful organization of knowledge about thinking, and facilitates answering questions such as these:

• What do we know about students—their developmental paths, needs, and interests?
• What is in the nature of the subject matter that can help to shape objectives?
• What does the psychology of learning tell us about the appropriate placement of objectives in the learning sequence? Do the ways that students learn suggest a series of steps that must be mastered?

Many educators believe that the elegant simplicity of Bloom's logic and the detailed presentation of the various categories of the taxonomy have not been fully utilized. With today's interest in teaching thinking skills, many concerned teachers and administrators have again turned to Bloom's categories of analysis, synthesis, and evaluation as the best means available for organizing the teaching of higher-order thinking skills.

Using Questions to Improve Thinking Skills

Even before Socrates, questioning was one of teaching's most common and most effective techniques. Some teachers ask hundreds of questions, especially when teaching science, geography, history, or literature. Using questions is a specific example of how teachers can help students to improve their thinking skills. In 1966, Sanders analyzed classroom questions and identified seven levels.

1. *Memory*—recall or recognize previously learned ideas
2. *Translation*—restate an idea in a different manner
3. *Interpretation*—compare ideas or use an idea to solve a problem when told to do so
4. *Application*—use an idea to solve a problem when not told to do so but when the problem requires it
5. *Analysis*—solve a problem following logical steps
6. *Synthesis*—create something with data you are given
7. *Evaluation*—make a value judgment

Now identify the levels of the following questions based on this notice.

> *Wanted: Thinking Students*
> *Are you tired of being frustrated during examinations?*
> *Do you refuse to settle for second best?*
> *Do you want to succeed?*
> *Do you know how to analyze a problem?*
> *Do you even know how to begin to attack a problem?*
> *If your answers to these questions indicate that you are unhappy with your present level of thinking skills, meet me in Room 211 at 3:00 p.m.*

Indicate the levels of the following questions by filling in the blanks.

1. Imagine that you saw this notice taped to the classroom bulletin board. How would you reply? _____
2. Who wrote this notice? _____
3. Do you think this is an appealing notice? _____
4. How would you rewrite it to make it more attractive? _____
5. What type of student do you think would respond to this notice? _____
6. What type of problem do you see in using the questions in the notice? _____
7. When the interested students report to Room 211, what will they be told? _____

Here are the question levels: 6, 1, 7, 2, 3, 5, 4. By using an exercise like this and similar techniques, you can help your students to achieve higher levels of thinking and improve their methods of attacking problems.

Questions take different forms and place different demands on students. Some questions require only factual recall and do not provoke analysis. For example, of more than 61,000 questions found in the teacher guides, student workbooks, and tests for nine history textbooks, more than 95 percent were devoted to factual recall. This is not to say that questions meant to elicit facts are unimportant. Students need basic information to engage in higher-level thinking processes and discussions. Such questions also promote class participation and provide a high success rate in answering questions correctly.

The difference between factual and thought-provoking questions is the difference between asking, "Where did Lincoln deliver the Gettysburg Address?" and asking, "Why was Lincoln's Gettysburg Address an important speech?". Each kind of question has its place, but the second question requires the student to analyze the speech according to the issues of the Civil War.

Although both kinds of questions are important, students achieve more when teachers ask thought-provoking questions and insist on thoughtful answers. Students' answers may also improve if teachers wait longer for responses, giving students more time to think. Table 9.1 provides several examples of questions that require varying levels of thinking.

Table 9.1

Using Bloom's Taxonomy of Thinking Skills to Guide the Development of Questions for Students

Level of thinking	Examples of questions
Knowledge	Who did _____ ?
	When was _____ completed?
	Identify the _____ in the list.
	What does 2 + 6 equal?
Comprehension	Provide a good title for the story you read.
	In your own words, what was the main theme of the story?
Application	Use the word correctly in a sentence.
	Design a model that illustrates your understanding of the concept.
Analysis	Categorize all of the elements of the problem.
	What is the function of _____ ?
	How is A related to B?
Synthesis	Identify the common pattern resulting from all of the pictures.
	Summarize the various points that were made by stating a rule.
	Integrate the various pieces of information to create a profile of the person.
Evaluate	Judge the best method for testing the hypothesis.
	Rank order the projects, using stated criteria, from best to worst.
	Decide which problems were solved correctly.

Improving Teachers' Questions

Worried about their students' inability to draw inferences, two elementary school administrators, Falkoff and Moss (1984), turned to the improvement of teacher questions. Beginning with a series of workshops, they introduced their teachers to several theorists, beginning with Bloom. Next, they matched types of questions with the categories from the taxonomy.

Question	**Taxonomy**
1. Factual	Knowledge, comprehension
2. Interpretative	Application, analysis
3. Creative	Synthesis
4. Evaluative	Evaluation

Students then had to be taught to respond appropriately to the various types of questions. Working with both students and teachers, they found that interpretative questions served as the best vehicles to achieve higher-order thinking. They also discovered that if students were to answer such questions, they must be taught to make inferences: sensory inferences, visual inferences, and relationship inferences.

Therefore, they initiated a three-stage sequence to help their students achieve higher-order thinking skills.

• *Inferences from sensory cues* involve such techniques as standing in front of students with tight lips and folded arms. Ask students how you are feeling; then, ask them, "Why?".

Which type of question, interpretative or evaluative, is generally the most difficult for you to answer? Why?

- *Inferences from visual cues* require attention to details. For example, ask students what they can tell about a culture from some artifacts, like old coins.
- *Inferences about relationships* force students to conceptualize attributes and then search for common themes. Students are also required to discuss their rationales for making relationships. They then can be encouraged to compare and contrast.

Use of these strategies is an excellent example of building Bloom's ideas into the teaching of thinking skills. Let's now examine a second approach to teaching critical thinking skills.

Costa and Thinking Skills

Costa's (1985) rationale for his discussion of thinking skills is as simple as it is far-reaching: thinking is hard work, but with proper instruction, human thought processes can be more broadly applied, more spontaneously generated, more precisely focused, more intricately complex, more metaphorically abstract, and more insightfully divergent. With this statement, Costa took a firm stand in favor of *direct instruction* of thinking skills.

Teaching about thinking can be divided into three components: *brain functioning, metacognition,* and *epistemic cognition.* Knowing how our brains work, being conscious of our own thinking, and learning how knowledge is produced by studying the lives of great composers, scientists, or writers all contribute to our teaching for, of, and about thinking.

Following this introductory work, Costa turned his attention to a model of human intellectual functioning, since he believes that an information-processing model should be the basis for any definition of thinking, instructional strategies, and teaching behaviors. The main features of any such model are as follows:

- Processing through the senses implies that students are alert to problems, consider as many variables as possible, identify pertinent data, and devise a system for collecting vital information.
- Students derive meaning from data by defining problems, determining goals, searching for relationships, and formulating strategies.
- Students apply and evaluate decisions by communicating them to others after checking them against possible alternative solutions.
- Students become aware of their own behaviors as they attempt to reach decisions.

Costa's next step is to suggest a four-level hierarchy of thinking skills that should be helpful in teaching, curriculum construction, and development of instructional materials. The four levels are as follows:

Level I: The Discrete Level of Thinking. This level of thinking involves individual skills prerequisite to more complex thinking. The teacher could ask, What demands are made on students' vocabulary? Can students comprehend the material?

Level II: Strategies of Thinking. This second level of thinking skills involves the combination of individual, discrete skills to formulate strategies. The teacher could ask, Do students understand the ideas presented, and can they combine them in a way that leads to problem solving?

Level III: Creative Thinking. This level of thinking skills requires the use of strategies to create new thought patterns and innovative solutions. For example, the teacher might ask, Can students apply what they have learned about America's original break with England to the current changes in Eastern Europe?

Level IV: The Cognitive Spirit. Although we can generate numerous lists of skills, that alone is insufficient. Thus, this level of thinking requires students' willingness, disposition, inclination, and commitment to think.

What can teachers do to foster thinking skills? Costa believes that certain teacher behaviors can be quite effective in their impact on thinking skills. Four categories of teaching behavior seem particularly relevant: questioning, structuring, responding, and modeling—all of which should occur within a discussion format.

Questioning Costa (1985, p. 126) stated that students derive their cues for expected behavior almost totally from teacher questions and statements. If we assume a relationship between the level of thinking in a teacher's statements and questions and the level of student thinking, then questions containing higher-order thinking will require students to use higher-order thinking skills to answer them.

Questions can activate each part of Costa's model of intellectual functioning. For example, to aid input, questions that require students to name, describe, define, and observe are effective tools. To help students process data, questions that require students to search for relationships, synthesize, analyze, compare, and contrast are appropriate. Questions that force students to apply data in a novel manner should have them evaluate, judge, imagine, and predict.

Structuring Costa used the term *structuring* in the traditional manner, to mean how teachers control the classroom environment. We have long known that teaching success is tightly linked to a well-structured classroom. Note: Well-structured and controlled does not imply rigid and unbending rules and discipline; rather, the term applies to a situation in which both teacher and students know what the structure is (firm, tight, relaxed, friendly), and in which the structure remains consistent.

Structuring your classroom to improve your students' thinking skills demands clear objectives that they can understand. Costa believes that such structure emerges from three instructional goals: (a) instructional clarity, (b) structuring time and energy, and (c) carefully organizing your interactions with your students.

Responding In attempting to create a climate conducive to developing student thinking skills, Costa focused on the nature of teacher responses. Teacher responses, which are extremely influential in shaping student behavior, fall into two major categories: closed responses and open responses. *Closed responses* include criticism and praise. Critical responses (in the sense of "put-downs") add little to the attainment of thinking skills. Praise must be used judiciously; otherwise it is relatively ineffective. If used carefully with students experiencing difficulty and if matched with clear standards of achievement for all students, praise seems to be positive. We will emphasize in chapter 10, on motivation, that intrinsic motivation should be our constant goal. *Open responses* include silence, accepting, clarifying, and facilitating. We can summarize this category by stating that you should give students time to answer your questions, be nonjudgmental, clearly indicate when you do not understand an answer, and provide feedback.

Modeling Avoid any inconsistencies between what you say and what you do. Students are remarkably perceptive and will quickly discern any discrepancies. If you want students to improve their thinking skills, you must show them that you place a high value on these behaviors. If you truly appreciate innovative solutions, careful inferences, and well-planned predictions, demonstrate your enthusiasm by your own behavior. Look for challenges and welcome obstacles.

What you say and do greatly influences students; show how much you value thinking skills. Try to do this in a way that reflects the thoughtful analysis of the strengths of good programs, as did Superintendent Grimes and his colleagues at the chapter's opening.

Thinking Skills and Multicultural Students

You may occasionally be thwarted by what appear to be unrelated answers by multicultural students, but remember one guiding principle: their perception of the problem may be quite different from yours (Rogoff, 1990). For example, Greenfield (1966) conducted a series of studies among the Wolof of Senegal, in which she investigated their attainment of Piagetian conservation abilities. Greenfield found that the manner of questioning influenced children's answers. When children were asked about the amount of water in two identical beakers, Greenfield noticed that if the question was asked directly—"Why do you think this glass has more than the other?"—she seldom received an answer. When she asked the question in a less personal manner—"Why is this true?"—the children answered easily and correctly.

Greenfield also discovered that the children's reasoning for nonconservation answers was related to the person who poured the water, and not to the logic of the problem. When the experimenter poured the liquid into a new container, 25 percent of the youngsters said the new container had more in it, because the adult had poured it. When the children themselves poured the liquid, 70 percent of the 6- and 7-year-olds gave conservation answers. Thus, when children poured the water, their conservation answers didn't reflect a cultural tendency to attribute power to an adult.

Research consistently has upheld this finding: No matter how diverse the cultural group, evidence testifies to the existence of commonly held cognitive abilities (Miller-Jones, 1989). What previously obscured this fact was a failure to recognize the importance of the experimental method, a recognition we have just seen in Greenfield's work. Once a cognitive task was presented in a culturally appropriate way, similar cognitive skills (memory, classification) appeared.

When we translate these and similar findings to our classrooms, we find the same cultural tendencies at work. Problems with language, trouble with standardized tests, and difficulties with a novel environment all translate into behavior that can too easily be interpreted as deficient.

What is needed? We need educators who accept diversity; encourage and integrate the cultures, languages, and backgrounds of their students; and incorporate the curriculum and teaching strategies appropriate to the vast range of learning styles and cultures that are found in our multiethnic, multiracial society (Olsen, 1988, p. 218).

SELECTED THINKING SKILLS PROGRAMS

With these taxonomies of thinking skills and an awareness of the influence of cultural differences on problem solving as background, we can now turn our attention to how "thinking skills" have been translated into programs. We shall again discuss only well-documented, carefully researched programs. Three programs will be discussed here: Sternberg and Gardner's *Practical Intelligence for School,* Feuerstein's *Instrumental Enrichment,* and deBono's *CoRT Thinking Program.* Other potentially worthwhile programs will be summarized briefly.

Practical Intelligence for School

practical intelligence *Tactical knowledge necessary for success both inside and outside of school.*

Students must learn to use their **practical intelligence** effectively in school, because that is where so much of their lives take place. Yet, according to Sternberg and his colleagues, many teachers neither make explicit their expectations nor share the tacit knowledge that is necessary for success, both inside and outside school (Sternberg, Okagaki, & Jackson, 1990). Since 1987, Sternberg and his team of researchers have worked in cooperation with Gardner's research team to develop a theory-based curriculum called *Practical Intelligence for School* (PIFS).

The PIFS program is an outgrowth of the combination of Sternberg's triarchic model of intelligence and Gardner's multiple intelligences model. Figure 9.2 illustrates how these models of intelligence, which we discussed earlier in this chapter, are combined in the PIFS program. Note that Gardner's theory expresses the domains in which intelligence manifests itself (linguistic, logical-mathematical, musical, etc.), whereas Sternberg's componential subtheory identifies the mental processes

teacher – student

Intelligence and Thinking Skills Exercises

1. The triarchic theory of intelligence consists of componential, experiential, and contextual elements.

   • You can help students improve their thinking skills by combining their preferred learning styles with their inclinations to pattern matching. Ask individual students to give you directions to their houses from the school. Some students will tell you, others will write out directions, and still others will draw you maps. Make them aware of these differences and encourage them to capitalize on their strengths.

   • Give students a list of words in which each word is somehow related to another. You are encouraging them to infer relationships. For example:

      heel

      train

      liar

      track

      feel

      rail

      ——

      heel–feel

      train–track

      liar–rail (liar backwards)

   • Encourage your students to focus only on relevant information. Try analogies such as the following:

      Beds have sheets.

      Building is to dome as bed is to: pillow, canopy, hotel room.

      Help students see that the first statement (beds have sheets) is not relevant to the problem.

   • Frame your questions in a way that encourages your students to think creatively and hypothetically and that leads them to make judgments.

2. The theory of multiple intelligences has attracted considerable attention.

   • Help students to become comfortable with language by giving examples of how the arrangement of words can change meaning. Why are these sentences the same? Why are they different?

      The cow was hit by the helicopter.

      The helicopter hit the cow.

   • Appeal to the use of as many intelligences as possible. Assign your students to groups and ask them to draw the shape of an island. Have them put in rivers, lakes, valleys, crops, mineral deposits, and any other data you think are important. Now ask them to put in cities, transportation facilities, occupations, etc. You can use similar activities at the various grade levels by using more abstract and sophisticated analyses but, in each case, you are asking students to use their spatial, logical-mathematical, language, and personal intelligences.

   • Use varied activities that require your students to apply their different intelligences. For example:

      Play charades to reinforce the learning of people, places, and events in social studies classes.

      Start a collection of twentieth-century heroes: List specific achievements, background, and relevance to the topic you're studying; defend your selections to the class.

      Select a different period of American history and have groups explain what it would have been like for a family to live in those times.

      Do the same thing for different cultures.

3. Teaching thinking skills is a means of improving tactical intelligence.

   • Don't be satisfied with questions and assignments that are restricted to data collection. Pose themes or problems that require students to make judgments, hypothesize, and react creatively.

   • Ask your students to predict what the community they're living in will be like in twenty years. Have them hypothesize, collect data, and then justify their predictions.

   • Pick a sport with which your students are familiar— for example, baseball. Divide them into teams and have each member of each team write a question about the subject(s) they're studying. You then assign a value to each question: single, double, triple, home run. Each team member takes a turn as the pitcher and "throws" a question at the opposition. You can act as scorekeeper. The students are working together, collecting data for their questions, writing the questions, and reviewing material for their answers.

	Componential ──────→ Contextual ──────→ Experiential		
Intellectual domains (Multiple Intelligences)	*Examples of mental processes:*	*Practical application:*	*Transfer to new situations:*
Linguistic	Selecting the steps needed to solve a problem.	How to organize your thoughts in order to write a book report.	Writing a history report. Writing a letter. Giving directions to someone.
Logical-mathematical	Ordering the components of problem solving.	How to complete a math worksheet accurately.	Figuring out the steps for balancing a budget.
Musical	Selecting relevant information.	How to pick out the melody from the harmony.	Recognizing the main theme in a musical work.
Spatial	Selecting a mental representation for information.	How to make pictures in your mind to help you remember what you read.	Using a schematic to assemble a piece of electronic equipment. Reading a map.
Bodily-kinesthetic	Allocating your resources.	How to pace yourself throughout a long-distance run.	Adjusting your physical exertion during a basketball game or ballet performance.
Interpersonal	Solution monitoring.	How to understand your teacher's comments on your history report.	Restating what someone is telling you to be sure you understand him or her.
Intrapersonal	Identifying a problem.	Figuring out that something bothers you in school.	Figuring out that you are getting annoyed by your brother's teasing.

Figure 9.2

Intellectual operations resulting from Gardner's and Sternberg's models of intelligence.

From R. J. Sternberg, et al., "Practical Intelligence for Success in School" in Educational Leadership, *48, 1:35–39. Copyright © 1990 Association for Supervision and Curriculum Development. Reprinted by permission. All rights reserved.*

involved in these domains. His contextual subtheory defines the practical ways in which the processes are applied, and his experiential subtheory deals with the transfer of skills to new situations.

The total PIFS curriculum is comprised of two parts: (a) the Yale portion, designed to teach skills used across content areas, and (b) the Harvard portion, designed to teach specific skills within a subject. The organization of the PIFS curriculum is based on three kinds of tacit knowledge: managing oneself, managing tasks, and working with others. Figure 9.3 illustrates the three types of tacit knowledge, along with seven subdivisions and forty-eight specific skills.

The forty-eight practical intelligence skills are systematically taught. First, instruction focuses on the "managing yourself" skills. Once these are mastered, instruction turns to the "managing tasks" skills. Finally, the "cooperating with others" skills are taught. Teachers are provided a guide that emphasizes learning in a social context. Thus, students work together in a large group (class) initially, to discuss a skill, and then move to small groups to apply that skill. At the end of each session, students evaluate their use of the new knowledge and material. Later, teachers provide integrative activities that encourage students to apply their new learning in their lives.

According to Sternberg and his associates, teaching practical intelligence for schools is not easy. For those teachers who were evaluated in their project, successfully teaching the PIFS curriculum required a fundamental reorientation of attitudes and teaching style. "In particular, teachers need to come to value a kind of knowledge that they usually do not teach, despite expecting students to somehow learn it" (Sternberg, Okagaki, & Jackson, 1990, p. 38). The authors argued that teaching practical intelligence skills like those in the PIFS curriculum can foster success in all students.

I. Managing yourself	II. Managing tasks	III. Cooperating with others
A. Overview of managing yourself	A. Overview of solving problems	A. Communication
1. Introductory Lesson	22. Is There a Problem?	38. Class Discussions
2. Kinds of Intelligence: Definitions and Principles	23. What Strategies Are You Using?	39. What to Say
3. Kinds of Intelligence: Multiple Intelligences	24. A Process to Help You Solve Problems	40. Tuning Your Conversation
4. Kinds of Intelligence: Academic or Practical Intelligence	25. Planning a Way to Prevent Problems	41. Putting Yourself in Another's Place
5. Understanding Test Scores	26. Breaking Habits	42. Solving Problems in Communication
6. Exploring What You May Do	27. Help with Our Problems	
7. Accepting Responsibility		B. Fitting into school
8. Collecting Your Thoughts and Setting Goals	B. Specific school problems	43. Making Choices—Adapting, Shaping, Selecting
	28. Taking Notes	44. Understanding Social Networks
B. Learning styles	29. Getting Organized	45. Seeing the Network: Different Roles
9. What's Your Learning Style?	30. Understanding Questions	46. Seeing the Network: Figuring Out the Rules
10. Taking In New Information	31. Following Directions	47. Seeing the Relationship Between Now and Later
11. Showing What You Learned	32. Underlining—Finding the Main Idea	48. What Does School Mean to You?
12. Knowing How You Work Best	33. Noticing the Way Things Are Written	
13. Recognizing the Whole and the Parts	34. Choosing Between Mapping and Outlining	
	35. Taking Tests	
C. Improving your own learning	36. Seeing Likenesses and Differences in Subjects	
14. Memory	37. Getting It Done on Time	
15. Using What You Already Know		
16. Making Pictures in Your Mind		
17. Using Your Eyes—A Good Way to Learn		
18. Recognizing the Point of View		
19. Looking for the Best Way to Learn		
20. Listening for Meaning		
21. Learning by Doing		

Figure 9.3
Practical intelligence for school curriculum.

From R. J. Sternberg, et al., "Practical Intelligence for Success in School" in Educational Leadership, *48, 1:35–39. Copyright © 1990 Association for Supervision and Curriculum Development. Reprinted by permission. All rights reserved.*

Instrumental Enrichment

Originally proposed by Reuven Feuerstein (1980), **instrumental enrichment** rests on the assumption that we can modify our cognitive structures. Feuerstein believes that the root problem of poor learners is the reduced level of modifiability that such students exhibit. Cognitive growth occurs as a result of both **incidental learning** (learning that results from exposure to a changing environment) and **mediated learning** (the training given to learners by experienced adults). Of the two, mediated learning is by far the most important. By scheduling, sequencing, and grouping stimuli, adults order and regulate the learner's environment, thus forming the *Mediated Learning Experience (MLE)*. The program is intended to improve the cognitive performance of low-achieving adolescents by enhancing their modifiability as a result of exposure to new experiences.

Specifically, the IE program consists of a series of paper-and-pencil exercises that take two to three hundred hours to complete over two or three years. Feuerstein calls these exercises "instruments" rather than lessons, because they are intended to be content-free. The various tasks are clustered into 20 instruments, which comprise a total program. Each instrument focuses on one or more cognitive functions, while simultaneously promoting others. The program takes about three to five hours per week and is presented by a specially trained teacher who is a regular staff member.

Among the instruments used are the following:

- *Organization of dots,* a technique that is divorced from any school subject, and one that forces students to break a task into parts and search for relationships among the reorganized parts. The cognitive processes needed in this task also will transfer to other thinking skills.

instrumental enrichment
Feuerstein's program designed to help students acquire thinking skills.

incidental learning *Feuerstein's term for cognitive growth that results from a changing environment and is accomplished unintentionally.*

mediated learning *Feuerstein's term for the training given to learners by experienced adults.*

- *Orientation in space I* is designed to promote the formation of specific strategies that will help students acquire frames of reference for spatial relations, gradually culminating in each student's personal frame of reference. Students learn that perception of an object, event, or person depends on their personal vantage points, and that relationships can shift depending on a person's position.
- *Temporal relations,* which first furnishes systems whereby students can understand time as a fixed, measurable interval, and then slowly introduces the relative qualities of present, past, and future. This instrument encourages students to search for proper starting points and consider all relevant information, thus reducing impulsivity.
- *Transitive relations,* a more advanced instrument that concentrates on drawing inferences from relations that can be described as larger than, equal to, or smaller than.

These are but a few of the twenty instruments Feuerstein and his colleagues devised. They illustrate, however, the type of learning experience provided: one that is essentially content-free and based upon the mediated learning experience.

The rationale, instruments, and theoretical concepts are sharply focused on one goal: to develop thinking and problem-solving abilities in students so that they become autonomous learners. The program assumes that intelligence is dynamic and that cognitive development demands direct and mediated intervention to build the mental processes for learning. It is a complicated system, one in which teachers need careful training. This program is intended for upper elementary, middle, and secondary levels.

The CoRT Thinking Program

Cognitive Research Trust (CoRT)
de Bono's program that is intended to help students acquire thinking skills.

As our final example of a thinking skills program, we turn to de Bono's work on **Cognitive Research Trust (CoRT),** which has a different objective from Feuerstein's program. Whereas the latter program concentrates on the means of acquiring thinking skills, de Bono is more concerned with problem-solving ability. Linking his theory of thinking skills to a neurological and information-processing base, de Bono (1985a) argued for the direct teaching of thinking skills to students. The CoRT program has several objectives.

- The program should be *simple and practical.* A successful program must be teachable for instructors and understandable for students. Expensive materials and special audiovisual materials are unnecessary.
- The program should *apply to a wide range of ages,* since de Bono believes that thinking processes are fundamental.
- The thinking skills taught should be *those required in real life;* for this reason the program emphasizes "projective" thinking: gathering information, inferring from it, and acting on it.
- The program should be *independent of any detailed knowledge base.* Thinking skills needed throughout our lives aren't tied to a specific subject; we need vital thinking skills in all subjects and problem areas.
- Students should be able to *transfer the thinking skills* they acquire to all of life's situations. By the mixture of items in the CoRT program, de Bono believes that students' attention can be directed at necessary thinking processes.

So what is the CoRT method? It is best to illustrate this method with an example from de Bono (1985a).

I was teaching a class of thirty boys, all eleven years of age, in Sydney, Australia. I asked if they would each like to be given $5 a week for coming to school. All thirty thought this was a fine idea. "We could buy sweets or chewing gum. . . . We could buy comics. . . . We could get toys without having to ask Mum or Dad."

I then introduced and explained a simple tool called the PMI (which I will describe later). The explanation took about four minutes. In groups of five, the boys applied the PMI tool to the suggestion that they should be given $5 a week for coming to school. For three to four minutes

they talked and thought on their own. At no time did I interfere. I never discussed the $5 suggestion, other than to state it. I did not suggest that the youngsters consider this, think of that, and so forth. At the end of their thinking time, the groups reported back to me: The bigger boys would beat us up and take the money. . . . The school would raise its charges for meals. . . . Our parents would not buy us presents. . . . Who would decide how much money different ages received? . . . There would be less money to pay teachers. . . . There would be less money for a school minibus.

When they had finished their report, I again asked the boys to express their views on the suggestion of pay for attending school. This time, twenty-nine of the thirty had completely reversed their opinion and thought it a bad idea. We subsequently learned that the one holdout received no pocket money at home. The important point is that my contribution was minimal. I did not interact with the boys. I simply explained the PMI tool, and the boys then used it on their own—as their tool. My "superior" intelligence and broader experiences were not influences. The boys did their own thinking. (de Bono, 1985a)

The *PMI* acronym de Bono referred to represents *plus* (the good points in a situation), *minus* (the negative features), and *interesting* (things worth noting). In de Bono's usage, PMI becomes a scoring tool, one that students find easy to remember, easy to pronounce, and easy to use.

The CoRT method encompasses the following features as major concepts of the system:

- *The role of perception in thinking.* The intent of the program is to enable students to view things more clearly by providing a "perceptual map" to guide behavior.
- *CoRT attention tools.* The PMI is an example of an attention tool, since it forces students to go beyond their initial reactions. Using such a tool provides students with a frame that highlights details and enriches perception.
- *CoRT practice items.* The important point here is de Bono's insistence that thinking skills, not the content, are to be practiced.
- *Strategies for encouraging transfer.* Once students learn to focus attention on their thinking skills, the program has them use these skills in a variety of situations.
- *Identification of skills* in which to offer instruction. Each lesson in the program focuses on a different thinking skill that was selected because of its applicability to a wide variety of situations.

For students who enter a CoRT program, de Bono's expectation is that they will reach one of four levels of achievement.

- *Level 1.* A general awareness of thinking as a skill, a willingness to explore and think about a topic.
- *Level 2.* A more structured approach to thinking that considers the consequences of a plan or action and searches for alternatives.
- *Level 3.* Focused and deliberate use of several of the CoRT tools.
- *Level 4.* Fluid and appropriate use of such metacognitive processes as thinking about thinking.

Thus the main goal of the CoRT program is to teach thinking skills that are useful in and out of school. It assumes that lateral thinking is unconventional and nonsequential and may not always be right. Intelligent people aren't necessarily skillful thinkers. Finally, the CoRT program is supposedly useful for students of all ability levels, ranging in ages from 8 to 22.

PROBLEM SOLVING

Educators are concerned with how they can improve the abilities of their students to solve problems at school. They are also worried, however, about students' abilities to engage in productive problem-solving behavior outside the classroom. The problem to be solved, the activities involved, and the strategies that we adopt all represent problem-solving behavior.

Thanks to recent research, especially into information-processing and thinking skills, we are now more aware of the procedures involved in solving problems. From increased knowledge have come insights into various strategies that can improve our abilities to solve problems. For example, different kinds of memory techniques are better suited for different types of content. Not only will such knowledge aid us in solving our own problems, but we can teach these techniques and strategies to our students.

In a sense, the remainder of this chapter is about **metacognition,** the ability we develop to "think about thinking." We not only know something, but we also begin to think about what we can do with this knowledge. We develop strategies to solve the problems we face. In the remainder of this chapter, we will discuss the nature of problem solving, the reasons some of us avoid problems, and the typical kinds of strategies we use when we attempt problem solving. Then we'll examine the details of the DUPE model, which presents a formula for determining the dimensions of a problem, understanding its nature, planning for its solution, and finally, evaluating the success of the solution. We will also present several interesting problems to help you learn about your own problem-solving ability and to help you understand the techniques that your future students must master to become good problem solvers.

metacognition *The ability to think about thinking.*

What Is a Problem?

Have you ever sat baffled while you read an arithmetic word problem? Have you ever been assigned a term paper and been bewildered about where to start? In each of these instances, you had a problem; you could not get where you wanted to go. There was a void, a gap, that you had to cross to solve your problem. When dealing with students' learning or behavior problems, *we like to think of a problem as a significant discrepancy between the actual behavior and the desired behavior.*

Using this definition, some problems concern deficits (actual behavior is problematic and is below the desired standard). Other problems concern excesses (actual behavior is problematic and exceeds the desired standard of behavior). As we shall see later when we examine the nature of a problem in more detail, problem solving requires that we understand the meaning of the gap or discrepancy (i.e., we try to represent it in some manner), and then construct ways of bridging the gap.

To understand what is meant by representing the gap and then bridging it, try to solve this problem.

Students need time to reflect on problems and to apply knowledge. Problem solving requires careful observation, interpretation of information, and the enactment of a strategy.

Two motorcyclists are 100 miles apart. At exactly the same moment they begin to drive toward each other for a meeting. Just as they leave, a bird flies from the front of the first cyclist to the front of the second cyclist. When it reaches the second cyclist, it turns around and flies back to the first. The bird continues flying in this manner until the cyclists meet. The cyclists both travel at the rate of 50 miles per hour, while the bird maintains a constant speed of 75 miles per hour. How many miles will the bird have flown when the cyclists meet?

Many readers, examining this problem, will immediately begin to calculate distance, miles per hour, and constancy of speed. Actually, this is not a mathematical problem; it is a word problem. Carefully look at it again. Both riders will travel for one hour before they meet; the bird flies at 75 miles per hour; therefore, the bird will have flown 75 miles. No formulae or calculations are needed, just a close examination of what is given.

Improving Problem-Solving Skills

You may scoff and state that any problem is easy when you know the answer. True, but there is another lesson here. Regardless of how you react to problems, it is possible to improve your ability to solve them. If such a possibility exists for you, it also holds true for your students. This is an exciting prospect, because regardless of a student's intelligence or socioeconomic level, or other characteristic, the student can develop enhanced learning skills.

Individual differences in problem-solving ability exist; some of us are simply better at solving problems than others. There are many explanations for these differences. Some have had previous experience in similar activities; some, with more enriching educations, bring more knowledge to a problem; and some are motivated to solve problems. These factors are not the issue. Regardless of advantages, there is probably no such person as the perfect problem solver. There are, however, individuals who can improve their skills by attending more closely to the nature of each problem that faces them, by better understanding their own thinking processes, and by using mistakes to improve their skills.

Those of you reading this text have already had the benefit of considerable education. To have been successful thus far, you must be a fairly competent problem solver, even though you may not have thought of yourself in just this way. An example of how you can improve your skills is the fact that you will do better with the problems you encounter in the remainder of this chapter, because you will be more cautious and attentive after having analyzed the problem of the bird and the motorcyclists. Try this.

There are 3 separate, equally sized boxes, and inside each box there are 2 separate small boxes, and inside each of the small boxes there are 4 even smaller boxes. How many boxes are there altogether?

Your attempt to solve this problem is another excellent example of individual differences in problem solving, especially those differences that relate to problem-solving style. Though many readers will try to solve it "in their heads" (with some form of internal representation), others will immediately turn to paper and pencil and draw the various stages (using external representation). Our guess would be that more readers solved the second problem than the first. You attended to it more carefully and considered as many alternatives as possible. (The answer is 33: 3 large boxes + 6 small boxes + 24 smaller boxes.)

When you directly teach learning strategies and tactics to your students, it is reasonable to expect that their ability to solve problems, both in and out of the classroom, will improve. Although efforts to incorporate problem-solving activities and content within the curriculum are increasing, this is still, for the most part, a solitary effort by individual teachers. Rarely are students taught to think; typically the focus is on what to learn. This is unfortunate, since most teachers are good problem solvers. However, as noted earlier in this chapter, several psychologists and educators are developing programs for children designed to teach critical thinking skills. Unfortunately, many teachers have never been taught to scrutinize thought processes; consequently, they tend to overlook these abilities as valuable tools for their students to master.

What are some of the common sources of error you experience when trying to solve a problem?

Sources of Error

Whimbey and Lochhead (1985) believe that we can improve our analytical skills by becoming aware of the kinds of errors that we frequently make in attempting to solve problems. As these authors noted, most errors are not because people lack information about the problems. Even with the necessary facts present, individuals have difficulty with problems because they do not attend well or fully employ their reasoning processes. As an example of the type of error that ensnares many problem solvers, the authors offer the following example.

In a different language *liro cas* means red tomato, *dum cas dan* means big red barn, and *xer dan* means big horse. What is the word for barn in this language? (a) dum (b) liro (c) cas (d) dan (e) xer

Here we have a fairly simple problem, but one that demands that we make a systematic comparison of phrases and a careful matching of words. Poor problem solvers often jump at the first clue, with the result that they choose b, c, d, or e. Aside from mechanical mistakes in problem-solving procedures, emotional elements can also be influential.

Among the most common sources of error are the following:

- Failure to observe and use all the relevant facts of a problem. Did you account for each word in the language problem?
- Failure to adopt systematic, step-by-step procedures. The problem solver may skip steps, ignore vital information, and leap to a faulty conclusion. Did you make a check, or some other mark, against each word?
- Failure to perceive vital relationships in the problem. Did you discover the order of the words?
- Frequent use of sloppy techniques in acquiring information and using one's reasoning processes. Did you guess at the meanings of any of the words?

Retreating from Problems

None of us enjoys having to cope with difficult situations. It is much easier to ignore or avoid problems that demand considerable effort to solve. If motivated individuals feel this way, imagine how much more difficult it must be for those students who constantly experience frustration in school and who are more accustomed to failure than to success. These students can react only negatively to any problems that they encounter in the classroom, and as we shall see, they transfer this attitude to other problems they meet. Mathematics is an example of a subject that produces negative reactions in many, even in experienced adult learners. For whatever reason—poor instruction, poor materials, lack of motivation at a critical time—these individuals either avoid or simply refuse to attempt to solve math problems. As an example of this reaction, try to solve the following problem.

Group these numbers in such a way that when you total the groups, they add up to the sum of 1,000.

88888888

Some elementary school youngsters will find the solution almost immediately, but there will be many readers who simply ignore the problem and continue their reading. Others will routinely read the problem while their thoughts are on something totally different. Still others react in an almost reflex manner by saying, "Math—that's not for me."

Your inability to solve a problem may not be solely the result of faulty attention, dislike of math, or even lack of motivation. You may have acquired a general feeling of anxiety about certain types of problems, or all problems. If this is true of successful students, why should less mature students, who may have a history of failure and lack problem-solving skills, even try to solve any educational problems? Their experiences, which probably have contributed to feelings of futility, can generate only a negative reaction to anything resembling a problem, both in and out of school.

(In case you are still searching for the answer, try this line of reasoning. How many groups are required to produce a 0 in the units column when you add them? This is the key to solving the problem, since five is the first number that will result in 0: $5 \times 8 = 40$. Try working with five groups.

(Solution: 888 + 88 + 8 + 8 + 8.)

Excuses, Excuses, Excuses

There are those who will not attempt to search for solutions. As Lewis and Greene (1982) noted, too many people just give up or decide immediately that they would be unsuccessful. Lewis and Greene attribute these attitudes to several myths about mental abilities, the most prominent of which are the following:

- *I just wasn't born smart.* This myth retains its popularity because it shifts responsibility for failure from the individual to some genetic blueprint (Lewis & Greene, 1982). But current interpretations of intelligence have led us to conclude that it is primarily a collection of experiences. Enrich the experiences; improve the performance. This in no way, of course, ignores the inherited ability that establishes a ceiling for potential. However, since potential is rarely, if ever, approached, there exists ample opportunity to improve performance and enhance self-esteem.
- *I have a terrible memory.* Another misleading belief is that our storage capacity for memory is severely restricted, when studies have clearly shown that our ability to retain is much greater than is commonly realized. Retrieval is undoubtedly the issue here: under hypnosis or through the use of electric brain probes, the average person's memory has been proven to be amazingly detailed.
- *You can't teach an old dog new tricks.* The third myth refers to the belief that mental ability declines with age. Again, research has demonstrated that aside from physical damage or disease, there is little actual decline in brain functioning. Too often we live up to stereotypes: if you're old, you're forgetful, or would find it difficult to learn anything new.

Regardless of the reasons people have for retreating from problems, it is a difficult task to help anyone, adult or student, break away from customary attitudes and beliefs. Creative thinking (searching for alternatives to solve problems) is concerned with breaking away from old ideas. This leads to changes in both attitudes and approach: we look differently at situations. If an approach is novel, most people feel uncomfortable trying it. It is much easier to do the same things, even if they have previously led to failure. If, however, you can teach your students to use the strategies discussed in this chapter, the chances are that they will experience greater success, which will in turn encourage them to try again.

Problem-Solving Strategies

What are these strategies that would help your students in their work? They range from general problem-solving techniques to specific and simple tactics. For example, you are probably now cautious about any problem that you meet in this chapter: you are attending more carefully to detail—a simple practice, but one that can be enormously helpful. Try this problem, one that appears in almost any analysis of problem solving.

What day followed the day before yesterday if three days from now it will be Monday?

Good problem solvers analyze details with considerable care and usually break a problem into sections. They might proceed as follows:

- If three days from now it will be Monday, today must be Friday.

- If today is Friday, yesterday was Thursday.
- Then the day before yesterday was Wednesday.
- The following day was Thursday.

Although superficially simple, attending to detail is a powerful tool in solving problems. It makes no difference if the strategy is general or specific; *attending must be the initial step,* and it is from this beginning that strategies take shape. A problem-solving strategy is a means of putting things in place carefully and with a great deal of thought, which is just the opposite of hoping something will happen or taking a wild guess (deBono, 1984).

Problem-solving strategies are usually divided into two categories: *general* (also called *weak*) and *strong* (also called *specific* or *detailed*).

1. *General strategies.* A general strategy, according to deBono (1984), is a set of principles and guidelines that may apply to any situation. De Bono used the example of an interviewer who always selects people who are rated number two: they achieve almost as well as those who rank first, but temperamentally they are less likely to be difficult to work with. Operational structures seem to be the basis of general problem solving, and lead to a set of highly general methods that constitute the core of problem-solving behavior.

   Bransford and Stein (1984) likewise offered specific examples of general strategies. Working a problem backwards is a general strategy that eases problem solution. If you have a 9:00 A.M. examination and you can't be late, one technique would be to decide that you want to arrive at 8:45 A.M.; it takes thirty minutes for the trip; you want to allow fifteen minutes for potential traffic slowdowns; therefore, you should leave at 8:00 A.M. Bransford and Stein believe that working backwards is especially helpful whenever the goal is clear and the initial state of the problem is vague.

strong strategy *A problem-solving strategy designed for a specific subject.*

2. *Strong strategies.* A **strong strategy** is one designed for a specific purpose, that is, a strategy that seems to be unique to a particular subject. Anyone familiar with the core concept of a subject is better able to initiate steps to solve a problem involving that knowledge. The most powerful approach to problem solving is to become familiar with concepts that others have invented (Bransford & Stein, 1984). These concepts, then, provide the tools for representing and solving problems. For example, researchers who are thoroughly versed in the basic concepts of genetics and molecular biology are also the most suitably equipped to explore the biological frontiers where ultimately the problems of cancer and heart disease will be solved.

The Good Problem Solver

Are there discernible characteristics that identify a good problem solver? Whimbey and Lochhead (1985) believe that an accumulation of research has resulted in the identification of the following characteristics that identify the "good problem solver."

- *Positive attitude.* Good problem solvers believe that they can solve problems by careful, persistent analysis. Poor problem solvers, on the other hand, believe that you either know the answer or you don't; if you don't, why bother trying? They have not learned that a problem that at first appears confusing can be broken down into parts and gradually analyzed. Poor problem solvers have not learned how to analyze, and thus they have little experience with successful solutions and even less self-confidence.

- *Concern for accuracy.* The good problem solver takes pains to grasp the facts and relationships that the problem presents. Poor problem solvers are rather casual; their method is a quick reading, an immediate reaction, little concern for details. Here is an excellent example of what was previously mentioned about improving performance: simply by teaching students to read more carefully, to reread, and to look for the details that are given, you can help them grasp a problem more accurately, thus improving their problem-solving skills.

Annual **Edition**

- *Habit of breaking the problem into parts.* Good problem solvers consistently try to break a problem into parts, analyze each part, and then integrate the parts in an attempt to reach a solution. Poor problem solvers fail to see any sequence in a problem; they view it as total confusion. By teaching them to search for parts and then to try to understand the parts, we can ensure that poor problem solvers will increase their chances for success.
- *Avoidance of guessing.* Poor problem solvers tend to jump at the first answer that comes to mind. They frequently "play a hunch" (with few facts) or simply stop in the hunt for a solution; both of these tendencies reflect a lack of the first three qualities of good problem solvers and are major sources of errors for students.
- *Active problem solving.* Good problem solvers just do more things than poor problem solvers as they search for a solution. If the problem is wordy, they may outline; if the problem is complicated, they may draw a diagram; they will continuously ask themselves questions about the problem. Each of these activities improves accuracy and sharpens focus on the problem.

Different Cultures—Different Perspectives

Problem-solving strategies provide unique insights into the cultural differences you will find in your classroom and what they mean for learning. Consider these statements (taken from First & Carrera, 1988).

- Don't take offense if Southeast Asian or Hispanic children don't look you in the eye—it's a sign of respect.
- Don't pat Southeast Asian children on the head—that's insulting.
- If you cross your fingers (considered good luck by Americans), many Southeast Asians think you have made an obscene gesture.
- Cambodians are insulted by anyone who calls to them by hand gestures.

These are but a few examples of cultural variation that can affect interpersonal relations. We also must avoid stereotypes: African American students will fail; Asian American students will succeed. Remember that *Asian* describes people from Korea, Vietnam, the Philippines, Cambodia, China, and many other countries of origin and that remarkably few studies have been done on Asian American students who fail (Slaughter-Defoe et al., 1990).

The differences we have described may affect the way that students from different cultures attack problems. Remember that students from different cultures may initially differ in what they identify as problems. What you consider highly significant may appear irrelevant to them (Goodnow, 1990). For example, Cole and Scribner (1974) described differences in the ways that children from different cultures attempt to solve problems. In one experiment, a metal box is divided into three sections—A, B, and C—and the subject is taught to push a button in the middle of door A to obtain a marble. Next, the subject learns to push door C to receive a ball bearing. Then the subject can acquire a piece of candy by putting the marble in section B. Finally, all three doors are opened together, and the subject is told to do whatever is necessary to get the candy. Note that the subject must combine two learned acts to get the candy: get the marble and then put it in box B. Liberian children had great difficulty with this task, but most American youngsters mastered it quickly. You can see how easy it would be to jump to conclusions about the problem-solving abilities of American and Liberian children.

When the authors changed the task by using materials more familiar to the Liberian youngsters (using keys painted red and black instead of pushing buttons to open the boxes), their success rate jumped to about 80 percent, and with prompting, to about 90 percent. The lesson should be clear: *By adjusting the circumstances surrounding a task, we can help students from different cultures to use their abilities and thus improve their achievement.*

In teaching multicultural students, try to detect any characteristics in their learning history that could affect problem solving (as we have just seen in the above experiment). The following are especially significant differences among students of varied cultures (Grossman, 1990):

- whether your students rely on internal clues (ideas, feelings, values) to learn and solve problems, or tend to use information from their environments
- whether they prefer working alone or with others
- whether they function better in competitive or cooperative situations
- whether they prefer to work independently or seek feedback and guidance from others
- whether they prefer abstract activities (such as math or science) or are interested in more affective subjects, such as history
- whether they respond to praise or criticism from others or are relatively indifferent to the opinions of others

Keeping in mind the characteristics of a good problem solver and the nature of tasks, we propose several strategies to help individuals, regardless of their cultural backgrounds to master effective problem-solving techniques.

THE DUPE MODEL

Many models have been proposed to help people solve a wide variety of problems. Often they use a series of steps in the form of an acronym (a letter combination like SAC—Strategic Air Command; NATO—North Atlantic Treaty Organization; or HOMES—The names of the Great Lakes: Huron, Ontario, Michigan, Erie, Superior). We will use an acronym that you can pass on to your students, one that they should be able to remember easily and that they can transfer to any problems. The acronym is **DUPE.** In its full form, its intent is to convey the message, *Don't let yourself be deceived.* The meaning of each letter is as follows:

DUPE *An acronym for a problem-solving model. Intended to mean "Don't let yourself be deceived."*

> D—*Determine* just exactly what is the nature of the problem. Too often we are deceived by meaningless elements in the problem situation; it is here that attention to detail is so important.
>
> U—*Understand* the nature of the problem. It is not enough to realize that a particular problem exists; you must also comprehend the essence of the problem if your plan for solution is to be accurate. For example, teachers frequently state that a student's classroom difficulties are the result of hyperactivity. The problem has been identified, but to understand the cause of the hyperactivity—physical, social, psychological—additional information is required.
>
> P—*Plan* your solution. Now that you know that a problem exists and you understand its nature, you must select strategies that are appropriate for the problem. It is here that memory plays such an important role.
>
> E—*Evaluate* your plan; this usually entails two phases. First you should examine the plan itself in an attempt to determine its suitability. Then you must decide how successful your solution was.

The model you are about to analyze offers several metacognitive strategies that you can pass on to your students. The first step in the DUPE model is to determine the nature of the problem.

Determining the Nature of a Problem

How do we know that a problem exists? Students are often baffled when confronted by a problem; they have no idea of how to begin, since they are unable to identify the nature of the problem. They have a vague sense that they "just can't do something." In the classroom they are usually told about the problem or read about it, and yet even these clues may offer little tangible help, because the nature of the problem still eludes them.

They are not alone in their bewilderment. How would you go about solving this problem?

> **There is a super psychic who can predict the score of any game before it is played. Explain how this is possible.**

This problem, taken from Bransford and Stein (1984), poses a challenge to most of us because, as the authors noted, it is difficult to generate a reasonable explanation. If you are having difficulty, it is probably because you have made a faulty assumption about the nature of the problem. You were not asked about the final score; the score of any game before it is played is 0 to 0. We deliberately presented a tricky problem to stress that you must attend to details.

The Elements of a Problem

Psychologists usually divide problems into two classes: well-defined and ill-defined. A well-defined problem is one in which the steps to solution are specified clearly in the problem's statement. The major focus in the solution of such problems is on the sequence of steps needed.

> **If 3 oranges cost 99¢, how much does each orange cost?**
> **The facts are clearly stated; what is needed are the steps.**
> 1. **3 cost 99¢**
> 2. **To find the cost of one, divide 99 by 3**
> 3. **Answer: 33**

An ill-defined problem is one in which the givens are much more vague and the steps to solution more elusive. As Sternberg (1987) noted, such problems require one or two insights into their nature, insights that usually are difficult to achieve. Once they are achieved, however, the problem is quickly resolved.

The problems presented earlier in this chapter are examples of this type. If you had difficulty with the eight 8s, you could not solve the problem until you achieved the insight that there must be five groups. In the problem with the motorcycles and the bird, once you realized that the solution depended on the bird's speed per hour (since the cyclists traveled for one hour), the answer came quickly.

In his classic study of problem solving, Wickelgren (1974) stated that problems provide three types of information: givens, operations, and goals.

Givens   These are the facts that are presented in a problem as we commence work, including representations of objects, things, and events, as well as expressions representing assumptions, definitions, and facts. For example, you were given eight 8s to work with. A kind of implicit given is that you may need additional knowledge from other sources. As Wickelgren noted, you should be alert to this type of implicit information (again the importance of attention is reinforced). Carefully attending to the details in the problem helps you to grasp its nature and decide if you need additional information, and if you do, from what source.

Wickelgren's advice is excellent; even recognizing the relevant properties of the givens, with no additional background information needed, human beings still often fail to explore the possible uses of these properties to solve problems. This failure is especially detrimental in efforts to solve insight problems, for which the relationships among the properties are often critical for solution. The opposite advice to this, of course, is not to become dazzled by the irrelevant givens that appear in a problem. For example, in the motorcycle and bird problem, to concentrate on how many times the bird flew back and forth between the cyclists would be merely distracting.

Operations By *operations,* Wickelgren means the actions that you can perform on the givens. These are the actions that are permitted within the framework of a problem. How do you solve the following problem?

> **The perimeter of a rectangle is 25 feet greater than the sum of its length and width. If the length is 15 feet longer than the width, what are its dimensions?**
> 1. **What is required? (The rectangle's dimensions.)**
> 2. **What am I asked to do? (Solve for length and width.)**
> 3. **What am I given? (The perimeter and the length.)**
> 4. **What shall I do? (Use the given data: The perimeter**
> $P = x + (x + 15) + x + (x + 15)$ **is 25 feet greater than the sum of length and width.**
> 5. **Solve:**
> $$x + (x + 15) + x + (x + 15) = x + (x + 15) + 25$$
> $$4x + 30 = 2x + 15 + 25$$
> $$4x + 30 = 2x + 40$$
> $$2x = 10$$
> $$x = 5$$

The solution to this problem demonstrates all that we have been discussing thus far:

- What is required? (Attend to detail)
- What am I asked to do? (Understand the nature of the problem)
- What are the givens? (Decide if additional information is needed)
- What shall I do? (Plan and represent the solution)

With regard to operations, certain mathematical rules that are essential to the problem's solution determine your actions. You must remove parentheses and change signs when you move an item from one side of the equation to the other. Most of us are quite familiar with these operations, but other actions, which are almost as familiar, can remain tantalizingly elusive. Try to solve this much-used balance problem.

> **In a collection of 12 cans of soda, 11 cans have exactly the same weight, while one is heavier than the others. How would you determine which is the heavy can if you are provided with a balance scale that will weigh as many cans as you wish to put on each side of the scale? The problem is that you must discover the heavy can in the least number of weighings.**

A quick reaction to this problem is to divide the 12 cans into 2 sets of 6, select the set of 6 that is heavier, and divide this into 2 sets of 3. It is here that your strategy breaks down. How will you assess the final set of 3: 1 against 1, and then a final set of 1 versus 1?

Actually, however, the scale offers three options for solution: heavier, lighter, or equal. Consequently, by dividing the original 12 cans into 3 sets of 4, you can weigh one set of 4 against the other, thus immediately determining which set of 4 contains the heavy can. If the first two sets balance, then the heavy can is in the third set. Now balance 2 against 2, and finally 1 against 1. You have solved the problem in three steps.

By carefully considering the operations required and understanding the most efficient way that they can be employed, you can avoid miscalculations that frustrate problem solution.

Goals When you cannot get where you want to go—you can't immediately solve the problem—you must devise a means of bridging the gap as economically as possible. Accurately representing the information contained in a problem depends on a precise and correct definition of the goal. You should have a clear, precise statement of the goal, rather than some vague formulation, which may do considerable harm when you attempt to solve a problem (Wickelgren, 1974, p. 37).

The goal must be perfectly clear in your mind, because it influences the choice of strategies that you select for solution. Questions like these are helpful: What is the goal as stated in the problem or posed by the situation? What do I need to attain the goal? Was I successful? It is here that we see the value of categorizing problems as ill- or well-structured. Although the basic strategies that lead to solution are probably the same for both problem types, surface differences affect the ease and quality of solution. For ill-structured problems that require more background information, your perspective on the problem continues to change as you secure new data. But it is your definition of the goal that shapes all else that follows.

We now realize that a problem exists and have determined its basic dimensions; the second stage of the DUPE model takes us more deeply into the nature of problems.

Understanding the Nature of the Problem

Understanding the nature of a problem implies that you can both define and represent it, an assumption that has several significant implications. Before you define a problem you must have a sufficient amount of knowledge to recognize the givens. To represent it, you must also have adequate problem-solving skills. Both of these prerequisites suggest the relevance of categorizing problems as ill- or well-defined. Many of life's daily problems are vague; we can label them as ill-defined. If we lack problem-solving strategies, then our task is next to impossible. Here is one of the major reasons why there is growing pressure for schools to teach problem-solving skills, either as a separate course or as part of a course's content.

As an example of the value of teaching problem-solving strategies, consider the following.

> **Tom either walks to work and rides his bicycle home or rides his bicycle to work and walks home. The round trip takes one hour. If he were to ride both ways, it would take 30 minutes. If Tom walked both ways, how long would a round trip take?**

This problem (based on Wickelgren, 1974, p. 104) illustrates the basic problem-solving strategy of dividing the givens into subgoals. Think for a moment: What are the givens? How long would it take to ride one way? (15 minutes.) How long is a round trip? (One hour.) How long does it take to walk one way? (45 minutes.) How long is the round trip if Tom walked both ways? (45 + 45 = 90 minutes.)

The Knowledge Base

Compare the givens of the above problem with the example Hayes (1989) used to stress the importance of prior knowledge.

> **Liquid water at 212° F and 1 atm has an internal energy (on an arbitrary basis) of 180.02 BTU/lb. The specific volume of liquid water at these conditions is 0.01672 ft/lb. What is the enthalpy?**

For anyone with a knowledge of thermodynamics, this is not a particularly difficult problem. If you lack the necessary prior knowledge, however, you are defeated before you start. If you are missing relevant knowledge, an easy problem may appear difficult, if not impossible. *Remember: Much that passes for cleverness or innate quickness of mind actually depends on specialized knowledge* (Hayes, 1989). This helps to explain the current interest in the role of prior knowledge in problem solving.

Recent cognitive research demonstrates that an understanding of cognitive processes demands recognition of the role of knowledge and its internal representation. In their studies of expert chess players, Chase and Simon (1973) discovered that experts differ from novices in playing chess not by employing different processes but in the knowledge bases that they use for their strategies. What also has become more apparent is that the acquisition of knowledge in itself is not enough; what also is critical is the availability of knowledge when needed. (Retrieval from memory, which we will discuss later in this chapter, is an example of getting at and using information that we have previously stored.)

Available knowledge also serves another function, that of assisting the individual in deciding what information provided by the problem is pertinent. Analyzing the givens that we have discussed previously illustrates this function. In the problem of the eight

8s, the number of digits is obviously pertinent; what is not as equally pertinent is the manner in which the 8s must be grouped. In this problem, pertinence must emerge from background knowledge, demonstrating that both pertinence and availability of knowledge are key issues in problem solving.

Problem Representation

The first and most basic step in problem solving is to represent the information in either symbolic or diagrammatic form. Symbolic form casts the problem's information in words, letters, or numbers, while diagrammatic form expresses the information by some collection of lines, dots, or angles. The first step, then, in solving a problem is to take the givens and cast them in some form that is more personally meaningful.

Representation may be either internal or external. When we initially begin problem solving, we mentally visualize and arrange the givens, so that all representation commences as internal. There can be as many diverse schemes of internal representation as there are people. First, however, let us examine **external representation.**

external representation *A method of problem solving in which a person uses symbols or some other observable type of representation.*

Following this beginning phase, some of us with almost all problems and all of us with complex problems turn to external representation (drawing parts; expressing the givens as symbols). The value and applicability of our external representation is highly dependent on the quality and perceptiveness of the internal representation.

Lewis and Greene (1982, p. 204) offered the following problem as an example of using internal or external representation, or both.

> **As principal of a school with 1,000 students, you have the task of ordering textbooks for each course. Students can elect to study either a language or a science, and this semester you learn from the language department that 400 students have elected to take Spanish and 300 will take French. One hundred and fifty of the language students want to take both. How many science books must you order to be sure that each student not electing language will have one?**

Once again we have a problem that incorporates much of what we have discussed. It is well-structured, but the givens require careful attention. Although some readers will derive the solution in their heads, others will immediately reach for paper and pencil. A quick reading of the problem might lead you to conclude that 300 science books should be ordered. But note that 150 students are taking both French and Spanish.

Representing the givens externally, you could proceed as follows.

Total number of students	1,000
Taking Spanish	400
Taking French	300
Taking both	150

The total number taking French and Spanish is 700, but 150 of these are the same students; thus, 550 students will take language, leaving 450 students needing science books.

Here we have an excellent example of how external representation can help in problem solving. Wickelgren (1974, pp. 186–187) offered several reasons for the use of external representation.

- Writing down a problem's givens focuses your attention on the most important concepts.
- You begin to see relationships among the givens.
- If the problem is complex, representing the intermediate steps aids memory.
- Some givens, such as tables or graphs, are quite difficult to visualize in detail.

internal representation *A mental model of how to solve a problem.*

In no way is the emphasis on external representation intended to diminish the vital role of **internal representation,** which is the basis of all symbolic and diagrammatic forms.

It is a mistake to conceive of internal representation as an internal copy of an external situation, because internal representation entails adding details to and eliminating details from the original interpretation of information (Hayes, 1989). As a simple

teacher – student

Teaching Students to Construct Graphic Representations

Graphic representations are visual illustrations of verbal statements and can be helpful in understanding problems and in mapping solutions to problems. Many researchers have discussed the uses and effects of graphic representations in problem solving (Bransford, Sherwood, Vye, & Rieser, 1986; Silver, 1987) and in creative thinking (McTighe & Lyman, 1988).

Undoubtedly you are familiar with graphic representations such as flow charts, pie charts, and family trees. Figure A presents other graphic representations that are useful in facilitating students' comprehension, summarizations, and synthesis of complex ideas.

Students who used graphic structures like these were better able to select important ideas and recall details, as well as detect missing information and unrelated connections from the material they read (Jones, Pierce, & Hunter, 1988–1989). These researchers also noted that the use of graphic representations seemed to foster nonlinear thinking and provide input into both visual and verbal modes of pro-

cessing information. Thus, an effective graphic representation can show at a glance the key parts of a whole and their relations, thereby allowing a holistic understanding that words alone can't convey.

Jones and her colleagues recommend a five-step procedure for teaching students to use graphic representations in their work. The five steps are these:

1. Present at least one good example of a graphic outline that matches the type of outline you will teach.
2. Model how to construct either the same graphic outline or the one to be introduced.
3. Provide procedural knowledge about when and why they should use a particular type of graphic structure.
4. Coach students in the use of graphic structures by asking them to explain the structures they choose and then give them feedback about their choices.
5. Give students opportunities to practice outlining with graphic structures and provide them feedback.

"Here's your problem; you had a fold in your plans."

© Dave Carpenter.

Spider map

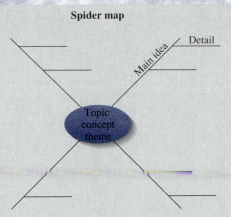

Used to describe a central idea: a thing (a geographic region), process (meiosis), concept (altruism), or proposition with support (experimental drugs should be available to AIDS victims). Key frame questions: What is the central idea? What are its attributes? What are its functions?

Series of events chain

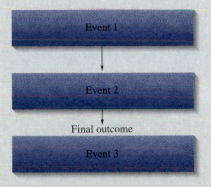

Used to describe the stages of something (the life cycle of a primate); the steps in a linear procedure (how to neutralize an acid); a sequence of events (how feudalism led to the formation of nation states); or the goals, actions, and outcomes of a historical figure or character in a novel (the rise and fall of Napoleon). Key frame questions: What is the object, procedure, or initiating event? What are the stages or steps? How do they lead to one another? What is the final outcome?

Continuum/Scale

Low   High

Used for time lines showing historical events or ages (grade levels in school), degrees of something (weight), shades of meaning (Likert scales), or ratings scales (achievement in school). Key frame questions: What is being scaled? What are the end points?

Compare/Contrast matrix

	Name 1	Name 2
Attribute 1		
Attribute 2		
Attribute 3		

Used to show similarities and differences between two things (people, places, events, ideas, etc.). Key frame questions: What things are being compared? How are they similar? How are they different?

Problem/Solution outline

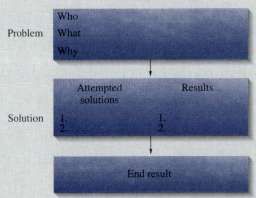

Used to represent a problem, attempted solutions, and results (the national debt). Key frame questions: What was the problem? Who had the problem? Why was it a problem? What attempts were made to solve the problem? Did those attempts succeed?

Figure A

Graphic forms with corresponding text frames. Graphic representations are visual illustrations of verbal statements. Frames are sets of questions or categories that are fundamental to understanding a given topic. Here are shown nine "generic" forms with their corresponding frames. Also given are examples of topics that could be represented by each graphic form. These graphics show at a glance the key parts of the whole and their relations, helping the learner to comprehend text and solve problems.

From B. F. Jones, in Educational Leadership. *Copyright © 1988 B. F. Jones. Reprinted by permission.*

Continued on next page

Network tree

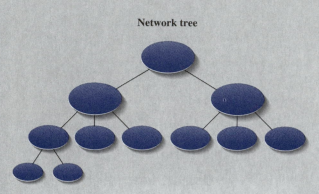

Used to show causal information (causes of poverty), a hierarchy (types of insects), or branching procedures (the circulatory system). Key frame questions: What is the superordinate category? What are the subordinate categories? How are they related? How many levels are there?

Fishbone map

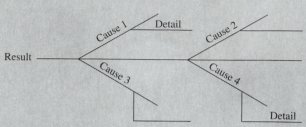

Used to show causal interaction of a complex event (an election, a nuclear explosion) or complex phenomenon (juvenile delinquency, learning disabilities). Key frame questions: What are the factors that cause X? How do they interrelate? Are the factors that cause X the same as those that cause X to persist?

Human interaction outline

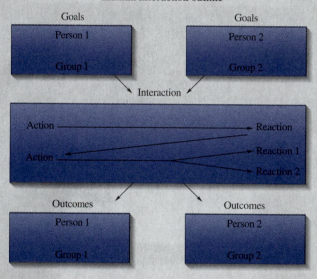

Used to show the nature of an interaction between persons or groups (European settlers and American Indians). Key frame questions: Who are the persons or groups? What are their goals? Did they conflict or cooperate? What was the outcome for each person or group?

Cycle

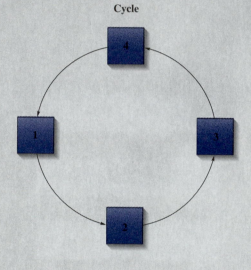

Used to show how a series of events interact to produce a set of results again and again (weather phenomena, cycles of achievement and failure, the life cycle). Key frame questions: What are the critical events in the cycle? How are they related? In what ways are they self-reinforcing?

Figure A concluded

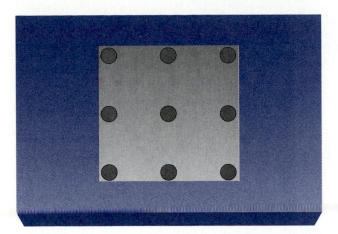

Nine Dots Problem: Without taking your pencil from the paper, connect each of the dots by using four straight lines. Each dot must be touched.

example of Hayes' intent, close your eyes for a moment and picture some location in which you typically relax and enjoy yourself, such as a particular beach. You probably added details that are not part of the beach; people, boats, parasols. You undoubtedly omitted some details that usually are present, such as seaweed. Finally, you probably experienced pleasant feelings as you thought about the beach: you interpreted the data.

Each of us also forms a unique representation of the same circumstances; some of us tend to represent visually and others verbally, while still others may use auditory images. There are no rigid distinctions among these various kinds of representations, although one form is usually dominant; teachers, for example, tend to be quite verbal.

The manner in which we represent a problem determines the ease or difficulty with which we solve it, if we do. A good example of the importance of representation is seen in the classic nine dots problem.

Difficulty arises for those who attempt the following solution.

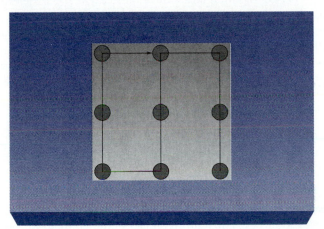

There are variations of this strategy, but they always reach the same conclusion: one dot remains untouched. *You will never solve the nine dots problem until you change your representation,* which you can do if you attend to the givens in the instructions. Nowhere were you told to remain within the confines of a square. (We too often impose limits on ourselves when we face problems!) Once you change your representation, the solution follows easily.

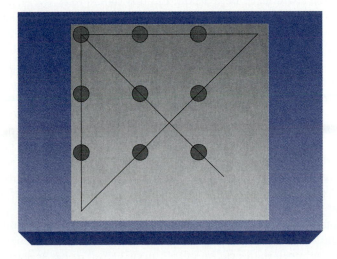

Representation, then, is basic for planning an accurate solution: you should remember, and encourage your students to remember, this advice. If you are having difficulty in solving a problem, consider changing your representation.

Planning the Solution

Once you have a workable representation of the problem, you must devise a plan for its solution, which involves two critical aspects. First, there is the need to be familiar with the core concepts required for solution. If the problem demands basic arithmetic facts, then your students must be able to do the addition or division that is required. We have seen the necessity for conceptual tools in the problem concerning thermodynamics: for those of us lacking prior knowledge in this field, the problem remains insoluble, since we lack the strong strategies.

Second, there is the need to apply certain general strategies that seem appropriate. We have mentioned some of these, such as working backwards, which can be helpful if the goal and givens are stated clearly. Means-end analysis is another general strategy that aids solution when the goal is obvious. Assume that your house needs painting and you decide to do it yourself. The goal is clear, but the means to achieve it requires additional planning.

If the old paint is peeling, then it first must be scraped and roughed up with a wire brush. You must then decide if these spots need priming. Is there hardware you should remove? What kind of paint is best suited to the weather conditions in your area: latex or oil? How you answer this question dictates the kind of paintbrush you should use. Though these steps seem simple, if you omit one—such as scraping—the solution is faulty.

Helping You Plan

Now that you have done the basic preparation for attacking the problem, you can select an array of learning strategies that will help you to formulate a plan for solution. Hayes (1989) suggested seven learning strategies that reflect much of the work we have discussed thus far in this chapter, especially the role of memory.

1. **The Structuring Strategy.** The strategy of structuring is intended to have you search for relations within the learning material; it is a method for discovering structures. What is the relationship among the eight 8s that will enable you to solve the problem? Once you uncover these relations, they may reveal categories, hierarchies, or networks that will help you to understand the material. The use of graphic representations, as described in the previous teacher-student interactions box, is an illustration of a structuring strategy.

   structuring   *The strategy of searching for relations in learning materials.*

2. **The Context Strategy.** In the context strategy, you are again urged to search for relations in the material to be learned. But this differs from the structuring strategy in that the relations may be between the learning material and what we already know. You know that $8 \times 5 = 40$; therefore, you realize that five groups are needed. To repair a two-barrel carburetor is much easier if you have learned how to disassemble a one-barrel carburetor than if you have had no experience whatsoever.

   context   *For Hayes, the strategy of searching for relationships between new material and material that is already known.*

3. **Monitoring.** Monitoring requires that you constantly teach yourself to see what you have or have not learned. In problem solving you can constantly question yourself to determine if each detail of your plan is moving you closer to solution: "Now that I know I need five groups, how many 8s should be in each group?"

   monitoring   *The learning strategy of examining or monitoring one's own learning.*

4. **Inferencing.** Inferencing also involves asking yourself questions, but the questions are not merely factual. They are intended to generate inferences about the material to evaluate its importance or implications for problem solution. In the nine dots problem, you may well begin to wonder, "What would happen if I extended the lines outside the square?" Or in the eight 8s problem, you might ask, "Can I use more than one 8 in each group? How many 8s should be in the first group?"

   inferencing   *A learning strategy involving questioning oneself about the implications of material one has learned.*

instantiation *The strategy of furnishing an example.*

5. **Instantiation.** Instantiation means to furnish an example. Are there problems similar to the one I am attempting to solve? We may also try to create examples for ourselves or others. If you were trying to explain a foul in baseball, your listeners might find it helpful if you told them that if the baseball stayed outside the white lines before it reached either first or third bases, the hit would be called a foul.

multiple coding *Mental representation of a problem in more than one way—for example, verbally and visually.*

6. **Multiple Coding.** Can we represent the information—the givens in our problem—in more than one way: verbally or through mental imagery? Such a process is called multiple coding. As you attempted to solve the problem of the cyclists and the bird, you may have made the givens more meaningful by using them in a story or by forming mental pictures of the cyclists moving toward each other and the bird racing between them.

attention management *A term that refers to the effective use of time.*

7. **Attention Management.** What do you do with your time? If you face a problem, do you find yourself daydreaming? Hayes suggests that you allow yourself enough time to study a problem, organize your schedule, and stay with it.

The Role of Memory

As we saw in chapter 8, one of the most powerful strategies in solving problems is the efficient use of memory. All memory strategies, however, are not equally effective. The appropriateness of the strategy depends on the level of material involved and the conditions under which the information must be remembered. Try this memory problem.

> The following list contains 25 words. Take 90 seconds to study the following words. When time runs out, write as many of the words as you can without looking at the list.

book	light	leaf	pear	tire
page	net	basket	truck	minutes
wheel	orange	referee	court	minutes
ball	branch	word	wrench	brake
apple	sneaker	mirror	tree	column

How did you do? Or more importantly from our perspective, how did you do it? Were these among the strategies you used?

- Rehearse (repeat) each word until you were sure you had memorized it: tire, tire, tire; book, book, book; branch, branch, branch.
- Rehearse several words: ball, apple, referee; ball, apple, referee.
- Organize the words by category. Note that several words related to cars; others could be grouped as fruit; still others could be categorized as relating to books.
- Construct a story to relate as many of the words as possible.
- Form images of words or groups of words.

You may have tried one or a combination of these strategies, but note that you were not told to memorize them in any particular manner. If you had received specific instructions, each of these strategies would not have been equally as effective. When we are asked to remember a particular telephone number, our tendency is to rehearse it for as long as we need to in order to recall it. But if you attempted to memorize these 25 words by straight rehearsal—not by grouping or any other technique—then you undoubtedly could recall only from 5 to 9 words; the average memory span for familiar words is 5.86. If you had been directed to memorize the words in a certain order (the way that they were presented), grouping items by categories would not have been efficient; thinking of a story to link them in the correct order would have been much more efficient (Kail, 1984; Levin, 1993).

Retrieval Aids

storing *The ability to hold information in memory.*

retrieving *Ability to access information in stored memory.*

A major issue for most of us is what psychologists call **storing** and **retrieving.** Much too frequently we have something in memory (we have stored it), but we cannot get at it (we cannot retrieve it). We know what the answer is, but just can't recall it. "It's on the tip of my tongue" is a common expression for a familiar experience, that can't immediately be retrieved.

Think for a moment about the list of words you were asked to memorize. A few of them were probably on the "tip of your tongue." If an instructor were to ask you, "Who is Larry Bird?" you may hesitate. Then the instructor adds, "Boston." It is as if the teacher had opened a door: Bird, Boston, Boston Celtics, basketball, most valuable player.

There are several techniques that can help us to trigger our memory. Among the most effective retrieval aids are the following.

Cues   Although you were supplied with the cue (Boston) in the above example (Larry Bird), the most effective **cues** for your students, as for all of us, are those that they generate themselves. Regardless of the task that we face, we almost always believe that we have learned more than we can recall; we simply cannot "get at" the material. Try this memory problem.

cues   Techniques to help us recall; particularly effective if we generate them ourselves.

Read each of the following sentences once, spending about (no more than) three seconds on each. As soon as you are finished, put the list out of sight and write as many of the sentences as you can recall.

> Thomas Jefferson was a Virginian.
> The tide was high at 10:45 A.M.
> Evergreens are not deciduous.
> Our new car is a turbo diesel.
> The lawnmower has a rotary construction.
> Light travels at the rate of 186 million miles/second.
> John F. Kennedy was born in Brookline, Massachusetts.
> Richard Feynman won the Nobel Prize for physics in 1965.
> In the colder climates, lobsters usually shed their shells in July.
> The new generation of printers is based on laser principles.

Most readers will recall six or seven of these ten sentences. Our interest is in what happened to the other three or four. Did you fail to encode them? Did you lose them almost immediately? Use these words as retrieval cues for the sentences you cannot recall.

laser	rotary
Virginian	deciduous
tide	lobsters
Brookline	light
turbo	Nobel

This time you probably remembered most, if not all, the sentences that you initially failed to retrieve. With instruction and guidance, your students can easily master this technique and will improve not only their problem-solving skills but also their memory in all subjects. Initially, you can teach them how to utilize this technique by providing them with tangible cues for the material you are presenting. Your ultimate objective is to help them devise their own cues for any subject they encounter.

A particularly effective cue is the use of acronyms and acrostics. As mentioned earlier, an acronym is a word consisting of the initial letters in a series of words (DUPE). There is a two-fold value to acronyms: (a) the compression of several facts into a smaller number (recall Miller's magic number of 7 ± 2), and (b) the cues they provide for remembering large amounts of data (DUPE acts as a trigger, releasing the facts incorporated under each letter).

A second strategy is to devise a sentence or phrase with words whose first letters are the cues for certain information. Most of us who are nonmusicians have relied on an acrostic to recall the lines in the G clef.

E very
G ood
B oy
D oes
F ine

Using an acrostic is an effective strategy, as long as the material is not too complicated or unique. The strategy should never be more difficult than the task; the goal is to simplify!

Imagery   Some students—as well as readers—tend to visualize objects or events; they function more efficiently in this mode, rather than relying on verbal processes that are less dependent on concreteness. You can encourage the use of **imagery** in all students, and they will find it helpful.

Urge them to form a picture that links the items that they are to remember. For example, if students must remember that John Adams was the second president of the United States, ask them to picture Adams standing for a portrait and holding a large card with the number 2 on it. For those students who function best in this mode, and even for those who are more verbal, the use of imagery can aid retention and recall.

imagery   *The ability to visualize objects or events.*

The Method of Loci   The above techniques are excellent, provided that the retrieval cues are appropriate. Lacking appropriate stimuli, however, you still can devise personal cues to help you remember and recall unrelated items. The **method of loci**—using familiar locations—was originally used by the Greeks and Romans to recall items in a fixed sequence. By utilizing a series of familiar visual images and linking each image to an object to be retained, you will have formulated your personal retrieval cues.

method of loci   *The use of familiar locations to help one visually store things in memory and retrieve them more easily.*

Since the rooms in your house are firmly locked in your memory, they are suitable "locations" in which to place the items to be remembered. First, form an image of the object that you must recall; second, place it somewhere in one of the rooms. Use each location only once; if you placed the word "educational psychology" on the couch in the living room, do not use that specific location again. Try using the method of loci.

Here are several words that I would like you to be able to define and use. Map out a path that you would take in your home, arranging the rooms along the path in the most economical manner possible. Now "picture" each word and place it somewhere on your route.

> assimilation
> concrete operations
> learning
> locus of control
> cognitive
> attribution
> value
> strategy
> iconic
> accommodation

Elaboration   To elaborate is to add information to what you are trying to learn so that the material becomes more personally meaningful. According to Weinstein and others (1988/1989), "Elaboration involves using what we already know to help make sense of what we are trying to learn. 'What we already know' includes our prior knowledge, our experiences, our attitudes, our beliefs, and our values" (Weinstein et al., 1988/1989, pp. 17–18).

Elaboration strategies that improve students' recall of material are effective because they produce an increased depth of processing (more involvement with material). Elaboration also facilitates storage of new information with related information that is well known to the learner (Weinstein & Mayer, 1986). The effective use of elaboration strategies depends on students' relating what they are trying to learn to what they already know. The way learners enact this strategy can involve a number of specific tactics, such as creating analogies, paraphrasing, summarizing in their own words, transforming information into other forms, such as charts or diagrams, using comparison and contrast methods, and trying to teach what they are learning to someone else.

elaboration   *The adding of information to what one is trying to learn so the material becomes more personally meaningful.*

Teachers can help students develop fluent and flexible elaboration tactics by encouraging them to answer questions about the material they are learning. Questions that have been shown to be helpful include these:

• What is the main idea of this story?
• What does this material remind me of?
• How can I put this into my own words?
• What is a good example of this that I am familiar with?
• How does this apply to my life?

Teachers can help students to use elaboration tactics by creating opportunities for students to answer questions like those above and then test their recall of the information they have acquired.

These are the most prominent of several techniques designed to improve retention and recall. They can be extremely helpful to you and your students if you remember two warnings: (a) be sure that the strategy itself is not so complex and cumbersome that it requires more effort to remember than the content does; (b) be sure that you and your students adopt techniques that are best suited to you. Your personal style should determine the strategy with which you are most comfortable.

Finally, try to devise your own method of improving retention. When you are faced with the task of mastering material, how do you go about it? What is your general strategy? Now, apply the suggestions just offered to refine and improve your strategy.

For example, a student will occasionally describe a strategy of attempting to visualize the page on which the material to be memorized is located. If this is successful, the words on that particular page seem to come alive in memory. Performance could be aided by suggesting the use of cues within this student's preferred general strategy.

You can improve your memory by:

• knowing as much about different techniques as possible
• discovering those techniques that seem to work particularly well for you
• practicing, practicing, practicing

These techniques for improving memory are intended to be used with other strategies discussed in this section, so that you have a wide variety of choices to help you select the most effective plan possible, one that is most pertinent for a particular problem. With this accomplished, it is time to move to the evaluation stage of the DUPE model.

Evaluating the Solution

If all has gone well, you have formulated a plan that incorporates careful attention to the givens, either an internal or an external representation of the problem (or both), and a plan that you can effectively use. Evaluation now plays an important role in your search for a solution.

Examining Your Plan and Solution

Two aspects of evaluation seem especially pertinent:

1. *The necessity to stop here and evaluate the plan.* Does it include all of the vital givens? Does your representation account for the givens in a way that reflects the essence of the problem? Does your plan use both the vital facts and your representation of the problem so that it is calculated to reach the required solution?

2. *A second evaluative phase, after the plan has been tried.* If your answers to the question above and similar questions are affirmative, then the first evaluative phase is complete, and you should activate your plan. After you have worked through the plan, the second evaluative phase allows you to decide if you have found a solution or if you are totally satisfied with the solution that you have achieved. As Hayes (1989, p. 46) noted, the critical question in evaluation is this: Does the answer I proposed meet all of the goals and conditions set by the problem? If you were told to solve for x, the mere fact that you have x on one side of your equation and everything else on the other does not necessarily mean that you are right.

As one means of addressing the issues raised by evaluation, Sternberg (1982) introduced the concept of "component," which he defines as an elementary information process that operates upon internal representations of objects or symbols. One class of the derivatives of components is what Sternberg designated as *metacomponents,* higher-order control processes used in planning, determining alternate courses of action, and monitoring the success of the plan. Metacomponents activate and receive feedback from other components, thus insuring a constant monitoring process. Though the existence of metacomponents may be highly speculative, Sternberg's work indicates intense interest in the evaluative phase of problem solving.

What happens if you negatively answer the evaluative question just posed: "No, I have not reached the correct solution." You must continue the search process and not let frustration halt your continued search. We are all creative to a certain extent, and knowledge about the creative process may help you through these periods of frustration.

Creativity and Evaluation

Have you ever done something totally novel, at least for you? Have you fit a part into a toaster or iron so that it works? Have you discovered a solution to a math problem, a solution that was not in the back of the book? Creative behavior involves acts that are both novel and of value. Thus creativity can be a critical part of the problem-solving evaluation process. As Perkins noted (1981), there is nothing odd or novel about the idea of inventing behavior to help with thinking, problem solving, or invention. Discussing the notion of generating novel solutions when other efforts are blocked, Perkins described the results of research on heuristics that has emerged from recent analyses of "teaching thinking."

Heuristics

Assume that you are frustrated in your efforts to solve a particular problem. You have used all the suggested techniques: attention to detail, breaking into parts, forming representations, searching for relationships. None of these well-known techniques helps. *Therefore, you must generate new solutions.* One way is by teaching yourself (and your students) to use alternative search strategies in a process called **heuristics.**

Perkins contrasts heuristics with algorithms. An algorithm is a precise series of steps that leads to a solution. Solving for the perimeter of a rectangle is a good example; you must place the correct expressions on the proper side of the equation and then solve for x by a series of definite steps. Using algorithms to solve many (if not most) of your problems is impossible, especially with ill-defined daily problems. Consequently, we tend to use heuristics and engage in searches that are highly selective (that is, highly individualistic) and usually incomplete. Then why use them?

Identify characteristics of a "good problem solver" and explain how you can help a student acquire these characteristics.

heuristics *The use of alternative search patterns to solve problems; the generation of new possible solutions.*

Heuristics are personal guidelines based on your knowledge, your experiences, your learning style, and your choice of strategies. They are effective when they call your attention to overlooked facts, hidden relationships, ties to something you already know. They can be effective even while being incomplete, because they initiate a different kind of effort, a different type of search. All the evidence need not be present before you reach a solution. Recall the Gestalt principle of closure and examine the drawing to the right. You instantly identified a circle. Heuristics function in exactly the same way. What do we know about creative individuals that could help us in our work with students?

The Creative Student

Who are the creative students? Remember that *creative* is not identical with *gifted*. Giftedness is too restricted an interpretation of creativity, since it has been amply demonstrated that intelligence test items have a low correlation with creativity (Dacey, 1989a). Among the characteristics of creative people are the following:

- *Cognitive Skills*. Certain cognitive elements are necessary for creative thinking. These include memory and evaluation. Divergent elements, such as originality, flexibility, and sensitivity, are indispensable. Another outstanding characteristic of the creative thinker is the ability to sense problems, the realization that some ambiguity exists.
- *Motivation-Interest*. Creative people are curious; they like to manipulate ideas. They have a high achievement need that is linked with an intellectual persistence. They seek challenges, prefer the complex, and can tolerate uncertainty. They like to look at things in a new way (Dacey, 1989a). An inevitable conclusion is that creative thinkers have an intense commitment to their work.
- *Personality*. Creative persons are independent, inclined to take risks, resourceful, adventurous, and complex. They also possess an excellent sense of humor and see themselves as getting along well with others (Dacey, 1989a).

As a teacher, you are probably most interested in discovering if there are any links between age and creativity. There seem to be three stages of creative change (Lesner & Hillman, 1983):

1. *From birth to 11 years old* is a period of "creative internal enrichment," during which children develop their own distinct personalities;
2. *From 12 to 60 years old* is a time of "creative external enrichment," during which there occurs a transition to a more outward, socially aware orientation;
3. *From age 60 to death* is a period of "creative self-evaluation," during which individuals assess their life accomplishments.

Dacey (1989b) made a more recent attempt to address this issue. Noting that most people, under the right circumstances, can greatly improve their creative ability, Dacey (1989b) argued that there are six peak periods in the growth of creativity, which follow these general age guidelines:

For Males	For Females
1. 0–5 years	0–5 years
2. 11–14 years	10–13 years
3. 18–20 years	18–20 years
4. 29–31 years	29–31 years
5. 40–45 years	40–45 years
6. 60–65 years	60–65 years

These are the periods that seem more intellectually volatile than others, and Dacey argued that substantial increases in creativity are less likely with each succeeding period. For our purposes, note how the first three periods include both preschool and school years. Of particular importance is the 10- to 14-year-old period. Noting that students of this age are attempting to define their self-concepts, Dacey asserted that this is an ideal time to foster creativity, because these students are open to new ideas as they intensify their searches for their identities.

How can you help your students to fulfill their creative potential? There is nothing trivial about any discussion of creativity: society urgently needs a steady supply of creative minds to insure not only its progress but its very survival. Creativity by its very nature requires fertile grounds in which to flourish, one of which, and perhaps the most important of which, is the classroom. To help you think about your classroom as a stimulating environment for creative behavior, consider the following general suggestions.

- *Try to ensure that the material you use to encourage creativity in the classroom matches the developmental level of the child.* If you recall Piaget's stages of cognitive development, you will remember that young children can have difficulty with material that is too abstract; at these early stages, although you can encourage them to be innovative, you must also use content suitable for their cognitive abilities.
- *Give children experience in deriving as many different responses to a problem as possible.* Select an item such as a book and ask students to think of as many uses as possible for it. List them on the board and then ask the children for more uses. You are fostering divergent thinking, not just requiring one correct answer. What can you do with a book? Obviously, read it. But you can also use it as a doorstop, a weight, or even a ruler in an emergency.
- *Ask students to imagine, to go beyond the data.* For example, assume that the class is studying the opening of the American West. They could write essays that incorporate the basic facts but go far beyond them. A popular book takes the life of General Custer, presents the facts, and then asks the reader to assume that Custer, critically wounded, survived Little Big Horn and had to stand trial for his role in the massacre. *The Trial of George Armstrong Custer* is a lesson in creativity. Try something like it.
- *Encourage your students to search for relationships.* Creativity tests often ask you to name one word that can be linked to others. Devise lists that are appropriate for your students and that require similar thinking.
- *Help your students to tolerate ambiguity.* This ability is one of the most important aspects of creativity. Fear of failure and fear of the unknown usually drive individuals (especially children) to reach some solution, suitable or not. Directly teach students that it is better to pause, to muse, to think of alternatives, to search for the better way.

In addition to fostering creative behavior, you can encourage students to become more flexible in their approaches to problem solving by using techniques that teach them about themselves. Here is one fairly simple method.

How can you foster creative behavior in a young student?

TEACHING PROBLEM-SOLVING TECHNIQUES

Strategies that cut across situations and that are not confined to specific subjects are those that will concern us in this section, which introduces the topic of the transfer of learning.

Helping Students to Transfer Their Learning

Once you have taught students basic knowledge, learning strategies, and problem-solving techniques, you want them to use these tools in a variety of situations and not to think of them as applying only to the classroom. *Transfer of learning* refers to attempts to understand how learning one topic influences later learning.

Solving interpersonal problems is a challenge that confronts all students and adults. Learning how to get along with others, how to communicate successfully to avoid disputes, and how to help in ways that do not hinder others requires many of the same problem-solving skills that we have presented as relevant to solving academic problems. Teaching students to be good social problem solvers has become an important part of social skills, drug prevention, and sexual awareness programs in many schools today. The basis for many of these programs is the work on *Interpersonal Cognitive Problem Solving* or *ICPS* (Spivak & Shure, 1974).

Interpersonal Cognitive Problem Solving (ICPS) was originally designed to teach young children how to think, not what to think. In other words, the goal was to teach children a process for thinking about problems they would encounter, not the solutions to the problems. Teaching solutions would be an endless task for even the best teacher, so the goal of any ICPS program is to teach students to identify alternative solutions to problems and to evaluate each solution on the basis of its potential consequences. Six specific problem-solving skills constitute the major instructional components of ICPS.

- *Alternative solution thinking*. This component stimulates students to search for new solutions by combining old solutions or by inventing truly new solutions.
- *Consequential thinking*. This component involves students making predictions about possible outcomes of various actions they might take and evaluating the outcomes.
- *Causal thinking*. This component stresses the relationships between events and requires students to have the ability to relate one event to another over time. Causal thinking is a more direct or exacting extension of consequential thinking.
- *Interpersonal sensitivity*. This component concerns one's awareness that an interpersonal problem actually exists. Given that students (and adults) do not always perceive that a problem exists between themselves and others, it is necessary to teach them to listen to and observe others' actions and attitudes.
- *Means-ends thinking*. This component involves planning a step-by-step plan to achieve a given goal. Students initially must identify their goal and then consider systematically the resources and skills needed to reach their goal. Finally, they must plan for setbacks and not being able to reach a goal immediately.
- *Perspective taking*. This component emphasizes that different people have different motives and viewpoints, and thus may respond differently in any given situation. Perspective taking involves role taking and empathy, and thus is a complex cognitive skill for many students.

Research investigating the application of ICPS has been conducted with mixed results. Most of the major reservations about ICPS concern research methodology (e.g., absence of control groups, bias in evaluations of teachers who have been actively involved in ICPS training, the use of many other training components such as modeling and coaching along with ICPS). It is widely agreed, however, that the thinking and acting skills stressed in the ICPS approach are meaningful and are significantly related to successful interpersonal relationships. Research and the application of ICPS and its problem-solving subcomponents will most certainly continue in schools.

The original ICPS work of Spivack and Shure has influenced many psychologists and educators interested in the development of students' social competence. For example, ICPS is a major component in the popular *Think Aloud* classroom program (Camp & Bosh, 1981) and in *The Prepare Curriculum* (Goldstein, 1988). The problem-solving components of ICPS are also evident in a parenting program entitled *Teach Your Child Decision Making* (Clabby and Elias, 1987). Figure A is from the *Think Aloud* classroom program and illustrates a basic four-step problem-solving sequence: state the problem, think about alternative plans, select a plan and carry it out, and self-evaluate the plan's success. Programs like *Think Aloud* and *The Prepare Curriculum* originally were designed for use with aggressive and impulsive students, but as they have been used more, teachers are finding that all students can benefit from learning how to be good problem solvers.

The think aloud classroom program

1 — What is my problem?
2 — How can I do it?
3 — Am I using my plan?
4 — How did I do?

Figure A
"What is my problem?"

From Think Aloud: Increasing Social and Cognitive Skills—A Problem-Solving Program for Children *(Primary Level: pp. 43–46) by M. A. S. Bash and B. W. Camp, 1985, Champaign, IL: Research Press. Copyright 1985 by the authors. Reprinted by permission.*

Transfer may be positive, such as when learning one topic helps students to learn another: knowing how to add and subtract helps them to master long division. It may also be negative, however, such as when learning one topic hinders the learning of another: knowing one word processing program may interfere with the learning of a new, more powerful program.

Influences on Transfer

Certain conditions influence what and how much will be transferred. Among these are the following (Ellis & Hunt, 1989).

- *Task similarity exercises a strong influence on transfer.* Imagine changing the color of the traffic lights that govern our driving. Instead of stopping at a red light, we must now stop at the orange signal. Would this bother us? Not too much, because orange is similar to red, and it would be relatively easy to transfer the stopping habit. Learning to make the same response to new but similar stimuli usually produces positive transfer.

   Now let's change the conditions. Instead of stopping at red, we must stop at green and go on red. The pattern will be completely reversed. What will happen? Drivers, making new and opposite responses to red and green, will undoubtedly get into more accidents. Here we see an instance of negative transfer: what was previously learned interferes with the new learning. Is it any wonder that students can have difficulty with some English sounds? How will you sound *ou:* as it is pronounced in *though,* in *tough,* or in *ouch?* In your teaching, be alert to the impact that similarity can have on transfer.

- *The degree of original learning is an important element in transfer.* More practice on and greater familiarity with the original material produces more positive transfer. If students are thoroughly familiar with multiplication, for example, they have little trouble determining how much 8 apples at 9¢ each will cost them while shopping.

- *Personal variables such as intelligence, motivation, and past experiences are important, but difficult-to-control, influences on transfer.* Your personal knowledge of your students will help you to ensure transfer, since you know something about the extent of their past learning. You can usually relate some aspect of their experiences to new material, thus facilitating transfer. For example, knowing places that your students have visited can make a social studies lesson more meaningful for an entire class.

For the Classroom

For transfer to occur, students must see similar elements in both situations and must have a good grasp of the original material. Courses in driver education should produce students who in fact obtain their driving licenses and have good safety records. If algebra is intended to be used in physics and chemistry classes, then students should demonstrate this transfer in their science classes. Here are several suggestions that will help your students to be aware of the value of transfer.

- *Teach to overlearning.* The more experience students have with the material to be transferred, the more successful will be the transfer. A good idea is to give verbal examples of how material can be transferred and then provide circumstances that encourage your students to use the material. In class discussions, assignments, and quizzes, urge your students to search for transfer.

- *Be certain that the material you teach is well organized.* Meaningful material is more easily transferred. We have previously mentioned how important it is for students to recognize the organization and structure of material. If you can bring them to this realization, they will discover principles and generalizations that they can use in many situations. For example, if students thoroughly grasp the reasons for Lincoln's desire not to punish the Southern states, they will transfer this knowledge to modern times and appreciate why presidents tolerate dissent for the sake of national unity.

- *Use advance organizers if possible.* When you are about to teach abstract material, it may be useful to furnish your students with Ausubel's "advance organizers." These general principles will help your students to see that the abstract material they are encountering possesses more structure than it would if they met it unprepared. You must know both your students and the subject to formulate effective advance organizers: your introductory work reflects what you think is important, and it must match your students' ability level.

- *Emphasize the similarity between classroom work and the transfer situation.* If you are concerned with transfer, you must attempt to make the classroom condition similar to the transfer situation. For example, most algebra tests involve word problems; consequently, as soon as possible have your students work with word problems, perhaps incorporating terms from chemistry and physics. If you teach reading, be sure that the letters and words you teach have the same forms that the youngsters will see in their readers. Sometime during your teaching, students should receive practice under conditions similar to those in the working or transfer environment.

- *Specify what is important in the task.* Identifying the important features of a task helps youngsters to transfer these elements or to guard against potential difficulties. For example, children frequently confuse *b* with *d,* so teachers should stress the distinction and give them considerable experience with words containing these letters. In algebra, students consistently forget to change signs (+, −) when moving terms from one side of an equation to the other. Instructors should constantly call students' attention to the required change of sign, while providing numerous instances that require transposition.

- *Try to understand how students perceive the possibility of transfer.* Instructors teach what they know and have organized. But how do students view the process? Is it meaningful to them? Do they see how they can use the material in different circumstances? If you attempt to see your teaching and the subject from your students' viewpoint, you may present it quite differently, capitalizing more on their backgrounds, and offering more practical possibilities of transfer. This is more easily said than done, but once you try it, you will be more conscious of the need for emphasizing strategies, meaning, organization, and structure.

Using Problem-Solving Strategies

Among the many suggestions for achieving the goal of using problem-solving strategies are the following:

- *Problem-solving instruction should begin with content that students are comfortable with;* only gradually should you introduce slightly different notions (Rummelhart & Norman, 1981). For example, before you ask students what they think caused the changing political climate in Eastern Europe, they should have a basic knowledge of the geography and history of these nations.

- *Consciously choose direct or indirect instruction.* In his discussion of problem-solving methods, Doyle (1983) distinguished between direct and indirect instruction; in direct instruction, the tasks are clearly defined, with definite steps for mastering each step for solution. Indirect instruction involves less clearly defined tasks, and students use considerable self-discovery in their striving for solution. Instruction is intended to provide opportunities for students to initiate their own generalizations and procedures.

For those students who need help in solving problems, direct instruction is probably best. You could begin by asking them for reasons why an oppressed people would risk overthrowing their government, after first discussing with them ideas of freedom, self-determination, and the like. Then, as their problem-solving abilities grow, switch to more indirect methods by posing more general questions, such as asking them to consider what neighboring countries would do in this situation.

Doyle believes direct instruction is most suitable for teaching elementary school students, those with low ability, and those who lack expertise in a particular

teacher – student

Using Problem-Solving Strategies in the Classroom

From our discussion thus far we can be encouraged by the knowledge that our students can improve their problem-solving methods. Here are a few pertinent suggestions based on the work reviewed in this chapter that you should find useful.

1. *Analyze the difficulties in individual student's problem-solving behavior.* These difficulties usually result from any or all of five causes:
   a. *Intelligence.* Even if some students have relatively low ability, you can still improve their problem-solving technique, but keep the problem manageable for them; that is, the problem cannot be too abstract. For those of greater ability, problems should become progressively more abstract. Show these students films and filmstrips about England; show them pictures of, and discuss the merits of, some of England's great leaders over the years. In this way, gradually lead them to understand England's emergence as a world leader.
   b. *Motivation.* Often students are so discouraged by previous attempts to solve problems that they either stop immediately or guess. No one has taken the time to help them. If you provide tangible help and manageable problems, they will show immediate improvement. Keep the problems simple at first, such as tracing the factors that led to England's rise. Combine a manageable problem with teaching the problem-solving strategies that we have discussed in this chapter.
   c. *Information.* Either the problem does not provide sufficient data, or students cannot relate information they possess to the problem. You must know your students so that you can satisfactorily match problem with student. In working with your students, be sure that the problem has sufficient "givens" for them to recognize. A good technique to use here is means-end analysis: do I have the means to solve this problem?
   d. *Experience.* In initially attempting to solve problems, students are usually bewildered. You must actively demonstrate techniques and then let them practice with simple problems. Once you have brought your students to a realization that

they have solved a problem–England's status, for example–then emphasize the techniques that they used and point out how they can be used in different situations.
   e. *Mind-set.* Teach students to look initially for several possible solutions and to test them mentally to determine which is most feasible. Emphasize that they should not necessarily use the first solution they think of. For example, if the class is mature enough, you could have them try both the nine-dot and the cyclists problems.

2. *Correct students' difficulties.* Teach students to search diligently for clues that organize the problem and to use their existing knowledge, plus the problem's data, to solve it. By urging students to separate the problem into meaningful parts, you not only aid analysis by helping them to simplify it, but also encourage a more positive attitude about their ability to solve problems. In this way, you have taught them to think, not only of England, but *about ways of solving a problem.*

3. *Teach–directly teach–problem-solving techniques.* Do not assume that presenting a problem to students will automatically activate some problem-solving mechanism. Teach the ideas discussed here and stress the use of errors. Help them to use their errors. "No, Betty. It wasn't just its army that helped England. When you look at all that water around it, it must have needed what?"

   Students must learn to expect errors, but not to cease searching for a solution. Why was it an error? At what stage? Do I need more information? Can I use here what I learned elsewhere? These are the questions that can help students to use errors intelligently.

4. *Give your students the opportunity to solve problems.* Success in life is determined by the ability to see, to analyze, and to solve problems. Admittedly it is a time-consuming process, and it would be much easier to tell students the answer. But that offers little support when they meet other, different obstacles. It is the technique that will transfer and assist your students in all situations. Nowhere in your teaching can you better serve your students than by helping them to remove those intellectual blocks that both frustrate and defeat.

subject. Indirect instruction is best suited for those students who possess the required knowledge base and general strategies.

- *Institute a good instructional program.* Frederiksen (1984) commented that among the attributes of such a program are the following: instruction in the necessary knowledge base (teach your students what they need to know about England's rise to great power status); instruction in strategies for developing internal representations (picture this string of small islands that became powerful); and finally, linking of what is known about problem-solving processes to teaching techniques (teach according to the DUPE model), using such techniques as means-end analysis, identifying goals and subgoals, and changing internal representations. These general strategies resist application without considerable domain-specific knowledge.

APPLICATIONS AND REFLECTIONS

Chapter Highlights

Thinking Skills

- Educators today believe that students need more than facts; they need those skills and strategies that enable them to adapt to constant change.

Intelligence and Thinking

- Given the more restricted view that educators and psychologists now have of intelligence tests, new theories of intelligence have appeared that offer considerable support for the role of thinking skills in the curriculum.
- Sternberg's triarchic model attempts to explain what intelligence "should do." By recognizing a range of intelligence encompassing many skills, from metacognitive to contextual, he provided a qualitative means of devising thinking skills programs for each segment of the model.
- Many psychologists have long sought an explanation of intelligence that accounts for its varied nature. Gardner proposed a theory of multiple intelligences to address this issue; his theory contains clear implications for teaching and learning.
- Concerned about narrow views of intelligence, Perkins has concentrated upon thinking skills that are designed to supplement his view of tactical intelligence. Perkins introduced the term "thinking frames" to indicate those representations that guide our thought processes.

Thinking Skills: An Analysis

- Bloom's Taxonomy of Educational Objectives is intended to specify desirable cognitive objectives in behavioral terms, to suggest means of evaluating the attainment of these goals, and to aid in curriculum construction.
- Costa's Thinking Skills program is based upon knowledge of how the brain works, humans' awareness of their own thinking, and the acquiring of knowledge. He urged that an information processing model should be the basis for teaching, learning, and curriculum construction.

Problem Solving

- Though some students are probably better than others at solving problems, the problem-solving ability of all students can be improved.
- Difficulty in solving problems can come from simple mistakes, such as failing to use all of the clues present in the problem.
- Problem-solving strategies can be divided into general and specific (also called strong) techniques. General strategies are those that may be used in any situation, while specific strategies are used for particular topics.
- Multicultural students may possess particular problem-solving skills that cultural differences mask and that may remain hidden unless teachers are aware of a culture's expectations.
- Various models, such as DUPE, have been proposed to help in solving problems. DUPE stands for determining the nature of the problem, understanding the nature of the problem, planning the solution, and evaluating the solution.

- Identifying the "givens" of a problem and then deciding what actions can be performed on them helps to specify the problem's goal, that is, to "bridge the gap" between where one is and where one wants to go.
- Understanding the nature of a problem means identifying the nature of the problem and also representing it.
- Representing a problem means casting its information in either symbolic (internal) or graphic (external) form.
- Evaluation of a problem-solving plan can occur at two stages: after the plan is devised (is it adequate?) and after the solution is proposed (did it work?).

Teaching Problem-Solving Techniques

- If you are well-versed in the various problem-solving strategies, you can teach them to your students as a form of knowledge. Perhaps the best advice to remember is this: Directly teach problem-solving techniques.

Connections

1. Think about how you learn and describe how one of the major concepts discussed in this chapter is part of your learning activities or approach.

2. Identify at least one learning situation (e.g., classroom instruction, self-study, taking a test, small-group work) and describe how you would apply one of the key concepts examined in this chapter *if you were a teacher*.

Getting the Picture and Drawing Relationships

Think about the various learning concepts and variables discussed in this chapter. Create pictures, graphics, or figures that highlight relationships among the key components.

Personal Journal

What I really learned in this chapter was _____

_____

_____

_____

What this means to me is _____

_____

_____

_____

Questions that were stimulated by this chapter include _____

_____

_____

_____

Key Terms

attention management	313	incidental learning	294	multiple coding	313
cognitive research trust		inferencing	312	multiple intelligences	282
(CoRT)	295	instantiation	313	performance components	281
context	312	instrumental enrichment	294	practical intelligence	291
critical thinking	280	internal representation	307	retrieving	313
cues	314	knowledge-acquisition		storing	313
DUPE	303	components	281	strong strategy	301
elaboration	315	mediated learning	294	structuring	312
enculturation	285	metacognition	297	thinking frames	285
external representation	307	metacomponents	281	thinking skills	280
heuristics	317	method of loci	315	triarchic theory of	
imagery	315	monitoring	312	intelligence	281

Barbara Cotter, the senior high English teacher we met earlier, was worried about the motivational level of one of her classes, which lacked the "spark" that she felt with other classes. There were twenty-five students, some of whom would finish their formal academic work at high school graduation; the others would go on to college.

What particularly bothered her was that she was excited about this new course, entitled "Contemporary American Authors," but her students weren't. It wasn't that the class was troublesome; they just sat there passively. She considered this course to be her favorite and believed she knew the material as well as any-

lish major in college, was quite frank. "You know, Ms. Cotter, we all thought we would like this class, but I'm not sure that the direction it's going in meets my needs for college. What's the purpose of the stories we're reading? What are they related to?"

At that, Susan, a quiet student who usually said little but who did well on her written work, shyly raised her hand and said, "If I'm going to be able to go to college, I'll need as much financial support as possible. So I need good marks—but I find it hard to study for this class. I know you're excited about the stories. But as Tom said, where are we going with them? What are we expected to get out of our work?"

chapter 10

motivation in the classroom

one. She had a wealth of knowledge and could present the material in considerable detail.

She was a good teacher. During five years of teaching English at this level, she had received favorable evaluations from both students and administrators. She had been an English major in college and was continuing her English studies in a graduate Master of Arts program.

Barbara was honest enough with herself to realize that the students probably weren't the only source of the problem. Even her best students, those who planned to major in English in college, were indifferent. They seemed unable to share her enthusiasm about the stories they discussed in class. "Let's face it," Barbara said to herself, "there's really no discussion. It's turned out to be a forty-minute lecture."

"What can I do to motivate them? I know; I know," she thought, "I can't motivate them. They have to become motivated themselves. Still, I have to do something."

First, she decided that she should be brutally honest with herself and with her students. Consequently, at the beginning of the next class she mentioned to her students that she was concerned about their lack of enthusiasm. She was surprised at their immediate response. Tom, a good student who planned to be an Eng-

Le Yang, who had entered this school in November, stood up. "I know my English isn't perfect," he said carefully, "and perhaps I don't understand what's needed for class discussion. But I study a lot and pay attention in class. I just don't know why I'm not doing better."

Zack, an outstanding athlete who the teacher felt could do much better, surprised her by saying, "You're a good teacher, Ms. Cotter. You can tell from what's been said that we all like you. But something about the class bothers us. We just seem to pick apart the stories. You know so much about them that I'm afraid to ask questions; I'd probably sound stupid. I just don't know what I'm supposed to get out of them. Are the stories supposed to teach us how to write? Or are the themes of the stories what's important? Should we relate them to current events?"

Elaine, who often was dramatic, sighed and said, "I would love to be a writer. Maybe if we used more examples of today's writers, I would be more excited." ∎

As you read this chapter, keep in mind the dilemma of the teacher in the chapter's opening. Faced with a class of unresponsive students—many of whom she admitted were good students—Barbara Cotter was perplexed. What was keeping them from participating in class discussions? Why were they simply "going

Motivation: Meaning and Myths 330
What Are the Myths About Motivation? 330
Motivation to Learn 331
Intrinsic and Extrinsic Motivation 332

What Causes Motivation? 334
Humanistic Psychology and Motivation 334
Cognitive Psychology and Motivation 336
Achievement and Motivation 336
Attribution Theory and Motivation 337
Behavioral Psychology and Motivation 339
Social Cognitive Learning and Motivation 340

What Affects Students' Motivation? 342
Anxiety 342
Attitudes 344
Curiosity 346
Locus of Control 347
Learned Helplessness 348
Self-Efficacy and Motivation 350
Cooperative Learning and Motivation 354
Motivation and Multicultural Students 355

Educational Implications of Motivation 357
The Beginning of Learning 357
During Learning 359
When Learning Ends 360

Applications and Reflections 361

through the motions"? How could she get at the roots of the problem? Reading about the importance and critical role of motivation in learning will help you to assume the role of either teacher or student when you return to this case after finishing the chapter, and to offer suggestions for improvement.

Motivation is a subject that intrigues teachers, because they realize—both through their professional training and instinctively—that this is an issue that can mean the difference between success and failure in the classroom. The study of motivation also illustrates how educational psychology can reach into classrooms and offer significant direction to everyone interested in improving the quality of education. For example, in his history of motivational research, Weiner (1990a) noted that psychologists recently have focused on clarifying classroom goals (both teachers' and stu-

dents') in an attempt to improve student achievement.

When you complete your reading of this chapter, you should be able to answer these questions about motives, students, and the classroom.

- What causes motivation? We will examine some theories that attempt to explain the nature of motivation.
- What affects students' motives? This section will concentrate on those states (anxiety, curiosity, attitudes) that influence student behavior.
- What are the effects of motivation? We will relate motivational knowledge to a positive classroom atmosphere.
- What are the educational implications of motivation? We will examine the specific relationship of motivation to both teaching and learning.

MOTIVATION: MEANING AND MYTHS

When teachers ask about motivation, they want to know what causes a student to act in a particular way. To answer this question, we must first attempt to understand what is meant by motivation, a central construct in both educational and psychological research for the past sixty years (Weiner, 1990a). No single best definition of motivation is recognized; we will think of motivation as consisting of three interrelated components: *personal goals, personal agency beliefs,* and *emotions* (Ford, 1992).

Although we'll discuss goals in greater length later in the chapter, here we are using the term *goal* to signify what students find personally meaningful. This may help to explain part of Barbara Cotter's problem in the chapter opening. Her excitement and enthusiasm about the new English course obviously were not shared by her students. *Goals assigned by teachers become motivational only if they are adopted by students as their personal goals* (Ford, 1992, pp. 73–74).

Personal agency beliefs refer to your students' beliefs that they have the abilities to attain goals. They must be realistic beliefs, based on your helping them to identify the means to attain goals. For example, one of your students decides to enter an essay contest on "The Changing Face of America." Motivated by her belief that this is something she can do, plus her willingness to work at it, she feels more confident because of your support: your guidance in a computer search for appropriate immigration data and your agreeing to edit the final version of the paper. Consequently, both her own assessment of her ability and her realization that she will receive important assistance from her teacher should help this student to feel confident about submitting an essay worthy of careful consideration.

You are probably aware of the role of *emotions* in arousing behavior, but less familiar with the close association between goals and emotions (Ford, 1992). How does this relate to motivation? Think for a moment about how you feel when you attain something that you have worked hard for. You *feel* good; your subjective emotional reaction reflects the degree of success or failure that you think you have achieved. Students react in the same way: they *feel* pleased and competent when they have achieved a worthwhile goal.

We can now use these ideas to define motivation. *Motivation arouses, sustains, directs, and integrates behavior.* When you are motivated, or when you observe that your students are motivated, you usually can discover the source of the motivation. Something acts on you, or on your students, to produce a certain kind of behavior, which is maintained at a certain level of intensity and directed toward a definite goal. For example, one of your students may be promised a ticket to a rock concert for passing an algebra course. You may wish for a good grade in your educational psychology course so that your transcript will be attractive to a future employer. In both examples, a certain type of behavior is aroused and maintained long enough for the achievement of a specific goal. How do these facts relate to some of the more popular myths that surround the concept of motivation?

What Are the Myths About Motivation?

In analyzing the nature of motivation, several issues have arisen concerning what is fact and what is fiction. Wlodkowski (1986) and Grossnickle and Thiel (1988) believe that the concept of motivation is shrouded in myths that can mislead and confuse. Some of these myths focus on students, while others concern teachers. Among the most damaging are the following.

- *When students are not actively involved in their work, they are unmotivated.* Nothing could be more misleading; if students are doing anything, they are motivated. They may not be motivated to learn, but they are motivated to do something, and that "something" could lead to a serious discipline problem.

Which of the myths of motivation do you believe? How has this belief affected your learning behavior?

- *Failure is a good motivator.* Experience may be a valuable teacher, but chronic failure often begets more of the same, unless a better way is substituted. Success, even a small success, is a more potent motivator for most students.

- *Learning is more important than motivation.* Some would say that because students must learn to survive, schools must force students to learn, regardless of the conditions. Though this belief may produce immediate learning, the ultimate consequences may be negative. Students may not use their learning, since it was meaningless; worse, they simply may be repelled by the thought of any additional learning (Moses, 1991b).

- *Teachers motivate students.* Realistically, the best we can do as teachers is to make conditions as attractive and stimulating as possible. Your students' perceptions, values, personalities, and judgments ultimately determine their motivation (Ford, 1992; Wlodkowski, 1986). By matching task with ability under meaningful and pleasant conditions (including teacher encouragement), we can encourage students' self-motivation (Thorkildsen, 1988).

- *Threats increase motivation.* By using the threat of low grades, retention, and parental notification, some teachers (especially new teachers) believe that they motivate students. Although stern measures are occasionally necessary and must be used, to build a classroom atmosphere around threats is counterproductive.

- *Learning automatically improves with increased student motivation.* Positive evidence is lacking to show that motivation always improves learning. Motivation is certainly a condition for learning, but if other vital conditions are lacking, we must question the extent of the learning. For example, a teacher may have motivated students, but if the lesson is not well planned, if the teacher cannot control the class, or if the teacher's presentation is vague, then motivated students will probably learn less than they would if conditions were more favorable. How do the ideas we have discussed thus far apply to learning?

Motivation to Learn

If you were asked to provide a list of highly motivated individuals, the chances are that your list would include the names of some great athletes. These gifted people did not arrive at their present lofty positions by ability alone. Talent plus dedicated determination helped them to attain their "world-class" accomplishments.

Psychologists are convinced that many of today's great athletes have not yet reached their physiological limitations, and that any restraints on their performance are psychological. In their efforts to help athletes overcome these restraints, sports psychologists have devised techniques that can help not only athletes, but also classroom teachers.

For example, runners are urged to imagine the noise of the crowd, the sound of their own breathing, their position at the starting line, the starter's gun, their first steps, the encouragement of their teammates, and the feeling of the track under their spikes. They are likewise directed to see themselves crossing the finish line first and receiving a victory medal. They are instructed to *imagine* how they feel when they win.

The intent of the sports psychologists is to produce in the athletes a feeling of their own competence as a strong motivating force—that is, to ensure that they not only can do it, but want to do it. Similar techniques can be effective in the classroom. It is entirely possible that if you match a task with a student's ability, having that student imagine successful performance will produce more effective behavior, which then will aid motivation for the next task. For example, urge students to visualize themselves understanding the material to be covered. Then have them see themselves in the classroom, relaxed and ready for work. Finally, have them see the desired A grades on their papers.

Will students learn what we want them to learn even if they are poorly motivated? Everything that we know about learning indicates that if motivation is faulty, learning will suffer. Attention is limited; behavior is not directed at objectives; discipline may become a problem; learning goes awry.

What motivational strategies do you use to get yourself to invest more time and energy in studying?

To avoid these problems, try to analyze the motives of your students (or your class-mates in this course), much as the teacher in the chapter opening did. Do they want to come to class? Observe them carefully: determine the needs that they bring to your classroom, and identify what interests them. Do they enjoy learning, or try to avoid it and dread coming to school? Why do they feel as they do? If they enjoy the work, try to discover what they like, and link it to the classroom atmosphere. If they are reluctant scholars, try to discover what has gone wrong. Is there anything in the classroom atmosphere that explains what has happened?

Attempting to answer these and similar questions, Brophy (1987b) argued that no motivational strategies will succeed if certain preconditions are not met. One of these is a supportive, warm, and encouraging classroom atmosphere, so that pupils are sufficiently secure to take risks without fear of criticism. A related requirement is that teachers know and understand their pupils, and set worthwhile, meaningful objectives that are clearly understood by their classes. Finally, motivational strategies should be moderate and monitored; that is, students should not be kept at motivation levels that are too high or too low.

Because motivational strategies are designed to enhance student motivation and achievement, teachers should be able to turn these motivational concepts and strategies into classroom practices (Ames, 1990). Doing this means structuring the learning environment to influence students' views of the nature and process of learning. Several motivational categories have been identified that can be used to develop specific motivational strategies for your students (Ames, 1990; Blumenfeld, 1992; Epstein, 1988; Maehr & Midgley, 1991). Among these categories are task, authority, recognition, grouping, evaluation, and time. Note that together, the first letters of the category names form the acronym TARGET.

T   *Task* refers to those decisions schools and teachers make about what tasks their students will do.
A   *Authority* means the manner in which teachers define and use their authority.
R   *Recognition* emphasizes the significance of careful and pertinent rewards and reinforcement.
G   *Grouping* refers to the way students are grouped in a classroom, which can encourage either cooperation or competition.
E   *Evaluation* focuses on the type and basis of evaluation, which has particular relevance for motivation.
T   *Time* means those class periods that teachers have available and the ways they use this time.

As Maehr and Midgley (1991) noted, these categories can help students to understand the purpose of learning in given situations, and may incorporate both intrinsic and extrinsic motivation.

Intrinsic and Extrinsic Motivation

Psychologists have long argued about the relative merits of intrinsic and extrinsic motivation. Should our students always be intrinsically motivated? Should teachers avoid extrinsic motivation, since it works against the development of intrinsic motivation? Or should teachers stress the role of the environment and learn as much as possible about the use of rewards to further learning?

Graded work provides many students with valuable feedback and an opportunity for reinforcement.

▶ **Should Teachers Be Generous When Grading Their Students' Work?**

Many teachers will admit that assigning grades to students' work is the part of teaching they like least of all. Mrs. Smyth has the reputation among her students of being a great teacher. When faced with the "close call" decision of whether to give a C+ or a B–, she usually opts for the B–, reasoning that the higher grade will motivate the student in the future.

Issue

A higher grade motivates a student to remain successfully engaged with the material.

Answer: Pro   A good grade certainly gives a student a feeling of accomplishment and increased self-esteem. We know that these factors can contribute to motivation in learners.

Answer: Con   The better grade might result in the student's feeling no need to work any harder in the future. The B– might be a better grade than the student feels is deserved.

Issue

How students perceive the B– influences their motivation in the future. If the B– is viewed as *earned,* motivation is likely to lead to improved success. If the grade is seen as a *gift,* it could negatively affect motivation.

Answer: Pro   A better grade will always be a positive motivational factor. Even if a student expects a lower grade, the B– will send the message that the teacher still has confidence in the student's ability.

Answer: Con   If students receive what they perceive as undeserved grades, the teacher will be seen as dishonest and drop in the students' estimation. This can have a drastic impact on their motivation to engage with the material in the future.

Issue

Some teachers confer with each student before assigning term grades. Together they come to an agreement on a fair assessment of the child's work. This would seem to be a sensible and equitable approach to this required and necessary task.

Answer: Pro   Such a conference gives both students and the teacher an opportunity to talk in some depth about the many factors that go into evaluation. When students are engaged in the evaluation process, and have input into it as well, they can better understand and accept the grade. Partial ownership and empowerment argue for sustained and even increased motivation in the future.

Answer: Con   Students cannot be expected to objectively evaluate their own work. Teachers should feel confident that their grading systems are fair and objective. There is little real merit in bringing students into this process.

Today's educational psychologists believe that there is no real difference between the two (Chance, 1992); any apparent differences are a matter of interpretation (Deci & Ryan, 1990). For example, Ford (1992) argued that it is a mistake to believe that motivation resides in the activities in which students engage: *motivation is in the person.* Drawing is *not* intrinsically motivating; the *student* is intrinsically motivated to draw. Nevertheless, the two types of motivation are dynamically different, and it may help you to keep the differences in mind when you decide on motivational strategies (Deci & Ryan, 1990). For example, use extrinsic motivation (rewards such as praise, grades, and candy) to further intrinsic motivation (wanting to do something, such as read, for the enjoyment or value of it).

Intrinsic motivation means the desire of students themselves to learn in order to achieve specific objectives. Obviously, this is an ideal state that results in considerable learning and a minimum of discipline problems. You can help your pupils acquire intrinsic motivation by relating your knowledge of their abilities, needs, and interests to meaningful goals. Knowing that a student is interested in the medical field and knowing that student's ability enables you to channel that interest in an appropriate direction.

While this is the ideal, intrinsic motivation can be elusive. Consequently, marks, prizes, and other tangible rewards are used. Because rewards and inducements are external to a student, they are characterized as **extrinsic motivation.** Even when using these methods, you should always attempt to have students translate these temporary external devices into intrinsic motives. How? By making sure that your students succeed at some level and being there to reinforce their efforts.

intrinsic motivation   *The desire of students themselves to learn, without the need for external inducements.*

extrinsic motivation   *Those rewards and inducements external to students.*

Maintaining Motivation

Watch your students for signs of restlessness. If you detect these, change the pace; introduce something new; move swiftly to involve students actively in the classroom activities. Motivated students possess certain identifiable characteristics that you can learn to recognize. Motivated students see their classroom work as *personally meaningful:* they believe that what they are doing in school matches their interests and goals. They also believe they have the *capability of achieving relevant goals.* (As noted earlier, one of your chief motivational tasks is to help your students make realistic assessments about their abilities.)

Motivated students likewise realize that they are *personally responsible* for defining and attaining personal goals. As Corno (1992) noted, even elementary school students can acquire strategies that encourage personal responsibility for learning. In doing so, they learn to *control those emotions* that aid or distract from motivation and learning; otherwise, frustration and other emotions can quickly undermine motivation.

Finally, motivated students actually *demonstrate those behaviors that indicate successful goal attainment,* which leads to recognition and reinforcement, both powerful motivating agents.

Now let us turn our attention to several explanations that have been proposed to clarify the meaning of motivation.

Distinguish between intrinsic and extrinsic motivation. Which form best characterizes your motivation for success in school?

WHAT CAUSES MOTIVATION?

Because motivated students obviously are the most desirable to teach, it is well worth the time and effort for teachers (and future teachers) to learn as much as possible about motivation. For example, Serna (1989) discovered motivation was needed for students actually to use study skills. Providing a rationale, setting goals, using shaping procedures, and aiming for errorless learning all encouraged pupils to apply the study skills.

One way of coming to grips with the nature and meaning of motivation is to examine several motivational theories. Although there are numerous theoretical explanations of motivation—biological, learning, and cognitive—we will include only those that have direct classroom application. If you grasp the theories, you will be in a much better position to understand motivation, or its lack, in your individual students. A good beginning is to examine humanistic interpretations of motivation, especially the needs hierarchy of Abraham Maslow.

Humanistic Psychology and Motivation

Tom, the student who was concerned about whether Barbara Cotter's English class was meeting his needs, reminds us of the importance of need satisfaction. One of Maslow's (1987) most famous concepts is that of *self-actualization,* or the use of one's abilities to the limit of one's potentialities. If we can convince students that they should—and can—fulfill their promises, they then will be on the path to self-actualization. *Self-actualization is a growth concept;* students move toward this goal as they satisfy their basic needs. It is movement toward physical and psychological health.

Need Satisfaction

Growth toward self-actualization requires the satisfaction of a hierarchy of needs. There are five basic types of needs in Maslow's theory: *physiological, safety, love and belonging, esteem,* and *self-actualization.* Figure 10.1 illustrates the hierarchy of needs, with those needs at the base of the hierarchy assumed to be more basic than the needs above them in the hierarchy.

1. *Physiological Needs.* Physiological needs, such as hunger and sleep, are dominant and are basic to motivation. Unless they are satisfied, everything else recedes. For example, students who frequently do not eat breakfast or suffer from poor

Figure 10.1

Maslow's hierarchy of needs.

Data for diagram based on Hierarchy of Needs from Motivation and Personality, *Third Edition, by Abraham H. Maslow. Revised by Robert Frager, et al., Harper & Row, Inc. 1954, 1987.*

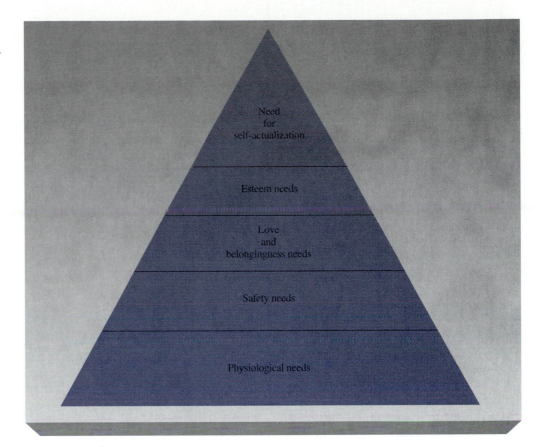

nutrition generally become lethargic and stop interacting; their learning potential is severely lowered. Note: this is particularly true of adolescents, who can be failing to eat out of extreme sensitivity about their weight.

2. *Safety Needs.* These are needs for security, protection, stability, and freedom from fear and anxiety, and also for structure and limits in our lives. Any of your students who are afraid of school, of their peers, of a teacher, or of their parents' reactions have their safety needs threatened, and their classroom performance can be affected.

3. *Love and Belongingness Needs.* This category refers to the human need for family and friends. Healthy, motivated people wish to avoid feelings of loneliness and isolation. Students who feel alone—not part of the group—or who lack any sense of belongingness usually have poor relationships with others, which can then affect their classroom learning.

4. *Esteem Needs.* These needs encompass the reactions of others to us as individuals, and also our own opinions of ourselves. We want favorable judgments from others, which should be based on honest achievement. Our own sense of competence combines with the reactions of others to produce our sense of self-esteem. As a teacher, be sure to provide opportunities for students to satisfy this need: help students to achieve and receive *deserved* reinforcement.

5. *Need for Self-Actualization.* This is Maslow's term for the tendency, in spite of the satisfaction of the lower needs, to feel restless unless we are doing what we think we are capable of doing. Encourage your students to recognize their potential, and guide them into activities that will enable them to feel both competent and fulfilled.

For the Classroom

Clearly, a deficit in any one need category in Maslow's hierarchy will affect student performance. Hungry students, for example, usually are not scholars; their hunger overwhelms all other concerns. Similarly, students who are fearful (for whatever reason) may find it difficult to concentrate on their studies. Students who feel rejected and isolated may refuse to participate fully in class activities. Teacher-student relationships are significant in satisfying student needs (Whisler, 1991).

Teachers experience similar needs. Ratliff (1988) compared the perceived-need differences between teachers and workers in government, retail sales, and industry. He discovered that many teachers had significantly higher physiological, safety, and love and belongingness needs, and lower needs for self-esteem and self-actualization, than did the other workers.

Like all human beings, students need to feel that they are worthy of respect, from both themselves and others. This respect must be based on actual achievement. Teachers frequently are accused of using excessive praise, to the point where it becomes meaningless. Students recognize this and resent it; they often see it as insulting. To avoid making this mistake, target specific student behaviors, so they understand exactly why they are being reinforced. And remember that unless students believe that they are doing all that they could be doing, they will be plagued by feelings of restlessness and even discontent. As you can see, Maslow's remarkably perceptive analysis of human needs furnishes us with rich general insights into human behavior—insights easily applied to the classroom.

Cognitive Psychology and Motivation

Although there are several cognitive explanations of motivation, none are so closely related to the classroom as are those of Jerome Bruner. In his little classic, *The Process of Education* (1960), Bruner stated that any attempt to improve education inevitably begins with the motives for learning. He questioned the results from an emphasis upon examinations, grades, and promotion. Does it intensify motivation? How intense should motivation be? Bruner believed that there is some ideal level of arousal that falls between apathy and wild excitement, because passivity causes boredom, and intense activity leaves little time for reflection and generalization.

One possible key to arousing motivation is Bruner's notion of **discovery learning,** which has captured many educators' imaginations with its insights into classroom motivation. The result is that students learn to manipulate their environments more actively and achieve considerable gratification from personally coping with problems. We know that students like tasks that have them respond actively by interacting with teachers or with each other (Brophy, 1987a). That is, students see meaning in knowledge, skills, and attitudes when they themselves discover these things.

discovery learning *Bruner's term for learning that involves the rearrangement and transformation of material in a way that leads to insight.*

Finally, Bruner noted that knowledge of results (feedback, reinforcement) is valuable if it comes when learners compare their results with what they have attempted to achieve. Even then, learners use feedback according to their internal states, that is, their interests, attitudes, anxieties, and the like. Information is least useful when a learner is highly anxious or focuses on only one aspect of a problem too closely. For Bruner, information is most helpful when it is at the learner's level and encourages self-activity and intrinsic motivation.

Achievement and Motivation

Students differ in their need achievement, that is, in how much achievement means to them. We also know that achievement motivation is related to standards of excellence: to doing well, or wanting to do well. As Dweck (1990) discovered, some children (those designated as helpless) react to failure as if they were being judged and discredited, while others (those designated as mastery-oriented) view failure as an opportunity for learning. Dweck believed that the two groups of children focus on different goals and thus react to similar events in totally different manners. Consequently, be aware of feelings of helplessness in your students and try to help them keep from becoming discouraged and frustrated by making sure that they experience successes that can be legitimately rewarded. You can then use these triumphs to help them meet and overcome failure on their own terms.

need achievement theory *An explanation of motivation that is related to competence: judging it and increasing it.*

A practical example of how you can help students improve their need achievement can be seen in the work of David McClelland on **need achievement theory.** Defining the need to achieve as *a spontaneously occurring concern to do things better,* McClelland (1987) stated that such individuals seek out challenging, moderately difficult tasks, do well at them, want all possible feedback, and become bored with steady success. To measure the need for achievement (nAch), McClelland gave his subjects achievement-oriented tasks. For example, male college students were told the tests they were taking would reflect their intelligence and reliably discriminate people of high ability. The students thus were motivated to do as well as possible.

When the tests were completed, the subjects' fantasies were studied by having them respond to pictures (depicting work) that were flashed on a screen. The subjects were given five minutes to write stories about the pictures. The themes of their stories were then compared with those of similar subjects who had not been given the test and the accompanying instructions. The stories of the test subjects showed many more references to standards of excellence, doing well, or wanting to do well.

For the Classroom

McClelland (1987) determined that some individuals have a higher inner need to achieve than others. After demonstrating that adult levels of achievement can be raised, McClelland (1987) next turned his attention to students. He taught children how to think, talk, and act like persons who had the spontaneously occurring need to do better (nAch). What conclusions emerged from these studies that could benefit classroom teachers?

Important gender differences appeared. Girls benefited more when the training was structured, while boys showed improvement when they were given more freedom within the training. A forced restructuring, however, produced few results. Having teachers specifically include achievement motivation instruction in their regular work seems more effective. Teachers become more alert to the need to involve their students actively, to encourage all students to participate, and, finally, to provide tangible feedback to student responses.

Don't be discouraged if your efforts are not successful with all students. Certain students are unconcerned about achievement. But these same students may be intensely interested in task mastery for its own sake. For example, students who consistently work on vocabulary to improve their reading and use their free time to go to the library table are *task-focused:* they are concerned with understanding, insight, and skill. Other students seem to be *ability-focused:* they are more concerned with the judgment of others, and want to obtain favorable judgments by outperforming other students.

Attribution Theory and Motivation

Even with a need to achieve, students will either succeed or fail. As they do, they search for reasons for their success or failure, attributing their performance to specific causes. "The test was difficult." "The teacher dislikes me." "I'm good in this subject." Students' attributions then serve as a guide to their expectations for future success or failure in a subject (Moses, 1991b). Le Yang, the student in the chapter opener, may have attributed his performance to language difficulties. Like most of us, he was searching for a cause to explain his behavior.

Human beings are all similar in this respect. If, when you are with a certain person, you consistently have an enjoyable time, then your expectation is that you will continue to have a good time in the future. Students who consistently do poorly in a subject expect to continue to do poorly. But before you can hope to have success in changing a student's performance, you must know to what factor that student attributes subpar performance.

attribution theory *A motivational theory that assumes people want to know the causes of their behavior.*

Attribution theory rests on three basic assumptions (Petri, 1991). First, people want to know the causes of their own and others' behavior, particularly of behavior that is important to them. Second, they do not randomly assign causes to their behavior.

There are logical explanations for the causes to which humans attribute behavior. Third, the causes that individuals assign to behavior influence their subsequent behavior. If we attribute our failure to a particular person, we may come to dislike that person. The student who believes this—"No matter what I do, Mr. Smith won't give me a good grade"—will come to dislike Mr. Smith.

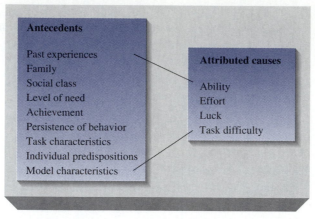

Figure 10.2

Conditions and characteristics that often influence students' attributions about successes or failures.

Weiner believed that when achievement is aroused, we tend to attribute our performance to one of four elements: ability, effort, task difficulty, or luck. Of these attributions, ability and effort are the most important (Weiner, 1980, 1984, 1990a, & 1990b). Thus, success is attributed to high ability or high effort, and failure is seen as resulting from low ability or low effort. Figure 10.2 presents an expanded version of the attribution concept and the many factors that influence students' attributions.

Ability

These attributions of success and failure have important implications for teaching, because students' assumptions about their abilities are usually based upon past experiences. It is precisely here that we may find explanations for math phobia, reading problems, or dislike of science. Students who have a history of failure often make the devastating assumption that they lack ability. This tendency is particularly true if others have done well on the task in question. Once students question their abilities, this doubt spreads to other subjects and other tasks. Soon, there is a generalized feeling of incompetence that paralyzes initiative and activates an expectation of failure.

Students who consistently question their own abilities pose a serious challenge, because their histories of failure and feelings of incompetence undercut motivation and learning. Your initial assumption about these students should be that there must be something that they can do well. Consequently, search for tasks that they can perform with competence and publicly reward them for their success. Remember: avoid attributing their initial failure to a lack of ability and search for alternate explanations.

Effort

Weiner (1990a) also made the interesting discovery that students usually have no idea how hard they try to succeed. Students (like the rest of us) judge their efforts by how well they have done particular tasks. Even in tasks involving pure chance, successful students believed that they had tried harder than those who were unsuccessful. An important cycle is thus established: success increases effort; effort produces more success.

The educational implications are real and significant. If a skill is to be mastered and your teaching is consistent for your entire group, then your students' performances, given their individual differences, will vary because of motivation. Here again, we note the importance of insuring success as a means of encouraging further effort.

Task Difficulty

Task difficulty usually is judged by the performance of others on a task. If many succeed, the task is perceived as easy, and vice versa. An interesting phenomenon can develop here. If a student consistently succeeds on a task at which others fail, that student will attribute success to ability. But if individual success is matched by the success of others, then the source of the success is considered to be the easiness of the task. Weiner's findings emphasize once again the importance of matching a task with a student's ability, thus enhancing ability and increasing effort.

Luck

Finally, if there is no tangible link between behavior and goal attainment, the tendency is to attribute success to luck. Those students who have little faith in their abilities attribute their success on almost all tasks to luck, thus short-circuiting the motivational network just described. Success in this case will not increase effort; lack of effort does nothing to bolster a belief in one's ability; and tasks remain overwhelming obstacles.

For the Classroom

In applying his interpretation of attribution theory to the classroom, Weiner (1990b) stated that there are relationships between students' attributions (ability, luck, effort, task difficulty), and their various underlying dimensions: the stability of an attribution, its locus (either within or external to the student), and its controllability (whether the student can control the cause).

Consequently, in achievement-related situations, students experience cognitive and emotional reactions such as the following: "I just failed this exam," accompanied by feelings of frustration and upset.

- "I failed the exam because I didn't try hard enough," followed by feelings of shame and guilt.
- "I just don't have the right stuff," followed by feelings of low self-esteem, lack of worth, and hopelessness.

Examining the subtleties of motivation leads to the conclusion that certain motivational aspects involve learning. Some motivation is learned: we learn to want definite objects; we learn to expect certain outcomes; we learn to fear certain things. But the relationship between learning and motivation is bidirectional: new learning also depends upon motivation. Motivation is heightened for many students when new, interesting learning opportunities are presented.

We have already seen that learning theorists view learning quite differently; their explanations of motivation reflect these differences. Among the most prominent of the learning theorists is B. F. Skinner, whose work with operant or instrumental conditioning was examined in chapter 7.

Behavioral Psychology and Motivation

If you asked people why they went to the theater and they replied simply that they felt like going, you probably would be satisfied. Their answer would be more revealing, however, if they told you what had happened when they previously had attended the theater, what they had read beforehand about a given play, and what other factors had induced them to go (Skinner, 1971). According to Skinner, behavior is shaped and maintained by its consequences. Thus, the consequences of previous behavior influence students. There may be no major internal or intrinsic motivational component in the process. For example, in a study of 301 secondary school students—African American, Hispanic American, and white—Goodenow (1992) found that the students' social context had a powerful effect on their sense of belongingness, which then affected both motivation and achievement.

Skinner believed that motivated behavior results from the consequences of similar previous behavior. If students obtain reinforcement for certain behavior, they tend to repeat it with vigor. If they don't, as in the case of Zack, the athlete we described in the chapter opening, students tend to lose interest and their performance suffers. Yet Chance (1992) noted that in spite of strong experimental support, the systematic use of reinforcement has never been widespread in American schools.

For the Classroom

Students should not study merely to avoid the consequences of not studying, which may be aversive (i.e., punishment.) Under aversive conditions, students will engage in truancy, vandalism, disruptive behavior, or apathy. How can teachers improve their control over the classroom, not abandon it? Skinner believed that the answer lies in the appropriate use of *positive reinforcement schedules*.

With this method, students are immediately encouraged upon giving correct responses, not merely punished for incorrect responses. Such students come to feel free and happy both in the classroom and outside school, because they have established behavioral patterns that produce success, pleasant relations with others, and a deserved sense of accomplishment. Skinner believed that this is an important component in learning with understanding. If you or your students have been fortunate enough to have received such positive reinforcement, you can understand what Skinner meant by self-motivation. (Much more about Skinner's views of motivation and human behavior will appear in chap. 13, "Classroom Management," because many of the most challenging issues facing teachers in the classroom pertain to students' motivation.)

Social Cognitive Learning and Motivation

The final theorist we will consider is Albert Bandura (1977, 1981, 1986, 1990, 1993), who has combined both cognitive and behavioristic elements in his explanation of motivation. Bandura's social learning theory has particular relevance for motivation. Of the students who come to your classroom, all are able, and some are willing, to imitate. A more lasting impression is made on pupils by setting an example for them, rather than telling them what to do. Teachers should be models as much as possible, since their behavior can be a powerful motivating force for student behavior.

Observation of models can produce some significant changes in students' behavior. For example, observing models helps in the acquisition of new responses, strengthens or weakens existing responses, and may cue the appearance of apparently forgotten responses.

Obtaining Information About Oneself

If modeling is to be a motivational force, then your students' self-knowledge is crucial. A student's self-knowledge is gained from information conveyed by either personal or socially mediated experiences (see chap. 7). Bandura believes that people motivate themselves and guide their actions by planning ahead. Consequently, we should help students to set realistic goals for themselves, plan courses of action to attain their goals, and anticipate the likely outcomes of their behavior (Bandura, 1986, 1990, 1993).

Bandura believes that to obtain this kind of knowledge, students (and all of us) use four sources of information. *Performance accomplishments* enable us to acquire personal and effective information from what we do. *Vicarious experiences,* which students have when they watch others perform tasks successfully, help them to feel more optimistic when they begin. *Verbal persuasion* can cause students to believe that they can overcome obstacles and improve their performance. Finally, the *emotional arousal* inherent in stressful situations constitutes a source of personal information when a student learns from such experiences how to remain "cool under fire."

Receiving data from these sources enables us to judge the extent of our self-efficacy (the belief that we *can* do this); that is, success raises our sense of self-efficacy, while failure diminishes it. Clearly, feedback can have a powerful effect on students' feelings of competency. As a respected model, your evaluations carry significant weight. When you say, "Of course you can do it, Heather," you are providing strong verbal persuasion. You should then follow through on this encouragement by ensuring that the student's performance accomplishment meets your (and your students') expectations.

For the Classroom

The role of imitation in motivation and learning has direct classroom implications. Students' successful imitation of what they see and hear in the classroom is partially influenced by how you as the model respond to them. Effective modeling requires *attention, retention,* and *reinforcement.*

Students must *attend* if they are going to imitate; they must *remember* what they have imitated if they are to reproduce it in the future; and their imitating behavior must have been *reinforced* for them to remember and later use it. We can thus conclude that students will imitate when you provide incentives for them to do so, and when you attend to what they have done. Note the two-way influence process described here (Bandura, 1986). Your students attend to and imitate you; you then attend to and reinforce them. Imitative performance reflects not only the competencies of students, but also the reactions of the model (the teacher). If you respond equally to performances that are markedly different in quality, your students will not imitate successfully. But if you attend to their behavior and reinforce them appropriately, they will accurately reproduce behavior.

As students grow older and move through the grades, their intellectual capacities increase and they become capable of delayed imitation. They can witness modeled performances and later perform those tasks without having practiced them. Recall from our discussion of Piaget's cognitive development theory that the growth of cognitive structures permits students to cope with increasingly more abstract material, retain that material, conserve it, and finally use it.

Now, apply these concepts to Bandura's work to consider that students can mentally rehearse what they view. With this increasing cognitive sophistication, they can escape the limitations of direct imitation and form new patterns of modeled behavior. This is especially true when students become comfortable with verbal symbols.

You can describe a course of action to them; *they will attend, retain, rehearse, and imitate* according to the verbal stimuli that you have presented to them. For example, before assembling equipment necessary for a science project, you can describe it and draw pictures of it, thus helping your students in the actual assembly. As we conclude our discussion of Bandura's work, remember this: students who observe enthusiastic, knowledgeable teachers tend to imitate that behavior and become enthusiastic and knowledgeable themselves.

Table 10.1 summarizes the major ideas of the motivational theorists we have reviewed. Which theory is most compatible with your thoughts about motivation and learning?

As we apply these ideas to the classroom, certain factors appear that have direct impact on the motivation of students.

Table 10.1

Motivational Theorists and Their Basic Ideas

Name	Theory	Central element of theory	Explanation of motivation
Maslow	Humanistic	Needs hierarchy	Need satisfaction
Bruner	Cognitive	Intrinsic processes	Mixed motives
McClelland	Achievement	Need to achieve	Changes in need achievement
Weiner	Attribution	Causes of behavior	Identifying perceived causes of behavior
Skinner	Operant conditioning	Reinforcement	Schedules of reinforcement
Bandura	Social cognitive	Imitation	Modeling

teacher – student

interactions

Motivation and Learning

1. Intrinsic motivation is the ideal state for student learning.
   - Provide a comfortable area and adequate time in your classroom for students to lose themselves in books of *their* choice. The joy of reading, then, will be its own reward.
   - Establish a learning center with "hands-on" science materials (e.g., shells, rocks, etc.), so that students will find pleasure in identifying the various specimens and explaining them to classmates.
   - Have at your students' fingertips reference books they can use to do their own research (or just browse through when they have free time).
2. Understanding students' needs is a critical factor in facilitating teaching and learning.
   - Be aware of any "hidden" difficulties of your students (e.g., slight hearing loss, minor eye problems, etc.) when writing on the board, giving directions, assigning seats, etc.
   - Develop the skill of "sweeping" your classroom regularly to discern how your students react to one another, to new work, to interruptions.
   - Take time to talk individually to your students often about outside activities and events that are important to them.

3. Explanations of motivation help teachers, not only in understanding the motivational process, but also in their practical classroom work.
   - Use your knowledge of Bandura's theory to be the model your students will imitate. Your enthusiasm for your subject and your encouraging attitude will help them to overcome their fear of attempting new assignments.
   - Use your knowledge of Skinner's theory to praise and reward students' good work. One technique to use throughout the year is a series of attractive bulletin boards that recognize your students' good behavior or improved work; another is the presentation of awards for accomplishments.
   - Use your knowledge of attribution theory to assess students' abilities, understand their efforts, and acknowledge that sometimes luck does play a part in a person's success. Your ability to admit that you too can make a mistake will encourage your students to apologize for theirs, correct them, and continue to succeed.

WHAT AFFECTS STUDENTS' MOTIVATION?

The teacher in the vignette at the chapter's opening reflected a real concern for implementing motivational techniques and demonstrated her understanding of how motives affect pupils. Given the importance of motivation to learning, you should be aware of several of the most crucial influences on motives. Among them are anxiety, attitudes, curiosity, locus of control, learned helplessness, self-efficacy, and, finally, cooperative learning.

Anxiety

Were you anxious before your last exam? How do you feel when you must speak in public? Are there certain situations in which you feel particularly anxious, regardless of your preparation? We are all alike in this regard: anxious in some conditions, not in others. Terms to describe this condition are *state, normal,* or **situational anxiety.** There are other individuals, however, who are almost constantly in a state of anxiety, which is called *neurotic* or *trait anxiety.*

situational anxiety *A tendency to be anxious in some situations and not in others.*

    Within the classroom setting there are numerous sources of anxiety for students: teachers, examinations, peers, social relations, achievement settings, what girls think of boys, what boys think of girls, like or dislike of subjects, and distance from home (for younger pupils). Regardless of the cause or level of anxiety, you can be sure of one thing: anxiety will affect student performance. Keep in mind, however, that anxiety at relatively low to moderate levels can be constructive, while anxiety at relatively high levels can be destructive and nonadaptive.

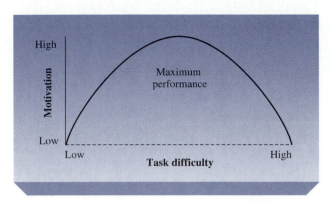

Figure 10.3
The Yerkes-Dodson law, explaining
the relationship between motivation
and task difficulty.

Yerkes-Dodson law   *The*
principle that ideal
motivation for learning
decreases in intensity with
increasing task difficulty.

Our concern is primarily with anxiety's effect on achievement; it is important to realize that extremely intense motivation that produces high anxiety has a negative effect on performance. Moderate motivation seems to be the desirable state for learning complex tasks. For example, in a study of sixty classes of junior high school students, Hecht and Tittle (1992) found that anxiety improved mathematics performance for high achievers who displayed moderate levels of anxiety.

These results are best explained by referring to the **Yerkes-Dodson law,** which states that ideal motivation for learning decreases in intensity with increasing task difficulty. Figure 10.3 illustrates this concept.

Note how increasing difficulty improves performance only to a certain level, beyond which continued task intensity results in a deteriorating performance. Think about some task that you generally do well; now, think about your motivation for it. Would you characterize it as high or low? Usually, as tasks become more difficult, students have fewer successes and subsequently become less motivated to continue the tasks.

Classroom Conditions

You will encounter exactly the same phenomenon in your classroom; this means that your knowledge about anxiety can benefit both you and your students. Anxiety may appear at any time. It may be confined to one situation, or generalize widely. Think of anxiety as a feeling of uneasiness, apprehension, or fear that has a vague or unknown source (Craig, 1992, p. 293).

This general overview has many classroom implications. One is the distinct possibility that anxiety may generalize from one subject or teacher to another. Older students may develop a distaste for school that affects their overall achievement. Younger students could develop school phobia, a psychological condition producing such physical manifestations as crying and vomiting before school in the morning, in the hope of avoiding school attendance.

Several personality and behavioral characteristics are typical of anxious students and are reflected in opinions about these students on the part of themselves, other classmates, teachers, and parents. For example, anxious students develop *negative attitudes about themselves* and persistently blame only themselves for any failures. They tend to become dependent and are reluctant to display curiosity. Their *peers view anxious classmates negatively* and may take advantage of them. Anxious students usually are not popular pupils; they are rarely chosen by either peers or teachers for leading roles in classroom activities. Also, *teachers typically perceive anxious students as more poorly adjusted* than their classmates, and as displaying more negative personality characteristics. These students are seen as less secure and less task oriented. Even *their parents, especially their fathers, see their anxious children as less mature, less well adjusted, and more dependent.*

It is clear from this brief summary that anxious students carry a heavy burden, which, as we have seen, can affect their classroom performance, especially in test-taking. Although anxiety affects all aspects of behavior, no topic has been more carefully researched in educational psychology than test anxiety.

Test Anxiety

test anxiety   *Anxiety*
generated by planning for and
taking tests.

The construct of **test anxiety** has been used for well over four decades to describe the behavior and emotions of students who find preparing for and taking tests stressful. These students see any test as difficult, challenging, and threatening, and themselves as ineffective or inadequate in handling the task. Test anxiety may appear at an early age—perhaps as early as age 7—and persist well into high school (Hembree, 1988). Estimates are that as many as 30 percent of school children suffer from debilitative test anxiety (Hill & Wigfield, 1984). This translates into a figure of eight to nine million children in American schools who may experience debilitating anxiety in academic performance situations. Approximately 20 percent of all test-anxious children will drop out of school because of repeated academic failure (see, for example, Julkunen, 1992).

Females seem to exhibit more test anxiety than males, although as a group females are more likely to admit and self-report test anxiety. Average students, as measured by standardized tests, experience higher levels of test anxiety than do both higher- and lower-ability students. High test-anxious students perform better under conditions that include low-stress instructions, provisions for memory supports, performance incentives, and minimal classroom distractions (Hembree, 1988).

Test anxiety is directly related to fears of negative evaluation, dislike of tests, cognitive self-preoccupation, and less effective study skills. Also, high test-anxious students hold themselves in lower esteem than do low test-anxious students. These students spend more time than low-anxious students attending to task-irrelevant behaviors such as negative self-statements, attention toward physical discomfort, and watching others in the classroom; as a result, their performance suffers. Finally, test anxiety affects all sociocultural groups in our society.

Attitudes

Psychologists typically define an *attitude* as a relatively permanent way of feeling, thinking, and behaving toward something or somebody. Your perceptions of situations or of persons, like those of your students, typically reflect these feelings, thoughts, and actions. The implications for teaching in this analysis are important: the more you know and the more strongly you feel about somebody or something, the less likely you are to change your attitude.

Pause for a moment to consider what this means for the classroom. If other teachers, especially those you respect, have spoken negatively and with feeling about a student, your attitude toward that student will probably be negative, and will be difficult to change. Also, if you have had difficulty with one member of a family, you must guard against being negative about any brothers or sisters that you may teach later.

Attitude Change

Any instance of attitude change involves persuasion. The student who enters your classroom with a negative attitude toward you, the subject you teach, or both must be persuaded to change that attitude. Persuasive communication (or attitude change) involves four main elements: the communicator, the message, the audience, and the audience-communicator feedback loop.

The *communicators* in our example are teachers. Certain characteristics of communicators contribute to (or detract from) their ability to persuade: power, attractiveness, likeableness, and similarity to those receiving the message. If it is fairly administered, power, in the sense of maintaining discipline and assigning grades, enhances a teacher's ability to persuade. Teacher attractiveness and likeableness are composed of many features: fairness, a sense of humor, consistent behavior in all situations and toward all students, and an ability to relate to students, among others. Finally, it is almost a truism that we tend to believe and be drawn to those who are like us.

Nevertheless, the one feature that seems to mark the effective communicator is credibility. In a classic study, Hovland, Janis, and Kelley (1953) wrote a statement about the importance of atomic submarines and attributed it to two sources, one of high credibility and the other of low credibility. The source of the message strongly affected the subjects' attitudes: subjects given the message from the high-credibility source tended to accept the argument, while the other group rejected it.

A month later the investigators retested their subjects. They were amazed to discover that the high-credibility group had become less positive, while the low-credibility group had become more positive. What had happened was that the subjects had begun to forget the sources of their information and to concentrate on the information itself. If we translate these findings into suggestions for the classroom, it seems that teachers as

Define the Yerkes-Dodson law. How does this apply to your learning in this course?

the sources of information have an immediate and strong effect on students, but that if the effect is to be long-lasting, the information itself should be accurate, pertinent, and interesting.

The *message* refers to the information that you transmit to your class. Assuming the accuracy of the material that you are presenting to your class, your next concern should be the manner in which you present it. This isn't merely a matter of the methods that you select: the emotional accompaniments of the message are a critical aspect of its persuasiveness.

Do you present material with a "do it, or else" attitude, hoping that fear will be a strong motivating force? If you do, consider follow-up studies about the television film *Scared Straight*. This film showed prison inmates telling young people in graphic detail about prison brutality. Follow-up studies showed that more offenses were later committed by those who had participated in the study (watched the film) than by subjects in a control group. Yelling and frightening young people for a brief time does not provide them with the skills necessary to cope with their environments. What seems to be much more effective is teaching those skills that promise success and that promote self-esteem.

The *audience* in our example is a class of students. Several audience characteristics seem to determine the effectiveness of a message: age, gender, and self-esteem. Younger students, for example, generally are easier to persuade than older ones; females are often more willing to change their attitudes than are males; and self-esteem also seems to be significant. Learn to know your students and translate this knowledge into classroom action. For example, you may identify a student with a negative attitude toward history. Determine the cause of the attitude (find out to what the student attributes such behavior) and arrange for successful experiences, all the while carefully shaping classroom material to the student's needs.

Another influential feature of attitude change is the *audience-communicator feedback loop* (McConnell, 1990), which refers to the response that a class actually makes to a teacher. You can deceive yourself by thinking that your students fully understood a lesson simply because you presented it in what you thought was a stimulating manner. You must take the time to determine if the students can respond cognitively (do they understand what you have taught?) and what their affective reaction is (do they enjoy this work?). Seeking and reviewing feedback about your performance is a critical component of communication and teaching that reaches *all* students in our multicultural classrooms.

For the Classroom

Students' attitudes toward school arise from a number of sources: parents, siblings, peers, their own performance, and teachers, among others. Because students' attitudes toward school are a given when they arrive at school, one's chances of successfully changing those attitudes will come from directly working with the students, as seen in the following examples.

Students' Attitudes Toward Teachers. Here are several strategies for fostering positive attitudes toward teachers.

- Make every effort to share something with individual students. By giving students time on an individual basis (not forced, but in as natural a way as possible), you convey a sense of caring that even students with negative attitudes appreciate. If teachers combine this with an obvious liking for the subjects they teach, students begin to think of teachers as something more than distant figures in the front of the room.
- There is a cliche (true, as are most cliches) that warns teachers to accept students, but not necessarily their behavior. Such acceptance is not always easy; there are some students who are difficult to like. Students with negative attitudes are expecting rejection. When we accept their positive behavior, it frustrates their expectations and may provide the opportunity for attitude change.

Students' Attitudes Toward Subjects. Rare indeed is the student without a negative attitude toward some subject. This is to be expected; even teachers like some subjects better than others. But an overall negative attitude is damaging to a student and can, if unchecked, affect an entire classroom. Learning suffers and cynicism becomes rampant, especially in older pupils. Suggestions to improve attitudes toward subjects include the following.

• Show enthusiasm about your subject (Fouts & Myers, 1992). You can accomplish this by becoming expert in your field and permitting your students to see how much you like what you are doing. Relate the subject to your students' knowledge—about home, community, activities, sports, or anything else that your class is interested in.

• Be careful about what you teach indirectly about your subject. Be aware of anything negative that could have an impact on your teaching. For example, avoid using extra assignments in your subject as punishment.

• Demonstrate how meaningful your subject is. For example, many students dislike anything about geography because of past experiences—being forced to memorize capitals, products, rivers, and the like. But if geography is linked to such current events as environmental pollution or tense world situations, the subject takes on new meaning.

Students' Attitudes Toward Themselves. Poor self-opinions can have devastating consequences for motivation. Here are several suggestions that you may find helpful.

• Guarantee success. However you do it, make certain that students with poor self-concepts experience earned success. Honesty is fundamental here, because if a student discovers that the achievement was unwarranted, self-esteem and trust in the teacher diminish sharply.

• Be prepared to offer nearly constant encouragement. It is insufficient to structure a learning situation for these students. If their self-esteem is low, they may not have the motivation to commence the task. Initially, you must be with them to recognize any effort and any success. Work closely with them at the beginning of the task to minimize the possibility of any mistakes. Then, stress learning from mistakes and reinforce effort.

Curiosity

If students are relatively relaxed and willing to work (as are most of them), you can reasonably expect them to have some interest in their environments. Curiosity can be one of a teacher's best friends, because it signals motivated, eager-to-learn students, and applies to both males and females. Studying male and female elementary school students, Johnson and Beer (1992) found no significant differences in curiosity between the sexes. Your task as a teacher, then, is to capitalize on this interest by further stimulating students and maintaining an optimal level of curiosity. But first, it is necessary to explain what we mean by curiosity.

What Is Curiosity?

Curious behavior is often described by other similar terms, such as exploratory, manipulative, or active. To identify the origin of curiosity is difficult. Explanations have focused on external factors (something in the pupil's environment is attractive), or on internal ones (human beings need stimulation). Current interpretations include both.

Curiosity is a meaningful component of motivation. Try to set up learning events that allow for "discoveries" and fuel curiosity.

Researchers have established that certain correlates of curiosity appear consistently, although not with high significance. For example, there seems to be a low to moderate correlation between intelligence and curiosity; measures of achievement also relate somewhat to curiosity. However, the most significant relationship is between curiosity and creativity (Dacey, 1989b).

For the Classroom

Curiosity is a natural phenomenon that should be encouraged within the limits that you establish for your class. A relaxed atmosphere, freedom to explore, and an acceptance of the unusual all inspire curiosity. The development of curiosity should be encouraged as early as possible: during the preschool and elementary years. In their study of 156 male and 142 female elementary school students, Engelhard and Monsaas (1988) found a decrease in student curiosity with increasing grade level. These findings pose a challenge for teachers: to help their students maintain a sense of curiosity. Recall from your earlier developmental reading (chap. 4) that the early years are a time for the formation of cognitive structures that furnish a basis for future cognitive activity. Students not only acquire knowledge, but also learn about learning; they also become curious if their environments are stimulating.

Youngsters are naturally curious, and if their curiosity is encouraged, it will probably last a lifetime. Here are some suggestions for engaging students' curiosity.

- *Let your students see your enthusiasm for a subject.* Then, by using questions related to the material, "tease" students into exploring new vistas.
- *Stimulate cognitive conflicts,* based upon students' levels of sophistication: cause some apparent confusion, but simultaneously provide clues to solutions. Some of the problems we posed in chapter 9 (on problem solving) are good examples of stimulating and potentially confusing problems that many curious students like.
- *Allow students to select topics* that they are curious about, whenever possible. Give them the freedom, and the direction, to explore for themselves.
- *Model curious, inquiring behavior.* Tell students the things you are curious about and model some of the resourceful behavior that curious people use to solve problems.

Locus of Control

Did you do well in your last test in this course? Why? Were you well prepared? Or does the instructor like you? Or were you just plain lucky? If you think about your answers to these questions, you can discern possible patterns that identify your **locus of control.**

Internals versus Externals

locus of control *The cause of behavior; some individuals believe it resides within them, while others believe it resides outside themselves.*

internals *Individuals who attribute the causes of their behavior to themselves.*

externals *Individuals who attribute the causes of their behavior to factors outside themselves.*

Some students' answers to these questions suggest that anything good that happens to them is caused by chance; the replies of other students indicate that they deserve anything good that happens to them. For most of us, our responses follow a definite form. If we attribute responsibility to ourselves, we are called **internals;** if we attribute the causes of our behavior to somebody or something outside of ourselves, we are called **externals.**

Parents, peers, and a student's total environment subtly interact to produce these feelings of confidence or uncertainty about life's challenges. Using more refined and sophisticated versions of this basic theme, Rotter (1966, 1975) and Phares (1973) analyzed individuals to determine their loci of control. If students believe they have little control over the consequences of their actions, they are said to have external loci of control; if they believe they can control what happens to them, they are thought to have internal loci of control.

An example of the classroom implications of this work can be found in a study of secondary school students by Nunn and Parish (1992), in which they discovered that students identified as externals were at greater risk for academic failure. If students believe that success and rewards come from skill and not from luck, they then assume that they have control over their own destinies. On the other hand, if students believe that rewards come from luck and not from skill, they assume that they have little control over their own destinies. In general, as students mature and experience more success, they become more internal (Chance, 1992).

Internals and Externals in the Classroom

Understanding the concept of locus of control provides another opportunity to improve your relationships with your students. By getting to know and understand them, you can assess their self-concepts, then build on their strengths and work on their weaknesses. An individual is neither all internal nor all external, but will have one of these traits typically dominant. This raises the issue of desirability. Because internals are seen as independent, alert, competent, and self-confident, it is difficult to avoid the conclusion that internality is the desired personality characteristic. Rotter (1975) cautioned against such speculation, however, noting that internals may be too confident or withdrawn, while externals can be quite appealing and socially attractive.

Externality may also help some students to adapt successfully in situations where internality could cause problems. For example, some students with extremely authoritarian parents realistically assume that they have little control over their actions. Students from impoverished environments may also realistically assume that their well-being depends on others.

Rotter was not making a value judgment here, but simply offering a practical assessment of how things often are in our society. Do you agree with his position on this issue? In any case, an examination of the characteristics of internality and externality makes it clear why internality is favored.

Internals	**Externals**
Alert	Less attentive
Competent	Erratic in performance
Able to resist influence	Influenced by status
Domineering	Influenced by peers
Achievement oriented	Controlled by others
Independent	Low confidence in their abilities
Self-confident	Random in reactions
Skillful	

For the Classroom

Make every attempt to present your students with realistic challenges; this implies that you must know the students, so that you can determine what is achievable for them. Then you can carefully reward their accomplishments, or at least their efforts; external students perform better when they receive specific comments about teachers' expectations. Reinforcement must be based on actual accomplishment; otherwise, students will quickly identify it as a sham. If students think that their success resulted from a teacher's manipulation of their work, there will be little change in their locus of control. It is only when they perceive that their actions were instrumental in achieving success that real change may occur.

Be sure to reinforce their effort; be specific in noting that you realize that *they* have taken responsibility (Dacey, 1989b). Use any initial successes and attempt to foster in students a habit of trying and taking responsibility for their actions. (Teachers are often more impressed by the initial performances of students than by recent performances.) Finally, remember that teachers tend to attribute negative characteristics more frequently to external students than to internals, and that external students describe their teachers more negatively than do internals.

Learned Helplessness

For some students, the best opportunity for change may be in the classroom; if this chance is lost, they may experience a condition that Seligman (1975) called **learned helplessness** (see chap. 7). What seems to happen is that after repeated failure students become frustrated and simply will not try. The evidence—both in animals and in humans—strongly supports this conclusion.

learned helplessness *The reaction on the part of some individuals to become frustrated and simply give up after repeated failure.*

In a series of experiments by Seligman and Maier (1967), harnessed dogs encountered one of three conditions. An *escape* group learned to escape shock while harnessed by pressing a panel with their noses. A *yoked* group received precisely the same shocks as the escape group, but they could do nothing to reduce or escape them. A *naive* group received no shocks while in the harness. After twenty-four hours all three groups were moved to a shuttle box, where they could escape the shocks by jumping over a barrier. Both the escape and the naive groups quickly learned to escape the shocks—but the yoked group showed little, if any, ability to learn how to avoid the shocks. The animals refused even to try to escape, and also exhibited signs of stress and depression. It could not have been the shocks themselves that made the yoked dogs unable to learn the escape response, because dogs in the escape group had been equally shocked. Rather, their lack of control sealed their fates when they were later in a position to control the shocks.

The yoked group's response when presented with a situation that they could control—yet did not—is called *learned helplessness*. It appears to be a subtle combination of cognitive, motivational, and emotional elements causing the subject to fail to see the necessary relationships.

Learned helplessness also applies to humans, as seen in the work of Hiroto (1974). Hiroto subjected three groups of people to a loud, unpleasant noise. The escape group could stop the noise by pushing a button. The yoked group experienced the same noise, but had no way of reducing or eliminating it. The third group initially heard no noise. In the follow-up condition, members of all groups could escape the noise by moving one of their hands in a shuttle box from one side to the other. Again, the escape and naive groups did well, but those who had experienced unavoidable noise simply sat and made no move to eliminate the noise.

If for noise we substitute failing grades, sarcasm at home and school, and ridicule, then it becomes possible to trace a possible developmental path of learned helplessness. Students who experience nothing but failure and abuse at home and school have little positive reinforcement for their behavior. If you discover such students, make every effort to combat this habit of "giving up."

Helplessness and Success

In discussing the impact of helplessness on achievement, Seligman (1990) noted that the traditional view of achievement rests on the assumption that success depends on talent and desire. That is, students do poorly because they lack the ability or the motivation to succeed. As long as success was measured by such instruments as the well-known IQ tests, there could be little argument with the belief that talent is everything. Students who did poorly on IQ tests typically demonstrated low achievement in their academic work. (We shall discuss the details of these tests in chap. 16.)

When these results were linked to the hereditarian view of intelligence, then the issue could be clearly stated: talent was something you either had or didn't have because of the accident of birth. Following this logic, talent was inborn and could be assessed by IQ tests. This assumption also dictated school success. Labeling, for example, was a direct outgrowth of IQ tests: students who did poorly on them were labeled slow or learning disabled, and placed on specific (general or industrial) curriculum tracks.

Only slowly did psychologists realize that another issue was involved: the environment also exercises a powerful effect on the appearance of whatever talent a student possesses. Psychologists such as Martin Seligman (1990) and Carol Dweck (1990) began to raise questions about the influence students' thoughts about their abilities also had on the degree to which their talents would be expressed.

Seligman (1990, p. 5) described helplessness as the state of affairs in which nothing you choose to do affects what happens to you. Many things in our lives are beyond our control, but in most matters we either take control or surrender control to others. We realize today that even our thoughts are not mere responses; they can also change events.

Students who feel helpless when presented with math problems are often frozen into inaction. Frequently in our educational psychology classes, we use problems that demand some fairly simple calculations. It is fascinating to observe those students who won't even attempt the problems! Their beliefs that they can't do them prevent them from even trying. As Seligman stated (1990, p. 7), when students overestimate their helplessness, other forces take control and shape their futures. They believe they can't do tasks; they don't do them; grades suffer; labels are applied; curriculum tracks are solidified.

For the Classroom

In a series of studies analyzing the differences between helpless and mastery-oriented children, Dweck (1990) traced discernible patterns of behavior in each group of students. Investigating learned helplessness in fifth-graders, Dweck and Repucci (1973) had one teacher give solvable problems and another teacher give unsolvable problems to their students. Later, when the teacher who had given the unsolvable problems instead gave students solvable problems (like those given by the other teacher), the researchers observed that many students could not solve the problems, even though they had previously done so with the other teacher.

In a follow-up to the Dweck and Repucci study, Diener and Dweck (1978, 1980) investigated the differences in students' reactions to failure. They identified two groups of students, "helpless" and "mastery-oriented." When the helpless students failed, they tended to ruminate about the causes of their lack of success. In contrast, when the mastery-oriented students failed, they focused on finding solutions to the problems they had failed at. Diener and Dweck also reported that the helpless students underestimated the number of their successes and overestimated that of their failures. When the helpless students had successes, they often reported that they didn't expect them to continue.

Summarizing these findings, Dweck (1990) identified distinct patterns of behavior that characterized the helpless and mastery-oriented children (even though the two groups had shown similar reactions to success problems). The strategies that the helpless children used quickly deteriorated. They almost immediately defined themselves as failures and began to offer excuses for their performances: they just didn't have the "right stuff"; they never could do these things; they wouldn't be any better in the future. Interestingly, they seemed to dismiss their past successes.

The mastery-oriented students, on the other hand, didn't blame themselves or offer excuses. They didn't see themselves as having failed; they wasted no time in devising new strategies and furnishing themselves with new self-instructions. They remained highly positive in predicting future success; many of them indicated their pleasure at the thoughts of future challenges. Dweck (1990, p. 203) summarized their reactions nicely: they saw any present failures as interludes between past and future successes.

In summary, the concept of learned helplessness has provided a meaningful way to understand the behavior of some students who have repeatedly over several years experienced many more failures than successes. It does not appear that simply increasing the number of their successes will significantly influence their outlook on learning. These conclusions point to a powerful teaching strategy: help students to realistically assess their failures and focus on increasing their efforts to achieve success and overcome feelings of helplessness.

Self-Efficacy and Motivation

In 1986, Bandura defined **self-efficacy** as "people's judgments of their capabilities to organize and execute courses of action to attain designated types of performances" (p. 391). What is important for us is Bandura's belief (1990) that self-efficacy is crucial for a student's *control* over motivation. Students who have a strong sense of efficacy tend to focus their attention and effort on the demands of tasks and to minimize potential difficulties (Bandura, 1986).

self-efficacy *Individuals' beliefs in their abilities to exert control over their lives; feelings of competency.*

Figure 10.4

Representation of the difference between efficacy expectations and outcome expectations within Bandura's (1977) theory of self-efficacy.

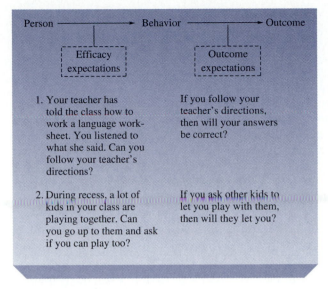

Person ⟶ Behavior ⟶ Outcome

Efficacy expectations

Outcome expectations

1. Your teacher has told the class how to work a language worksheet. You listened to what she said. Can you follow your teacher's directions?

2. During recess, a lot of kids in your class are playing together. Can you go up to them and ask if you can play too?

If you follow your teacher's directions, then will your answers be correct?

If you ask other kids to let you play with them, then will they let you?

efficacy expectation *The belief that one can perform the behavior or behaviors required to produce a certain outcome.*

outcome expectation *The belief that a given behavior will lead to a specific outcome.*

In self-efficacy theory, an **efficacy expectation** is differentiated from an **outcome expectation.** An outcome expectation represents a person's estimate that a given behavior will lead to a certain outcome; an efficacy expectation is an individual's belief that he or she can perform the behavior or behaviors required to produce certain outcomes. Outcome and efficacy expectations are differentiated because a student may believe that certain behaviors will produce an outcome, but may not believe that she or he can execute the behaviors which will produce the outcome. An illustration of this difference is provided in figure 10.4.

Students' feelings of efficacy influence what challenges they will face, how much effort they will expend, how long they will persevere, and how much stress they are willing to accept (Bandura, 1990). Deciding to try out for a part in the senior high school play, a student auditions, attends rehearsals, studies lines, and practices at home, all the time believing that she is qualified for the role and will do well in it. In other words, this student has selected a reasonably difficult goal (being in the play), processed information about the nature of the task and her ability (made decisions about self-efficacy), observed others succeeding at similar tasks (modeling), and begun to receive praise for her performance (feedback and reinforcement). All of these activities are linked to the notion of self-efficacy.

Students will accept only those goals that are meaningful to them and that they believe they have the capability to attain. For example, is the reading assignment in science relevant? Equally as important, is the reading level of the assignment manageable for students? If the answer is yes to both of these questions, a teacher can expect students to persist in their efforts and to tolerate inevitable frustration for lengthy periods. In other words, such students will remain motivated.

Students may possess low perceptions of efficacy in one skill domain (e.g., academics) and high perceptions of efficacy in other skill domains (e.g., sports). Moreover, self-perceptions of efficacy often vary from setting to setting. Research has shown that many handicapped children have higher self-concepts in self-contained special education classrooms than in regular education classrooms (Kaufman, Agard, & Semmel, 1985).

In the development of a scale to measure students' self-efficacy, Gresham, Evans, and Elliott (1988) found that the self-efficacy ratings of gifted, nonhandicapped, and mainstreamed mildly handicapped students varied in consistent patterns. Social, physical, and academic variations were observed. As expected, the handicapped students rated themselves as less efficacious in the academic skill domain than in the other domains, and in comparison to the nonhandicapped and gifted students. The gifted students rated themselves on average highest in the academic domain and lowest in the social domain. In some cases, the gifted students also rated themselves as less efficacious in the social and physical domains than did the nonhandicapped students. Thus, students' perceptions of their self-efficacy vary across skill domains and in comparison to fellow students who are known to function at different levels academically, socially, and physically.

Students and Help-Seeking Behavior

Researchers interested in the role of self-efficacy in teacher-student interactions have reported some important findings about students' help-seeking behaviors (Newman, 1990) and teachers' help-giving behaviors (Graham & Barker, 1990). Let us examine several of these studies in detail, given the important role that asking and giving help plays in the classroom. As Newman (1990) noted, the student who asks questions and obtains assistance when it is required alleviates immediate learning difficulties and also acquires knowledge and skills which can be used for self-help later. Despite the obvious importance of help-seeking in the classroom, many students do not ask teachers for help or avail themselves of help when it is needed (Good, Slavings, Harel, & Emerson, 1987).

Newman studied 177 third-, fifth-, and seventh-graders to examine why children often are reluctant to seek academic assistance from teachers. He assessed the students' perceived academic competence, intrinsic orientation, and attitudes and intentions regarding help-seeking in math class. The data from these assessments were used to answer this question: How do students' efforts at academic help-seeking vary according to characteristics of the students and social-interactional conditions in the classroom? Newman found (1990) that the influence of motivational factors on the children's intentions to seek help with academic problems was stronger for the third- and fifth-graders than for the seventh-graders. A student's expressed likelihood of seeking help increased with the strength of the student's belief that help-seeking is beneficial and with the weakness of the student's belief that it has associated costs.

Another finding was that, for all grades, the greater the student's perceived competence was, the less strongly the student felt that there were costs associated with seeking help. The implication regarding students with low perceived competence is the same as that regarding low achievers: those most in need of help may be those most reluctant to seek help.

Giving help to students is not always easy; nor is it without some possible negative side effects for students. According to a recent investigation by Graham and Barker (1990) of children ranging in age from 4 to 12 years, unsolicited teacher assistance signaled low ability to students. Compared with a nonhelped peer, a student receiving teacher assistance was judged less smart, less proud of success, more grateful, less likely to be successful in the future, and less preferable as a workmate. This study has important implications for help-givers, and emphasizes how instructional practices affect not only students' acquisition of skills, but also their motivation and efficacy for learning.

For the Classroom

Drawing heavily from the teacher expectancy literature, Alderman (1990) emphasized that teachers must show students that they want them to succeed and also that they expect students to achieve the major learning objectives for a class. Referring to her work as *The Link Model,* Alderman stressed that students need to see a link between what they do and a given learning outcome.

Figure 10.5 illustrates Alderman's link model and highlights its four main linking components: proximal goals, learning strategies, successful experiences, and attributions for success. Let's briefly explore each of these components.

- *Link 1: Proximal goals.* Goals play an important role in the development of self-motivation by establishing targets by which students can evaluate their own progress. To be effective, goals should be specific rather than general; attainable; and proximal, or close at hand, rather than long-term. Figure 10.6 illustrates the steps involved in planning and evaluating one's goals.
- *Link 2: Learning strategies.* Low achievers often are inefficient learners—that is, they fail to apply learning strategies that would facilitate their performance. In link 2, students are asked to identify effective learning strategies that will help them to accomplish their goals.

Figure 10.5
Motivational links to success.

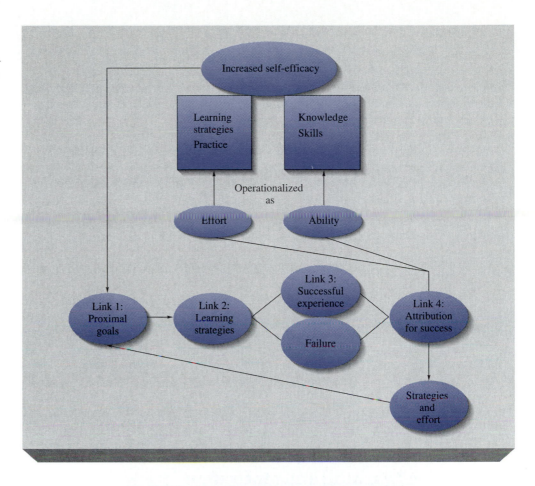

Figure 10.6
Proximal goals and progress.

Make your goals as specific as possible:

Planning

1. My specific learning goals for this week (today) are:

2. I will know I have accomplished my goals by:

3. Actions or steps I will take to accomplish these goals:

4. Possible blocks, both personal and outside, that may interfere with my goals:

5. If I need help, I can go to:

6. My confidence in reaching my goals is:

No confidence	Very confident
0	25

Evaluating

7. My satisfaction with my goal attainment is:

Very unsatisfied	Very satisfied
0	25

8. Reasons for attaining or not attaining my goals:

- *Link 3: Successful experiences.* A learning goal is the key to success in this component. Students measure their success using the proximal goals as the criteria. Teachers play a valuable role by creating opportunities for students to work on their goals and fostering effective learning conditions.
- *Link 4: Attributions for success.* Students are encouraged to attribute their success to their personal efforts or abilities. Teachers can help students make appropriate attributions; for example, they might ask, "What happened when you tried?" For difficult tasks, teachers' attributional feedback should begin with a focus on effort and then shift to students' abilities.

The link model for fostering motivation goes "full circle." Students who have succeeded and attributed their success to their own effort and ability have concrete performance feedback that will lead them to increased self-efficacy, which in turn will lead to increased confidence about goal accomplishments. All students will not consistently experience success; some failures will always occur.

When failure does occur, students' attributions for it are important determinants of their future expectations for success. Students who attribute failure to the use of weak or inappropriate strategies are more likely to try again. Attributing failure to a lack of effort when students feel they have put forth a strong effort can be damaging. Working closely with students to assess their performance and helping them to make realistic attributions about their successes and failures is an important task for teachers and parents. The link model provides a useful organizer for working with students who are at risk for motivation problems.

Although not specifically designed to facilitate self-efficacy, instructional techniques based on cooperative learning principles have been used effectively with a wide range of students. Let us examine this popular methodology next.

Cooperative Learning and Motivation

The dynamics of a classroom are deeply enmeshed in the give-and-take among classroom members—between student and student, and between students and teacher. Classroom atmosphere—especially the impact of competition and cooperation—powerfully affects motivation and learning. Recent research on cooperative learning offers several interesting and potentially useful classroom applications.

Cooperative learning is a set of instructional methods in which students are encouraged or required to work together on academic tasks, to help one another learn (Slavin, 1991). Such methods may include having students sit together for discussion or having them help each other with assignments and complex tasks. Slavin distinguished cooperative learning from peer tutoring by noting that in the former method, all students learn the same material, there is no tutor, and the initial information comes from the teacher.

cooperative learning *A set of instructional methods in which students are encouraged or required to work together on academic tasks.*

Increases in student achievement depend on the conditions of cooperative learning, which have important motivational consequences. For example, Johnson and Engelhard (1992) demonstrated that girls prefer cooperative learning more than boys do; this must be considered in forming groups. Motivation for cooperative learning is associated with the goal structures and potential rewards for group members (Cosden & Haring, 1992). Group members can attain their personal goals only if *the group* is successful. Consequently, two conditions must be met for cooperative learning to be effective. First, each cooperating group must have a *group goal* that is meaningful to its members (a prize, recognition, free time). Second, the group's success must emerge from the individual learning of *all* group members (Slavin, 1988). If these two conditions—identification of a group goal and individual accountability—are met, students are motivated to help each other learn.

Cooperative learning involves two aspects of classroom organization: *task structure* and *reward structure* (Slavin, 1987b). In cooperative learning, the task structures insure that group members work with one another. Reward structures may depend on the performance of the total group (such as a product they produce), or on the sum of the individual learning performances.

In an attempt to develop techniques designed to further cooperative learning, Slavin (1987b) proposed that students should work in small (four-member) groups of mixed ability, including one high achiever, two average achievers, and one low achiever. He also urged that students in each group be responsible for the material taught under regular classroom conditions, and for helping other group members to learn and to achieve the group goal.

One such technique is the *Student Teams-Achievement Division (STAD),* which consists of a definite cycle of activities. The teacher initially presents a lesson under regular classroom conditions. Students then attempt to master the material in their four-member groups. For example, if the subject is math, students may work on problems, compare their answers, and attack any difficulties that arise. Students now take individual tests, during which they cannot help each other.

The teacher next sums the results of the quizzes to obtain team scores. Since this is cooperative learning, the focus is on improvement for all group members. So the teacher compares students' scores on the test with their average scores on previous tests. For example, a student whose score is ten percent above the average earns three points for the group. An improvement of five to nine points earns two points; four points above to four points below the average earns one point; and anything below five points receives zero points.

Stating that research supports the superiority of this technique over other methods, Slavin (1987a) warned that simply putting students together will not produce learning gains. Students need to work toward a group goal, and all members must contribute, not just the smartest. Slavin (1991) emphasized that the most successful approaches to cooperative learning incorporate two key elements: group goals and individual responsibility. When these two features are used, achievement effects are consistently positive. For example, 37 of 44 experimental/control studies of at least four weeks' duration had significantly positive results. These positive effects were about the same at all grade levels, in all major subjects, in urban, rural, and suburban schools, and for high, average, and low achievers. Positive effects also have been found on such outcomes as self-esteem, intergroup relations, acceptance of academically handicapped students, and attitudes toward school (Slavin, 1991).

Cooperative learning seems to be a technique whose time has come. You may want to experiment with it in your classes, because, if properly handled, it can enhance motivation, encourage students of all races to work together, and introduce an element of tolerance into multicultural classrooms that might otherwise be lacking.

Motivation and Multicultural Students

One of the major contributions teachers can make to the successful integration and accomplishments of multicultural students is to provide an understanding, supportive environment. Garibaldi (1992), in discussing the motivation of African American males to succeed, urged that teachers publicly recognize the successful academic experiences of young African American men, thus helping them to improve their self-concepts, self-esteem, and academic confidence. Treating *all* students with respect and dignity is a vital first step. To be especially alert to the needs of those students whose physical appearance, speech, and behavior may differ from those of other students, you must be familiar with their cultural backgrounds.

Describe cooperative, competitive, and individualistic goal structures. Which goal structure do you work best under?

Annual **Edition**

➤ Will a Multicultural Curriculum Better Motivate Minority Children?

Is it important to give voice to the distinctions that exist within our schools and classrooms by revising curricula to include faces and ideas reflecting a multitude of colors, ethnicities, and cultures? Included in Jerome Bruner's *Acts of Meaning* is the following quotation, which argues for a multicultural approach to the school curriculum.

> When someone with the authority of a teacher, say, describes the world and you are not in it, there is a moment of psychic disequilibrium, as if you looked into a mirror and saw nothing. (Bruner, 1990, p. 32)

Issue

Students will better relate to and assimilate information that is meaningful to them.

Answer: Pro Cognitive learning theory tells us that students learn by assimilating new information into already existing schemata. David Ausubel describes this process when he talks about *meaningful learning*. For Ausubel, meaningful learning takes place when the material to be learned is related to what the learner already knows. Making a concept or topic relevant to a student's previous experience sets the stage for the acquisition of new meaning, which is a good description of learning.

Answer: Con Cognitive learning theory is only one way of explaining how we learn. There are many times when we are faced with information for which we have no reference point, but learn in spite of this. Behaviorists would attribute learning to positive reinforcement, to the positive consequences of similar behavior resulting in an enthusiastic repeat performance. This theory is not sensitive to the nature of the material itself, but rather to the circumstances in which it is presented. Consequently, a good teacher could motivate learners even if the students were all children of color learning to read from a basal text filled with stories and pictures of white suburban children.

Issue

A multicultural curriculum sends a message to the school community that all kinds of people are valued within the school. By modeling acceptable behavior in our culture, administrators and teachers can set an example that has a strong motivational influence on student behavior.

Answer: Pro Modeling on the part of the teacher and other people of authority within a school can be an effective way to influence behavior. Teachers' enthusiasm for the material goes a long way to motivate student interest. Teachers who wholeheartedly embrace a multicultural curriculum send a strong message of endorsement for such a program.

Answer: Con There is always the danger that a multicultural curriculum might not include all the learners in the classroom. To be left out of a program that promises to reflect everyone can be very damaging. Teachers who are less vigilant might not offer all students the opportunity to see themselves reflected in the material. A commitment to this curriculum that is less than enthusiastic, knowledgeable, and serious would do all learners a great disservice.

Issue

Once out in the world children must succeed in the mainstream culture, which is still predominantly white and Eurocentric. Doesn't a multicultural approach delude, if not ill serve, students of color?

Answer: Pro Teachers already feel there is not enough time to accomplish all the work that needs to be done in any school year. To study minor writers, scientists, or historical figures would take even more time out of an already compromised schedule. While the major figures in Western history and culture are for the most part white, male, and of European descent, this doesn't change the fact that they are the people who have shaped our culture. Our young people, to be considered educated, must be aware of mainstream history and accomplishments.

Answer: Con Only one part of a child's education consists of names and deeds and dates. The other part is the *process* that stands behind every thought and product of our culture. It is the discussion of the *how* that offers limitless opportunity to give reflection and voice to all of our citizens:

> The Asian, the Hispanic, the Jew
>
> The African, the Native American, the Sioux
>
> The Catholic, the Muslim, the French, the Greek
>
> The Irish, the Rabbi, the Priest, the Sheik
>
> The Gay, the Straight, the Preacher
>
> The privileged, the homeless, the teacher . . . .
>
> (Angelou, 1993)

Discussing strategies that help to meet the needs of multicultural students, Gary and Booker (1992) suggested several techniques to empower African American students to achieve academic success. Help these students to establish goals early in life. Recognize and foster their early interests, to help them engage in long-term thinking and avoid seeking immediate gratification. Recognize the need for racial pride. Be aware of distinct learning styles: remember that many African American students learn best in environments that encourage human interaction and verbal dialogue. Finally, try to foster in students a sense of self-control, and cultivate academic motivation as much as possible.

Language can also be a serious obstacle to acceptance for many students. A practical technique for helping students overcome language barriers was described by First (1988). Called the *English Plus* program, it was developed for the Washington, D.C. schools, and involves special strategies to supplement other language programs. For example, while multicultural students are learning English, the program uses peers and adults to work with students in their native languages. This and similar strategies can motivate and improve learning by providing both subject-matter help and role modeling.

No class is completely homogeneous. Teachers learn to expect differences among their students and search for ways to best reach their multicultural students. Make sure these students experience immediate success by assigning tasks within their capability and rewarding them for successful performance. Individualize instruction as much as possible by sequencing and pacing the programs carefully for individual children. Consider using a classwide peer tutoring program or cooperative learning groups (Sleeter & Grant, 1988, p. 55).

What does all of this motivational work mean for teaching and learning?

EDUCATIONAL IMPLICATIONS OF MOTIVATION

In a perceptive analysis of motivation and teaching, Wlodkowski (1986) noted that in any learning event, motivational strategies exercise a decisive influence at the beginning of learning, during learning, and at the end of learning.

The Beginning of Learning

There are two key motivational factors involved at this stage: attitudes and needs.

Attitudes

What are students' feelings about themselves, school, their teachers, and their subjects? As we discussed earlier in this chapter, you as the communicator bear great responsibility for student attitudes. You must identify what exactly is causing a student's negative attitude. Is the student uncomfortable with a subject because of either its novelty, or unsuccessful previous experiences with it? Has a student missed the fundamentals that are necessary for work in your class? Once you have located the problem, then you can precisely direct your efforts toward its solution.

For example, if some students believe that they simply lack the ability to succeed in a subject, your task will be to assess their level of competence and then construct a base from which they can experience success. If their difficulty seems to be mainly affective—they simply don't like the material—you might assign them to a group that enjoys the subject.

Needs

Students behave to satisfy all of their needs, and the need that is predominant at any moment will be a student's primary concern. For example, you may have prepared an

teacher – student

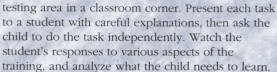

Motivation and Learning

1. Identifying the natural incentives of the age group you are teaching helps to initiate and sustain motivation.
   - Establish interest centers like a "Kids Did It" corner for elementary and middle-age students. Students can bring in projects they have made or display awards or accomplishments. A student who has won a medal at the state fair, for example, could bring it in and write about the experience. Such descriptions could be in a special folder for others to read.
   - Ask a student with a special hobby to write a report or make an oral presentation demonstrating it. Encourage other students to seek more information about that hobby (or others) by going to the library and reading books about it.
   - Divide your class into small heterogenous groups to research a topic of their choice: animals, sports, costumes, underwater adventure, etc. Then have them choose the method by which they will present their findings to the class: by using the overhead projector, making a filmstrip, a video, a movie, a model, etc.
2. In the initial phase of learning, be sure to identify the attitudes and needs of your students.
   - Examine your students carefully to make sure their negative attitudes and needs are not causing them to fail. They may have phobic reactions to particular subjects (like math, spelling, computers). Discuss with them how these fears could interfere with their success. If they persist, suggest counseling, remedial work, or even academic therapy.
   - Learn as much as possible about your students' attitudes and needs. You may want to use a temporary divider in your classroom to create a testing area in a classroom corner. Present each task to a student with careful explanations, then ask the child to do the task independently. Watch the student's responses to various aspects of the training, and analyze what the child needs to learn.
3. Knowing your students well enables you to determine the appropriate level of stimulation to be used in your teaching.
   - In the lower elementary grades, encourage your students to talk about their families. Discuss family concepts with them, pointing out ways that you as a teacher and the children in your class care for one another at school, and ways family members show care at home. By doing such things you become a friend of the very young student.
   - In the lower grades, take a photograph of each child and mount it on a sheet of construction paper. Have children write (or dictate) several sentences telling you about their likes or dislikes and other information. Keep this information in a folder and refer to it from time to time as a means of getting acquainted with your students and offering them the stimulation they need to become motivated students.
   - In middle school especially, look for clues that will help you to get to know students who are erratic and difficult to stimulate. Do they like to work alone or in small groups? Do they have rigid thought patterns and need structure to succeed, or do they thrive on change and novelty? Examine your teaching style. Are you highly structured or relaxed? Do you rely heavily on verbal instruction, or do you use lots of visuals? You may find clues that will help you to coordinate your teaching style with the learning style of these students.

extremely stimulating lesson that is lost on the student who skipped breakfast and is ravenous by eleven o'clock. It is well to be guided by the indisputable fact that for most of us, physiological needs demand our immediate consideration.

Safety needs require a different type of response. Most students have had their fundamental safety needs met at home. This is not to say, however, that they are incapable of feeling anxiety. High anxiety does not correlate with high achievement; consequently, anything you can do to relieve this condition will help the student.

Classroom work can help to combat the fears that accompany each developmental stage. For example, young children are afraid of the dark, the unknown, animals, and loud noises; from ages 9 to 18, fears relate to school failure and social relations. Probably the best advice to be offered with regard to students' needs is this: Make your classroom as physically and psychologically safe as possible.

During Learning

The key motivational processes involved during the middle stage of learning are stimulation and affect.

Stimulation

To what are the students attending during the learning experience? Are there elements in the material or in the environment that attract—and distract—their attention? One of the most effective means of ensuring that students find a lesson stimulating is to involve their need for achievement. Working from the assumption that personal motives and increased individual effort can be stimulated in the classroom, deCharms (1976) asserted that motivation is tightly linked to students' identification of the origin of their actions.

Origins and *pawns* are terms used to distinguish the two motivational states that are basic to personal causation. Origins are those who believe that they control their own fate; pawns believe they are at the mercy of everyone and everything. A given person is not always an origin or a pawn, but one of these feelings usually predominates. (This concept is similar to that of locus of control, but deCharms believes that locus of control emphasizes reinforcement, while the origin-pawn concept stresses students' determination of their own goals and the courses of action needed to attain them.)

To enhance the motivation of teachers, the first step is to have them focus on their own motives. In his workshops, deCharms asked teachers to write imaginative stories in response to six pictures. This was intended to assess individuals' needs for achievement. The teachers were then asked to write essays in response to the question, "Who am I?" The teachers were encouraged to tell the group something about themselves: their goals, values, hobbies, lifestyles. As the group members became more comfortable with one another, discussion became more open.

While this was going on, each teacher was asked to step outside and prepare to play a ring-toss game. A stake was set up at one end of the room, with three-foot distances marked off from it. Each participant was given four rings to toss from any distance desired. The only stipulation was that all rings had to be thrown from the same distance. The objective of the game was to demonstrate the level of an individual's need achievement. Interestingly, those individuals who stood far from the stake and those who stood quite close had lower need achievement than those who selected intermediate distances. The rationale is that the intermediate group realistically decided that certain distances posed a challenge for them, indicating a high need for achievement.

Another technique used was the blindfold game. Here, one teacher was blindfolded and a partner was chosen to be the guide. The guide was responsible for taking the blindfolded member to dinner and back to the meeting room. The purpose of this exercise was to demonstrate individual differences in giving and receiving help, and to make the teachers aware of feelings of power and control.

Similar techniques were suggested to the teachers for use with their students. For example, the teachers were urged to have their students write stories with achievement themes that they elicited from the children. A class could be told that they were to think about a story that they would write on Friday. The discussion during the week would focus on a main character's efforts to do better (thus indicating the objective). The stories could then be used in a weekly essay contest and judged by the students.

Affect

How do students feel about their classroom work? If affect is a constant companion of learning, actually an integral part of the process, then student attributions have practical implications for the classroom. When students assign a cause to behavior, that assignment carries with it strong emotional overtones. For example, in one study, Weiner and his colleagues (1978) had subjects read brief stories about success and failure that also contained the reasons for the successes and failures. Here is one of the stories.

Francis studied intensely for a test he took. It was very important for Francis to record a high score on this exam. Francis received a very high score on the test. Francis felt that he received this high score because he studied so intensely. How do you think Francis felt upon receiving this score?

Subjects were asked to give the emotional reaction of the person in the story by selecting affective words from a list presented to them. There were ten different stories, with ten different reasons for success. Some words, such as *pleased* and *happy,* appeared in almost all of the attributions for success. But the reasons for the success influenced many of the words chosen. For example, if subjects attributed success to an unstable effort, they chose words like *ecstatic* and *uproarious.*

Eleven other stories attributed failure to luck, ability, and fatigue. When ability was mentioned, subjects chose words such as *incompetent* and *inadequate;* when the cause was given as luck, their responses were *stunned* and *overwhelmed.* Thus it seemed possible to discriminate between subjects' attributions by the affective words they chose.

These studies have direct implications for teachers: different emotions are associated with different attributions for success and failure. If students think that they have succeeded at a task because they were lucky, they will have no feeling of pride at the outcome. Similarly, if their failure is attributed to lack of effort and not lack of ability, they may experience feelings of shame, but no loss of confidence.

When Learning Ends

The key motivational processes involved during the last stage of learning are competence and reinforcement.

Competence

If by competence we mean a feeling of controlling our environment, then competence is a powerful motive in our lives. You can help your students achieve competence by making sure that they have the skills necessary to attain desired goals. By doing this, you also communicate to them that their classroom environment will support them in their work (Ford, 1992). In this way, you provide them with skill mastery and feelings of classroom acceptance.

Retention is aided by having pupils actually practice the behavior whenever possible: "*Watch how I'm adjusting the microscope. Don't move it too quickly. OK, now you try it.*" Be sure that your students have the capability of acquiring the behavior that you are modeling; when the desired behavior appears, arrange for immediate reinforcement. A sense of competence not only reduces fear and anxiety for a task, but also increases the effort expended; thus, *self-efficacy* becomes a powerful motivating force (Bandura, 1977, 1986).

Reinforcement

Since the theoretical aspects of reinforcement were thoroughly discussed in chapter 7, our focus here is on specific classroom use. Remember to reinforce immediately. Whenever possible, provide reinforcement while students are still learning. Reinforce with small amounts rather than large amounts. Use reinforcers—praise, stars, points, etc.—frequently, but in sufficiently small amounts to avoid having them become meaningless for students. Finally, reinforce small improvements in learning and motivation. A common mistake of teachers is to demand too much before they reinforce, thus discouraging students and interrupting the flow of learning.

APPLICATIONS AND REFLECTIONS

Chapter Highlights

Motivation: Meaning and Myths
- Motivation arouses, sustains, and integrates behavior.
- Several myths have grown up around motivation that can obscure its actual meaning and cause classroom difficulty.
- Recognizing the distinction between intrinsic and extrinsic motivation can help you to devise techniques that improve learning in your classes.

What Causes Motivation?
- Of the various attempts to explain motivation, Maslow's needs hierarchy has had a lasting impact, due to the appeal of its theoretical and practical implications.
- McClelland's explanation of need achievement has direct classroom bearing, especially its identification of the importance of your students' expectations and values.
- Students search for the causes of their behaviors just as teachers do. To explain this phenomenon, Weiner has been a leader in the development of attribution theory. Knowing whether students attribute their behaviors to ability, effort, task difficulty, or luck can help you to improve their self-concepts, by realistically examining their abilities in light of the tasks, thus furthering learning.
- Skinner has long believed that the proper use of schedules of reinforcement (see chap. 7) can improve motivation and, in general, enhance classroom performance.
- According to Bandura, your performance in the classroom can be a powerful model for your students to imitate. Once you recognize desirable behavior in your students, act swiftly to reinforce that behavior.

What Affects Students' Motivation?
- Among the most potent influences on motivation are anxiety, attitudes, curiosity, and locus of control.
- Anxiety, either situational or trait, affects classroom performance either positively or negatively. Increasing anxiety lessens performance as task complexity increases.
- A positive attitude toward school and learning increases achievement. Be particularly concerned with not only your students' attitudes toward you and the subjects you are teaching, but also their attitudes about themselves.
- All of your students possess a certain degree of curiosity that, if capitalized upon, can lead to richer and more insightful learning. Structured but relaxed classroom conditions that allow for an acceptance of students' ideas can encourage the creative use of curiosity.

- The locus of control concept can be useful in improving the achievement of your pupils, especially the "externals." By carefully providing reinforcement for selected behaviors, you not only improve their learning, but also help them to develop more positive self-concepts.
- Repeated criticism and failure can produce learned helplessness, a form of behavior that causes pupils to give up, just refusing to try. If you find such students, your first task will be to persuade them to make an effort so that you can begin to reinforce them.

Educational Implications of Motivation

- Considering various stages of learning—the beginning, the middle, and the end— leads to the direct application of motivational theory and research in the classroom, for both you and your students.

Connections

1. Think about how you learn and describe how one of the major concepts discussed in this chapter is part of your learning activities or approach.

_____

_____

_____

_____

_____

_____

2. Identify at least one learning situation (classroom instruction, self-study, taking a test, small-group work) and describe how you would apply one of the key concepts examined in this chapter *if you were a teacher*.

_____

_____

_____

_____

_____

_____

Getting the Picture and Drawing Relationships

Think about the various learning concepts and variables discussed in this chapter. Create pictures, graphics, or figures that highlight the relationships among key components.

Personal Journal

What I really learned in this chapter was _____

_____

_____

_____

_____

_____

What this means to me is _____

_____

_____

_____

_____

_____

Questions that were stimulated by this chapter include _____

_____

_____

_____

_____

_____

Key Terms

attribution theory	337	internals	347	outcome expectation	351
cooperative learning	354	intrinsic motivation	333	self-efficacy	350
discovery learning	336	learned helplessness	348	situational anxiety	342
efficacy expectation	351	locus of control	347	test anxiety	343
externals	347	need achievement theory	337	Yerkes-Dodson law	343
extrinsic motivation	333				

section

4

design and management of classroom instruction

Barbara Cotter, the high school English teacher we met earlier, was one of two teachers just elected to the school council at the Senior high school. Recent state legislation had mandated the formation of these groups, and individual schools across the state were wrestling with their missions. As this council's first meeting approached, Barbara was attempting to identify what her role would be. The other teacher elected, Kevin Jones, was a popular instructor in mathematics. He had stopped Barbara in the corridor yesterday and suggested they meet before the first scheduled group session.

In thinking about what she would say to Kevin, and mulling over her role on the school

elementary, junior high, and senior high schools. She also recalled that in the days of her professional training, her instructor in educational psychology had mentioned the need for teachers to have both general and specific ideas about what they want to accomplish.

When she met Kevin the next day, he was less than enthusiastic. "Barbara, I don't have a clue about what's expected of us. Why don't we let Joe Greene (the principal) spell out what he wants us to do? That will save us time and probably a lot of trouble."

Barbara hesitated and then said, "I know, Kevin. It would save a hassle and probably win us some points. But I'm not sure I want to let Joe call

chapter 11

planning for essential learning outcomes

council, Barbara was perplexed. "I'm pleased the faculty trusts me to represent them, but I'd like to feel better about what I can contribute. I suppose the first step would be to look at the literature distributed to the new members." As she read the guidelines, Barbara noticed the council had four major responsibilities: adopt relevant educational goals, identify the needs of their students, review the annual school budget, and formulate a school improvement plan. "Well, it certainly makes sense to start with goals," Barbara said to herself. "If we don't know where we're going, it's hard to figure out a way to get there."

After reading the guidelines, she realized this was a unique opportunity to think about the role of the high school today, to identify what students should know when they left, to suggest means of assessing students, and, finally, to examine as critically and objectively as possible how good a job the high school was doing with its students. She laughed as she wrote down this last task. "What's the latest name for this? Oh, yes: school delivery standards. Well, this won't leave me much time to get into trouble."

As she thought about her responsibility to be a productive member of the school council, she remembered that a recent edition of a national educational journal had been devoted to the issue of what skills and knowledge students of all ages needed to have upon completing

the shots. After all, the faculty elected us to represent them. I like Joe—he's a good principal—but he's got a different perspective. After all, we're the ones on the firing line every day. Let's see if we can work something out ourselves."

Of the millions of words written about education, perhaps none are so true as those that apply to goals, objectives, and plans. As you read this chapter, remember that *your* objectives are one part of a much larger scenario. While there is as yet no set of national standards, specialists in the various disciplines are devising criteria you can use as *standards* to assess your students.

Having analyzed the major features and theories of development and having examined the intricacies of the learning process, we come now to the teaching act itself—what you do in the classroom. Before commencing our work, it would be well to step back and ask ourselves, "Why am I doing this? What do I hope to attain? What should students take from their endeavors?" In other words, our concern in this chapter will be with the objectives of instruction.

First, we must make the distinction between the **goals** of education— the broad, general aims of schooling that are desirable for all of our citizens—and those more narrowly defined **objectives** of instruction that are suited to individuals and classes. These distinctions are

goals *Clear, precise statements of educational priorities.*

objectives *Those instructional and learning outcomes deemed worthy of attainment.*

Educational Standards 368
Standards for Disciplines 368

Deciding on Educational Objectives 368
Classroom Objectives 369
What Place Schooling? 370

The Role of Objectives in Instruction 371
Why Bother with Objectives? 371
Descriptions, Goals, and Objectives 373
Goals and Multicultural Students 374
What Are Good Objectives? 376
Writing Acceptable Objectives 377
Sources of Objectives 378

Instructional Objectives and School Subjects 380
Reading 381
Mathematics 385
Science 388

Applications and Reflections 391

provided here along with definitions that will guide our work throughout the remainder of the chapter.

Goals: Those broad, general aims that identify educational priorities for a society (e.g., Learns to read, write, and do basic mathematical processes)

Objectives: Those instructional outcomes that together describe the range of student learning (e.g., Uses the computer as a word processor)

Learning Outcomes: Instructional outcomes stated as specific student behaviors (e.g., Can insert and delete material by using the correct computer commands)

Second, we will focus on specific objectives, illustrating the "good" objective and suggesting several sources that you would find helpful in learning to state objectives that are pertinent for your purposes.

Third, our concern will shift to the role of educational psychology in helping you formulate valuable objectives. One way of accomplishing this task is to present problems identified by educational psychologists in various subjects. For example, such concepts as the coding process in reading, the nature of error in mathematics, and the role of knowledge structures in science all can help you to focus your instructional objectives.

When you have finished reading this chapter, you should be able to

- recall the proposals in the discussion of national standards
- identify the role of your classroom objectives in relation to educational standards
- recall the benefits of formulating pertinent objectives
- recognize the characteristics of good objectives
- recognize suitable methods for deriving relevant and important objectives
- acquire information about the major published sources of objectives
- acquire information about the challenges to learning that are inherent in the subject you are teaching

EDUCATIONAL STANDARDS

To identify your role in the overall scheme of standards, goals, and objectives, you can visualize your planning activities from different perspectives. The primary task for all of us, at all levels, is to improve our schools. Many are beginning to view this challenge from a national perspective: What should American children acquire in their schooling? If you think of your role in establishing objectives for your students in this larger setting, you will begin to sense, perhaps more clearly than you have in the past, how important your identification of specific objectives is for your students.

In a thoughtful analysis of the mission of our schools, Gardner (1991) noted that in addition to a multitude of responsibilities (teaching of the basics, administrative chores, addressing of social issues), our schools also face the formidable task of presenting the fundamental concepts and burgeoning discoveries of specific disciplines. When he initially became interested in educational reform, Gardner recalled, he soon realized that it was necessary to involve four critical elements: assessment, curriculum, teacher education, and community support—all of which relate to the purposes of education.

If you were in a teachers' meeting and were asked about standards in your field, how would you define standard? How would you include the ideas of quality and excellence?

Standards for Disciplines

The national concern about identifying and raising standards in our schools is seen in the question that most educators are now addressing: Are there some things that *all* students should know? This concern with standards reflects the growing national unease with the current state of American education. It also reflects the desires of professionals to bring improvement to the classroom. For example, several reports in recent years have identified what students should know in specific disciplines: *Science For All Americans* presents what educated citizens should know about science, mathematics, and technology; *Civitas* outlines what is needed to be a good citizen; the widely heralded *Curriculum and Evaluation Standards For School Mathematics* suggests objectives for the mathematics curriculum (O'Neil, 1993).

Although the notion of national standards may be an idea whose time has come, the path to attaining these standards may be rocky. As O'Neil (1993) noted, we are not yet sure of what is meant by the term *standard*. Does it imply simply "what is good enough"? Or is it an attempt to identify a standard of excellence (Sizer & Rogers, 1993)? In an attempt to clarify the issues surrounding standards, the National Council on Education Standards and Testing recommended that national standards should include **content standards** (identification of material that should be taught), **performance standards** (the level of mastery required), **system performance standards** (how well the school system is doing its job), and **school delivery standards** (the effectiveness of instruction). The council also urged that a national assessment system be developed to measure standards (see also Simmons & Resnick, 1993). These concerns about standards should alert teachers to the value of their own classroom planning.

content standards *Material that should be taught*

performance standards *The level of mastery required for a task.*

system performance standards *Measures of how well a school system is doing its job.*

school delivery standards *A school's effectiveness in instruction.*

DECIDING ON EDUCATIONAL OBJECTIVES

When you turn to the classroom, how will you define your teaching as successful? The only answer to this question can be that your teaching is successful if your students learn. The next question is this: What is it my students are expected to learn? And the answer: Students are supposed to learn specified content, which must be clearly understood by *both* teacher and pupils. When students don't know what is called for, their performance suffers. A teacher's effectiveness in the classroom can falter when the focus of instruction is dissipated. What precisely do you want your students to accomplish in a particular lesson, a unit, a course? These concerns take us into the world of objectives.

"I'm usually three days ahead of a regular class, one day ahead of the fast learners and two days behind a classful of them."

Learning suffers when objectives are missing or poorly stated.

© 1992 by Sidney Harris.

Throughout this chapter we will concentrate on the role of objectives in instruction, discussing why we should take the time to think about them, write them, and attempt to achieve them. Before we do so, however, it would be helpful to concentrate on some practical benefits that come to both teachers and students from the concern with objectives.

Remember: this relates to *you and your students*. It's deceptively easy to become enmeshed in *this* day's work, *this* lesson, and *this* test. There's nothing wrong with such planning; in fact, you won't do a good job on any particular day if you don't devote thought to your work for that day. But research has shown that most teachers are not initially concerned with specific objectives to be attained by their pupils at the end of a unit. Experienced teachers seem to engage in about eight types of planning: weekly, daily, long-range, short-range, term, and yearly planning; lesson planning; and unit planning. Note that six of these relate to time (Clark & Peterson, 1986). Teachers usually plan activities to fill available instructional time. They also use teachers' editions of textbooks and curriculum guides, but it is only after teaching that they measure their work against objectives (Brown, 1988).

Although research is scanty about the planning of secondary school teachers, elementary teachers' planning seems to focus on daily plans within the context of weekly, unit, term, and yearly plans. The organizational context (materials, tests, and curriculum guides) greatly influences teachers.

Studying the planning of twelve middle school (seventh- and eighth-grade) teachers by interviews and by analysis of their plans, Brown (1988) found that their planning involved "nested" decision making (general to specific, yearly to daily). One of the most interesting findings was the teachers' tendencies to rely on experience: their own notes, handouts, worksheets, audiovisual materials, and tests. In other words, the teachers turned to what they had successfully used in the past. This interesting finding requires more research in an attempt to discover what guides teachers in their initial planning.

The basis of their planning included the following:

- What topics to cover the next day
- What materials to prepare for the next day
- How to conduct lessons
- What topics to review from the day before
- How to sequence activities
- What kinds of discussions to have with students
- What to use for written activities
- What homework to assign
- When to schedule tests
- How to test

As a result of this study, Brown (1988) concluded that teachers act as curriculum facilitators and not curriculum planners. Also, teachers seem to depend heavily on their unit notebooks; it would be well to determine the reasons why teachers include what they do in these planning books. Finally, it seems clear that teachers have limited purposes in their planning that gradually broaden to include long-term objectives.

Classroom Objectives

In any discussion of objectives, there is inevitably controversy concerning student objectives versus teacher objectives. Do you see the two as identical? Should they be? Should you attempt to merge the two? Is that possible?

Our task, then, is to encourage teachers to formulate specific objectives that will encompass their daily concerns. By relating what your students are doing now to what they will be doing in the future, and to the greater reason they are learning this material,

Focus ◄ High-Achieving African American Schools

Sizemore (1990) graphically traced in her description of a primarily African American school in the Pittsburgh, Pennsylvania system what goes into the making of a high-achieving school. In 1979, of Pittsburgh's 21 African American elementary schools (schools with 70 percent or more African American students), 5 were considered to be "high achieving." High achievement was determined by reading and math scores. The board of education was forced to search for an explanation of these different outcomes.

Sizemore first compared the differences between the low- and the high-achieving schools. She found that in the high-achieving schools, parents were treated as equal members in a partnership and were welcome in the school; principals were more authoritarian, were more independent of the central office (which enabled them to respond more quickly to community needs), and assumed responsibility for student discipline; and there was a consensus among teachers, parents, and principals that high achievement should be the priority.

In the low-achieving school examined by Sizemore, there was no such consensus. The principal felt restrained by the central office, did not stand with teachers in discipline problems, and tended to retain unsatisfactory teachers rather than undertake the sometimes difficult task of "persuading" them to leave. The principal also spent less time interacting with students than did the principals of the high-achieving schools. Not only student achievement but also morale was lower than in the other schools, while absenteeism was higher.

When Sizemore returned to this school five years later, a new, systemwide school improvement had been put into practice, a new principal was in place, and excellence had become the major objective. The new principal, who was mildly authoritarian, had convinced staff and community that high achievement was the top priority. This had not been done without a struggle. Weak teachers had been persuaded to leave; revolts against the principal had occurred, but had failed, because of the support of the majority of the staff and community; questionable programs had been eliminated, thus providing more time on task for students. The principal devoted considerable time to student interactions and also helped teachers with their discipline problems, not hesitating to refer for suspension those students who had committed serious breaches of discipline. Once this policy of student responsibility for their actions was recognized, the number of serious problems decreased dramatically.

As a result of these changes, Sizemore (1990) identified the following features as characterizing those schools with high-achieving African American students.

- A moderately authoritarian principal
- A principal who does not fear to be different in order to help students achieve to the best of their ability
- Agreement between school and community concerning high achievement as the top-priority objective
- An educational environment contributing to high expectations for student achievement
- Clearly stated rules and regulations intended to help students realize their goals
- The willingness of teachers and principals to fight for those policies and programs that lead to high achievement

you take your work to another level. This process links practical and theoretical considerations in a way that makes learning more meaningful and useful. A path is charted that can help your students to learn more meaningfully, and also to use and apply present learning to their future work. They can address questions like this: How does today's lesson on *Hamlet* relate to the goals of the unit? Is there any potential transfer to history or current events classes?

To maintain this higher level of instruction, you must continually decide exactly what you want your students to accomplish. If there is one indispensable guideline for formulating objectives, it is this: Be precise. Learning will improve because students will know exactly what is expected of them and, consequently, will understand the basis of their marks and grades. In their excellent analysis of objectives, Bloom, Madaus, and Hastings (1981) noted that statements of educational objectives describe, in a relatively specific manner, what students should be able to produce or do, or what characteristics students should possess after the learning.

In our analysis, we'll move from discussing the general lofty goals that society assigns to our schools to examining specific objectives in specific subjects.

What Place Schooling?

In 1984, John Goodlad's widely discussed text, *A Place Called School*, was published. In it, he asked a simple but unsettling question: Can we have effective schools? The implication, of course, is that popular opinion is skeptical, if not downright hostile, toward public education. But as Goodlad notes, such negative reactions appear to be directed at "education" in general. Most of the parents surveyed stated that while schools across the country were doing a poor job, *their own* child's school was doing just fine. This is an interesting distinction and one that leads to an analysis of our expectations—that is, our goals—for our public schools.

Tracing educational literature for more than three hundred years, Goodlad and his colleagues concluded that four broad areas of school goals have emerged:

academic goals *Those goals that include intellectual skills and domains of knowledge.*

vocational goals *Those goals intended to enhance responsibility by focusing on the search for gainful employment.*

social and civic goals *Those goals intended to prepare students for socialization into a complex society.*

personal goals *Those goals that emphasize the development of individual responsibility, talent, and free expression.*

1. **Academic goals.** These include all intellectual skills and domains of knowledge.
2. **Vocational goals.** These are intended to enhance self-responsibility by aiding the search for gainful employment.
3. **Social and civic goals.** These are intended to prepare the student for socialization into a complex society;
4. **Personal goals.** These emphasize the development of individual responsibility, talent, and free expression.

Given the variety of tasks that we expect our schools to accomplish (see chap. 1), articulation of clear and nationally accepted goals is no easy assignment, even with widespread recognition of certain broad, desirable educational concerns—for example, that the school should do a good job in academic matters. Goodlad (1984) asserted that two prerequisites must be met if today's schools are to succeed: (a) society's charge to the schools must be understood by those the school serves, as well as by professional educators; and (b) new conditions, similar to those that gave rise to our present system, must emerge. Otherwise, educators will lack a clear mandate, and the attainment of goals will remain elusive.

But for our purposes, the next task is to discover the means by which you can implement in your classroom those goals that Americans do agree on. As Borich (1992) noted, your objectives must reflect clearly identified goals if you are to justify them to parents, students, school administrators, and the community. Let us turn our attention to instructional objectives.

THE ROLE OF OBJECTIVES IN INSTRUCTION

It is the end of August and you know that on the Wednesday after Labor Day you will be facing your class(es) for the first time. Whether you are in an elementary school teaching subtraction or in a secondary school teaching Biology 1, you are faced with the same question: What exactly do I want these students to learn?

You quickly realize, however, that this is not the only question. What behaviors will you accept in your students as evidence that they have learned? Having determined what you want to accomplish and what your students should know, you now turn your attention to the techniques and materials you will use (Lovell-Troy, 1989). Finally, since you need some evidence that your students have learned, you must devise some means of evaluating their performance.

In short, you must have clearly defined *instructional objectives* that form an integrated whole to guide all of your teaching: *planning, teaching,* and *testing.* As Airasian (1994, p. 81) noted, the intent of stating an educational objective is to identify student outcomes in order to select appropriate instructional methods and resources, to communicate to others the purposes of instruction, and to help plan assessments.

Why Bother with Objectives?

To write good objectives is a time-consuming, absorbing task. Why should you bother? Before considering specific reasons, you should be aware that given the current decrease in dependence on textbooks and curriculum guides for the identification of objectives (particularly in such subjects as language arts), teacher planning is assuming greater importance. This is just one example of a deeper teacher involvement in the decision-making process. Although positive, this trend could cause conflict within a school system unless it was carefully handled. Everyone involved—parents, teachers, students, and administrators—must recognize the need for both individual and collective decision making. *Teachers must make decisions based on the needs of the individual learners in their classrooms.*

The diversity found in any classroom testifies to the critical role that teachers play in formulating any plans about their students. Maxim's plea (1991) that teachers plan for individuals is rooted in the differences among the students in any classroom in age, sex, height, weight, personality, race, achievement level, values, interests, and learning styles, among other factors. Airasian (1994) addressed much the same issue when he noted that classroom characteristics range from the number of students in the classroom and the size of the library to such individual differences as parental interest.

There are many reasons for writing thoughtful objectives. One of these is that many pupils simply don't know what teachers expect. By writing clearly stated objectives, teachers keep their instruction focused and students quickly learn what is expected of them. They also recall more information (Muth et al., 1988).

Many school districts have established **expected learner outcomes (ELOs)** for each primary grade. Originating in the basic competency movement in education, ELOs are used to communicate a school district's learning expectations to parents, teachers, and students. Well-written ELOs list curriculum-referenced cognitive and behavior objectives that can be empirically assessed.

expected learner outcomes (ELOs) *Cognitive and behavioral objectives used to express learning expectations to students, teachers, and parents.*

Many school districts use their ELOs in making decisions about school entry and grade retentions. Ideally, preschool screening tests should be highly congruent with a school's kindergarten ELOs. Thus, those selecting preschool screening measures can assess their content validity by systematically comparing them to the ELOs developed by the schools the children will attend. A representative set of kindergarten ELOs for reading, writing, and mathematics is illustrated in Table 11.1.

One specific method of linking objectives to content is called **task analysis.** This method breaks down a body of material into distinct attainable tasks. For example, in a unit on American history, after students had studied about the American presidents, a teacher might say, "This week we're going to see how some former presidents led the country in times of peril. We'll discuss Washington, Lincoln, and Franklin Roosevelt."

task analysis *The breaking of a task into its essential elements.*

Task analysis would require this teacher to decide first how these lessons related to the unit's objectives. Next, the teacher would have to be sure that the pupils had the skills to carry out any assignments. Did they have the necessary reading skills? Did they know how to do independent research? Had they been taught outlining skills? Could they write research papers? Next, the teacher would have to decide on materials and methods. Different stimuli would be used (pictures, stories, movies), in both direct teaching and group activities. Finally, the teacher would determine what kinds of pupil behavior would be accepted as evidence of learning.

If there is some hierarchical order to a component task, students should understand the logical sequence, and the necessity to integrate all components for achievement of the completed task. The teaching of the separate elements requires constant reference to the whole task to furnish direction and meaning to the learning. In a geography class, for example, a student needs to know fundamental facts about a country, but the teacher should relate these to an ultimate objective: determining the causes of the country's foreign policy, for example, and attempting to predict future action.

Questions like these can help a teacher identify and evaluate component tasks. Exactly what is it that we wish our pupils to achieve? (For example, knowledge of the actions of presidents in troubled times.) What tasks must pupils undertake to gain these goals? (For example, reading, writing, outlining, research.) What stimuli must be provided to insure the necessary knowledge and skill to complete these tasks? (For example, books, films, group discussion.) Using present information about varied curricula, techniques of grouping, assessment of capacity, and the like, students could progress by a graded series of discernible stages.

Table 11.1

Kindergarten ELOs	
Subject	**Expected learner outcomes**
Reading	1. Identify common objects or pictures in the environment. 2. Identify these positions: above-below, behind–in front, top-bottom, and left-right. 3. Distinguish likenesses and differences. 4. Identify lowercase manuscript letters. 5. Identify uppercase manuscript letters. 6. Identify rhyming pictures. 7. Match upper- and lowercase manuscript letters. 8. Sequence pictures. 9. Select pictures that show story endings. 10. Recognize words that begin with the same sound.
Writing	1. Identify these positions: above-below, behind–in front, top-bottom, and left-right. 2. Distinguish likenesses and differences. 3. Identify lowercase manuscript letters. 4. Identify uppercase manuscript letters. 5. Match upper- and lowercase manuscript letters. 6. Sequence pictures.
Mathematics	1. Identify elements of a set. 2. Identify the smaller or larger object. 3. Identify these simple closed figures: circle, triangle, and square. 4. Compare the number of elements in two sets and indicate which is greater. 5. Classify objects or pictures according to color and shape. 6. Count concrete objects. 7. Count to ten by ones. 8. Identify one-half of a concrete object. 9. Identify these coins: penny, nickel, dime and quarter. 10. Identify sets with an equal number of elements. 11. Identify the cardinal number of a set of not more than ten elements. 12. Identify the primary colors.

Source: Modeled after the New Orleans' Public Schools Kindergarten ELOS, Fall 1984.

Descriptions, Goals, and Objectives

Although we have moved from a consideration of broad educational goals to the level of more restricted, attainable instructional objectives, further distinctions can still be made.

Educational psychology is a course designed to familiarize students with the basic processes of development, learning, and instruction.

Stop for a moment to think about this statement. Is it an educational goal? Why? Why not? Is it an instructional objective? Why? Obviously, it is neither. It is a course description that could appear in any university catalog in the country.

Students should develop respect for members of different ethnic groups, people of different colors, and individuals of different religious beliefs.

How would you categorize this statement—as description, goal, or objective? You probably realized immediately that this is one of those broad educational goals we previously discussed.

As you read this text in educational psychology, you should use those learning strategies discussed in chapter 7.

Focus — An Example of Task Analysis

Usually, the task analysis approach requires that an algorithm of instruction be specified in constructing the task components. An example of this requirement is seen in the work of Salvia and Hughes (1990), who illustrated the teaching of division to elementary school students. As noted in the picture below, there are three methods for teaching simple division. The first strategy is called the *goes into* method and involves this sequence: 3 goes into 21 exactly 7 times. The second method, sometimes used in special classes, involves a subtraction algorithm, and is sometimes called *cumulative subtraction:* subtract 3 from 21, 3 from 18, etc.; count the tallies; and arrive at the answer of 7. The third algorithm for teaching division is the *button to button* method. The students are usually taught to use hand calculators to solve the problem sequence, by learning the appropriate order of pushing buttons on the device.

Different algorithms for teaching division.

How would you classify this statement? As a general educational goal? No. As a course description? No. What we see here is a statement regarding the processes you should be using; it says nothing about product.

> *When you complete this text, you should be familiar with those topics that comprise educational psychology.*

Is this an objective? Yes. What kind of objective? Here is an example of what Gronlund (1985) called a general instructional objective, which is stated as a broad learning outcome.

> *When you complete this text, you should be able to list and explain Skinner's two dimensions of punishment.*

At this point, we have become much more specific about an expected learning outcome and indicated exactly what behaviors are anticipated. You can see how precisely stated objectives define and improve evaluation.

Goals and Multicultural Students

Before we complete this section on goals and objectives, we should review the recommendations made by the National Coalition of Advocates for Students (NCAS), since these are a good example of goal statements. As the authors noted (First & Carrera, 1988), most young immigrants to the United States bring with them a passion for freedom, for education, and for gaining economic and personal security. Unless our schools are ready to capitalize on these motivations, most pupils will be unable to attain their goals.

Focus

Teachers, Students, and Objectives

In his little classic, *Preparing Instructional Objectives,* Robert Mager (1975) noted that without clearly defined goals, it is impossible to evaluate a lesson, course, or program efficiently. How can you evaluate your teaching and your students' performance unless you measure outcome against stated objectives?

Bloom, Madaus, and Hastings (1981) have identified a variety of benefits derived from formulating and selecting pertinent objectives.

- Writing clear, specific behavioral statements of objectives requires you to think about the changes you want to accomplish.
- The process helps you discover any nonessentials that might obscure your main objectives.
- Clearly stated objectives help you to group students more efficiently.
- Stating objectives helps you in selecting proper methods and materials.
- Once you recognize exactly what you want to achieve, your evaluative techniques become more precise and meaningful.

- Stated objectives can facilitate communication among teachers, since, in a sense, you are "talking the same language." Such commonality facilitates the exchange of ideas among teachers as they attempt to improve courses or programs.
- When both you and your students clearly understand what is to be attained, communication improves and learning increases.
- Precisely stated objectives also improve communication between teachers and parents. When parents know just what is expected of their children, they better understand their children's strengths and weaknesses, and can help them to join with teachers in combatting weaknesses.

Focusing on objectives in this manner improves the quality of the entire learning environment. Students clearly recognize what is expected of them and they understand the basis of your marks and grades. Precisely defined objectives thus help to establish and maintain positive teacher-student relationships.

To help these students, the NCAS suggests several goals. For example, *be sure that everyone (parents, other pupils, and school personnel) understands that immigrant children have a legal right to a free, public education.* This right belongs to all students—male and female, exceptional, and culturally diverse. Also, *help your students acquire respect for each pupil's native language and culture.* In this way, you'll help all students develop positive attitudes toward different cultural, racial, ethnic, and religious groups.

Be sure that there are sufficient resources for immigrant students. See that appropriate assessment and placement is available for immigrant students. This implies that ESL and/or bilingual programs are in place to ensure that immigrant students can become competent in the use of English. By using these techniques, you will promote the success of immigrant pupils by offering as much support as possible. Finally, *work hard to ensure that your classroom is free of harassment and conflict,* that you have provided a warm and supportive environment.

Noting that youthful immigrants tend to be a group without a constituency, the NCAS report urges that community agencies work together to support the welfare of potentially vulnerable pupils. In addition, you can help these students to develop and maintain a strong sense of their personal and cultural self-esteem by aiding them to recognize those influences that have shaped their thinking and behavior (Tiedt & Tiedt, 1990). Emphasize that any differences in the ways that they dress or act reflect their traditions and heritages, which can enrich—and have enriched—American culture.

Summarizing the goals of multicultural education, Willis (1993) noted that they are remarkably diverse. They include the need for accurate information, the desirability of reducing prejudice and fostering tolerance, the improvement of the academic achievement of minority students, and the building of a commitment to the American ideals of pluralism and democracy. To accomplish these goals, Willis urged that multicultural education permeate the curriculum rather than consist of added separate units about individual topics. Willis's suggestion leads us to a discussion of how objectives should be expressed.

What Are Good Objectives?

Once you have determined the type of objectives needed, you must express them in such a way that they are clearly understood by all. In other words, they must be meaningful in the sense that they are worth the time and effort they take to achieve. They should also be expressed in behavioral terms that can guide your teaching and enable you to assess whether students have or have not attained them. Answering several questions will help you to formulate worthwhile objectives.

Do your objectives include all important outcomes? You should be cautious that your teaching and testing does not focus on one type of objective, a trap that can lure us all. Typically we focus on the cognitive outcomes (especially knowledge of facts) that are most familiar to us. Don't forget those affective outcomes that can be so important to the total learning environment, as well as any essential psychomotor skills.

Are your objectives consistent with the general goals of the school? One of the difficulties in answering this question relates to the usual lack of clearly stated school goals. In most cases you are on your own, and must determine if the community's and school's aims for the children are in harmony with yours.

Are your objectives in harmony with sound principles of learning? Be sure that your desired learning outcomes match your pupils' developmental levels, are attainable, and can help your students in other situations as well as in your class.

Are your objectives realistic when you consider your pupils' abilities and the time and facilities available? This question reflects our earlier concern that the objectives you formulate be worthwhile. Realistic objectives apply to multicultural as well as typical students. Your knowledge and understanding of multicultural pupils will give you confidence in helping them fulfill their needs, which then become part of your objectives (Gronlund, 1985).

With these guidelines in mind, we can now turn our attention to those specific instructional objectives that will guide your teaching. An instructional objective is an intent communicated by a statement describing a proposed change in the learner: a statement of what the learner is to be able to do upon completion of the learning experience (Kim & Kellough, 1991). Thus an instructional objective requires a demonstrable behavioral change in the learner. Consequently, we can tell that learning has occurred only when we observe a change in behavior.

Note the essential ingredients of this description: *an objective is student-centered and involves learning outcomes* and *observable behavior*. In other words, your objective states what the student is expected to accomplish, the products of that learning (not the activities), and clearly defined student levels of performance.

Evaluating Objectives

Your reading thus far should help you to be aware of the characteristics of good objectives. How would you evaluate these four according to the criteria just discussed?

1. To appreciate the insights offered by educational psychology.
2. To present to you, the reader, several examples of clearly stated objectives.
3. To study the "Chapter Highlights" summary at the end of the chapter and refer back to the appropriate parts of the chapter.
4. To write ten instructional objectives that reflect the content of educational psychology described in this book.

Let us look at each of these "objectives."

1. This objective is so vague as to be meaningless. What is meant by "appreciate"? What insights?
2. Here we have an objective for the teacher and not for students.
3. This objective tells students what to do (a learning activity), and does not refer to a learning outcome. Be careful of objectives like this; although they are student-centered, they lack any reference to performance.
4. This meets the criteria of the good objective: it is student-centered, identifies a learning outcome, and is observable.

You need some type of formula to help you write your objectives. Think of the suggestions that are offered here, such as the ABCD format and Bloom's taxonomy. Which do you find most helpful? Can you use the best features of several? Discuss this topic in class and try to obtain other ideas.

Table 11.2

Desired Characteristics of Objectives	
Characteristic	**Meaning**
Specified content	Content should be precisely stated in behavioral terms.
Specified outcome	Students' behavior, as a result of learning, should be stated as observable outcomes.
Specified level of performance	Not only should expected student behavior be specified, but the exact degree of attainment should be clear to both teacher and students.
Specified outcome in clear, exact terms	Verbs such as *name, identify, classify, order, avoid,* and *understand* should be used.

As you turn your attention to the actual writing of objectives, consider Robert Mager's (1975) reminders that desirable objectives have three characteristics. First, *what is the behavior that should result?* Here you are concerned with identifying the specific behavior that signals that the learner has achieved the objective. Remember that your statement of the desired behavior also should specify an acceptable level. For example, if you give students ten problems, you might decide that seven correct solutions is an acceptable performance level. This description is sometimes called performance-based or outcome-based instruction (Kim & Kellough, 1991).

Second, *what are the conditions under which the specific behavior should occur?* For example, calculating with paper and pencil differs from calculating by a computer. Mager also strongly urged that you describe enough conditions for the objective to write appropriate test items.

Third, *what are the criteria that inform you that students have achieved an objective at the proper level?* In other words, how well must a student perform to be judged successful? Is the criterion the number of items correct? Is it time? Be sure that students understand all criteria for a minimal acceptable level of performance.

Writing Acceptable Objectives

Keeping in mind the essential characteristics of good objectives, you can now begin to formulate your own objectives. *First,* decide on the content that you wish your students to learn. What are the major concepts that need to be included? Are they appropriate for your course, the curriculum, and your students? *Second,* determine the general goals for this course. What are the goals for the individual sections or units of the course? Answering these questions leads you to consider the general instructional objectives mentioned earlier, and the manner in which you will sequence the objectives (Nesbit & Hunka, 1987). *Third,* break down these general goals into specific, observable outcomes. Recall the general goal that referred to the "topics of educational psychology." If we moved to a more specific, observable level, our objective might read as follows:

> **Given that "learning" is an essential topic in educational psychology, students should be able to identify five cognitive theorists and the concepts that are central to their theories.**

Fourth, be sure your objectives are clear and appropriate.

Table 11.2 summarizes the characteristics of appropriately stated instructional objectives as suggested by Bloom, Madaus, and Hastings (1981) and Gronlund (1985).

As we begin to translate these ideas into action, we should remember to use precise terminology. As Gronlund noted (1985, p. 45), the action verbs you use should satisfy two criteria: *they should convey clearly your instructional intent, and they should state precisely the behavior and level of performance expected of pupils* (use action verbs such as *identify* and *name*).

Table 11.3

How Verbs Specify Response		
Action verb	**Types of response**	**Sample test task**
Identify*	Point to, touch, mark, encircle, match, pick up.	"Put an X under the right triangle."
Name*	Supply verbal label (orally or in writing).	"What is this type of angle called?"
Distinguish	Identify as separate or different by marking, separating into classes, or selecting out a common kind.	"Which of the following statements are facts (encircle F) and which are opinions (encircle O)?"
Define	Supply a verbal description (orally or in writing) that gives the precise meaning or essential qualities.	"Define each of the following terms."
Describe*	Supply a verbal account (orally or in writing) that gives the essential categories, properties, and relationships.	"Describe a procedure for measuring relative humidity in the atmosphere."
Classify	Place into groups having common characteristics, assign to a particular category.	"Write the name of each type of pronoun used in each of the following sentences."
Order*	List in order, place in sequence, arrange, rearrange.	"Arrange the following historical events in chronological order."
Construct*	Draw, make, design, assemble, prepare, build.	"Draw a bar graph using the following data."
Demonstrate*	Perform a set of procedures with or without a verbal explanation.	"Set up the laboratory equipment for this experiment."

Reprinted with the permission of Simon & Schuster, Inc. from the Macmillan College text *Measurement and Evaluation in Teaching,* 7/E by Norman E. Gronlund and Robert L. Linn. Copyright © 1995 by Macmillan College Publishing Company.

*Sullivan states that these six action verbs (and their synonyms) encompass nearly all cognitive learning outcomes in the school. See H. J. Sullivan, "Objectives, Evaluation, and Improved Learner Achievement," in *Instructional Objectives.* AERA Monograph Series on Curriculum Evaluation, No. 3 (Chicago: Rand McNally, 1969).

Writing objectives can become more focused by following the suggestions offered by Armstrong and Savage (1983). Their **ABCD format** includes four elements:

A The audience for which the objectives are intended
B The behavior that indicates learning
C The conditions under which the behavior is to appear
D The degree of competency that will be accepted

ABCD format   *A technique for writing objectives that includes Audience, Behavior, Conditions, and Degree of Competency.*

Although these elements are similar to those already discussed, the familiar ABCD format provides a helpful reminder. For example, in the following objective—"Each student will be able to define 8 of the 10 items in the reading passage of the unit test"—A refers to the audience ("each student"), B defines the behavior ("will be able to define"), C refers to the condition ("in the reading passage of the unit test"), and D establishes the degree of competency ("8 of 10 items," or 80 percent). The order in which these elements appear can vary; the important thing is that all four elements must be present.

Table 11.3 illustrates the manner in which an objective by the use of an action verb can specify a student response.

Sources of Objectives

As you begin to consider the importance of good objectives for your teaching, you may want to turn to established sources of objectives and then commence writing your own. There are many sources you can use to guide your own work. *Published materials* such as your own texts and the instructor manuals that accompany them make a good beginning. They usually contain a wealth of valuable materials. You might also consider the annual yearbooks published by the national associations of teachers of your subjects. *The Encyclopedia of Educational Research* is another excellent source. *Your colleagues,* such as teachers of the same subject or grade, can often help you, thinking of outcomes you might forget. Finally, you will find *specialized sources,* such as *The Taxonomy of Educational Objectives,* extremely valuable.

The Taxonomy of Educational Objectives

taxonomy of educational objectives *Bloom's hierarchy of objectives, intended to clarify the terminology often used in formulating objectives.*

Benjamin Bloom (1913–), Professor Emeritus of Education at the University of Chicago, has long been interested in taxonomies of educational objectives, Bloom and his colleagues devised the **taxonomy of educational objectives,** which is an endeavor to clarify some of the vague terminology often used in the social sciences (Bloom, 1956). The main purpose of the taxonomy is to provide a classification of the goals of our educational system (Bloom, 1956, p. 1). There are three taxonomies: *cognitive, affective,* and *psychomotor.* The cognitive taxonomy, which has greatly influenced American education, is divided into six major classes:

- *Knowledge.* The recall of pertinent facts when needed (Who were the first astronauts to reach the moon?)
- *Comprehension.* Understanding the meaning of what is presented (Can you explain the causes of World War II?)
- *Application.* Use of ideas and rules where needed (Does final *e* make the preceding vowel long?)
- *Analysis.* Separating a unit into its parts (How many subfields make up educational psychology?)
- *Synthesis.* Constructing a whole from parts (Write a paper about a topic combining class work, films, and a field visit)
- *Evaluation.* Making judgments (Can you justify—or not—a particular nation's aggressive policies?)

Each category is further subdivided into other, more specific objectives. The authors state that these six classes represent an hierarchical order of the different classes of objectives. The objectives of each class usually depend on the preceding classes (Bloom, 1956, p. 18).

The great value of the taxonomy is its general application. Experts in curriculum construction can study it to refine the objectives of any school. Inexperienced teachers can turn to the taxonomy as a guide to the kinds of objectives for which pupils should be striving. Both expert and neophyte can profit by the wide range of test items that the authors offer to ascertain if students are actually achieving these goals.

When the authors suggest typical objectives and test items, they offer an invaluable service to teachers. For example, in the main class of *knowledge,* one of the objectives is *knowledge of specific facts.* This is followed by an explanation of what is meant by the heading, and then the authors present illustrative educational objectives for this category, as follows:

Knowledge of Specific Facts—Illustrative Educational Objectives:

- The recall of major facts about particular cultures
- The possession of a minimum knowledge about the organisms studied in the laboratory
- Knowledge of biological facts important to a systematic understanding of biological processes
- Recall and recognition of factual information about contemporary society
- Knowledge of practical biological facts important to health, citizenship, and other human needs
- Acquiring information about major natural resources
- Acquiring information about various important aspects of nutrition
- Recall and recognition of what is characteristic of particular periods

Table 11.4

Guidelines for Achieving Educational Objectives	
Knowledge of the learner	**Educational import**
1. The learner possesses a unique capacity for achievement.	Schools must recognize and provide for individual differences among students.
2. The learner's achievement is affected by the nature of the environmental contacts.	Learning experiences furnished by the school must enhance, or enrich, the learner's background.
3. The learner's developmental pattern should suggest classroom materials and methods.	A wide assortment of learning experiences should afford maximum opportunity for achievement at all ages.
4. The learner's intellectual level is not fixed and is capable of change.	Administrative procedures and organization should account for a variable expression of intellectual capacity.
5. The learner's emotions exercise a decisive effect, either positive or negative, upon learning.	The classroom atmosphere should be sufficiently stable to afford security and sufficiently stimulating to offer challenge.
6. The learner is a social being who requires satisfactory relations with other humans.	Emphasis upon the individual should not cause neglect of the interaction with peers, which is necessary to develop the mature personality.
7. The learner is an active, motivated individual who is capable of responses that range from the concrete to the abstract.	Self-activity in pursuit of an attainable goal is essential for learning. The learner should have educational experiences that require motor responses, thinking, problem solving, and creative thought.

- Knowledge of physical and chemical properties of common elements and their compounds
- An acquaintance with the more significant names, places, and events in the news
- A knowledge of the reputation of a given author for presenting and interpreting facts on governmental problems
- A knowledge of reliable sources of information for wise purchasing (Bloom, 1956, pp. 66–67)

The taxonomy (often referred to as Bloom's taxonomy) is a remarkably flexible tool. Not only does it offer reliable insights into the formation of acceptable objectives, but it also can be used as the basis for teaching thinking skills (see chap. 9). To support the contention that properly stated instructional objectives are well worthwhile, consider the research of Boulanger (1981). Examining eleven preinstructional strategies used with science classes, he found that eight of these strategies produced statistically significant cognitive effects, and among the most powerful contributions to the positive effects were the five studies that used behavioral objectives.

Finally, it would be well here to return to the broader themes with which we initiated our discussion of objectives. Combining your knowledge of development and learning, remember those basic principles that will guide you in your selection and formulation of specific objectives suited for your pupils. Table 11.4 illustrates these features.

INSTRUCTIONAL OBJECTIVES AND SCHOOL SUBJECTS

One of the general objectives of educational psychology is to help you identify those obstacles that are inherent in teaching any subject. You can then formulate specific instructional objectives that reflect the suggestions presented in this chapter. The subjects we shall examine, from the perspective of educational psychology, are reading, mathematics, and science.

teacher – student

interactions

Thinking About Objectives

1. Be sure you understand the distinction between goals and instructional objectives.
   - Write down what you think are the goals of a course that you are teaching now or will teach. Discuss them in class and then compare them with those of your classmates.
   - Within the framework of the general goals for this course, narrow your aims and write several general instructional objectives, as defined by Gronlund.
   - Finally, write several specific objectives that you think you want your students to attain in your course.
2. Good objectives should be clearly written and expressed in behavioral terms.
   - Examine the texts that you use in your teaching. Do they present objectives for the chapter or unit?
   - Examine the objectives if they have been written. Are they phrased in a way that your students find helpful? Be sure that your pupils understand them and use them as guides for their reading.
   - Write your own objectives for chapters or units, if they have not been written. Begin with general instructional objectives and then move to those specific objectives that reflect your pupils' needs.
3. In writing objectives, be sure that you include the student behavior that should result, the conditions under which the behavior should appear, and the criteria that satisfy the objective.
   - When your work in this course is complete, you should be able to write instructional objectives for this text. For example:
   a. Identify three learning strategies discussed in chapter 8 and give examples of each.
   b. Name the stages of development in Piaget's cognitive theory and give four characteristics of each stage.
   c. Identify three motivational theorists and list two essential concepts for each theory.
   - Write four or five objectives for the subject(s) you teach, using the same format.

Reading

In a widely read report, *Becoming A Nation Of Readers* (1984), reading was compared to the performance of a symphony orchestra. This analogy illustrates three points. *First,* like the performance of a symphony, reading is a holistic act. In other words, while reading can be analyzed into subskills such as discriminating letters and identifying words, performing the subskills one at a time does not constitute reading. Reading can be said to take place only when the parts are put together in a smooth, integrated performance. *Second,* success in reading comes from practice over long periods of time. *Third,* readers interpret text differently, depending on their backgrounds, the purposes for their reading, and the contexts in which reading occurs.

A topic that seems to have educators in a constant state of crisis, the teaching of reading has probably attracted more speculation, research, attacks, and apparent "breakthroughs" than that of any other school subject. No one questions its primacy in school, or, indeed, its critical function in an individual's adaptation to a technological society. What is argued over is the technique that will produce the best results for the most children. Determining the most suitable methods requires a consideration of objectives.

For example, consider the following plan for an intermediary reading lesson.

1. *Subject and Grade:*
   Reading
   Grade 5
2. *Lesson Topic:*
   Enjoyment of Literature
3. *Lesson Objectives:*
   Students can read the story aloud.
   Students can state the main idea of the story.
   Students can place the main parts of the story in the correct sequence.
   Students can explain the motivation of the characters.
   Students can relate the story's ideas to other stories they have read.

Focus — How Clear Objectives Can Help

In one example of the efforts being made to aid students with comprehension problems, Palinscar and Brown (1984), working with junior high school pupils, identified six major objectives that reflect Gronlund's general instructional objectives:

- Understand the purposes of reading, both explicit and implicit
- Activate relevant background knowledge
- Allocate attention so that concentration can be focused on the major content at the expense of trivia
- Evaluate content critically for internal consistency and compatibility with prior knowledge and common sense
- Monitor ongoing activities to see if comprehension is occurring, by engaging in such activities as periodic review and self-interrogation
- Draw and test inferences of many kinds including interpretations, predictions, and conclusions

They then selected four procedures that would enable the pupils to focus on these objectives: *summarizing, questioning, clarifying,* and *predicting.* The instructional technique began with a teacher's modeling of the activity. Then each pupil performed the activity with a teacher; finally, the student performed independently of any teacher.

Note the attempt to engage many of the processes discussed in the learning section of this book: attending, monitoring, predicting, evaluating. The results were impressive: students went from low comprehension levels to about the 70th percentile on standardized comprehension tests. Most noteworthy about the learning accomplished in this study, however, have been its lasting effect and its transfer to new tasks.

4. *Lesson Content:*
   Be sure students can read the story.
   Have students read aloud the various parts.
   Be sure students understand the story's theme.
   Take paragraphs out of context and ask students to place them in correct sequence.

5. *Closure:*
   Ask students to relate the story's ideas to their personal experiences.
   Point out how a good story can hold your attention and bring satisfaction and enjoyment.

6. *Materials needed:*
   Individual copies of the story; cut-out paragraphs; overhead projector.

7. *Evaluation:*
   Have students write a summary of the story that will be corrected during the next reading period and that will become part of their reading portfolio.

Although the plans presented in this chapter are necessarily quite general, they reflect the major stages of the instructional process: *planning instruction* (identifying desired pupil behavior changes, selecting materials, organizing the learning experiences); *delivering instruction;* and *assessing pupil outcomes* (Airasian, 1994). These three components of instruction have a complicated relationship. You cannot make decisions about pupil behavior without knowing the needs of your individual pupils and the resources you need to meet these needs. You can see, then, that good planning demands knowledge of your pupils, appropriate objectives, pertinent activities, and informative assessment measures.

To help you in your planning, here are some common errors to avoid (Airasian, 1994).

- Ignoring students' needs when planning
- Relying solely on texts and curriculum guidelines for your planning
- Concentrating on lower-level objectives
- Restricting the use of instructional strategies and activities
- Overlooking the relationship between instructional strategies and objectives
- Failing to utilize worthwhile assessment techniques

Use this list of common errors as a basis to devise a method—reflecting your own learning style—that permits you to devise a list of positive "things to do" in the classroom.

We can examine several of the key elements of reading within the context of our discussion thus far to see more clearly how the use of objectives—both general and specific—can aid your teaching and help your students to avoid reading problems. Here are several key characteristics to consider.

- *Reading is a constructive process.* This clearly implies that readers construct meaning from what they read (Mason & Au, 1990). The meaning that your students glean from their reading also depends upon their previous experiences, which may be rich or deficient. A related problem here is that even if your pupils possess relevant knowledge about what they are reading, they may not use it.
- *Reading must be fluent.* This means that your students must be able to decode quickly and accurately. Are you sufficiently familiar with the coding process to determine where your pupils may be having difficulties? Does your knowledge of attention help here?
- *Reading must be strategic.* This means that good readers, for example, adapt their reading techniques to the difficulty of the text and the purpose of their reading (Mason & Au, 1990). What do you see as the role of prereading suggestions? Can you treat a reading assignment as problem solving and adjust your teaching accordingly?
- *Reading requires motivation.* This demands that teaching be innovative and challenging. See if you can apply ideas from the motivation chapter to reading instruction. Can you suggest reading materials that help to satisfy the needs of a particular pupil?
- *Reading is a continuously developing skill.* This suggests that instruction and materials must match the changing abilities and skills of pupils.

Educational Psychology and Reading

You can better understand the relationship between educational psychology and reading by applying several psychological concepts to the topics we have just discussed. For example, you could view reading as an example of problem solving and help students use the DUPE model. With this model, readers must first determine what is required—comprehension; understanding the meaning of the beginning, middle and end of a story; or understanding the motivation of the characters? Have you decided upon the type of reinforcement you will use? How will you apply positive reinforcement? Do you think extinction will be necessary? What will cause you to decide on a particular technique? What form of motivation will you use, and why?

Because reading is an active, constructive process, the cognitive work we have discussed can offer insights into methodology. For example, recent analyses of reading processes have viewed reading within the framework of **parallel distributed processing.** That is, skillful reading depends not just on the appearance of words, but also on their meaning and pronunciation. These three sources of information are not processed independently. Rather, skillful reading results from the coordinated and interactive processing of all three: spelling + sound + meaning (Adams, 1990).

In other words, teaching reading is not simply teaching a system for translating speech into print, but instilling an understanding of the conventions for thinking and communicating in the modern world. Among the topics occupying the time and attention of reading researchers are the following (Calfee & Drum, 1986).

parallel distributed processing
Processing of information according to its appearance, meaning, and pronunciation.

decoding *A listener's use of the sounds and grammar of a language to interpret it.*

- **Decoding** refers to the technique by which we recognize words. This is a controversial and elusive topic. Two interpretations divide reading theorists: some argue that instruction should focus on the whole word, and others fervently believe that individual letters must be taught through the phonics method. Research today indicates that early phonics instruction produces the most satisfactory results.

Issues & Answers

Should Schools Replace a Skills Approach to Teaching Reading with a Whole Language Approach?

Schools today find themselves moving from a skills model to a more wholistic approach to teaching reading. This trend comes in response to years of literacy learning in which instructors taught each skill separately. In the mid-1980s the U. S. ranked 49th out of 159 United Nations members in level of literacy (Goodman, 1986). The skills approach to reading has been indicted by some as a contributing factor to our nation's poor literacy standing.

Issue

Should basal reading series, which have traditionally promoted a skills model, be replaced by authentic reading materials?

Answer: Pro Learning based on authentic materials like children's literature or children's own writing is more stimulating and will foster a more lasting positive attitude toward reading.

Answer: Con Basal readers offer teachers a comprehensive and structured approach to skills and vocabulary learning. Teachers don't have to worry that the literature they choose will not be appropriate or that it will not demonstrate the exact skills they want their students to learn.

Issue

Should learning to read be considered a natural process like learning to speak, and should we therefore allow children to learn to read in the same manner in which they learn to speak?

Answer: Pro We all learned to speak by being surrounded by speech and by being given every opportunity to practice and perfect the skill. When children learn to read they should enjoy a similar environment, in which they are immersed in print and are given numerous opportunities to experience reading and writing.

Answer: Con Many children who are extremely verbal have difficulty with reading. It cannot be assumed that learning to read exactly parallels how we learn to speak. Therefore we cannot assume that the best way to learn to read is the same way we learn to speak.

Issue

When teaching children to learn to read, should our objective be the construction of meaning?

Answer: Pro Meaning should be the engine driving all literacy learning. A whole language approach emphasizes the reader's background knowledge and experience. This, not the text, is seen as the starting point of the process.

Answer: Con Readers must attend to the print and basics should precede refinement. Children can never hope to make meaning without first understanding letters, words, sentences, and so on.

- **Vocabulary** refers to the meaning of a word, and not merely its pronunciation. It is interesting to pause for a moment to consider the ramifications of this statement. Knowledge of vocabulary is highly correlated with intelligence, which is highly correlated with reading performance and school success. Is it any wonder, then, that the acquisition of vocabulary rates high on any list of reading priorities?

- **Reading comprehension,** which is the ultimate objective in any type of reading instruction, means that a reader not only recognizes words, but understands the concepts that the words represent. Reading a text, comprehending it, and later recalling it involve complex strategies (perceptual, linguistic, and conceptual operations) that take years to develop (Mason & Au, 1990). Letters on the printed page must be encoded, text references must be comprehended, and the theme of the content must be followed (Beck & Carpenter, 1986, p. 1098).

   Clearly, the current concern with reading is an example of educational psychology's achievement of a general objective—identifying problems in a critical school subject—and provision of insights to help teachers identify specific instructional objectives that meet their (and their students') individual needs.

vocabulary *The extent to which students recognize, pronounce, and understand words.*

reading comprehension *The skill by which readers not only recognize words but understand the concepts that the words represent.*

Mathematics

The public's persistent concern with mathematics has been well documented and needs no additional comment here. Some individuals experience problems with numbers as early as the first grade and develop anxieties, even phobias, about mathematics that remain with them throughout their lives. Given the pervasive role of mathematics in modern life, such individuals will probably encounter constant frustration.

There are also cultural differences in math achievement scores. Comparing the mathematical performance of Chinese pupils in Beijing and American pupils in Chicago, Stevenson and his colleagues (1990) found that American pupils did more poorly, *but that neither the children nor their mothers realized it*. Both mothers and pupils viewed their performance favorably. The investigators speculate that the reasons for this discrepancy may be lower standards for the American youngsters and American teachers' deemphasis of mathematics.

Gaps also appear between the scores of black students and white students; the causes of this discrepancy are unclear. Entwiste and Alexander (1990) examined the mathematical abilities of 785 black and white pupils at school entrance in Baltimore and found little difference. (This doesn't necessarily mean that these abilities had developed in the same way.) The pupils were of similar ability when they started school.

By the end of the first grade, differences had appeared with the white pupils showing superior scores and black males surpassing black females. The authors conclude that while family type was not a factor, parental expectations and social class were both influential. Thus, important differences were appearing in the first year of school.

To address these, and similar problems, the National Council of Teachers of Mathematics (NCTM) drafted a set of standards for curriculum development and assessment measures that was published in 1989 as *Curriculum and Evaluation Standards for School Mathematics*. The goal of the NCTM's standards is quite clear: Teach math to all students in such a way that they understand and not just memorize, thus becoming confident in their ability to use math.

Students should come to value math when they see it as something they can use in different situations. To achieve this goal, planning must involve everyone in the school system, so that together educators can translate new ideas into practice and produce appropriate curriculum (Romberg, 1993). In other words, learning math is doing math. *What* students learn depends on *how* they learn it. Smith, Smith, and Romberg (1993) gave the example of an algebra class's study of the exchange rate between U.S. dollars and Dutch guilders, rather than merely of symbols and notations, thus emphasizing process and the interactions between instructor and students.

How can educational psychology help in the teaching of mathematics? As in our discussion of teaching reading, we should be able to identify key functions in mathematics learning, point out potential trouble spots, and suggest ways in which instruction can utilize this psychological probing, beginning with the formulation of clear objectives. Remember these questions: What do you want your students to acquire? Under what conditions? What criteria will you use to determine that they have acquired this desired behavior?

Skill and/or Understanding

Recent work in the psychology of mathematics has emphasized the relationship between computational skills and understanding, the role of mental representations in learning, and the way in which new knowledge is constructed by learners; all of these topics point to a more interactive process than has been used previously. The relationship between computational skill and understanding has intrigued psychologists, who have urged that procedural errors should be examined more closely than by simply calling them "right" or "wrong." Recall from our previous discussions of both development and learning that human beings are rule-learners. We learn rules and apply them as widely as possible to solve routine problems—*but,* we also adapt our rules, searching for innovative solutions when needed.

Our repeated use of arithmetic procedures (also called algorithms) can be good or bad, depending on the purposes for which the procedures are used. For example, try these simple problems.

$$\begin{array}{cccc} 33 & 58 & 314 & 8218 \\ -19 & -24 & -182 & -4742 \\ \hline \end{array}$$

What were your answers? Assuming that you refused to panic, you undoubtedly answered

$$\begin{array}{cccc} 14 & 34 & 132 & 3476 \end{array}$$

But sometimes a pupil, given the identical subtraction problems, will respond this way:

$$\begin{array}{cccc} 26 & 34 & 272 & 4536 \end{array}$$

What has happened? Can you identify the student's problem? Here we have an example of a fairly common mathematical problem that, upon analysis, clearly indicates that many such errors are rule-governed.

Note the repeated mistake: in each example, the pupil subtracts the smaller number from the larger, regardless of position. It is not that this student has failed to learn an algorithm, but rather that the algorithm is misapplied. Called "buggy algorithms," such processes indicate that students do not recognize the limitations of applications. The name comes from a computer program (Buggy) originally devised by Brown and Burton (1978) to aid teachers with their diagnoses.

As Romberg and Carpenter (1986) stated, the reason for using the common buggy algorithms is to discover how and why these misapplications are acquired. Note how this objective will guide the instruction to follow. What too often happens is that students are confronted with problems for which their learned algorithms are incorrect. But if they don't understand the mismatch and have nothing else to use, they will apply the buggy algorithm anyway. Thus, their understanding does not match their skills, which were learned mechanically. Teach your pupils to avoid mere mechanical application of the procedures; otherwise, they cannot use their knowledge.

Using Mathematical Knowledge

Students too frequently cannot transform mathematical meaning from the concrete level to the abstract. A similar difficulty exists with word problems, which link mathematics with language understanding. Nesher (1986) summarized the issue by noting that word problems should occupy a unique category, since they require employment of a student's language knowledge as well as a special interpretation in mathematical contexts. Often the text's complexity obscures the needed mathematical processing.

Students can experience difficulties when they are forced to use their mathematical skills either in practical, everyday situations or to solve word problems (Hughes, 1986). For example, for 11-year-olds to solve a simple division problem proved fairly simple.

A bar of chocolate can be broken into 18 squares. There are six squares in each row. How many rows are there?

Seventy-three percent of the students answered correctly.

But if the question took a slightly different approach, the results would change dramatically. You can test this by asking pupils of this age to determine your batting average.

To determine a batting average, divide the number of times at bat into the number of base hits.

Name	Times at bat	Base hits	Average
(*your name*)	40	12	?

Reporting the response to a similar problem, Hughes stated that only 25 percent of the students answered correctly, while 38 percent wouldn't even attempt the problem.

Perhaps even more startling were the results of this problem, presented to 11- to 13-year-old pupils.

> *The Green family has to drive the 252 miles from Boston to New York. After driving 98 miles, they stop for lunch. How do you figure the remaining distance they have to drive? Select the correct calculation.*

84×3	$252 + 98$	$252 - 98$
252×98	$154 + 98$	$252 \div 98$

Note: the youngsters are asked only to select the correct calculation, not to compute it. Only 60 percent of the students selected the correct answer.

Educational Psychology and Mathematics

There is nothing startling in the examples we have just discussed. If pupils are not expected to apply their learned behavior under real conditions, many, if not most, will react as the students in this study did. Can educational psychology help? Nesher (1986) suggested that we turn to the notion of schema for guidance. (Recall that a schema is hypothesized to be a cognitive structure, a way of organizing knowledge.) She identified the following three types of schemata.

dynamic schema *A cognitive structure describing changes in an original situation.*

static schema *A cognitive structure describing relationships among elements.*

comparative schema *A cognitive structure describing one situation in relation to another.*

- The **dynamic schema,** in which changes in an initial situation are described. For example, John had 9 marbles. He lost 3 of them. How many are left?
- The **static schema,** in which relationships, involving no action, are described. There are 6 oranges and 3 apples on the table. How many pieces of fruit are there?
- The **comparative schema,** in which one situation is described in relation to another. John has 9 marbles and Jim has 5. How many more marbles does John have than Jim?

Again, we see the usefulness of critical educational psychology topics in the mathematics classroom. As one final example, consider a conversation one of the authors recently had with a first-grade teacher about these ideas. Miss Shippe has taught first grade for more than fifteen years. She has seen and been a part of many changes in approaches to fostering learning during that time. However, when a student teacher recently asked her in which area she had seen the greatest change, Miss Shippe replied quickly and without hesitation, "Mathematics."

> *When I began to teach, there was only one accepted way to approach any mathematical process. For example, when we began to carry in addition I would have written a problem on the board—for example, 26 plus 7—and walked my students through this problem and others like it several times before asking them to solve it. Those lessons were teacher-centered: the children were asked to mimic my language and my method. Today, when we begin to learn to "carry," I usually put a problem on the board. Then, before I say a word as to the solution, I ask the children to try to solve it with their own methods and rationales. I also ask that they share their ideas with the rest of the class. All of this happens before I ever take up a piece of chalk.*
>
> *The objectives for mathematics and consequently for each of my lessons have changed radically. Today my lessons stress independent thought, discussion, questioning, justification for thinking, and cooperation. It is a far cry from the rote-practice, one-correct-answer, one-method, teaching-by-telling lessons of the past.*

Concern with teaching mathematics has frequently focused on the "basics," and so often directed our attention to the elementary school years. With the appearance of the NCTM's curriculum and evaluation standards, however, effort has been directed at the whole curriculum—from kindergarten through high school. "More mathematics" implies that students need to learn more than the basics. All students should be comfortable with concepts from algebra, geometry, trigonometry, statistics, probability theory, discrete mathematics, and even calculus. Romberg (1993) nicely summarized this position when he stated that students need to value mathematics, to reason and communicate mathematically, and to become confident in their power to use mathematics.

One secondary school teacher has described his geometry class in a way that illustrates the joys and frustrations of teaching.

> **I begin with a concrete example. When we were ready to start parallelism, I raised the question of the parking lot at the high school, whether it could be restriped to hold more cars. The kids measured lines, turning radii, angles. Then they proposed ideas. They were doing a heck of a lot of math.**
>
> **But I have to give a departmental exam, and sometimes it's a real challenge to get to the right point at the right time. Also, it's hard to give a grade to projects submitted by groups. Is it fair to give a high grade to someone who is a marginal member of a productive group?**

From this brief review of some of the issues facing mathematics educators, it may be possible for you to formulate specific objectives that meet your needs. Several instructional implications seem to arise from our discussion. *The mathematical knowledge that pupils bring to your classroom needs to be more carefully evaluated.* As we have repeatedly seen, prior knowledge can be a potent influence on later learning.

Careful diagnosis for the meaning of error seems to be a likely source of objectives. This technique can be particularly helpful if you are familiar with developmental changes and levels of cognitive development, which can help you appropriately match instruction with ability level.

Assess carefully the relationship between understanding and skill usage in your class. The results may more accurately shape your instruction and encourage your efforts to integrate mathematics with other subjects, resulting in "mathematics across the curriculum" (Kleiman, 1991).

Science

Project 2061—a committee for constructing goals for science, mathematics, and technology education—was formed in 1985 to identify what is needed to achieve scientific literacy. The committee defined "science" quite broadly: the natural sciences, the social sciences, mathematics, and technology. One of its first products was the influential publication *Science for All Americans* (Hoffman & Stage, 1993). The content recommended by this publication came about after three years of disciplined discussion; content was included only if it was essential, enduring, and learnable (Ahlgren, 1993). Any suggestions for new content had to include proposals and the rationale for what was to be dropped. Particularly interesting from an educational psychology perspective was the suggestion of cognitive psychologists that certain subjects should be omitted because they were not developmentally appropriate.

The contribution of educational psychology to science instruction parallels that of its input to the other subjects discussed. As you have probably discerned by now, understanding is a critical objective. Students reading a science text or listening to a science teacher must gain understanding by relating what they read to what they know, in an interactive process. Still, this may be more difficult than expected because students often lack the necessary schema that is at the heart of understanding (Carey, 1986).

Science and the Schools

Discussing the qualifications of science teachers, Trowbridge and Bybee (1986) identified several important characteristics. Although directed mainly at secondary school science teachers, their work has relevance for elementary school teachers also. For example, they noted that science teachers should have a good general background, specific scientific knowledge, and the ability to apply science to new situations. *They must understand science*—not only the basics, but also where science is today. *Their science instruction should be well organized.* As a science teacher, you should build the sequence of your program within this framework, which implies that you know both the basics and the frontiers in scientific study. As you do, be aware of the interpersonal relationships in your classroom and use them to foster a positive attitude toward science. Help your students to derive as much personal meaning as possible from science by your enthusiasm for both them and the subject. You can see how

Carefully defined objectives help teachers to organize material in a way that encourages students' understanding.

important this is in any successful science classroom from the following statement by a professor of astronomy.

> *My first experience with science was through a four-year high school sequence, general science through physics, all taught by Mr. Brown. I loved the courses. I loved Mr. Brown, and I almost never asked why. I took a standard interest test my junior year and it showed I liked science. "So much for the insights available through modern psychological testing," I thought. But I did wonder why I liked science (Trowbridge & Bybee, 1986, p. 10).*

Today we are rightly concerned about the scientific skills of our students at a time when understanding science and technology is needed for various types of decision making, such as voting on environmental and technical matters. Unless conditions in the nation's schools change radically, it is unlikely that today's 9- and 13-year-olds will perform much better when they are the 17-year-olds of tomorrow (Mullis & Jenkins, 1988, p. 7).

If the task of science is to develop new schemata, what can be used as a basis for understanding? Here is the source of many of the difficulties that students experience with science. A typical junior or senior high school text often contains more new words per page than a foreign language text. But students at least understand the concepts foreign language words represent, which is not the case in science. The full force of what students *do not understand* has just begun to be appreciated (Carey, 1986).

To help remedy this condition, research into science instruction has focused on the manner in which scientific knowledge is organized and accessed. Science educators have also concentrated on the relationship between the ability to reason scientifically and the development of Piaget's stages of cognitive growth. As one example of these efforts, *Benchmarks for Science Literacy,* an extension of *Science for All Americans,* offers a detailed outline of what students should know by the ends of grades 2, 5, 8, and 12 (Ahlgren & Rutherford, 1993).

> **By the end of grade 2, students will know that different kinds of plants and animals living in different environments have characteristics that help them to live there.**
> **By the end of grade 5, students will know that some characteristics of individual organisms are inherited and some are acquired.**
> **By the end of grade 8, students will know that differences in inherited characteristics permit some organisms to survive and reproduce more successfully than others.**
> **By the end of grade 12, students will know that differing survival values of inherited characteristics may explain how populations of organisms change over time.**

These recent publications have been widely accepted by scientists and will have a significant impact on science teaching in the future.

Your identification of *specific instructional objectives* in your science classes would probably benefit from your knowledge of these recommendations, *and* from close scrutiny of the developmental sequence discussed in chapter 4. For example, what cognitive abilities do your students require if they are to master needed scientific concepts? If these abilities are lacking, how will you alter your objectives? When an elementary school pupil asks, "If the earth is round, why don't the people in Australia fall off?" developmental knowledge will help to shape your answer and methods.

As another example of educational psychology's role, consider the following plan. During the summer, Mr. McIntyre attended a conference for elementary teachers on emphasizing higher-level thinking skills in the curriculum. At the conference, he became familiar with Bloom's seven levels of thinking: memory, translation, interpretation, application, analysis, synthesis, and evaluation. Mr. McIntyre found his thoughts returning to that conference as he began to prepare for the start of another school year in three weeks' time. He reviewed the lessons for his unit on mammals and decided that they really did not stress higher-order and divergent thinking skills such as synthesis and evaluation. He decided to rework his introductory lesson based upon the recent conference, making certain that the children had an opportunity to experience all seven levels of thinking as described by Bloom. His lesson plan looked like this:

Unit topic: Mammals/Intro
Subject: Science
Time: 2 45-minute lessons a week/ 4–5 weeks
Whole class

Whole Unit Content Generalizations:
Mammals are animals.
Mammals live all over the world.
There are many kinds (species) of mammals.
All mammals have certain characteristics in common.

Whole Unit Behavioral Objectives:
Children will be able to list characteristics of mammals.
Children will be able to identify mammals and parts of the world in which they
    are found.
Children will be able to identify mammals from other groups of animals and
    support decisions.
Children will begin to understand "mammals" as a way we classify animals.

Lesson Content Generalizations:
Animals that share four specific characteristics are called mammals.
All mammals have four characteristics in common.

Lesson Behavioral Objectives
Children will be able to identify the four characteristics of mammals and based
    on this knowledge distinguish mammals from other animals.

Direct Instruction—Memory:
1. Begin lesson by showing class poster with many photos of mammals on it,
   i.e., baby, whale, monkey, lion, dog, cat, dolphin, skunk.
2. Ask children to name the animals.

Direct Instruction—Interpretation:
3. Ask children what all these things have in common (what is the same about
   them?) Web answers on board.

Direct Instruction—Application:
4. Ask children what we might call this group of things in the picture with so
   many things in common.

Direct Instruction—Synthesis and Evaluation:
5. Write "mammals" on the board; say the word together with class.
6. Ask children what they already know about mammals (point to web).
7. Identify any of those characteristics that define mammals and add any to
   the web that are needed (defining characteristics should be in another color
   of chalk).
8. Point out that these particular characteristics define mammals.

teacher – student

interactions

Objectives in the Classroom

Educational psychology can help in identifying desirable objectives in the various subjects.

- Try to discover what your pupils think about reading. In your discussion with your pupils, ask questions similar to the following. (By using appropriate language, you can do this at almost any level.)

1. Why is it important to read well?
2. What do people do when they read?
3. When you're reading and you come to something you don't know, what do you do? Does everyone here do the same thing?
4. Do you know anyone who is a good reader?
5. What makes them a good reader?
6. Do you think you are a good reader? Why?
7. What would you like to improve in your reading?

- Now that you have some idea of how your students feel about reading, use the ABCD format to write objectives for the subject(s) you teach. Discuss them in class to determine if there is agreement about what you have designated as audience, behavior, conditions, and degree of competence.

- Knowing that repeated mathematical errors produce frustration, a lack of a willingness to apply mathematical principles, and decreasing motivation, use the ABCD method to write specific objectives that are realistic for your pupils. For example, Each student (A) will solve (B) 8 of 10 word problems (D) on the weekly test (C).

- Since some students have nothing in their backgrounds to which they can relate any given scientific concept, consider whether you want to teach a concept in isolation before they meet it in context, or treat it as it appears in the flow of your lesson. Whatever you decide, write specific objectives that indicate what you expect from your pupils; be sure to specify behavior, conditions, and criteria.

- Request that your school obtain a copy of *Benchmarks for Science Literacy* (in press) and familiarize yourself with the standards for each grade. Now examine your long-range goals to see how they "fit." As a final step, determine if your unit and lesson plans form a logical progression with regard to school system and national standards.

Group Work—Interpretation:

9. Present pictures of animals to each group; ask children to work together to decide which pictures show mammals and why.
10. Ask children to take out their science notebooks, draw a picture of any mammal, and list its characteristics (model this at easel).

Together with your knowledge of cognitive psychology, the pertinent features of the work on learning discussed in this text—proper use of reinforcement, rule learning, memory cues, the interactive role of the learner during problem solving—will help you to form pertinent objectives. A field trip designed to obtain seeds from trees and bushes provides opportunities for students to recall, to interact with the teacher and other pupils, and to be reinforced.

Science teachers, like all teachers, want to improve; contributing significantly to any improvement are better plans and skillful classroom organization.

APPLICATIONS AND REFLECTIONS

Chapter Highlights

Educational Standards

- The quest for national standards in the various disciplines is a growing phenomenon with significant implications for all teachers.
- Mathematicians and scientists have led the field in formulating standards for their disciplines.

Deciding on Educational Objectives

- Long-range goals and objectives in the various disciplines help teachers to structure their teaching in a manner that meets the individual needs of their students, but within a framework that identifies the frontiers of their fields.
- Clearly articulated objectives make learning more meaningful and useful.
- The public's expectations for its schools reflect a concern for the attainment of specific objectives. Are our graduates as well prepared as possible for the life of their choosing?

The Role of Objectives in Instruction

- Objectives guide classroom work with regard to planning, teaching, and testing.
- Writing clear behavioral objectives forces the teacher to think about what exactly needs to be accomplished.
- When you begin to concentrate on what you want to accomplish, distinguish among descriptions, goals, and objectives.
- As you think about your objectives, remember the difference between general and specific instructional objectives, deciding what you wish to use and when each type seems most appropriate.
- Your objectives must be clear and realistic, indicating exactly what students must accomplish and at what level.
- You should specify the behavior to be acquired, the conditions under which the behavior occurs, and the criteria informing an observer that the objective has been achieved.
- Don't hesitate to use established sources of objectives that you can readily apply to your work.

Instructional Objectives and School Subjects

- Educational psychology is particularly well suited to help you devise appropriate objectives, because of the insights it offers into the teaching and learning processes. In this chapter, three subjects are used to illustrate educational psychology's role: reading, mathematics, science.
- In each of these disciplines (as with all subjects), the ability to state meaningful objectives depends on a cluster of factors: national standards, community needs, school goals, and classroom objectives.

Connections

1. Think about how you learn and describe how one of the major concepts discussed in this chapter is part of your learning activities or approach.

_____

_____

_____

2. Identify at least one learning situation (classroom instruction, self-study, taking a test, small-group work) and describe how you would apply one of the key concepts examined in this chapter _if you were a teacher_.

_____

_____

_____

Getting the Picture and Drawing Relationships

Think about the various learning concepts and variables discussed in this chapter. Create pictures, graphics, or figures that highlight the relationships among key components.

Personal Journal

What I really learned in this chapter was _____

_____

_____

_____

What this means to me is _____

_____

_____

_____

Questions that were stimulated by this chapter include _____

_____

_____

_____

Key Terms

ABCD format	378	**objectives**	366	**static schema**	387
academic goals	371	**parallel distributed**		**system performance**	
comparative schema	387	processing	383	standards	368
content standards	368	**performance standards**	368	**task analysis**	372
decoding	383	**personal goals**	371	**taxonomy of educational**	
dynamic schema	387	**reading comprehension**	384	objectives	379
expected learner		**school delivery standards**	368	**vocabulary**	384
outcomes (ELOs)	372	**social and civic goals**	371	**vocational goals**	371
goals	366				

When Kevin Roche, the Junior High West math teacher we met earlier, arrived at school on a warm, sunny morning in late September, he found a note in his mailbox asking him to see Joe Allan, the principal. "What have I done now?" Kevin wondered. "It's too early in the year for me to be in real trouble." On the way to his homeroom, he stopped at the principal's office and made an appointment to see him after school.

After his last student left, Kevin went to his appointment with Joe Allan. "Come in, Kevin, come in. How are the classes going?" asked the principal. "Fine," said Kevin. "A good group. A few seem lost, but they should catch up with a

"I know this is unexpected; we haven't tried it before. But this year we have several nervous new teachers and I think we could help each other by a pooling of ideas. Look, Kevin. It's only ninety minutes. What I had in mind was to have you suggest ways that teachers can get and keep attention, different ways of presenting various materials, how to get feedback, topics like that. By the way, both Kim and Alice have agreed—not that I want to put any pressure on you, of course. What do you say?"

Kevin knew he had to agree. Besides, it could really be productive for everyone. As he walked out of the building to his car, his mind was racing. "Joe wants me to go first, at the beginning

chapter 12

effective teaching strategies and the design of instruction

little help. Thankfully, there aren't any serious discipline problems. Jerry Kale still wants to be the class clown, but he's really a good kid."

"Well, that's good to hear, Kevin. You do a nice job, and that's what I want to talk to you about." Kevin, who was on good terms with the principal, groaned loudly. Joe Allan laughed. "No, Kevin. I'm not trying to set you up. I want to ask you to do me a favor."

Kevin watched the principal closely. In spite of his small talk and easy relationship with his faculty, Kevin knew, Allan was an exceptional principal and very sharp. The principal, now quite serious, said, "We have an unusually talented faculty and I'd like to use their talents in a way that would benefit everyone."

"I'd like to have a series of in-service workshops run by the faculty. For example, you know how good Kim is with media; Alice is outstanding with computers and makes excellent use of them in her classes." (Kim Fraser was the English teacher we met previously; Alice West was a social studies teacher.) Joe continued, "I thought each of them could lead a session—no more than ninety minutes long—right after school. I'll furnish coffee and cookies and we'll keep it as informal as possible. I'd like you to lead one session devoted to teaching strategies, Kevin. I know you've taken some courses on this subject and you're good with students.

of October, so I'll have to start on this right away. Perhaps the best way would be to list some of the things that we know about effective teaching— the ideas first, and then the applications."

Later that day, Kevin sat at his desk at home and started to outline his presentation. "How should I begin?" he asked himself. ∎

When we examine the situation facing Kevin Roche, we realize that personal characteristics affect both teacher performance and student learning. Students may react to different teaching techniques in remarkably diverse ways. Some students may resent the exciting lecturer who dominates every moment of a class; others may achieve admirably under such stimulation. Some students thrive in an atmosphere where discussion is the technique; others, due to their individual personalities, avoid participation.

Students bring their attitudes, interests, prejudices, values, and opinions into the classroom with them. So do teachers. Realizing that these variables combine in the teaching-learning process will help you to appreciate more readily the complicated nature of teaching.

To help you understand the intricacies of teaching, in this chapter we will discuss "teaching" as the public thinks of it, and teaching as it really is. Next we will examine various theories and designs of instruction that reveal

The Meaning of Teaching 396
What Makes an Effective
Teacher? 396
Direct Instruction 399
Indirect Instruction 403
Teaching and Subject
Matter 408

The Design of Instruction 410
Skinner and the Technology of
Teaching 411
Markle and Programed
Instruction 414
Gagne and Instructional
Design 415

**Adapting Instruction to the
Individual Differences of
Learners 418**
Bloom and School Learning 418
Students and Study Skills 421
The Role of Homework 424
Adapting Instruction in a
Multicultural Classroom 425
Teacher Expectations 427

Applications and Reflections 429

how teaching can be analyzed. This should help you to adopt, and adapt, different strategies for your purposes. But these adaptations should be made in light of the individual differences of your pupils, which will occupy us in the final section of the chapter.

When you complete this chapter, you should be able to

- identify the common features of teaching
- distinguish between direct and inquiry teaching

- use praise in the classroom effectively
- apply the research findings concerning teaching to improve your own instruction
- distinguish instructional theory from instructional design and apply the appropriate features of both to your own teaching
- furnish examples of how you could adapt your teaching to the needs of your students

First, let's try to grasp the meaning of "teaching."

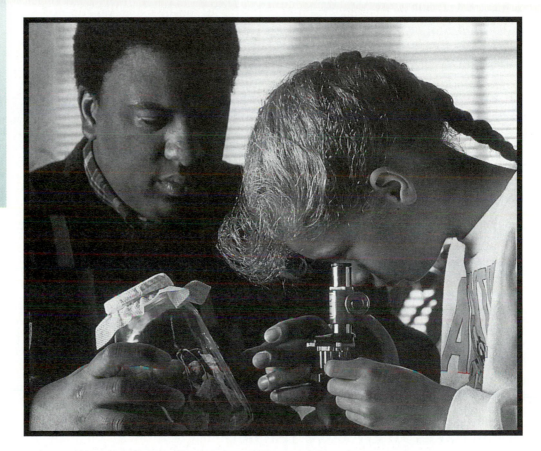

THE MEANING OF TEACHING ←

The moment of truth is at hand. You have closed the classroom door behind you, and as you slowly turn to meet the eager (and perhaps not-so-eager) faces watching your every move, you're probably wondering how to begin. Nervous? Right. Uncertain? Right. Never have done this before? Wrong!

As a reminder that we all have had more teaching experience than we realize, try answering these questions.

- Have you ever been a babysitter? If so, you had to give directions, explain a word, show a child how to do something.
- Have you ever coached? If so, you instructed, explained, demonstrated, and evaluated.
- Have you ever been a summer counselor? If so, you managed, directed, lectured, demonstrated, and led group discussions.
- Have you ever held a job? If so, at some time you undoubtedly explained procedures to a new employee.

Consequently, you have experience with the four "common features" of teaching: teachers, learners, subject matter, and context (Posner, 1989). Let's briefly examine each of these features of teaching.

Teachers. What kind of person were you in whatever teaching experience you had? Were you permissive or authoritarian? What did you see as the best role for you? What were the tasks you faced? When you enter a typical classroom you must answer the same questions. Think about the circumstances in which you expect to teach (elementary or secondary school, the subject(s), the kind of community) and try to determine how well your perspective of teaching "fits" these circumstances.

Learners. Everyone is a learner, but age, objectives, backgrounds, and experiences vary enormously. We have discussed learning in several of the preceding chapters; here, note simply that one of the most important ways to encourage student learning is to discover what they already know and use this as building blocks for your new work.

Subject Matter. How much material do you think your pupils should cover? How much time can be devoted to a particular topic? Are you going to emphasize facts, comprehension, or both in a particular unit?

Context. Any analysis of the impact of teaching must account for more than the immediate classroom. Parents, community, and a changing cultural blend all influence the success of the teaching-learning interaction.

With this brief introduction, let us turn our attention to what is meant by effective teaching.

Have you ever had any type of teaching experience (as described here)? Did it "fit" the characteristics of teaching presented here? What types of learning did you encourage?

What Makes an Effective Teacher?

Reflecting on several outstanding teachers that he had in school, Ernest Boyer (1990), a respected commentator on American education, stated that there were several characteristics that made them great. First was the way in which they used language. Think about it for a moment; the use of symbols is a constant in classrooms. Your writing and your use of oral language helps students to learn, while your ability to communicate effectively shapes your relationships with your class. Boyer next mentioned the knowledge that these teachers possessed. Being well informed and able to move freely in the disciplines is essential if you are to prepare students to succeed in a complex world. Finally, effective teaching implies that the teacher meaningfully relates what is known to the students so that they become aware of the power of knowledge.

Key Behaviors of Effective Teachers

In a similar, but more specific analysis, Borich (1992) reviewed recent research on teaching effectiveness and concluded that five key behaviors characterize effective teachers: lesson clarity, instructional variety, task orientation, engagement in the

Effective teaching takes place throughout a school and requires flexibility on the part of teachers and students.

learning process, and student success. *Lesson clarity* refers to how clear you make your presentations to your class; do your students understand you? Once you have decided on objectives (see chap. 11), step back to ask yourself, as if you were a student, if you could understand what it is you are asking the class to do. Some "dos and don'ts" are helpful here. *Don't* be vague; don't talk over the heads of your students; don't be too complicated. *Do* organize material carefully; do be precise in your directions; do use easily comprehended speech; do link the present lesson to past work; do use instructional strategies that are appropriate to the material and to the ages and cognitive levels of your students. All of these practices will help to maintain clarity.

Instructional variety means that your teaching techniques remain flexible during the presentation of a lesson. Use different materials; switch from a recitation to a discussion technique; be precise in your reinforcement of student behaviors. Work hard to become a skilled questioner so that you can integrate questions into your lesson; this helps to keep student interest high. Vary your use of reading materials, audiovisual aids, reference tools, and any other learning resources.

Task orientation and *engagement in the learning process* refer to the time spent in learning academic subjects. When students' academic learning time is increased, their achievement improves; this is especially true for low-achieving or at-risk students (Berliner, 1988). Students must be engaged in appropriate academic activities with a good probability of success. For example, the **beginning teacher evaluation studies (BTES)** inspired by John Carroll's model of school learning (1963) represented an effort to identify a mediating variable between teaching behavior and student performance (Shulman, 1986). Carroll's model shifted the research emphasis from teacher behavior

beginning teacher evaluation studies (BTES) *An effort to evaluate beginning teachers by focusing on student activities.*

Focus   Multicultural Teaching

If you were asked to summarize the general attitude of teachers, you would say that teachers want to be helpful; they want to help their students in as many ways as possible. One means of being helpful is to improve multicultural relationships in their classrooms and teach for transfer of these ideas to situations outside of the school (Sleeter & Grant, 1993). There are several ways you can go about this.

In attempting to help teachers achieve this goal, Willis (1993) summarized several specific issues that teachers should find useful. For example, a question you will have to face immediately is what groups you should teach about. Any multicultural curriculum should include at least the five major groups in America: Native Americans, African Americans, Hispanics, Asians, and Europeans. Even here you must be careful in your discussions. "Asian Americans" is too sweeping a category, given the differences among Chinese Americans, Japanese Americans, and Korean Americans, for example.

The question of which groups to study should not dominate your thinking, however. Underlying concepts—immigration, intercultural interactions, racism—can be applied to the experiences of any group and used to further multicultural relationships. These concepts are applicable throughout the curriculum, and you can apply them to many subjects. For example, in teaching about World War II, you could discuss the consequences of internment for Japanese Americans, of women's employment for the defense industry, and of segregated military units.

Another point to remember is the need to illustrate the role of social, economic, and cultural history, and not to concentrate solely on individuals. For example, while it is tempting to focus on the leaders of the American revolution (Washington, Jefferson, etc.), acknowledge that there were many other powerful forces at work. This also helps you to avoid labeling groups as either victims or heroes (Willis, 1993). In this way, you will be able to identify such important influences as class, gender, and religion as contributors to the trials and accomplishments of the group you are discussing.

Finally, to be honest, you will find yourself presenting behavior that you find offensive but that is culturally rooted; for example, the oppression of women in some cultures is seen as a means of strengthening the family. There are, however, some behaviors that defy explanation and must be condemned: rape, murder, torture, infanticide. As you face these new responsibilities, remember that the goal of your instruction is to improve relationships among diverse peoples whose common bond is their humanity.

---

to student activities: what were students doing with their tasks? Explanations of student achievement that focused solely on teachers seemed lacking in predictive power. For example, how could the number and quality of teacher praise statements in the fall influence student achievement in spring examinations? Researchers raising such questions, then turned their attention to a more meaningful subject: the time that a student spent on particular content. Figure 12.1 illustrates the various times—allocated time, instructional time, engaged time, and academic learning time—that teachers need to be aware of and manage. Is there anything you can do to improve the academic learning time of your students?

To encourage the efficient use of time, Borich (1992) suggested that teachers make sure students know the classroom rules, so that they don't have to ask each time they want to do something. Monitor seatwork carefully to be sure that students remain engaged. Independent assignments should be interesting and worthwhile so that you don't have to spend time in constantly giving directions. The time you devote to these matters will actually provide more time on task for your students.

By *success rate,* Borich (1992) meant the rate at which students understand and correctly complete their work. As you would expect, if your instruction produces a moderate to high success rate, your students' achievement will increase. Time is a major contributor here. If students spend *more* than an average amount of time working toward high success, their achievement scores rise and retention improves—both changes that are accompanied by a more positive attitude toward school.

Finally, *be careful how you use praise.* Teacher praise, as a function of teacher effectiveness, has recently received mixed reviews as a means of facilitating student achievement. Praise has a more intense meaning than feedback, conveying as it does an affective commitment by the instructor; in other words, we go beyond "That's right" to "Right, good thinking, John; keep up the good work." Examining the praise research, Brophy and Good (1986) found that teacher praise usually is infrequent, noncontingent

Do you agree that "time on task" is an essential criterion for learning to occur? How to accomplish this goal can be difficult. What content and activities would you bring to your classroom to increase time on task? Be specific in your suggestions.

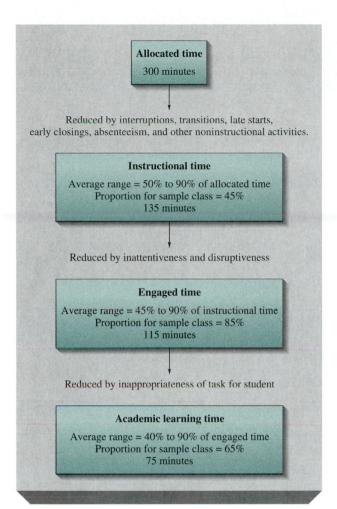

Allocated time
300 minutes

Reduced by interruptions, transitions, late starts,
early closings, absenteeism, and other noninstructional activities.

Instructional time
Average range = 50% to 90% of allocated time
Proportion for sample class = 45%
135 minutes

Reduced by inattentiveness and disruptiveness

Engaged time
Average range = 45% to 90% of instructional time
Proportion for sample class = 85%
115 minutes

Reduced by inappropriateness of task for student

Academic learning time
Average range = 40% to 90% of engaged time
Proportion for sample class = 65%
75 minutes

Figure 12.1
Components of academic
learning time.

From Maribeth Gettinger, Best Practices.
*Copyright © 1990 the National
Association of School Psychologists.
Reprinted by permission of the publisher.*

Annual **Edition**

Clinical Theory of Instruction (CTI)
*Hunter's theory that the teacher
is a decision-making professional.*

(not always based on a student's appropriate behavior), global rather than specific, and determined more by students' personal qualities than by students' achievement. To help you in your use of praise, consider the guidelines for the effective use of praise presented in table 12.1.

Now that you are thinking about teaching effectiveness, don't hesitate to evaluate yourself; your reactions to your own performance are usually quite accurate. You *know* when you've had a good class. Try something like this, using S (satisfactory) or U (unsatisfactory) as labels. (These are the behaviors we have discussed; add other items that may be more pertinent for your classroom.)

Key Behaviors	Evaluation (S or U)	
Lesson clarity	S	U
Instructional variety	S	U
Task orientation	S	U
Engagement in the learning process	S	U
Student success rate	S	U

The final aspect of effectiveness we wish to mention here involves reflection. Step back occasionally to think about what you are doing—not to evaluate scores or your maintenance of an orderly environment (both desirable accomplishments, by the way), but to ask yourself if what you are doing is worthwhile. Try to assume the perspective of an objective observer of your actions; this is a form of "knowing-in-action" (Schon, 1988). As Tremmel (1993) noted, the process of learning to teach does not end at graduation or even after the first few years of teaching. Reflective and mindful teachers are aware of the workings of their own minds as they engage in the practice of instruction.

As a teacher, your goal is to have your instruction help your students achieve as well as their ability permits. Consequently, you should be aware of those circumstances that require either direct or indirect instruction.

Direct Instruction

Students achieve at a higher level in classes where they are directly taught by their teachers rather than working on their own (Blair, 1988). With direct instruction, teachers tell, demonstrate, explain, and assume the major responsibility for a lesson's progress, and adapt the work to their students' age and abilities. Student achievement seems to be superior with direct instruction, particularly with regard to factual information. Table 12.2 summarizes many of the activities involved in direct instruction. These include giving class presentations, guiding practice, grading work, providing feedback, and monitoring students' work.

An example of direct instruction can be found in Madeline Hunter's work.

Madeline Hunter's Clinical Theory of Instruction

Working on the assumption that the teacher is a decision-making professional, Hunter, in her **Clinical Theory of Instruction (CTI)** (Hunter, 1991; Hunter & Russell, 1981), claimed universal application, regardless of content, school organization, learner's age, or socioeconomic status. CTI is derived from research on human learning and based on the notion that instructional decisions are made consciously or by default.

Table 12.1

Guidelines for Effective Praise	
Effective praise	**Ineffective praise**
1. Is delivered contingently	1. Is delivered randomly or unsystematically
2. Specifies the particulars of the accomplishment	2. Is restricted to global positive reactions
3. Shows spontaneity, variety, and other signs of credibility; suggests clear attention to the student's accomplishment	3. Shows a bland uniformity, which suggests a conditioned response made with minimal attention
4. Rewards attainment of specified performance criteria (which can include effort criteria, however)	4. Rewards mere participation, without consideration of performance processes or outcomes
5. Provides information to students about their competence or the value of their accomplishments	5. Provides no information at all or gives students information about their status
6. Orients students towards better appreciation of their own task-related behavior and thinking about problem solving	6. Orients students toward comparing themselves with others and thinking about competing
7. Uses students' own prior accomplishments as the context for describing present accomplishments	7. Uses the accomplishments of peers as the context for describing students' present accomplishments
8. Is given in recognition of noteworthy effort or success at difficult (for *this* student) tasks	8. Is given without regard to the effort expended or the meaning of the accomplishment (for *this* student)
9. Attributes success to effort and ability, implying that similar successes can be expected in the future	9. Attributes success to ability alone or to external factors such as luck or easy task
10. Fosters endogenous attributions (students believe that they expend effort on the task because they enjoy the task and/or want to develop task-relevant skills)	10. Fosters exogenous attributions (students believe that they expend effort on the task for external reasons—to please the teacher, win a competition or reward, etc.)
11. Focuses students' attention on their own task-relevant behavior	11. Focuses students' attention on the teacher as an external authority figure who is manipulating them
12. Fosters appreciation of and desirable attributions about task-relevant behavior after the process is completed	12. Intrudes into the ongoing process, distracting attention from task-relevant behavior

Source: Jere Brophy, "Teacher Praise: A Functional Analysis" in *Review of Educational Research,* Spring 1981, 5–32. Copyright 1981 by the American Educational Research Association.

Planning for Effective Instruction The careful design of lessons continues to be one of the most important elements in successful teaching, and the CTI model suggests the following steps to achieve your objectives.

> *Step 1. Anticipatory Set.* Here Hunter was chiefly concerned with readiness and attention, and suggested using a brief period to practice previous learning, then focusing students' attention on what is to be learned. You should not continue this activity beyond the time needed to "set" your students, that is, to make sure that they are ready for the new learning.
> *Step 2. The Objective and Its Purpose.* Hunter asserted that teachers must clearly inform students of what they should be able to do by the end of the instruction and why it is important that they master the lesson's content. Step 2 reflects our previous discussion of classroom objectives.
> *Step 3. Instructional Input.* You must decide just what information your students need to attain the lesson's objective. How are you going to do this? The content of this chapter should be helpful: determine the readiness of students, the reinforcements needed, the degree of understanding required, the necessary design, and any specific steps.
> *Step 4. Modeling.* We have discussed modeling in several preceding chapters sufficiently for you to realize its value to students in allowing them to see

In several places throughout this chapter, you have read warnings about the use of praise. What is your reaction to these cautions? What has your experience been? Has your opinion changed as a result of your reading?

Issues & Answers

Will Reflective Teaching Lead to Higher Student Achievement Scores?

Teachers are often criticized for "teaching to the test," a charge many teachers would confirm. Many teachers would tell you that in spite of lip service to "fulfilling student potential," their students are expected to do well on standardized tests, and that the teachers themselves are judged by the success of their students. Such circumstances almost dictate a policy of direct instruction.

Teachers are also bound by technical constraints that limit their thinking about what they are doing; that is, they are bound by a set of sequential steps that they have learned constitutes the correct way to present a lesson. Teaching viewed in this manner impedes their ability to guide their students to more meaningful learning. Critics agree strongly that reflective teaching can help to correct this condition.

Issue

Reflective teaching is another "in" trend that will soon disappear and may actually have a negative impact on students.

Answer: Pro   The history of teaching is filled with radical, temporarily fashionable ideas that typically fade after doing more harm than good. Research has repeatedly shown that the best results—improvement in students' achievement, classroom discipline, and positive attitudes toward school—are found in those classrooms using direct instructional techniques. The open-ended strategy leads to sloppy thinking, poor study habits, and students who are not ready to compete in a highly technological society.

Answer: Con   Anyone agreeing with this statement does not understand the meaning of reflective teaching. The narrow-minded approach to instruction that is prevalent today actually works against our students. Merely telling them something leaves them grossly ill-equipped to solve the problems they must inevitably meet. Students must learn to think on their feet, to respond as the situation demands, and not to be bound by a limited perspective. Reflective teaching, also called "knowing-in-action" (Schon,1987), offers the means to help students truly use their abilities.

Issue

Reflective teaching is better suited to help students to adapt to a rapidly changing society.

Answer: Pro   Reflective teaching fosters a positive attitude toward problem solving and a willingness to apply variable techniques in a search for solutions both in and out of the classroom. As the issues facing all citizens become more complicated and global, there is a corresponding need to deal with them with considerable creativity and flexibility. If our students are not taught critical thinking skills by reflective teachers, they will be unable to comprehend, let alone judge, the meaning of issues they must vote on. Narrow thinking and an inability to weigh competing claims jeopardizes the future of all of us.

Answer: Con   Students who face the complexity of modern society need a tested methodology and a feeling of security. The frustration of facing problems with no discernible solution and no sense of guidance, far from preparing students to adapt, can leave them fearful and unwilling to face novel situations. We see this far too frequently with students who, when challenged, simply give up. Our students need a basic frame of reference. The knowledge, the experience, and the expertise of teachers must be brought to bear on the classroom in the form of direct instruction. Only in this way can we help our students to use their abilities; under other conditions they may never recognize, let alone use, their talents.

actual examples of an acceptable finished product. Whenever you model, be sure to combine both visual and verbal stimuli, so that your students will concentrate on the essential features that you wish them to learn.

Step 5. Checking for Understanding. If you are to make accurate adjustments in your instruction, you must continuously assess your students' level of understanding.

Step 6. Guided Practice. Be alert to your students' efforts in their initial attempts at new learning. Circulate among your students to be sure that students are performing satisfactorily. Students must practice their skills, but they require monitoring in case clarification or remediation is needed.

Step 7. Independent Practice. Once students have eliminated major errors, they can then apply the skills in some appropriate task: homework, research papers, reading assignments.

Table 12.2

Instructional Functions

1. Daily Review and Checking Homework
   Checking homework (routines for students to check each other's papers)
   Reteaching when necessary
   Reviewing relevant past learning (may include questioning)
   Review prerequisite skills (if applicable)

2. Presentation
   Provide short statement of objectives
   Provide overview and structuring
   Proceed in small steps but at a rapid pace
   Intersperse questions within the demonstration to check for understanding
   Highlight main points
   Provide sufficient illustrations and concrete examples
   Provide demonstrations and models
   When necessary, give detailed and redundant instructions and examples

3. Guided Practice
   Initial student practice takes place with teacher guidance
   High frequency of questions and overt student practice (from teacher and/or materials)
   Questions are directly relevant to the new content or skill
   Teacher checks for understanding (CFU) by evaluating student responses
   During CFU teacher gives additional explanation, process feedback, or repeats explanation—where necessary
   All students have a chance to respond and receive feedback; teacher ensures that all students participate
   Prompts are provided during guided practice (where appropriate)
   Initial student practice is sufficient so that students can work independently
   Guided practice continues until students are firm
   Guided practice is continued (usually) until a success rate of 80 percent is achieved

4. Correctives and Feedback
   Quick, firm, and correct responses can be followed by a question or a short acknowledgement of correctness ("That's right")
   Hesitant correct answers might be followed by process feedback (i.e., "Yes, Linda, that's right because . . . ")
   Student errors indicate a need for more practice
   Monitor students for systematic errors
   Try to obtain a substantive response to each question
   Corrections can include sustaining feedback (i.e., simplifying the question, giving clues), explaining or reviewing steps, giving process feedback, or reteaching the last steps
   Try to elicit an improved response when the first one is incorrect
   Guided practice and corrections continue until the teacher feels that the group can meet the objectives of the lesson
   Praise should be used in moderation, and specific praise is more effective than general praise

5. Independent Practice (Seatwork)
   Sufficient practice
   Practice is directly relevant to skills/content taught
   Practice to overlearning
   Practice until responses are firm, quick, and automatic
   Ninety-five percent correct rate during independent practice
   Students alerted that seatwork will be checked
   Student held accountable for seatwork
   Actively supervise students, when possible

6. Weekly and Monthly Reviews
   Systematic review of previously learned material
   Include review in homework
   Frequent tests
   Reteaching of material missed in tests

From Barak Rosenshine and Robert Stevens, "Teaching Functions." Reprinted with permission of Simon & Schuster Macmillan *Handbook of Research on Teaching,* Third Edition, Merlin C. Wittrock, Editor. Copyright © 1986 by the American Educational Research Association.

Note: With older, more mature learners, or learners with more knowledge of the subject, the following adjustments can be made: (1) the size of the step in presentation can be larger (more material is presented at one time), (2) there is less time spent on teacher-guided practice and (3) the amount of overt practice can be decreased, replacing it with covert rehearsal, restating and reviewing.

Although Hunter's ideas have received considerable publicity, not all educators support her work.

Some Dos and Don'ts for Direct Instruction

Properly used, direct instruction can be extremely effective, especially if the information it conveys is not easily available elsewhere. It can also be preferable to textbook readings, workbook exercises, and the like as a way to maintain student interest. Students can see your enthusiasm for material that you are presenting in an exciting manner (Borich, 1992).

It is a good idea to begin your teaching by using an advance organizer. (This is a summary of the ideas that you will be presenting, in which you attempt to link new concepts with prior knowledge; see the chap. 8 discussion of meaningful learning.) Be sure your students understand any new words that they need. Present your ideas in a

Focus ← To Be "Hunterized" or Not?

In an article entitled "Teachers Ask: Is There Life After Madeline Hunter?" (Garman and Hazi, 1988), the authors identify several pros and cons of Hunter's system. Examining the movement in Pennsylvania, the authors note that state officials, responding to national concerns about education, turned to a search for some means of evaluating and rewarding good teaching. Impressed by its seven identifiable steps, the Pennsylvania State Department of Education proposed a series of workshops featuring the Hunter model.

After interviewing more than two hundred Pennsylvania teachers who were involved in the Hunter training program, the authors first mentioned the "good news." There is no denying the attention that the model has brought to teaching, nor the sense of professionalism that accompanies such attention. Teachers also felt that their careers were enhanced by participating (financial rewards, promotions). Finally, through standardization of the seven steps, teachers could be held more accountable.

The "bad news" (expressed by about two-thirds of the teachers) focused on such negative features as being forced to adopt a single method, whether they agreed with it or not. Many teachers were angry: they felt that if they didn't use Hunter, they weren't rewarded. To some, the seven steps seemed like a game; many felt the charges for the workshops were excessive. Most of the teachers interviewed rejected the notion that the Hunter model made them any better teachers.

One major criticism from participants and observers alike was the increasing rigidity of the system. Regardless of the technique adopted, teachers must have the freedom to experiment and to explore, adapting methods to their own personalities.

Responding to these and similar criticisms, Hunter (1987) denied that her model is a recipe for successful teaching; rather, she considers it a decision-making model. Where her model has not produced any effects different from those of other techniques, Hunter believes that CTI has been used poorly. She insisted that there is no such thing as a "Madeline Hunter–type lesson," no one way to teach. She argued that her work presents basic instructional knowledge that teachers can use to make their classroom decisions.

carefully prepared and logical sequence that is appropriate for their level. As you proceed, use questions to keep the class motivated and to check their understanding. Give your students immediate feedback so that they know if their comprehension of the ideas you're discussing is right or wrong. Be alert for any signs of wandering attention or boredom, and engage these students immediately. Finally, follow up your presentation with activities designed to help retention and transfer. A good rule to remember for direct instruction is this: Tell them what you're going to tell them; tell them; and then remind them of what you've told them (Callahan, Clark, & Kellough, 1992).

Guard against talking too much, a habit easily acquired in direct instruction. If you think this is happening, stop, ask questions, or pose a relevant problem. Another danger inherent in direct instruction is to assume that just because you have told your students something, they have learned it. Constantly check for misinterpretations. Finally, as you review the content of the lesson that you are to teach, be sure that the material lends itself to direct instruction. For example, assume that in a biology class, you want your students to comprehend the extent and possible application of the discoveries of the *Human Genome Project*. Simply lecturing them is not the most productive way to accomplish this. Rather, you will want them to read, explore, discuss with one another, and suggest creative possibilities. If you want your students to integrate subject matter that is fairly complex for their level, you may well decide to turn to more indirect methods.

Indirect Instruction

Given the complexities of a modern society, teachers are aware that their students need to be adaptive and creative as they adjust to their changing environments. Consequently, the acquisition of facts and knowledge as the sole tools of teaching and learning is not enough. Teaching that encourages inquiry learning (let us call this *indirect* or *inquiry teaching*) is less structured and more informal. You will find yourself arranging classroom conditions in a way that encourages students to think about the means of solving problems, and working from the assumption that students should actively seek information rather than passively accepting it in lectures, recitation, or demonstrations (Callahan, Clark, & Kellough, 1992).

To assist students in such active exploration provides advance organizers and conceptual frameworks that can serve as "pegs" on which to hang key points that guide and channel thinking to the most productive areas. Use questions to guide the search and discovery process: raise contradictions, probe for deeper-level responses, pass responsibility for learning to each individual learner. Encourage students to use examples and references from their own experience, to seek clarification, and to draw parallels and associations that aid understanding and retention. Relate ideas to past learning and to students' own sphere of interests, concerns, and problems. Finally, provide cues, questions, or hints as needed to call their attention to inappropriate responses. Use discussion to encourage critical thinking and help students to examine alternatives, judge solutions, make predictions, and discover generalizations. Your task during discussion is to orient students, provide new content, review and summarize, alter the flow of information, and combine areas to promote the most productive discussion (Borich, 1992). An example of indirect instruction can be found in the work of Jerome Bruner.

Have you formed any opinions about the effectiveness of direct and indirect instruction? Think about your answer for a moment. Why did you answer as you did? Because of what you have read? Because of research? How much will your teaching methods be influenced by your answer to this question?

Bruner and Instructional Theory

In a wide-ranging series of essays from the cognitive perspective, Bruner (1960, 1966, 1971) afforded us penetrating insights into both **inquiry teaching** and learning. Examining the classroom functions of the instructor, he noted three sources of teacher behavior. First, teachers are *communicators of knowledge;* this implies mastery of both the knowledge to be communicated and the effective methods of its communication: you must know what to teach and how to teach it. Second, teachers are *models;* they should be competent and exciting individuals who will inspire in students a love of learning. Your behavior in the classroom is an important source of knowledge, guidance, and motivation for your students. We saw this clearly demonstrated in Bandura's work on modeling in chapters 7 and 10. Third, teachers are *symbols,* the immediate representatives of "education," and can be particularly persuasive figures in shaping students' attitudes, interests, opinions, and values, not to mention their intellectual achievement.

inquiry teaching *Bruner's term for teaching that permits students to be active partners in the search for knowledge, thus enhancing the meaning of what they learn.*

Principles of Instructional Theory

Bruner noted that learning is closely linked to cognitive structures, readiness, motivation, and interaction with the environment. He raised this question: since psychology already contains theories of learning and development, why is a theory of instruction needed? His answer is that theories of learning and development are *descriptive rather than prescriptive;* that is, they tell us what has happened, rather than what should happen. For example, from Piaget's theory we know that a child of 6 usually has not achieved the cognitive ability of reversibility. A theory of instruction prescribes how teachers can help a child acquire this. It outlines the materials and the methods best suited to help these pupils move to a higher cognitive level.

Bruner believes that there are four elements in any theory of instruction or inquiry teaching.

1. The theory should specify those experiences that *predispose* a youngster toward learning. What is there in the classroom or the materials that will make pupils want to learn? How can I get my pupils to want to learn long division, for example?
2. The theory should clearly delineate the *structure* of any subject to aid learning. Teachers must determine whether the subject is best presented *enactively,* that is, by emphasizing psychomotor learning (you might want preschoolers to actually mix the ingredients of a cake they are to bake); *iconically,* that is, by using images and other visuals to represent concepts (you might show a picture of a Civil War battlefield and ask your students to picture a row of Confederate soldiers behind the stone wall); or *symbolically,* that is, by using rules, logic, and propositions. Here you act as a decision maker, deciding whether the materials and methods are appropriate for a youngster's developmental level.

Figure 12.2

The spiral curriculum illustrated with an example: content concerning World War II.

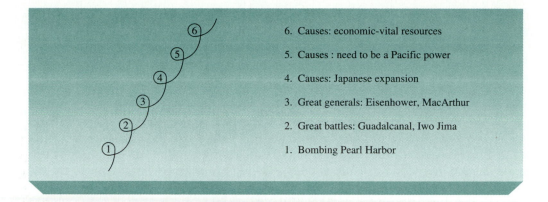

6. Causes: economic-vital resources

5. Causes : need to be a Pacific power

4. Causes: Japanese expansion

3. Great generals: Eisenhower, MacArthur

2. Great battles: Guadalcanal, Iwo Jima

1. Bombing Pearl Harbor

3. The theory should specify the *optimal sequence* for presenting materials. Is it always better to proceed from concrete to abstract, simple to complex, part to whole? Or is it better to present the entire structure and then fill in the pieces? Since teachers must lead students through some predetermined sequence, they again must act as decision makers. Your decision may have a powerful influence on the ease or difficulty with which a student learns.

4. The theory should specify the *nature and pacing of rewards and punishments*. Learning depends on knowledge of results, and the theory should indicate where, when, and under what circumstances correction and praise will occur. Teachers then become actively engaged in instructing pupils to both use error and apply information correctly.

Bruner concluded that a theory of instruction must accept that a curriculum reflects the nature of knowledge, the nature of the learner, and the learning process. To be successful, a teaching theory must erase the lines of distinction separating these three dimensions. The theory should have as its ultimate goal teaching students to participate in the entire process of acquiring and using knowledge.

Bruner and the Process of Education

Bruner developed four major themes in analyzing learning: structure, readiness, intuition, and motivation.

Understanding a subject's structure is central in Bruner's thinking. The first object of any act of learning, over and beyond the pleasure it may give, is that it should serve us in the future. Learning should not only take us somewhere, but also allow us later to go further more easily (Bruner, 1960, p. 17).

As Bruner noted, grasping a subject's structure is understanding it so that many other things can be related to it meaningfully; to learn structure is to learn how things are related. Students can grasp a subject's structure only if they understand its basic ideas. The more basic is the idea that students learn, the more they can apply it to other topics. If students understand a subject's fundamental structure, the subject itself becomes more comprehensible, aids memory, facilitates transfer, and helps to build the "spiral curriculum." For example, learning to identify and understand the causes of the Civil War can help your students to look beyond the mere names of the battles in any other war they study.

spiral curriculum *Bruner's term for teaching a subject in an ever more abstract manner; tied to his interpretation of readiness.*

The **spiral curriculum**, an excellent example of an attempt to develop structure, is closely linked to *Bruner's second theme: readiness.* For example, World War II has become a major topic in contemporary history. Using the principles of the spiral curriculum, it is taught at successively higher grade levels in an increasingly abstract manner. Figure 12.2 illustrates the process. Note the increasing abstraction and complexity of the presentation. Completing their study, pupils should have a good grasp of the subject.

Bruner's famous statement that any subject can be taught effectively in some intellectually honest form to any child at any stage of development implies that the basic ideas of science, mathematics, and literature are as simple as they are powerful. If teachers begin teaching the foundations of these subjects in an appropriate manner consistent with pupils' intellectual levels, as described by Piaget, pupils can learn important basics at any stage of mental development. Then, by applying the principles of the spiral curriculum, they can steadily proceed to more complex forms of the subject.

Once students obtain a detailed knowledge of a subject, they can begin to expand their hypothetical abilities; that is, they can make informed guesses. Knowing a topic deeply and widely enables them to proceed by implicit perception; they can grasp something without detailed analysis. They can make their informed guesses and then subject them to critical scrutiny, thus fostering both problem-solving and creative behavior. An understanding of the geography and history of the countries of Eastern Europe can help students speculate about the reasons for their independence movements.

Motivation is Bruner's final indispensable learning ingredient. He questions the value of excessive emphasis upon examinations, grades, and promotions with respect to a desirable lifetime commitment to learning. Children always have mixed motives for learning: pleasing parents and teachers, competing with peers, and acquiring a sense of self-mastery. Inspiring intrinsic motivation is difficult in children; Bruner realistically stated that if you teach well and if what you teach is worth learning, forces at work in our society will augment your efforts with an external prod, with the combined result that pupils will become more involved in their learning processes.

Modes of Representation

How can these ideas of Bruner's help us in teaching? Bruner believes that if teachers understand the mental stages that a child passes through, they can adapt their teaching accordingly. He calls these stages **modes of representation.** The first level is the **enactive** mode of representation. The infant knows the world only by acting on it; otherwise, the object does not exist for the child. As Bruner noted, even in an adult's life, there are times when words simply cannot express an experience (1966a, p. 10). For example, how can you tell someone about the "feel" of a golf or tennis swing?

The second level is the **iconic** mode of representation, Bruner's term for perceptual organization. For an individual faced with a series of apparently unrelated tasks, the discovery of a pattern makes the work easier. Word problems are a good example. Once students see the steps (the pattern) necessary to solve the problem, it then becomes more realistic and easier to solve.

The third level is the **symbolic** mode of representation. At this level the child engages in symbolic activities, such as language and mathematics. Bruner (1966a, p. 14) stated that when children translate experience into language, they enter the world of possibilities, enabling them to solve problems and engage in creative thinking.

Students learn according to their mode of representation. For Bruner, learning a subject involves three almost simultaneous processes: acquisition of new information, transformation, and evaluation.

modes of representation
Bruner's term for the mental stages a child passes through.

enactive *Bruner's term for the mental stage of knowing the world by acting on it; usually refers to the infancy period.*

iconic *Bruner's term for the perceptual organization of the world; a mode of representation.*

symbolic *Bruner's term for the ability to represent, to consider possibilities.*

- *Acquisition of new information* that replaces or expands what the pupil already knows is the initial phase. Here the child incorporates environmental stimuli according to the existing mode of representation: by physical action, by forming images, or by abstracting, comparing, and judging. Before students can understand the surge toward freedom and independence among the countries of Eastern Europe, they must know the history of these countries, especially since World War II.
- *Transformation* is the second phase. Once youngsters or adults acquire new information, they must manipulate or change it to meet new tasks. Bruner often uses the illustration of going beyond the information given. For example, your friend passes by the door and says, "Hi, Janie." You do not see her, but immediately think, "There goes Liz." You have manipulated verbal stimuli to form the idea of your friend.

Focus — Teaching and Learning—Bruner in the Classroom

Bruner described a junior high school course he taught that illustrated these principles (1966a, p. 109). One unit related Caesar's decision to cross the Rubicon and drive for Rome. The class read Caesar's commentaries and some letters from Cicero, but knew nothing about his opponent Pompey. The class immediately divided into Caesarians and Pompeyans and tried to obtain more information about strategy. Would Caesar move his army through a narrow valley unless he had had previous reassurance that the inhabitants were friendly? Bruner stated that the pupils reasoned like politicians.

One group of troublesome students provided an excellent analysis of the corrupt Roman political system and sympathized totally with Caesar. Pompey "had no guts." When these students compared Roman politicians to current ones and equated Roman governmental problems with current difficulties, the course came alive.

Here you see an excellent example of theory translated into practice. Remember Bruner's belief that any act of learning involves three processes:

1. *The acquisition of new information.* What was the political situation in the valley?
2. *The transformation,* or manipulation, of existing knowledge to make it fit new tasks. Was the Roman political situation similar to contemporary American politics?
3. *The evaluation,* or determination if the manipulation of knowledge was adequate. Did understanding and applying current information help students to comprehend the Roman issues?

A learning episode occurred that reflected what had gone before it, and that permitted generalization beyond it. Anyone at any age is ready to learn. Bruner would advise you to allow children to explore and make educated guesses; allow them to make mistakes; and teach them the structure of a subject, not minute and isolated facts.

• *Evaluation* is the final phase. Students ask themselves if they have successfully manipulated the information. Was it adequate? Was it correct?

Bruner joins mental growth, modes of representation, and learning processes to support his model of the spiral curriculum. He stated (1960) that if teachers respect a pupil's thinking process and translate material into meaningful units (that is, if they match the subject matter to the pupil's mode of representation), they can introduce great ideas to children at different times and with increasing abstractness. For example, a discussion of freedom in the first grade differs from a junior high school discussion of slavery, which differs from a high school discussion of the meaning of the Constitution—hence the spiral curriculum.

Bruner also made specific teaching recommendations, especially related to the continued use of discovery teaching and learning (Wilcox, 1987). He noted that despite the many mechanical aids for teachers (films, television, programmed instruction), the chief facilitator of learning is still the teacher. If you believe in cognitive learning principles, consider the following.

First, if you desire to teach effectively, you must master the material to be taught. (There probably is no better way to learn a subject than to teach it.) Second, remember that you are a model. Unimaginative, uninspiring, and insecure teachers are hardly likely to spark a love of learning, especially since students quickly sense a lack of commitment. Recognize that students will identify with you as a model, and often compare themselves to you. This is a sobering thought, but it can motivate you to search constantly for ways to better your teaching and furnish a stimulating classroom atmosphere.

Some Dos and Don'ts for Indirect Instruction

Indirect (inquiry) instruction has a distinctive place in the classroom, since it helps students not only to learn concepts, but to move beyond memorization to draw conclusions and form generalizations. The knowledge that is acquired by this process may be more meaningful for your students because of their self-involvement, which aids them in discovering the structure of the subject they're studying. They can also see how *this* topic relates to others. Both motivation and retention seem to be better with this type of instruction.

Remember, however, that there are also disadvantages with this method. The content and situation must be appropriate; devising a strategy to bring relief to a beleaguered nation requires a different process from mastering the vocabulary of a language. Considerable time and effort is required, and the results may be totally unexpected. For example, your students will be much more noisy and active; this may lead to control problems unless you monitor their activities closely. Also, as a consequence of their independent work, they may reach conclusions totally at odds with your goals (which may not be bad!).

There are some "dos" to remember when you use this technique. Perhaps most important, be supportive: your students inevitably will make false starts, make incorrect assumptions, and reach sometimes startling conclusions. As you work with them, reinforce what they do correctly (but don't give general praise; you might reinforce an incorrect response). Since they will be working independently, be sure that you have provided adequate clues for them to use. By "adequate," we mean directions, reading, and materials that are suited to your students' abilities. Encourage your students to work cooperatively, which helps them to discover new ideas and also fosters positive relationships.

Both direct and indirect instruction are needed in the classroom, since pupils need to acquire facts before they attempt to solve problems, but must also be urged to learn those adaptive skills that carry beyond the classroom. At this point, you may well ask this: What do teachers themselves need to know?

Teaching and Subject Matter

In analyzing the basic data teachers need, our first consideration should be the knowledge base of teaching. In a thoughtful essay, Good (1990) identified several topics with which teachers should be comfortable enough to use them almost automatically in assessing their instruction. These include motivation, classroom management, teacher expectations, student misconception research, and learning strategies (topics that are at the heart of this book).

If you are familiar with this rich teacher knowledge base, you can then use it while your lesson is in progress. For example, in the middle of a lesson, you might decide that things aren't going as well as you had anticipated, determining perhaps that motivation is the reason, or that the strategy you had decided on just isn't reaching your students. You can then make changes while the lesson is going on. You can do this, however, only if you are completely at ease with the tools of teaching.

Along with these ideas about good teaching, you also need to be confident about the subject you are teaching. To help you identify what content you need to know to be an effective teacher, Shulman (1986) distinguished three types of content knowledge: subject matter knowledge, pedagogical knowledge, and curriculum knowledge.

Subject matter knowledge refers to a teacher's comprehension of a subject when compared to that of a specialist. How comfortable am I with this subject? Can I answer students' questions accurately and in a relaxed manner? *Pedagogical knowledge* refers to how the basic principles and strategies of a subject are best acquired and retained. Am I sufficiently prepared in this subject to know the best way to introduce it? What is the best way to teach its core elements? What is the best way to evaluate my students? *Curriculum knowledge* refers to the optimal manner in which knowledge of a subject can be organized and presented: in texts, programs, media, and workbooks. Am I aware of the supplementary materials that can broaden my students' knowledge of this subject?

For example, assume that you are teaching one of Faulkner's stories and students are having difficulty. What do you do? Do you yourself turn to the story and attempt to clarify themes, or do you search for an outside interpretation? Let us explore some deciding factors.

How does your knowledge of a subject affect the manner in which you teach it. Subject matter knowledge cuts both ways. If you feel shaky about material, you may attempt to brush by it quickly. Conversely, if you have depth of knowledge, you may do

The Instructional Environment

Many educational psychologists have been reaching a more complete understanding of the instructional environment than has been possible in the past. In fact, methods have been devised to measure specific components of the instructional environment. One of these techniques is *TIES, or The Instructional Environment Scale,* developed by Ysseldyke and Christenson (1987) at the University of Minnesota. Teachers and other school professionals can use the scale to aid them in designing effective instruction in their classrooms. Working with colleagues or requesting the assistance of a master or resource teacher or psychologist can help teachers to better understand their contribution to the instructional environment. Basically, TIES assesses various domains of instruction in the classroom.

Twelve components were selected for inclusion in TIES; they are presented in figure A. The twelve components are said to be relevant across different types of classrooms (e.g., regular and special education) and across different grades (e.g., kindergarten through high school).

The meaning of each of the twelve components follows.

1. *Instructional Presentation.* Instructional presentation greatly influences quality teaching, with lesson development being the most important component.

2. *Classroom Environment.* Effective classroom management that incorporates behavioral rules and organizational routines is essential to quality teaching.

3. *Teacher Expectations.* Teachers should have high academic expectations for their students and hold them accountable for academic performance; these standards should also be made clear to students.

4. *Cognitive Emphasis.* By cognitive emphasis, the authors mean that students should understand how to solve problems and how to approach tasks.

5. *Motivational Strategies.* Effective instruction depends upon motivated instructional lessons or other strategies (e.g., praise).

6. *Relevant Practice.* Two types of practice are necessary, controlled (guided) and independent (seat work); both must be present to promote student achievement. Practice must be on appropriate tasks.

7. *Academic Engaged Time.* The time that students spend engaged in learning predicts academic achievement moderately; other components noted above are designed to increase academic engaged time.

8. *Informed Feedback.* Feedback that is task-specific and explicit as well as that which provides students with increased opportunity to respond is important to student achievement.

9. *Adaptive Instruction.* Based on application with handicapped children, adaptive instruction that incorporates clearly communicated instructional goals at an appropriate difficulty level, careful monitoring of feedback, a comprehensive feedback system, and student responsibility for task completion has been found to increase student achievement.

10. *Progress Evaluation.* Monitoring of student performance with the explicit purpose of providing student correction opportunities and time needed to achieve mastery aids student achievement.

11. *Instructional Planning.* It is essential that the teacher match student characteristics with the instruction delivered in the classroom.

12. *Student Understanding.* Students' accurate perception of tasks and directions is critical for increasing engaged time and achievement.

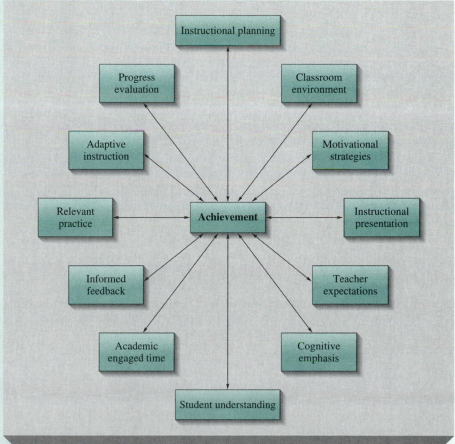

Figure A

Important components of an instructional environment as conceptualized in The Instructional Environmental Scale (TIES).

From J. Ysseldyke and S. Christianson, The Instructional Environment Scale. Copyright © 1987 Pro-Ed, Austin, Texas. Reprinted by permission of the authors.

too much with your pupils. Generally, though, research indicates that knowledgeable teachers can better detect student misconceptions and exploit opportunities for meaningful learning. Teachers who are less knowledgeable in subject matter may avoid presenting critical material if they are uncomfortable with it, and may misinterpret students' learning (Dill, 1990).

In attempting to answer the question of how much and what teachers should know of the material they teach, researchers are just beginning the task of unraveling teacher cognition. Shulman's three categories help us to discover where teachers turn when students experience difficulty, and whether differences in the knowledge that teachers bring to a subject produce differences in the way that they organize that topic.

Nevertheless, it all comes down to one fundamental question: *How much and what should teachers know of what they teach* (Shulman, 1986, p. 26)? The best approach is to know as much as possible about your subject, to present it as dynamically as possible, and to be prepared to answer all kinds of questions about what you teach.

What does all of this mean for you? You should remember one guiding principle: *Your task is to help your pupils learn as much as their potential permits.* To help you comprehend the relevance of the remaining work of this chapter, here are several principles of learning proposed by Bower and Hilgard (1981) that have direct instructional implications.

Be sure you know what you want to accomplish; that is, keep clearly defined objectives in sight at all times (see chap. 11). In this way, you can recognize the necessary stages in any task that are necessary for mastery. If you know your subject, you are aware of the sequence in the content that students need to progress at their level. For example, pupils can't do long division until they can add, subtract, and do short division.

Encourage as much student activity as possible. Student involvement may range from reading a text with comprehension, to class discussion and research projects. As your students become engaged, provide reinforcement, but be sure it is both specific and deserved. Students need encouragement; just be sure it is appropriate, and don't use praise carelessly.

Guard against student anxiety, which can have many causes. Constantly monitor the classroom atmosphere so that it remains challenging but not overwhelming. Remember that tried-and-true cliche: match the mix. That is, use teaching techniques and materials that are appropriate for the level of your students.

Teach for understanding and encourage the use of learning strategies (see chap. 9). What do we mean by "understanding"? To answer this question, Perkins and Blythe (1994, pp. 5–6) stated that understanding is being able to do a variety of thought-demanding things with a topic—explaining, finding evidence and examples, applying, and representing the topic in new ways. For example, understanding is needed to discuss everything from why skates need to be sharp if one is to skate well to the pros and cons of a superpower's invasion of a small country to restore order.

As Gardner noted (in Brandt, 1993), the cognitive research of the last twenty years is quite compelling: Students really don't understand what they learn. They master facts, but their comprehension lags far behind. To rectify this is difficult for many reasons. Schools are often more interested in how their students do on standardized tests, and there is disagreement about the best materials and strategies to reach understanding (Perkins & Blythe, 1994).

As you proceed with your reading, remember the principles we have established. Also, keep these questions in mind: What will help me to teach more effectively and my students to learn better? Which teaching theories and models best fit my teaching style, the level of my students, and the subject(s) I teach?

THE DESIGN OF INSTRUCTION

Thus far we have discussed the characteristics of effective teaching and analyzed the two basic methods of direct and indirect instruction. We have also examined the different kinds of knowledge that a teacher should possess. It is time now to introduce the work of those who focus on instructional design, that is, those who concentrate on the specific steps needed to achieve particular learning objectives. Thus, we now turn our attention to the leading exponents of instructional design: B. F. Skinner, Susan Markle, and Robert Gagne.

Skinner and the Technology of Teaching

We examined Skinner's presentation of instrumental learning in chapter 7. Now we will follow his theoretical beliefs into the classroom to see how he has steadfastly applied the principles of operant conditioning to both learning and teaching, in a procedure called **programmed instruction.**

programmed instruction
Skinner's classroom application of the principles of operant conditioning; a method of instruction.

Recall Skinner's argument that teachers depend too heavily upon punishment while neglecting their use of positive reinforcement. Insisting that special techniques can arrange contingencies of reinforcement—resulting from the relationship between behavior and the consequences of that behavior—Skinner stated that teachers now can effectively control behavior. This assumption is the basis of operant conditioning (Skinner, 1968).

Annual **Edition**

Skinner in the Classroom

In the modern educational environment, where control of behavior is critical, Skinner believed that all was chaos. As an example, he turned to one of his favorite subjects: the teaching of arithmetic. Here, the responses are verbal—speaking and writing figures, words, and signs—and it is necessary to bring them under stimulus control. How do teachers accomplish this? They should use reinforcers. Traditionally, this has meant reliance on negative consequences. Skinner noted that although yesterday's physical punishment is mostly gone, teachers still rely too much on sarcasm, ridicule, and low marks. So arithmetic, like most subjects, has become mired in a maze of dislike, anxiety, and ultimately, boredom.

Improvement is possible, since there are general characteristics of teaching that, if practiced, cultivate both teaching and learning. For example, Skinner urged teachers to *define the* **terminal behavior:** they must decide what students should be able to do after having been taught. Statements like "be a good citizen" are both inadequate and unworthy; they do not describe behavior. "Knowledge" is another deceptive goal of education. Students have learned something when they behave. That is, they respond to stimuli differently than they did before instruction. Students "know" when teachers can specifically identify their behavior; that is, teachers have taught them to behave in certain ways. What they know is what they do; therefore, teachers must objectively and concretely state their objectives.

terminal behavior *Skinner's term for what students should be able to do after instruction.*

Teachers must also *solve the problem of the* **first instance.** Once you have determined the terminal behavior (what you want students to do after teaching), you must strengthen it by reinforcement. But you cannot reinforce what does not appear. The problem of the first instance means the need for pupils to exhibit some aspect of the desired behavior. One option is to induce it, as in physically taking a child's hand and guiding it to form letters. Another option is to have pupils imitate the teacher or some example of excellent work. Simply telling pupils what to do and then reinforcing them when they do it is yet another possibility. Learning, however, does not occur because the teacher has primed the behavior; it occurs only when behavior is reinforced. The above examples illustrate only the first step in the process.

first instance *For Skinner, some aspect of desired behavior, initially exhibited by a student.*

Skinner also stated that teachers should *decide what they will use to prompt behavior.* One reinforcement will hardly free a response from priming stimuli. When do you stop priming students? If you continue too long, you are inefficient; if you stop too soon, you may cause error. Use only as much as is necessary. For example, you may wish students to be able to identify the Midwestern states, their major cities, and their principal industries. You may begin by using maps and reading materials. Some cities may be near water and thus be port cities. Later, when students should know which cities do what, you may ask them to locate a city without using maps or texts. You thus have supplied various prompts as part of the original priming behavior.

Be sure that you *program complex behavior*. Priming and prompting evoke a behavior to be reinforced in the presence of required stimuli. Some behavior, however, is so complex that you cannot reinforce it as a unit. You must program (or structure) it, which does not mean teaching one thing at a time in an isolated manner and as a collection of responses. What a student does halfway through a program may not be a part of the terminal behavior. Small steps are needed to ensure constant reinforcement.

Finally, teachers must *decide on not only the proper size but also the most effective sequence of steps for the program*. You must ensure proper student preparation for each step, as well as an orderly arrangement of steps. You cannot always depend upon a subject's inherent logic. A good example is our work with Piaget. Usually students are well advised to read original sources and trace the author's work. This may not work with Piaget, because his ideas are so complex and his writing so tortuous that students, trying to proceed logically, may become hopelessly confused. Instructors are better advised to select and test basic ideas (such as Piaget's notion of the functional invariants) before presenting the entire system (his theory of cognitive development).

An example that reflects many of these principles is the highly structured Bereiter-Englemann program, designed to prescribe teaching procedures for disadvantaged children. Bereiter and Englemann (1966) stated that new teachers like to work with "ideas." Good teaching, however, employs much smaller and more intricate units than ideas; it involves specific information modules and specific techniques. Teaching is the interplay between information, pace, discipline, rewards, and drama as they relate to curriculum (1966, p. 105).

Acquiring these techniques comes gradually—a motivational trick here, an attention-getting device there. According to Bereiter and Englemann, teachers are good not because of what they are but because of what they do. Good teachers do the "right thing" because they have learned to do so slowly—even painfully. They were not naturally proficient; they achieved proficiency through practice.

Bereiter and Englemann devised several teaching strategies to use in an intensive preschool program for disadvantaged children. Nevertheless, they have broad applicability. One suggestion is to *be careful when you vary your presentation methods*. Variations may confuse the culturally disadvantaged child, who ordinarily experiences considerable language difficulty. Excessive variation bothers and bewilders all children, who need to feel psychologically secure in the classroom.

Still, youngsters, disadvantaged or not, must respond in a variety of situations and should be ready to respond to variation outside of the classroom. Although the authors' suggestion is pertinent, remember also to consider variation in relation to the readiness of your students. Whatever you do, *give children sufficient time to respond*. Time has been a recurring theme in this text. You previously encountered it in Bloom's work on mastery learning. In their work, Bereiter and Englemann urged that a lesson's tempo be such that the youngster can respond thoughtfully.

They also suggested that teachers use questions liberally. Questions are important because they help students attend to relevant cues. You must consider the question's difficulty: is the student capable of answering it? The value of questioning is clear from countless studies. Subjects tend to remember more about material on which they are questioned, and to retain it longer. The direct instructional effect of questioning is substantial.

Try using multiple examples. When presenting a new concept, avoid talking too much about it. The authors advise that you "stretch" the concept. For example, if you are teaching the concept of the color red, give numerous examples of different objects whose sizes, shapes, and other characteristics are all different, with the one exception of their shared color: red. Remember, however, to *try to prevent incorrect responses*. Helping children avoid error will help them to avoid mistake patterns. Always assume that children will repeat mistakes in similar situations, and try to forestall them. Use prevention techniques.

Table 12.3

Research on Closing the Gap Between Special Education and General Education Students

Reasoning	1. On a variety of measures of argument construction and critiquing, high school students with mild handicaps in a higher-order-thinking intervention scored as high as or higher than high school students in an honors English class and college students enrolled in a teacher certification program (Grossen & Carnine, 1990).
	2. In constructing arguments, high school students with learning disabilities in a higher-order-thinking intervention scored significantly higher than college students enrolled in a teacher certification program and scored at the same level as general education high school students and college students enrolled in a logic course. In critiquing arguments, the students with learning disabilities scored at the same level as the general education high school students and the college students enrolled in a teacher certification program. All of these groups had scores significantly lower than those of the college students enrolled in a logic course (Collins & Carnine, 1988).
Understanding Science Concepts	1. High school students with learning disabilities were mainstreamed for a higher-order-thinking intervention in science. On a chemistry test that required applying concepts such as bonding, equilibrium, energy of activation, atomic structure, and organic compounds, the students' scores did not differ significantly from control students' in an advanced placement chemistry course (Hofmeister, Englemann, & Carnine, 1989).
	2. Middle school students with learning disabilities were mainstreamed for a higher-order-thinking intervention in science. On a test of misconceptions in earth science, the students showed better conceptual understanding than Harvard graduates interviewed in Schnep's 1987 film, *A Private Universe* (Muthukvishna, Carnine, Grossen, & Miller, 1990).
Problem Solving	1. On a test of problem solving in health promotion, high school students with mild handicaps in a higher-order-thinking intervention scored significantly higher than nonhandicapped students who had completed a traditional high school health class (Woodward, Carnine, & Gersten, 1989).
	2. Middle school students with learning disabilities were mainstreamed for a higher-order-thinking intervention in science. On a test of earth science problem solving, the students scored significantly higher than nonhandicapped students who received traditional science instruction (Woodward & Noell, this series).
	3. High school special education students were mainstreamed for a higher-order-thinking intervention in math. On a test of problem solving requiring the use of ratios and proportions, the students scored as well as nonhandicapped high school students who received traditional math instruction (Moore & Carnine, 1989).
	4. Middle school students with mild handicaps were mainstreamed for a higher-order-thinking intervention in earth science. Most of the students with handicaps scored higher than the nonhandicapped control students in problem solving involving earth science content (Neidelman, 1991).

From D. Carnine, "Curricular Interventions for Teaching Higher Order Thinking to all Students: Introduction to the Special Series." in *Journal of Learning Disabilities*, Vol. No. 24, pp. 261–269. Copyright 1991 by PRO-ED, Inc. Reprinted by permission.

Finally, *be clear in responding to correct and incorrect answers*. If a child brings a blue crayon when asked to bring a red one, do not praise the youngster for bringing a crayon. Youngsters cannot understand the subtle distinction. Teachers should provide nonthreatening but clear feedback. This suggestion is similar to our earlier warnings about nonpertinent praise.

Bereiter and Englemann furnished several more suggestions that indicate the nature of their program: carefully controlled stimuli, judicious application of reinforcement, and the avoidance of error. The Bereiter-Englemann program is an example of behavioral principles put to action.

Recent work derived from the Bereiter-Englemann program has focused on curricular interventions and been applied to all students with great promise, especially with regard to higher-order thinking skills (Carnine, 1991). Table 12.3 presents research that may close the gap between special and regular education, and, as Carnine (1991) argued, should encourage educators to teach higher-order thinking skills in reasoning, science, and problem solving through curricular interventions.

Markle and Programed Instruction

Adapting Skinner's technology of teaching while remaining faithful to the basic principles of operant conditioning, Susan Markle (1990; Tiemann & Markle, 1990) built her concept of "programed" (note the one *m*) instruction around the principle of active responding (the student learns what the student does—Markle, 1990, p. 1). Although the original programmed instruction movement enjoyed great initial success, Markle believes that too rigid adherence to these early views—small steps, heavy prompting, verbatim student responses to oft-repeated sentences—all contributed to criticism of the system as excessively sterile.

The Basic Programing Principles

Three programing principles—active responding, errorless learning, and immediate feedback—form the basis of Markle's model of instructional design.

The Principle of Active Responding

Here Markle refers not to random student activity, but rather to meaningful responses that are covert, overt, psychomotor, or verbal. Students who think through an answer are active in the sense that Markle intends. To indicate how meaningful activity can be incorporated into programed instruction, Markle used the following example.

> The symbol for "less than" is < , and the symbol for "greater than" is >. Which of these questions is more meaningful, 1 or 2?
> 1. Write the symbol for "less than" _____
>   Write the symbol for "greater than" _____
> 2. Make these arithmetic statements true by writing the correct symbol:
>   a. 8 ? 3   b. 2 × 2 ? 5   c. 3+7 ? 8

The second statement is more meaningful. Each of these frames requires student activity, but in the second (meaningful) frame, the student reads the instruction, examines the problems, decides which quantities are greater (making computations, if necessary), and writes the symbol in the blank space.

Note that the amount of processing required and the amount of overt activity needed are not identical. Return to the two math frames; you notice immediately that task (2) requires far more thought. What the student is asked to do determines what information the student will notice and retain. Information that isn't needed, that is not processed at a meaningful level, is likely to go unnoticed. Telling the student and causing the student to process are not the same things.

Must students respond overtly? Note: this does not call into question the necessity of responding, but that of responding overtly. No one questions the need for active responding—but if a response remains covert (that is, inside a student's head), how can you be sure that the student knows the correct answer? Programers are often split on this issue; what you decide will reflect your personal preference. Incidentally, this issue is by no means restricted to programed instruction; all instructional theories and designs face the same question.

To illustrate the problem, examine the following statements and decide if you would want your students to respond covertly or overtly.

1. The student is learning how to write numbers.
2. The student is learning to sing the notes of the scale.
3. The student is learning how to play first base.
4. The student is learning Spanish names for familiar objects.
5. The student is learning to distinguish the music of Handel from that of Mozart.

You may decide that all statements require an overt response. Most readers would agree that 1, 2, and 3 demand overt activity; most would agree that learning is probably enhanced by overt responses in number 4; there would be less agreement about the last statement. Active responding, yes; overt responding, maybe. Note that active, overt responding provides rich opportunities for feedback and reinforcement, which is particularly important in the beginning stages of acquiring new knowledge or skills.

The Principle of Errorless Learning   Markle attempted to define more precisely the meaning of error. As we saw in chapter 7, Skinner was urgently concerned with the control exerted by the environment, stating that lack of control and not the theory itself is responsible for unexpected results. Although we all make mistakes, the goal of instruction should be to reduce error as much as possible.

If learners respond actively, they tend to remember the circumstances surrounding the learning: your teaching, the stimuli, the response, any feedback that was provided. If they give an incorrect response, what do they learn? They learn the error. Markle, then, questioned the manner in which we treat error. If we tell a student "No, that's wrong," or make a red X on the paper, will the student suppress the mistake? No. The student will simply try some other response. However, nothing will have been done to reinforce the correct answers, in working toward errorless learning. If you say, "No, John, 9 × 7 is not 56; it's 63," then the student does not respond actively. Does it follow, then, that students should never be allowed to make mistakes? Not in this system. Errors serve many functions. They can be signals that instruction needs improvement; they are a reliable guide for diagnosis; they aid programers in shaping the final form of a program.

There may also be good reasons for getting a mistake out in the open, such as diagnosing a lack of background information that is needed for a topic. Students should also be permitted to "mess around" with the subject matter, as in a lab or in simulated lab situations in computer-assisted instruction.

The Principle of Immediate Feedback   Markle linked the need for feedback to the manner in which the statement is framed. For example, there are instances in which feedback would add nothing to the learning. If I ask you how much 2 + 2 equals, you don't need me or the text to tell you that you are right. You have that information from your personal knowledge. Challenging situations, however, cause students to make more errors and learn less when feedback is lacking.

Gagne and Instructional Design

Since 1979, Robert Gagne has established himself as a leader in the field of instructional design (Gagne & Briggs, 1979; Gagne & Driscoll, 1988; Gagne, Briggs, & Wager, 1988). His influential work has been based upon Gagne's views of five learning outcomes: verbal information, intellectual skills, cognitive strategies, attitudes, and motor skills. Each of these five learning outcomes demands a different set of conditions for optimizing learning, retention, and transferability. The "optimal conditions" refer to a particular set of external events surrounding the learner: *the instruction that students receive.*

Here we see the great value of Gagne's work: the close relationship between teaching and learning. In his tightly organized view of teaching and learning, Gagne has identified several instructional events that he believes help students to learn meaningfully.

First, you must gain the attention of your students. Instruction terminates immediately if attention falters. What you have read in chapters 7 and 8 (on learning) applies here. Watch the conditions of your class (time of the day, hunger, fatigue); use stimulating materials that are appropriate for your students; appeal to as many senses as possible (read, listen, discuss, touch, manipulate); be sure that stimuli are biologically and psychologically appropriate. *Informing learners of the objective* of the lesson is another way of helping them focus their attention. What precisely is to be learned? Students should know the criteria for mastery and when they have achieved it.

teacher – student

interactions

The Functions of Teaching

1. Any type of instruction involves certain functions of teaching.
   - To help you diversify your instruction, describe, in concrete terms, the kinds of students and types of content that you think require direct instruction. Do the same for inquiry instruction.
   - To determine your students' prior knowledge in a subject, devise a brief (6- to 10-item) diagnostic pretest that assesses skills you think are needed for a successful introduction to new work. This type of device can be used at all levels and for almost any subject.
   - Analyze the texts that you are using to determine if they present subject matter effectively. Use questions such as these as a guide:
     a. What is the main purpose of the text?
     b. Is the reading level appropriate for my students?
     c. Is the format designed to hold a pupil's attention and to sustain motivation?
     d. Is the subject matter presented in a clear and orderly manner?
     e. Is there adequate subject matter coverage?
     These five points will also serve as guidelines if you serve on curriculum committees or textbook evaluation committees.
   - Keep a journal in which you list the community resources that you could use: social agencies, recreational facilities, businesses that offer field trips, cultural organizations that offer speakers.

2. One of the major findings regarding teaching relates to the quantity and pacing of instruction.
   - Be sure that you remain involved with your students; it is the key to successful time on task and enables you to furnish necessary feedback.
   - For a quick check of how your students spend their time during any lesson or with any subject, have an observer (even one of your students) make two observations. Give your observer a list of your students' names next to two columns headed "off-task" and "on-task." At each observation point, the observer puts a check in the appropriate box.
   - To review your own use of class time, make a list of the functions that you perform in the classroom (directly instructing, monitoring seatwork, checking homework, conducting drills, encouraging student inquiry). For each lesson taught, put a check next to the appropriate function. Are you making the best use of your time?
   - It is an excellent idea to tape some of your classes occasionally. When you listen to the tape, use a device such as the Bloom taxonomy to evaluate your questions.

     Did they mainly demand facts?

     Did they pursue students' comprehension of their work?

     Did they prod students to use their facts to solve problems?

Gagne recommends that you *stimulate recall of prerequisites,* that is, appeal to your students' prior knowledge. Students may need a simple reminder of previous learning, or they might require detailed help. This will help you when you *present the stimulus material.* Use techniques that are as attractive and exciting as possible, whether verbal, demonstrative, or media-related. Make the material interesting and pertinent to facilitate attention and to spark inquiry.

You may have to *provide learning guidance.* By this Gagne means you must ensure that students acquire the details involved in the learning objective; if a series of steps is needed for mastery, then students must know what these steps are and how to master them. Learn the geography; learn the history; finally, speculate about politics. This guidance in turn helps to *elicit the performance.* You cannot be certain that your students have learned unless they perform the behavior. (Recall the discussion at the beginning of the learning section concerning learning versus performance.) Be certain students' behavior is that demanded in the objective. For example, can your students identify the specific causes of an independence movement?

Part of your task is to *provide appropriate feedback.* Your reinforcement should be carefully considered. Give students accurate, detailed comments or notes about their performance, specifying what was done well and what needs improvement. Does your feedback match a specific response? Is it appropriate for the quality of the response? Again, do not overpraise. Finally, check to see if students understand the feedback and are able to use it to improve future performance.

Did they urge students to think about relations?

Did they require students to integrate facts and then make judgments?

3. Other major findings about teaching focus on the quality of instruction.
   • Once you decide on your objectives, apply the main features of direct instruction by listing them on the board, explaining them to your pupils, and then acting on them. For example,
     a. Be sure that all pupils are actively engaged on task
     b. Use several concrete examples to illustrate your lesson
     c. Be sure that vocabulary and level of difficulty are correct for your students
     d. Monitor your pace by watching your pupils and slow down or pick up accordingly
     e. Stop to ask questions and provide appropriate feedback
     f. Give a clear summary
   • If you have taped any of your lessons, listen to them again and evaluate the way that you use praise. A good technique is to have the "Guidelines for Effective Praise" (see table 12.1 on page 400) in front of you as you listen to the tape and to check your responses against the criteria for effective and ineffective praise.

• Once students have acquired needed information—by either direct or inquiry instruction—question them about their knowledge. Pick one topic that you will teach (for example, photosynthesis). Now decide
   a. How you will respond to correct answers. "What does a green plant make from water and gas?" "Sugar." If you find yourself frequently saying "That's right," you're probably asking too many factual questions.
   b. How you will respond to incorrect answers. You must tell students immediately that they are wrong. If they can't answer a factual question, tell them what they need to know. If they are wrong on a higher-level question (synthesis or evaluation), say something like this: "You're almost right, but . . . ." At this point, you can either give them the needed information or use additional questioning to lead them to the correct answer.
   c. How you will respond to incomplete answers. You may ask another question that acts as a probe to the student, thus requiring the student to answer. You may also ask another student to complete the first student's answer.

Small work groups and teacher inquiry are two critical elements that promote motivation and learning.

Table 12.4

Best Practices to Increase Academic Learning Time	
Increase time used for instruction:	Establish contingencies for school attendance and punctuality. Minimize interruptions. Program for smooth transitions. Maintain an academic focus.
Increase engaged time:	Clarify instructions and expectations regarding performance. Keep instruction fast-paced. Maintain an interactive teaching style and frequent student responding. Adopt seating arrangements to maximize attending.
Increase productive learning time:	Use seatwork effectively. Provide immediate, appropriate feedback. Diagnose, prescribe, and monitor performance accurately.

From Maribeth Gettinger, *Best Practices*. Copyright 1990 the National Association of School Psychologists. Reprinted by permission of the publisher.

Assess the performance of your students in an accurate manner designed to determine if they have attained the objectives of the work. Assessment of student performance can occur in several ways. Assessment and testing of classroom performance are discussed in detail in chapters 15 and 16. Finally, if you have followed Gagne's suggestions to this point, you will want to *enhance retention and transfer*. You simply cannot assume that students will automatically transfer their learning from one class to another; you must include in your instructional plans provisions for both review and the use of the material in novel situations.

Gagne believes that this nine-step model is a new theory of learning and memory. It also utilizes existing theory as a basis for designing instruction and attempts to include all types of learning outcomes that are typically the objectives of instruction. Finally, the model provides an instructional basis for analyzing the interaction of internal events with external events; this makes the model applicable to instruction of many forms in a wide variety of settings, while simultaneously appealing to the individual differences of learners.

ADAPTING INSTRUCTION TO THE INDIVIDUAL DIFFERENCES OF LEARNERS

Although our focus has been on teachers and teaching strategies, you should not overlook the necessity of adapting your teaching to the characteristics of your students. Adapting instruction means attempting to "match the mix" between student aptitudes and the methods and materials you use. A good example of this can be seen in the work of Benjamin Bloom.

Bloom and School Learning

Benjamin Bloom's ideas on learning have received the careful attention of psychologists and educators. Bloom, long a leader in American education and a fervent advocate of educational research guidance of classroom policy, has devised an explanation of school learning that is a sophisticated mix of theory and research. Bloom (1981) identified several variables that influence the teaching-learning process.

Time on task has always been recognized as a critical factor in learning, whether the term refers to years a subject appears in a curriculum, number of days in the school year, number of hours per day, or number of minutes per class. These are relatively fixed times, which tell us little about how much time students are actively engaged in learning. As Bloom stated (1981, p. 3), if one student is actively engaged 90 percent of the time while another is thus engaged only 30 percent of the time, we should not be surprised at their different achievement levels. As for teachers, studies of cues (what is to be learned), reinforcement (rewards for learning), and participation (active student engagement in learning) provide valuable clues as to just what teachers are doing with their time. What is most important to remember, however, is that *time on task can be altered*.

Using Bloom's work as a basis, Gettinger (1990) identified three aspects of learning time that could be increased. The first is the time used for instruction, the second is engaged time, and the third is productive learning time. Table 12.4 summarizes the methods that have been found to increase the various aspects of learning time.

Bloom argued that we must make a distinction between *intelligence* and *cognitive entry behaviors*. Although researchers repeatedly have demonstrated a link between intelligence and aptitude tests and later achievement, Bloom reasoned that these findings do not determine a student's potential for learning. Cognitive entry characteristics, which is knowledge essential for learning a particular subject (what we have referred to as "prior knowledge"), also show a close relationship with achievement and can be altered. These characteristics are subject to change because they contain specific content and skills that can be learned.

The purpose and uses of assessment are crucial. Here, Bloom turned to *summative* versus *formative testing*. While the customary use of classroom tests has been to measure a student's achievement at the completion of a block of work **(summative evaluation),** they have also been used to assess the quality of learning, as well as the quality of the learner. **Formative evaluation,** on the other hand, is primarily intended to aid in the formation of learning by providing feedback about what has been learned and what still remains to be learned. Bloom believes that when tests are used in this manner, the number of students who achieve mastery increases dramatically, chiefly because the necessary prerequisite skills have been identified for each student, student motivation intensifies, and more time is spent on task.

Mastery Learning

Mastery learning is probably the key element in Bloom's work, for it is this goal that all other means are intended to achieve. As Bloom noted (1981), most teachers begin a school year with the entrenched expectation that about one-third of the students will adequately learn, one-third will pass, and one-third will achieve a marginal pass or fail. Bloom finds this condition one of the most wasteful in all of education, especially since he believes that about 90 percent of all students can learn to mastery if properly instructed.

A few students (1 to 5 percent) will show special talent for any subject; that is, they will show an *aptitude for particular learning*. Another small group (1 to 5 percent) will show a special disability for a given subject. This leaves the majority 90 percent. Here is the basis for Bloom's belief that 95 percent of our students can achieve mastery, with some requiring more time, effort, and help than others.

Mastery learning is tied closely to the *quality of instruction*. We begin with the assumption that individual students need individual instruction to reach mastery. You may argue that teachers have always attempted to adapt their teaching to individuals. In a classroom of thirty students to one teacher, this goal often remains elusive, reinforcing Bloom's idea that the quality of instruction must be considered in light of *individual* learners. This leads us to a student's *ability to understand instruction*. Do your students understand what they are to learn and how they are to learn it? It is precisely here that student ability interacts with quality of instruction and curricular material. Since our schools are highly verbal, ability to understand is linked to language ability and reading comprehension. Modifying your instruction by using a variety of techniques—tutorial, group, text, and media—can benefit their comprehension.

---

summative evaluation
Measurement of a student's achievement at the completion of a block of work.

formative evaluation
Assessment intended to aid learning by providing feedback about what has been learned and what remains to be learned.

mastery learning *Learning in which instructor and student decide on time needed and what is necessary for mastery, usually about 90 percent of the possible achievement score.*

Do your students show *perseverance?* How much time is a student willing to spend in learning? We know that student perseverance varies from subject to subject. Adapting instruction and using appropriate content has been shown to increase perseverance. Bloom emphasized the significance of perseverance by commenting on students' variability in the amount of time they are willing to spend on a task. Some students give up quickly on math problems, but will work indefinitely on faulty automobile engines. Bloom also believes that the key to increasing perseverance is appropriate design in instruction and learning materials.

If aptitude determines the rate of learning, then the *time allowed for learning can produce mastery.* Bloom believes that some students spend as much as six times longer on homework than others—yet time spent on homework often has little relationship to final grades. Homework with the correct structure and conditions for learning, however, can be quite effective (see section later in this chapter). The time spent on task can be altered by following mastery principles and allowing students the time they need to reach mastery in particular subjects. This in turn depends on aptitude, verbal ability, quality of instruction, and quality of help received outside of school.

If you are to help your students achieve mastery, first be certain what you mean by mastery, and know when students reach it. Use formative evaluation techniques as frequently as you think they are needed: divide a subject into meaningful sections, and then construct diagnostic tests to discover if students have mastered the material. You will then know where specific weaknesses lie and what steps need to be taken to overcome any difficulties.

Not only does Bloom's work on mastery learning recommend itself for its obvious cognitive benefits, but students usually show an increased interest in subject matter, and, perhaps most important of all, an increased sense of self-worth. They do better on teacher-made tests, earn higher grades, and attain higher scores on standardized tests. Their retention and transfer of material learned under mastery learning conditions also improves substantially (Guskey, 1986).

Teachers also experience positive effects. When they see the improvement in their students' learning, they gain a sense of professional renewal; they feel better about themselves and their work. Teachers using this approach tend to see learning as a cooperative venture in which their role is that of facilitators in helping their students reach the highest level of learning possible (Guskey, 1986).

A Model of School Learning

How can Bloom's basic ideas help to improve classroom learning? Individual differences in learning ability may not be alterable, but individual differences in learning can be predicted, explained, and improved. For example, much of the variation in school learning can be traced to environmental conditions in the home and school, both of which are subject to modification if teachers work closely with parents.

Three interdependent variables, which can be phrased as questions, form the foundation of Bloom's theory.

- To what extent has a student learned the necessary prerequisites for the new learning to be attempted?
- To what extent can a student be motivated to engage in the learning process?
- To what extent is instruction appropriate to the learner?

The theory addresses student characteristics, instruction, and learning outcomes. The student characteristics deemed to be most significant for learning are **cognitive entry behaviors** (the necessary prerequisite skills) and **affective entry characteristics** (motivation to learn new material). **Quality of instruction,** as we have seen, refers to needed cues, practice, and reinforcement. Learning outcomes can be designated by level and type of achievement, rate of learning, and affective results. The interaction of these variables can be seen in figure 12.3. By *learning task* Bloom means a learning unit in a course, a chapter in a textbook, or a topic in the curriculum. Such a task usually takes from 1 to 5 hours to master.

cognitive entry behaviors
Bloom's term for the prerequisite learning skills needed before attempting new learning.

affective entry characteristics
Bloom's phrase to describe a student's motivation to learn new material.

quality of instruction *Bloom's term for the cues, practice, and reinforcement necessary to make learning meaningful for students.*

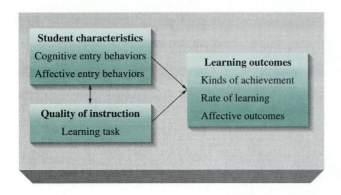

Figure 12.3
Bloom's theory of school learning.

Cognitive entry behavior is the prerequisite learning needed for mastery of new tasks, and, as such, represents one aspect of a student's history. While it is possible that all the students have had an opportunity to acquire the prerequisite learning, and it is even possible that all the students have acquired it, the critical point is the availability of the prerequisite learning *at the time it is required* for the specific new learning task. That is, the student remembers and can use these prior learnings when and where they are required in a specific new task. How much of the background of the Eastern European countries does a student bring to an analysis of the independence movements there?

Cognitive entry behaviors fall into two categories: those that are *specific* to a specific subject (addition, subtraction, and multiplication are necessary prerequisites for division), and those that are *general,* such as verbal ability and reading comprehension. Both types of entry behaviors are alterable.

Affective entry characteristics refer to the differences among students in what they are emotionally prepared to learn as expressed in their interests, attitudes, and self-views. All students have different histories that color their reactions to specific subjects and to school in general. A brother or sister may have been unhappy in school or disliked a particular teacher. Such feelings rub off on younger pupils.

Especially interesting in Bloom's analysis of affect is the notion of age change: the correlation between affect toward school and achievement in a particular subject is relatively low up to grade 5, but *increases* sharply at the junior and senior high levels. Bloom estimates that affect toward school accounts for as much as 25 percent of the variation in achievement. Again, affect toward both school and subject can be altered.

Bloom has focused on teaching and not on the teacher; thus, his analysis of quality of instruction focuses on the interactions that occur in the classroom. Cognitive entry behaviors and affective entry characteristics can account for about 65 percent of the achievement variation on a new learning task. The quality of instruction can do little to overcome the input of cognitive entry behaviors unless it is remedial, which is not usually the case. Affective entry characteristics can be altered by the quality of instruction; in spite of the significant contribution made by cognitive entry behaviors, quality of instruction can have a powerful effect on learning a particular task.

We can perhaps best conclude Bloom's excellent analysis of school learning by noting that with this system most students become quite similar with regard to learning ability, rate of learning, and motivation for further learning when provided with favorable learning conditions (Bloom, 1981, p. 135).

In this chapter, we have examined teaching from several theoretical perspectives. Each of them has much to offer; you probably would be well advised to take from each those aspects that are best suited to your beliefs and objectives. That is, you may analyze a task from a cognitive perspective, yet find much to use in the work of Skinner concerning the best means of using reinforcement, or in Bloom's concern with cognitive entry behavior. To help you separate and compare the various components of these theories, see table 12.5.

Although our focus has been on teachers and teaching strategies, we should remember that adapting instruction can involve many techniques. One way of accomplishing this goal is to help your students develop efficient study skills.

Students and Study Skills

The ability to study effectively is important for a student's success in school. Many capable students at all grade levels may experience frustration and even failure in school *not* because they lack ability, but because they do not have adequate study skills. Good study skills benefit students beyond improving their academic performance. Children

Table 12.5

Instructional Theories: A Summary			
Name	**Basis**	**Emphasis**	**Application**
Bloom	Educational research	Mastery learning Entry behaviors Time on task Learning outcomes	Prerequisite skills Learning tasks Achievement levels Instructional processes
Bruner	Cognitive development	Theoretical base Optimal sequence Modes of representation	Readiness, motivation, acquisition, transformation, evaluation
Gagne	Information processing	Instructional events Learning outcomes	Learning Retention Transfer
Hunter	Decision making	Adaptive teaching Instructional decisions	Formulating objectives Direct instruction Enhanced achievement
Markle	Operant conditioning	Active responding Errorless learning Immediate feedback	Programed instruction Behavior analysis
Skinner	Operant conditioning	Defined objectives First instance Sequential steps Controlled responses Reinforcement	Programmed instruction All aspects of behavior

who have developed good study skills are also more likely to experience an increase in their feelings of competence and confidence as they learn. They tend to approach their schoolwork with a positive attitude, rather than a negative and anxious one.

Developing Study Skills

Study skills may be viewed as basic learning tools; they enable students to acquire and retain information presented in textbooks and classrooms. More specifically, study skills include listening and reading, notetaking, outlining, managing time, and taking tests. Study skills may be organized according to four general stages of learning that are common to all students. The first stage of studying involves taking in information from books, lectures, or presentations. Study behaviors that are associated with success at this stage include listening and reading. The second stage entails some organization of the information. Study behaviors that facilitate organization of the information include underlining, notetaking, outlining, making lists, and asking oneself questions about the material. Stage three involves practicing or rehearsing the organized material and requires some type of review or discussion on the part of the learner. The final stage is the actual remembering or application of information. Skills in taking tests, writing, and preparing reports are used in this stage.

How Parents Can Help

Parents need to remember that there is no simple formula for improving study skills for all children. More important than following any one particular method are building good habits, developing a system that works for a given child, and using the system effectively and consistently. Learning styles vary from student to student. Study habits that work for one person may not work well for another person—even when both children come from the same family. Students need to discover how they learn and then work out study systems that fit in best with the way they learn. Here are some tips parents can pass on to their children for helping them develop good study skills. Without pressuring, parents may encourage children to:

- *Establish a study routine.* Children should pick a place, find a time, and build a routine. Studying should be a part of the daily family routine. Students find that they learn more if they get into the habit of studying at the same time and in the same place each day. Of course, special family events or sudden demands will force them to break that routine from time to time, but they should try to stay in the routine as much as possible.
- *Make sure study surroundings allow children to concentrate.* To concentrate on studies, some children may require total quiet, while others may need a little background noise (such as music). Children should find the atmosphere that helps them focus on what they have to study without being distracted by other activities or being so relaxed that they fall asleep. Children may need some cooperation from the family to do this (not disturbing them, taking phone messages, etc.).
- *Keep assignments in one folder.* Students may have a separate notebook for each class, but they should keep all homework assignments in one folder. That way, they will be able to see all of the things they have to do and divide their study time accordingly.
- *Work out a study system.* Rather than just reading straight through an assignment, most students find that they learn more if they work out a systematic method. This may involve skimming the material, underlining or taking notes, reviewing major ideas, and so on. Two key elements are to *read with a question in mind* and *take notes in their own words.* One popular system, known as the SQ3R method, involves these steps: (a) *Survey:* Quickly scan the reading assignment (look at headings, graphs, summaries, etc.); (b) *Question:* Make up a question to keep in mind as they read (Manzo & Manzo, 1990); (c) *Read:* Read actively to answer the questions they have formulated; (d) *Recite:* Try to answer questions without looking at the reading assignment; and (e) *Review:* Immediately review the material to make certain notes are organized and major ideas are understood. The best way to begin using this method with your students is to model it for them and then have the whole class try it before using it independently (Reutzel & Cooper, 1992).
- *Expand concentration time.* At first, children may be able to concentrate only for short time periods (ten minutes is typical, since it is the time between commercials on TV programs). Parents can help children work on building this up to longer stretches without breaks, so it will take less time to get through assignments. Most children need to work up slowly and steadily, just as one does in weight training or aerobics.
- *Develop time estimation skill.* One key to good studying is being able to estimate how long it will take to complete each assignment. Start by having children make an estimate for each assignment, then note how long it really took to do the work, and note how well they did on the assignment (or on the test for which they studied). Most students must keep adjusting and evaluating estimates until they become routinely accurate.
- *Plan ahead.* Athletes cannot get in shape in one or two nights; they need to "work out" for several weeks. Studying works the same way. Students should start working on major assignments or reviewing for major tests well ahead, planning their strategy for finishing the assignment on time.
- *Set goals.* Before they begin work on an assignment, help children decide how well they want to do on it and how much effort it will take to do that well. This will help them learn to divide study time effectively so they do not spend too much time on relatively unimportant assignments.

Table 12.6

Suggested Effects of Homework	
Positive Effects	**Negative Effects**
Immediate achievement and learning	*Satiation*
Better retention of factual knowledge	Loss of interest in academic material
Increased understanding	Physical and emotional fatigue
Better critical thinking, concept	
information, information processing	*Denial of access to leisure-time and*
Curriculum enrichment	*community activities*
Long-term academic effects	*Parental interference*
Willingness to learn during leisure time	Pressure to complete assignments and
Improved attitude toward school	perform well
Better study habits and skills	Confusion of instructional techniques
Nonacademic effects	*Cheating*
Greater self-direction	Copying from other students
Greater self-discipline	Help beyond tutoring
Better time organization	
More inquisitiveness	*Increased differences between high and*
More independent problem solving	*low achievers*
Greater parental appreciation of and	
involvement in schooling	

From Harris Cooper, *Homework*. Copyright © 1989 Longman Publications. Reprinted by permission of Harris Cooper.

•*Reward achievements.* When children achieve one of their study goals, give them a little reward: make a snack, allow them to call a friend, etc. Often children want someone (parent or friend) to congratulate them on their achievements and with whom they can share what they have learned.

The Role of Homework

Another means of adapting your instruction to the needs of your students is by the use of carefully assigned homework. Homework engenders many different responses from students, teachers, and parents. Many students hate it; still, a significant number think it's important. Some teachers think it is useless; others see it as essential. Some parents think it is just busywork, yet many think it is an indication of the quality of the school and is critical for their child. By homework, we mean "tasks assigned to students by school teachers that are meant to be carried out during non-school hours" (Cooper, 1989, p. 86).

In a thorough review of research on homework, Cooper (1989) concluded that homework has positive effects on achievement, especially for junior and senior high school students. Several other authors, although with far less empirical orientation than that of Cooper, have touted the benefits of homework for children in the 1980s and 1990s. Books such as *Homework Without Tears* (Canter & Hausner, 1987) and *Hassle Free Homework* (Clark & Clark, 1989) have been promoted in bookstores across the country to parents as guides for helping their children. Thus, homework currently seems to be perceived positively, as an important instructional adjunct that involves students, teachers, and parents. Homework deserves your attention, so let's scrutinize some of the points that Cooper (1989) made in his synthesis of research on homework.

Cooper's review of the research literature identified numerous potential positive and negative effects of homework on students. Table 12.6 documents many of the suggested effects of homework. Note that homework is seen as having some important "side effects" on student-parent relations and self-management. Based on your own experiences with homework, can you add possible positive or negative effects to the list in table 12.6?

What is your view on homework—that is, should it be given at all? If so, how much? (Link your answer to student age.) Should it be done in study or library periods? How much time should teachers devote to correcting homework?

Exogenous factors	Assignment characteristics	Initial classroom factors	Home-community factors	Classroom follow-up	Outcomes or effects

Student characteristics
  Ability
  Motivation
  Study habits
Subject matter
Grade level
	Amount
	Purpose
	Skill area utilized
	Degree of
	  individualization
	Degree of
	  student choice
	Completion
	  deadlines
	Social content
		Provision of
		  materials
		Facilitators
		  Suggested
		    approaches
		Links to curriculum
		Other rationales
			Competitors for
			  student time
			Home environment
			  Space
			  Light
			  Quiet
			  Materials
			Others' involvement
			  Parents
			  Siblings
			  Other students
				Feedback
				  Written
				    comments
				  Grading
				  Incentives
				Testing or related
				  content
				Use in class
				  discussion
					Assignment
					  completion
					Assignment
					  performance
					Positive effects
					  Immediate
					    academic
					  Long-term
					    academic
					  Nonacademic
					  Parental
					Negative effects
					  Satiation
					  Denial of leisure
					    time
					  Parental
					    interference
					  Cheating
					  Increased student
					    differences

Figure 12.4

A model of factors influencing the effects of homework.

From Harris Cooper, Homework. *Copyright © 1989 Longman Publications. Reprinted by permission of Harris Cooper.*

In addition to examining the effects of homework, Cooper formulated a "model" of the factors that influence homework outcomes. He identified over 20 specific factors (e.g. student characteristics, home environment, testing of related work, parents' involvement) and organized these specific factors into 6 general factors. These general and specific factors, which influence the effects of homework, are displayed in figure 12.4. Of all the factors, grade level was perhaps the most significant one. Specifically, Cooper found the effect of homework on achievement to be only negligible for elementary students, moderately important for junior high students, and very important for high school students. Although the effects of homework on elementary students' achievement were small or nonexistent, Cooper still recommended some homework for elementary students. He believes it can help them to develop good study habits, fosters positive attitudes toward school, and communicates the idea that learning takes place at home as well as at school.

Cooper also concluded that in-class study supervised by a teacher was as good as or better than homework, especially for younger students. As noted by Cooper, however, the allocation of time for in-class study versus other learning activities becomes the issue.

 ## Adapting Instruction in a Multicultural Classroom

Multicultural education is a concern affecting every phase and aspect of teaching, enabling teachers to scrutinize their options and choices to clarify what social information they are conveying overtly and covertly to their students. It also is a means of challenging and expanding the goals and values that underlie a curriculum, its materials, and its activities (Ramsey, 1987, p. 6).

In a multicultural curriculum, pupils learn about themselves and others as they study various cultures. They analyze the beliefs, attitudes, values, and behaviors that are characteristic of particular cultures. As they do, members of those cultures should have an increase in self-esteem and simultaneously develop an appreciation and understanding of other cultures. In this way, your instruction in a classroom dedicated to multicultural understanding can help raise the academic expectations of minority students and combat any negative stereotypes. A good guiding principle here is this: Challenge

Issues & Answers

Can Homework Bring Home and School Closer Together?

Homework is a topic of interest for all involved, including teachers, students, and parents. When used effectively, it can enhance learning and send a strong message that learning also takes place outside of the classroom. It also offers parents the opportunity to participate in the education of their children (Schiefflin & Gallimore, 1993).

Parental involvement in a child's education is an increasingly provocative topic among educators and parents. Traditionally, parental involvement has been relegated to PTA social activities, but a closer look at successful schools shows a high level of parental involvement. One way parents can participate in their children's education is to support the schoolwork they do at home.

Issue

Homework offers parents a real opportunity to become involved on many different levels with their children's schoolwork—as coaches, tutors, and resource persons.

Answer: Pro Through their working together, a student's skills improve and parental attention sends a strong message that schoolwork is valued.

Answer: Con Parents can run the risk of becoming too involved in their child's school life. In some cases, they may become too critical; in other cases, they may actually do the child's work.

Issue

Teachers often complain that there aren't enough hours in the day to cover all they would like to accomplish. Homework is a good way to extend the day's learning time.

Answer: Pro Homework, when used effectively, can offer opportunities to add depth and breadth to a topic, allowing learners to explore at length subjects that are of interest to them.

Answer: Con Not all children have access to materials or an environment that allows them to concentrate on schoolwork. Depending on work outside of the classroom to acquire needed skills can put these students at a disadvantage.

Issue

Homework is a valuable adjunct to the curriculum. As to any other part of the curriculum, teachers must devote thought and creativity to their homework assignments.

Answer: Pro Interesting homework can supplement skills, and also challenge and excite students.

Answer: Con Homework assignments are not always carefully planned by teachers. When they are used only for rote activities (memorizing math facts and spelling words), students can come to dislike not only homework, but also the subject and school itself.

minority students (Spencer & Dornbusch, 1990). Minority students are no different in this respect from any others; that is, they respond best to teacher support and warmth and to appropriate, challenging standards.

In presenting multicultural topics, teachers proceed exactly as they would with their other subjects. They establish the necessary knowledge base, utilize effective instructional methods, and base their instruction on their students' needs. As we have emphasized throughout this chapter, teaching is not telling—a warning that is particularly timely when you are attempting to further multicultural understanding. You must help your students construct their own positive attitudes toward different races (Tiedt & Tiedt, 1990). Involve families as much as possible. Try to arrange school events (academic and social) in a manner that enables parents to visit the school without major interruptions in their schedules (Comer, 1988).

This is actually a continuation of a theme initially presented in chapter 1: Teachers must be sensitive to the unique needs of multicultural students (Rogoff, 1990). Although your recognition of students' individual differences is not confined to cultural diversity, nevertheless, the classroom challenges of minority students may have quite different roots than those of your other students. Minority students may bring distinctive behavioral and communication styles to your classroom that you must recognize if these students are to achieve as well as possible. For example, Shade and New (1993) noted that many African American students are movement oriented, and appear less responsive to direct verbal questioning in the classroom. Yet these same students may be leaders on the playground, and be able to explain the rules of a game in some detail.

As a dramatic illustration of these differences, consider the following.

In a San Francisco elementary school, a teacher plays *Hangman* with her students to enliven a spelling lesson. As the class eagerly shouts out letters, one child bursts into tears. A Cambodian immigrant recently arrived from a Thai refugee camp, the child speaks little English. Another child is found who can interpret, and the hysterical child finally manages to communicate that she had witnessed the hanging of her father in Cambodia (Olsen, 1988, p. 211).

It is not difficult to envision this student having learning difficulties linked to the emotional trauma she is experiencing.

Although you may not have the language skills to communicate fully with some of your students, you can nevertheless be sensitive to their origins and customs, help these students to see themselves as part of the larger society, encourage respect and appreciation for the ways of others, urge students to develop positive relationships with children of all cultures, and learn as much as possible about the heritage of all your students.

Teacher Expectations

In adapting your instruction, you must avoid certain pitfalls, particularly that of being blinded by your expectations for any student, since these may have powerful effects on that student's achievement. In 1968, Rosenthal and Jacobson reported the results of a study that fascinated both educators and psychologists. Beginning in 1964, the authors had teachers in an elementary school administer an imposing test, the Harvard Test of Inflected Acquisition, that actually was a nonverbal IQ test. It was administered to youngsters who would return in the fall. Teachers were told that the test would predict which youngsters would show an academic spurt in the coming year. These would be the "intellectual bloomers." The tests had supposed predictive value and the youngsters so identified were imaginary.

Teachers believed that they were taking part in a study to validate a test predicting the likelihood that a child would show an inflection point or "spurt" in the near future. The test would predict which youngsters were most likely to show academic spurts. Teachers were told that students with scores on these tests in the top 20 percent (approximately) would probably be found at various levels of present academic functioning (Rosenthal & Jacobson, 1968, p. 66).

In the fall, the teachers were told which youngsters had scored in the top 20 percent, and the investigators suggested that these children would probably show remarkable progress during the year. Actually, there was no difference between these children and the control group. All the youngsters were retested at the end of the school year, using the same test. The experimental group (the "bloomers") all scored higher than the control group. The investigators interpreted the results to indicate that when teachers expected more of children, the youngsters met their expectations, in a **self-fulfilling prophecy** referred to as "Pygmalion in the classroom."

self-fulfilling prophecy *The phenomenon that when teachers expect more of children, the students tend to meet the expectations, and vice versa.*

The news media and general public seized upon the results and the study received enormous publicity. Uncritically accepted, the results were interpreted as heralding a breakthrough in the classroom. Many educators and investigators remained skeptical, and their skepticism was confirmed when attempts to replicate the Rosenthal and Jacobson study produced conflicting evidence. Other critics attacked the study's methodology. Carefully controlled studies, in which teachers received varied information (IQ scores, no IQ scores, IQ scores inflated by 16 points, or designation of some students as academic bloomers) did not duplicate Rosenthal's findings. These findings cast serious doubt on the Rosenthal hypothesis.

Perhaps it is safest to conclude that teachers' expectations make a difference, but not as uniformly and in a much more complex manner than they were originally believed to. Answering his critics, Rosenthal stated that expectations produce effects because teachers provide a favorable social and emotional atmosphere for the selected

teacher – student

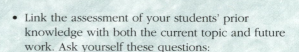

Adapting Your Teaching

1. When you attempt to adapt your teaching, you are "matching the mix"; this introduces the notion of aptitude-treatment interaction.
   - One way of helping both you and your students to adapt classroom materials is to be sure that your students have good study habits. Prepare a chart that you distribute to your students (using appropriate language) on which you have listed those habits that you think are important for the success of your students. Then have them check *always* or *seldom* after each item. (Use terms with which your students are comfortable.) For example:

	Always	Seldom
Have a regular place to study		
Do my homework at the same time		
Have TV off when studying		

   - Be sure you know what your students are capable of before introducing a new topic. Use a pretest to assess their current level of knowledge. Once you know the extent of their prior knowledge, make a simple chart of each pupil's weaknesses. For example, on a scale of 1 to 10, rate each student on key topics.

American History: The Civil War

	Politicians	Geography	Products	Battles
John	4	2	1	8
Heather	4	4	3	6
Tim	2	1	0	2
Diana	1	1	1	5

   You can then individualize your instruction and help each student to attain the unit's objectives.
   - Try independent work with some of those students whose weaknesses you have identified. (These students must be able to work without constant supervision; not all students can do this, but selected students are capable of it.) Be sure they understand exactly what they are to do and provide, or direct them to, the proper materials that will bring them up to class level. You may want to set up a learning center in your classroom, enlist the school librarian's aid, or have your pupils go to the community library.

   - Link the assessment of your students' prior knowledge with both the current topic and future work. Ask yourself these questions:

     Can I assume that my pupils have enough background data to begin work, or must I pretest?

     Does the difficulty level of the subject matter, the materials, and the activities match the ability level of my pupils?

     Am I sufficiently familiar with the subject's content, the materials, and the activities to adapt them to meet the needs of my pupils?

     Do my students understand that what they are doing now is related to the unit's objectives?

2. Teachers' decisions and actions are deliberately designed to increase the probability of student learning.
   - Here are some decisions you must make.

     Will I lecture, assign teams to projects, use class activities such as debates, or set up independent work assignments?

     Will I have one group compete against another?

     Will I have groups cooperate?

     Will I try to prevent my students from making any mistakes by breaking the material into small, easy-to-master steps?

     Will I encourage students to use their mistakes as a means of teaching problem solving?

   - Remember: the activities that you use are those in which the *learners* are engaged. Among student activities that lead to learning are the following.

     Have your students solve problems, not just memorize facts.

     Have them play roles in various classes.

     Have them debate various issues.

     Have them look up information.

     Have them *read, read, read!*

     Have them *write, write, write!*

students. These pupils receive more attention, and thus are furnished carefully controlled reinforcement. Teachers spend more time with them, demand more from these students, and usually receive it.

If teacher expectations do produce differences in a student's achievement, the process may be as follows. Because of what they have heard or read about these students, teachers develop certain expectations about them. Teachers then behave differently with these students. Students infer from a teacher's behavior that they are or are not good achievers, and frequently behave accordingly. If a student understands the meaning of the teacher's behavior, achievement may follow the direction of the teacher's expectations (Hamachek, 1987).

How do these expectations translate into teacher behavior in the classroom? Teachers often tend to

- seat low-expectation students farther from the teacher
- pay less attention to low-expectation students in academic activities
- call on these students less often to answer questions
- wait less time and then interrupt those students whom they perceive as less capable
- criticize those students for whom they have low expectations more frequently, praising them less often
- provide lower-quality feedback to their low-expectation students

Not all teachers, of course, treat low- and high-expectation students differently. Yet the evidence continues to indicate the existence of expectations that influence teacher behavior. The solution is not to form expectations, but to use a reliable and valid process to assess students.

APPLICATIONS AND REFLECTIONS

Chapter Highlights

The Meaning of Teaching

- Recent analyses of teaching have several pertinent findings, such as the importance of pacing (especially the need for quality student-engaged time).
- Effective teaching is characterized by identifiable behaviors.
- John Carroll's model of school learning has guided several research efforts into the variables of teaching behavior and student performance.
- Direct and indirect, or inquiry, instruction must be compatible with both objectives and materials.
- A well-known example of direct instruction is Madeline Hunter's Clinical Theory of Instruction.
- A well-known example of inquiry instruction is Jerome Bruner's cognitive theory.
- Teachers' use of praise has been carefully analyzed in attempts to make it a more meaningful and forceful element in the classroom.
- Teachers' mastery of their subject(s), including the teacher knowledge base, is a necessity.

The Design of Instruction

- B. F. Skinner applied the principles of operant conditioning (see chap. 7) to the classroom as he consistently advocated a technology of teaching.
- Skinner urged that teachers first decide what their students should be able to do after instruction, carefully determine the steps needed to achieve that behavior, and skillfully use appropriate reinforcers.
- Susan Markle, using a programed instruction model ("programed" with one *m*), concentrated on a pupil's active responding.
- Robert Gagne, employing an instructional design technique, formulated a plan that accounts for learning outcomes as they are related to specific conditions for that learning.

Adapting Instruction to the Individual Differences of Learners

- Your teaching success will depend on how successfully you adapt your instruction to the individual differences of the learners in your class.
- Benjamin Bloom believes that studies of teaching must take into account the time pupils need for a task, their cognitive entry behaviors, and the proper use of testing, among other aspects.

- Bloom's concern with mastery learning led him to propose a model of school learning with such core concepts as cognitive entry behaviors, affective entry characteristics, and quality of instruction.
- You can increase the effectiveness of your instruction by the skillful use of study skills and homework.
- The "Pygmalion in the classroom" effect—letting your expectations about pupils affect your assessment of them—is a danger to be aware of and avoid.
- Your students' behavior must be your sole concern in the judgments you make.

Connections

1. Think about how you learn and describe how one of the major concepts discussed in this chapter is part of your learning activities or approach.

_____

_____

_____

_____

2. Identify at least one learning situation (classroom instruction, self-study, taking a test, small-group work) and describe how you would apply one of the key concepts examined in this chapter *if you were a teacher*.

_____

_____

_____

_____

Getting the Picture and Drawing Relationships

Think about the various learning concepts and variables discussed in this chapter. Create pictures, graphics, or figures that highlight the relationships among key components.

Personal Journal

What I really learned in this chapter was _____

_____

_____

_____

_____

_____

_____

What this means to me is _____

_____

_____

_____

_____

_____

_____

Questions that were stimulated by this chapter include _____

_____

_____

_____

_____

_____

_____

Key Terms

affective entry characteristics	420	enactive	406	quality of instruction	420
beginning teacher evaluation studies (BTES)	397	first instance	411	self-fulfilling prophecy	427
		formative evaluation	419	spiral curriculum	405
		iconic	406	summative evaluation	419
Clinical Theory of Instruction (CTI)	399	inquiry teaching	404	symbolic	406
		mastery learning	419	terminal behavior	411
cognitive entry behaviors	420	modes of representation	406		
		programmed instruction	411		

It was 8:15 A.M. on an October morning, and Virginia Allan's fifth-grade class came swirling into her classroom. Some went to hang up their jackets, others went immediately to their desks, and others stood around talking at the back of the room. Jimmy, an energetic, likeable 11-year-old boy, came through the doorway and bumped into Tommy, one of the boys talking at the back of the room. The boys began to shout and push each other.

"Stop that, Jimmy!" shouted Mrs. Allan. "Don't do any more pushing and shoving."

Suddenly, Jimmy turned and shouted back, "Don't yell at me! Don't blame me! You're always picking on me."

students? Jimmy may indeed have given earlier warnings that something was bothering him. This incident reinforces the belief that a smoothly running classroom will do much to cut down on discipline problems. To help you understand the importance of classroom management, we will open this chapter by describing what most concerns teachers, then turn to an analysis of life in the classroom—what really happens when you close the classroom door. Next, we will examine models such as QAIT, to help you identify critical classroom features that lead to successful classroom management. We then will move to specific techniques for organizing the classroom, discussing rules that

chapter 13

classroom management: organization and control

Mrs. Allan was stunned. She had encountered cases of misbehavior from the first day, but this was the most flagrant. Also, Jimmy hadn't caused any previous serious problems.

Mrs. Allan separated the boys and told Jimmy to see her after school, but the incident still bothered her throughout the day. Was it something she had done, or not done? Had she missed or misread clues that Jimmy had given?▪

How would you answer these questions? Before you try look at the words that were used to describe the students' behavior: "swirling," "standing around talking," "no previous serious problems." If you were to advise this teacher, you would probably direct her attention to the manner in which she was managing her classroom. Did her students know what they were to do when they entered the classroom? Did they have work to occupy them immediately? Had she been attentive enough to the individual

help, and what kinds of behavior you can expect at different age levels. Finally, we will offer clear and specific suggestions for maintaining control in your classroom by analyzing three well-known methods. These techniques differ in philosophy and in efficiency. You will want to select those that will give you the most support for effective management of your unique classroom.

When you finish reading this chapter, you should be able to

- describe the significance of time in mastery of classroom material
- match developmental tasks with appropriate management techniques
- identify those rules that are needed for a smoothly functioning classroom
- use methods that maintain productive classroom control

Management Concerns in the Classroom 434
Preventing Classroom
    Problems 434
Time and Teachers: The Carroll
    Model 435
Developmental Tasks and
    Classroom Management 436
Management and Control of
    Problem Students 438

Life in the Classroom 439
When You Close the Classroom
    Door 439
Classroom Activities 441
The QAIT Model 443
Classroom Contexts 445

Managing the Classroom 447
Rule Setting and Classroom
    Procedures 447
Rules and Classroom
    Activities 448
Management and Control 449
Aggression in the Classroom 449
Searching for the Causes of
    Classroom Problems 451

Methods of Control 451
Misbehavior in the
    Classroom 452
Multicultural Students and
    Discipline 453
Effective Teacher
    Behaviors 454
Using Behavior Modification 455

**Don't Cause Any Problems
Yourself 467**
Teacher-Parent
    Collaboration 468
You Are Not Alone 469

**Applications and
Reflections 472**

MANAGEMENT CONCERNS IN THE CLASSROOM

Many readers may believe that this is the most important chapter in the book. Managing a classroom means more than avoiding chaos; it means establishing a routine that enables learning activities to proceed smoothly. It also helps to prevent many unnecessary discipline problems. We can only guess at the amount of learning that was lost after the boys' fight described in the chapter's opening.

Students must know what is expected of them. This is true from a practical standpoint: they must know what various signals mean and what they should do (this bell means a fire drill, that buzzer signals an assembly). It is true from an affective standpoint: teachers who give the impression of knowing what they are doing and who act decisively establish that someone is in control, thus providing a sense of security.

And it is true from a pedagogical standpoint. Learning can occur only in an orderly classroom. "Orderly," however, does not imply quiet or rigid. The classroom whose hum and flow indicates youngsters engaged in meaningful activity can be more orderly than the classroom in which you can hear a clock tick. Students may be in various groups around the classroom, perhaps talking over projects, or moving to the library area for research materials, or reading or writing in the group area. An orderly environment is one in which everyone—teacher and students—knows exactly what is going on. Do not minimize the importance of routine: a smoothly running classroom can prevent discipline problems.

Although management issues most concern beginning teachers, they actually keep all teachers on the alert, regardless of our experience—and "management" is by no means confined to discipline alone. We can define classroom management as the use of rules and procedures to maintain order so that learning may result. In this light, *organizing the classroom is the first step in effective classroom management.*

"Sure there's a way to discipline them. Yell at them."

© *1990 by Sidney Harris*—Phi Delta Kappan.
There are, however, better ways of guiding student behavior.

Annual **Edition**

Preventing Classroom Problems

Educational psychologists recently have begun to shift their focus from merely managing student behavior in the classroom to the *prevention* of behavioral problems by using instructional and managerial procedures. Increasingly, psychologists and educators have realized that the prevention of problems should be a national priority, not just in schools but across the life span in all types of community settings. Reflecting this perspective, the American Psychological Association commissioned a task force to examine existing prevention programs and identify those that could be considered outstanding (Price, Cowen, Lorion, & Ramos-McKay, 1988).

In this chapter, we have adopted a dual focus: on strategies that you can use to respond to problems as they occur in your classroom, as well as techniques to prevent problems from occurring. A comprehensive classroom management program includes both reactive responding to problems and proactive planning for productive behavior, an approach that has been labeled **proactive classroom management.** Proactive classroom management has three characteristics that distinguish it from other management techniques (Gettinger, 1988):

- It is preventive rather than reactive.
- It integrates methods that facilitate appropriate student behavior with procedures that promote achievement, using effective classroom instructional techniques.
- It emphasizes the group dimensions of classroom management.

proactive classroom management
Classroom management including both reactive responding to problems and proactive planning for productive behavior.

Focus ◀ Classroom Activities to Manage

Stop for a moment to think what you mean by "classroom management." List six activities that you believe fall into this category.

1.
2.
3.
4.
5.
6.

Did you include discipline as one of your topics? You probably did, and rightly so. But consider any of the routine procedures that, if not closely monitored, can lead to discipline problems. For example, do your students have assigned seats? If not, the ensuing "musical chairs" could likely lead to pandemonium at any given moment. Who is in charge of attendance, you or a designated student?

At the elementary school level, do students know their groups for various subjects? Have you assigned seats for each group? Does each student have paper? pencil? crayons? How did students get them? Do students have a clear understanding of what they are to do while you work with one of the groups?

Though you may initially react to these examples as trivial, remember that mastery of the simple routine of your classroom will save you countless problems in the future. If you have a well-ordered classroom, you will keep your discipline problems to a minimum. These examples also point to a basic distinction that is made throughout the remainder of the chapter: Classroom management consists of two parts, organization and control.

Proactive classroom management means that you should have a program that includes reactive responding to problems and a plan for productive learning.

engaged time *The time during which students are actively involved in their work.*

Maintaining sufficient order requires that you have students enter your classroom and move to their seats with no disruption. Once they are seated, be certain that they have the needed materials and understand what they are to do with them. Your plan for any lesson must provide for engaged time for all your students. Finally, see that your students leave in an orderly fashion. Let's use a general example here. Your students enter your room. They immediately check the board to see what they are to do for the first part of the period. Two assigned students may move around the room collecting homework. Note: The students know what is expected of them; they know the rules (the classroom organization). While this is going on, you may devote your time to individuals, checking on one or two students who could have problems. Notice how you are heading off potential trouble, a practice that in itself is a form of classroom control. At the same time, all of your students are productively engaged. Remember that **engaged time** is not the time allotted to any class; it is the time during which students are actively involved in their work.

Thus, effective teaching and fruitful learning are tightly linked to classroom organization and management. Doyle (1986) noted that although *learning* is served by an *instructional* function, *order* is served by a *managerial* function: the forming of groups, establishment of rules and procedures, reaction to misbehavior, and in general, monitoring of classroom activities. Individuals learn; order applies to groups.

Time and Teachers: The Carroll Model

In Chapter 12, we mentioned the pervasive influence that John Carroll has exercised over recent research into the improvement of students' achievement. (His 1963 article, "A Model of School Learning," was the basis of Bloom's work on school learning.) Discussing classroom organization and management, Carroll noted that the primary job of the educational psychologist is to develop and apply knowledge concerning why students succeed or fail in their learning at school, and to assist in the prevention and remediation of learning difficulties (1963, p. 723).

Using this guideline, Carroll stated that a learner will succeed in learning a task to the extent that the needed time is spent for that student to learn the task. Time (actual time spent on learning) becomes the key feature. The Carroll model uses two categories to analyze time.

1. *The determinants of time needed for learning.* There are three important aspects in this category. (a) *Aptitude* refers to the amount of time any student will need to learn a task. Be on the watch for those students who do well, except perhaps in one subject (science, math, art, music); be sure to give them additional time in the subject that causes them difficulty. (b) *Ability to understand instruction* refers to the effects of general intelligence and verbal ability. (c) *Quality of instruction* refers to the teacher's ability to present appropriate material in an interesting manner. You should not only be aware of a student's understanding, but also think of your own teaching: Was it clear? Was it to the point? How many failed to understand? Be honest with yourself.

2. *Time spent in learning.* Carroll focused on two important features of this category: (a) *the time allowed for learning,* which refers to the opportunity that individual schools allow for learning; and (b) *perseverance,* which refers to the amount of time students are willing to spend in learning.

We also may divide the five features included in these two categories by identifying those that reside within the student, those that stem from external conditions, and the one that results from the interplay of external with internal. Those conditions over which a teacher has little control are aptitude and ability to understand instruction; time allowed for learning and quality of instruction are both under the control of the instructor; perseverance, or the motivational aspect, reflects both student characteristics and the classroom situation.

If we now link Carroll's model of school learning to an effectively managed classroom, we can draw three conclusions. First is the inescapable link between learning and order. Simply put, learning rarely emerges from chaos. Second, a disorganized classroom substantially reduces time for learning; too much time is spent in trying to achieve order. Third, quality of instruction is tightly bound to efficiency of classroom management. In this instance, good intentions are not enough; you cannot teach effectively if students are out of control.

A strong relationship exists between the way in which you manage your classroom and the effectiveness of your teaching. Both these functions must be appropriate for the ages and levels of the children you teach. Let us use the developmental task model to review important developmental principles.

Developmental Tasks and Classroom Management

The developmental changes students experience will require teachers of different grade levels to adopt different types of management techniques. Stop for a moment to think of the developmental characteristics of the elementary school child that we discussed in chapters 4 and 5; now, compare these with those of the adolescent. The developmental sequence alone dictates changing management techniques.

As we have seen in chapter 10 on motivation, when natural motivators can be linked with educational requirements, tasks are more easily mastered. Examine table 13.1 carefully to distinguish those tasks that are significant for the different age groups. (Note the appearance of developmental tasks in more than one category, emphasizing the integrated nature of development.) Now think about the classroom techniques you would use in teaching 5-year-olds to read, compared to those you would use in working with adolescents in a current events class.

Describing schools as different social contexts at the preschool, elementary, and secondary levels, Minuchin and Shapiro (1983) stated that they are organized differently, children perceive them differently, and different aspects of social behavior appear to meet students' changing needs. *Preschool experiences* are more protective and caring than educational, with children interacting with one or two teachers,

Table 13.1

Developmental Tasks—Guidelines for Teachers			
	Infancy–early childhood	**Middle childhood**	**Adolescence**
Physical	Learning to walk Learning to take solid foods Learning to talk Learning to control eliminations	Learning physical skills necessary for games	Accepting one's physique
Cognitive	Learning to talk Acquiring concepts Preparing for reading Learning to distinguish right from wrong Learning sex differences	Building a healthy self-concept Learning an appropriate sex role Developing the fundamental skills—reading, writing, arithmetic Developing concepts for everyday living	Preparing for a career
Social	Learning to distinguish right from wrong Learning sex differences	Learning to get along with others Learning an appropriate sex role Developing acceptable attitudes toward society	Developing a satisfactory social role Achieving mature relations with both sexes Preparing for marriage and family
Personal-emotional	Learning to distinguish right from wrong Learing sex differences	Building a healthy self-concept Developing attitudes and values Achieving independence	Preparing for a career Achieving emotional independence from adults Preparing for marriage and family Acquiring systems to guide behavior Achieving socially responsible behavior

perhaps an equal number of aides, and several peers. Socialization and communication needs are paramount and experiences are shaped by adults with two important, often unarticulated goals: desirable socialization (necessary conformity) and individuation (self-expression).

The *elementary school classroom* is more of a true social unit, with more intense interactions between teacher and student and among peers. Teachers, as authority figures, establish the climate of the classroom and the kind of relationships permitted. Peer-group relationships stress friendship, belongingness, and status. In *high school,* the entire school, rather than a particular classroom, becomes the social context. Heterosexual relationships assume considerable importance, and social behavior becomes the standard of acceptance. Extracurricular activities now are a greater and more significant part of the student's life.

With a child's age, then, the school environment broadens in scope and complexity, producing changes in self-concept, gender differentiation, and interpersonal relationships. With these inevitable changes, it is little wonder that management techniques change accordingly. For example, during the kindergarten and early elementary school grades, students are being socialized—learning to respond to teachers and get along with their peers—and instructed in the basic skills. Discipline typically is not a major concern, since youngsters of this age usually react well to authority and seek teacher praise and rewards. Adjustment to the school as a major socializing agent and mastery of the fundamentals are the two chief tasks teachers should incorporate into their classroom management.

Table 13.2

Management and Development	
Level	**Desirable qualities**
Lower elementary	Patience Nurturance skills Socialization skills Instructional skills
Middle elementary	Patience Diagnostic skills Instructional skills Understanding Developmental awareness
Upper elementary-junior high	Motivating skills Firmness Management skills Patience Understanding of concerns of early adolescence
Senior high	Subject matter expertise Relationship skills Ability to have control yet give freedom

Students in the middle elementary school grades know a school's routine and have worked out their relationships with their peers. Teachers should be able to concentrate on curricular tasks, provided that they maintain a clearly defined classroom atmosphere. The upper elementary and lower high school years are times when peer pressure mounts, and most students are concerned with pleasing friends rather than teachers. The teacher's role as an authority figure is often challenged by students, and classroom control becomes more of an issue. Students should have mastered the basics and be able to function, to a certain extent, independently. Classroom procedures and rules should be distinct, understandable, and fair. Once students of these ages know the boundaries and what is expected of them, the teacher's major tasks include subject matter expertise and motivation.

In the upper high school grades, the teacher is working with more mature students, a majority of whom probably are beginning to think of college and/or careers. Thus, these students are more responsible, and concern with management decreases after the beginning of the year, when the teacher informs students what is expected of them in the class. Wildly disruptive students (a small minority) often either have dropped out of school by these years or have been placed elsewhere.

The developmental characteristics that affect teacher management techniques should influence your decision as to the age group you would like to teach. Table 13.2 summarizes these features.

Classrooms are remarkably complex settings, and the activities that occur within them are subject to the likes and dislikes, feelings, and motivations of a large number of people. Many students have a tendency to "fool around" when their attention wavers; they require tasks to prevent classroom problems and loss of learning. What are some of these problems?

What age group would you like to teach? The developmental characteristics that affect teacher management techniques will influence your decision. Do you hold the desirable qualities of teacher management for your desired grade level?

Management and Control of Problem Students

We have stressed that any analysis of classroom management cannot be confined to a discussion of discipline alone. For example, in the chapter's opening vignette, if the students had known exactly what they had to do when they came into the classroom, no one would have been standing in the back of the room, and the incident may have been avoided.

Throughout the remainder of this chapter, we will mention a wide variety of factors that contribute to good classroom management; however, control remains central to our discussion. To help you put this issue in perspective, examples of student behavior problems (based on empirical classification studies) will be identified. Thus, you will have a frame of reference to use in determining what kinds of management techniques may be most effective with each type of problem.

In thinking about managing classrooms, it is useful to know something about the kinds of students who will be exhibiting problem behaviors. Over the years researchers have used a variety of checklists and rating scales to measure the types of problems that parents and teachers report children experiencing. Table 13.3 displays some of the various patterns of child problems that have emerged. Remember, however, that although each category is presented separately, any one student may have more than one particular behavior problem. As you read through the categories, try to answer the following questions:

- What do you see as the core of each of these problems?
- How would this problem affect the rest of the class?
- How would you handle each of these problems?
- Would you need help in working with this student?

Remember your answers; we will return to them at the end of the chapter. Now let us examine what is actually going on in the classroom.

"Heckuva day, wasn't it, Ms. Carpenter? No hard feelings?"
© James Estes.

LIFE IN THE CLASSROOM

Much has been written about the necessity of adapting general management techniques for classroom use. Management, which is essential in all organizations for goal attainment, involves three basic functions: *planning,* by which objectives and procedures are selected; *communication,* by which information is transferred; and *control,* by which performance is matched to plans.

Note how these three basic functions identify the major topics in the remainder of the chapter.

1. *Planning* concerns ongoing activities and how they can best be organized.
2. *Communication* underscores the necessity to tell students what is expected of them, and thus is a major element in effective management.
3. *Control* expresses the need to maintain a classroom atmosphere conducive to learning. Although planning, communication, and control are essentials for all classrooms, they appear in different guises in different classrooms. The chief reason for this is the uniqueness of the classroom environment.

When You Close the Classroom Door

Philip Jackson, in his *Life in Classrooms* (1968), presented a charming and enduring essay on "life as it is" in the classroom. Noting that although schools are places where skills are acquired, tests are given, and amusing and maddening things happen, they also are places where young people come together, make friends, learn, and engage in all sorts of routine activities. Jackson adds that if we total the number of hours that a youngster spends in kindergarten and elementary school, we obtain a figure of seven thousand hours. If you were to spend an equal amount of time in church, you would have to attend a one-hour service one day a week for 150 years!

Table 13.3

Dimensions of Behavior Arising in Multivariate Statistical Analysis with Frequently Associated Characteristics of Each

Conduct	Socialized aggression
Fighting, hitting	"Bad" companions
Disobedience, defiance	Truancy from home
Temper tantrums	Truancy from school
Destructiveness	Stealing in company of others
Impertinence, impudence	Loyalty to delinquent friends
Uncooperativeness, resistance	Membership in a gang
Attention problems	*Anxious-depressed withdrawal*
Poor concentration, short attention span	Anxious, fearful, tense behavior
Daydreaming	Shyness, timidity, bashfulness
Clumsiness, poor coordination	Withdrawn, seclusive behavior
Preoccupation, staring into space	Depression, sadness, disturbance
Failing to finish, lack of perseverance	Hypersensitivity, being easily hurt
Impulsiveness	Feelings of inferiority, worthlessness
Motor overactivity	*Schizoid-unresponsive*
Restlessness, overactivity	Refusal to talk
Excitability, impulsiveness	Withdrawn behavior
Squirmy, jittery movements	Sadness
Overtalkativeness	Staring blankly
Humming and other odd noises	Confusion

From Herbert C. Quay, "A Critical Analysis of DSM III as a Taxonomy of Psychopathology in Childhood and Adolescence" in *Contemporary Directions in Psychopathology,* edited by T. Millon and G. Klerman. Copyright © 1986 Guilford Press, New York. Used with permission.

Shouldn't this amount of time be translated into meaningful outcomes? Although the classroom is a stable environment and its activities are spinoffs of certain set procedures—seatwork, group discussion, teacher demonstration, questions and answers—we must also remember that young people are in school because they must be. Given the reality of time and coercion, Jackson turned to three features of classroom life not typically mentioned: *crowds, praise,* and *power.*

Spending time in a classroom means learning to live with others, which can entail delay, denial, interruptions, and social distraction. During this time, and in the presence of others, a student experiences the pain of failure and the joy of success, which then become part of that student's official record. Finally, there is a vast gulf between a powerful teacher and the students; how that teacher's authority is used tells us much about the atmosphere of any classroom.

It is difficult to determine how students react to classroom conditions. Realistically, everyone can be temporarily unhappy, including achieving, seemingly happy students. Jackson (1968) stated that students' attitudes toward school are complicated and puzzling. Summarizing data from previous studies, he demonstrated considerable negative feelings among basically satisfied students. Following are some of the negative terms students used to describe their feelings toward classroom life: bored, uncertain, dull, restless, inadequate, unnoticed, unhelped, angry, restrained, misunderstood, rejected.

Jackson summarized student feelings nicely in this way:

The number of students who become ecstatic when the school bell rings and who remain that way all day is probably very small, as is the number who sit in the back of the room and grind their teeth in anger from opening exercise to dismissal. One way of interpreting the data we have reviewed so far is to suggest that most students do not feel too strongly about their classroom experience, one way or the other. (Jackson, 1968, p. 60)

Note how the adjectives students used reflected not only the material learned in the classroom, but also planning, communication, and control. For example, "bored" and "uncertain" probably related to poor planning and communication, as well as to uncertainty about what was expected of them.

Students' feelings about school have not changed much since Jackson's report in 1968. Junior high school students asked about their thoughts on good teaching gave the following responses:

- Don't assign extra work to students who finish their work early.
- Don't be overconfident.
- Correct papers with appropriate comments.
- Be versatile.
- Don't yell.
- Be patient.
- Don't give up on students.
- Let students go to the bathroom.
- Be supportive and reassuring.
- Have a sense of humor.
- Don't leave the classroom.
- Check on students while they work.
- Be qualified in your subject area.
- Teach at our level.
- Use textbooks.
- Don't have class favorites.
- Don't complain.
- Dress neatly and stay young.

Classroom Activities

In a more formal analysis of the classroom, classroom activities emerge as the basic unit of organization. Doyle (1986) described activities as relatively short blocks of classroom time (about 10 to 20 minutes) during which students are arranged and taught in a particular way. For example, most activities involve seatwork, recitation, small groups, and/or presentations. Again we note the importance of engaged time. If students aren't "hooked" immediately, valuable learning time is lost.

Types of Activities

Berliner (1983), studying 75 classrooms from kindergarten to grade 6, identified 11 activities that consistently appear:

- Reading circle
- Seatwork
- One-way presentations
- Two-way presentations
- Use of media
- Silent reading
- Construction
- Games
- Play
- Transitions
- Housekeeping

You can probably determine at a glance that a few of these activities consume most of the time: about 60 percent of classroom time is spent in seatwork, and about 30 percent in recitation or whole-class presentations. These numbers vary because at any given time transitions and housekeeping may intrude.

Focus

Student Engagement During Class

Considerable research has been done on student behavior during classroom activities. You should find these data pertinent when planning activities for a class. In one of the most comprehensive studies yet undertaken, Gump (1982) studied third-graders by using time-lapse photography. He found that student involvement (time on task) was highest in teacher-led small groups and lowest during student presentations.

Between these two extremes, engagement was high during whole-class recitations, tests, and teacher presentations but dropped during independent seatwork and supervised study. Research has continued to support this study, with studies indicating student involvement during recitation at 85 percent and 65 percent for seatwork.

Student involvement during the beginning phases of a lesson seems to be significantly lower than that during the remainder of the activity. The lowest involvement scores of all occur during the beginning phase of seatwork, while highest involvement occurs during the remaining phase of recitations.

Remember that your students will be most actively engaged when you lead small groups and least actively engaged during student presentations. These results have received tentative support in high school studies as well as studies of the elementary grades. (For further information, see Doyle, 1986.)

Note that activities with different labels are similar in structure. All seatwork, for example, is alike, regardless of subject matter. Also, lectures, demonstrations, and audiovisual presentations share many similarities.

Doyle (1986) estimated that a teacher's involvement during a class seems to consist mainly of

- Actual instruction (questions, feedback, imparting knowledge)—about 51 percent;
- Organizing students—about 23 percent;
- Dealing with deviant behavior—about 14 percent;
- Handling individual problems and social tasks—about 12 percent.

The findings we have been discussing are consistent with the emphasis placed on such topics as time on task and student engagement, in the learning and teaching sections of this book. School outcome variables are not divorced from variables of "climate," the atmosphere to which students are exposed. For example, Brookover and associates (1979) studied 68 schools drawn from a pool of Michigan fourth and fifth grades. Using a variety of assessment techniques, they examined such variables as social composition of the student body, school social structure, and school climate. They assessed as outcomes student achievement, self-concept with regard to academic ability, and self-reliance. The investigators discovered that many of the outcome differences could be attributed to the school's social characteristics. Teachers in the higher-achieving schools spent more time on instruction and had more academic interactions with their students than those in the low-achieving schools. The authors concluded that student characteristics do not predict outcome independently from classroom processes. Schools with comparable resources may have very different climates and quite different student outcomes. From this brief glimpse of the varied and complex life of the classroom, you can understand the need for careful organization of its activities.

Organizing Classroom Activities

Recall the distinctions that have been made throughout the chapter thus far: good classroom management entails more than gimmicks or entertainment devices to keep students under control. The first element to consider is that of classroom atmosphere. What is the "climate" of your classroom? Is it conducive to learning?

High work involvement with a minimum of deviant behaviors does not appear by accident. Laslett and Smith (1984) identified four "rules"—actually, skills—that should help your classroom organization.

1. *Get them in.* Lessons should start on time, and teacher attention should not be diverted by routines that should have been attended to earlier. The authors believe that classwork begins smoothly when teachers are present before the class arrives and have checked to see that everything is in proper order. Your being there early simply reinforces your authority as you decide when you want the class to enter, assign seats, and have work available to occupy each student immediately.

2. *Get them out.* Laslett and Smith (1984) recommended that before teachers decide what they will teach, they consider the ideal method for concluding the lesson and dismissing the class. They argued that there is nothing strange about these priorities, since carefully won and maintained control can be quickly lost at the conclusion of a lesson. Such planning is only one factor ensuring the smooth transitional processes constantly needed. Control is not the only reason for thinking about concluding your lesson. If you do not provide time for some reinforcement at the end of the lesson, learning can be lost in the rush toward dismissal.

3. *Get on with it.* Here your focus should be on the lesson itself—its content, your manner, and its organization. To maintain motivation, assure that class activities are complete, well structured, and as interesting as you can make them. Balance your work by making your classes as varied as possible. Mix the familiar with the new, the interesting with what you know is necessary but might be boring, and seatwork with recitation. As these authors note, however, be sure that variety does not become confusion.

4. *Get on with them.* Classroom disruptions are infrequent when teacher-student interactions are positive. Your success as a teacher hinges on your relationships with your students. Several techniques to further these relationships are suggested throughout this chapter; for now, remember that you should know your students as well as you can, as they are both in and out of school. Constantly be aware of what is going on in your class.

Though these four "rules" will not guarantee the absence of discipline problems, following them carefully should help to eliminate misbehaviors that result from classroom disorganization. Let us now consider one technique for integrating the many ideas we have discussed. This is the QAIT model developed by Slavin (1987d).

The QAIT Model

Teachers must adapt instruction to students' levels of knowledge, motivate students to learn, manage student behavior, group students for instruction, and test and evaluate students. These functions are carried out at two levels. At the school level, the principal and/or central administrators may establish policies concerning grouping of students (e.g. tracking); provision and allocation of special education and remedial resources; and grading, evaluation, and promotion practices. At the classroom level, teachers control the grouping of students within the class, teaching techniques, classroom management methods, informal incentives, frequency and form of quizzes and tests, and so on. These elements of school and classroom organization are at least as important for student achievement as the quality of teachers' lessons (Slavin, 1987d, p. 90).

QAIT *An instructional model proposed by Slavin that emphasizes the quality of instruction, appropriate levels of instruction, incentive, and time.*

Building on Carroll's model of school learning, Slavin (1987d) proposed an instructional model focused on the alterable elements of Carroll's model. Called **QAIT,** the model encompasses four components: quality of instruction, appropriate levels of instruction, incentive, and time.

Quality of instruction depends on both the curriculum and the lesson presentation. Slavin stated that when quality instruction occurs, the information presented makes sense to students, is interesting, and is easy to both remember and apply. Above all else, however, Slavin argued instruction must make sense to students. For this to happen, the teacher must (a) present information in an orderly, systematic fashion; (b) provide smooth transitions to new topics; (c) use vivid images and concrete examples; and (d) ensure necessary repetition and reinforcement.

Appropriate levels of instruction implies that the teacher know that the students are ready to learn new material. The lesson cannot be either too easy or too difficult. One of your most challenging tasks will be to accommodate your teaching to the individual differences and needs of your students. Though most of the methods schools and teachers use to provide appropriate levels of instruction (remedial grouping, tracking, special education) have serious drawbacks, given the diversity of your students, there can be no avoiding the issue. Slavin (1987d) identified the following methods as most common:

1. *Ability groups,* in which elementary students remain in heterogeneous classes most of the day but are grouped for certain subjects such as reading and mathematics, can be effective.
2. *Group-based mastery learning* (see chap. 12) does not require permanent ability groups; students regroup after each skill is taught. The danger here is that in the traditional class period, corrective instruction can slow down the entire class.
3. *Individualized instruction* provides for accommodation and can be effective if coupled with personalized contact with an instructor and some group work.

Summarizing what is currently known about the results of grouping practices, Slavin (1988a) separated the results into two categories:

- *Within-class groupings.* The research suggests that the evidence for the value of mastery learning remains inconclusive, while analyses of cooperative learning methods indicate consistent gains in student achievement if properly managed.
- *Between-class groupings.* Such groupings (ability groups, special classes) have little effect on student achievement, although acceleration may possibly benefit some gifted students. Departmentalization at the upper elementary and middle school levels probably should be avoided, although regrouping strategies (for certain subjects such as math and/or reading) can be effective.

Incentive refers to the degree of student motivation. As much as we desire intrinsic motivation for our students (see chap. 10), not all students will be ecstatic about all subjects at all times. One of the best incentives you can offer is to ensure that students be held accountable for what they do. Give them time to respond to your questions; check their homework. Don't rely solely on individual praise and reward; cooperative learning methods in which groups are rewarded because of their learning consistently have shown increases in student achievement.

Time refers to sufficient time for learning to occur. But don't be satisfied with "time" as a general concept. Remember the distinction between allocated time and engaged time.

The four elements of QAIT (quality, appropriateness, incentive, and time) share one critical characteristic: each element must be adequate if instruction is to be effective (Slavin, 1987d, p. 92). Figure 13.1 illustrates the QAIT model.

Note the independent variables in Figure 13.1. Students bring to your classroom certain abilities and motivational dispositions over which the school has little control. The alterable variables are QAIT, and they influence achievement by two time-related variables seen in the middle column—instructional efficiency and engaged time. Note how instructional efficiency in turn is related to quality of instruction, appropriate levels of instruction, and incentive.

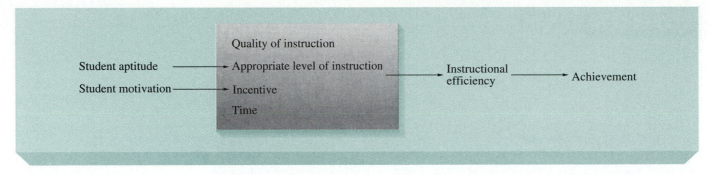

Figure 13.1
The QAIT model.

Describe the four components of the QAIT model. Apply the model to a problem that you will face in the classroom.

Slavin argued that his model accounts for many of the variables through which classroom organization affects learning outcomes. The QAIT model is not bound by any particular theory, but can be adopted as a method for understanding instruction and learning in any classroom context.

Classroom Contexts

We have identified several common classroom activities and examined ways to improve performance in many of them. Now let us consider two of these activities in greater detail.

Recitation

Recitation entails calling on individual students who give answers publicly before the rest of the class, usually for a brief time. Recitation has several purposes: review, introduction of new material, checking of assigned work, practice, and ensuring of comprehension (Doyle, 1986). The purpose of the recitation dictates the type of question and opportunity for participation.

Recitation involves the use of questions; you must ask these in a manner calculated to sustain the attention of the entire class. Try to systematize your questions so that all members have the chance to participate. Think about your questions. Do you intend them for review? Will you be satisfied with a yes-or-no answer, or are you looking for a thoughtful reply? Remember:

- *Ask your question of the entire class,* give them all time to think of the answer, and then call on an individual student. Do not indicate a student and then ask your question.
- *Wait for the answer.* Give the student time to think and respond. Use your best judgment; if the delay continues, rephrase the question, perhaps supplying prompts. If the student answers incorrectly, correct the answer impersonally, explaining as you do. Discourage any type of student calling-out behavior while another student is thinking of an answer, as such behavior can quickly produce chaos.

Seatwork

Two types of seatwork are used most commonly. The first is *supervised study,* during which all students are assigned independent work and the teacher moves around the room, monitoring each student's work. The second is *independent work,* when the teacher is busy with another task and does not monitor each student's work.

Estimates are that students in grades 1 through 7 spend from 50 to 75 percent of their time working alone on seatwork. Since students are less engaged during seatwork than they are in group or individual work with the teacher, you should be alert to techniques that improve engaged time. Here are several suggestions to guide seatwork:

Focus

The Native American Student: Core Values and the Teaching Process

Disproportionate numbers of Native American students have experienced difficulties with school. The dropout rate remains alarmingly high, enrollment in higher education is low, and teen pregnancy, suicide, and substance abuse continue at rates significantly higher than those for their Anglo peers. Many educators have observed that Native American students often have poor self-esteem and lack pride in being "Indian."

In a recent article in *Phi Delta Kappan* (1989) a leading educational publication, Lee Little Soldier reviewed some of the major core values of Native Americans that he believes educators should recognize and use constructively. While noting some vast differences among the many North American tribes of Native Americans, Soldier cited the following five core values as being relevant to the education of Native American students:

1. Native Americans respect and value the dignity of the individual, and (subsequently) children are afforded the same respect as adults.
2. Traditional Indian families encourage children to develop independence, to make wise decisions, and to abide by them. Thus, the locus of control of Indian children is (more) internal than external, and they are not accustomed to viewing adults as authorities who impose their will on others.
3. Cooperation and sharing are important values. Native Americans are thought to be more group-centered than

self-centered. They are accustomed to sharing whatever they have with many family members. Soldier perceives sharing as a habit that often bothers teachers who emphasize labeling possessions and taking care of one's own belongings.

4. Harmony is another core value of Native Americans according to Soldier: harmony with self, with others, and with nature.
5. The perception of time by Native Americans traditionally differs from that of the Anglo world. It appears that Native Americans view time as a continuum with no real beginning or end. There is an emphasis on living in the present and not worrying much about the future. Native Americans generally are patient individuals. Strict adherence to rigid schedules may prove to be difficult for many Native Americans.

Thus, a significant problem facing educators who wish to teach Native American students effectively is to develop supportive learning environments without compromising educational goals. According to Soldier, the answer to this problem may lie partly in the concept of instruction that is currently being characterized as cooperative learning. Instructional approaches that emphasize the group and the values of sharing and cooperating are consistent with many Native Americans' basic values.

Source: L. L. Soldier, "Cooperative Learning and the Native American Student" in Phi Delta Kappan, *October 1989; 161–163.*

- You should spend sufficient time explaining, discussing, and even practicing before your students commence work on their own.
- Practicing should immediately precede the seatwork.
- The exercises assigned to your students should flow directly from your explanations and the practice.
- You should guide your students through the first few exercises.

A good clue to the success you can expect from assignments lies in the number of questions you receive during the actual seatwork. If you find yourself giving multiple explanations during the seatwork, you can anticipate multiple errors (Rosenshine & Stevens, 1986). Establish a set routine that your students are to follow any time they engage in seatwork. In this way, they will know what to do when they have questions and when they finish, and how to get help. Even if you are working with another group, arrange seating so that you can monitor both groups adequately. If possible, try to move around to check on the seatwork group. Teacher contact greatly increases engaged time, since feedback and follow-up are as related to achievement as praise or reward.

Although teachers can easily overuse seatwork, if the assignment is interesting, clearly explained, and not just busy-work, seatwork can be a valuable classroom tool—as it should be, given the amount of time students spend at it.

MANAGING THE CLASSROOM

Good class management begins with a clear understanding of rules, preferably rules that are worded positively.

The next two sections, on managing the classroom and methods of control, are actually subdivisions of the same topic. They are separated here because of their individual importance and in order to give you both general and specific approaches to classroom control. Remember that the initial meetings that you have with your class during the first two weeks of school are probably the most important with regard to classroom control. During these sessions, you will set the classroom atmosphere by the rules and procedures you establish.

Rule Setting and Classroom Procedures

Any time people—adults or children—come together to achieve a particular goal, their behavior must be subject to rules. Otherwise, goal attainment is doomed. You may have had experience in attempting to learn in a setting where individual misbehavior constantly disrupted the class. If you were intent on learning, you probably became frustrated very quickly.

Many rules are explicit and openly discussed. Behaviors such as tardiness, fighting, talking in class, and other similar activities cannot be tolerated for the good of the entire group. Policies on other behaviors, such as leaving the room, sharpening pencils, or getting a drink of water are more implicit; that is, they are known and require little discussion once the rules are established. For a student to leave the room, you may require hand-raising or some other routine, such as the student's walking to a chalkboard, writing his or her name on the board, leaving the room, and upon reentering, erasing the name from the board.

Good Managers

Emmer and colleagues (1980), after studying elementary school teachers designated as "good managers," stated that all these teachers made known their rules and procedures on the first day of class, and also quite deliberately integrated them into a system, which they taught. Their rules were explicit, concrete, and functional, and these teachers gave students examples of the signals they would use for various activities.

The "good managers" did not initially overburden their students with rules—a tendency of many beginning teachers—but began with those that they considered basic and then gradually introduced more as they were needed. They also periodically reminded their students of the rules. By monitoring their classes closely, they were able to notice any rule violations almost instantly and attempt to correct them before minor violations developed into major problems.

Effective secondary school teachers also clearly and unmistakably stated the desired behaviors for their classes, gave precise indications of the expected work standards in their classes, and acted immediately to check disruptive behavior (Evortson & Emmer, 1982). Soon after the opening of school, less effective managers experienced more talking out in class and unapproved movement around the room. The main difference between the elementary and secondary "good managers" was that the secondary school instructors spent less time teaching and rehearsing the rules and procedures. Remember these points:

- Decide on as few important rules as possible.
- Make rules absolutely clear to all.
- Enforce rules for all.
- Avoid playing favorites.

Rules and Classroom Activities

As we have seen, classroom activities run in cycles in which students' behaviors are defined by rules. Once the teacher and other students repeatedly perform and reinforce behaviors specified by the rules, the rules become a part of the regular classroom routine. When this happens, the pieces are in place for efficient instruction. Medland and Vitale (1984) suggested the following five steps will help formulate meaningful rules for many classroom activities:

1. *Define the class activity.* We have previously commented on general classroom rules (for example, no calling out), but specific activities require specific rules. When you are working with one reading group, other group members must occupy themselves with seatwork. Efficient laboratory sessions demand orderly retrieving and storing of equipment. Physical education classes necessitate proper dress, equipment, and warm-up, certainly requirements that need structure and rules.

2. *Determine the social behaviors necessary for activities.* What is it that you want your students to accomplish during the activity? How should they go about it? Answering these two questions should help you to identify the needed behaviors. Also, consider what is inappropriate for the activity.

3. *Determine which activities need lists of rules.* Several guidelines can help you here (Medland & Vitale, 1984).

   a. Are there many social behaviors associated with the activity?

   b. Does the activity require considerable time?

   c. Are special classroom rules needed to cover the activity's behaviors?

   d. Have misbehaviors been associated with this activity?

   Answering any of these questions in the affirmative would seem to suggest the need for appropriate rules.

4. *Make a set of rules for the selected activities.* Rules add structure to any activity and enhance learning by providing a means of coordinated movement. If you think for a moment about the rules that function when you are with one group, and the rules that apply to those doing seatwork, you can understand the necessity for coordination.

   Since rules describe the behaviors necessary to accomplish an activity, try these suggestions:

   - Keep rules short.
   - Phrase rules in a positive way.
   - Don't use too many rules.

5. *Be sure to formulate a set of general activity rules.* We have previously commented on the need for such rules, and you can understand the necessity for being certain that your specific activity rules are consistent with the general rules. Otherwise, students become confused, and any contradiction could lead to misbehavior.

From this discussion it should be clear that successful teachers establish a classroom work system with rules and procedures designed to keep the system in good order. Successful teachers set these rules at the beginning of the school year, even though their students previously have learned those general rules that apply to school behavior. Experience has shown that unless rules are reinforced, student behavior deteriorates. The quality of rule setting, even at the secondary level, determines the order that will prevail in any class for its duration (Doyle, 1986).

Finally, although classroom order depends on your ability to have your students understand classroom procedures, you must also be ready to cope with rule violations. Your students expect a certain minimum level of competence in making the system work.

Management and Control

You should also take into account several developmental considerations in managing your classroom. Students exhibit a wide range of difficulties in development, but many problems are not serious enough to be of great concern. Kazdin (1988) stated that the following developmental issues are noteworthy in considering students' problems.

- Some of the behaviors that characterize maladjustment are relatively common in childhood. As most students mature, they do not experience severe problems.
- As students develop and undergo rapid changes, problem behaviors wax and wane at different ages. Such behaviors as lying and destructiveness are frequent from 4 to 9 years of age, but decline by 10 to 11 years of age.
- As a result of rapid changes as development continues, a problem of one type may be replaced by another problem at a later age.

There probably is no such thing as the "normal" youngster; all students usually exhibit troublesome behavior during development. They may be anxious, insecure, or aggressive—but these characteristics bother teachers only when they persist and become severe. For most children, problems do not persist. Youngsters typically show decreases in such behavior and progress to more mature stages of development.

Be alert to developmental problems and know when and where to refer students. Remember, however, that all children experience stress, and their reaction may be to exhibit maladaptive behavior. Your role (shared with their parents) in helping your students to master developmental crises is vital, because the manner in which they meet these difficulties shapes the way that they will face future dilemmas. You are teaching your students problem-solving behavior, and what they learn may last a lifetime. Constant failure, punishment, and ridicule destroy confidence and can cause a low self-concept that may result in a worrisome elementary school student who becomes a sullen, rebellious secondary school student. Estimates are that about 5 percent of all school-age youngsters show serious symptoms, and about 10 percent manifest milder behavioral disturbances. Thus, 85 percent of students proceed normally, perhaps causing teachers some anxieties with temporary maladaptive behavior (J. Travers, 1982). Your students, then, will inevitably experience growth problems and bring these to the classroom. They usually pass fairly quickly; only when they persist should you become concerned.

Aggression in the Classroom

An aggressive student not only can be a classroom problem but also may require special treatment. You may find it helpful to consider this problem developmentally, so that you can identify those classroom situations that could trigger outbursts.

A completely satisfactory theory of aggression still eludes us, but research interest has turned recently to the social encounters of infancy and early childhood to discover the roots of aggression. (See Parke & Slaby, 1983, for a particularly thoughtful analysis of aggressive behavior.) Investigators have discovered that as early as 12 to 18 months, half of the interchanges among children in a nursery involved conflict. By 2½ years, such disruptive interchanges had dropped to 20 percent, and by 42 months, to 5 percent. Between the ages of 2 and 4 years, physical aggression decreases and verbal aggression increases; by age 7, aggressive behavior becomes much more person-oriented. Aggressive students present behaviors that are typically classified as externalizing.

Focus   The Bully

Is there any reader who did not have nightmares sometime during school about that "monster" who loved to tease, humiliate, threaten, and fight? Even today most middle school principals will list bullying among their major worries.

Who is the bully? Most bullies seem to be students who have been treated violently themselves, attend schools that treat violence ineffectively, or are members of peer groups that encourage aggression. When we couple this kind of student with others who are almost "natural victims" (small, underweight, perhaps differently dressed, or having an obvious personal problem, such as anxiety), then conditions are ripe for bullying.

Olweus (1982) has identified four causes in the development of a bully:

1. *Indifference* (usually by the mother), which Olweus terms silent violence;
2. Parents who are *permissive* with an aggressive child;
3. Parents who typically resort to *physical punishment;*
4. A *temperamentally* aggressive child.

Be alert for this type of behavior; often teachers and parents are the last to know, since the victim is reluctant to talk about it. Among Olweus's suggestions for dealing with bullies are the following:

- Supervise recreation periods more closely.
- Intervene immediately to stop bullying.
- Talk to both bully and victim privately, and insist that if such behavior does not stop, both school and parents will become involved.
- If the problem persists, suggest therapy.

It is interesting to note that bullying is not just a concern in the United States. In Japan, bullying (or *ijime*) is a major social problem of concern to the entire nation (Prewitt, 1988). Remember: Prevent bullying, reinforce a child for not acting as a bully, and work with the victim to build self-confidence and success.

Table A Development and Aggression

Age	Type of aggression	Cause
Birth–2 yrs.	General upset	Possession of object
2–4	Physical Some verbal	Frustration
4–8	Verbal Physical	Hostility towards others
8–12	Verbal Some physical	Peers Authority Insecurity

As students continue to age and greater cognitive ability develops, their understanding of other students' intentions becomes important. There seem to be clear developmental changes involved. Seven-year-olds respond aggressively to both accidental and intentional provocation, while 9- and 12-year-olds react less aggressively to accidental provocation. Twelve-year-olds also respond less aggressively to intentional verbal than to intentional physical provocations, in contrast to 7- and 9-year-olds. Table 13.A in the focus box illustrates a general developmental sequence of aggressive behavior.

Remember that there are clear sex differences in aggression, with boys generally being much more aggressive. Impressive evidence exists that aggression in males is remarkably stable. Studying subjects from 2 to 18 years of age, Olweus (1982) reported that male aggression and acting-out behaviors showed substantial persistence over long periods of time.

Some students who exhibit aggressive behavior may need professional services focused on the school and family (Horne & Sayger, 1990). In dealing with most cases of aggression, however, try these suggestions:

- *Stop trouble before it starts.* Knowing the right moment to interrupt behavior is a valuable asset; interrupting too soon makes a teacher appear fussy, while intervening too late may produce an uproar. If a youngster is not stopping voluntarily, then a teacher should act decisively.

- *Use signal interference*. A skillful teacher instantly notices the signs that lead to trouble: fidgeting in one youngster, rigidity in another. Watch youngsters and then act. Let the student know you are aware of them by moving closer, staring, coughing. Discover those mannerisms that signal difficulty. The results will make your time and efforts worthwhile.
- *Avoid the tribal dance,* which usually involves a dare. Trouble starts; the teacher acts; the student reacts, to protect status. The tribal dance has begun. The student dares the teacher to do something, and the teacher must accept the dare or retreat and lose status. Teachers must know which students are susceptible to the tribal dance, and must act quickly to avoid the ritual, either by ignoring the behavior or by instantly suppressing it. The truly tough youngsters are not usually susceptible; they are not forced to prove their courage. The lesson here is that you should know the danger signals and not put yourself in an impossible situation.
- *Watch for hidden effects*. Though a student may do what you want, there are usually side effects, and the wise teacher will work with a youngster who must be disciplined to prevent feelings of hostility and isolation. We may have to live with aggression, but we should not breed it by exposing normal youngsters to classroom experiences that produce frustration.
- *Recognize your own aggression*. Though your hostility may be justified, your maturity and your professional obligation demand that your behavior reduce classroom tension and lessen the opportunities for student aggression.
- *Evaluate your classroom procedures*. Emmer and colleagues (1984) suggested that you frequently check your classroom's organization and decide if you should make changes in your management procedures.

Searching for the Causes of Classroom Problems

Once you recognize that a problem exists, the next step is to identify its cause. If you answer these questions objectively, you may well discover significant clues.

- Is your room arrangement causing any problems, such as congestion, bumping, or limited visibility for some students?
- Are your rules and procedures clear? Some disruptive behavior may not be included under your rules, or you may be forgetting to enforce one or more rules.
- Are you managing student work carefully? Be sure that your directions are clear and understood by all and that students realize that they will be accountable for their work.
- Are you satisfied with your consequences for appropriate and inappropriate behavior? Review your own behavior to be sure that your rewards and penalties are still effective and that you are not punishing or praising students too freely.
- Are you detecting misbehavior in its early stages? You may need to work on your monitoring ability for dealing with misbehaviors in their early stages, before they become major problems.
- Is your teaching effective? Check to be certain that students are not confused during your instruction and that transitions from one activity to another are smooth and uneventful.

METHODS OF CONTROL

Annual **Edition**

You have now reached the point at which you can better understand specific suggestions about classroom control. All the topics discussed in this chapter point to one basic conclusion: a smoothly running classroom blocks most problems before they can get started. You must always relate your present classroom situation to your students' needs and developmental changes. If your classroom is well organized, and you have followed the management ideas presented here but are still not satisfied, you may want to adopt specific control techniques.

Issues & Answers

➤ Do Discipline Programs Promote Ethical Behavior?

As we have noted in this chapter, classroom discipline is one of the major challenges facing American education. Virtually all teachers are faced with maintaining an effective instructional environment—on this issue there is general consensus. Yet, the methods that are used to discipline students remain controversial. Some critics of behavior modification programs have argued that these programs (such as Cantor's *Assertive Discipline*) must do more than merely control behavior. Discipline programs, they argue, must also teach our children to be moral and engage in ethical behavior.

Issue

Should discipline programs teach the moral and ethical concepts that undergird appropriate behavior?

Answer: Pro Discipline programs should include a focus that promotes moral and ethical behavior, so that our children grow up to be good citizens and not merely good students in school.

Answer: Con Discipline programs are designed to control student behavior in schools and to promote effective instructional environments for students. They should not include curricula to teach moral and ethical behavior.

Answer: Pro Children must be taught the concepts underlying the rules and behavior that they are to display in classrooms. That is, they must understand that some forms of inappropriate behavior are morally and ethically wrong. With this understanding they can leave our schools and become moral and ethical citizens.

Answer: Con Discipline programs that focus on rules and control of behavior through contingencies, in effect, do teach appropriate ethical and moral behavior in children. When children behave in appropriate ways, they will receive feedback from significant adults and eventually learn the standards that guide our culture.

Answer: Pro Children must develop internal consciences during the school years that they take with them into our culture. Moral and ethical citizens have an understanding of the reasons behind their actions, not just a knowledge that they will be rewarded and punished for their actions.

Answer: Con Discipline programs that rely on rules, standards, and contingencies for appropriate behavior do create a culture for the development of moral and ethical behavior. The real challenge is to generalize these standards to the greater culture when children leave the schools.

Where do you stand on these important issues? What focus do you think our discipline programs should take to create better moral and ethical individuals?

Misbehavior in the Classroom

The acts of school violence that you read or hear about in the news are infrequent and seldom occur in most effective schools. We do not wish to minimize, however, the growing concern in this country with crime and violence in the schools. The key to understanding misbehavior is to be alert to what students do while in the classroom. What may appear to be misbehavior may actually aid a class. For example, the student who talks out in eagerness may generate an enthusiasm and motivation that spreads to other class members. However, a student's refusal to do what you request or insistence on answering you back constitutes true misbehavior (Doyle, 1986).

You must also be aware of any difference in your responses when different students demonstrate the same behaviors. Some students seem to be particularly skilled in irritating and frustrating teachers. These are not usually the overtly unruly, but those who walk the thin line between acceptable behavior and insolence. Others see any teacher as an authority figure who must be challenged.

Some teachers will ignore the student who practices insolence and concentrate on any unruliness; others will see both types of behavior as inappropriate. Remember, however, that you and you alone will establish the rules of acceptable behavior in your classroom. As long as your students do not violate school codes, you are responsible for setting standards. You should never become a teacher who intervenes frequently to check misbehavior. Such behavior characterizes the least effective teachers, and is a clear signal that something is wrong.

Multicultural Students and Discipline

There must be order in a classroom. Otherwise, chaos prevails and learning declines. It makes no difference which students are involved in disruptive behavior; you must determine the degree of control necessary for efficient learning. Our discussion is intended to remind you to treat all students fairly and equally. Evidence indicates that larger numbers of minority students are disciplined and suspended, a situation that causes additional problems, because the time lost from school hurts both motivation and achievement (Children's Defense Fund, 1975).

About two million students are suspended from school each year, with African American and Hispanic students more than twice as likely as white students to be suspended. The dropout rate for all Hispanics remains high (80 percent in New York, 70 percent in Chicago, and 50 percent in Los Angeles—Grossman, 1984). Dropping out is likely the result, in part, of discipline problems that are related to academic skill difficulties (Casas, Furlong, Solberg, & Carranza, 1990).

> Think about this statement. Teachers have absolutely no knowledge, not only of the language but about the culture of the children that they are working with. . . . Haitian children are very physical. We express . . . we use our hands . . . we talk. This doesn't mean that we are creating a scene or disrupting. If the child wants to speak, instead of saying: "Hi, Johnny," he will touch the other child automatically. In the classroom, if the teacher said you were supposed to be quiet, or "You don't move," it quickly turns into a discipline thing. They don't understand that we use a lot of body language. (First & Carrera, 1988, p. 62)

You must keep order in your classroom—that's a given. Some behavior, however, that is natural for particular students could lead to problems. Take these students aside, explain what could happen if the entire class acted like this, and work out some signal that would let you know when they needed help. Occasionally a minority student may have difficulty understanding what is going on in the classroom, and in an effort to keep up with the others, may appear to act in a disruptive fashion. "Calling out" is a good example of this situation. For example, a Spanish-speaking student may call out for a translation. If intervention programs are available for minority students during the elementary school years, these students may acquire those academic skills that will ultimately reduce discipline problems (Miranda & Santos de Barona, 1990). The point here is to make a concerted effort to understand your students. To help you to understand your students better, use the following questions as a guideline (Grossman, 1990):

- How much reinforcement and punishment are students accustomed to receive from the adults in their culture? For example, Hawaiian children respond well to considerable attention, while Navajo students prefer to work independently.
- What kinds of consequences work best for particular students? Are given students used to physical punishment, loss of attention, removal (such as being sent to their rooms), or loss of privileges? Mexican American students, for example, do not react well to persistent questioning by well-intentioned teachers intent on having them give correct answers. This technique violates their sense of tolerance.
- How much initiative can you expect newly arrived students to display? Japanese students may at first be reluctant to express their opinions and resist answering questions or raising issues for discussion. They may depend solely on memorization and be confused by attempts to have them solve problems on their own.

If you think about these situations and others that you may encounter, you will become more sensitive to the relationship between cultural background and classroom behavior.

Maintaining Classroom Control

While teaching a college mental hygiene course, Kounin (1970) noticed a student reading a newspaper in the back of the room. He immediately and angrily reprimanded him. The discipline succeeded; the student's attention returned to the lecturer. But the reprimand had also affected other class members. Attention was rigid, and a depressing silence settled on the room. This was Kounin's first experience with the **ripple effect.** Punishment was not confined to one student; its effects spread to other class members. Kounin decided to study ripple effects and what he calls **desists:** a teacher's actions to stop misbehavior. To avoid experimental contamination, Kounin and his colleagues videotaped 30 actual classrooms. They analyzed the tapes and coded teachers' desist techniques for clarity, firmness, intensity, focus, and student treatment. They then attempted to relate the desist techniques to managerial success, which they defined as the degree of student work involvement in that teacher's class, the amount of student deviancy in that class, and the degree to which deviancy spread to other class members. They found that there was no relationship between the qualities of a teacher's desists and that teacher's success in handling deviant behavior.

Does this mean that misbehavior is insignificant and of no concern to others? Absolutely not; discipline heads any list of teachers', administrators', and parents' educational concerns. The problem is to isolate those techniques that contain misbehavior and prevent it from spreading. The question should be this: What is it that teachers do that makes a difference in how students behave?

ripple effect *The phenomenon in which punishment is not confined to one student; its effects spread to other class members.*

desists *A teacher's actions to stop misbehavior.*

Effective Teacher Behaviors

Additional study convinced Kounin that some teachers' behaviors correlated highly with managerial success. These behaviors were effective not only with specific children, but also with entire classes. In this second study, Kounin videotaped 50 first- and second-grade classes for a full day each. Realizing that the clarity, firmness, intensity, and focus of a teacher's desists are not critical in maintaining classroom control, Kounin searched for other factors. From continued replaying of the tapes, certain characteristics emerged.

1. *Withitness.* The first was **withitness,** which means teachers' knowledge and understanding of what is occurring in their classrooms. Some teachers clearly demonstrated that they knew what was going on in their classrooms. These teachers selected the correct targets for their desists; that is, they knew who had misbehaved and how serious it was. They also timed their interventions so that the misbehavior did not spread and become more serious.

2. *Overlapping.* Some teachers had no difficulty in attending to two issues simultaneously. For example, imagine what would you do in the following situation. You are with a group in which one youngster is reading aloud, when two other youngsters in another group, who are supposedly doing seatwork, become noisy. Do you leave the reading group and attempt to check the noisy twosome? Or do you tell the youngster to continue reading while simultaneously telling the other youngsters to stop talking and get to work? Kounin refers to the latter technique as **overlapping:** a teacher's ability to handle two events simultaneously. As he notes, a learning event and misbehavior simultaneously present a teacher with two issues; the two events overlap.

Although both withitness and overlapping are associated with managerial success, Kounin believes that withitness seems to be more important. Teachers who demonstrate withitness can simultaneously handle two issues (overlapping). What can you learn from Kounin's discussion of these two topics? Work at widening your attention; force yourself to try to be aware of everything that is occurring in your classroom, so that you acquire withitness. When this happens,

withitness *Teachers' knowledge and understanding of what is happening in their classrooms.*

overlapping *A teacher's ability to handle two or more classroom issues simultaneously.*

you are almost compelled to use overlapping to attend to multiple events. Since these teacher behaviors relate closely to managerial success, they are well worth the effort.

3. *Transition smoothness.* The next characteristic Kounin discovered was **transition smoothness.** Some teachers had no trouble in handling activity and movement in their classes. The classes he videotaped averaged 33.2 major changes in learning activities during the day. If such transitions are not handled smoothly, chaos can result. Teachers must initiate, sustain, and terminate many activities involving many materials. If you are to maintain smooth movement, you must avoid jerkiness and slowdowns, those teacher behaviors that abruptly introduce one activity by interrupting another: "Close your books, return to your desks, and do your arithmetic." There is no smoothness here; the youngsters are not ready to interpret and act on the teacher's directions. Also avoid "dangles"—leaving some direction unfinished—and changes from one activity to another and then back again.

A *slowdown* occurs when a teacher's behavior slows an activity's movement. Kounin identified two kinds of slowdown: *overdwelling,* when a teacher spends excessive time—beyond that needed for student understanding—on a topic; and *fragmentation,* when a teacher has individual students do something it would be better to have the group do—for example, have children come to the reading group one by one instead of as a group. Kounin concluded that avoiding jerkiness and slowdowns is a significant aspect of successful classroom management.

4. *Group alertness.* For Kounin, **group alertness** refers to programming for "learning-related" variety. As mentioned previously, be honest with yourself: Am I an interesting teacher? Are my classes lively? Do I keep all of my students involved? To help you minimize misbehavior, remember to

- watch all of your students while one is responding.
- keep on the move; don't stay in one spot; let students know that you are interested in what they are doing.
- call on students randomly; avoid any set patterns.
- keep interest high by leading up to a question: "You haven't heard about this before, but I think you can answer it."

Finally, Kounin emphasized that teachers are not tutors; that is, they work with groups, either the class as a whole, or subunits within the class. How, then, can you keep your classes alert? Kounin observed teacher behaviors that he designated as *positive group alerting cues,* such as creating suspense before calling on a student, and consistently calling on different students. *Negative group alerting cues* included a teacher's concentration on only one student, designation of a student to answer before asking the question, and practice of having youngsters recite in a predetermined sequence.

transition smoothness *Teachers have no difficulty in handling activities and movement in their classes.*

group alertness *Use of instructional methods that maintain interest and contribute to lively classes.*

What effective teacher behaviors did Kounin identify regarding maintaining classroom control? How could you use these procedures in your classroom?

Using Behavior Modification

As we now focus our discussion on specific techniques for handling misbehavior, you must make a decision concerning the method with which you feel most comfortable. In a survey of teachers' classroom management techniques, Rosen and others (1991) found distinctions between teachers' responses to appropriate and inappropriate academic behaviors and their responses to comparable social behaviors. Note from tables 13.4 and 13.5 that more teachers reported using management techniques to control inappropriate social behavior than reported their use for inappropriate academic behavior.

Although there were a few exceptions, the percentage of teachers using management techniques to address appropriate social behaviors was equivalent to the percentage

Table 13.4

Procedures for Appropriate Social and Academic Behavior: Percentage of Teachers Reporting Use, and Mean Frequency of Reported Use

Procedure	Appropriate social behavior		Appropriate academic behavior	
	% Reporting (SD)	Mean freq. (SD)	% Reporting (SD)	Mean freq. (SD)
1. Praise or compliment	100 (0.0)	2.5 (0.18)	100 (0.0)	2.6 (0.11)
2. Hug, pat on back, wink, etc.	92 (8.2)	1.9 (0.27)	89 (10.9)	1.8 (0.31)
3. Friendly/encouraging teasing	84 (11.8)	1.7 (0.34)	85 (13.3)	1.7 (0.35)
4. Show others the good work	78 (9.5)	1.5 (0.19)	87 (4.4)	1.5 (0.17)
5. Send note or call parents	72 (15.8)	1.3 (0.36)	79 (9.8)	1.3 (0.28)
6. Special time with teacher	69 (6.0)	1.1 (0.17)	76 (9.7)	1.1 (0.24)
7. Use special materials/objects	67 (13.7)	1.2 (0.27)	66 (16.6)	1.2 (0.32)
8. Give happy face, star, or other symbolic reward	65 (22.5)	1.5 (0.64)	82 (20.6)	1.9 (0.69)
9. Give sticker, food, or other material reward	63 (17.4)	1.3 (0.49)	71 (13.6)	1.5 (0.48)
10. Allow to run errands	63 (11.0)	1.1 (0.29)	59 (12.5)	1.0 (0.21)
11. Allow child to tutor	55 (12.2)	0.9 (0.27)	78 (11.7)	1.2 (0.24)
12. Stories, movies, parties	50 (8.5)	0.9 (0.26)	42 (10.7)	0.8 (0.24)
13. Give free time, less classwork or homework	49 (11.4)	0.8 (0.28)	51 (13.1)	0.7 (0.25)
14. Post progress/work	48 (9.8)	0.9 (0.28)	93 (4.7)	1.9 (0.23)
15. Assign as monitor/line leader	41 (14.4)	0.8 (0.28)	37 (11.3)	0.7 (0.21)
16. Do nothing special (ignore)	39 (12.0)	0.7 (0.27)	32 (7.0)	0.5 (0.08)
17. Bonus points/extra credit	38 (11.2)	0.7 (0.23)	61 (20.3)	1.1 (0.43)
18. Eat in room/talk to neighbor	36 (10.6)	0.6 (0.14)	31 (9.1)	0.5 (0.12)
19. Allow to choose own seat	34 (12.8)	0.6 (0.26)	34 (8.3)	0.5 (0.21)
20. Allow to skip ahead in work	29 (7.5)	0.4 (0.12)	56 (6.8)	0.9 (0.22)
21. Points given toward earning privileges	28 (12.6)	0.5 (0.23)	32 (8.9)	0.5 (0.24)

Reprinted from L. A. Rosen, et al., "A Survey of Classroom Management Practices" in *Journal of School Psychology,* 28:1991, with kind permission from Elsevier Science Ltd., The Boulevard, Langford Lane, Kidlington 0X5 1GB, UK.

Note. Percentages are averages of responses across all grades, K–6.

using the same techniques for appropriate academic behavior. Moreover, verbal management techniques (for example, praise or reprimands) were used more than techniques based on concrete consequences (for example, a pat on the back or the sending of a note home). A second study by the authors using direct observations of the teachers also verified that the teachers used verbal techniques more than those based on concrete consequences. Interestingly, most of the interactions that teachers had with their students were classified as neutral and were not designed to control behavior. The authors concluded that the choice of a management technique appears to depend greatly on the teacher's acceptance of the procedure.

In a sense, this chapter's discussion of control reflects many of the choices that you faced in the learning section (see especially chapters 7 and 8). Which basic theoretical position should you follow: cognitive, behavioral, or some combination of

Table 13.5

Procedures for Inappropriate Social and Academic Behavior: Percentage of Teachers Reporting Use, and Mean Frequency of Reported Use				
	Inappropriate social behavior		Inappropriate academic behavior	
Procedure	% Reporting (SD)	Mean freq. (SD)	% Reporting (SD)	Mean freq. (SD)
1. Reprimand privately	99 (1.9)	2.4 (0.18)	94 (5.9)	2.0 (0.27)
2. Send notice or call parents	95 (4.3)	2.1 (0.18)	96 (4.1)	2.0 (0.16)
3. Reassure/discuss with child	94 (3.9)	2.2 (0.29)	97 (3.1)	2.3 (0.13)
4. Take away a privilege	83 (6.3)	1.5 (0.34)	62 (9.1)	1.0 (0.22)
5. Reprimand loudly in class	77 (13.5)	1.1 (0.26)	48 (12.4)	0.5 (0.16)
6. Move desk by teacher, in corner, in hall	72 (7.6)	1.2 (0.22)	56 (7.8)	0.8 (0.31)
7. Threaten to punish	63 (13.3)	0.9 (0.24)	39 (9.5)	0.5 (0.12)
8. Take away snack or recess	47 (12.7)	0.8 (0.33)	46 (13.1)	0.7 (0.25)
9. Tell child to put work away or head down	46 (16.8)	0.7 (0.33)	25 (16.1)	0.3 (0.20)
10. Send to principal	45 (8.8)	0.5 (0.15)	18 (10.4)	0.2 (0.13)
11. Do nothing special (ignore)	43 (15.8)	0.5 (0.21)	29 (14.9)	0.4 (0.19)
12. Detention/stay after school	42 (21.1)	0.8 (0.39)	36 (23.5)	0.6 (0.41)
13. Assign extra work or sentences to write	32 (15.8)	0.4 (0.24)	30 (10.9)	0.4 (0.18)
14. Bang book/ruler on desk	29 (9.9)	0.4 (0.16)	N/A	N/A
15. Write negative comment on academic work	23 (6.7)	0.4 (0.14)	61 (4.3)	0.8 (0.23)
16. Take chair away	23 (12.4)	0.3 (0.15)	9 (8.7)	0.1 (0.10)
17. Rip up papers, work, etc.	18 (6.0)	0.2 (0.08)	28 (10.7)	0.3 (0.10)
18. Shake or use other firm physical contact	16 (9.7)	0.2 (0.12)	4 (3.2)	0.1 (0.05)
19. Send to different or lower classroom	13 (8.9)	0.2 (0.15)	8 (4.6)	0.1 (0.04)
20. Take points off grade	7 (2.4)	0.1 (0.08)	43 (18.3)	0.8 (0.39)
21. Publically post demerits	7 (8.9)	0.1 (0.14)	3 (3.2)	0.0 (0.0)
22. Take away gym, art, etc.	6 (5.7)	0.1 (0.08)	4 (4.0)	0.1 (0.05)

Reprinted from L. A. Rosen, et al., "A Survey of Classroom Management Practices" in *Journal of School Psychology,* 28:1991, with kind permission from Elsevier Science Ltd., The Boulevard, Langford Lane, Kidlington 0X5 1GB, UK.

Note. Percentages are averages of responses across all grades, K–6.

both? Most of us are not bound by rigid adherence to a particular approach; nevertheless, we tend to favor one while incorporating material from others.

You may well believe that behavioral techniques are best suited for all aspects of the classroom, or decide that certain types of student behavior (perhaps hyperactivity or aggression) are best addressed by behavior modification. In fact, behavioral techniques are among the most widely evaluated procedures in psychology and education. Remember that behaviorism's basic assumptions are that both adaptive and maladaptive behavior are learned, and that the best means for treating problems is to structure a student's classroom environment so that you can reinforce desirable behavior. (You may want to reread chapter 7 to refresh your knowledge of behaviorism.)

Table 13.6

Summary of Basic Principles of Operant Conditioning

Principle	Characteristic procedure and its effect on behavior
Reinforcement	Presentation or removal of an event after a response that increases the frequency of the response.
Punishment	Presentation or removal of an event after a response that decreases the frequency of the response.
Extinction	No longer presenting a reinforcing event after a response that decreases the frequency of the previously reinforced response.
Stimulus control and discrimination training	Reinforcing the response in the presence of one stimulus but not in the presence of another. This procedure increases the frequency of the response in the presence of the former stimulus and decreases the frequency of the response in the presence of the latter stimulus.

From *Behavior Modification in Applied Settings,* pp. 11, 26, by Alan E. Kazdin. Copyright © 1994, 1989, 1984, 1980, 1975 by Brooks Cole Publishing Company, a division of Thomson Publishing, Inc., Pacific Grove, CA 93950. Reprinted by permission of the publisher.

Definition of Terms

Although behavior modification is the general label that identifies those management techniques emerging from behavioral theory, certain distinctions should be made.

- *Behavior influence.* **Behavior influence** occurs whenever one person exercises some control over another. It is a constant occurrence in home, work, politics, and schools where teachers are constantly involved with behavior.

  behavior influence   *The exercise of some control by one person over another.*

- *Behavior modification.* **Behavior modification** is a deliberate attempt to apply certain principles derived from experimental research in order to enhance human functioning. Its techniques are designed to better a student's self-control by improving skills, abilities, and independence. One basic assumption guides the total process: People are influenced by the consequences of their behavior. A critical assumption is that the current environment controls behavior more directly than an individual's early experience, internal conflicts, or personality structure.

  behavior modification   *A deliberate attempt, using learning principles, to control student behavior.*

- *Behavior therapy.* Behavior modification and behavior therapy are often used synonymously, but behavior modification is the more general term. **Behavior therapy** usually applies to a one-to-one client-therapist relationship. So, technically, behavior therapy is only one aspect of behavior modification.

  behavior therapy   *An attempt to change behavior in a client-therapist relationship.*

Teachers using behavior modification attempt to influence their students' behavior by changing the environments and the way that youngsters interact with their environments, rather than by probing into backgrounds, or referring the children for medical treatment (usually medications), or expelling them. To be successful, the teacher must clearly specify the problem behavior. What is it, precisely, that you wish a student to do, or not to do? Try to determine the consequences of children's behavior—that is, what they obtain by it. Then decide what you are going to do. Will you ignore it, hoping for extinction; will you punish it; or will you reward some other form of behavior?

Decisions about how to manage behavior (for example, punishing an undesired behavior or reinforcing a desired one) and which behavioral techniques to use are important and often complex. Table 13.6 summarizes much of what was stated in chapter 7 by highlighting the critical dimensions of applied behavioral techniques.

- *Positive reinforcement.* As we have seen in chapter 7, **positive reinforcement** can be defined as any event following a response that increases the possibility of recurrence of that response. Good examples would be money, food, praise, attention, and pleasurable activities. You must be careful in using positive

  positive reinforcement   *A procedure wherein the rate of a response increases as a function of the consequences and presentation of a positive reinforcer.*

Table 13.7

Intermittent Rewards Suitable for Secondary Students

- Writing a note to the student's parents
- Writing a note to the student
- Calling the student's parents
- Calling the student
- Complimenting the student in front of another staff member
- Asking one of the administrators to reward the student's behavior
- Privately praising the student's classroom performance in a nonclassroom setting such as in the hall after school
- Give the student a responsibility
- Tokens for a video arcade
- Tickets to a school activity
- Food
- Coupon to rent a movie
- Let the student choose an activity for the class
- Check out a book the student might be interested in

From R. S. Sprick and V. Nolet, "Prevention and Management of Secondary-Level Behavior Problems" in *Interventions for Achievement and Behavior Problems*, G. Stoner, et al., eds. Copyright © 1991 the National Association of School Psychologists. Reprinted by permission of the publisher.

reinforcement with your students; what may be pleasurable (providing positive reinforcement) for one student may not be for another. Rewards for secondary students will not be the same as those for elementary or preschool students. Table 13.7 provides examples of rewards that are effective with secondary school students. Here is the value of knowing your students—what they like and dislike. Students will have different preferences among the items in the table. Positive reinforcement is a powerful tool in changing behavior; presenting youngsters with things they like can produce consistently desirable results.

- *Token economy.* The **token economy** technique has been widely used in managing groups. For example, students, patients, and other group members receive tokens when they exhibit desirable behavior; collect them; and when they have attained an accepted number, exchange them for something pleasurable. For example, talkative students may receive tokens for every 15 or 20 minutes they are silent; when they have enough tokens, they may trade them for extra recreation or something else they like.
- *Shaping.* In **shaping,** the teacher first determines the successive steps in the desired behavior and teaches them separately, reinforcing each until students master it. The students then move to the next phase, where the procedure is repeated. Ultimately, they acquire the total behavior by these progressive approximations.
- *Contingency contracting.* In **contingency contracting,** a teacher and a student decide on a behavioral goal and what the student will receive after attaining the goal. For example, the goal may be successfully completing 20 division problems; the positive reinforcement may be an extra art period, if this is the child's favorite school activity. Contracts involve an exchange; both teacher and student agree on what each will do.
- *Aversive control.* Students maintain some undesirable behavior because the consequences are reinforcing. To eliminate the behavior, a teacher might apply an aversive stimulus (for example, remaining after school). The removal of positive reinforcement is another example of **aversive control.** (Recall the definition of punishment: the introduction of aversive stimuli, *or* the withdrawal of positive reinforcement.) You have read about the possible negative consequences of punishment; use care in the selection of an aversive stimulus, and try to have students do something desirable so that you can positively reinforce them.
- *Overcorrection.* **Overcorrection** combines both restitution and positive practice. For example, a child may deliberately knock things off another student's desk while moving about the room. The teacher has the student not only remedy the situation (put the things back on the desk) as restitution, but also straighten all the other desks in the room, in positive practice.

token economy *A form of classroom management in which students receive tokens for desirable behavior. These may then be exchanged for something pleasurable.*

shaping *A form of classroom management in which teachers determine the successive steps needed to master a task and then teach them separately, reinforcing each step.*

contingency contracting *Joint decision by a teacher and a student on a behavioral goal and what the student will receive when the goal is achieved.*

aversive control *A technique to eliminate undesirable student behavior, either by introducing an unpleasant event or removing a pleasurable one.*

overcorrection *A form of classroom management involving both restitution and positive practice.*

Behavior Modification and the Causes of Behavior

As noted in previous chapters, behavioral techniques are often called *applied behavior analysis* when used in educational settings. Applied behavior analysis involves a "systematic performance-based, self-evaluative method of studying and changing socially important behavior" (Sulzer-Azaroff & Mayer, 1991, p. 4). Table 13.8 provides a list of the characteristics of applied behavior analysis. As you examine this table, note the emphasis on the environment as the cause of behavior.

Why should teachers concentrate on student behavior and not on the causes of the behavior? Behavior therapists argue that teachers are not analysts. They are not trained to explore the special circumstances that influence behavior. Since the multiple and interactive causes of behavior can elude detection even by highly trained and skilled professional psychologists and counselors, busy teachers, who often do not have the required time, training, or experience, are less likely to detect them.

Even if teachers can identify the causes of maladaptive behavior, they frequently can do little about them. If the trouble lies in the home, a teacher's options are limited. Consequently, the teacher must focus on the child's behavior, and if necessary, obtain professional consultation. Occasionally, however, the causes of maladaptive behavior are discerned and treated, but the behavior remains. An example is a reading problem caused by poor vision; when the physical difficulty is corrected, the reading deficiency remains.

Noting the concern that all teachers share in maintaining discipline, Wielkiewicz (1986) suggested the need for several steps in any behavior management program.

Table 13.8

Characteristics of Applied Behavior Analysis

- Focus on behaviors of applied (social or clinical) significance.
- Search for marked intervention effects that make a clear difference to the everyday functioning of the individual.
- Focus on overt behaviors.
- Focus on the behaviors of one or a small number of individuals over time.
- Assessment of behavior through direct observation, as in counting the frequency of responses.
- Assessment continuously over time for extended periods (hours, days, weeks).
- Use of environmental (and observable) events to influence the frequency of behavior.
- Evaluation and demonstration of the factors (e.g., events) that are responsible for behavior change.

From *Behavior Modification in Applied Settings*, pp. 11, 26, by Alan E. Kazdin. Copyright © 1994, 1989, 1984, 1980, 1975 by Brooks Cole Publishing Company, a division of Thomson Publishing, Inc., Pacific Grove, CA 93950. Reprinted by permission of the publisher.

- *Identify the problem.* Usually a general problem is identified—this boy is hostile—and then additional assessment helps to identify the circumstances that trigger the problem (the hostility).
- *Refine the target behavior.* A general label such as "hostility" is not much help. Recall that one of the major objectives of applied behavior analysis is the accurate presentation of reinforcement; you must identify precise behavior (the target behavior) if reinforcement is to be effective. What is the problem behavior? Under what circumstances is the behavior to be reinforced?
- *Assess the baseline rate.* If you obtain a baseline rate before intervention, then you can assess the success of the program. What is the rate of occurrence when behavior management is not in effect? How does it compare to intervals when behavioral techniques are at work?
- *Identify the reinforcer and the contingency.* You must know your students well to discover just what reinforces them; this is not always an easy task with some students in a classroom setting. You may have to link tokens earned at school with reinforcement at home.
- *Begin the program.* In a manner they can understand, tell students what they need to know.
- *Modify the program when necessary.* If the program does not appear to be as successful as you anticipated, step back to evaluate your steps. Perhaps more time is necessary, or some other element interferes, such as a brother or sister who attempts to subvert the program at home.
- *Fade out the program.* The good program puts itself out of business. The desired behavior appears at a steady rate with ever-increasing frequency between reinforcements.
- *Ensure generalization.* A good program includes procedures that will facilitate transfer and maintenance of behavior change over time and across settings.

Provide examples of how you could use these behavioral techniques in the classroom: token economy, shaping, contingency contracting, aversive control, and overcorrection.

Suppose seventh-grader Dale is late for school almost every day. Identify steps of a behavior management program that you could use to solve this problem.

Focus ← Using Behavior Modification

Below are several widely accepted strategies for using behavior modification:

- *Know your target.* Just what behaviors do you wish to change? Specify precisely what the behavior is and what you want it to become. Do not attempt too much. For example, some students may be unable to tolerate inattention too long; consequently, they frequently use maladaptive, disruptive behavior to secure attention. You will not immediately change that behavior for an entire day, but you may quickly change it for a period and gradually extend it over an entire school day.

- *Know the circumstances surrounding the behavior.* When maladaptive behavior occurs, try to discover what happened immediately preceding and following it. A girl consistently misbehaves just before reading period. She may have a reading problem, while her friends read smoothly and effortlessly. By being disruptive, she secures satisfaction and successfully directs attention from her difficulty. The teacher should strive for Kounin's "transition smoothness" by providing positive reinforcement just before the reading class, and then either ignoring (if possible) her behavior in reading or planning for her some reading task that ensures positive reinforcement.

Many teachers and parents have found helpful the use of a simple model—referred to as the ABC model—to organize information about the events surrounding a target behavior. The A in the model refers to antecedents, the B to behavior, and the C to consequences. By focusing on those events that surround the target behavior—both antecedents and consequences—we gain knowledge about events that are likely to influence a student's behavior. Table A illustrates the use of the ABC model by a school psychologist who was trying to understand the events that controlled an aggressive third-grader's behavior.

You can see that Jim, the classmate on the other team, and the teacher influenced John's behavior. Jim's successes served to stimulate negative comments from John, but the teacher's close physical proximity to John appeared to reduce/stop John's teasing. One can conclude from this analysis that teacher proximity was an important element in managing John's behavior.

- *Know your students so that you know what reinforces them.* Although the primary reinforcers, such as food and physical stimulation, are powerful shapers of behavior, they are hardly appropriate for the classroom. Teachers must search for those things, objects, events, that individual students find reinforcing. For example, some students find adult attention a strong positive reinforcement. Other youngsters, because of unpleasant experiences with adults, think their attention is aversive. You must know your students to use reinforcers effectively.

- *Select appropriate strategies.* Select techniques that effectively encourage desirable behavior and discourage undesirable behavior.

- *Use feedback wisely.* Make sure that students understand the link between behavior and reinforcement. Your goal should be a gradual reduction in external reinforcement and increasing self-control.

Thoughtfully used, behavior modification techniques can help you attain a constructive classroom atmosphere.

Table A   The ABC Model Used to Understand Aggressive Behavior

Antecedents	Behavior	Consequences
Jim makes a good play.	John calls Jim a bad name.	Jim ignores John.
Jim's teammates congratulate him.	John calls Jim another name and challenges him with the statement, "I can beat you any day."	Jim says, "Not today," in response.
Teacher moves close to John.	John stops teasing Jim.	Teacher praises John for controlling his temper.

Cognition and Behavior Change

Our third and final explanation of maintaining classroom control differs distinctly from that in Kounin's work, which focused on teachers' behaviors, and from behavior modification, which focuses on the careful application of the principles and procedures of behavior change. Here the search concentrates more on the cognitive than on overt behavior. The classic works of Dreikurs and his associates (1971) and of Redl and Wattenberg (1959) are good examples of this kind of analysis.

Social Discipline and Goal Seeking

Goal seeking, a frequent theme in the motivational literature, is especially important for teachers, since a student seeking a positive goal is a joy in the classroom. Dreikurs and his colleagues (1971) raised several provocative issues about discipline, and their discussion of goals is especially pertinent here. Their basic premise is that behavior is purposive and that correcting goals is possible, while correcting deficiencies is a fantasy. They believe that the force behind every human action is its goal and that all our actions are efforts to find a place for ourselves. Students are not driven through life; they seek their own goals.

The following assumptions are associated with Dreikurs' **social discipline** model:

- Students are social beings and desire to belong to social groups.
- Students are decision makers.
- All behavior is purposeful and directed toward social goals.
- Students see reality as they perceive it to be.
- A student is a whole being who cannot be understood by isolated characteristics.
- A student's misbehavior results from faulty reasoning on how to achieve social recognition (Wolfgang & Glickman, 1986, p. 190).

social discipline *A theory of classroom management based on the conviction that misbehavior can be eliminated by changing a student's goals.*

Once students establish goals, their behavior manifests a certain consistency and stability that is threatened by crises and frustrations. All youngsters want attention; when they do not receive it through socially acceptable means, they try anything to obtain it. Punishment is preferable to being ignored: it reinforces one's presence. Some children feel accepted only when they do what they want, and not what they are supposed to do.

Parents and teachers who engage in power struggles with children are eventually doomed to failure. Once power struggles begin, youngsters want to get even with those who punish them. They seek revenge, and the turmoil they create provides feelings of satisfaction. If students experience constant struggle and failure, they finally withdraw, desiring only to be left alone.

Discipline should not be considered an either-or proposition (either students obey instantly or they rule the classroom, causing chaos). Discipline does not mean control by punishment. The authors believe that self-discipline comes from freedom with responsibility, while only forced discipline comes from the use of force, power, and fear (Dreikurs et al., 1971).

The classroom atmosphere must be positive, accepting, and nonthreatening. Students need limits, however, and discipline means teaching them that certain rules exist that everyone must follow. Students and teachers should agree on the rules for classroom behavior; this increases students' appreciation of the necessity for rules, especially when they have cooperated in formulating them. Discussing rules on borrowing, using equipment, name calling, or classroom manners is excellent training in discipline. (You can find further information on Dreikurs' social discipline model in Wolfgang & Glickman, 1986.)

Good class management requires direct communication characterized by attention, a soft controlled voice, and specific feedback about the student's misbehavior.

Mutual Respect in the Classroom

Dreikurs and his colleagues believe that both teachers and students need inner freedom, which results from cooperating with each other, accepting responsibility for behavior, speaking truthfully, respecting each other, and agreeing on common behavioral rules. Here are some of their practical suggestions.

- *Do not nag or scold.* Frequently, this response gives students just the attention they want.
- *Do not ask a student to promise anything.* Children will agree to almost anything to extricate themselves from an uncomfortable situation. You just waste your time.

Focus ← Glasser's Control Theory

The work of William Glasser (1986) has attracted considerable attention. Advocating a similar perspective to that of Redl and Wattenberg—searching for the causes of misbehavior—Glasser argues that under the best of conditions, teaching is a hard job, but when students make no effort to learn, it becomes an impossible task.

Glasser's beliefs, which he calls **control theory,** attempt to explain how our behavior is always our best attempt to satisfy powerful forces at work within us. If nothing outside us, including school, can ever fulfill our needs, a good school could be defined as a place where almost all students believe that if they do some work, they will be able to satisfy their needs enough so that it makes sense to keep working (Glasser, 1986, p. 15).

The following basic assumptions, which are derived from Glasser's Reality Therapy, help to explain his views on discipline:

- Relevance, responsibility, and reality are necessary for schools without failure.
- A student is rational and capable of responsibility.
- Students must meet their own needs in a way that does not infringe on the rights of others.
- Each student has two basic needs, a need for love and a need for self-worth.
- Misbehavior results when these two basic needs are not met.
- Students must make their own behavior logical and productive and behave in a responsible manner (Wolfgang & Glickman, 1986).

Arguing that we attempt to satisfy five basic needs—to survive and reproduce, to belong and love, to gain power, to be free, to have fun—Glasser believes that we (and our students) always choose to do what is most satisfying to us at the time. Immediately after birth we begin to learn what satisfies our needs and then form pictures of what produces need satisfaction. Glasser then states that the pictures in students' heads determine what they do in school.

None of us satisfies our needs directly; rather we behave to satisfy the "pictures in our heads," as Glasser says. *When we act it is always our best effort to gain effective control of our lives.* Glasser believes that students have a much greater opportunity to satisfy the pictures in their heads during

William Glasser, M.D., President, Institute for Reality Therapy, Los Angeles.

Photograph courtesy of the Institute for Reality Therapy.

school time if they are taught by a *learning-team* model. The team concept can be a powerful motivator because:

- students gain a sense of belonging by working together in learning teams of two to five students.
- a sense of belongingness provides the initial impetus to work, and successful students become excellent role models.
- stronger students find need-fulfillment in helping weaker peers; power and friendship become a united force.
- weaker students find need fulfillment by contributing as much as possible.
- students learn to work together and apart from the teacher, giving a sense of power and freedom.
- learning teams offer meaningful structure.

Notice that each of these statements refers to satisfaction of the pictures that fulfill needs and to an ever-increasing degree of control. Glasser's work is thoughtful and could furnish you with practical techniques for improving classroom control.

---

control theory *A theory suggesting that behavior is always the attempt to satisfy powerful forces at work within.*

- *Do not reward good behavior.* The child may work only for the reward and stop immediately. Also, children come to expect something whenever they behave correctly. (Note how this differs from behavior modification techniques.)
- *Avoid double standards.* What is right for the student (politeness, punctuality) is right for the teacher. (Here, Dreikurs' work approximates the modeling of social learning theory.)
- *Avoid threats and intimidation.* Students cannot learn or acquire self-discipline in a tense, hostile environment.
- *Try to understand the purpose of misbehavior.* Why do students clown during arithmetic? Is it to get attention, or to demonstrate to peers that they are powerful by daring to defy adult pressure?

"I'm your teacher, Mrs. Gridley. Learn to read, write, and do arithmetic, and nobody will get hurt."

- *Establish a relationship based on trust and mutual respect.* If you treat your students as "nearly equal," they soon will respect you and believe that you truly want to help them. Thus, they often will discuss their problems with you, and thus help you devise ways to correct them.
- *Emphasize the positive.* Refuse to take misbehavior personally, to avoid causing a ripple effect to permeate the classroom. Try to make your behavior kind but firm.

These techniques of control reflect the theme of teacher-student cooperation that has been a continuous theme throughout our work. What happens between a teacher and student constitutes a relationship, one that must be positive if teaching and learning are to attain desired objectives.

Packaged Discipline Programs

Some school districts have adopted "packaged discipline programs" which are designed to give teachers and administrators comprehensive procedures for managing student behavior and addressing various discipline issues. Teachers are always looking for discipline programs that can be used in their classrooms. Yet, selection of a program is not straightforward, and requires consideration of a number of important issues. Chard, Smith, and Sugai (1992) reviewed package discipline programs to provide a consumers' guide for selection of such programs. During their review, they found eight programs, but had to exclude three from the list. Glasser's programs *Schools Without Failure* and *Control Theory in the Classroom* were excluded, because Glasser's program is based on theoretical considerations rather than specific strategies. Algozzine's program *Behavior Management* is based on topic modules; because it was not considered an integrated program, it also was excluded.

The authors reviewed the discipline programs within the context of the five general categories that appear in figure 13.2: they include foundation, features, implementation, staff and school development, and resources. The presence of the critical features in each of the five programs that were reviewed is summarized in figure 13.3.

Some interesting trends emerged in the analysis of the five discipline programs. First of all, most programs embraced a behavioral perspective, although in some cases

Figure 13.2

Discipline Program Analysis Form.

From D. Chard, S. Smith, and G. Sugai, "Packaged Discipline Programs: A Consumer's Guide" in J. Marr and G. Tindal, (eds.), The Oregon Conference Monograph, *19-26, 1992. Copyright © 1992 University of Oregon, Eugene OR.*

Discipline Program Analysis Form

Foundation

Y N 1. Description of theoretical foundation stated?

2. Program's technical adequacy available to validate:

Y N   a. problem diagnosis?
Y N   b. treatment?
Y N   c. generalization?
Y N   d. maintenance?

3. Social validity indicated for the program:

Y N   a. in schools (i.e., teachers, administrators)?
Y N   b. in communities (i.e., parents, public agencies)?
Y N   c. among students?

Features

Y N 1. Description of program's goals, outcomes, and focus?

2. Systematic approach to management at the:

Y N   a. school level?
Y N   b. classroom level?
Y N   c. individual student level?

3. Definition of participants' roles for:

Y N   a. teachers?
Y N   b. students?
Y N   c. parents?
Y N   d. administrators?
Y N   e. outside agencies (i.e., public officials, police)?

Y N 4. Program's limitations of the behavior types that the program can effect described?

Implementation

Y N 1. Description of the environmental (i.e., physical context, setting) prescriptions stated?

2. Effective instructional strategies for expected behavior explicitly addressed for:

Y N   a. preskill assessment?
Y N   b. effective teaching strategies?
Y N   c. error correction procedures?
Y N   d. adequate skill practice?
Y N   e. generalization strategies?

Y N 3. Consequences strategies for inappropriate behaviors stated?

Y N 4. Description of summative and formative monitoring procedures stated?

Staff and school development

Y N 1. Description of staff development model stated?

Y N 2. Empirical support for the model given?

Y N 3. Identification of the person to implement the training stated?

Y N 4. Description of the personnel and resources required for training stated?

Y N 5. Description of the orientation and training of students, parents, and community stated?

Resources

Y N 1. Description of the amount of time required for implementation stated?

Y N 2. Description of the material resources to be provided by the school district stated?

Y N 3. Description of the required support personnel for implementation of the program stated?

this was not made explicit in the materials. More important, none of the five programs included any data regarding the program integrity or its effectiveness. As in many traditional discipline approaches, the authors of these programs also did not emphasize environmental or instructional prescriptions. With the exception of *The Solution Book,* generally, the programs did not include orientation and procedural guidelines for training individuals in the discipline systems. A more crucial omission was that none of the programs provided specific guidelines for how the program would be implemented and maintained in a schoolwide system of discipline. Where can a teacher obtain this kind of guidance? Perhaps the best option would be to talk to other school professionals who may have experience in establishing such programs. These individuals include school psychologists, school counselors, and sometimes special education program administrators or directors.

Critical features \ Programs	Assertive discipline	Cooperative discipline	Positive discipline	Discipline with dignity	The solution book
Description of theoretical foundation	Present	Present	Present	Not present	Not present
Technical adequacy	Not present	Not present	Not present	Not present	Not present
Social validity	Present	Present	Partially present	Partially present	Not present
Description of program goals, outcomes, and focus	Present	Present	Present	Present	Present
Systematic approach to classroom management	Present	Present	Partially present	Present	Present
Systematic approach to schoolwide discipline	Not present	Not present	Not present	Present	Present
Systematic approach to dealing with individual children	Present	Present	Partially present	Present	Present
Definition of participant's roles	Partially present	Partially present	Partially present	Present	Present
Program's limitations	Not present	Not present	Not present	Present	Present
Clear description of environmental prescriptions	Not present	Partially present	Partially present	Not present	Present
Effective instructional strategies for expected behaviors	Not present	Partially present	Not present	Partially present	Present
Consequence strategy for inappropriate behaviors	Present	Present	Present	Present	Present
Models and strategies for staff development	Partially present	Partially present	Partially present	Partially present	Partially present
Orientation for students, parents, and community	Not present	Partially present	Partially present	Not present	Partially present
Description of necessary resources	Not present	Not present	Not present	Not present	Not present

Legend: ● Present   ● Partially present   ○ Not present

Figure 13.3

Summary of results from the review of five discipline programs using the Discipline Program Analysis Form.

From D. Chard, S. Smith, and G. Sugai, "Packaged Discipline Programs: A Consumer's Guide" in J. Marr and G. Tindal, (eds.), The Oregon Conference Monograph, *19-26, 1992. Copyright © 1992 University of Oregon, Eugene OR.*

DON'T CAUSE ANY PROBLEMS YOURSELF

Your first task in establishing a desirable classroom atmosphere is not to cause any problems yourself. Your initial reaction undoubtedly will be to place all responsibility for discipline problems on students, but closer inspection may suggest that some responsibility falls "on the infallible side of the desk." Though experience may eliminate many of the self-generated problems, to be aware of them early is to minimize their repercussions. How would you honestly answer the following seven questions?

- *Are you unfair?* Students probably react more intensely to this issue than to any other. You must treat all students equally, a task that may be difficult, because some students will seem to provoke you deliberately. But if you punish one student for disrespect, then you must punish all for disrespect. If you equivocate, a student's attitude toward you will quickly degenerate into personal resentment, with serious consequences.

- *Are you inconsistent?* You must react to similar conditions in a similar manner. If you scold or punish students for talking one day, then ignore this behavior the next, you are inconsistent. If you expect students to do papers or reports carefully in October and November, and then ignore these standards in January and February, you are inconsistent. Students are bewildered; they do not know how to act. Their behavior and work soon become erratic, and these conditions encourage trouble.

- *Are you boring?* This is a blunt question that deserves a frank answer. If you maintain the same pace and procedure every day, students eventually will search for excitement. Break your routine: use games, stories, the playground, audiovisual techniques, discussions, lectures, group work, guests, and any relevant source or technique that will make your classroom exciting and inviting.

- *Have you established routine?* You cannot break routine unless you have established it. Make no mistake; routine is one of your best safeguards against discipline problems. Students must know what they are to do, when they are to do it, and where they are to do it. If you betray uncertainty about school rules, classroom procedures, location of materials, the meaning of bells, the function of machinery, or any aspect of daily planning, you only invite trouble. Master routine; when you break it, your students will perceive the change as a real treat.

- *Do you know your subject?* Woe to the teacher who consistently cannot answer questions, who demonstrates a lesson only to arrive at the wrong answer. Students quickly sense incompetence and lose respect.

- *Can you control your temper?* A common mistake is to interpret all challenges personally. Some problems are personal attacks, but these are usually infrequent; most arise from the daily give-and-take of the classroom. If you respond spitefully, you provoke a sharp personal confrontation. Although it is difficult not to see misbehavior as a personal challenge, work at this; eventually an objective perspective will serve you well.

- *Have you considered how you should best respond?* If you require considerable personal control over the class, your disciplinary methods should focus on students' behavior, either rewarding, ignoring, or punishing it. If you are less concerned about control, you probably are more interested in a search for the causes of problems, in an understanding of the behavior. Adapt your techniques to your personality and beliefs; do what you do best.

If you are still concerned about classroom control and want to be certain that you are not responsible for any upsets, try the following exercise. First, identify a classroom problem. Next, evaluate your answers to the seven questions on the previous page to discover if you were the cause. If you honestly and objectively conclude that there was trouble, but that you did not cause it, then search elsewhere. What were you teaching? How were you doing it? What was the time of day? The problem could be a lack of specific control techniques, one or two particularly disruptive students, a topic that didn't interest students, or a restless class at a particular time of the day. Even if you're tired and unhappy after a class, try this exercise, being ruthlessly honest with yourself. You may want to do it for a full week, thus capturing all times and all classes.

Class	On-task Engaged	On-task Not Engaged	Off-task Distracted	Off-task Disruptive
One (Arithmetic)				
Two (Reading)				
Three (Social Science)				
Four (Art)				
Five (Music)				

After checking your students' behavior for each class, assess how much you contributed to that behavior.

Your behavior	Yes	No
Showed fairness		
Was interesting		
Had knowledge		
Controlled temper		
Required appropriate responses		
Established routine		

List your classes (1–5 for secondary school subjects, subject name for elementary). Check the box that best describes students' behavior during each class. Now, focus on the class that you are concerned about. Use the second checklist to analyze your behavior objectively. You can use this technique for both classes and individual students.

Now return to table 13.3 and reexamine the problem types discussed there. As a result of your reading, would you now handle any of these problems differently? Compare your answers now to those you gave when you first read about the problems.

Teacher-Parent Collaboration

Virtually all of the management strategies that we have introduced in this chapter involve what you as a teacher can do in the school setting. But students also spend a considerable amount of time at home and in the greater community. Parents still greatly influence students, and some parents have major roles in establishing effective management programs in the classroom. In fact, there is a considerable amount of research to support the successful outcomes that occur with students when parents are involved in academic and behavioral programs (Christenson & Conoley, 1992; Kramer, 1990).

What are some examples of the way that parents can be involved? One illustration of how parent involvement can make a difference is a project by Sheridan,

Kratochwill, and Elliott (1990). In the study, two forms of consultation with teachers for the purpose of establishing intervention programs for students demonstrating social withdrawal were implemented. In one form of consultation, the teacher and psychologist developed a program to improve social interaction skills in the school only. In the second form of consultation, the teacher met with the psychologist and the parent. The parent established the same program in the home setting as the teacher did in the classroom. What do you think the outcome of this study was? Results indicated that the students who received the teacher-only services improved only in the classroom. Students who received the services of both the teacher and the parent improved in both the home and the school. Also, the changes in the students in both home and school settings were maintained better in the dual teacher-and-parent program. Thus, there were direct benefits to the students in the intervention when it was implemented by the teacher, but the program had greater impact when both teacher and parent were involved.

Similar programs have been established by teachers who make contact with parents in the hopes of improving behavior in school. Many of these programs involve home-based reinforcement delivered by the parent (Kelley, 1990; Kelley & Carper, 1988) or a combination of a home note system with back-up contingencies administered by the parent. Figure 13.4 provides an example of a home note for use with adolescents and older students. Such a note system is designed to be used by the teacher to monitor certain classroom behaviors and to communicate the information to the parents. Parents are responsible for establishing and delivering the consequences.

Here are several guidelines for implementing a school-home note system that will be useful to you.

• Plan a parent-teacher conference to communicate your concerns, agree on the nature of the problem, and secure the commitment of the parent.
• Define the problem behaviors that both you and the parent agree need to be changed, being as specific as possible.
• Set small goals to change the problem behavior.
• Design the school-home note (like the example in fig. 13.4).
• Establish responsibilities for you, the parent(s) and the student. The parent will complete the note, and it is the responsibility of the student to return the note to you.
• Collect baseline information to determine the nature of the problem.
• Establish the reward system and how consequences will be delivered.
• Implement the program with the stipulated consequences.
• Fade out the note system as the student's behavior improves.

Kelley and Carper (1988) suggested that cooperation is the key to success in any program when school-home notes are used. It is important for teachers to communicate with parents and urge them to assist with their child, since parents can be extremely helpful in a comprehensive classroom management program.

You Are Not Alone

In thinking about the task of managing your classroom, don't feel overwhelmed. In this chapter we have presented new information that can have a bearing on effective classroom management. You will need time, however, to think about the issues in classroom management, and you will need experience in putting the various techniques into practice. Here are some practices that will make the task of classroom management easier.

• Read more about classroom management techniques.
• Take courses that focus on classroom management techniques. Typically, courses in classroom management are offered in schools of education through the departments of educational psychology or special education.

School–Home Note

Name _____   Date _____

CLASS _____   Assignment:

    Completed Classwork   Yes   So-So   No   NA
    Obeyed Classroom Rules   Yes   So-So   No   NA
    Handed in Homework   Yes   So-So   No   NA

Comments: Initials _____
_____

CLASS _____   Assignment:

    Completed Classwork   Yes   So-So   No   NA
    Obeyed Classroom Rules   Yes   So-So   No   NA
    Handed in Homework   Yes   So-So   No   NA

Comments: Initials _____
_____

CLASS _____   Assignment:

    Completed Classwork   Yes   So-So   No   NA
    Obeyed Classroom Rules   Yes   So-So   No   NA
    Handed in Homework   Yes   So-So   No   NA

Comments: Initials _____
_____

CLASS _____   Assignment:

    Completed Classwork   Yes   So-So   No   NA
    Obeyed Classroom Rules   Yes   So-So   No   NA
    Handed in Homework   Yes   So-So   No   NA

Comments: Initials _____
_____

Parent Comments:
_____

Figure 13.4
To improve school-home relations and to keep parents informed of progress, many schools have adopted home notes as a means of communication.

- Use your time in practice teaching to sharpen your classroom management skills. Seek out effective teachers and visit their classrooms to observe skillful classroom management in action.
- Participate in pre-service and in-service experiences that focus on developing successful classroom management skills.
- Discuss a student's problem with the parents when possible. Sometimes the parents can provide insights into the problem and may be able to assist in a discipline program (as noted previously).
- Consult other professionals who will be able to offer you advice on solving specific discipline problems and suggest ways to improve your classroom management tactics. Individuals in the school who may be able to assist you include lead teachers, special education resource teachers, school psychologists, and counselors.

teacher – student

Maintaining Order in the Classroom

1. Be alert to what your students are doing in the classroom.
   - Watch your students carefully during class, and when you sense their attention is wandering, pose unexpected questions, stop and have students question each other, or suddenly become quiet to regain their attention.
   - Involve the group: "Who'll get this first?" Look at one student, then another, and then another, creating the impression that you expect them all to be first.
   - When you detect student restlessness or fading attention, act immediately; stare at the student; use the student's name. Build a repertoire of these mild behavioral countermeasures to prevent, if possible, serious misbehavior.
   - Make this repertoire a sequence of responses that ranges from less to more serious: standing next to the student, staring at the student, calling attention to the behavior by using the student's name, reprimanding more sharply, talking to the student after school, holding a conference with the parents (perhaps including the principal), making a referral, and finally, recommending formal school action.
   - Know your students well enough so that you can detect something outside the class that may be influencing a student's behavior in class. This strategy could include family financial problems, family illness, or a pending parental divorce. By talking to such students, you may be able to help them adjust to the stress and to prevent any emotional spillover to the classroom.
2. Certain teacher behaviors lead to a smoothly running classroom.
   - Communicate with the entire class even while you are working with one student; use body language, facial expressions, and verbal statements and questions.
   - Be sensitive to your students' span of interest and when it's lost, shift to another medium (hold a discussion, watch a filmstrip, listen to a tape recording), or another activity ("OK, stand up and let's stretch"), or another subject.
   - Don't overdwell; sometimes teachers are so concerned about learning that they continue to the point of boredom; watch for the signs.
   - Act immediately when you detect the first signs of misbehavior, no matter how small; be sure that your reaction is appropriate for the seriousness of the misbehavior.
   - Make sure that your behavior is consistent with what you expect from your students; in this respect you are a constant model: speech, dress, clarity, courtesy, promptness.
   - Don't be afraid to use humor; when appropriate, it can be an effective change of pace in the classroom. Be careful, however; don't let it become sarcastic, don't let any one student become the butt of jokes, and don't overdo it.
3. Use those control techniques that are best suited for you and a particular class.
   - Be natural; keep your voice and body movements as relaxed as possible. In this way, you can create a positive learning environment. Occasionally teachers, by the shrillness of their voices and tense, rapid movements, can overstimulate a class.
   - Use as much positive reinforcement as possible; identify desirable student behavior and respond to it immediately. If you "get along" with your students, most of them will want to receive similar recognition from you.
   - At times it may be difficult not to take misbehavior personally, but make every effort to understand why students respond as they do. Sometimes students can misinterpret your behavior and can't understand why they are punished.
   - Try to help your students to develop inner controls. After students have misbehaved and you have reacted, talk to them to discover why the misbehavior occurred. Do they know why they acted as they did? Were they angry for some reason? Did some classmates urge them on? Help them to recognize the signs of trouble and suggest ways of avoiding it: remind them that they can always talk to you if something is bothering them; if you know your students well, you can use those that they admire as models for handling difficult situations.
   - Rules, control measures, and appropriate disciplinary techniques all add up to good classroom management and a minimum of problems.

APPLICATIONS AND REFLECTIONS

Chapter Highlights

Management Concerns in the Classroom

- Your students' learning depends on the orderly routine that you establish in the classroom. Remember that "orderly" does not imply an atmosphere of quiet terror. It means an atmosphere in which all students (and teachers) know exactly what is expected of them.
- Organizing your classroom in a way that satisfies you and that your students understand is the first step in providing effective teaching and learning.
- John Carroll's ideas on the use of time have had a significant impact on the way that teachers structure their classrooms. His basic thesis is that students will learn to the extent that time (that is, time on task) is available for learning.
- The developmental characteristics of your students affect the management techniques you use and influence your decision about the age group you would like to teach.

Life in the Classroom

- Students' attitudes toward school seem to be a mixture of happiness and unhappiness. The causes of these mixed feelings seem to be rooted in the conditions of the individual classrooms, that is, how you manage your work.
- Student engagement, that is, what students are doing at any time, is related to your activity. Student engagement seems to be highest when teachers lead small groups and lowest during student presentations.
- Teachers in "higher-achieving schools" spend more time in actual teaching and in academic interactions with their students than do teachers in "lower-achieving schools."
- As you decide how to organize your classroom, what to teach, and how to teach it, remember that you must adapt your techniques—both instructional and organizational—to the needs of your students.

Managing the Classroom

- The rules you establish for organizing your classroom are critical, since they establish the conduct that you think is important. Unless your students' behavior conforms to these rules, learning will be negatively affected.
- Good managers make their rules known on the first day of class and combine the teaching of the rules with a demonstration of the signals they would use for various activities.
- Good managers use as few initial rules as possible and then introduce others as needed. They also occasionally remind their students of these rules and act immediately when they see rule violations. Such action usually prevents minor difficulties from becoming major problems.
- By understanding the developmental characteristics of the students you are teaching, you can anticipate many of the sources of potential problems and formulate rules that will help you to prevent them.

Methods of Control

- You and you alone can determine what is misbehavior, since individual differences apply to teachers as well as students. What one teacher may judge to be misbehavior, another may ignore.
- Among teacher behaviors that contribute to the successful management of their classrooms are withitness, overlapping, transition smoothness, and group alertness.
- Behavior modification, as a means of classroom control, relies on changing the classroom environment and the manner in which students interact with the environment to influence students' behavior.
- Understanding the causes of a student's misbehavior requires that teachers realize that their students' behavior has a purpose. Consequently, if teachers can identify the goal that a particular behavior is intended to achieve, they can correct problem behavior.
- Most teachers are eclectic in the manner in which they manage their classes, selecting and choosing from all of the techniques discussed in this chapter as the need arises.

Connections

1. Think about how you learn and describe how one of the major concepts discussed in this chapter is part of your learning activities or approach.

_____

_____

_____

_____

_____

2. Identify at least one learning situation (e.g., classroom instruction, self-study, taking a test, small-group work) and describe how you would apply one of the key concepts examined in this chapter _if you were a teacher_.

_____

_____

_____

_____

_____

_____

Getting the Picture and Drawing Relationships

Think about the various learning concepts and variables discussed in this chapter. Create pictures, graphics, or figures that highlight relationships among the key components.

Personal Journal

What I really learned in this chapter was _____

_____

_____

_____

_____

_____

What this means to me is _____

_____

_____

_____

_____

_____

Questions that were stimulated by this chapter include _____

_____

_____

_____

_____

_____

Key Terms

aversive control	459	engaged time	435	QAIT	443
behavior influence	458	group alertness	455	ripple effect	454
behavior modification	458	overcorrection	459	shaping	459
behavior therapy	458	overlapping	454	social discipline	462
contingency contracting	459	positive reinforcement	458	token economy	459
control theory	463	proactive classroom		transition smoothness	455
desists	454	management	434	withitness	454

Marty Bandan looked around the display room at the technology conference. She was amazed at the variety of things available. This was her third year teaching the fifth grade. Her teacher training program had included information on technology in education, but vast changes had taken place in the brief time since she had left school. She walked up to one of the presenters and said, "I know a little about laser videodiscs; how could I use that knowledge to enhance my fifth-graders' science lessons?"

"In lots of ways," the presenter said. She showed Marty the machine and how it worked, then said, "This particular videodisc series was carefully designed to help students learn about

students spontaneously bring up relevant and interesting additional principles, and you as the teacher can encourage and guide this process. As far as grading goes, you can certainly assess the content and principles learned with traditional assessments. But many teachers and experts are working toward developing newer kinds of assessments when using teaching tools like this. Students are learning different kinds of things and tests should reflect that. For example, if students are learning to solve complex, realistic problems, then assessments might be made up of having them solve such problems and observing progress in how they approach the problems and the strategies they use."

chapter 14

teaching and technology

science as well as about several mathematical principles. We feel it's important for students to encounter and learn to solve larger-scope, more complex and realistic problems, so the issues presented on this videodisc are made up of numerous smaller problems. To solve them, students need to notice and use the relevant information from the videodisc. In the research we've done, students quite often go beyond the information presented in the video to search for other resources as well. This helps them learn how to seek out and find information in many different sources. So students are learning not only the content of mathematics and science, but also how to seek out information and solve complex problems, skills that the experts in education and psychology feel should get much more emphasis in our students' educations."

"That sounds interesting. I'm sure my students would be interested and have fun with it. I would too! But how will I know if we've covered the material we're supposed to cover in a given unit, and how will I grade students if I use a system like this?" Marty replied.

"Good questions!" The presenter smiled. "You've hit on two of the biggest issues. This system targets several specific scientific and mathematical principles, so of course you can be sure that these particular ones are covered. Others can be incorporated, though, by doing follow-up questioning and having students develop projects based on the series. Often

Marty nodded her head. "Yes, I think the ways of assessing students' knowledge will have to change. Now, what can you tell me about the equipment needed to use this system and how much it costs? And do you have any information with suggestions about how to set this up in a classroom? My students work in groups quite often—would a set-up like that work with this series?"

Marty and the presenter talked a little while longer, then she went on to other exhibits. She was amazed at the variety of technological innovations at the conference and the ways in which they were being used in classrooms. Several exhibits showed the use of CD-ROMs in different content areas and exemplified how they could be used to individualize instruction. Others explained networking and its advantages for teaching, connecting learners across districts or across the world. One exhibit even demonstrated a "virtual reality" system in which Marty could "browse" through the Library of Congress even "selecting" and reading a document on the Declaration of Independence, and then another on the space shuttle!

When Marty left the conference, she was very excited about all the possibilities she had seen, but she was also a bit overwhelmed. "Where would I even start to learn about all these things?" she wondered. "And how do I know which types of technology will be most beneficial for my students? The cost is sure to be a factor

**What Is Educational
Technology? 478**
Questions to Answer When
    Considering Technology 478

**A Brief History of Technology in
Education 480**

**How Is Technology Currently
Used in Classrooms? 481**
Quantitative Aspects 481
Qualitative Aspects 484
Why Don't More Teachers Use
    Technology? 485

**Students' Perceptions of
Technology in the
Classroom 488**
Attitude Surveys 488
Novelty Effects? 488
Gender Differences in
    Attitudes 489

**Types and Uses of Technology in
Education 489**
Administrative and Managerial
    Uses 491
Audiovisual Aids for
    Instruction 491
Teaching of the Technology 493
Computer-Assisted
    Instruction 494
Using Technology to Teach
    Thinking 498
Intelligent Tutoring Systems 501
Multimedia Uses 503
Recent Developments in
    Educational Technology 506

Issues in Technology Use 509
Access 509
Security 509
Role of the Teacher 510
Selection of Hardware and
    Software 511
Classroom Set-Up of
    Technology 511
Effect of Computers on Social
    Interactions 512
Consideration of Individual
    Differences 512

**Applications and
Reflections 513**

too, though the district has said it's committed to increasing our use of educational technology. I think I'll talk to some of the other teachers in my building about what they know and have used. We could talk to Larissa's mom, too—she works with a lot of technology at the university and may be interested in doing an in-service with us to overview some of these ideas."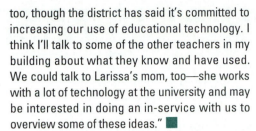

As Marty found, there are many ways that technology can be used in classrooms. Many teachers, particularly those whose teacher training didn't include much information on technology, find themselves overwhelmed when trying to incorporate new technological advances into their teaching. From simple items like the overhead projector and television to complex computerized intelligent tutoring systems, teachers have a tremendous array from which to choose. But how should you go about selecting the type of technology to include in your teaching? How do you select computer programs that will enhance, rather than detract from, your instruction? The first step is to become familiar with the types of technology available and the purposes to which they can be put. This chapter will help you get started.

When you finish this chapter, you should be able to

- define "educational technology"

- give a brief description of the history of educational technology, identifying changes in the underlying theories of learning and teaching which have influenced the form and uses of the technology
- describe how technology is currently used in classrooms
- discuss several reasons why technology is not used as widely as it could be, and offer suggestions for how this situation could be changed
- summarize how students feel about technology use in the classroom
- define, provide an example of, summarize the effects of, and discuss the pros and cons of each of the categories of technology usage, including identification of the major theory of learning and instruction underlying each category
- summarize the major issues in technology use and offer suggestions as to how you would deal with these issues in your classroom
- discuss your opinion as to the best use(s) of technology in teaching, how you as a classroom teacher will or will not make use of technology, and your reasons for the latter
- identify ways to utilize the maximum potential of each category of technology

WHAT IS EDUCATIONAL TECHNOLOGY?

The term **educational technology** refers to technology applied to the teaching and learning processes. This includes not only the particular media used to deliver instruction (televisions, computers, CD-ROMs, etc.), but also the processes involved in analyzing instructional problems and devising, implementing, evaluating, and managing solutions to those problems. The term is quite broad and can include many things that you may not have considered particularly technological. For example, the typical classroom has available and uses on a fairly regular basis an overhead projector. While clearly not *high*-tech, this simple machine can greatly improve your teaching simply by providing an easy way to present outlines, give examples, or keep a record of brainstorming ideas. Similarly, many classrooms in our country today have televisions permanently installed. Wisely used, television can be an impressive learning tool. Many of you probably had your first lessons in letters and numbers presented via such TV programs as *Sesame Street*. TV programs, educational films, and videos can certainly be useful for older students as well, presenting information on practically all topics.

While this chapter will discuss some of these "lower-tech" versions of technology, we will spend most of the time discussing newer types and uses of technology, all of which are computer-based. One reason is that more and more computers are becoming available in classrooms. Teachers often do not take full advantage of computers, however, often simply because they do not have access to newer software or because they have not been made aware of the vast array of possible uses. A second reason for focusing on the newer technologies is that if and when the "information superhighway" being discussed in technological and political circles is realized, teachers and schools must be ready to take advantage of its tremendous potential for affecting instruction. The video accompanying this text shows an example of how classrooms can be networked via computers with one another, with other schools, and with databases and experts worldwide. This is one example of how technology can have a tremendous impact on your instruction. It is a vastly different way of teaching, based on fairly recent cognitive and problem-solving theories of learning, and it is one you should be ready to take advantage of.

Questions to Answer When Considering Technology

The first question you must answer is whether to use technology at all in your classroom. Overall, the research available at this point gives us a resounding "yes," and points to several advantages. First, the technologies available can help you manage your instruction by assisting you in record keeping, grade tracking, lesson planning, and determining whether individual students have met their instructional goals. Of course, teachers have been doing these tasks without technology for decades, but technology offers improved ways of accomplishing these goals.

Second, technology allows some activities that simply would not be possible otherwise. For example, Stewart and colleagues (1992) developed a computerized genetics simulation program that involves high school students in thinking about genetics and science as the construction, revision, and use of explanatory models. Labs on humans, fruit flies, and other organisms allow students to do specified crosses given certain genetic characteristics and principles (e.g., simple dominance, codominance, gene interaction, etc.) and to observe patterns of phenotypes across generations. The software is an important part of this instructional program, allowing the student to perform crosses and see the resulting offspring for several generations immediately, without waiting for those fruit flies to hatch (or the babies to be born!). This compression of time helps students understand the underlying principles of genetics as well as notions about the probability of certain events' occurrence in both the near and the more distant future.

How has technology been used in your educational experience? Analyze the pros and cons of the ways it has been used. After reading this chapter, come back to this question and see if you can think of ways that your experiences with technology could have been even more positive and productive.

educational technology
Technology applied to the teaching and learning processes. Includes the particular media used to deliver instruction, as well as the processes involved in analyzing instructional problems and devising, implementing, evaluating, and managing solutions to those problems.

Focus ◄ A Computer Glossary

You may find it helpful to pause here and consider some of the more common terms associated with computer usage.

ASCII—American Standard Code for Information Interchange, a code whereby numbers are used to represent letters and symbols.

Bit—Acronym for binary digit, the smallest unit of information used by the computer (either 0 or 1).

Byte—The number of bits required to store one character, usually, eight bits.

Cathode Ray Tube (CRT)—The monitor.

Central Processing Unit (CPU)—The heart of the computer; controls operations.

Compact Disc-Read Only Memory (CD-ROM)—An optical disk technology that allows storage of very large amounts of any type of digital data, including text, digital sound and graphics, and digital movies.

Computer-Assisted Instruction (CAI)—Use of a computer to aid classroom instruction.

Computer-Managed Instruction (CMI)—Use of a computer to aid in classroom management—record keeping, for example.

Disk drive—A peripheral that stores information on disks, which you can then use or save; transmits information on disks to and from the computer.

Hardware—The collection of devices that constitute the computer system.

Internet—The international system that connects networks, allowing users of different networks to communicate with one another; a network of networks.

Laser videodisc—An optical disk containing digital movies.

Local Area Network (LAN)—An interconnected group of computers that share software, peripherals, etc. over a limited geographic area. Connections are made through direct cables or over telephone lines.

Microcomputer—Those computers whose CPUs are microprocessors.

Microprocessor—Silicon chip containing the computer's basic control functions.

Modem—A device enabling one to transmit computer signals over telephone lines.

Networking—Communication among two or more computers.

Peripherals—Devices that enable one to communicate with a computer (disk drive, printer, keyboard).

Printer—The output peripheral that enables you to put characters on paper.

Random Access Memory (RAM)—Information presented to or read from a computer; it is nonpermanent, and may be lost when the computer is shut off unless previously saved to tape or disk.

Read Only Memory (ROM)—Information, locked into a computer, that is stored permanently. It cannot be changed.

Software—Computer programs; those instructions that tell the computer to perform specific tasks.

Wide Area Network (WAN)—A computer network that spans a large geographic area. Connections are made through telephone lines.

The software also allows students to formulate and systematically test hypotheses about the genetic principles at work, contributing to their abilities to explain and predict patterns in the data, tasks which real geneticists engage in daily.

Third, technology can allow students to work on problems that, although possible, would not be feasible in the real world, either due to safety considerations or because the problems are rare occurrences. For example, one computerized avionics tutoring system, called Sherlock, presents students with problems similar to those they encounter when working on avionics equipment (Lesgold, Lajoie, Bunzo, & Eggan, 1992). The system allows students to engage in activities like taking measurements of voltage at various points in a high-voltage electrical system. If students, especially beginning ones, happened to measure incorrectly or at the wrong place, the results could be quite dangerous—but the system allows students to take such measurements and see the consequences without doing harm to themselves or equipment.

Fourth, newer forms of technology such as CD-ROMs and laser videodiscs offer students the advantage of not only reading and hearing about processes and changes, but actually seeing the dynamics of such changes. These technologies, unlike slides or videotapes, allow students to control precisely how quickly the changes progress, so that they can more carefully examine and understand the changes, their causes, and their results. Many cognitive psychologists argue that the combination of different sources of information (e.g., visual, auditory, dynamic movement), along with increased control over such changes, results in students' development of clearer and more correct "mental models" of the information being learned. Put another way, technology helps students reach a more detailed and more accurate understanding of what they are learning.

Finally, increasingly sophisticated technology allows students and teachers to use computer networks to communicate with others in their school or district, or across the country or world. Via networks, students can share their views on a wide range of issues, or even collaborate on academic projects, much as top-level experts do. Both teachers and students can also gain access to resources and expertise that otherwise would not be available (e.g., software packages, national databases, encyclopedias). Thus, educators can have high-speed access to up-to-date and accurate information about virtually any topic of interest.

The next questions to consider, after deciding to use technology in your teaching, are what kind of technology to use, and for what goals. The remainder of this chapter will help you in answering these questions. First, though, a brief overview of the history of technology in education is provided; we will briefly review the ways in which technology is currently being used in classrooms. Most of the chapter will focus on a categorization of different types of technology, the uses they have, and the research results indicating how well each type works. This categorization is useful, but is clearly not the only way to group the types. Finally, we will discuss some of the controversies surrounding the uses of technology in education. Where possible, we will provide research results to help you form your own opinions about these issues. In several cases, however, the best we can do is to help you clearly frame the issue, since research results are either unavailable or in conflict. Perhaps you will be the teachers/researchers to resolve these issues!

A BRIEF HISTORY OF TECHNOLOGY IN EDUCATION

Though it hasn't always used the same label, educational technology has quite a long history. The focus box on the history of educational technology gives a brief overview of the major theorists and events in the development of educational technology. As you will notice as you read it, many of the people who contributed to the development of educational technology are already familiar to you. E. L. Thorndike's emphasis on empirical investigation strongly influenced the way in which many aspects of educational technology were and still are developed and evaluated. B. F. Skinner developed and helped popularize one approach that provided an empirical basis for a science of education, programmed instruction. Other important contributors include Gagne (contributing the use of task analysis and hierarchical sequencing of skill instruction); Tyler (contributing information on how to develop clear, specific behavioral objectives that could form the basis of a programmed instructional system); and Bloom (contributing the idea that there are different levels of objectives which should be addressed in any system of instruction).

One point to note when reviewing the changes across the history of educational technology concerns the theoretical bases which govern the forms of technology developed and the ways in which the technology has been used. The forms and uses of educational technology have been heavily influenced by changes in theories of learning and teaching in the fields of psychology and educational psychology. Earlier developments in educational technology, particularly in the audiovisual devices view, were consistent with Piagetian cognitive theory (though they predated Piaget in some cases), in that they emphasized providing students with concrete examples. This audiovisual devices view proposed that learning proceeds best when it moves from the more concrete to the more abstract, and that utilizing concrete objects in instruction facilitates

Annual **Edition**

cognitive constructivism *A cognitive theory of learning and teaching that underlies much of the current work on technology in education. It holds that students actively construct their own knowledge, and that reality is determined by the experiences of the knower rather than existing as an objective truth distinct from the individual. The teacher is seen as a facilitator of knowledge and skill acquisition, and the learner takes on a high degree of responsibility for his or her own learning.*

the learning process. However, the predominant view in educational technology (as in most of psychology) came to be strongly behavioristic, and the emphasis for many years was on the development of programs that clearly defined and specified behavioral instructional objectives, and provided instruction and reinforcement for each step along the way to accomplishing the objectives.

In keeping with changes in the predominant theories of teaching and learning, more recent innovations in educational technology are almost exclusively based on cognitive theories. One particularly influential perspective has been that of **cognitive constructivism,** which holds that students actively construct their own knowledge, and that reality is determined by the experiences of the knower, rather than existing as an objective truth distinct from the individual (Jonassen, 1991). From this perspective, the teacher acts as a facilitator of knowledge and skill acquisition, as a guide or resource person whose role is to structure the learning environment to help each student come to an individual understanding of the information. Learning is very individualized and personalized for each student, taking into account each student's prior knowledge, interests, cognitive level, and skills. The teacher relinquishes some degree of control over what and how the students learn, since the most appropriate ways to explore information and develop understanding can differ substantially from one student to another. As a result, a teacher should not prepare a single lecture or set of learning exercises for an entire class, but must respond to each student's individual needs. The teacher is very often a fellow student, in that the teacher is exploring and learning along with the students, facing real problems and challenges for which even the teacher does not have a ready answer. Students play much more active and self-directive roles, taking on much of the responsibility for their own learning, and making choices as to how, if not what, they are learning. Many of the current uses of educational technology also incorporate cooperative learning groups, often with small groups of students working on large-scale, long-term projects of their own design. The cooperative learning aspect of current uses is consistent with both cognitive constructivism and Vygotsky's theory of cognitive development. As you will recall from chapter 4, Vygotsky stressed the role of other people in an individual's cognitive development. Clearly, present and earlier uses of educational technology and their underlying theoretical bases differ considerably.

HOW IS TECHNOLOGY CURRENTLY USED IN CLASSROOMS?

Computers can play a valuable role in the teaching-learning process. They increase the opportunities to respond, expand academic engaged time, provide specific feedback and reinforcement, and often involve students in projects of their own design—all of which are fundamental activities for effective teaching and effective learning.

The vast majority of the information available concerning current uses of technology deals exclusively with computers, thus making it difficult to determine how other, less sophisticated forms of technology are used (e.g., overheads, slide projectors, televisions). Most teachers have these simpler forms of technology readily available and seem to feel comfortable using them, though there is little information on exactly how these technologies are utilized. Several national surveys have estimated the availability and usage of computers in schools. Ely (1993) summed up the results of these surveys by concluding the "virtually every student, teacher, and administrator has computer access but beyond that one similarity, all other aspects are different" (p. 53).

Quantitative Aspects

Several surveys were done by the Center for Social Organization of Schools at Johns Hopkins University throughout the 1980s to track changes in computer usage (Becker, 1991). In 1983, few schools provided in-depth experience on computers for many of their students, primarily because they had large numbers of students and very few machines. Most schools had to severely limit the amount of time any individual student spent working with computers, with

Focus

A Brief History of Educational Technology

Rieser (1987) identified three views of educational technology and traced their development:

1. Audiovisual devices view. Focuses on the type of instructional medium employed (i.e., the equipment itself).
2. Systems approach process view. Focuses on a systematic way of designing, carrying out, and evaluating the total process of learning and teaching.
3. Individual differences view. Focuses on using technology to meet the individual needs of individual learners.

The following timeline gives you a sense of the history of each view and the people and events that influenced each.

Audiovisual devices view	Systems process view	Individual differences view
1600s–1800s Various theorists advocated use of concrete objects and a sensory component (vision; audition) to aid instruction, and moving from the concrete to the abstract in instruction.		Instruction very individualized until mid-1800s. Then graded schools became popular. Soon afterwards, however, educators began searching for ways to individualize instruction within the graded system.
Early 1900s School museums developed, giving educators access to AV aids and guidance as to how to incorporate them into their teaching.	E. L. Thorndike's emphasis on empirical investigation laid groundwork for the process of developing instructional systems.	
1940s Military training during World War II made extensive and successful use of AV aids. A variety of media types were developed and used for various training purposes.		*1940s, 1950s, 1960s, and early 1970s* A variety of programs to individualize instruction were developed and tested including • systems for grouping students within the larger graded school • mastery-based systems • Skinner's programmed instruction • the Keller Personal System of Instruction • Bloom's learning for mastery • Klausmeier's Individually Guided Education system
1950s Due to their success in military training, AV aids became popular in schools.	B. F. Skinner developed one method that used an empirical basis for a science of education, programmed instruction. Such instruction, offered on teaching machines, would allow students to learn "twice as much in half the time" as they would using conventional teaching methods.	
1960s The USSR's launching of Sputnik caused the U.S. government to drastically increase funding for educational media and technology development and dissemination. New media forms were developed (esp. educational uses of television), and information on uses of educational technology widely disseminated and encouraged.	The Sputnik launching led to increased government funding to develop and test educational systems (esp. in math and science). A "team of experts" approach was used, in which content, programming, psychology, and instructional experts collaborated to develop the systems. This approach is still commonly used in educational technology today.	

the result that most students learned more about the equipment and software available at that time than about academic content and skills. By 1992, however, 98 percent of the schools in the United States had computers of some sort available, with 30 percent of the schools surveyed having one computer for every 10 to 19 students (Ely, 1993). It seems, then, that one of the major problems faced in 1983, the lack of enough machines to go around, is being addressed by schools across the country.

Audiovisual devices view	Systems process view	Individual differences view
1960s (continued) The focus in educational technology shifted from the media forms used to the more complex systems involved in the development and successful use of the technology.	R. Gagne contributed the use of task analysis and hierarchical sequencing of skill instruction. R. Tyler contributed information on how to develop clear, specific behavioral objectives that could form the basis of a system. B. Bloom contributed the idea that there are different levels of objectives that should be addressed in any system of instruction.	
	1960s and 1970s A gradual shift in underlying theoretical orientation took place, with increasing emphasis on cognitive theories of learning and teaching and decreasing emphasis on behavioristic theory. Educational technology systems today are predominantly cognitively based.	*Early 1970s* Interest in these individualized systems was fading somewhat due to decreases in funding and administrative support and the perception by some that the systems were too cumbersome.
		Mid–late 1970s Developments in computer technology led to renewed interest in individualized systems, and computer-assisted instruction (CAI) systems were developed.
		Late 1970s Development of and widespread access to the microcomputer led to increased popularity of CAI systems.

1980s and 1990s
- Vast increases in access to computers and other forms of technology
- Vast increases in the power of the technology available
- Vast increases in the types of technology available (e.g., CD-ROM, laser videodiscs, digitalization of information allowing phone line transmission of data and networking, virtual reality)
- Changes in the underlying theories of teaching and learning, with increased emphasis on cognitive constructivism, cooperative learning, and project/design-oriented instruction
- Changes in the role of the teacher, from that of an expert imparting knowledge to that of a guide or facilitator of learning and collaborator
- Changes in the role of the student, to a participant who has greater control over own learning, more self-regulation, and more self-direction

It is also informative to know what kinds of computers schools have. It is probably not surprising that Apple II operating systems are the most common, accounting for about 77 percent of the computers at the elementary level (kindergarten through sixth grade) and 47 percent at the high school level (Becker, 1991). IBM-compatible MS-DOS machines were the next most common, accounting for 29 percent of the high school machines, but only 9 percent of the elementary school machines. It is important to note that the majority of these machines, especially the Apple IIs, have very limited power.

This makes it difficult for teachers to take advantage of some of the newer developments in educational research because such small machines simply do not have the memories and processing capacities to run the programs. The situation seems to be improving, but progress is slow.

Qualitative Aspects

What about how teachers currently use the technology that is available to them? Sheingold and Hadley (1990) asked 608 computer-using elementary and secondary teachers what software they used. The teachers reported the percentages shown in table 14.1. As the table clearly shows, text processing tools are by far the applications most commonly used by these teachers, while multimedia uses come in a distant last. There are a variety of instructional software packages used as well, with the most common being problem-solving programs, tutorial programs, and drill and practice programs.

Though the overall number of teachers using computers for instruction has doubled since 1985, there are substantial differences in their usage by elementary and secondary teachers. Many more elementary than secondary teachers reported using computers regularly in their instruction. Becker (1991) reported that most of the computer time of elementary school students was spent in academic subject areas, especially mathematics and reading/language arts activities. The emphasis, however, was still on drill and practice of computational skills in mathematics and of language mechanics and vocabulary, rather than on higher-level problem solving and application of knowledge. High-schoolers spent only 25 percent of their computer time on work in academic content areas. Instead, half of their computer time was spent learning "computer-specific skills": these students were being taught how to use software packages (e.g., word processing programs, database programs, etc.), keyboarding skills, and programming, and not how to use these tools to learn subject matter or to solve problems in any content area (Becker, 1991). So although both elementary and secondary students are spending more time working with computers than did students in earlier years, the kind of work they are doing is typically not geared toward developing higher-level problem-solving skills, or learning to use the computer and its software as tools to achieve such higher-level ends. This trend was expected to continue in the near future, with the computer coordinators surveyed saying they expected to see increases in the use of computers to teach students how to use word processing programs, databases, and spreadsheets, and how to practice basic skills. Few foresaw increases in teaching students how software packages might be used as "conceptual tools" to solve problems or improve quality and productivity in subject areas.

What can we conclude from all these statistics? First, many teachers do not use technology at all in their teaching. Even though schools have continued to make acquisition of machines a priority, teachers, especially at the secondary level, are not using them. Second, when computers are used consistently as part of instruction, they are utilized at the lowest level of their capacity.

Why is there such an emphasis on instructing students in how to use computers rather than having them use the machines as ways to learn content or as problem-solving aids? Although the surveys do not speculate about this, let us examine some possibilities. First, perhaps the basics simply must come first. Before a student can use a computer to solve a complex genetics problem or to write an insightful essay, that student needs to know how to type and how to input, manipulate, and store data. This is certainly reasonable. To stop at this point, however, is to miss the major educational

Table 14.1

Software Used by Computer-Using Teachers	
Software type	**Use (percentage of teachers)**
Text processing tools	95
Instruction software	89
Problem-solving programs	75
Tutorial programs	73
Drill and practice programs	72
Software accompanying textbooks	37
Conceptual tools	30
Analytic and information tools	87
Programming and operating systems	84
Games and simulations	81
Graphics and operating tools	81
Communications programs	49
Multimedia uses	25

Data from K. Sheingold and M. Hadley (1990), *Accomplished Teachers: Integrating Computers into Classroom Practice*. New York: Center for Technology in Education, Bank Street College of Education. Table in Ely, D. P. (1993), Computers in Schools and Universities in the United States of America, *Educational Technology, 33,* 53–57.

advantage of technology: fostering students' learning and understanding, improving the quality of their thinking and their products. Second, it is undoubtedly easier to teach the basics and mechanics. Teaching students to engage in quality thinking is a formidable task (as we discussed in chap. 9). Doing this via technology offers many advantages, but it is still difficult. Third, many of the machines available to teachers are of limited capacity, as we noted earlier, and may not be able to handle the programs being developed that focus on higher-level goals. Fourth, much of the software available, at least until recently, has not been geared toward higher-level problem solving, making it necessary for teachers to develop their own (a difficult task to accomplish on top of everything else teachers are asked to do). However, this argument doesn't hold up when we consider word processing, database, and spreadsheet packages. Instruction in any of these could combine learning about the tool with use of the tool to solve problems. Finally, teachers may simply not be aware of, or alternatively may be resistant to, different uses of technology. Time constraints, fear of being replaced, or feelings of discomfort with the new role the teacher may need to take on when using technology to introduce content or teach problem solving may all be involved. These possibilities will be discussed in more detail below.

Why Don't More Teachers Use Technology?

The statistics on the increasing availability of computers and the seeming emphasis on them by our society leads us to ask why more teachers do not use computers in their classrooms. There appear to be a number of reasons (Ely, 1993).

- *Poor software and no development time.* Many teachers feel that software is often poorly designed. They may have neither the time nor the programming skill necessary to develop their own software (Rieser & Dick, 1990). Some of the newer software packages (e.g., Hypercard, Supercard) help teachers develop their own courseware without having to be skilled programmers, but these too take time to learn.
- *Belief that computers don't help.* Some teachers don't believe that the computer improves instruction, but think instead that students can become dependent upon it. Using word processing in writing, for example, "some students tend to hand in poorly written first drafts that still look 'neat' and are free of obvious spelling errors. . . . WP software seems to result in less processing time but inferior writing" (Ely, 1993, p. 27).
- *Lack of long-range planning.* Some teachers report that there is often no process for long-range planning concerning technology in their schools, so they are unsure of what kind of technology will be available, how they are expected to use it, how widespread it will be, and the degree of support that will be available. In addition, when long-range plans are formulated, some teachers report that they are not included in the process, but are excluded from making decisions about the degree and direction of technological implementation (Brennan, 1991).
- *The computer as a competitor.* The computer may be seen as a competitor for students' attention (McMahon, 1990). Computer software, when done well, can be informative, individualized, colorful, and fun. Teachers can feel threatened and fear that their typical teaching styles can no longer hold students' attention.
- *Lack of administrative support* (Cuban, 1989). Some teachers who might otherwise be willing to invest the time and energy to integrate computers into their instruction do not see such activities as being rewarded or valued by their superiors. Or, even worse, they may fear being perceived by the administration as teachers who are always asking for something (more equipment, more time, more materials) to develop technological resources, and fear developing negative reputations. In fact, according to Sheingold and Hadley (1990), teachers who use technology consistently in their teaching receive a great deal of support in their efforts. They also note that "although barriers to the integration of computers have lessened for most of these teachers over the years, significant barriers still remain" (pp. vii–viii).

Are Today's Teachers Prepared to Teach in a Technological Classroom?

The pace of technological development is astonishing, and exciting opportunities for improved instruction are becoming readily available to the average classroom teacher. Yet, as recent surveys have indicated, many classroom teachers do not use technology at all in their teaching, and those who do use technology do not take full advantage of its potential.

Issue

Many teachers do not use technology because they are afraid of it, either of the machines themselves or of the theories underlying some of the more recent innovations.

Answer: Pro   Fear is often based on ignorance and inexperience. Many teachers are afraid of technology simply because they have not had the opportunity to learn about it in a meaningful way. Most would welcome the chance to grow as professionals if only the opportunities and support to do so were provided. Greater numbers of colleges of education are requiring some computer literacy for teachers in training. While this is a step in the right direction, technology is often not integrated with the rest of their training, but is seen as a separate class to be taken. Much of the debate on this issue focuses on the lack of use of technology by teachers already in the classroom, but more attention needs to be paid to familiarizing those in training with technology as an integral part of their own learning. Fear of the theories underlying newer uses of technology is a reality among teachers and administrators. A noisy classroom in which students are not in their seats completing assignments is seen by many as a classroom out of control, rather than a place where students are so enthusiastic in their learning that they can't sit still! Clearly, teachers need to be in control in the sense that they are guiding students toward meaningful learning and eliminating time off task, but there are multiple ways to achieve this goal.

Answer: Con   While some teachers do fear technology, many have thoughtfully considered the integration of its use into their classrooms and have opted for a limited role of technology. There is a risk of students becoming dependent on the technology, thus limiting their ability to reason and solve problems when the machines are not available. Extensive use of technology can also seduce students into believing that if an assignment or project looks good, it is good, rather than helping them focus on an in-depth analysis of the information. Others say that technology reinforces students' expectation that learning must be entertaining to be useful, an expectation that makes it difficult to get students to persevere if their interest is not immediately captured. Finally, some authors argue that students need to know certain facts to be successfully functioning members of our society. It is the school's job to ensure that students learn these facts, and an orderly, teacher-directed classroom is the most effective and efficient way to ensure mastery of them. Otherwise, classes become chaotic and children do not learn.

Issue

Extensive use of technology in the classroom can result in a loss of control over what is being learned, and students' achievement suffers as a result.

Answer: Pro   Teachers are not taught how to manage technologically rich classrooms. Students are often left on their own in the development of special projects. Teachers cannot ensure that all students will choose projects and topics within a given domain. It is also difficult to control how much time is spent on specific parts of the domain, because students can choose to move quickly through parts of programs, or, in some cases, bypass some parts completely. Grading becomes problematic, since it is difficult to put together assessments for all students.

Answer: Con   Teachers can choose what types of technology to use in their classrooms. Intelligent tutoring systems (ITS) programs actually can ensure a more adequate coverage of common material for all students, though such systems are not widely available yet. It is true that much of the newer technology being introduced in classrooms today places much more responsibility on the learner to direct his or her own learning. While the teacher does not control what is presented, how, and to whom, proponents of these technologies argue that students develop a deeper understanding of the content covered because they have chosen to cover it and are more interested in it and motivated to learn it. Students also develop self-regulation skills along with content knowledge, and problem-solving skills as they develop and follow through on longer-term and in-depth projects.

- *Increased time and effort required* (Cuban, 1989). When an individual is first learning a skill, the time required to complete tasks may actually increase a bit, even though the initial time investment often pays off in terms of time saved (or instruction improved) in the long term. Teachers' enthusiasm for computers, not surprisingly, depends on how much work the computer will do for them as well as how much time and effort it takes to get the computer to do the work. Time investment is a legitimate concern. Sheingold and Hadley (1990) reported that teachers who use computers regularly in their instruction devote a great deal of time and effort to learning how best to use computers in their classrooms, and that it may take as long as six years of using computers in instruction to master computer-based approaches.

- *Fear.* Teachers often report being afraid that they will look stupid in front of their students if they try using computers (Wiske et al., 1990). Some teachers may begin developing such fears before they even begin their professional careers (Kay, 1990; Summers, 1990). In some cases, students know more about the machines than their teachers do, a situation that can be intimidating. Other teachers say they fear losing control of the group when substantial aspects of instruction are done using computers. They can't control what is presented when and to whom as well as they can with more traditional instructional methods. Ironically, this is precisely one of the major potential advantages that all experts in educational technology cite: that instruction can be more responsive to the individual needs of students.

  Many of these fears have their roots in teachers' lack of knowledge about technology. One study of a teacher-training program showed that over half the future teachers in the program had never used a computer in any course during any of their college training (Beaver, 1990). Courses that both familiarize teachers with technology and provide specific instruction in how and why to integrate technology into teaching go a long way toward relieving beginning teachers' fears. Fortunately, increasing numbers of colleges of education are making such courses requirements for their teacher preparation programs. Other studies point to the lack of in-service training opportunities for those already teaching. These studies indicate that the in-services that are offered often seem to deal with basic literacy issues or specifics of particular pieces of software, rather than more general methodology (Brennan, 1991).

- *Different role for teachers.* Fears such as those discussed above say something about what many teachers see as the teacher's role in the classroom: that of an expert responsible for imparting knowledge to students, rather than a collaborator working with students to solve problems and discover information (Hannafin & Savenye, 1993). It seems that those teachers who successfully integrate technology into their instruction experience a significant change in how they teach and in how they view teaching (Fawson & Smellie, 1990; Hannafin & Savenye, 1993; Sheingold & Hadley, 1990). These teachers begin to view themselves less as experts imparting knowledge and more as guides or facilitators as students themselves acquire knowledge. This new role can be a difficult one to assume, particularly given the training that many teachers have received.

- *Societal resistance.* Some researchers argue that, surprisingly, it is not just teachers who may be resistant to a new role for the teacher (Hannafin & Savenye, 1993; Leuhrmann, 1985; Tobin & Dawson, 1992). Society at large may have trouble with this. While this idea at first seems to contradict our society's ever-increasing emphasis on technology, it may be that the society expects classrooms to be orderly and controlled, with teachers teaching and students learning the facts. This image reflects a view that knowledge exists in discrete chunks that teachers are expected to give to students. If more and more responsibility is given to students to control their own learning, and if students begin to learn that facts aren't always what they seem and knowledge isn't as orderly and "chunk-like" as we thought, this may meet with a negative societal reaction. If society doesn't accept these new views of knowledge, teaching, and learning, then the culture as a whole, while not resistant to technology per se, may resist the shift in the definition of learning and the changes in the teacher-student relationship which seem to be required. Such barriers are subtle, "but these views may form a powerful unseen and unobserved force capable of blocking even the most promising of innovations" (Hannafin & Savenye, 1993, p. 29).

Some of the newer uses of technology in teaching call for a different role of the teacher, that of a guide and at times a collaborator with students, rather than an expert. What is your opinion of this role? Will it be easy or difficult for you to assume such a role? Do you think you will encounter resistance to it, and if so, from whom?

STUDENTS' PERCEPTIONS OF TECHNOLOGY IN THE CLASSROOM

What about the impact of technology on students? Most of the literature relevant to this question focuses on one of two outcomes: changes in student achievement (e.g., unit tests, standardized achievement tests, tests of problem solving, increased quality of products) or in student attitudes as a result of using technology. Changes in student achievement vary according to the way in which technology is used, and so this work will be discussed in the next section.

Attitude Surveys

In general, most studies assessing students' attitudes report positive changes when technology is used in classrooms; students seem to like using computers to learn (Martin, Heller, & Mahmoud, 1992; Todman & Dick, 1993). These results seem to hold for students of varying ages (K through 12th grade), though there is evidence that older students are less favorable than younger students toward computers (Krendl & Broihier, 1992). In a review of some of the early work on attitudes, Lawton and Gerschner (1982) found that children generally had positive attitudes toward computers and computerized instruction, saying that computers had infinite patience, never got tired, never forgot to correct or praise them, were impartial to ethnicity, and were great motivators. Negative attitudes and fears about computers were found mostly among teachers rather than students.

Novelty Effects?

Other researchers are not so convinced of the wonderful effects of computers on student attitudes. One issue that is just beginning to be addressed concerns the **novelty effect.** That is, perhaps one reason for such positive student attitudes is simply that computers are new to students. It is a well-known finding in the literature that when a tool or program is new, it tends to get more attention and often is rated as being highly enjoyable and acceptable. Salomon and Gardner (1986) argued that much of the research done to examine the effects of computers in schools on students' attitudes is too simplistic, using short-term computer interventions or one-time surveys. Often the reports are vague about the software used, role of the teacher, description of the learning environment, and other important details. Attitudes may reasonably be expected to vary considerably with any or all of these details of implementation.

More and more studies are being done to address the claim of a novelty effect, with mixed results. For example, Krendl and Broihier (1992) evaluated fourth- through tenth-graders' perceptions about computers along three dimensions (preference, perceived learning, and perceived difficulty) for three years. They found clear evidence of a novelty effect for preference and perceived learning, with ratings for these two dimensions declining each year. Students were more stable in their ratings of perceived difficulty, a finding that surprised the researchers. They had reasoned that the more familiar students became with computer technology across the three-year span, the easier they would find computer work to be, but this did not happen. Perceived difficulty remained the same across the three years, even though there was a vast increase in the number of students who gained computer experience

novelty effect *The tendency to give more attention to, give higher ratings to, and in general find more positive effects of an educational tool or instructional program simply because it is new.*

"I don't have my homework. My dog deleted it."

© *Randy Glasbergen.*

during the time of the study. Other studies do not find such clear-cut evidence of a novelty effect, though most of these are not as long in duration as the Krendl and Broihier study just described. At this point, the literature seems to indicate that novelty may play some role in how favorable student attitudes are toward computers, though the existence and degree of novelty effect is probably related to how the technology is used in the classroom.

What difference does a novelty effect mean for teachers using technology in their classrooms? If the effect is real and complete (meaning that it accounts for all of the positive effects seen when computers are used), then the positive effects attributed to using computers as a medium for instruction might be expected to occur simply by changing the way one teaches. Thus, there would be no need to invest in costly computers and spend the time and effort to learn to use them. Such a finding would also mean that teachers, if they did choose to use computers in their instruction, might expect great things to happen at first, but that there would be a diminished effect as time went on and students became more used to the technology. They might become less interested and motivated, to the point that the "computer work" became just another academic assignment that they had to complete.

Gender Differences in Attitudes

Another finding regarding student attitudes toward computers is better established in the literature. In most studies in which gender differences were assessed, girls tended to show less favorable attitudes than boys (Chen, 1985; Collis & Williams, 1987; Krendl & Broihier, 1992; Martin, Heller, & Mahmoud, 1992; Todman & Dick, 1993). This finding holds across elementary, middle, and high schools, and even across countries (the U.S., Britain, Canada, China, and the former Soviet Union)! It holds for such aspects of attitudes as computer preference, difficulty, and perceived learning (Krendl & Broihier, 1992), and also for fun and usefulness (Todman & Dick, 1993).

The reasons for the effect are a bit harder to pin down. Some studies claim that girls tend to have less experience with computers and technology in general than boys do, and so show more negative attitudes toward them (Martin, Heller, & Mahmoud, 1992). Others point to the disturbing possibility that both girls and boys see computers as male-oriented and their use as more of a "male-appropriate" than a "female-appropriate" activity (Chen, 1986; Clarke, 1985; Wilder, Mackie, & Cooper, 1985). Another possibility concerns the attitudes of teachers. Some studies suggest that many times teachers have more negative attitudes toward computers than students do. Given that many teachers, particularly at the elementary level, are female, it is possible that girls are using these teachers as models in their attitudes and behavior toward computers.

Although the finding of gender differences is consistent, not all the news is bad. If experience with computers is an important factor, then the proliferation of computers in classrooms is good news for girls, since it will give them increased opportunities to work with the machines. However, girls and boys alike need to be encouraged from an early age to view computer use as an appropriate activity for girls as well as boys. Teachers and parents alike can go a long way toward decreasing the gender gap with respect to computers by modeling positive attitudes themselves and reinforcing both genders for their interest in and work on computers and other forms of technology.

We have reviewed the historical development of educational technology and have a sense of how technology is currently used. The next step in understanding educational technology is to get a sense of the variety of ways this educational tool can be used.

Have you observed gender or cultural differences in attitudes toward computer usage? If so, what do you think are the causes and effects of such differences? How will you deal with them as a teacher?

TYPES AND USES OF TECHNOLOGY IN EDUCATION

We have organized the uses and types of technology into the categories summarized in table 14.2. This categorization provides a convenient way to present information about each type, but it is clearly not the only (or necessarily the best) way to categorize the

Table 14.2

Categories of Educational Technology		
Category	**Definition**	**Example**
Administrative/managerial	Using technology to collect, analyze, and report information concerning students or instruction.	Computerized gradebooks Word processing used to record lesson plans, student goal attainment Spreadsheets used to graph student progress
Audiovisual aids	Using technology to present information in several formats (vision, audition). Usually supplements a teacher- or text-based presentation.	Overhead projectors Slide projectors Television
Teaching technology	Teaching students the basics of how to use the technology itself, particularly how to use word processing packages, spreadsheets, graphing programs, etc.	Computer literacy Teaching programming basics Teaching how to use word processing software Teaching how to use spreadsheets
Computer-assisted instruction	Using technology to present material to students initially and to assist them in mastering it. Included are programs with a predominantly behavioristic theoretical basis, emphasizing progressive shaping of behavior toward a final goal via small steps and positive reinforcement. More cognitively based programs are included in other categories.	Programmed instruction Drill and practice software
Teaching of thinking using technology	Using technology to foster the development, use, and transfer of students' general thinking and problem-solving skills.	Teaching programming (e.g., Logo) Using word processing to improve writing and thinking skills (especially when computerized prompting systems are incorporated)
Intelligent Tutoring Systems	Using technology to provide an individualized tutor for each student. The system presents new material in a way that is comprehensible to each student, provides examples and practice problems, tracks student performance, identifies errors and misconceptions, and provides appropriate guidance and feedback.	Sherlock (an avionics tutor)
Multimedia uses	Using technology to integrate and simultaneously use several different types of technology. Often based on cognitive constructivist theory, and often involves students in collaborative, large-scale projects.	Laser videodisc series (e.g., Jasper Woodbury) CD-ROM (e.g., National Geographic Society series)
Other recent developments Networks	Connecting computers to one another through telephone lines or cables so that information and/or equipment can be shared. Includes local area networks (LANs), wide area networks (WANs), and the Internet.	WaterNet project Intercultural Learning Network National Geographic Kids Network
Virtual reality (VR)	A computer-generated environment that is three-dimensional and involves the user in real-time, multisensory interactions.	

work in this domain. There will certainly be overlap between some of the categories. In general, the categories reflect a developmental timeline; i.e., the work on TV and computer-assisted instruction (CAI) came before the teaching of the technology, and the work on intelligent tutoring systems (ITS), multimedia, and networking is most recent. As we noted in the brief historical review of technology in education, earlier work tended to be based on a behavioristic theory of learning and teaching. The vast majority of the more recent work (especially teaching thinking, ITS, and multimedia, along with some of the newer CAI programs) is firmly rooted in cognitive theory. As you

Is your personal underlying theory of learning and instruction more behavioristic or cognitive? How will your underlying theory affect how you use technology? As you read about the uses of technology described in this chapter, think about which ones seem most reasonable to you, given your personal theory.

computer-managed instruction (CMI) *Use of the computer to collect, analyze, and report information concerning students in an educational program. Can include information on students' academic performance, attendance, background information, teachers' lesson plans, etc.*

read, keep in mind the theoretical assumptions of these two approaches to better understand the differences between the categories. For each category we will describe the type of technology involved, discuss how it is used, summarize the research results, and provide some information about how teachers might incorporate this particular type or use of technology into their teaching.

Administrative and Managerial Uses

To say that teachers spend considerable time in keeping track of student activities, grades, and records is a gross understatement. Grades, attendance records, text assignments, and auxiliary equipment are but a few of the types of records that teachers must keep. It is precisely here that computer-managed instruction (CMI) can help in tracking and documenting classroom activities, thus making manageable the necessary paperwork.

Computer-managed instruction is the use of the computer to collect, analyze, and report information concerning the performance of students in an educational program. Most teachers have available word processing packages and printers that can be used to produce notes and memos to parents, permission slips, notices about upcoming events, etc. Beyond this simple use, you may decide to create a file for each student in your class, beginning with the student's name. You may then continually add data to the file: test scores, results of standardized tests, any special work, pertinent health data, need for any type of special attention (e.g., medication).

Technology can also make it easier to compute grades and keep track of student progress during a school year. An increasing number of software and textbook companies are developing easy-to-use computerized gradebooks which allow teachers to enter students' names and grades, then compute final grades in a variety of different ways. Teachers can also use either regular word processing packages or specialized software to write and keep track of lesson plans and instructional goals (for individuals and for the class) throughout the school year, updating and adding notes as the year progresses. Such detailed record keeping can be especially helpful when meeting with parents: the teacher can simply print out the goals, plans, and progress notes, and have these available for parent-teacher conferences. It may also be useful for *students* to have access to such information, perhaps letting them see the overall instructional goals, as well as specific instructional objectives for each unit and lesson.

The trend in many of the newer instructional systems is to incorporate within them CMI that can provide constant evaluation of students' progress. Indeed, many of these systems must include such tracking elements, because the specific material presented and its timing is designed to be dependent upon how well a student has done on the last material presented. When CMI is incorporated within other systems, there are five major functions which are served:

- Assessment—collecting vital information
- Diagnosis—a continuing evaluation of learner needs
- Learning prescription—matching students' needs with appropriate instruction
- Record keeping—maintaining all kinds of student records, from final answers on specific exercises to small steps students took in solving each problem
- Reporting—supplying needed information for both teachers and students

As you can see, the goals of CMI are not restricted solely to course management, but also apply to learner performance, the learning sequence, and selection of appropriate learning activities.

Audiovisual Aids for Instruction

audiovisual aids *Use of technology to present information in several different formats (e.g., visual, auditory), usually supplementing a teacher- or text-based presentation. Examples include overhead projectors, slide projectors, and television.*

Another quite frequent use of technology in education is in **audiovisual aids.** Many of the machines in this category are geared toward the visual presentation of information, which supplements an auditory presentation by a teacher or a written presentation from a textbook. This category includes such things as simple overhead projectors, slide projectors, and televisions. Laser videodisc players and CD-ROM, relatively recent innovations in educational technology, could also be included here, but will be discussed later. As we noted earlier in talking about the history of technology in education, AV aids were some of the earliest forms of technology, and most teachers have ready access to many types.

The main idea underlying the use of AV aids is that presenting information in several formats offers students the advantage of not only hearing about information (from a teacher or a textbook), but also seeing it, thus receiving a "dual presentation." Recall Paivio's work, discussed in chapter 8 on cognitive theories. Use of AV aids allows information to be presented in two different modalities, with the assumption that more information can be processed.

Some theorists also assert that information presented in a visual format is more integrated—that it is easier to see the relations among the pieces and how they all fit together when it is presented via a drawing (Mayer & Gallini, 1990; Mayer & Sims, 1994). Videotapes, films, laser videodiscs, and CD-ROMs also offer the advantage of being able to show movement: students can readily see the dynamic changes occurring over time in a process, rather than only hearing or reading about them. Slow motion capabilities on videos allow students to slow down the movement to examine it and the changes that occur more closely. Such techniques have been used extensively for improvement of physical skills (e.g., learning how to play tennis, ski, or read a defense in football) and in the biological sciences (e.g., watching the process of cell division in slow motion to see how chromosomes line up and then separate).

One piece of AV technology that has stirred and continues to stir controversy in the classroom is the use of television. There is little doubt that most of the students you will work with are quite familiar with TV. *Sesame Street,* along with other programs, such as *3-2-1 Contact, Mr. Rogers' Neighborhood, Square One TV,* and *Reading Rainbow,* is for many students the first systematic introduction to numbers, letters, reading, reasoning, and problem-solving skills. Critics claim that television has a number of negative effects on students, ranging from reduced attention spans and expectations that teachers must "entertain" them to increased aggression. Wisely used, however, television can have positive influences on students (Howe, 1983; Sammur, 1990). For example, the program *Sesame Street* appears to affect positively a variety of academic and social skills (e.g., vocabulary development, achievement, school readiness, letter and number recognition, word identification, and cooperative behavior), though it clearly has not erased the academic differences between children growing up in enriched circumstances and those who are less advantaged (Children's Television Workshop, 1990; Howe, 1983; Rice et al., 1990). Educational television programs specifically designed for elementary and secondary classrooms are readily available to most teachers free of charge or at little cost, and the array of documentaries available on specific topics is ever increasing.

Other uses of television in the classroom are more controversial. For example, *Channel One Television* is a national television show developed for high-schoolers by Whittle Communications (Brodinsky, 1993; Bruder, 1989). Whittle sought to beam the program directly into high schools across the country, providing current news events for students and teachers to use for instructional purposes. Since many of the classrooms involved in early pilots did not have televisions, much less VCR recording equipment and satellite dishes to receive the program, Whittle provided the equipment. The cost was quite high. Advertising was sold on the channel to finance the project, starting a tremendous controversy in educational, political, and business circles. Shortly after Channel One was started, Turner Broadcasting Company and the Discovery Channel both began producing programs intended for educational use, but these companies do not supply equipment and do not include advertising. Results are not yet in on the effects of these systems or on the most effective ways to use them.

Teaching of the Technology

As we have seen from the survey results presented earlier, one of the most common uses of technology currently is in the teaching of how to use the technology itself, particularly how to use the variety of word processing packages available. It is certainly reasonable to spend time teaching our students how to use such tools, since much of their working lives will presumably be spent utilizing these tools to accomplish the tasks required in their professions. As we noted above, however, many educational experts feel that we must move beyond simply teaching students how to use the tools, to teaching students to use these software packages to develop higher-level skills. That being said, however, let us review a few of the types of programs that students are learning about.

Word Processing

word processing *Use of computer software for writing, editing, revising, formatting, and printing text. If combined with instruction in text production and revision, use of word processing may have positive effects on the quality of students' writing.*

Students are frequently taught how to use **word processing** packages. Sometimes use of word processing begins as early as first or second grade, when students begin writing essays and stories. More and more high school and college teachers require that students produce their papers on word processors rather than turning in handwritten copies. The advantage of such a policy to teachers is obvious: no more time spent trying to decipher what each poorly handwritten word is! But what are the advantages to students of using word processing?

The major advantage that word processing offers is the opportunity to do significant revisions and editing. "Significant" here means not just doing a lot of it, though that is certainly possible, but making changes that significantly improve the quality of the message being conveyed. Think back to the days when you wrote papers in longhand, then perhaps typed them on a typewriter to be turned in. As you reread a paper, what would you do if you thought of a better way to express a certain thought, one that required a few more sentences? Or if you realized after rereading it that a different organization would clarify the points you wanted to make? Or that adding an example would help clarify a point? It's quite likely that if you had to rewrite or retype the entire paper (or resort to "cutting and pasting" by hand), the changes would not be made, and the paper would not be as clear, well organized, and high in quality as it could be. Word processing makes all these types of changes quite easy, and so offers students the opportunity to improve the quality of their writing.

Unfortunately, students often do not take advantage of this powerful capability, sometimes because they are not taught to do so. The instruction offered in word processing programs tends not to emphasize these types of revision and editing skills, so the real power of word processing is often not realized. In these cases, the fear expressed by many teachers comes true: students come to believe that if a paper "looks pretty," then it must be of high quality. The different fonts and formats offered by the word processor are used to produce a professional-looking document, but not a high-quality product. (We will talk about some studies that do seek to use this capability of word processors to improve the quality of students' writing, as well as their general thinking skills, in a later section.)

The teacher can address this problem by consistently prompting students to focus not just on what their compositions look like, but on what they actually say. Helpful approaches are to have students write in pairs after receiving instruction and to provide examples of well-written and poorly written papers, as well as spacing deadlines for the subtasks involved in writing a quality paper throughout the semester. For example, if students are asked to write a term paper that is due at the end of the semester, the teacher may set a deadline for a one-paragraph summary of the topic one month into the class. A detailed outline might be due during the second month, then a rough draft a few weeks later, then finally the end product. For this to be effective, of course, the students must receive detailed feedback about strong and weak points at each step along the way. This procedure may help students understand that it is the quality and depth of thought that goes into a composition that determines its quality. Word processing is simply a tool that makes it easier to implement the revised, improved thinking that underlies changes. There are also software packages available that help students analyze the grammatical aspects of their writing (e.g., presence of run-on sentences; subject-verb agreement, etc.) and their spelling. These packages offer some advantage over teacher corrections of such things, since they give immediate feedback and often ask students to decide what to do about their errors. This forces students to become aware of the individual error patterns they have, as well as forcing them to learn how to correct such errors.

Spreadsheets

Less often used are spreadsheets, or programs that allow students to enter numerical data and perform calculations on them. Most of these packages also offer graphing capability: students can select all or some of the data entered and display these in a variety of different graphing formats (e.g., in bar graphs, pie charts, line graphs, etc.). These programs offer students the opportunity to "play with numbers" by entering different data points and looking at the effects on the end result. For example, have you ever tried to figure out precisely how well you had to do on a final exam to get an A in the course? Spreadsheets would allow you easily to try out different numbers to answer this question, assuming that the course is graded on a point basis and you know how the teacher is weighting different test and assignment scores.

The graphing capability of these programs also allows students to see a visual representation of the numbers entered, which can be very helpful in identifying patterns in the numbers. For example, students could use spreadsheets to graph functions so they could more easily see the connection between the graph produced and the equation. They could also see instantly the effect of altering part of the equation, and could play with systematic alterations to see which changes had a big impact on the size and shape of the graph, and which had little impact. However, the same caution we gave regarding word processing applies to the use of these packages. That is, students can be taught how to use them without being taught how to use them to improve their thinking and reasoning about numerical information and patterns. This is unfortunate, since the real educational power of spreadsheets lies in helping students better understand the relations among data, formulas, graphs, and conclusions that can validly be drawn.

Computer-Assisted Instruction

Of course, most of the categories we discuss in this chapter could be considered part of this one; most are in a very real sense instruction assisted by the computer. We present the following examples in a separate category, however, because of their common theoretical perspective and their history in education. The other categories in this chapter either do not have a clear underlying theoretical perspective per se (e.g., they are simply using the technology to aid in management tasks or teaching students the basics of specific types of software), or come from a different theoretical perspective (e.g., cognitive constructivism). The types of **computer-assisted instruction** included in the present category come from a predominantly behavioristic theoretical tradition and tend to focus on systematic presentation of material in small steps. They follow behaviorism in their emphasis on progressive shaping of behavior toward a final goal through small steps that offer students the opportunity to be correct most of the time and to receive positive reinforcement quite frequently.

computer-assisted instruction (CAI) *Use of the computer initially to present material to students and then to assist them in mastering it. Earlier versions were based in behaviorist theory; more recent programs are based in cognitive theory.*

Programmed Instruction

programmed instruction   *A set of instructional materials that students can use to teach themselves about a particular topic, skill, or content area. Based on Skinner's theory of operant conditioning, such a program is designed so that instruction progresses in small steps toward a well-defined final goal, is sequenced so that students give correct answers most of the time, and relies heavily on positive reinforcement of correct answers.*

In general, **programmed instruction** consists of a set of instructional materials that students can use to teach themselves about a particular topic, skill, or content area. One of the earliest proponents of this approach was, not surprisingly, B. F. Skinner (Skinner, 1968). He argued that teachers depend too heavily upon punishment while neglecting their use of positive reinforcement. Instruction should be designed to progress in small steps toward a well-defined final goal, and sequenced so that students can give correct responses the majority of the time, thereby allowing the teacher to use positive reinforcement more frequently. Early versions of programmed instruction were often either not computerized or presented on "teaching machines". Programmed instruction has evolved into a variety of types of computer-assisted instruction, all of which are computer-based, that incorporate the underlying principles Skinner developed.

Skinner (1984) reviewed what he felt was wrong with our educational system and offered his proposal for how to improve the situation. His prescription for our educational ills was programmed instruction, which, he argued, would result in teaching "what is now taught in American schools in half the time with half the effort" (Skinner, 1984, p. 948). He cited a study in which eighth-grade students were taught algebra by instruction programmed on "crude teaching machines"—machines nowhere near the power of those available today. The students went through the entire eighth- and ninth-grade curricula in one semester. Tests of comprehension and use of the information indicated that these eighth-graders met ninth-grade norms for recall and use of the information. Many critical details are left out of Skinner's account of the algebra study (e.g., Was this a typical, run-of-the-mill class of students, or were they specially selected for their interest, aptitude, or motivation in some way? What was the teacher like? What was the comparison group like?), but Skinner's description does point out that programmed instruction can be quite effective even when implemented on relatively simple machines.

In chapter 12 we reviewed the instructional principles that Skinner argued are necessary to improve teaching and learning. These principles are important to consider in programmed instruction, whether it is computerized or not.

- Clearly define the final goal, or terminal behavior, stating it in objective and concrete terms.
- Solve the problem of the first instance; i.e., induce the student to exhibit some aspect of the desired behavior so that positive reinforcement can be provided. Initial responses must be ones that the student is capable of making.
- Sequence instruction carefully and thoughtfully, with careful definition of subgoals that the student should progress through on the way to achieving the final desired behavior. This is critically important for complex behaviors, such as those desired in most academic subjects. In essence, the program will be reinforcing progress toward the final goal, or shaping the student's behavior.
- As far as possible, prevent incorrect responses, so that punishment can be avoided and positive reinforcement used.
- Provide immediate, nonthreatening, but clear feedback in responding to correct and incorrect answers.

There are several types of programmed instruction. An earlier, more traditional type is called *linear programmed instruction*. A student is presented with an exercise or problem and required to respond. If the response is correct, the student is told so, and the next problem in the sequence is presented. If the answer is incorrect, the student is simply told that the answer was not correct and is given the correct answer;

then the next problem in the sequence is presented. The sequence of problems is the same, regardless of whether the answers were correct or not, and no instruction is given to explain why the answer the student provided was wrong. It may seem odd that incorrect responses are not explored, but the reasoning behind this type of programming is that time spent exploring or explaining incorrect responses in essence reinforces those incorrect responses. Students need to be corrected and told the right answer, but no more time and attention than necessary should be paid to wrong answers, to avoid reinforcing mistakes.

A second, more recent type of programmed instruction is a *branching program*. In this method, the student receives an example or problem for which a response is required. If the answer is correct, the student is positively reinforced and the next problem in the sequence is presented. If the answer is incorrect, however, the student is "branched," or sent to, a different part of the program to receive instruction as to why the response was incorrect, additional instruction in the correct answer, and/or additional problems or examples dealing with the same concept. This type of programmed instruction incorporates aspects of a cognitive approach to instruction, in that it involves helping students explore their current understanding of concepts; still, it retains many aspects of behaviorism in its emphasis on sequencing for correct answers and positive reinforcement.

Drill and Practice Software

As the name implies, programs designed for this purpose have as their objective helping students master the basic elements in mathematics, reading, spelling, and any other subjects in which they must acquire fundamental facts. The computer presents a stimulus, elicits a response, and provides reinforcement. Whereas programmed instruction is intended to provide the initial introduction to and instruction in skills and knowledge, **drill and practice** programs are intended to help students practice and master the skills *after* they have already received initial instruction in them. For example, many drill and practice programs are available to help master and automatize (i.e., be able to quickly recall) basic math facts, or to help students master spelling of vocabulary words.

drill and practice   *Use of the computer to help students master the basic elements in a given domain after they have already received initial instruction. The computer presents a stimulus, elicits a response, and provides feedback and reinforcement.*

Among teachers who use computers, particularly in elementary schools, drill and practice programs are quite common. There are many drill and practice programs readily available, and they can be incorporated easily into many teachers' existing styles of teaching. Students can be introduced initially to the material in the teacher's customary way, then do short amounts of individual practice (e.g., 15 to 20 minutes) with the program during spare moments.

Lockard, Abrams, and Many (1994) described several levels of drill and practice programs. At the basic level, a program may offer students a fixed number of problems to solve. All students face the same tasks, and only after successful completion can they move on to a higher level. They spend as much time as needed to work to mastery. Next is the program that has an arbitrary mastery criterion: six successive successful completions may be required, for example. Note that some students may well meet this criterion on their initial effort, while others might need several attempts. A more adaptive program could require students to reach mastery after relatively few responses, or increase the difficulty of the materials, or even force students to switch the operations needed—for example, from multiplication to division. For a student experiencing difficulty, the program would then branch to a less difficult context, or return the user to a lower level. As Lockard and associates (1994) noted, such constant adjustments are intended to develop mastery without causing either boredom or frustration.

Opponents of using computers for drill argue that

- Programs are boring.
- All students receive the same content, regardless of ability.
- Programs may provide undesirable feedback.

- Some teachers use computers for primary instruction, rather than as tools to practice and automatize material to which students have already been introduced. While using the computer for primary instruction is generally viewed by experts in the field as a good use of technology, these particular types of programs are not designed for this task. There are other programs that do a much better job of this.
- Using computers for drill is an expensive waste of money.
- Drill and practice results in memorized knowledge, but does nothing to help students understand the meaning behind the knowledge or how and why it is important to learn.

On the other hand, proponents argue that

- Extra practice is provided where it is needed most.
- Attention can be maintained during practice sessions.
- Where problems exist, they are usually the result of poorly designed programs.
- Unexpected bonuses, such as a student's fascination with the computer itself or interest in programming, can often result.

The effectiveness of CAI (the two types we have discussed as well as others) has been examined in many studies. Two recent meta-analyses have been conducted to synthesize the research on CAI and reach conclusions about the literature (Kulik & Kulik, 1991; Ryan, 1991). (Recall our discussion of this analysis technique in chap. 2.) These two analyses included students ranging from kindergarten age to adulthood, and together analyzed almost 300 individual studies. Both meta-analyses indicated that students using CAI showed achievement gains of approximately .30 standard deviations over students taught without CAI. The advantage in achievement gain is equivalent to about three months in a school year (Ryan, 1991), or an increase from the 50th to the 62nd percentile (Kulik & Kulik, 1991). Interestingly, the CAI in the Kulik and Kulik analysis was very effective when the duration of treatments was limited to four weeks or less. When treatments were continued for several months or longer, the effects were less robust, raising the clear possibility of the novelty effect we discussed earlier in this chapter.

Ryan's analysis (1991) also pointed to an important factor in reaching the achievement gains: teacher training. The amount of training provided to teachers was significantly related to the academic achievement of students in the CAI treatment groups. It is important to note that short-term training (less than 10 hours) was actually *counterproductive,* with students in CAI treatment groups whose teachers had 1 to 10 hours of training showing smaller effect sizes than students in CAI groups whose teachers had no training. This is a critical point for teachers and administrators attempting to integrate CAI in their classrooms, and it underscores the need for strong and continuing administrative support for such efforts.

What can you conclude about using CAI in the classroom? First, be aware that the results will be only as good as the quality of the program used. It is true that such programs are readily available and usually fairly inexpensive, but you must carefully examine the software. Critics argue that much of it is not of good quality. Second, it appears that using CAI can help students master basic skills, particularly when the skills are of the types that require automatic recall of basic facts (e.g., arithmetic facts, spelling vocabulary). Third, keep in mind the possible novelty effect. It may be that students are simply enamored with this new activity rather than anything inherent in the program itself. You may want to take advantage of the novelty—after all, if students are increasing their attention, practicing and learning, then that's the ultimate objective—but you may see decreases in all these outcomes after a period of time. Finally, teachers and administrators alike must keep in mind the need for continuing support and training for teachers using CAI in their classrooms, remembering that too little training not only appears to not help, but may actually be harmful.

Using Technology to Teach Thinking

One of the main goals that most educators have for their students is improvement of their critical thinking abilities. A number of researchers have investigated how this might be done using technology. When technology is used for this purpose, it is the student who is giving directions, making decisions, and in essence instructing the computer. Proponents of this approach argue that when students are calling the shots and telling the computer what to do, they are forced to clarify their own thinking, since any mistakes cannot be blamed on the computer—it only does what they tell it to!

How do you foresee using technology in your future classrooms? Why do those uses seem particularly appropriate to you?

Learning to Program

We've already discussed one reason to teach programming to students: so that they can learn the programming language to produce a desired output and accomplish a given computing task. But another reason for teaching programming hopefully has a more long-lasting impact: to help students improve their general thinking and problem-solving skills. One well-known proponent of this use of technology is Seymour Papert (1993). Papert argued that programming requires programmers to think about their own thinking, clarify it, examine it for flaws in logic, and be extremely precise in expressing the goal and steps needed. He felt that programming not only requires these skills, but can help students develop them as well.

Papert and his colleagues at Massachusetts Institute of Technology developed the programming language **Logo,** specifically designing it so that even preschool children could use it. Since its initial development, it has been revised a number of times and is now available in a number of different forms. Although Logo includes powerful graphics and text processing components, it is often introduced to young children through its turtle graphics component. This component allows students to be quickly introduced to programming and lets them begin to be able to produce drawings on the computer screen almost immediately. (For introductions to Logo, see Delclos, 1986; Lehrer, et al., 1993.)

Logo *A computer programming language derived from the artificial intelligence language LISP. It was designed so that students could easily learn its basics and begin programming computers from an early age, with the idea that programming would be beneficial for students' cognitive development.*

How might Logo enhance children's thinking skills? First, programming the computer forces children to think carefully about their own thinking (the most important benefit, according to Papert). They cannot write a slipshod, vague program: the program will not run and the desired product (graphic or text) won't be produced. Second, proponents argue that programming requires the consistent use of a number of important problem-solving skills, thus providing a realistic and motivating context in which children can develop and practice these skills. For example, the most efficient way to program in Logo (as in many languages) is to use subprocedures, which requires that children define new words (i.e., procedures) for the various subparts of a desired product, then tell the turtle how to put these new procedures together. To write the subprocedures, a child must analyze the product desired and break it down into subcomponents. The literature on problem solving indicates that the ability to decompose problems is an important skill for solving complex problems, and Logo may provide a very good context in which to develop and practice problem decomposition.

A third aspect of Logo and programming in general that may contribute to improved problem-solving skills is the need to "debug," or to notice the existence of, identify the nature of, and correct errors. As anyone who has done any programming knows all too well, programs rarely work perfectly the first time! Most often, the programmer must compare the output the program gives to the desired output, then analyze the program code to identify precisely what the mismatches are and what parts of the program code caused them. Debugging is clearly an important skill to learn, and Papert and others have argued that Logo is a very good vehicle for enhancing such skills in children.

Fourth, Littlefield and her colleagues (1989) noted that Logo, and programming in general, is a "problem-rich" environment. That is, "real-life," meaningful, and complex problems occur frequently in the course of writing a program, so there is no need to manufacture problems for students to solve. These naturally occurring problems are likely to be more motivating and interesting to students than any a teacher could come up with, since they arise from and block progress toward goals the students are presumably quite interested in reaching. Finally, Logo seems to be a motivating and interesting context for students, because it is easily accessible by even young students, as noted previously, and because the projects are ones that students come up with on their own and thus they probably feel more personal involvement with and ownership of these problems.

How could you as a teacher use Logo to enhance problem-solving skills? The literature indicates several things teachers need to consider (Clements & Gullo, 1984; Lehrer et al., 1989; Littlefield et al., 1989; Pea, Kurland, & Hawkins, 1985). First, teachers need to provide a certain degree of structure in the learning environment; simply teaching children the basics of the language then letting them play with it in a free discovery manner keeps them clearly engaged and on task, but this does not mean they will necessarily master the language itself, or develop any of the important skills mentioned previously. Second, there needs to be consistent and thoughtful mediation on the part of the teacher. *Mediation* is a Vygotskian term for an adult's or more advanced peer's help of a learner in structuring and interpreting the information being learned. This help often consists of helping students choose certain tasks that are within their zones of proximal development, then providing "scaffolding" as students attempt the tasks (i.e., providing a supportive structure through hints, guidance, assistance, prompts, even pieces of programming code, etc. while learning to do new things), and gradually fading this support as the student develops greater programming skill.

Third, recent work with Logo indicates that working on larger-scale projects, or "designs," may be helpful in fostering thinking skills and achievement when learning programming (Harel & Papert, 1991). These designs involve students from the initial conception of a project through to its completion, most often in collaboration with other students or adults. The students decide what they want to produce, discuss alternative ways to approach the problem, and deal with problems and issues that arise during the course of programming. Programming the designs usually requires a great time investment, spread out over many weeks or even months. This process is quite similar to what expert programmers do and requires the use of just the sort of general thinking and problem-solving skills we wish students to develop.

One additional caveat is in order when discussing teaching programming to improve thinking and problem-solving skills. Several studies of a medium duration (Littlefield et al., 1989; Pea et al., 1985) found that with good mediation, certain problem-solving skills can show improvement and transfer to tasks that are fairly similar to those in the Logo environment (i.e., to tasks that also involve giving spatially oriented directions). In other words, students show "near transfer" of the skills, However, these studies do not show consistent evidence of "far transfer," or use of the skills on problems that are not obviously similar to the Logo environment. As you might recall from chapter 9, teaching students problem-solving skills is a difficult task in and of itself, but getting them to actually transfer and use the skills spontaneously on other problems and in other contexts is more difficult still. The Logo studies clearly agree about one thing: if far transfer is to be found, the teacher's role will be of great importance in bringing it about. Teachers in the Logo context, as in any other, must carefully mediate the skills they want students to learn and transfer, explicitly and systematically helping them identify situations in which the problem-solving skills under consideration might be useful.

Improving Thinking Skills Through Writing Instruction

A great deal of research has been conducted on the effects of word processing. Investigators note two aspects of word processing that may result in improved thinking. First, word processing allows students to focus on higher-level aspects of writing (e.g., conceptualization, organization) rather than mechanical aspects (e.g., grammar, spelling).

Table 14.3

The Effects of Word Processing

1. When student writers use word processing in classroom or computer laboratory situations, some of their composing processes are affected.
   a. Students often make a greater number of revisions (i.e., changes of any kind) in their writing than they do with paper and pencil.
   b. Without instructional intervention, students using word processing often make more surface-level revisions and error corrections, but they do not necessarily make more meaning-level changes. They do not tend to change their existing models of composition or their revision strategies. Those with already well-developed writing and revising skills use word processing more effectively than those who do not already have such skills.
   c. When accompanied by instruction in the form of computer prompting, students tend to produce longer and more error-free texts. When accompanied by instruction that focuses on writing as a meaning-making activity, use of word processing may facilitate the production of discovery-centered texts and increase meaning-level revisions.
2. When students use word processing in classroom or computer laboratory situations, the quality and quantity of their written products are affected. However, using word processing in and of itself generally does not improve the overall quality of students' writing. Many students produce slightly longer texts than they do when writing with paper and pencil, produce a greater quantity of writing and/or spend more time writing, and produce neater, more error-free texts.
3. Using word processing for writing in individual classrooms is a practice that is social as well as technical. The ways that word processing is used, the social organization of classroom learning environments, and the goals and strategies of individual teachers and students are interactively related.
4. Student writers of all ages have generally positive attitudes toward using word processing for writing.
5. Student writers of all ages are able to master keyboarding and word processing strategies for use in age-appropriate writing activities.

From M. Cochran-Smith, "Word Processing and Writing in Elementary Classrooms: A Critical Review of Related Literature" in *Review of Educational Research, 61* (1), 107–155, 1991. Copyright © 1991 by the American Educational Research Association.

Second, as we noted earlier, word processing provides students the opportunity to make substantial, meaningful revisions to their text. This capability allows students to improve the quality of thought in their writing by allowing them easily to change their text as they think about and rework their compositions.

Table 14.3 summarizes the conclusions of a recent review of the literature on the effects of word processing (Cochran-Smith, 1991). The table shows that, although the use of word processing *can* have positive effects on several aspects of students' writing, it often does not. When using word processing, students often do make more revisions and produce slightly longer and neater texts. But the overall quality of students' writing is generally not improved just by their use of word processing; nor do students seem to change their strategies for text production and revision.

What must happen for positive changes to occur in the quality of writing and of the thinking underlying the text? Cochran-Smith's review indicates that some kind of instruction in text production and revision must accompany the use of word processors. Several researchers have developed computerized prompting systems that are integrated within the word processing systems (Bonk, 1989; Daiute, 1985; Daiute, 1986; Woodruff, Bereiter, & Scardamalia, 1981–82). Such prompting "may be an effective instructional approach, perhaps especially for writers without well-developed writing and revising skills" (Cochran-Smith, 1991, p. 131). Students can invoke a variety of different kinds of prompts as they plan or compose a paper. Some prompts focus on helping students organize or evaluate their thinking (e.g., "This point is relevant to the main theme in that . . ."; "This point is important to include because . . ."; "Evidence supporting this point includes . . ."), while others are geared toward helping students produce more and better-quality ideas to write about (e.g., "Another idea is that . . . "; "The main point is . . ."). The developers of these systems argue that improvements in writing quality after students have worked on prompting systems indicate improvements in the thinking that underlies their papers: if the quality of thought is not good, then the paper cannot be.

Of course, prompts can certainly be given in a nontechnological way through written comments on the paper made by the teacher or a peer reviewer, but the technology offers the advantage of immediate feedback and advice during the composition process. The scope and depth of prompts in many of these systems is also quite impressive, perhaps surpassing the comments the average teacher or peer reviewer might have the time, inclination, or expertise to offer.

Though the literature on such prompting systems indicates improved writing and presumably improved thinking skills, the degree to which students internalize the prompts is not clear (Bonk, 1989). This is an important point, since the goal of such systems is to help students eventually become able to regulate their own thinking and writing so that they are not dependent on the system to evaluate and prompt their thinking.

Cochran-Smith's review makes another point important for teachers to keep in mind when using word processing in their classrooms: Using word processing in a classroom is a *social* as well as a technical innovation. Teachers' and students' interpretations of the technology, its use, and the existing instructional program and goals must all be considered, because all these factors influence the success of using word processing. In other words, as in the literature on programming, the role of the teacher and interactions between the teacher and students in the existing classroom environment are quite important for determining whether and how students' writing and thinking skills will be affected.

These are only two examples of ways in which technology has been used to improve thinking and problem-solving skills. Technological applications in the next two categories also often seek to do this, but we have kept these separate to emphasize the tremendous increase in complexity which is required to implement them, and also because these last two categories include some of the latest work in applying technology to education.

Intelligent Tutoring Systems

intelligent tutoring system (ITS)
Use of technology to provide an individualized tutor for each student. The computer presents new material, provides examples and practice problems, tracks student performance, identifies errors and misconceptions, and provides appropriate guidance and feedback.

One of the newer uses of technology in education is the **intelligent tutoring system (ITS),** sometimes also called intelligent computer-assisted instruction (ICAI). The goal of such a system is in effect to provide an individual tutor to teach a student about a given domain. The system must present new material in a way that is comprehensible to the student, provide examples, and supply problems so that the student can practice the knowledge and skills being taught. Most important, it must be capable of tracking a student's performance, identifying errors and misconceptions, and providing appropriate guidance and feedback. It is this last aspect that often proves to be the most difficult, because it involves programming into the system decision rules for when to intervene as well as how to intervene, and when to allow the student to continue to the next set of skills or concepts.

An ITS typically has three components (Barr & Feigenbaum, 1982). First, the system must contain an expert component that is able to solve the problems the system will present to the student. Second, there must be a diagnostician, which tracks a student's performance and diagnoses the student's misconceptions and errors. This component also must identify discrepancies between the student's and the expert's knowledge and strategies. Finally, there must be a tutorial component that is responsible for determining and providing appropriate feedback and guidance for the student.

Originally, such systems were developed for training in industry and the military. They have not been used in elementary and secondary instruction until recently. There are several reasons for this (Anderson, Boyle, & Rieser, 1985). First, an ITS generally requires a very powerful computer to be implemented; such computers were not available in microcomputer form and at a feasible cost for most school systems until recently. Second, a great deal of time and money is needed to develop such systems. By some early estimates, as many as hundreds or even thousands of hours were required to create one hour's worth of ITS instruction (more recent estimates of time requirements are somewhat lower, however). The development of an ITS usually requires the collaboration of a team of experts in various fields, as well. For example, to develop an ITS in algebra, the team would need to include a mathematician as the content expert, several experienced programmers, an instructional design expert, an expert in human cognition, and an expert in instructional methods and teaching, at the least! Third, those developing early ITS programs often did not work from an integrated theory of human cognition, learning, and instruction, and as a result were less effective than they perhaps could have been. More recent ITS programs are based on some form of cognitive theory.

What are the advantages of the ITS? First, such systems, when well-programmed, can individualize instruction to a degree not seen before in educational technology. They track students' performance, provide different problems and explanations of content based on students' current understanding, intervene and reinstruct when appropriate, and give immediate feedback. Suppes (1966) described the advantage this way: "Millions of school children will have access to what Philip of Macedon's son Alexander enjoyed as a royal prerogative: the personal services of a tutor as well-informed and responsive as Aristotle" (p. 207).

A second advantage is that an ITS often can allow a type of instruction that would otherwise be quite difficult if not impossible, using examples that are either rarely occurring but quite important, or dangerous. For example, Lesgold and colleagues (1992) developed Sherlock, an avionics ITS, to assist in the training of air force mechanics whose job would be to maintain and repair jets and fighters. The traditional way of training these students is to give them intensive work in the classroom, consisting of lectures and workbook exercises on the many systems in these planes (e.g., electrical, mechanical, fuel, etc.). This classroom instruction is followed by on-the-job training in which the students work under the guidance of experienced mechanics to diagnose and repair planes. The avionics tutor was developed to improve the training these students receive. The tutor can present to the student very rarely occurring, but catastrophic, problems in the planes so that the students can learn to recognize the warning signs of such catastrophes. The computer can also allow the students to make mistakes, even quite dangerous and possibly deadly ones, while working on the problems. Feedback from the computer on the results of these errors allows the students to learn in a very memorable way to avoid these errors in the future. In a series of controlled experiments, the computerized system was quite effective in teaching basic information and how to solve problems. It was also a tremendous time-saver. After four months of classroom instruction and use of the tutor, students were solving problems on a par with students who had spent years in traditional training.

A third advantage of the ITS is that in some cases, the level of content expertise programmed into the system far exceeds that which a classroom teacher can be expected to have. This becomes especially important in trying to identify students' misconceptions about content, i.e., those underlying and often quite ingrained and enduring ways of understanding and knowing about concepts that make sense to the students, but that are not correct. It can be quite difficult to identify such misconceptions, but they have a tremendous impact on students' abilities to understand, remember, and use new information (Roth, 1990). In some cases, teachers may share the same misconceptions, making it quite difficult to identify and change them. An ITS provides a high-level expert for a given content area, thus making it more likely that such misconceptions will be identified and corrected. The expertise inherent in such systems includes an understanding of the importance of certain kinds of errors; the ITS "knows" when it is necessary to intervene to avoid the development of future misconceptions and when the errors are likely to have less of an impact on future learning.

Finally, an ITS offers students the opportunity to move through content at their own pace. As with the CAI programs we have already discussed, this alone can be a big advantage, in that students do not feel the need either to keep up with everyone else even if they're not ready to move on, or to slow down so they don't get too far ahead.

What are the disadvantages of this use of technology? Several have to do with the current state of ITS development and the costs entailed in such development. It is rare to find an ITS system currently available that is geared toward the kindergarten through twelfth-grade levels, though this situation is changing rapidly. As we noted above, each ITS requires a significant amount of time and effort on the part of a number of experts; this, of course, makes development costs high. The potential savings in instructional time and costs will depend on ITS quality and on how widespread its use eventually becomes. Some experts believe that our educational system will include increasingly greater amounts of "distance education," or education of students at locations separate from their instructors. In such situations, if a computer network is available, the ITS could play a major role.

Another potential disadvantage of the ITS has to do with the tutorial component. Some researchers argue that this component focuses almost exclusively on the cognitive aspects of the tutoring process, i.e., identifying and programming the rules that govern when and how a tutor should intervene. Lepper and Chabay (1988) pointed out that motivational as well as cognitive components of tutoring must be considered in developing a truly personalized instructional system. They stressed that an ITS must display not only intelligent tutoring, but empathetic tutoring as well. The literature on the tutoring process is only beginning to acknowledge the importance of motivational and other affective variables. How to program this kind of expertise is an issue that has yet to be addressed in the ongoing development of the ITS.

Multimedia Uses

multimedia uses *The integration and simultaneous use of several different types of technology (e.g., computers, CD-ROMs, laser videodiscs). This use of technology in teaching is often based on cognitive constructivist theory and often involves students in collaborative, large-scale projects.*

In our final category of technology uses are multimedia forms. **Multimedia uses** of technology involve the integration and simultaneous use of several different types of technology to improve instruction. For example, a computer software program might be written using some specialized language (e.g., Handy, Hypercard) that controls not only the presentation of text and graphics on the computer screen, but also the use of a laser videodisc, an audio compact disc, a videotape, an audiotape, voice synthesis, digitized voice, or animated graphics (Nix & Spiro, 1990). Many are interactive, in that the user does not just listen and view them, but can manipulate them in some way.

The current work on multimedia technology in education clearly is based on a cognitive perspective, specifically the cognitive constructivist view that we described earlier in this chapter. Students often work on complex projects of their own design in collaboration with other students and teachers. In doing the projects, which often require months of work, students come to a deeper understanding not only of the subject matter, but also of themselves as learners and of what it means to "know" something. In other words, they not only gain content knowledge, but also gain experience about what knowledge in a given domain consists of, how it is accumulated, and how it may change over time.

Working on such projects also allows students to integrate several different formats of information, thus presenting and learning information in several different "notational systems" (Lehrer, 1994, p. 200). That is, the students use several different formats in storing and understanding knowledge (e.g., visual, verbal, auditory), presumably thus creating a more in-depth, more accessible, and better-integrated base of knowledge and skills. Multimedia programs are often designed to encourage students to integrate different types of content as well (e.g., science, mathematics, history), so that students will begin to see the interconnections between these areas. Integration such as this is thought to help students understand how to use knowledge and skills as cognitive tools for solving realistic problems, rather than seeing knowledge as a collection of unrelated, often useless facts (Bransford et al., 1990).

Laser Videodisc Series

One multimedia project designed to integrate several content areas was developed by the Cognition and Technology group at Vanderbilt University (Cognition and Technology Group at Vanderbilt, 1990; Van Haneghan et al., 1992). This group has designed a **laser videodisc** series that depicts a character named Jasper Woodbury who is involved in several complex, realistic problem situations. For example, in one disc, Jasper travels to look over an old cruiser that he is considering buying. The videodisc shows Jasper setting out in his motorboat, looking over a map of the area, listening to the marine radio, and buying gas. He breaks a shear pin of his propeller and must get to a repair shop to have it fixed, then continues. He arrives at the dock where the cruiser is kept, test-drives it, and decides to buy it. At the end of the video, Jasper is asking himself whether he can make it home without running out of gas and when he needs to leave. Students are challenged to identify Jasper's major goal, generate the subproblems that must be solved to meet the goal, find relevant information presented in the videodisc, and come up with strategies to solve the subproblems and achieve the major goal.

The developers note several aspects of this videodisc that make it a useful context for learning both content knowledge and general problem-solving skills, and that encourage students to integrate knowledge across content areas (Bransford, Sherwood, et al., 1990). First, the problem presented is quite complex, requiring students to generate and solve approximately fifteen subgoals. The authors argue that students need experience generating problems and solving complex problems, but they are often not given such opportunities in classrooms, because it can be quite difficult to design and present problems that are complex and interesting, but that students are capable of understanding and working with.

Second, the problems encountered are realistic, allowing students the opportunity to make decisions in realistic settings. This realism also conveys information to students that might be important in solving the problems, but is difficult to fully describe verbally. For example, a student can be told verbally that the highest sustained wind speed of an approaching storm is 68 mph, but many students will not really grasp just how fast this is and will not realize the implications of such a speed. Seeing the wind buffeting a boat and hearing the howl of a high-speed wind may help them grasp the fuller meaning and implications of such verbally presented information (Steinberg, 1991).

Third, the videodiscs use an embedded data design in which students view the videodisc and generate the subproblems, then must go back to find the relevant information that is embedded in the story. All necessary data are included, but as in many real-life situations, the students are not told that the information is relevant for solving a problem when they first encounter it. Students must learn how to search information sources (including their memories!) for potentially useful information.

Finally, the video encourages students to integrate such content areas as mathematics and science. For example, Jasper must determine whether he has enough gas to make it home. This requires taking into account such scientific information as the wind speed, the rate of the current, whether he is going with or against the current, the effect of the boat's weight on travel time, etc. It also requires that students be able to use such mathematical information as ratios and probabilities. Probably most important, the videodisc encourages students to view these scientific and mathematical skills as tools to be used in the service of solving a problem, rather than just as facts and formulae to be memorized.

A number of other multimedia studies have been conducted, including some in which children design and develop projects about the Civil War (Lehrer, 1994) or Victorian England, and some in which they write stories (Bransford, Vye, et al., 1990). Initial results are encouraging, with studies reporting positive effects of multimedia design projects on student comprehension, retention, and use of new knowledge. In addition, several of the studies have reported positive affective results, with students (both those who are academically successful and those who are less successful) reporting increased feelings of ownership and greater student involvement and engagement in the design and production process (Cognition and Technology Group at Vanderbilt, 1990; Lehrer, 1994).

laser videodisc *An optical disk technology that stores digital movies and allows instantaneous access to any frame on the disc. The data are read from the disc by a laser beam.*

What are the disadvantages of or potential problems associated with using multimedia for educational purposes? As with several of the other categories we've discussed, one potential disadvantage is the cost. Though not nearly as expensive as an ITS, instruction using multimedia still requires that teachers have available a variety of different types of technology (computers, videodisc players, audio disc players, etc.) and software capable of interfacing the different machines. Obviously, if a school cannot afford the equipment, then a teacher cannot teach using multimedia.

A bigger disadvantage to many teachers' minds, however, is the loss of control over what students are learning. As we noted earlier in this chapter, allowing students to design their own multimedia projects turns over the control and responsibility for learning to the students themselves. This may have the result that students do not cover the material the teacher (or school system) thinks they ought to cover. Proponents argue that students may well cover much of the "required" material, but in a very different and (they claim) superior way.

Finally, a potential problem with this use of technology has to do with how a teacher determines exactly what a student has learned. As with many new instructional methods, old ways of assessing learning may not be valid. For example, many of the proponents of multimedia uses advocate emphasizing not just the learning of factual information, but the learning of problem-solving skills, the use of factual knowledge to solve problems, self-regulation of learning, and a change in the way students view knowledge: from a collection of facts to a repertoire of useful, dynamically changing information. But how does a teacher assess students' views of knowledge, degree of self-regulation, and problem-solving skills? Assessment of motivational aspects and the degree to which students feel more involved in their own learning are also seen as important, and these too can present thorny assessment issues. Chapter 15 in this text presents information on new approaches to assessment that should help teachers with this problem.

CD-ROM (Compact Disc–Read Only Memory)

CD-ROM *Compact disc–read only memory. An optical disk technology that allows storage of very large amounts of any type of digital data, including text, digital sound and graphics, and digital movies. The data are read from the disc by a laser beam.*

CD-ROM is an increasingly popular form of technology in education. Like the audio compact disc, **CD-ROM** uses an optical disk technology, but CD-ROMs allow the storage of very large amounts of any type of digital data, including text, digital sound and graphics, and digital movies. CD-ROMs have been used in school libraries for quite some time, providing fast and easy access to large databases. At the college level, you might be familiar with CD-ROM versions of *Psychological Abstracts* or the ERIC system, both of which contain listings of thousands of references on psychological or educational topics.

One well-known CD-ROM system for use at the elementary and secondary level is Compton's *Multimedia Encyclopedia,* which allows users to access any topic included in the entire encyclopedia within seconds. CD-ROM encyclopedias such as Compton's are more than computerized pages of text, however. They also include both static and dynamic visual information and sound, often in the form of news footage or animation with and without narration, giving the user much richer information than a printed text is capable of. Advocates argue that richer information allows students to better visualize and comprehend information with which they have no direct experience. Using special types of software, students can also interface the CD-ROM database with their classroom computers and develop projects, reports, and stories that include text about certain topics as well as motion picture and audio historical information. This ability to manipulate the information from the database, easily choosing which parts of the database to include, and when, where, and how to use them, can help students personalize the information and thus understand and remember it more effectively. For example, if students are preparing a multimedia presentation about the Civil Rights movement, they could combine text they wrote with video clips of actual news footage from the time and with video and audio clips of Martin Luther King, Jr.'s "I have a dream" speech, all integrated into one presentation.

Thus far, the major educational use of CD-ROM has been as an economical, multimedia way to access large databases. Other uses focused more on initial instruction of skills are being developed, and also include animation, music, narration which can be turned on or off, and bilingual options. For example, the National Geographic Society has produced a series of CD-ROMs focusing on different topics for use in teaching reading. One set of CD-ROMs, *Animals and How They Grow,* is a content-based reading series. Students select one of five different "books" to access from the CD-ROM. Information is presented about different kinds of animals and how they develop, including animated sequences and video clips. Students can follow the stories both on the screen and in accompanying hard copy of the text. The teacher has a number of different options in the way the information is presented. These include having a digitized voice read all or part of the story to the student; having the voice read only certain phrases and allowing the student to read other parts; presenting the information in English or Spanish; or presenting vocabulary words in one language, then in the other, for those just learning one language or the other. The system can also be set up to ask students questions about what they have read and seen. Thus, this series fosters students' reading and comprehension skills, and can also be used to teach students either English or Spanish. Some CD-ROMs also have the capability to allow students to use the images, vocabulary, and audio features to write their own stories, which the program then "reads" aloud. Clearly, CD-ROMs hold a great deal of promise for instruction. However, at this point little empirical work has been done to evaluate their impact on students' knowledge and skill development.

Recent Developments in Educational Technology

Educational technology is a rapidly expanding field, with each year bringing new and exciting developments. One technological innovation that is rapidly gaining acceptance in classrooms is the **computer network.** Another development sure to have a substantial impact in the future is virtual reality (VR).

computer network *The connection of computers to one another through telephone lines or cables so that information and/or equipment can be shared.*

Networks

Increasing numbers of schools are discovering the advantages of networking, or connecting computers to one another through telephone lines or cables so that information and/or equipment can be shared. In part, the increase is occurring because networks are becoming easier to install and operate. But educators are also coming to realize that networks can be quite helpful in instruction as well as management tasks.

In general, there are three levels of networks. A local area network (LAN) connects computers in a limited geographic area and allows users to share software applications, data files, and peripheral computer equipment (e.g., printers). A wide area network (WAN) connects users across larger geographic areas and is done through the use of telephone lines. WANs allow users to communicate with other computer users across the country or the world, and allow fast and easy access to a vast array of different databases. Finally, there is the Internet, which is not a single network at all, but the interconnection of many different networks to allow global communications—a network of networks.

One of the most exciting educational advantages of networking is that it facilitates group work by allowing students at different computers to work on different aspects of one problem, then share their work with group members. Such collaborative research projects are "where student science becomes real science" (Roberts et al., 1990, p. 122): when students collaborate on real problems and share ideas, data, insights on conclusions, and recommendations, they are engaging in the same activities as professional scientists. Students at different locations in a school, district, city, or country can easily access and add to a database their group is developing, make revisions on a project and report they are writing, or discuss the project with one another.

A number of these collaborative research projects span different countries. For example, the WaterNet project involved high school students from the United States and

Germany in a collaborative research project to assess and discuss water quality, factors affecting it, and ways to improve it, in various rivers in both countries (Berger & Wolf, 1988). The Intercultural Learning Network involves several projects connecting students from various countries in collaborative projects that integrate science, social studies, and language arts. Some of the topics addressed thus far include studies of severe weather conditions, animal and insect pests, pollution, and energy. Some of the countries involved include the United States, Mexico, Japan, and Israel (Waugh & Levin, 1989). The National Geographic Kids Network connects hundreds of schools in several countries in a networked science curriculum for fourth- through sixth-graders.

Another, more administrative, advantage of networking concerns management of student records (McCarthy, 1989). Educators can have instant access to accurate information on any student in a district whenever it is needed, and can add various kinds of information to the record easily and quickly (e.g., attendance information, necessary medical information, grades, notes). Teachers also can share files easily about curricular content and activities, student progress, or even scheduling. A third advantage is that networks can save money: they can cut the cost of software (by buying one piece of the software along with a site license, rather than buying multiple copies of the software) and of peripherals (by having multiple computers networked to one high-quality printer rather than buying multiple printers).

Students and teachers involved in networked projects seem to enjoy the projects and feel they learn about different cultures as well as academic content (Lockard, Abrams, & Many, 1994; Roberts et al., 1990). One study of usage of the Internet indicated that, along with enthusiasm toward using Internet, students showed development of leadership skills, and teachers showed changes in teaching style toward a facilitator and/or motivator role (Department of Engineering & Public Policy et al., 1993). However, at this time there is little information concerning the effects of networking on students' comprehension, achievement levels, problem-solving skills, or classroom interactions.

Virtual reality (VR)

virtual reality (VR) *A computer-generated environment that is three-dimensional and involves the user in real-time, multisensory interactions.*

A second recent development in technology sure to have a substantial impact on education is **virtual reality (VR).** This is a computer-generated environment which is three-dimensional and involves the user in real-time, multisensory interactions (Ferrington & Loge, 1992). The user wears a special viewing helmet that generates three-dimensional visual and auditory experiences, and a wired glove (or a full-body data suit, in some newer systems) that allows the user to "move about" in the virtual space. As the user moves the glove, the computer updates the position in the virtual space and provides appropriate changes in the visual and sound information provided in the viewing helmet.

The exciting aspect of VR systems for learning is that students will be able to engage in interactive learning that will combine cognitive, affective, and psychomotor skills (Walser, 1990). For example, students will not be limited to imagining what it is like to live on Mars; they will be able to *experience* this within a VR simulation of Mars' environment. Biology and medical students could perform operations on "virtual" patients to learn about various organ systems and the effects of different treatments, learning activities which are clearly not possible in "real" reality. Though virtual reality systems are not yet being used in elementary and secondary education, the military and higher education institutions are experimenting with their uses for training and education. As more information about VR's educational usefulness is gathered and as the cost of the VR systems decreases, it is likely that such systems will begin to be used in lower-level classrooms.

There are a number of different ways in which technology can be used in teaching. Our categorization is not meant to be definitive or exhaustive, but only to provide a framework for some examples of how technology might enrich your teaching. This area of education changes almost daily; expect new and even more exciting developments

Will the "Information Superhighway" Change the Nature of Teaching and Learning?

There has been much discussion recently about a coming "information superhighway" to electronically connect schools, homes, businesses, and government across our country. While it is not a reality as yet, many educators are quite excited about the possibilities the information superhighway will offer for meaningful long-distance collaboration among students, increased access to resources of many types, and the further development of higher-level thinking and problem-solving skills. Others are more wary, citing the possibility that this superhighway will not rid our system of intolerance, and may actually increase students' frustration when learning.

Issue

The information superhighway will help foster an understanding of and appreciation for individual differences as students collaborate long-distance on projects.

Answer: Pro One of the best ways to foster acceptance and understanding, and to learn to value those different from ourselves, is to work together to achieve a common goal. In doing so, students are exposed to different models of thinking and come to understand that different individuals possess different skills which, when combined with their own skills, contribute to a better result. In the past students have been limited to working with those in their immediate classes and schools. The information superhighway will allow easy, fast collaboration across long distances, either for work on academic projects or simply for socializing and learning about different cultures. It will also allow students access to numerous resources that are currently unavailable (e.g., libraries, museums) to experience the ideas, literature, music, art, etc., of people from not only different cultures, but different historical time periods. In addition to teaching content in history, English, art, and music, such access can foster greater understanding of the conventions of contemporary people in different cultures.

Answer: Con The information superhighway will allow students access to the conventions and ideas of different cultures, but it clearly does not guarantee acceptance and appreciation of individual differences. Students learn toler-

ance and acceptance by example, and if teachers and parents do not actively support the use of the information superhighway for this goal, then increased knowledge may provide students with more detailed bases for prejudice. Knowledge of the advantages that others have may even increase feelings of jealousy and discomfort if a student's own situation is compared to those of others and is found to be lacking in some way, whether that lack is real or exaggerated. Money is also an important consideration. Students in schools that are not able to fund easy access to the information superhighway may become the "new underclass," discriminated against in subtle ways because of their lack of knowledge and technological skill.

Issue

The information superhighway will change the types of skills students develop from recall and comprehension of factual information to learning how to define and solve self-generated problems.

Answer: Pro Because the information superhighway will allow access to much more information and different resources than before, students will need to be taught different kinds of skills. It is already fast becoming impossible to identify the specific pieces of knowledge that students will need to function effectively in the future, much less remember them all! Students can be encouraged to use the information superhighway to develop projects of their own choosing, then further refine and develop them. Such projects will offer unique opportunities to develop skills such as goal definition and information search and selection—skills that are absolutely essential in our information age.

Answer: Con The information superhighway will allow access to numerous types of resources and tremendous amounts of information. But students often are overwhelmed already with the choices of information they have, and have difficulty figuring out where to start when asked to do a project of their own choosing. Information overload, frustration at not knowing how to start, and losing track of the overall goal in the midst of a myriad of detail may well result.

with each passing year. One final point we urge you to keep in mind, however, is that technology is a *tool* to be used to enhance quality education. It is the creativity, planning, and commitment of the teacher that determines the degree to which the ever-more-sophisticated technologies will impact students. Teachers must be willing to try new things and spend time learning the most effective ways to use technology for their instructional goals in order for the power of educational technology to be fully utilized.

ISSUES IN TECHNOLOGY USE

When we began this chapter, we proposed several questions that a teacher must answer in deciding whether to use and how to use technology. After reading the chapter to this point, you know how technology is currently being used, and have some idea of the variety of ways in which it can be used. There are several remaining issues that are important when considering using technology in your classroom. Some reflect problems that we know exist, while others concern potential problems we anticipate as technology use becomes even more widespread.

Access

As we have noted several times, certain uses of technology can be quite expensive. Even the more common uses, such as teaching students how to use various software packages, involve substantial cost in acquiring appropriate machines and software. In times of economic hardship, some poorer school districts begin to cut supplies and expense budgets, resulting in the purchase of fewer and less sophisticated machines and software. What is the effect of this on the so-called "technology gap," i.e., the gulf between schools that can afford more sophisticated equipment and supplies and those that cannot? An even more important question will arise if educational technology does prove to improve teaching and learning, as its proponents claim and many studies seem to indicate: What will unequal access to technology do to the already existing gap in quality of schooling between those schools in poorer areas and those in wealthier ones? There are no easy answers to this issue, even though it is one that is faced daily with respect to many educational issues.

A second problem related to access to technology is a bit different in nature. Recall that the literature indicated a clear gender gap in how technology is viewed. Computers are often reported as being gender-appropriate for boys but not for girls, and girls are often less likely to enjoy and seek out computer work. We don't fully understand the reasons for this trend, but experts are quite disturbed by it, particularly in light of its implications for future career opportunities for girls. Teachers who choose to use technology in their teaching need to be mindful of how they are using it, and with whom. They also should try to become aware of the subtle messages they may send through their own enthusiasm (or lack thereof) for technology. Girls may benefit from having positive female role models and from being explicitly encouraged to engage in computer and other technology-related tasks.

Security

As more and more schools begin to network their computers, assuring security is becoming increasingly important. While easy access to other students' work fosters student collaboration, there will certainly still be times when individual work is required and students should not be able to access others' work. Easy access to student records can also be problematic, and schools must develop policies and procedures to ensure that only those with legitimate needs for information have access to student files, especially confidential testing and evaluation information. As students become able to access more and more information sources via networks, the issue of access to age- and grade-inappropriate information is also raised. Should students have ready and virtually unlimited access to all databases and information available on the networks, or should there be some way to limit access to educationally relevant and age-appropriate materials? Educators must develop policies on access and use of information, and establish procedures to limit access, if that is what they decide is necessary.

Issues & Answers

Will Increased Emphasis on Educational Technology Further Widen the Technology Gap?

Many educators argue that technology needs to be strongly emphasized in classrooms. In addition to providing technology-related knowledge and skills that will increase their job marketability, technology will enable students to experience educational opportunities they otherwise would not be able to. Others are more wary, citing the possibility that increasing the emphasis on technology may actually increase the already-existing inequities in our educational system.

Issue

Girls are already reluctant to use computers. Increasing the emphasis will cause them to fall farther behind in yet another domain important for future academic and occupational success.

Answer: Pro Surveys indicate that computer use is seen by both girls and boys as a male- rather than a female-appropriate activity. Increasing the importance of computer-related skills and knowledge will result in even more instructional time being focused on an area that many girls are not interested in, thus reducing the amount of class time during which they are actively engaged with information and materials they feel comfortable with and are motivated to pursue. Many computer programs are set up in an educational game format that readily fosters a competition between students for the highest scores. This may further decrease girls' interest and comfort with computers, since the literature indicates that girls often prefer more cooperative learning environments. The end result will be lack of knowledge and skills for girls, and ultimately decreased opportunities for higher-level, better-paying, and more valued occupations.

Answer: Con The literature does indicate that girls like computers less, use them less often, and think of their use as a male-appropriate activity. But the literature also suggests that part of this reaction is due to the way in which technology is currently presented and used. When computers and technology are emphasized, presented as everyday activities and as tools to accomplish various ends, all students will become more comfortable with them and experienced in their use. Teachers must also be taught how to use computers in various ways in their classrooms, sometimes using competitive games, but also incorporating cooperative and individual work, so that students with differing learning preferences all develop feelings of confidence and competence when using technology.

Issue

Increased emphasis on technology in education will affect students in wealthy schools differently from those in poor schools, and will further widen the "technology gap".

Answer: Pro Technology requires money. Federal and state governments cannot pay for everything needed to place a strong emphasis on technology in education. At the least, individual schools will be responsible for supplying some of the equipment, materials, and instruction in how to use technology effectively. Whenever money is involved, poorer schools are obviously at an automatic disadvantage. If the effect of an increased emphasis on technology is to open new, exciting avenues for learning, then poorer schools and students will be denied yet another opportunity for academic advancement.

Answer: Con Though it is hard to estimate the initial costs of a strongly technological educational system, it is sure to be expensive. However, technology, particularly electronic connections like networks, could serve eventually to reduce the technology gap. Students in poorer schools could "travel" to places and have access to resources they could not afford otherwise, thus widening their range of experiences and opportunities for learning. Increased emphasis on technology should also serve to help these students develop strong technological skills, which will enable them to compete for higher-paying and higher-status jobs, and improve the economic status of the next generation.

Role of the Teacher

As we noted earlier, one of the biggest roadblocks to innovative uses of technology in the classroom, uses that take fuller advantage of its potential, is discomfort with the new role the teacher often must assume. Teachers may have difficulty adjusting to not being the ones in charge and not making all the decisions in the classroom (this difficulty might be reflected in society in general, as well). Some teachers may feel a bit uncomfortable when first using technology, and will need time to adjust to this different role. In addition, these teachers could greatly benefit from a supportive network of other teachers who are integrating technology into their teaching. Setting up or joining groups of other teachers both within the school and in other schools is quite helpful in providing technical and moral support, as well as providing ideas for dealing with instructional or management issues. Support from administrators and parents is also quite important. More and better-quality in-service training should be made available, and district technology services and experts widely publicized, so that teachers do not feel that they are going it alone.

Selection of Hardware and Software

A very practical issue is how to select appropriate hardware and software for your school. Some general aspects to consider in software selection are listed in the focus box on this topic. A variety of educator-oriented journals and magazines are available that provide reviews of new products, and several organizations exist that have the sole purpose of providing up-to-date and easily understandable reviews of new hardware and software (e.g., Minnesota Area Computing Consortium, with reviews available nationwide). Again, the school district as a whole can be quite helpful in solving this problem by hiring a school- and/or districtwide technology expert who can answer questions for teachers and collect software for teachers to preview or use. Many districts now have software libraries where teachers can preview different packages (some on loan from software companies) and look up information. Most of these libraries, however, contain only CAI and some applications packages (e.g., word processing software). They often do not have access to multimedia equipment and software or to ITS, nor do they often have a repository of information about more and less effective ways to use the packages.

Some communities do have such information available at nearby colleges and universities with faculty knowledgeable in the use of educational technology. Often, researchers will "trade" their expertise in return for the opportunity to implement technological innovations and collect data in local schools; this is probably the best way to get access to the newest uses of technology. Obviously, teachers can also make use of these resources by attending classes on educational technology at local colleges and universities and by inviting faculty knowledgeable about educational technology to present in-service workshops.

Classroom Set-Up of Technology

There is controversy surrounding how technology, specifically computers, should be set up in schools (Salomon, 1990). Those in favor of placing machines directly in individual classrooms argue that this arrangement encourages regular use and integration of the machines with everyday instruction. They also argue that the alternative, separate computer labs, creates scheduling headaches, and encourages students to view computers as a separate content domain, rather than as tools to be used to learn about other domains. Those in favor of computer labs argue that with only one or two machines in each classroom, students are forced to use the computers during "free time," and for very limited durations. Regardless of whether machines are set up in a computer lab or in classrooms, experts recommend that they be networked so that software, databases, and so forth can be easily accessed from any location.

Another issue concerning how computers should be set up concerns whether students will use the machines individually or cooperatively. Some uses have as their explicit goal the individualization of learning, and so it makes sense that students work on their own (e.g., many forms of CAI; ITS). Many other uses can be and have been implemented quite successfully with students working in pairs or small groups. For example, the multimedia design projects are often quite complex and best accomplished in small groups, with students sharing both ideas and labor in putting the projects together. Using the computer to teach thinking skills is also often done using pairs or small groups of students, with the students providing one another with constructive criticism, as well as brainstorming about problems and their potential solutions. If technology is used cooperatively, it is important to remember that the work must be truly cooperative—i.e., the students must understand how to offer constructive criticism to help one another, rather than simply dividing chores with little or no discussion of why the project or problem is being approached in a certain fashion.

Focus — **Selection of Software**

Selection of software can be quite confusing. The following questions might be helpful when reviewing software for classroom use.

1. General criteria to consider, similar to those you would use to evaluate any curricular materials:
   - Is the subject matter covered accurately?
   - Is the material written at an appropriate reading level?
   - Are the activities of appropriate length?
   - Are clear, concise instructions given for students?
   - Are the activities sequenced logically?
   - Is the layout of the material appealing?
   - Is correct grammar used in the materials?
   - Are the activities motivating for the students?
   - Are the materials socially acceptable?
   - Are the support materials complete?
   - Is the cost reasonable?
2. Criteria specifically related to computers and computing:
   - Is the program easy to operate?
   - Is the program versatile to use?
   - Is the program attractive and motivating?

- Is the package well documented?
- Is the interactive capability of the computer used to advantage?
- Are special capabilities, such as the ability to produce random events, used to advantage?
- Does the use of features such as graphics, animation, and sound enhance instruction rather than distracting students?
- Does the software allow appropriate control over the activity by providing options for movement through the materials?
- Does the computer handle input from the student effectively, so that excessive typing is avoided and unexpected responses do not disrupt the activity?
- Is feedback for correct and incorrect responses and performance provided effectively and appropriately?
- Does the program produce realistic and valid results?
- Do the materials allow for appropriate teacher-student and student-student interaction (e.g., collaborative learning)?

Source: Adapted from David Squires and Anne McDougall, Choosing and Using Educational Software: A Teacher's Guide, *Falmer Press, London, 1194.*

Effect of Computers on Social Interactions

When computers were first being implemented in classrooms, many educators worried that students' social development would suffer, and that classroom interactions would be adversely affected. This was of particular concern for younger students who were still in the process of developing strategies for appropriate social interactions. A recent review of computer usage in young children (preschool through elementary age) indicated that contrary to these fears, students working on the computer often showed a higher amount of social interaction than students working on noncomputer activities such as art projects or reading (Clements & Nastasi, 1992). The type of interaction varied with the type of software used and with the children's ages, with some students showing increases in turn-taking, while others showed increases in providing explanations to other students. The reason for these results isn't clear; it may be that students are forced to interact more often due to limits in the number of computers available. The nature of the computer activities may also play a role, with some computer activities (e.g., programming large-scale projects in Logo) being quite difficult to accomplish alone. Proponents of networking argue that involvement in networked research projects will be quite beneficial to students' social development, in particular improving their knowledge and acceptance of students of different cultures. The work we reviewed earlier on international collaboration among students over a network seems to support this assertion, though more work is needed.

Consideration of Individual Differences

Finally, teachers must think about whether the forms of technology they are considering for their classrooms meet the individual needs of their students. Clearly, some uses of technology will do this, since that is one of the main purposes for their development (e.g., CAI, ITS). However, even these systems were developed with individual differences in *cognition* in mind: differences in knowledge base, existing cognitive skills, and rate of advancement through the material. Most existing technology has not really taken other types of individual differences into account. For example, perhaps some forms of technology are better suited to some cognitive styles than to others.

Other aspects of individual differences concern social and affective characteristics that we know are important for learning, but that we don't know how to account for in educational technology. One example is a student's preference for learning alone versus with a group. Some students simply prefer working in a social setting, while others find this quite distracting and detrimental to learning. Another example is some students' preference to work predominantly with textual material, while others work much more effectively with audio or visual forms. And a third example concerns an individual student's degree of motivation. Many proponents of various uses of technology assert that students will be more motivated to learn when using technology instead of traditional methods to do so. Though this may be true, we don't know if the effect is long-lasting (recall the evidence for a novelty effect of technology), and there will certainly still be differences between individual students in their degree of motivation and enthusiasm for technological forms of instruction (recall, for example, the gender differences we discussed earlier).

The best advice for addressing this issue is to use common sense. It is probably best to provide students with a variety of different learning activities and media, including several different forms of technological as well as nontechnological methods of instruction, and to ask students to work cooperatively on some projects and individually on others. We hope that this book has at least provided a start in developing your repertoire of both technological and more traditional teaching methods and skills—a source that we hope you can draw on again and again as you progress through your teaching career.

APPLICATIONS AND REFLECTIONS

Chapter Highlights

What is Educational Technology?

- Educational technology (or instructional technology) takes many different forms and includes simple kinds of machines (e.g., overhead projectors, slide projectors) as well as complex, powerful computers and software.
- Research indicates that using technology in your classroom can significantly improve instruction and students' learning. Educational technology offers a number of advantages for instruction, from providing simple audiovisual demonstrations of concepts to allowing students to interact with concepts and materials in a way that would otherwise be difficult, dangerous, or impossible, and to collaborate with students across the world.

A Brief History of Technology in Education

- Historically, the theoretical basis for educational technology has shifted from an emphasis on the media used to behaviorist theory, and then to cognitive theory. Newer forms and uses of educational technology are often based on cognitive constructivist theory.

How Is Technology Currently Used in Classrooms?

- Recent surveys indicate that although computers are increasingly available to teachers, the machines are often of limited computing power. Although more teachers are incorporating technology into instruction in some way, teachers who regularly use computers are still very much in the minority. When technology is used regularly, it is often used for "lower-level" purposes.

Students' Perceptions of Technology in the Classroom

*   In general, students surveyed seem to enjoy using technology. However, some research indicates that a novelty effect may account for some of the positive attitude changes, and there is a strong and consistent finding that girls are generally less positive toward computer technology than boys are.

Types and Uses of Technology in Education

*   We categorize technology and teaching according to seven types and/or uses.
*   Administrative and/or managerial uses involve technology to collect, analyze, and report information concerning students or instruction. Examples include computerized gradebooks, word processing for record keeping, and spreadsheets to graph student progress.
*   Audiovisual aids use technology to present information in several formats, and include overhead and slide projectors, and television.
*   Teaching the technology provides hands-on learning of the basics of using technology, particularly how to use word processing packages, spreadsheets, and graphing programs.
*   Computer-assisted instruction uses technology to present material to students or assist them in mastering it. Examples are computerized programmed instruction and drill and practice software.
*   Teaching thinking using technology attempts to foster the development, use, and transfer of students' general thinking and problem-solving skills. Examples are teaching programming and using word processing to improve thinking skills.
*   Intelligent tutoring systems use technology to provide an individualized tutor for each student.
*   Multimedia uses technology to integrate and simultaneously use several different types of technology. Laser videodiscs and CD-ROMs are examples.
*   Recent developments in technology that are impacting education include networks and virtual reality environments.

Issues in Technology Use

*   The effect of unequal access to technology, caused either by economic factors or differential interest and encouragement of boys versus girls, has yet to be addressed.
*   Security of computerized information is a growing problem.
*   Discomfort with a changing role of the teacher can be problematic and hinder the most effective use of technology.
*   Selection of hardware and software is difficult and time-consuming, and questions about the best way to set up classrooms for technology use (e.g., computers distributed throughout classrooms versus in a centralized computer laboratory) are controversial.
*   The effect of computer use on students' social interactions appears to be more positive than initially expected.
*   Teachers must also think about whether the uses of technology they choose for their classes meet the individual needs, both academic and affective, of their students.
*   The role of the "information superhighway" and how to best take advantage of it to improve instruction is an issue on which there is little information as of yet.

Connections

1. Think about how you learn and describe how one of the major concepts discussed in this chapter is part of your learning activities or approach.

_____

_____

_____

_____

2. Identify at least one learning situation (e.g., classroom instruction, self-study, taking a test, small-group work) and describe how you would apply one of the key concepts examined in this chapter *if you were a teacher*.

_____

_____

_____

_____

Getting the Picture and Drawing Relationships

Think about the various learning concepts and variables discussed in this chapter. Create pictures, graphics, or figures that highlight relationships among the key components.

Personal Journal

What I really learned in this chapter was _____

_____

_____

_____

_____

_____

What this means to me is _____

_____

_____

_____

_____

_____

_____

_____

Questions that were stimulated by this chapter include _____

_____

_____

_____

Key Terms

audiovisual aids	491	computer-managed		laser videodisc	504
CD-ROM	505	instruction (CMI)	491	Logo	498
cognitive constructivism	481	control theory	463	multimedia uses	503
computer network	506	drill and practice	496	novelty effect	488
computer-assisted		educational technology	478	programmed instruction	495
instruction (CAI)	494	intelligent tutoring		virtual reality (VR)	507
		system (ITS)	501	word processing	493

section 5

assessing learning and evaluating education

How will we know if our children are really learning material that is essential for their continued success in school and college? This was a question that the teachers at Verona Middle School were frequently asked by parents. Jayne Bischoff, like her colleagues at VMS, often found this question difficult to answer with a brief, meaningful response. In addition, the teachers were aware that some parents really liked to get individual standardized test results of their children's achievement, while others thought that the most important achievement data resulted from classroom work samples and time-intense small-group projects.

Just remember, Jim, that we do assessment to facilitate communication. Because we have to communicate with many people—parents, students, and administrators—we have to use a variety of assessment tools. Be flexible in the data you use to communicate a student's academic functioning. Also, try to compare the student's performance to a set of criteria, rather than just saying the student is above average, at the top of the class, or some other comparative statement concerning classmates. Although parents like to know where their children rank among their peers, they need to understand even more the criteria we use to judge progress!" stated Jayne confidently.

chapter 15

teacher-constructed tests and performance assessment methods

When Jim Lasso, a second-year math and science teacher, was preparing for teacher-parent conferences, he decided he would ask Jayne how she typically answered the question about determining student's academic progress. It seemed like Jim had "tons" of information about his students, but given the brief time allotted for a conference and the concern that many parents had about their children's progress, he felt a little overwhelmed when it came to summarizing a student's progress. "How do you do it, Jayne? How do you tell parents about their child's academic progress without giving them standardized test scores and grade point averages?" asked Jim. Jayne smiled and responded succinctly, "I don't."

"What do you mean?" responded Jim with surprise.

Jayne continued, "I do give them grades, and standardized test scores when they are available, but I do a lot more. I share the student's work portfolio with them and the student's self-assessment ratings. Then I outline the major class goals or outcomes that I am teaching toward and conclude with a general statement about the student's accomplishments. Something like 'The major learning outcomes have been mastered' or 'The major learning outcomes need additional work; however, clear evidence of progress is present.'

After reflecting for a moment, Jim responded, "That sounds like very good advice. I'll try to put it into practice next week with parents during conferences." ■

The process of assessing students' learning is central to instruction, and is most frequently accomplished with either teacher-made or commercially published standardized tests. To help you construct or select fair tests and at the same time help your students prepare for them, we will explore the world of testing and measurement in this chapter. A major theme will be the role of testing and assessment in the teaching-learning process. In other words, testing is not an isolated activity to be done because students "need a grade"; sound instruction requires sound classroom-level assessment of students' achievement and behavior. A second theme highlights students' need to be helped in preparing for tests so that their performance accurately reflects their learning.

To understand these themes and integrate them into your thinking about testing, you will be introduced to the terminology of testing and assessment, examine basic issues in measuring human performance, and confront several of the issues that you will face in constructing your own tests. You must plan assessments carefully and give thought to the kinds of tests and the kinds of items that will best sample your

Assessment: Terminology and Assumptions 520
Uses and Users of Classroom Assessment Information 521
Multicultural Students and Testing 522

Integrating Learning and Assessment 522
Teachers and Testing 523

Methods and Technical Issues in the Assessment of Students 524
Teacher-Constructed Tests 525
Planning a Teacher-Constructed Test 529

Alternative Methods and New Assessment Trends 536
Behavioral Assessment Fundamentals 537
Curriculum-Based Assessment (CBA) 539
Authentic/Performance Assessment 540

Using Data From Teacher-Constructed Tests and Classroom Assessments 547
Marking 548
Grading 549
Reporting 551

Research on Teachers' Judgments of Students' Achievement 552

Helping Students Take Tests 552

Applications and Reflections 553

students' learning. You must also use test data to give marks, assign grades, and report on the progress of your students. You should feel much more comfortable discussing grades with students, parents, and school officials if your grades are based on well-constructed tests.

When you have completed reading this chapter, you should be able to

- plan for tests that serve specific purposes
- write appropriate test items
- assess the role of testing in your classroom
- evaluate how successfully students have attained desired objectives
- evaluate your instructional effectiveness by the results of your testing
- discuss the use of authentic/performance assessment methods to guide instruction and document students' learning

ASSESSMENT: TERMINOLOGY AND ASSUMPTIONS

Effective communication about tests and the assessment process requires us to know the distinctive meanings of such terms as *assessment, testing, tests, measurement,* and *grading*. These are *not* synonymous, although they are related terms. By **assessment,** we mean the process of gathering information about a student's abilities or behavior for the purpose of making decisions about the student. There are many tools or methods a teacher can use to assess a student, such as paper-and-pencil tests, published tests, rating scales or checklists, interviews, and observations. Thus, assessment is more than testing.

Testing is simply one procedure through which we obtain evidence about a student's learning or behavior. **Teacher-constructed tests,** as well as commercially published tests, have played and will continue to play a major role in the education of students. Such tests are assumed to provide reliable and valid means to measure students' progress. But note that *a test is a sample of behavior. It tells us something, not everything, about some class or type of behavior.* Well-designed tests provide representative samples of knowledge or behavior.

Measurement is quantifying, or placing a number on, a student's performance. Not all performances demonstrating learning can or need to be quantified (for example, art or musical exhibitions). The science of measurement in itself includes many concepts—reliability, validity, standard scores—that are important for teachers and others responsible for assessing students. We will consider these psychometric concepts later in this chapter.

A final term that deserves definition is **grading.** Grading is the assignment of a symbol to a student's performance. A grade is not an assessment; rather, it is often an interpretation of the assessment process. As you well know, it most frequently takes the form of a letter (e.g., A, B, C) and indicates some relative level of performance to other students or stated criteria. Remember, however, that you can assess your students' work, effort, attitude, and countless other behaviors without ever assigning a grade.

Now that we have defined several key assessment terms, here are four assumptions that we believe are fundamental to the assessment of students. Read them carefully and think about the implications of these fundamental assumptions.

1. Tests are samples of behavior and serve as aids to decision making.
2. A primary reason to conduct an assessment is to improve instructional activities for a student.
3. The person conducting the assessment is properly trained.
4. All forms of assessment contain error.

These assumptions are rather straightforward; however, each deserves additional commentary. The first assumption stresses that tests do not reveal everything a student does or does not know; they provide snapshots of a student's knowledge or behavior. When a test is well constructed, it can give us representative and useful information about a student that can be helpful in making decisions about the student.

This information leads us to the second assumption, which emphasizes that the primary educational reason for using tests is to guide instructional activities. Good tests can furnish teachers with information about what to teach next and under what conditions the content might best be taught.

This point leads to the third assumption: A teacher must be properly trained to use tests and the information they yield. A poor test or the misuse of a well-constructed test can significantly damage the teaching-learning process.

assessment *The process of gathering information about a student's abilities and using such information to make decisions about the student.*

teacher-constructed tests *One method for assessing a student's learning or behavior that is developed by the teacher.*

measurement *To quantify, or place a number on, student performance.*

grading *The assigning of a symbol to a student's performance.*

The final assumption—that all forms of assessment contain some error—is a cautionary note to all persons involved in assessing human performance, and stresses the need for frequent assessment of students with a variety of methods. This final assumption also emphasizes that teachers are trusted to make important and difficult decisions about all of their students.

Uses and Users of Classroom Assessment Information

Research suggests that teachers spend as much as one-third of their time involved in some type of assessment. Teachers are continually making decisions about the most effective means of interacting with their students. These decisions are usually based on information they have gathered from observing their students' behavior and performances on learning tasks in the classroom (Witt, Elliott, Kramer, & Gresham, 1994).

Many individuals have a vested interest in student learning and in assessment information about such learning. Clearly, teachers, students, and parents should have great interest in the results of student assessments. School administrators and community leaders also voice keen interest in assessment results that document students' performances. No single assessment technique or testing procedure can serve all these potential users of assessment results. Thus, the purpose of one's assessment must be clear, for it influences assessment activities and, consequently, the interpretation of any results.

Teachers have three main purposes for assessing students: (a) to form specific decisions about a student or a group of students; (b) to guide their own instructional planning and subsequent activities with the entire class; and (c) to control student behavior.

Teachers use assessment results for specific decisions, including diagnosing student strengths and weaknesses, grouping students for instruction, identifying students who might benefit from special services, and grading student performances. Assessments also provide teachers with valuable feedback about how successful they have been in achieving their instructional objectives, and thus help them to chart the sequence and pace of future instructional activities.

Teachers can also use assessment activities and results to inform students about teacher expectations. In other words, the assessment process can provide students with information about the kind of performance that they need in order to be successful in a given classroom. Tests become a critical link in teaching when teachers provide to students clear feedback about results.

Teachers can use tests and the assessment of students to facilitate classroom management, as well. For example, the anticipation of a forthcoming assessment can serve to encourage students to increase their studying and classroom participation.

Students also are decision makers, and use classroom assessment information to guide many of their decisions. For example, many students set personal academic expectations for themselves based on teachers' assessments of prior achievement. Feedback they receive from teachers about their performance on classroom tests directly affects other students' decisions about whether, what, when, and with whom to study.

The assessment activities and decisions of teachers affect parents as well as students. For example, many parents communicate educational and behavioral expectations to their children. Some parents also plan educational resources and establish home study environments to assist their children. Feedback from teachers about daily achievement, communicated using homework, classroom tests, annual standardized tests, report cards, and school conferences, often significantly influences these parental actions.

Testing results also provide parents (and others in the community) with information about the school's performance. Does the school equip students with the basic skills of reading, writing, and calculating? This is only one issue parents use assessments to

In your opinion, what is the most important reason for giving a test?

judge. Teachers' assessments of children greatly influence parents' attitudes about many aspects of their children and their schooling. Clearly, the enterprise of assessing students is crucial in the lives of teachers, students, and many parents.

Multicultural Students and Testing

Of all the topics discussed in the next two chapters, none is more practically important than your ability to help students take tests. Tests often make students anxious. Regardless of the reason for test anxiety—parental pressure, their own prior experience, or the testing atmosphere—merely taking a test can affect a student's performance. This is especially true for those students who find your classroom a different cultural experience. Language (both oral and written), expectations, and student and teacher behavior all may be new to multicultural students; all may influence test performance (Stigler et al., 1990). One publication, *New Voices: Immigrant Students in U.S. Public Schools* (1988), describes many of these students as having experienced war, political oppression, economic deprivation, and long, difficult journeys before coming to the United States.

These students want to succeed. Interviews with immigrant students showed that almost 50 percent were doing one to two hours' homework every night (25 percent of the Southeast Asian students reported more than three hours' homework each night) (First & Carrera, 1988). We have mentioned throughout this book the need for sensitive responsiveness. Here is an instance in which being sensitive to the needs of multicultural students can aid both teaching and learning.

We have commented earlier on the need for a positive and receptive classroom environment. When students feel comfortable, they do better. When students are prepared adequately to take a test, they do better. Try to help any student who is uncertain about "the test." Provide information about why the test is being given, when it is being given, what material will be tested, and what kind of items will be used. These are just a few topics to consider. You also will want to be sure that language is not a barrier to performance. Take some time to explain the terms in the directions of your test. Tell them or illustrate what "analyze" means, what you are looking for when you ask them to "compare," what "discuss" means.

If you were responsible for assessing a student with a primary language other than English who was from a different culture than your own, what adjustments in your assessment would you make?

Helping multicultural students in this way will take extra time and effort. But it is teaching, just as teaching English or history is teaching. As more and more multicultural students take classroom tests, you will be helping them to do well and to avoid being limited by the mechanics of the test.

INTEGRATING LEARNING AND ASSESSMENT

Assessment of students' learning traditionally has been conducted using tests. Tests don't exist in a vacuum. Good tests are designed and used to discover if objectives have been met and if learning has occurred; they are also a means of communication. They are a valuable and powerful tool, not only in assessing student progress, but also as a means of examining teaching efforts. Today other techniques, such as teacher observation, student portfolios, and student exhibits, also have been proposed as means of evaluating student performance (Archbald & Newmann, 1988). This collection of techniques is referred to as authentic/performance assessment.

Educators can defend the success of teaching, the value of a curriculum, or the amount of learning only by some demonstrable evidence. In education such evidence is obtained through assessment, often by testing. Our work in chapters 11 and 12 was concerned with identifying and attaining worthwhile objectives and instructional methods. Here we discuss your third major task: assessing students' learning. Figure 15.1 illustrates the integrated nature of the three enterprises of identifying learning objectives, selecting teaching methods, and assessing learning.

Figure 15.1 graphically illustrates the key position of assessment of students' learning in the teaching-learning process. You have formulated desirable objectives,

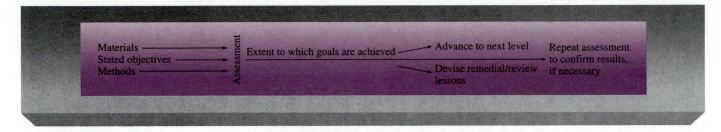

Figure 15.1

The integration of teaching and assessment activities.

selected methods and materials to attain these objectives, and used the results of assessment to discover whether learning has occurred. If it has, students advance to more difficult materials; if it has not, then you should initiate review and repetition.

The above procedure, which is most commonly completed by using a classroom test, focuses upon student achievement. What have students learned as manifested on the test? Have they achieved enough objectives to move on to the next level? The vital role of objectives is clear once more. That is, objectives must be sharply defined and stated in language that permits measurement and specifies behavioral change.

Testing, however, also has a guidance function. Depending upon the nature of the test scores, the results will portray the specific type of remedial work required, or the kind of advanced material that would be most suitable for continued growth. Careful interpretation of test scores also furthers the diagnosis of learning difficulties, in both an individual and a class. If an individual or your class has failed to attain objectives, you will search for the cause. There are three immediate possibilities: *the student* (e.g., physical illness at the time of testing, a personal problem, etc.), *the difficulty of the material,* or *your methods*. If the class is typical and the material has been proven to be successful with other similar groups, then you can consider several possibilities: lack of background information, too rapid a presentation, or limited student activity when the material demanded more personal involvement. There is another lesson here. Professional teachers will also use test results as a form of self-evaluation; that is, *testing results inform teaching*.

Testing can likewise help teachers and administrators in their search for appropriate subject matter. If students consistently fail, experience difficulty, or score unusually high, you may question the nature of the subject matter. The influence of assessment on objectives, methods, and materials reinforces the belief that the assessment of students is at the vital core of education.

Teachers and Testing

Teachers frequently feel that testing is an added burden that interferes with real teaching and learning. It frequently is, unless the tests are carefully constructed and the content is relevant. Can you assess the quality of materials, the effectiveness of your teaching, and the worthiness of objectives without testing?

If teachers avoid, or merely tolerate, testing, it is impossible for them to judge these issues without resorting to guessing. When one realizes that tests, both teacher-made and standardized, may alter students' futures, it is apparent that poorly made and questionably interpreted tests can cause lasting damage. Grades, promotion, college acceptance, and employment opportunities all reflect the results of testing. Why then are teachers frequently careless in the construction of tests and the interpretation of test results?

One reason may be that teachers are confident about their judgment of students (Marso & Pigge, 1989). They "know" what their students can do; in many instances they view testing as superfluous. Another reason is that a good test is extremely difficult and time-consuming to construct.

Admittedly, each and every one of these contributing factors to carelessness can influence student test scores. The primary purpose of this chapter is to alert you to these

Focus

A Teacher's Professional Role and Responsibilities for Student Assessment

Professional educators have long been concerned that the potential benefits of student assessment were not being fully realized. In 1990, educators representing the American Federation of Teachers, the National Council on Measurement in Education, and the National Education Association completed work on a set of seven standards for teacher competence in student assessment. The seven standards or professional principles are as follows:

1. Teachers should be skilled in *choosing* assessment methods appropriate for instructional decisions.
2. Teachers should be skilled in *developing* assessment methods appropriate for instructional decisions.
3. Teachers should be skilled in *administering, scoring, and interpreting the results* of both externally-produced and teacher-produced assessment methods.
4. Teachers should be skilled in *using assessment results* when making decisions about individual students, planning teaching, developing curriculum, and improving schools.
5. Teachers should be skilled in *developing valid pupil grading procedures* that use pupil assessments.
6. Teachers should be skilled in *communicating assessment results* to students, parents, other lay audiences, and other educators.
7. Teachers should be skilled in *recognizing unethical, illegal, and otherwise inappropriate assessment methods and uses of assessment information.*

These standards clearly indicate that assessment competencies are an "essential part of teaching and that good teaching cannot exist without good student assessment" (American Federation of Teachers, 1990, p. 1). The enactment of these standards requires a range of activities by teachers prior to instruction, during instruction, and after instruction. Some examples follow:

Assessment-Related Activities Occurring Prior to Instruction

1. Understanding students' cultural backgrounds, interests, skills, and abilities as they apply across a range of learning domains and subject areas.
2. Understanding students' motivations and their interest in specific class content.
3. Clarifying and articulating the performance outcomes expected of pupils.
4. Planning instruction for individuals or groups of students.

Assessment-Related Activities Occurring During Instruction

1. Monitoring pupil progress toward instructional goals.
2. Identifying gains and difficulties pupils are experiencing in learning and performing.
3. Adjusting instruction.
4. Giving contingent, specific, and credible praise and feedback.
5. Motivating students to learn.
6. Judging the extent of pupil attainment of instructional outcomes.

Assessment Activities Occurring After Instruction

1. Describing the extent to which each pupil has attained both short- and long-term instructional goals.
2. Communicating strengths and weaknesses based on assessment results to students and to parents or guardians.
3. Recording and reporting assessment results for school-level analysis, evaluation, and decision making.
4. Analyzing assessment information gathered before and during instruction to understand each student's progress to date and to inform future instructional planning.
5. Evaluating the effectiveness of instruction.
6. Evaluating the effectiveness of the curriculum and materials in use.

As you can see, the professional expectations for teachers are high: they must be competent and proactive in the assessment of their students! Study and guided experience beyond the knowledge acquired in this chapter is essential for competent practice.

---

obstacles and to suggest techniques for limiting any negative effects they could have on students' performance. Let us now examine some of the various methods teachers use to assess students.

METHODS AND TECHNICAL ISSUES IN THE ASSESSMENT OF STUDENTS

The assessment of students' classroom performances can take many forms. Some assessment methods are formal, others informal; some are administered to individuals, others to groups; some are standardized for all classrooms, others designed for specific classroom contexts. Typically, educators have used four primary methods for assessing students' classroom performances: paper-and-pencil tests, oral questions, performance tests, and standardized tests. The first three methods are teacher-constructed, whereas **standardized tests** are commercially constructed.

Annual **Edition**

standardized tests *Tests that are commercially constructed and administered under uniform conditions.*

Table 15.1

Comparative Advantages of Standardized and Informal Classroom Tests of Achievement

	Standardized achievement tests	Informal achievement tests
Learning outcomes and content measured	Measure outcomes and content common to majority of United States schools. Tests of basic skills and complex outcomes adaptable to many local situations; content-oriented tests seldom reflect emphasis or timeliness of local curriculum.	Well adapted to outcomes and content of local curriculum. Flexibility affords continuous adaptation of measurement to new materials and changes in procedure. Adaptable to various-sized work units. Tend to neglect complex learning outcomes.
Quality of test items	General quality of items high. Written by specialists, pretested, and selected on basis of effectiveness.	Quality of items unknown unless test item file is used. Quality typically lower than that of standardized because of teacher's limited time and skill.
Reliability	Reliability high, commonly between .80 and .95; frequently above .90.	Reliability usually unknown; can be high if carefully constructed.
Administration and scoring	Procedures *standardized;* specific instructions provided.	Uniform procedures favored but may be flexible.
Interpretation of scores	Scores can be compared with those of norm groups. Test manual and other guides aid interpretation and use.	Score comparisons and interpretations limited to local school situation.

Reprinted with the permission of Simon & Schuster, Inc. from the Macmillan College text *Measurement and Evaluation in Teaching,* 7th ed. by Norman E. Gronlund and Robert L. Linn. Copyright © 1995 by Macmillan College Publishing Company.

In this chapter, we will focus on teacher-constructed tests, which are the most frequently used methods for assessing students. We will also examine some emerging alternative assessment strategies (i.e., authentic/performance assessment) that are assuming a more salient role in the classroom. Chapter 16 will be devoted to an analysis of standardized tests. Before examining details of both teacher-constructed and standardized tests, note the major advantages of each as summarized in table 15.1.

Teacher-Constructed Tests

Although teachers use many techniques in evaluating students, probably the most popular is the written paper-and-pencil test that they construct. These usually consist of essay questions or **multiple-choice items.**

The multiple-choice pencil-and-paper test is probably the most frequently used kind of test, with other types, such as essay and performance tests and tests containing **true-false questions,** also quite popular with teachers. Good multiple-choice items are difficult to prepare, but can be scored easily and objectively. **Essay tests,** on the other hand, are relatively easy to prepare, but difficult to score reliably.

Tests, measurements, and **evaluation** are needed for successful education, but that need should not blind you to several difficulties. First, all measurement is subject to error. The testing conditions, the person giving the test, the person taking the test, and the test itself are all potential sources of error. These reservations should not discourage you; test-making has become quite precise, and statistical techniques have become more sophisticated and yield more information from test scores than they once could. Yet, realistically, problems remain. For example, consider the limitations of the test itself: the lack of a true "zero" is apparent. If a student scores zero on a geography test, does this imply no geographical knowledge? Obviously not. It means that knowledge is zero on the geographical material that the particular test is measuring, but it tells us nothing more about the student's knowledge of geography.

Another difficulty is that of teacher influence on the results of any examination. The disciplinary attitude toward assessment, the "life or death" view, or the indifferent

multiple-choice items
Questions or incomplete statements that are followed by several possible responses. One of these responses is correct.

true-false questions *Test questions that present subjects with statements that must be judged true or false.*

essay tests *Teacher-constructed tests that allow students considerable latitude in their answers to questions.*

evaluation *The interpretion of data obtained from tests and measurements.*

approach, all affect results. Testing has not yet been subjected to the complete control that measurement experts desire. As continued efforts add to knowledge of the classroom's psychological atmosphere, testing itself will undoubtedly improve.

The individuality of students and the need to meet those individual needs, however, remain the chief concerns in our analysis of measurement problems. It is crucial to provide the opportunity for all of the diverse students in the class to demonstrate the knowledge they have. Part of this attention to student individuality is reflected in the teacher's attempts to use teacher-made tests to further learning. The student's outlook on testing is important. If a test is only the measure of achievement, the learning process is distorted. Tests that tell what should be reviewed, or where the student can next progress, are constructive and serve a valuable motivational purpose.

Individuals interested in constructing tests are confronted with challenges concerning *what* to assess, *how* to assess it, and whether they are measuring it in a reliable and valid manner. These are fundamental challenges to teachers who construct their own tests and to professionals who design standardized tests.

"But isn't it more important to learn how to be a decent human being?"

H. Schwadron *in* Phi Delta Kappan.

Teachers deciding what to test must be guided by the principle that *the test must measure what was taught*. Tests will be reliable and valid to the same degree that test constructors are successful in relating test items to what was taught. You may question whether teacher-made tests could have any difficulty testing what was taught. After all, students were exposed to the same teacher, methods, and materials. The answer is not that simple.

Let us temporarily ignore the conditions of testing: classroom atmosphere, student health, and related factors. The test itself may fail to assess a student's learning. Did you know why you were teaching—that is, were the objectives stated in objective terms that permitted measurement? Did the test adequately sample the material that was taught? Did it stress the content that you emphasized as important?

Teachers occasionally stress certain aspects of a subject and then test other sections. This strategy supposedly ensures broader coverage. Yet it is obviously unfair to the student. Did you construct items that concentrated only upon a small amount of the material that was taught? Were the items comprehensible to the students?

You should also be alert to other issues. The essay test, for example, allows students to express their own ideas in a creative fashion and permits them to demonstrate such elements as organization and grasp of a subject, and its application to a particular problem. It also is deceptively easy to construct. But it samples only a limited amount of material (unless you increase the time for assessment), favors the articulate student, and is difficult to mark. Conversely, an objective or multiple-choice test samples much more subject matter than the essay examination, has greater objectivity of scoring, and reduces the verbal element in a student's response. Measuring problem-solving and creative behavior, however, is difficult. These tests also emphasize factual information, frequently promote guessing, and are time-consuming to prepare.

Determining what to measure and deciding how to measure it are genuine concerns for teachers. Avoid absolute standards. If most students in a heterogenous class receive A's on a test, or almost all fail another test, you can assume that the test is at fault. Examine figure 15.2 to see the key role that assessment plays in the teaching-learning process, a role that incorporates all that we have examined thus far in our work. With these ideas in mind, let us now examine the important topics of reliability and validity.

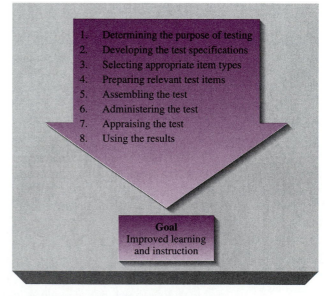

1. Determining the purpose of testing
2. Developing the test specifications
3. Selecting appropriate item types
4. Preparing relevant test items
5. Assembling the test
6. Administering the test
7. Appraising the test
8. Using the results

Goal
Improved learning and instruction

Figure 15.2

Planning a test.

Reliability

A test is reliable to the extent that a student's scores are nearly the same in repeated measurements. A test is reliable if it is consistent (Frisbie, 1988). Do two forms of a test yield similar results? If the test is repeated after a certain interval, how consistent are the results? Some error exists in any test, since fluctuations in human behavior are uncontrollable, and the test itself may contain possibilities of error (Matarazzo, 1990). For example, its language may be so ambiguous as to be misleading. The wide range of acceptable responses to essay examinations also introduces the chance of error (Griswold, 1990).

Note carefully the distinction between **reliability** (consistency) and validity (meaningfulness). A valid test must be reliable, but a reliable test need not be valid. In other words, reliability is a necessary but not sufficient condition for validity. For example, a test may have an error built into it. Giving an algebra test to first-graders would produce consistent results, but the results would not be meaningful for 6-year-olds. Thus, the test would be reliable, but would not be valid.

Suppose, for instance, that Miss Jones had just given an achievement test to her students. How similar would the students' scores have been if she had tested them yesterday, or would they be if she tested them tomorrow, or next week? How would the scores have varied had she selected a different sample of equivalent items? If it were an essay test, how much would the scores have differed had a different teacher scored it? These are the types of questions with which reliability is concerned (Gronlund, 1985, p. 87).

The reliability of a test is often operationalized by the computing of a correlation statistic between scores. In the case of a test-retest approach to reliability, this approach is straightforward, as illustrated in table 15.2. Correlations technically can range between +1.0 and −1.0, where +1.0 indicates perfect agreement between the magnitudes of the scores for the same individual. Given that most teachers do not repeatedly administer the same test, alternative methods of estimating the reliability of a test, such as internal consistency, must be used. The latter method uses a slightly different formula for calculating a reliability coefficient (referred to as a *coefficient alpha*). Regardless of the method for quantifying the reliability of a test, most experienced users of teacher-constructed tests consider reliability coefficients in the +.80 or higher range to be essential. Many published tests have reliability coefficients in the +.90 or higher range.

We conclude that unless a test is reasonably consistent on different occasions or with different samples of the same behavior, the teacher can have very little confidence in its results (Griswold, 1990). A variety of factors, some concerning the individual taking the test and others inherent in the design and content of the test itself, can affect the reliability of a test. Student characteristics affecting a test's reliability include guessing, test anxiety, and practice in answering items like those on the test (Witt et al., 1994). Characteristics of the test that can influence reliability include its length (longer tests are generally more reliable), the homogeneity or similarity of items (more homogeneous tests are usually more reliable), and the time required to take the test (speed tests are typically more reliable than unbound tests).

reliability *Characteristic of a test for which a student's scores are nearly the same in repeated measurements, and of a test that consistently measures what it says it measures.*

Table 15.2

Test-Retest Reliability of a Kindergarten Screening Test

	Number of Answers Correct	
Student	Test	Retest
1	9	10
2	7	6
3	5	1
4	3	5
5	1	3

$$r_{xy} = \frac{N \Sigma XY - (\Sigma X)(\Sigma Y)}{\sqrt{[N \Sigma X^2 - (\Sigma X)^2][N \Sigma Y^2 - (\Sigma Y)^2]}}$$

$$r = \frac{150}{\sqrt{(200)(230)}}$$

$$r = .70$$

From J. C. Witt, S. N. Elliott, J. J. Kramer, and F. M. Gresham (1994), *Assessment of Children: Fundamental Methods and Practices*. Dubuque, IA: Brown & Benchmark.

What are two major sources of error in the assessment of students?

Validity

When you test a student in arithmetic, you are testing a sample of that student's arithmetic knowledge. From the score of a subtraction test, for example, you infer that a student knows or does not know how to subtract. *Your inference depends on the truthfulness or meaning of the test: its validity*. **Validity** is the extent to which a test measures what it is supposed to measure. Of all the essential characteristics of a good test, none surpasses validity. If a test is not valid for the purpose used, it has no value.

validity *The extent to which a test measures what it is supposed to measure.*

For example, if a test designed to measure academic achievement in a particular subject uses questions that are phrased in difficult language, it does not test geography or history as much as it does reading. The test does not measure what it claims to. Validity is specific. A test may be valid for one purpose and no other. To administer a spelling test for the purpose of determining a student's achievement in grammar is invalid.

Traditionally, test developers examine three major kinds of validity: content validity, criterion-related validity, and construct validity.

1. A test has **content validity** if it adequately samples behavior that has been the goal of instruction. Does the test adequately represent the material that was taught? Testing on a minor portion of a unit on *Hamlet* after stressing the unity of the total play violates content validity. Determining whether a test has content validity is somewhat subjective. It usually is established when subject-matter experts agree that the content covered is representative of the tested domain of knowledge. Content validity also is referred to as *face validity,* because judgments about content are based on reading or looking at the content.

   content validity *Validity of a test based on its ability adequately to sample behavior that has been the goal of instruction.*

2. A test has **criterion-related validity** if its results parallel some other, external criteria. Thus, test results are similar or not similar to another sample of a student's behavior (or some other criterion for comparison). If students do well on a standardized reading test that measures all aspects of reading, they should likewise do well at understanding and completing geography and history assignments. Some authors refer to this type of validity as *predictive validity.* You can understand how this kind of validity is valuable for the teacher, particularly in assessing the validity of teacher-made achievement tests. Some other measure is taken as the criterion of success.

   criterion-related validity *Validity of a test based on its results' similarity to some other, external criteria.*

3. A test has **construct validity** when the particular knowledge domain or behavior purported to be measured is actually measured. For example, you may claim that your test measures understanding and not facts. If the results of your test agree with ratings of your students on understanding, then your test is, indeed, measuring the construct of understanding. If a test claims to measure anxiety, then its results should match judgments that given people are anxious. Construct validity is a complex issue, and is increasingly coming to refer to the entire body of research about what a test measures (Lyman, 1986).

   construct validity *Validity of a test based on its actually measuring the knowledge domain or behavior it claims to measure.*

It makes no sense to prepare or select a classroom test designed to measure something other than what has been taught. We don't measure height by using a bathroom scale. Therefore teachers and others should work hard to ensure that a test does the job it is designed to do.

Central to the development and use of any assessment instrument is one's conceptualization of validity. Judgments about the validity of an assessment are concerned with the degree to which the adequacy and appropriateness of the interpretations and uses of assessment results are supported by empirical evidence and logical analysis. Thus, validation of an assessment instrument and process requires an evaluation of interpretations of assessment results, as well as the intended and unintended consequences from using the assessment. As one focuses on the consequences of an assessment, it becomes apparent that validity issues are in many ways issues of values!

Criteria for evaluating the validity of tests and related assessment instruments have been written about extensively (e.g., Cronbach, 1970; Wiggins, 1993). A joint committee of the American Educational Research Association, the American Psychological Association, and the National Council on Measurement in Education (American Psychological Association, 1985) developed a comprehensive list of standards for tests that stressed the importance of construct validity. Extrapolating from this document, Baker and her associates (1993) enumerated five internal characteristics that valid assessments should exhibit:

1. Have meaning for students and teachers and motivate high performance.
2. Require the demonstration of complex cognitions applicable to important problem areas.
3. Exemplify current standards of content or subject matter quality.
4. Minimize the effects of ancillary skills that are irrelevant to the focus of assessment.
5. Possess explicit standards of content or subject-matter quality.

Evidence for the validity of a test or assessment instrument takes two forms: how the test or assessment instrument "behaves" given the content covered, and the effects of using the test or assessment instrument. Questions commonly asked about a test's "behavior" concern its relation to other measures of a similar construct, its ability to predict future performances, and its coverage of a content domain. Questions about the use of a test typically focus on the test's abilities to differentiate individuals into groups reliably and to guide teachers' instructional actions with regard to the subject matter covered by the test. Some questions also arise about unintended uses of a test or assessment instrument: Does use of the instrument result in discriminatory practices against various groups of individuals? Is the test used to evaluate others (e.g., parents or teachers) not directly assessed by the test?

Messick (1988) best captured the complexities of judging the validity of a test or assessment instrument, characterizing validity as "an inductive summary of both the adequacy of existing evidence for and the appropriateness of potential consequences of test interpretation and use" (p. 34). Thus, Messick corrected the common misconception that validity lies *within* a test, and went on to conceptualize validity as resting on four bases. These are as follows:

> **(1) an inductive summary of convergent and discriminant evidence that the test scores have a plausible meaning or construct interpretation, (2) an appraisal of the value implications of the test interpretation, (3) a rationale and evidence for the relevance of the construct and the utility of the scores in particular applications, and (4) an appraisal of the potential social consequences of the proposed use and of the actual consequences when used. (Messick, 1988, p. 42)**

Planning a Teacher-Constructed Test

With these fundamentals of testing in mind, we turn now to the process of constructing those tests that you need to devise for your students. The first step in the process is planning. Constructing a "good" test remains a challenge, one that demands time and effort. Teachers are busy and may well be tempted to ask, "Why bother?" Nitko (1983) summarized the benefits of developing skill in test construction.

- Developing a test helps you to identify more precisely those behaviors important for students to learn.
- As you develop a test, your perspective on both teaching and learning broadens as you distinguish conditions and sequences of learning.
- As you gain skill in constructing your own tests, you become more critical of published testing material.
- A carefully constructed test furnishes you with fair and objective information for the evaluation of students.

Test Planning and Objectives

The first step in planning the test is to review the objectives of the unit or subject. A clear understanding and statement of your specific instructional objectives will significantly improve the quality of the tests that you construct (Gentry, 1989). At this point you might want to review the objectives section of chapter 11.

Some of the questions that you should answer in this planning stage include the following. What exactly is the purpose of this test? Is it a pretest to discover weaknesses and strengths, or will the results be used as a basis for evaluating a student's academic achievement? How many and what kind of questions should be used? Does the test reflect the emphasis of instruction? Will the test give evidence of the degree to which the students have achieved given goals? Refer again to figure 15.2 for a summary of the various steps in the process of planning a test, keeping in mind that the goal of classroom testing is improved instruction.

As you plan your tests, be guided by several considerations:

- Be sure you know why you are testing, that is, the purpose of your test. For example, "giving a test" merely because you need marks for your students reflects the lack of a clear rationale for testing.
- Consider what type of item will best serve your purposes. Should you use essay or objective items?
- Devote time to preparing relevant items.

Earlier in this book (in chap. 9), the importance of teaching thinking skills was stressed. It logically follows that the assessment of a student's knowledge should be sensitive to the various levels of thinking skills that can be used to solve problems. Both multiple-choice and essay test items can be written to assess recall, analysis, comparison, inference, or evaluation skills. By carefully wording your questions, you can influence the thinking-skill level needed to answer the question. Table 15.3 illustrates action words to consider when you want to assess various levels of thinking skills in your students.

Taking tests involves both subject-matter knowledge and knowledge of test-taking skills. Teachers can do much to facilitate students' test-taking.

Selecting Test Items

You should consider carefully those aspects of testing that need your attention before the test. Once you have determined the purpose of your test and identified those behaviors that are critical for mastery, you need to give thought to those items that will best serve your purpose.

What type of test item should you use? Although some readers will use performance items or interviews, most will be concerned with either objective or essay items. We will discuss these in some detail; first, here are a few distinguishing characteristics of each.

- Objective test items are usually separated into two classes: **supply items,** which require students to give answers, and *selection items,* which require students to choose from among several alternatives. Selection items are more highly structured and restrict the types of responses students can make.
- *Essay questions* permit students greater latitude of expression and are divided into two types. The **extended response** type allows students complete freedom to choose any kinds of responses. The **restricted response** type asks for specific information, thus restricting students' responses somewhat.

Be careful of the number of items you use. How much time have you allotted for testing? Here you face a rather delicate issue, since an increase in the number of items increases your test's reliability. But students should have enough time to answer each item. Also, be conscious of the difficulty of the items you use, since complexity obviously affects time and number of items.

supply items *Questions on objective tests that require students to give the answers (as opposed to choosing from among possible answers).*

extended response *A form of essay question that permits a student to make any kind of answer the student desires.*

restricted response *A form of essay question that asks for specific information.*

Table 15.3

Using Action Words to Assess Thinking Skills			
Thinking skill	**Action words**		**Example**
Analysis	Subdivide Break down Separate	Categorize Sort	Break the story down into different parts.
Comparison	Compare Contrast Relate	Differentiate Distinguish	Compare the two approaches to government.
Evaluation	Evaluate Judge Assess Appraise Defend	Argue Recommend Debate Critique	Evaluate this picture. Is it well-drawn?
Inference	Deduce Predict Infer Speculate	Anticipate What if Apply Conclude	If there were twice as many people, how might they change the shape of the room to accommodate them?
Recall	Define Identify Label List Name	Repeat What When Who	List the names of three states that produce wheat.

Before we consider the specifics of writing both types of items, examine table 15.4. This table provides a comparative summary of teacher-constructed tests and may help you to decide which type of item would best suit your purposes.

Writing Essay Tests

Teachers have long claimed advantages for the essay examination that are not subject to either proof or disproof. Whether they evaluate higher thought processes more effectively than the objective test is an unanswered question. Essay tests have both advantages and disadvantages. Since teachers place so much value on essay tests, they remain the most widely used type of classroom test, and deserve your careful study and thought. Here are some general considerations you may find helpful.

- *Determine the level of thought you want the students to use.* For example, if a political science teacher wants students to think critically about election processes, then an essay question should force students to weigh TV commercials against fact, to question emotional appeals to an electorate, and to examine conflicting interpretations of issues. Responses should reflect these criteria.
- *Phrase your questions so that they demand some novelty in students' responses.* Students often complain that essay questions make them reproduce material. Novel questions enable them to integrate and apply their knowledge. If you begin questions with verbs such as *compare, contrast, predict,* and *illustrate,* you are asking students to select, organize, and use their knowledge.
- *Write essay questions that clearly and unambiguously define the students' task.* For example, this item is poorly phrased: *Discuss the organizations that contribute to the health of the community.* What does "discuss" mean? Should students list, criticize, or evaluate? What kinds of organizations? What types of contributions? This item and items like it force students to guess.
- *Be certain that your question specifies the behavior you want.* If you phrase your questions accurately, you will help your students to display what they really know, and you will make your scoring of the answers easier and more exact. The pertinence and phrasing of the question is critical in an essay test; this is one of the reasons that the simplicity of essay test construction is deceptive.

Table 15.4

Characteristics of Test Items		
	Objective test	**Essay test**
Learning outcomes measured	Is efficient for measuring knowledge of facts. Some types (e.g., multiple-choice) can also measure understanding, thinking skills, and other complex outcomes. Inefficient or inappropriate for measuring ability to select and organize ideas, writing abilities, and some types of problem-solving skills.	Is inefficient for measuring knowledge of facts. Can measure understanding, thinking skills, and other complex learning outcomes (especially useful where originality of response is desired). Appropriate for measuring ability to select and organize ideas, writing abilities, and problem-solving skills requiring originality.
Preparation of questions	A relatively large number of questions is needed for a test. Preparation is difficult and time-consuming.	Only a few questions are needed for a test. Preparation is relatively easy (but more difficult than generally assumed).
Sampling of course content	Provides an extensive sampling of course content because of the large number of questions that can be included in a test.	Sampling of course content is usually limited because of the small number of questions that can be included in a test.
Control of a student's response	Complete structuring of task limits student to type of response called for. Prevents bluffing and avoids influence of writing skill, though selection-type items are subject to guessing.	Freedom to respond in own words enables bluffing and writing skill to influence the score, though guessing is minimized.
Scoring	Objective scoring that can be quick, easy, and consistent.	Subjective scoring that can be slow, difficult, and inconsistent.
Influence on learning	Usually encourages student to develop a comprehensive knowledge of specific facts and the ability to make fine discriminations among them. Can encourage the development of understanding, thinking skills, and other complex outcomes if properly constructed.	Encourages students to concentrate on larger units of subject matter, with special emphasis on the ability to organize, integrate, and express ideas effectively. May encourage poor writing habits if time pressure is a factor (it almost always is).
Reliability	High reliability is possible and is typically obtained with well-constructed tests.	Reliability is typically low, primarily because of inconsistent scoring.

Reprinted with the permission of Simon & Schuster, Inc. from the Macmillan College text *Measurement and Evaluation in Teaching,* 7th ed. by Norman E. Gronlund and Robert L. Linn. Copyright © 1995 by Macmillan College Publishing Company.

Suggestions for Writing Essay Questions

In this section, we will discuss several guidelines that will help you write more precise essay questions. Remember, however, that when students take these tests, they bring with them their fears and anxieties about test-taking. Their perceptions of what it means to take your tests will affect their performance. Perhaps you can help them by acting on some of the suggestions that focus on students in this section.

Here are some general suggestions that you may find helpful for writing essay questions.

• Be sure that your questions reflect the material that you have taught and that your students have read.
• Be precise in your wording so that your students clearly understand what is expected of them. Vague, ambiguous questions not only are unfair to students, but can only add to the difficulty of scoring.
• Use your questions, when possible and when you deem it advisable, to have students explain new situations or solve problems; do not restrict them to purely factual material.

Focus | Essay Tests—Pros and Cons

There are pros and cons about the essay test. Among the advantages are these:

- It is fairly easy to construct.
- It may be administered simply: questions may be written on the blackboard.
- It emphasizes wholes rather than parts.
- It better illustrates a student's ability to recall, organize, reorganize, and apply knowledge. Also a student's expression of ideas may well reflect learning that is impossible to measure objectively.

Among the disadvantages are these:

- Its validity is questionable because of the small amount of material it samples.
- Teachers are often tempted to grade other factors than content, for example, spelling or grammar. Also, if a student is more articulate than his or her classmates, it is often troublesome to distinguish between fact and form.
- Scoring answers to essay questions can be difficult. Study after study has shown wide differences among teachers in grading essay tests. It is a true saying that students often pass or fail essay tests depending on who marks the paper and who takes the test.

Essay tests will continue to be used widely, so you should be aware of several precautions that you can take to improve your essay questions. Here are examples of the various kinds of essay questions and the purposes they serve. A classic, yet still valid source is Weidmann (1933, 1941), who classified essay questions as follows:

1. Who, what, when, which, where
2. List
3. Outline
4. Describe
5. Contrast
6. Compare
7. Explain
8. Discuss
9. Develop
10. Summarize
11. Evaluate

Give your test plenty of thought; your students deserve a fair opportunity to display what they have learned.

- Avoid optional questions. If you provide such alternatives—for extra credit or for another reason—not all students take the same test, so it is almost impossible for you to compare them.
- Write sensible questions that permit your students to read, interpret, and answer them in the allotted time.

Writing clear and purposeful essay questions should enable you to assess your students' factual knowledge and their ability to organize, interpret, and apply their learning.

Suggestions for Scoring Essay Tests   You can increase the reliability of your test before you actually administer it by giving thought to your scoring. We have previously touched on several important but general considerations. Are you assessing objectives? How wide a range of responses will you accept? Specifically, you might consider the following:

- Decide what major points must be in an answer for full credit. Must they all be there? If not, how many are required? How many points will you assign to each? How much weight will you give to each question?
- Read all answers to one question; do not read all the answers on a single student's test. By reading all answers to a single question, you increase the reliability of your scoring. You are more accurately comparing your students' responses, thus giving you a sense of how your class has achieved as a group. If all or most of your students—bright, average, and slow—failed one question, then you can be quite sure that either the question was at fault, or your teaching was misinterpreted or not understood at all.
- Do not associate a name with a test, since your previous knowledge and feelings about a student could possibly bias your scoring. If possible, have students use identification numbers instead of their names. You can match names to numbers after you have finished scoring the tests.

Finally, remember that essays are a good means of obtaining more than factual material from your students. They can tell you how students organize, interpret, and apply data, and whether they can use data they know to solve problems. But also remember that scoring can be unreliable unless you are careful.

Writing Objective Tests

Objective tests are better suited than essay examinations for some purposes. Objective tests' range of coverage in a relatively brief period and the objectivity of their scoring make them an attractive tool, although you must consider the time and care that go into the construction of the items.

One of the major criticisms constantly directed at the objective test is its apparent emphasis on fragmented, factual knowledge. Consequently, psychologists and educators have labored to devise test items that sample a student's depth and understanding of knowledge. Objective items fall into two general categories: the supply type (free response, simple recall, completion) and the selection type (alternative response, multiple-choice, matching).

Suggestions for Writing Supply Items Simple recall and completion items are fundamentally the same. In both instances, the subject responds with either one or a few words. The simple recall type usually takes the form of a direct question, while the completion item normally uses a sentence with one or several key words missing. For example:

1. Who is the present president of the United States? (simple recall)
2. The next election for president of the United States will be held in the year
   _____ . (completion)

The teacher needs to take care to make directions sufficiently clear so that students know exactly what is expected, without "leading" them. Some helpful points are to avoid textbook language, phrase a question to offer only one possible correct answer, and avoid excessive blanks in completion items.

Although supply items appear to be easy to write, you must be sure that the items serve the purpose for which they are intended.

- *Don't be fancy with the wording of items.* Since only one response can be correct, your phrasing must be sufficiently precise so that students understand its intent.
- *Avoid using the exact wording from a text in your item,* since direct quotations often become vague when removed from context.
- *Avoid giving clues.* The giving of clues is almost always inadvertent and occurs because of phrasing, answers from preceding questions, or the format of the item (using the same number of blanks as of letters in the correct response).

Suggestions for Writing Selection Items The selection type (alternative response, multiple-choice, matching) restricts the student's answers to those that are presented in the item.

The most common *alternative response item* is the true-false, right-wrong, yes-no variety. A declarative sentence is the usual form of a true-false item, and the subject indicates whether the statement is T (true) or F (false).
Directions: Mark each of the following statements true or false. If the statement is true, circle the T; if it is false, circle the F.

    T   F   Jimmy Carter became president of the United States in 1977.

As you can see, you are asking students to judge the correctness of a statement. Try to avoid opinion statements, since students are unaware if a statement is your opinion or not. Attribute any opinion to a definite source.

    T   F   Bill Clinton supported aid to the Contras.

teacher – student

Helping Students Prepare for Essay Tests

1. Some students, when faced with questions and a blank piece of paper, have no idea how to begin. Tell them first, to read the question carefully, not only for what content is called for but also for the exact meaning of what's asked. For example, you are taking an educational psychology exam and one of the questions is: Compare the basics of essay tests with those of objective tests. Your instructor has asked you to examine the qualities or characteristics of both types of tests and show similarities and differences.
   - To help your students, teach them what certain words mean:

     compare—show similarities and differences

     classify—assign to a category

     evaluate—make a value judgment

     summarize—present the main points briefly.

   You know what words will appear most frequently in your questions, so be sure that your students know exactly what you're asking for.

2. If you can impress the following guidelines on your students, you can help them to relax a little more and focus on the test itself, thus giving you a better idea of their actual knowledge.
   - Read all of the questions carefully. If you have to choose,*think before you choose.* Pick those questions you are comfortable answering. As you read each question, jot down next to the question the ideas that you think of immediately. In this way you won't forget what's important for question 4 after you've spent time on the first three.
   - Indicate clearly which question you're answering.
   - Plan the amount of time you'll spend on each question. If the period is one hour and there are four questions, you should spend about fifteen minutes on each. The "about" is cautionary; leave some time at the end to check your work.
   - General suggestions: write as clearly as possible; use complete sentences; try to use words you know (so you can spell them correctly); devote one topic to each paragraph.

Since your chief objective in writing true-false items will be to state them in clear and unambiguous terms, try to remember these guidelines:

- Be certain that the statement is definitely true or definitely false.
- Avoid writing irrelevant and trivial items.
- Avoid any obvious patterns: two true and then two false statements.
- Avoid using negative statements.
- Avoid textbook phrasing.
- Avoid terms such as *always* and *never*.
- Keep the length of true statements about the same as that of false statements.

The *multiple-choice item* presents students with a question or incomplete statement and several possible responses, one of which is correct (unless more than one response to each item is permitted, in what is called the *multiple-response* type). A typical multiple-choice item reads as follows:

Directions: For each of the following questions, there are several possible answers. Select the response that you think is correct for each question, and write the number of that answer in the blank space to the right of the question.

1. **Who is considered to be the "founder" of operant conditioning?** _____
   a. **Lewin**
   b. **Watson**
   c. **Skinner**
   d. **Thorndike**

You present your students a problem followed by several solutions. Note that in the above item, there is one correct answer (which one?) with three "distractors." The manner in which the problem is stated (called the *stem*) may be either a question or an incomplete statement. The multiple-choice item is thought to be the best of the objective items. When it is used, the direct question is the preferred form. At least four possible responses are needed (all of which should be plausible); all possible answers must be consistent and of equal length.

Here are some suggestions for writing multiple-choice items:

- The stem should present the problem in a clear and definite manner.
- Again, avoid negative statements where possible.
- Be sure that all distractors are plausible.
- See that the correct answer is clearly distinguishable from the incorrect distractors.
- Be sure that the correct answer appears in a different position from item to item.
- Avoid using "all of the above" or "none of the above" responses.
- Avoid clues, that is, words such as *always* or *never*.

The **matching item** usually utilizes two columns, such that each item in the first column is to be matched with an item in the second column. Here is a typical matching item.

matching item *A test item utilizing two columns, such that each item in the first column is to be matched with an item in the second column.*

Directions: Below are two lists, one containing the names of individual psychologists, and the other the names of schools of psychology. Match the individual with a school of psychology by writing the number of the school before the name of the appropriate individual in the space provided.

_____ Watson	1. Gestalt
_____ Skinner	2. Functionalism
_____ Thorndike	3. Dynamic psychology
_____ Koffka	4. Behaviorism
_____ Woodworth	5. Topological
	6. Connectionism
	7. Programming
	8. Structuralism
	9. Contiguity

In writing the matching item, the instructions should be simple, clear, and precise; otherwise they can confuse students. Also, take care to include more than the required number of responses, keep homogeneous material in each column, and keep the list of responses fairly short. The matching item is best suited for a test of factual material.

Here are some suggestions for writing matching items.

- Use more possible responses than items to be matched, thus reducing the likelihood of successful guessing.
- Arrange the list of responses logically.
- Be sure your students know the reasons for matching specific items.

Objective items should be selected for a particular purpose, carefully written to suit the appropriate reading level of a class, and free from ambiguity. You must rely on your own judgment, based on your knowledge of a class, to allot sufficient time for the objective test. There is no other reliable guide, although a rule of thumb is that 100 true-false items or 75 multiple-choice items are appropriate for a 50-minute period.

ALTERNATIVE METHODS AND NEW ASSESSMENT TRENDS

During the past decade we have witnessed an immense growth in the application of behavioral assessment methods. These methods emphasize observation techniques to describe a person's overt behavior and are useful in linking assessment results to interventions (Kratochwill & Sheridan, 1990; Shapiro, 1988). Progress in the application of behavioral assessment methods in psychology, along with the school restructuring

teacher – student

Helping Students Prepare for Objective Tests

1. You can help your students prepare for objective tests by impressing on them how searching and analytical objective items can be. You can use the *Taxonomy of Educational Objectives* (Bloom, 1956, p. 156), for example, to assess the complexity of your questions. (See chap. 9 for a detailed explanation of the taxonomy.)

   - Questions reflecting *knowledge* search for
     facts
     definitions
     results
     techniques.
   Start your questions with words such as *list, write, recall,* or *name.*

   - Questions reflecting *comprehension* search for
     understanding
     interpretation
     explanation.
   Start your questions with words such as *explain, transform, retell,* or *expand.*

   - Questions reflecting *application* search for
     usage
     demonstration
     specification
     prediction.
   Start your questions with words such as *use, construct, apply,* or *utilize.*

   - Questions reflecting *analysis* search for
     identification
     recognition
     classification
     inference.
   Start your questions with words such as *divide, examine, simplify,* or *classify.*

   - Questions reflecting *synthesis* search for
     integration
     realignment
     novelty.
   Start your questions with words such as *create, design, develop,* or *compare.*

   - Questions reflecting *evaluation* search for
     decisions
     judgments.
   Start your questions with words such as *rank, award, justify, evaluate.*

2. Here are some specific suggestions to give as you help students to prepare for objective tests.
   - If it's to be a machine-scored test, understand the mechanics of taking this kind of test; name in the right place, filling in the blocks carefully, correct type of pencil.
   - Find out if you're to be penalized for guessing.
   - Read all the possible answers to each question; don't jump at the response you think is right.
   - Go through the test quickly, answering those items you're sure about; then go back to those you're doubtful about.
   - On those items giving you trouble, try to eliminate any response you know is wrong. Then use any clues (wording, contradictions) to eliminate any other false responses.
   - Remember that true-false items that use such terms as "always" or "never" are usually false.
   - Remember that if a true-false statement is lengthy, it's usually true.
   - Be sure to understand the directions in matching items, and look for any theme connecting the question list and the answer list.
   - Always look for verbal clues.

curriculum-based assessment (CBA) *As assessment technique linked to curriculum and instruction in which a student's success is evaluated by that student's progress in the curriculum and whose purpose is to determine further instructional needs.*

movement, has fostered the development of two new (and related) assessment methods for evaluating students' learning. These techniques are referred to as **curriculum-based assessment (CBA)** and authentic assessment. Before examining these new techniques in detail, we want to discuss the basic assumptions underlying behavioral assessment and highlight their practicality in assessing students' academic and social behavior.

Behavioral Assessment Fundamentals

In behavioral assessment it is assumed that assessment of people's behavior at any time is merely a sample of their behavior, one that may or may not be representative of their behavior in other situations or at other times. Therefore, repeated assessments of a person's behavior over time and in different situations is typical of behavior assessment. As stated earlier, observation is the primary method used to conduct a behavioral assessment. There are, however, several forms of observation and related techniques that are used to do so. These techniques include interviews, self-reports, ratings by others, and role plays or performances, in addition to naturalistic observations (at home, in the schoolyard, and in the classroom). Gresham (1985) used a "directness continuum" to classify these various assessment methods; "direct" methods are those used at the same time and in the same place as the actual behavior. Methods such as naturalistic observations and self-monitoring are considered to be direct assessment methods. Indirect methods are removed in time and place from the actual occurrence of the target behavior. Interviews with students, self-reports from students, ratings by others (i.e., parents and teachers), and behavioral role plays are all examples of indirect methods of behavioral assessment (Witt, Elliott, Kramer, & Gresham, 1994).

Given the central role of observations in behavioral assessment and their frequent use by classroom teachers, we briefly will examine three fundamental aspects of a good observational assessment: an operational definition of a behavior, the dimensions of a behavior, and the methods for recording one's observations.

The first step in planning an observation of a student's behavior is to define the behavior in objective, observable terms. General descriptions such as "hyperactive," "depressed," or "learning difficulty" are unlikely to communicate the same behavior to different observers. Using an operational definition of behavior means defining behavior in clear, unambiguous, and explicit terms so that more than one person could reliably observe the behavior. For instance, an operational definition of the behavior of noncompliance would be as follows: *Noncompliance is defined as the student not complying with a verbal request or direction from the teacher within five seconds after the request or direction has been given. Examples of verbal requests or directions are being told to sit down, begin work, be quiet, come to the teacher's desk, etc.*

Behavior can be described and measured along four dimensions: frequency, temporality, intensity, and permanent products. The *frequency* of behavior refers to how often a behavior occurs (e.g., the number of correct oral responses, the number of temper tantrums). The temporality of behavior can be characterized by duration or latency. *Duration* refers to how long a behavior lasts (e.g., the child cried for 4 minutes), whereas *latency* describes the amount of time that elapses between an event and a behavior (e.g., 3 minutes after the teacher made the request, the boy brought his paper to her). *Intensity* refers to the amount of force with which a behavior is performed; intensity is not as easily measured as frequency or temporality. An example involving intensity might be one in which a student is yelling or a student is hitting another student. Technically, these examples could be scientifically measured in a lab, but in classrooms their intensity is judged by the teacher or observer.

Many behaviors leave **permanent products** in the environment. These might be called behavior by-products. Examples include number of worksheets completed, number of correct written responses to math problems, and number of paper wads on the floor. Of course, you realize that behavior by-products are not really measures of behavior; rather, they are measures of the results of some behaviors.

The method you use to record observations will depend on the dimension of behavior you are interested in measuring: frequency, temporality, intensity, or permanent products. Possible methods are event recording, interval recording, time-based recording, and permanent product recording. **Event recording** is designed to measure the frequency of behavior. It refers to the measurement of the number of times a behavior occurs. Event recording is best used with behaviors that are discrete in nature (i.e., they have clear beginnings and endings) and occur at a low to moderate rate. **Interval recording** is designed to record behaviors as occurring or not occurring during specified time intervals. A time unit such as 1 minute might be divided into six 10-second intervals. The behavior would be observed as occurring or not occurring during each of the six intervals. An interval recording method is best used for behaviors that

permanent products *Physical by-products of a person's behavior.*

event recording *Method of direct observation designed to measure the frequency of behavior; it refers to the number of times a behavior occurs and is best used with behaviors that have a clear beginning and ending.*

interval recording *A method for recording observations of a given behavior that occur during a specified time period; typically, the time period is 15 to 30 seconds long.*

time-based recording *The measurement through direct observation of the temporal aspects of behavior, such as duration, latency, and interresponse times.*

permanent product recording *A method of recording the by-products (e.g., worksheets, homework, pages written) of a person's behavior.*

are more continuous (i.e., that do not have specific beginnings and endings) and occur at relatively high rates. **Time-based recording** methods measure the temporal aspects of behavior, such as duration or latency. The number of behaviors is not measured with time-based recording; rather, this method measures the amount of time a behavior lasts or the amount of time between an environmental event and the beginning of a target behavior. **Permanent product recording** methods measure the actual physical by-products of behavior. Most often this involves the number of products or some quantifiable quality (e.g., percent accuracy) of a product.

During the past several years, much has been written about behavioral assessment and its application in schools to assess the academic and behavior functioning of children (Kratochwill & Sheridan, 1990). Interested readers are encouraged to consult these basic sources for more information. With this as background on behavioral assessment, let us now turn to an examination of curriculum-based assessment.

Curriculum-Based Assessment (CBA)

Curriculum-based assessment is a relatively new approach to educational assessment, although as noted by Shapiro and Derr (1990), "its basic idea is as old as education itself: using the curricula to assess student learning." CBA may be defined as a methodology in which (a) assessment is linked to the curriculum and instruction, (b) educational success is evaluated by student progress in the curriculum, and (c) the purpose is to determine students' instructional needs (p. 365). The impetus for the acceptance of CBA is the growing dissatisfaction among educators with the incongruence between what is taught in the classroom and what is tested by standardized achievement tests. If assessment results are to guide instructional intervention, then any assessment method must cover material and tasks representative of what has been or will be taught. Unfortunately, the content of many standardized **achievement tests** does not adequately assess what is taught in basal curricula (Jenkins & Pany, 1978; Shapiro & Derr, 1990). So CBA was born and has been developed by several researchers around the country.

achievement tests *Tests that measure accomplishment in such specific subjects as reading, arithmetic, etc. Developed by testing specialists. Concern today is that these tests may not adequately reflect what is actually taught in the classroom.*

Several forms of CBA have developed concurrently (e.g., *Curriculum-Based Evaluation,* by Howell, 1986; *Curriculum-Based Measurement,* by Deno, 1985; and *Criterion-Referenced-Curriculum-Based Assessment,* by Blankenship, 1985). Although each form of CBA has some unique characteristic, they are more alike than different. CBA has been used primarily at the elementary level for the basal curricula in reading and math. The heart of a CBA assessment is the development of brief (3- to 5-minute), frequent (weekly) "tests" or probes on material that has come directly from the curriculum. Most of these tests or samples of behavior are of the pencil-and-paper variety.

The results of several CBA assessments yield information about (a) what material from the curriculum students know and what material they do not know (or at least have not mastered) and (b) the rate at which a student is acquiring new knowledge. With this kind of information, the content of a remedial program can be readily identified and some reasonable prediction about the amount of time needed to master the material can be rendered. These are essential ingredients in the development of an intervention for a student who is experiencing academic problems.

The logic of CBA, using specific curriculum content for assessing what students know, is very appealing to many teachers and school psychologists who evaluate children. Yet CBA is hard work and still must meet the criteria for reliability and validity. At this time, CBA is enjoying increasing popularity among school practitioners, especially school psychologists, who often are responsible for assessing students with academic difficulties (Rosenfield & Shinn, 1989). When considering teacher-directed assessments, however, you should know that the trend in classroom assessment is toward authentic assessment, a more comprehensive and flexible approach to assessment than that offered by CBA approaches.

Focus ◄ Conducting a Classroom Observation

Ten Steps to Conducting Classroom Observations

The conduct of classroom observation involves ten essential components. Each of these components is described.

1. *Definition(s) of the target behavior(s).* The first step is to define the target behaviors. One good way to decide what is appropriate behavior in the classroom is to use the classroom rules posted by the teacher. However, the rules used by the teachers are frequently not well operationalized. Even more frequently, teachers have no rules posted. If that is the case, then you can utilize some standard observational categories. A simple system will consist of the following:

   On-task: Eye contact with teacher or task and performing the requested task.

   Verbal off-task: Inappropriate verbalization or making sounds with object, mouth, or body.

   Motor off-task: Student fully or partially out of assigned seat without teacher permission, or playing with objects.

   Passive off-task: Student not engaged with assigned task and passively waiting, sitting, daydreaming, etc.

   Occasionally, a student will exhibit unusual behaviors that would not be picked up using a standard coding system. In these cases, you will need to define the behavior yourself. For example, a child with Tourette's disorder who exhibits verbal and motor tics may require a special "tic" category.

2. *Observation of the teacher's interaction with the target student.* Frequently, student behavior is a function of teacher reaction to the behavior. Hence, examining teacher behavior is an essential aspect of any classroom observation. Examples follow:

   Positive teacher attention: Positive comments, smiling, touching, or gesturing directed toward target student.

   Negative teacher attention: Reprimands, negative consequences, or negative gestures directed toward target student.

   Neutral teacher attention: Teacher attends to student but there is neither negative nor positive valence associated with the attention (e.g., teacher looks at student).

3. *Class activity.* The basic activity in which the class is engaged should be noted on the observational form. Some examples follow:

   teacher directed whole class activity

   teacher directed small group activity

   independent seat work

   other

4. *Observation interval.* To structure the observation period, an *interval* observational system is most often used. Hence, if you observe for 20 minutes, the entire observational period would be broken down into many smaller intervals. The length of these smaller intervals depends on the type and frequency of the behavior being observed. For example, if you are observing a high frequency of behavior, you would choose a small interval (10 seconds). Alternatively, if you are observing a low frequency behavior such as fighting, you would choose a longer interval.

5. *Alternative measures.* Although the interval recording (described above) is useful in most cases, it is occasionally necessary to monitor some behaviors using different methods. The two methods most commonly used as an alternative to interval recording are event and duration systems.

   Event recording allows you to note *every* instance of a behavior. Students who are self-abusive, for example, may strike themselves 20 to 30 times in 30 seconds. An interval system would not accurately convey the intensity of the behavior.

   Duration recording allows one to note how long a behavior occurs. A child who has trouble paying attention, for example, may be on task and off task several times during a 30-second interval, but

Source: Adapted from J. C. Witt, S. N. Elliott, J. J. Kramer, and F. M. Gresham (1994), Assessment of Children: Fundamental Methods and Practices. *Dubuque, IA: Brown & Benchmark.*

Authentic/Performance Assessment

Authentic/performance assessment is a philosophy about classroom assessment as well as a combination of practical data collection techniques. As such, it is a central piece of many school restructuring efforts in the United States and in several foreign countries. Consequently, authentic/performance assessment methods are being proposed by some educators as replacements for both standardized tests and typical pencil-and-paper classroom tests.

What exactly is **authentic/performance assessment**? Although no standard definition of authentic assessment has been offered, this statement by Archbald and

authentic/performance assessment *The securing of information about a student's success or failure through meaningful and significant (authentic) tasks.*

using an interval system would be marked as off task only once. With duration recording, you simply record the length of time the child is either off-task or on-task.

6. *Observation of a peer for comparison.* To determine whether the behavior you observe is a problem you can compare the target student's behavior with that of a "normal" peer. To accomplish this, you simply record the behavior of a peer in the classroom using the same system you chose for the target student. You should choose a same sex peer who has been nominated by the teacher as "normal." This can help you in consulting with the teacher because you can present the data for the target student and the comparison student.

7. *Class scan check.* To characterize the classroom context, it is beneficial to conduct periodic (i.e., every 3–5 minutes) classroom scans. The purpose here is to note relevant features of the classroom environment. In particular, it is important to determine the degree to which other students in the classroom are on-task, following teacher's directions, etc. The scan is an informal procedure that will end up later in your notes to help you characterize the classroom. It is informal in that there is no need to precisely quantify the amount of on-task activity. For example, you could provide a rough estimate of the percentage of students who are on-task.

8. *Necessary equipment.* At a minimum, classroom observations require the following equipment:

> *Wristwatch*—watch with a second hand needed to monitor intervals and length of observation sessions.
>
> *Observation form*—see attached form, for example.
>
> *Stopwatch*—to monitor duration.

9. *Calculation of the data.* It is useful to determine the percentage of time a student is on-task. To accomplish

this, you divide the number of on-task intervals by the total number of intervals observed and multiply by 100 as follows:

$$\frac{\text{\# of on-task intervals}}{\text{Total intervals observed}} \times 100$$

10. *Interpretation and report of the data.* To summarize and report the data, you should begin by describing the context of the observation. Here you can report observations from the classroom scan check and you can note ongoing classroom activities during observation (e.g., teacher-directed small group activity). Next, you can report the percentage of on-task behavior for the target student and tell how this contrasts with the comparison student. The idea is to determine whether the target students exhibited behavior that is markedly different from the norm or from what would be reasonably expected in that particular classroom context. What follows is an example of how to report data:

> Kevin was observed for 30 minutes during Mrs. Wickstrom's English class. During the observation session, the class was engaged in teacher-directed large group instruction. In a classroom where students were generally very well behaved, Kevin's behavior was quite noticeable. He was off-task approximately 88% of the time. This off-task behavior consisted of mostly verbal off-task and motor off-task behaviors. That is, he was talking and out of his seat a great deal. By comparison, a peer nominated by Mrs. Wickstrom as being "normal" was only off-task 7% of the time.

For classification of a student as behavior disordered, at least three different observation sessions should be used. The reason for observing on multiple occasions and preferably multiple settings is to increase the validity of your results.

Newmann (1988) will serve as a beginning: "A valid assessment system provides information about particular tasks on which students succeed or fail, but more important, it also presents tasks that are worthwhile, significant, and meaningful—in short, authentic" (p. 1). Performance assessment is a closely related approach, and in fact, often is conceptualized as a subset of authentic assessment. Thus, the definition of performance assessment is also offered to facilitate understanding of the nature of authentic assessment. Specifically, Airasian (1991) defines performance assessment as "assessments in which the teacher observes and makes a judgment about a pupil's skill in carrying out an activity or producing a product" (p. 252). Table 15.5 illustrates the dimensions on which performance-based assessments differ from the typical classroom methods of objective test, essay test, and oral questioning by a teacher. A careful review of this table should give you a clear understanding of the types of

Table 15.5

Comparison of Various Types of Assessment

	Objective test	Essay test	Oral question	Performance assessment
Purpose	Sample knowledge with maximum efficiency and reliability	Assess thinking skills and/or mastery of a structure of knowledge	Assess knowledge during instruction	Assess ability to translate knowledge and understanding into action
Typical exercise	Test items: Multiple-choice True/false Fill-in Matching	Writing task	Open-ended question	Written prompt or natural event framing the kind of performance required
Student's response	Read, evaluate, select	Organize, compose	Oral answer	Plan, construct, and deliver original response
Scoring	Count correct answers	Judge understanding	Determine correctness of answer	Check attributes present, rate proficiency demonstrated, or describe performance via anecdote
Major advantage	Efficiency—can administer many items per unit of testing time	Can measure complex cognitive outcomes	Joins assessment and instruction	Provides rich evidence of performance skills
Potential sources of inaccurate assessment	Poorly written items, overemphasis on recall of facts, poor test-taking skills, failure to sample content representatively	Poorly written exercises, writing skill confounded with knowledge of content, poor scoring procedures	Poor questions, students' lack of willingness to respond, too few questions	Poor exercises, too few samples of performance, vague criteria, poor rating procedures, poor test conditions
Influence on learning	Overemphasis on recall encourages memorization; can encourage thinking skills if properly constructed	Encourages thinking and development of writing skills	Stimulates participation in instruction, provides teacher immediate feedback on effectiveness of teaching	Emphasizes use of available skill and knowledge in relevant problem contexts
Keys to success	Clear test blueprint or specifications that match instruction, skill in item writing, time to write items	Carefully prepared writing exercises, preparation of model answers, time to read and score	Clear questions, representative sample of questions to each student, adequate time provided for student response	Carefully prepared performance exercises; clear performance expectations; careful, thoughtful rating; time to rate performance

Source: R. J. Stiggins, "Design Development of Performance Assessments" in *Educational Measurement: Issues and Practice*, 6:35, 1987. Copyright © 1987 by National Center on Measurement in Education, Washington, D. C.

Assessing children's understanding of common school situations and their problem-solving strategies for dealing with these situations is an important focus for educators interested in the social and emotional functioning of students.

activities expected of teachers in an authentic/performance assessment-oriented classroom.

Authentic/performance assessment involves assessment activities like those commonly used in the world outside the classroom: work samples, performances, exhibitions, and self-evaluation reports. With an authentic assessment, the learner must produce something new, rather than simply reproducing prior knowledge. Authentic/performance assessments can guide teaching and provide evidence that a student has achieved significant learning objectives. Multiple-choice and many standardized tests rarely accomplish these goals, and in most cases are inconsistent with the spirit of authentic/performance assessment.

Some educational subjects have a long history of using authentic performances or products as a means of assessing students' learning. For example, physical education, art, music, and vocational and technological arts all use, to a large extent, students' products or performances to determine whether the learning objectives of a class have been met. Thus, many educators are already aware of the importance of authentic/performance assessment and are actively using it.

Authentic/performance assessment often requires students to apply knowledge and skills resulting in some type of *performance* or *demonstration* (Coalition of Essential Schools, 1990). A performance is a recital, a debate, a play, a game, an oral report in front of a class, or any event at which a student can be observed to use acquired knowledge or skills. Some performances may be videotaped to provide feedback to students and to allow others to evaluate the performance.

Performance assessment is best understood as a continuum of assessment formats, ranging from the simplest student-constructed responses to comprehensive demonstrations or collections of work over time. Regardless of the format, common features of performance assessments involve (a) students' construction rather than selection of responses, (b) direct observation of student behavior on tasks resembling those commonly required for functioning in the world outside school, and (c) illumination of students' learning and thinking processes along with their answers (Office of Technology Assessment, 1992).

"I'll have to count off for the missing heart."

Reprinted by permission of James Warren.

As Coutinho and Malouf (1992) noted in their article on performance assessment of students with disabilities, writers have used a variety of terms (e.g., *authentic, portfolio, alternative*) to refer to assessment methods featuring student-generated responses. The term *performance* emphasizes *a student's active generation of a response* and highlights the fact that the response is observable, either directly or indirectly, in the form of a permanent product. By contrast, the term *authentic* (which perhaps is used as often as is *performance*) refers to the nature of the *task* and *context* in which an assessment occurs. The authenticity dimension of assessment has become a very salient issue for at least two reasons. First, most educators assume that the more realistic or authentic a task is, the more interesting it is to students. Thus, students' motivation to engage in and perform authentic tasks is perceived to be much higher than it would be for tasks whose relevance to "real-world" problems or issues they had trouble seeing. Second, educators who espouse an outcomes-oriented approach to education want to focus assessments on complex sets of skills and conditions that are like those to which they wish to generalize their educational efforts.

Figure 15.3 is designed to highlight the performance and authenticity dimensions of the emerging conceptualization of educational assessment tasks. It also indicates that a common third dimension of a valid assessment task is that the content assessed represents the content taught. Figure 15.3 synthesizes three key aspects that educators want to manipulate in their assessments of students' achievement: *student response, nature of the task,* and *relevance to instruction.* As indicated in the figure, assessment tasks can be characterized as varying in the *level of performance they require* (low performance: filling in a bubble sheet, or selecting the best answer by circling a letter; high performance: writing and presenting a report on research, or conducting a scientific experiment in a lab); their *authenticity* (low authenticity: reading isolated nonsense words, or writing a list of teacher-generated spelling words; high authenticity: reading a newspaper article or the directions for installing a phone recording system, or writing a letter to a friend using words that are important to the student); and their *alignment with curriculum outcomes* (low alignment: teaching facts and concepts, but assessing application; high alignment: both teaching and assessing application of facts and concepts). Many educators are searching for assessments that are relatively high on all three dimensions. That is, they want highly authentic, or "real-world," tasks that clearly are connected to their instructional curricula and that require students to produce, rather than select, responses. Conceptually, such tasks would lie within the HIGH circle in figure 15.3.

Many educators already use some **weak performance assessment** in some form. That is, (a) they ask students to apply their knowledge and skills by producing a product, and (b) they provide students feedback about their performances in the form of grades. Besides these two traditional elements of performance assessment, the new, pedagogically "stronger" forms of performance assessment take steps to influence students' performances. **Strong performance assessment** uses these methods:

1. Selecting assessment tasks that are clearly aligned or connected to what has been taught
2. Sharing the scoring criteria for an assessment task with students prior to their work on the task

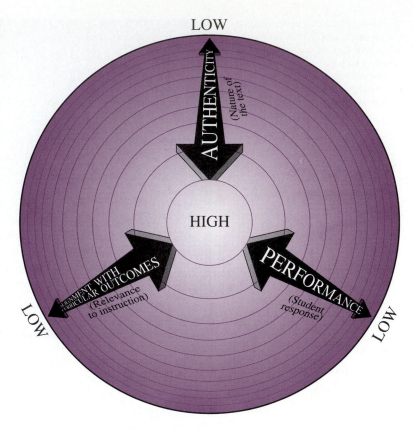

Figure 15.3
The Relationships Among Performance, Authenticity, and the Classroom Curriculum in an Assessment Task.
Courtesy Stephen N. Elliott.

weak performance assessment
An assessment in which students are asked to apply their knowledge and skills by producing a product and then a teacher provides feedback in the form of a grade.

strong performance assessment
An assessment in which students who are asked to apply knowledge and skills are provided scoring criteria before they produce products, and are also encouraged to assess themselves after they have completed the products.

3. Providing students with clear statements of standards and/or several models of acceptable and exemplary performances prior to their attempting a task,

4. Encouraging students to complete self-assessments of their performances, and

5. Interpreting students' performances by comparing them to consensus standards that are developmentally appropriate, as well as possibly comparing them to other students' performances.

As described here, the stronger forms of performance assessment interact in visible ways with instruction that precedes *and* follows an assessment task. This approach to assessment emphasizes the point that *the central purposes of most educational assessments are to facilitate communication among educational stakeholders—teachers, students, parents, administrators, employers—and to guide instruction!* Let us now examine some of the typical performance assessment methods.

Portfolios are a common feature of an authentic/performance approach to assessment (referred to as **portfolio assessment**). A portfolio is a revealing collection of a student's work that a teacher, a student, or both judge to be important evidence of the student's learning (Paulson, Paulson, & Meyer, 1991). A portfolio often serves two purposes: documentation and evaluation. Some teachers, particularly those involved with language and communication arts, already use writing portfolios as a means of collecting and analyzing students' growth in written communication skills.

Exhibitions are one of the most frequently discussed components of an authentic/performance assessment system. Exhibitions require integration of a broad range of competencies and ever-increasing student initiative and responsibility. Gibbons (1974, 1984) is credited with stimulating educators to apply to schooling the philosophy of the "walkabout," an Australian aborigine rite of passage to adulthood. In many cases, the educational application of the walkabout has been the development of rite-of-passage or exit exhibitions in which students are required to demonstrate the integration and application of knowledge and skills in targeted areas of outcome competencies. In some school systems, rite-of-passage exhibitions serve as gateways to the next levels (e.g., an exhibition of essential skills must be demonstrated to move to junior high school; another exhibition of even more sophisticated skills must be passed to earn a diploma). Figure 15.4 illustrates the content and activities required in a twelfth-grade exhibition referred to as a "ROPE" or "rite-of-passage experience."

Performances, portfolios, and exhibitions all can be rich sources of information about a student and the teaching-learning process. To interpret the results of these assessment methods, a set of evaluation criteria is required that provides meaningful feedback about a student's academic and behavioral strengths and weaknesses. In an authentic/performance assessment approach, evaluative criteria are referred to as **rubrics.** Meaningful rubrics are developed by expert teachers and provide clearly articulated criteria that allow reliable judgments about students' demonstrated levels of proficiency. The development of rubrics to evaluate and score students' performances is perhaps the most challenging implementation aspect of authentic/performance assessment. An example of an evaluation and scoring rubric for students' written reports is provided in figure 15.5; one for mathematics problem solving is illustrated in figure 15.6.

Rubrics are useful for evaluating discrete performances and products of students; however, a comprehensive system for evaluating students' progress also is needed. Grades traditionally have been used to accomplish this goal. In an authentic/performance assessment system, **performance-based grading benchmarks** provide the standards by which students' accomplishments are evaluated. Grading is unnecessary, if not inconsistent, in an authentic/performance assessment system. Instead, students' progress toward mastery of the agreed-upon learning outcomes is evaluated by comparing their work to the terminal learning objectives for any given subject or school year. Students' work and accomplishments are compared to a standard of performance (using **criterion-referenced tests** in a mastery approach), rather than to other students.

A final common component of an authentic/performance assessment system is **student self-assessment.** In theory, self-assessments by students could be part of

portfolio assessment
Assessment of a student's behavior based upon a collection of the student's work that the teacher, the student, or both believe to be important evidence of learning.

exhibitions *A form of authentic assessment in which students are required to demonstrate the integration of the knowledge and skills they have acquired.*

rubrics *Authoritative or established criteria used to evaluate student performance; usually consists of a fixed scale and a list of characteristics describing performances for each point on the scale.*

performance-based grading benchmarks *The use of objective standards by which students' accomplishments are evaluated.*

criterion-referenced tests *A type of testing used to determine if a student has achieved predetermined behavioral or learning objectives. A student's performance is interpreted by comparing the performance to a set of objective criteria.*

student self-assessment
Students are encouraged to review and analyze their own performance.

All seniors must demonstrate mastery in fifteen areas of knowledge and competence by completing a portfolio, a project, and six other presentations before a ROPE committee consisting of staff members (including the student's home-room teacher), a student from the grade below, and an adult from the community. Nine of the presentations are based on the materials in the portfolio and the project; the remaining six presentations are developed especially for the presentation process.

The Portfolio. The portfolio, developed during the first semester of the senior year, is intended to be "a reflection and analysis of the graduating senior's own life and times." Its requirements are:

1. *A written autobiography,* descriptive, introspective, and analytical. School records and other indicators of participation may be included.

2. *A reflection on work,* including an analysis of the significance of the work experiences for the graduating senior's life. A resume can be included.

3. *Two letters of recommendation* (at minimum) from any sources chosen by the student.

4. *A reading record,* including a bibliography, annotated if desired, and two mini-book reports. Reading test scores may be included.

5. *An essay of ethics* exhibiting contemplation of the subject and describing the student's own ethical code.

6. *An artistic product* or written report on art and an essay on artistic standards for judging quality in a chosen area of art.

7. *A written report analyzing mass media:* who or what controls mass media, toward what ends, and with what effects. Evidence of experience with mass media may be included.

8. *A written summary and evaluation of the student's course work in science/technology; a written description of a scientific experiment* illustrating the application of the scientific method; an *analytical essay* (with examples) on social consequences of science and technology; and *an essay on the nature and use of computers* in modern society.

The Project. Every graduating senior must write a library research-based paper that analyzes an event, set of events, or theme in American history. A national comparative approach can be used in the analysis. The student must be prepared to field questions about both the paper and an overview of American history during the presentations, which are given in the second semester of the senior year.

> To graduate from Walden III you must complete a portfolio, a written project, and fifteen oral presentations before two teachers, a peer, and an outside adult.

The Presentations. Each of the eight components of the portfolio, plus the project, must be presented orally and in writing to the ROPE committee.

Six additional oral presentations are also required. For these, however, no written reports or new products are required by the committee. Supporting documents or other forms of evidence may be used. Assessment of proficiency is based on the demonstration of knowledge and skills during the presentations in each of the following areas:

1. *Mathematics knowledge and skills* is demonstrated by a combination of course evaluations, test results, and worksheets presented before the committee, and by the ability to competently field mathematics questions asked during the demonstration.

2. *Knowledge of American government* should be demonstrated by discussion of the purpose of government; the individual's relation to the state; the ideals, functions, and problems of American political institutions; and selected contemporary issues and political events. Supporting materials can be used.

3. The *personal proficiency* demonstration requires the student to think about and organize a presentation about the requirements of adult living in our society in terms of personal fulfillment, social skills, and practical competencies; and to discuss his or her own strengths and weaknesses in everyday living skills (health, home economics, mechanics, etc.) and interpersonal relations.

4. *Knowledge of geography* should be demonstrated in a presentation that covers the basic principles and questions of the discipline; identification of basic landforms, places, and names; and the scientific and social significance of geographical information.

5. Evidence of the graduating senior's successful *completion of a physical challenge* must be presented to the ROPE committee.

6. A demonstration of *competency in English (written and spoken)* is provided in virtually all the portfolio and project requirements. These, and any additional evidence the graduating senior may wish to present to the committee, fulfill the requirements of the presentation in the English competency area.

The above is drawn from the 1984 student handbook, "Walden III's Rite of Passage Experience," by Thomas Feeney, a teacher at Walden III, an alternative public school in Racine, Wisconsin. Preliminary annotations are by Grant Wiggins.

Figure 15.4
Walden III's rite of passage experience (ROPE).

Courtesy Charles Kent, Principal, Walden III, Racine, Wisconsin.

Figure 15.5

A grading grid for essays.

Adams County Schools, District I.

	1	2	3	4	5	
O	Little or nothing is written. Essay is disorganized and poorly developed. Does not stay on topic		Essay is incomplete. It lacks an introduction, well-developed body, or conclusion. Coherence and logic are attempted but are inadequate		The essay is well-organized. It is coherent, ordered logically, and fully developed	×6
S	The student writes frequent run-ons or fragments		Occasional errors in sentence structure. Little variety in sentence length and structure		Sentences are complete and varied in length and structure	×5
U	Student makes frequent errors in word choice and agreement		Student makes occasional errors in word choice and agreement		Usage is correct. Word choice is appropriate	×4
M	Student makes frequent errors in spelling, punctuation, and capitalization		Student makes an occasional error in mechanics		Spelling, capitalization, and punctuation are correct	×4
F	Format is sloppy. There are no margins or indents. Handwriting is inconsistent		The margins and indents have inconsistencies— there is no title or title is inappropriate		The format is correct. The title is appropriate. The margins and indents are consistent	×1

O = Organization
S = Sentence structure
U = Usage
M = Mechanics
F = Format

The essays are scored using a 1–5 scale. The numbers in the boxes to the far right indicate the relative importance of each factor in the overall grade. Thus, organization is valued most, and counts 30% of the grade; format counts 5% of the grade.

any approach to assessment. In practice, they are infrequently used, because the evaluation criteria and the expected learning outcomes rarely are explained to students. In an authentic assessment system, learning outcomes are made explicit, and students are encouraged to review and analyze their performances, their portfolios, and other activities that provide feedback about their learning. Thus, student understanding of their strengths and weaknesses is an important outcome of this form of assessment and schooling.

In conclusion, authentic/performance assessment is an ambitious approach to both assessing and teaching students that places heavy emphasis on teachers' judgments. Few teachers will use all the procedural components reviewed here for any given class, yet some of the procedures would appear to be very useful and easily can be integrated into almost any class—elementary through high school.

> If you could select the method by which you would be assessed for this course, what would it be like?

USING DATA FROM TEACHER-CONSTRUCTED TESTS AND CLASSROOM ASSESSMENTS

marking *The summary assessment of a test or an oral or written report.*

Some of the purposes of classroom testing and assessment have been mentioned: assessing ability, measuring achievement, determining the degree to which objectives have been attained, and guiding educational decisions. But educators also use test data in marking, grading, and reporting. **Marking** refers to assessment of a test or an oral or written report; *grading* refers to a cumulative evaluation of tests, reports, essays;

reporting refers to the manner in which an educator communicates the results of marking and grading to children and parents.

Remember Jayne Bischoff's words of wisdom to Jim Lasso in this chapter's opening vignette: "Assessment is communication!" It is time now to examine each of the end products of assessment: marks, grades, and reports.

Marking

A mark—at any educational level—is a judgment of one person by another. Sometimes your judgment may be informal, as when you discuss an oral report with a student, or mark and comment on an essay examination. Occasionally your mark may be quite mechanical, as when you simply total the number of correct items in an objective test and assign a mark on the basis of the number right.

Our concern here is with the mark you assign to a test or report. Are you more comfortable with percentage figures or letters? How will you use this mark? Will your students understand a letter grade if they've taken an objective test? How will you relate numbers to letters? What contributes to a letter grade?

Although students understand both A and 95 as a judgment of how they have performed, they may better understand a number as reflecting exactly what they did on a test. Letter grades may include many variables, such as spelling and writing ability. Depending on your likes and dislikes, you may discriminate more fairly by using numbers: 66, 68, 71, as opposed to C-, C, C+. What can you do to improve your marking technique?

- *Be sure to mark (or somehow respond to) any work you assign.* Nothing frustrates students more than spending substantial time on a project and not having teachers react to it. Your assignments are quickly labeled "busywork," and if done at all, contribute little to learning. The best rule of thumb is this: if you assign written work, mark it. If you assign readings, discuss them. In this way, all students will feel involved and realize that you always respond to assignments.
- *Return work promptly, or as soon as possible.* Unless students receive feedback, they often forget, or worse, remember error. Giving a test one day and not returning it for a week or two is poor teaching. If you believe that tests aid teaching and learning, they will become an integral part of your work, not something added at the end of a unit or course. If you delay furnishing test results, students find it difficult to use your corrections; too much has happened since the tests. If serious weaknesses are uncovered, students probably should not commence new work. If they do well, they could possibly bypass the introductory work of the next topic. All these benefits are lost if you return the tests two weeks after they are written.

Mathematics Scoring Rubric

4   **Exemplary response**
4.1 Complete in every way, with clear, coherent, unambiguous, and insightful explanation
4.2 Shows understanding of underlying mathematical concepts, procedures, and structures
4.3 Examines and satisfies all essential conditions of the problem
4.4 Presents strong supporting arguments with examples and counterexamples as appropriate
4.5 Solution and work is efficient and shows evidence of reflection and checking of work
4.6 Appropriately applies mathematics to the situation

3   **Competent response**
3.1 Gives a fairly complete response with reasonably clear explanations
3.2 Shows understanding of underlying mathematical concepts, procedures, and structures
3.3 Examines and satisfies most essential conditions of the problem
3.4 Presents adequate supporting arguments with examples and counterexamples as appropriate
3.5 Solution and work show some evidence of reflection and checking of work
3.6 Appropriately applies mathematics to the situation

2   **Minimal response**
2.1 Gives response, but explanations may be unclear or lack detail
2.2 Exhibits minor flaws in underlying mathematical concepts, procedures, and structures
2.3 Examines and satisfies some essential conditions of the problem
2.4 Draws some accurate conclusions, but reasoning may be faulty or incomplete
2.5 Shows little evidence of reflection and checking of work
2.6 Some attempt to apply mathematics to the situation

1   **Inadequate response**
1.1 Response is incomplete and explanation is insufficient or not understandable
1.2 Exhibits major flaws in underlying mathematical concepts, procedures, and structures
1.3 Fails to address essential conditions of the problem
1.4 Uses faulty reasoning and draws incorrect conclusions
1.5 Shows no evidence of reflection and checking of work
1.6 Fails to apply mathematics to the situation

0   **No attempt**
0.1 Provides irrelevant or no response
0.2 Copies part of the problem but does not attempt a solution
0.3 Illegible response

NOTE: To receive a particular score, a significant number of the associated criteria must be met.

Figure 15.6
Mathematics scoring rubric.

- *If possible, personally comment on the test.* On an objective test, students appreciate some remark, even if it is only, "You did quite well on this test." Essay tests provide more freedom to comment.
- *Be specific in your comments.* Telling students they are wrong has little effect. Your comments should indicate precisely where their errors are and, if necessary, how to correct them. Also tell students exactly where their answers are superior so that they can capitalize on their strengths.
- *Mark the student's work, not the student.* In this chapter, we have cautioned constantly against using tests for personal reasons. This is especially dangerous in objective marking.
- *Avoid sarcasm and belittling or ridiculing remarks.* You have the experience, the authority, and the power in the classroom. Use it wisely and not to enhance self-importance. Be careful of your remarks; they can hurt and discourage sensitive, developing personalities. A successful teacher works with students.
- *Make a personal decision whether to have students repeat their work and correct errors.* This decision is often based on available time. Merely mentioning mistakes does not remedy them. If possible, have students actually rework their errors after they have determined where they blundered.

Annual Edition

Grading

Most schools insist that teachers periodically grade their students; this means that you must judge a student's work for two or three months and decide upon A or B, 90 or 72. What contributes to the grade? Is it the mere average of all test scores, or should it also include students' attitude, improvement, or participation? Only you can answer this question by determining the purpose of grading for you.

If a grade is intended to indicate competence in algebra, then it should probably consist essentially of marks assigned to subject matter: tests, reports, a final examination. Specialized schools or programs can then strictly interpret a grade and judge a student's readiness for a course or program. Such grades characterize most secondary schools, while elementary school grades often represent some combination of competence, effort, and general attitude. A combination is difficult to interpret, and even at the elementary level it is better to assign a competence grade and to report on attitude, interest, or comprehension in some other way.

One danger in assigning grades, at both the elementary and the secondary levels, is using grades to discipline or punish unruly students. This can be more subtly done in grading than in marking. If you mark harshly on a test, it is obvious that you are not marking content. Something else is influencing the mark. But unless a grade represents competence alone—and students, parents, teachers, and administrators have agreed on this—many other factors may affect a final grade.

As you can see from this brief discussion, the more variables that are included in a grade, the less effective it is as an indication of achievement. Your grades will represent true achievement to the extent that they reflect objectives and satisfactory test construction.

In a perceptive and now classic essay, Palmer (1962) identified several dishonest grading habits.

- *Abdicating.* The first, and most indefensible, way of grading dishonestly is by abdication. Some teachers may doubt the role of testing in teaching and learning. Consequently, they use either hastily devised tests or none at all. It is hard to decide which is more harmful to students. With no testing, everyone understands that a course grade represents a teacher's personal opinion. No one is sure of what a disorganized collection of test scores represents.
- *Using the "carrots and clubs" system.* This is another dishonest method, wherein grades represent many different things for different teachers: tests, entire course

Focus ← **Writing Comments on Tests**

Ellis Page (1958) conducted a famous study of marks and the effects of teacher comments. He wanted to determine if teachers' comments improve student performance and which comments were effective. Previous similar studies had inherent difficulties: outsiders conducted the experiments, tests were contrived to mask the treatment, and praise or reproof was often random (classroom comments are definite and specific). Page's study eliminated these problems by leaving classroom procedures untouched, except for written comments upon the tests.

Seventy-four teachers randomly selected one of their classes as an experimental group. The total student group consisted of 2,139 secondary school students. The teachers initially administered whatever test came next in the course. They then scored the tests as usual—A, B, C, D, or F—and then randomly assigned each paper to one of three groups. The *no comment* group received a mark and nothing else. The *free comment* group received whatever comment the teacher deemed appropriate. The *specified comment* group received uniform comments previously designated for each mark:

A. Excellent! Keep it up.
B. Good Work. Keep at it.
C. Perhaps try to do still better?
D. Let's bring this up.
F. Let's raise this grade.

The teachers returned the tests with no unusual attention. The effects of these comments were judged by the scores the same students achieved on the next scheduled test. The results were:

- The free comment students achieved higher scores than the specified comment group, which did better than the no comment students.
- The results were consistent for all schools in the sample.
- Although teachers had expected the better students to profit more from their comments, no evidence supported their expectations.

Page concluded that when secondary school teachers write truthful but encouraging remarks on student papers, they have a measurable and potent effect on students so that learning improves.

---

work, spelling mistakes in history tests, personal likes and dislikes. Enough has been said about the purpose of grading to alert you to the dangers of marking something other than merit.

- *Defaulting.* Grading by default was briefly popular in the 1960s, when many instructors and schools were reluctant to grade students. Many college professors refused to give tests and assigned everyone an A. Secondary and elementary teachers gave as few tests as possible. Academic dishonesty soon became apparent, because no one could determine whether students were prepared for new, more difficult, work. Many students, at all levels, found themselves progressing into programs or schools for which they lacked the necessary interest, competence, or ability. Today there is intense national interest in improving tests, marks, and grades.

- *Being a zealot.* Test, test, test! These teachers turn their classes into a nightmarish endurance contest. The danger here is so obvious it needs little comment, but consider the possible outcome: student dislike of the course, teacher, and school.

- *Changing rules in midstream.* The "tough" teacher eases standards. Easy markers panic when the principal mentions how well their students are doing. When an established pattern is reversed, students are bewildered, and the learning atmosphere becomes tense and mistrustful.

- *Psychic testing.* This is an alarming extension of abdication and default. "They do not require tests; they know who will receive A's or F's." Most students are frightened by this type of teacher; in college, especially, they will shun the course.

- *Being a perfectionist.* Some teachers, striving for impossible perfection, inform their classes that no one receives an A and only geniuses need expect B. Failure is rampant.

Unfortunately, you have probably been a victim of one, or several, of the above approaches. How can you avoid these pitfalls in your own grading efforts? Decide specifically what the grade is to represent and have it firmly in mind when you assign grades. You should share this information, or whatever criteria you use, with your students, and your decision should be accepted by other teachers and administrators and communicated to parents.

Reporting

Parents wish to be informed of their children's educational progress; this is one rationale for report cards. Teachers know how their students are progressing. Students and parents, however, need extra communication. The main benefit of any reporting system is that it strengthens the link between home and school. Schools and teachers should know how much support they will receive from parents, what advantages or disadvantages a child has, and what the parents' attitude is toward education. Parents should know what the objectives of teachers and schools are, how their child meets these objectives, and what they should reasonably expect their child to attain.

In addition to informing parents and students of progress, a reporting system should bring together parents and teachers so that they can combine efforts to encourage and help children. Unfortunately, most new teachers dread these conferences. They often report feeling insecure and defensive, especially if a child has earned poor grades. To evade or to be vague can be disastrous. Honest and hopeful evaluation, based on student work and observation of behavior, is the only rule. A teacher's portrayal of an average child as superior in both ability and performance frustrates everyone. Parents' expectations are unduly heightened; children quickly sense adult dishonesty; teachers avoid a crucial task. If home and school are to work together, there must be honesty, tempered by mature judgment.

No reporting system is completely satisfactory. Either the report of academic progress is slighted ("John is doing very nicely"), or there is excessive emphasis upon a grade ("John: C–"). For example, the traditional report card supplies letter or numerical grades—A, B, C, 95, 85, 75—with little interpretation. It may also include one column where the teacher identifies attitudes as satisfactory or unsatisfactory. Such cards are more typical of elementary than of secondary schools.

A less rigid system may use the two categories "satisfactory" and "unsatisfactory" to report on all behavior, including academic behavior. Doubts persist about such reports. The behavior is satisfactory or unsatisfactory—compared to what? Little realistic information is conveyed to parents in this system.

A third, equally unsatisfactory, technique is to use even broader categories: "John is progressing." "John has shown improvement since the last report." "It is necessary to discuss John's progress, so please arrange a conference."

Given these conditions, what can you do?

- *Recognize that it makes little difference which system you prefer; you probably will be required to use the school's system.* The best advice is to study it thoroughly so that you can report objectively and carefully.
- *Know exactly what constitutes your evaluation of a student.* If you assign a C, or a 75, or "satisfactory," or "progressing normally," be sure that you realize exactly what contributes to the grade: tests, homework assignments, class participation, library research, reports, etc.
- *Beware of personal opinion in any objective reporting.* When you judge a student's work to be unsatisfactory or nonprogressing, or even assign a C, avoid any personal prejudices. Separate the subjective from the objective, even if the report involves just a comment. For example, state precisely what the student has accomplished, and then relate it to ability or aptitude. Answer this question: Can you objectively defend your grade as free from bias?
- *Use any subjective evaluation cautiously but honestly.* Whether it is a written comment or an attitude checklist, make your judgment as fair as possible, while

telling parents and students exactly what you think. For example, if a student is not working up to ability, tell the student; if a student's classroom behavior is damaging achievement, tell the student.

- *Use the parent-teacher conference wisely.* Here you have a unique opportunity to improve home-school cooperation. If you are prepared, if you can justify your grades and comments, then the conference is no longer something to dread, but a tool to help students. But you must be able to produce test scores, marks, essays and reports, and a record of completed assignments to support objective grades. You must be prepared to furnish detailed reasons for your personal evaluation. There is no greater persuasive argument than the facts.

Gronlund (1985) suggested that schools and teachers adopt guidelines for their grading and reporting practices and then follow these procedures. For example, a grading and reporting system functions effectively when it results from the efforts of students, parents, and school personnel. The system itself should be sufficiently detailed to be helpful in diagnosis, yet not overly complicated. It also should reflect those educational objectives that guide learning, grading, and reporting.

Evaluating and reporting students' academic progress is a challenging endeavor and one that evokes high interest from teachers and students alike. Although many people have questioned teachers' ability to accurately evaluate students' achievement, recent research indicates that teachers are highly accurate judges! Let us examine this important area more closely.

RESEARCH ON TEACHERS' JUDGMENTS OF STUDENTS' ACHIEVEMENT

In 1989, Robert Hoge and Theodore Coladarci published a data-based review of research examining the match between teacher-based assessments of student achievement levels and objective measures of student learning. As a rationale for their work, they noted that (a) many decisions about students are influenced by teachers' judgments of the students' academic functioning, and (b) historically, there seems to have been a widespread assumption that teachers generally are poor judges of the attributes of their students.

Hoge and Coladarci identified 16 studies that were methodologically sound and featured comparisons between teachers' judgments of their students' academic performance and the students' actual performance on achievement criteria. They found generally "high levels of agreement between teachers' judgmental measures and the standardized achievement test scores" (p. 308). The range of correlations was from a low of .28 to a high of .92, with the median being .65. (Note: A perfect correlation would be 1.00.) The median correlation certainly exceeds the convergent and concurrent validity coefficients typically reported for psychological tests.

This review of research has an important implication for practitioners and researchers alike: Teachers, in general, can provide valid performance judgments of their students. This result is comforting and should not be surprising, given the number of hours that teachers have to observe their students' performances.

HELPING STUDENTS TAKE TESTS

A final concern in this chapter is **test-wiseness,** or the ability of students to take tests. Don't confuse test-wiseness with coaching. *Coaching* means preparing students to take a specific test, that is, familiarizing them with the content of a particular test. *Test-wiseness,* however, means helping students to take all kinds of tests. If you think of test-wiseness as preparing students to demonstrate what they know, then you become

test-wiseness *Knowing how to take tests; can be improved by teaching.*

Talking to students about their test-taking strategies and coaching them to use good problem-solving skills are important teaching activities that enhance student performances on tests.

How can teachers help students to improve their test-taking skills?

more sensitive to the importance of this skill. You can help students to improve their test-taking skills by giving them these suggestions (Dobbin, 1984):

- *Find out what the test is like beforehand.* This is one of the most productive strategies in test-taking. There is a lot of information and practice material available about such exams as the Scholastic Aptitude Test. If a test is teacher-made, *ask the teacher any questions you may have.* There's no better source. For example, what will the test cover? Where will it begin? Where will it end? Will it be multiple-choice or essay? How long will it be? (Students should know if they're expected to finish it. Speed can be a factor affecting a mark.) Should I guess? (Some tests penalize students for guessing.) Will anything else other than content be scored? (Students have a right to know if handwriting and spelling will count.)

- *Decide how to study for the test.* What are you going to study? If you have a good idea of what the test will be like, then concentrate on that content and any needed skills. Get all the relevant material together and try to remember what the teacher emphasized in class. You could even make an outline of these topics. Combine reading your notes with reading the text; underline anything you think is critical. As Dobbin (1984) noted, *cram with a plan!*

 You have identified the critical content, the necessary facts and meanings; now you have to study with intensity. Since cramming is best done with facts—Who was the U.S. president during the first World War?—why not make out questions about the facts? Put one question and its answer on each card. Vary the cards; get someone else to ask you the questions. After a while, close your eyes and try to visualize the card, including both question and answer. Finish up the night before the exam, if possible.

- *Make sure you're physically prepared to take the test.* This includes your own physical condition: Get plenty of sleep, don't take any stimulants, don't eat too much before the test (you could get drowsy). It also includes other practical details. Give yourself plenty of time; try to get to the test early.

 We have covered many facets of teacher-constructed tests and classroom assessment because this is a topic of immense importance to instruction. Good assessment and good instruction fit together like a hand in a glove. As your understanding of assessment grows, so does your potential to communicate effectively with students, parents, and fellow educators. In the next chapter, we will continue to look at educational assessment, this time from the perspective of standardized tests.

APPLICATIONS AND REFLECTIONS

Chapter Highlights

Assessment: Terminology and Assumptions

- Assessment is the process of gathering pertinent information to help make decisions about students.
- Testing is one means of obtaining evidence about a student's learning or behavior.
- Measurement means to place a number on a student's performance.
- Grading is the assignment of a symbol to a student's performance.

- Careful analysis of testing results aids educators in improving their instruction, revising curricula, guiding students to realistic decisions, judging the appropriateness of subject matter, and assessing the conditions of learning.
- Educators today are sensitive to the needs of multicultural students in taking tests. In giving tests to these students, teachers should help them with the test-taking skills, such as language comprehension, that could influence their test results.
- All forms of assessment contain error; this implies that we must assess students frequently and with a variety of methods.

Integrating Learning and Assessment

- Assessment techniques should help you to determine if your objectives have been met.
- If objectives remain unattained, then you must search for the cause and attempt to discover whether it lies in the student(s), the material, or your methods.
- The evidence provided by assessment enables teachers and administrators to present appropriate materials that serve the needs of their students.
- Test-wiseness refers to familiarity with test-taking procedures that students can learn.

Methods and Technical Issues in the Assessment of Students

- Assessing classroom performance typically entails four methods: pencil-and-paper tests, oral questions, performance tests, and standardized tests.
- Teacher-constructed tests usually consist of essay questions or multiple-choice items.
- Reliability refers to a test's consistency, which can be affected by an individual's characteristics and by the design of the test. Reliability typically is operationalized with a correlation statistic.
- Validity refers to a test's meaningfulness, that is, its ability to measure what it is supposed to measure. Evidence for validity is based on the accuracy and utility of the results and the consequences of using the test.

Planning a Teacher-Constructed Test

- Test items should reflect the objectives of a subject or unit.
- The teacher should think carefully about the test, taking the time to construct relevant items. A few questions hastily thrown together are not fair to the teacher, given the amount of time spent on teaching, and certainly are not fair to the students, who deserve a thoughtful assessment of their achievement.
- Next the teacher must decide what kind of test—essay or objective—best serves the instructional purpose. Both of these types have strengths and weaknesses. The teacher could consider carefully which type of test is better suited to obtain the information needed to evaluate students' achievement.

Writing Essay Tests

- Writing essay questions is more difficult than it initially appears. Attention to the level of thought needed to answer, clarity of expression, and a degree of objectivity are required.
- Scoring the answers to essay questions requires a clear understanding of the major points in the answer. Teachers should try to ensure that they do not know which student's paper they are marking. Reading all answers to one question rather than reading all of one student's answers at one time also enhances objectivity.

Writing Objective Tests

- Objective tests sample a wide range of material, and if carefully formulated, can also assess comprehension as well as knowledge.
- Teachers should be sure their students are ready for objective tests: Are there any mechanics they should be familiar with? Do they have strategies for taking the test? Can they find the clues an item furnishes? Do they know the rules for guessing?

Alternative Methods and New Assessment Trends

- Advances in behavioral assessment and the school restructuring movement have led to the development of two new assessment approaches: curriculum-based assessment and authentic/performance assessment.
- Behavioral assessment emphasizes observational techniques to characterize a student's overt behavior or performance.
- Good observational procedures require an operational definition of the behavior to be observed, a clear sense of which dimension (i.e., frequency, temporality, intensity, or permanent product) of behavior is being measured, and a recording method (i.e., event, interval, time-based, or permanent product) that fits the behavior dimension.
- Behavioral assessment assumes that a student's assessed behavior is merely a sample of that student's behavior. Therefore, repeated assessments over time and in different situations is typical of a behavioral approach to assessment.
- Curriculum-based assessment (CBA) grew out of the concern that many standardized tests do not adequately test what is taught in a student's curriculum. Although several approaches to CBA have been developed, they all use the content from the curriculum in the classroom to develop brief probes or tests that provide information on what a student knows or doesn't know, and on the rate at which the student is acquiring new information.
- Authentic/performance assessment is a collection of assessment techniques (i.e., portfolios, performances, exhibitions) and interpretative tools (i.e., scoring rubrics and self-ratings) that are designed to link teaching and assessment.
- Authentic/performance assessment focuses on authentic classroom performances rather than typical multiple-choice or essay pencil-and-paper tests. The integration of "real-world" skills is stressed.
- Authentic/performance assessment places a heavy emphasis on teacher judgments of students' performances.

Using Data from Teacher-Constructed Tests and Classroom Assessments

- After assigning work, teachers should mark it and return it as soon as possible with appropriate remarks.
- When grading students (that is, judging their work over a period of time), teachers must be sure that their grades represent their work, not their behavior or attitudes.
- Teachers have been shown generally to be highly accurate judges of students' academic performances, when their judgments have been compared to standardized test results of the students' knowledge.
- One of the main reasons for reporting, if not the main reason, is to strengthen the association between home and school. Remember: Assessment is communication.

Connections

1. Think about how you learn and describe how one of the major concepts discussed in this chapter is part of your learning activities or approach.

_____

_____

_____

_____

2. Identify at least one learning situation (e.g., classroom instruction, self-study, taking a test, small-group work) and describe how you would apply one of the key concepts examined in this chapter _if you were a teacher_.

_____

_____

_____

_____

Getting the Picture and Drawing Relationships

Think about the various learning concepts and variables discussed in this chapter. Create pictures, graphics, or figures that highlight the relationships among key components.

Personal Journal

What I really learned in this chapter was _____

_____

_____

_____

_____

What this means to me is _____

_____

_____

_____

_____

Questions that were stimulated by this chapter include _____

_____

_____

_____

_____

Key Terms

achievement tests	539	extended response	530
assessment	520	grading	520
authentic/performance		interval recording	538
assessment	540	marking	547
construct validity	528	matching item	536
content validity	528	measurement	520
criterion-referenced		multiple-choice items	525
tests	545	performance-based	
criterion-related validity	528	grading benchmarks	545
curriculum-based		permanent product	
assessment (CBA)	537	recording	539
essay tests	525	permanent products	538
evaluation	525	portfolio assessment	545
event recording	538	reliability	527
exhibitions	545	restricted response	530

rubrics	545
standardized tests	524
strong performance	
assessment	544
student self-assessment	545
supply items	530
teacher-constructed	
tests	520
test-wiseness	552
time-based recording	539
true-false questions	525
validity	527
weak performance	
assessment	544

It was that time of the year again; Hugh Taylor, who taught sixth grade at Bailey School, knew that his students were about to take their standardized achievement tests. He always worried that any students who were not "test-wise" might not do as well as they could. So this year he decided to discuss these tests with his class.

He started by asking them, "Why do you have to take these tests, anyway?"

"So the teachers can have a day off, Mr. Taylor," laughed Phil, a happy-go-lucky 12-year-old.

"Hardly that, Phil. We're here with you all the way. But seriously, what good comes from them? Alice?"

With the basics of classroom assessment and test construction behind us, we turn now to the world of standardized tests. Though teachers occasionally may have the responsibility of selecting standardized tests for particular purposes, the chances are that their major tasks with regard to these tests will be as advisors in the selection process. Standardized tests are a major part of many schools' testing programs, and teachers must be informed professionals. It should be noted, however, that some school systems are seriously questioning the value of standardized testing today. Yet, at a national level, many educational leaders are urging a national examination to assess students' academic

chapter 16

standardized tests and rating scales in the classroom

"Well, Mr. Taylor, I suppose it helps you to find out what we're not good at."

"Good, Alice. That's probably the most important reason: to discover what areas you have to work on to improve."

"For example, if anyone seemed to have trouble finding out what the main idea of a story or passage was, we could focus on that skill area in some of our lessons. If you work on it now, you'll reduce the possibility of having any trouble in junior high school." He knew that his students were looking ahead to junior high with a little anxiety.

He then turned to Phil. "Okay, Phil. You were being funny a little while ago. Now, seriously, tell us what you do when you take one of these tests—what do you look for, what do you skip, and what do you think is important."

Phil grinned sheepishly and said, "Well, Mr. Taylor, I look for give-aways."

"That's interesting, Phil. What do you mean?"

"Little clues that tip the answer; words like 'always' or 'never.' "

"Good, Phil. Any other tips? Anybody have any ideas to add?"

The discussion between Mr. Taylor and his students demonstrates the concern that many teachers and students have about standardized tests. ■

progress (Gawronski, 1991). Thus, it is important to examine the advantages and disadvantages of standardized tests and rating scales, as we will do in this chapter.

Standardized tests have become "big business." When you consider that about 45 million students are enrolled in kindergarten through grade 12, you begin to sense the enormous dimensions of "testing." The multibattery nature of most standardized tests makes the number of tests potentially administered very large; the need for prudent and knowledgeable guardians of students' interests is apparent.

Standardized tests used as classroom tests must be appropriate for the educational purposes of the system, the school, and the students. Giving tests simply because "it's the thing to do" is a futile and expensive exercise. The best, and perhaps the only, safeguard against such a practice is knowledge: knowledge of test construction in general, of specific tests, of your students, and of the educational goals of your school.

First, we will discuss the objectives of a school's testing program, and then begin our examination of standardized tests with a description of these tests. Next we will examine how the results of standardized tests can help teachers in the classroom. As with most topics in education, controversy exists about these

A School's Testing Program 560
Standardized Tests 561
Developing a Standardized
    Test 562

Types of Standardized Tests 564
Standardized Achievement
    Tests 564
Standardized Aptitude Tests 566
Behavior Rating Scales 573
Preschool Screening 576

Interpreting Standardized Test Scores 579
Kinds of Scores 579

Using Standardized Tests 583
Educational Applications of
    Standardized Testing 583
Multicultural Students and
    Standardized Testing 584
Common Criticisms of
    Standardized Tests 584
Best Practices 586

**Applications and
Reflections 585**

**Appendix: The Code of Fair
Testing Practices in
Education 589**

tests, so both pros and cons will be presented. Since there are several types of standardized tests, we will sort out the differences. Finally, we will examine several current issues that are swirling about standardized testing.

When you finish reading this chapter, you should be able to

- distinguish between the purposes of standardized tests and teacher-made tests
- appraise the various interpretations of intelligence and intelligence tests
- describe the uses of behavior rating scales and state criteria for interpreting them
- use basic statistical techniques to interpret test results
- evaluate standardized test scores
- apply the results of standardized testing to improve teaching and learning
- make informed decisions concerning current testing issues

A SCHOOL'S TESTING PROGRAM

Before beginning a specific analysis of standardized tests, let us again recall how significant the relationship is between learning objectives and testing. Schools are designed to change students' behavior. The ideal means of accomplishing this change largely determines the choice of administrative structure (e.g., self-contained classroom vs. team teaching), methods, materials, and curriculum. We can't make reliable decisions about these matters unless they are based upon an accurate **assessment** of student capacity. All of these issues—administration, assessment, counseling, teaching, and learning—involve educational objectives.

What do we need to know about a student, and how can we acquire this knowledge? Once we have the needed information, what does it mean? Little value is derived from a series of achievement tests unless the results can be used to improve the instruction offered students. Unless teachers and administrators understand exactly what a test score does and does not mean, tests are of little value, and may, in fact, be detrimental.

The use of group intelligence testing during World War I, the more sophisticated selection tests developed during World War II, and both state and federal legislation (such as P.L. 94–142; the *Individuals with Disabilities Act*) have combined to establish an important place for testing at all levels of education. When selecting and using instruments in a school testing program, remember that any program implies the systematic use at all levels, and in all disciplines, of several tests.

The selection, administration, and interpretation of standardized tests should be linked closely to the educational objectives of a particular school system. A given testing program usually involves *readiness tests* before school entrance, *subject-matter achievement tests* at all levels, occasional *cognitive tests* for students with special needs, and other tests, such as *interest inventories, personality questionnaires,* and *academic diagnostic tests,* as needed in individual cases (see table 16.1). Thus, a variety of tests are available to educators. In some cases, these tests are administered to individual students by specialists such as school psychologists or counselors.

The choice of an appropriate testing program depends upon the chooser's knowledge about the nature of standardized tests and how they aid in the attainment of educational objectives. Testing programs generally have three major purposes: instructional, guidance, and administrative.

assessment *The process of gathering information about a student's abilities and using such information to make decisions about the student.*

Table 16.1

School Testing Programs	
Level	**Type of test**
Preschool	Psychomotor and readiness
Primary	Basic skills
	Reading
Elementary	Achievement
	Basic skills
	Personality/behavior
Junior high	Aptitude
	Achievement
	Basic skills
	Personality/behavior
Senior high	Aptitude
	Achievement
	Basic skills
	Personality/behavior
	Vocational/interest
	College entrance

1. *Instructional.* Achievement tests administered in the fall help teachers to commence instruction at a point where students can logically expect both challenge and success. In other words, some achievement tests answer these questions: Where are my students right now? Where can I begin instruction?
2. *Guidance.* The results of some testing programs enable instructors to adapt the curriculum more efficiently to individual students, and to aid students in choosing specialized courses, thus serving a guidance function. These tests help to answer such questions as these: What do they need? Are special services needed, such as gifted/talented programs, remedial reading programs, or special education programs?
3. *Administrative.* Administrators are often interested in how groups of students are performing. Good tests can help them to make suitable decisions about curriculum and placement, based on substantial data comparing their students to others in the region or the nation.

Standardized tests often are directly administered to students in one-to-one situations. Some standardized rating scales are administered through interviews with adults who know the students well.

Remember that an achievement test is designed to indicate how much one can now accomplish as a result of training. An aptitude test reveals an individual's potential for learning (as in a general intelligence test), or an individual's specific abilities, in such areas as music and art. These two types are the basic ingredients of a school's testing program. The next question to be answered is this: What is meant by standardized tests?

Standardized Tests

standardized tests *Tests that are commercially constructed and administered under uniform conditions.*

Standardized tests are commercially prepared and sample behavior under uniform procedures. Procedures are uniform when the same fixed set of questions is administered to all students; the directions are the same for all; the time requirement is the same for all; and the scoring procedure is the same for all. Testing experts usually administer the test to a norm group (usually a large national sample) so that any one student's performance can be compared to those of others throughout the country. Standardized tests are usually classified according to what they measure. There are two general categories: aptitude and achievement tests.

aptitude tests *Tests that assess students' general or specific abilities.*

1. **Aptitude tests** are intended to assess students' general or specific abilities; for example, an intelligence test supposedly assesses a student's total ability. (The current controversy over what intelligence tests measure will be discussed later.) There are other, more specific, aptitude tests that measure mechanical, musical, artistic, and many other aptitudes.

achievement tests *Measures of accomplishment in such specific subjects as reading, arithmetic, etc. Developed by testing specialists; concern today is that these tests may not reflect what is actually taught in the classroom.*

2. **Achievement tests** measure accomplishment in such subjects as reading, arithmetic, language, and science. Gronlund (1985) noted that carefully constructed standardized achievement tests possess the following characteristics:

   - the test items are of high technical quality, developed by test specialists, pretested, and selected according to precise requirements;
   - directions for administering and scoring are rigidly controlled to ensure uniformity;
   - norms are provided to help interpret test scores;
   - equivalent forms of the test are typically available;
   - a variety of materials, including a test manual, are included to aid in administering, scoring, and interpreting scores.

You can see, then, that uniformity is a critical element in these tests, so that legitimate comparisons can be made. How does a fourth-grade student in Maine compare to a fourth-grade student in California? Standardization is the degree to which the observational procedures, administrative procedures, equipment and materials, and scoring rules have been fixed, so that exactly the same testing procedure occurs at different times and in different places.

Many standardized tests allow the teacher to compare a given student with a representative group (referred to as a norm group) of students. Such tests are called *norm-referenced tests*. A norm-referenced test (NRT) yields a score that can be compared with the scores of others who have taken the same test. When you grade an essay test, you might compare each student's answers to those of other students and decide that the student's answers, compared to the others, warrant a B. You have given a norm-referenced test at the classroom level. A score on a standardized achievement test informs you how a student compares to some national group that has taken the test.

There are several advantages of the norm-referenced test.

- It can assess a broad range of knowledge and understanding.
- It reflects common goals for learning.
- It can assess achievement at all levels of attainment—high, medium, or low.
- It can sample achievement more widely.
- It reflects the belief that achievement is "more or less," not "all or nothing."
- It furnishes a single score that summarizes a student's general level of achievement.
- It provides summative evaluation information.
- It identifies learning as the primary responsibility of the student.

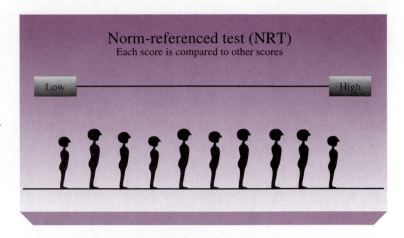

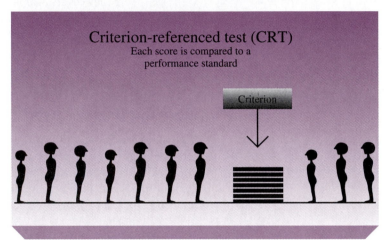

Madaus (1989) told of a student's bringing home a score of 38 on an English test. The parents were upset until they discovered that the highest score was 58, and that their child's score ranked tenth highest in a class of forty.

There are other tests that provide scores informing teachers of the extent to which students have achieved predetermined objectives. These are called *criterion-referenced tests* (CRTs). Criterion-referenced tests are increasingly popular because of renewed emphasis on individualized instruction, behavior objectives, and mastery learning. No question arises as to whether one student is better or worse than another; the focus is on reaching a particular standard of performance. Figure 16.1 illustrates the differences in the interpretations of a norm-referenced test and a criterion-referenced test.

Typically, skills within a subject are hierarchically arranged, so that the skills that are learned initially are tested first. In math, for example, addition skills are taught and evaluated before multiplication skills. These tests are usually criterion-referenced, because a student must achieve competence at one level before being taught at a higher level. Thus, criterion-referenced tests help teachers to determine if a student is ready to move on to the next level. The major characteristics of criterion-referenced and norm-referenced tests are presented in table 16.2.

Developing a Standardized Test

The term *standardization* implies consistency or sameness, the greatest contribution of the standardized test. If students' scores are to be compared, the test and the testing circumstances must remain uniform at any and all test administrations. The standardized test contains detailed directions that the tester must follow faithfully. If test administrators varied the testing conditions, they would introduce an unaccountable source of error, and comparison of these scores with others would become less meaningful.

Figure 16.1

Simplified illustration of the nature of norm-referenced and criterion-referenced test scores.

From F. L. Finch, Ed., Educational Performance Assessment. *Copyright © 1991. Reproduced with permission of The Riverside Publishing Company, Chicago, Illinois.*

Annual **Edition**

Identify at least one advantage that criterion-referenced tests have over norm-referenced tests.

Table 16.2

Comparison of Norm-Referenced Tests (NRTs) and Criterion-Referenced Tests (CRTs)

Common characteristics of NRTs and CRTs

1. Both require specification of the achievement domain to be measured.

2. Both require a relevant and representative sample of test items.

3. Both use the same types of test items.

4. Both use the same rules for item writing (except for item difficulty).

5. Both are judged by the same qualities of goodness (reliability and validity).

6. Both are useful in educational measurement.

Differences between NRTs and CRTs (but it is only a matter of emphasis)

1. NRT—Typically covers a *large* domain of learning tasks, with just a few items measuring each specific task.
   CRT—Typically focuses on a *delimited* domain of learning tasks, with a relatively large number of items measuring each specific task.

2. NRT—Emphasizes *discrimination* among individuals in terms of relative level of learning.
   CRT—Emphasizes *description* of what learning tasks individuals can and cannot perform.

3. NRT—Favors items of average difficulty and typically omits easy items.
   CRT—Matches item difficulty to learning tasks, without altering item difficulty or omitting easy items.

4. NRT—Used primarily (but not exclusively) for *survey* testing.
   CRT—Used primarily (but not exclusively) for *mastery* testing.

5. NRT—Interpretation requires a clearly defined group.
   CRT—Interpretation requires a clearly defined and delimited achievement domain.

Reprinted with permission of Simon & Schuster, Inc. from the Macmillan College text *Measurement and Evaluation in Teaching,* 7th ed. by Norman E. Gronlund and Robert L. Linn. Copyright © 1995 by Macmillan College Publishing Company.

All administrations of a given standardized test are identical in material, oral directions, time, or demonstrations. Testing conditions should be as comfortable as possible, with adequate seating, lighting, and ventilation. As much as possible, the tester should establish rapport with the subjects, to reduce the inevitable tension and anxiety that accompany any test.

The construction of the standardized test is an involved and complicated process. Unlike the teacher-made test, a standardized test is usually fashioned by a measurement expert, or team of experts, in a particular field. A team usually includes both subject-matter and testing specialists. Considerable care is taken to insure comprehensive coverage of a subject (content validity) and to avoid ambiguity in the writing of the individual items. The test initially is given experimental trials with representative groups to ascertain its suitability, reliability, and validity. As a result of these trials, revisions are made that should result in a highly accurate instrument. Authors of good tests may spend from four to five years developing and refining a test.

norms *Scores on a given test that are derived from an identified sample, and are then used as a basis for comparison (and therefore interpretation) of scores on the same test.*

Probably the most desirable feature of standardized tests is the **norms** supplied with them. Norms enable you to interpret the test scores of your class by comparing them with many other scores derived from a national sample. In the process of standardizing a test, researchers give it to large numbers of subjects who represent the population of students for whom it is ultimately intended. These norm groups should represent the total population with regard to age, sex, and socioeconomic status.

If a test is intended as a fifth-grade arithmetic achievement instrument, it is tried out with as many fifth-graders as possible who represent the age range of the typical fifth-grade population, and who also represent urban and rural populations, multicultural students, and the like. Norms, then, provide the normal range of scores for a

Table 16.3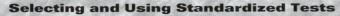

Selecting and Using Standardized Tests

1. At some point in your career you may be a member of a test selection committee. Here are some guidelines to consider when reviewing tests for possible use with your students.
    - Be sure the test is a fair assessment of those objectives that teacher-made tests cannot effectively measure.
    - Study the test literature, such as *The Mental Measurements Yearbook* (Mitchell, 1985), to determine the most promising tests.
    - Carefully analyze the specimen sets (inexpensive or free samples of test items) with which many publishers provide potential purchasers.
    - Select those tests that most closely approximate the school's goals.
    - Consider cost, time for administration, and ease of administration, scoring, and interpretation.
    - Remember that any test battery may only partially assess the objectives formulated for your classroom.
    - Remember that test material can become quickly outdated, especially in subjects such as science and social studies.
    - Examine format, content, the manual, and instructional suggestions carefully.
    - Combine test results with other means of student evaluation (teacher-made tests, observation, and aptitude assessment).

2. To achieve positive outcomes with a testing program, you must treat the test properly.
    - Take into consideration such general characteristics as student worry and anxiety, motivation, and rapport.
    - Do not use standardized achievement tests of students to evaluate teachers. Too many conditions elude control, and more direct methods for evaluating teachers are recommended.
    - Don't make the test the intentional objective of instruction. If teachers teach for the test, a desired breadth of learning may be lost.
    - Be careful in how you interpret test scores, particularly intelligence test scores. Again we see the value of norms; you are urged to look to these, and not to compare the scores of a given student on different IQ tests. If similar misuses are shunned, and if test scores are interpreted properly, they are useful tools in the guidance of learning.

given population. If a test consists of 100 items, and the typical 12-year-old correctly answers 60 of these items, the 12-year-old's average on this test is 60.

When selecting a standardized test, ask questions such as these: Why is testing necessary? What objective information is known about the test being examined? What technical information about the test is provided? Table 16.3 summarizes the main aspects of test selection and use.

TYPES OF STANDARDIZED TESTS

Standardized tests are classified according to what they measure. Teachers generally are concerned with two overall test categories: achievement and aptitude tests. As we have mentioned, an achievement test measures accomplishment in a subject such as reading, arithmetic, language, or science. Aptitude tests are designed to assess students' general and specific abilities. We will examine both types of test in some detail.

Standardized Achievement Tests

Achievement tests attempt to assess the knowledge and skills taught by the school. A standardized achievement test has certain distinctive features, including a fixed set of test items designed to measure a clearly defined achievement domain, specific directions for administering and scoring the test, and norms based on representative groups: groups containing individuals like those for whom the test was designed (Gronlund, 1985, p. 264). Thus, the same content and procedure permit the identical testing of individuals in different places at different times. Students tested in Madison, Wisconsin, can be compared on the same test to students in Hillsdale, Michigan, or San Francisco, California. Norms, then, enable us to compare an individual's score with those of members of known groups who also have taken the test.

Achievement tests have one main objective: to discover how much individuals have learned from educational experiences. They may be prepared for use throughout the entire system (for example, everyone studying American history would take the same examination, most likely at the end of the school year), or be prepared by specialists and standardized for national use. Some achievement tests (actually, batteries of tests) cover a number of subjects, like reading, mathematics, and social studies; and others cover specific subjects, such as French or American history.

When achievement tests fit the goals of learning and measure with acceptable accuracy, they have many desirable uses. Probably the most important of these is to assess the development of individual learners. Once you have determined students' potential and decided on the objectives of instruction, you should check your students' learning progress, usually with teacher-made tests and occasionally with standardized tests.

Standardized achievement tests aid both in the academic guidance of students and in planning curriculum changes. Standardized achievement tests also help in decisions about promotion and admission, since they yield additional evidence from objective sources.

The value of the standardized achievement test is that of all standardized tests: it samples an extensive range of subject matter, and it affords norms that enable school systems to evaluate themselves. If such tests are selected in accordance with learning objectives, they can be helpful tools for any school system, because they can stimulate creative thinking about the effectiveness of the curriculum, materials, and instruction.

multilevel survey batteries

Series of tests that assess separate curricular topics over a wide range of grades.

Two types of standardized achievement tests currently are popular: **multilevel survey batteries,** which assess separate curricular topics over a wide range of grades, and those designed to measure specific subjects, such as reading or mathematics (see Witt et al., 1994).

Among the most popular of the achievement test batteries are the Metropolitan Achievement Tests, which range in level from grade 1 to grade 12. These tests, available in alternate forms, measure achievement in reading, arithmetic, language, social studies, science, and study skills. The format is attractive, the test content is adequate, and the test items are carefully written. Another example of a multilevel survey battery is the California Achievement Tests, which also are applicable to children from kindergarten through grade 12. These tests measure reading, arithmetic, language, spelling, and reference skills. Reliabilities of total scores are good, and the difficulty of the items is appropriate for the level. Table 16.4 describes several other widely used and well-regarded batteries.

Other types of standardized achievement tests measure readiness, or achievement in specific subjects. Still others measure vocational achievement, or determine persons' qualifications for graduate training. The Metropolitan Readiness Tests are a good illustration of more specific measures. They measure children's abilities to acquire first-grade skills, including items that assess auditory memory, letter recognition, and visual matching, among other skills.

Tests of achievement in reading are a particularly popular type of specific standardized test. They typically are used to assess the efficiency of reading instruction in a system, to diagnose particular problems, and to identify underachievement in related subjects. The Iowa Silent Reading Tests have been widely adopted for both elementary and secondary usage. These assess subjects' rates of reading, comprehension, vocabulary, word and sentence meaning, and ability to locate information. At the advanced level, they also include tests on poetry comprehension and directed reading. These tests encompass the various skills needed in reading, and a weakness in any one of them could conceivably cause reading difficulties.

Table 16.4

Widely Used and Highly Regarded Group-Administered Comprehensive Achievement Batteries

Battery	Grades	Subject areas
Iowa Tests of Basic Skills	K.1–1.5	Listening, Vocabulary, Word Analysis, Language, Mathematics
(Forms G and H)	K.8–1.9	Listening, Vocabulary, Word Analysis, Reading, Language, Mathematics
(Hieronymus et al., 1986)	1.7–2.6	Vocabulary, Word Analysis, Reading Comprehension, Spelling, Mathematics Concepts, Mathematics Problems, Mathematics Computation, Listening, Capitalization, Punctuation, Usage and Expression, Visual Materials, Reference Materials, Social Studies, Science
Note: At older grade levels not all subject areas need to be administered to all children as subtests are divided into Basic, Complete, and Complete Plus Supplemental batteries of tests. Schools	2.5–3.5	Vocabulary, Word Analysis, Reading Comprehension, Spelling, Mathematics Concepts, Mathematics Problems, Mathematics Computation, Listening, Capitalization, Punctuation, Usage and Expression, Visual Materials, Reference Materials, Social Studies, Science
may choose whichever battery they believe best meets their need.	3–9	Vocabulary, Word Analysis, Reading Comprehension, Spelling, Mathematics Concepts, Mathematics Problems, Mathematics Computation, Listening, Capitalization, Punctuation, Usage and Expression, Visual Materials, Reference Materials, Supplemental Social Studies/Science Test
Metropolitan Achievement Tests	K.0–K.5	Reading, Mathematics, Language, Total
(Sixth Edition) (Prescott, Balow,	K.5–1.9	Reading, Mathematics, Language, Total
Hogan & Farr, 1987)	1.5–2.9	Reading, Mathematics, Language, Basic Total, Science, Social Studies, Complete Total
(Survey Battery)	2.5–3.9	Reading, Mathematics, Language, Basic Total, Science, Social Studies, Complete Total
Note: At older grade levels some subject areas (e.g., Reading) contain a number of	3.5–4.9	Reading, Mathematics, Language, Basic Total, Science, Social Studies, Complete Total, Research Skills
different subtests (e.g., at grades 3.5–4.9 Reading	5.0–6.9	Reading, Mathematics, Language, Basic Total, Science, Social Studies, Complete Total, Research Skills
consists of vocabulary, word recognition, reading	7.0–9.9	Reading, Mathematics, Language, Basic Total, Science, Social Studies, Complete Total, Research Skills
comprehension, and total reading).	10.0–12.9	Reading, Mathematics, Language, Basic Total, Science, Social Studies, Complete Total, Research Skills

From J. C. Witt, S. N. Elliott, J. J. Kramer, and F. M. Gresham (1994), *Assessment of Children: Fundamental Methods and Practices.* Dubuque, IA: Brown & Benchmark.

Standardized Aptitude Tests

Aptitude tests (for both individuals and groups) are used to predict what students can learn. Aptitude tests do not measure native capacity or learning potential directly; rather, they measure performance based on learning abilities (Gronlund, 1985, p. 295). It is interesting to note some differences between aptitude and achievement tests. An aptitude test predicts an individual's performance in a certain task or in a particular job by sampling the cumulative effect on the individual of many experiences in daily living, including definite educational experiences. Make no assumption, however, that aptitude tests measure only innate capacity, while achievement tests measure only the effects of learning. Any psychological test reflects the influence of past experiences upon present performance. Memory and transfer ensure that there is no escape from the past.

While research supports the relationship between intelligence and achievement (general measures of ability predict learning performance), specific abilities (an aptitude for mathematics, for example) vary within each individual. Personal experience testifies to specific strengths and weaknesses within one person. Some readers of this

"After 20 years of schooling, your aptitude test shows that you're skilled at just one thing—taking tests."

H. Schwadron in Phi Delta Kappan.

Battery	Grades	Subject areas
SRA Achievement Series (Forms 1 and 2) (Science Research Associates, 1987) *Note:* At all age levels some subject areas (e.g., Mathematics) contain a number of different subtests (e.g., at grades 6.5–8.5 Math consists of math computations, math concepts, math problem solving). The Verbal, Nonverbal, and Total tests are referred to as Educational Ability Scales.	K.5–1.5	Reading, Mathematics, Composite, Verbal, Nonverbal, Total
	1.5–2.5	Reading, Mathematics, Composite, Verbal, Nonverbal, Total
	2.5–3.5	Reading, Mathematics, Language Arts, Composite, Verbal, Nonverbal, Total
	3.5–4.5	Reading, Mathematics, Language Arts, Composite, Verbal, Nonverbal, Total
	4.5–6.5	Reading, Mathematics, Language Arts, Reference Materials, Social Studies, Science, Composite, Verbal, Nonverbal, Total
	6.5–8.5	Reading, Mathematics, Language Arts, Reference Materials, Social Studies, Science, Composite, Verbal, Nonverbal, Total
	8.5–10.5	Reading, Mathematics, Language Arts, Reference Materials, Social Studies, Science, Composite, Verbal, Nonverbal, Total
	9.0–12.9	Reading, Mathematics, Language Arts, Reference Materials, Social Studies, Science, Survey of Applied Skills, Composite, Verbal, Nonverbal, Total
Stanford Achievement Test (Eighth Edition) (The Psychological Corporation, 1990) *Note:* At all grade levels some subject areas (e.g., Language) contain a number of different subtests (e.g., at grades 3.5–4.5 Language consists of mechanics, expression, and total scores).	1.5–2.5	Reading, Mathematics, Language, Spelling, Listening, Environment, Basic Battery, Complete Battery
	2.5–3.5	Reading, Mathematics, Language, Spelling, Listening, Environment, Basic Battery, Complete Battery
	3.5–4.5	Reading, Mathematics, Language, Listening, Spelling, Study Skills, Science, Social Studies, Listening, Using Information, Thinking Skills, Basic Battery, Complete Battery
	4.5–5.5	Reading, Mathematics, Language, Listening, Spelling, Study Skills, Science, Social Studies, Listening, Using Information, Thinking Skills, Basic Battery, Complete Battery
	5.5–6.5	Reading, Mathematics, Language, Listening, Spelling, Study Skills, Science, Social Studies, Listening, Using Information, Thinking Skills, Basic Battery, Complete Battery
	6.5–7.5	Reading, Mathematics, Language, Listening, Spelling, Study Skills, Science, Social Studies, Listening, Using Information, Thinking Skills, Basic Battery, Complete Battery
	7.5–8.5	Reading, Mathematics, Language, Listening, Spelling, Study Skills, Science, Social Studies, Listening, Using Information, Thinking Skills, Basic Battery, Complete Battery
	8.5–9.9	Reading, Mathematics, Language, Listening, Spelling, Study Skills, Science, Social Studies, Listening, Using Information, Thinking Skills, Basic Battery, Complete Battery

chapter undoubtedly freeze at the sight of numbers, while others possess little, if any, artistic ability. It is the totality or pattern of performance on measures of general ability that is significant for understanding the achievement-intelligence relationship. Before discussing the various intelligence tests, we will examine the conditions that led to their use and general acceptance.

The Measurement of Intelligence

Any attempt to analyze an issue or problem should commence with a clear definition of terms. A satisfactory definition of intelligence or cognitive ability, however, has always been elusive. Another obstacle to understanding intelligence is that our experience is not with intelligence in the abstract but with intelligent behavior. Some individuals can solve problems rapidly; others master certain kinds of tasks easily; still others are remarkably well adjusted. Each of these examples represents a form of intelligence; together, they explain why there are so many different definitions of intelligence.

Focus   Testing Young Children

If you administer standardized achievement tests to young children, remember certain developmental considerations. In a thoughtful essay, Ludlow (1989) noted that youngsters from kindergarten to grade 2 (about 4½ to 7 years of age) interpret assessment tasks in a highly personal manner. (Recall that children of this age are struggling to overcome egocentrism—see chap. 4 and 5.) Developmental factors, then, may influence how such children interpret questions. The younger the child, the greater the measurement problem. Several questions must be considered when testing young children.

- Are these tests technically inadequate? No, the tests are constructed following the same safeguards as tests for older subjects, but they cannot control for an important source of variation: the manner in which a child's cognitive, social, and affective development may interact and influence test scores.

- Do young children possess the skills necessary to answer the range of questions presented? Not always. For some children, a picture as part of a question may elicit highly individual responses because of their experiences. Other youngsters may lack such test-taking skills as patience, task persistence, or reading ability. You should also be careful in interpreting test norms, since your system may vary significantly from national norms.

- Do youngsters interpret test instructions similarly? Obviously not, given several of the developmental characteristics just mentioned: lack of attention, reading difficulties, lack of ability to make the correct written response (especially important if the test is machine-scored).

Nevertheless, carefully selected, properly administered, judiciously interpreted standardized achievement tests for young children may yield needed data. More will be said about assessing preschoolers later in this chapter.

Definitions of Intelligence

Definitions of Intelligence L. M. Terman (1956) characterized intelligence as the ability to carry on abstract thinking. David Wechsler (1958) characterized it as the aggregate or global capacity of the individual to act purposefully, to think rationally, and to deal effectively with the environment. These statements represent the most widely held class of definitions, which describes intelligence as unitary. Other theoretical explanations define intelligence quite differently. Researchers view it not as an all-inclusive, global concept, but as a cluster of several factors or abilities. J. P. Guilford (1967), for example, stated that although some psychologists still view intelligence as a monolith, there is overwhelming evidence to indicate that many elements or factors are involved. Differences in abilities within one person, differing patterns of intellectual growth and decline, the instability of individual IQ scores over the years, and the different symptoms of brain damage all suggest that intelligence may be multifaceted. B. F. Skinner (1953) offered an even more radical analysis. He noted that we can designate almost any characteristic as a dimension of personality, but that this adds little to our knowledge until something beyond mere naming is achieved. We may easily coin the term "intelligence" or even neatly define it, but this alone does little to increase our practical understanding of the concept. Skinner stated that we must define intelligence by its behavior.

More recent attempts to analyze intelligence have likewise resulted in a movement away from accepting intelligence as a unitary concept. The concept of intelligence as a dynamic process involving individual competencies (musical, artistic, logical) was proposed by Kornhaber, Krechevsky, and Gardner (1990). These theorists also stressed the interactions between individuals and the societies in which they function, in a contextual interpretation. (Gardner's belief in multiple intelligences and Sternberg's triarchic interpretation of intelligence were discussed in detail in chap. 9.)

Urging that an all-purpose intelligence test should be a thing of the past, Hunt (1990) argued that three different views of intelligence are necessary to understand intellectual functioning: intelligence as general reasoning ability, intelligence as domain-specific skills, and intelligence as information processing. Clearly, there is no universally accepted definition of intelligence, although, as we have seen, current efforts (e.g., those of Sternberg and Gardner) stress the multiple qualities of intelligence and the role of context (Davidson, 1990).

Individuals have intelligence to the extent that they behave intelligently. This statement resembles the definition of intelligence that many psychologists believe to be the only one acceptable: Intelligence is that quantity that an intelligence test measures. But this is unsatisfactory as well. Before a test is constructed, decisions must be made about the nature of what is to be measured. In the instance of intelligence testing, what is to be measured obviously is "intelligence." Consequently, items are chosen that are best suited to measure the author's concept of intelligence.

Background of the Intelligence Testing Movement

Intelligence, that fascinating yet enigmatic "something" that promised to discriminate the able from the less able, defied definition, but perhaps could be quantified. With the advent of the twentieth century and the influx of immigrants to American shores, there appeared to be a need to devise some means of classifying individuals for education, for work, and ultimately for military service. This social context helps to explain the ready, almost eager, acceptance that the mental testing movement received. Here at last was a tool (so went the claim) that cut through the outer psychological barriers and laid bare the untarnished portrait of a person's innate capacity. The circumstances that led to the development and acceptance of the Binet and Wechsler tests provide helpful background for understanding the methods investigators adopted to assess native ability by individual intelligence tests.

The story of Alfred Binet and his search for the meaning and measurement of intelligence is a major chronicle in the history of psychology. Binet, who was born on July 8, 1857, and died in Paris on October 18, 1911, originally trained for law. Later, his interests changed, and he received a doctorate in science from the Sorbonne, where he remained as director of the psychological laboratory. Much of his early work on the intellectual and emotional lives of children was the result of studies of his daughters. He was cofounder, in 1895, of *L'Annee Psychologique*, the journal in which his early studies on intelligence were published.

In 1904, Binet was asked by the Parisian Minister of Public Instruction to formulate techniques for identifying the children most likely to fail in school. This challenging problem required finding some means of separating the normal from the truly retarded, of determining the lazy but bright who were simply poor achievers, and of eliminating the halo effect which occurs when an unwarranted high rating is assigned to youngsters because they are neat or attractive (Gould, 1981). To devise such an instrument, Binet had to begin with a preconceived notion of intelligence, since it is impossible to measure something without knowing what that something is. In a series of articles published in *L'Annee Psychologique*, Binet outlined his idea of the nature of intelligence. It consisted of three elements:

1. *Any mental process possesses direction*. It is directed toward achievement of a particular goal and toward the discovery of adequate means of attaining the goal. In the preparation of a term paper, for example, a student selects a suitable topic and the books and journals necessary to complete it.
2. *The ability to adapt by the use of tentative solutions*. Here the individual selects and utilizes some stimuli and tests their relevance while proceeding toward the goal. Before writing a term paper, the student may make a field trip to the area being discussed, or to save time, may decide to use library resources.
3. *The ability to make judgments and to criticize solutions*. Frequently called "autocriticism," this implies an objective evaluation of solutions. The student may complete the paper, reread it, decide that one topic included is irrelevant, and then exclude that topic.

The items in Binet's early test reflected these beliefs. When an item seemed to differentiate between normal and subnormal, he retained it; if no discrimination appeared, he rejected it. Binet defined normality as the ability to do the things that others of the same age usually do. Fortunately for the children of Paris, Binet was devoted to his task. The fruits of his and his coworkers' endeavors was the publication in 1905 of the Metrical Scale of Intelligence.

Since its publication, Binet's mental age scale has led the way in intelligence testing, and its success motivated a prominent American psychologist, Lewis Terman, to adapt it for American usage. Terman's revision, called the **Stanford-Binet Intelligence Test,** first appeared in 1916. It was revised in 1937, 1960, and 1972, and was both revised and renormed in 1986 by Hagan, Sattler, and Thorndike.

As a result of his studies, Binet arrived at certain conclusions about the nature of intelligence. One of these was that nearly all psychological data relates to intelligence. Another was that intelligence involves the fundamental faculty of judgment (sometimes called "common sense" or adaptation). To judge well, to comprehend well, and to reason well are the essential functions of intelligence.

Binet's orientation was practical; he did not become entangled in problems of definition. For Binet, children and adults simply had something that distinguished them from one another and that enabled them to perform well or poorly on any given task. Call it what you will, it existed and therefore could be measured. Here Binet's practical side again manifested itself. Age must be a key element, he reasoned, since older children generally do better than younger children on the same task. So the researcher must find tasks that are appropriate for a given age and determine if a youngster does about the same, better, or worse on these tasks than others of the same age.

But even if we can measure it on a scale, exactly what meaning are we to give intelligence? Since Binet considered almost all psychological data as intellectual phenomena, to him the fundamental faculty of judgment was critical. All other intellectual faculties were of little importance in comparison with judgment. What was of utmost significance to him in the measurement of intelligence was not whether the youngsters made mistakes, but the kinds of mistakes that they made; the absurd error resulting from a lack of judgment tells much about the student.

Dissatisfied with previous attempts to measure adult intelligence, David Wechsler, a clinical psychologist at New York's Bellevue Hospital, greatly influenced thought about the nature and measurement of intelligence. As part of his hospital work, Wechsler needed some reliable means for identifying the truly subnormal in his examination of criminals, neurotics, and psychotics. The Binet scales, effective through the early teens, did not accurately assess adult intelligence.

Sympathetic to Binet's views of intelligence, Wechsler likewise considered intelligence a general capacity. He defined intelligence as the aggregate or global capacity of the individual to act purposefully, to think rationally, and to deal effectively with the environment (Wechsler, 1958), in a definition that closely approximates Binet's reasoning.

Wechsler made a classic comparison of electricity and intelligence. We do not confuse the nature of electricity with our techniques for measuring it; exactly the same holds true for intelligence. General intelligence, like electricity, is a kind of energy. We do not fully understand its fundamental nature; we understand it by the things it does and enables us to do. According to Wechsler, intelligence produces associations, understandings, and problem-solving abilities in much the same way that electricity produces heat and magnetic fields. Consequently, we know intelligence by what it enables us to do.

As we have noted, once a definition of intelligence has been formulated, then a researcher can devise tests to meet those criteria. Wechsler first stated that intelligence is a global concept composed of interdependent elements. This led him to construct a test that best measured the various elements and that combined these measures to give a comprehensive view of intelligence.

After years of investigation, Wechsler reached the conclusion that intelligence tests measure a quantity that is far from simple. It cannot be expressed in a single figure (a general factor), since it includes more than just a single ability. Intelligence is the ability to use the previously mentioned energy in a context that has form, meaning, content, and purpose.

There are three forms of the Wechsler test, designed to measure the intelligence of human beings throughout the life span, beginning at the age of 4 years.

1. The Wechsler Adult Intelligence Scale–Revised, WAIS–III, is a revised form of Wechsler's first test, published in 1939, 1955, and 1980. It consists of eleven subtests, six comprising the verbal scale and five forming the performance scale.

Stanford-Binet Intelligence Test
Binet's famous measure of human intelligence, revised for American use originally by Terman, and most recently by Thorndike and colleagues. Presently called the Stanford-Binet Intelligence Scale.

Consequently, there are three possible intelligence scores: *verbal, performance,* and *total IQ*. Many clinicians have found the separation into verbal and performance assessments to be particularly valuable for diagnostic purposes.

2. The Wechsler Intelligence Scale for Children–III, WISC–III, first appeared in 1949, was renormed in 1974, and was renormed again in 1991. It attempts to assess the intelligence of children from 5 to 15 years old.

3. The Wechsler Preschool and Primary Scale of Intelligence, WPPSI–R, is designed to measure the intelligence of children from 4 to 6½ years of age.

Particularly significant in Wechsler's speculation (1958) was his firm belief that the definition of general intelligence, far from being merely interesting theorizing, is at the heart of the measurement of intelligence. Although Wechsler was a firm adherent of intelligence as a general capacity (as his definition shows), he stated that there are other important aspects of intelligence, such as *motivation* and *persistence at a task*. For example, individuals achieving precisely the same score on the same intelligence test defy identical classification. One youngster with a Binet IQ of 75 may require institutional care, while another child with the same IQ may function adequately in the home. Clearly, other elements, such as behavior adaptation and persistence, are significant in assessing intelligence.

The Wechsler and Binet scales were the forerunners of a movement that caught, and held, the attention of psychologists and educators for decades. Only gradually, as the claims of these test-makers were weighed against growing insights into learning and development and concerns about racial bias, did doubts arise about their efficacy.

Problems in Measuring Intelligence   Measurement difficulties have plagued the testing movement from its inception. Intrigued by numbers, investigators have long felt that if it is possible to quantify a given concept, then the results must be precise and beyond challenge. The application of such a rationale to the measurement of intelligence—a concept that has staunchly resisted definition for over a century—has produced some insights, some moments of comic relief, and also much damage.

In a biting criticism, Gould (1981) noted that mental tests evolved from hereditarian belief that head size was an excellent indication of intelligence. In the latter part of the nineteenth century, brain size also was thought to be directly related to intelligence; Paul Broca's work was an outstanding example of efforts to measure cranial capacity. If it was at all possible, Broca removed subjects' brains after autopsy and weighed them.

In interpreting his results, Broca carefully allowed for an increase in brain size with body size and a decrease with age and disease. Broca's data have rarely been questioned; his assumptions, however, are another story. White males, especially French white males, were assumed to be intellectually superior, with brain sizes greater than any others. Embarrassing results almost immediately posed a challenge to these assumptions: many eminent men were found to have quite small brains (Broca's brain later was discovered to be only slightly larger than normal; it is interesting to speculate how he would have explained this finding.) Another embarrassment was that many criminals were found to have large brains.

Perhaps the most intriguing of Broca's methods was the excavation of cemeteries to exhume bodies buried during different centuries. Broca hypothesized that brain size should increase as civilization progressed. His arduous efforts produced yet another embarrassment. Obtaining twelfth-, eighteenth-, and nineteenth-century samples from Parisian cemeteries, Broca was initially chagrined to find the cranial capacities of the twelfth-century sample to be larger than those from the eighteenth century. There was actually little difference among the three samples. Undaunted, Broca explained away this finding by that convenient variable: socioeconomic status. The twelfth-century sample was from a churchyard; therefore, its occupants must have been high on the social ladder. The eighteenth-century sample was from a common grave; consequently, the cranial capacity of its occupants was smaller. So much for science.

Binet's Lost Legacy Originally, Binet followed Broca's methods, believing that skull measurement was the surest way to assess intelligence. But Binet was a scholar, not intent on forcing data to match assumptions, and he quickly dismissed Broca's techniques, turning to the scales just described.

If the followers of Binet had remained faithful to his rationale, considerable anguish would have been avoided. Binet never defined intelligence: he felt intelligence was too complex to be defined by a single number, and flatly refused to label individuals. Binet's intent was clear: to provide a means of identifying those Parisian students who needed help.

It was during the early decades of the twentieth century that Binet's objectives were subverted, so that IQ scores were seen as unchanging figures that precisely portrayed innate abilities. Individuals were labelled, and the IQ label was fixed forever. Heredity had become destiny. As concern grew about America's swelling immigration population and their supposed mental deficiencies (unfortunately, language differences were rarely considered), Henry Goddard visited Ellis Island in 1912 armed with translations of Binet's scale. As immigrants came ashore, Goddard and his colleagues visually inspected them, instantly identified those who might be defective, and tested these people on the spot. Needless to say, few, if any, of the subjects did well; the vast majority were judged "feeble-minded." The disregard for language and cultural differences was not an issue then, but is a serious concern today. Tests must be nonbiased and used by well-trained professionals.

Similar results were obtained when group intelligence tests, based on the Binet scales, were given during World War I. The average mental age of white American males barely surpassed moronic: 13 years. The results puzzled the test designers, but rather than admit that test results were powerfully influenced by education and environment, they confessed uncertainty as to their true meaning.

In the never-ending dispute over the importance of heredity versus environment (often referred to as the "nature vs. nurture" controversy), the test-makers clearly sided with the hereditarians. Those now attempting to link intelligence to learning must realize this. If an individual does poorly on a mental test, what does this suggest for learning ability? Today, the answer to such a question would address the contributions of both heredity and environment to mental test performance. Thus, a low score on an aptitude test may not be a precise indication of poor education, or of poor motivation, or of difficulty with specific topics (math, reading). Most likely, it is the result of a combination of these and other causes.

Stability of the IQ One of the most pervasive ideas about intelligence, one that has become entrenched in the minds of many, is that infants are born with a certain amount of "intelligence," which does not change as the child grows. Misinterpretations of research on the stability of performances on intelligence tests has fed this misconception. In general, most research has suggested that IQ tests tend to yield scores that are fairly stable (Elliott, Piersel, Witt, Argulewicz, Gutkin & Galvin, 1985). However, this same research indicates that IQs are more stable over shorter periods than over longer ones, and more stable for older children and adults than for children under 6 years of age. There is a good deal of evidence to indicate that IQ scores obtained before children enter kindergarten or first grade are not highly reliable.

Based on these readings, what is your definition of intelligence?

Data on the relative stability of IQ can be deceiving and must be interpreted with care. When considering the IQ scores of large groups of individuals, a researcher could expect that most of those within the group would receive similar scores if retested. It is not unusual, however, for particular individuals to show a great deal of variability in their scores. Changes of 8, 10, 15, or even 30 IQ points are not unheard of.

Bias in Cognitive Abilities Testing No issue related to the assessment of cognitive abilities has generated so much heated debate as the question of whether IQ tests are biased against individuals from minority cultures. There is no universally accepted definition of bias; however, according to Brown and Campione

(1986), most definitions hold that a test can be considered biased if it differentiates between members of various groups on bases other than the characteristic being measured (p. 224). Discussions in the popular press have vehemently assailed most aptitude and achievement tests as being unfair to children from backgrounds different from those of most middle-class white Americans. Numerous researchers have investigated the issue of bias in mental tests, with the greatest attention focused on the differences between the performances of blacks and those of whites (e.g., Jensen, 1981). Some have turned to the courts for help in determining whether IQ tests are biased and whether they should be used in the assessment of minority children. Courts, however, have not been consistent in their findings (*Larry P. v. Riles,* 1979/1986; *PASE v. Hannon,* 1980).

The technical evidence overwhelmingly indicates that the vast majority of items used on tests like the WISC-R and Binet are not biased; these tests tend to measure the same factors (verbal, perceptual, performance, etc.), and to predict success equally well for all racial groups (Reynolds & Kaiser, 1990). This last point is critical, for it is important to remember that IQ tests do *not* measure the quantity of some innate, immutable ability that we all possess, but *provide a general measure of expected school achievement,* just as they were designed to do in the early 1900s. The predictive validity evidence suggests that race does not really matter. An individual with an IQ score of 60 from a reliable test is at risk of failing in almost every public educational system, and an individual with a score of 140 is likely to do well in that same system. It is worth repeating that these tests do not measure innate ability, but attempt to predict school achievement.

Behavior Rating Scales

Up to this point in our examination of testing and assessment, we have focused on the evaluation of children's academic and cognitive skills. As you know, however, children's social skills and emotional characteristics also influence their schooling. Teachers and parents, given their many opportunities to observe and interact with children, have often played a significant role in the assessment of children's inter- and intrapersonal skills. Behavior rating scales have become one of the most popular and efficient assessment methods for gathering input from teachers and parents about a child's social-emotional functioning. Rating scales such as the Child Behavior Checklist (Achenbach & Edelbrock, 1986) and the Social Skills Rating System (Gresham & Elliott, 1990) are used in many schools with students from kindergarten through twelfth grade. Both these instruments are well developed, focus on a wide range of behaviors, and provide normative information about the social-emotional functioning of students. Many other rating scales that are used in schools focus on specific areas of functioning (e.g., adaptive behavior, self-concept, motivation) or problems (e.g., depression, anxiety, fears, hyperactivity) (Witt, Elliott, Kramer & Gresham, 1994).

A typical behavior rating scale includes a list of items that clearly describe particular behaviors (e.g., Shares materials with friends willingly; Follows directions; Teases other children) and asks a respondent to indicate how frequently (e.g., 0 = Never; 1 = Sometimes; 2 = Very Often; 3 = Always) the child exhibits the behaviors. Table 16.5 illustrates two items from a social skills rating scale. In addition to requesting information about the frequency of the described behavior, this rating scale asks the teacher-respondent also to provide information about "how important" the behaviors are to functioning in that person's classroom. Most rating scales like the one illustrated provide norms, so the results for a child can be compared to those of a sample of students of a similar age and the same sex. Well-constructed rating scales have the potential to facilitate communication among individuals interested in the assessment of particular children and to provide useful diagnostic information. Although rating scales appear straightforward, a closer look is required, to ensure that their strengths and weaknesses are understood.

Behavior rating scales have proliferated during the past ten years. This growth in objective rating scales seems to have been fueled by a variety of service delivery and

Table 16.5

	How often?			**How important?**		
Example of Items and Rating Format on a Behavioral Rating Scale						
	Never	*Sometimes*	*Very often*	*Not important*	*Important*	*Critical*
Shows empathy for peers.	0	1	②	0	①	2
Asks questions of you when unsure of what to do in schoolwork.	0	①	2	0	1	②

This student *very often* shows empathy for classmates. Also, this student *sometimes* asks questions when unsure of schoolwork. This teacher thinks that showing empathy is *important* for success in his or her classroom and that asking questions is *critical* for success.

From Graham and Elliott, *Social Studies Rating System*. Copyright © 1990 American Guidance Service, Circle Pines, Minnesota.

technological factors. Major factors affecting the increased use of rating scales include their rather brief time demands, their user-friendly administration and scoring, the need for more regular educator and parent involvement in assessment and intervention activities, and generally improved reliability and validity information (Edelbrock, 1983; Wilson & Bullock, 1989).

Uses of Rating Scales

Traditionally, rating scales have been used primarily as part of the screening and identification process for children referred for possible special education services. Secondarily, rating scales have been used, albeit often inappropriately, to monitor behavior changes as a result of an intervention. Rating scales also have played a central role in taxonomic efforts concerning childhood social-emotional disorders (e.g., Achenbach & Edelbrock, 1983; Elliott & Gresham, 1989) and the validity of teachers' judgments of students' achievement (e.g., Hoge & Coladarci, 1989). In addition to these well-established uses of behavior rating scales, they can have other uses, depending on the qualities of a scale and one's approach to service delivery. Practitioners who emphasize a prereferral intervention and/or consultation approach to service delivery should find rating scales to be a primary assessment tool (Witt, Elliott, Kramer & Gresham, 1994). For example, a rating scale can be used to facilitate a prompt reaction to a referral from a teacher or parent. This practice of having a rating scale completed and interpreted before a meeting with a teacher (or a parent) often has several positive side effects. These include more precise, behavior-specific communications and more time-efficient interviews that focus more on problem analysis than on problem identification. When the rating scale used has sound, representative norms, it also facilitates understanding of the social validity of the referral problem. A final use is for purposes of documentation and accountability regarding regular teacher and parent involvement in the identification of a child's problem. In some cases, the child also is able to play an active role in the problem identification process through self-ratings.

Rating scales, of course, have some limitations or disadvantages, of which all users should be cognizant. McConaughy's list of disadvantages (1993) represents a good summary that deserves some comment and elaboration. She accurately noted that rating scales are measures of current or recent functioning, but do not provide information on causes of problems. She also noted that scores on existing problem-focused rating scales do not dictate choices for intervention. Although this latter disadvantage generally is characteristic of rating scales, there are some published rating scales (e.g., the Social Skills Rating System) that have direct conceptual and practical links to interventions. A third disadvantage that McConaughy indicated as characteristic of rating scales is that they involve perceptions of problems rather than truly "objective" measures of such problems. The practical ramification of this distinction is that one must confirm any rating scale results with an additional form of assessment, such as direct observation and/or clinical interviews. Multiple assessment methods and sources, however, are always recommended best practices in addressing social-emotional difficulties.

In summary, rating scales have many potential positive uses in the delivery of psychoeducational services in schools. These uses involve primarily the enhancement of problem-identification activities involving teachers and parents. Rating scales also often contribute positively to a scientific understanding of the co-occurrence of childhood problem behaviors. The use of any rating scale is influenced by its particular characteristics and by some basic interpretive issues. Hence, we explore these next.

Characteristics and Interpretation Guidelines

Most rating scales have a misleading appearance of simplicity due to the ease with which they can be administered and scored. But in terms of reliability and validity characteristics and of interpretation, rating scales are decidedly complex instruments. For example, the standards concerning reliability and validity that are used for cognitive abilities tests should apply equally to rating scales. In fact, issues of reliability, especially inter-rater reliability, are even more complex for rating scales than for cognitive abilities tests. With regard to validity, developers of rating scales are subject to great demands to establish the social validity of their items. **Social validity** is achieved when the items on a scale adequately sample the intended domain of behavior, and are deemed important to social functioning by individuals who regulate significant portions of a child's life.

social validity *The applied, or social, importance of exhibiting certain behaviors in particular situations.*

To conclude this section on behavior rating scales, we focus on five issues influencing use and interpretation of behavior rating scales.

1. *Ratings are summaries of observations of the relative frequency of specific behaviors.* In reality, for example, one student may exhibit turn-taking behavior three times a day, whereas a second student may exhibit the same turn-taking behavior one time a day. These students exhibit different rates of turn-taking behavior, yet their teacher, when asked to complete a 3-point rating scale (0 = Never; 1 = Sometimes; 2 = Very Often), is likely to characterize both students with a rating of 1. The teacher would characterize the turn-taking behavior of a third student, who is observed to exhibit such behavior on the average of six times a day, as occurring "very often," as evidenced by a frequency rating of 2. As illustrated, the precision of measurement with rating scales is relative, not exact, and needs to be supplemented by more direct methods if specific frequency counts of a given behavior are necessary.

2. *Ratings of social behavior are evaluative judgments affected by the subject's environment and the rater's standards for behavior.* Researchers and lay persons alike are aware that an individual's social behaviors may change depending on the situation in which the person is functioning. Such variability in behavior highlights the role one's environment (i.e., people and places) plays in determining behavior. This has led researchers to characterize many social behaviors as situationally specific behaviors rather than traits (Achenbach, McConaughy & Howell, 1987; Kazdin, 1979). In addition to environmental influences, the standards of behavior established by the adults who regulate the settings largely determine the social behaviors deemed more important in one setting than in another. Given that different situations and raters' standards of behavior potentially influence ratings of social skills, the use of multiple raters (e.g., teachers, parents, even the student) to observe a student's behavior across many situations and settings is desirable.

3. *The social validity of the behaviors one assesses and eventually treats should be understood.* Behaviors that are socially valid are those that society reinforces. The social validity of a behavior is reflected in the importance attributed to it by significant members of society (i.e., teachers, parents, peers). Direct assessment of the social validity of specific prosocial behaviors by means of importance

ratings can be done concurrently with assessment of their frequency. This provides a sense of item content validity, as well as allowing for a documentation of the most salient behaviors to treat, should they be deficient. When focusing on problem behaviors, one becomes interested in the tolerance the rater has for the behavior, as opposed to the importance of the behavior.

4. *Multiple assessors of the same child's social behavior may agree only moderately.* This guideline is based on the facts that many social behaviors are situationally specific, that all measures of behavior have error in them, and that rating scales use rather simple frequency scales for quantifying behaviors that actually may vary widely in frequency, intensity, and duration. The work of Achenbach and his associates (1987) and McConaughy (1993) provides empirical support for this position of moderate agreement among raters of the same behaviors. This degree of agreement should not be taken as an indictment of the use of multiple raters. In fact, it suggests that different raters perceive behaviors in varying settings differently. Collectively, such ratings can tell us more about a child than can only one rater from a single setting.

5. *Many characteristics of a student may influence the child's social behavior; however, the student's sex is a particularly salient variable.* Researchers interested in children's social competence and social-emotional functioning have identified variables such as physical attractiveness, athletic abilities, language skills, family background, and gender as variables that can influence the judgments of others when evaluating social behaviors (Halle, 1985; Hops & Finch, 1985). Of all these characteristics, a student's gender is the one that consistently appears to be associated with differences in social behavior. This fact has been supported by the standardization samples of several major social behavior rating scales, and has resulted in separate male and female norms for these instruments. Consequently, interpretation of most child social behavior rating scales should be done with norms that demonstrate sensitivity to gender differences.

Preschool Screening

Throughout this chapter, we have noted that the primary purpose of assessment is to determine if a problem exists and how it should be resolved. In other words, assessment stimulates and guides actions. Given that substantial numbers of young children are struggling and even failing in school, **preschool assessment** tools are needed to identify these children early and to establish intervention methods to improve their lives at school.

preschool assessment *A method of identifying children who need help before they enter formal schooling.*

Many different sets of developmental categories or skills, such as perceptual processing, cognitive, language, speech/articulation, gross motor, fine motor, self-help, social-emotional, and school readiness, are important targets of assessment (Lichtenstein & Ireton, 1984). Researchers have developed a variety of standardized tests, both multidimensional and unidimensional in nature, that can be used to assess the skills and abilities of preschoolers. Though space does not allow us to describe such tests in detail, we have reprinted two useful tables from Witt et al. (1994) that document over fifty tests that have been designed to provide meaningful information about the functioning of young children at school and home (see tables 16.6 and 16.7).

In theory, preschool screening should aim to recognize early problem warning signs and to make a comprehensive assessment for identification and treatment. The utility of preschool screening, however, is influenced by several factors, including the provision of follow-up services, timing of screening, and involvement of parents. Before concluding this section, let us examine each of these factors briefly.

Provision of Follow-Up Services

Implementation of a screening program without the provision of follow-up assessment and treatment services is an irresponsible policy and poor educational practice. We believe the development of preschool screening procedures should be

Table 16.6

Multidimensional Preschool Screening Instruments

Name of instrument	Age range	Administration time	T = Test	P = Parent record	E = Professional examiner	Cognitive	Language	Speech	Fine motor	Gross motor	Self-help	Social-emotional	Reliability data	Validity data	Normative data
ABC Inventory	3–6 to 6–6	10 min.	T			x			x				–	+	+
BRIGANCE® Diagnostic Inventory of Basic Skills	4–5 to 12–0	15 min.	T		E	x	x	x	x	x			–	–	–
BRIGANCE® Diagnostic Inventory of Early Development	0–1 to 6–0	15–30 min.	T	P	E	x	x	x	x	x	x		–	–	–
Comprehensive Identification Process	2–6 to 5–6	30 min.	T	P		x	x	x	x	x		x	–	–	–
Cooperative Preschool Inventory, Revised Edition	3–0 to 6–0	15–20 min.	T			x	x		x				+	+	+
Daberon: A Screening Device for School Readiness	4–0 to 6–0	20–40 min.	T			x	x		x	x			+	+	+
Dallas Preschool Screening Test	3–0 to 6–0	15 min.	T			x	x	x	x	x			+	+	+
Denver Developmental Screening Test	0–1 to 6–0	15–20 min.	T	P		x	x		x	x	x		+	+	+
Denver Prescreening Developmental Questionnaire	0–3 to 6–0	5 min.		P		x	x		x	x	x		–	+	+
Developmental Indicators for the Assessment of Learning (DIAL-R)	2–0 to 5–1	25–30 min.		P	E	x	x	x	x	x		x	+	+	+
Developmental Profile II (Developmental Profile)	0–0 to 9–0	30–40 min.		P		x	x		x	x	x	x	+	+	+
Developmental Tasks for Kindergarten Readiness	4–6 to 6–2	20–30 min.	T			x	x		x			x	+	+	+
Early Detection Inventory	3–6 to 7–6	15–30 min.	T	P		x	x	x	x	x		x	–	+	+
Early Screening Inventory (Eliot-Pearson Screening Inventory)	4–0 to 6–0	15 min.	T			x	x	x	x	x			+	+	+
Hannah-Gardner Test of Verbal and Nonverbal Language Functioning	3–6 to 5–6	25–35 min.	T			x	x	x					+	+	+
Kaufman Infant and Preschool Scale	0–1 to 4–0	25–30 min.	T	P		x	x						–	–	+
Kindergarten Questionnaire	4–0 to 6–0	20–30 min.	T	P		x	x		x	x		x		+	–
Lexington Developmental Scale, Short Form	0–3 to 6–0	30–45 min.	T			x	x		x	x		x	+	+	–
Lollipop Test: A Diagnostic Screening Test of School Readiness	4–0 to 6–0	15–20 min.	T		E	x	x		x				+	+	+
McCarthy Screening Test	4–0 to 6–5	20 min.	T			x	x		x	x			+	+	+
Minneapolis Preschool Screening Instrument	3–7 to 5–1	10–15 min.	T			x	x	x	x	x			+	+	+
Minnesota Preschool Inventory	4–8 to 5–7	15 min.		P		x	x	x	x	x	x	x	–	+	+
Preschool Attainment Record, Research Edition	0–6 to 7–0	20–30 min.		P	E	x	x	x	x	x	x	x	–	–	–
Preschool Screening Instrument	4–0 to 5–0	5–10 min.	T	P		x	x	x	x	x		x	+	+	–
Preschool Screening System (PSS Field Trial Edition)	2–6 to 5–9	15–20 min.	T	P		x	x	x	x	x		x	+	+	+
Riley Preschool Developmental Screening Inventory	3–0 to 6–0	5–10 min.	T			x			x				–	–	+
School Readiness Checklist—Ready or Not?	4–0 to 7–0	10–15 min.		P		x	x		x	x	x	x	–	+	+
School Readiness Survey	4–0 to 6–0	25–35 min.	T	P		x	x						+	+	+
Slosson Intelligence Test	0–1 to adult	10–20 min.	T			x	x						–	+	+

From Robert Lichtenstein and Harry Ireton, *Preschool Screening*. Copyright © 1984 Allyn & Bacon, Inc. Reprinted by permission.

Table 16.7

Selected Unidimensional Preschool Screening Measures

Name of instrument	Age range	Administration time	T = Test	P = Parent report	E = Professional examiner	Reliability data	Validity data	Normative data
Language and vocabulary measures								
Assessment of Children's Language Comprehension[a]	3–0 to 6–6	10–20 min.	T		E	–	–	+
Bankson Language Screening Test[c]	4–1 to 8–0	25 min.	T			+	+	+
Del Rio Language Screening Test[c]	3–0 to 6–11		T			–	+	+
Peabody Picture Vocabulary Test–Revised[a]	2–6 to adult	10–20 min.	T		E	+	+	+
Pictorial Test of Bilingualism and Language Development[b]	4–0 to 8–0	15 min.	T			+	+	–
Preschool Language Assessment Instrument[c]	3–0 to 6–0	20 min.	T			+	–	+
Screening Test for Auditory Comprehension of Language[a]	3–0 to 6–0	5–10 min.	T		E	+	–	+
Test of Early Language Development[c]	3–0 to 7–11	15–20 min.	T			+	+	+
Verbal Language Development Scale[c]	0–1 to 16–0	20 min.		P	E	+	+	–
Social-emotional measures								
Burks' Behavior Rating Scales: Preschool and Kindergarten	3–0 to 6–11	10 min.		P	E	+	–	–
Child Behavior Rating Scale	4–0 to 9–0	10 min.		P		+	+	+
Children's Self-Social Construct Tests: Preschool Form	3–6 to 10–0	10–15 min.	T			–	–	–
Joseph Preschool and Primary Self Concept Screening Test	3–6 to 9–11	5–7 min.	T			+	+	+
Speech/articulation measures								
Denver Articulation Screening Test	2–6 to 7–0	5 min.	T			+	+	+
Photo Articulation	3–0 to 12–0	5 min.	T		E	+	+	+
Perceptual-motor measures								
Developmental Test of Visual-Motor Integration	2–0 to 15–0	5–10 min.	T			+	+	+
Riley Motor Problems Inventory	4–0 to 9–0	10 min.	T		E	+	+	–
Tree/Bee Test of Auditory Discrimination	3–0 to adult	10–15 min.	T			+	+	+
Observational instruments for classroom use								
Basic School Skills Inventory-Screen	4–0 to 6–11	5–10 min.				+	+	+
Preschool Behavior Rating Scale	3–0 to 5–11	5–10 min.				+	+	+
Classroom Behavior Inventory, Preschool Form	2–0 to 6–0	10–15 min.				–	+	–

From Robert Lichtenstein and Harry Ireton, *Preschool Screening*. Copyright © 1984 Allyn & Bacon, Inc. Reprinted by permission.

[a]Measures receptive language only.

[b]Measures expressive language only.

[c]Measures both expressive and receptive language.

concurrently coordinated with a comprehensive assessment and treatment program. In fact, the instructional objectives of a treatment program provide the primary basis for determining the content validity of assessment procedures.

Timing of Screening

The issue of timing of screening has two components: (a) the age of the child, and (b) the time of year when screening is done. A guiding principle in all assessment activities is that the more recent an assessment is, the more accurately it predicts behavior. This is particularly true with preschoolers, because within a few months, a child may demonstrate quantitative and qualitative advances in development across several domains. A corollary principle of preschool assessment is that identification must be made soon enough to permit early intervention, especially for sensory problems and with "disadvantaged" children. Thus, the critical question is this: At what age can reliable and valid measures of skills and abilities that are relevant to successful performance in school first be obtained?

Generally, research indicates that by the age of 4 or 5, a child's developmental gains in language, fine motor, and cognitive skills begin to stabilize and correlate significantly with school-age measures of achievement. Earlier assessments, except those of children with severe handicaps, generally do not have substantial predictive validity. Thus, there exists a dilemma: the educator wants to intervene as early as possible, but is limited by the reliability and validity of the assessment tools that exist for preschoolers.

What role can standardized tests play in the education of preschool children?

Several schedules for preschool screening programs exist, including testing children (a) once, in the spring or fall prior to school entry; (b) more than once during the years preceding school or kindergarten; or (c) once, immediately before or during the first few weeks of kindergarten. Each of these schedules for testing has some advantages. In general, however, periodic, repeated assessments offer greater reliability and more information than a one-time approach.

Involvement of Parents

Although parental involvement is the last topic discussed here, it is by no means the least important. Parents play a critical role in the assessment and treatment of young, at-risk, or handicapped children. Also, as a result of recent amendments to the Public Law 94–142 (such as P.L. 99–457), not only is working with parents considered good educational practice, it is the law.

Entire books have been written to describe standardized tests. Obviously, we have provided you with only a sample of tests in our discussion of achievement, intelligence, and preschool tests. With this as background information, we turn now to the important topic of test interpretation.

INTERPRETING STANDARDIZED TEST SCORES

Let us assume that your students recently have taken a standardized achievement test, and a copy of the results is sent to you. You will receive several kinds of scores: raw scores, percentiles, grade equivalents, and standard scores. Since these scores are probably unfamiliar to most readers, this section will examine the meaning of the various scores and the uses to which they can be put.

If these results are to provide the best information possible, then you must have some means of telling whether a score is good or poor. You usually cannot do this by looking at the raw score (the number of correct items on each of the subtests), although this gives some information, as we will see. Raw scores are converted into derived scores, which are more meaningful and tell you more about a student's performance.

Kinds of Scores

raw score *Uninterpreted data; often, the number of correct items.*

A **raw score** may be difficult to interpret. If an arithmetic test contains 50 items and a student scores 32, that student's raw score is 32. What does this tell you? You probably think immediately that at least this student knew more than half the answers. But how did the other students do? You don't know. Was it an easy or difficult test? You don't know—unless you can compare scores. To help you make sense of the raw scores of all your students, you could rank them from highest to lowest. This ranking would enable you to interpret a score in relation to other scores.

Assume that the score of 32 is the average raw score for the group taking this test. These are fifth-grade students. The month is September. Thus, 32 is the *grade equivalent* score of 5.0 for that test. It is a mistake to assume that a student who has a grade equivalent score of 7.2 on this test should be working at a seventh-grade level. The score means that this student's performance on fifth-grade material is equal to the performance of a student in the second month of the seventh grade on fifth-grade material (Bloom, Madaus & Hastings, 1981). It tells you that your fifth-grade student knows this subject thoroughly. It does not say that this same student has mastered seventh-grade or even sixth-grade material. These scores seem easy to interpret, but they are just as easily (and often) misinterpreted. Of greater interpretative value are derived standard scores, which we will examine shortly.

You probably are comfortable with a scoring system that assigns the highest score a rank of 1, the second-highest a rank of 2, and the like. Percentiles work in a way similar to this, except that the lowest percentile rank appears at the bottom of the scores. For example, a **percentile score** of 74 means that this student has done as well as or better than 74 percent of all the other students taking the test. If the student's raw score mentioned earlier—32—placed that student 40th from the bottom in a class of 50, the percentile rank would be computed thus:

$$40/50 \times 100 = 80$$

This student would be at the 80th percentile, having done as well as or better than 80 percent of the students. Be careful how you use this score with parents who may interpret it as a grade of 80 percent.

> **percentile score** *A score that tells the percentage of individuals taking a test who are at or below a particular score; a percentile rank of 74 means that this student did as well or better than 74 percent of those taking the test.*

Working with many numbers is cumbersome, time-consuming, and prone to misinterpretation. Consequently, we should search for techniques to organize our data. A good way to begin is with a **frequency distribution.** You often want to organize and summarize data. The first step usually entails constructing a frequency distribution, which indicates the frequency with which a particular score appears in a score category. In the preparation of a frequency distribution, the scores typically are grouped by intervals, and each test score is assigned to the proper interval. Table 16.8 illustrates this procedure; here, the scores range from a low of 10 to a high of 21, and the number of individuals achieving each score is provided in the frequency column.

> **frequency distribution** *A record of how often a score appears in a score category.*

Table 16.8

A Typical Frequency Distribution

Scores	Frequency
21	2
20	1
19	6
18	10
17	20
16	19
15	16
14	22
13	5
12	27
11	36
10	27

Now that we have grouped the data, we want to use the groupings. A basic way of describing the scores is to give the average score. Are you of "average height"? Although most people understand the meaning of "average," there are three *measures of central tendency* (or average): mode, median, and mean.

The **mode** is that score obtained by the largest number of students. Once you have finished a frequency distribution, you can determine the mode simply by looking at the frequency column. In table 16.8, the mode is 11, which 36 individuals earned.

> **mode** *The score obtained by the largest number of individuals taking a test.*

The **median** is that point in the distribution above which exactly 50 percent and below which exactly 50 percent of the cases lie. In table 16.8, look up the frequency column until you find half the scores accounted for. What is the median score? (Answer: 13.5.)

> **median** *That point in the distribution above which 50 percent and below which 50 percent of the scores lie.*

The **mean** is the average of the raw scores, arrived at by adding all the scores and dividing by the number of scores. The formula for calculating the mean is this:

> **mean** *The average of the raw scores.*

$$X = \Sigma X/N,$$

where X is the mean score, Σ is the sum of all the scores, and N is the total number of scores. Table 16.9 illustrates the process using a sample data set.

Table 16.9

Calculating the Mean

9
4
4
3
3
3
1
9
7
7
——
50

Using the formula for the mean:

$$\Sigma \frac{X}{N} = \overline{X}$$

then $\qquad \overline{X} = \frac{50}{10} = 5$

standard scores *Any of several derived scores (any score other than a raw score) based on the number of standard deviations between a specified raw score and the mean of the distribution.*

standard deviation unit *Measure of how much a score varies from the mean.*

z-score *A score that tells the distance of a student's raw score from the mean in standard deviation units; has a mean equal to 0 and a standard deviation equal to 1.*

These measures of central tendency provide a good idea of how any student has done in relation to the average score of the group. When the scores are normally distributed, all three measures of central tendency are equal. When the distribution of scores is skewed or unbalanced (for example, when there are two or three very high scores and the remainder of the scores in a typical class are much lower), the median is a more representative score than the mean.

To further our understanding of any score, we need some method that will provide constancy, that is, a score not affected by the length of the test or the difficulty of the items. Glasnapp and Poggio (1985) defined *standard* as constant across different times and situations. **Standard scores** have this quality; they offer a constant definition and interpretation. How is this possible? Standard scores relate to the normal curve, a theoretical mathematical model based on the assumption that most human characteristics are distributed normally. The normal curve is a representation showing the normal distribution of a particular trait. Figure 16.2 illustrates the normal curve.

Look at the baseline of the normal curve. You see a series of numbers ranging from +1 to +3 and from –1 to –3. Each number represents a **standard deviation unit.** These tell us how much a score varies from the mean. Look again at figure 16.2: note that about 68 percent of the scores fall between +1 and –1 standard deviation units from the mean; 95 percent of the scores fall between +2 and –2 standard deviation units from the mean. Once the mean and standard deviation are computed, we can use them to derive several standard scores: z-scores, t-scores, and stanine scores.

A **z-score** is the fundamental standard score, which tells us the distance of a student's raw score from the mean in standard deviation units. Here is an example: the raw score on a reading test was 78; the mean was 72; the standard deviation was 24. The raw score minus the mean equalled 6; it was divided by a standard deviation of 24 to equal +.25. This student had a z-score of +.25. The z-score informs us that the raw score was a little above average (¼ of a standard deviation unit). Thus, by looking at a z-score, you can tell quickly how a student has done on a test, and can compare students across classes.

Figure 16.2
The normal curve.

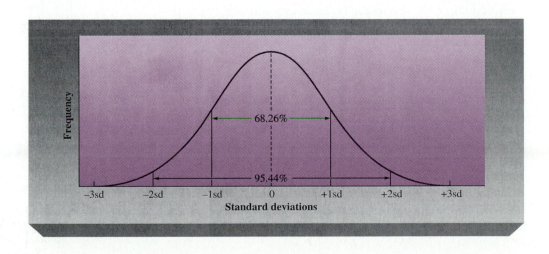

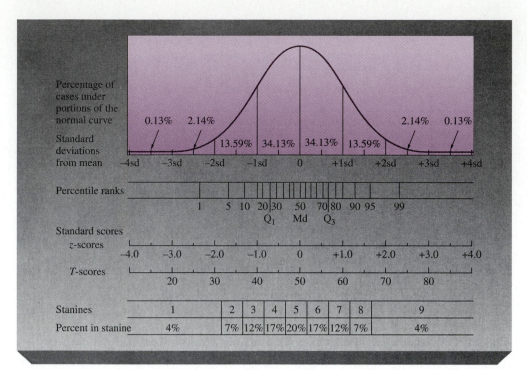

Figure 16.3
Relationships among standardized
test scores.

From Howard Lyman, Test Scores and
What They Mean. *Copyright © 1986
Allyn and Bacon, Needham Heights, MA.
Reprinted by permission.*

The **t-score** offers an alternative method of computing standard scores that avoids negative z scores and decimals. T-scores are computed by multiplying the standard score by 10 and adding 50. Let us take a z score of −1.5. The result would be this: $10 \times (-1.5) + 50 = 35$.

Stanine scores (the term is derived from "standard nine") were devised during World War II to classify pilots as quickly as possible. Those taking the tests would be classified into one of nine groups. A stanine has a mean of 5 and a standard deviation of 2. Stanine 5 includes the middle 20 percent of the scores. The ideal percentage for each stanine is as follows (Lyman, 1986):

t-score *A standard score with a mean of 50 and a standard deviation of 10.*

stanine scores *A standard score that classifies those taking a test into one of nine groups.*

	Lowest 4%	Next 7%	Next 12%	Next 17%	Middle 20%	Next 17%	Next 12%	Next 7%	Highest 4%
Stanine	1	2	3	4	5	6	7	8	9

As you can see, this is a quick means of classification, and is easily understood. If you tell parents that their child is in the ninth stanine, with nine as the highest, they can readily grasp the meaning. Figure 16.3 illustrates how these various scores relate to one another.

Assume that one of your students has a raw score of 300 on a particular test and that the mean for the test is also 300. This can be transformed into a percentile rank of 50, a z-score of 0.00, a t-score of 50, and a stanine of 5. You would be wise to familiarize yourself with these scores, since almost all standardized tests use one or more of them.

"I thought there was supposed to be safety in numbers."

© Reprinted by permission of James Warren.

USING STANDARDIZED TESTS

A major concern about standardized tests should be how to obtain the most helpful information from them to aid your students. One way of accomplishing this is to compare the results with the learning objectives of your school or classroom. Understanding the potential uses of test results is a major step in actively applying their results to your classroom.

We have previously seen how standardized tests such as the Scholastic Aptitude Test are used to form opinions about the state of education. The SAT recently was revised to include longer reading passages, vocabulary testing in the context of reading, interpretation of mathematical data, and the opportunity to work out mathematical problems rather than select options from a multiple-choice format, among other changes (Moses, 1991). Yet, in general, standardized tests have changed very little, in spite of widespread usage, continuing controversy about usage and interpretation, advances in statistical techniques, and improved test construction (Linn, 1986; Wiggins, 1994).

Educational Applications of Standardized Testing

Other forces, such as institutional concerns about efficiency, tracking, and selection have been mainly responsible for the popularity of standardized tests. One of the more prominent causes of the acceptance of standardized tests has been their educational application. Five major uses have been identified (Linn, 1986).

1. *Special education placement.* Tests that predict academic achievement (IQ tests) have played central roles in decision making about student placement. Though many questions have been raised about this policy, particular concern has been expressed about the large number of minorities in special education classes. Do these tests lead to bias in decision making about minorities? Recent court decisions have both affirmed (*Larry P. v. Riles,* 1979/1986) and denied (*PASE v. Hannon,* 1980) that IQ tests are biased; the question is still unanswered.

2. *Student certification.* At one time, a high school diploma was a sign that, based on teacher grades and the satisfaction of course requirements, the school testified to a student's ability to perform adequately at a satisfactory level. Now, more and more states are turning to **minimum competency tests** to provide evidence for certification. Here, our interest lies in the ability of these tests to furnish convincing evidence concerning students' minimal satisfactory performance. Although student scores in those states using minimum competency tests (MCTs) have risen rather dramatically, several questions remain. Would other tests of the same content produce the same results? Have thinking skills improved similarly? Are teachers teaching for the test?

3. *Teacher testing.* Recently, national concern has been expressed over teacher competency, with regard not only to initial certification but also to continued employment. Heated political debates have emerged in the wake of questions about teacher competency, which are not our concern here. Our interest focuses on the means used to judge instructional ability. Should the means be a national test, or the judgment of others? In both instances, the key requirement must be that the knowledge and skills assessed are actually those required for competent job performance.

4. *Educational assessment.* This idea—making decisions about schools based on testing students—is far from new. The comparison of students from a particular school to national norms traditionally has appealed to many educators. Though student scores may seem a fragile foundation on which to make judgments, sophisticated item analysis techniques have greatly enhanced and lent support to such a use of test scores.

minimum competency tests
Tests to determine whether students minimally can produce a satisfactory performance.

5. *Instructional guidance.* As testing technology has improved, standardized tests more frequently have been used as diagnostic guides. When a combination of tests providing more detailed information is enriched with insights derived from cognitive psychology (see chap. 8), sharper diagnostic distinctions are possible.

Multicultural Students and Standardized Testing

We previously have commented on the importance of style for both teaching and learning. Cognitive style is thought to be rooted at a deep structural level and influences the way in which humans organize and use the environment (Hilliard, 1983). Cognitive style, in turn, leads to expectations; if teachers are unaware of the impact of style on learning, educational outcomes—as measured by tests—can be negatively affected. What do cognitive styles, especially those of multicultural students, have to do with standardized tests? Our concern is with the response of these students to such tests.

As students get older, they often take tests that help them identify vocational or career interests.

Probably no one has more thoughtfully considered how multicultural students react to standardized testing than Anastasi (1982). Noting that cultural conditions may produce low scores, she stated that test results can have a negative influence on motivation, interests, and attitudes. Distinguishing between cultural factors that can affect test performance and test elements that also influence test results, Anastasi stated that it is the test-related elements that reduce validity. Among these elements are previous testing experience, motivation to do well on a particular type of test, and rapport with the examiner. Every effort should be made to familiarize all students, especially minority students, with the test-taking procedures described in chapter 15.

Cultural context also must be taken into consideration. A test's use of names or pictures unfamiliar to a student, or portrayal of an affluent middle-class family, or representation of a single racial type may have adverse effects on a student. Students benefit from the evaluations of those who have common ground with them (Rogoff, 1990). Most test publishers are working diligently to consider implications for minorities as they construct their tests.

The interpretation and the use of standardized test scores—major considerations in this chapter—need sensitive attention for minority students (Jones, 1988). If a student's scores are quite low, the tester should investigate why this has happened. Does it reflect factors just mentioned: motivation, reading ability, or lack of familiarity with test-taking?

Our discussion of standardized tests need not be all negative. Standardized tests can be a safeguard against racism or favoritism. The tests cannot see color or hear language. Also, if a disproportionate number in a minority group do poorly, a clear warning flag is raised, and steps must be taken to improve conditions contributing to these scores.

Common Criticisms of Standardized Tests

Though we have emphasized the positive aspects of these tests, standardized testing has had its share of criticism. The most common criticisms of standardized tests come from classroom teachers. These criticisms seem to focus on the pressure that tests exert on the curriculum, the danger of labeling students, and the accompanying side effects of worry and anxiety. Criticisms of standardized academic and cognitive tests in the classroom can be summarized by eight statements (Kellaghan, Madaus & Airasian, 1980; Wiggins, 1994).

What kind of information from tests can help you teach students?

1. *Testing limits teaching,* in the sense that instructors teach for the test, thus restricting students' experiences.
2. *Testing produces rigid grouping practices.* Students are assessed, and the resulting label causes an inflexible classification.

teacher – student

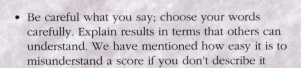

Communicating Test Results

Your first concern is with the kinds of people who have a right to receive test information. As mentioned previously, the Buckley amendment (The Family Education Rights and Privacy Act of 1975) provides that adult students and the parents of minors have access to test results. Your school may also have its own policy with regard to those who have access to test results, those who can release test scores, and those who can interpret scores to students and parents. You may find these suggestions helpful in discussing test results.

- Try to link the test score to an educational objective, such as improving reading skills or class placement.
- Know what you're talking about. What do the scores mean? How do they relate to the school? the class? a particular student?
- If you're discussing test results with parents, try to establish a comfortable basis for your talk; tie it specifically to improving their child's achievement.

- Be careful what you say; choose your words carefully. Explain results in terms that others can understand. We have mentioned how easy it is to misunderstand a score if you don't describe it precisely yet simply.
- If you think it's called for, explain what the score means in relation to others who took the test—the norm group.
- Ask parents how they think their child is doing and then link their answer to test results to show that the student should be doing better, or is currently doing well.
- If you tell parents, or a student, about a low score, use considerable sensitivity. Try something like this.

This grade is low and could keep you from being promoted. But I think if you work hard, you still have time to bring it up.

3. *Testing lowers student achievement.* Testing takes time from instruction, especially if time is taken to practice for the test. Some teachers also have a tendency to concentrate on bright students, since their scores appear easier to raise.

4. *Tests lead to labeling students.* This common danger can easily influence teacher expectations, and leads also to the difficulties posed in statement 2.

5. *Testing arouses negative emotional feelings.* We have commented frequently on such test accompaniments as fear, anxiety, and competitiveness for some students.

6. *Testing may negatively affect a student's self-concept.* Given the reality of students who "freeze" during testing, test results may not reflect actual ability. Yet, students will believe "the score," causing lowered self-esteem, with all its attendant consequences.

7. *Test scores do not directly influence teaching.* Test scores provide little relevant information about individual students, revealing only how they compare to other similar students. We have mentioned this previously, when noting the efforts of test publishers to provide more penetrating diagnostic tools.

8. *Tests often do not measure what was taught.* This statement, which is a common criticism by teachers and students, reinforces criticism 1: teachers frequently feel compelled to teach for the test.

Given the advantages and disadvantages of standardized tests that we have reviewed in this chapter, it is now time to focus on the resulting "best practices." We believe that standardized tests have a significant role in educational psychology and effective teaching. As with almost anything else, however, one must be cautious and use good judgment to achieve maximum results from the use of standardized tests.

Best Practices

From your perspective, what is the most salient criticism of standardized tests?

Standardized tests have generated concerns on the part of many educators. The authors believe, however, that many of the concerns are the result of poor testing practices or misunderstanding of the purposes of tests, and that standardized tests will continue to have a central place in students' education. Recognizing this, a joint committee on testing practices from major educational and psychological associations developed the

Code of Fair Testing Practices in Education (1988). The Code contains standards for educational test developers and users in four categories: developing/selecting tests, interpreting scores, striving for fairness, and informing test-takers.

The Code is meant for the general public and is limited to educational tests. It supplements the more technical *Standards for Educational and Psychological Testing* (AERA, APA, NCME, 1985). We have reprinted the four sections of the Code in their entirety in an appendix to this chapter. It serves as an appropriate conclusion to this chapter on standardized testing, for it reminds us that tests affect everybody (developers, users, and students), and that their use requires significant knowledge and skill on the part of educators.

APPLICATIONS AND REFLECTIONS

Chapter Highlights

A School's Testing Program

- The use of standardized tests is integral to the educational purposes of the entire school system and should serve the needs of its students at all levels.
- A well-designed standardized testing program serves three purposes: instructional, guidance, and administrative.
- The value of standardized tests lies in their consistency or sameness, which provides a means of comparing students.
- The norms that accompany standardized tests enable teachers, counselors, and other educators to interpret test scores by comparing them to the scores of other students, taken from a comparison sample.
- A norm-referenced test enables the teacher to compare a student with a representative group of students who have already taken the test.
- A criterion-referenced test enables the teacher to determine if a student has achieved competence at one level of knowledge or skills before moving on to the next higher level of content.

Types of Standardized Tests

- Standardized achievement tests are designed to assess the knowledge and skills taught by the schools. The value of these tests is in their assessment of the development of individual learners at different ages and in different subjects.
- Standardized aptitude tests are used to predict what students can learn; they provide assessments of performance based on learning abilities.
- Although a clear definition of intelligence has remained elusive, attempts to measure it have produced some of psychology's most colorful, damaging, and useful insights into human behavior.
- In spite of the problems that have been encountered in attempts to measure intelligence, several reasonable suggestions have been made as to fruitful uses of the results of intelligence testing. Properly interpreted, these scores can help teachers to improve their instruction; they are a good guide for initial efforts at grouping students; several of these tests can be used to identify students' needs; teachers can use test results to monitor school progress—to determine if these students are doing as well as possible, given what the tests indicate about their abilities.
- Behavior rating scales are commonly used to identify potential problem behaviors in students referred for special services. Teachers and parents are frequently asked to complete scales concerning a wide range of intrapersonal and interpersonal behaviors exhibited by children in situations at school and in the community.
- A behavior rating scale provides information about the frequency of potential problem behaviors and often compares the summative ratings of a student to those of a comparison group of students of the same age and sex. Thus, some behavior rating scales are used to classify children's problems.
- Preschool screening tests and assessment methods have become an important part of the assessment scene in schools today. The early identification of problems allows educators greater opportunities to remedy them sooner.

Interpreting Standardized Test Scores

- To utilize the results of standardized testing as fully as possible, the teacher must have some means of interpreting students' scores. Several meaningful techniques are available that can help the teacher to analyze scores and organize data so that the results of testing can be applied to classroom work. These include standard scores, percentile ranks, and knowledge of the normal distribution.

Using Standardized Tests

- The possible uses of standardized tests include student certification, special education placement, the testing of teachers, and assessing the success of a school, and instructional assistance.
- Many warnings have appeared about the potential negative effects of standardized testing on multicultural students as a result of language difficulties, previous testing experiences, or motivation. Standardized tests, however, are not necessarily a negative experience for these students; they can be a safeguard against racism or favoritism.
- Clear standards as guides to the best practices in test construction have been proposed for test developers.

Connections

1. Think about how you learn and describe how one of the major concepts discussed in this chapter is part of your learning activities or approach.

_____

_____

_____

2. Identify at least one learning situation (e.g., classroom instruction, self-study, taking a test, small-group work) and describe how you would apply one of the key concepts examined in this chapter *if you were a teacher*.

_____

_____

_____

Getting the Picture and Drawing Relationships

Think about the various learning concepts and variables discussed in this chapter. Create pictures, graphics, or figures that highlight relationships among the key components.

Personal Journal

What I really learned in this chapter was _____

_____

_____

_____

_____

What this means to me is _____

_____

_____

_____

_____

Questions that were stimulated by this chapter include _____

_____

_____

_____

_____

Key Terms

achievement tests	561	mode	580	standard deviation unit	581
aptitude tests	561	multilevel survey		standardized tests	561
assessment	560	batteries	565	standard scores	581
frequency distribution	580	norms	563	Stanford-Binet	
mean	580	percentile score	580	Intelligence Test	570
median	580	preschool assessment	576	stanine scores	582
minimum competency		raw score	579	t-score	582
tests	583	social validity	575	z-score	581

The Code of Fair Testing Practices in Education

Prepared by the Joint Committee on Testing Practices

The Code of Fair Testing Practices in Education states the major obligations to test takers and professionals who develop or use educational tests. The Code is meant to apply broadly to the use of tests in education (admissions, educational assessment, education diagnosis, and student placement). The Code is not designed to cover employment testing, licensure or certification testing, or other types of testing. Although the Code has relevance to many types of educational tests, it is directed primarily at professionally developed tests such as those sold by commercial test publishers or used in formally administered testing programs. The Code is not intended to cover tests made by individual teachers for use in their own classrooms.

The Code addresses the roles of test developers and test users separately. Test users are people who select tests, commission test development services, or make decisions on the basis of test scores. Test developers are people who actually construct tests as well as those who set policies for particular testing programs. The roles may, of course, overlap as when a state education agency commissions test development services, sets policies that control the test development process, and makes decisions on the basis of the test scores.

The Code presents standards for educational test developers and users in four areas:

A. Developing/Selecting Tests
B. Interpreting Scores
C. Striving for Fairness
D. Informing Test Takers

Organizations, institutions, and individual professionals who endorse the Code commit themselves to safeguarding the rights of test takers by following the principles listed. The Code is intended to be consistent with the relevant parts of the *Standards for Educational and Psychological Testing* (AERA, APA, NCME, 1985). However, the Code differs from the Standards in both audience and purpose. The Code is meant to be understood by the general public; it is limited to educational tests; and the primary focus is on those issues that affect the proper use of tests. The Code is not meant to add new principles over and above those in the Standards or to change the meaning of the Standards. The goal is rather to represent the spirit of a selected portion of the Standards in a way that is meaningful to test takers and/or their parents or guardians. It is the hope of the Joint Committee that the Code will also be judged to be consistent with existing codes of conduct and standards of other professional groups who use education tests.

Developing/Selecting Appropriate Tests*

Test developers should provide the information that test users need to select appropriate tests.

Test Developers Should:

1. Define what each test measures and what the test should be used for. Describe the population(s) for which the test is appropriate.
2. Accurately represent the characteristics, usefulness, and limitations of tests for their intended purposes.
3. Explain relevant measurement concepts as necessary for clarity at the level of detail that is appropriate for the intended audience(s).
4. Describe the process of test development. Explain how the content and skills to be tested were selected.
5. Provide evidence that the test meets its intended purpose(s).
6. Provide either representative samples or complete copies of test questions, answer sheets, manuals, and score reports to qualified users.
7. Indicate the nature of the evidence obtained concerning the appropriateness of each test for groups of different racial, ethnic, or linguistic backgrounds who are likely to be tested.
8. Identify and publish any specialized skills needed to administer each test and to interpret scores correctly.

Test users should select tests that meet the purpose for which they are to be used and that are appropriate for the intended test-taking populations.

Test Users Should:

1. First define the purpose for testing and the population to be tested. Then, select a test for that purpose and that population based on a thorough review of the available information.
2. Investigate potentially useful sources of information, in addition to test scores, to corroborate the information provided by tests.
3. Read the materials provided by test developers and avoid using tests for which unclear or incomplete information is provided.
4. Become familiar with how and when the test was developed and tried out.

---

*Many of the statements in the Code refer to the selection of existing tests. However, in customized testing programs test developers are engaged to construct new tests. In those situations, the test development process should be designed to help ensure that the completed tests will be in compliance with the Code.

5. Read independent evaluations of a test and of possible alternative measures. Look for evidence required to support the claims of test developers.
6. Examine specimen sets, disclosed tests or samples of questions, directions, answer sheets, manuals, and score reports before selecting a test.
7. Ascertain whether the test content and norms group(s) or comparison group(s) are appropriate for the intended test takers.
8. Select and use only those tests for which the skills needed to administer the test and interpret scores correctly are available.

Interpreting Scores

Test developers should help users interpret scores correctly.

Test Developers Should:

9. Provide timely and easily understood score reports that describe test performance clearly and accurately. Also explain the meaning and limitations of reported scores.
10. Describe the population(s) represented by any norms or comparison group(s), the dates the data were gathered, and the process used to select the samples of test takers.
11. Warn users to avoid specific, reasonably anticipated misuses of test scores.
12. Provide information that will help users follow reasonable procedures for setting passing scores when it is appropriate to use such scores with the test.
13. Provide information that will help users gather evidence to show that the test is meeting its intended purpose(s).

Test users should interpret scores correctly.

Test Users Should:

9. Obtain information about the scale used for reporting scores, the characteristics of any norms or comparison group(s), and the limitations of the scores.
10. Interpret scores taking into account any major differences between the norms or comparison groups and the actual test takers. Also take into account any differences in test administration practices or familiarity with the specific questions in the test.
11. Avoid using tests for purposes not specifically recommended by the test developer unless evidence is obtained to support the intended use.
12. Explain how any passing scores were set and gather evidence to support the appropriateness of the scores.
13. Obtain evidence to help show that the test is meeting its intended purpose(s).

Striving for Fairness

Test developers should strive to make tests that are as fair as possible for test takers of different races, gender, ethnic backgrounds, or handicapping conditions.

Test Developers Should:

14. Review and revise test questions and related materials to avoid potentially insensitive content or language.
15. Investigate the performance of test takers of different races, gender, and ethnic backgrounds when samples of sufficient size are available. Enact procedures that help to ensure that differences in performance are related primarily to the skills under assessment rather than to irrelevant factors.
16. When feasible, make appropriately modified forms of tests or administration procedures available for test takers with handicapping conditions. Warn test users of potential problems in using standard norms with modified tests or administration procedures that result in non-comparable scores.

Test users should select tests that have been developed in ways that attempt to make them as fair as possible for test takers of different races, gender, ethnic backgrounds, or handicapping conditions.

Test Users Should:

14. Evaluate the procedures used by test developers to avoid potentially insensitive content or language.
15. Review the performance of test takers of different races, gender, and ethnic backgrounds when samples of sufficient size are available. Evaluate the extent to which performance differences may have been caused by inappropriate characteristics of the test.
16. When necessary and feasible, use appropriately modified forms of tests or administration procedures for test takers with handicapping conditions. Interpret standard norms with care in the light of the modifications that were made.

The Code has been developed by the Joint Committee on Testing Practices, a cooperative effort of several professional organizations, that has as its aim the advancement, in the public interest, of the quality of testing practices. The Joint Committee was initiated by the American Educational Research Association, the American Psychological Association, and the National Council on Measurement in Education. In addition to these three groups, the American Association for Counseling and Development/Association for Measurement and Evaluation in Counseling and Development, and the American Speech-Language-Hearing Association are now also sponsors of the Joint Committee. This is not copyrighted material. Reproduction and dissemination are encouraged. Please cite this document as follows:
Code of Fair Testing Practices in Education. (1988) Washington, D.C.: Joint Committee on Testing Practices
(Mailing Address: Joint Committee on Testing Practices, American Psychological Association, 1200 17th Street, NW, Washington, D.C. 20036.)

glossary

ABCD format   A technique for writing objectives that includes Audience, Behavior, Conditions, and Degree of Competency.   378

ability grouping   The technique of helping students achieve individual goals by placing those of similar ability together, either by groups in the same classroom (homogeneous grouping) or in separate classrooms (tracking).   153

academic goals   Those goals that include intellectual skills and domains of knowledge.   371

acceleration   A change in the regular school program that permits a gifted student to complete a program in less time or at an earlier age than usual.   158

accommodation   Piaget's term for a change in cognitive structures that produces corresponding behavioral changes; one part of adaptation.   84

achievement tests   Tests that measure accomplishment in such specific subjects as reading, arithmetic, etc. Developed by testing specialists. Concern today is that these tests may not adequately reflect what is actually taught in the classroom.   539, 561

activity reinforcers   High-frequency behaviors used to reinforce low-frequency behaviors.   223

adaptation   Piaget's term for one of the two psychological mechanisms used to explain cognitive development (organization is the other). Refers to the two complementary processes of assimilation and accommodation.   84

advance organizers   Ausubel's term for an abstract, general overview of new information before the actual learning is expected.   246

affective entry characteristics   Bloom's phrase to describe a student's motivation to learn new material.   420

animism   Piaget's term for a child's tendency to attribute life to inert objects.   91

appreciation   Knowing when you have done a good job in your teaching.   12

aptitude tests   Tests that assess students' general or specific abilities.   561

artificialism   Piaget's term for a preoperational child's tendency to assume that everything is the product of human creation.   91

assessment   The process of gathering information about a student's abilities and using such information to make decisions about the student.   520, 560

assimilation   Piaget's term to describe the way human beings take things into their minds; one part of adaptation.   84

at risk   A term used to describe those children who have a high probability of becoming handicapped.   152

attachment   Behavior intended to keep a child (or adult) in close proximity to a significant other.   121

attention-deficit/hyperactivity disorder (ADHD)   A disorder usually appearing in childhood that is characterized by various symptoms of inattention and/or hyperactivity-impulsivity.   168

attention management   A term that refers to the effective use of time.   313

attribution theory   A motivational theory that assumes people want to know the causes of their behavior.   337

audiovisual aids   Use of technology to present information in several different formats (e.g., visual, auditory), usually supplementing a teacher- or text-based presentation. Examples include overhead projectors, slide projectors, and television.   491

authentic/performance assessment   The securing of information about a student's success or failure through meaningful and significant (authentic) tasks.   540

autonomy   Erikson's term for a child's growing sense of independence. Attained in stage 2 (Autonomy versus Shame and Doubt).   121

aversive control   A technique to eliminate undesirable student behavior, either by introducing an unpleasant event or removing a pleasurable one.   459

beginning teacher evaluation studies (BTES)   An effort to evaluate beginning teachers by focusing on student activities.   397

behavior disorders   Any conditions in which environmental conflicts and personal disturbance persist and negatively affect academic performance.   167

behavior influence   The exercise of some control by one person over another.   458

behavior modification   A deliberate attempt, using learning principles, to control student behavior.   458

behavior therapy   An attempt to change behavior in a client-therapist relationship.   458

bilingual education   Instruction using programs designed to help those with limited English proficiency (LEP) to acquire English by teaching them partly in English and partly in their own languages.   191

bilingualism   The condition of using, with facility, two or more languages.   109

case study   The evaluation and report of research on an individual subject, usually of an anecdotal nature.   31

CD-ROM   Compact disc-read only memory. An optical disk technology that allows storage of very large amounts of any type of digital data, including text, digital sound and graphics, and digital movies. The data are read from the disc by a laser beam.   505

centering   Piaget's term for a child's tendency to concentrate on only part of an object or activity.   90

classical conditioning   Pavlov's explanation of conditioning in which a neutral (conditioned) stimulus gradually gains the ability to elicit a response because of its pairing with a natural (unconditioned) stimulus.   200

classification   Piaget's term for the ability to group objects with some similarities within a larger category.   93

Clinical Theory of Instruction (CTI) Hunter's theory that the teacher is a decision-making professional. 399

cognitive constructivism A cognitive theory of learning and teaching that underlies much of the current work on technology in education. It holds that students actively construct their own knowledge, and that reality is determined by the experiences of the knower rather than existing as an objective truth distinct from the individual. The teacher is seen as a facilitator of knowledge and skill acquisition, and the learner takes on a high degree of responsibility for his or her own learning. 481

cognitive entry behaviors Bloom's term for the prerequisite learning skills needed before attempting new learning. 420

cognitive research trust (CoRT) de Bono's program that is intended to help students acquire thinking skills. 295

communication Imparting of a message not only verbally, but also through body language and use of space, voice intonation, and eye contact. Vital in teaching as an art. 12

comparative research Research in which the investigator searches for direct relations among variables that are compared with one another. 36

comparative schema A cognitive structure describing one situation in relation to another. 387

computer-assisted instruction (CAI) Use of the computer initially to present material to students and then to assist them in mastering it. Earlier versions were based in behaviorist theory; more recent programs are based in cognitive theory. 494

computer-managed instruction (CMI) Use of the computer to collect, analyze, and report information concerning students in an educational program. Can include information on students' academic performance, attendance, background information, teachers' lesson plans, etc. 491

computer network The connection of computers to one another through telephone lines or cables so that information and/or equipment can be shared. 506

conditioned reflex A response that is elicited by a conditioned stimulus when the unconditioned stimulus is not present. 200

conditioned stimulus A previously neutral stimulus that has acquired the power to elicit a response. 200

connectionism Thorndike's explanation of learning (by selecting and connecting). 202

conservation Piaget's term for the realization that the essence of something remains constant, although surface features may change. 92

construct validity Validity of a test based on its actually measuring the knowledge domain or behavior it claims to measure. 528

content Piaget's term for behavior. 85

content standards Material that should be taught 368

content validity Validity of a test based on its ability adequately to sample behavior that has been the goal of instruction. 528

context For Hayes, the strategy of searching for relationships between new material and material that is already known. 312

contingency contracting Joint decision by a teacher and a student on a behavioral goal and what the student will receive when the goal is achieved. 459

control theory A theory suggesting that behavior is always the attempt to satisfy powerful forces at work within. 463

conventional level Kohlberg's second level of moral development (from about 10 to 13 years of age), when children desire approval from both others and society. 138

cooperation Situation in which students and teachers get along well together, so that a classroom functions smoothly. 12

cooperative learning A set of instructional methods in which students are encouraged or required to work together on academic tasks. 354

correlational research Research in which the researcher attempts to determine if a relation exists between two or more variables. 35

criterion-referenced tests A type of testing used to determine if a student has achieved predetermined behavioral or learning objectives. A student's performance is interpreted by comparing the performance to a set of objective criteria. 545

criterion-related validity Validity of a test based on its results' similarity to some other, external criteria. 528

critical thinking The use of mental strategies to solve problems. 280

cross-cultural research Research conducted across different cultures to determine which factors are related to a particular culture. 42

cross-sectional research Research involving data collection at one point in time from a sample containing two or more subgroups that are then compared on variables of interest. 41

cues Techniques to help us recall; particularly effective if we generate them ourselves. 314

cultural compatibility Compatibility of instruction with the cultural patterns of students. 56

curriculum-based assessment (CBA) As assessment technique linked to curriculum and instruction in which a student's success is evaluated by that student's progress in the curriculum and whose purpose is to determine further instructional needs. 537

decoding A listener's use of the sounds and grammar of a language to interpret it. 383

dependent variable The variable on which subjects respond to the manipulation of the independent variable. 36

descriptive research Research in which the investigator examines and reports things the way they are. 34

desists A teacher's actions to stop misbehavior. 454

discovery learning Bruner's term for learning that involves the rearrangement and transformation of material in a way that leads to insight. 247, 336

discrimination The process by which we learn not to respond to similar stimuli in an identical manner. 201

drill and practice Use of the computer to help students master the basic elements in a given domain after they have already received initial instruction. The computer presents a stimulus, elicits a response, and provides feedback and reinforcement. 496

DUPE An acronym for a problem-solving model. Intended to mean "Don't let yourself be deceived." 303

dynamic schema A cognitive structure describing changes in an original situation. 387

educational psychology The application of psychology to the study of development, learning, motivation, instruction, and related issues. 3

educational technology Technology applied to the teaching and learning processes. Includes the particular media used to deliver instruction, as well as the processes involved in analyzing instructional problems and devising, implementing, evaluating, and managing solutions to those problems. 478

efficacy expectation The belief that one can perform the behavior or behaviors required to produce a certain outcome. 351

egocentrism Piaget's term for children's tendency to see things as they want them to be. 88

elaboration The adding of information to what one is trying to learn so the material becomes more personally meaningful. 315

enactive Bruner's term for the mental stage of knowing the world by acting on it; usually refers to the infancy period. 406

enculturation   The broad and complex process of acquiring knowledge.   285

engaged time   The time during which students are actively involved in their work.   435

enrichment   A method of instruction for gifted students in which they are furnished with additional, challenging experiences.   159

episodic memory   The recall of personal experiences within a specific context or period of time.   263

equilibration   Piaget's term for the balance between assimilation and accommodation.   84

essay tests   Teacher-constructed tests that allow students considerable latitude in their answers to questions.   525

evaluation   The interpretation of data obtained from tests and measurements.   525

event recording   Method of direct observation designed to measure the frequency of behavior; it refers to the number of times a behavior occurs and is best used with behaviors that have a clear beginning and ending.   538

exceptional   A term that refers to one or more kinds of special needs or characteristics in children.   150

exclusion component   A means of accurately identifying students with learning disabilities.   172

exhibitions   A form of authentic assessment in which students are required to demonstrate the integration of the knowledge and skills they have acquired.   545

expected learner outcomes (ELOs)   Cognitive and behavioral objectives used to express learning expectations to students, teachers, and parents.   372

experimental research   Research in which the researcher actively manipulates an independent variable to observe changes in the dependent variable.   36

extended response   A form of essay question that permits a student to make any kind of answer the student desires.   530

external representation   A method of problem solving in which a person uses symbols or some other observable type of representation.   307

externals   Individuals who attribute the causes of their behavior to factors outside themselves.   347

extinction   Refers to the process by which conditioned responses are lost.   202

extrinsic motivation   Those rewards and inducements external to students.   333

first instance   For Skinner, some aspect of desired behavior, initially exhibited by a student.   411

fixed interval   Term describing a schedule in which a response results in reinforcement only after a definite length of time.   208

fixed ratio   Term describing a schedule in which reinforcement depends on a definite number of responses.   208

forgetting   The loss of previously acquired material from memory.   266

forgiveness   A special application of mercy; focuses on the individual who forgives, not on the one seeking forgiveness.   143

formative evaluation   Assessment intended to aid learning by providing feedback about what has been learned and what remains to be learned.   419

frame   Present material in a certain manner; here, refers to teachers.   272

frequency distribution   A record of how often a score appears in a score category.   580

functional invariants   Piaget's term for the cognitive mechanisms of adaptation and organization.   84

gender identity   The conviction that one belongs to the sex of birth.   65

gender role   Culturally acceptable sexual behavior.   65

gender schema   A mental blueprint for organizing information about gender.   69

gender stereotypes   Beliefs about the characteristics associated with males or females.   65

generativity   Erikson's term for productive and creative responsibility for the next generation. Attained in stage 7 (Generativity versus Stagnation).   135

gifted   A term describing those with abilities that give evidence of high performance capabilities.   156

goals   Clear, precise statements of educational priorities.   366

grading   The assigning of a symbol to a student's performance.   520

group alertness   Use of instructional methods that maintain interest and contribute to lively classes.   455

hard of hearing   A term describing those individuals with sufficient hearing potential (with hearing aids) to process linguistic information through audition.   164

Head Start   An intervention program intended to provide educational and developmental services to preschool children from low-income families.   62

hearing impairment   A term referring to any type of hearing loss, from mild to profound.   164

heuristics   The use of alternative search patterns to solve problems; the generation of new possible solutions.   317

historical research   The study, understanding, and explanation of past events.   34

iconic   Bruner's term for the perceptual organization of the world; a mode of representation.   406

identity achievement   Committing oneself to choices about identity and maintaining that commitment.   132

identity confusion   The state of human beings who experience doubt and uncertainty about who they are.   130

identity crisis   Erikson's term for those situations, usually in adolescence, that cause humans to make major decisions about their identities.   130

identity diffusion   An inability to commit oneself to choices; the lack of a sense of direction.   132

identity foreclosure   The making of a commitment under pressure, not as the result of the resolution of a crisis.   132

identity moratorium   The desire to make a choice but the inability to do so.   132

imagery   The ability to visualize objects or events.   315

incidental learning   Feuerstein's term for cognitive growth that results from a changing environment and is accomplished unintentionally.   294

inclusion   The movement to place all handicapped children in regular classrooms regardless of the nature and severity of the handicaps.   178

independent variable   The experimental or treatment condition variable.   36

industry   Erikson's term to describe a child's sense of being able to do things well and desire to win recognition in this way. Attained in stage 4 (Industry versus Inferiority).   126

inferencing   A learning strategy involving questioning oneself about the implications of material one has learned.   312

initiative   Erikson's term for children's ability to explore the environment and test their world. Attained in stage 3 (Initiative versus Guilt).   123

inquiry teaching   Bruner's term for teaching that permits students to be active partners in the search for knowledge, thus enhancing the meaning of what they learn.   404

instantiation   The strategy of furnishing an example.   313

instrumental enrichment   Feuerstein's program designed to help students acquire thinking skills.   294

integrity Erikson's term for the ability to look back and see meaning in life. Attained in stage 8 (Integrity versus Despair). 135

intelligent tutoring system (ITS) Use of technology to provide an individualized tutor for each student. The computer presents new material, provides examples and practice problems, tracks student performance, identifies errors and misconceptions, and provides appropriate guidance and feedback. 501

intermittent reinforcement Reinforcement in which reinforcers occasionally are implemented. 208

internal representation A mental model of how to solve a problem. 307

internals Individuals who attribute the causes of their behavior to themselves. 347

interval recording A method for recording observations of a given behavior that occur during a specified time period; typically, the time period is 15 to 30 seconds long. 538

interval reinforcement Scheduled reinforcement, in which the reinforcement occurs at definite established time intervals. 207

interviews A research method in which an investigator asks another individual questions designed to obtain answers relevant to a research problem. 39

intimacy Erikson's term for the ability to be involved with another without fearing a loss of self-identity. Attained in stage 6 (Intimacy versus Isolation). 134

intrinsic motivation The desire of students themselves to learn, without the need for external inducements. 333

irreversibility Piaget's term for children's inability to reverse their thinking. 90

knowledge-acquisition components Humans' ability to acquire and use language, thus helping them solve problems. A major component in Sternberg's triarchic model. 281

Language Acquisition Device (LAD) Chomsky's term for the mechanism in humans that, he believes, gives them an innate knowledge of language. 113

laser videodisc An optical disk technology that stores digital movies and allows instantaneous access to any frame on the disc. The data are read from the disc by a laser beam. 504

learned helplessness The reaction on the part of some individuals to become frustrated and simply give up after repeated failure. 348

learning disabilities A term referring to a handicapping condition characterized by a discrepancy between ability and achievement, most commonly manifested in reading, writing, reasoning, and/or mathematics. 171

least restrictive environment A learning environment or classroom situation that provides necessary support for a handicapped student's continuing educational progress while also minimizing the time the student is removed from a normalized educational environment. In many ways, it has the same philosophical base as the practice of mainstreaming. 154

legally blind A term referring to those individuals with vision of 20/200 or less in the better eye (after correction). 163

levels of processing Describes analysis of memory focusing on the depth at which humans process information. 264

locus of control The cause of behavior; some individuals believe it resides within them, while others believe it resides outside themselves. 347

Logo A computer programming language derived from the artificial intelligence language LISP. It was designed so that students could easily learn its basics and begin programming computers from an early age, with the idea that programming would be beneficial for students' cognitive development. 498

longitudinal research A research method in which subjects are assessed repeatedly over a lengthy period of time. 42

long-term store The aspect of memory that holds both conscious and unconscious data for long periods of time; related to meaningfulness of material. 264

mainstreaming Integrating physically, mentally, and behaviorally handicapped students into regular classes. 150

marking The summary assessment of a test or an oral or written report. 547

mastery learning Learning in which instructor and student decide on time needed and what is necessary for mastery, usually about 90 percent of the possible achievement score. 419

matching item A test item utilizing two columns, such that each item in the first column is to be matched with an item in the second column. 536

mean The average of the raw scores. 580

meaningful learning Ausubel's term to describe the acquisition of new meanings. 245

measurement To quantify, or place a number on, student performance. 520

median That point in the distribution above which 50 percent and below which 50 percent of the scores lie. 580

mediated learning Feuerstein's term for the training given to learners by experienced adults. 294

mental representation The coding of external events so they are retrievable in an internal form. 238

mental retardation Significantly subaverage general intellectual functioning. 174

meta-analysis A statistical technique used to synthesize and interpret the results of multiple data-based studies. 45

metacognition The ability to think about thinking. 269, 297

metacognitive experiences Cognitive or affective experiences that relate to cognitive activities. 270

metacognitive knowledge An individual's knowledge and beliefs about cognitive matters, gained from experiences and stored in long-term memory. 269

metacomponents Higher-order control processes used to evaluate a planned course of action; the executive components of intelligence. A major component in Sternberg's triarchic model. 281

method of loci The use of familiar locations to help one visually store things in memory and retrieve them more easily. 315

minimum competency tests Tests to determine whether students minimally can produce a satisfactory performance. 583

mode The score obtained by the largest number of individuals taking a test. 580

modes of representation Bruner's term for the mental stages a child passes through. 406

monitoring The learning strategy of examining or monitoring one's own learning. 312

moral dilemma A conflict causing subjects to justify the morality of their choices. 143

morpheme The smallest unit of language to have meaning; may be a whole word or part of a word (old,er). 103

multicultural classrooms Classrooms with students and teachers from different ethnic or cultural groups. 14

multilevel survey batteries Series of tests that assess separate curricular topics over a wide range of grades. 565

multimedia uses The integration and simultaneous use of several different types of technology (e.g., computers, CD-ROMs, laser videodiscs). This use of technology in teaching is often based on cognitive constructivist theory and often involves students in collaborative, large-scale projects. 503

multiple-choice items Questions or incomplete statements that are followed by several possible responses. One of these responses is correct. 525

multiple coding Mental representation of a problem in more than one way—for example, verbally and visually. 313

multiple intelligences Gardner's seven relatively autonomous intelligences. These include linguistic, musical, logical-mathematical, spatial, bodily-kinesthetic, interpersonal, and intrapersonal intelligence. 282

need achievement theory An explanation of motivation that is related to competence: judging it and increasing it. 337

negative reinforcers Stimuli whose withdrawal strengthens behavior. 209

neverstreaming A term introduced by Slavin that refers to a determined effort to keep students functioning within normal limits by preventing academic problems. 187

norms Scores on a given test that are derived from an identified sample, and are then used as a basis for comparison (and therefore interpretation) of scores on the same test. 563

novelty effect The tendency to give more attention to, give higher ratings to, and in general find more positive effects of an educational tool or instructional program simply because it is new. 488

number concept Piaget's term for the ability to understand numbers. 94

objectives Those instructional and learning outcomes deemed worthy of attainment. 366

object permanence Piaget's term for an infant's ability to realize that an object or person not within sight still exists. 88

observation A research method in which trained observers assess individuals in as natural a setting as possible. 41

operant conditioning Skinner's explanation of learning, which emphasizes the consequences of behavior. 205

operations Piaget's term for actions that we perform mentally in order to gain knowledge. 90

organization Piaget's term for the connections among cognitive structures. 85

outcome expectation The belief that a given behavior will lead to a specific outcome. 351

overcorrection A form of classroom management involving both restitution and positive practice. 210, 459

overlapping A teacher's ability to handle two or more classroom issues simultaneously. 454

parallel distributed processing Processing of information according to its appearance, meaning, and pronunciation. 383

percentile score A score that tells the percentage of individuals taking a test who are at or below a particular score; a percentile rank of 74 means that this student did as well or better than 74 percent of those taking the test. 580

perception (1) Insight of teachers into the moods of their classes, prompting them to adapt their methods. 12 (2) The ability to recognize familiar persons, objects, or events with meaning and expectations. 255

performance-based grading benchmarks The use of objective standards by which students' accomplishments are evaluated. 545

performance components The implementation aspect of intelligence in Sternberg's triarchic model of intelligence. 281

performance standards The level of mastery required for a task. 368

permanent product recording A method of recording the by-products (e.g., worksheets, homework, pages written) of a person's behavior. 539

permanent products Physical by-products of a person's behavior. 538

personal goals Those goals that emphasize the development of individual responsibility, talent, and free expression. 371

personalized system of instruction (PSI) Kellers technique for individualized instruction. 208

phonemes The distinctive, fundamental sounds of a language. 103

phonology The use of sounds to form words. 102

portfolio assessment Assessment of a student's behavior based upon a collection of the student's work that the teacher, the student, or both believe to be important evidence of learning. 545

positive reinforcers Those stimuli whose presentations increase the rates of responses. 209

postconventional level Kohlberg's third level of moral development when individuals act according to an enlightened conscience. 140

practical intelligence Tactical knowledge necessary for success both inside and outside of school. 291

pragmatics The ability to take part in a conversation, using language in a socially correct manner. 102

preconventional level Kohlberg's first level of moral development, from about 4 to 10 years of age, when children respond mainly to rewards and punishment. 138

Premack principle The theory that access to high-frequency behaviors acts as a reinforcer for the performance of low-frequency behaviors. 214

preschool assessment A method of identifying children who need help before they enter formal schooling. 576

proactive classroom management Classroom management including both reactive responding to problems and proactive planning for productive behavior. 434

programmed instruction A set of instructional materials that students can use to teach themselves about a particular topic, skill, or content area. Based on Skinner's theory of operant conditioning, such a program is designed so that instruction progresses in small steps toward a well-defined final goal, is sequenced so that students give correct answers most of the time, and relies heavily on positive reinforcement of correct answers. 411, 495

psycholinguistics The combined study of psychology and linguistics; refers most often to Chomsky's work on language development. 113

punishment Refers to the presentation of an aversive stimulus or removal of a positive stimulus contingent upon a response which decreases the probability of the response. 209

QAIT An instructional model proposed by Slavin that emphasizes the quality of instruction, appropriate levels of instruction, incentive, and time. 443

quality of instruction Bloom's term for the cues, practice, and reinforcement necessary to make learning meaningful for students. 420

ratio reinforcement Reinforcement occurring after a certain number of responses. 208

raw score Uninterpreted data; often, the number of correct items. 579

reading comprehension The skill by which readers not only recognize words but understand the concepts that the words represent. 384

realism Piaget's term for a child's growing ability to distinguish and accept the real world. 90

reciprocal interactions Process in which we respond to those around us and they change; their changed behavior then causes changes in us. In the classroom, emphasizes a student's active involvement in teacher-student interactions; that is, students are not merely passive recipients in any exchange. 121

recognition The act of comparing an incoming representation with a representation already in memory. 265

Regular Education Initiative (REI) A movement to include more of the mildly handicapped in regular classrooms. 185

reinforcer A consequential stimulus that occurs contingent on a behavior and increases the behavior. 205

reliability Characteristic of a test for which a student's scores are nearly the same in repeated measurements, and of a test that consistently measures what it says it measures. 527

reminiscence The phenomenon that after rest, memory seems to improve. 268

representation The manner in which information is recorded or expressed. 253

response cost A form of punishment involving the loss of a positive reinforcer (e.g., after misbehavior, a student may no longer be a classroom monitor). 210

restricted response A form of essay question that asks for specific information. 530

retrieval The act of recognizing, recalling, and reconstructing what we have previously stored in memory. 265

retrieving Ability to access information in stored memory. 313

ripple effect The phenomenon in which punishment is not confined to one student; its effects spread to other class members. 454

rubrics Authoritative or established criteria used to evaluate student performance; usually consists of a fixed scale and a list of characteristics describing performances for each point on the scale. 545

schemata Mental frameworks that modify incoming data; plural of schema. 242

schemes Piaget's term for organized patterns of thought. 85

school delivery standards A school's effectiveness in instruction. 368

self-efficacy Individuals' beliefs in their abilities to exert control over their lives; feelings of competency. 218, 350

self-fulfilling prophecy The phenomenon that when teachers expect more of children, the students tend to meet the expectations, and vice versa. 427

self-regulated Describing an individual's ability to control his or her own learning or behavior through cognitive processes. 272

semantic memory Memory necessary for the use of language. 263

semantics The meaning of words; the relationship between ideas and words. 102

sensory register The ability, which is highly selective, to hold information in memory for a brief period. 264

seriation Piaget's term for the ability to arrange objects by increasing or decreasing size. 93

sex cleavage The tendency of children of the same sex to play together. 68

shaping A form of classroom management in which teachers determine the successive steps needed to master a task and then teach them separately, reinforcing each step. 459

short-term store The working memory; consciousness is involved. 264

single-case research Research designed to evaluate the effect of an intervention on a single case, usually one individual. 43

situational anxiety A tendency to be anxious in some situations and not in others. 342

social and civic goals Those goals intended to prepare students for socialization into a complex society. 371

social cognitive learning According to Bandura's theory, the process whereby the information we glean from observing others influences our behavior. 216

social discipline A theory of classroom management based on the conviction that misbehavior can be eliminated by changing a student's goals. 462

social validity The applied, or social, importance of exhibiting certain behaviors in particular situations. 575

spiral curriculum Bruner's term for teaching a subject in an ever more abstract manner; tied to his interpretation of readiness. 405

standard deviation unit Measure of how much a score varies from the mean. 581

standardized tests Tests that are commercially constructed and administered under uniform conditions. 524, 561

standard scores Any of several derived scores (any score other than a raw score) based on the number of standard deviations between a specified raw score and the mean of the distribution. 581

Stanford-Binet Intelligence Test Binet's famous measure of human intelligence, revised for American use originally by Terman, and most recently by Thorndike and colleagues. Presently called the Stanford-Binet Intelligence Scale. 570

stanine scores A standard score that classifies those taking a test into one of nine groups. 582

static schema A cognitive structure describing relationships among elements. 387

stimulus generalization The process by which a conditioned response transfers to other stimuli. 201

storage The act of putting information into memory. 265

storing The ability to hold information in memory. 313

strong performance assessment An assessment in which students who are asked to apply knowledge and skills are provided scoring criteria before they produce products, and are also encouraged to assess themselves after they have completed the products. 544

strong strategy A problem-solving strategy designed for a specific subject. 301

structures Piaget's term for the psychological units of the mind that enable us to think and know. 84

structuring The strategy of searching for relations in learning materials. 312

student self-assessment Students are encouraged to review and analyze their own performance. 545

summative evaluation Measurement of a student's achievement at the completion of a block of work. 419

supply items Questions on objective tests that require students to give the answers (as opposed to choosing from among possible answers). 530

surveys A research technique in which the investigator asks subjects questions about a particular issue, usually with structured questionnaires. 37

symbolic Bruner's term for the ability to represent, to consider possibilities. 406

syntax The grammar of a language; the system used to put words together to form sentences. 102

system performance standards Measures of how well a school system is doing its job. 368

task analysis The breaking of a task into its essential elements. 372

taxonomy of educational objectives Bloom's hierarchy of objectives, intended to clarify the terminology often used in formulating objectives. 379

teacher-constructed tests One method for assessing a student's learning or behavior that is developed by the teacher. 520

teaching Those actions designed to help one or more students learn. 6

telegraphic speech The use of two- or three-word phrases to convey more sophisticated meanings ("milk gone" means "my milk is all gone"). 105

terminal behavior Skinner's term for what students should be able to do after instruction. 411

test anxiety Anxiety generated by planning for and taking tests. 343

test-wiseness Knowing how to take tests; can be improved by teaching. 552

thinking frames Perkins' term for those representations that guide the thought process. 285

thinking skills Skills and strategies that enable students to adapt to constant change. 280

time-based recording The measurement through direct observation of the temporal aspects of behavior, such as duration, latency, and interresponse times. 539

time out A form of punishment in which a student loses something desirable for a period of time. 210

token economy A form of classroom management in which students receive tokens for desirable behavior. These may then be exchanged for something pleasurable. 459

TQM (Total Quality Management) Name for a conceptual framework for understanding the complexity of systems. 17

transductive reasoning Piaget's term for a preoperational child's reasoning technique: moving from particular to particular in a non-logical manner. 91

transition smoothness Teachers have no difficulty in handling activities and movement in their classes. 455

triad model Renzulli's enrichment model for working with the gifted. 159

triarchic theory of intelligence Sternberg's view of intelligence as consisting of three elements: componential, experiential, and contextual. 281

true-false questions Test questions that present subjects with statements that must be judged true or false. 525

t-score A standard score with a mean of 50 and a standard deviation of 10. 582

validity The extent to which a test measures what it is supposed to measure. 527

variable interval Term describing a schedule in which the time between reinforcements varies. 208

variable ratio Term describing a schedule in which the number of responses needed for reinforcement varies from one reinforcement to the next. 208

virtual reality (VR) A computer-generated environment that is three-dimensional and involves the user in real-time, multisensory interactions. 507

visually impaired Those individuals subject to any type of reduction in vision. 162

visually limited Those who have difficulty seeing under ordinary conditions but who can adapt with glasses. 163

vocabulary The extent to which students recognize, pronounce, and understand words. 384

vocational goals Those goals intended to enhance responsibility by focusing on the search for gainful employment. 371

weak performance assessment An assessment in which students are asked to apply their knowledge and skills by producing a product and then a teacher provides feedback in the form of a grade. 544

whole language A technique in which all language processes are studied together in a natural context (as a whole, and not as a series of possibly unrelated facts). 8, 107

withitness Teachers' knowledge and understanding of what is happening in their classrooms. 454

word processing Use of computer software for writing, editing, revising, formatting, and printing text. If combined with instruction in text production and revision, use of word processing may have positive effects on the quality of students' writing. 493

Yerkes-Dodson law The principle that ideal motivation for learning decreases in intensity with increasing task difficulty. 343

zone of proximal development The distance between a child's actual developmental level, as determined by independent problem solving, and that child's potential developmental level, as determined by problem solving under adult guidance or in collaboration with more capable peers. 54, 82

z-score A score that tells the distance of a student's raw score from the mean in standard deviation units; has a mean equal to 0 and a standard deviation equal to 1. 581

references

Achenbach, T., & Edelbrock, C. (1983). *Manual for the child behavior checklist and revised child behavior profile.* Burlington: University of Vermont, Department of Psychiatry.

Achenbach, T., McConaughy, S., and Howell, C. (1987). Child/adolescent behavioral and emotional problems: Implications of cross-informant correlations for situational specificity. *Psychological Bulletin, 101,* 213–232.

Adams, M. J. (1990). *Beginning to read: Thinking and learning about print.* Cambridge, MA: MIT Press.

Agne, K. (1992). Caring: The expert teacher's edge. *Educational Horizons, 70*(3), 120–124.

Ahlgren, A. (1993). Creating benchmarks for science education. *Educational Leadership, 50*(5), 46–49.

Ainsworth, M. (1979). Infant-mother attachment. *American Psychologist, 34,* 932–937.

Airasian, P. W. (1991). *Classroom assessment.* New York: McGraw-Hill.

Airasian, P. W. (1994). *Classroom assessment.* New York: McGraw-Hill.

Alberto, P., & Troutman, A. (1986). *Applied behavioral analysis for teachers.* Columbus, OH: Merrill.

Alderman, M. K. (1990, September). Motivation for at-risk students. *Educational Leadership,* pp. 27–30.

American Association of University Women (AAUW) Educational Foundation. (1992). *How schools shortchange girls: The AAUW report.* Washington, DC: Author.

American Educational Research Association. (1988). *Code of fair testing practices in education.* Washington, DC: Author.

American Federation of Teachers. (1990). *Standards for teacher competence in educational assessment of students.* Washington, DC: Author.

American Psychiatric Association. (1994). *Diagnostic and statistical manual of mental disorders* (4th ed.). Washington, DC: Author.

American Psychological Association. (1985). *Standards for educational and psychological testing.* Washington, DC: Author.

Ames, C. (1990). Motivation: What teachers need to know. *Teachers College Record, 91*(3), 409–421.

Anastasi, A. (1982). *Psychological testing.* New York: Macmillan.

Anderson, J. (1985). *Cognitive psychology and its implications.* San Francisco: W. H. Freeman.

Anderson, J. R., Boyle, C. F., & Rieser, B. J. (1985). Intelligent tutoring systems. *Science, 228,* 456–462.

Anderson, L. W., & Burns, R. B. (1989). *Research in classrooms: The study of teachers, teaching, and instruction.* New York: Pergamon.

Archbald, D. A., & Newmann, F. M. (1988). *Beyond standardized testing: Assessing authentic academic achievement in the secondary school.* Reston, VA: National Association of Secondary School Principals.

Armstrong, D., & Savage, T. (1983). *Secondary education: An introduction.* New York: Macmillan.

Asher, W. (1990). Educational psychology, research methodology, and meta-analysis. *Educational Psychologist, 25,* 143–158.

Atkinson, R. C., & Shiffrin, R. M. (1968). Human memory: A proposed system and its control processes. In K. W. Spence & J. T. Spence (Eds.), *The psychology of learning and motivation.* New York: Academic Press.

Ausubel, D. (1960). The use of advance organizers in the learning and retention of meaningful verbal material. *Journal of Educational Psychology, 51,* 267–272.

Ausubel, D. (1968). *Educational psychology: A cognitive view.* New York: Holt, Rinehart & Winston.

Ausubel, D. (1977). The facilitation of meaningful verbal learning in the classroom. *Educational Psychologist, 12,* 162–178.

Ausubel, D. (1980). Schemata, cognitive structures, and advance organizers: A reply to Anderson, Spiro, and Anderson. *American Educational Research Journal, 17,* 400–404.

Ausubel, D., Novak, J., & Hanesian, H. (1978). *Educational psychology: A cognitive view.* New York: Holt, Rinehart & Winston.

Baddeley, A. (1988). Cognitive psychology and human memory. Trends in Neurosciences, 11, 176–181.

Baddeley, A. (1990). *Human memory: Theory and practice.* Boston: Allyn & Bacon.

Bailey, D. B., & Wolery, W. (1984). *Teaching infants and preschoolers with handicaps.* Columbus, OH: Merrill.

Baillargeon, R. (1987). Object permanence in 3 1/2 and 4 month old infants. *Developmental Psychology, 23,* 655–664.

Baker, E. L., O'Neil, H. F., Jr., & Linn, R. L. (1993). Policy and validity prospects for performance-based assessment. *American Psychologist, 48,* 1210–1218.

Bales, J. (1990). Skinner gets award, ovations at APA talk. *The APA Monitor, 21,* 10, 1, 6.

Bandura, A. (1977). *Social learning theory.* Englewood Cliffs, NJ: Prentice Hall.

Bandura, A. (1981). Self-referent thought: A developmental analysis of self-efficacy. In J. Flavell & L. Ross (Eds.), *Social cognitive development.* New York: Cambridge University Press.

Bandura, A. (1986). *Social foundations of thought and action: A social-cognitive theory.* Englewood Cliffs, NJ: Prentice Hall.

Bandura, A. (1990). Self-regulation of motivation through anticipatory and self-reactive mechanisms. In R. Dienstbier (Ed.), *Nebraska symposium on motivation: Perspectives on motivation.* Lincoln, NE: University of Nebraska Press.

Bandura, A. (1993). Perceived self-efficacy in cognitive development and functioning. *Educational Psychologist, 28,* 117–148.

Bandura, A., Ross, D., & Ross, S. (1963). Imitation of film-mediated aggressive models. *Journal of Abnormal and Social Psychology, 66,* 3–11.

Banks, J. (1993a). Multicultural education: Characteristics and goals. In J. Banks & C. Banks (Eds.), *Multicultural education: Issues and perspectives.* Boston: Allyn & Bacon.

Banks, J. (1993b, September). Multicultural education: Development, dimensions, and challenges. *Phi Delta Kappan*, pp. 22–28.

Banks, J., & Banks, C. A. (1989). *Multicultural education: Issues and perspectives*. Boston: Allyn & Bacon.

Barker, R. G. (1968). *Ecological psychology*. Stanford: Stanford University Press.

Barker, R. G., & Associates. (1978). *Habitats, environments, and human behavior*. San Francisco: Jossey-Bass.

Barlow, D. H., Hayes, S. C., & Nelson, R. O. (1984). *The scientist practitioner: Research and accountability in clinical and educational settings*. New York: Pergamon.

Barlow, D. H., & Hersen, M. (1984). *Single case experimental designs: Strategies for studying behavior change* (2nd ed.). New York: Pergamon Press.

Barr, A., & Feigenbaum, E. A. (1982). Applications-oriented AI research: Education. In A. Barr & E. Feigenbaum (Eds.), *The handbook of artificial intelligence* (Vol. 2, pp. 229–235). Los Altos, CA: William Kaufmann.

Bartlett, F. C. (1932). *Remembering: A study in experimental and social psychology*. London: Cambridge University Press.

Beaver, J. F. (1990). *A profile of undergraduate educational technology competence: Are we preparing today's education graduates for teaching in the 90's?* Unpublished study conducted at the State University of New York, Buffalo, October, 1990. Cited in Hannafin, R. D., & Savenye, W. C. (1993).

Beck, I., & Carpenter, P. (1986). Cognitive approaches to understanding reading: Implications for instructional practice. *American Psychologist, 41*, 1098–1105.

Becker, H. J. (1991). How computers are used in United States schools: Basic data from the 1989 I.E.A. Computers in education survey. *Journal of Educational Computing Research, 7*(4), 385–406. *Becoming a nation of readers: The report of the commission on reading*. (1985). Washington, DC: National Academy of Education, National Institute of Education, and Center for the Study of Reading.

Belsky, J., & Rovine, M. (1988). Nonmaternal care in the first year of life and the security of infant-parent attachment. *Child Development, 59*, 157–167. *Benchmarks for Science Literacy*. (in press). Washington, DC: American Association for the Advancement of Science.

Benninga, J. (1988, February). An emerging synthesis in moral education. *Phi Delta Kappan, 69*, 415–418.

Bereiter, C., & Englemann, S. (1966). *Teaching disadvantaged children in the preschool*. Englewood Cliffs, NJ: Prentice Hall.

Berger, C. F., & Wolf, C. J. (1988). *Using technology to manage complexity: Water monitoring in local streams and rivers*. Paper presented at the International Association for Computing in Education. Cited in N. Roberts, G. Blakeslee, M. Brown, & C. Lenk (1990), *Integrating telecommunications into education*. Englewood Cliffs, NJ: Prentice Hall.

Berk, L. (1994). *Child development*. Boston: Allyn & Bacon.

Berliner, D. (1983). Developing conceptions of classroom environments. *Educational Psychologist, 18*, 1–13.

Berliner, D. C. (1988). The half-full glass: A review of research on teaching. In E. L. Meyer, G. V. Vergason, & R. L. Whelan (Eds.), *Effective instructional strategies for exceptional children* (pp. 7–31). Denver, CO: Love.

Billingsley, A. (1992). *Climbing Jacob's ladder: The enduring legacy of African American families*. New York: Simon & Schuster.

Bjorklund, D., & Bjorklund, B. (1992). *Looking at children*. Pacific Grove, CA: Brooks/Cole.

Blair, T. (1988). *Emerging patterns of teaching*. Columbus, OH: Merrill.

Blankenship, C. (1985). Using curriculum-based assessment data to make instructional decisions. *Exceptional Children, 52*, 233–238.

Block, J. (1983). Differential premises arising from differential socialization of the sexes: Some conjectures. *Child Development, 54*, 1335–1354.

Bloom, B. (1981). *All our children learning*. New York: McGraw-Hill.

Bloom, B. (1985). *Developing talent in young people*. New York: McGraw-Hill.

Bloom, B. (Ed.). (1956). *Taxonomy of educational objectives. Handbook 1: Cognitive domain*. New York: McKay.

Bloom, B., Madaus, G., & Hastings, J. T. (1981). *Evaluation to improve learning*. New York: McGraw-Hill.

Blumenfeld, P. (1992). Classroom learning and motivation: Clarifying and expanding goal theory. *Journal of Educational Psychology, 84*(3), 272–281.

Bobbitt, S., & Rohr, C. (1993). *What are the most serious problems in school?* Washington, DC: National Center for Educational Statistics.

Bonk, C. J. (1989). *The effects of generative and evaluative computerized prompting strategies on the development of children's writing awareness and performance*. Doctoral dissertation, University of Wisconsin–Madison.

Bonstingl, J. (1992, November). The quality revolution in education. *Phi Delta Kappan*, pp. 4–9.

Borich, G. (1992). *Effective teaching methods*. New York: Merrill.

Borland, J. (1989). *Planning and implementing programs for the gifted*. New York: Teachers College Press, Columbia University.

Bos, C., & Vaughn, S. (1988). *Strategies for teaching students with learning and behavior problems*. Boston: Allyn & Bacon.

Boulanger, F. D. (1981). Instruction and science learning: A quantitative synthesis. *Journal of Research in Science Teaching, 18*, 311–327.

Bower, G., & Hilgard, E. (1981). *Theories of learning*. New York: Appleton-Century-Crofts.

Bowlby, J. (1969). *Attachment*. New York: Basic Books.

Boyer, E. (1990). Introduction: Giving dignity to the teaching profession. In D. Dill & Associates (Eds.), *What teachers need to know*. San Francisco: Jossey-Bass.

Bragstad, B. J., & Stumpf, S. (1984). *A guidebook for teaching study skills and motivation*. Boston: Allyn & Bacon.

Brandt, R. (1990). On research on teaching: A conversation with Lee Shulman. *Educational Leadership, 49*(7), 14–19.

Brandt, R. (1992). On Deming and school quality: A conversation with Enid Brown. *Educational Leadership, 50*(3), 28–31.

Brandt, R. (1993). On teaching for understanding: A conversation with Howard Gardner. *Educational Leadership, 50*(7), 4–7.

Bransford, J., & Stein, B. (1984). *The IDEAL problem solver*. New York: Freeman.

Bransford, J. D., Sherwood, R., Vye, N., & Rieser, J. (1986). Teaching thinking and problem solving. *American Psychologist, 41*, 1078–1089.

Bransford, J. D., Sherwood, R. D., Hasselbring, T. S., Kinzer, C. K., & Williams, S. M. (1990). Anchored instruction: Why we need it and how technology can help. In D. Nix & R. Spiro (Eds.), *Cognition, education, and multimedia: Exploring ideas in high technology*. Hillsdale, NJ: Erlbaum.

Bransford, J. D., Vye, N. J., Kinzer, C., & Risko, V. (1990). Teaching thinking and content knowledge: Toward an integrated approach. In B. F. Jones & L. Idol (Eds.), *Dimensions of thinking and cognitive instruction* (pp. 381–413). Hillsdale, NJ: Erlbaum.

Braswell, L., & Bloomquist, M. L. (1991). *Cognitive-behavioral therapy with ADHD children*. New York: Guilford Press.

Brennan, E. C. (1991). *Improving elementary teachers' comfort and skill with instructional technology through school-based training*. Doctoral Dissertation, Nova University, Fort Lauderdale. (ERIC Document Reproduction Service No. ED 339 348)

Brislin, R. (Ed.). (1990). *Applied cross-cultural psychology*. Newbury Park, CA: Sage.

Brodinsky, B. (1993, March). How 'new' will the 'new' Whittle American school be? A case study in privatization. *Phi Delta Kappan*, pp. 540–543, 546–547.

Bronson, M., Pierson, D., & Tivnan, T. (1984). The effects of early education on children's competence in elementary school. *Evaluation Review, 8*, 615–627.

Brookhart, S., & Freeman, D. (1992). Characteristics of entering teacher candidates. *Review of Educational Research, 62*(1), 37–60.

Brookover, W. B., Beady, C., Flood, P., Schweitzer, J., & Weisenbaker, J. (1979). *School social systems and student achievement*. New York: Praeger.

Brooks, D., & Kann, M. (1993). What makes character education programs work? *Educational Leadership, 51*(3), 19–21.

Brophy, J. (1981, Spring). Teacher praise: A functional analysis. *Review of Educational Research, 51*, 5–32.

Brophy, J. (1983a). Fostering student learning and motivation in the elementary school classroom. In S. Paris, G. Olson, & H. Stevenson (Eds.), *Learning and motivation in the classroom*. Hillsdale, NJ: Erlbaum.

Brophy, J. (1987a, October). Synthesis of research on strategies for motivating students to learn. *Educational Leadership*, pp. 40–48.

Brophy, J. (1987b). Teacher influences on student achievement. *American Psychologist, 41*, 1069–1077.

Brophy, J., & Good, T. (1986). Teacher behavior and student achievement. In M. Wittrock (Ed.), *Handbook of research on teaching*. New York: Macmillan.

Brown, A., & Campione, J. (1986). Psychological theory and the study of learning disabilities. *American Psychologist, 41*, 1059–1068.

Brown, D. S. (1988). Twelve middle-school teachers' planning. *The Elementary School Journal, 89*, 69–87.

Brown, J. S., & Burton, R. R. (1978). Diagnostic models for procedural bugs in basic mathematical skills. *Cognitive Science, 2*, 153–192.

Brown, R. (1988). Model youth: Excelling despite the odds. *Ebony, 43*, 40–48.

Brown, R., & Lennenberg, E. (1954). A study in language and cognition. *Journal of Abnormal and Social Psychology, 44*, 454–462.

Bruder, I. (1989). Whittle moves to install educational network in schools nationwide. *Electronic Learning, 9*(1), 10.

Bruner, J. (1960). *The process of education*. Cambridge, MA: Harvard University Press.

Bruner, J. (1966a). *Studies in cognitive growth*. New York: Wiley.

Bruner, J. (1966b). *Toward a theory of instruction*. New York: John Wiley & Sons.

Bruner, J. (1971). *The relevance of education*. New York: Norton.

Bruner, J. (1983). *In search of mind*. New York: Harper & Row.

Bruner, J. (1986). *Actual minds, possible worlds*. Cambridge, MA: Harvard University Press.

Bruner, J. (1990). *Acts of meaning*. Cambridge, MA: Harvard University Press.

Bruner, J., & Goodman, C. (1947). Value and need as organizing factors in perception. *Journal of Abnormal and Social Psychology, 42*, 33–44.

Bruner, J., Goodnow, J., & Austin, G. (1956). *A study of thinking*. New York: Wiley.

Bullinger, A., & Chatillon, J. (1983). Recent theory and research of the Genevan school. In P. Mussen (Ed.), *Handbook of child psychology*. New York: Wiley.

Burke, J. (1991). Teenagers, clothes, and gang violence. *Educational Leadership, 49*(1), 11–13.

Caine, R., & Caine, G. (1990). Understanding a brain-based approach to learning and teaching. *Educational Leadership, 48*, 66–70.

Calfee, R., & Drum, P. (1986). Research on teaching reading. In M. Wittrock (Ed.), *Handbook of research on teaching*. New York: Macmillan.

Callahan, J., Clark, L., & Kellough, R. (1992). *Teaching in the middle and secondary schools*. New York: Macmillan.

Calvert, P. (1986). *Responses to guidelines for developmentally appropriate practice for young children and Montessori*. Paper presented at the Annual Meeting of the National Association for the Education of Young Children, Washington, DC.

Camp, B. W., & Bosh, M. A. (1981). *Think aloud*. Champaign, IL: Research Press.

Canter, L., & Hausner, L. (1987). *Homework without tears: A parents' guide for motivating children to do homework and to succeed in school*. New York: Harper & Row.

Capelli, C., Nakagawa, N., & Madden, C. (1990). How children understand sarcasm: The role of context and intonation. *Child Development, 61*, 1824–1841.

Carey, S. (1986). Cognitive science and science education. *American Psychologist, 41*, 1123–1130.

Carnine, D. (1991). Curricular interventions for teaching higher order thinking to all students: Introduction to the special series. *Journal of Learning Disabilities, 24*, 261–269.

Carroll, J. (1963). A model of school learning. *Teachers College Record, 64*, 723–733.

Casas, J. M., Furlong, M., Solberg, U. S., & Carranza, O. (1990). An examination of individual factors associated with the academic success and failure of Mexican-Americans and Anglo students. In D. Barona & E. E. Garcia (Eds.), *Children at risk: Poverty, minority status, and other issues in educational equity* (pp. 103–118). Washington, DC: National Association of School Psychologists.

Case, R. (1985). *Intellectual development: Birth to adulthood*. New York: Academic Press.

Ceci, S., & Bronfenbrenner, U. (1991). On the demise of everyday memory: "The rumors of my death are much exaggerated" (Mark Twain). *American Psychologist, 46*, 27–31.

Chance, P. (1992, November). The rewards of learning. *Phi Delta Kappan*, pp. 200–207.

Chaney, C. (1990). Evaluating the whole language approach to language arts: The pros and cons. *Language, Speech, and Hearing Services in Schools, 21*(4), 244–249.

Chard, D., Smith, S., & Sugai, G. (1992). Packaged discipline programs: A consumer's guide. In J. Marr & G. Tindal (Eds.), *The Oregon Conference Monograph: 1992* (pp. 19–26). Eugene: University of Oregon Press.

Chase, W., & Simon, H. (1973). Perception in chess. *Cognitive Psychology, 4*, 55–81.

Chen, M. (1985). A macro-focus on microcomputers: Eight utilization and effects issues. In M. Chen & W. Paisley (Eds.), *Children and microcomputers* (pp. 37–58). Beverly Hills, CA: Sage.

Chen, M. (1986). Gender and computers: The beneficial effects of experience on attitudes. *Journal of Educational Computing Research, 2*(3), 265–282.

Children's Defense Fund. (1975). *School supervisors: Are they helping children?* Washington, DC: Author.

Children's Television Workshop. (1990). What research indicates about the educational effects of "Sesame Street." New York: Children's Television Workshop. (ERIC Document Reproduction Service No. ED 340 498)

Choi, S. (1991). Children's answers to yes-no questions: A developmental study in English, French, and Korean. *Developmental Psychology, 27*(3), 407–420.

Chomsky, N. (1965). *The development of syntax in children 5 to 10 years*. Cambridge, MA: MIT.

Chomsky, N. (1985). *Reflections on language*. New York: Pantheon.

Christenson, S. L., & Conoley, J. C. (Eds.). (1992). *Home-school collaboration: Enhancing children's academic and social competence*. Silver Springs, MD: National Association of School Psychologists.

Clabby, J. F., & Elias, M. J. (1987). *Teaching your child decision making*. Garden City, NY: Doubleday.

Clark, C., & Peterson, P. (1986). Teachers' thought processes. In M. Wittrock (Ed.), *Handbook of research on teaching*. New York: Macmillan.

Clark, F., & Clark, C. (1989). *Hassle-free homework: A six-week plan for parents and children to take the pain out of homework.* New York: Doubleday.

Clarke, V. A. (1985). When attitudes count. *Proceedings of the LOGO/85 Conference* (pp. 73–74). Boston: MIT.

Clarke-Stewart, A. (1993). *Daycare.* Cambridge, MA: Harvard University Press.

Clements, D. H., & Gullo, D. F. (1984). Effects of computer programming on young children's cognition. *Journal of Educational Psychology, 76,* 1051–1058.

Clements, D. H., & Nastasi, B. K. (1992). Computers and early childhood education. In M. Gettinger, S. N. Elliott, & T.R. Kratochwill (Eds.), *Preschool and early childhood treatment directions: Advances in school psychology* (pp. 187–246). Hillsdale, NJ: Erlbaum.

Coalition of Essential Schools. (1990). Performances and exhibitions: The demonstration of mastery. *Horace, 6,* 1–9 .

Cochran-Smith, M. (1991). Word processing and writing in elementary classrooms: A critical review of related literature. *Review of Educational Research, 61*(1), 107–155. *Code of fair testing practices in education.* (1988). Washington, DC: Joint Committee on Testing Practices.

Cognition & Technology Group at Vanderbilt. (1990). Anchored instruction and its relationship to situated cognition. *Educational Researcher, 19*(6), 2–10.

Cohen, R. (1992). *A lifetime of teaching: Portraits of five veteran high school teachers.* New York: Teachers College Press.

Colby, A., Kohlberg, L., Gibbs, J., & Lieberman, A. (1983). A longitudinal study of moral judgment. *Monographs of the Society for Research in Child Development, 48* (Serial No. 200).

Cole, M., & Scribner, S. (1974). *Culture and thought.* New York: Wiley.

Collins, M., & Carnine, D. (1988). Evaluating the field test process by comparing two versions of a reasoning skills CAI program. *Journal of Learning Disabilities, 21,* 375–379.

Collis, B. A., & Williams, R. L. (1987). Differences in adolescents' attitudes toward computers and selected school subjects. *Journal of Educational Research, 8*(1), 17–27.

Comer, J. (1988). Educating poor minority children. *Scientific American, 259,* 42–48.

Conway, M. (1991). In defense of everyday memory. *American Psychologist, 46,* 19–26.

Cook, T. D. (1974). The potential and limitations of secondary evaluations. In M. W. Apple, H. C. Subkoviak, & J. R. Lufler (Eds.), *Educational evaluation: Analysis and responsibilities.* Berkeley, CA: McCutchan.

Cooledge, N. (1992). Rescuing your rookie teachers. *Principal, 72*(2), 28–29.

Cooper, H. (1989a). *Homework.* White Plains, NY: Longman.

Cooper, H. (1989b, November). Synthesis of research on homework. *Educational Leadership,* pp. 85–91.

Cooper, J. J., Heron, T. E., & Heward, W. L. (1987). *Applied behavior analysis.* Columbus, OH: Merrill.

Corkill, A. J., Glover, J. A., Bruning, R. H., & Krug, D. (1989). Advance organizers: Retrieval hypotheses. *Journal of Educational Psychology, 81,* 43–51.

Corno, L. (1992). Encouraging students to take responsibility for learning and performance. *The Elementary School Journal, 93*(1), 69–83.

Corno, L., & Snow, R. (1986). Adapting teaching to individual differences. In M. Wittrock (Ed.), *Handbook of research on teaching.* New York: Macmillan.

Cosden, M., & Haring, T. (1992). Cooperative learning in the classroom: Contingencies, group interactions, and students with special needs. *Journal of Behavioral Education, 2*(1), 53–71.

Costa, A. (Ed.). (1985). *Developing minds.* Alexandria, VA: Association for Supervision and Curriculum Development.

Coutinho, M., & Malouf, D. (1992, November). *Performance assessment and children with disabilities: Issues and possibilities.* Washington, DC: Division of Innovation and Development, U.S. Department of Education.

Craig, G. (1992). *Human development.* Englewood Cliffs, NJ: Prentice-Hall.

Craik, F. I., & Lockhart, R. S. (1972). Levels of processing: A framework for memory research. *Journal of Verbal Learning and Verbal Behavior, 11,* 671–684.

Craske, M. L. (1985). Improving persistence through observational learning and attribution retraining. *British Journal of Educational Psychology, 55,* 138–147.

Cronbach, L. (1970). *Essentials of psychological testing.* New York: Harper & Row.

Cuban, L. (1989). Neoprogressive visions and organizational realities. *Harvard Educational Review, 59*(2), 217–222.

Dacey, J. (1989a). Discriminating characteristics of the families of highly creative adolescents. The Journal of Creative Behavior, 23, 263–273.

Dacey, J. (1989b). *Fundamentals of creativity.* Lexington, MA: D.C. Heath/Lexington Books.

Dacey, J. (1989c). Peak periods of creative growth across the lifespan. *The Journal of Creative Behavior, 23*(4), 224–247.

Daiute, C. (1985). *Writing and computers.* Reading, MA: Addison-Wesley.

Daiute, C. (1986). Physical and cognitive factors in revising: Insights from studies with computers. *Research in the Teaching of English, 20,* 141–159.

Darling-Hammond, L. (1994). Performance-based assessment and educational equity. *Harvard Educational Review, 64*(1), 5–30.

Dash, U., & Mohanty, A. (1992, July). Relationship of reading comprehension with metalinguistic awareness. *Social Science International, 8*(1), 5–13.

Davidson, J. (1990). Intelligence recreated. *Educational Psychologist, 25,* 337–354.

deBono, E. (1984). *The art and science of success.* Boston: Little, Brown.

deBono, E. (1985). The CoRT thinking program. In A. Costa (Ed.), *Developing minds.* Alexandria, VA: Association for Supervision and Curriculum Development.

de Charms, R. (1976). *Enhancing motivation: Change in the classroom.* New York: Irvington.

Deci, E., & Ryan, R. (1990). A motivational approach to self: Integration in personality. In R. Dienstbier (Ed.), *Nebraska Symposium on Motivation: Perspectives on motivation.* Lincoln, NE: University of Nebraska Press.

deCuevas, J. (1990). "No, she holded them loosely." *Harvard Magazine, 93,* 60–67.

de Jong, T., & Ferguson-Hassler, M. (1986). Cognitive structures of good and poor novice problem solvers in physics. *Journal of Educational Psychology, 78,* 279–288.

Delclos, V. R. (1986). An introduction to programming in LOGO. In C. K. Kinzer, R. D. Sherwood, & J. D. Bransford (Eds.), *Computer strategies for education: Foundations and content-area applications* (pp. 81–101). Columbus, OH: Merrill.

Deno, S. (1985). Curriculum-based measurement: The emerging alternative. *Exceptional Children, 52,* 219–232.

Department of Engineering & Public Policy, H. John Heinz III School of Public Policy and Management, & Department of Social and Decision Sciences. (1993). *The Internet in K–12 education.* Pittsburgh, PA: The Internet in K-12 Project Team, Carnegie Mellon University.

Derry, S. J. (1989, December/January). Putting learning strategies to work. *Educational Leadership,* pp. 4–10.

Diener, C., & Dweck, C. (1978). An analysis of learned helplessness: Continuous changes in performance, strategy, and achievement cognitions following failure. *Journal of Personality and Social Psychology, 36,* 451–462.

Diener, C., & Dweck, C. (1980). An analysis of learned helplessness: 2. The processing of success. *Journal of Personality and Social Psychology, 39,* 940–952.

Dill, D., & Associates. (1990). *What teachers need to know.* San Francisco: Jossey-Bass.

Dobbin, J. (1984). *How to take a test: Doing your best*. Princeton, NJ: Educational Testing Service.

Donnellan, A. M., & LaVigna, G. W. (1990). Myths about punishment. In A. C. Repp & N. N. Singh (Eds.), *Perspectives on the use of nonaversive and aversive interventions for persons with developmental disabilities* (pp. 33–57). Sycamore, IL: Sycamore.

Doris, J. (Ed.). (1991). *The suggestibility of children's recollections: Implications for eyewitness testimony*. Washington, DC: American Psychological Association.

Doyle, W. (1983). Paradigms for research on teacher effectiveness. In L. S. Shulman (Ed.), *Review of Research in Education* (Vol. 5). Itasca, IL: F. E. Peacock.

Doyle, W. (1986). Classroom organization and management. In M. Wittrock (Ed.), *Handbook of research on teaching*. New York: Macmillan.

Dreikurs, R., Grunwald, B., & Pepper, F. (1971). *Maintaining sanity in the classroom*. New York: Harper & Row.

Dresher, M., & Zenge, S. (1990). Using metalinguistic awareness in the first grade to predict reading achievement in third and fifth grades. *Journal of Educational Research, 84*(1), 13–21.

Dreyfus, H. L. (1979). *What computers can't do: The limits of artificial intelligence*. New York: Harper & Row.

Dukes, W. F. (1965). N-1. *Psychological Bulletin, 64*, 74–79.

Dunn, J. (1983). Sibling relationships in early childhood. *Child Development, 54*, 787–811.

Dunn, R. (1987). Research on instructional environments: Implications for student achievement and attitudes. *Professional School Psychology, 3*, 43–52.

Dunn, R. (1990). Rita Dunn answers questions on learning styles. *Educational Leadership, 48*(2), 15–18.

Dweck, C. (1990). Self-theories and goals: Their role in motivation, personality, and development. In R. Dienstbier (Ed.), *Nebraska Symposium on Motivation: Perspectives on motivation*. Lincoln, NE: University of Nebraska Press.

Dweck, C., & Repucci, N. D. (1973). Learned helplessness and reinforcement of responsibility in children. *Journal of Personality and Social Psychology, 25*, 109–116.

Ebbinghaus, H. (1885). On memory. New York: Teachers College Press.

Edelbrock, C. (1983). Problems and issues in using rating scales to assess child personality and psychopathology. *School Psychology Review, 12* 253–299.

Elkind, D. (1981). *The hurried child*. Reading, MA: Addison-Wesley.

Elliott, S. N., & Gresham, F. M. (1989). Teacher and self-ratings of popular and rejected adolescent boys' behavior. *Journal of Psychoeducational Assessment, 7*, 308–322.

Elliott, S. N., & Gresham, F. M. (1991). *Social skills intervention guide*. Circle Pines, MN: American Guidance Service.

Elliott, S. N., Piersel, W., Witt, J. C., Argulewicz, E., Gutkin, T. B., & Galvin, G. (1985). Three year stability of WISC-R IQs for handicapped children from three racial/ethnic groups. *Journal of Psychoeducational Assessment, 3*, 233–244.

Ellis, H., & Hunt, R. (1989). *Fundamentals of human memory and cognition*. Madison, WI: Brown & Benchmark.

Ellis, H., & Hunt, R. (1993). *Fundamentals of cognitive psychology* (5th ed.). Madison, WI: Brown & Benchmark.

Ely, D. P. (1993). Computers in schools and universities in the United States of America. *Educational Technology, 33*, 53–57.

Emmer, E., Evertson, C., & Anderson, L. (1980). Effective classroom management at the beginning of the school year. *Elementary School Journal, 80*, 219–231.

Emmer, E., Evertson, C., Sanford, J., Clements, B., & Worsham, M. (1984). *Classroom management for secondary teachers*. Englewood Cliffs, NJ: Prentice Hall.

Engelhard, G., & Monsaas, J. (1988). Grade level, gender, and school-related curiosity in urban elementary schools. *Journal of Educational Research, 82*(1), 22–26.

Ennis, R. (1987). A taxonomy of critical thinking dispositions and abilities. In J. Barron & R. Sternberg (Eds.), *Teaching thinking skills*. New York: Freeman.

Enright, R. D., & the Human Development Study Group. (1991). The moral development of forgiveness. In W. Kurtines & J. Gewitz (Eds.), *Handbook of moral behavior and development* (Vol. 1, pp. 123–152). Hillsdale, NJ: Erlbaum.

Entwiste, D., & Alexander, K. (1990). Beginning school math competence: Minority and majority comparisons. *Child Development, 61*, 454–471.

Epstein, J. (1988). Effects on student achievement of teachers' practices of parent involvement. In S. Silvern (Ed.), *Literacy through family, community, and school interaction*. Greenwich, CT: JAI Press.

Erikson, E. (1950). *Childhood and society*. New York: Norton.

Erikson, E. (1968). *Identity: Youth and crisis*. New York: Norton.

Esveldt-Dawson, K., & Kazdin, A. E. (1982). *How to use self-control*. Lawrence, KS: H & H Enterprises.

Evertson, C., & Emmer, E. (1982). Effective management at the beginning of the school year in junior high classes. *Journal of Educational Research, 74*, 485–498.

Evertson, C., & Green, J. (1986). Observation as inquiry and method. In M. Wittrock (Ed.), *Handbook of research on teaching*. New York: Macmillan.

Fagot, B. (1985). Changes in thinking about early sex role development. *Developmental Review, 5*, 83–98.

Fagot, B., & Hagan, R. (1991). Observations of parent reactions to sex-stereotyped behaviors: Age and sex effects. *Child Development, 62*, 617–628.

Fagot, B., Leinbach, M., & O'Boyle, C. (1992). Gender labeling, gender stereotyping, and parenting behaviors. *Developmental Psychology, 28*, 225–230.

Falkof, L., & Moss, J. (1984). When teachers tackle thinking skills. *Educational Leadership, 42*, 4–10.

Fantz, R. (1961). The origin of form perception. *Scientific American, 204*, 66–72.

Fantz, R. (1963). Pattern vision in newborn infants. *Science, 140*, 296–297.

Fawson, E. C., & Smellie, D. C. (1990). Technology transfer: A model for public education. *Educational Technology, 30*, 19–25.

Ferrington, G., & Loge, K. (1992). Virtual reality: A new learning environment. *The Computing Teacher, 19*(7), 16–19.

Ferster, C. B., & Skinner, B. F. (1957). *Schedules of reinforcement*. New York: Appleton-Century-Crofts.

Feuerstein, R. (1980). *Instrumental enrichment*. Baltimore: University Park Press.

Field, D. (1987). A review of preschool conservation training: An analysis of analyses. *Developmental Review, 7*, 210–251.

Fillmore, L., & Valadez, C. (1986). Teaching bilingual learners. In M. Wittrock (Ed.), *Handbook of research on teaching*. New York: Macmillan.

Finch, C. L. (Ed.). (1991). *Educational performance assessment: The free-response alternative*. Chicago: Riverside.

First, J. (1988). Immigrant students in U.S. public schools: Challenges with solutions. *Phi Delta Kappan, 70*, 205–210.

First, J. M., & Carrera, J. W. (Eds.). (1988). *New voices: Immigrant students in U.S. public schools*. Boston: The National Coalition of Advocates for Students.

Fischer, K., & Silvern, L. (1985). Stages and individual differences in cognitive development. In M. Rosenzweig & P. Porter (Eds.), *Annual review of psychology*. Palo Alto: Annual Reviews.

Flavell, J. (1985). *Cognitive development*. Englewood Cliffs, NJ: Prentice Hall.

Flavell, J. H. (1963). *The developmental psychology of Jean Piaget*. Princeton: Van Nostrand.

Flinders, D. (1989, May). Does the "Art of Teaching" have a future? *Educational Leadership*, pp. 16–22.

Ford, M. (1992). *Motivating humans*. Newbury Park, CA: Sage.

Foster, S. (1986). Ten principles of learning revised in accordance with cognitive psychology: With implications for teaching. *Educational Psychologist, 21*, 235–243.

Fouts, J., & Myers, R. (1992). Classroom environments and middle school students' views of science. *Journal of Educational Research, 85*(6), 356–361.

Fox, L. H., & Washington, J. (1985). Programs for the gifted and talented: Past, present, and future. In F. D. Horowitz & M. O'Brien (Eds.), *The gifted and talented*. Washington, DC: American Psychological Association.

Fraenkel, J. R., & Wallen, N. E. (1990). *How to design and evaluate research in education*. New York: McGraw-Hill.

Frasier, M. (1989). Poor and minority students can be gifted, too. *Educational Leadership, 46*, 16–18.

Frederiksen, N. (1984). Implications of cognitive theory for instruction in problem solving. *Review of Educational Research, 54*, 363–408.

Frisbie, D. (1988). NCME instructional module on reliability of scores from teacher-made tests. *Educational Measurement, 7*, 25–33.

Fromberg, D., & Driscoll, M. (1985). *The successful classroom*. New York: Teachers College Press.

Gage, N. L. (1977). The scientific basis of the art of teaching. New York: Teachers College Press.

Gage, N. L. (1985). *Hard gains in the soft sciences: The case of pedagogy*. Bloomington, IN: Phi Delta Kappan.

Gagne, R., & Briggs, L. (1979). *Principles of instructional design*. New York: Holt, Rinehart & Winston.

Gagne, R., Briggs, L., & Wager, W. (1988). *Principles of instructional design* (3rd ed.). New York: Holt, Rinehart & Winston.

Gagne, R., & Driscoll, M. (1988). *Essentials of learning for instruction* (2nd ed.). Englewood Cliffs, NJ: Prentice Hall.

Garbarino, J., & Benn, J. (1992). The ecology of childbearing and childrearing. In J. Garbarino (Ed.), *Children and families in the social environment*. New York: Aldine.

Garcia Coll, C. (1990). Developmental outcome of minority infants: A process-oriented look into our beginnings. *Child Development, 61*, 270–289.

Gardner, H. (1982). *Developmental psychology*. Boston: Little, Brown.

Gardner, H. (1983). *Frames of mind*. New York: Basic Books.

Gardner, H. (1985). *The mind's new science*. New York: Basic Books.

Gardner, H. (1987). Developing the spectrum of human intelligences. *Harvard Educational Review, 57*, 187–193.

Gardner, H. (1991). *The unschooled mind*. New York: Basic Books.

Garger, S. (1990). Is there a link between learning style and neurophysiology? *Educational Leadership, 48*, 63–65.

Garibaldi, A. (1992). Educating and motivating African American males to succeed. *Journal of Negro Education, 61*(4), 4–11.

Garman, N., & Hazi, H. (1988). Is there life after Madeline Hunter? *Phi Delta Kappan, 69*, 669–672.

Gary, L., & Booker, C. (1992). Empowering African Americans to achieve academic success. *Urban Education*, 51–55.

Gawronski, J. D. (1991, October). National assessment: Ready or not—here it comes. *Thrust for Educational Leadership*, pp. 12–16.

Gelfand, D. M., & Hartmann, D. P. (1986). *Child behavior analysis and therapy* (2nd ed.). New York: Pergamon.

Gelman, R., & Baillargeon, P. (1983). A review of some Piagetian concepts. In P. Mussen (Ed.), *Handbook of child psychology*. New York: Wiley.

Genshaft, J. (1991). The gifted adolescent in perspective. In M. Birely & J. Genshaft (Eds.), *Understanding the gifted adolescent: Educational development and multicultural issues* (pp. 259–262). New York: Teachers College Press.

Gentry, D. (1989). *Teacher-made test construction*. Paper presented at the annual meeting of the Mid-South Educational Research Association, Little Rock, AR.

Gettinger, M. (1988). Methods of proactive classroom management. *School Psychology Review, 17*, 227–242.

Gettinger, M. (1990). Best practices in increasing academic learning time. In A. Thomas & J. Grimes (Eds.), *Best practices in school psychology-II* (pp. 393–405). Washington, DC: National Association of School Psychologists.

Gibbons, M. (1974). Walkabout: Searching for the right of passage from childhood and school. *Phi Delta Kappan, 9*, 596–602.

Gibbons, M. (1984). Walkabout ten years later: Searching for a renewed vision of education. *Phi Delta Kappan, 9*, 591–600.

Giddings, L. (1992). Literature-based reading instruction: An analysis. *Reading Research and Instruction, 31* (2), 18–30.

Gilligan, C. (1977). In a different voice: Women's conception of self and of morality. *Harvard Educational Review, 47*, 481–517.

Gilligan, C. (1982). *In a different voice*. Cambridge, MA: Harvard University Press.

Gilligan, C., Ward, J., & Taylor, J. (1988). *Mapping the moral domain*. Cambridge, MA: Harvard University Press.

Gilman, D. (1992). Correlates of a defective school. *Contemporary Education, 53*(2), 89–90.

Ginsberg, H., & Opper, S. (1988). *Piaget's theory of intellectual development*. Englewood Cliffs, NJ: Prentice-Hall.

Glaser, R. (1991). The reemergence of learning theory within instructional research. *American Psychologist, 45*, 29–39.

Glasnapp, D., & Poggio, J. (1985). *Essentials of statistical analysis for the behavioral sciences*. Columbus, OH: Merrill.

Glass, A., Holyoak, K., & Santa, J. (1987). *Cognition*. Reading, MA: Addison-Wesley.

Glass, G., McGaw, V., & Smith, M. L. (1981). *Meta-analysis in social research*. Beverly Hills: Sage.

Glasser, W. (1986). *Control theory in the classroom*. New York: Harper & Row.

Gleason, J. B. (1985). Studying language development. In J. B. Gleason (Ed.), *The development of language*. Columbus, OH: Merrill.

Glover, J. A., & Ronning, R. R. (1987). Introduction. In J. A. Glover & R. R. Ronning (Eds.), *Historical foundations of educational psychology* (pp. 3–15). New York: Plenum Press.

Glover, J. A., Ronning, R. R., & Bruning, R. H. (1990). *Cognitive psychology for teachers*. New York: Macmillan.

Goldstein, A. P. (1988). *The prepare curriculum: Teaching prosocial competencies*. Champaign, IL: Research Press.

Good, T. (1990). Building the knowledge base of teaching. In D. Dill & Associates (Eds.), *What teachers need to know*. San Francisco: Jossey-Bass.

Good, T., Slavings, R., Harel, K., & Emerson, H. (1987). A study of question asking in K–12 classrooms. *Sociology of Education, 60*(3), 181–199.

Goodenow, C. (1992, April). *School motivation, engagement, and sense of belonging among urban adolescent students*. Paper presented at the annual meeting of the American Educational Research Association, San Francisco.

Goodlad, J. (1984). *A place called school*. New York: McGraw-Hill.

Goodlad, J. (1991). Why we need a complete redesign of teacher education. *Educational Leadership, 49*(3), 4–10.

Goodman, K. (1986). *What's whole in whole language?* Portsmouth, NH: Heinemann.

Goodman, Y. (1989). Roots of the whole language movement. *Elementary School Journal, 90*, 113–127.

Goodnow, J. (1990). The socialization of cognition. In J. Stigler, R. Shweder, & G. Herdt (Eds.), *Cultural psychology*. New York: Cambridge University Press.

Gould, S. (1981). *The mismeasure of man.* Cambridge: Harvard University Press.

Grady, M. (1984). *Teaching and brain research.* New York: Longman.

Graham, S., & Barker, G. (1990). The down side of help: An attributional-developmental analysis of helping behavior as a low-ability cue. *Journal of Educational Psychology, 82,* 7–14.

Grant, C., & Sleeter, C. (1993). Race, class, gender, and disability in the classroom. In J. Banks & C. Banks (Eds.), *Multicultural education: Issues and perspectives.* Boston: Allyn & Bacon.

Greene, L. (1987). *Learning disabilities and your child.* New York: Fawcett Columbine.

Greenfield, P. (1966). On culture and conservation. In J. Bruner, R. Oliver, & P. Greenfield (Eds.), *Studies in cognitive growth.* New York: Wiley.

Greer, R. D. (in press). The teacher as strategic scientist: A solution to the educational crisis? *Behavior and Social Issues.*

Gresham, F. M. (1985). Behavior disorder assessment: Conceptual, dysfunctional, and practical considerations. *School Psychology Review, 14,* 495–509.

Gresham, F. M., & Elliott, S. N. (1990). *Social skills rating system.* Circle Pines, MN: American Guidance Service.

Gresham, F. M., Evans, S., & Elliott, S. N. (1988). Self-efficacy differences among mildly handicapped, gifted, and nonhandicapped students. *The Journal of Special Education, 22,* 231–241.

Griswold, P. (1990). Assessing relevance and reliability to improve the quality of teacher-made tests. *NASSP Bulletin, 74,* 18–24.

Gronlund, N. (1985). *Measurement and evaluation in learning.* New York: Macmillan.

Gronlund, N. E., & Linn, R. L. (1990). *Measurement and evaluation in teaching* (6th ed.). New York: Macmillan.

Grossen, B., & Carnine, D. (1990). Diagramming a logical strategy: Effects in difficult problem types and transfer. *Learning Disability Quarterly, 13,* 168–182.

Grossman, H. (1983). *Classification in mental retardation.* Washington, DC: American Association on Mental Deficiency.

Grossman, H. (1984). *Educating Hispanic students: Cultural implications for instruction, classroom management, counseling, and assessment.* Springfield, IL: Charles C Thomas.

Grossman, H. (1990). *Trouble-free teaching.* Mountain View, CA: Mayfield.

Grossnickle, D. R., & Thiel, W. B. (1988). *Promoting effective student motivation in school and classrooms: A practitioner's perspective.* Reston, VA: National Association of Secondary School Principals.

Guilford, J. (1967). *The nature of human intelligence.* New York: McGraw-Hill.

Gump, P. (1982). School settings and their keeping. In D. L. Duke (Ed.), *Helping teachers manage classrooms.* Alexandria, VA: Association for Supervision and Curriculum Development.

Guskey, T. (1986, Winter). Bloom's mastery learning: A legacy of effectiveness. *Educational Horizons,* pp. 80–86.

Hakuta, K. (1986). Mirror of language: The debate of bilingualism. New York: Basic Books.

Hale-Benson, J. (1986). *Black children: Their roots, culture, and learning styles.* Baltimore: The Johns Hopkins University Press.

Halford, G. S. (1989). Reflection on 25 years of Piagetian cognitive developmental psychology: 1963–1988. *Human Development, 32,* 325–357.

Hallahan, D., & Kauffman, J. (1988). *Exceptional children: Introduction to special education.* Englewood Cliffs, NJ: Prentice Hall.

Halle, J. W. (1985). Enhancing social competence through language: An experimental analysis of a practical procedure for teachers. *Topics in Early Childhood Special Education, 4,* 77–92.

Hamachek, D. (1987). *Encounters with the self.* New York: Holt, Rinehart & Winston.

Hammill, D. D. (1990). On defining learning disabilities: An emerging consensus. *Journal of Learning Disabilities, 23,* 74–84.

Hammill, D., Leigh, J., McNutt, G., & Larsen, S. (1981). A new definition of learning disabilities. *Learning Disability Quarterly, 4,* 336–342.

Hannafin, R. D., & Savenye, W. C. (1993). Technology in the classroom: The teacher's new role and resistance to it. *Educational Technology, 33,* 26–31.

Harel, I., & Papert, S. (1991). *Constructionism.* Norwood, NJ: Ablex.

Haring, N., & McCormick, L. (1986). *Exceptional children and youth.* Columbus, OH: Merrill.

Harre, R., & Lamb, R. (1983). *The encyclopedic dictionary of psychology.* Cambridge, MA: MIT Press.

Hart, L. (1983). *Human brain and human learning.* New York: Longman.

Hauser-Cram, P., Pierson, D., Klein Walker, D., & Tivnan, T. (1991). *Early education in the public schools.* San Francisco: Jossey-Bass.

Hayes, J. (1989). *The complete problem solver.* Philadelphia: Franklin Institute Press.

Hayes, L. (1992). Building schools for tomorrow. *Phi Delta Kappan, 73*(5), 412–413.

Hecht, D., & Tittle, C. (1992, April). *Affective and motivational characteristics of 60 urban JHS math classrooms: A class-level analysis of student beliefs in three instructional activity settings.* Paper presented at the American Educational Research Association, San Francisco.

Hembree, H. (1988). Correlates, causes, effects, and treatment of test anxiety. *Review of Educational Research, 58,* 41–77.

Hendrick, J. (1992). *The whole child.* New York: Macmillan.

Herbert, B. (1993, December 1). America's job disaster. *New York Times,* Section A, p. 23.

Hergenhahn, B. R. (1988). *An introduction to theories of learning.* Englewood Cliffs, NJ: Prentice Hall.

Hetherington, E. M. (1991). The role of individual differences and family relationships in children's coping with divorce and remarriage. In P. A. Cowan & E. M. Hetherington (Eds.), *Family transitions.* Hillsdale, NJ: Erlbaum.

Hetherington, E. M., & Clingempeel, W. G. (1992). Coping with marital transitions. *Monographs of the Society for Research in Child Development, 57* (No. 227), 2–3.

Hetherington, E. M., Cox, M., & Cox, R. (1985). Long term effects of divorce and remarriage on the adjustment of children. *Journal of the American Academy of Child Psychiatry, 5,* 518–530.

Hetherington, E. M., & Parke, R. D. (1993). *Child psychology* (4th ed.). New York: McGraw-Hill.

Hetherington, E. M., Stanley-Hagan, M., & Anderson, E. (1989). Marital transitions: A child's perspective. *American Psychologist, 44,* 303–312.

Heward, W. L., & Orlansky, M. D. (1988). *Exceptional children.* Columbus, OH: Merrill.

Highet, G. (1950). *The art of teaching.* New York: Knopf.

Hill, K. T., & Wigfield, A. (1984). Test anxiety: A major educational problem and what can be done about it. *Elementary School Journal, 85,* 105–126.

Hilliard, A. (1983). Psychological factors associated with language in the education of the African-American child. *Journal of Negro Education, 52,* 24–34.

Hinde, R. A. (1979). *Towards understanding relationships.* New York: Academic Press.

Hiroto, D. S. (1974). Locus of control and learned helplessness. *Journal of Experimental Psychology, 102,* 187–193.

Hodgkinson, H. (1993, April). American education: The good, the bad, and the task. *Phi Delta Kappan,* pp. 619–623.

Hoffman, K., & Stage, E. (1993). Science for all: Getting it right for the 21st century. *Educational Leadership, 50*(5), 27–31.

Hofmeister, A., Engelmann, S., & Carnine, D. (1989). Developing and validating science education videodiscs. *Journal of Research in Science Teaching, 26,* 665–677.

Hoge, R. D., & Coladarci, T. (1989). Teacher based judgment of academic achievement: A review of the literature. *Review of Educational Research, 59,* 297–313.

Holmes, C. T. (1990). Grade level retention efforts. A meta-analysis of research studies. In L. A. Shepard & M. L. Smith (Eds.), *Flunking grades: Research and policies on retention.* New York: Falmer Press.

Hops, H., & Finch, M. (1985). Social competence and skill: A reassessment. In B. H. Schneider, K. H. Rubin, & J. E. Ledingham (Eds.), *Children's peer relations: Issues in assessment and intervention* (pp. 24–40). New York: Springer-Verlag.

Horne, A. M., & Sayger, T. V. (1990). *Treating conduct and oppositional defiant disorders in children.* New York: Pergamon Press.

Hovland, C., Janis, S., & Kelley, J. (1953). *Communication and persuasion: Psychological studies of opinion change.* New Haven: Yale University Press.

Howard, G. (1991). Culture tales: A narrative approach to thinking, cross-cultural psychology, and psychotherapy. *American Psychologist, 46,* 187–197.

Howe, M. J. A. (1983). *Learning from television: Psychological and educational research.* London: Academic Press.

Howell, K. W. (1986). Direct assessment of academic performance. *School Psychology Review, 15,* 324–335.

Hubel, D. (1979). The brain. *Scientific American, 241,* 44–53.

Huck, S. W., & Sandler, H. M. (1979). *Rival hypotheses: Alternative interpretations of data based conclusions.* New York: Harper & Row.

Hughes, M. (1986). *Children and number.* New York: Blackwell.

Hulse, S., Egeth, H., & Deese, J. (1980). *The psychology of learning.* New York: McGraw-Hill.

Hunt, E. (1990). A modern arsenal for mental assessment. *Educational Psychologist, 25,* 223–242.

Hunter, M. (1987, April). The Hunterization of America's schools. *Instructor,* pp. 56–58, 60.

Hunter, M. (1991). Hunter design helps achieve the goals of science instruction. *Educational Leadership, 48*(4), 79–81.

Hunter, M., & Russell, D. (1981). Planning for effective instruction: Lesson design. In *Increasing your teaching effectiveness.* Palo Alto, CA: The Learning Institute.

Huttenlocher, J., Haight, W., Bryk, A., Seltzer, M., & Lyons, T. (1991). Early vocabulary growth: Relation to language input and gender. *Developmental Psychology, 27,* 236–248.

Hyden, H. (1985). The brain, learning and values. In J. Eccles (Ed.), *Mind and brain.* New York: Pergamon.

Ingersoll, B. (1988). Your hyperactive child. New York: Doubleday.

Irvine, J. T. (1978). Wolof "magical thinking": Culture and conservation revisited. *Journal of Cross-Cultural Psychology, 9,* 300–310.

Isenberg, J. (1987, June). Societal influences on children. *Childhood Education,* pp. 341–348.

Jackson, P. (1968). Life in classrooms. New York: Holt, Rinehart & Winston.

Jaynes, G., & Williams, R. (1989). *A common destiny: Blacks and American society.* Washington, DC: National Academy Press.

Jenkins, J., & Pany, D. (1978). Standardized achievement tests: How useful for special education? *Exceptional Children, 44,* 448–453.

Jensen, A. (1981). *Bias in mental testing.* San Francisco: Free Press.

Johnson, C., & Engelhard, G. (1992). Gender, academic achievement, and preferences for cooperative, competitive, and individualistic learning among African-American adolescents. *Journal of Psychology, 126*(4), 385–392.

Johnson, L., & Beer, J. (1992). Specific and diverse curiosity in elementary students. *Perceptual and Motor Skills, 75*(2), 463–466.

Jonassen, D. H. (1991). Objectivism versus constructivism: Do we need a new philosophical paradigm? *Educational Technology Research and Development, 39*(3), 5–14.

Jones, B. F., Pierce, J., & Hunter, B. (1988–1989, December/January). Teaching students to construct graphic representations. *Educational Leadership,* pp. 20–25.

Jones, M. (1989). Gender bias in classroom interactions. *Contemporary Education, 14,* 216–222.

Jones, R. L. (Ed.). (1988). *Psychological assessment of minority group children: A casebook.* Berkeley, CA: Cobb & Henry.

Julkunen, K. (1992, January). *Train and test anxiety in the foreign language classroom.* Paper presented at the Teaching Symposium, Helsinki, Finland.

Kagan, J. (1989). Unstable ideas. Cambridge, MA: Harvard University Press.

Kagan, J., & Moss, H. (1962). *Birth to maturity.* New York: Wiley.

Kail, R. (1984). *The development of memory in children* (2nd ed.). San Francisco: W. H. Freeman.

Kalish, H. (1981). *From behavioral science to behavior modification.* New York: McGraw-Hill.

Kane, P. (Ed.). (1992). *The first year of teaching: Real world stories from American teachers.* New York: Walker.

Kassenbaum, N. (1994). Head Start: Only the best for America's children. *American Psychologist, 49*(2), 123–126.

Kauffman, J., Gerber, M., & Semmel, M. (1988). Arguable assumptions underlying the regular education initiative. *Journal of Learning Disabilities, 21,* 6–11.

Kaufman, M., Agard, J. A., & Semmel, M. I. (1985). *Mainstreaming: Learners and their environments.* Cambridge, MA: Brookline Books.

Kay, R. H. (1990). Predicting student teacher commitment to the use of computers. *Journal of Educational Computing Research, 6*(3), 299–309.

Kazdin, A. (1989). *Behavior modification in applied settings* (4th ed.). Pacific Grove, CA: Brooks/Cole.

Kazdin, A. E. (1979). Situational specificity: The two-edged sword of behavioral assessment. *Behavioral Assessment, 6,* 57–76.

Kazdin, A. E. (1982). *Single-case research designs: Methods for clinical and applied settings.* New York: Oxford University Press.

Kazdin, A. E. (1988). *Child psychotherapy: Developing and evaluating effective treatments.* New York: Pergamon Press.

Kazdin, A. E. (1993). Evaluation in clinical practice: Clinically sensitive and systematic methods in treatment delivery. *Behavior Therapy, 24,* 11–45.

Kazdin, A. E. (1994). *Behavior modification in applied settings* (5th ed.). Pacific Grove, CA: Brooks/Cole.

Kellaghan, T., Madaus, G., & Airasian, P. (1980). *Standardized testing in elementary schools: Effect on schools, teachers, and students.* Washington, DC: National Education Association.

Keller, F. S. (1968). Good-bye teacher. *Journal of Applied Behavior Analysis, 1,* 69–89.

Kelley, M. L. (1990). *School-home notes: Promoting children's classroom success.* New York: Guilford Press.

Kelley, M. L., & Carper, L. B. (1988). Home-based reinforcement procedures. In J. C. Witt, S. N. Elliott, & F. M. Greshman (Eds.), *Handbook of behavior therapy in education* (pp. 419–438). New York: Plenum.

Kellogg, J. (1988). Forces of change. *Phi Delta Kappan, 70,* 109–204.

Kerlinger, F. (1973). *Foundations of behavioral research.* New York: Holt, Rinehart & Winston.

Kim, E., & Kellough, R. (1991). *A resource guide for secondary school teaching.* New York: Macmillan.

Kim, U. (1990). Indigenous psychology: Science and applications. In R. Brislin (Ed.), *Applied cross-cultural psychology*. Newbury Park, CA: Sage.

Kinsbourne, M. (1986). Systematizing cognitive psychology. *Behavioral and Brain Sciences, 9,* 567.

Kleiman, G. (1991). Mathematics across the curriculum. *Educational Leadership, 48,* 49–51.

Kohlberg, L. (1975). The cognitive-developmental approach to moral education. *Phi Delta Kappan, 56,* 670–677.

Kohlberg, L. (1976). Moral stages and moralization: The cognitive developmental approach. In T. Lickona (Ed.), *Moral development and behavior: Theory, research, and social issues*. New York: Holt, Rinehart & Winston.

Kornhaber, M., Krechevsky, M., & Gardner, H. (1990). Engaging intelligence. *Educational Psychologist, 25,* 177–200.

Kosslyn, S. (1980). *Image and mind*. Cambridge, MA: Harvard University Press.

Kounin, J. (1970). *Discipline and group management in classrooms*. New York: Holt, Rinehart & Winston.

Kozol, J. (1991). *Savage inequalities*. New York: Crown.

Kramer, J. J. (1990). Training parents as behavior change agents: Successes, failures and suggestions for school psychologists. In T. B. Gutkin & C. R. Reynolds (Eds.), *Handbook of school psychology* (2nd ed., pp. 683–702). New York: Wiley.

Krathwohl, D. R. (1993). *Methods of educational and social science research: An integrated approach*. New York: Longman.

Kratochwill, T. R. (Ed.). (1978). *Single subject research: Strategies for evaluating change*. New York: Academic Press.

Kratochwill, T. R., & Goldman, J. A. (1973). Developmental changes in children's judgments of age. *Developmental Psychology, 9,* 358–362.

Kratochwill, T. R., & Levin, J. R. (Eds.). (1992). *Single-case design and analysis: New developments for psychology and education*. Hillsdale, NJ: Erlbaum.

Kratochwill, T. R., & Sheridan, S. (1990). Advances in behavioral assessment. In T. B. Gutkin & C. R. Reynolds (Eds.), *The handbook of school psychology* (2nd ed., pp. 328–369). New York: John Wiley & Sons.

Krendl, K. A., & Broihier, M. (1992). Student responses to computers: A longitudinal study. *Journal of Educational Computing Research, 8*(2), 215–227.

Krouse, H. (1986). Use of decision frames by elementary school children. *Perceptual and Motor Skills, 63,* 1107–1112.

Kulik, C. C., & Kulik, J. A. (1991). Effectiveness of computer-based instruction: An upgraded analysis. *Computers in Human Behavior, 7,* 75–94.

Langlois, J., & Downs, A. C. (1980). Peer relations as a function of physical attractiveness: The eye of the beholder or behavioral reality? *Child Development, 50,* 409–418.

Larry P. et al. v. Wilson Riles et al. (1979). United States District Court. Northern District of California. Case No. C-71-2270 RFP. Injunction in 1972 & 1974. Opinion in October 1979.

Larry P. v. Riles, 343 F. Supp. 1306 (N.D. Cal. 1972) (preliminary injunction). Aff'd 502 F. 2d 963 (9th cir. 1974); 495 F. Supp. 926 (N.D. Cal. 1979) (decision on merits). (Aff'd (9th cir. no. 80-427 Jan. 23, 1984). Order modifying judgment, C-71-2270 RFP, Sept. 25, 1986.

Laslett, R., & Smith, C. (1984). *Effective classroom management*. New York: Nichols.

Lau v Nichols, 414 U.S. 563 (1974).

LaVigna, G. W., & Donnellan, A. M. (1986). *Alternatives to punishment: Solving behavior problems with non-aversive strategies*. New York: Irvington Publishers.

Lawton, J., & Gerschner, V. T. (1982). A review of literature on attitudes towards computers and computerized instruction. *Journal of Research and Development in Education, 16*(1), 50–55.

Lazar, I., & Darlington, R. (1982). Lasting effects of early education: A report from the consortium for longitudinal studies. *Monographs of the Society for Research in Child Development, 47*(Serial No. 195).

Leahey, D., & Harris, T. (1985). *Human learning*. Englewood Cliffs, NJ: Prentice Hall.

Lehrer, R. (1994). Authors of knowledge: Patterns of hypermedia design. In S. Lajoie & S. Derry (Eds.), *Computers as cognitive tools* (pp. 197–227). Hillsdale, NJ: Erlbaum.

Lehrer, R., Guckenberg, T., & Sancilio, L. (1989). Influences of Logo on children's intellectual development. In R. E. Mayer (Ed.), *Teaching and learning computer programming: Multiple research perspectives* (pp. 75–110). Hillsdale, NJ: Erlbaum.

Lehrer, R., Littlefield, J., Wottreng, B., & Youngerman, N. (1993). *Seeding mindstorms with LogoWriter: Using Logo in the elementary classroom* (2nd ed.). Fontana, WI: Interactive Education Technologies.

Lenneberg, E. (1967). *Biological foundations of language*. New York: Wiley.

Lepper, M. R., & Chabay, R. W. (1988). Socializing the intelligent tutor: Bringing empathy to computer tutors. In H. Mandl & A. Lesgold (Eds.), *Learning issues for intelligent tutoring systems* (pp. 242–257). New York: Springer-Verlag.

Lesgold, A., Lajoie, S. P., Bunzo, M., & Eggan, G. (1992). A coached practice environment for an electronics troubleshooting job. In J. Larkin & R. Chabay (Eds.), *Computer assisted instruction and intelligent tutoring systems: Shared goals and complementary approaches* (pp. 201–238). Hillsdale, NJ: Erlbaum.

Lesner, W. J., & Hillman, D. (1983). A developmental schema of creativity. *The Journal of Creative Behavior, 17,* 1–11.

Leuhrmann, A. (1985). School of the future—School of the past. Adopting microcomputers in ways that will and won't work. *Peabody Journal of Education, 62*(2), 42–51.

Levin, J. R. (1993). Estimating the knowledge base for school learning. *Review of Educational Research, 63,* 335–343.

Levine, M., Brooks, R., & Shonkoff, J. (1980). *A pediatric approach to learning disorders*. New York: Wiley.

Lewis, D., & Greene, J. (1982). *Thinking better*. New York: Holt.

Lichtenstein, R., & Ireton, H. (1984). *Preschool screening: Identifying young children with developmental and educational problems*. New York: Grune and Stratton.

Lickona, T. (1983). *Raising good children*. New York: Bantam.

Lickona, T. (1991). *Educating for character: How our schools can teach respect and responsibility*. New York: Bantam Books.

Lickona, T. (1993). The return of character education. *Educational Leadership, 51*(3), 6–11.

Liebert, R. M., Sprafkin, J. N., & Davidson, E. (1988). *The early window*. New York: Pergamon.

Lindholm, K. J. (1990). Bilingual immersion education: Educational equity for language minority students. In A. Barona & E. E. Garcia (Eds.), *Children at risk: Poverty, minority status, and other issues in educational equity* (pp. 77–89). Washington, DC: National Association of School Psychologists.

Linn, R. (1986). Educational testing and assessment. *American Psychologist, 41,* 1153–1160.

Lipman, M. (1987, September). Critical thinking: What can it be? *Educational Leadership,* pp. 38–43.

Lips, H. (1993). *Sex and gender*. Mountain View, CA: Mayfield.

Lipsey, M. W., & Wilson, D. B. (1993). The efficacy of psychological, educational, and behavioral treatment: Confirmation from meta-analysis. *American Psychologist, 48,* 1181–1209.

Littlefield, J., Delclos, V. R., Lever, S., Clayton, K. N., Bransford, J. D., & Franks, J. J. (1989). Learning Logo: Method of teaching, transfer of general skills, and attitudes toward school and computers. In R. E. Mayer (Ed.), *Teaching and learning computer programming: Multiple research perspectives* (pp. 111–135). Hillsdale, NJ: Erlbaum.

Livingston, R. (1986). Visual impairments. In N. Haring & L. McCormick (Eds.), *Exceptional children and youth*. Columbus, OH: Merrill.

Lloyd, J. W., Singh, N. N., & Repp, A. C. (Eds.). (1991). *The regular education initiative: Alternative perspectives on concepts, issues, and models*. Sycamore, IL: Sycamore.

Lockard, J., Abrams, P. D., & Many, W. A. (1994). *Microcomputers for twenty-first century educators*. New York: HarperCollins.

Loftus, E. F., & Palmer, J. C. (1974). Reconstruction of automobile destruction: An example of the interaction between language and memory. *Journal of Verbal Learning and Verbal Behavior, 13,* 585–589.

Lonner, W., & Malpass, R. (1994). *Psychology and culture*. Needham, MA: Allyn & Bacon.

Looft, W. R. (1971). Children's judgments of age. *Child Development, 42,* 1282–1284.

Looft, W. R., Raymond, J. R., & Raymond, B. B. (1972). Children's judgments of age in Sarawak. *Journal of Social Psychology, 86,* 181–185.

Lott, B. (1987). *Women's lives*. Monterey, CA: Brooks/Cole.

Lovell-Troy, L. (1989). Teaching techniques for instructional goals: A partial review of the literature. *Teaching Sociology, 17,* 28–37.

Lovinger, S. L., Brandell, M. E., & Seesdedt-Stanford, L. (1991). *Language learning disabilities: A new and practical approach for those who work with children and their families*. New York: Continuum.

Lowenbraun, S., & Thompson, M. (1986). Hearing impairments. In N. Haring & L. McCormick (Eds.), *Exceptional children and youth*. Columbus, OH: Merrill.

Ludlow, L. (1989). *Testing young children*. Unpublished manuscript.

Luria, A. (1973). *The working brain*. New York: Basic Books.

Luria, A. (1980). *Higher cortical functions in man*. New York: Basic Books.

Lyman, H. (1986). *Test scores and what they mean*. Englewood Cliffs, NJ: Prentice Hall.

Maccoby, E. E., & Jacklin, C. N. (1974). *The psychology of sex differences*. Palo Alto, CA: Stanford University Press.

Madaus, G. (1989). *Teach them well*. Boston: Allyn & Bacon.

Madaus, G. (1994). A technological and historical consideration of equity issues associated with proposals to change the nation's testing policy. *Harvard Educational Review, 64*(1), 76–95.

Maehr, M., & Midgley, C. (1991). Enhancing school motivation: A schoolwide approach. *Educational Psychologist, 26*(3, 4), 399–427.

Mager, R. (1975). *Preparing instructional objectives*. Palo Alto, CA: Fearon.

Magid, K., & McKelvey, C. (1987). *High risk: Children without a conscience*. New York: Bantam Books.

Malone, M. (1984). *An analysis of difference in cognitive development in selected African and Western societies*. Unpublished manuscript.

Manaster, G. J. (1989). *Adolescent development*. Itasca, IL: Peacock.

Manzo, A., & Manzo, U. (1990). *Content area reading: A heuristic approach*. Columbus, OH: Merrill.

Marcia, J. (1966). Development and validation of ego identity status. *Journal of Personality and Social Psychology, 3,* 551–558.

Marcia, J. (1980). Identity formation in adolescence. In J. Adelson (Ed.), *Handbook of adolescent psychology*. New York: Wiley.

Markle, S. (1990). *Designs for instructional designers* (2nd ed.). Champaign, IL: Stipes.

Marschark, M. (1993). *Psychological development of deaf children*. New York: Oxford University Press.

Marso, R., & Pigge, F. (1989). *The status of classroom teachers' test construction proficiencies*. Paper presented at the annual meeting of the National Council of Measurement in Education, San Francisco.

Martin, C., Wood, C., & Little, J. (1990). The development of gender stereotype components. *Child Development, 61,* 1891–1904.

Martin, C. D., Heller, R. S., & Mahmoud, E. (1992). American and Soviet children's attitudes toward computers. *Journal of Educational Computing Research, 8*(2), 155–185.

Maslow, A. (1987). *Motivation and personality*. New York: Harper & Row.

Mason, J., & Au, K. (1990). *Reading instruction for today*. Glenview, IL: Scott, Foresman/Little, Brown.

Matarazzo, J. (1990). Psychological assessment versus psychological testing: Validation from Binet to the school, clinic, and courtroom. *American Psychologist, 45,* 999–1017.

Matsumoto, D. (1994). *People: Psychology from a cultural perspective*. Belmont, CA: Brooks/Cole.

Maxim, G. (1991). *Social studies and the elementary school child*. New York: Merrill.

Mayer, R. (1992). *Thinking, problem solving, cognition*. San Francisco: W. H. Freeman.

Mayer, R. E., & Gallini, J. K. (1990). When is an illustration worth ten thousand words? *Journal of Educational Psychology, 82,* 715–726.

Mayer, R. E., & Sims, V. K. (1994). For whom is a picture worth a thousand words? Extensions of a dual-coding theory of multimedia learning. *Journal of Educational Psychology, 86*(3), 389–401.

McBay, S. (1990, January 10). Plan unveiled for improving minority education. *New York Times*, p. B8.

McCarthy, R. (1989). The advantages of using a network. *Electronic Learning, 9*(1), 32–38.

McCaslin, M. (1989). Theory, instruction, and future implementation. *Elementary School Journal, 90,* 223–229.

McClelland, D. (1987). *Human motivation*. New York: Cambridge University Press.

McConaughy, S. H. (1993). Advances in empirically based assessment of children's behavioral and emotional problems. *School Psychology Review, 2,* 285–307.

McConnell, J. V. (1990). *Understanding human behavior. An introduction to psychology* (6th ed.). New York: Holt, Rinehart & Winston.

McLaughlin, B. (1990). Development of bilingualism: Myth and reality. In A. Barona & E. E. Garcia (Eds.), *Children at risk: Poverty, minority status, and other issues in educational equity* (pp. 65–75). Washington, DC: National Association of School Psychologists.

McLoyd, V. (1990). Minority children. *Child Development, 61,* 263–266.

McMahon, H. (1990). Collaborating with computers. *Journal of Computer Assisted Learning, 6*(3), 149–167.

McNamara, E., Evans, M., & Hill, W. (1986). The reduction of disruptive behavior in two secondary school classes. *British Journal of Educational Psychology, 36,* 209–215.

McTighe, J., & Lyman, F. T. (1988). Aiding thinking in the classroom: The promise of theory-embedded tools. *Educational Leadership, 47,* 18–24.

Medland, M., & Vitale, M. (1984). *Management of classrooms*. New York: Holt, Rinehart & Winston.

Medway, F. J., & Rose, J. S. (1986). Grade retention. In T. R. Kratochwill (Ed.), *Advances in school psychology* (Vol. 5, pp. 141–175). Hillsdale, NJ: Erlbaum.

Mervis, C. B., & Rosch, E. (1981). Categorization of natural objects. *Annual Review of Psychology, 32,* 89–115.

Messick, S. (1988). The once and future issues of validity: Assessing the meaning and consequences of measurement. In H. Wainer & H. Braun (Eds.), *Test validity* (pp. 33–45). Hillsdale, NJ: Erlbaum.

Miller, G. A. (1956). The magical number seven, plus or minus two: Some limits on our capacity for processing information. *Psychological Review, 63,* 81–97.

Miller, P. (1989). *Theories of developmental psychology*. New York: Freeman.

Miller-Jones, D. (1989). Culture and testing. *American Psychologist, 4,* 360–367.

Minuchin, P., & Shapiro, E. (1983). The school as a context for social development. In P. Mussen (Ed.), *Handbook of child psychology*. New York: Wiley.

Miranda, A. H., & Santos de Barona, M. (1990). A model for interventions with low achieving minority students. In A. Barona & E. E. Garcia (Eds.), *Children at risk: Poverty, minority students, and other issues in educational equity* (pp. 119–134). Washington, DC: National Association of School Psychologists.

Mitchell, J. (Ed.). (1985). *The ninth mental measurements yearbook.* Lincoln: University of Nebraska Press.

Money, J. (1980). *Love and love sickness.* Baltimore: Johns Hopkins Press.

Moore, G. (1983). *Developing and evaluating educational research.* Boston: Little, Brown.

Moore, L., & Carnine, D. (1989). Evaluating curriculum design in the context of active teaching. *Remedial and Special Education, 10,* 28–37.

Morris, R. J., & Kratochwill, T. R. (1983). *Treating children's fears and phobias.* New York: Pergamon.

Morsink, C. (1985). Learning disabilities. In W. Berdine & A. E. Blackhurst (Eds.), *An introduction to special education.* Boston: Little, Brown.

Moses, S. (1991). Major revision of SAT goes into effect in 1994. *The APA Monitor, 22,* 1, 34–35.

Mullis, I., & Jenkins, L. (1988). *The science report card.* Princeton, NJ: Educational Testing Service.

Murphy, J. (1993, April). What's in? What's out? American education in the nineties. *Phi Delta Kappan,* pp. 641–646.

Muth, D., Glynn, S., Britton, B., & Graves, M. (1988). Thinking out loud while studying text: Rehearsing new ideas. *Journal of Educational Psychology, 80,* 315–318.

Muthukvishna, N., Carnine, D., Grossen, B., & Miller, S. (1990). *Children's alternative frameworks: Should they be directly addressed in science?* Unpublished manuscript, University of Oregon at Eugene.

Myers, P. I., & Hammill, D. D. (1990). *Learning disabilities: Basic concepts, assessment practices, and instructional strategies* (4th ed.). Austin, TX: PRO-ED.

Nagin, D., & Farrington, D. (1992). The stability of criminal potential from childhood to adulthood. *Criminology, 30,* 235–260.

Narayan, J., Heward, W. L., & Gardner, R. (1990). Using response cards to increase student participation in an elementary classroom. *Journal of Applied Behavior Analysis, 23,* 483–490.

National Commission on Testing and Public Policy. (1990). *From gatekeeper to gateway: Transforming testing in America.* Chestnut Hill, MA: Boston College.

National Council of Teachers of Mathematics. (1989). *Curriculum and evaluation standards for school mathematics.* Reston, VA: Author.

National Council on Education Standards and Testing (NCEST). (1992). *Raising standards for American education: A report to Congress, the Secretary of Education, the National Education Goals Panel, and the American people.* Washington, DC: U.S. Government Printing Office.

Neisser, U. (1982). *Memory observed.* San Francisco: Freeman.

Nesbit, J., & Hunka, S. (1987). A method for sequencing instructional objectives which minimizes memory load. *Instructional Science, 16,* 137–150.

Nesher, P. (1986). Learning mathematics: A cognitive perspective. *American Psychologist, 41,* 1114–1122.

Newman, R. S. (1990). Children's help-seeking in the classroom: The role of motivational factors and attitudes. *Journal of Educational Psychology, 82,* 71–80.

New Voices. (1988). *Immigrant students in U.S. public schools.* Boston: The National Coalition of Advocates for Students.

Niedelman, M. (1991). Problem solving and transfer. *Journal of Learning Disabilities, 24*(6), 322–329.

Nitko, A. (1983). *Educational tests and measurement: An introduction.* New York: Macmillan.

Nix, D., & Spiro, R. (1990). *Cognition, education, and multimedia: Exploring ideas in high technology.* Hillsdale, NJ: Erlbaum.

Nunn, G., & Parish, T. (1992). The psychosocial characteristics of at-risk high school students. *Adolescence, 27*(106), 435–440.

Office of Technology Assessment. (1992, February). *Testing in the American schools: Asking the right questions.* (OTA-SET-519). Washington, DC: U.S. Government Printing Office.

Olsen, L. (1988). Crossing the school-house border: Immigrant children in California. *Phi Delta Kappan, 70,* 211–218.

Olweus, D. (1982). Development of stable aggressive reaction patterns in males. In R. Blanchard & C. Blanchard (Eds.), *Advances in the study of aggression* (Vol. 1). New York: Academic Press.

O'Neil, J. (1993). Can national standards make a difference? *Educational Leadership, 50*(5), 4–8.

Page, E. (1958). Teacher comments and student performance. *Journal of Educational Psychology, 49,* 173–181.

Paivio, A. (1974). Comparisons of mental clocks. *Journal of Experimental Psychology, 4,* 61–71.

Palincer, A. S., & Brown, A. (1984). Reciprocal teaching of comprehension—fostering and monitoring activities. *Cognition and Instruction, 1,* 117–175.

Palmer, O. (1962). Seven classic ways of grading dishonestly. *The English Journal, 51,* 464–467.

Papert, S. (1993). *Mindstorms: Children, computers, and powerful ideas* (2nd ed.). New York: Basic Books.

Paris, S., Cross, D., & Lipson, M. (1984). Informed strategies for learning: A program to improve children's reading awareness and comprehension. *Journal of Educational Psychology, 76,* 1239–1252.

Parke, R., & Slaby, R. (1983). The development of aggression. In P. Mussen (Ed.), *Handbook of child psychology.* New York: Wiley.

Parker, J., & Asher, S. (1993). Friendship and friendship quality in middle childhood: Links with peer group acceptance and feelings of loneliness and social dissatisfaction. *Developmental Psychology, 29*(4), 611–621.

Pase (Parents in Action on Special Education) v Joseph P. Hannon. U.S. District Court, Northern District of Illinois, Eastern Division, No. 74 (3586), July, 1980. Also 506 F. Supp. 831 (N.D. Ill. 1980).

Paulos, J. (1988). *Innumeracy.* New York: Hill & Wang.

Paulson, F. L., Paulson, P. R., & Meyer, C. A. (1991, February). What makes a portfolio a portfolio? *Educational Leadership,* pp. 60–63.

Pavlov, I. P. (1927). *Conditioned reflexes.* London: Oxford University Press.

Pavlov, I. P. (1928). *Lectures on conditioned reflexes.* London: Oxford University Press.

Pea, R. D., Kurland, D. M., & Hawkins, J. (1985). LOGO and the development of thinking skills. In M. Chen & W. Paisley (Eds.), *Children and microcomputers: Research on the newest medium* (pp. 193–212). Newbury Park, CA: Sage.

Pease, D., & Gleason, J. B. (1985). Getting meaning: Semantic development. In J. B. Gleason (Ed.), *The development of language.* Columbus, OH: Merrill.

Perkins, D. (1981). *The mind's best work.* Cambridge: Harvard University Press.

Perkins, D. (1986). Thinking frames. *Educational Leadership, 43,* 4–10.

Perkins, D. (1987). Thinking frames. In J. Baron & R. Sternberg (Eds.), *Teaching thinking skills.* New York: Freeman.

Perkins, D., Jay, E., & Tishman, S. (1993). New conceptions of thinking: From ontology to education. *Educational Psychologist, 28,* 67–85.

Perkins, D. N., & Blythe, T. (1994). Putting understanding up front. *Educational Leadership, 51*(5), 4–7.

Petri, H. (1991). *Motivation: Theory and research*. Belmont, CA: Wadsworth.

Phares, E. J. (1973). *Locus of control: A personality determinant of behavior.* Morristown, NJ: General Learning Press.

Phillips, D. C. (1983). On describing a student's cognitive structure. *Educational Psychologist, 18,* 59–74.

Phye, G., & Andre, T. (1986). *Classroom cognitive learning.* New York: Academic Press.

Piaget, J. (1926). *The language and thought of the child*. New York: Harcourt, Brace, and World.

Piaget, J. (1952). *The origin of intelligence in children.* New York: International Universities Press.

Piaget, J. (1964). Development and learning. In R. Ripple & V. Rockcastle (Eds.), *Piaget rediscovered.* Washington, DC: U.S. Office of Education, National Science Foundation.

Piaget, J. (1969). *Science of education and the psychology of the child.* New York: Viking.

Piaget, J. (1973). *The child and reality.* New York: Grossman.

Piaget, J., & Inhelder, B. (1969). *The psychology of the child.* New York: Basic Books.

Piersel, W., & Kratochwill, T. R. (1979). Self-observation and behavior change: Applications to academic and adjustment problems through behavioral consultation. *Journal of School Psychology, 17,* 151–161.

Pinker, S. (1994). *The language instinct.* New York: Morrow.

Pompi, K. F., & Lachman, R. (1967). Surrogate processes in the short-term retention of connected discourse. *Journal of Experimental Psychology, 75,* 143–150.

Posner, G. (1989). Field experience: Methods of reflective teaching. New York: Longmans.

Premack, D. (1965). Reinforcement theory. In David Levine (Ed.), *Nebraska Symposium on Motivation* (Vol. 13). Lincoln: University of Nebraska Press.

Pressley, M., & Harris, K. R. (1990, September). What we really know about strategy instruction. *Educational Leadership,* pp. 31–34.

Prewitt, P. W. (1988). Dealing with Ijime (bullying) among Japanese students. *School Psychology International, 9,* 189–195.

Price, R. H., Cowen, E. L., Lorion, R. P., & Ramos-McKay, A. (1988). *14 ounces of prevention.* Washington, DC: American Psychological Association.

Pugach, M. (1985). The limitations of federal special education policy: The role of classroom teachers in determining who is handicapped. *The Journal of Special Education, 19,* 123–137.

Pulido, J. (1991). High retention rates, no dropouts among Hispanic students in California high schools. *Journal of School Leadership, 1*(3), 212–221.

Pullin, D. (1994). Learning to work: The impact of curriculum and assessment standards in educational opportunity. *Harvard Educational Review, 64*(1), 31–54.

Quackenbush, M., & Villarreal, S. (1988). *Does AIDS hurt?* Santa Cruz: Network Publications.

Quay, H. C. (1986). A critical analysis of DSM II as a taxonomy of psychopathology in childhood and adolescence. In T. Millon & G. Klerman (Eds.), *Contemporary directions in psychopathology.* New York: Guilford Press.

Rafferty, M., & Shinn, M. (1991). The impact of homelessness on children. *American Psychologist, 46,* 1170–1179.

Rahman, R., & Bisanz, G. (1986). Reading ability and use of a story schema in recalling and reconstructing information. *Journal of Educational Psychology, 75,* 323–333.

Ramsey, P. (1987). *Teaching and learning in a diverse world.* New York: Teachers College Press.

Ratliff, J. D. (1988). Motivation and the perceived need deficiencies of secondary teachers. *High School Journal, 72,* 8–16.

Rauth, M. (1981). What can be expected of the regular teacher? Ideals and realities. *Exceptional Education Quarterly, 2,* 27–36.

Redl, F., & Wattenberg, W. (1959). *Mental hygiene in teaching.* New York: Harcourt, Brace and Jovanovich.

Reis, S. (1989). Reflections on policy affecting the education of gifted and talented students. *American Psychologist, 44,* 399–408.

Renyi, J. (1993). *Going public: Schooling for a diverse democracy.* New York: The New Press.

Renzulli, J. (1986). *The enrichment triad model.* Mansfield Center, CT: Creative Learning Press.

Renzulli, J. (Ed.). (1986). *Systems and models for developing programs for the gifted and talented.* Mansfield Center, CT: Creative Learning Press.

Repp, A. C., & Singh, N. N. (Eds.). (1990). *Perspectives on the use of non-aversive and aversive interventions for persons with developmental disabilities.* Sycamore, IL: Sycamore.

Rest, J. (1983). Morality. In P. Mussen (Ed.), *Handbook of child psychology.* New York: John Wiley.

Reutzel, R., & Cooper, R. (1992). *Teaching children to read: From basics to books.* New York: Macmillan.

Reynolds, C. R., & Kaiser, S. M. (1990). Test bias in psychological assessment. In T. B. Gutkin & C. R. Reynolds (Eds.),

The handbook of school psychology (2nd ed., pp. 487–525). New York: John Wiley & Sons.

Rice, M. L., Huston, A. C., Truglio, R., and Wright, J. (1990). Words from "Sesame Street": Learning vocabulary while viewing. *Developmental Psychology, 26*(3), 421–428.

Rieser, R. A. (1987). Instructional technology: A history. In R. M. Gagne (Ed.), *Instructional technology: Foundations* (pp. 11–48). Hillsdale, NJ: Erlbaum.

Rieser, R. A., & Dick, W. A. (1990). Evaluating instructional software. *Educational Technology Research and Development, 38*(3), 43–50.

Roberts, N., Blakeslee, G., Brown, M., & Lenk, C. (1990). *Integrating telecommunications into education.* Englewood Cliffs, NJ: Prentice-Hall.

Robinson, N., & Magliocca, L. (1991). *Identifying and modeling the problem situated expertise of the regular class teacher in the instruction of at-risk and mildly handicapped students.* Paper presented at the annual meeting of the American Educational Research Association, Chicago.

Rogoff, B. (1990). *Apprenticeship in thinking.* New York: Oxford University Press.

Romberg, T. (1993). NCTM's Standards: A rallying flag for mathematics teachers. *Educational Leadership, 50*(5), 36–41.

Romberg, T., & Carpenter, T. (1986). Research on teaching and learning mathematics. In M. Wittrock (Ed.), *Handbook of research on teaching* (3rd ed.). New York: Macmillan.

Rose, S. (1987). *The conscious brain.* New York: Knopf.

Rose, T. L. (1984). Current uses of corporal punishment in American schools. *Journal of Educational Psychology, 76,* 427–441.

Rosen, L. A., Taylor, S. A., O'Leary, S. G., & Sanderson, W. (1991). A survey of classroom management practices. *Journal of School Psychology, 28,* 257–269.

Rosenfield, S., & Shinn, M. R. (Eds.). (1989). Mini-series on curriculum-based assessment. *School Psychology Review, 18*(3), 297–370.

Rosenshine, B., & Stevens, R. (1986). Teaching functions. In M. Wittrock (Ed.), *Handbook of research on teaching* (3rd ed.). New York: Macmillan.

Rosenthal, R., & Jacobson, L. (1968). *Pygmalion in the classroom.* New York: Holt, Rinehart & Winston.

Rosser, P. (1989). *Gender and testing.* Berkeley, CA: National Commission on Testing and Public Policy.

Roth, K. J. (1990). Developing meaningful conceptual understanding in science. In B. F. Jones & L. Idol (Eds.), *Dimensions of thinking and cognitive instruction* (pp. 139–175). Hillsdale, NJ: Erlbaum.

Rotter, J. (1966). Generalized expectancies for internal versus external control of reinforcement. *Psychological Monographs, 80*(No. 609).

Rotter, J. (1975). Some problems and misconceptions related to the construct of internal versus external control of reinforcement. *Journal of Consulting and Clinical Psychology, 43,* 56–67.

Rourke, B., Bakker, D., Fisk, J., & Strang, J. (1983). *Child neuropsychology.* New York: Guilford.

Rummelhart, D., & Norman, D. (1981). Analogical processes in learning. In J. R. Anderson (Ed.), *Cognitive skills and their acquisition.* Hillsdale, NJ: Erlbaum.

Rutter, M. (1975). *Helping troubled children.* New York: Plenum.

Rutter, M. (1980). *Changing youth in a changing society.* Cambridge, MA: Harvard University Press.

Ryan, A. W. (1991). Meta-analysis of achievement effects of microcomputer applications in elementary schools. *Educational Administration Quarterly, 27*(2), 161–184.

Sadker, M., & Sadker, D. (1994). *Failing at fairness: How America's schools cheat girls.* New York: Charles Scribner's Sons.

Salomon, G. (1990, October). The computer lab: A bad idea now sanctified. *Educational Technology, 30*(10), 50–52.

Salomon, G., & Gardner, H. (1986). The computer as educator: Lessons from television research. *Educational Researcher, 15*(1), 13–19.

Salvia, J., & Hughes, C. (1990). *Curriculum-based assessment: Testing what is taught.* New York: Macmillan.

Sammur, G. B. (1990). Selected bibiography of research on programming at the Children's Television Workshop. *Educational Technology: Research and Development, 38*(4), 81–92.

Sanders, N. (1966). *Classroom questions: What kinds?* New York: Harper & Row.

Santrock, J. (1995). *Children* (4th ed.). Dubuque, IA: Brown & Benchmark.

Scarr, S. (1992). Developmental theories for the 1990s: Development and individual differences. *Child Development, 63*(1), 1–19.

Scarr, S., Weinberg, R., & Levine, A. (1986). *Understanding development.* New York: Harcourt Brace Jovanovich.

Schab, F. (1991). Schooling without learning: Thirty years of cheating in high school. *Adolescence, 26,* 839–848.

Schiefflen, B., & Gallimore, P. (1993). *The acquisition of literacy: An ethnographic perspective.* Norwood, NJ: Ablex.

Schon, D. A. (1988). *Educating the reflective practitioner: Toward a new design for teaching and learning in the professions.* San Francisco: Jossey-Bass.

Schunk, D. (1989). Self-efficacy and cognitive skill learning. In C. Ames & R. Ames (Eds.), *Research on motivation in education: Vol. 3. Goals and cognitions.* San Diego, CA: Academic Press.

Schunk, D., Hanson, A., & Cox, P. (1987). Peer model attributes and children's achievement behaviors. *Journal of Educational Psychology, 79,* 54–61.

Science for All Americans. (1989). Washington, DC: American Association for the Advancement of Science.

Secretary's Commission on Achieving Necessary Skills (SCANS). (1992). *Learning a living. A blueprint for high performance.* Washington, DC: U.S. Department of Labor.

Seligman, M. (1990). *Learned optimism.* New York: Knopf.

Seligman, M. E. (1975). *Helplessness: On depressions, development, and death.* San Francisco: Freeman.

Seligman, M. E., & Maier, S. F. (1967). Failure to escape traumatic shock. *Journal of Experimental Psychology, 74,* 1–9.

Selinske, J. E., Greer, R. D., & Lodhi, S. (1991). A functional analysis of the comprehensive application of behavior analyses to schooling. *Journal of Applied Behavior Analysis, 24,* 107–117.

Serbin, L., Powlishta, K., & Gulko, J. (1993). The development of sex typing in middle childhood. *Monographs of the Society for Research in Child Development, 58*(2, Serial No. 232).

Serna, L. (1989). Implications of student motivation on study skills instruction. *Elementary School Journal, 24,* 503–514.

Shade, B. (1987). Ecological correlates of the educative style of Afro-American children. *Journal of Negro Education, 56,* 88–99.

Shade, B., & New, C. (1993). Cultural influences on learning: Teaching implications. In J. Banks & C. Banks (Eds.), *Multicultural education: Issues and perspectives.* Boston: Allyn & Bacon.

Shapiro, E. S. (1988). Behavioral assessment. In J. C. Witt, S. N. Elliott, & F. M. Gresham (Eds.), *The handbook of behavior therapy in education* (pp. 67–98). New York: Plenum.

Shapiro, E. S., & Derr, T. F. (1990). Curriculum-based assessment. In T. B. Gutkin & C. R. Reynolds (Eds.), *The handbook of school psychology* (2nd ed., pp. 365–387). New York: John Wiley & Sons.

Sheingold, K., & Hadley, M. (1990). *Accomplished teachers: Integrating computers into classroom practice.* New York: Center for Technology in Education, Bank Street College of Education.

Sheridan, S. W., Kratochwill, T. R., & Elliott, S. N. (1990). Behavioral consultation with parents and teachers: Delivering treatment for socially withdrawn children at home and school. *School Psychology Review, 19,* 33–52.

Sherry, D., & Schachter, D. (1987). The evolution of multiple memory systems. *Psychological Review, 94,* 439–454.

Shuell, T. (1986). Cognitive conceptions of learning. *Review of Educational Research, 56,* 411–436.

Shulman, L. (1986). Paradigms and research programs in the study of teaching. In M. Wittrock (Ed.), *The handbook of research on teaching.* New York: Macmillan.

Shweder, R. (1991). *Thinking through cultures.* Cambridge, MA: Harvard University Press.

Siegler, R. (1983). Information processing approaches to development. In P. Mussen (Ed.), *Handbook of child psychology.* New York: John Wiley.

Silver, A. (1987).*Learning disabilities: A report to the MS Congress.* Washington, DC: U.S. Department of Health and Human Services, Intergroup Committee on Learning.

Simmons, W., & Resnick, L. (1993). Assessment as the catalyst of school reform. *Educational Leadership, 50*(5), 11–16.

Sizemore, B. (1990). The Madison elementary school: A turnaround case. In K. Lomotey (Ed.), *Going to school: The African-American experience.* New York: State University of New York Press.

Sizer, T., & Rogers, B. (1993). Designing standards: Achieving the delicate balance. *Educational Leadership, 50*(5), 24–26.

Skinner, B. F. (1938). *The behavior of organisms.* New York: Macmillan.

Skinner, B. F. (1953). *Science and human nature.* New York: Macmillan.

Skinner, B. F. (1957). *Verbal behavior.* New York: Appleton-Century-Crofts.

Skinner, B. F. (1968). *The technology of teaching.* New York: Appleton-Century-Crofts.

Skinner, B. F. (1971). *Beyond freedom and dignity.* New York: Knopf.

Skinner, B. F. (1974). *About behaviorism.* New York: Knopf.

Skinner, B. F. (1983). *A matter of consequences.* New York: Knopf.

Skinner, B. F. (1984, September). The shame of American education. *American Psychologist, 39*(9) 947–954.

Skinner, B. F. (1986, March). Some thoughts about the future. *Journal of the Experimental Analysis of Behavior,* pp. 229–235.

Skinner, B. F. (1990). Remarks after receiving a lifetime achievement award at the 98th Annual Convention of the American Psychological Association, Boston. Cited in E. Scott Geller, The Editor's Page. *Journal of Applied Behavior Analysis, 23,* 399–402.

Slaughter-Defoe, D., Nakagawa, K., Takanishi, R., & Johnson, D. (1990). Toward cultural/ecological perspectives on schooling and achievement in African-American and Asian-American children. *Child Development, 61,* 361–383.

Slavin, R. (1987a, November). Cooperative learning and the cooperative school. *Educational Leadership,* pp. 7–13.

Slavin, R. (1987b). Developmental and motivational perspectives on cooperative learning: A reconciliation. *Child Development, 58,* 1161–1167.

Slavin, R. (1987d). A theory of school and classroom organization. *Educational Psychologist, 22,* 90–99.

Slavin, R. (1988a, September). Synthesis of research on grouping in elementary and secondary schools. *Educational Leadership,* pp. 67–77.

Slavin, R. (1988b, October). Cooperative learning and student achievement. *Educational Leadership,* pp. 31–33.

Slavin, R. (1991a). Cooperative learning and group contingencies. *Journal of Behavioral Education, 1*(1), 105–115.

Slavin, R. (1991b). *Educational psychology* (3rd ed.). Englewood Cliffs, NJ: Prentice Hall.

Slavin, R. E. (1989). Students at risk of school failure: The problem and its dimensions. In R. E. Slavin, N. L. Karweit, & N. A. Madden (Eds.), *Effective programs for students at risk.* Needham Heights, MA: Allyn & Bacon.

Slavin, R. E., & Madden, N. A. (1989, February). What works for students at risk: A research synthesis. *Educational Leadership,* pp. 4–13.

Slavin, R. E., Madden, N. A., Korweit, N. L., Dolan, L., Wasik, B. A., Shaw, A., Mainzer, K. L., & Haxby, B. (1991). Neverstreaming: Prevention and early intervention as an alternative to special education. *Journal of Learning Disabilities, 24,* 373–378.

Sleeter, C., & Grant, C. (1993). *Making choices for multicultural education.* Columbus, OH: Merrill.

Smith, M. (1984). Learning about learning: The contributions of Ausubel's assimilation theory to a teacher education program. *Journal of Learning Skills, 3,* 33–36.

Smith, M. L., & Glass, G. J. (1980). Meta-analysis of psychotherapy outcome studies. *American Psychologist, 32,* 752–760.

Smith, S., Smith, M., & Romberg, T. (1993). What the NCTM standards look like in one classroom. *Educational Leadership, 50*(8), 4–7.

Snow, R. (1986). Individual differences and the design of educational programs. *American Psychologist, 41,* 1029–1039.

Soldier, L. L. (1989, October). Cooperative learning and the Native American student. *Phi Delta Kappan,* pp. 161–163.

Spencer, M., & Dornbusch, S. (1990). Challenges in studying minority youth. In S. Feldman & G. Elliott (Eds.), *At the threshold: The developing adolescent.* Cambridge, MA: Harvard University Press.

Spencer, M., & Markstrom-Adams, C. (1990). Identity processes among racial and ethnic minority children in America. *Child Development, 61,* 290–310.

Speth, C., & Brown, R. (1988). Study approaches, processes and strategies. Are three perspectives better than one? *British Journal of Educational Psychology, 58,* 247–257.

Spivak, G., & Shure, M. B. (1974). *Social adjustment of young children.* San Francisco: Jossey-Bass.

Sprick, R. S., & Nolet, V. (1991). Prevention and management of secondary-level behavior problems. In G. Stoner, M. R. Shinn, & H. M. Walker (Eds.), *Interventions for achievement and behavior problems* (pp. 519–538). Washington, DC: National Association of School Psychologists.

Squires, D., & McDougall, A. (1994). *Choosing and using educational software: A teacher's guide.* London: The Falmer Press.

Sroufe, L. A., Cooper, R., & DeHart, G. (1992). *Child development.* New York: Knopf.

Stallings, J., & Stipek, D. (1986). Research on early childhood and elementary school teaching programs. In M. Wittrock (Ed.), *Handbook of research on teaching.* New York: Macmillan.

Stanley, J., & Davidson, J. E. (Eds.). (1986). *Conceptions of giftedness.* New York: Cambridge University Press.

Steinberg, E. R. (1991). Interactive videodisc instruction. In *Teaching computers to teach* (2nd ed., pp. 187–206). Hillsdale, NJ: Erlbaum.

Sternberg, R. (1985). Critical thinking. In F. Link (Ed.), *Essays on the intellect.* Alexandria, VA: Association for Supervision and Curriculum Development.

Sternberg, R. (1986). *Intelligence applied.* New York: Harcourt Brace Jovanovich.

Sternberg, R. (1987). Teaching intelligence. In J. Baron & R. Sternberg (Eds.), *Teaching thinking skills.* New York: Freeman.

Sternberg, R. (1988). *Mechanics of cognitive development.* Prospect Heights, IL: Waveland Press.

Sternberg, R., & Davidson, J. E. (Eds.). (1986). *Conceptions of giftedness.* New York: Cambridge University Press.

Sternberg, R., Okagaki, L., & Jackson, L. (1990). Practical intelligence for success in school. *Educational Leadership, 48,* 35–39.

Stevenson, H., Lee, S., Chen, C., Lummis, M., Stigler, J., Fan, L., & Ge, F. (1990). Mathematics achievement of children in China and the United States. *Child Development, 61,* 1053–1066.

Stewart, J., Hafner, R., Johnson, S., & Finkel, E. (1992). Science as model building: Computers and high-school genetics. *Educational Psychologist, 27*(3), 317–336.

Stiggins, R. J. (1987). Design and development of performance assessments. *Educational Measurement: Issues and Practice, 6,* 33–42.

Stiggins, R. J. (1991). Facing the challenges of a new era of educational assessment. *Applied Measurement in Education, 4,* 263–274.

Stigler, J., Shweder, R., & Herdt, G. (Eds.). (1990). *Cultural psychology.* New York: Cambridge University Press.

Stokes, T. F., & Baer, D. M. (1977). An implicit knowledge of generalization. *Journal of Applied Behavior Analysis, 11,* 285–303.

Sue, S., & Okazaki, S. (1990). Asian-American educational achievements: A phenomenon in search of an explanation. *American Psychologist, 45,* 913–920.

Sullivan, H. J. (1969). Objectives, evaluation, and improved learner achievement. *Instructional Objectives.* AERA Monograph Series on Curriculum Evaluation (3). Chicago: Rand McNally.

Sulzer-Azaroff, B., & Mayer, G. R. (1991). *Behavior analysis for lasting change.* Fort Worth: Holt, Rinehart & Winston.

Sulzer-Azaroff, B., & Reese, E. (1982). *Applying behavior analysis.* New York: CBS Publishing.

Summers, M. (1990). New student-teachers and computers: An investigation of experiences and feelings. *Educational Review, 42*(3), 261–271.

Suppes, P. (1966). The uses of computers in education. *Scientific American, 215,* 206–221.

Swanson, H. L. (1990). An information processing analysis of expert and novice teachers' problem solving. *American Educational Research Journal, 27*(3), 533–556.

Symons, S., Woloshyn, V., & Pressley, M. (Eds.). (1994). The scientific evaluation of the whole-language approach to literacy development. *Educational Psychologist, 29*(4), 173–222.

Takaki, R. (1989). *Strangers from a different shore.* Boston: Little, Brown.

Tennure, J. (1986). Instruction and cognitive development: Coordinating communication and cues. *Exceptional Children, 53,* 109–117.

Terman, L. (1956). In symposium: Intelligence and its measurement. *Journal of Educational Psychology, 12,* 127–133.

Terman, L., & Oden, M. (1959). *Genetic studies of genius: The gifted group at mid-life.* Stanford, CA: Stanford University Press.

References **613**

Tharp, R. (1989). Psychocultural variables and constants: Effects on teaching and learning in schools. *American Psychologist, 44,* 349–359.

Thorkildsen, T. (1988). Theories of education among academically able adolescents. *Contemporary Educational Psychology, 13,* 323–330.

Thorndike, E. (1913). *Educational psychology* (Vol. 1). New York: Teachers College Press.

Thorndike, E. L. (1932). *The fundamentals of learning.* New York: Teachers College Press.

Tiedt, P., & Tiedt, I. (1990). *Multicultural teaching.* Boston: Allyn & Bacon.

Tiemann, P., & Markle, S. (1990). *Analyzing instructional content: A guide to instruction and evaluation.* Champaign, IL: Stipes.

Tobin, J., Wu, D., & Davidson, D. (1989, April). How three key countries shape their children. *World Monitor,* pp. 36–45.

Tobin, T., & Dawson, G. (1992). Constraints to curriculum reform: Teachers and the myths of schooling. *Educational Technology Research and Development, 40*(1), 81–92.

Todman, J., & Dick, G. (1993). Primary children and teachers' attitudes to computers. *Computers in Education, 20*(2), 199–203.

Travers, J. (1982). *The growing child.* Glenview, IL: Scott, Foresman.

Tremmel, R. (1993). Zen and the art of reflective practice in teacher education. *Harvard Educational Review, 63*(4), 434–458.

Triandis, H. (1990). Theoretical concepts that are applicable to the analysis of ethnocentrism. In R. Brislin (Ed.), *Applied cross-cultural psychology.* Newbury Park, CA: Sage.

Trowbridge, L., & Bybee, R. (1986). *Becoming a secondary school science teacher.* Columbus, OH: Merrill.

Tulving, E. (1972). Episodic and semantic memory. In E. Tulving & W. Donaldson (Eds.), *Organization and memory.* New York: Academic Press.

Tversky, A., & Kahneman, D. (1981). The framing of decisions and the psychology of choice. *Science, 211,* 453–458.

Twardosz, S., Cataldo, M. F., & Risley, T. R. (1974). An open environment design for infant and toddler daycare. *Journal of Applied Behavior Analysis, 7,* 529–546.

Unger, R. (1979). Toward a redefinition of sex and gender. *American Psychologist, 34,* 1085–1094.

Vandegrift, J., & Greene, A. (1992). Rethinking parent involvement. *Educational Leadership, 50*(1), 57–59.

Van Haneghan, J., Barron, L., Young, M., Williams, S., Vye, N., & Bransford, J. D. (1992). The *Jasper* series: An experiment with new ways to enhance mathematical thinking. In D. F. Halpern (Ed.), *Enhancing thinking skills in the sciences and mathematics* (pp. 15–38). Hillsdale, NJ: Erlbaum.

Veroff, J., & Veroff, J. (1980). *Social incentives.* New York: Academic Press.

Vygotsky, L. (1962). *Thought and language.* New York: Wiley.

Vygotsky, L. (1978). *Mind in society.* Cambridge, MA: Harvard University Press.

Walberg, H. J. (1986). Synthesis of research on teaching. In M. Wittrock (Ed.), *Handbook of research on teaching.* New York: Macmillan.

Walker, H., & Sylvester, R. (1991). Where is school along the path to prison? *Educational Leadership, 49*(1), 14–16.

Wallerstein, J., & Blakeslee, S. (1989). *Second chances: Men, women and children a decade after divorce.* New York: Ticknor & Fields.

Walser, R. (1990). *Virtual reality: Theory, practice, and promise.* New York: Meckler Press.

Walsh, M. (1992). *Moving to nowhere.* New York: Auburn House.

Walsh, M. E., & Bibace, R. (1990). Developmentally-based AIDS/HIV education. *Journal of School Health, 60,* 256–261.

Wang, M., & Baker, E. (1985/1986). Mainstreaming programs: Design features and effects. *The Journal of Special Education, 19,* 503–521.

Wang, M. C., Huertel, G. D., & Walberg, H. J. (1993). Toward a knowledge base for school learning. *Review of Educational Research, 63,* 249–294.

Waugh, M., & Levin, J. (1989). TeleScience activities: Educational use of electronic networks. *The Journal of Computers in Mathematics and Science Teaching, 8*(2), 29–33.

Wechsler, D. (1958). *The measurement and appraisal of adult intelligence* (4th ed.). Baltimore: Williams & Wilkins.

Weidmann, C. (1933, November). Written examination procedures. *Phi Delta Kappan,* pp. 78–83.

Weidmann, C. (1941). Review of essay test studies. *Journal of Higher Education, 12,* 41–44.

Weiner, B. (1980). *Human motivation.* New York: Holt, Rinehart & Winston.

Weiner, B. (1984). Principles for a theory of student motivation and their application within an attributional framework. In R. Ames & C. Ames (Eds.), *Research on motivation in education* (Vol. 1). New York: Academic Press.

Weiner, B. (1990a). History of motivational research in education. *Journal of Educational Psychology, 82,* 616–622.

Weiner, B. (1990b). On perceiving the other as responsible. In R. Dienstbier (Ed.), *Nebraska Symposium on Motivation: Perspectives on motivation.* Lincoln, NE: University of Nebraska Press.

Weiner, B., Russell, D., & Lerman, D. (1978). Affective consequences of causal ascriptions. In J. H. Harvey et al. (Eds.), *New directions in attribution research.* Hillsdale, NJ: Erlbaum.

Weinstein, C. E., & Mayer, R. E. (1986). The teaching of learning strategies. In M. C. Wittrock (Eds.), *Handbook of research on teaching* (3rd ed.). New York: Macmillan.

Weinstein, C. E., Ridley, D. S., Dahl, T., & Weber, E. S. (1988/1989, December/January). Helping students develop strategies for effective learning. *Educational Leadership,* pp. 17–19.

Weiss, L., Farrar, E., & Petrie, H. (1989). *Dropouts from school: Issues, dilemmas, and solutions.* Albany: State University of New York Press.

Wertheimer, M. (1985). A Gestalt perspective on computer simulations of cognitive processes. *Computers in Human Behavior, 1,* 19–33.

Wertsch, J. (1985). *Vygotsky and the growth of mind.* Cambridge, MA: Harvard University Press.

Wertsch, J., & Tulviste, P. (1992). L. S. Vygotsky and contemporary developmental psychology. *Developmental Psychology, 28*(4), 558–565.

Whimbey, A., & Lochhead, T. (1985). *Problem solving and comprehension: A short course in analytical reasoning.* Philadelphia: Franklin Institute Press.

Whisler, J. (1991). The impact of teacher relationships and interactors on self-development and motivation. *Journal of Experimental Education, 60*(1), 15–30.

White, O. R., & Associates. (1988). Review and analysis of strategies for generalization. In N. G. Haring (Ed.), *Generalization for students with severe handicaps: Strategies and solutions* (pp. 15–51). Seattle: University of Washington Press.

Wickelgren, W. (1974). *How to solve problems.* San Francisco: W. H. Freeman.

Wielkiewicz, R. (1986). *Behavior management in the schools.* New York: Pergamon.

Wiggins, G. P. (1993). *Assessing student performance: Exploring the purpose and limits of testing.* San Francisco: Jossey-Bass.

Wigginton, E. (1992). Culture begins at home. *Educational Leadership, 49*(4), 60–64.

Wilcox, R. (1987, October). Rediscovering discovery learning. *The Clearing House,* pp. 53–56.

Wilder, G., Mackie, D., & Cooper, J. (1985). Gender and computers: Two surveys of computer-related attitudes. *Sex Roles, 13*(3, 4), 215–228.

Will, J., Self, P., & Datan, N. (1976). Maternal behavior and perceived sex of infant. *American Journal of Orthopsychiatry, 46,* 135–139.

Williams, J. (1986). Teaching children to identify the main idea of expository text. *Exceptional Children, 53,* 163–168.

Willis, S. (1993). Multicultural teaching. *Curriculum update.* Alexandria, VA: Association for Supervision and Curriculum Development.

Wilson, B. (1987). What is a concept? Concept teaching and cognitive psychology. *Performance and Instruction, 25,* 16–18.

Wilson, J. (1993). *A moral sense.* New York: Free Press.

Wilson, J., & Herrnstein, R. (1985). *Crime and human nature.* New York: Simon & Schuster.

Wilson, M. J., & Bullock, L. M. (1989). Psychometric characteristics of behavior rating scales: Definitions, problems, and solutions. *Behavioral Disorders, 14,* 186–200.

Wiske, M. S., Zodhiates, P., Wilson, B., Gordon, M., Harvey, W., Krensky, L., Lord, B., Watt, M., & Williams, K. (1990). *How technology affects teaching.* Cambridge, MA: Harvard Graduate School of Education, Educational Technology Center.

Witt, J. C., Elliott, S. N., Kramer, J. J., & Gresham, F. M. (1988). *Assessment of special children: Tests and the problem solving process.* Glenview, IL: Scott, Foresman.

Witt, J. C., Elliott, S. N., Kramer, J. J., & Gresham, F. M. (1994). *Assessment of children: Fundamental methods and practices.* Dubuque, IA: Brown & Benchmark.

Wlodkowski, R. (1986). *Motivation and teaching.* Washington, DC: National Education Association.

Wolfgang, C. H., & Glickman, C. D. (1986). *Solving discipline problems: Strategies for classroom teachers* (2nd ed.). Boston: Allyn & Bacon.

Woodruff, E., Bereiter, C., & Scardamalia, M. (1981/82). On the road to computer assisted compositions. *Journal of Educational Technology Systems, 10,* 133–148.

Woodward, J., Carnine, D., & Gersten, R. (1988). Teaching problem solving through a computer simulator. *American Educational Research Journal, 25,* 72–86.

Woodward, J., & Noell, J. (1991). Science instruction at the secondary level: Implications for students with learning disabilities. *Journal of Learning Disabilities, 24,* 277–284.

Workman, E. A. (1982). *Teaching behavioral self-control to students.* Austin, TX: Pro-Ed.

Wynne, E. (1988, February). Balancing character development and academics in the elementary school. *Phi Delta Kappan,* pp. 424–426.

Yao, E. L. (1988, November). Working effectively with Asian immigrant parents. *Phi Delta Kappan,* pp. 223–225.

Ysseldyke, J. E., & Algozzine, B. (1990). *Introduction to special education* (2nd ed.). Boston: Houghton Mifflin.

Ysseldyke, J. E., Algozzine, B., & Thurlow, M. L. (1992). *Critical issues in special education* (2nd ed.). Boston: Houghton Mifflin Co.

Ysseldyke, J. E., & Christenson, S. L. (1987). *The instructional environment scale: A comprehensive methodology for assessing an individual student's instruction.* Austin, TX: Pro-Ed.

Ysseldyke, J. E., Christenson, S. L., Thurlow, M. L., & Bakewell, D. (1989). Are different kinds of instructional tasks used by different categories of students in different settings? *School Psychology Review, 18,* 98–111.

Zigler, E., & Lang, M. (1991). *Child care choices: Balancing the needs of children, family and society.* New York: The Free Press.

Zigler, E., & Muenchow, S. (1992). *Head Start.* New York: Crown.

Zigler, E., & Styfco, S. (1994). Head Start: Criticisms in a constructive context. *American Psychologist, 49*(2), 127–132.

Zigler, E., Taussig, C., & Black, K. (1992). Early childhood intervention: A promising preventative for juvenile delinquency. *American Psychologist, 47*(8), 997–1006.

Zimmerman, B. J. (1989). A social cognitive view of self-regulated academic learning. *Journal of Educational Psychology, 81,* 329–339.

Zimmerman, B. J. (in press). Dimensions of academic self-regulation: A conceptual framework for education. In D. H. Schunk & B. A. Zimmerman (Eds.), *Self-regulation of learning and performance: Issues and educational applications.* Hillsdale, NJ: Erlbaum.

credits

Photographs

Section Openers

Section 1: © Daemmrich/The Image Works; **Section 2:** © Michael Siluk; **Section 3:** © Superstock, Inc.; **Section 4:** © Karen Halsinger Mullen/Unicorn Stock Photos; **Section 5:** © Superstock, Inc.

Chapter 1

Opener: © Tom McCarthy Photos/Unicorn Stock Photos; **p. 6 a & b:** © James L. Shaffer; **p. 11:** © Nancy Anne Dawe; **p. 14:** © Tom McCarthy/Unicorn Stock Photos; **p. 15:** © James L. Shaffer

Chapter 2

Opener: © R. Llewellyn/Superstock, Inc.; **p. 29:** © Michael Siluk; **2.2 left & right:** Tom Kratochwill

Chapter 3

Opener: © Eric Berndt/Unicorn Stock Photos; **p. 54:** © Nancy Anne Dawe; **p. 59:** © Skjold Photographs; **p. 62 (left):** © Jean Higgins/Unicorn Stock Photos; **(right):** © Paul Barton/The Stock Market; **p. 69:** © Elizabeth Crews/The Image Works

Chapter 4

Opener: © T. Rosenthal/Superstock, Inc.; **p. 81 a:** John Travers; **p. 81 b, c, & d:** © Michael Siluk; **p. 84:** © The Bettman Archive; **p. 87 a:** © Michael Siluk; **p. 87 b & d:** © James L. Shaffer; **p. 87 c:** © Will & Deni McIntyre/Photo Researchers, Inc.; **p. 103 (top left & right):** © Michael Siluk; **(bottom):** © Steve Bourgeois/Unicorn Stock Photos

Chapter 5

Opener: © Martin R. Jones/Unicorn Stock Photos; **p. 120:** The Bettman Archive; **p. 122:** © Michael Siluk; **p. 125:** © Lawrence Migdale/Photo Researchers, Inc.; **p. 130:** © Jeff Greenberg/Unicorn Stock Photos; **p. 135:** © Skjold Photographs

Chapter 6

Opener: © Superstock, Inc.; **p. 152:** © Bob Daemmrich/The Image Works; **p. 154:** Courtesy of Samuel A. Kirk, University of Arizona, Professor of Special Education; **p. 157:** © James L. Shaffer; **p. 161:** © Sheryl Siegel; **p. 179:** © James L. Shaffer; **p. 190:** © Bob Daemmrich/The Image Works

Chapter 7

Opener: © Nancy Anne Dawe; **p. 200:** The Bettman Archive; **p. 202:** Archives of the History of American Psychology; **p. 204:** Photo by G. K. Hare, Fred S. Keller, "Burrhus Frederick Skinner" in Journal of Applied Behavior Analysis, Vol. 23, No. 4, Winter 1990, Society for the Experimental Analysis of Behavior; **p. 216:** © Skjold Photographs; **p. 218:** A. Bandura, D. Ross & S. Ross, Imitation of Film-Mediated Aggressive Models, Journal of Abnormal and Social Psych., Vol. 66, 1963, fig. 2-2, pg. 3–11; **p. 219:** A. Bandura, D. Ross & S. Ross, Imitation of Film-Mediated Aggressive Models, *Journal of Abnormal and Social Psych.*, Vol. 66, 1963, fig. 2-2, pg. 3–11; **p. 220:** © Will McIntyre/Photo Researchers, Inc.

Chapter 8

Opener: © Superstock, Inc.; **p. 238:** © Michael Siluk; **p. 254 (top left and right):** © James L. Shaffer; **(bottom):** © Will & Deni McIntyre/Photo Researchers, Inc.

Chapter 9

Opener: © T. Rosenthal/Superstock, Inc.; **p. 281:** Courtesy of Robert Sternberg; **p. 282:** Courtesy of Howard Gardner, Harvard University; **p. 284:** Courtesy of David Perkins, Harvard University; **p. 297 (left):** © Michael Siluk; **(middle):** © Skjold Photographs; **(right):** © Betts Anderson/Unicorn Stock Photos

Chapter 10

Opener: © Sheryl Siegel; **p. 332:** © MacDonald Photography/Unicorn Stock Photos; **p. 346:** © Lawrence Migdale/Photo Researchers, Inc.

Chapter 11

Opener: © Superstock, Inc.; **p. 389:** © Gabe Palmer/The Stock Market

Chapter 12

Opener: © R. Heinzen/Superstock, Inc.; **p. 397 a & d:** © Michael Siluk; **b:** © Frank Pedrick/The Image Works; **c:** © David Frazier Photolibrary; **p. 417 (left):** © James L. Shaffer; **(right):** © Jeff Greenberg/Unicorn Stock Photos

Chapter 13

Opener: © Michael Siluk; **p. 435:** © James L. Shaffer; **p. 447:** © James L. Shaffer; **p. 462:** © Michael Siluk; **p. 463:** Photograph courtesy of the Institute for Reality Therapy

Chapter 14

Opener: © Gabe Palmer/The Stock Market; **p. 481:** © Daemmrich/The Image Works

Chapter 15

Opener: © Jeff Greenberg/Unicorn Stock Photos; **p. 530:** © Michael Siluk; **p. 543:** AGS Catalog, 1991, American Guidance Service, Circle Pines, MN; **p. 553:** © Bob Daemmrich/The Image Works

Chapter 16

Opener: © R. Llewellyn/Superstock Inc.; **p. 561 (left):** © Dennis MacDonald/Unicorn Stock Photos; **(right):** © Nancy A. Dawe; **p. 584:** © Elizabeth Crews/The Image Works

name index

Abrams, P. D., 496, 507
Achenbach, T., 573, 574, 575, 576
Adams, M., 383
Agard, J. A., 351
Agne, K., 19
Ahlgren, A., 388
Ainsworth, M., 121
Airasian, P. W., 371, 372, 382, 541, 584
Alberto, P., 223, 224, 225, 226, 231
Alderman, M. K., 352, 353
Alexander, K., 385
Algozzine, B., 153, 154, 168, 178, 181,
    182, 190
American Association of University Women
    Educational Foundation, 72, 73, 131
American Educational Research Association,
    586, 589
American Federation of Teachers, 524
American Psychiatric Association, 168,
    169, 178
American Psychological Association, 47, 528,
    586, 589
Ames, C., 332
Anastasi, A., 584
Anderson, J., 254
Anderson, J. R., 501
Anderson, L. W., 6, 7
Andre, T., 238, 242, 243
Archbald, D. A., 522, 540–541
Argulewicz, E., 572
Armstrong, D., 378
Asher, S., 129
Asher, W., 46
Atkinson, R. C., 263
Au, K., 383, 384
Austin, G., 247, 261
Ausubel, D., 245, 246

Baddeley, A., 243, 263, 264
Baer, D. M., 227
Bailey, D. B., 166
Baillargeon, P., 96, 97, 98
Baillargeon, R., 97
Baker, E., 186, 529
Bakker, D., 251
Bales, J., 205
Bandura, A., 216, 217, 218, 220, 221, 222, 340,
    341, 350, 351, 360
Banks, C., 14, 83
Banks, J., 14, 55, 72, 73, 83
Barker, G., 352
Barker, R. G., 41
Barlow, D. H., 32, 44, 46
Barr, A., 501
Bartlett, F. C., 239, 242
Beaver, J. F., 487
Beck, I., 384

Becker, H. J., 481, 483, 484
Beer, J., 346
Belsky, J., 122
Benchmarks for Science Literacy, 391
Benn, J., 57, 62
Benninga, J., 142
Bereiter, C., 412, 500
Berger, C. F., 507
Berk, L., 70, 128
Berliner, D., 441
Berliner, D. C., 397
Bibace, R., 99, 100
Billingsley, A., 57
Bisanz, G., 244
Bjorklund, B., 80
Bjorklund, D., 80
Black, K., 133
Blair, T., 399
Blakeslee, S., 126
Blankenship, C., 539
Block, J., 67
Bloom, B., 159, 286, 377, 379, 380, 418, 419,
    421, 537, 580
Bloomquist, M. L., 168
Blumenfeld, P., 332
Blythe, T., 410
Bobbitt, S., 132
Bonk, C. J., 500, 501
Bonstingl, J., 7, 17
Booker, C., 57, 357
Borich, G., 72, 371, 396, 398, 402, 404
Borland, J., 156
Bos, C., 157
Bosh, M. A., 320
Boulanger, F. D., 380
Bower, G., 410
Bowlby, J., 121
Boyer, E., 396
Boyle, C. F., 501
Bragstad, B. J., 19
Brandell, M. E., 168
Brandt, R., 17, 18, 410
Bransford, J., 301, 304
Bransford, J. D., 308, 503, 504
Braswell, L., 168
Brennan, E. C., 485, 487
Briggs, L., 415
Brislin, R., 52
Brodinsky, B., 492
Broihier, M., 488, 489
Bronfenbrenner, U., 265
Bronson, M., 35
Brookhart, S., 8
Brookover, W. B., 442
Brooks, D., 144
Brooks, R., 172, 173
Brophy, J., 153, 230, 332, 336, 398, 400
Brown, A., 173, 382, 572–573

Brown, D. S., 369
Brown, J. S., 386
Brown, R., 158, 256, 261
Bruder, I., 492
Bruner, J., 52, 54, 247, 256, 261, 275, 336, 356,
    404, 405, 406, 407
Bruning, R. H., 246
Bryk, A., 105
Bullinger, A., 98, 107
Bullock, L. M., 574
Bunzo, M., 479
Burke, J., 133
Burns, R. B., 6, 7
Burton, R. R., 386
Bybee, R., 388, 389

Caine, G., 250, 251, 252
Caine, R., 250, 251, 252
Calfee, R., 383
Callahan, J., 403
Calvert, P., 126
Camp, B. W., 320
Campione, J., 173, 572–573
Canter, L., 424
Capelli, C., 110
Carey, S., 388, 389
Carnine, D., 413
Carpenter, P., 384
Carpenter, T., 386
Carper, L. B., 469
Carranza, O., 453
Carrera, J. W., 190, 302, 374, 453, 522
Carroll, J., 397, 435
Casas, J. M., 453
Case, R., 101
Cataldo, M. F., 32
Ceci, S., 265
Chabay, R. W., 503
Chance, P., 333, 339, 347
Chaney, C., 108
Chard, D., 464, 465, 466
Chase, W., 306
Chatillon, J., 98, 107
Chen, M., 489
Children's Defense Fund, 453
Children's Television Workshop, 492
Choi, S., 5
Chomsky, N., 113
Christenson, S. L., 409, 468
Clabby, J. F., 320
Clark, C., 369, 424
Clark, F., 424
Clark, L., 403
Clarke, V. A., 489
Clarke-Stewart, A., 122
Clements, D. H., 499, 512

Clingempeel, W. G., 126
Coalition of Essential Schools, 543
Cochran-Smith, M., 500
Code of fair testing practices in education, 586, 590
Cognition & Technology Group at Vanderbilt, 504
Cohen, R., 11
Coladarci, T., 552, 574
Colby, A., 137, 140
Cole, M., 274, 302
Collins, M., 413
Collis, B. A., 489
Comer, J., 426
Conoley, J. C., 468
Conway, M., 264
Cook, T. D., 44
Cooledge, N., 8
Cooper, H., 10, 424, 425
Cooper, J., 489
Cooper, J. J., 198
Cooper, R., 60, 423
Corkill, A. J., 246
Corno, L., 153, 334
Cosden, M., 354
Costa, A., 289, 290
Coutinho, M., 544
Cowen, E. L., 434
Cox, P., 219
Craig, G., 343
Craik, F. I., 264
Craske, M. L., 222
Cronbach, L., 528
Cross, D., 219
Cuban, L., 485, 486

Dacey, J., 318, 346, 348
Daiute, C., 500
Darling-Hammond, L., 59
Darlington, R., 63
Dash, U., 107
Datan, N., 67
Davidson, D., 54
Davidson, J., 568
Davidson, J. E., 156, 158
Dawson, G., 487
deBono, E., 295, 296, 301
de Charms, R., 359
Deci, E., 333
deCuevas, J., 102
Deese, J., 201, 205
DeHart, G., 60
de Jong, T., 244
Delclos, V. R., 498
Deno, S., 539
Department of Engineering & Public Policy, 507
Derr, T. F., 539
Derry, S. J., 270
Dick, G., 488, 489
Dick, W. A., 485
Diener, C., 350
Dill, D., 410
Dobbin, J., 553
Donnellan, A. M., 212, 225
Doris, J., 243
Dornbusch, S., 426
Downs, A. C., 68
Doyle, W., 322, 435, 441, 442, 445, 449, 452
Dreikurs, R., 461, 462
Dresher, M., 107
Dreyfus, H. L., 240
Driscoll, M., 231, 415

Drum, P., 383
Dukes, W. F., 32
Dunn, J., 67, 68
Dunn, R., 32
Dweck, C., 336, 349, 350

Ebbinghaus, H., 266
Edelbrock, C., 573, 574
Egeth, H., 201, 205
Eggan, G., 479
Elias, M. J., 320
Elkind, D., 95
Elliott, S. N., 64, 351, 468–469, 572, 573, 574
Ellis, H., 240, 241, 267, 321
Ely, D. P., 481, 482, 484, 485
Emerson, H., 352
Emmer, E., 447, 451
Engelhard, G., 347, 354
Engelmann, 412, 413
Ennis, R., 280
Entwiste, D., 385
Epstein, J., 332
Erikson, E., 120, 121, 135
Esveldt-Dawson, K., 229
Evans, M., 214
Evans, S., 351
Evertson, C., 41, 447

Fagot, B., 67
Falkof, L., 288
Fantz, R., 256
Farrar, E., 60
Farrington, D., 132
Fawson, E. C., 487
Feigenbaum, E. A., 501
Ferguson-Hassler, M., 244
Ferrington, G., 507
Ferster, C. B., 208
Feuerstein, R., 294
Field, D., 97
Fillmore, L., 191
Finch, C. L., 562
Finch, M., 576
First, J., 190, 302, 357, 374, 453, 522
Fischer, K., 98, 100
Fisk, J., 251
Flavell, J. H., 87, 95, 269, 270
Flinders, D., 12
Ford, M., 330, 331, 333, 360
Foster, S., 245, 253, 258
Fouts, J., 346
Fox, L. H., 160
Fraenkel, J. R., 37
Frasier, M., 157, 158
Frederiksen, N., 323
Freeman, D., 8
Frisbie, D., 527
Fromberg, D., 231
Furlong, M., 453

Gage, N. L., 13
Gagne, R., 415
Gallimore, P., 426
Gallini, J. K., 492
Garbarino, J., 57, 62
Garcia Coll, C., 109
Gardner, H., 113, 238, 239, 240, 241, 247, 261, 270, 282, 284, 368, 488, 568
Gardner, R., 44
Garger, S., 253

Garibaldi, A., 355
Garman, N., 403
Gary, L., 57, 357
Gawronski, J. D., 558
Gelfand, D. M., 231
Gelman, R., 96, 97, 98
Genshaft, J., 157
Gentry, D., 530
Gerber, M., 185
Gerschner, V. T., 488
Gersten, R., 413
Gettinger, M., 399, 418, 419, 434
Gibbons, M., 545
Giddings, L., 107, 108
Gilligan, C., 141
Gilman, D., 18
Ginsberg, H., 90, 95
Glasnapp, D., 581
Glass, A., 238, 253, 262
Glass, G. J., 45
Glasser, W., 241, 463
Gleason, J. B., 102, 104
Glickman, C. D., 462, 463
Glover, J. A., 3, 246
Goldman, J. A., 41, 42, 43
Goldstein, A. P., 320
Good, T., 153, 352, 398, 408
Goodenow, C., 339
Goodlad, J., 18, 371
Goodman, C., 256
Goodman, K., 384
Goodman, Y., 81, 107
Goodnow, J., 247, 261
Gould, S., 569, 571
Grady, M., 251
Graham, S., 352
Grant, C., 55, 357, 398
Green, J., 41
Greene, A., 20
Greene, J., 300, 307
Greene, L., 170
Greenfield, P., 291
Greer, R. D., 230, 231
Gresham, F. M., 64, 351, 538, 573, 574
Griswold, P., 527
Gronlund, N., 374, 376, 377, 527, 552, 561, 564, 566
Gronlund, N. E., 378, 525, 532, 563
Grossen, B., 413
Grossman, H., 174, 274, 303, 453
Grossnickle, D. R., 330
Guilford, J., 568
Gullo, D. F., 499
Gump, P., 442
Guskey, T., 420
Gutkin, T. B., 572

Hadley, M., 484, 485, 487
Hagan, R., 67
Haight, W., 105
Hakuta, K., 113, 191
Hale-Benson, J., 83
Halford, G. S., 97
Hallahan, D., 155, 172, 184
Hallan, D. D., 171
Hamachek, D., 429
Hammill, D. D., 171
Hannafin, R. D., 487
Hanson, A., 219
Harel, I., 499
Harel, K., 352
Haring, N., 179
Haring, T., 354

Harre, R., 3
Harris, K. R., 267
Harris, T., 243
Hart, L., 252
Hartmann, D. P., 231
Hastings, J. T., 370, 375, 377, 580
Hauser-Cram, P., 62, 63
Hausner, L., 424
Hawkins, J., 499
Hayes, J., 306, 307, 312, 317
Hayes, L., 61
Hayes, S. C., 44, 46
Hazi, H., 403
Hecht, D., 343
Heller, R. S., 488, 489
Hembree, H., 343, 344
Hendrick, J., 100
Herbert, B., 134
Hergenhahn, B. R., 204, 208
Heron, T. E., 198
Herrnstein, R., 132
Hersen, M., 32
Hetherington, E. M., 60, 62, 126
Heward, W. L., 44, 152, 198
Hilgard, E., 410
Hill, K. T., 343
Hill, W., 214
Hilliard, A., 584
Hillman, D., 318
Hinde, R. A., 74
Hiroto, D. S., 349
Hodgkinson, H., 3
Hoffman, K., 388
Hofmeister, A., 413
Hoge, R. D., 552, 574
Holmes, C. T., 10
Holyoak, K., 238, 253, 262
Hops, H., 576
Horne, A. M., 450
Hovland, C., 344
Howard, G., 275
Howe, M. J. A., 492
Howell, C., 575
Howell, K. W., 539
Hubel, D., 252
Huck, S. W., 30, 31
Huertel, G. D., 46
Hughes, C., 374
Hughes, M., 386
Hulse, S., 201, 205
Hunka, S., 377
Hunt, E., 568
Hunt, R., 240, 241, 267, 321
Hunter, B., 308
Hunter, M., 399, 403
Huttenlocher, J., 105
Hyden, H., 253

Ingersoll, B., 170
Inhelder, B., 86, 88, 91, 95
Ireton, H., 576, 577, 578
Irvine, J. T., 98
Isenberg, J., 120

Jacklin, C. N., 70
Jackson, L., 291, 293
Jackson, P., 18, 439, 440, 441
Jacobson, L., 427
Janis, S., 344
Jay, E., 285
Jaynes, G., 57
Jenkins, J., 539

Jenkins, L., 389
Jensen, A., 573
Johnson, C., 354
Johnson, L., 346
Jonassen, D. H., 481
Jones, B. F., 308, 309
Jones, M., 131
Jones, R. L., 584
Julkunen, K., 344

Kagan, J., 42, 121
Kahneman, D., 269
Kail, R., 313
Kaiser, S. M., 573
Kalish, H., 201
Kane, P., 8
Kann, M., 144
Kassenbaum, N., 63
Kauffman, J., 155, 172, 184, 185
Kaufman, M., 351
Kay, R. H., 487
Kazdin, A., 205, 206, 209, 210, 211, 458
Kazdin, A. E., 32, 46, 229, 449, 458, 460, 575
Kellaghan, T., 584
Keller, F. S., 208
Kelley, J., 344
Kelley, M. L., 469
Kellogg, J., 15, 16
Kellough, R., 376, 377, 403
Kerlinger, F., 30
Kim, E., 376, 377
Kim, U., 52, 56
Kinsbourne, M., 241
Kleiman, G., 388
Kohlberg, L., 69, 137, 138, 139, 143
Kornhaber, M., 568
Kosslyn, S., 254
Kounin, J., 454
Kozol, J., 61, 62
Kramer, J. J., 468
Krathwohl, D. R., 37
Kratochwill, T. R., 41, 42, 43, 44, 123, 124, 229, 468–469, 536, 539
Krechevsky, M., 568
Krendl, K. A., 488, 489
Krouse, H., 270, 272
Krug, D., 246
Kulik, C. C., 497
Kulik, J. A., 497
Kurland, D. M., 499

Lachman, R., 242
Lajoie, S. P., 479
Lamb, R., 3
Lang, M., 122
Langlois, J., 68
Larry P. v. Riles, 573, 583
Larsen, S., 171
Laslett, R., 443
LaVigna, G. W., 212, 225
Lawton, J., 488
Lazar, I., 63
Leahey, D., 243
Lehrer, R., 498, 499, 503, 504
Leigh, J., 171
Leinbach, M., 67
Lenneberg, E., 111, 261
Lepper, M. R., 503
Lesgold, A., 479, 502
Lesner, W. J., 318
Leuhrmann, A., 487
Levin, J., 507

Levin, J. R., 44, 46, 313
Levine, M., 172, 173
Lewis, D., 300, 307
Lichtenstein, R., 576, 577, 578
Lickona, T., 138, 141, 144, 147
Liebert, R. M., 68
Lindholm, K. J., 108
Linn, R., 583
Linn, R. L., 378, 525, 532, 563
Lipman, M., 280
Lips, H., 67, 68
Lipsey, M. W., 46
Lipson, M., 219
Little, J., 67
Littlefield, J., 498, 499
Livingston, R., 162
Lloyd, J. W., 171, 183
Lochhead, T., 299, 301
Lockard, J., 496, 507
Lockhart, R. S., 264
Lodhi, S., 230
Loftus, E. F., 243
Loge, K., 507
Lonner, W., 14
Looft, W. R., 41, 42, 43
Lorion, R. P., 434
Lott, B., 67
Lovell-Troy, L., 371
Lovinger, S. L., 168
Lowenbraun, S., 164
Ludlow, L., 568
Luria, A., 249
Lyman, F. T., 308
Lyman, H., 528, 582
Lyons, T., 105

Maccoby, E. E., 70
Mackie, D., 489
Madaus, G., 58, 59, 73, 370, 375, 377, 562, 580, 584
Madden, N. A., 152, 153
Maehr, M., 332
Mager, R., 375, 377
Magid, K., 132
Magliocca, L., 20
Mahmoud, E., 488, 489
Maier, S. F., 349
Malone, M., 98
Malouf, D., 544
Malpass, R., 14
Manaster, G. J., 95
Many, W. A., 496, 507
Manzo, A., 423
Manzo, U., 423
Marcia, J., 132
Markle, S., 414
Markstrom-Adams, C., 130
Marschark, M., 164
Marso, R., 523
Martin, C., 67
Martin, C. D., 488, 489
Maslow, A., 334, 335
Mason, J., 383, 384
Matarazzo, J., 527
Matsumoto, D., 14
Maxim, G., 372
Mayer, G. R., 231, 460
Mayer, R., 21
Mayer, R. E., 315, 492
McBay, S., 16
McCarthy, R., 507
McCaslin, M., 107
McClelland, D., 337

McConaughy, S., 575
McConaughy, S. H., 574, 576
McConnell, J. V., 345
McCormick, L., 179
McDougall, A., 512
McGraw, V., 45
McKelvey, C., 132
McLaughlin, B., 110
McLoyd, V., 16
McMahon, H., 485
McNamara, E., 214
McNutt, G., 171
McTighe, J., 308
Medland, M., 448
Medway, F. J., 10
Mervis, C. B., 261
Messick, S., 529
Meyer, C. A., 545
Midgley, C., 332
Miller, G. A., 247
Miller, P., 101
Miller, S., 413
Miller-Jones, D., 291
Minuchin, P., 436
Miranda, A. H., 453
Mohanty, A., 107
Money, J., 66
Monsaas, J., 347
Moore, G., 35
Moore, L., 413
Morris, R. J., 123, 124
Morsink, C., 171
Moses, S., 331, 337, 583
Moss, H., 42
Moss, J., 288
Muenchow, S., 63
Mullis, I., 389
Murphy, J., 7
Muth, D., 372
Muthukvishna, N., 413
Myers, P. I., 171
Myers, R., 346

Nagin, D., 132
Narayan, J., 44
Nastasi, B. K., 512
National Commission on Testing and Public
    Policy, 73
National Council of Teachers of Mathematics,
    385
Neisser, U., 265
Nelson, R. O., 44, 46
Nesbit, J., 377
Nesher, P., 386, 387
New, C., 83, 426
Newman, R. S., 352
Newmann, F. M., 522, 540–541
Niedelman, M., 413
Nitko, A., 529
Nix, D., 503
Noell, J., 413
Nolet, V., 459
Norman, D., 322
Nunn, G., 347

O'Boyle, C., 67
Oden, M., 160
Office of Technology Assessment, 543
Okagaki, L., 291, 293
Okazaki, S., 158
Olsen, L., 16, 291, 427

Olweus, D., 450
O'Neil, J., 368
Opper, S., 90, 95
Orlansky, M. D., 152

Page, E., 550
Paivio, A., 254
Palincer, A. S., 382
Palmer, J. C., 243
Palmer, O., 549
Pany, D., 539
Papert, S., 498, 499
Paris, S., 219
Parish, T., 347
Parke, R., 449
Parke, R. D., 60, 62
Parker, J., 129
Pase (Parents in Action on Special Education),
    573, 583
Paulos, J., 9
Paulson, F. L., 545
Paulson, P. R., 545
Pavlov, I. P., 200
Pea, R. D., 499
Pease, D., 104
Perkins, D., 284, 285, 317
Perkins, D. N., 410
Peterson, P., 369
Petri, H., 337
Petrie, H., 60
Phares, E. J., 347
Phillips, D. C., 253
Phye, G., 238, 242, 243
Piaget, J., 84, 85, 86, 88, 90, 91, 93, 95,
    112, 136
Pierce, J., 308
Piersel, W., 229, 572
Pierson, D., 35
Pigge, F., 523
Pinker, S., 70
Poggio, J., 581
Pompi, K. F., 242
Posner, G., 396
Premack, D., 214
Pressley, M., 107, 267
Prewitt, P. W., 450
Price, R. H., 434
Pugach, M., 179
Pulido, J., 18
Pullin, D., 54, 59, 73

Quackenbush, M., 100
Quay, H. C., 440

Rafferty, M., 125
Rahman, R., 244
Ramos-McKay, A., 434
Ramsey, P., 58, 425
Ratliff, J. D., 336
Rauth, M., 155
Raymond, B. B., 42
Raymond, J. R., 42
Redl, F., 461
Reese, E., 231
Reis, S., 156
Renyi, J., 61
Renzuli, J., 159
Repp, A. C., 171, 185, 225
Repucci, N. D., 350

Resnick, L., 368
Rest, J., 96
Reutzel, R., 423
Reynolds, C. R., 573
Rice, M. L., 492
Rieser, B. J., 501
Rieser, J., 308
Rieser, R. A., 482, 485
Risley, T. R., 32
Roberts, N., 506, 507
Robinson, N., 20
Rogers, B., 368
Rogoff, B., 54, 55, 98, 99, 216, 291, 426, 584
Rohr, C., 132
Romberg, T., 385, 386, 387
Ronning, R. R., 3
Rosch, E., 261
Rose, J. S., 10
Rose, S., 249
Rose, T. L., 38, 39
Rosen, L. A., 455, 456, 457
Rosenfield, S., 539
Rosenshine, B., 402, 446
Rosenthal, R., 427
Rosser, P., 73
Roth, K. J., 502
Rotter, J., 347, 348
Rourke, B., 251
Rovine, M., 122
Rummelhart, D., 322
Russell, D., 399
Rutter, M., 120, 176
Ryan, A. W., 497
Ryan, R., 333

Sadker, D., 66, 70, 71, 72
Sadker, M., 66, 70, 71, 72
Salomon, G., 488, 511
Salvia, J., 374
Sammur, G. B., 492
Sanders, N., 287
Sandler, H. M., 30, 31
Santa, J., 238, 253, 262
Santos de Barona, M., 453
Santrock, J., 95
Savage, T., 378
Savenye, W. C., 487
Sayger, T. V., 450
Scardamalia, M., 500
Scarr, S., 96, 125
Schab, F., 136
Schachter, D., 264, 266
Schiefflen, B., 426
Schon, D. A., 399, 401
Schunk, D., 217, 219
Scribner, S., 274, 302
Seesdedt-Stanford, L., 168
Self, P., 67
Seligman, M., 349, 350
Seligman, M. E., 348, 349
Selinske, J. E., 230, 231
Seltzer, M., 105
Semmel, M., 185
Semmel, M. I., 351
Serbin, L., 66
Serna, L., 334
Shade, B., 83, 426
Shapiro, E., 436
Shapiro, E. S., 536, 539
Sheingold, K., 484, 485, 487
Sheridan, S., 536, 539
Sheridan, S. W., 468–469

Sherry, D., 264, 266
Sherwood, R., 308
Sherwood, R. D., 504
Shiffrin, R. M., 263
Shinn, M., 125
Shinn, M. R., 539
Shonkoff, J., 172, 173
Shuell, T., 241, 255
Shulman, L., 397, 408, 410
Shure, M. B., 320
Shweder, R., 53
Skinner, B. F., 29
Siegler, R., 241
Silver, A., 308
Silvern, L., 98, 100
Simmons, W., 368
Simon, H., 306
Sims, V. K., 492
Singh, N. N., 171, 185, 225
Sizemore, B., 370
Sizer, T., 368
Skinner, B. F., 29, 204, 205, 206, 207, 208, 209,
    212, 213, 230, 232, 339, 411, 495, 568
Slaby, R., 449
Slaughter-Defoe, D., 302
Slavin, R., 45, 354, 355, 443, 444
Slavin, R. E., 152, 153, 187
Slavings, R., 352
Sleeter, C., 55, 357, 398
Smellie, D. C., 487
Smith, C., 443
Smith, M., 246, 385
Smith, M. L., 45
Smith, S., 385, 464, 465, 466
Snow, R., 152, 153
Solberg, U. S., 453
Soldier, L. L., 446
Spencer, M., 130, 426
Speth, C., 256
Spiro, R., 503
Spivak, G., 320
Sprick, R. S., 459
Squires, D., 512
Sroufe, L. A., 60
Stage, E., 388
Stallings, J., 208
Stanley, J., 158
Stein, B., 301, 304
Steinberg, E. R., 504
Sternberg, R., 156, 280, 281, 282, 291, 293,
    294, 304, 317
Stevens, R., 402, 446
Stevenson, H., 57, 385
Stewart, J., 478
Stiggins, R. J., 542
Stigler, J., 58, 98, 136, 522
Stipek, D., 208
Stokes, T. F., 227
Strang, J., 251

Stumpf, S., 19
Styfco, S., 63
Sue, S., 158
Sugai, G., 464, 465, 466
Sullivan, H. J., 378
Sulzer-Azaroff, B., 230, 231, 460
Summers, M., 487
Suppes, P., 502
Swanson, H. L., 20
Sylvester, R., 133
Symons, S., 107

Takaki, R., 16
Taussig, C., 133
Tennure, L., 271
Terman, L., 160, 568
Tharp, R., 56, 57, 274, 275
Thiel, W. B., 330
Thompson, M., 164
Thorkildsen, T., 331
Thorndike, E., 202
Thurlow, M. L., 178
Tiedt, I., 14, 128, 375, 426
Tiedt, P., 14, 128, 375, 426
Tiemann, P., 414
Tishman, S., 285
Tittle, C., 343
Tivnan, T., 35
Tobin, J., 54
Tobin, T., 487
Todman, J., 488, 489
Travers, J., 449
Tremmel, R., 399
Triandis, H., 52
Troutman, A., 223, 224, 225, 226, 231
Trowbridge, L., 388, 389
Tulving, E., 263
Tulviste, P., 52
Tversky, A., 269
Twardosz, S., 32, 33

Unger, R., 64

Valadez, C., 191
Vandegrift, J., 20
Van Haneghan, J., 504
Vaughn, S., 157
Villarreal, S., 100
Vitale, M., 448
Vye, N. J., 308, 504
Vygotsky, L., 52, 54, 82

Wager, W., 415
Walberg, H. J., 46

Walker, H., 133
Wallen, N. E., 37
Wallerstein, J., 126
Walser, R., 507
Walsh, M., 99, 100, 125
Wang, M., 186
Wang, M. C., 46
Washington, J., 160
Wattenberg, W., 461
Waugh, M., 507
Wechsler, D., 568, 570, 571
Weiner, B., 329, 330, 338, 339, 360
Weinstein, C. E., 315
Weiss, L., 60
Wertheimer, M., 242
Wertsch, J., 52, 82
Whimbey, A., 299, 301
Whisler, J., 336
White, O. R., 227
Wickelgren, W., 304, 305, 306, 307
Wielkiewicz, R., 460
Wigfield, A., 343
Wiggins, G. P., 528, 583, 584
Wigginton, E., 83
Wilcox, R., 407
Wilder, G., 489
Will, J., 67
Williams, J., 246
Williams, R., 57
Williams, R. L., 489
Willis, S., 375, 398
Wilson, B., 262
Wilson, D. B., 46
Wilson, J., 132
Wilson, M. J., 574
Wiske, M. S., 487
Witt, J. C., 521, 527, 538, 540, 565, 567, 572,
    573, 574, 576
Wlodkowski, R., 330, 331, 357
Wolery, W., 166
Wolf, C. J., 507
Wolfgang, C. H., 462, 463
Woloshyn, V., 107
Wood, C., 67
Woodruff, E., 500
Woodward, J., 413
Workman, E. A., 229
Wu, D., 54
Wynne, E., 144

Yao, E. L., 58
Ysseldyke, J. E., 153, 154, 168, 177, 178, 181,
    182, 185, 190, 409

Zenge, S., 107
Zigler, E., 63, 122, 133

subject index

Ability, attribution theory and, 338
Ability grouping, 153–155, 444
About Behaviorism (Skinner), 204
Academic achievement. *See* Achievement;
    Achievement tests
Academic diagnostic tests, 560
Academic goals, 371
Acceleration, 158–159
Access, to technology, 509
Accommodation, 84, 246
Accuracy, problem solving and, 301
Achievement
    culture and, 55
    gender and, 70–72
    motivation and, 336–337
    social class and, 59–63
Achievement tests, 539, 560, 561, 564–565
    reflective teaching and, 401
Acquisition, as thinking frame, 285
Active problem solving, 302
Active responding, in programmed instruction,
    414–415
Activities. *See* Classroom activities
Activity reinforcers, 223
Acts of Meaning (Bruner), 356
Acuity, perceptual, helping students with,
    258–259
Adaptation, 84
    to individual differences. *See* Individual
        differences
Additive approach, to gender material, 72
ADHD (attention-deficit/hyperactivity
    disorder), 168–170
Administration
    standardized tests uses for, 560
    technology use by, 491
Adolescence
    classroom management and, 437–438
    cognitive development in, 95–96, 97
    moral development in, 140–141
    psychosocial development in, 130–134
Advance organizers, 246–247
Affect
    motivation and, 360
    speech and, 104
Affective entry characteristics, 420, 421
African American students, 14
    cultural compatibility of, 56
    environmental aspects important to, 83
    exceptional, 190
    high-achieving schools and, 370

    interactions in classrooms and, 57
    poverty among, 60
    problem solving and, 302
Aggression. *See* Violence
AIDS prevention, cognitive development and,
    99–100
Alternative response items, 534–535
Alternative solution thinking, 320
Amputations, 167
Animism, 91
Anxiety
    classroom conditions and, 343
    motivation and, 342–344
    test, 343–344
Applied behavior analysis, 460
Appreciation, art of teaching and, 12
Apraxia, 166
Aptitude tests, 561, 566–573
    intelligence measurement using, 567–573
Argument of compensation, 93
Argument of identity, 93
Argument of reversibility, 93
Artificialism, 91
Art of Teaching (Highet), 12
ASCII, 479
Asian American students, 14
    cognition and, 274
    cultural compatibility of, 56, 57
    exceptional, 190
    poverty among, 60
    problem solving and, 302
Assessment, 583. *See also* Test(s)
    assumptions of, 520–521
    authentic/performance, 540–547
    behavioral, 537–539
    curriculum-based, 539
    definition of, 520
    of exceptional students, 176–178
    grading and, 547–548, 549–551
    integrating with learning, 522–524
    marking and, 547, 548–549
    of multicultural students, 522
    reporting and, 551–552
    standardized tests for. *See* Achievement
        tests; Aptitude tests; Standardized
        tests
    teacher-constructed tests for. *See* Teacher-
        constructed tests
    of teachers, 583
    teachers and, 523–524
    teachers' judgments and, 552

    terminology for, 520
    uses and users of information and,
        521–522
Assimilation, 84, 246
Asthma, 167
Attachment, in infancy, 121
Attention
    selective, learning disabilities and, 172
    social cognitive learning and, 217
Attention-deficit/hyperactivity disorder
    (ADHD), 168–170
Attention management, for problem
    solving, 313
Attitudes
    changing, 344–345
    classroom implications of, 345–346
    motivation and, 344–346, 357
    problem solving and, 301
Attributions for success, in Link Model, 354
Attribution theory
    classroom implications of, 339
    motivation and, 337–339
Audience, attitude change and, 345
Audience-communicator feedback loop,
    attitude change and, 345
Audiovisual aids, 491–492
Authentic/performance assessment, 540–547
Authority, as source of knowledge, 28
Autonomy versus shame and doubt stage,
    121–123
Aversive control, 459
Aversive stimulus, 209
Avoidance behavior, 212

Babbling, 104–105
Baby and Child Care (Spock), 29
Baby biographies, 30–31
Becoming a Nation of Readers, 381
Beginning teacher evaluation studies
    (BTES), 397
Behavior
    language and, 111–112
    principle of, 205
    recording, 231
    terminal, 411
    violent. *See* Violence
Behavioral assessment, 537–539
Behavioral psychology, 198–235
    application to schooling, 230–233

classical conditioning and. *See* Classical conditioning
classroom implications of, 340
connectionism and, 202, 204
motivation and, 339–340
operant conditioning and. *See* Operant conditioning
social cognitive learning and. *See* Social cognitive learning
techniques of self-control and, 228–230
techniques to decrease behavior and, 224–226
techniques to increase behavior and, 222–224
techniques to maintain behavior and, 227–228
Behavior change procedure, 205
Behavior disorders, 154, 167–170
characteristics of, 167–168
Behavior influence, 458
Behaviorist psychology, 20
Behavior Management, 464
Behavior modification, 455–461
causes of behavior and, 460
terminology for, 458–459
Behavior of Organisms (Skinner), 204
Behavior rating scales, 573–576
characteristics and interpretation of, 575–576
uses of, 574–575
Behavior therapy, 458
Belongingness needs, 335
Benchmarks for Science Literacy (Ahlgren and Rutherford), 389, 391
Beyond Freedom and Dignity (Skinner), 204
Bias, testing. *See* Test bias
Bilingual Act of 1988, 191
Bilingual education, 190–192
Bilingualism, 108–110
Bilingual technique, 191–192
Binet's measures of intelligence, 572
Biographical Sketch of an Infant, A (Darwin), 31
Bit, 479
Blind students, 154, 162–164
Bloom, B.
educational taxonomy of, 286–289, 379–380
on school learning, 418–421
Bodily-kinesthetic intelligence, 283
Brain, 249–253
functioning of, 289
lateralization of, 250–251
learning and, 252–253
pattern matching and, 252
relationship with mind, 249–250
Branching programs, 496
Bruner, J.
contribution to cognitive psychology, 247–248
on indirect instruction, 404–407
BTES (beginning teacher evaluation studies), 397
Bullies, 450
Button to button method, 374
Byte, 479

CAI. *See* Computer-assisted instruction (CAI)
California Achievement Tests, 565
Case studies, 31–32, 33
Categorization, 259–263
classroom implications of, 262–263
forming categories and, 261–262

Cathode ray tube (CRT), 479
Causality, 88
Causal thinking, 320
CBA (curriculum-based assessment), 537, 539
CD-ROM (compact disc-read only memory), 479, 505–506
Centering, 90
Central processing unit (CPU), 479
Central tendency measures, 580–581
Cerebral palsy, 167
Channel One Television, 492
Childhood and Society (Erikson), 120
Children at risk, 152–153
Chomsky's theory of language acquisition, 113
Civic goals, 371
Civitas, 368
Classical conditioning, 200–202, 203
classroom applications of, 203
features of, 201–202
Pavlov's work on, 200
Classification, 93–94
of exceptional students, 176–178
Classroom(s)
activities in. *See* Classroom activities
anxiety and, 343
contexts of, 445–446
cultural compatibility in, 56–57
educational psychology and, 21–22
educational technology in. *See* Educational technology
interactions in, 57–58
life in, 439–446
management of. *See* Classroom control; Classroom management
multicultural. *See* Culture(s); Multicultural *entries*
objectives of, 369–370
observation in, 540–541
respect in, 462–464
technology set-up in, 511
Classroom activities, 441–443
for management, 435
organizing, 442–443
recitation, 445
rules for, 448–449
seatwork, 445–446
types of, 441–442
Classroom control, 449, 451–465
behavior modification for, 455–461
cognition and, 461
effective teacher behaviors for, 454–455
maintaining, 454
of misbehavior, 452
multicultural students and, 453–454
mutual respect for, 462–464
packaged discipline programs for, 464–465
of problem students, 438–439
social discipline and goal seeking for, 462
Classroom management, 432–475
activities for, 435
aggression and, 449–451
assistance with, 469–470
avoiding causing problems oneself and, 467–470
Carroll model for, 435–436
classroom activities and, 441–443
classroom contexts and, 445–446
control and. *See* Classroom control
developmental tasks and, 436–438
proactive, 434–435
problem prevention and, 434–435
problem student control and, 438–439
QAIT model for, 443–445
rules for classroom activities and, 448–449

rules for classroom procedures and, 447–448
student engagement and, 442
Classroom objectives, 369–370
Classroom observation, 540–541
Clinical Theory of Instruction (CTI), 399–402
evaluation of, 403
planning for, 400–402
CMI (computer-managed instruction), 479, 491
Coaching, 552
Code of Fair Testing Practices in Education, 585
Codification of rules, stage of, 136
Cognition. *See also* Aptitude tests; Cognitive constructivism; Cognitive development; Cognitive psychology; Intelligence; Intelligence measurement; IQ scores; Metacognition; Social cognitive learning; Thinking skills
behavior change and, 461
creativity and, 318
cultural compatibility and cognitive functioning and, 57
epistemic, 289
Cognitive constructivism, 481
Cognitive development, 82–102
in adolescence, 95–96, 97
AIDS prevention and, 99–100
culture and, 53–55
in early childhood, 90–92
in infancy, 87–90
language and, 54–55
in middle childhood, 92–95
Piaget's theory of. *See* Piaget's theory of cognitive development
Vygotsky's theory of, 82–83
Cognitive disabilities. *See* Mental retardation
Cognitive entry behaviors, 420, 421
intelligence contrasted with, 419
Cognitive psychology, 20, 236–277
brain and, 249–253
Bruner's contribution to, 247–248
categorization and, 259–263
classroom implications of, 244–245
computers and, 240
culture and, 274–275
decision making and reasoning and, 270–272
emergence of, 241–245
Gestaltists and, 241–242
information processing and, 253–255
meaningful learning and, 245–247
memory and, 263–269
metacognition and, 269–270
motivation and, 336
nature of, 238–241
perception and, 255–259
schemata and, 242–244
Cognitive Research Trust (CoRT), 295
Cognitive taxonomy of educational objectives, 379
Cognitive tests, 560
Collective monologues, 112
Communication. *See also* Language; Speech
art of teaching and, 12
definition of, 165
of test results, 585
Communication disorders, 154, 165–166
Communicators, attitude change and, 344–345
Compact disc-read only memory (CD-ROM), 479, 505–506
Comparative research, 36
Comparative schema, 387
Comparison, selective, 281

Compensation, argument of, 93
Competence, motivation and, 360
Complex behavior, programming, 412
Componential intelligence, 281
Computer(s). *See also* Educational technology
  cognitive psychology and, 240
  learning to program, 498–499
  networks of, 506–507
Computer-assisted instruction (CAI), 479, 494–497
  drill and practice software for, 496–497
  intelligent, 501–503
  programmed instruction, 495–496
Computer-managed instruction (CMI), 479, 491
Concepts, types of, 247
Concrete operational period, 92–95
Conditioned reflexes, 200
Conditioned Reflexes (Pavlov), 200
Conditioned response, 200
Conditioned stimulus, 200
Conditioning. *See* Classical conditioning; Operant conditioning
Conjunctive concepts, 247
Connectionism. *See* Thorndike's connectionism
Conscience, in early childhood, 124
Consequential thinking, 320
Conservation, cognitive, 92–93
Construct validity, of teacher-constructed tests, 528
Content, schemes and, 85
Content standards, 368
Content theory of intelligence, 284
Content validity, of teacher-constructed tests, 528
Context
  recognition and, 266
  of teaching, 396
Context strategy, for problem solving, 312
Contextual intelligence, 282
Contextualized instruction, 274
Contextual psychology, 20
Contingency contracting, 459
Contributions approach, to gender materials, 72
Control
  aversive, 459
  of classroom. *See* Classroom control
  in experimental research, 36
  locus of, motivation and, 347–348
Control theory, 463, 464
Control Theory in the Classroom, 464
Conventional level of morality, 138–140
Convulsions, 167
Cooing, 104
Cooperation
  art of teaching and, 12
  morality of, 137
Cooperative learning, motivation and, 354–355
Correlational research, 35
CoRT (Cognitive Research Trust), 295
Costa's levels of thinking skills, 289–290
CPU (central processing unit), 479
Creativity, 317, 318–319
Criterion-referenced tests (CRTs), 545, 562
Criterion-related validity, of teacher-constructed tests, 528
Critical thinking. *See* Thinking skills
Cross-cultural studies, 42–43
Cross-sectional studies, 41–42
CRT (cathode ray tube), 479
CRTs (criterion-referenced tests), 545, 562
CTI. *See* Clinical Theory of Instruction (CTI)

Cues
  for group alertness, 455
  as retrieval aids, 314–315
Cultural compatibility, 56–57
  psychocultural variables affecting, 56–57
Cultural exemplars, 285
Culture(s), 14, 52–59. *See also* Multicultural *entries; specific cultural groups*
  bilingualism and, 108–110
  cognition and, 274–275
  cognitive development and, 53–55
  cross-cultural research and, 42–43
  goals and, 374–375
  merging, 52–53
  motivation and, 355–357
  multicultural teaching and, 398
  Piaget's theory of cognitive development and, 98
  problem solving and, 302–303
  standardized testing and, 584
  testing and, 522
  testing practices and, 58–59
  thinking skills and, 290–291
Cumulative subtraction, 374
Curiosity
  classroom implications of, 347
  definition of, 346
  motivation and, 346–347
Curriculum
  gender and, 72–74
  knowledge of, 408
  Piaget's theory of cognitive development and, 101
  spiral, 405–406
Curriculum and Evaluation Standards for School Mathematics, 368, 385
Curriculum-based assessment (CBA), 537, 539

Day care, psychosocial development and, 122–123
Deafness, 164
Decision making, 270–272
  classroom implications of, 271–273
  representativeness and, 270–271
Decoding, 165, 383
Descriptions, goals and objectives compared with, 373–374
Descriptive research, 34–35
Desists, 454
Development, 80–82
  classroom management and, 436–438
  cognitive. *See* Cognitive development; Piaget's theory of cognitive development
  of language. *See* Language development
  learning disabilities and, 172–173
  moral. *See* Kohlberg's theory of moral development; Moral development
  psychosocial. *See* Erikson's theory of psychosocial development; Psychosocial development
Differential reinforcement, 224–225
Direct instruction, 399–403
  dos and don'ts for, 402–403
  Hunter's Clinical Theory of Instruction and. *See* Clinical Theory of Instruction (CTI)
  of thinking skills, 289
Discipline. *See also* Classroom control; Classroom management
  during infancy, 123
  packaged programs for, 464–465
  social, 462

Disciplines. *See* Institutional objectives; Subject matter; *specific disciplines*
Discovery learning, 247, 336
Discrimination, 201–202, 203
Dishonest grading, 549–551
Disjunctive concepts, 247
Disk drive, 479
Divorce, psychosocial development and, 126
Documentation as source of knowledge, 30
Drill and practice software, 496
DUPE model, 303–319
  creativity and, 318–319
  determining nature of problem and, 303–306
  evaluating solutions and, 316–318
  memory and, 313–316
  planning solutions and, 312–313
  reading and, 383
  understanding nature of problem and, 306–312
Dynamic schema, 387

Early adulthood, psychosocial development in, 134–135
Early childhood
  classroom management and, 436–437
  cognitive development in, 90–92
  language development in, 106–110
  psychosocial development in, 123–126
Ecological psychology, 41
Educating Americans for the 21st Century, 280
Education. *See also* Special education
  of females, 66
  motivation during, 359–360
  social class and, 60–61
Educational objectives. *See* Instructional objectives
Educational process, Bruner on, 405–406
Educational psychology
  core concepts of, 20–22
  definition of, 3
Educational standards, 368
Educational technology, 476–516
  access to, 509
  administrative and managerial uses of, 491
  amount of use of, 481–484
  audiovisual aids, 491–492
  classroom set-up of, 511
  computer-assisted instruction, 494–497
  computer terminology and, 479
  gender and, 489
  hardware and software selection and, 511, 512
  historical background of, 480–481, 482–483
  individual differences and, 512–513
  information superhighway, 508
  intelligent tutoring systems, 501–503
  lack of use of, 485–487, 510–511
  manner of use of, 484–485
  multimedia, 503–506
  networks, 506–507
  novelty of, 488–489
  questions to answer when considering, 478–480
  security and, 509
  social interactions and, 512
  student attitudes toward, 488–489
  teacher's role and, 510–511
  teaching of, 493–494
  for teaching thinking, 498–501
  technology gap and, 510
  virtual reality, 507–508

Education for All Handicapped Children Act, 153, 178–180
Effect, law of, 204
Effective schools, 17–20, 370–371
Effective teachers, 19–20
   behaviors of, 454–455
   key behaviors of, 396–399
Efficacy expectation, 351
Effort, attribution theory and, 338
Egocentric speech, 112
Egocentric stage of moral development, 136
Egocentrism, 88, 90, 95
Elaboration, as retrieval aid, 315–316
ELOs (expected learner outcomes), 372
Emotion, motivation and, 330, 340
Emotional disturbances. *See* Behavior
   disorders
Enactive mode of representation, 406
Encoding, 165
   selective, 281
Enculturation, 285
Engaged time, 435
Engagement in the learning process, 397–398
English as a Second Language (ESL), 191–192
Enrichment, 159
   instructional, 294–295
Epilepsy, 167
Episodic memory, 263
Epistemic cognition, 289
Equilibration, 84, 86
Erikson's theory of psychosocial development, 120–136
   autonomy versus shame and doubt stage and, 121–123
   classroom implications of, 135–136
   generativity versus stagnation stage and, 135
   identity versus identity confusion stage and, 130–134
   industry versus inferiority stage and, 126–130
   initiative versus guilt stage and, 123–126
   integrity versus despair stage and, 135
   intimacy versus isolation stage and, 134–135
   trust versus mistrust stage and, 120–121
Errorless learning in programmed instruction, 415
Escape behavior, 212
Escape group, 349
ESL (English as a Second Language), 191–192
Essay tests, 525, 530
   helping students prepare for, 535
   scoring, 533–534
   writing, 531–534
Ethical behavior, discipline problems and, 452
Ethics, research and, 47
Ethnic groups, 14. *See also* Culture(s);
   Multicultural *entries; specific groups*
Evaluation, 407, 525. *See also* Assessment;
   Teacher-constructed tests; Test(s)
Event recording, 538
Exceptional students, 150–195
   ability grouping and, 153–155
   assessment and classification of, 176–178
   behavior disorders and, 154, 167–170
   children at risk and, 152–153
   cognitively disabled, 154, 174–176
   communication disorders and, 154, 165–166
   education and, 187–188
   gifted/talented. *See* Gifted/talented
      students
   hearing impaired, 154, 164–165

   labeling of, 177, 178
   learning disabled, 154, 171–174
   mainstreaming. *See* Mainstreaming
   multicultural, 188–192
   physically and health impaired, 154, 166–167
   prevalence of, 155–156
   referral of, 179
   visually impaired, 153, 154, 162–164
Exclusion component, learning disabilities and, 172
Executive control structures, 101
Exercise, law of, 202
Exhibitions, 545
Expectation(s)
   recognition and, 266
   of teachers, 427–429
Expected learner outcomes (ELOs), 372
Experience(s)
   metacognitive, 270
   Piaget's view of, 86
   as source of knowledge, 29–30
   successful, in Link Model, 354
Experience, prior. *See* Prior experience,
   recognition and
Experiential intelligence, 281–282
Experimental research, 36–37
Expert opinion as source of knowledge, 29
Exploration, in triad model, 159
Expressive language function, learning
   disabilities and, 173
Extended response, 530
External(s), 347–348
External representation of problems, 307
External validity of research findings, 37
Extinction, 202, 203
   forgetting and, 267
   resistance to, 225
Extrinsic motivation, 332–334
Eyewitnesses, 243

Family, psychosocial development and, 126
Feedback in programmed instruction, 415
Figure-ground relationship, 255–256
First instance, 411
First words, 105
Fixed interval, 208
Fixed ratio, 208
Fluency disorders, 166
Forgetting, 266–268
Forgiveness, 145
Formal operational period, 95–96, 97
Formative evaluation, 419
Fragmentation, 455
Framing, 272
Frequency distributions, 580
Functional invariants, 84–86

Gagne's instructional design, 415–416, 418
Gardner's multiple intelligences, 282–284
Gender, 64–75
   achievement need and, 337
   attitudes toward technology and, 489
   brain lateralization and, 251
   classroom achievement and, 70–72
   curriculum and, 72–74
   definition of, 64–65
   development of. *See* Gender development
   educational inequality and, 131
   education and, 66
   interaction patterns and, 70–72
   similarities and differences and, 70

Gender development
   biological factors and, 66
   environmental factors and, 66–67
   family influences on, 67
   media impact on, 68
   peer influences on, 67–68
   theories of, 68–69
Gender identity, 65
Gender role, 65
Gender stereotypes, 65, 69–70
Generality power, of research findings, 37
Generalization, 201, 203
   facilitating, 227–228
Generalized reinforcers, 207, 223
Generativity versus stagnation stage, 135
Genetic Studies of Genius (Terman), 160
Genius, genetic studies of, 160
Gestalt processing, learning disabilities
   and, 173
Gestalt psychologists, cognitive psychology
   and, 241–242
Gifted and Talented Children's Education Act
   of 1978, 156
Gifted/talented students, 156–162
   acceleration of, 158–159
   developing talent in, 159–162
   enrichment for, 159
   special grouping for, 159
   triad model and, 159
Glaser's control theory, 463
Goals
   academic, 371
   civic, 371
   descriptions and objectives compared with, 373–374
   group, cooperative learning and, 354–355
   motivation and, 330
   personal, 330, 371
   proximal, in Link Model, 352
   social, 371
   vocational, 371
Goal seeking, 462
Grade(s), motivation and, 333
Grade equivalent scores, 579–580
Grading, 520, 547–548, 549–551
   dishonest, 549–551
   performance-based benchmarks for, 545
Grammar, 102, 103–104, 165
Graphic representations, teaching students to
   construct, 308–310
Group alertness, of effective teachers, 455
Group goals, cooperative learning and, 354–355
Guidance, as purpose of tests, 560

Hardness of hearing, 164
Hardware, 479
   selection of, 511
Hassle Free Homework (Clark and Clark), 424
Head Start program, 62–63
Health impairment, 154, 166–167
Hearing impaired students, 154, 164–165
Hearing loss, 164
Helplessness, learned, 348–350
Help-seeking behavior, 352
Heuristics, 317–318
Hispanic American students, 14
   cultural compatibility of, 56
   exceptional, 190
   poverty among, 60
Historical research, 34
Holophrastic speech, 105
Homelessness, in early childhood, 125

Homework, 10, 424–425, 426
Homework Without Tears (Canter and Hausner), 424
How Children Fail (Holt), 29
How to Parent (Dodson), 29
How to Raise Independent and Professionally Successful Daughters (Dunn and Dunn), 29
Humanistic psychology, 20
    motivation and, 334–336
Hyperactivity, 168–170
    learning disabilities and, 172
Hypothetical abilities, 406

ICAI (intelligent computer-assisted instruction), 501–503
Iconic mode of representation, 406
ICPS (Interpersonal Cognitive Problem Solving), 320
IDEA (Individuals with Disabilities Education Act), 153, 178–180
Identical elements, 204
Identity
    argument of, 93
    gender, 65
Identity achievement, 132
Identity confusion, 130
Identity crisis, 130
Identity diffusion, 132
Identity foreclosure, 132
Identity moratorium, 132
Identity versus identity confusion stage, 130–134
Imagery, 254–255, 260
    for increasing comprehension, 267
    as retrieval aid, 315
Incidence, 155
Incipient cooperation, stage of, 136
Inclusion, 178
Independent variable, 36
Indirect instruction, 403–408
    Bruner's inquiry teaching, 404
    Bruner's process of education and, 405–406
    dos and don'ts for, 407–408
    principles of, 404–405
    representation modes and, 406–407
Individual differences, 152, 418–429
    Bloom's view of, 418–421
    homework and, 424–425
    in multicultural classrooms, 425–427
    study skills and, 421–424
    teacher expectations and, 427–429
    technology and, 512–513
Individualized education program, 182–183
Individualized instruction, 444
Individuals with Disabilities Education Act (IDEA), 153, 178–180
Industry versus inferiority stage, 126–130
Infancy
    cognitive development in, 87–90
    language development in, 104–106
    moral development in, 138
    psychosocial development in, 120–123
Inferencing for problem solving, 312
Information. *See also* Experience(s); Knowledge
    acquisition of, 406
    obtaining about oneself, 340
Information processing, 253–255
    classroom implications of, 260
    mental imagery and pictures and, 254–255, 260
    representation and, 253

verbal, 255, 260
Information superhighway, 508
Initiative versus guilt stage, 123–126
Inquiry teaching. *See* Indirect instruction
Instantiation, for problem solving, 313
Instruction. *See also* Teaching
    adapting to individual differences of learners. *See* Individual differences
    audiovisual aids for, 491–492
    contextualized, 274
    direct, 399–403
    indirect. *See* Indirect instruction
    individualized, 444
    programmed. *See* Programmed instruction
    as purpose of tests, 560
    quality of, 420, 444
Instructional design, 410–418
    Gagne's view of, 415–416, 418
    Markle's view of, 414–415
    Skinner's view of, 411–413
Instructional enrichment, 294–295
Instructional Environmental Scale, The (TIES), 409
Instructional guidance, testing for, 584
Instructional level, QAIT model and, 444
Instructional objectives, 368–371, 380–391
    for classroom, 369–370
    effective schools and, 370–371
    for mathematics, 385–388
    for reading, 381–384
    for science, 388–391
Instructional theory
    Bruner on, 404–407
    principles of, 404–405
Instructional variety, 397
Instrumental learning, 294
Integrity versus despair stage, 135
Intelligence, 280–285
    cognitive entry behaviors contrasted with, 419
    Gardner's multiple intelligences and, 282–284
    identifying, 282–283
    Perkins' thinking frames and, 284–285
    practical, 291, 293
    Sternberg's triarchic model of, 281–282
Intelligence measurement, 567–573. *See also* IQ scores
    bias in, 572–573
    Binet's approach to, 572
    definitions of intelligence and, 568–569
    historical background of intelligence testing movement and, 569–571
    problems in, 571
    stability of IQ scores and, 572
Intelligent computer-assisted instruction (ICAI), 501–503
Intelligent tutoring systems (ITSs), 501–503
Interactions. *See* Social interactions; Teacher-student relationships
Intercultural Learning Network, 507
Interest, creativity and, 318
Interest inventories, 560
Interference, forgetting and, 267
Intermittent reinforcement, 207
Internal(s), 347–348
Internalization, as thinking frame, 285
Internal representation, of problems, 307, 311
Internal validity, of research findings, 37
Internet, 479
Interpersonal Cognitive Problem Solving (ICPS), 320
Interpersonal intelligence, 284
Interpersonal sensitivity, 320

Interval recording, 538–539
Interval reinforcement, 207
Interviews, as research technique, 39, 41
Intimacy versus isolation stage, 134–135
Intrapersonal intelligence, 284
Intrinsic motivation, 332–334
Iowa Silent Reading Tests, 565
IQ scores. *See also* Intelligence measurement
    Head Start program and, 63
    learned helplessness and, 349
    mental retardation and, 174
    stability of, 572
    zone of proximal development and, 53
Irreversibility, 90
ITSs (intelligent tutoring systems), 501–503

Kamehameha Early Education Program (KEEP), 56
KEEP (Kamehameha Early Education Program), 56
Keller plan, 208
Knowledge. *See also* Experience(s); Information
    in Bloom's taxonomy of educational objectives, 379–380
    of curriculum, 408
    mathematical, using, 386–388
    metacognitive, 269–270
    pedagogical, 408
    prior. *See* Prior knowledge, activation of, for increasing comprehension
    sources of, 28–30
    of subject matter, 408
Knowledge acquisition components of intelligence, 281
Kohlberg's theory of moral development, 137–145
    classroom implications of, 142–145
    conventional morality and, 138–140
    criticisms of, 141–142
    postconventional morality and, 140–141
    preconventional morality and, 138

Labeling, of exceptional students, 177, 178
LAD (Language Acquisition Device), 113
LAN (local area network), 479, 506
Language. *See also* Bilingual education; Bilingualism
    acquisition of. *See* Language acquisition
    behavior and, 111–112
    classroom implications of, 113–114
    cognitive development and, 54–55
    definition of, 165
    development of. *See* Language development
    disorders of, 166
    as educational issue, 8–9
    learning disabilities and, 173
    native, 180
    whole. *See* Whole language approach
Language acquisition, 111–113
    Chomsky's theory of, 113
    Lenneberg's biological explanation of, 111–112
    Piaget's theory of, 112–113
Language Acquisition Device (LAD), 113
Language development, 102–111
    accomplishments and, 102
    components of language and, 102–104
    in early childhood, 106–110
    facilitating, 114
    in infancy, 104–106
    in middle childhood, 110–111

Language disorders, 166
Language explosion, 105
Language spurt, 111
Laser videodiscs, 479, 504–505
Late adulthood, psychosocial development in, 135
Lateralization, of brain, 250–251
Law of effect, 204
Law of exercise, 202
Law of readiness, 202
Learned helplessness, 348–350
    classroom implications of, 350
    motivation and, 348–350
    success and, 349–350
Learners. *See* Student(s)
Learning. *See also* Classical conditioning;
        Operant conditioning
    beginning of, motivation and, 357–358
    brain and, 252–253
    cognitive, social. *See* Social cognitive learning
    cooperative, 354–355
    discovery, 247, 336
    end of, motivation and, 360–361
    errorless, in programmed instruction, 415
    helping students transfer, 319, 321
    information superhighway and, 508
    instrumental, 294
    integrating with assessment, 522–523
    mastery, 419–420, 444
    meaningful, 245–247
    mediated, 294
    motivation for, 331–332
    to program, 498–499
    school. *See* School learning
    social class and, 61–63
Learning disabilities, 171–174
    development and, 172–173
    previous knowledge and, 173–174
Learning strategies, in Link Model, 352
Learning tasks, 420
Least restrictive environment, 154, 164
Lectures on Conditioned Reflexes (Pavlov), 200
Legally blind students, 163
Lenneberg's theory of language acquisition, 111–112
LEP (limited English proficiency), 190–192
Lessons, clarity of, 397
Levels of processing, 264
Limited English proficiency (LEP), 190–192
Linear programmed instruction, 495–496
Linguistic intelligence, 283
Linking power, of research findings, 37
Link Model, 352–354
Local area network (LAN), 479, 506
Locus of control, motivation and, 347–348
Logical-mathematical intelligence, 283
Logical thinking, 275
Longitudinal studies, 42
Long-term store, 264
Love needs, 335
Luck, attribution theory and, 339
Luria's work on brain-mind relationship, 249–250

Mainstreaming, 178–187
    classroom support for students and, 180, 184–186
    definition of, 178–180
    or inclusion, 178
    results of, 186–187
Management, technology use by, 491
Marking, 547, 548–549

Markle's programmed instruction model, 413–415
    active responding and, 414–415
    errorless learning and, 415
    immediate feedback and, 415
Mastery learning, 419–420
    group-based, 444
Matching items, 536
Mathematics
    as educational issue, 9
    instructional objectives for, 385–388
    skill and understanding and, 385–386
    using mathematical knowledge and, 386–388
Maturation, Piaget's view of, 86
MCTs (minimum competency tests), 583
Mean, 580
Meaningful learning, 245–247
    advance organizers and, 246–247
Means-end thinking, 320
Measurement, 520
Median, 580
Mediated learning, 294
Mediated Learning Experience (MLE), 294
Mediation, 499
Memory, 239, 263–269
    classroom implications of, 268–269
    forgetting and, 266–268
    learning disabilities and, 173
    problem solving and, 313–316
    recall and, 266
    recognition and, 265–266
    research on, 264–265
    structure and, 259
    types of, 263
Mental growth, 53–54
    zone of proximal development and, 53–54
Mental imagery. *See* Imagery
Mental representations. *See* Representations
Mental retardation, 154, 174–176
    adaptation and, 175
    problems associated with, 175–176
Messages, attitude change and, 345
Meta-analysis, 45–46
Metacognition, 107, 269–270, 289, 297
Metacognitive experiences, 270
Metacognitive knowledge, 269–270
Metacomponents of intelligence, 281, 317
Metalinguistic awareness, 107
Method of loci, as retrieval aid, 315
Metropolitan Achievement Tests, 565
Metropolitan Readiness Tests, 565
Microcomputers, 479
Microprocessors, 479
Middle adulthood, psychosocial development in, 135
Middle childhood
    classroom management and, 437
    cognitive development in, 92–95
    language development in, 110–111
    moral development in, 138–140
    psychosocial development in, 126–130
Mind, relationship with brain, 249–250
Minimum competency tests (MCTs), 583
Minority groups. *See* Culture(s); Multicultural *entries; specific groups*
Misarticulation, 166
Misbehavior, control of, 452
MLE (Mediated Learning Experience), 294
Mode, 580
Modeling. *See also* Social cognitive learning
    as thinking skill, 290
"Model of School Learning, A" (Carroll), 435
Modems, 479

Moderate mental retardation, 174
Modes of representation, 406
Monitoring, for problem solving, 312
Monologues, 112
Moral development, 136–145. *See also*
        Kohlberg's theory of moral development
    in adolescence, 140–141
    forgiveness and, 145
    in infancy, 138
    in middle childhood, 138–140
    Piaget's theory of, 136
    schools and, 144
Moral dilemmas, 143–145
Moral education, violence in schools and, 140
Morality of cooperation, 137
Morphemes, 103, 165–166
Morphology, 165
Motivated forgetting, 266
Motivation, 328–364, 406
    achievement and, 336–337
    anxiety and, 342–344
    attitudes and, 344–346
    attribution theory and, 337–339
    beginning of learning and, 357–358
    behavioral psychology and, 339–340
    classroom implications of, 357–361
    cognitive psychology and, 336
    cooperative learning and, 354–355
    creativity and, 318
    cultural compatibility and, 57
    curiosity and, 346–347
    during education, 359–360
    end of learning and, 360–361
    grades and, 333
    humanistic psychology and, 334–336
    intrinsic and extrinsic, 332–334
    to learn, 331–332
    learned helplessness and, 348–350
    locus of control and, 347–348
    maintaining, 334
    multicultural students and, 355–357
    myths about, 330–331
    QAIT model and, 444
    self-efficacy and, 350–354
    social cognitive learning and, 217, 340–341
Motor reproduction, social cognitive learning and, 217
Motor rules, stage of, 136
M-space, 101
Multicultural classrooms, 14–16, 55–58
    adapting instruction in, 425–427
Multicultural models, 220
Multicultural students. *See also* Culture(s);
        Multicultural *entries; specific groups*
    discipline and, 453–454
    motivation and, 355–357
    special education and, 188–192
Multicultural teaching, 398. *See also*
        Multicultural *entries*
Multilevel survey batteries, 565
Multimedia, 503–506
Multiple-choice items, 525, 535–536
Multiple coding, for problem solving, 313
Multiple intelligences, 282–284
Muscular dystrophy, 167
Musical intelligence, 283

Naive group, 349
Narrative thinking, 275
National Geographic Kids Network, 507
Native American students, 14
    cognition and, 274

core values and teaching process and, 446
cultural compatibility of, 56–57
exceptional, 190
Native language, 180
Need(s)
classroom implications of, 335–336
motivation and, 334–335, 357–358
Need achievement theory, 337
Negative group alerting cues, 455
Negative reinforcement, 206, 209
Negative reinforcers, 209
Network(s), computer, 506–507
Networking, 479
Neurotic anxiety, 342
Neverstreaming, 187
*New Voices: Immigrant Students in U.S. Public
    Schools,* 522
Nonseclusionary time out, 226
Norm(s), 563–564
Norm-referenced tests (NRTs), 562
Novelty effect, of technology, 488–489
NRTs (norm-referenced tests), 562
Number concept, 94

Objectives, 371–380
descriptions and goals compared with,
    373–374
educational. *See* Instructional objectives
evaluating, 376–377
good, 376–377
instructional. *See* Instructional objectives
multicultural students and, 374–375
need for, 371–372
sources of, 378–380
of teacher-constructed tests, 530
usefulness of, 382
writing, 377–378
Objective tests. *See also* Standardized tests
helping students prepare for, 537
writing, 534
Object permanence, 88
Observation
classroom, 540–541
as research technique, 41
Operant conditioning, 204–216
classroom implications of, 212–216
programmed instruction and, 411–415
Skinner's views on, 204–206
Organization, cognitive, 85
Origins, motivation and, 359
Orthopedic impairment, 166
Outcome expectation, 351
Overcorrection, 210, 459
Overdwelling, 455
Overextension, 106
Overlapping, of effective teachers, 454–455
Overregularities, 106

Parallel distributed processing, 383
Parents
involvement in preschool screening, 579
reporting progress to, 550
study skills and, 422–424
Pattern matching, brain and, 252
Pavlov's classical conditioning, 200
Pawns, motivation and, 359
Pedagogical knowledge, 408
Percentile scores, 580
Perception, 255–259
art of teaching and, 12
classroom implications of, 256–259
disorders of, 162–165

helping students with acuity and, 258–259
patterns of stimuli and, 256–258
Perceptive language function, learning
    disabilities and, 173
Performance accomplishments, 340
Performance assessment, 540–547
Performance-based grading benchmarks, 545
Performance components of intelligence, 281
Performance standards, 368
Peripherals, 479
Perkins' thinking frames, 284–285
Permanent product(s), 538
Permanent product recording, 539
Personal agency beliefs, motivation and, 330
Personal goals, 371
motivation and, 330
Personality, creativity and, 310
Personality questionnaires, 560
Personalized system of instruction (PSI), 208
Perspective taking, 320
Persuasion, verbal, 340
Phi phenomenon, 242
Phonemes, 103
Phonology, 102, 103, 165
Physical and health impairment, 154, 166–167
Physiological needs, 334–335
Piaget's theory of cognitive development,
    83–102
alternatives to, 100–102
classroom implications of, 98–100, 101
concrete operational period and, 92–95
criticisms of, 96–98
cultural differences and, 98
formal operational period and, 95–96, 97
functional invariants and, 84–86
preoperational period and, 90–92
sensorimotor period and, 87–90
Piaget's theory of language acquisition,
    112–113
Piaget's theory of moral development, 136
PIFS (Practical Intelligence for School), 291,
    293
Planning, of teacher-constructed tests, 529–536
Plasticity, 252
Play, in early childhood, 124–125
Portfolio assessment, 545
Positive attitude, problem solving and, 301
Positive group alerting cues, 455
Positive reinforcement, 209, 458–459
motivation and, 340
time out from, 210
Positive reinforcers, 209
Postconventional level of morality, 140–141
Poverty, 60
Power theory of intelligence, 284
Practical Intelligence for School (PIFS), 291,
    293
Pragmatics, of language, 102, 104
Praise, cautions regarding use of, 398–399
Preconventional level of morality, 138
Premack principle, 214
Preoperational period, 90–92
Prepare Curriculum, 320
Preparing Instructional Objectives (Mager),
    375
Preschool screening, 576–579
follow-up services and, 576, 578
parental involvement in, 579
timing of, 578–579
Prevalence, 155–156
Previous knowledge, learning disabilities and,
    173–174
Primary analysis, 44
Primary reinforcers, 207

Principle of behavior, 205
Principle of reinforcement, 205
Printers, 479
Prior experience, recognition and, 266
Prior knowledge, activation of, for increasing
    comprehension, 267
Proactive classroom management, 434–435
Proactive interference, 267
Problems in classrooms
causes of, 451
preventing, 434–435
Problem solving, 296–324
characteristics of good problem solvers
    and, 301–302
classroom implications of, 321–324
culture and, 302–303
DUPE model for. *See* DUPE model
during formal operational period, 96
helping students transfer learning
    for, 319, 321
improving skills for, 298
problems and, 297–298
retreating from problems and, 299–300
social, 320
sources of error in, 299
strategies for, 300–301, 322–324
Profound mental retardation, 174
Programmed instruction, 411–415, 495–496
linear, 495–496
Markle's view of, 413–415
Skinner's view of, 411–413
Programming, learning, 498–499
Propositional thinking, 96
Prototypes, 262
Proximal goals, in Link Model, 352
PSI (personalized system of instruction), 208
Psycholinguistics, 113
Psychosocial development. *See also* Erikson's
    theory of psychosocial development
in adolescence, 130–134
in early adulthood, 134–135
in early childhood, 123–126
in infancy, 120–123
in late adulthood, 135
in middle adulthood, 135
in middle childhood, 126–130
Public Law 94-142, 153, 178–180
Punishment, 209–212
alternatives to, 225
categories of, 210
effectiveness of, 211–212
excessive use of, 212

QAIT model, 443–445
Quality of instruction, 420
QAIT model and, 444
Question(s)
to improve thinking skills, 286–287
for increasing comprehension, 267
for teacher-constructed tests, 530–531
of teachers, improving, 288–289
Questioning, as thinking skill, 290

Race, 14. *See also* Culture(s); Multicultural
    entries; specific groups
RAM (random access memory), 479
Random access memory (RAM), 479
Random assignment, in experimental
    research, 36
Rating scales. *See* Behavior rating scales
Ratio reinforcement, 208
Raw scores, 579

Readiness, 405–406
  law of, 202
Readiness tests, 560, 565
Reading
  instructional objectives for, 381–384
  skill versus whole language approach to
    teaching, 384
Reading comprehension, 384
Read only memory (ROM), 479
Realism, 90–91
Reasoning. *See also* Decision making; Problem
    solving
  transductive, 91
Recall, 266
Recitation, 445
Recognition, 265–266
Recording, of student behavior, 231
Reflective teaching, achievement scores and,
    401
Reflexes, conditioned, 200
Regular Education Initiative (REI), 185
REI (Regular Education Initiative), 185
Reinforcement, 205–209
  differential, 224–225
  motivation and, 361
  negative, 206, 209
  positive, 458–459
  principle of, 205
  programmed instruction and, 411–415
  reinforcers and, 205, 207
  schedules of, 207–209
  using, 206–207
  withholding, 225
Reinforcers, 205, 223
  negative, 209
  primary, 207, 209
  secondary, 207, 223
  types of, 207
Relational concepts, 247
Reliability, of teacher-constructed tests, 527
Reminiscence, 268
Reorganization, forgetting and, 267
Repetition, 112
Reporting, 551–552
Representational codes, 253
Representations, 238, 241, 253
  modes of, 406–407
  of problems, 307–312
Representativeness, decision making and
    reasoning and, 270–271
Research, 26–49
  on children, emergence of, 30–34
  effective schooling and, 28–30
  ethics and, 47
  methods of. *See* Research methods
  primary, secondary, and meta-analysis and,
    44–46
  on teachers' judgments of students'
    achievement, 552
  techniques in. *See* Research techniques
  in triad model, 159
Research articles, 35
Research methods, 30–32, 33, 34–37
  baby biographies, 30–31
  case study, 31–32, 33
  comparative research, 36
  correlational research, 35
  descriptive research, 34–35
  experimental research, 36–37
  historical research, 34
Research techniques, 37–44
  cross-cultural studies, 42–43
  cross-sectional studies, 41–42
  interviews, 39, 41

longitudinal studies, 42
observation, 41
single-case studies, 43–44, 46
surveys, 37–39
Respect, in classroom, 462–464
Responding
  active, in programmed instruction, 414–415
  as thinking skill, 290
Response
  conditioned, 200
  unconditioned, 200
Response cost, 210
Restricted response, 530
Retention, social cognitive learning and, 217
Retention in grade, as educational issue, 9–10
Retrieval, 265
  aids for, for problem solving, 313–316
Retroactive interference, 267
Reversibility, argument of, 93
Reward structure, cooperative learning
    and, 355
Ripple effect, 454
Roles, gender, 65
ROM (read only memory), 479
Rubrics, 545
Rules
  for classroom activities, 448–449
  for classroom procedures, 447–448
  stage of codification of, 136

Safety needs, 335
Schedules of reinforcement, 207–209
Schemata
  cognitive psychology and, 242–244
  mathematics and, 387
  in Piaget's theory of cognitive
    development, 85–86
Scholastic Achievement Test (SAT), gender
    bias of, 73–74
School(s). *See also* Classroom(s)
  effective, 17–20, 370–371
  moral development and, 144
  violence in, 132
School delivery standards, 368
School learning
  Bloom's view of, 418–421
  Carroll's model of, 435–436
Schools Without Failure, 464
Science
  as educational issue, 9
  instructional objectives for, 388–391
Science and Human Behavior (Skinner), 204
Science For All Americans, 368
Science for All Americans, 388
Scientific method, 13, 32–34
Scientific research. *See also* Research
  as source of knowledge, 30
Scores. *See also* IQ scores
  on standardized tests, 579–582
Scoring, of essay tests, 533–534
Screening. *See* Preschool screening
Seatwork, 445–446
Seclusionary time out, 226
Secondary analysis, 44
Secondary reinforcers, 207, 223
Security, educational technology and, 509
Segmental processing, learning disabilities
    and, 173
Seizures, 167
Selection items, 530
  writing, 534–536
Selective attention, learning disabilities
    and, 172

Selective combination, 281
Selective comparison, 281
Selective encoding, 281
Self-actualization, 334
  need for, 335
Self-assessment, by students, 545, 547
Self-control
  teaching, 229–230
  techniques of, 228–230
Self-efficacy
  classroom implications of, 352–354
  help-seeking behavior and, 352
  motivation and, 350–354
  social cognitive learning and, 217–220
Self-esteem, in middle childhood, 128–129
Self-fulfilling prophecy, 427
Self-regulated training, 272–273
Semantic(s), 102
Semantic memory, 263
Semantics, 104
Sensorimotor period, 87–90
Sensory impairments
  hearing, 154, 164–165
  visual, 153, 154, 162–164
Sensory register, 264
Sentences, simple, 105
Seriation, 93
Severe mental retardation, 174
Sex, definition of, 64
Shaping, 459
Short-term store, 264
Simple sentences, 105
Single-case studies, 43–44, 46
Single words, 105
Situational anxiety, 342
Skill approach, to reading instruction, 384
Skill building, in triad model, 159
Skinner's operant conditioning. *See* Operant
    conditioning
Slowdowns, 455
Social action approach to gender material, 73
Social class, 59–63
  education and, 60–61
  poverty and, 60
  teaching and learning and, 61–63
Social cognitive learning, 216–222
  classroom implications of, 220–222, 341
  motivation and, 340–341
  multicultural models and, 220
  self-efficacy and, 217–220
Social discipline, 462
Social goals, 371
Social interactions. *See also* Teacher-student
    relationships
  in classrooms, 57–58
  culture and, 57–58
  Piaget's view of, 86
  technology and, 512
Socialized speech, 112–113
Social organization, cultural compatibility
    and, 56
Social problem solving, 320
Social reinforcers, 223
Social skills, teaching, 64–65
Socioeconomic status. *See* Social class
Sociolinguistics, cultural compatibility and,
    56–57
Software, 479
  selection of, 511, 512
Solution Book, The, 465
Space, concept of, 88
Spatial intelligence, 283
Special education
  multicultural students and, 188–192

process of, 181
testing for placement in, 583
Special grouping, 159
Speech. *See also* Communication; Language
affective nature of, 104
definition of, 165
egocentric, 112
holophrastic, 105
irregularities of, during infancy, 105–106
problems with, 165, 166
socialized, 112–113
telegraphic, 105
Speech disorders, 166
Speech impairment, 165
Spiral curriculum, 405–406
Spontaneous recovery, 225
Spreadsheets, teaching of, 494
STAD (Student Teams-Achievement Division), 355
Stage of codification of rules, 136
Stage of incipient cooperation, 136
Stage of motor rules, 136
Standard(s), educational, 368
Standard deviation unit, 581
Standardized interviews, 39
Standardized tests, 524, 558–588
achievement. *See* Achievement tests
aptitude. *See* Aptitude tests
behavior rating scales, 573–576
communicating results of, 585
criterion-referenced, 545, 562
criticisms of, 584–585
developing, 562–564
educational applications of, 583–584
multicultural students and, 584
norm-referenced, 562
for preschool screening, 576–579
school testing program and, 560–564
scores on, 579–582. *See also* IQ scores
testing practices and, 585–586
Standard scores, 581
Stanford-Binet Intelligence Test, 570
Stanine scores, 582
State anxiety, 342
Static schema, 387
Stereotypes, gender, 65, 69–70
Sternberg's triarchic model of intelligence, 281–282
Stimulation, motivation and, 359
Stimuli
aversive, 209
conditioned, 200
patterns of, 256–258
unconditioned, 200
Stimulus generalization, 201, 203
Storage, 265, 313
Story grammar, for increasing comprehension, 267
Strong performance assessment, 544–545
Strong strategies, 301
Structure(s), cognitive, 84
Structure, memory and, 259
Structured interviews, 39
Structuring, as thinking skill, 290
Structuring strategy, for problem solving, 312
Student(s)
attitudes toward technology, 488–489
engagement of, 442
exceptional. *See* Exceptional students; Gifted/talented students; Mainstreaming
multicultural. *See* Culture(s)
problem, control of, 438–439
recording behavior of, 231

relationships with teachers. *See* Teacher-student relationships
teaching and, 396
Student certification, testing for, 583
Student self-assessment, 545, 547
Student Teams-Achievement Division (STAD), 355
Study skills, 421–424
developing, 422
parental help with, 422–424
Subject matter. *See also specific subjects*
instructional objectives for. *See* Instructional objectives
standards for, 368
teaching and, 396, 408, 410
Successful experiences, in Link Model, 354
Summarization, for increasing comprehension, 267
Summative evaluation, 419
Supply items, 530
writing, 534
Surveys, as research technique, 37–39
Symbolic mode of representation, 406
Syntax, 102, 103–104, 165
System performance standards, 368

Tactical theory of intelligence, 284
Talented students. *See* Gifted/talented students
Task analysis, 372
Task difficulty, attribution theory and, 338–339
Task orientation, 397–398
Task structure, cooperative learning and, 355
Taxonomy of educational objectives, 286–289, 379–380
questions and, 286–289
Taxonomy of Educational Objectives, Handbook 1: Cognitive Domain (Bloom), 286
Teacher(s)
avoidance of causing problems, 467–470
beginning, characteristics of, 8
Bruner's view of roles of, 404
effective. *See* Effective teachers
expectations of, 427–429
failure to use technology, 485–487, 510–511
grading by. *See* Grading
improving questions of, 288–289
judgments of students' achievement, 552
questions asked by, 13–14
reasons for becoming teachers, 18–19
referral of exceptional children and, 179
relationships with students. *See* Teacher-student relationships
teaching and, 396. *See also* Instruction; Teaching
testing and, 523–524. *See also* Teacher-constructed tests
testing of, 583
Teacher-constructed tests, 525–529
definition of, 520
essay. *See* Essay tests
objective. *See* Objective tests
objectives of, 530
planning, 529–536
reliability of, 527
selecting items for, 530–531
validity of, 527–529
Teacher-student relationships, 10, 74–75
adapting instruction and, 428
behavior disorders and, 168
checking on, 58
classical conditioning and, 203

classroom management and, 471
cognitive psychology and, 248, 271
during concrete operational period, 94
effective teaching and, 20
during Erikson's adolescent year stages, 134
during Erikson's early stages, 127
during Erikson's elementary school year stages, 128–129
exceptional students and, 157
facilitating language skills and, 114
during formal operational period, 97
functions of teaching and, 416–417
gifted/talented students and, 162
hearing impaired students and, 164
information processing and, 260
intelligence and thinking skills exercises and, 292
mentally retarded students and, 176
moral development and, 139
motivation and, 342
objectives and, 381
operant conditioning and, 215
physically and health impaired students, 167
during preoperational period, 92
problem-solving strategies and, 323
during sensorimotor period, 89
social cognitive learning and, 221
teaching social skills and, 64–65
teaching students to construct graphic representations and, 308–310
value of, 74
visually impaired students and, 163
Teaching, 396–400. *See also* Instruction
as art, 11–12
behavioral theories and. *See* Behavioral psychology
core values and, 446
educational issues and, 8–10
functions of, 416–417
information superhighway and, 508
inquiry. *See* Indirect instruction
multicultural, 398
nature of, 6–7
reflective, achievement scores and, 401
as science, 12–13
social class and, 61–63
subject matter and, 408, 410
of technology, 493–494
of thinking skills, 498–501
Teaching machines, 213
Teach Your Child Decision making, 320
Technology. *See* Educational technology
Technology of Teaching, The (Skinner), 204
Telegraphic speech, 105
Television, for instruction, 492
Temporal-sequential organization, learning disabilities and, 173
Terminal behavior, 411
Test(s)
achievement. *See* Achievement tests
Code of Fair Testing Practices in Education and, 585
comments on, 550
criterion-referenced, 545
cultural differences and, 58–59
essay. *See* Essay tests
grading. *See* Grading
helping students prepare for, 535
helping students take, 552–553
objective. *See* Objective tests
standardized. *See* Aptitude tests; Standardized tests

summative and formative, 419
teacher-constructed. *See* Teacher-constructed tests
Test anxiety, 343–344
Test bias
gender-based, 73–74
against racial and ethnic minorities, 572–573
Test items, for teacher-constructed tests, 530–531
Test-wiseness, 552–553
Think Aloud classroom program, 320
Thinking. *See also* Thinking skills
brain and. *See* Brain
Bruner's study of, 247–248
culture and, 275
technology for teaching, 498–501
Thinking frames, 284–285
Thinking skills, 280–296
Bloom's taxonomy and, 286–289
Cognitive Research Trust program and, 295–296
Costa view of, 289–290
definition of, 280
improving through writing instruction, 499–501
instrumental enrichment and, 294–295
intelligence and, 280–285
multicultural students and, 290–291
Practical Intelligence for School program and, 291, 293
questions to improve, 286–287
Thinning, 224
Thorndike's connectionism, 202, 204
law of effect and, 204
law of exercise and, 202
law of readiness and, 202
TIES (The Instructional Environmental Scale), 409
Time
Carroll model for classroom management and, 436
concept of, 88
engaged, 435
QAIT model and, 444
on task, 418–419
Time-based recording, 539
Time out, 210, 226
Token economies, 459
Total quality management (TQM), 17
Tradition, as source of knowledge, 29

Trait anxiety, 342
Transductive reasoning, 91
Transfer, as thinking frame, 285
Transfer of learning
classroom implications of, 321–324
factors influencing, 321
helping students with, 319, 321
Transformation, 406
Transformational approach, to gender material, 73
Transition smoothness, of effective teachers, 455
Transmission, of messages, 165
Triad model, 159
Triarchic theory of intelligence, 281–282
True-false questions, 525
Trust versus mistrust stage, 120–121
t-scores, 582
Tutoring systems, intelligent, 501–503
Type R conditioning, 206
Type S conditioning, 206

Unconditioned response, 200
Unconditioned stimulus, 200
Unstandardized interviews, 39
Unstructured interviews, 39

Validity
of research findings, 37
of teacher-constructed tests, 527–529
Values, teaching process and, 446
Variable(s), 36
Variable interval, 208
Variable ratio, 208
Verbal Behavior (Skinner), 204
Verbal persuasion, 340
Verbal processing, 255, 260
Vicarious experiences, 340
Videodiscs, laser, 479, 504–505
Violence
control of, 449–451
moral education and, 140
roots of, 132–133
in schools, 132, 140
Virtual reality (VR), 507–508
Visually impaired students, 153, 154, 162–164
myths about, 163–164
Visually limited students, 163

Visual-spatial processing, learning disabilities and, 173
Vocables, 105
Vocabulary, 384
expansion of, 105
Vocational goals, 371
Voice disorders, 166
Voluntary motor function, learning disabilities and, 173
VR (virtual reality), 507–508
Vygotsky's theory of cognitive development, 82–83
zone of proximal development and, 53–54, 82–83

WAIS-III (Wechsler Adult Intelligence Scale-Revised), 570–571
WAN (wide area network), 479, 506
Weak performance assessment, 544
Wechsler Adult Intelligence Scale-Revised (WAIS-III), 570–571
Wechsler Intelligence Scale for Children—III (WISC-III), 571
Wechsler Preschool and Primary Scale of Intelligence (WPPSI-R), 571
What Computers Can't Do (Dreyfus), 240
Whole language approach, 107–108
as educational issue, 8–9
to reading instruction, 384
Wide area network (WAN), 479, 506
WISC-III (Wechsler Intelligence Scale for Children—III), 571
Withitness, of effective teachers, 454
Word(s)
first, 105
single, 105
Word processing, teaching of, 493–494
WPPSI-II (Wechsler Preschool and Primary Scale of Intelligence), 571
Writing, for improving thinking skills, 499–501

Yoked group, 349

Zone of proximal development, 53–54, 82–83
z-scores, 581